Java™ 2 Enterprise Edition 1.4 Bible

**James McGovern, Rahim Adatia, Yakov Fain,
Jason Gordon, Ethan Henry, Walter Hurst,
Ashish Jain, Mark Little, Vaidyanathan Nagarajan,
Harshad Oak, Lee Anne Phillips**

WILEY

Wiley Publishing, Inc.

Java™ 2 Enterprise Edition 1.4 Bible

Published by
Wiley Publishing, Inc.
10475 Crosspoint Boulevard
Indianapolis, IN 46256
www.wiley.com

ISBN: 0-7645-3966-3

Manufactured in the United States of America

10 9 8 7 6 5 4 3 2 1

1O/RS/QY/QT/IN

For general information on our other products and services or to obtain technical support, please contact our Customer Care Department within the U.S. at (800) 762-2974, outside the U.S. at (317) 572-3993 or fax (317) 572-4002.

Wiley also publishes its books in a variety of electronic formats. Some content that appears in print may not be available in electronic books.

Library of Congress Control Number: 2003101921

About the Authors

James McGovern is currently employed as an enterprise architect for Hartford Financial Services. He is the coauthor of *The Practical Guide to Enterprise Architecture* (Prentice Hall, 2003), *Java Web Services Architecture* (Morgan Kaufmann, 2003), and *Xquery — Kick Start* (Sams Publishing, 2003). James has 16 years of experience in information technology. He is a member of the Java Community Process, the IEEE, and the Worldwide Institute of Software Architects. He holds industry certifications from Microsoft, Cisco, and Sun.

Rahim Adatia has been programming since he got his first computer — a TRS-80 — way back in the beginning of the '80s. Fortunately, he didn't stagnate there and progressed on to developing large-scale enterprise architectures using C/C++, UML, CORBA, J2EE/EJB/Java, and now C# and .NET. He has applied his more than 15 years of experience to leading implementations at Charles Schwab, Williams Communications, Valtech, Nortel Networks, Corel Corporation, Lokah Limited, and T-Mobile International, to name a few. Most recently, he has focused on the wireless middleware market, where he has led product development using Web services, J2EE, and .NET. He is also a delegate for T-Mobile International at the Open Mobile Alliance standards body. Rahim has contributed to numerous books and articles throughout his career, including the books *Professional EJB* and *J#,* and is actively reviewing other titles. He can be reached at rahimadatia@yahoo.com.

Yakov Fain has more than 20 years of experience in information technology and is an experienced architect, developer, instructor, and mentor. He is the author of *The Java Tutorial for the Real World*. Yakov is the principal of Smart Data Processing, Inc. (http://www.smartdataprocessing.com), whose clients include major Wall Street companies. He is a Sun Certified Java 2 Programmer and a Sybase Certified Powerbuilder Developer.

Jason Gordon is a software engineer for Verizon and serves as lead for the Global Email system team. While at Verizon he has played a variety of roles, including systems architect for the eBusiness Technology Integration and eInfrastructure group and key developer of the EDGE project, which helped provide a Web-based infrastructure to facilitate the merger of Bell Atlantic and GTE into Verizon. Jason also served as a member of Verizon's XML-Task Force and collaborated on several wireless and Web-services initiatives within the company. In addition to being an active technical author, Jason also currently serves as the national technology coordinator for the National Society of Black Engineers. He can be reached at jasontgordon@hotmail.com or http://www.jtgordon.com.

Ethan Henry has most recently worked as the manager of training services at Sitraka. In previous positions he was a developer, product manager, and Java evangelist. He has written numerous articles for *Java Report, Dr. Dobbs Journal, Java Developers Journal,* and *Web Techniques.* He has been a technical reviewer of multiple books, including *Enterprise Java Beans* by Valesky, *Java How to Program* by Dietel and Dietel, *Professional JSP* by Wrox, and *Java Language API Superbible* from the Waite Group all the way back in 1996.

Walter Hurst is the chief technology officer and founder of Wakesoft. He is widely recognized as a leader in the design and implementation of large-scale distributed enterprise applications. At Wakesoft, Walter was the product architect and author before becoming more involved in company strategy and industry leadership. He is a frequent speaker at conferences and often writes for technical publications. During his career he has been involved in the design, architecture, and implementation of distributed business systems for many Fortune 1000 companies as an independent consultant and also, while at Xpedior and Andersen Consulting, Walter received a B.S. in computer engineering from the University of Michigan. When he needs a break from technology, Walter volunteers as a scuba diver for the Steinhart Aquarium in San Francisco, where he cleans the shark tank.

Ashish Jain is an enterprise consultant/architect with over ten years of IT experience. He currently works for BEA Systems Professional Services. In this capacity, Ashish assists BEA customers in designing and implementing their e-business strategies using solutions based on J2EE. He holds several industry certifications from SUN and BEA. He is an active member of local J2EE-user groups and a board member of the Denver BEA-user group. He holds a degree in electronics engineering from BITS Pilani, India.

Mark Little is Head of Transactions Technology for Arjuna Technologies Limited, a company that spun off from Hewlett-Packard to concentrate on developing transactions technologies for J2EE and Web services. Prior to this, Mark was a distinguished engineer/architect in HP's Arjuna Labs in England, where he led the HP Transaction Service and HP Web Services Transaction teams. He is one of the primary authors of the OMG Activity Service Specification. He is a member of the expert group for the work in J2EE: JSR 95 and JSR 117, and is the specification lead for JSR 156 (Java API for XML Transactions). Mark is active on the OTS Revision Task Force and the OASIS Business Transactions Protocol specification. He is the coauthor of an upcoming book, *Transaction and Java for Systems Professionals* (Prentice Hall). He has been published in many industry magazines, including *Doctor Dobbs, The Java Developers Journal,* the *Web Services Journal, Developer.com,* and *Application Development Advisor.* Mark holds a Ph.D. in computer science from the University of Newcastle.

Vaidyanathan Nagarajan, a.k.a Nathan, is the coauthor of a recent book, *Xquery — Kick Start* (Sams Publishing). He coauthored *Professional EJB* for Wrox in summer of 2001. He has seven years of experience in information technology. Prior to joining Hartford Life Insurance as an enterprise developer, he worked as a consultant to Netscape Professional Services. He has an M.B.A. in General Management from a leading business school in the New England area. He is a former student of the Indian Institute of Technology, Mumbai, India. His main interests include programming in Java, robotics using Lego Mindstorms, writing, reading, and cartooning. If he is not thinking about design patterns or Java, he will be modeling a robot in his robotic lab. He can be reached at vnathan@hotmail.com.

Harshad Oak holds a master's degree in computer management and is a Sun Certified Java Programmer and a Sun Certified Web Component Developer. He has been part of several J2EE projects at i-flex Solutions and Cognizant Technology Solutions. He is also a regular contributor of articles to developer Web sites like http://www.builder.com.

Lee Anne Phillips has a long history in computer networking and interface design, having created beaucoup systems-firmware and machine-language hardware-interface routines before the appearance of Java and other sensible tools to relieve the burdens of a suffering humanity. She attended the University of California at Berkeley. Lee Anne is the author of many books and articles on computer-related subjects, including *Special Edition Using XML, Practical HTML 4*, and about a fifth of *HTML 4.0 Unleashed Professional Reference Edition*. An extended list may be seen on her Web site: www.leeanne.com.

Credits

Acquisitions Editor
Jim Minatel

Project Editors
Valerie H. Perry
Neil Romanosky
Mark Enochs

Technical Editor
Kunal Mittal

Copy Editor
S. B. Kleinman

Editorial Manager
Mary Beth Wakefield

Vice President & Executive Group Publisher
Richard Swadley

Vice President and Executive Publisher
Bob Ipsen

Vice President and Publisher
Joseph B. Wikert

Executive Editorial Director
Mary Bednarek

Project Coordinator
Kristie Rees

Graphics and Production Specialists
Beth Brooks
Jennifer Click
Sean Decker
Heather Pope

Quality Control Technicians
Laura Albert
John Greenough
Brian H.Walls

Media Development Specialist
Angela Denny

Proofreading and Indexing
TECHBOOKS Production Services

Foreword

Something about this book needs to be short, so I guess it's going to have to be the foreword. Seriously, though, this is a very good book. In fact, it's the best introduction to J2EE that I've seen. It's well written, covering all the information you need to succeed with J2EE. And it's presented in an order that makes sense — the chapters provide an end-to-end overview of J2EE. The book starts by showing you how to build the frontend of your application, then describes your connectivity options, then shows you how to build your business logic using Enterprise JavaBeans (EJB), and finally explains how to connect to the backend databases. In other words, this book is architecturally layered.

Why should you read this book? First, because the authors know what they're talking about and can explain it in ways that you can understand. Second, because it really does cover the fundamentals of J2EE incredibly well. The first five parts of this book are oriented toward people learning to work with J2EE technology, and in my opinion they do an incredibly good job of explaining exactly what you need to know. Third, because the book goes beyond J2EE. Part VI is a great overview of using Web services with J2EE, a critical issue most developers need to understand. Part VII is a great overview of common J2EE patterns, and Part VIII covers such important topics as performance and frameworks. In many ways this book is a "one-stop shop" for J2EE information.

In the end the thing that I like most about this book is that it's practical. Yes, it's pretty darn big, but as a result it provides a significant amount of real-world advice. Isn't that what good books are supposed to do?

Scott W. Ambler
Senior consultant, Ronin International, Inc. (`http://www.ronin-intl.com`)
Author, *Agile Modeling, Agile Database Techniques*
Coauthor, *Mastering EJB 2/e*

To our peers in the industry who maintain a sense of speed, agility, and balance

Acknowledgments

The process of writing a book is more time-consuming than anyone could ever imagine. Luckily, the author team was composed of very talented people who made the experience enjoyable. Some doubted that we could complete a book of this magnitude on schedule without sacrificing quality. That you are reading it now means that we were successful in our undertakings.

This book is the result of many people's efforts. We would first like to thank our acquisitions editor, Jim Minatel, for providing insight into the publishing industry in general, and for allowing us to challenge the typical book-production process and to focus on writing a good book instead of simply following a publishing formula. The team would also like to thank Neil Romanosky for his efforts in making Wiley a little more agile.

We would also like to acknowledge authors we have worked with in the past and hope to work with in the future, including Sameer Tyagi, Martin Fowler, Sunil Mathew, James Linn, Michael Stevens, Elias Jo, Vikas Sharan, John Crupi, Steven Graham, Erich Gamma, Paul Reed, Tim Howes, Kent Beck, Jeff Sutherland, Marty Biggs, Alistair Cockburn, Ed Roman, Nitin Narayan, Marty Biggs, Chris Caserio, Kurt Cagle, Per Bothner, and Jeff Ryan.

James McGovern — First, I must thank my wife, Sherry, and my son, little James, for putting up with me for the past several months while I've kidnapped and held myself hostage in my dungeon (office) working on this book. I know they would have liked to have me around more, but writing this book is something I really needed to do. Thank you for your support.

I would like to acknowledge my Connecticut family: Daisy May, Pamela, Annika, Demesha, Aunt Jesse, and the little doggie Pinto. Universal greetings to my Trinidad family: Soogia, Kello Ricky (Kenrick), Robby (Kiley), Kelon, and Keifer, and to my United Kingdom family: Nicholas, Ian, and Alex.

Finally, thanks to my father James Sr. and mother Mattie Lee, who gave me the courage to start and the discipline to finish.

Rahim Adatia — I would like to thank James McGovern, Jim Minatel, and Mark Enochs for all their hard work in developing this book. Thank you for your patience. I would also like to thank the professors and colleagues I have worked with at the University of Ottawa, Valtech (U.K. and U.S.A.!), BEA, and T-Mobile International. Last but not least, I would like to thank my family and friends who have been there to support and encourage me — I know that I can be difficult at times (did I say that?). Thank you for your strength.

Yakov Fain — I'd like to thank my family — Natalia, Yuri, and David — for their love and support. I'd also like to thank a wonderful teacher and a lovely lady, Dr. Alice S. Koutkova, and close friends of our family, Dora and Felix Rubinchik.

Jason Gordon — I would like to thank GOD for giving me guidance and strength. I would also like to acknowledge the following people: Abby, Jerry, Marvin, Charlie Lindahl, Beth, Mitch, Kyle, Lisa, The Jamisons, and my entire family. A special thanks to my Mother who has been there every time I needed her. I would like to thank MaryKim for her encouraging words and advice. I would like to thank Lee Felts who gave me the inspiration to write. I would like to thank Kyle for his support and guidance. Last but not least . . . thanks to Mr. Starbucks and his friend Mr. Caffeine! You guys are awesome!

Ethan Henry — I'd like to thank my family, especially my wonderful wife Margit, for helping me work on this book, my colleagues at Sitraka (now Quest Software), the rest of the author team, and the fine people at Wiley who helped pull everything together.

Walter Hurst — For all the effort required writing my chapter, I would first like to thank my wife, Christine. This chapter is just one more instance where I had to work hard on nights and weekends, and her cheerful support is what made it all possible. I would also like to thank James McGovern for inviting me to write the chapter; this book would not be possible without a lead author organizing the many required writers, which is a task probably very akin to herding cats. The concepts contained within this chapter I have learned indirectly from thought leaders in the industry, directly from my time at Sage IT Partners, and even more definitely since founding Wakesoft. There are too many individuals to list them, but they know who they are. Thank you.

Ashish Jain — I would like to thank my wife Nishma and our son Eshan for their love and patience and support. I would also like to thank my colleagues at BEA, Chris John and Bob Webster, for their useful and insightful comments.

Mark Little — I would like to thank my wife Paula and two sons, Daniel and Adam (who was born during the writing of this book) for their support and love. They have put up with my disappearances into the book-writing world many times over the past few months, and I know it can't have been easy. My entire family has given all the effort over the many years meaning and ensured that I stayed sane. Lots of love to Adam, who thinks his rattle and toys are far more important than Java and J2EE!

Vaidyanathan Nagarajan — I would like to thank my wife Padma and my parents, Nagarajan and Geetha, for encouraging me to put in my best effort in contributing to this book. This book is dedicated to Padma, Geetha, Nagarajan, Vedham, all my family members, and my best friends the Srinivasans (Arun and Sujata) who have supported me in being what I am. A special mention goes to James McGovern for giving me an opportunity to work with him and for introducing me to the world of writing technical books. Thanks to those Asterix comics (by the time I completed writing this book, I have collected all the Asterix collection except for one) and Dilbert strips for making the creative juices run fresh in me every morning. I would also like to take a moment to thank my friend and colleague, Thomas Nordlund, for prototyping the source code for the session-authenticator pattern.

Harshad Oak — I wish to thank my father, Baba, without whose affection, support, inspiration, and experiments at the art of cooking Indian food, nothing would have been possible. I also wish to thank my dear sister Charu for always being there for me, and Sangeeta for helping me with my writing and painstakingly reviewing my work. Thanks to Jim and Mark for being a big help throughout this project and to Laura and Stacey for playing an important part in my writing endeavors.

Lee Anne Phillips — My deepest thanks to Alison Eve Ulman, who provided needed support and advice throughout the development of the chapter on JAAS, and to my editors, whose tactful suggestions rarely failed to be either right on the mark or an indication of a needed new direction for the phrase or discussion in question. Any remaining errors or infelicitous explanations are entirely my own responsibility, the creation of a book being a cooperative enterprise, especially this one that ultimately depends on the imagination and skill of the author.

Contents at a Glance

Foreword vii
Acknowledgments viii
Introduction xxix

Part I: Introduction 1
Chapter 1: Understanding Java and the J2EE Platform 3
Chapter 2: Reviewing XML Fundamentals 17
Chapter 3: Introducing Application Servers 43
Chapter 4: Understanding Remote Method Invocation 55

Part II: The Presentation Tier 75
Chapter 5: Studying Servlet Programming 77
Chapter 6: Going Over JSP Basics 113
Chapter 7: Using JSP Tag Extensions 143

Part III: The Enterprise Information System Tier 179
Chapter 8: Working with JavaMail 181
Chapter 9: Understanding the Java Messaging Service 231
Chapter 10: Introducing Java Transactions 255
Chapter 11: Examining JNDI and Directory Services 303
Chapter 12: Understanding Java Authentication and Authorization Services . . . 347
Chapter 13: Exploring Java Cryptography Extensions 409

Part IV: The Service Tier 427
Chapter 14: Understanding EJB Architecture and Design 429
Chapter 15: Explaining Session Beans and Business Logic 483
Chapter 16: Working with Entity Beans 511
Chapter 17: Using Message-Driven Beans 565

Part V: The Data Tier 579
Chapter 18: Reviewing Java Database Connectivity 581
Chapter 19: Understanding the J2EE Connector Architecture 607

Part VI: Web Services **645**

Chapter 20: Introducing Web Services 647
Chapter 21: Digging Deeper into SOAP, WSDL, and UDDI 665
Chapter 22: Understanding J2EE Web Services 711

Part VII: Patterns **727**

Chapter 23: Reviewing Presentation-Tier Patterns 729
Chapter 24: Working with Service-Tier Patterns 763
Chapter 25: Using Data-Tier Patterns 797

Part VIII: Advanced Topics **817**

Chapter 26: Exploring Frameworks and Application Architecture 819
Chapter 27: Using ANT to Build and Deploy Applications 857
Chapter 28: Creating High-Performance Java Applications 881

Appendix A: Airline Reservations Business Case 915
Appendix B: Magazine Publisher Business Case 923
Appendix C: Additional Reading and References 927

Index 935

Contents

Foreword vii

Acknowledgments viii

Introduction xxix

Part I: Introduction   1

Chapter 1: Understanding Java and the J2EE Platform 3

Reviewing a Brief History of Java 3
Understanding J2SE 5
Examining the Origin of (J2EE) 5
    Application components 6
    Roles 7
Working with the Model-View-Controller 9
    The model 9
    The view 10
    The control 10
Understanding J2EE APIs 10
    J2EE standard services 11
    Application component APIs 13
Discovering What's New in J2EE 1.4 13
Looking toward the Future of J2EE 14
Understanding the Java Community Process (JCP) 14
Summary 15

Chapter 2: Reviewing XML Fundamentals 17

Explaining XML 17
    Well-formed XML 18
    Valid XML 18
Understanding XML Document Structure 20
    Prologue 20
    Elements 20
    Attributes 21

Examining XML Parsers 21
  DOM parsers 22
  SAX parsers 22
  DOM versus SAX 23
Implementing XML DTDs 24
Understanding XML Namespaces 26
Exploring XML Schema 30
Working with eXtensible Stylesheet
  Language Transformations (XSLT) 34
  Producing simple HTML with XSLT 35
  Producing a Wireless Markup Language (WML) Document
    with XML 38
Introducing J2EE XML–Based APIs 40
Summary 41

Chapter 3: Introducing Application Servers **43**
Implementing the J2EE Platform 43
Understanding the Features of an Application Server 45
  Scalability 46
  Client agnosticism 46
  Server management 47
  Development 47
Examining Full J2EE Implementations 47
  BEA WebLogic 48
  Borland Enterprise Server 48
  IBM WebSphere 48
  JBoss 49
  Oracle 9iAS 49
  Orion 50
  Sun ONE Application Server 50
Examining Partial J2EE Implementations 51
  Apache Tomcat 52
  Resin 52
  ServletExec 52
Avoiding Vendor Lock-In 53
Summary 54

Chapter 4: Understanding Remote Method Invocation **55**
Providing an Overview of RMI 55
Developing Applications with RMI 57
  Declaring remote interfaces 57
  Implementing remote interfaces 58
  Stubs and skeletons 60
  Registering remote objects 61
  Writing RMI clients 63
  Setting up the Flight Server example 65

Pushing Data from the RMI Server 68
RMI over Inter-ORB Protocol (IIOP) 72
Summary 73

Part II: The Presentation Tier   75

Chapter 5: Studying Servlet Programming 77

Creating a Magazine Publisher Application Using Servlets 77
   The server side 78
   The client side 79
   Creating an HTML login screen 79
Using the Servlet Context 84
Performing URL Redirection 85
   Using RequestDispatcher 86
   Using sendRedirect( ) 86
   The Lost Password screen example 87
   Session tracking with servlets 88
   Cookies 88
   URL rewriting 90
   Hidden fields 90
   The session-tracking API with HttpSession object 91
   Example of a LoginServlet with an access counter 93
   Listeners 94
   Filters 97
   Deploying servlets 103
   The Web-application archive 103
Examining the web.xml Deployment Descriptor 104
   Mandatory servlet elements 104
   Servlet listener elements 105
   Servlet filter elements 106
   Applet-servlet communication 107
What's New in the Servlet 2.4 Specification 111
Summary 112

Chapter 6: Going Over JSP Basics 113

Introducing JSP 113
Examining MVC and JSP 115
JSP Scripting Elements and Directives 116
   Declarations 117
   Expressions 117
   Directives 118
   Scriptlets 119
   Comments 119
   Actions 120
   Implicit JSP objects 121

Working with Variable Scopes 122
Error Pages 123
Using JavaBeans 124
    Using JavaBeans in JSP 125
    The scope of JavaBeans 127
    Creating a login JSP using a JavaBean 127
    Deploying the Login JSP example using Tomcat 129
Designing an Online Store with JSP 130
Airline Reservations Business Case 133
Summary 141

Chapter 7: Using JSP Tag Extensions **143**
Why Use Tag Extensions? 143
Explaining Custom-Tag Concepts 144
    Working with the JSP Standard Tag Library 145
    Importing a tag library 147
    The Tag Library Descriptor 148
    The tag-library-descriptor location 151
Explaining taglib Mapping 152
Understanding Tag Handlers 153
    Classic tag handlers 153
    Simple tag handlers 170
Exploring Dynamic Attributes 174
Summary 177

Part III: The Enterprise Information System Tier   **179**

Chapter 8: Working with JavaMail **181**
Exploring the "Hello World" of JavaMail 181
Understanding the Protocols for JavaMail 183
    SMTP 183
    POP3 184
    IMAP 184
    MIME 185
JavaMail Components 185
    Session management 186
    Message manipulation 190
    Message content 199
    Mail storage and retrieval 205
    Transportation with javax.mail.Transport 216
Using the JavaMail API 218
    Sending e-mail and attachments 218
    Receiving e-mail 223
Integrating JavaMail into J2EE 229
Summary 230

Chapter 9: Understanding the Java Messaging Service 231

Explaining Messaging 231
Introducing JMS 232
    JMS versus RMI 232
    Message structure 234
Examining Messaging Models 235
    Point-to-point messaging 235
    Publish-and-subscribe messaging 236
Understanding the Major JMS Components 236
    Destinations 237
    Connections 237
    Connection factories 237
    Sessions 238
    Producers 238
    Consumers 238
Configuring JMS 239
Connexia Airlines Point-to-Point Messaging Business Case 240
Magazine-Publisher Publish-Subscribe Messaging Business Case 248
Explaining Reliable Messaging 252
    Autonomous messages 252
    Persistent messages 252
    Synchronous acknowledgments 253
    Transactions 253
Introducing Message-Driven Enterprise JavaBeans 254
Summary 254

Chapter 10: Introducing Java Transactions 255

What Are Atomic Transactions? 255
Examining Transactional Objects and Participants 257
Reviewing Atomicity and the Two-Phase Commit Protocol 259
    Optimizations 260
    Heuristics and removing the two-phase block 261
Understanding Local and Distributed Transactions 262
    Local transactions 262
    Distributed transactions 264
    Interposition 265
Understanding Consistency 267
Introducing Isolation (Serializability) 268
    Optimistic versus pessimistic concurrency control 269
    Degrees of isolation 270
Understanding the Role of Durability 272
Performing Failure Recovery 273
Using Transaction-Processing Monitors 274
Transaction Models 275
    Nested transactions 276
    Nested top-level transactions 277
    Extended transaction models and the J2EE Activity Service 278

Understanding Transaction Standards 283
  X/Open Distributed Transaction Processing 284
  The Object Transaction Service 285
Understanding the Java Transaction API 288
  The JTA's relationship to the JTS 289
  The UserTransaction interface 290
  The TransactionManager interface 291
  Suspending and resuming a transaction 292
  The Transaction interface 293
  The XAResource interface 294
  Enrolling participants with the transaction 295
  Transaction synchronization 296
  Transaction equality 297
  The XID interface 297
Airline Reservation Using Transactions Business Case 297
Summary 301

Chapter 11: Examining JNDI and Directory Services **303**
Explaining Naming Services and Directory Services 303
Providing an Overview of X.500 and LDAP 305
  LDAP implementations 305
  Configuring OpenLDAP 306
  LDAP schema 308
Reviewing the JNDI Structure 309
  Directories and entries 310
  Names and attributes 310
  Binding and references 311
  Contexts and subcontexts 311
  File systems 311
  DNS naming conventions 311
  LDAP mapping 312
Using JNDI and LDAP 312
  Connecting to the server 312
  Specifying environment properties 313
  Implementing authentication 316
  Performing simple LDAP lookups 316
  Performing searches and comparing entries 318
  Modifying the directory 322
  Adding objects to a directory 323
Connecting to DNS 328
  DNS environment properties 330
  DNS lookups 331
  Reverse DNS lookups 332

Considering Other JNDI Service Providers 332
    File systems 333
    COS naming for CORBA 333
    Network Information System 333
    Directory Services Markup Language 334
    Application-server providers 334
Exploring the Enterprise JavaBean Environment 335
Airline Reservations Business Case 337
Magazine Publisher Business Case 342
Summary 346

**Chapter 12: Understanding Java Authentication and
Authorization Services** **347**
Examining the Importance of Java Security 348
    Typical Java security weaknesses 349
    Providing an overview of JAAS 353
Understanding Security Realms 355
    Single login across security domains 356
    Setting up for JAAS 358
    Callback handlers 358
    Pluggable/stackable authentication 360
Examining the Java Subject Class 362
Authenticating Users 364
    Authorizing users 368
    JAAS policy files 368
    Compiling the example 369
Debugging the Simple JAAS Module 372
    Hiding JAAS 375
    Predefined JAAS login callbacks and their handlers 375
    Custom login modules 384
    Writing your own login handler 385
    Writing your own callback handler 394
    Authenticating a Web user against a Windows NT domain 397
    Brief security analysis 397
    Security limitations 398
    Implementation 398
    Alternative methods 403
Connexia Airlines Business Case 404
    Authenticating a Web user against a directory service 404
    Brief security analysis 404
    Security limitations 405
    Implementation 405
Summary 407

Chapter 13: Exploring Java Cryptography Extensions **409**

Grasping the Basic Terminology 410
One-way encryption versus two-way encryption 410
Algorithms 412
Shared-key cryptography 415
Public-key cryptography 416
Digital certificates 417
Protocols 417
Reviewing the Java Cryptography Package 420
Writing a Java Program Using JCE 421
Magazine Publisher Business Case 422
Airline Reservations Business Case 424
Summary 426

Part IV: The Service Tier   427

Chapter 14: Understanding EJB Architecture and Design **429**

Explaining the EJB Component Model 429
Reviewing Roles, Relationships, and Responsibilities 432
The deployment descriptor 432
The bean provider 433
The server/container provider 433
The application assembler 434
The EJB deployer 435
The system administrator 435
The Enterprise JavaBean 436
Entity beans 436
Session beans 440
Entity beans versus session beans 441
Message-driven beans (MDB) 442
What does an EJB contain? 443
Understanding EJB Container Functionality 446
Restrictions on the bean provider 447
Achieving scalability by pooling resources 450
The life of an entity bean 451
The life of a session bean 454
Transactions and EJBs 456
Container-managed transactions 456
Examining a transactional EJB example 462
Naming objects 463
The security infrastructure 464
The Timer service 464
Persistence in BMP and CMP 466
Distribution support 466
Integrating with CORBA 467
Why is CORBA important to J2EE? 468
When J2EE met CORBA 469

Performance and Scalability Issues 472
   Application-server availability strategies 473
   Transaction concerns 475
   Threading model 476
   Tools 479
Summary 481

Chapter 15: Explaining Session Beans and Business Logic **483**
Writing a Session EJB 484
   The home interface 484
   The component interface 485
   The session bean class 487
   The deployment descriptor 488
   The stateless session bean 489
Connexia Airlines Business Case 492
   FlightServiceHome — The home interface 493
   FlightService — The remote interface 493
   FlightServiceBean — The bean class 494
   The ejb-jar.xml deployment descriptor 495
   Deployment 496
   Writing an EJB client 496
   Stateful-session-bean model 499
   The lifecycle of the stateful session bean 500
   Passivation and activation 502
Implementing the Session Synchronization Interface 503
Storing a Handle 503
Collecting Payment Business Case 504
   WorkFlowHome — The home interface 504
   WorkFlow — The remote interface 504
   WorkFlowBean — The bean class 505
Choosing between Stateless and Stateful Beans 509
   The stateless model 510
   The stateful model 510
Summary 510

Chapter 16: Working with Entity Beans **511**
Understanding Entity Beans 511
   Remote and local client views 512
   Entity-bean components 513
   The entity-container contract 517
   Container-managed persistence (CMP) 526
   Bean-managed persistence (BMP) 552
   Exceptions 562
Summary 563

Chapter 17: Using Message-Driven Beans **565**

Understanding the Need for MDB 565
Reviewing MDB Lifecycle Methods 569
Examining MDB Deployment Descriptors 570
    Deployment descriptors as per EJB 2.0 570
    Changes in MDB 2.1 deployment descriptors 572
    Internal messaging within EJB applications 573
Understanding Clients and MDB 575
Working with EJBs Asynchronously 576
Summary 577

Part V: The Data Tier **579**

Chapter 18: Reviewing Java Database Connectivity **581**

Introducing JDBC Driver Types 582
Creating Your First JDBC Program 583
    Retrieving data 585
    Database-error processing 587
    Processing result sets 587
    The ResultSetMetaData class 589
    Scrollable result sets 591
    The PreparedStatement class 592
    The CallableStatement class 592
Performing Batch Updates 593
Using Savepoints 594
Configuring the JDBC-ODBC Bridge 594
Explaining Database Connection Pools and Data Sources 596
    Configuring connection pools 597
    Creating Data Source objects 597
Revisiting DBProcessor 599
Using the RowSet Interface 601
    Working with CachedRowSet 602
    The WebRowSet class 606
Summary 606

Chapter 19: Understanding the J2EE Connector Architecture **607**

Examining the Contracts 608
    The lifecycle-management contract 610
    Work management contract 612
    Outbound communication 616
    Inbound communication 631
The Common Client Interface (CCI) 633
    Connection interfaces 634
    Interaction interfaces 635
    Data interfaces 635

Metadata interfaces 636
Using the CCI 636
Packaging and Deployment 640
Summary 643

Part VI: Web Services   645

Chapter 20: Introducing Web Services 647

Defining Web Services 648
Universal Resource Identifiers 648
XML-based technologies 648
Why Do We Need Web Services? 649
Remote Method Invocation 649
DCOM 650
CORBA 650
Web-service architecture 650
Advantages of Web services 652
Examining Some Web-Service Scenarios 653
Enterprise-application integration (EAI) 654
Understanding the Technologies behind Web Services 656
SOAP 657
WSDL 657
UDDI 658
Web services in a service-oriented architecture 659
Summary 663

Chapter 21: Digging Deeper into SOAP, WSDL, and UDDI 665

Understanding the SOAP Message Architecture 666
The header 666
The body 667
XML schemas and SOAP data types 668
Arrays 670
SOAP RPC 672
SOAP messaging 675
SOAP and Java 676
Explaining WSDL 681
SOAP binding 686
HTTP GET and POST binding 687
MIME binding 688
WSDL and Java 689
Examining UDDI 689
UDDI versions 1, 2, and 3 689
Searching with UDDI 698
Publishing with UDDI 700
Subscribing with UDDI 703
UDDI and Java 704
Summary 709

Chapter 22: Understanding J2EE Web Services 711

Integrating J2EE and Web Services 711
    Using Java servlets in a Web-services architecture 712
    Exposing EJBs as Web services 713
    Using JMS as a transport layer 714
    Exploring Products and Tools for Web Services 715
JSR 109 — J2EE Web Services 717
    The client-side programming model 719
    The server-side programming model 721
    Web-service deployment descriptors 725
Summary 725

Part VII: Patterns   727

Chapter 23: Reviewing Presentation-Tier Patterns 729

Providing an Overview of Patterns 729
Explaining the Session Pattern 731
    Forces 732
    Implementation 732
    Strategies 734
    Results 735
    Session pattern — UML diagram and sample code 735
    Related patterns 735
Understanding the Router Pattern 736
    Forces 736
    Implementation 736
    Strategies 738
    Results 738
    The router pattern — sample code 738
    Related patterns 740
Reviewing the Model-View-Controller Pattern 740
    Forces 741
    Implementation 742
    Strategies 743
    Results 743
    The model-view-controller pattern — sample code 744
    Related patterns 745
Using the Front-Controller Pattern 746
    Forces 746
    Implementation 746
    Strategies 748
    Results 749
    The front-controller pattern — sample code 749
    Related patterns 750

Working with the View-Helper Pattern 750
  Forces 750
  Implementation 751
  Strategies 752
  Results 753
  The view-helper pattern — sample code 753
  Related patterns 753
Using the Composite-View Pattern 754
  Forces 754
  Implementation 754
  Strategies 756
  Results 757
  The composite-view pattern — sample code 757
  Related patterns 757
Using the Intercepting-Filter Pattern 758
  Forces 758
  Implementation 758
  Strategies 760
  Results 760
  The intercepting-filter pattern — sample code 761
  Related patterns 761
Summary 762

Chapter 24: Working with Service-Tier Patterns 763

Introducing Service-Tier Patterns 763
Using the Business-Delegate Pattern 765
  Forces 765
  Implementation 765
  Structure 765
  Strategies 767
  Results 767
  Business-delegate pattern — sample code 768
  Related patterns 769
Understanding the Value-Object Pattern 769
  Forces 769
  Implementation 770
  Strategies 771
  Results 772
  Value-object pattern — sample code 772
  Related patterns 773
Exploring the Session-Facade Pattern 774
  Forces 774
  Implementation 774
  Structure 774
  Strategies 776

Results 776
Session-facade pattern — sample code 776
Related patterns 777
Explaining the Composite-Entity Pattern 777
Forces 778
Implementation 778
Strategies 779
Results 780
Composite-entity pattern — sample code 780
Related patterns 781
Using the Service-Locator Pattern 781
Forces 782
Implementation 782
Strategies 783
Results 784
Service-locator pattern — sample code 784
Related patterns 785
Working with the Half-Object-Plus-Protocol Pattern 785
Forces 786
Implementation 786
Strategies 787
Results 788
Half-object-plus-protocol pattern — sample code 788
Related patterns 788
Summary 796

Chapter 25: Using Data-Tier Patterns **797**
Introducing the Data-Access-Object Pattern 797
Implementation 799
Implementing the Data-Access-Object Pattern 801
Applying the data-access-object pattern 803
Applying related patterns 805
Using the Service-Activator Pattern 805
Implementation 806
Implementing the Service-Activator Pattern 809
The service-activator-server strategy 809
The EJB-server strategy 809
The EJB-client strategy 809
Applying the service-activator pattern 810
Applying related patterns 810
Examining the Transfer-Object Pattern 811
Implementation 812
Implementing the transfer-object pattern 813
Applying the transfer-object pattern 814
Applying related patterns 815
Summary 816

Part VIII: Advanced Topics · 817

Chapter 26: Exploring Frameworks and Application Architecture 819

What are Frameworks? 820
    Frameworks versus class libraries 821
    The pains of J2EE 821
Understanding Framework Principles 823
    Inversion of control 823
    Separation of concerns 823
    Loose coupling 824
    Extensibility 824
    Configurability 824
    Alignment 825
    Design patterns 826
    Examining the Struts framework example 827
Understanding Framework Objectives and Benefits 835
    Design 835
    Development and testing 836
    Production and maintenance 836
    Application portfolios 837
Reviewing Application Architecture beyond Frameworks . . . 837
    Overview of architectures 837
    Traditional application architecture 838
    Services-oriented architecture 839
    Application architecture versus frameworks 841
Building Your Own Framework 841
    Building versus buying 841
    Open source 842
    Software vendor 843
    System Integrators (SIs) 844
Predicting the Future of Frameworks 845
Alternatives to Frameworks 846
    All-in-one proprietary environments 846
    Model-driven architecture 847
    Minimal J2EE 848
    Advanced Integrated Development Environments 848
Evaluating Frameworks 850
    Requirements 850
    Cost 850
    Framework checklist 851
    Vendor questions 853
Summary 854

Chapter 27: Using ANT to Build and Deploy Applications **857**

   Introducing ANT 857
   Getting Comfortable with ANT Vocabulary 863
      Projects 864
      Properties 864
      Targets 865
      File matching 867
      Tasks 868
   Putting It All Together 877
   Summary 879

Chapter 28: Creating High-Performance Java Applications **881**

   Understanding Different Types of Problems 881
      Functional problems 882
      Performance problems 882
   Isolating Problems 886
      Critical-path analysis 886
      Load testing 886
      Benchmarking 887
      Tunable parameters 889
      Profiling 892
   Logging 893
      Logging APIs 894
   Managing Memory-Usage Problems 906
      Loiterers 908
      Loiterer anti-patterns 910
   Summary 914

Appendix A: Airline Reservations Business Case **915**

Appendix B: Magazine Publisher Business Case **923**

Appendix C: Additional Reading and References **927**

Index 935

Introduction

The world of information technology is evolving rapidly. Enterprise applications must deliver services that meet the needs of the global business environment, ensure that users' data remains private, protect the integrity of enterprise data, and ensure that business transactions are accurate and processed quickly. Enterprises today need to extend their reach, reduce their costs, and lower the response times of their services to customers, employers, and suppliers. Typically, applications that do these things must combine enterprise information systems (EIS) with new business functions that deliver services to a broad range of users.

J2EE reduces the cost and complexity of developing multi-tier enterprise services. J2EE applications can be rapidly deployed and easily enhanced as the enterprise responds to competitive pressures.

This book provides leading-edge but practical examples to illustrate how J2EE can be applied to existing business and technology initiatives. The book focuses on thinking concretely about the specifications that comprise J2EE, while providing solutions to today's problems.

This book is ideal for those who prefer personal interaction to processes and tools, responding to change to following a plan, and techniques that work to comprehensive documentation. Some of the respective authors' anecdotal experiences will periodically appear. This will make for an easier read and allow the reader to connect and become involved.

Whom this book is for

J2EE is the foundation of many large-scale application-development projects. As major corporations shift away from expanding the spaghetti code contained within their monolithic mainframe systems, they are looking for an architecture that will prevent them from making past mistakes again. J2EE is the answer. The author team, as writers and buyers of many of today's information-technology books, wanted to write something different from what is currently on the shelves. This book is targeted toward architects and senior developers who understand the fundamentals of Java and want to take the next step. The driving goals are to provide a complete overview of the major J2EE technologies and to show how they can be used to solve non-trivial business problems.

If you are a developer, an architect, or even a project manager, you will appreciate our attempt to bring you a no-frills introduction to J2EE. The author team has worked many long hours to bring you the ultimate guide that explains everything you need to know about J2EE. This book provides examples that clearly illustrate how the technologies contained within can be applied to existing business and technology undertakings. Where appropriate, this book will provide additional sources of information.

Each author has enjoyed the freedom to provide anecdotal experiences where appropriate, as all knowledge is beneficial. This book should be considered a trusted advisor and an authoritative source of J2EE information.

What this book covers

The Java 2 Platform, Enterprise Edition (J2EE) defines the standard for developing *n*-tier enterprise applications using Java. J2EE simplifies enterprise applications by basing them on standardized modular components and providing for those components a complete set of services that handle the complexities automatically.

N-tier applications are difficult to build. Usually building such an application requires people with a variety of skills and an understanding of both modern and legacy code and data. Enterprise applications typically use heterogeneous approaches to systems development and require the integration of tools from a variety of vendors and the merging of disparate application models and standards.

This book covers the various components of J2EE that are used to build enterprise *n*-tier applications, including the following:

+ JavaServer Pages (JSP)
+ Enterprise JavaBeans (EJB)
+ Java Messaging Service (JMS)
+ Java Naming and Directory Interface (JNDI)
+ Java Authentication and Authorization Service (JAAS)
+ Java Connector Architecture (JCA)
+ And more . . .

The author team recommends that the chapters in this book be read in order, as each chapter builds upon previous chapters. If reading the chapters in order is not viable, reading a particular section in a single sitting may be a better choice.

What this book is not!

The purpose of this book is to cover the various components of J2EE. Understanding J2EE requires a working knowledge of the basics of Java. This book's coverage of Java will be limited to coverage of the APIs required for advanced J2EE features. All the examples within this book use Java, so it is important to minimally understand the principles of another object-oriented language such as C++ or Smalltalk.

The authors have avoided recommending software-development processes, project-management discipline, software architecture, or naming conventions. We believe that our readers are better served by other books that cover these topics.

What you'll need

To gain the most benefit from this book, you'll need a workstation loaded up with the following software:

+ An application server that supports Sun's J2EE SDK, version 1.4

+ A relational database, such as Microsoft SQL Server or Oracle

+ An integrated development environment (IDE) for Java, such as Borland JBuilder (http://www.borland.com) or Eclipse (http://www.eclipse.org)

+ An SMTP-compliant mail server, if you plan to write applications that will process incoming or outgoing electronic mail

Conventions used in this book

This book uses the following conventions when it explains how to do something on your computer:

+ *Italic type* introduces new technical terms.

+ **Bold type** indicates a new section of code that has been introduced into an existing code listing, or something you should type.

+ Monospace font is for output you see on your computer.

+ Keystroke combinations are separated by plus signs (+). For example, Ctrl+Alt+Del means "press the Ctrl, Alt, and Delete keys together."

+ When using the mouse, assuming you're right-handed, the term *click* refers to pressing the left mouse button once. The term *double-click* refers to pressing the left mouse button twice. The term *right-click* refers to pressing the right mouse button once. The term *drag* refers to holding down the left mouse button and pulling the pointer to where you want it to be. If you are left-handed, adjust these instructions to match your mouse setup.

The companion Web site

Be sure to visit the companion Web site for this book at `http://www.wiley.com/compbooks/mcgovern`, where you can download code listings and program examples covered in this book. These are also available at `http://www.j2eebible.com`.

Disclaimer

Any source code shown in the examples is free, and you may use it as your heart desires, with the sole restriction that you may not claim you are the author. Neither the publisher, the authors, or their respective employers provide any form of warranty on the code contained within this book, nor do they guarantee its usefulness for any particular purpose.

The author team and editors have worked long hours to bring you a comprehensive guide to J2EE. If you find any mistakes in this book, we would appreciate your contacting us at our respective e-mail addresses. We equally appreciate any comments, suggestions, praise, or letters of admiration you have for this book.

This book will use for its examples a fictitious airline company and magazine publisher. Any example companies, organizations, products, domain names, e-mail addresses, people, places, and events depicted in these examples are fictitious. No association with any real company, organization, product, domain name, e-mail address, person, place, or events is intended or should be inferred.

Introduction

✦ ✦ ✦ ✦

In This Part

Chapter 1
Understanding Java
and the J2EE Platform

Chapter 2
Reviewing XML
Fundamentals

Chapter 3
Introducing
Application Servers

Chapter 4
Understanding
Remote Method
Invocation

✦ ✦ ✦ ✦

Understanding Java and the J2EE Platform

◆ ◆ ◆ ◆

In This Chapter

Reviewing a brief
history of Java

Understanding J2SE

Examining the
origin of J2EE

Working with
the Model-View-
Controller (MVC)

Understanding
the J2EE APIs

Discovering what's
new in J2EE 1.4

Looking toward
the future of J2EE

Understanding the
Java Community
Process

◆ ◆ ◆ ◆

Java 2 Enterprise Edition, or J2EE, is a package of specifications aligned to enable the development of multi-tier enterprise applications. The specifications outline the various components needed within a J2EE enterprise system, the technologies for accessing and providing services, and even the roles played during the development, deployment, and runtime lifecycle. The combination of these specifications introduced faster and more streamlined development processes, to the software industry, that have been mapped onto common software methodologies such as RUP, XP, and others.

J2EE has fast become the *de facto* standard for developing and deploying enterprise systems. It represents Sun's attempt to take their Java mantra of "Write Once, Run Anywhere" to the next level and make it "Write Once, Deploy Anywhere." While using it is not as easy as dropping new code fragments into existing code, J2EE has made significant strides in easing the burden on the developers and deployers of a system.

This chapter will introduce J2EE. At the time of this writing J2EE 1.4 is in beta but it should be in public release by the time this book is published.

Reviewing a Brief History of Java

In 1995, Sun released Java, a fully object-oriented programming language. While most of the concepts within Java were not new, it did meld many features, such as memory management and garbage collection from Smalltalk and the syntax of C/C++, into a new easy-to-learn programming language.

Java brought the concept of a virtual machine into the mainstream. Traditionally, programs written in a particular language, such as C, were compiled directly for the operating system on which the program would run. In order for companies to support multiple-target runtime environments, a new build environment became necessary for each target—for example, Windows95, HP-UX, Solaris, and so on. However, Java is not compiled completely, but instead is compiled to an intermediary stage as Java bytecodes. At runtime, the Java bytecodes are executed within a *virtual machine*, which is a piece of software that interprets the bytecodes in runtime into the native binary for the operating system.

The virtual machine is responsible for allocating and releasing memory, ensuring security, and optimizing the execution of the Java bytecodes, among other functions. This has indeed created a new market simply for virtual machines for various operating systems. As long as a virtual machine is available for a particular operating system, the Java bytecodes should be able to be executed on it, assuming that all the Java APIs are implemented. Figure 1-1 shows the stages that Java code must go through before being executed on a target machine.

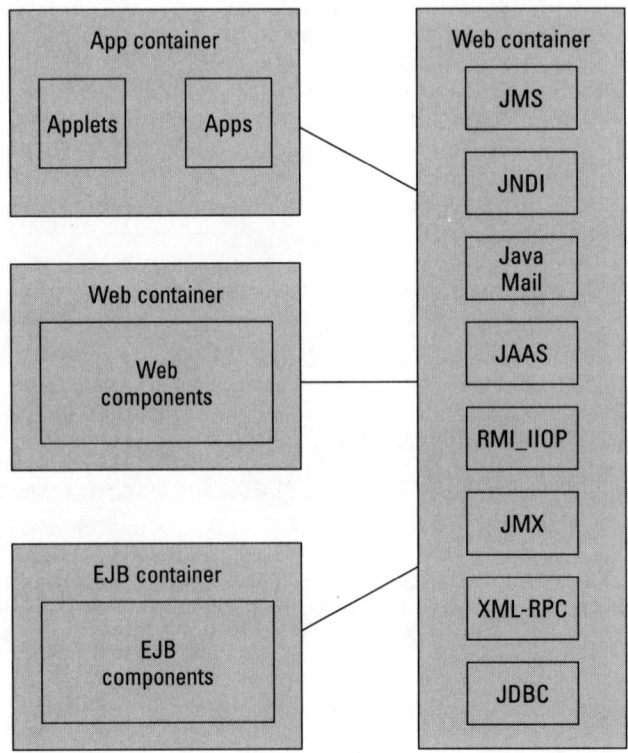

* Not all APIs shown

Figure 1-1: Java Virtual Machine compilation

Understanding J2SE

Around 1998, Sun updated the Java specification and introduced Java 1.2 along with the accompanying libraries, making Java not only a language, but also a platform — Java 2 Standard Edition (J2SE). Prior to the release of J2SE, Java had gone through the number of revisions and new libraries were not necessarily introduced in a concerted manner, making it difficult for developers to understand. Prior to the J2SE, the Java Development Kit (JDK) was the primary package that was installed, and developers would choose which additional libraries they would want such as Java Database Connectivity (JDBC) or Swing. This led to inconsistent environments making it difficult to port code since the deploying party would not be guaranteed of the libraries on the deployment platform.

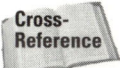 **Cross-Reference**　　JDBC is the topic of Chapter 18.

With J2SE, Sun attempted to fix the problem by bundling the various libraries into a single unit. J2SE provided libraries for GUI support, networking, database access, and more. J2SE is also the foundation for the J2EE.

Examining the Origin of (J2EE)

J2SE was sufficient for developing stand-alone applications, but what was missing was a standard way to develop and deploy enterprise applications — one similar to the standard method for using the Common Object Request Broker Architecture (CORBA). While J2SE already included enterprise-level APIs such as Remote Method Invocations (RMI), too much was still left undefined — such as persistence, transaction management, security, and so on. This resulted in a plethora of architectures being developed.

J2EE, introduced in 1998, defines a multi-tier architecture for enterprise information systems (EIS). By defining the way in which multi-tier applications should be developed, J2EE reduces the costs, in both time and money, of developing large-scale enterprise systems. Figure 1-2 illustrates the J2EE architecture, highlighting the new additions within the 1.4 release.

The J2EE platform specifies the logical application components within a system and defines the roles played in the development process.

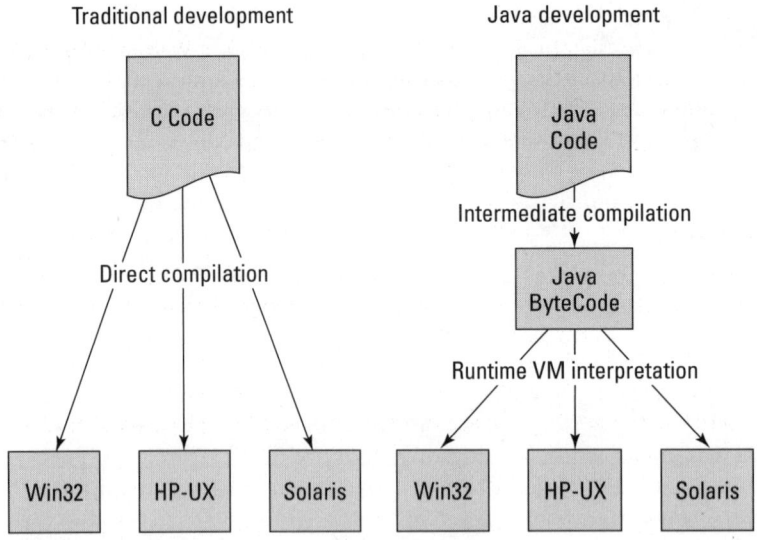

Figure 1-2: J2EE Architecture (source: Javasoft)

Application components

Four application components are defined within the J2EE platform. They are as follows:

✦ Application clients (Standalone Java clients)

✦ Applets (Java code which executes within a browser)

✦ Web components (JSPs, Servlets)

✦ Server components (EJBs, J2EE API implementations)

A product does not need to support all types of components; the norm is to provide an implementation to support a particular component type. However, all components are similar in that they run within a *container*. The container is responsible for providing the runtime environment, the mechanism for identifying and understanding the file formats used for deployment, and the standard services for application components to use.

The four application components are discussed in the following sections.

Application clients

Clients are generally stand-alone applications written in Java. They run within a virtual machine and can use the J2EE standard services to access components located within another tier. The J2EE standard services are usually provided on the client via an installation of J2SE, or along with the distribution of the application itself.

Applets

Applets are similar to application clients, but execute within a Web browser. Initially applets garnered extensive attention, as they were seen as a means of making Web pages more dynamic. Most Web browsers have an embedded Java Virtual Machine (JVM); however, the Java plugin can be used to force the browser to use a particular version of JVM.

Web components

Although the term can be misleading, Web components do not execute on the client side. Web components are server-side components, generally used to provide the presentation layer to be returned to a client. Two types of Web components exist: Java Server Pages (JSPs) and Java servlets. Very basically, JSPs are similar to regular HTML pages but contain embedded Java code while Java servlets are Java classes that use Java's I/O application programming interfaces (APIs) to output HTML to the client. Both JSPs and servlets can be used to output other format types.

Server components

Server components come in the form of Enterprise JavaBeans (EJBs). EJBs execute within a container that manages the runtime behavior of the EJB. EJBs are usually where the business logic for an enterprise system resides.

Roles

The *roles* specified within the J2EE are those played during the development and deployment cycles of an enterprise application. While the roles are distinct, in reality multiple roles tend to be filled by the same organization. The following roles are discussed in this section:

- ✦ J2EE product provider
- ✦ Application component provider
- ✦ Application assembler
- ✦ Deployer
- ✦ System administrator
- ✦ Tool provider
- ✦ System component provider

The J2EE product provider

A J2EE product provider is a company that provides a product that implements a part of the J2EE specification. For example, one company may provide a product that implements the J2EE container for EJBs, and another may provide a product that provides an implementation for a JMS server.

The application component provider

An application component provider is a developer who creates a component that is intended to reside within one of the J2EE containers. The application component provider develops application components adhering to the J2EE API specifications with the intention that the component will be deployed within a J2EE Server. This enables a developer to select a different J2EE product provider without modifying the component. Application component providers develop a range of components, including EJBs, HTML pages, and other Web components.

The application assembler

An application assembler generally uses various application components to create a single application for distribution. Generally, in a large project, one team will be responsible for developing the Web components, another for the business-logic components, and perhaps another for the data-object components. The application assembler would package the various components and then distribute them as an enterprise archive (.ear) file.

The deployer

The deployment of an enterprise application nearly always requires a different configuration for each rollout. J2EE has taken this into consideration by specifying the role of deployer. The deployer is responsible for configuring the applications developed by the application assembler for execution within a platform provided by the J2EE product provider.

The system administrator

A *system administrator* generally uses tools provided by a tool provider to monitor the runtime environment and to ensure that services are performing optimally. Various tools are available on the market, ranging from those which allow for monitoring the system as a whole, to runtime inspection on individual services to help determine where bottlenecks may reside.

The tool provider

The J2EE specification also provides tools to make development easier and to monitor the runtime environment. Tools vary from integrated development environments to runtime-performance products.

The system-component provider

Many system components are available for the J2EE architecture. The J2EE architecture provides ways to introduce these new components for accessing services such as existing messaging systems, transaction services, and others, such as billing systems that may be industry-specific. Using the connector architecture is one way to introduce these new components.

In addition to specifying the lifecycle roles, the J2EE also recommends the usage of the model-view-controller (MVC) design pattern to ease the burden on developing long-lived applications.

Working with the Model-View-Controller

The MVC paradigm provides a pattern for separating the presentation logic (view), business logic (control), and data objects (model). J2EE's architecture maps onto the MVC nicely. Typically, entity beans are used to provide the model logic, while a mix of entity beans and session beans are used to provide the control logic, and Web components are used to implement both control and presentation logic. In practice, however, the separation of the three types of logic is not as distinct, and additional patterns are often needed to support the development cycle. Figure 1-3 shows how the three different logical functional blocks work together.

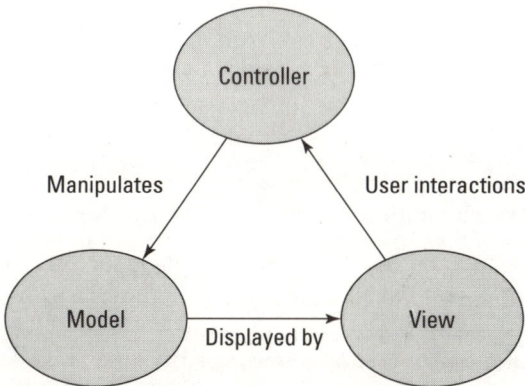

Figure 1-3: MVC pattern

Sun has provided guidelines in the form of Java BluePrints. A sample application, Java Adventure Builder, has been developed specifically for J2EE 1.4 and you can download it from http://www.javasoft.com.

The model

The *M* in MVC refers to the data object model. For example, in an airline ticketing service you may have the concept of a booking, which in the real world is represented by a paper ticket. The model deals with issues such as how the booking is represented within the software system, where it is persisted, and how it is accessed. For example, the booking may be held within a relational database within a table named Bookings with the fields `PassengerName`, `DepartureCity`, `DestinationCity`, `TravelDate`, and `DepartureTime`. This data may be accessed via JDBC using Entity Beans (which we will discuss in detail later in the chapter).

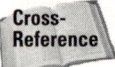

Cross-Reference   Entity beans and JDBC are discussed in Chapters 16 and 18, respectively.

The view

The view is responsible for presentation issues. It handles how the client will see the application, and so HTML issues are usually dealt with here. However, other markup languages such as Wireless Markup Language (WML) and Extensible Markup Language (XML) are increasingly being used to support more varied types of clients. The Booking example may be displayed in various ways. For example, on a wireless device only the most relevant information might be displayed due to the limited screen size. In fact, the term *view* may be misleading, implying that it is meant for visual display only; the view may also be used to present the model via an audio interface if desired. The method in which the model is presented is abstracted from the underlying data.

The control

The control part of the paradigm deals with the business logic of the application. It handles how and when a client interacting with the view is able to access the model. The control layer usually interacts with authorization and authentication services, other J2EE services, and external systems to enforce the business rules to be applied to the application. In our Booking example, the control would determine whether the view can actually display the model. This may be based on whether the user is logged in, if he or she has appropriate authorization and so on. It would also hold the business logic of what to do if the user attempts to view a booking that no longer exists — for example, should an error be presented to the user? Should the user be prompted with a screen asking for additional information? These are rules that change within the business but they do not necessarily force a change on the view or model.

To support the MVC, the J2EE architecture also provides a varied set of APIs to help facilitate the separation between the model, view, and control functional blocks within an application.

Understanding J2EE APIs

The J2EE specification stipulates a number of different APIs, not all of which are mandatory for every application component type. In some cases, for example the Java Database Connectivity (JDBC) API, the API may only be mandatory for the some components, while other APIs may be optional for all components.

The J2EE specifies a set of standard services, which are listed in the next section with an accompanying chart. The standard services have been used within other APIs, such as EJB, JSP, and Java servlets.

J2EE standard services

Included in the J2EE are the following standard services. Some of these services are provided by J2SE, while others are termed "optional packages," meaning that they are optional within a J2SE implementation, but not within a J2EE implementation.

✦ **HyperText Transfer Protocol/HyperText Transfer Protocol Secure sockets (HTTP/HTTPS)** — Both of these protocols must be supported by J2EE servers.

✦ **Java Transaction API (JTA) 1.0** — JTA provides an interface for demarcating transactions. It enables the developer to attach transaction-processing systems.

✦ **Remote Method Invocation to Internet Inter-ORB Protocol (RMI-IIOP)** — EJB components use this service for communication. The underlying IIOP protocol can be used to access compliant CORBA objects residing in external systems.

✦ **Java Database Connectivity (JDBC) 3.0** — JDBC provides a Java interface for executing SQL statements without understanding the specifics of the underlying data store. JDBC 3.0 merged with the previously optional JDBC Extension package.

✦ **Java Message Service (JMS) 1.1** — JMS is an asynchronous messaging service that enables the user to send and receive messages via point-to-point or publish-subscribe models.

✦ **JavaMail 1.3** — JavaMail enables the delivery and retrieval of e-mail via message transports and message stores, respectively.

✦ **Java Naming and Directory Interface (JNDI) 1.2** — JNDI is used to access directories such as Lightweight Directory Access Protocol (LDAP). Typically, components use the API to obtain references to other components.

✦ **JavaBeans Activation Framework (JAF) 1.0** — JavaMail uses JAF to handle various different Multipurpose Internet Mail Extensions (MIME) types that may be included within an e-mail message. It converts MIME byte streams into Java objects that can than be handled by assigned JavaBeans.

✦ **Java API for XML Parsing (JAXP) 1.2** — JAXP includes both Simple API for XML (SAX) and Document Object Model (DOM) APIs for manipulating XML documents. The JAXP API also enables Extensible Stylesheet Language Transformation (XSLT) engines to be plugged in.

✦ **J2EE Connector Architecture 1.5** — The connector architecture specifies a mechanism by which to attach new resource adaptors to a J2EE server. Resource adaptors can be used to provide access to services that are not specified through other APIs.

✦ **Security Services** — These are provided via Java Authentication and Authorization Service (JAAS) 1.0, which allows J2EE servers to control access to services.

✦ **Web Services** — Support for Web services is provided via Simple Object Access Protocol (SOAP) for attachments; API for Java (SAAJ) 1.1 for handling of SOAP messages; Java API for XML Registries (JAXR) 1.0 for access to Universal Description, Discovery, and Integration (UDDI); and Java API for XML-based RPC (JAX-RPC) 1.0 to specify how clients can use Web services.

✦ **Management** — The Java 2 Platform, Enterprise Edition Management API 1.0, and Java Management Extensions (JMX) 1.2 are used to provide management support for querying a server during runtime.

✦ **Deployment** — The Java 2 Platform, Enterprise Edition Deployment API 1.1 allows tools to plug into a J2EE server for deployment purposes.

✦ **Java Authorization Service Provider Contract for Containers (JACC) 1.0** — JACC is the interface between application servers and authorization policy providers.

Table 1-1 gives a list of the various J2EE Standard Services APIs and indicates which APIs are required for each component type.

Table 1-1
J2EE Standard Services APIs

Standard Service	Version	App Client	Web	EJB
HTTP/HTTPS	1.0, SSL 3.0, TLS 1.0	Required	Required	Required
JTA	1.0	Not Required	Required	Required
RMI-IIOP		Required	Required	Required
JDBC	3.0	Required	Required	Required
JMS	1.1	Required	Required	Required
JavaMail	1.3	Required	Required	Required
JNDI	1.2	Required	Required	Required
JAF	1.0	Required	Required	Required
JAXP	1.2	Required	Required	Required
Connecture Architecture	1.5	Not Required	Required	Required
JAAS	1.0	Required	Required	Required

Standard Service	Version	App Client	Web	EJB
SAAJ	1.2	Required	Required	Required
JAXR	1.0	Required	Required	Required
JAX-RPC	1.1	Required	Required	Required
JMX	1.2	Required	Required	Required
JACC	1.0	Not Required	Required	Required

Application component APIs

The standard services described in the previous section are used to provide additional J2EE application-component specifications as Web and server components. The following is a list of the application component APIs specified in J2EE.

✦ **Enterprise JavaBeans (EJB) 2.1** — EJBs are similar to CORBA components and typically encapsulate business-logic code or data-model code. They execute within a container, which manages their interactions with other components, including resources and security. Three different types of EJBs exist:

- Entity beans

- Message-driven beans

- Session beans, which come in two flavors — either stateless or stateful.

✦ **Java Servlet 2.4** — Servlets are classes that reside on the server and are typically used to respond to incoming requests via HTTP. They are often used to return the presentation layer to a client.

✦ **JavaServer Pages (JSP) 2.0** — JSP pages are very similar to HTML pages, except that they have embedded Java code. The pages are parsed and executed on the server prior to being returned to the requesting client. JSPs can make use of additional APIs, such as JSP tag extensions, to allow for more complex logic.

 **Note**   Not all of the preceding APIs will be discussed in this book, as many of them are fairly straightforward.

Discovering What's New in J2EE 1.4

Version 1.4 introduces significant improvements in J2EE's support for Web services and XML. Until now J2EE lagged behind the recently introduced Microsoft .NET, which provided extensive support for XML from its initial release in 2000. However,

J2EE 1.4 has dramatically changed that with the introduction of XML-RPC, JAXR, SAAJ, and modifications within the Enterprise JavaBeans (EJB) specification, as well as with the manner in which new libraries are deployed. XML and support for Web services are now an integral part of J2EE, providing another level of abstraction for the decoupling of systems.

In addition, J2EE 1.4 has improved tools support via the J2EE Management and J2EE Deployment APIs, and many of the other individual APIs have been enhanced as well. The following chapters will discuss the various APIs and their capabilities in greater detail.

Looking toward the Future of J2EE

Java has progressed incredibly since its inception, as has J2EE. While the needs of today and those of the near future are being met by the current release of J2EE, it is not complete, nor will it ever be. Like all enterprise systems, J2EE is constantly evolving.

Some of the innovations planned for the future are an XML data-binding API, enhanced security APIs, support for JDBC RowSets, and more. For a full list of potential future enhancements, review "Future Directions" in the specification document. Alternatively, you can follow the Java Community Process, which is discussed next.

Understanding the Java Community Process (JCP)

The JCP is an initiative similar to a standardization body, put in place by Sun to allow for an unbiased approach to the development of Java. While it is not an official standards body, it is open to the public. All the Java APIs, along with the various distributions (J2EE, J2SE, and J2ME), are covered with the JCP.

Generally, the process works as follows:

1. A member (or group of members) within the JCP submits a Java Specification Request (JSR) which requests either a new specification or modifications to an existing one.

2. Following the acceptance of the JSR by the JCP, an expert group is formed and specification development begins.

3. Final acceptance of the specification is made via a vote by an executive committee.

The JCP Web site lists over 500 members working on 90 outstanding JSRs as of the start of 2003. If you would like to be a part of the ongoing development of Java, sign up and start contributing to one of the existing JSRs at `http://www.jcp.org`.

Summary

This chapter has given a brief introduction to Java and to the J2EE platform. It is by no means exhaustive but is more intended to give a basic grasp of the concepts. You learned about Java and the Java Virtual Machine. You took a look at the evolution of the Java platform from J2SE to J2EE and examined the various component types within the J2EE architecture. Using this information, you will be able to take advantage of the following chapters, which will discuss the various APIs and their usage in greater detail.

✦   ✦   ✦

Reviewing XML Fundamentals

✦ ✦ ✦ ✦

In This Chapter

Explaining XML

Understanding XML
document structure

Examining
XML parsers

Implementing
XML DTDs

Understanding
XML namespaces

Exploring
XML schemas

Working with
eXtensible Stylesheet
Language
Transformations
(XSLT)

Introducing J2EE
XML-based APIs

✦ ✦ ✦ ✦

One of the most significant recent additions to J2EE is its support for Web services and its integration of the eXtensible Markup Language (XML) to facilitate faster development of enterprise applications. To support Web services, new application-programming interfaces (APIs) such as Java API for XML-based Remote Procedure Calls (JAX-RPC) have been added. This chapter will briefly discuss the history and structure of XML. It will introduce key concepts such as DTDs, XML Schemas, and XML Namespaces. It will also give examples of how to use XML efficiently.

Within this chapter, we will touch on some of the applications of XML, going into greater detail in other parts of this book. We will see that XML is a very flexible yet simple technology that is well suited for electronic data interchange due to its characteristics of being extensible and easy to use.

Explaining XML

XML was accepted as a standard by the World Wide Web Consortium (W3C) in 1996 and was immediately heralded as the wave of the future. This was because of its promise to improve the Web experience by replacing HTML with XML, making it possible to improve its presentation and redefine the way in which documents and data were exchanged. In the initial days, XML was primarily used as a more flexible markup language for use in Web pages; however, as developers familiarized themselves with XML and its related technologies, a whole host of new uses such as database manipulation, configuration manipulation, and service description have been presented.

While XML is helping to revolutionize the software industry by introducing a new document exchange format, it is a relatively simple technology. However its terminology is beginning to be misused; for example, XSLT, which is an application of XML, is sometime compared directly with XML itself. That, along with new functionality such as XML-Schema or XML Namespaces continuously being introduced to fulfill XML's promise, can make the task of fully grasping XML a seemingly daunting task.

XML has its roots in the *Standard Generalized Markup Language* (SGML) and *Hypertext Markup Language* (HTML). SGML was the industry's first standardized markup language, but it was far too complex and did not get widespread acceptance since the required supporting software tended to be expensive. XML represented a concerted effort to take the best principles from SGML and develop a simpler and more generic markup language. The basic concept of XML is to use *tags* similar to the markup tags used in HTML, to identify data in order to make it easier for another application to understand the context of the data. Unlike HTML, XML's flexibility allows for the tagging of any type of data.

If you have ever written an HTML document, you have also written an XML document. Unlike HTML documents, though, XML documents must adhere strictly to the rules, which we will discuss in this chapter. To begin with, let's look at two of the most important restrictions on XML documents. First, all XML documents must be *well formed*. Next, they must be *valid*.

Well-formed XML

A well-formed XML document is simply one that is correct syntactically and that contains tags that are used properly. Here's an example:

```
<myXML>
  <nestedTag>
    contained content
  </nestedTag>
</myXML>
```

For example, use of correct case, correct nesting, and the presence of start and end tags account for a well-formed XML document. XML documents must always be well formed. An XML browser will only be able to view an XML document if no syntactical errors are present; this forces developers to produce higher-quality documents.

Valid XML

An XML document is said to be valid if it follows the rules laid out by the Document Tag Definition (DTD) or XML Schema for that document. (We will discuss DTDs and XML-Schemas later in this chapter.) These rules specify which tags can be used and what type of content they may contain. Before taking a more detailed look at how XML is structured, let's take a look at how HTML handles these issues.

In HTML, the schema for HTML would be the HTML language definition itself. Unfortunately, HTML browsers are lax in their enforcement of HTML guidelines, thus perpetuating lazy development. This has led to poorly developed HTML containing tags that are neither valid nor well formed. Listing 2-1 provides an example of a bad HTML page.

Listing 2-1: **An example of bad HTML**

```
<html>
Hello, this is my <b><i>web page</b></i><br>
And this is a tag that will be ignored. <myTAG>
</body>
</HTML>
```

The preceding HTML code will display in your browser without any problems, but you can see that it contains a tag called <myTAG> that is not a valid tag within HTML. More seriously, it does not have a beginning <body> tag.

Listing 2-2 gives an example of a well-formed HTML document; however, it is still lacking.

Listing 2-2: **A well-formed HTML document**

```
<html>
<head
  ><title>A better HTML page</title>
</head>

<body>
Hello, this is my <b><i>web page</i></b><br>
And this is a tag that will still be ignored. <myTAG>

</body>
</html>
```

The preceding HTML example still has a lot wrong with it, including that it does not separate presentation logic from content logic. In fact, HTML does not provide the ability to convey the context of content. In Listing 2-2 the text contained within the ... tags will be presented in bold. However, the actual meaning of that content is not conveyed

In addition, HTML is not extensible (meaning that new tags cannot be defined and introduced into the document). In Listing 2-1 and Listing 2-2 the HTML browser ignored the `<myTAG>` element. Typically, HTML browsers will ignore tags that they do not understand. This may not be too serious in HTML; however, for document exchange within more complex and critical systems, it could have disastrous effects. Now that we have taken a look at the limitations of HTML, let's consider the structure of an XML document.

Understanding XML Document Structure

XML documents consist of several elements that are similar to the tags used to make up an HTML document. These elements are used to provide context to the information that they surround. XML documents can be developed to be *document-centric*, meaning that they are intended to be used by humans. However, XML documents can also be *data-centric*, meaning that they are intended to be used by another application and will generally contain data extracted from a database or data that will be submitted to an API.

XML documents consist of the three following components:

- ✦ Prologue
- ✦ Elements
- ✦ Attributes

Prologue

Usually XML documents begin with a *prologue* like the following:

```
<? xml version="1.0" encoding="UTF-8"?>
```

The prologue, always enclosed within angle brackets (<>), declares the version of XML being used (the current version is 1.0) and the encoding standard. If the prologue is not present, the defaults (XML version 1.0 and an encoding standard of UTF-8) are assumed; however, for interoperability purposes you should always included the prologue. The prologue is the only element that has a slightly different syntax from the others: It begins with a question mark (?).

Elements

The rest of an XML document is made up of a sequence of *elements*. Typically an XML element will have the following format:

```
<element_tag_name attribute1_name="attribute_value"
attribute2_na...>element_content</element_tag_name>
```

Elements may contain either data or other nested elements; however, note that unlike in HTML documents, in XML documents all element tags must have a closing tag. Thus the HTML tags for a line break, `<BR>`, and for a horizontal line, `<HR>` would not be valid by themselves; they need to be closed with `</BR>` or `</HR>` respectively. However, if no content needs to be enclosed, the start and end tags may be compressed as `<BR/>` or `<HR/>`.

Attributes

Within the element tag declaration it is also possible to include *attributes* that may be used to further qualify the tag. Unlike in HTML, in XML the possible attributes and their values can be defined in an accompanying DTD or schema. (DTDs and schemas are covered later in this chapter.) Also, in XML documents tag and attribute definitions are case-sensitive. Thus `<important>` and `<IMPORTANT>` are viewed as different tags in XML because they are different cases. Let's now take a look at how XML documents are processed.

Examining XML Parsers

Much as HTML is parsed within an HTML browser, XML is parsed by a piece of software called an *XML parser* (sometimes referred to as an *XML processor*). The functionality required of an XML parser has been defined by the W3C, so it is fairly easy to swap among different parsers. Basically, an XML parser provides an application with access to the elements within a document, thus becoming the link between the document and the application. The parser is responsible for making sure that the XML document is well formed and (optionally) if it is valid.

Figure 2-1 provides a high-level overview of the processing of an XML document. An XML document along with its associated schema is input into an XML parser. The parser checks that the document is well formed and, if the schema is also available, checks that the XML is valid according to what has been defined in the schema. Because the schema is also an XML document, it is validated recursively against another schema, respectively. The parser then provides access methods for another application to access the data that was contained within the original XML document.

A document can be parsed in one of two ways: via the Document Object Model (DOM) specified by the W3C, or via the Simple API for XML (SAX), which is also popular.

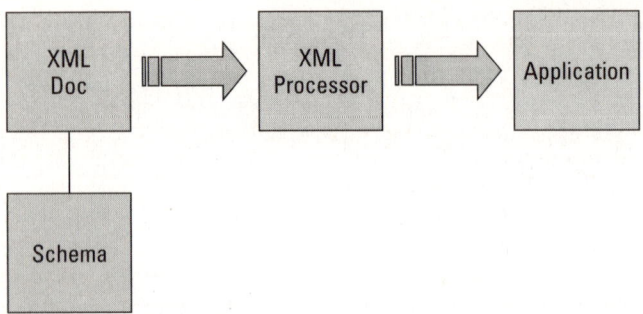

Figure 2-1: XML processing

DOM parsers

A DOM parser reads an entire document at once and holds a corresponding tree-like structure in memory. Each element within the document is a node in the tree. Using the `org.w3c.dom.Node` interface specified by the W3C, another application can traverse or modify the tree. In Figure 2-2, the XML on the left is parsed into memory to have a similar structure tree on the right. The XML is read line by line. The prologue indicates the XML version and the encoding that is being used to process the rest of the document. As the elements are encountered, the processor develops the associated tree. For example, when it encounters the first `<customerName>` tag, it knows that any elements encountered within are children elements until a corresponding `</customerName>` tag is encountered. This document does not have a schema or DTD associated with it, thus the processor will not check for validity. We will see in a later section how we can enforce the validity of a document using a schema or DTD.

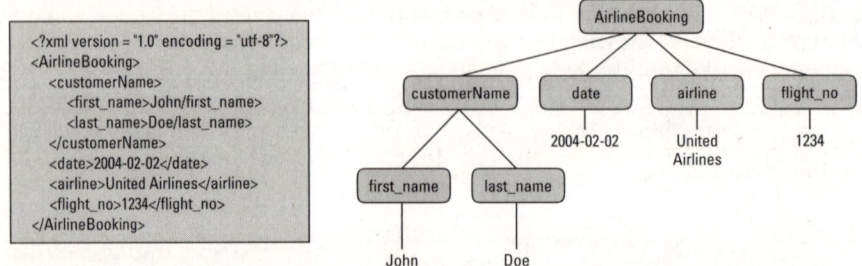

Figure 2-2: A DOM parser's memory structure

SAX parsers

A SAX parser is an event-driven parser. It reads the document sequentially without storing the structure into memory, thus making SAX more efficient than DOM. At the start of the document, the SAX parser begins by making callback functions based on the tags it encounters. Most XML parsers support SAX, although the W3C standards group has not officially accepted it.

In Figure 2-3, the SAX processor issues events for the start and end of the XML document, for the start and end of each tag, and for each piece of character data. In most instances the XML document will also include processing instructions such as namespaces and schema instructions, each of which will also result in a SAX event. In the following example, when the XML document is processed by the SAX parser, an event is triggered by the start of the document, and then for each contained element. The first element encountered is the `<carRental>` tag, which causes a start element event. The corresponding end element tag is not triggered until all of the other elements have been processed and the final element `</carRental>` tag is encountered.

```
<?xml version = "1.0" encoding = "utf-8"?>
<CarRental>
    <customerName>JohnDoe
    </customerName>
    <date>2004-02-02</date>
    <model>Oldsmobile Alero</model>
</CarRental>
```

Start Document
Start Element "CarRental"
Start Element "customerName"
Character Data "John Doe"
End Element "customerName"
Start Element "date"
Character Data "2004-02-02"
End Element "date"
Start Element "model"
Character Data "Oldsmobile Alero"
End Element "model"
End Element "CarRental"
End Document

Figure 2-3: Event sequence via SAX processing

DOM versus SAX

Both DOM and SAX have their benefits and drawbacks. Because DOM stores the structure of the document into memory, it requires more resources and is therefore less efficient; however, it enables easy traversal between elements, making it more suitable than SAX for modifying documents.

SAX, on the other hand, is more lightweight, retaining no memory of the structure of the document; this makes it less memory-intensive. SAX is more suitable than DOM when applications are more concerned with individual elements than with where those elements reside within the document. Choosing a parser is an important decision and the expected needs of the application should be considered wisely.

Note   J2EE provides an API for handling XML parsing in the form of JAXP (Java API for XML Processing), which enables you to use either DOM or SAX.

So far, we have only looked at how to create a well-formed XML document. However, to create a valid XML document, you need to specify a DTD or an XML Schema, which describes the valid tags and their constraints permitted for the accompanying XML document. We will first look at DTDs and compare them with XML Schema.

Implementing XML DTDs

Document Tag Definitions (DTDs) were the initial mechanism defined by the W3C for specifying the validity of an XML document. A corresponding DTD specifies the elements that an XML document may contain — its attributes, child elements, and content type. Prior to XML Schemas, if an XML document did not have a DTD, it would have been up to the consuming application to ensure that the document was valid. This is not a maintainable approach since it would require modification to the consuming application whenever the structure of the XML document would change. With a DTD, the XML parser can check that the corresponding XML is valid, thus reducing the burden on applications.

You can specify a DTD in one of two ways. The first is by defining it within the XML document itself, and the second is by specifying the location of the DTD within the prologue. A DTD for a TravelInformation element might look like this:

```
<!DOCTYPE TravelInformation [
<!ELEMENT TravelInformation (Item+)>
<!ELEMENT Item (CDATA)>
]>
```

The initial tag declares the root element for the document. The enclosing brackets ([ ]) list the possible elements, their attributes, the order and number of allowed occurrences, and the possible values. In the preceding example, the first element is stated to be TravelInformation and it must include at least one Item element. The plus (+) character denotes that the Item element must be present. An asterisk (*) would denote that the corresponding element could occur any number times (including none), and a question mark (?) would denote that it could occur only either zero or one times. The following table summarizes these special characters:

Special Character	Effect on Preceding Element D
+	Must occur at least once
*	May occur any amount of times (including zero)
?	May only appear zero or one times

The keyword CDATA specifies that the element data may be any character data. The other possible values that a tag may specify for the data enclosed are #PCDATA (parsed character data), which allows any character data other than markup or special characters, or the tag may specify that another element can be contained as the TravelInformation tag declared.

Attributes may also be declared by means of the following syntax:

```
<!ATTLIST element-name attribute-name attribute-type
default-value>
```

The default value can be specified to have a value, to require that it must be given by the producer of the XML document, or to be a fixed value. In the current example we could specify an attribute for the Item element as follows:

```
<!ATTLIST Item status (confirmed|paid) "confirmed">
```

This declaration specifies that the status attribute must be present with a value of confirmed or paid. If the author of the XML page does not explicitly include the attribute, a default value of confirmed will be included by the DTD.

In order to internally specify the DTD, we can list the DTD specification directly into the XML document as shown in Listing 2-3.

Listing 2-3: **TravelInfo_InternalDTD.xml**

```
<?xml version="1.0" encoding="UTF-8"?>
<!DOCTYPE TravelInformation [
<!ELEMENT TravelInformation (Item+)>
<!ELEMENT Item (#PCDATA)>
<!ATTLIST Item status (confirmed|paid) "confirmed">
]>

<TravelInformation>
  <Item>
...
  </Item>
  <Item status="paid">
  ...
  </Item>
</TravelInformation>
```

As you can see, in the preceding example only the second Item element declares the status attribute; however, when you view the document in a browser the status attribute for the first Item element will be included with a default value of confirmed.

To externally specify the DTD, modify the document-type tag element at the beginning of the XML document to what you see in Listing 2-4, where `TravelInformation.dtd` is the name of the file that contains the remaining DTD. That DTD appears in Listing 2-5.

Listing 2-4: **TravelInfo_External.xml**

```
<?xml version="1.0" encoding="UTF-8"?>
<!DOCTYPE TravelInformation SYSTEM "TravelInformation.dtd">
<TravelInformation>
  <Item>
    ...
  </Item>
  <Item status="paid">  ...
  </Item>
</TravelInformation>
```

Listing 2-5: **TravelInformation.dtd**

```
<?xml version="1.0" encoding="UTF-8"?>
<!ELEMENT TravelInformation (Item+)>
<!ELEMENT Item (#PCDATA)>
  <!ATTLIST Item
  status (confirmed | paid) "confirmed"
>
```

The preceding examples should give you a beginner's grasp of using DTDs; after playing around a bit you will see how they are lacking. DTDs grew from SGML, but the limitation of using DTDs in XML was quickly evident. The primary limitation is that DTDs require XML parsers to understand a second syntax because DTDs are not specified in XML. In addition, DTDs do not support namespaces very well. Enter XML schemas. However, before we look at XML Schemas, let's take a look at namespaces.

Understanding XML Namespaces

Namespaces are similar to those in C++ or packages within Java. They provide a way to distinguish among tags in order to make them globally unique. For example, imagine the airline-ticket example from the DOM parser section earlier in this chapter. We also have another travel plan for a car rental, and both reservations may need to be included in an overall itinerary that uses the TravelInformation schema. Because the Item tag allows any character data to be included we can embed our AirlineBooking and CarRental XML element examples from the XML Parser section within it.

The code shown in Listing 2-6 may be used to deliver a message between systems in order to relay all reservations.

Listing 2-6: **Delivering the message**

```
<?xml version="1.0" encoding="utf-8"?>
<TravelInformation>
  <Item>
    <AirlineBooking>
      <customerName>John Doe</customerName>
      <date>2004-02-02</date>
      <airline>United Airlines</airline>
      <flight_no>1234</flight_no>
    </AirlineBooking>
  </Item>
  <Item>
    <CarRental>
      <customerName>John Doe</customerName>
      <date>2003-02-02</date>
      <model>Oldsmobile Alero</model>
    </CarRental>
  </Item>
</TravelInformation>
```

The problem with this is that it provides no way for the receiving application to distinguish which tags are for which reservation. For example, customerName and date appear within both AirlineBooking and CarRental. If we add the tag <notes> to both Item and AirlineBooking, the problem will be compounded since there will now be a tag with the same name in two different locations of the document and there is no way for the processing application to distinguish between them when they are encountered. Listing 2-7 shows the new XML document with the new <notes> tag entered in the two different locations.

Listing 2-7: **The new XML document**

```
<?xml version="1.0" encoding="UTF-8"?>
<TravelInformation>
  <Item>
    <note>A note added to the Item tag</note>
```

Continued

Listing 2-7 *(continued)*

```
    <AirlineBooking>
      <customerName>John Doe</customerName>
      <date>2004-02-02</date>
      <airline>United Airlines</airline>
      <flight_no>1234</flight_no>
      <note>A note for the AirlineBooking tag</note>
   </AirlineBooking>
  </Item>
  <Item>
    <CarRental>
      <customerName>John Doe</customerName>
      <date>2003-02-02</date>
      <model>Oldsmobile Alero</model>
    </CarRental>
  </Item>
</TravelInformation>
```

Namespaces provide a way to separate tags into groups using Uniform Resource Identifiers (URIs). Namespaces can be identified within the prologue of the document, which allows subsequent tags to make use of them. Using namespaces, we can make the TravelInformation XML document more comprehensible. In Listing 2-8, we have added namespace declarations to distinguish the different tags.

Listing 2-8: **TravelInformationNS.xml**

```
<?xml version="1.0" encoding="UTF-8"?>

<TravelInformation
  xmlns="http://www.j2eebible.com/chap02/TravelInformation"
  xmlns:flight="http://www.j2eebible.com/chap02/Flight"
  xmlns:car="http://www.j2eebible.com/chap02/Car">

  <Item>
    <note>A note added to the Item tag</note>
    <flight:AirlineBooking>
      <flight:customerName>John Doe</flight:customerName>
      <flight:airline>United Airlines</flight:airline>
      <flight:flight_no>1234</flight:flight_no>
      <flight:note>A note for the AirlineBooking tag
      </flight:note>
    </flight:AirlineBooking>
  </Item>
  <Item>
    <note>Another note added to Item</note>
    <car:CarRental>
```

```
        <car:customerName>John Doe</car:customerName>
        <car:date>2003-02-02</car:date>
        <car:model>Oldsmobile Alero</car:model>
      </car:CarRental>
    </Item>
</TravelInformation>
```

The preceding listing contains three namespaces. The first specified namespace, `xmlns="http://www.j2eebible.com/chap02/TravelInformation"` is the default and is not given a name. The other two namespaces are `flight` and `car`. Any tag can specify that it belongs to a particular namespace by prefixing its declaration with the namespace name and a colon. For example, the `AirlineBooking` tag is now prefixed by `flight:`, which indicates that it belongs to that namespace. In the current example it is necessary to explicitly specify that all tags contained within `AirlineBooking` also belong to the `flight` namespace.

An alternate syntax can be used to remove the need to explicitly add the namespace to every tag. Namespaces can be included directly in a tag to specify a different default until the tag has been closed, as shown in Listing 2-9.

Listing 2-9: **TravelInformationNS2.xml**

```
<?xml version="1.0" encoding="UTF-8"?>
<TravelInformation
  xmlns="http://www.j2eebible.com/chap02/TravelInformation">

  <Item>
    <note>A note added to the Item tag</note>
    <AirlineBooking
      xmlns="http://www.j2eebible.com/chap02/Flight">
      <customerName>John Doe</customerName>
      <airline>United Airlines</airline>
      <flight_no>1234</flight_no>
      <note>A note for the AirlineBooking tag
      </note>
    </AirlineBooking>
  </Item>
  <Item>
    <note>Another note added to Item</note>
    <CarRental
      xmlns="http://www.j2eebible.com/chap02/Car">
      <customerName>John Doe</customerName>
      <date>2003-02-02</date>
      <model>Oldsmobile Alero</model>
    </CarRental>
  </Item>
</TravelInformation>
```

The preceding listing may be possible in a scenario in which the application creating the `TravelInformation` document is not the same application that has developed the other documents and does not know about their respective contents or their namespaces. The validation of the individual documents needs to be performed; however, because DTDs do not support namespaces very well, XML Schema is the preferred mechanism for such validation.

Exploring XML Schema

The XML Schema, compared to DTDs, is a more flexible and powerful means of specifying the validity of an XML document. Schemas are superior in part because they are also specified in XML, and thus are extensible. The XML Schema specification is an extremely large and complex specification, and so DTDs continue to be used.

A complete tutorial on XML Schema is beyond the scope of this book. However, we can look at the simple schema shown in Listing 2-10.

Listing 2-10: **SimpleExample.xsd**

```xml
<?xml version="1.0" encoding="UTF-8"?>
<xsd:schema xmlns:xsd="http://www.w3.org/2001/XMLSchema">

<xsd:element name="myTag">
  <xsd:complexType>
    <xsd:sequence>
      <xsd:element name="FirstName" type="xsd:string"/>
      <xsd:element name="LastName" type="xsd:string"/>
    </xsd:sequence>
  </xsd:complexType>
</xsd:element>

  <xsd:annotation>
    <xsd:documentation xml:lang="en">
      This is a simple example of a schema.
    </xsd:documentation>
  </xsd:annotation>
</xsd:schema>
```

The preceding schema is pretty straightforward. Like all XML files, it begins with the prologue declaration. That is immediately followed by the first tag `schema`, prefixed by the namespace `xsd`, which is defined to point at the URI `http://www.w3.org/2001/XMLSchema`. XML Schema defines the `schema` tag, along with all the other tags in the preceding document that are prefixed by `xsd`. The first `xsd:element` tag defines a new tag with the name `myTag` and the first enclosing tag defines it to be of type `complexType`. This means that it is a tag that may hold both other element tags and attributes. The enclosed `xsd:element` tags define simple elements — *simple* meaning that that they cannot contain other element tags or attributes. They must be of one of the data types defined within XML Schema. The most common data types are as follows:

✦ `string`

✦ `normalizedString`

✦ `token`

✦ `byte`

✦ `int`

✦ `long`

✦ `short`

✦ `float`

✦ `double`

✦ `decimal`

✦ `time`

✦ `dateTime`

✦ `date`

The `string` data type is quite useful for enabling the embedding of tags or other XML documents.

The XML Schema data types are far more powerful than those provided in DTDs, in that they enable you to define specific types of character data. In DTDs, for example, the definition `<!ELEMENT date (#PCDATA)>` leaves room for failure in interoperability because the date entry may be given as 2004-04-06, which could mean April 6, 2004 to one application and June 4, 2004 to another. In XML Schema, the format of the `date` data type has been strictly defined as `YYYY-MM-DD`.

Lastly, in the preceding schema example is a new way of inserting comments — by means of the tags `xsd:annotation` and `xsd:documentation`. This mechanism for adding comments is very useful in that it allows XML tools to access the comments as needed.

To use the preceding schema definition in a XML document you can simply add two new attributes to the root element, as shown in Listing 2-11.

Listing 2-11: **SimpleExample.xml**

```xml
<?xml version="1.0" encoding="UTF-8"?>
<myTag
        xmlns:xsi="http://www.w3.org/2001/XMLSchema-instance"

   xsi:noNamespaceSchemaLocation="SimpleExample.xsd">

   <FirstName>John</FirstName>
   <LastName>Doe</LastName>
</myTag>
```

The first added attribute defines a namespace, xsi, associated with http://www.
w3.org/2001/XMLSchema-instance, and then defines the qualified attribute xsi:
noNamespaceSchemaLocation with the schema document simpleExample.xsd. The
declaration noNamespaceSchemaLocation declares that in absence of a namespace,
this schema should be used as the default. Alternatively, you can use the attribute
schemaLocation to associate specific namespaces with different schemas, which
we will demonstrate in Listing 2-12.

Listing 2-12: **TravelInformationSchema.xml**

```xml
<?xml version="1.0" encoding="UTF-8"?>

<TravelInformation
   xmlns="http://www.j2eebible.com/chap02/TravelInformation"
   xmlns:xsi="http://www.w3.org/2001/XMLSchema-instance"
   xsi:noNamespaceSchemaLocation="TravelInformationSchema.xsd">

   <Item>
     <note>A note added to the Item tag</note>
     <AirlineBooking
      xmlns="http://www.j2eebible.com/chap02/AirlineBooking"
      xmlns:xsi="http://www.w3.org/2001/XMLSchema-instance"
      xsi:schemaLocation=
"http://www.j2eebible.com/chap02/AirlineBooking
AirlineBooking.xsd">

         <customerName>John Doe</customerName>
         <airline>United Airlines</airline>
         <flight_no>1234</flight_no>
         <note>A note for the AirlineBooking tag
         </note>
     </AirlineBooking>
   </Item>
```

```
<Item>
  <note>Another note added to Item</note>
  <CarRental
    xmlns="http://www.j2eebible.com/chap02/Car"
    xmlns:xsi="http://www.w3.org/2001/XMLSchema-instance"

xsi:schemaLocation="http://www.j2eebible.com/chap02/CarRental
CarRental.xsd">

    <customerName>John Doe</customerName>
    <date>2003-02-02</date>
    <model>Oldsmobile Alero</model>
  </CarRental>
</Item>

</TravelInformation>
```

Listing 2-12 specifies that the `TravelInformation` namespace is associated with `TravelInformation.xsd`. Listing 2-13 displays `TravelInformation.xsd`.

Listing 2-13: **TravelInformationSchema.xsd**

```
<?xml version="1.0" encoding="UTF-8"?>
<xsd:schema
  xmlns:xsd="http://www.w3.org/2001/XMLSchema"

targetNamespace="http://www.j2eebible.com/chap02/TravelInformat
ion"
  xmlns="http://www.j2eebible.com/chap02/TravelInformation"
  elementFormDefault="qualified">

  <xsd:element name="Item">
    <xsd:complexType mixed="true">
      <xsd:sequence>
        <xsd:any/>
      </xsd:sequence>
      <xsd:attribute name="status" type="xsd:string"
default="confirmed"/>
    </xsd:complexType>
  </xsd:element>

  <xsd:element name="TravelInformation">
    <xsd:complexType>
      <xsd:sequence>
        <xsd:element ref="Item" minOccurs="0"
maxOccurs="unbounded"/>
```

Continued

Listing 2-13 *(continued)*

```
      </xsd:sequence>
    </xsd:complexType>
  </xsd:element>

  <xsd:annotation>
    <xsd:documentation xml:lang="en">
      TravelInformation schema for J2EEBible Chapter.
    </xsd:documentation>
  </xsd:annotation>
</xsd:schema>
```

The XSD in Listing 2-13 describes two different `complexType`s. The first is the `Item` tag. It specifies that it may have any type of content within itself — meaning that it may contain another XML document — and it also specifies that it may include the `status` attribute. The second `complexType` is the `TravelInformation` tag, which is simply defined as an unbounded sequence of `Item` tags.

We have also specified the file for the `http://www.j2eebible.com/chap02/TravelInformation` namespace using the `targetNamespace` keyword.

Working with eXtensible Stylesheet Language Transformations (XSLT)

So far we have not distinguished between documents intended to be read by humans and those developed for machines. If documents are intended to be read by humans, presentation must be considered. XML itself does not necessarily contain any presentation logic. In keeping with the methodology of the model-view-control (MVC) pattern, in which presentation logic is separated from the model and the control logic, the W3C has defined Extensible Stylesheet Language Transformations (XSLT) for presentation.

In the example that we are using of arranging travel schedules, the data are being described without our knowing how it is going to be presented. Depending upon the medium that will be used to view the information (a desktop, PDA, or a mobile phone), the presentation may vary. We can use XSLT to define a *stylesheet* that will make the presentation decisions.

A stylesheet is a document that can be applied to another document to add presentation logic. Within the browser world, Cascading StyleSheets (CSS) has proliferated in order to alter the presentation of HTML pages. Similarly, XSLT can be applied to

XML documents in order to alter their presentation; however, XSLT is far more powerful than CSS. XSLT can be used not only to convey to a browser how to display an XML file, but also to transform an XML document into another XML document altogether. Furthermore, XSLT documents are defined in XML, and therefore can take advantage of all the benefits of XML.

Consider our current example, wherein we have travel details embedded in a single document. The application will need to transform the document so that it can be read by the device requesting it.

XSLT is a great example of the power of XML. An XSLT document has a defined schema and is processed by a specialized XML processor that understands that schema, matching the XSLT tags to instructions for XSLT transformation. While the XSLT specification is far too large to include here, we will step through some basic examples to give you a feel for them.

Producing simple HTML with XSLT

You can apply an XSL file to a document by including a tag of the format

```
<?xml-stylesheet type="text/xsl" href="<docLocation>"?>
```

in the XML document to be transformed. In the preceding code fragment, `<docLocation>` should be replaced by the location of the XSL file. Alternatively, the XSL file can be applied externally.

For example, if you know that the XSL file to be applied will always have the name `TravelInformation.xsl`, you can add the following name to the `TravelInformationSchema.xml` document:

```
<?xml-stylesheet type="text/xsl" href="TravelInformation.xsl"?>
```

This is not to say that the contents of that XSL document cannot change.

For example, `TravelInformation.xsl` may look like Listing 2-14.

Listing 2-14: **TravelInformation.xsl**

```
<?xml version="1.0" encoding="UTF-8"?>
<xsl:stylesheet version="1.0"
xmlns:xsl="http://www.w3.org/1999/XSL/Transform"
xmlns:def="http://www.j2eebible.com/chap02/TravelInformation"
xmlns:car="http://www.j2eebible.com/chap02/CarRental"
xmlns:flight="http://www.j2eebible.com/chap02/AirlineBooking">
  <xsl:output method="html" version="1.0" encoding="UTF-8"/>
```

Continued

Listing 2-14 *(continued)*

```
<xsl:template match="/">
  <html>
    <head>
      <title>XSLT Sample</title>
    </head>
    <body>
      <table border="1" bgcolor="yellow">
        <thead>
          <tr>
            <th>Type</th>
            <th>Date</th>
            <th>Name</th>
            <th>Operator</th>
            <th>Details</th>
          </tr>
        </thead>
        <xsl:apply-templates/>
      </table>
    </body>
  </html>
</xsl:template>
<xsl:template match="car:CarRental">
  <tr>
    <td>Car Rental</td>
    <td><xsl:value-of select="car:date"/></td>
    <td><xsl:value-of select="car:customerName"/></td>
    <td><xsl:value-of select="car:model"/></td>
  </tr>
</xsl:template>
<xsl:template match="flight:AirlineBooking">
  <tr>
    <td>Flight</td>
    <td><xsl:value-of select="flight:date"/></td>
    <td><xsl:value-of select="flight:customerName"/></td>
    <td><xsl:value-of select="flight:airline"/></td>
    <td><xsl:value-of select="flight:flight_no"/></td>
  </tr>
</xsl:template>
<xsl:template match="def:note"/>
</xsl:stylesheet>
```

Like all XML files, the XSL file begins with the prologue declaration, which is followed by `<xsl:stylesheet>`, the first tag specific to XSLT. This is the root tag for XSLT. You can specify other namespaces in addition to `xsl=http://www.w3.org/1999/XSL/Transform` if you know something about the document to be transformed. In this case, you know that three namespaces will be present: the default one from the source XML document, the namespace corresponding to the `CarRental` XML, and the namespace corresponding to the `AirlineBooking` XML. It is only necessary, though, to include the namespaces if you want the XSL document to manipulate the content of the XML.

The `<xsl:output>` tag specifies the output method to be `xml`. Alternatively, the method could have been set to `html`, `text`, or the like. Much like an explicit prologue declaration, the output has been defined to be of version 1.0 with an encoding of UTF-8.

The only other tag embedded within the `xsl:stylesheet` tag is the `xsl:template` tag. Templates contain the core logic for an XSL document. They enable processing based either on encountered tags or on the content embedded within.

The `xsl:template` tag includes a match indicating where to apply the template. In the current example the first template tag contains the phrase `match="/"`, which specifies that the template should be applied to the root. When the XSL processor encounters the `TravelInformation` tag of the XML document being transformed, it realizes that it is the root element and it is matched in the XSL file by the slash (/) qualifier.

The embedded content is then delivered to the output, unless it is a tag belonging to the `xsl` namespace. Tags in the `xsl` namespace are also interpreted to commands by the XSLT processor. The first tag encountered is the `apply-templates` tag. This indicates to the processor that it should apply all the additional templates to the current tag in the original XML document or optionally to a sub-node if the `select` attribute is specified.

In the current example there are three additional templates:

✦ `match="car:CarRental"`

✦ `match="flight:AirlineBooking"`

✦ `match="def:note"`

The original template started the setup of an HTML table. The `CarRental` and `AirlineBooking` templates simply cycle through the contents of the corresponding matching nodes and search for sub-nodes that match the tags specified by the `select` attribute in the `<xsl:value-of...>` tags and processor output their values.

If you view the preceding document within a browser, you will see a simple HTML document with a table listing the two different bookings. The notes will not be displayed because no action will be taken in the corresponding template. Listing 2-15 shows the output of viewing the above XML document with the XSLT directive added.

Listing 2-15: Resulting HTML

```
<html xmlns:car="http://www.j2eebible.com/chap02/CarRental"
xmlns:def="http://www.j2eebible.com/chap02/TravelInformation"
xmlns:flight="http://www.j2eebible.com/chap02/AirlineBooking">
<head>
<META http-equiv="Content-Type" content="text/html;
charset=UTF-8">
<title>XSLT Sample</title></head>
<body><table border="1" bgcolor="blue">
<thead>
<tr><th>Type</th>
<th>Date</th><th>Name</th>
<th>Service Provider</th>
<th>Details</th></tr>
</thead>
<tr><td>Flight</td>
<td>2004-02-02</td>
<td>John Doe</td>
<td>United Airlines</td>
<td>1234</td></tr>
<tr><td>Car Rental</td>
<td>2004-02-02</td>
<td>John Doe</td>
<td>Oldsmobile Alero</td>
</tr>
</table>
</body></html>
```

Note that matches will work for every instance of the expression. For example, in the preceding XSL document, replace the match in the first template with `def:Item`. If you transform the XML document now, you will see that two tables are present in the resulting page — one for each entry in the original document. When it encounters the first `def:Item` tag the XSLT processor outputs the initial table elements, and then matches with the `flight:AirlineBooking` tag with the XSLT's apply-templates tag, completing the first table. When it encounters the second Item tag the processor outputs the second table.

Producing a Wireless Markup Language (WML) Document with XML

The power of XSLT is that it can modify presentation based on the context of the request. For example, if the request for the preceding `TravelInformation` XML were to be made using a mobile phone, the request would need to be formatted with WML in order to be displayed on the device (though if the device were WAP 2.0–compliant, XHTML might make more sense).

Listing 2-16 is an example of an XSL file for transforming TravelInformation into WML.

Listing 2-16: **XSL to produce WML**

```xml
<?xml version="1.0" encoding="UTF-8"?>
<xsl:stylesheet version="1.0"
xmlns:xsl="http://www.w3.org/1999/XSL/Transform"
xmlns="http://http://www.w3.org/TR/xhtml1"
xmlns:def="http://www.j2eebible.com/chap02/TravelInformation"
xmlns:car="http://www.j2eebible.com/chap02/CarRental"
xmlns:flight="http://www.j2eebible.com/chap02/AirlineBooking">
  <xsl:output method="xml" encoding="UTF-8"/>
  <xsl:template match="/">
    <wml>
      <card>Welcome!<br/></card>
    <xsl:apply-templates/>
    </wml>
  </xsl:template>
  <xsl:template match="def:note"/>
  <xsl:template match="car:CarRental">
    <card>
      <b>Car Rental</b>
      <ul>
        <li><b>Date:</b>
            <xsl:value-of select="car:date"/></li>
        <li><b>Name:</b>
            <xsl:value-of select="car:customerName"/></li>
        <li><b>Car Model:</b>
            <xsl:value-of select="car:model"/></li>
      </ul>
    </card>
  </xsl:template>
  <xsl:template match="flight:AirlineBooking">
    <card>
      <b>Flight</b>
      <ul>
        <li><b>Date:</b>
            <xsl:value-of select="flight:date"/></li>
        <li><b>Name:</b>
            <xsl:value-of select="flight:customerName"/>
</li>
        <li><b>Airline:</b>
            <xsl:value-of select="flight:airline"/></li>
        <li><b>Flight Number:</b>
            <xsl:value-of select="flight:flight_no"/></li>
      </ul>
    </card>
  </xsl:template>
</xsl:stylesheet>
```

The preceding XSL is very straightforward. It begins with the prologue and the opening XSL tag `<xsl:stylesheet>`, within which are the necessary namespaces. Following this are the same `xsl:output` and `xsl:template` tags that were in the previous example, with the formatting changed so that WML is created instead of HTML.

When you're applying an XSL, it is important to understand the way in which the XSLT processor will progress through the XML document. In XSLT processing, the order in which the matching occurs can affect the way in which documents are transformed, if the XSL tags are applied in an unexpected order.

The previous two examples are a good introduction to XSLT, but you should be aware that they hardly scratch the surface of its capabilities. For more information on the XSLT spec, visit `http://www.w3.org/Style/XSL/`.

Introducing J2EE XML–Based APIs

A number of Java APIs are available to facilitate the manipulation, development, and usage of XML. Table 2-1 identifies each of them.

Table 2-1 Java XMLAPIs		
API	**Full API Name**	**Description**
JAXP	Java API for XML Processing	JAXP enables the processing of XML documents by either DOM or SAX. It also provides APIs to apply XSL Transformations.
JAXM	Java API for XML Messaging	JAXM is an easy-to-use API that enables you to develop XML-based messages using SOAP.
JAX-RPC	Java API for XML–Remote Procedure Call	JAX-RPC also uses SOAP but specifically for the construction of calls to be made when Web services are being used.
JAXB	Java API XML Binding	JAXB facilitates the development of Java classes to represent XML schemas, making XML documents easier to process.
JAXR	Java API for XML Registries	JAXR makes the deployment and discovery of Web services easier.

Summary

In this chapter we took a look at XML, its origins, and some of its uses. In doing so we contrasted it with HTML and highlighted XML's strict enforcement to be well formed and valid. We provided a brief introduction to DOM and SAX, comparing their uses and their benefits and drawbacks. Key concepts such as DTDs, XML Schemas, and XML Namespaces were introduced in this chapter along with their syntax and application to XML documents.

Finally, we discussed XSLT, a great example of an XML-based application, which allows for transforming XML documents, usually for presentation purposes. You should now be well armed to delve into APIs that utilize XML. Within other chapters in this book, we will take a look at the Java XML APIs in further detail and see how they fit into the J2EE architecture.

✦   ✦   ✦

Introducing Application Servers

In This Chapter

Implementing the
J2EE platform

Understanding
the features of an
application server

Examining full J2EE
implementations

Examining partial
J2EE implementations

Avoiding vendor
lock-in

Discussing the ins and outs of the various APIs within the J2EE platform is all well and good, but at some point someone has to actually do the work and provide the functionality behind the method calls your code so heavily relies on. For example, when your servlet is invoked via its `service()` method, who invokes this call? Who manages the request and response? This is where the application server fits in, providing the housekeeping for your business logic.

By all accounts your firm's choice of application server should not influence your design in the slightest. You should always design for the J2EE platform and resist the urge to use any libraries that may tie you to a particular vendor's platform. That said, sometimes a vendor will offer a very attractive library that you can't resist. While this pretty much ties you to that particular vendor, we'll take a look at a technique that will make this tie less painful and easier to undo should you decide to port to another vendor.

This chapter will explain the role the application server plays in the Java space and the characteristics that define an official J2EE application server.

Implementing the J2EE Platform

The *J2EE platform* is a large collection of APIs, all working together to provide a unified platform for enterprise development.

The J2EE platform consists of various components and services that are available and operate in the following containers:

✦ Applet container

✦ Applet client container

✦ Web container

✦ Enterprise JavaBeans (EJB) container

J2EE components and services are as follows:

✦ Applets

✦ Servlets

✦ JSP (JavaServer Pages)

✦ EJB (Enterprise JavaBeans)

✦ JavaMail

✦ JMS (Java Messaging Service)

✦ Connectors

✦ JMX (Java Management Extensions)

✦ JTA (Java Transaction API)

✦ JNDI (Java Naming and Directory Interface)

✦ JDBC (Java Database Connectivity)

✦ Management tools

✦ Web services

✦ Java IDL

✦ RMI-IIOP protocol

✦ JAXP (Java API for XML Parsing)

✦ JAXR (Java API for XML Registries)

✦ JACC (Java Authorization Service Provider Contract for Containers)

✦ JAX_RPC (Java API for XML-based RPC)

✦ SAAJ (SOAP Attachments API for Java)

✦ JAF (JavaBeans Activation Framework)

✦ Security Services

A J2EE platform requires a database, accessible from these components, using JDBC API. However, J2EE itself does not actually implement these components but relies on third-party vendors (*licensees*) to provide the actual implementation. Because the whole underpinning of J2EE is "develop once, deploy anywhere," it is very important to ensure that implementation is tightly monitored with no areas open for misinterpretation. This is where the *J2EE Compatibility Test Suite* (CTS) fits in. This is a comprehensive suite of tests that an application server must pass before it can carry the official "J2EE Certified" branding. The CTS consists of the following types of tests:

Signature tests check that all required elements of all J2EE components are included.

API tests check that all required API are implemented and each individual API meets all requirements of specification.

End-to-end integration tests check compatibility of components, for example the client application has to access a database using Enterprise JavaBeans components.

Passing these tests ensures that any application developed to the J2EE APIs will run on any server that has been certified as J2EE-compliant.

But how do you know if the application you have written is indeed J2EE-compliant? As a developer you can have your application checked under the *Java Verification Program*. This program, much like "100% Java,"(a set of guidelines to ensure that your program is portable) has been designed to allow companies to determine whether their enterprise applications are truly compliant to J2EE and thus deployable to any of the Java application servers. You can download the program from `http://java.sun.com/j2ee/verified/`. It is not free. You must also pay Sun a license fee for permission to use the testing software and all the branding that goes with it should your application pass the tests.

Each J2EE application server provides developers with a number of features that will be discussed in the next section.

Understanding the Features of an Application Server

The previous section dealt with the implementation of an application server and the various APIs it has to provide for before being considered a J2EE platform. This section discusses the following features that an application server should provide:

✦ Scalability

✦ Client agnosticism

✦ Server management

✦ Development

Scalability

A *scalable* piece of software is thought to be able to cope equally well with one client or a much larger number of concurrent Web clients, without requiring complete re-design of the software. More resources might be required for more clients, but only on the systems side, not in the application software.

Of course, we are discussing this from the perspective of the client programs access-ing distributed applications that run under control of the application servers but scaling software is not exclusive to such applications. Consider writing a text editor. What upper limit will you impose on the size of file you can edit? 1MB? 10MB? 100MB? At what point will you say, "Enough is enough?" If you write your text editor with a limit, the editor will not be considered scalable.

The same logic applies when it comes to processing clients in a J2EE application server. At what number does the number of clients become too many? Answer: You should not establish a limit. The J2EE framework has been designed with scalability in mind; therefore, assuming you have adhered to the best practices and design patterns, your enterprise application should be able to scale to service thousands of concurrent clients.

An application server should provide the infrastructure to permit this scalability, managing a server farm of potentially many hundreds, or even thousands, of inde-pendent servers all working together to present a unified front. The application server should make adding or removing servers a trivial matter. The load balancing and sharing of session data amongst the various worker-servers should also be eas-ily configurable.

The most important thing when scaling is to ensure that you stick to the recom-mended practices so you don't inadvertently create any bottlenecks in your own software. Java, contrary to popular belief, doesn't provide any magic techniques to help you do this. It is still up to you, the developer. Java, with its inherent object-orientation and code reusability, certainly makes the job of designing and imple-menting scalable applications much easier, but it should by no means be taken for granted.

Client agnosticism

The official J2EE Blueprints states that a J2EE application can support many types of the clients running as independent applications as well as the clients running under control of a Web browser. For example, the application server should be as comfortable scaling thousands of RMI/IIOP requests as it would be scaling HTTP requests. The former case may require an increase in the number of concurrent Enterprise JavaBeans, while the scaling of the HTTP requests may be achieved by increased number of Java Servlets. It should not matter what protocol has been used to deliver a client's request to the application server.

Server management

As you probably realize, J2EE is quite an expansive framework. A multitude of different resources all work together to provide a single coherent system.

As an administrator you want to be in control of your server environment from one integrated console, configuring application and server resources. Using resources as benign as JDBC pools right up to deploying WAR (Web Application Archive) and EAR (Enterprise Application Archive) files that represent complete enterprise applications should be straightforward, and no server restarts should be necessary.

The administrator console should also provide up-to-the-second runtime information on the performance of all aspects of the system to enable you to plan for the future and avert any major disasters.

Development

Finally, the application server should make it easy for the J2EE developer to safely develop new applications without unduly affecting the existing applications executing. For example, a new application could be added by simple modification of the configuration files that are used during the server startup process. For example, to deploy a new application you can include additional WAR or EAR files to the configuration files. The application should also be compatible with the major IDE vendors; this ensures that the developer is free to choose his or her development platform, as opposed to being locked into the application server's particular choice. The next section will discuss the major vendors of the J2EE application servers.

Examining Full J2EE Implementations

This section will take a look at the available application servers that fully support the J2EE platform. They implement what is effectively a one-stop shop for your J2EE needs. Even though the J2EE platform is middleware and you may opt for one J2EE component, you are not tied to its whole implementation; you are still free to swap in third-party implementations to replace specific layers.

We'll take a look at the following application servers in this section:

✦ BEA WebLogic

✦ Borland Enterprise Server

✦ IBM WebSphere

✦ JBoss

✦ Oracle 9iAS

✦ Orion Application Server

✦ Sun ONE

The following sections are not meant to serve as product reviews, but instead to give you a flavor of each item's capabilities.

BEA WebLogic

BEA is one of the oldest players in the J2EE game with its WebLogic offering. The original developers of WebLogic were heavily involved with the first evolution of the Servlet API and have been major contributors to the enterprise specifications ever since. BEA in many respects set the precedent that the others followed; specifically, it was one of the first to implement its complete server in Java itself. BEA presently has one of the largest in the world deployment base of J2EE servers and continually pushes the threshold for ease of implementation and deployment. BEA's application server is available free for development at `http://www.bea.com/products/weblogic/server/`; it integrates with all the major IDEs with no problems.

BEA also provides, free of charge, one of the fastest JVMs: jRockit. This is a JVM designed specifically for the server side in which the virtual machine is expected to be executing for long periods of time. BEA has spent a lot of time working with Intel to optimize jRockit specifically for the Intel processors to ensure that WebLogic runs as fast as possible. BEA is leaving nothing to chance, by controlling the virtual machine its server heavily relies on. Incidentally, Oracle's Application Server also ships with jRockit.

Borland Enterprise Server

A company better known for its rich development tools, Borland is also a major player in the J2EE space with its Enterprise AppServer Edition (see `http://www.borland.com/besappserver`). This application server integrates tightly with its JBuilder IDE, but is open to all J2EE development tools. Supporting all the latest APIs, Borland has integrated rather than innovated with its enterprise server. The Enterprise Server brings together and enhances technology from the likes of Apache (Axis/HTTP Server/Tomcat) and Sonic Software (SonicMQ for JMS).

IBM WebSphere

After BEA, IBM has the biggest J2EE market share with its WebSphere application server (see `http://www.ibm.com/software/webservers/appserv/was/`). IBM offers a number of different WebSphere editions for different budgets and levels of functionality. WebSphere Express is basically a complete Web-hosting system including servlets and JSP. The 5.0 edition of WebSphere is available in Base, Network Deployment, and Enterprise versions.

IBM is not renowned for its speed in implementing new releases. In fact it is famed for lagging significantly behind the others when it comes to providing implementations of the latest J2EE specification.

IBM has poured a significant amount of resources into Java over the years and much of its technology is available to the community in one shape or another. A great example is its development environment, Eclipse, which is now available at `http://www.eclipse.org/` as a free open-source download.

JBoss

One of the oldest and most popular open-source implementations of the J2EE framework is from the JBoss group (see `http://www.jboss.org/`). JBoss has taken a slightly different approach to the implementation compared to other application server vendors by building a sophisticated API model that enables you to (for example) swap out the servlet engine for Tomcat as opposed to using JBoss' Jetty engine. This swap feature applies to all the major J2EE components.

JBoss is free for development and deployment and is a very straightforward application server.

Oracle 9iAS

Contrary to popular belief, Oracle is more than just a database company. It has been making significant inroads in providing all the software that you need on the server side. When Oracle decided to enter the Java marketplace a number of years ago, it went on a shopping spree, buying up all the necessary components to ensure it wouldn't be starting from scratch.

Oracle's core application server is based on code licensed from IronFlare's Orion application server. Its development environment, JDeveloper, was originally a code snapshot of Borland's JBuilder. However, it is fair to note that Oracle recently announced that it has developed all the code currently contained in JDeveloper and that it has broken free of the code of Borland. Oracle's HTTP server is the popular Apache Server. It recently purchased TopLink from ailing WebGain to round out its Java offering.

But Oracle has done more than just put these components together. It has designed all the components, recoding where necessary to meet its demanding company standard of "unbreakable code." Oracle 9iAS is the result of these efforts. It is a pure Java implementation with a very small memory footprint. An application server that is increasingly gaining market share, it fully implements the J2EE framework, providing all the necessary facilities for large-scale deployment.

The server is available as a free download from `http://www.oracle.com/` for development only.

Orion

One of the application servers that seems to be gaining significant popularity in the development community is the Orion application server from IronFlare in Sweden. One of the primary reasons for IronFlare's success is how easy it is to get this server up and running. Simply download and run; `java -jar orion.jar` and that's it. It is written purely in Java and uses the existing JVM installed on your system without having to drag its own along.

The server has been designed to be very developer-centric, enabling easy deployment, simple configuration, and very short startup, execution, and deployment times. The server can be configured through its Java Swing GUI or by means of directly manipulating the XML files, depending on your own preference.

Orion also attempts to support the latest APIs. The server is free for development and non-commercial projects. You can obtain it from `http://www.orionserver.com/`

Sun ONE Application Server

Sun's Open Net Environment (ONE) Application Server (version 7) forms the heart of Sun's J2EE offering. Built from the legacy of the iPlanet server, Sun's application server comes in two primary editions, Platform (see `http://wwws.sun.com/ software/download/products/Sun_ONE_App_Svr_7,_Platform_Edition.html`) and Standard (see `http://wwws.sun.com/software/products/appsrvr/ appsrvr_download.html`). Each one implements the latest EJB, JSP, and JMS APIs and ships on the latest JVM. As you might imagine, Sun ONE is one of the first application servers to incorporate the latest releases of the JDK, which for better or worse allows Sun to prove to the community that it has total faith in their own technology by "eating in its own kitchen." At the time of this writing Sun ONE officially supports version 1.3 of J2EE, but expect version 1.4 soon.

Sun's Platform edition is designed for development and limited deployment for mid-sized applications. It is free, which makes it attractive, especially when you consider that it now ships as standard with all releases of Sun's Solaris operating system.

The Standard edition is a fuller product offering, featuring a richer suite of tools specially aimed at providing the necessary tools for a complete Web-serviced platform. This edition handles mid-sized to enterprise applications and is designed to handle high loads.

Sun also offers a development environment based on the NetBeans technology, called Studio 4. This integrates with the Sun ONE application server, simplifying development and deployment in Sun ONE as well as other application servers.

Examining Partial J2EE Implementations

Without a doubt, the J2EE platform is large. Many developers will only ever use servlets and JSP; the requirement to install the full J2EE server is overkill for them. The Servlet API is one of the oldest and best-established APIs of the J2EE platform. It was on the scene years before J2EE was available, and thanks largely to its success Java at the server side became not only an option but a serious contender for the best technology for development of the Web applications.

From the Servlet API grew the JSP specification, which essentially takes embedded Java inside an HTML page, converts it into a servlet, and compiles and runs it. This results in a very powerful partnership. The Servlet API gave the world the WAR format, which enables you to deploy servlet applications very easily by packaging up all the files into one easily managed file that you can then drop into an application server for execution.

Many servlet engines on the market provide support for the full Servlet API and JSP specifications, and in this section we'll look at some of the more popular ones:

- ✦ Apache Tomcat
- ✦ Resin
- ✦ ServletExec

Table 3-1 provides an overview of the major features of the three servlet containers mentioned in this chapter.

Table 3-1
Major features of the servlet containers

Category	Apache Tomcat	Resin	ServletExec
Servlet API	2.3	2.3	2.3
JSP specification	1.2	1.2	1.2
Built-in HTTP server	Yes	Yes	No
Development cost	None	None	None
Deployment costs	None	$500	$695
Configuration	File-based	File-based	Web-based

Apache Tomcat

It's difficult to be involved with Java servlets or JSP and not have run into Tomcat from Apache. This is the official servlet and JSP reference implementation that Sun uses. Tomcat is free to use and deploy and is an open-source implementation that you can download from the main Apache site at `http://jakarta.apache.org/ tomcat/`.

Tomcat comes in many versions. The reason for the multiversion approach is that each major version represents the corresponding Servlet API version that it implements. For example, at the time of this writing, Tomcat 5 was being discussed as the official implementation of the Servlet API 2.4 and the JSP 2.0 specification.

Tomcat does not come with any fancy administration tools and all settings are controlled via XML files, which may put off some developers. Tomcat also ships with its own Web server but works better in conjunction with the Apache Web Server. Because Tomcat requires you to administer the XML files manually, you will get a better understanding of how the Servlet API operates. Tomcat also serves as an excellent first-step, hands-on servlet engine.

Resin

Resin is a no-frills Servlet engine from Caucho Technology (see `http://www.caucho. com/resin/`). Resin has been around for a number of years now and has a good reputation among the developer community. The engine itself can stand on its own using the built-in HTTP server or provide servlet/JSP processing for a variety of Web servers, including Apache and Microsoft's Internet Information Server.

Resin offers many of the features that you would expect from a servlet engine, including load balancing and distributed sessions. Resin is free for developers and non-commercial applications.

ServletExec

One of the oldest and best-established players in this market space is ServletExec from New Atlanta (see `http://www.newatlanta.com/products/servletexec/`). The New Atlanta team has been involved in the evolution and design of the Servlet API from the start, and its ServletExec engine is one of the oldest servlet engines available. New Atlanta has stayed focused on the Servlet API and has resisted the urge to make ServletExec into a full-blown J2EE server.

ServletExec is an engine that bolts onto your existing Web server and takes over the processing of any servlet or JSP requests. It supports all the major Web servers (IIS, Netscape/iPlanet, Apache) and also operates on most of the major operating systems (Windows NT/2000/XP, Solaris, AIX, and Linux).

One of the great features of JSP is its accessibility. There's no need to worry about complicated IDEs or compilers; you just save an HTML page with embedded Java, trigger it with your browser, and you are done. New Atlanta has made the installation and administration of its servlet engine similarly straightforward. It has done all the hard work of figuring out what needs to be done with each Web server and the configuration of the server is very simple.

ServletExec (as well as ServletExec Debugger) is available for free as a development environment; only when you deploy you need to purchase a license.

We've introduced you to various vendors of the J2EE application servers. In the next section, we'll discuss how to avoid dependency on a particular vendor.

Avoiding Vendor Lock-In

While the J2EE framework has a lot to offer the developer, there is still a lot of room for improvement, which many vendors have been quick to provide through their own libraries. It can sometimes be frustrating when you come up against what seems like a brick wall. The framework has let you down in some way and the time has come to look elsewhere. You may be able to overcome the obstacle using a library that is native only to that application server.

You may think that this won't happen to you, but you might be surprised at how easy it is to drop into a particular vendor's API, especially if you are using an IDE that is quick to "sell" you easy-access classes. But if you use a method native to a particular server, you are effectively locked into that application server and won't be able to easily deploy to another server. You have thus rendered null and void the whole openness of J2EE. Fortunately, careful consideration of your design enables you to have the best of both worlds — openness and utility.

The best way to avoid lock-in is to develop your own proxy interface to act as a stepping stone between your code and the underlying library. Then, for each J2EE server you intend to deploy on, you simply provide the necessary class implementation that maps onto the underlying library.

Take a look at a quick example that is simple enough to illustrate the point. Here is a simple interface that defines a method to return a reference to a file that can be shared:

```
public interface myFileLibraryProxy {
  public File createSharedFile();
}
```

In your application code you would simply refer to the myFileLibraryProxy class, possibly using a factory pattern to obtain an instance of this class to use. For each server you would code an implementation that would map the call to an underlying method, as shown here:

```
public class beaFileLibrary implements myFileLibraryProxy {
public File createSharedFile(){
  //-- calls an underlying BEA method
}
}
```

In your deployment files you could include all the implementations and let the factory class decide which one to actually instantiate, depending on the underlying server platform. This method will work for the majority of instances in which you may feel the need to use a specific vendor's application code. The key thing to remember is that what may seem like a good idea today may not seem to be a good idea tomorrow. Try to avoid coding yourself into a corner, and adhere to the standards at all costs.

Note For a comprehensive and up-to-date look at the vendors that provide J2EE implementations, visit http://www.flashline.com/Components/appservermatrix.jsp.

Summary

In this chapter we took a look at the overall role the application server plays in J2EE. We also mentioned components that comprise the J2EE platform. These components will be discussed in greater detail in the subsequent chapters of this book. It is important to understand the difference between J2EE specification and specific implementations done by the vendors of the application servers. Any application server has to pass the J2EE Compatibility Test Suite to have a right for the "J2EE certified" brand.

We covered the dynamics of application servers and took a quick look at the major operators in this space. In addition to the major vendors we looked at the minor vendors that provide implementations for servlet engines.

✦   ✦   ✦

Understanding Remote Method Invocation

◆ ◆ ◆ ◆

In This Chapter

Using RMI in distributed Java applications

Understanding stubs and skeletons

Working through an airline flight information server example

Pushing data to clients

◆ ◆ ◆ ◆

Ultimately, J2EE is about distributed applications. In the following chapters of this book you'll learn various ways of designing software components that reside on multiple computers and communicate over the network. But before diving into the world of application servers, engines, and containers, take a look at a simple but powerful way of creating distributed Java applications using technology called *Remote Method Invocation* (RMI).

We decided to put this chapter toward the beginning of the book because RMI is not only the simplest way of creating distributed applications, but also gives us a chance to introduce you to naming services similar to the Java Naming and Directory Interface (JNDI). In this chapter we will also introduce such terms as *data marshalling, stubs,* and *skeletons,* which are also important for understanding Enterprise JavaBean (EJB) technology.

Providing an Overview of RMI

RMI is the action of invoking a method of a remote interface on a remote object. It enables Java clients to invoke methods on Java objects living on the remote computer's Java Virtual Machine (JVM). Both JVMs can be running on the same or different computers, but the most important thing is that the application has to be distributed, which in the case of RMI means that it should use at least two JVMs.

Since RMI is a part of J2SE, it's available on all platforms that support Java, and does not require any additional software. RMI is often compared with *Common Object Request Broker Architecture* (CORBA), which enables communication between distributed components written in different languages, but CORBA requires additional middleware called an object request broker to provide data translation from one language to another. While a discussion of CORBA is outside the scope of this book, later we'll introduce you to other J2EE technologies that allow communication between systems written in different languages and running on different platforms.

Any RMI application consists of the following components:

✦ Client

✦ Server

✦ Registry

The registry is the naming service. The RMI components usually run on separate networked computers. The server creates some Java objects, registers them with the naming service, and waits for remote clients to invoke methods on these objects. A client application gets a reference to a remote-server object from the registry and then invokes methods on this remote object. The main concept of RMI is that even though the methods are being called in the client's JVM, they are executed on the server's JVM.

The best part of RMI applications is that a developer does not have to program the network communications — the programming is done automatically by a special tool called an *RMI compiler* (rmic). This tool generates two additional classes, stub and skeleton, that will take care of data exchange over the network by using *data marshalling* — presentation of Java objects as a set of bytes — and serialization.

RMI technology is useful for many business applications written in Java. Some of the typical applications are listed here:

✦ Getting stock-market price quotes

✦ Obtaining flight information

✦ Requesting and downloading music files

✦ Performing inventory maintenance

Usually an RMI server works in the wait mode: It "listens" to requests on a particular port. A Java RMI client does not work directly with the server's database(s) or other resources — it just sends a request for the information or updates in a form of a Java class, XML, or the like. That's why the underlying infrastructure of a system is hidden from the client and no database drivers or other third-party software must be installed on the client's machines.

After giving a brief overview of the RMI technology, the next several sections of this chapter will define the process of creation of an RMI application step-by-step.

Developing Applications with RMI

Writing distributed RMI applications usually consists of the following steps:

1. Declaring a remote interface for the client
2. Implementing a remote interface on the server
3. Writing a client program that uses this remote interface to connect to a server and call its methods
4. Generating stubs (client proxies) and skeletons (server entities)
5. Starting the registry on the server and registering remote objects with it
6. Starting the server application on the remote machine
7. Starting the Java application that is either located on the client machine or downloaded as a Java applet

You'll learn how to perform each of these steps by developing the Flight Information Application, which provides a client with the latest flight departure/arrival information for Connexia Airlines, which is explained fully in Appendix A.

Declaring remote interfaces

A remote interface defines method(s) that can be invoked remotely by a client. Like any Java interfaces, the remote interfaces describe the behavior of remote objects and do not contain the implementation of this behavior. The client program will "have a feeling" that it calls local methods, but actually these calls will be redirected to a remote server.

The following are the rules for creation of remote interfaces:

An application's remote interface must declare business methods having `public` access that will enable clients to communicate with the server.

An application's remote interface must extend the `java.rmi.Remote` interface. The `Remote` interface does not have any methods — just declare the required methods there.

Each method must declare a `java.rmi.RemoteException` or one of its ancestors.

Method arguments and return data types must be serializable.

Let's apply all these rules while writing the code for the `FlightServer` interface that will be used on the client side of our sample application. Since Java interfaces just declare methods and cannot contain code in the method bodies, our interface will declare two business methods — `getDepartureTime()` and `getArrivalTime()`. Please note that the `FlightServer` interface from Listing 4-1 extends the `Remote` interface and that its methods declare `RemoteException`.

Listing 4-1: **The FlightServer interface**

```
import java.rmi.*;
          public interface FlightServer extends java.rmi.Remote {
    public String getDepartureTime(String flightNo)
                        throws java.rmi.RemoteException;
    public String getArrivalTime(String flightNo)
                        throws java.rmi.RemoteException;
}
```

These two methods constitute the only API that is available for the client. The class that implements these methods may have other methods as well, but those are hidden from the client.

Implementing remote interfaces

In RMI, the interface and implementations are completely separated. While the remote interface just declares the methods used by the client, the actual class that provides the implementation for these methods will run on the server side in a separate JVM. These methods must have exactly the same signatures as their proxies on the client, otherwise the RMI clients won't find them.

You can make the implementation class visible to remote Java clients declaring that this class is inherited from the java.rmi.server.UnicastRemoteObject class, as in the FlightServerImpl class derived from Listing 4-2. This class will respond to and process the client's requests. The implementation class can also initiate the data feed to the client, as explained in the section "Pushing Data from the RMI Server," later in this chapter.

In real life flight information should be retrieved from a database or other data source, but for simplicity's sake we'll just create two hard-coded Hashtable objects containing arrival and departure information. After reading Chapter 18, you should be able to replace the hardcoded flight information with dynamic data coming from a database.

When a client calls the method getArrivalTime() or getDepartureTime(), this call will be received by a local object (the stub), which converts it into a method-invocation on the remote class FlightServerImpl. Listing 4-2 contains the code for this remote class.

Listing 4-2: **The FlightServerImpl class**

```
import java.rmi.*;
import java.rmi.server.*;
import java.util.Hashtable;
public class FlightServerImpl extends UnicastRemoteObject
                                implements FlightServer {
  private Hashtable arrivals = new Hashtable();
  private Hashtable departures = new Hashtable();
  public FlighterverImpl() throws RemoteException {
    super();
   // Define some hard-coded arrival and departure times
   // The key in the Hashtable represents a flight number
    arrivals.put("C01208","3:20PM");
    arrivals.put ("C01331","8:00PM");
    arrivals.put ("C03450","6:05PM");
    departures.put ("C01209","4:20PM");
    departures.put ("C01200","9:15PM");
    departures.put("C00456","10:05PM");
  }

  public String getArrivalTime(String flightNo)
                         throws RemoteException {
    String arrTime=null;

   // Throw an exception if the flight number does not exist
    arrTime= (String) arrivals.get(flightNo);
    if (arrTime==null)  {
      throw new RemoteException("Flight number "+ flightNo +
                        " does not exist");
    }
    return arrTime;
  }
public String getDepartureTime(String flightNo)
                         throws RemoteException {
    String depTime=null;

   // Throw an exception if the flight number does not exist
    depTime= (String) departures.get(flightNo);
    if (depTime==null)  {
      throw new RemoteException("Flight number "+ flightNo +
                        " does not exist");
    }
    return depTime;
  }
}
```

If the `FlightServerImpl` class cannot be inherited from the `UnicastRemoteObject` because it's already derived from some other business class, you can just declare that this class implements the `Remote` interface. You would then make it available to the remote clients by exporting it. Here's how you would do this:

```
FlightServerImpl fsi = new FlightServerImpl();
UnicastRemoteObject.exportObject(fsi);
```

Remote exceptions

In RMI applications, all remote methods must declare `java.rmi.RemoteException`. (See method declarations in Listing 4-2.) This exception will be thrown by the server application in such cases as communication failures, marshalling or unmarshalling errors, and so on. Because a `RemoteException` is a checked exception, it has to be handled in the client code. (See the `FlightClient`-class example later in this chapter in the section "Writing RMI Clients.")

Besides the `RemoteException`, a remote application can throw any other exceptions to be handled by the client exactly as if they were thrown locally.

Stubs and skeletons

After the remote interface and its implementation are created, you need to generate the objects responsible for the network communications between them. The stub is a client-side object that represents the remote object. When a client calls a remote method, such as `getFlightArrivals()`, the stub method is invoked and it does the following:

✦ Initiates a connection with the remote JVM

✦ Marshals (prepares and transmits) the parameters to the server

✦ Waits for the result of the method invocation

✦ Unmarshals (reads) the return value or exception returned

✦ Returns the value to the client

All the background work (serialization and networking) is hidden from developers — they just need to write local method calls!

An RMI server may have a similar object called a skeleton to process the client's network calls. It performs the following operations for each received call:

✦ Unmarshals (reads) the parameters for the remote method

✦ Invokes the method on the actual remote-object implementation

✦ Marshals the result to the caller

The skeleton is responsible for dispatching the client call to the actual object implementation. The skeletons are deprecated starting from Java 1.2 onwards. They are not replaced by any other classes and can be just ignored. But if at least one of the JVMs participating in the RMI application uses Java version 1.1 or older, the skeleton class must exist on the server side.

J2SE comes with the RMI compiler called `rmic`, which generates stubs and skeletons from the existing implementation class. You can start the `rmic` program like this:

```
c:>rmic FlightServerImpl
```

This command will create two more classes — one (`FlightServerImpl_stub.class`) for the client side and the other (`FlightServerImpl_skel.class`) for the server.

The stub implements only remote interfaces. When the client calls a remote method the stub marshals and serializes the data over the network to the skeleton (or to the server application). The skeleton, in turn unmarshals and deserializes the data on the remote machine and passes the data to the actual implementation of the method. After the method completes, the return value is delivered back to the client in the reverse order. Obviously, the remote method parameters and returned values of the remote methods must be serializable.

If you want to know what's under the hood, run the `rmic` with the `-keepgenerated` flag to see the source code of the stub and skeleton in the files `FlightServerImpl_stub.java` and `FlightServerImpl_skel.java`.

If the application does not use JVMs older than version 1.2, you can inform the RMI compiler that the stub does not have to be generated by issuing the following command:

```
c:>rmic -v1.2 FlightServerImpl
```

Registering remote objects

Before a client program can invoke a particular method on the remote object, it has to find this object on the network. A server makes remote objects visible to the clients by registering these objects with a naming service. The `rmiregistry` is a simple naming service that comes with J2SE. The process of registering an object with the RMI registry is called *binding*. The RMI registry is nothing but a naming service that knows where to find the server's objects, and it will enable clients to look up an object in the network by name. While the class name can be long and include the package name, the registry name is usually short and descriptive.

Two methods in the `java.rmi.Naming` class can bind an object to the registry. The `bind()` method binds an object to a name. It throws the `AlreadyBoundException` if the binding already exists under the specified name.

The `rebind()` method replaces any preexisting registry entry with the new one. The `unbind()` method removes an object from the registry.

The registry must be up and running by the time you bind the objects. To start the registry, open a command window and type the following:

```
c:\>rmiregistry
```

This command will start the registry on the default RMI port 1099. If you need to specify another port, provide the port's number as a command-line parameter. For example, to start the registry on port 6000 use the following command:

```
c:\>rmiregistry 6000
```

The `StartFlightServer` program shown in Listing 4-3 binds the `FlightServerImpl` class under the name `FlightService` to the registry that runs on the same machine as the server (`localhost`) on port 6000.

Listing 4-3: **The StartFlightServer class**

```
import java.rmi.*;
import java.rmi.registry.LocateRegistry;
public class StartFlightServer {
  public static void main (String args[]) {
    try {
      FlightServerImpl fsi = new FlightServerImpl();
      Naming.rebind("rmi://localhost:6000/FlightService",fsi);
      System.out.println(
        "FlightService is waiting for the requests on port
6000...");
    } catch(Exception ex) {
        ex.printStackTrace();
    }
  }
  }
```

If the specified port is being used by another program, the `rmiregistry` will throw an exception that may look like the following:

```
java.rmi.server.ExportException: Port already in use: 6000;
   nested exception is: java.net.BindException: Address already in
                                            use: JVM_Bind
```

In this case, start the server on a different port and specify the new port number in the `StartFlightServer` program and in the `FlightClient` class shown in Listing 4-4.

Listing 4-4: **The FlightClient class**

```
import java.rmi.*;
import java.util.Vector;
public class FlightClient {
   public static void main.(String args[]) {
  if (args.length == 0) {
   System.out.println("\nUsage: java " +
   "-Djava.security.policy=security.policy FlightClient
flightNo");
      System.exit(0);
  }
  try {
       if (System.getSecurityManager() == null) {
            System.setSecurityManager(new
RMISecurityManager());
       }
       FlightServer myServer = (FlightServer)
           Naming.lookup("rmi://localhost:6000/FlightService");
       // this example searches for the arrival info only
       String arrival = myServer.getArrivalTime(args[0]);
       System.out.println("Arrival time of " + args[0] +
                           " is " + arrival);
   } catch (NotBoundException nbe) {
         System.out.println(nbe.getMessage());
   } catch (java.net.MalformedURLException mfue) {
         System.out.println(mfue.getMessage());
   } catch (RemoteException re) {
         System.out.println(re.getMessage());
   }
  }
}
```

Instead of starting the registry manually, you could have also started it from within the `StartFlightServer` program itself. Just add the following line at the beginning of the `main()` method in Listing 4-3:

```
LocateRegistry.createRegistry(6000);
```

To bring the flight server up, open a command window and start the `StartFlightServer` class from your working directory. Here's an example:

```
C:\>java StartFlightServer
```

Writing RMI clients

The client has to perform a lookup in the registry on the server's machine and obtain a remote reference to the object listed under the specified name. The `lookup()` method of the `java.rmi.Naming` class locates the remote object on the specified host and port, as shown in Listing 4-4:

```
FlightServer myServer = (FlightServer)
        Naming.lookup("rmi://localhost:6000/FlightService");
```

Please note the casting of the `Object` from the `lookup()` method to the `FlightServer` type. Even though the `FlightService` registry entry represents the `FlightServerImpl` class, we cast it to the `FlightServer` remote interface. Java allows you to cast a class to any interface it implements, and the `FlightServerImpl` class implements the `FlightServer` interface. This Java feature also enables you to keep on the client side only the thin `FlightServer` interface instead of the much fatter implementation class. The `myServer` variable in Listing 4-4 will "see" only the methods defined in this interface, while the `FlightServerImpl` class may implement many other interfaces as well, and may have other public methods.

Recall that a remote class can start its own registry that supports the naming services for the RMI clients. The registry API is defined by the `java.rmi.registry.Registry` interface.

The RMI registry runs by default on port 1099, unless another port number is specified. When the client wants to invoke methods on the remote object it obtains a reference to that object by looking up the name. The lookup returns to the client a stub of the remote object.

The method takes the object's URL as an argument in this format:

```
rmi://<hostname>[:<name_service_port>]/<service_name>
```

These components are described as follows:

✦ *hostname* is the name of the computer on the local area network (LAN) or a DNS name on the Internet.

✦ *name_service_port* has to be specified only if the naming service is running on a port other than the default one (1099).

✦ *service_name* is the name of the remote object that should have been bound to the registry.

Cross-Reference   More advanced naming services that are widely used in J2EE applications are described in Chapter 11.

The `main()` method in the class from Listing 4-4 loads the instance of the `java.rmi.RMISecurityManager` method (a subclass of the `SecurityManager` class) that allows access to a specified port.

```
System.setSecurityManager(new RMISecurityManager());
```

If the RMI client is an applet, `RMISecurityManager` is not needed—just make sure that the RMI implementation classes exist on the same server that the applet is coming from. If the Web server and RMI server are running on different hosts, the applets have to be digitally signed.

`FlightClient` can be started as follows:

```
c:>java -Djava.security.policy=security.policy FlightClient C01208
```

Policy files contain permissions granted to users of this application. A sample security file is shown in Listing 4-5. Detailed explanations of how to write security-policy files can be found at `http://java.sun.com/j2se/1.4/docs/guide/security/PolicyFiles.html`

Listing 4-5: **The security.policy file**

```
grant {
    // Allow the client to connect to any port above 1024
    permission java.net.SocketPermission "*:1024-", "connect";
};
```

An absence of granted access permissions will prevent the `FlightClient` from accessing the RMI server and will generate the following exception:

```
java.security.AccessControlException: access denied
(java.net.SocketPermission 127.0.0.1:6000 connect,resolve)
```

Setting up the Flight Server example

This section will bring all the RMI pieces of our sample application together. Figure 4-1 shows the RMI components of our flight server. It depicts the client, server, and the registry. The client and the server use different classes and interfaces that are listed below the JVM1 and JVM2 boxes, respectively. The client (JVM1) performs a lookup of the server in the registry and calls remote methods on the server. The server (JVM2) has to register the remote object with the registry. The stubs and skeletons perform both marshalling and unmarshalling.

Follow the steps below to install and run the RMI Flight Server application. Doing so will enable you to emulate a distributed environment on a stand-alone machine. We'll open multiple command windows—one for the RMI server, one for the registry, and one or more for the client(s). If you have access to a network, start the server and the clients on separate machines and replace the `localhost` in Listing 4-3 and Listing 4-4 with the actual IP address or network name of the workstation. For the sake of this example we assume that all required classes are created in the directory called `chapter4`.

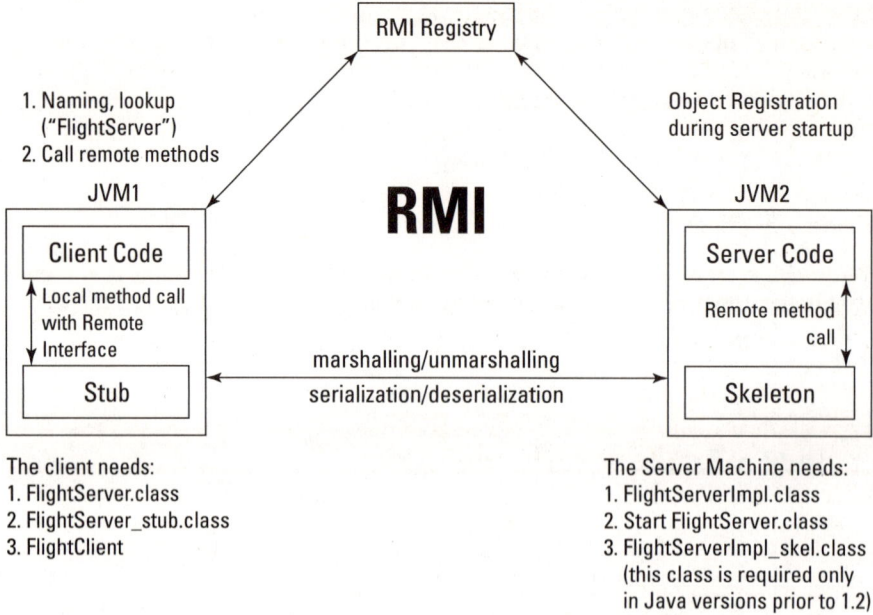

Figure 4-1: The Flight Server example contains these RMI components.

1. Create the `FlightServer.java` file containing the remote interface from Listing 4-1.

2. Create the `FlightServerImpl.java` server class based on the code shown in Listing 4-2.

3. Create the `StartFlightServer.java` class according to Listing 4-3.

4. Create the `FlightClient.java` class according to Listing 4-4.

5. Compile all of the preceding classes as follows:

        c:\chapter4>javac *.java

6. Create stub and skeleton classes from `FlightServerImpl` using the `rmic` compiler, as follows:

        c:\chapter4>rmic StockServerImpl

7. Open three command windows emulating separate machines.

8. Start the RMI registry on port 6000 from the first command window. Your screen should resemble Figure 4-2.

Do not expect to see any confirmation that the `rmi` registry has been successfully started. The very fact that no error messages are shown in this command window is your confirmation.

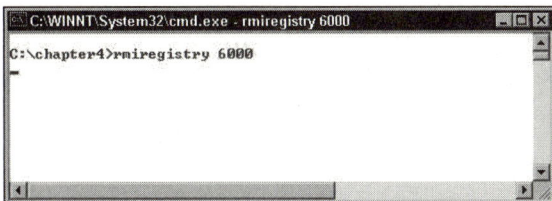

Figure 4-2: Starting the RMI registry

Register `FlightService` with the naming service from the second command window, as shown in Figure 4-3:

Figure 4-3: Starting the Flight Server

What can go wrong at this point? If the registry does not run on the host and port specified in Listing 4-3, the program will throw an exception that may look like this:

```
java.rmi.ConnectException: Connection refused to host:
      localhost; nested exception
is:java.net.ConnectException:
                 Connection refused: no further information
```

Depending on the settings of your LAN, the loopback IP address `127.0.0.1` (`localhost`) may or may not work. If it does not work, replace `localhost` with the network name or IP address of your computer.

Run the `FlightClient` from the third command window, as shown in Figure 4-4. Pass the flight number as a command-line argument and the client will connect to the "remote" server and receive the flight information. Do not forget to create a `security.policy` file, as shown in Listing 4-5.

Figure 4-4: Running the Flight Client

To deploy this application within Connexia Airlines, create the `FlightInfoClient.jar` file containing the `FlightClient.class`, `FlightServer.class`, and `FlightServerImpl_stub.class` files and install this jar on each customer service representative's workstation.

If Connexia Airlines is ready to provide its customers on the Web with flight information, create an applet with a simple GUI containing a text field in which the user can enter a flight number, a Submit button, and a text field to display the result. Besides the GUI part, the applet should contain code similar to that of the `FlightClient`, but that does not create `RMISecurityManager`. When it's ready, add the applet's class to the `FlightInfoClient.jar` and add the applet HTML tag to the Web page. Here's an example:

```
<HTML>
<BODY>
  <APPLET code="FlightInfoApplet.class"
    archive="FlightInfoClient.jar" width=100 height=100>
  </APPLET>
</BODY>
</HTML>
```

Up till now, we've been using the client-server terminology in this chapter. We've also assumed that the client is a program that requests services from another program (the server). The next section will explain how an RMI server can initiate the data exchange with an RMI client.

Pushing Data from the RMI Server

In our airline example requests for the flight information were originated by the client application. Now try to visualize yourself in the arrival area of the Connexia terminal waiting for your friend's arrival. There are plenty of monitors everywhere with flight-arrival information that is updated at a specified time interval. All these monitors are the clients that receive the data feed from some remote server. Our flight-information application that we developed earlier in this chapter could be used for automation of such airport terminal. There is a major difference though — in this case not the client but the server has to initiate updates of the information on the clients' monitors!

In this section we'll show you how to treat the RMI server and the client as peers so either of them can "start the conversation." This is how it works. The RMI client(s) has to register itself with the server, and it also has to implement an interface that contains the code refreshing the screen. Periodically the RMI server will call the method that refreshes the screen on each registered client. In other words, instead of the client pulling the data from the server, the server is pushing the data to the client.

Let's discuss the modifications that should be done to our flight-information application. First, the client has to implement an additional interface (which may look like the one shown in Listing 4-6). This interface contains only one method, `refreshFlightInfo()`, which should be implemented by the client. The server will call this method on the client, passing a collection of flight number/time pairs that have to be updated on the screen.

Listing 4-6: **The RefreshScreen interface**

```
import java.rmi.*;
public interface RefreshScreen extends java.rmi.Remote {
    void updateFlightInfo(Hashtable flightsInfo)
                                    throws RemoteException;
}
```

The new version of the flight client is shown in Listing 4-7.

Listing 4-7: **The FlightClient2 class**

```
import java.rmi.*;
import java.rmi.server.UnicastRemoteObject;
import java.util.Vector;
import java.util.Hashtable;
import java.util.Date;
import java.io.Serializable;

public class FlightClient2 implements RefreshScreen {

    public FlightClient2(){
    }

    public void updateFlightInfo(Hashtable flightInfo){
        System.out.println("Flight data as of " + new Date() +
                                    ": "+flightInfo);
    }

    public static void main (String args[]) {

        FlightClient2 fc=new FlightClient2();
        try {
        if (System.getSecurityManager() == null) {
            System.setSecurityManager(
                    new RMISecurityManager());
```

Continued

Listing 4-7 *(continued)*

```
        }

UnicastRemoteObject.exportObject(fc);

        FlightServer myServer = (FlightServer)
            Naming.lookup("rmi://localhost:6000/FlightService");

    // register the client for automatic flight info updates
        myServer.registerClient(fc);

    } catch (Exception e) {
        System.out.println(e.getMessage());
    }

    System.out.println("FlightClient2 is waiting for the " +
                "flight info updates from the server... ");

        while(true){} // keep the client alive...
    }
}
```

Let's discuss the important changes that will allow the remote server to call the updateFlightInfo() method on the client and execute this method in the client's JVM:

1. The client registers itself with the server using the method registerClient(fc).

2. The client also makes itself visible to the remote server by exporting itself with the help of UnicastRemoteObject.

3. The client also has to be processed by the rmic compiler. The following command will create two pairs of stubs and skeletons:

   c:>rmic FlightServerImpl FlightClient2

4. At the end of the main() method you can see an endless loop that will keep the client alive so that it can receive updates from the server.

5. To simplify the example, the updateFlightInfo() method just prints the current date and time and the content of the received Hashtable with the flight information. We just want to see that the client receives the data feed from the server. It should not be too difficult to improve the look of the client by creating a Java Swing screen with a JTable that displays the received data.

The server from Listing 4-2 also needs some changes. The modified version of the FlightServerImpl class will have a new member variable to store the reference to the client. Here's the code:

```
private RefreshScreen client;
```

The registerClient() method will store the reference to the client and will start sending "update" flight information as soon as the client registers. Here's the code:

```
public void registerClient(RefreshScreen client)
                        throws java.rmi.RemoteException{
    this.client=client;
    startClientUpdates();
}
private void startClientUpdates()
                    throws  java.rmi.RemoteException{
    while(true){
    // Send the arrivals info every 10 seconds
    try{
        Thread.sleep(10000);
    } catch(InterruptedException e){
      e.printStackTrace();
    }
    client.updateFlightInfo(arrivals);
  }
}
```

Please note that the registerClient() method has an argument of type RefreshScreen, which is perfectly legal because our client implements this interface. Of course, we could have used the argument of type FlightClient2, but our method is more flexible because it'll work for different clients as long as they implement the interface RefreshScreen. This is polymorphism in action! Start this application in a different command window as you did before, and the messages with the flight information will be refreshed in the client's window every 10 seconds.

It's very important to understand that the server-side method call client. updateFlightInfo(arrivals) is actually executed on the client side! The reference variable client, with the help of the stub, points at the object on the client's JVM. If you need proof that this is the case, perform the following experiment with FlightClient2:

1. Remove the client's stub.

2. Comment out the line that exports the client.

3. Declare that the client also implements the Serializable interface.

Run this example again and you'll see that the messages with the flight information are now printed in the server's window. In this wrong version the whole client has been serialized to the server and the updateFlightInfo() method works in the server's JVM. This wrong version of the client would not be able to update the monitors in the Connexia terminal.

This example demonstrates a simple method for use when the server needs to push the data to the client — either at specified intervals or when an important event occurs. Another example in which such technology could be used is the stock-market data feed. Just create an applet as an RMI client, register it with the server that will feed it with real-time price quotes, and enjoy the earnings.

However, there are situations when Java RMI applications need to communicate with non-Java applications. The next section will introduce you to another protocol that can be considered for the RMI-based solutions.

RMI over Inter-ORB Protocol (IIOP)

The RMI technology internally uses the Java Remote Method Protocol (JRMP), which can be used for communications between Java programs only. On the other hand, CORBA technology can be used in distributed applications whose components are written in different languages, but CORBA uses the Internet Inter-ORB Protocol (IIOP). Back in 1997, IBM and Sun Microsystems created RMI-IIOP protocol, which allows write Java client programs that are communicating with non-Java objects. RMI-IIOP supports both JRMP and IIOP protocols.

CORBA uses the Interface Definition Language (IDL) to define objects, and the RMI compiler supports mapping between Java and IDL objects. The `-iiop` flag causes `rmic` to generate stubs and ties (CORBA specific delegation mechanism) for remote objects using the IIOP protocol, rather than stubs and skeletons. Some other differences in the development of RMI-IIOP applications (as opposed to CORBA applications) are listed here:

The server-implementation class must extend the `javax.rmi.PortableRemoteObject` class.

JSDK includes the `tnameserv.exe` program, which is used as a naming service.

The JNDI lookup has a different appearance. It looks like this:

```
Object obj=ctx.lookup("FlightService");
        FlightServer fs = (FlightServer)

PortableRemoteObject.narrow(obj,FlightServer.class);
```

`rmic` must be run one extra time with the `-idl` option to generate IDL for CORBA clients.

While RMI is a lot simpler than CORBA, the latter gives you more flexibility in creating distributed applications. As a matter of fact, you may not even have a choice if an application written in CORBA is already in production and you need to write a Java application that communicates with it.

RMI and RMI-IIOP protocols are also implemented in the Enterprise JavaBeans containers that are explained later in the book in Part IV.

Summary

In this chapter we've shown you the simplest way to create a distributed application using Remote Method Invocation. It's readily available on any platform where Java exists and does not require any third-party middleware. You should also consider RMI for any Web application in which a Java applet communicates with a remote RMI server.

RMI technology allows you to arrange communication between the client and the server JVM in a unique way when the client can locate the remote object and dynamically load the code (objects) to the server for processing. The details of communication between the client and the server are hidden for a developer by means of subs and skeletons. The RMI principles have been used in the EJB components described later in Part IV of this book.

✦   ✦   ✦

The Presentation Tier

In This Part

Chapter 5
Studying Servlet
Programming

Chapter 6
Going Over
JSP Basics

Chapter 7
Using JSP Tag
Extensions

Studying Servlet Programming

❖ ❖ ❖ ❖

In This Chapter

Creating Java
Web applications

Using servlets
for processing
HTML forms

Providing
session tracking

Using cookies

Applying listeners
and filters

❖ ❖ ❖ ❖

Java servlets, empowered by other J2EE components, enable you to create responsive, reliable, and scalable server-side Web applications. They run inside a servlet container that communicates with the user's Web browser by exchanging HTTP request and response objects. The servlet container processes each servlet's request in a separate thread, maintains user sessions, creates response objects and sends them back to the client. Servlets are easily portable to any application server or servlet engine — it comes down to copying a Web-application archive to the right disk directory (see the section, "Deploying Servlets," later in this chapter).

In this chapter you'll learn how to work with servlets by developing some of the screens for the Magazine Publisher application described in Appendix B.

Creating a Magazine Publisher Application Using Servlets

When you use an online store or bank or when you search for some information on the Internet, your request is usually processed on the server side. Only a limited number of operations, such as simple calculations and input validation, are performed on the client's machine using Java applets and JavaScript.

However, Java applets have security restrictions and depend on the version of the Web browser's JVM (for example, some of the Java classes or methods may not be available in older versions of JVM). Also, if a Web browser has to download large Java programs, the site's response time will substantially increase. That's why the better choice is to keep only light-weight HTML pages (a thin client) on the client's machine, while major processing should be done by the programs running on the server. The server computers could be more powerful than the client computers, have the proper version of JVM, and might be clustered, load-balanced, fail-overed, and so on. Also the network bandwidth requirements are lowered if the client just sends short requests.

Because the Magazine Publisher is a Web application, we need to decide what software runs where. Let's start with the server.

The server side

Web server software supporting the HTTP protocol has to run on the server side. This Web server will "listen" for the user's requests, usually on port 80. If the Web server receives a simple request for a static HTML page, it can handle this request without any additional software.

The server also needs to run a servlet engine (or an application server that has a servlet container that is a component that supports the life cycle of servlets). If a user requests some information that should be retrieved programmatically from a database or any other resource, we'll use Java servlets that will accommodate the request, build an output HTML page dynamically, and pass that page over to the user with the help of the Web server. When the user's Web browser displays the received page, it does not know if that page was a static HTML page or a fresh one right from the oven (servlet engine).

Even though HTML is just a markup language, it has some basic elements and GUI components, such as buttons, text fields, check boxes, and dropdown lists, that allow users to enter data, make some selections, and submit requests to a remote server. For example, the HTML <FORM> tag enables users to enter and submit data from a Web page. Since this is not an HTML tutorial we'll just mention some important elements of this tag:

Note   All GUI controls should be placed between the <FORM> and </FORM> tags.

A <FORM> tag has important attributes such as action and method. The action attribute contains the uniform resource locator (URL) of the server program to which the browser should send the user's input. The method attribute tells the browser how to send the data; this attribute is usually either Get or Post, as shown in the following example:

```
<form action= "http://www.mymagpublisher.com/servlet/LoginServlet"
                                        method=Get>
```

You can create a text field as follows:

```
<input type=Text name="id" >
```

The name of the text field will be passed by the browser to the servlet as a parameter name.

The button that sends the data is of type Submit, and the button that clears all fields is of type Reset:

```
<input type="Submit">
<input type="Reset">
```

The client side

Our Magazine Publisher wants to maximize the number of customers by minimizing requirements for the client's computer. The publisher wants to ensure that even the clients with older computers and slow Internet connections will not wait long. Our user should be able to work with any system, from an old PC to a Unix-based dumb terminal to an Apple computer — as long as the system has a Web browser installed. The user will interact with the publisher using HTML pages. Since we are not going to install any software on the client machine, the maintenance of the system becomes easy because all software and hardware upgrades will be done in one central location — the publisher's company.

Creating an HTML login screen

Let's create a simple HTML login screen containing two text fields for the user ID and the password, and two buttons: Reset and Submit. Listing 5-1 shows the code for this screen, pub_login.html.

Listing 5-1: **pub_login.html**

```
<html>
<head>
<title>Magazine Publisher Login</title>
</head>
<body>
<P>
<form action="http://www.mymagpublisher.com
              /servlet/LoginServlet" method=Post>
   Enter Login  ID:  <input type=Text name="id" >
   <P>
   Enter Password: <input type=Password name="pwd">
   <P>
   <input type="Submit" value="Login">
   <input type="Reset" >
</form>
</body>
</html>
```

If you open this page in your browser, the screen will look like the one shown in Figure 5-1.

Figure 5-1: The HTML client — pub_login.html

The client's part is ready, so let's work on the `LoginServlet`.

Servlet structure and life cycle methods

To create a servlet for a Web application we'll have to derive our class from the `javax.servlet.http.HttpServlet` class, which in turn is derived from the `javax.servlet.GenericServlet` class. The simplified class diagram in Figure 5-2 shows an example of a user-created servlet called `MyServlet`.

Figure 5-2: The servlet inheritance hierarchy

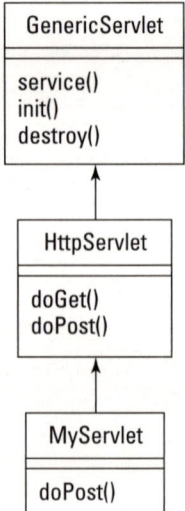

The servlet engine invokes methods such as `init`, `service`, and `destroy`. Application programmers can also create so-called *listener objects,* which are objects that are notified when some important events occur (as you'll see in "Listeners," later in this chapter).

Init()

The servlet container calls the `init()` method exactly once after instantiating the servlet. This method is called when the servlet is initially loaded by the container. When this happens depends on the deployment parameter — it may happen during the application server's startup, or when the servlet is being requested for the first time. This method is a good place to write code that creates non-user-specific resources, namely the creation of object pools. For example, you can create a pool of reusable connections objects to a messaging server (see Chapter 9). In general, object pooling could substantially improve performance of the application by minimizing the need of the Java garbage collection. The method `init` is overloaded and one of its versions receives the object `ServletConfig` as an argument. This object provides the method `getInitParameter()` to find the values of the configuration parameters, if any. For details, see "Examining the `web.xml` Deployment Descriptor," later in this chapter.

service()

The `service()` method is called on the servlet's ancestor every time the servlet receives a user's request. At this point the servlet container passes an instance of the class `ServletRequest`, which contains the client's data, to the servlet. The `service()` method creates the objects `HttpServletRequest` and `HttpServletResponse` and passes them as parameters to the `doGet()` or `doPost()` method of the descendent class.

destroy()

The method `destroy()` is called by the servlet container to notify the servlet that it's about to be removed from service. This method will be called only once, and developers should use it to program clean up of any resources that are being held, for example threads and file, `handlesdoPost()` and `doGet()`.

A programmer has to create a class derived from the `HttpServlet` and override the `doGet()` or `doPost()` method according to the `method` attribute used in the HTML form. The request object contains the information received from the Web browser, and the servlet's output will be sent back to the user as an instance of the response object.

Writing the servlet

Let's write the login servlet shown in Listing 5-2 that will be invoked by `pub_login. html`. This servlet checks the user's ID and, if it is correct, greets the user; otherwise it displays an error message. To stay focused on servlet-coding techniques we'll just compare the ID and a password with the hard-coded values `jsmith` and `spring12`.

Listing 5-2: **The LoginServlet.java class**

```java
import java.io.*;
import javax.servlet.*;
import javax.servlet.http.*;

public class LoginServlet extends
                javax.servlet.http.HttpServlet {

// Do not declare these variables on the
// class level - the same instance of
// LoginServlet is shared by all users


public void doPost(HttpServletRequest req,
                       HttpServletResponse res)
    throws ServletException, IOException  {

    res.setContentType("text/html");
    PrintWriter out = res.getWriter();

    String id = req.getParameter("id");
    String password = req.getParameter("pwd");

    out.println("<HTML><BODY>");

    if("jsmith".equalsIgnoreCase(id) &&
        "spring12".equalsIgnoreCase(password)){
    out.println("Hello "+ id +
                       ". Welcome to our magazines! ");
    } else {
        out.println("Id/Password combination is not valid");
    }

    out.println("</BODY></HTML>");
  }
}
```

When the doPost() method of LoginServlet is being called by the container, it receives references to the HttpServletRequest and HttpServletResponse objects. First the code calls the method setOutput() of the HttpServletResponse object to specify the output type text/html. Then it gets the reference to the servlet's output stream of type PrintWriter. The method println() of the PrintWriter's sends the text output to the user.

Note   The servlet sends to the browser text surrounded by the HTML <HTML> and <BODY> tags. Actually, our LoginServlet can send any mix of plain text and HTML tags.

Third, the servlet gets the parameters supplied by the user's browser from the request object. It can do this with the help of such methods as getParameter(), getParameterValues(), and getParameterNames().

Fourth, after applying some business rules, the servlet forms the content of the output page and sends it to the output stream PrintWriter.

At this point the servlet has to be compiled as any other Java class and deployed as described in the section "Deploying Servlets," later in this chapter.

Even though the code in Listing 5-2 looks simple, two invisible players are present here — the Web browser and the servlet container. In this example, two computers talk to each other and some of the methods are called by the servlet container. This is why it's very important to understand what happens and when in this example. The following is a list of the steps involved in the browser/servlet interaction, using LoginServlet as an example:

1. The user enters his or her ID and password and presses the Submit button on the Login Web page.

2. The Web browser tries to connect to http://www.mymagpublisher.com/ servlet/LoginServlet and sends the entered data using Post.

3. A servlet engine checks to see if the LoginServlet is already running.

4. If LoginServlet is not running the servlet container starts it and invokes its method init().

5. The servlet container calls the service() method of the servlet's superclass, passing HttpServletRequest and HTTPServletResponse to it as arguments.

6. The ancestor's method service() calls the doPost() method of the LoginServlet.

7. The code in LoginServlet.doPost() extracts the data entered by the user from HttpServletRequest.

8. After applying some application business logic contained in the doPost() method, the results are sent to the user's browser when the code invokes the method println() on the object PrintWriter. The method getWriter() gets the reference to this object from the HTTPServletResponse.

9. The user's Web browser displays the received HTML page.

Please note that we did not use instance variables in LoginServlet, because the same servlet is used by multiple users. If you want to ensure that only one thread processes the method service() at any given time, implement the interface SingleThreadModel in your servlet . This interface has no methods to implement. Its use is generally not recommended, as it slows down the servlet's performance.

HTTP Get and Post requests

If the HTML `<FORM>` tag has the attribute `method=Get`, the servlet has to override the method `doGet()`. In this case the Web browser will append the values entered by the user to the end of the URL string, using the question mark (?) as a delimiter. For example, if `pub_login` has the `method=GET` as its form attribute, the Web browser will create the following URL string:

```
http://www.mymagpublisher.com /servlet/LoginServlet?id=
"jsmith"&pwd="Spring12"
```

The HTML method `Get` has the following disadvantages:

The length of the URL string is limited.

Different browsers have different restrictions on the URL length.

The URL string can be used only for text/data exchange. The binary data are not passed as a part of the URL.

The data is not protected—the password is visible as it's a part of the URL.

If the HTML `<FORM>` tag uses the `method=Post` attribute, the servlet has to override the `doPost()` method. The `doPost()` method does not append the user's input to the URL string and can be used for sending and receiving various datatypes described in the Multipurpose Internet Mail Extensions (MIME).

If you'd like a servlet to handle both `Get` and `Post` requests, override both the `doGet()` and `doPost()` methods. If you place the application's code in the method `doGet()`, the method `doPost()` should look like this:

```
public void doPost(HttpServletRequest req,
                            HttpServletResponse res)
throws ServletException, IOException {

  doGet(req, res);  // execute the code from doGet()

}
```

We started this chapter with a detailed discussion of the login servlet example, to give you a feeling of basic data flow between the servlet and the Web client. The following sections will discuss more advanced topics such as servlet context and session tracking.

Using the Servlet Context

The servlet context is a place inside the container where the servlet(s) live. More than one Web application can be deployed in the servlet container, and each of them will have its own servlet context. The `ServletContext` class can be used by the servlet whenever it needs to use the services of the container.

Java does not have global variables, but in a stand-alone Java application you can use the `System.setProperty()` and `getProperty()` methods to create variables visible by all the application's classes. You can also do this by using the following methods of the `ServletContext` class:

✦ `setAttribute()`

✦ `getAttribute()`

✦ `getAttributeNames()`

✦ `removeAttribute()`

For example, a servlet can set the database name in the `init()` method, as follows:

```
getServletContext().setAttribute("com.mycompany.dbname","Alpha");
```

Another servlet from the same Web application can get this value as follows:

```
String dbName = getServletContext().getAttribute("com.mycompany.dbname");
```

Keep in mind that these attributes are local to a Java Virtual Machine (JVM), and that in a distributed environment such global parameters should be stored in the `HttpSession` object. This object is described in "Session Tracking with Servlets," later in this chapter, or in other persisted objects.

The `ServletContext` class allows a servlet to load shareable file resources such as HTML, GIF, and so on. Here's an example:

```
InputStream in = getServletContext().getResourceAsStream
("/myLogo.gif");
```

You'll see more examples of the `ServletContext` class usage later in the chapter in the sections "Using RequestDispatcher" and "Listeners."

The following section will explain how a servlet can re-direct the processing of the user request to a different Web resource.

Performing URL Redirection

Servlets often need to redirect the processing of the user's request to a different URL, servlet or a JavaServer Page JSP (see Chapter 6, "Going Over JSP Basics"). You can do this by using either of the following methods: `HttpServletResponse.sendRedirect()` or `RequestDispatcher.forward()` explained in the next two sections. The JavaScript language also has a mechanism for redirection on the client side, but the JavaScript language is beyond the scope of this book.

Using RequestDispatcher

Let's say `LoginServlet` needs to pass control to `LostPasswordServlet` if
the user enters the wrong password. The reference to the instance of the
`RequestDispatcher` can be obtained from the `ServletContext` by means of
either the `getRequestDispatcher()` or `getNamedRequestDispatcher()` method.
When this is done just call the dispatcher's `forward()` method, providing the
`HttpServletRequest` and `HttpServletResponse` as arguments. For example:

```
    ServletContext context = getServletContext();
    RequestDispatcher requestDisp = null;
    String password = req.getParameter("pwd");

      if (password.equals("spring12") {
        requestDisp =
context.getRequestDispatcher("MainServlet");
      }
      else {
        requestDisp =
context.getRequestDispatcher("LostPasswordServlet");
      }

      requestDisp.forward(req,res);
```

If the entered password is correct, the `forward()` method passes the request
and response objects from `LoginServlet` to `MainServlet`, and from then on
`MainServlet` interacts with the user. If the password is not correct, `LostPassword`
servlet will be in charge. (See "The Lost Password screen example," later in this
chapter, for details.)

If the first servlet needs to stay in control and include its own output to the
response object as well as the output produced by another servlet or JSP, the
`include()` method should be used instead of `forward()`. For example:

```
  requestDisp.include(req,res)
```

It's worth mentioning that an instance of `RequestDispatcher` can also be
obtained from the `ServletRequest` object. The difference between calling
`getRequestDispatcher()` on `ServletRequest` and calling `getRequestDispatcher()`
on `ServletContext` is that `ServletRequest` enables you to specify a relative path
as a method argument.

Using sendRedirect()

While the `forward()` method performs the redirection on the server side using
original request and response objects, the `sendRedirect()` method sends the
request with the new URL back to the client, which connects to this URL, thereby
creating a new pair of request/response objects:

```
response.sendRedirect("www.anothersite.com") ;
```

As you can guess, the sendRedirect() method is slower than forward(), but it gives you more flexibility because it can redirect the user to any URL, while forward() works only within the same Web application.

The Lost Password screen example

Listing 5-3 contains the source code of LostPasswordServlet and the output screen it generates appears in Figure 5-3. The screen enables users to enter their e-mail addresses. If the e-mail addresses are known to the magazine's publisher, PasswordMailerServlet will e-mail the forgotten password to the specified address. Please note that we are able to get the user's ID from the request object forwarded from LoginServlet.

Listing 5-3: **LostPassword.java**

```java
import javax.servlet.*;
import javax.servlet.http.*;
public class LostPasswordServlet extends HttpServlet {
 public void doPost(HttpServletRequest req,
                          HttpServletResponse res)
   throws ServletException, IOException  {
   PrintWriter out = res.getWriter();

   String id = req.getParameter("id");

   out.println("<head><title>");
   out.println("Magazine Publisher Lost Password");
   out.println("</title></head><body>");
   out.println("Dear " + id + "<P>");
   out.println("Please enter the email address you have ");
   out.println("registered with your Magazine Publisher");
   out.println("account. We will send instructions on ");
   out.println("how to reset your password ");
   out.println("to that address.<P>");
   out.println("<form action=\""http://");
   out.println(
       "www.mymagpublisher.com/PasswordMailerServlet");
   out.println("method=Get>");
   out.println("Enter e-mail: <input type=Text ");
   out.println("name="email">");
   out.println("<input type=\"Submit\"");
   out.println("value=\"Send\"></form></body></html>");
 }

}
```

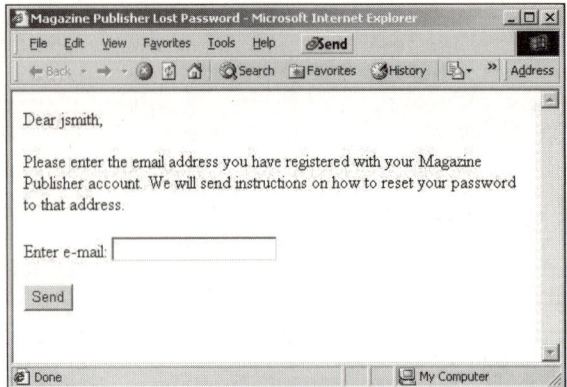

Figure 5-3: The Lost Password screen

As you can see from the lost password example, we may have situations when the user's request has to be processed by more than one Web resource. The following section will explain how to store and share the important information about the user's session between multiple servlet requests.

Session tracking with servlets

HTTP is a *stateless* protocol. This means that if a user inputs some data on a Web page and then goes to another page, the second page does not "know" what has been done on the first. *Session tracking* allows the server application to remember the user's input and carry it from page to page.

A *session* is some logical task that a user tries to accomplish on a Web site. Think of the so-called shopping cart application, for example, in which the process of buying a book may involve several steps — book selection, input of billing and shipping information, and so on. Multiple users connect to the same servlet, but each of them has a personal shopping cart.

Session information can be stored either in the client or in the server tier, and the Java Servlets API enables you to store the session data by using cookies, rewriting the URL, and using hidden form fields cookies or the session tracking API provided by the HTTPSession class. These alternatives are discussed in the following sections.

Cookies

A *cookie* is a small file that a Web server may send to the user's Web browser, which in turn saves it to the hard disk. This file contains an ID that is unique to the computer, so the server can identify the user when he or she connects to that particular Web site again. Obviously, your bank's site and a bookstore will send cookies with different data. Whenever you connect to a Web site, your browser finds all cookies for this site and sends them to the URL as part of the HttpServletRequest object.

Internet browsers give you the option to disable cookies. Your Web browser will store up to 20 cookies per Web site, and the size of a cookie cannot exceed 4K. A servlet can also specify the maximum lifetime of the cookie in seconds.

The following code snippet shows how a servlet can create and send a cookie that will store the user's account ID:

```
public void doGet(HttpServletRequest req,
                        HttpServletResponse res){

Cookie myCookie = new Cookie("acctID","12345");

// Set the lifetime of the cookie to 24 hours
myCookie.setMaxAge(60*60*24);
res.addCookie(myCookie);
}
```

When a user connects to the same site again, a servlet can retrieve the client's cookies from the HttpServletRequest object, as shown here:

```
Cookie [] cookies = req.getCookies();
for (i=0; i < cookies.length; i++){
  Cookie currentCookie = cookie[i];
  String name = currentCookie.getName();
  String value = currentCookie.getValue();

  if(name.equals("acctID")){
      // find some data about the user based in the account ID
and create a
      // personalized page. For example display the books which
user
      // has been looking for during the previous visit, etc.
  }

}
```

Cookies enable you to store the session information on the client side, which has the following advantages.

Cookies can survive server crashes because they are stored on the client's hard disk.

They lighten the load on the server's memory.

They simplify server fail-over procedure, because they may store the valuable data about the last user selections made before the server has crashed.

Cookies also have the following disadvantages:

Cookies can be read by unauthorized users.

They can increase the load on the network.

User can disable cookies in their Web browsers.

URL rewriting

URL rewriting allows the session ID to be attached to the end of the URL string to help the servlet container identify the client for subsequent requests. The session info is appended in the same way as the parameters in an HTTP GET request. The major advantage of URL rewriting is that it enables servlets to keep track of the session when a user disables cookies. The automatic switch between the use of cookies and URL rewriting is a configurable parameter of the servlet container.

When a servlet appends the session info to the URL, it should encode this URL using the HttpServletResponse method urlEncode(). This method will determine whether the Web browser supports cookies, and if not it'll attach the session ID to the URL. For example, if the original HTML page has the following link,

```
<a href="http://www.mymagpublisher.com/servlet/subscribeServlet">:
```

the servlet can rewrite this URL and append the session ID, if needed, as follows:

```
String newURL =
res.urlEncode("http://www.mymagpublisher.com/servlet/
subscribeServlet");
out.println("<a href=\""+newUrl + "\">Subscribe to
Magazine</a>");
```

The Web browser might get the URL http://www.mymagpublisher.com/servlet/subscribeServlet;jsessionid=657487.

Hidden fields

HTML form's hidden fields are yet another place for storing session data. The hidden type is one of the valid types for the input fields of the HTML tag, and when a servlet prepares an HTML page it may include one or more hidden fields.

The following is a code fragment from a servlet that creates an HTML page and stores selected magazines in the HTML code. Please note the bold code that creates and sends to the Web browser a hidden field:

```
out.println("<form action=
http://www.mymagpublisher.com/servlet/subscribeServlet>");
out println("Select another magazine: <input type=text
name=item");
out.println("<input type=submit value=Add>");
out.println("<input type=hidden name=item value=Smart
Cooking>");
out.println("</form>");
```

The user will see an empty text field with a button, but when you check the source of this page, you'll see the hidden field with the value Smart Cooking.

During subsequent requests the servlet can retrieve all the values from the hidden fields, as shown here:

```
String[] selectedItems=request.getParameterValues("item");
```

All previously selected magazines (as contained in our shopping cart) will be stored in the `selectedItems` array. Hidden fields give you more flexibility than URL rewriting, because no size restriction exists and your selections are not visible unless a knowledgeable user looks at the code of the HTML page.

The session-tracking API with HttpSession object

Instead of sending the shopping cart across the network to the client, you can keep it inside the `javax.servlet.http.HttpSession` object in the servlet container's memory. The container creates one `HttpSession` object per client, and the servlet can store any objects as key/value pairs there. These objects are the attributes of the `HttpSession` object. Figure 5-4 shows the interaction between the user and a servlet container. Please note that each client has a separate `HttpSession`.

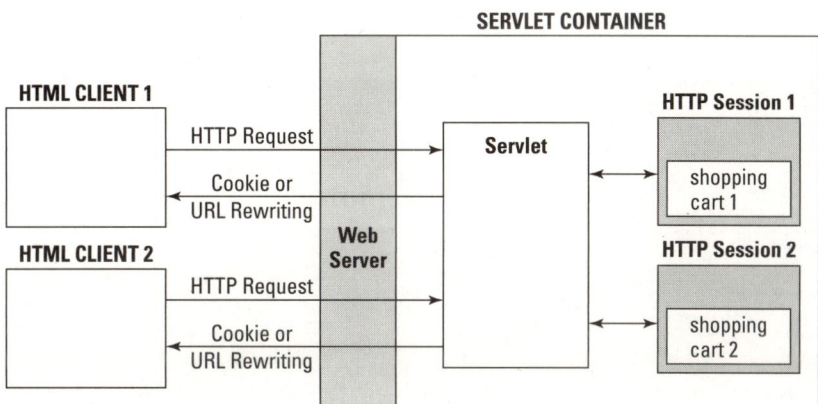

Figure 5-4: Session tracking

The following line of code creates or finds a session object:

```
HttpSession mySession = request.getSession(true);
```

The `getSession(true)` call means "Find my session object, or create a new one if not found." Usually any shopping process consists of a number of subsequent servlet calls, such as listing an inventory, adding an item to the shopping cart, entering the shipping information, and so on. The `getSession(true)` call should be used in the very first servlet. At this moment the application server generates a unique session ID and sends it to the user's Web browser as a cookie or by using URL rewriting.

The `getSession(false)` call means "find my session object," assuming that the object might have been created prior to this HTTP request. If this call returns `null`, the session object may have been destroyed, and you should display a message about the expired session to let the user start the process from scratch.

Now let's create a simple class that represents a magazine:

```
class Magazine {
    String title;
    double price;
}
```

This is what you can do in the `doGet()` method of the servlet:

```
...
// Find or create a session object
HttpSession session = request.getSession(true);

// We'll store selected magazines in a Vector.
// Find  the shopping cart that might have been
// created during previous calls to this servlet.

Vector myShoppingCart=session.getAttribute("shoppingCart");

if (myShoppingCart == null){
    // This is the first call - create a Vector
     myShoppingCart = new Vector();
}

// create an instance of a magazine object
Magazine  selectedMag = new Magazine();

selectedMag.title=request.getParameter("magTitle");
selectedMag.price=
        Double.parseDouble(request.getParameter("price"));

// Add the magazine to  shopping cart
myShoppingCart.addElement(selectedMag);

// Put the shopping cart back into the session object
session.setAttribute("shoppingCart", myShoppingCart);
...
```

After the order has been placed, the servlet should close the session by making the following call:

```
session.invalidate();
```

If the session has not been invalidated explicitly, the application server will invalidate it automatically after the time specified in the server's parameters has expired. (See the `<session-timeout>` parameter in the section, "Examining the web.xml

Deployment Descriptor," later in this chapter.) Application server vendors may provide a GUI tool to specify the session timeout. For example, if you use WebLogic or WebSphere, you can specify the time using the respective administration console. Idling sessions can also be programmatically invalidated after a specified period of time. For example, a program can perform the following call after creating a session object, in order to invalidate it in 120 seconds:

```
session.setMaxInactiveInterval(120); // invalidate in 2 minutes
```

Example of a LoginServlet with an access counter

Let's look at the "non-shopping" use of the sessions in Listing 5-4. Let's modify the `LoginServlet` to allow only a limited number of login attempts. A simple class-level variable counter that is incremented in every `doPost()` method call will not work for us because only one servlet exists for all users, and this counter would list the total number of login attempts. We need to maintain a separate counter for each user; hence the session object is the right tool.

Listing 5-4: **LoginServlet.java with the counter**

```java
import java.io.*;
import javax.servlet.*;
import javax.servlet.http.*;
public class LoginServlet extends
            javax.servlet.http.HttpServlet {

 public void doPost(HttpServletRequest req,
                    HttpServletResponse res)
   throws ServletException, IOException   {

  res.setContentType("text/html");
  PrintWriter out = res.getWriter();

  String id = req.getParameter("id");
  String password = req.getParameter("pwd");

  HttpSession session = request.getSession(true);

  Integer counter=session.getAttribute("logAttempt");

  if (counter == null){
   // This is the first call - create a counter
   counter=new Integer(1);
  } else {
    // do not allow more that 5 attempts
    if (counter.intValue()>5){
```

Continued

Listing 5-4 *(continued)*

```
        res.sendRedirect("BadLoginServlet");
    }
}

// Store the counter in the session object
session.setAttribute("logAttempt",counter);

out.println("<HTML><BODY>");

if("jsmith".equalsIgnoreCase(id) &&
    "spring12".equalsIgnoreCase(password)){
out.println("Welcome "+ id +"!");

    // store the user's ID for other servlets
    session.setAttribute("userID",id);
} else {
    out.println("Id/Password combination is not valid");
}

out.println("</BODY></HTML>");
    }
}
```

The next section will introduce you to servlet listeners — a feature that helps to keep track of important events that may happen during a servlet life cycle.

Listeners

Starting from the Servlet 2.3 specification developers have been able keep track of important ServletContext and HttpSession events. Listeners are Java classes that a programmer can write and deploy in the Web-application archive. (See "Deploying Servlets," later in this chapter, for details.) These listeners can be notified of lifecycle events and attribute changes. Servlet listeners are defined as Java interfaces; see Table 5-1 below.

Typically, a servlet-context creation event is used for the creation of such reusable objects as connections to the databases, messaging servers, and so on. When a servlet context is about to be shut down these objects should be gracefully closed. These interfaces are used in the same way as any other Java interface: Just write a class that implements one of them and specify its name in the deployment descriptor. (The web.xml deployment descriptor is discussed later in this chapter.) Each of the callback methods defined in these interfaces has one argument — an object describing an event. The classes that represent various events are listed in Table 5-2.

Table 5-1
Servlet listener interfaces

Interface Name	Event Description	Interface Methods

`ServletContextListener`
 	
Package: `javax.Servlet`
	Creation or shutdown of the servlet context	`contextInitialized()`
		
		`contextDestroyed()`

`ServletContextAttributeListener`
 	
Package: `javax.Servlet`
	Addition, replacement, or removal of the attributes of the `Servlet Context` object	`attributeAdded()`
		
		`attributeReplaced()`
		
		`attributeRemoved()`

`HttpSessionListener`
 	
Package: `javax.Servlet.http`
	Creation, invalidation, or timeout of the session	`sessionCreated()`
		
		`sessionDestroyed()`

`HttpSessionAttributeListener`
 	
Package: `javax.Servlet.http`
	Addition, replacement, or removal of the session attributes	`attributeAdded()`
		
		`attributeReplaced()`
		
		`attributeRemoved()`

Table 5-2
Servlet listener event classes

Class Name	Method(s)
`ServletContextEvent`	`getServletContext()`

`ServletContextAttributeEvent`
`extends ServletContextEvent`
	`getName()`
	
	`getValue()`

`HttpSessionEvent`	`getSession()`

`HttpSessionBindingEvent extends`
`HttpSessionEvent`
	`getName()`
	
	`getValue()`

The following code fragment demonstrates how to write a servlet-context listener that connects to an external messaging server when the servlet context is created. This listener closes the connection when the context is destroyed.

```
package com.magpub.listeners;
public class MagPublisherContextListener
            implements ServletContextListener {
    private ServletContext context = null;
    public void contextInitialized(ServletContextEvent e){
            this.context=e.getServletContext();

        // Establish a connection to the JMS server
            Connection mqCon = ....

        // Store connection to the messaging server in
        // the ServletContext object.
            context.setAttribute("mqConnection",mqCon);
    }

    public void contextDestroyed(ServletContextEvent e){

        // disconnect from the messaging server
            mqCon = (Connection)
                    context.getAttribute("mqConnection");

        mqCon.disconnect();
    }
}
```

Note   Do not forget to specify the `MagPublisherContextListener` class in the `web.xml` file as described in "Deploying Servlets," later in this chapter.

Session listeners can be implemented in a similar way. Say we need to create an administrative tool that displays all active users working with a `MagPublisher` servlet. Every time a user creates a session we can send a JMS message to a queue. These messages will be retrieved and displayed by another GUI program. For example:

```
public class MagPublisherSessionListener
            implements HttpSessionListener {

    public void sessionCreated(HttpSessionEvent e)
      {
        // The code sending a JMS message
        // to add a user goes here
      }

    public void sessionDestroyed(HttpSessionEvent e)
      {
        // The code sending a JMS message
        // to remove a user goes here
      }
}
```

The act of adding an object or attribute to, or removing it from, a session can be caught by implementing the `HttpSessionAttributeListener`. If this attribute/object also implements the `HttpSessionBindingListener` interface, the servlet container sends a notification to this object saying something like "Hey, you've been bound to (or unbound from) a session!" One more interface is worth mentioning here—`HttpSessionActivationListener`. The servlet container may decide to move session objects from one JVM to another, and it may passivate (temporarily remove from memory) and activate the session during this process. A container may also persist sessions and reactivate them after restart. A container is required to send a notification about these events to all attributes bound to sessions implementing `HttpSessionActivationListener`.

The next section will introduce you to yet another interesting feature of servlets called *filters*.

Filters

Servlet filters were first introduced in the Servlet 2.3 Specification and are used for additional processing or transformation of data contained in the request or response objects. Basically, filters allow you to plug in Java classes performing some business processing before or after the servlet. This is done without changing the servlet's code just by simple modification of the deployment descriptor elements located in the web.xml file. Please refer to the section, "Examining the web-xml Deployment Descriptor," later in this chapter for all configuration related examples. Filters add an ability to change the behavior of the servlets without changing the servlets' code. They act like pre- or post-processors. Let's looks at the example that shows how filters can make your code more elegant.

How can you write a servlet that performs a particular type of processing, but based on some deployment parameter sends its output either in HTML or XML format? In the pre-filter era you'd have to write an `if` statement in the method `doPost()`, like this:

```
// Get the value of the someInitParam in the method init() as
described above
...
if (someInitParam=='a'){
   out.println("<HTML>");
   ...
}else if (someInitParam =='b'){
   out.println("<?xml version=\"1.0\"?>");
   ...
}
```

However, if the output in the WML format is requested the servlet's code has to be modified to add yet another `else if` statement. Filters enable you to remove formatting or some other reusable processing of the incoming or outgoing datafrom the servlet's class. They act as plugins to the request and response objects and can perform additional processing for existing servlets without requiring modification to the servlets' code. The following reusable tasks are good candidates to be used in the filters rather than in the servlets themselves:

✦ Encryption

✦ Sign-on

✦ Auditing

✦ Data compressing

✦ Performance benchmarking

✦ Debug logging

Filters can also be chained to create a combination of functions without modifying the servlet's code—just add another <FILTER> section to the deployment descriptor file to turn the filter on. By modifying another configuration parameter <filter-mapping> you can apply the filter to one or multiple servlets.

The package javax.servlet provides three simple interfaces: Filter, FilterConfig, and FilterChain. To create a filter, write a Java class that implements the javax.servlet.Filter interface, which contains the methods listed in Table 5-3.

Table 5-3
The filter interface

Method Name	Description
doFilter(ServletRequest req, ServletResponse res, FilterChain chain)	Called by the container whenever a client requests a servlet that has this particular filter specified in the file web.xml. The third parameter allows the filter to pass these objects to the next filter in the chain, if any.
init(FilterConfig filtConfig)	Called by the container when the filter is loaded.
destroy()	Called when the filter is unloaded.

The interface FilterConfig provides an access to the initialization parameters of the servlet and to the object ServletContext. It has the following methods: getInitParameter(), getInitParameterNames(), getServletContext(), and getFilterName(). A reference to the FilterConfig object is given to the filter by the servlet container as an argument of the method init(), and it's a good idea to make it available for all filter methods by storing it in a class variable.

The interface `FilterChain` has only one method `doFilter()` with two parameters: `ServletRequest` and `ServletResponse`. In case of request filtering you call it to pass control to the next filter in a chain or a servlet. For response filters this method sends the output back to the user's Web browser.

The following code fragment illustrates the creation of a filter that will intercept and log all requests. After the `LogFilter` class is compiled, its name and mapping to the application resources has to be listed in the file `web.xml` (as explained in "Examining the web.xml Deployment Descriptor," later in this chapter).

```java
package com.magpub.filters;

import java.util.Date;

public class LogFilter implements Filter{
    private FilterConfig fConfig=null;
    private String custRepFile=null;

    public void init(FilterConfig filterConfig){
        fConfig=filterConfig;
        // Get an  initialization parameter CustRepFile
specified in
        // the <init> section of the  web.xml

        custRepFile = fConfig.getInitParameter("CustRepFile");
    }

    public void doFilter(ServletRequest req, ServletResponse
res,
                                        FilterChain
chain){
    // Log  IP addresses of user machines requesting a servlet.

        log("Received request from " + req.getRemoteHost());

    // Pass control to the next filter in chain or the servlet
      chain.doFilter(req,res);

    }

    public void destroy(){
        fConfig=null;
    }

    // A user-defined method
    public void log(String msg){
      Date date=new Date();
      System.out.println("Date:" + date+"," + msg)
    }

}
```

Say you want to notify security administrator about the IP addresses of the users who entered invalid credentials on the Login screen. The e-mail address of the security administrator could be retrieved in a filter from the initialization parameter, for example.

```
String email = fConfig.getInitParameter("SecAdminEmail");
String ipAddress = request.getRemoteHost();
```

Now you can add the code sending an e-mail as described in Chapter 8, "Working with JavaMail."

The following code fragment shows how to apply some encryption for all parameters that are being sent to a servlet:

```
    public void doFilter(ServletRequest req, ServletResponse res,
                                             FilterChain
chain){
   // Get all parameters from the request object and encrypt them
   // using some custom method encrypt()

   Enumeration params = request.getParameterNames();
   while(params.hasMoreElements()){
     String parName=(String)params.nextElement();
     String parValue= request.getParameter(parName);
     String encryptedValue = encrypt(parValue);

     req.setAttribute(parName,encryptedValue);

   }

   // Pass control to the next filter in chain or the servlet
     chain.doFilter(req,res);
   }
```

Please note that we set the encrypted values as attributes of the request object. The servlet or the next filter in the chain should retrieve these values using such methods as getAttributeNames() and getAttributes().

Now let's look at the filtering of the responses. This time we will actually modify the response object rather than just adding an attribute to it. Since the arguments of the method doFilter() have types ServletRequest and ServletResponse, you can create your own wrappers around the HttpServletRequest and HttpServletResponse to create more sophisticated filters. For this purpose Java servlets API provides the classes HttpServletRequestWrapper and HttpServletResponseWrapper.

Imagine that a servlet has to be implemented in multiple branches of a company. Each branch has to display a footer on the output HTML screen containing its own address, telephone and some other static information. This could be achieved by modifying the response object generated by the servlet.

First, we need to prevent a servlet from closing the output response stream so the filter could intercept and modify the output. This could be done by creating a customized response object that generates a so-called stand-in stream. Basically, the servlet's filter creates a wrapper response object and gives it to the servlet using the call similar to the following:

```
doFilter(request, wrapper);
```

where the `wrapper` is an instance of a subclass of `HttpServletResponseWrapper`.

When the servlet sends its response object using this wrapper, we'll intercept and modify it in the filter class as shown in the following code snippet. This technique is an example of a well-known design pattern called Decorator or Wrapper, when an instance of a class is modified to gain additional functionality. A wrapper class has the same interface as the object it contains, but provides an additional processing inside the interface method(s).

```
public class FooterFilter implements Filter{
    private FilterConfig fConfig=null;
    private String branchAddress =null;

   public void init(FilterConfig filterConfig){
       fConfig=filterConfig;
       // Get an  initialization parameter branchAddress
specified in
       // the <init> section of the  web.xml

       branchAddress =
fConfig.getInitParameter("BranchAddress");
       }

     public void doFilter(ServletRequest req, ServletResponse
res,
                                                 FilterChain
chain){
     PrintWriter out =  res.getWriter();


    // Pass the servlet's output to the Web browser or to the
next
    // filter in chain
     TextResponseWrapper wrapper = new TextResponseWrapper(

(HttpServletResponse)res);
    chain.doFilter(req,wrapper);

    // A response modification part
    java.io.CharArrayWriter caw = new
java.io.CharArrayWriter();

    // Get the servlet's output string up to the tag </body>
```

```
    String servletOutput = wrapper.toString();
    servletOutput= servletOutput.substring(0,

servletOutput.indexOf("</body>")-1);

    // Write the first part of the output to the buffer
    caw.write(servletOutput);

    // Append the address of the branch
    caw.write("<p>" + branchAddress);

    // Append  the closing tags of the HTML page
    caw.write("</body></html>");

    // Re-calculate and set the new length of the writer's
buffer
    res.setContentLength(caw.toString().length());

    // send the output to the Web browser
    out.write(caw.toString());
    out.close();
    }
  }
```

Following is the code of the response wrapper that has been used in the
FooterFilter. This class overrides the method getWriter() to substitute the
standard output stream with the customized one which is constructed in the filter.

```
public class TextResponseWrapper extends
HttpServletResponseWrapper {
    private java.io.CharArrayWriter buffer;
    public String toString() {
        return buffer.toString();
    }
    public TextResponseWrapper(HttpServletResponse res){
        super(res);
        buffer = new java.io.CharArrayWriter();
    }
    public PrintWriter getWriter(){
        return new PrintWriter(buffer);
    }
  }
}
```

We've mentioned various configuration parameters that can be used when a servlet
is deployed. In the next section we'll discuss in detail the process of servlet deployment and various parameters that can be used in the servlet's deployment descriptor file, web.xml.

Deploying servlets

Java Community Process provides the following definition of a Web application in the servlet specification: "A Web application is a collection of servlets, HTML pages, classes and other resources that make up a complete application on a Web server."

J2EE defines a standard way to deploy Web applications. It suggests that all components of a Web application should be packaged in the Web application archive (WAR) — the file with extension `.war`, which has the same format as `.jar` files. (The WAR is discussed next.) A Web application could be deployed either independently in the .war file, or it could be included in the Enterprise Application archive (.ear file) along with other application components, such as Enterprise JavaBeans. (See Part IV, "The Service Tier" for details.)

Multiple Web applications can be deployed on the same application server. Keep in mind though, that an application server assigns the same cookie name (`JSESSIONID`) for the session tracking cookies for all Web applications. If you use this name for the user authentication, refer to your vendor's documentation to see how to control the name of the cookie in the Web application. For example, the WebLogic application server provides a special deployment parameter `CookieName` for this.

The Web-application archive

Web-application archives are created with the Java jar utility, just like regular Java archives, which contain multiple files in a compressed form compatible with zip files. A sample jar command is shown at the end of this section. The WAR has to store deployed files using the following directory structure:

✦ The *top level* contains the resources that you'd put in a regular document root directory (HTML files, JavaServer Pages, and client-side resources).

✦ The *META-INF* subdirectory contains the file `manifest.mf`, which contains information about the files in this archive.

✦ The *WEB-INF directory* can contain the `web.xml` deployment descriptor and JSP tag library descriptors, if any.

✦ The *XML* `web.xml` *file* maps names of the deployed objects to full names of corresponding Java classes, and can contain some other application properties such as session configuration, security, and others.

✦ *Subdirectory classes* contain compiled servlets, beans, and utility classes.

✦ The `lib` *subdirectory* is for any additional jar files. If the same class exists in the subdirectory classes as well as in jar, the version from the `classes` directory is loaded.

✦ The `tlds` *subdirectory* is for JSP tag libraries (see Chapter 7, "Using JSP Tag Extensions"), if any.

A Web-application developer usually creates this directory structure on the local disk, and creates the WAR when the files are ready for deployment. The following command adds all the files from the current directory into the file `MagPublisher.war`:

```
jar cvf MagPublisher.war *
```

As long as your files are located in the directory structure described above, your Web application could be deployed even without creation of the WAR, which is typical for the development stage of the application.

As we've mentioned in the beginning of this chapter, static resources such as HTML files, images, jars and applets could be processed be the Web server alone, that's why you may leave these resources outside of the WAR in the document root directory.

Examining the web.xml Deployment Descriptor

The `web.xml` deployment descriptor is an XML file that can be prepared by any plain-text editor. The application-server vendor may provide a GUI tool for creation deployment descriptors. While `web.xml` is a required file for every Web application deployed in a J2EE compliant application server, vendors may also create additional deployment descriptor files. Please refer to your vendor's documentation describing the servlet deployment procedure.

The `web.xml` file should start with a `DOCTYPE` element pointing to the proper DTD file. For example, for the Servlet 2.3 Specification this element should look like this:

```
<!DOCTYPE web-app PUBLIC
  "-//Sun Microsystems, Inc.//DTD Web Application 2.3//EN"
     "http://java.sun.com/dtd/web-app_2_3.dtd">
```

Mandatory servlet elements

The following servlet names are mapped to actual servlet classes that might be located in packages:

```
<web-app>
  <servlet>
    <servlet-name>LoginServlet</servlet-name>
    <servlet-class>LoginServlet </servlet-class>
  </servlet>
  <servlet>
    <servlet-name>BadLoginServlet</servlet-name>
    <servlet-class>
         com.security.BadLoginServlet
```

```
        </servlet-class>
    </servlet>
</web-app>Optional Servlet Elements
```

While tags such as `<servlet-name>` and `<servlet-class>` are required elements, the following list includes some of the optional XML tags:

✦ `<init-param>` is a servlet-initialization parameter that can be accessed by means of `ServletConfig.getInitParameter()` — for example:

```
<init-param>
    <param-name>CustRepFile</param-name>
    <param-value>c:\custrep.ser</param-value>
</init-param>
```

✦ `<load-on-startup>` indicates a servlet that has to be loaded, and whose `init()` method has to be called on the Web-application startup. This tag may be empty or have an optional integer value that specifies the order in which the servlet must be loaded.

✦ `<session-config>` specifies the timeout for users' sessions. The following example specifies a 60-second timeout:

```
<session-config>
    <session-timeout>60</session-timeout>
</session-config>
```

✦ `<security-role-ref>` specifies the mapping between the hard-coded in the servlet security role and a `<security-role>` defined in the deployment descriptor, as shown here:

```
<security-role-ref>
    <role-name>DIRECT</role-name>
    <!--Name used in the servlet's code  -->
    <role-link>director</role-link>
</security-role-ref >
```

Servlet listener elements

If event listeners were created for this Web application, they should be listed in the `web.xml`. Here's an example:

```
<web-app>
    <listener>
        <listener-class>
            com.magpub.listeners.ContextListener
        </listener-class>
    </listener>
    <servlet>
        ...
    </servlet>
<web-app>
```

Servlet filter elements

To deploy filters, add the `<filter>` section to the `web.xml` file, and also map the filter to the servlet that will be using the filter. For example: `<filter>`

```
    <filter-name>LogFilter</filter-name>
    <filter-class>com.magpub.filters.LogFilter</filter-class>
</filter>
<filter-mapping>
    <filter-name>LogFilter</filter-name>
    <servlet-name>LoginServlet</servlet-name>
</filter-mapping>
```

To apply a filter to selected servlets repeat the `<filter-mapping>` section for each servlet.

If you'd like the filter to be used by all servlets of the Web application use the `<url-pattern>` section instead of the `<servlet-name>`, for example to apply the filter for all Web application objects use the following element:

```
    <url-pattern>/*</url-pattern>
```

The next example ensures that the filter will work only with JavaServer Pages (see Chapter 6):

```
    <url-pattern>/*.jsp</url-pattern>
```

To create a filter chain provide multiple `<filter-mapping>` sections. The following example ensures that request data will be logged and encrypted before reaching the `LoginServlet`:

```
<filter-mapping>
    <filter-name>LogFilter</filter-name>
    <servlet-name>LoginServlet</servlet-name>
</filter-mapping>
<filter-mapping>
    <filter-name>EncryptFilter</filter-name>
    <servlet-name>LoginServlet</servlet-name>
</filter-mapping>
```

The new deployment element `<dispatcher>` allows you to specify if the filter has to be applied, for example only when a control is redirected by a `forward()` or `include()` call of a request dispatcher. The following section ensures that the `LogFilter` will be invoked only when the request's generated by the call to a method `forward()` in the servlet `LoginServlet`:

```
<filter-mapping>
    <filter-name>LogFilter</filter-name>
    <servlet-name>LoginServlet</servlet-name>
    <dispatcher>FORWARD</dispacher>
</filter-mapping>
```

The next descriptor will apply the filter `MyFilter` only to requests that come directly from the client:

```
<filter-mapping>
  <filter-name>MyFilter</filter-name>
  <url-pattern>/*</url-pattern>
  <dispatcher>REQUEST</dispacher>
</filter-mapping>
```

The next section will show that not only HTML clients, but also Java applets could work with servlets.

Applet-servlet communication

Because HTML alone does not provide advanced GUI components, Java applets with AWT or Swing components can become handy. The main business processing should still be done by the servlets on the server side, but applets can take care of the presentation part. Let's take a look at the following applet/servlet design considerations:

Applets have to be downloaded to the client's machine, so we still want to keep them lightweight (small in size).

Applets should not connect directly to server databases — this will make them smaller, because they won't contain JDBC drivers.

In Internet applications applets do not access the user's disk, and therefore they should be used primarily for data entry, validation, display, and simple calculations.

Applets may not work properly if the user's Web browser has an outdated JVM.

While applets can connect to a remote computer using socket or RMI programming, there is an easier way — HTTP tunneling, which is a way of creating a sub-protocol for specific tasks on top of the existing protocol (HTTP). With the help of the HTTP protocol, applets can establish a communication channel with servlets and send and receive any text and binary objects using Java Serialization.

An applet can collect the user's input from the GUI components, package the data in a serializable object, and send the data to the servlet.

To receive data from a servlet, the applet has to play the role of a Web browser. It has to understand the data it receives and populate the appropriate GUI components. For example, if an applet expects to receive the magazine data as two values — the title and the price — it needs to get a reference to the servlet's input stream and read the received values, as shown here:

```
URL servet1URL = new
URL("http://www.mymagpublisher.com/ShowMagazines");
URLConnection  con = servletURL.openConnection();
InputStream in = con.getInputStream();
```

```
BufferedReader servletData = new BufferedReader(new
DataInputStream(in));

String magTitle = servletData.readLine();
String magPrice = servletData.readLine();

txtTitle.setText(magTitle);    // display the data in a AWT
TextField
  txtPrice.setText(magPrice);
```

What if a magazine is represented not by two, but by 50 values? Instead of performing 50 reads over the network we should pre-populate an object on the client side and send it to the servlet in one shot. Let's look at the applet/servlet communication using Java Serialization, which allows easy conversion of a Java object into a stream of bytes. Our applet is going to prepare the magazine-subscription order and send it over to a servlet, which will save the order in a database. We could implement this process by performing the following steps involved in applet/servlet object serialization:

1. Create a `SubscriptionOrder` class that implements the `Serializable` interface.

2. Using Java AWT or Swing components, create an applet to collect subscription info. Include a Send button to enable the user to submit the order to a servlet.

3. Create a database table for storing the orders, and a servlet that can work with the database using JDBC.

4. In the applet, under the `actionPerformed()` of the Send button do the following:

    a. Create an instance of `SubscriptionOrder` and initialize it with the values entered on the screen.

    b. Connect to a servlet using the `URLConnection` class.

    c. Obtain a reference to the `OutputStream` object of the servlet.

    d. Create an instance of `ObjectOutputStream`, chaining it with the servlet's `OutputStream`. Send the order to this stream using the `writeObject()` object.

    e. Close the streams.

5. In the servlet, do the following:

    a. Obtain a reference to the applet's `InputStream` using `request.getInputStream()`.

    b. Create an instance of the `ObjectInputStream`, chaining it with the applet's `InputStream`, and call the `readObject()` method to de-serialize the `SubscriptionOrder` instance.

    c. Connect to the database and save the order in the database.

    d. Close the streams.

Listings 5-5, 5-6, and 5-7 illustrate this process:

Listing 5-5: **Code fragment from SubscriptionOrder.java**

```
class SubscriptionOrder implements java.io.Serializable{
private String magazineID;
private int quantity;
private String promoCode;
private  String custID;

SubscriptionOrder(String magazineID, int quantity,
                      String promoCode, String custID){
  this. magazineID = magazineID;
  this.quantity=quantity;
  this.type=promocode;
  this.custID=custID;
}
public String getMagID (){return magazineID;}
public int getQuantity(){return quantity;}
...
```

Listing 5-6: **Code fragment from Client.java**

```
class Client extends java.applet.Applet implements
ActionListener {

  ObjectOutputStream out = null;

  // The GUI components should be created here
  ...
// The user  pressed a button
 public void actionPerformed (ActionEvent event){

  if (event.getSource() == buttonSend){
    SubscriptionOrder sOrd = new SubscriptionOrder(
listMagId.getSelectedItem(),

Integer.parseInt(txtQuantity.getText()),
                        txtPromo.getText(),
                        txtCustID.getText());
      try{
URL orderServlet =
new
URL("http://www.mymagpublisher.com/ShowMagazines/OrderServlet"
);
```

Continued

Listing 5-6 *(continued)*

```
URLConnection con = orderServlet.openConnection();

//We are only sending data ,otherwise call also the
setDoInput(true)
con.setDoOutput(true);

// We are sending the binary object, that's why the content
type
// should be application/octet-stream.
con.setRequestProperty ("Content-Type", "application/octet-
stream");

out = new ObjectOutputStream(con.getOutputStream());

// Send the order to the servlet
out.writeObject(sOrd);

    } catch(){
      ...
    } finally{
out.flush();
out.close();
    }
 }
}
```

Listing 5-7: Code fragment from OrderServlet.java

```
class OrderServlet extends HttpServlet{

// Since we are passing the binary data from the applet,
// we can't use doGet()

public void doPost(HttpServletRequest request,
                   HttpServletResponse response){

ObjectInputStream appletStream = null;
SubscriptionOrder  receivedOrder = null;

try{
   // get the applet's  input stream
  appletStream = new
           ObjectInputStream(request.getInputStream());

  //de-serialize the order  received from the applet
  receivedOrder = (SubscriptionOrder)
```

```
                           appletStream.readObject();

// connect do the database and save the received order

// If the servlet needs  to send some data to the
// applet, it  need s to call  create an instance of
// the ObjectOutputStream by using
// request.getOutputStream(),  and send a serializable //
object over there.

} catch(Exception e){
        e.printStackTrace();
} finally{
    ...
    appletStream.close();
}
}
}
```

A similar technique can be implemented to send data from a servlet back to the applet. For example, a servlet connects to the database, selects all orders of a given customer, puts the result set into a `Vector`, and serializes the result set into the applet's steam. The applet de-serializes the `Vector` and populates a `JTable`. Examples of working with relational databases using JDBC can be found in the Chapter 18.

The next section briefly lists some of the important new features of servlets that were introduced in the specification 2.4.

What's New in the Servlet 2.4 Specification

The Java Servlet Specification 2.4 is not a major upgrade of the servlet API, but some of the new features and changes are listed here:

✦ The ability to extend deployment descriptors will enable developers to insert application-specific configuration information into the deployment descriptor.

✦ New listeners will allow developers to use a `ServletRequestListener` instance to intercept events when a request comes in and out of scope (enters and exits the first filter in the filter chain). A `ServletRequestAttributeListener` instance will catch the events when attributes are being added to, removed from, or replaced on a `ServletRequest` instance.

✦ Filters can be configured and invoked under `RequestDispatcher forward()` and `include()` calls.

✦ Unhandled listener exceptions are propagated to the application's code.

Summary

In this chapter, we've introduced you to Java servlets that are widely used to create Web applications. While processing HTTP requests, servlet containers provide a concurrent multithreaded environment to improve the performance of such applications. Session management is yet another vital aspect of most of the Web applications, and you've learned various ways of storing session information.

✦   ✦   ✦

Going Over JSP Basics

In This Chapter

Introducing
JavaServer Pages

Applying the
model-view-controller
design pattern

Using JavaBeans
with JSP

Developing a sample
user-login application

Developing a sample
user-registration
application

JavaServer Pages (JSP) is a J2EE component that enables you to develop Web applications that work as if they had been created with Java servlets. The JSP specification defines JSP as "a technology for building the applications for generating dynamic Web content such as HTML, DHTML, SHTML, and XML." This chapter will teach you about the various JSP scripting elements and directives. You will also learn how to work with variable scopes and experiment with a few examples. Finally, you will design an online store and then apply JSP to the Airline Reservation business case.

Let's begin with some simple examples.

Introducing JSP

The first very basic examples discussed in this section will show the easy way of generating HTML content using JSP. Let's say you've created and deployed a servlet that displays the HelloWorld HTML page by using `println()` in its `doGet()` method. Here's that code:

```
out.println("<HTML><BODY>");
out.println("Hello World");
out.println("</BODY></HTML>");
```

What if you need to change the layout of this page — say you want to add a header and a footer? Because you've already learned about Java servlets, you can easily add several `out.println()` statements, and then recompile the servlet and deploy it again. A real Web application can generate dozens of Web pages and each of them may need to be modified. Fortunately, JSP enables you to separate screen design from business logic, so a Web designer can take care of the HTML part while the Java developer concentrates on the programming of business functions required by the application.

Now, to see how a simple HTML page could be converted into a JSP, type into any plain editor the HTML code shown in Listing 6-1, and save it in a file named `HelloWorld.jsp`.

Listing 6-1: **HelloWorld.jsp**

```
<HTML>
<BODY>
  Hello World
</BODY>
</HTML>
```

This file has to be placed into a document root directory on the application-server machine or deployed in the Web application-archive file (as explained in the previous chapter). Now users can access this JSP from the Web browser by entering a URL like this: `http://www.mydomainname.com/HelloWorld.jsp`. Upon the first request to this page, the JSP container will automatically generate, compile, and deploy a servlet that produces the output based on the content of the file `HelloWorld.jsp`. The container will automatically generate the `jspService()` method in the new servlet, which will have the same functionality and arguments as the servlet's `service()` method. The first request of the JSP will take longer than all single subsequent ones because of this generation process, but then the servlet will be up and running and will respond immediately.

It does not take a rocket scientist to understand that we could have achieved the same effect by creating a `HelloWorld.html` file without all these complications. This is true, as long as your page is a static one and does not need to perform any business processing.

Note   Remember, HTML is not a programming language, just a markup language. It could not perform even such a simple calculation as 2 + 2, but JSP can easily do it by using special tags that enable the programmer to embed Java code into an HTML page. During the servlet-generation process this Java code will also be included and executed as part of the servlet.

JSP elements are surrounded by angle brackets, like this: `<%=2+2%>`. The JSP container will replace these elements with the regular Java code. For example, the tag `<%=2+2%>` will be replaced with a Java statement similar to the following one:

```
out.println(2+2);
```

Listing 6-2 shows the code for the `MyFirstJSPPage.jsp` file.

Listing 6-2: My First JSP

```
<HTML>
<BODY>
   You may not know that 2 + 2 is  <%= 2 + 2%>
   <p>The code within the JSP tag was created by a Java
developer, while the rest of the page has been done by the HTML
person.
</BODY>
</HTML>
```

When this JSP is requested by the user, it will display the following text in the Web browser:

```
You may not know that 2 + 2 is 4
The code within the JSP tag was created by a Java
developer, while the rest of the page has been done
by the HTML person.
```

Please note that the expression `<%2 + 2%>` has been replaced by the value of 4. A JSP tag `<%= ... %>` from the preceding example can contain any Java expression that will be evaluated, and its result will be displayed in place of the expression by the JSP engine.

A JavaServer Page is nothing but a servlet that is automatically generated by a JSP container from a file containing valid HTML and JSP tags. The latest JSP specification is 2.0.The original Java Specification Request (JSR152) listed the version as 1.3. However, based on the scope of changes — such as introduction of the new Expression Language, the Standard Tags Library (JSTL), and some others — this specification has been released as version 2.0.

The following sections explain the various elements of JavaServer Pages, starting with a discussion of the design of the Web applications, and specifically, applying the model-view-controller to the JSP technology.

Examining MVC and JSP

The model-view-controller paradigm was briefly discussed in Chapter 1. Now, we will show you how to apply it in practice for Web applications. MVC suggests dividing the components of an application (or even an object!) into the three parts:

✦ *The model* — This component represents the application data and the business processing code.

✦ *The view* — This component is responsible for the presentation layer — Web pages or GUI screens, for example.

✦ *The controller* — This component provides a reaction to the user's input, "input" being such things as button clicks.

Even some of the Java Swing components were designed using the MVC pattern. For example, a JTable (the view) that looks like a spreadsheet can store its data in a different class, such as a descendent of the AbstractTableModel class (the model).

For Web applications the MVC pattern can work as follows:

The view portion is implemented by means of JSP, HTML, and JavaScript.

The model portion of an application can be developed with any Java (and non-Java) classes such as beans, EJB, and JMS. It can also provide data storage using a database-management system, flat files, and so on.

The controller is a navigation object that redirects control to appropriate classes based on the user's choices or some other events that may happen in the system. For example, the user makes a selection on a Web page that has to be processed by a Java class or JSP. A Java servlet is a good candidate for this role.

Any changes in page appearance (such as colors, fonts, or screen-real-estate allocation) can be made by the HTML person responsible for the presentation of the application. After the changes are applied and the modified JSP is deployed, the JSP will automatically be regenerated into a new servlet upon the first user's request. (See an example in the section "Deploying Login JSP Example Using Apache Tomcat," later in this chapter.) Since the business logic has not been changed (2 + 2 is still equal to 4), there is no need to change the model.

See the section "Designing an Online Store with JSP," later in this chapter, for a practical example of using the MVC paradigm.

The next section will introduce you to the basic JSP elements that control the servlet generation process and allow embedding of Java code into HTML pages.

JSP Scripting Elements and Directives

JSP elements (tags) can by grouped according to the functions they perform. For example, they can be referred to as variable declarations, expressions, page attributes, and so on. The tags are surrounded by angle brackets (<>), and like HTML and XML tags can have attributes. Everything else that can be contained in the JSP page but that cannot be known to the JSP translators (plain text, HTML tags, and so on) is called *template data*.

First we'll discuss the use of the following tags and other JSP elements:

✦ Declarations

✦ Expressions

✦ Directives

✦ Scriptlets

✦ Comments

✦ Actions

✦ Implicit JSP objects

✦ Error pages

✦ JavaBeans

Then we'll build the Login and Registration screens for the Connexia Airlines business case described in Appendix A.

Declarations

Declarations do not generate the output to the user's screen. They are used for declaring class variables and methods and start with <%! . The lastName variable declared in the following code is only available in the current page:

```
<%! String lastName; %>
If you need to declare a Java method called myMethod()  in a
JSP you could do it as follows:
<%! private  void myMethod(){
        ...
        }
%>
```

The code contained in the JSP declaration block will be located in the generated servlet outside any existing method.

Expressions

JSP expressions start with <%= and can contain any Java expression, which will be evaluated and its result inserted into the HTML page right where the expression is located. For example:

```
<HTML><BODY>
<%! double salary=50000; %>
Your new salary is <%= salary*1.2 %>
<HTML><BODY>
```

The next example shows how to display the current date on the Web page:

```
Today's date is <%= new java.util.Date() %>
```

Please note that there is no semicolon (;) at the end of the expression.

Directives

Directives do not generate screen output. They inform the JSP engine about the rules to be applied to the JSP. The page directive starts with `<%@ page` and will be applied during the servlet-generation process only to the current page. It's used with such attributes as `import`, `extends`, `session`, `errorPage`, and `contentType`. For example, an equivalent of the Java `import` statement looks like this:

```
<%@ page import="java.io.*" %>
```

With servlets you set the type of the output by code like `response.setContentType("text/html")`. The JSP version of this code is shown here:

```
<%@ page contentType="text/html" %>
```

Now consider the following example:

```
<%@ page session="true" %>
```

You can see that, as in servlets, the JSP containing this directive will try to find an existing session object, and if it does not find one will create a new one. You can find another example of the page directive in the section "Error Pages," later in this chapter.

The `include` directive allows inclusion of any text file or code from another JSP, at the time when the page is compiled into a servlet. For example, if every JSP in your application has to display the same header, you can place the code for the header in the file `TheHeader.jsp` and include it in every page. The following code fragment uses an HTML table to display a Web page with the content of the file `TheHeader.jsp` on top:

```
<table><tr>
<td><%@ include file="/TheHeader.jsp" %></td>
</tr>
<tr><td>
The rest of the web page content goes here
</td>
</table>
```

You can find out more about JSP directives at the following Web page: http://java.sun.com/products/jsp/tags/tags.html.

Scriptlets

Scriptlets can contain any valid Java code that will be included in the method `jspService` during servlet-code generation. For example, within scriptlets you can also insert variable and method declarations, Java expressions, and so on. Scriptlets start with `<%`. The `jspService` method is responsible for generating the Web-page output, as in the following example:

```
<% lastName = "Smith"; %>
```

The plain text and HTML tags should be placed outside of the scriptlets.

Next is an example of a mix of plain text, HTML, and JSP tags that uses scriptlets. Please note that before adding any text, HTML tags, or JSP elements, the scriptlet must be closed by adding the symbols `%>`, and then you can write the text and other JSP tags:

```
<% if (userID.equals("jSmith")) { %>
Hello <B>John</B>! You've got mail.
<% } else { %>
Please register or login.<P>
<% } %>
```

This mix will be converted into the Java code in the servlet, which may look like the following:

```
if (userID.equals("jSmith")) {
   out.println("Hello <B>John</B>! You've got mail.");
} else{
   out.println("Please register or login.<P>");
}
```

Even though the JSP syntax enables insertion of Java code fragments, variables, and method declarations, you should try to minimize the amount of Java code in the JSP body. Remember that the whole point of using JSP is to separate business processing from the presentation. That's why the best practice is either to move Java code into JavaBeans, as shown later in this chapter, or to use custom tag libraries, as shown in the next chapter.

Comments

JSP comments start with `<%--` and end with `--%>`, and are not included in the output Web page:

```
<%-- Some comments --%>
```

If you need to include comments in the source of the output page, use the HTML comments, which start with `<!--` and end with `-->`.

Actions

JSP actions provide runtime instructions to the JSP containers. For example, a JSP action can include a file, forward a request to another page, or create an instance of a JavaBean.

```
<jsp:include page "header.jsp" />
<jsp:forward page="someOther.jsp" />
<jsp:useBean  id="User" class="com.connexiaair.AirUser" />
```

JavaBeans and the use of the action `<jsp:useBean>` will be discussed later in this chapter in the section, "Using JavaBeans." I will briefly discuss the rest of the standard JSP action tags in this section.

forward

The `forward` action enables you to redirect the program flow to a different HTML file, JSP, or servlet while maintaining the same `request` and `response` objects. This directive works in the same way as the `forward()` method of the `RequestDispatcher class`, described in the previous chapter.

include versus jsp:include

Please note the following difference: the `include` directive adds the content of the included page at the time of compilation, while the `jsp:include` action does it at runtime. This adds flexibility to JSP, because the decision about what page to include can be made based on the user's actions or other events that may take place when the Web application is already running.

plugin

The `plugin` action ensures that if your JSP includes an applet, the Java plugin will be downloaded to the user's browser JVM to avoid version-compatibility problems. During code generation, the tag `<JSP:plugin>` will be replaced in the output stream by either an `<object>` or an `<embed>` tag, depending on the user's browser.

<jsp:param>

The `<jsp:param>` action can be used as a nested tag with such action tags as `<jsp:forward>`, `<jsp:include>`, and `<jsp:params>`. For example, it can be used to pass parameters to an applet like this:

```
<jsp:plugin type=applet code=Login.class>
  <jsp:params>
    <jsp:param name="userID" value="SCOTT" />
    <jsp:param name="password" value="TIGER" />
  </jsp:params>
```

</jsp:plugin>

The following example shows how a JSP can redirect control to a login servlet. The JSP could also contain the code that adds new parameters to the JSP that is being loaded. For example, a parameter called `password` was not part of the original request object but will be passed the JSP `LoginServlet`:

```
<jsp:forward page="LoginServlet">
    <jsp:param name="password" value="Spring" />
```

</jsp:forward>

Besides scripting elements, JSP also uses reserved variable names that point to *implicit objects*, which are discussed next.

Implicit JSP objects

In the previous chapter you learned how to use such objects as `HttpServletRequest`, `HttpServletResponse`, `HttpSession`, and `ServletContext`. Since JSPs live by the same rules as servlets, they also need to be able to get access to these objects. Fortunately, JSPs provide a number of predefined variables that give you access to these vital objects. Since all these objects were explained in Chapter 5, we'll just mention their names along with the corresponding JSP variables:

✦ `request` — This variable points at `HttpServletRequest`. The following example gets the flight destination entered by the user on the HTML page:

```
<% String dest=
        request.getParameter("destination"); %>
```

✦ `response` — Use this variable to access the `HttpServletResponse` object. For example:

```
<% response.setContentType("text/html"); %>
```

✦ `out` — This variable represents the `JspWriter` class, which has the same functionality as the `PrintWriter` class in servlets. Here's an example:

```
<% out.println("Enter flight destination"); %>
```

✦ `session` — This variable represents the instance of the `HTTPSession` object.

✦ `exception` — This variable represents an instance of the uncaught `Throwable` object and contains error information. This variable is only available from the JSP error page that contains the directive `isErrorPage=true`. See the section "Error Pages," later in this chapter, for details.

✦ `page` — This variable represents the instance of the JSP's Java class processing the current request.

✦ `pageContext` — This variable represents the `javax.servlet.jsp.PageContext` class, which contains methods for dealing with scoped data. See examples in the next section, "Working with Variable Scopes."

✦ application—This variable gives you access to the ServletContext object without your having to call getServletConfig().getContext().

✦ config—This variable provides access to the ServletConfig object.

Working with Variable Scopes

If a JSP variable is declared inside a scriptlet, it has a *local scope* (visible only within a method). The variable has to be declared by means of the declaration tag to have an *instance scope* (visible from any method of the generated servlet class).

JSP variables can also be stored in the PageContext and have the scope of a page, request, session, or application. If the data have the page scope, they are visible only within the current page. If they have the request scope the data are alive for as long as the request is not complete. Session-scoped variables are destroyed when the session is over. If the data have the application scope the variables die only when the Web application is destroyed.

You can prolong the lifetime of a variable by storing it as an attribute of the page context using an implicit JSP pageContext object. The following examples show you how to do it:

```
<%
pageContext.setAttribute("airline.flight", "704",
                                  PageContext.PAGE_SCOPE);
pageContext.setAttribute("airline.userID", "jsmith",
                                  PageContext.REQUEST_SCOPE);
pageContext.setAttribute("airline.flightOrigin", "JFK",
                                  PageContext.SESSION_SCOPE);
pageContext.setAttribute("airline.sysadmin",
"support@connexiaair.com", PageContext.APPLICATION_SCOPE);
%>
```

The following are examples of how to display these values, if you wish:

```
<%=pageContext.getAttribute("airline.flight",
                            PageContext.PAGE_SCOPE); %>
<%=pageContext.getAttribute("airline.userID",
                            PageContext.REQUEST_SCOPE); %>
<%=pageContext.getAttribute("airline.flightOrigin",
                            PageContext.SESSION_SCOPE); %>
<%=pageContext.getAttribute("airline.sysadmin",
                            PageContext.APPLICATION_SCOPE); %>
```

For additional scope information see the section "The scope of JavaBeans," later in this chapter.

Error Pages

Let's say we have a flight reservation page, `Reservation.jsp`, containing the code that may throw Java exceptions. Instead of scaring users with stack trace screens, we'd rather prepare a friendly `ReservationErrors.jsp` that explains the problem in plain English. Do not forget to mention the name of the custom error page that will display reservation errors, as shown in Listing 6-3.

Listing 6-3: Declaring a custom error page in a JSP

```
        <HTML>
            The code searching for seats availability and other
HTML stuff goes here
            ...
        <%@ page errorPage=RegistrationErrors.jsp %>

        </HTML>
```

Listing 6-4 shows `ReservationErrors.jsp`, which uses the predefined JSP variable `exception`, which in turn displays the error message in a user-friendly manner, and also contains the exception description for the technical-support team. The line `<%@ page isErrorPage="true" %>` must be present in the custom error page.

Listing 6-4: The error page, ReservationErrors.jsp

```
<HTML>
<BODY>
<%@ page isErrorPage="true" %>

Dear friend!
<P>
We are sorry to inform you that there was a little problem
during your flight reservation.
<P>
Make sure that the field Number of Passengers contains only
numeric values.
<P>
If this does not solve your problem please contact our award
winning technical support team at (999)100-0000 and provide
them with the following information:
<P>
<%=exception.toString() %>
</BODY>
</HTML>
```

You can have different error pages for different types of errors. The mapping between the error type and the name of the error page is specified in the deployment descriptor web-xml. These are probably the two most "popular" error codes:

✦ 404 — Resource not found

✦ 500 — Internal error

The error page for the "resource not found" error does not even have to be a JSP — it can be a static HTML page such as `Connexia404.html`. Most of the JSP compilation errors and Java exceptions generate a 500 error, which can be processed by `Connexia500.jsp`. To implement the error pages, you should create them and add the following section to the `web.xml` file:

```
<error-page>
    <error-code>404</error-code>
     <location>Connexia404.html</location>
</error-page>
<error-page>
    <error-code>500</error-code>
     <location>Connexia500.jsp</location>
</error-page>
```

You can even use the `<exception-type>` element of the deployment descriptor to define an error page to be displayed if a particular Java exception occurs. For example:

```
<error-page>
    <exception-type>java.sql.SQLException</exception-type>
     <location>ConnexiaDBError.jsp</location>
</error-page>
```

The next section discusses special JavaBean classes.

Using JavaBeans

A JavaBean is a Java class that has a `no-arguments` constructor, `private` or `protected` fields (properties) and public setter/getter methods accessing the bean's properties. If a bean has to support persistence, it should implement the `Serializable` interface. JavaBeans in the JSP world are used for data exchange, and they also help separate business processing from presentation.

 **Cross-Reference** See Chapter 7 for a discussion about tag libraries, which are an alternative means of creating reusable JSP components.

Listing 6-5 shows an example of a JavaBean representing a user of Connexia Airlines. Please note the naming conventions used in this listing for the setters and getters.

Listing 6-5: The JavaBean AirlineUser.java

```
package com.connexiaair;
class AirlineUser implements java.io.Serializable{
        private String lastName;
        private String firstName;
        private boolean employee;

        AirlineUser (){
            // some initialization code goes here
        }

        public String getLastName(){
            return lastName;
        }
        public String getFirstName(){
            return firstName;
        }
        public void setLastName(String value){
                lastName = value;
        }
        public void setFirstName (String value){
                firstName = value;
        }
        public void setEmployee(boolean value){
                employee = value;
        }

         public boolean isEmployee (){
                return employee;
        }

}
```

This class holds the first and last names of the user and also allows you to mark the user as an employee. Please note that we named the getter method isEmployee() rather than getEmployee() because it returns a boolean value.

Using JavaBeans in JSP

You declare a JavaBean in a JSP by specifying its name using the JSP action tag <jsp:useBean>. The syntax of this JSP element can vary depending on a bean's type, but in general you have to provide the bean's ID (nickname) and location. After that you can set or get its properties. The following JSP element instantiates the bean AirlineUser:

```
<jsp:useBean  id="AirUser"
            class="com.connexiaair.AirlineUser" />
```

If you need to use a bean that has been serialized, say into the file `AirUser.ser`, the syntax of the `useBean` action will look slightly different:

```
<jsp:useBean id="Student" beanName="AirUser.ser" type=
" com.connexiaair.AirlineUser" />
```

The next line shows how to assign the value `Smith` to the bean's `LastName` property:

```
<jsp:setProperty name=" AirUser" property="LastName"
                                      value="Smith"/>
```

You can get the value of a bean's property and insert it into the output page in two ways:

```
<jsp:getProperty name="AirUser" property="LastName" />
```

or

```
<%=AirUser.getLastName() %>
```

Typically, you will need to populate the bean's properties based on the data entered in the tag `<Form>` on the HTML page. For example:

```
<FORM ACTION=http://myServer:8080/Registration.jsp
                                      method =Post>
Enter the Last Name:<INPUT  TYPE="Text" name="LName">
Enter the First Name:<INPUT  TYPE="Text" name="FName">
</FORM>
```

The following is the code fragment from a `Registration.jsp` file that passes the values entered on the preceding form to the JavaBean and populates its properties:

```
<jsp:useBean  id="AirUser"
              class="com.connexiaair.AirlineUser" />
<jsp:setProperty name="AirUser" property="LastName" value=
    "<%= request.getParameter("LName") %>" />

<jsp:setProperty name=" AirUser" property="FirstName" value=
"<%=request.getParameter("FName") %>" />
```

If the bean property names are the same as the field names on the HTML form, all values entered on the HTML form can be passed to the bean in one shot by means of the wildcard (*):

```
<jsp:setProperty name="AirUser" property="*" />
```

The scope of JavaBeans

The bean's scope can be defined by means of the `scope` attribute of the `<jsp:useBean>` tag, as explained here. Only one of the following scopes could be specified as an attribute:

✦ `page` — This is the default scope and specifies that the bean is only available within the current page and will be destroyed as soon as the user exits the page. For example:

```
        <jsp:useBean  id="AirUser"
class="com.connexiaair.AirlineUser" scope="page" />
```

✦ `request` — Specifies that the bean will stay alive as long as the request object does. Even if control will be redirected to a different JSP with the `<jsp:forward>` tag, the bean will still be available on the new page, because the request object is alive. Here's an example:

```
        <jsp:useBean  id="AirUser"
class="com.connexiaair.AirUser" scope="request" />
```

✦ `session` — Specifies that the bean will be available for all pages until the session object expires. (Read about session tracking in the previous chapter.)

```
<jsp:useBean  id="AirUser"
        class="com.connexiaair.AirUser" scope="session" />
```

✦ `application` — Specifies that the bean is available for all users and all pages. A bean with this setting is a "global bean." For example:

```
        <jsp:useBean  id="AirUser"
class="com.connexiaair.AirUser"
                    scope="application" />
```

Creating a login JSP using a JavaBean

Let's redesign the login-screen example from Chapter 5 (see Listings 5-1 and 5-2) to demonstrate the use of JSP scriptlets, expressions, implicit objects, and JavaBeans.

Listing 6-6 shows the `Login.html` example. It invokes the `Welcome.jsp` page shown in Listing 6-7. That page uses the JavaBean `Login.java`, shown in Listing 6-8, to check the user's credentials.

Listing 6-6: **Login.html**

```
<html>
<head>
<title>Login</title>
</head>
```

Continued

Listing 6-6 *(continued)*

```
<body>
<P>
<form action="http://localhost:8080/Welcome.jsp" method=Post>
  Enter Login  ID:  <input type=Text name="id" >
  <P>
  Enter Password: <input type=Password name="pwd">
  <P>
  <input type="Submit" value="Login">
  <input type="Reset" >
</form>
</body>
</html>
```

Listing 6-7: **Welcome.jsp**

```
<jsp:useBean id="login" class="com.connexiaair.Login"
                                      scope="session"/>
<jsp:setProperty name="login" property="*"/>

<html>
<head>
<title>Connexia Airlines</title>
<body>

<%
if (login.checkCredentials())
{
%>
Welcome <%=request.getParameter("id") %> !
<% } else { %>
Invalid credentials.
<% } %>
</body></html>
```

Listing 6-8: **The Login.java JavaBean**

```
package com.connexiaair;

public class Login {
  // Bean's properties
  private String id;
  private String password;

  // Setters
```

```
public void setId(String value){
    id=value;
}
public void setPwd(String value){
    password=value;
}

// A no-argument constructor
public Login() {
}

// A method containing business logic
public boolean checkCredentials(){
    if("jsmith".equalsIgnoreCase(id) &&
       "spring12".equalsIgnoreCase(password)){
         return true;
    } else{
    return false;
    }
    }
}
```

If the user enters `jsmith` and `spring12` on the login page the `Welcome.jsp` will generate a Web page containing the message "Hello jsmith!" For any other user's input the `Welcome.jsp` will respond with the unfriendly "Invalid credentials." In a real-world application the method `checkCredentials()` could connect to a database, LDAP server or other resource to validate the user's credentials.

 **Cross-Reference**   See Chapter 18 for details about Java Database Connectivity.

The easiest way to deploy this simple application is to copy the `.html` and `.jsp` files to the document root directory of your application server and to put the compiled `Login` class into any directory listed in the `classpath` on the server (usually compiled classes are located in the directory called `classes`).

Deploying the Login JSP example using Tomcat

Apache Tomcat 5.0 is a servlet and JSP container used in the official implementation of the Java Servlets 2.4 and JSP 2.0 technologies. You can download it from `http://jakarta.apache.org/tomcat/`. The following steps describe the process of JSP deployment in Tomcat:

1. Install Tomcat. Then, copy the `Login.html` and `Welcome.jsp` files to the `webapps\ROOT` directory. You can place the `Login.class` file in the `webapps\ROOT\WEB-INF\classes\com\connexiaair` directory.

2. Now, start Tomcat by clicking the Start Tomcat option in Microsoft Window's start menu. For Unix installations, use the startup script.

3. To run the login example, start your Web browser and go to `http://localhost:8080/Login.html`.

   It'll be a couple of seconds during the first run before you see the output of the `Welcome.jsp` file, because Tomcat needs to generate and compile the JSP into a servlet, but all future requests will be processed a lot faster.

You can also deploy this example as a Web application using the `.war` file, as explained in Chapter 5.

If, out of curiosity, you'd like to see the Java code generated from `Welcome.jsp`, you can find it in the Tomcat directory `work`. We are now ready to discuss a more advanced example of JSP in real-world applications.

Designing an Online Store with JSP

Every purchasing process on the Internet consists of a few steps that are pretty much the same regardless of what goods or services you order. You, the online buyer, will usually perform the following actions:

1. Register or login to the online store, travel agency, airline, et cetera.

2. Browse the inventory of goods or services.

3. Select an item and add it to the shopping cart. After that, you may either proceed to checkout or keep browsing the inventory.

4. Once you have proceeded to checkout, enter (or confirm) your payment and shipping information.

5. Press that scary-looking button that says, "You are about to place THE ORDER! Are you 100% sure?"

At the end of the process, the order is saved in the vendor's database and a receipt is e-mailed to the buyer.

Online stores can be developed with such J2EE components as Java servlets, JSP, Java Database Connectivity (JDBC), and JavaMail, and this book explains all of them.

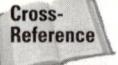 **Cross-Reference** Servlet programming is discussed in Chapter 5 and JDBC is covered in Chapter 18.

Let's discuss the Web-layer components that can be used for the development of such applications as online stores. This discussion can also serve as an example of how to apply the model-view-controller design pattern explained earlier in this chapter in the section "More On MVC." JavaBeans and other Java classes will represent the model, a servlet will represent the Controller, and several JSPs will represent the view.

Web sites usually consist of several screens with top and side panels that contain menus. The top panel may show the global menu and the company's logo. This global menu is usually displayed on every page. The side panel generally shows the navigational menu and may be different for each screen. These panels should be created as separate JSPs, and other screens (also JSPs) will include them by means of the <jsp:include> directive.

The shopping process consists of multiple steps, so we should take care of session tracking to remember every item that's been added to the shopping cart. A JavaBean is a good candidate to provide shopping-cart support, and the JSP's implicit session object will store this bean — let's call it ShoppingCartBean. The items placed into the shopping cart will be represented by the Item class, as shown in Listing 6-9:

Cross-Reference See Chapter 15 for a discussion of session beans.

Listing 6-9: **A Shopping-Cart Item**

```
class Item {
 long  productCode;
 String description;
 double unitPrice;
 int quantity;

 // Setters and getters go here
}
```

Since the shopping cart may contain more than one item, ShoppingCartBean has to be able to store a collection of items. For this let's use a Java Vector class.

```
import java.util.Vector;
import  java.uo.Serializable;

class  ShoppingCartBean implements Serializable{

   private Vector selectedItems = new Vector();

   ShoppingCartBean(){ }

   public Vector getItems(){
      return selectedItems;
   }

   public void addItem (Item selectedItem){
      selectedItems.add(selectedItem);
   }
}
```

You can create JSPs such as `ProductCatalog.jsp`, `Billing.jsp`, `Shipping.jsp`, and `Receipt.jsp` to interact with the online buyer. Each of these JSPs may generate a screen containing an HTML `<Form>` element with fields required by the next JSP, if needed.

A `MainServlet` servlet, shown in Listing 6-10, will process all user requests and load the appropriate JSP starting with `ProductCatalog.jsp`. For example, if the "Proceed To Checkout" button on the HTML form is clicked, the `MainServlet` should load `Billing.jsp`. If the user clicks the "Continue" button on the billing screen, the `MainServlet` will load `Shipping.jsp`. If the user clicks the "Return To Shopping" button, the servlet will load `ProductCatalog.jsp` again. The lightweight servlet `MainServlet` should perform only navigational functions. It can have an `if` statement to load the appropriate JSP with the help of the `RequestDispatcher` class, as was explained in the previous chapter.

Listing 6-10: **A partial controller servlet**

```
class MainServlet extends HTTPServlet{
    ...
    public void doGet(HttpServletRequest request,
                           HttpServletResponse response) {

HttpSession session = request.getSession(true);
RequestDispatcher disp = null;

// Find existing or create a  new Shopping Cart
ShoppingCartBean  shoppingCart =
  (ShoppingCartBean) session.getAttribute("ShoppingCart");

if(shoppingCart == null) {
    session.setAttribute("ShoppingCart",
                       new ShoppingCartBean ());
}

String nextScreen =
              request.getParameter("ScreenName");

if ("Billing".equals(nextScreen)) {
    disp = getServletConfig().getServletContext().
    getRequestDispatcher("Billing.jsp");
} else if ("Shipping".equals(nextScreen)) {
    disp = getServletConfig().getServletContext().
    getRequestDispatcher("Shipping.jsp");
}
  ...

if (disp != null) {
```

```
        disp.forward(request, response);
    }
  }
}
```

You can create a similar controller functionality using JSP, as shown in the next case study.

When the application starts, one more class can be instantiated and populated — the ProductCatalog class. This class connects to the database, as explained in Chapter 18, and retrieves and stores all available products. If the number of products is too big for all of them to be kept in memory, or if you'd like to show the real-time data, repopulate the product catalog from the database every time ProductCatalog.jsp is displayed. The next section contains the Airline Reservations example that illustrates interaction between such components of Web application as HTML pages, JSPs and JavaBeans.

Airline Reservations Business Case

Let's develop an airline-registration screen that will put together all the bits and pieces that you've learned in this chapter. This screen will allow agents, partners, consumers, and employees to register on the airline's Web site. A user will enter his or her name, e-mail address, and phone number. An employee will be required to enter his or her employee ID, an agent will be required to enter his or her agent ID, and a partner will be required to enter his or her partner ID.

During the reservation or registration process the user's input must be validated against the database. Because you have not yet learned how to access databases from Java, we'll throw an exception instead of saving user information in the database. Later on, in Chapter 18, we'll rewrite this code.

This example uses the following files:

✦ register.html

✦ register.jsp

✦ registerBean.java

✦ DBProcessor.java.

The file register.html, shown in Listing 6-11, contains an HTML form to be filled in by the user. Please note that all fields are located in an HTML table that simplifies filed alignment and ensures that the screen will look the same regardless of window sizes and screen resolution. Since the form tag has the attribute `action="register. jsp"`, the user's input will be sent to `register.jsp` when the "Register" button is clicked.

Listing 6-11: The registration page, register.html

```html
<html>
<head><title>Connexia Airline</title></head>
<body>
<form action="register.jsp" method=post>
<center>
<table bgcolor="#CCCCCC" border=0>

<th colspan=2>
<font size=5>Connexia Airline Registration</font></th>
<tr >
<td   valign=top>
<b>First Name<sup>*</sup></b><br>
<input type="text" name="firstName"  size=15></td>
<td   valign=top>
<b>Last Name<sup>*</sup></b><br>
<input type="text" name="lastName"  size=15></td>
</tr>

<tr>
<td valign=top>
<b>Address</b><sup>*</sup><br>
<input type="text" name="street" size=25>
<br></td>
<td   valign=top>
<b>Zip Code<sup>*</sup></b><br>
<input type="text" name="zip" size=5  maxlength=5></td>
</tr>

<tr >
<td valign=top>
<b>E-mail</b><br>
<input type="text" name="email" size=25></td>
</tr>

<tr>
<td valign=top colspan=2>
<b>User ID<sup>*</sup></b><br>
<input type="text" name="userName" size=10>
</td>
</tr>
<tr>

<td   valign=top colspan=2>
<b>Who are you?<sup>*</sup></b><br>
```

```
<input type="radio" name="userType" value="Cons" checked>
Consumer  
<input type="radio" name="userType" value="Empl">Employee
 
<input type="radio" name="userType" value="Agent">Agent 
<input type="radio" name="userType" value="Partner"> Partner
<br>
</td>
</tr>

<tr>
<td valign=top>
<b>Password<sup>*</sup></b><br>
<input type="password" name="pwd" size=12></td>
<td   valign=top>
<b>Confirm Password<sup>*</sup></b><br>
<input type="password" name="pwdConf" size=12></td><br>
</tr>

<tr>
<td   valign=top colspan=2>
<b>Would you like to receive Connexia Air newsletters?</b>
<br>
<input type="radio" name="sendLetter" value="Yes" checked>Yes
 
<input type="radio" name="sendLetter" value="No" > No
</td>
</tr><br>
<tr><td><sup>*</sup> Required Info</tr>
<tr>
<td   align=center colspan=2>
<input type="submit" value="Register"> <input type="reset"
value="Reset">
</td>
</tr>

</table>
</center>
</form>
</body>
</html>
```

Figure 6-1 shows the output of the file `register.html`.

After filling out the registration form the user clicks the "Register" button. At this point the browser creates the request object containing the user's data and sends it over to `register.jsp`. The content of this JSP depends on the functionality required. For example, if the registration of the agent, employee, and partner require additional registration information (screens), this JSP can play the role of a controller, much like the servlet shown earlier in Listing 6-10.

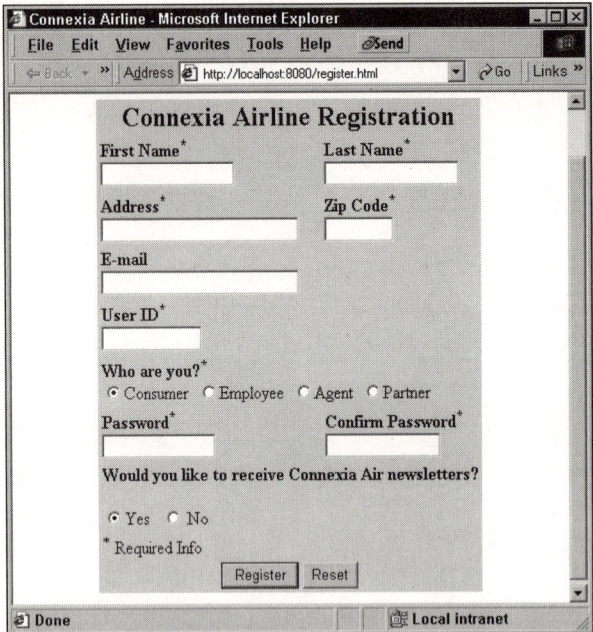

Figure 6-1: The registration screen

Listing 6-12 shows how to use a JSP as a controller in an MVC application.

Listing 6-12: **Code snippet from a controller JSP**

```
<%
  String userType =
                    request.getParameter("UserType");

  if ("Empl".equals(userType)) { %>
      <jsp:forward url="registerEmployee.jsp" />
<% } else if ("Agent".equals(userType)) { %>
      <jsp:forward url="registerAgent.jsp" />
<% } else if ("Partner".equals(userType)) { %>
      <jsp:forward url="registerPartner.jsp" />
<% } %>
```

Recall that the directive jsp:forward will pass the request object with all parameters to the next JSP. The code saving the user's registration information should be located in a JavaBean and utility classes — registerBean.java and DBProcessor.java, respectively.

To simplify the example we won't forward the registration request to other JSPs, but rather use the bean in the `register.jsp` shown in Listing 6-13. This JSP will demonstrate a data exchange between the JSP and the bean. Please note that this JSP declares the custom error page `myErrors.jsp` shown later in this section.

Listing 6-13: **register.jsp**

```
%-- instantiate the RegisterBean   --%>
<jsp:useBean id="registrar"
class="com.connexiaair.RegisterBean"
                                        scope="request"/>

<%-- pass the user's input to the RegisterBean   --%>
<jsp:setProperty name="registrar" property="*"/>

<%@ page errorPage="myErrors.jsp" %>

<html>
<head>
<title>Connexia Airline</title>
<body>

<%-- Initiate registration process --%>
<% registrar.registerUser(); %>

</body></html>
```

Listing 6-14 contains the source code for `RegisterBean.java`, which, besides getters and setters, has a `registerUser()` method. This method will instantiate a `DBProcessor` class that should save the registration information in the database.

Listing 6-14: **RegisterBean.java**

```
package com.connexiaair;

public class RegisterBean {
   // Bean's properties
   private String fName;
   private String lName;
   private String id;
   private String password;
   private String password2;
   private String street;
   private String zip;
```

Continued

Listing 6-14 *(continued)*

```java
    private String email;
    private String userType;
    private String sendLetter;

    // Setters and getters
    public void setFirstName(String value){fName=value;}
    public String getFirstName(){return fName;}
    public void setLastName(String value){lName=value;}
    public String getLastName(){return lName;}
    public void setStreet(String value){street=value;}
    public String getStreet(){return street;}
    public void setZip(String value){zip=value;}
    public String getZip(){return zip;}
    public void setEmail(String value){email=value;}
    public String getEmail(){return email;}
    public void setPwd(String value){password=value;}
    public String getPwd(){return password;}
    public void setPwdConf(String value){password2=value;}
    public String getPwdConf(){return password2;}
    public void setUserType(String value){userType=value;}
    public String getUserType(){return userType;}
    public void setSendLetter(String value){sendLetter=value;}
    public String getSendLetter(){return sendLetter;}

    // No-argument constructor
    public RegisterBean() {
    }

    // A method to save the registration info in the database
    public void registerUser() throws java.sql.SQLException{
        DBProcessor dbp = new DBProcessor();
        dbp.addUser(this);
    }
}
```

Listing 6-15 shows the DBProcessor class that should take care of database communications. At this point its addUser() method will just throw an exception, and this will give us a chance to demonstrate the use of the custom error page.

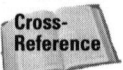

Cross-Reference   DBProcessor **will be explained in Chapter 18.**

Listing 6-15: **DBProcessor.java**

```java
package com.connexiaair;
import java.sql.SQLException;

public class DBProcessor {

  public DBProcessor() {
  }

  public void addUser(RegisterBean rb) throws SQLException{
    // The real code saving data in the database could be
    // found in Chapter 18.
    String errMessage="DBProcessor: I Do not know how to " +
      "work with databases - see you in  chapter 18. ";

    throw new SQLException(errMessage);
  }

}
```

Exceptions thrown by DBProcessor will be propagated to register.jsp, and myErrors.jsp, shown in Listing 6-16, will pick them up (see Figure 6-2).

Listing 6-16: **The custom error page, myErrors.jsp**

```jsp
%@ page isErrorPage="true" %>

<HTML><BODY>

<H2>
  Connexia Airline is experiencing the following problems:
</H2>

<%=exception.toString() %>

<H2>Please try again later </H2>

</BODY><HTML>
```

Figure 6-2: This is the output of the custom error page myErrors.jsp.

If you remove the line `<%@ page errorPage="myErrors.jsp" %>` from `register.jsp`, its output could look like what is shown in Figure 6-3.

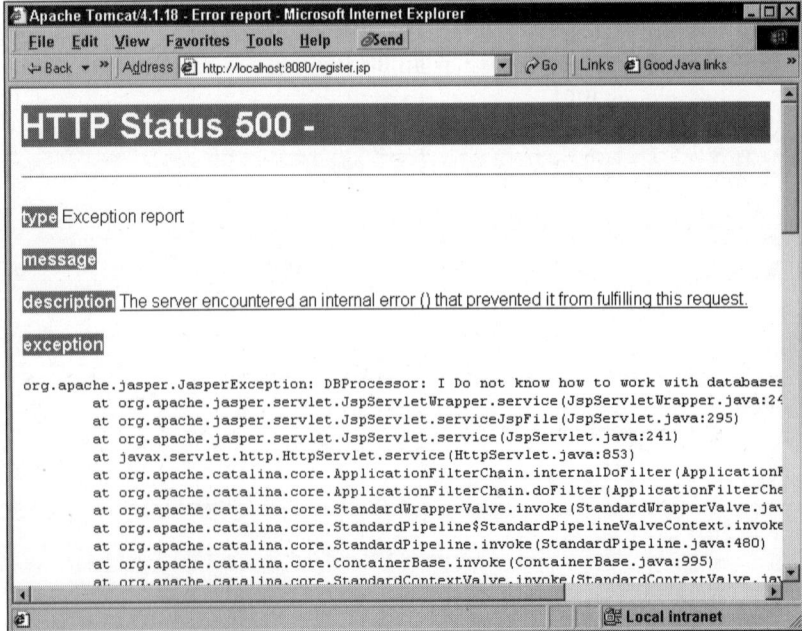

Figure 6-3: This is a fragment of the Tomcat default exception output.

The following steps will help you use Tomcat to deploy the Airline Registration example:

1. Copy `registration.html` and `register.jsp` and `myErrors.jsp` to the `webapps\ROOT` directory.

2. Place the compiled classes `RegisterBean` and `DBProcessor` in the `webapps\ROOT\WEB-INF\classes\com\connexiaair` directory.

3. Start Tomcat by clicking the Start Tomcat menu option in Microsoft Window's Start menu. For Unix installations, use the startup script.

4. To run the registration example, start your Web browser and enter the following URL: `http://localhost:8080/register.html`.

In general, JSPs are deployed the same way in any J2EE-compliant application server — just place JSPs and other static resources in the document root directory and make sure that compiled classes are located in the derectory listed in the `classpath` environment variable.

Summary

In this chapter we've introduced you to a simple but powerful Web technology — JavaServer Pages. JSP leads to a cleaner application design by separating Web components responsible for the presentation from the Java objects containing the business logic. Web designers can master relatively small sets of JSP tags while Java developers can concentrate on programming the processing logic of the application.

✦   ✦   ✦

Using JSP Tag Extensions

In This Chapter

Introducing tag
extensions

Working with
Tag Library
Descriptors (TLDs)

Explaining
taglib mapping

Using classic
tag handlers

Understanding
simple tag handlers

Exploring dynamic
attributes

In the previous chapter you were introduced to the basics of JSP and you even used some of the tags meant to simplify JavaBean usage in your JSP files. In this chapter we take JSP further and explore JSP tag extensions. We will first put forth the logic behind adopting custom tags; then we will check out a simple tag usage after which we will get to the actual nitty-gritty of the thing.

The proposed new version of JSP, version 2.0, has introduced quite a lot of changes to JSP and particularly in the domain of tag extensions. In this chapter we will explore these changes and also look at a technology that is rapidly growing in popularity—*JSP Standard Tag Libraries* (JSTL).

Why Use Tag Extensions?

One of the most talked-about aspects of development lately and one that is referred to very often in any discussion about design patterns and considerations is the separation of presentation and logic. The prevailing idea is that the presentation and the logic of your application should stay independent of each other and ideally even be capable of being managed by different people.

Taking this approach means that a Web designer should be responsible for your presentation while a Java developer handles the logic behind the presentation. As the Web designer, who presumably does not understand much Java, is responsible for your presentation, naturally you should not use Java in the JSPs responsible for the presentation. JSPs that have scriptlets used most liberally and have Java code appearing all over the JSP are a nightmare to maintain. The logic gets distributed between JSPs and the Java code, and becomes difficult to understand.

So if you do not want Java in your JSPs but you still want to make presentation decisions based on some logic, you need a technology as easily comprehensible as HTML that is still capable of invoking the power of Java where necessary.

This is why *custom tags* were created. Custom tags are HTML-like tags that you develop using Java and that are meant to provide some additional functionality. If we take HTML tags as an example, to create a new paragraph we use the `<p>` tag that HTML provides`<p>...</p>` tag. The reason that the text is displayed in a new paragraph is that the browser sees and understands these tags. Similarly, if we were to use the `<blue>...</blue>` `<blue></blue>` tag to display all numeric content within it in blue, would it work? Of course not, as the browser has no idea what the`<blue>` tag stands for.

But we can provide the implementation we want ourselves, using the power of Java. To take this example a step further, what we can do is tell the Web designers responsible for the presentation that whenever they encounter a case in which they want all numeric data in the text to be displayed in blue, they can use the `<blue></blue>` `<blue>` tag. If we weren't able to use this tag, we would have had to embed Java right in the JSP page. This would certainly have made the page a mess and would have been impossible for someone who does not know Java.

Here are the advantages of using custom tags:

✦ **Simplicity and ease of use** — Custom tags are very simple for even a nonprogrammer to use and using them makes the JSP page a lot easier to comprehend.

✦ **Code reusability** — Once you have the functionality in place as a custom tag, that code never has to repeat. The same piece of code can be reused over and over.

✦ **Ease of maintenance** — Any change you make to the core tag logic is reflected across all pages in which the tag is used. This can be a lifesaver. You do not have to touch any of the individual JSPs in which that particular tag was used.

Custom tags are the topic of the next section.

Note   Tag extensions are also often referred to as *custom tags* and are not new in JSP 2.0. They have been around right from JSP 1.1, although in JSP 2.0 they have undergone some significant changes.

Explaining Custom-Tag Concepts

Now that you have an understanding of what a custom tag is and the purpose that custom tags are meant to serve, we will introduce some of the terminology that you need to be aware of in order to understand and use custom tags. We will also dwell on some of the Web-application-configuration issues that you may need to handle.

✦ **Tag library** — A collection of tags. Most tags tend to be packaged as part of libraries containing many tags that might work independently or in coordination with each other. Being reusable components, tag libraries are generally distributed as JAR files.

✦ **Tag-library descriptor** — This is an XML file with `.tld` extension. This file contains the syntax of the tags and the instructions that the container requires in order to manage those tags.

✦ **Tag handler** — This is the Java class that contains the logic to perform the expected action for the tag. It is a container-managed object. The class has to implement one of the specified Java interfaces if it is to be treated as a valid tag handler by the container.

Before you begin developing your own tags and tag libraries, have a look at how tags are used in JSP and how you need to configure your Web application to get the tags to work properly. We'll examine a simple example of a tag so that the purpose and usage of custom tags becomes a little more apparent. For this example, we will introduce the JSP Standard Tag Library (JSTL) and use a tag from the library.

Working with the JSP Standard Tag Library

When custom tags first arrived on the scene they were heralded as an important step in simplifying JSP development. However, most developers (including me) found developing custom tags somewhat difficult. JSPs' support for scriptlets also led many developers to take the easy way out and go back to using scriptlets and embedding Java code in their JSPs.

Note   If you want to read the JSTL specification, check out `http://java.sun.com/products/jstl`. Apache Taglibs is the reference implementation for this specification and can be downloaded at `http://jakarta.apache.org`. Here you can also find tag libraries for string manipulation, working with dates, and so on that are not part of the specification but that could come in handy.

As a result, developing custom tags for specific project requirements never really caught on as much as it was expected to. However, custom tags that were meant to achieve basic functionality that was common across companies and projects were rapidly adopted. Look around the Web and you can find freely available tags that do specific tasks very well. It was a wise move to come up with a new specification for these common tags, and the JSTL is just that. It is a specification for developing custom tags that perform common tasks like formatting dates, parsing XML, and iterating through collections.

Note   JSTL is not specific to JSP version 2.0. JSTL should work fine with any container that supports JSP 1.2.

Let's have a look at a simple JSP, shown in Listing 7-1, which uses one of the tags in the JSTL.

Listing 7-1: **NumberFormat.jsp**

```
<%@ taglib prefix="fmt" uri="http://java.sun.com/jstl/fmt" %>
<html>
<body>
   <fmt:formatNumber value="00099765.4355" type="currency" currencySymbol="$"
maxFractionDigits="2"/>
</body>
</html>
```

NumberFormat.jsp on execution displays $99,765.44 as the output. Now let's dissect this simple code so you can see how the formatNumber tag has been used in this JSP.

The first line is the taglib directive that tells the container, which unique Uniform Resource Identifier (URI) identifies this tag and the prefix that you would be using while using any of the tags associated with this particular tag-library descriptor. So whenever the container finds in this JSP a tag with the prefix 'fmt', it will look for the associated tag-library descriptor to check the exact usage of the tag and the tag handler responsible for actually processing the tag and performing the required action. We will look at this process in more detail when we develop our own tags in the section, "Understanding Tag Handlers," later in this chapter.

Here we are using the formatNumber tag, which is part of the formatting library. The formatNumber tag is meant to format a numeric value as a number, currency, or percentage. Here we have used its capability to format a number based on the instructions provided and to convert that number to the format of the currency specified.

The value attribute conveys the value to be formatted while the type attribute tells the handler that the value is a currency amount. The currencySymbol attribute specifies the symbol for the currency. The maxFractionDigits attribute tells the handler that the value is to be rounded off so that only two digits exist after the decimal.

That is how simple tag usage is; the tag handler underneath does all the hard work to generate the expected results. The required functionality is now covered, the code underneath will be reused, and, most importantly, the JSP is now very easy to understand.

Many other tags much like the tag we just discussed are part of the library that covers functionality that is required very often in your JSPs. The JSTL as of version 1.0 consists of four tag libraries:

✦ **Core library** — This library consists of the tags that are used most often. These are tags that iterate through collections, perform if-logic, write output to the page, and so on.

✦ **XML library** — This library provides tags to parse XML, perform XSL transformations, and perform similar actions on your XML.

✦ **Formatting library** — This library is most useful for internationalization and performing date and number transformation.

✦ **SQL library** — This library consists of tags to connect to the database, fire SQL queries, and perform other database-related activities. Although very few applications these days have JSPs that talk directly to the database, this library is useful in that scenario.

Now that we have had a quick look at JSTL and a basic tag example, let's examine what you need to do in order to get your tags to work on a Web container like Tomcat.

Importing a tag library

A prerequisite for using custom tags in your JSP is that you must first tell the container that you are using them. This process is referred to as *importing* a tag library into a JSP. You can do this in one of two ways, one using the standard JSP syntax and the other using the XML syntax.

The JSP syntax

If you are using the JSP syntax, you need to put down a `taglib` directive. In Chapter 6, we discussed the purpose that JSP directives are meant to serve. The `taglib` directive tells the container that the JSP uses a tag library. The attributes of this directive specify the prefix that denotes usage of that particular library, and the URI that uniquely identifies that tag library.

In Listing 7-1, the `taglib` directive was as follows:

```
<%@ taglib prefix="fmt" uri="http://java.sun.com/jstl/fmt" %>
```

The `prefix` attribute specifies that all tags in the JSP file that begin with the prefix `fmt` should be associated with this tag library. All tags for this library that are used in this JSP page will be in the format `<fmt:XXX>`. The tag library does not dictate the prefix that you need to use. You can use the same tag library using any prefix you wish, as long as the prefix is unique to this JSP. The specification restricts usage of the following prefixes

✦ `jsp`

✦ `jspx`

✦ `java`

✦ `javax`

✦ `servlet`

✦ `sun`

✦ `sunw`

Note   Empty prefixes are also not permitted.

The `uri` attribute accepts either an absolute URI or a relative URI, and is meant to uniquely identify the tag-library descriptor associated with the prefix `fmt` that we used in Listing 7-1. That the URI has been specified does not mean that the container looks for the tag-library descriptor at that location. The URI is meant for mapping purposes only.

You can directly specify the actual location of the TLD file in the `uri` attribute. Use this option only for achieving quick results during development; do not use it in a real application, as your JSP now gets bound to the actual name and location of the TLD file.

The XML syntax

While writing a JSP page using the XML syntax, note that `taglib` does not have a corresponding tag form, unlike other directives, such as `page` and `include`, which are represented as `<jsp:directive.page>` and `<jsp:directive.include>` respectively. No `<jsp:directive.taglib>` tag exists.

To achieve the same purpose served by the `taglib` directive in Listing 7-1, we would place the code in this format:

```
<jsp:root xmlns:fmt="http://java.sun.com/jstl/fmt" version="2.0">
```

Here `<jsp:root>` is the root element for the JSP page. The preceding example is more typical of a JSP 1.2 page, as unlike in JSP 1.2, in JSP 2.0 it is not compulsory to introduce tag libraries right into the `<jsp:root>`. You now have the option of incorporating tag libraries wherever required using additional `xmlns` attributes.

Note   Until JSP 1.2 it was mandatory to have `<jsp:root>` as the top element of a JSP written using the XML syntax. With JSP version 2.0, using `<jsp:root>` is no longer mandatory.

The Tag Library Descriptor

The TLD plays an important role in the workings of all tags. The TLD is an XML file that contains information that the container needs to be able to process a tag. The container needs to be told things like the name of the tag, its attributes, the URI, and the tag-handler class. Without this information, the container is unable to validate the tag or properly execute the tag handler. TLD files also play an important part in enabling JSP-authoring tools to provide tag-related features.

 **Note** The JSP 2.0 specification lists XML schemas and the document-type definition (DTD) files for tag-library descriptors for JSP version 1.1 and above. All JSP 2.0 compatible containers must be able to parse and accept all these TLD formats. So all your JSP 1.2–compatible TLDs should work fine on any JSP 2.0 container.

The schema for the JSP 2.0 TLD file goes on for dozens of pages and talks about many elements. We will touch on some of the more common elements. For an in-depth understanding of the TLD file, do have a look at the TLD schema, which is part of the JSP 2.0 specification. The example in Listing 7-2 uses most of the common elements in the JSP 2.0 TLD file.

Listing 7-2: A sample TLD

```xml
<?xml version="1.0" encoding="UTF-8" ?>
<taglib xmlns="http://java.sun.com/xml/ns/j2ee"
    xmlns:xsi="http://www.w3.org/2001/XMLSchema-instance"
    xsi:schemaLocation="http://java.sun.com/xml/ns/j2ee web-
jsptaglibrary_2_0.xsd"
    version="2.0">
    <description>A maths utility tag library</description>
    <tlib-version>1.0</tlib-version>
    <short-name>util</short-name>
    <uri>/utiltag</uri>
    <tag>
        <description>Display the square of a number</description>
        <name>square</name>
        <tag-class>com.j2eebible.tags.SquareTag</tag-class>
        <body-content>scriptless</body-content>
        <variable>
            <description>Variable to display value</description>
            <name-given>val</name-given>
        </variable>
        <attribute>
            <name>rep</name>
            <required>true</required>
            <rtexprvalue>true</rtexprvalue>
        </attribute>
                    <dynamic-attributes>true</dynamic-attributes>
    </tag>
    <function>
      <description>Add Integers Function</description>
      <name>add</name>
        <function-class>jsp2.j2eebible.AdditionClass</function-class>
        <function-signature>java.lang.String add( int, int )</function-
signature>
    </function>
</taglib>
```

Listing 7-2 is a basic JSP 2.0 tag-library descriptor that provides the specification for a tag called 'square' and a function called 'add'. Table 7-1 lists some of the elements and their meanings in the order in which they appear.

<table>
<thead>
<tr><th colspan="2" align="center">Table 7-1
TLD methods</th></tr>
<tr><th>Method</th><th>Description</th></tr>
</thead>
<tbody>
<tr><td>description</td><td>A string describing the use and purpose of the entire tag library</td></tr>
<tr><td>version</td><td>The version of the tag-library implementation</td></tr>
<tr><td>short-name</td><td>The preferred prefix for the tag library</td></tr>
<tr><td>uri</td><td>A URI meant to uniquely identify that uniquely identifies this tag library</td></tr>
<tr><td>tag</td><td>One or more tag elements</td></tr>
<tr><td>description</td><td>The description of a particular tag functionality</td></tr>
<tr><td>name</td><td>An action name unique to a particular tag library</td></tr>
<tr><td>tag-class</td><td>The tag-handler class</td></tr>
<tr><td>body-content</td><td>The body-content type for the tag (default JSP)</td></tr>
<tr><td>variable</td><td>A variable that can be used in scripting and in expression-language expressions</td></tr>
<tr><td>description</td><td>The variable description</td></tr>
<tr><td>name-given</td><td>The name for the variable as a constant</td></tr>
<tr><td>attribute</td><td>The attributes for the tag</td></tr>
<tr><td>name</td><td>The attribute name</td></tr>
<tr><td>required</td><td>Whether the attribute is required or optional; takes the values true and false, default is false</td></tr>
<tr><td>rtexprvalue</td><td>Whether the attribute can take a runtime expression as value (default false)</td></tr>
<tr><td>dynamic-attributes</td><td>An element that denotes whether the tag supports dynamic attributes (new with JSP 2.0; default false)</td></tr>
<tr><td>function</td><td>The functions used in the expression language</td></tr>
<tr><td>description</td><td>The description of the function</td></tr>
<tr><td>name</td><td>The unique function name</td></tr>
<tr><td>function-class</td><td>The class that implements the function</td></tr>
<tr><td>function-signature</td><td>The function signature</td></tr>
</tbody>
</table>

The `<body-content>` element requires a special mention. With JSP 2.0 this element takes the four following values:

✦ `tagdependent` — The container will not interpret the tag body. It is the responsibility of the tag.

✦ `JSP` — The tag-body content is JSP and will be interpreted by the container. (This is the default value.)

✦ `empty` — The tag body is empty.

✦ `scriptless` — No scripting is accepted within the body of the tag. This value accepts template text, expression-language expressions and JSP action elements.

The tag-library-descriptor location

For any custom tag to work, the container must find and use the relevant TLD file. The TLD file can be maintained as an independent file in the application-directory structure, or it can be part of the `.jar` file that contains the tag library.

Independent files

With JSP 2.0, in the case of an independent TLD file the file must be present in the `WEB-INF` directory or some subdirectory of it. This TLD file also should not be placed in the `WEB-INF/classes` or `WEB-INF/lib` directories.

While developing your own tags, keep all your TLD files in a separate directory such as `WEB-INF/tlds`. This makes editing the files as you work on them a lot easier. Once you're done developing the tags you can package these TLDs into JAR files.

TLDs within JARs

The easiest way to distribute tag libraries is by packaging them into JAR files. Using a tag library packaged as a JAR file can be as simple as dumping that JAR file into the `WEB-INF/lib` directory of the application in which you intend to use the library.

For a tag library packaged as a JAR file the TLD files must reside in the `META-INF` directory within the JAR file or any of its subdirectories. A tag library packaged as a JAR file can have one or more tag-library descriptors.

If you develop a new tag library that would handle string manipulations, for example, you can package the library as a JAR file. Let's name it `stringtags.jar`. In this JAR file, the TLD files for the tags you have created would reside in the `META-INF` directory in the JAR file. To use this library in a Web application you are developing, all you would have to do is place the JAR file in the `lib` directory of your Web application and any container that supports JSP 2.0 will be able to load the library for use in your application.

In the next section, we will have a closer look at how tag library mappings work and how the container is able to figure out where to find a tag and how to execute it.

Explaining taglib Mapping

We have shown that in every JSP the container needs to be told the URI for a particular tag-library descriptor. Based on the tag-library descriptor that the container finds for a URI, the container is able to process the tags in the JSP. We showed that the TLD file can be placed in multiple locations. So to be able to associate a URI with the physical location of the tag-library descriptor, the container maintains a map of the URIs and the location of the TLD files.

The container creates the map in the following order of precedence:

1. The `taglib` map that is part of the Web-deployment descriptor (`web.xml`) file

2. The TLD files that the container finds in the `META-INF` directory of the JAR files found in the `WEB-INF/lib` directory and the TLD files that it finds in the `WEB-INF` directory and its subdirectories

3. Implicit map entries that the container might have anyway

For any `taglib` URI stated in the JSP file, the container has to find the associated TLD file. Let's consider an example in which you wish to use a tag in your JSP for which the tag-library descriptor is a file named `map.tld` located in the `WEB-INF/tlds` directory. The `taglib` directive in our JSP is as follows:

```
<%@ taglib prefix="xyz" uri="/mapTag" %>
```

The container will be able to locate all files with the `.tld` extension that exist in the `WEB-INF` directory and its subdirectories. It will then create mappings for these TLD files based on the URI specified in them. However, if you want your `web.xml` file to reflect all the tags your application uses, or if the TLD does not state the URI that would uniquely identify that particular tag library, you can explicitly provide all `taglib` mappings in your `web.xml`.

In the `web.xml` file, the `taglib` mapping for the preceding example needs to be in the following format:

```
<taglib>
    <taglib-uri>
        /mapTag
    </taglib-uri>
    <taglib-location>
        /WEB-INF/tlds/map.tld
    </taglib-location>
</taglib>
```

The `<taglib>` element must be a sub-element of `<jsp-config>`. Now that we have discussed the possible locations for the TLD files, let's get down to a discussion about what tag handlers are and the types of tag handlers.

Understanding Tag Handlers

Now that you have seen how tags are used and gotten a sense of the configuration issues you need to be aware of, let's get into the core of the topic, understanding the tag handlers.

Note Tag handlers are ordinary Java classes implementing certain interfaces. The way the container handles them is what makes them special. For all development purposes, treat them exactly like any other Java class.

With JSP 2.0, tag handlers have been classified into the two following types:

✦ **Classic** — These are the handlers that were present in JSP 1.2. Not much about these tags has changed.

✦ **Simple** — The development of these handlers can be called one of the most important in JSP 2.0. Simple tag handlers are an easier-to-use alternative to the classic tag handlers.

The primary reason for adding simple tag handlers was that it was hard to learn how to use the JSP 1.2–style tag handlers. In terms of functionality, simple tag handlers on their own do not offer anything that classic tag handlers do not. However, as their name suggests, simple tag handlers certainly are a lot easier to use than classic tag handlers.

Let's first deal with classic tag handlers. Once you understand these, simple tags are easy to grasp.

Classic tag handlers

The JSP 2.0 specification define a classic tag handler as follows:

A classic tag handler is a Java class that implements the `Tag`, `IterationTag`, or `BodyTag` interface, and is the runtime representation of a custom action.

A classic tag handler is just another Java class that implements the methods of the interface being implemented. Each of these three interfaces is meant to denote a different kind of tag handling.

Note Until JSP 1.2 the `Tag` interface, `javax.servlet.jsp.tagext.Tag`, was the top-level interface. The other interfaces were sub-interfaces of the `Tag` interface. However, with JSP 2.0 a new top-level interface, `javax.servlet.jsp.tagext.JspTag`, has been introduced. The `Tag` and `SimpleTag` interfaces both extend `JspTag`.

The Tag interface

The Tag interface is the base interface for all classic tag handlers. Figure 7-1 depicts the Tag hierarchy that you need to get familiar with before using tags. All classic tag handlers directly or indirectly implement this interface. This interface defines the methods required in all classic tag handlers. Tag handlers implementing just the Tag interface can be used for writing basic tags that do not involve any iterations or processing of the tag's body content. Table 7-2 lists the methods of the Tag interface while Table 7-3 lists the various constants defined.

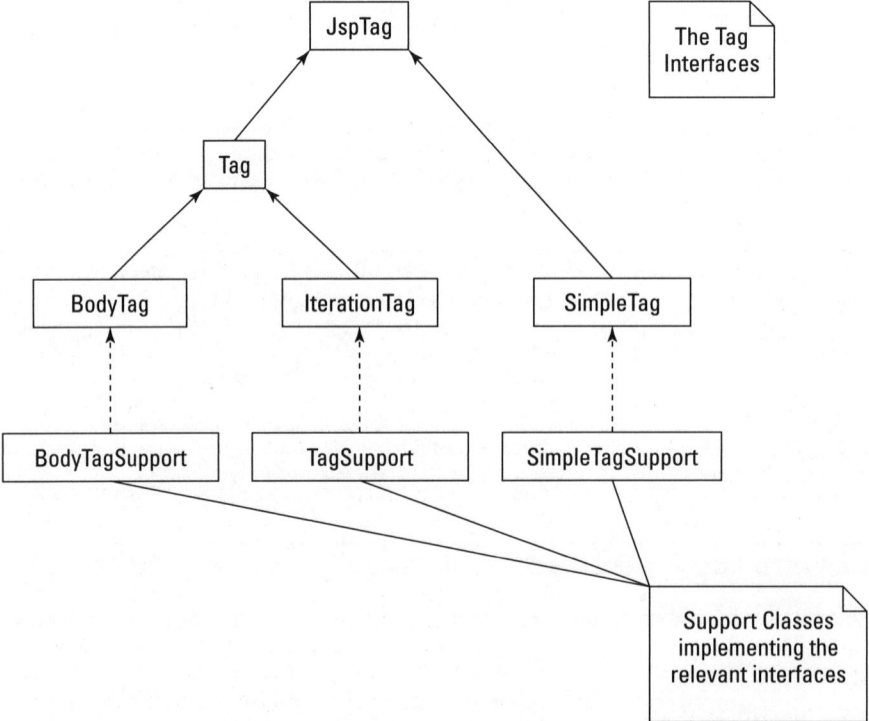

Figure 7-1: The Tag interfaces hierarchy and support classes implement the Tag interfaces.

	Table 7-2
	Tag methods

Method	Description
void setPageContext (PageContext)	The container calls this method to set the context for the current page.
void setParent(Tag)	The container sets the parent tag, and this is the closest enclosing tag handler of that tag.

Method	Description
`int doStartTag()`	The container invokes this method on encountering the start of the tag.
`int doEndTag()`	The container invokes this method on encountering the end of the tag.
`Tag getParent()`	This method gets the parent of the current tag handler. It is used primarily in the case of cooperating tags.
`void release()`	This method is called on the tag handler to release any resources held.

Table 7-3
Tag constants

Field	Description
`EVAL_BODY_INCLUDE`	The `doStartTag` method returns this value to tell the container to evaluate the body of the tag.
`SKIP_BODY`	The `doStartTag` method returns this value to tell the container to skip tag-body evaluation.
`EVAL_PAGE`	The `doEndTag` method returns this value to tell the container to evaluate the rest of the page.
`SKIP_PAGE`	The `doEndTag` returns this value to tell the container to skip evaluation of the rest of the page.

Let's take a look at a simple example that uses the `Tag` interface. In this example we'll use an empty tag that generates a `hello` message. The tag usage should look like the following:

```
<j2eebible:hello fname="MyFName" lname="MyLName"/>
```

This sample tag should generate the following content:

```
Hello MyFName MyLName! How do you do?
```

Let's get down to creating our first example. First, we need to create a separate Web application in the Tomcat `webapps` directory. Following the normal Web-application standards, we create the following new directories:

✦ `webapps/j2eeBible`
✦ `webapps/j2eeBible/WEB-INF`
✦ `webapps/j2eeBible/WEB-INF/lib`
✦ `webapps/j2eeBible/WEB-INF/classes`

Apart from these standard directories, we also create the new directory `webapps/j2eeBible/WEB-INF/tlds`, where we would be keeping all the TLD files. As you may recall, the container can find and use all `.tld`-extension files located in `WEB-INF` or any of its subdirectories.

As shown in Listing 7-3, we create a new `<tag>` node for our tag. It need not be the only tag in the TLD file; one TLD file can hold many distinct tags. As we have specified the URI in the TLD file, on finding this TLD file the container will be able to create a new `taglib` mapping on its own. With JSP 2.0, it is no longer mandatory to provide the mapping of the `web.xml` file. The URI we have specified is `/j2eebible`, so all JSPs that intend to use this TLD file can access it using this URI; they do not need to specify the location of the TLD file.

Listing 7-3: **j2eebible-taglib.tld**

```xml
<?xml version="1.0" encoding="UTF-8" ?>
<taglib xmlns="http://java.sun.com/xml/ns/j2ee"
    xmlns:xsi="http://www.w3.org/2001/XMLSchema-instance"
    xsi:schemaLocation="http://java.sun.com/xml/ns/j2ee web-
jsptaglibrary_2_0.xsd"
    version="2.0">
    <description>Samples for J2EEBible </description>
    <tlib-version>1.0</tlib-version>
    <short-name>j2eebible</short-name>
    <uri>/j2eeBible</uri>
    <tag>
        <description>Displays a Hello Message</description>
        <name>hello</name>
        <tag-class>com.j2eeBible.mytags.BasicTag</tag-class>
        <body-content>empty</body-content>
        <attribute>
            <name>fname</name>
            <required>true</required>
            <rtexprvalue>true</rtexprvalue>
        </attribute>
        <attribute>
            <name>lname</name>
            <required>true</required>
            <rtexprvalue>true</rtexprvalue>
        </attribute>
    </tag>
</taglib>
```

Next we specify the name of the tag as `hello` and the name of the tag-handler class as `com.j2eeBible.mytags.BasicTag`. As our tag is an empty tag and will have no body content, the body-content element's value is stated as `empty`. The two attributes, for the first name and the last name, are specified in Listing 7-4.

Listing 7-4: **Hello.jsp**

```
<%@ taglib prefix="j2eebible" uri="/j2eeBible" %>
<html>
  <head>
    <title>Hello Handler</title>
  </head>
  <body>
    <j2eebible:hello fname="George" lname="Bush"/>
  </body>
</html>
```

Listing 7-5 shows a bare-bones JSP in which we use the tag we have created. (Note that the URI specified here is exactly the same as the one we specified in the TLD file.) The prefix can of course change, and therefore this same tag, with different prefixes, can be used in different JSPs. Next let's look at the actual code that does the task for us.

Listing 7-5: **BasicTag.java**

```
package com.j2eeBible.mytags;

import javax.servlet.jsp.JspException;
import javax.servlet.jsp.PageContext;
import javax.servlet.jsp.tagext.Tag;

public class BasicTag implements Tag
{
    PageContext pageContext;
    Tag parent;
    String fname;
    String lname;
    int cnt=0;

    public BasicTag()
    {
        System.out.println((++cnt)+") >> IN CONSTRUCTOR");
    }
    public void setParent(Tag parent)
    {
        System.out.println((++cnt)+") >> IN SETPARENT");
        this.parent = parent;
    }
    public void setPageContext(PageContext pageContext)
    {
```

Continued

Listing 7-5 *(continued)*

```java
        System.out.println((++cnt)+") >> IN SETPAGECONTEXT");
        this.pageContext = pageContext;
    }
    public Tag getParent()
    {
        System.out.println((++cnt)+") >> IN GET PARENT");
        return this.parent;
    }
    public int doStartTag() throws JspException
    {
        System.out.println((++cnt)+") >> IN DO START");
        try
        {
          pageContext.getOut().write("Hello "+getFname()+" "+getLname()+"!
How do you do?");
        }
        catch(Exception e)
        {
          e.printStackTrace();
        }
        return SKIP_BODY;
    }
    public int doEndTag() throws JspException
    {
        System.out.println((++cnt)+") >> IN DO END \n");
        cnt=0;
        return EVAL_PAGE;
    }
    public void release()
    {
        System.out.println((++cnt)+") >> RELEASING RESOURCES");
        pageContext = null;
        parent = null;
    }
    public String getFname()
    {
        return fname;
    }
    public void setFname(String newFname)
    {
        System.out.println((++cnt)+") >> Setting FName");
        fname = newFname;
    }
    public String getLname()
    {
      return lname;
    }
```

```
public void setLname(String newLname)
{
   System.out.println((++cnt)+") >> Setting LName");
   lname = newLname;
}
}
```

The key to understanding custom tags is understanding the various flows based on
return values. Listing 7-5 depicts a trick that is particularly useful for understanding
tags. Look at the `System.out` lines in the code. Here we increment a counter while
printing out the location. On tag usage and execution by the container, we get a nice
little message on the Tomcat console showing exactly how things went. You should
get the following output on the Tomcat console:

```
1) IN CONSTRUCTOR
2) IN SETPAGECONTEXT
3) IN SETPARENT
4) Setting FName
5) Setting LName
6) IN DO START
7) IN DO END
```

What this output shows, first, is that the container called the constructor for our
tag handler. Next it set the `pageContext` and the parent tag for our tag. After this,
the container called the setter methods for the two attributes we have used. Only
after all these steps were executed successfully did we get to `doStartTag` and get
our piece of code generating the output expected. As for all classic tag handlers,
the container caches and reuses handler instances; the `release` method was not
called.

The IterationTag interface

The `IterationTag` interface extends the `Tag` interface and introduces just a single
new method to enable reevaluation of the body of the tag. All the concepts that
applied to the `Tag` interface also hold good for the `IterationTag` interface.
`IterationTag` is like a Tag on steroids. Refer to Table 7-4 and 7-5 for methods and
constants that are new to the `IterationTag` interface. The `IterationTag` interface
is used primarily in cases in which the tag content is to be repeatedly generated.

Table 7-4 IterationTag method	
Method	**Description**
`Int doAfterBody()`	This method is called after the body contents of the tag are evaluated.

Table 7-5 IterationTag constant	
Field	**Description**
EVAL_BODY_AGAIN	The doAfterBody method can return this value if the body of the tag needs to be reevaluated.

As shown in Listing 7-3, let's declare a new tag in the same tag-library descriptor that we used for earlier examples. We just put in this new tag into the existing TLD.

```
<tag>
<description>Iterates through an array</description>
<name>itrArray</name>
<tag-class>com.j2eeBible.mytags.TryIterationTag</tag-class>
<body-content>JSP</body-content>
</tag>
```

We now have a new tag called itrArray that takes JSP content as its body. Next, in Listing 7-6, we use a very basic JSP page that will display the output of this tag.

Listing 7-6: **Iterate.jsp**

```
<%@ taglib prefix="j2eebible" uri="/j2eeBible" %>
<html>
  <head>
    <title>Hello Handler</title>
  </head>
  <body>
    <j2eebible:itrArray>
    <br/>
    The Value is:
    </j2eebible:itrArray>
  </body>
</html>
```

The key difference between using the Tag interface and using the IterationTag interface is the presence of the doAfterBody method. If this method returns a value of EVAL_BODY_AGAIN the container reevaluates the body of the tag. This is what makes it possible for the tag to generate the output multiple times. In Listing 7-7, the doAfterBody method is where all the logic is. As long as the counter is less than the size of the array, the body content keeps getting reevaluated. When this condition stops being fulfilled, the method returns SKIP_BODY.

Note Reevaluation of the tag body does not mean that the `doStartTag` method is called every time. The `doStartTag` method is called only once.

Listing 7-7: **TryIterationTag.jsp**

```
package com.j2eeBible.mytags;
import javax.servlet.jsp.*;
import javax.servlet.jsp.tagext.*;

public class TryIterationTag implements IterationTag
{
    protected PageContext pageContext;
    protected Tag parent;
    int iTagCnt=0;
    int cnt=0;
    String []arTeam=new String[]{"One","Two","Three"};

    public TryIterationTag()
    {
       System.out.println((++cnt)+") **IN CONSTRUCTOR");
    }
    public void setParent(Tag parent)
    {
System.out.println((++cnt)+") **SET PARENT");
        this.parent = parent;
    }
    public void setPageContext(PageContext pageContext)
    {
        System.out.println((++cnt)+") **SET PAGECONTEXT");
        this.pageContext = pageContext;
    }
    public Tag getParent()
    {
        return this.parent;
    }
    public int doStartTag() throws JspException
    {
        System.out.println((++cnt)+") **IN DOSTARTTAG");
        return EVAL_BODY_INCLUDE;
    }
    public int doEndTag() throws JspException
    {
        System.out.println((++cnt)+") **IN DOENDTAG \n");
        return EVAL_PAGE;
public int doAfterBody() throws JspException
    {
        System.out.println((++cnt)+") **IN DOAFTERBODY");
        if(iTagCnt<arTeam.length)
        {
```

Continued

Listing 7-7 *(continued)*

```
         try
         {
           pageContext.getOut().write(arTeam[iTagCnt]);
           iTagCnt++;
         }
         catch(Exception e)
         {
           e.printStackTrace();
         }
         return EVAL_BODY_AGAIN;
      }
      else
      {
         iTagCnt=0;
         return SKIP_BODY;
      }
public void release()
    {
       System.out.println((++cnt)+") **RELEASE");
       pageContext = null;
       parent = null;
    }
}
```

Listing 7-8 shows the output expected. However, in this case, the output that we actually get is not as expected. We get an additional and unnecessary string at the end.

Listing 7-8: Actual output of using TryIterationTag example

```
The Value is: One
The Value is: Two
The Value is: Three
The Value is:
```

Although this iteration worked fine, we got an additional The Value is: string in our output. As you might have figured out, this problem has arisen because IterationTag does not offer the capability to buffer content.

The System.outs that we incorporated into our code will show that the doAfterBody method is called four times, while the array we have has only three values. So when doAfterBody is called the fourth time, the if condition fails and we return SKIP_BODY. This works fine. However, the problem here is that IterationTag does not buffer the content, so the string The Value is: has already been written to the stream by the time the doAfterBody method is called the fourth time.

To solve this problem and to get the expected output (listed in Listing 7-9), one solution is that in doAfterBody a new piece of code is put in, that would check if the counter has got to the last element in the array. If it has, the output is dumped to the stream and SKIP_BODY is returned. However, in this example we will go for another option. We buffer the contents of the tag body, so when we are done iterating through the array and have the string The Value is: in our buffer, we simply clear the contents of the buffer without writing to the output.

The BodyTag interface

The BodyTag interface extends the IterationTag interface and introduces two new methods and one new constant. The purpose of this interface is to enable buffering of the body content of a tag. The output of the tag can now be generated after the buffered body content is processed, modified or even rejected. Table 7-6 lists the new methods introduced by the BodyTag interface, and Table 7-7 lists the new constant.

Table 7-6
The BodyTag interface

Method	Description
void setBodyContent(BodyContent)	The container calls this method just before calling doInitBody. This method is called only if the tag has a body and the doStartTag has returned EVAL_BODY_BUFFERED.
void doInitBody ()	The container calls this method just before body-tag processing begins.

Table 7-7
The BodyTag-interface constant

Field	Description
EVAL_BODY_BUFFERED	The doStartTag method can return this value only if the handler class is implementing the BodyTag interface. This return value leads to the creation of a new buffer containing the body content.

The interfaces `IterationTag` and `BodyTag` are closely related, and `BodyTag` builds on the `IterationTag` capability, providing a content buffering capability that `IterationTag` does not provide. Let's take a look at an example of `IterationTag` usage wherein (although the iteration functionality will work fine) it will become obvious why the `BodyTag` interface is required. We will then use `BodyTag` to solve the problem that we face when using `IterationTag`.

In this example we have an array of values. (We are using a hardcoded array here, but in a real-life scenario you could use something similar that you have retrieved from a database or the user session.) The tag is meant to repeatedly display the tag-body content while iterating through the array of values and appending a value to the body content.

We declare the array to be used, in the following fashion:

```
String []arTeam=new String[]{"One","Two","Three"};
```

In the JSP file we have this tag:

```
<j2eebible:itrArray>
    <br/>
    The Value is:
</j2eebible:itrArray>
```

The expected output appears in Listing 7-9.

Listing 7-9: **Output expected from the itrArray tag**

```
The Value is: One
The Value is: Two
The Value is: Three
}
}
```

As shown in Table 7-7, the `BodyTag` interface introduces a new constant named `EVAL_BODY_BUFFERED`. When `doStartTag` returns this value, the container does not write the contents of the tag body to the output but instead buffers them. Therefore, in our code we always have the option of writing the buffered content to the output stream as is, or editing it, or even just getting rid of it.

For this example we again introduce a new tag, `itrBufArray`, into our tag-library descriptor.

```
<tag>
<description>BufferContent and Iterates through an array</description>
<name>itrBufArray</name>
```

```
<tag-class>com.j2eeBible.mytags.TryBodyTag</tag-class>
<body-content>JSP</body-content>
</tag>
```

The JSP we are using here is the same as the one we used for the `IterationTag` example. The only change is the tag name. Listing 7-10 shows the tag usage in a simple JSP file.

Listing 7-10: **IterateBuf.jsp**

```
<%@ taglib prefix="j2eebible" uri="/j2eeBible" %>
<html>
  <head>
    <title>Hello Handler</title>
  </head>
  <body>
    <j2eebible:itrBufArray>
    <br/>
    The Value is:
    </j2eebible:itrBufArray>
  </body>
</html>
```

As shown in Listing 7-11, the code for this example is also very similar to the code we used for the `IterationTag` example. The differences in this example are that the `doStartTag` method now returns `EVAL_BODY_BUFFERED`, that a new method, `doInitBody`, is introduced, and that changes are made to the `doAfterBody` method. The `doAfterBody` method is where we work with the buffered tag-body contents provided to us.

Note   The `doInit` method is not invoked if the tag body is empty. Even if the tag body is not empty, `doInit` is invoked only if `doStartTag` returns `EVAL_BODY_BUFFERED` and not if it returns any other values.

Listing 7-11: **TryBodyTag.java**

```
package com.j2eeBible.mytags;
import javax.servlet.jsp.*;
import javax.servlet.jsp.tagext.*;

public class TryBodyTag implements BodyTag
{
    protected BodyContent bodyOut;
    protected PageContext pageContext;
```

Continued

Listing 7-11 *(continued)*

```java
protected Tag parent;
int iTagCnt=0;
int cnt=0;
String []arTeam=new String[]{"One","Two","Three"};

public TryBodyTag()
{
  System.out.println((++cnt)+") $$IN CONSTRUCTOR");
}
public void setParent(Tag parent)
{
    System.out.println((++cnt)+") $$IN SETPARENT");
    this.parent = parent;
}
public void setBodyContent(BodyContent bodyOut)
{
    System.out.println((++cnt)+") $$IN SET BODYCONTENT");
    this.bodyOut = bodyOut;
}
public void setPageContext(PageContext pageContext)
{
    System.out.println((++cnt)+") $$IN SETPAGECONTEXT");
    this.pageContext = pageContext;
}
public Tag getParent()
{
    return this.parent;
}
public int doStartTag() throws JspException
{
    System.out.println((++cnt)+") $$IN DOSTARTTAG");
    return EVAL_BODY_BUFFERED;
}
public int doEndTag() throws JspException
{
    System.out.println((++cnt)+") $$IN DOENDTAG \n");
    return EVAL_PAGE;
}
public void doInitBody() throws JspException
{
    System.out.println((++cnt)+") $$IN DOINITBODY");
}
public int doAfterBody() throws JspException
{
    System.out.println((++cnt)+") $$IN DOAFTERBODY");
    try
    {
        JspWriter out=bodyOut.getEnclosingWriter();
```

```
                    String strStaticText=bodyOut.getString();

                     if(iTagCnt<arTeam.length)
                       {
                         try
                         {
                           String strWrite=strStaticText+
arTeam[iTagCnt];
                           System.out.println("iTagCnt "+ iTagCnt+"
Writing "+strWrite);
                           out.print(strWrite);
                           bodyOut.clearBody();
                           iTagCnt++;
                         }
                         catch(Exception e)
                         {
                           e.printStackTrace();
                         }
                         return EVAL_BODY_AGAIN;
                       }
                     else
                       {
                         iTagCnt=0;
                         bodyOut.clearBody();
                         return SKIP_BODY;
                       }
                }
            catch (Exception e)
            {
                e.printStackTrace();
            }
            return SKIP_BODY;
        }
    public void release()
    {
        System.out.println(((++cnt)+") $$IN RELEASE");
        bodyOut = null;
        pageContext = null;
        parent = null;
    }
}
```

TagSupport and BodyTagSupport

With all these interfaces, although we don't really need to write a lot of code, most of the classes are full of forced implementations of methods in the interface. We provide real implementations for very few methods, and so our code becomes unnecessarily lengthy and complex.

The idea behind the TagSupport and BodyTagSupport classes is to free the developer from having to write all that unnecessary code. They are utility classes that provide default implementations for the methods in the IterationTag and BodyTag interfaces, respectively.

Using these classes, we have the option of overriding only those methods for which we wish to provide some implementation. Now, the same result achieved by implementing the interface and overriding all the methods can be achieved with just a fraction of the code.

The TagSupport class implements the IterationTag interface. Table 7-8 lists the various methods of TagSupport. BodyTagSupport extends TagSupport and implements the BodyTag interface. Table 7-9 lists the various methods of BodyTagSupport.

Table 7-8
TagSupport methods

Method	Description
int doAfterBody ()	This method returns SKIP_BODY by default. You need to override this method only if repeated evaluation of the body is required.
int doEndTag ()	This method returns EVAL_PAGE by default. You do not need to override it in most cases.
int doStartTag()	This method returns SKIP_BODY by default.
static Tag findAncestor WithClass(Tag, Class)	This method finds the closest instance of the specified class. (Note that this is a static method.)
String getId()	This method returns the value of the id attribute of the tag.
Tag getParent()	This method gets the closest enclosing Tag instance.
Object getValue(String)	This method gets the value for a certain key from the Hashmap of tag attribute values maintained by the class.
Enumeration getValues()	This method gets an enumeration of all values.
void release()	The method is meant to have code that releases any resources that you use while processing the tag. You need to override it only if you wish to explicitly release any resources, instead of having the container handle it for you.

Method	Description
void removeValue(String)	This method removes from the Hashmap the value associated with the specified key.
void setId(String)	This method sets the ID for the tag.
void setParent(Tag)	This method sets the parent tag.
void setValue (String, Object)	This method sets a value against a key in the Hashmap.

Because BodyTagSupport extends TagSupport, it inherits a number of implementations from that interface. The additional methods in BodyTagSupport and the methods that differ from those of TagSupport are listed in Table 7-9.

Table 7-9
BodyTagSupport methods

Method	Description
void doInitBody	The default method performs no action.
int doStartTag()	This method returns EVAL_BODY_BUFFERED by default.
BodyContent getBodyContent()	This method gets the reference to the current BodyContent.
JspWriter getPreviousOut	This method gets the reference to JspWriter that underlies the BodyContent reference.
void setBodyContent(BodyContent)	This method sets the body content for the tag.

While you're using TagSupport classes, a big advantage is the Hashmap of attributes that is maintained by the class. This HashMap has key-value pairs of all attributes of the tag, where the key is the name of the attribute and the value is the value of the attribute. The underlying TagSupport and BodyTagSupport class has this functionality and nothing needs to be done by the class extending the support class. Using the name of the attribute as the key, these values can be fetched from the Hashmap when required.

With the support classes, you only need to extend a class; you do not need to implement an interface and then selectively provide implementations to the methods that would have your logic in them.

Simple tag handlers

Simple tag handlers are new in JSP 2.0. The classic tag handlers we discussed earlier can perform all the tasks that a simple tag handler can; the difference between the two kinds of handlers is that simple tag handlers are easier to use.

The `SimpleTag` interface extends the `JspTag` interface and is made up of just five methods as shown in Table 7-10. Within these methods, simple tags can do everything that classic tags can.

Table 7-10 SimpleTag methods	
Method	*Description*
`void doTag()`	This method is called by the container and is responsible for processing the tag.
`void setParent(JspTag)`	This method sets the parent of the tag.
`JspTag getParent()`	This method returns the parent of the tag.
`void setJspContext`	This method sets the `JspContext` into the protected field `jspContext`.
`void setJspBody(JspFragment)`	This method sets the body of the tag as a `JspFragment`.

The lifecycle of a simple tag handler is as follows:

1. For every use of the tag, the container creates a new instance of the tag handler. (In this the simple tag handler is unlike the classic tag handlers, which cache and reuse the same instance.) However, although the container now creates a lot more objects, it no longer has to waste time caching and maintaining them. As most new Java Virtual Machines (JVMs) are very good at garbage collection, the creation of a new handler instance for each tag usage should not affect performance.

2. The container calls the `setJspContext` and `setParent` methods.

3. The setter methods for the tag attributes are called in the order in which the attributes appear.

4. The `setJspBody` method is called. The body of the tag is set as a `JspFragment`.

5. The `doTag` method is called.

Compared to that of the classic tags, this is a drastically simple flow. The `doTag` is really the method to focus on, as the other methods are more or less enablers. So now let's get down to implementing with `SimpleTag` the same example we implemented earlier using `IterationTag` and `BodyTag`.

First, let's add a new tag to the TLD, as shown here:

```
<tag>
    <description>Iterate array using a Simple Tag</description>
    <name>itrSimple</name>
    <tag-class>com.j2eeBible.mytags.TrySimpleTag</tag-class>
    <body-content>JSP</body-content>
</tag>
```

We now slightly modify our earlier JSP and change the tag name to itrsample, as shown in Listing 7-12.

Listing 7-12: **IterateSimple.jsp**

```
<%@ taglib prefix="j2eebible" uri="/j2eeBible" %>
<html>
  <head>
    <title>Hello Handler</title>
  </head>
  <body>
    <j2eebible:itrSimple>
    <br/>
    The Value is:
    </j2eebible:itrSimple>
  </body>
</html>
```

The best part of using SimpleTag is the concise and easy-to-understand code. Listing 7-13 is how the code for the tag usage in Listing 7-12 will look.

Listing 7-13: **TrySimpleTag.jsp**

```
package com.j2eeBible.mytags;

import java.io.IOException;
import javax.servlet.jsp.JspContext;
import javax.servlet.jsp.JspException;
import javax.servlet.jsp.tagext.JspFragment;
import javax.servlet.jsp.tagext.JspTag;
import javax.servlet.jsp.tagext.SimpleTag;

public class TrySimpleTag implements SimpleTag
{
    JspTag parent;
```

Continued

Listing 7-13 *(continued)*

```java
JspContext jspContext;
JspFragment jspBody;
int cnt=0;

String []arTeam=new String[]{"One","Two","Three"};

public TrySimpleTag()
{
  System.out.println((++cnt)+") ## IN Constructor");
}
public void setParent(JspTag parent)
{
  System.out.println((++cnt)+") ## IN SetParent");
  this.parent=parent;
}
public JspTag getParent()
{
  return this.parent;
}
public void doTag() throws JspException, IOException
{
    System.out.println((++cnt)+") ## IN DOTAG \n");
    for(int iCnt=0; iCnt<arTeam.length; iCnt++)
    {
      jspBody.invoke(null);
      jspContext.getOut().write(arTeam[iCnt]);
    }
}
public void setJspContext(JspContext newJspContext)
{
    System.out.println((++cnt)+") ## IN Set JspContext");
    jspContext = newJspContext;
}
public void setJspBody(JspFragment newJspBody)
{
  System.out.println((++cnt)+") ## IN Set JSP Body");
  jspBody = newJspBody;
}
}
```

Note

The counter we have used in all the code in this chapter is an instance variable. In earlier examples we had to set it back to 0 when a particular tag usage was done. This was required as the same instance was getting reused and so the value of the instance variable was carried over across multiple tag usages. We do not do that in the code for the simple tag handler, yet the output for each invocation on the Tomcat console begins with 1, indicating that a new instance is being created for every tag usage, having a fresh counter starting with 0.

The `doTag` method is the only method that has some logic in it. The rest are methods forced by the interface and have pretty basic implementations. As `JspFragment` is an addition of JSP2.0 and plays a key role in making the tag code in Listing 7-13 so simple, let's delve a little further into what a `JspFragment` is.

JspFragment

The `JspFragment` interface (`javax.servlet.jsp.tagext.JspFragment`) is new to JSP 2.0 and is meant to encapsulate a portion of the code in one object. In addition to such scenarios as in Listing 7-13, where the tag-body content constitutes a `JspFragment`, `JspFragment` is used where tag attributes are declared by means of the `<jsp:attribute>` tag.

The `JspFragment` interface has just one method, whose signature is as follows:

```
public void invoke(java.io.Writer out)
```

Calling the `invoke` method executes the fragment, directing all output to the Writer stated. If a null Writer reference is passed, the output is directed to the `JspWriter` for the `JspContext` associate. Therefore, in our example in Listing 7-13 either of the following two lines of code could have been used to output the body content:

```
jspBody.invoke(null);
jspBody.invoke(jspContext.getOut());
```

SimpleTagSupport

Simple tag handlers do have the potential to drastically reduce custom-tag complexity. If you found the `SimpleTag` example in Listing 7-13 simple, we have an even better class to work with, the `SimpleTagSupport` class.

Much like `TagSupport` and `BodyTagSupport`, `SimpleTagSupport` is a utility class that provides default implementations for the methods in the `SimpleTag` interface. Table 7-11 lists the various methods of the `SimpleTagSupport`.

Table 7-11 SimpleTagSupport methods	
Method	**Description**
`void doTag()`	This method is an empty method and does nothing for you.
`static JspTag findAncestorWithClass (JspTag, Class)`	This is a static method that finds an instance of the specified class that is closest in the tag structure to the tag being used.

Continued

Table 7-11 *(continued)*

Method	Description
JspFragment getJspBody()	This method gets the body of the tag as a JspFragment.
JspContext getJspContext()	This method returns the page context.
JspTag getParent()	This method returns the parent of the tag.
void setJspBody (JspFragment)	This method is called by the container and sets the tag body in a protected field, jspBody.
void setJspContext (JspContext)	This method is called by the container and sets the jspContext in a protected field, jspContext.
void setParent(JspTag)	This method sets the parent for the tag.

Let's now explore *dynamic attributes,* which are new in JSP 2.0, and then take a look at a dynamic-attributes example in which we use the SimpleTagSupport class.

Exploring Dynamic Attributes

Dynamic attributes have emerged because it is not always possible to know the number and names of all the attributes that a tag would use. Dynamic attributes give you the flexibility to change the number and names of the attributes that the tag has without having to touch the tag definition in the TLD. In order for dynamic attributes to be used the tag handler must implement the DynamicAttributes interface and an additional <dynamic-attributes> tag must be introduced into the tag-library descriptor. The TLD element is what tells the container that a certain tag accepts dynamic attributes.

Note   Any tag handler can support dynamic attributes.

The DynamicAttributes interface declares the following method:

```
public void setDynamicAttribute(String uri, String localName, Object value)
```

Every time the container encounters an attribute that is not declared in the TLD for a tag that supports dynamic attributes, the container calls this method. The handler can store these values in a Hashmap or Arraylist that can be retrieved later.

For our example, we will create a tag that takes zero or more values as attributes and displays their sum. For this let's first declare the following tag:

```
<tag>
    <description>Add all attribute values</description>
    <name>addAttr</name>
    <tag-class>com.j2eeBible.mytags.TrySimpleDynamic</tag-class>
    <body-content>empty</body-content>
    <dynamic-attributes>true</dynamic-attributes>
</tag>
```

Note the addition of the new element `<dynamic-attributes>`. The default value for this element is `false`. Listing 7-14 is a JSP that will display the result of the tag execution.

Listing 7-14: **DynaAttribs.jsp**

```
<%@ taglib prefix="j2eebible" uri="/j2eeBible" %>
<html>
  <head>
    <title>Hello Handler</title>
  </head>
  <body>
    <j2eebible:addAttr x="2.0" y="3.0" z="5.0"/>
    <br/>
    <j2eebible:addAttr/>
  </body>
</html>
```

In Listing 7-15, we use the `SimpleTagSupport` class, which eliminates the need to write unnecessary code.

Listing 7-15: **TrySimpleDynamic.java**

```
package com.j2eeBible.mytags;

import java.io.IOException;

import javax.servlet.jsp.JspException;
import javax.servlet.jsp.JspWriter;
import javax.servlet.jsp.tagext.DynamicAttributes;
```

Continued

Listing 7-15 *(continued)*

```java
import javax.servlet.jsp.tagext.SimpleTagSupport;

public class TrySimpleDynamic extends SimpleTagSupport implements
DynamicAttributes
{
    double dblTotal=0.00;
    boolean blValidAttr=true;

    public void doTag() throws JspException, IOException
    {
      JspWriter out = getJspContext().getOut();
      if(blValidAttr)
      {
        out.write("The attributes add to:"+String.valueOf(dblTotal));
      }
      else

      {
        out.write("Invalid attributes provided.");
      }

    }

    public void setDynamicAttribute( String uri, String localName,Object value )
throws JspException
    {
      try
      {
        double dblAtrVal=Double.parseDouble((String)value);
        dblTotal+=dblAtrVal;
      }
      catch(NumberFormatException e)
      {
        blValidAttr=false;
      }
    }
}
```

The tag shown in Listing 7-15 generates the following output:

```
The attributes add to:10.0
The attributes add to:0.0
```

The attribute names have no relevance in this particular example. However, the
setDynamicAttributes method does pass the attribute name and can be used for
further processing.

Summary

In this chapter we looked at the usage and relevance of custom tags. With JSP 2.0, custom tags are certainly a far easier and more viable option then they ever were before. Although Classic tag handlers do confer the advantage of backward compatibility up to JSP version 1.1, simple tag handlers should be used wherever possible.

With an ever-growing number of freely available tag libraries on the Web, try and avoid developing new tags for tasks for which a tried and tested tag library might already exist. The JSP Standard Tag Libraries (JSTL) is another recent development that you must explore before taking up any tag development. If you find that you have too many complex situations to be tackled in your JSP, it is likely that a change of design is what is really required rather than creating new tags to handle complexities.

✦   ✦   ✦

The Enterprise Information System Tier

P A R T

III

◆ ◆ ◆ ◆

In This Part

Chapter 8
Working with
JavaMail

Chapter 9
Understanding the
Java Messaging
Service

Chapter 10
Introducing Java
Transactions

Chapter 11
Examining JNDI and
Directory Services

Chapter 12
Understanding Java
Authentication and
Authorization
Services

Chapter 13
Exploring Java
Cryptography
Extensions

◆ ◆ ◆ ◆

Working with JavaMail

In This Chapter

Understanding
the protocols
for JavaMail

Providing an
overview of JavaMail

Using the
JavaMail API

Implementing an
integrated JavaMail
within J2EE

The JavaMail API is an abstract suite of classes for handling message-based systems. It was first introduced as a stand-alone package but now ships as part of the core J2EE API, although it can still be downloaded as a separate package to be used with other applications outside of the J2EE space.

In this chapter we'll go through the logistics of using the JavaMail API to handle e-mail without having to worry too much about the underlying protocols. We'll look at the protocols briefly and take a look at how MIME operates. In addition, we'll be looking at how the JavaMail API has abstracted all the logistics away, with real examples of sending and receiving e-mail with a variety of different protocols. Finally, we'll take a look at harnessing the power of JavaMail within a J2EE application and how JavaMail integrates with the application server.

Exploring the "Hello World" of JavaMail

Before we take a detailed tour of the JavaMail API let's take a quick look at one of the most common tasks associated with e-mail: sending a single mail message via the Simple Mail Transport Protocol (SMTP). You might employ this routine, for example, to provide a feedback form on a Web page, or to report the status of some aspect of your application. Take a look at the code in Listing 8-1.

Listing 8-1: **Generating a HelloWorld e-mail**

```
import javax.mail.*;
import javax.activation.*;
import javax.mail.internet.*;

public class sendSMTP extends Object{
  public static String main(String args[]){
    try{
  //--[ Set up the default parameters       Properties p = new
Properties();
      p.put("mail.transport.protocol", "smtp" );
      p.put("mail.smtp.host", "yourmail.yourserver.com" );
      p.put("mail.smtp.port", "25" );

   //--[ Create the session and create a new mail message
      Session mailSession = Session.getInstance( p );
      Message msg = new MimeMessage( mailSession );

   //--[ Set the FROM, TO, DATE and SUBJECT fields
      msg.setFrom( new InternetAddress( "me@noah.com" ) );
      msg.setRecipients( Message.RecipientType.TO,

InternetAddress.parse("info@cormac.com") );
      msg.setSentDate( new Date() );
      msg.setSubject( "Hello World!" );

      //--[ Create the body of the mail
      msg.setText( "Hello from my first e-mail sent with
 JavaMail" );

   //--[ Ask the Transport class to send our mail message
      Transport.send( msg );

   }catch(Exception E){
        System.out.println( "Oops something has gone pear
shaped!");
     System.out.println( E );
   }
  }
 }
```

SMTP is discussed later in this chapter in the section of the same name.

This small program, although not very practical because the values are hardcoded, illustrates just how little you actually need to know about the underlying protocols in order to successfully send an e-mail.

This program assumes that either the server via which you are attempting to deliver the message has had relaying authorized for your client IP address, or the e-mail address you are sending is valid for that server. So don't panic if your e-mail isn't coming through; it may well be because of the forwarding SMTP server. Check with the administrator of that machine if you are authorized.

We won't go into too much detail here about the actual steps associated with sending the e-mail, as we will be taking a much closer look at the JavaMail API in subsequent sections. But it is fair to note that in this instance the majority of the work is involved with creating the actual mail message — setting its various properties such as the FROM, TO, and SUBJECT fields.

The JavaMail API helps the developer at each step of the process. Classes are there to aid in the production and validation of the e-mail components. For example, later on in this chapter, we'll look at classes designed to help us handle the complexities of working with e-mail addresses.

Listing 8-1 uses the SMTP protocol to deliver our message. The next section will discuss the protocols used by JavaMail in greater detail.

Understanding the Protocols for JavaMail

The protocols that underpin the workings of electronic mail are well established and very mature. Although it is not completely necessary, it is never a bad idea to get a feeling for what the JavaMail API is attempting to abstract for you. This section will take a quick a look at the following core protocol implementations that are bundled as part of the JavaMail distribution:

✦ Simple Mail Transport Protocol (SMTP)

✦ Post Office Protocol version 3 (POP3)

✦ Internet Message Access Protocol (IMAP)

Although Multipurpose Internet Mail Extensions (MIME) is not strictly a transport protocol because it packages mail content, we'll take a look at it as well.

SMTP

The *Simple Mail Transport Protocol* was first proposed back in 1982 and was designed for the delivery of mail messages to servers. Its staying power can be attributed to its extreme simplicity in moving (or *relaying*) messages. Note that SMTP is merely a delivery agent and is not used to read e-mail.

SMTP can act as a relay server by delivering e-mail on behalf of another server. For this reason, it has been abused by spammers to send large volumes of unsolicited e-mails to users all over the world. Consequently, many system administrators have blocked, or restricted, their SMTP server's capability, and will only accept e-mail that is specifically addressed to that server's user base.

Note It can appear that your JavaMail application isn't sending e-mail properly and you may be looking at your code for reasons why. Chances are that the SMTP server you are attempting to send e-mail to is not the host for that e-mail and has had its relaying capabilities significantly restricted. JavaMail will attempt to report these problems to you via exceptions if the server you are talking to gives back an error message. Many such servers do not, however, merely absorbing the message.

You can read more about the specifics of SMTP by referring to the RFC 821 document at `http://www.rfc-editor.org/rfc/rfc821.txt`.

POP3

The *Post Office Protocol* is the mechanism by which the majority of people collect their e-mail. It is then the responsibility of the user to take care of the e-mail by filing it in some logical storage. Much as with a mailbox at a real post office, a user comes along and collects, or downloads, his or her e-mail, storing it locally and removing it from the server. The POP server does not offer any storage facilities beyond the mailbox that new mail is delivered to. This setup can be a little confusing to new users because modern-day e-mail clients give the illusion that the server stores the messages.

POP has been in its present state, version 3.0, since late 1988, with it roots going back to 1984. Again, this is a very established protocol, and its staying power again can be attributed to the simplicity of its instruction set. You can read more about the specifics of SMTP by referring to the RFC 1939 document at `http://www.rfc-editor.org/rfc/rfc1939.txt`.

IMAP

The *Internet Message Access Protocol* is a protocol that many enterprise e-mail servers employ. It offers a far richer set of functions than POP. With POP the premise is that the user is responsible for the storage of e-mail, whereas with IMAP the server assumes this responsibility. IMAP offers a folder structure for the user to interact with and all messages are stored on the server. The user has no need to download e-mail to his or her local machine.

This setup has the major advantage, for the user, of keeping all of his or her e-mails in one place, irrespective of the client that user is using to log in with.

JavaMail supports this protocol. However, you should be aware that many of the features of IMAP are dependent solely on the mail server. JavaMail merely passes the request on through to the backend server and collates any results. It is on occasions like this that JavaMail resembles JDBC, which merely passes the processing through to the backend database and doesn't actually do any major processing by itself.

Although a far superior protocol to POP, IMAP is not as widely used as the others, so make sure your server supports it before attempting any communication using this protocol. IMAP is a communication protocol used between the user and the server and is only responsible for the reading and retrieval of messages. It is not used for the delivery of e-mail between servers.

You can read more about the specifics of IMAP by referring to the RFC 2060 document at `http://www.rfc-editor.org/rfc/rfc2060.txt`. To learn more about the various implementations of IMAP and to find out which e-mail servers support it, refer to the site `http://www.imap.org/`.

MIME

The *Multipurpose Internet Mail Extension* defines the translation of and all the rules that are associated with the transmission of binary-based e-mail. Internet mail is fundamentally based on pure American Standard Code for Information Interchange (ASCII) text, and on the whole does not permit non-ASCII data to be used. At first this may seem a little restrictive, but considering the wide variety of machine types that are exchanging e-mail with one another, it was important to choose the lowest common denominator to ensure data arrived safely. However, the need to start attaching non-ASCII files to mail messages soon became apparent and a standard was required to deal with the encoding of binary files into ASCII in such a way that they could be transported and, when received, decoded back out to their native binary representations.

The JavaMail API takes care of all this for us and ensures that all the necessary protocols and translations are handled correctly. For more information on MIME visit `http://www.oac.uci.edu/indiv/ehood/MIME/MIME.html`.

JavaMail Components

The JavaMail API is a collection of about one hundred classes and interfaces. That makes it sound tremendously complicated, but don't be intimidated by numbers. Fortunately you don't need to understand every single detail to be able to use the API. This is the power of an object-orientated system: It abstracts the implementation away and presents a clear and concise interface with the functionality.

In this section we'll take a look at the major components that make up the API. We'll delve into some of the more active classes to give you a feeling of just how flexible this API really is. It contains four major components:

✦ **Session management** — The session aspect of the API defines the interaction the mail client has with the network. It handles all aspects associated with the overall communication, including the protocol to use for transfer and any default values that may be required.

✦ **Message manipulation** — Because the whole premise of the JavaMail is to send and receive mail messages, it shouldn't come as any great surprise that there are many ways of creating and manipulating mail messages.

✦ **Mail storage and retrieval** — If a message isn't being sent or received, it is in storage. Messages are stored in hierarchies that are not unlike those of files and directories. The JavaMail API has a suite of classes for managing this storage, including classes for adding, deleting, and moving messages.

✦ **Transportation** — Last but not least is the delivery of the message. The API provides easy mechanisms for this.

After mentioning the major mail components we'll discuss their usage in detail in the subsequent sections of this chapter.

Session management

A *session*, in the JavaMail context, is merely used for storing information about the logistics of establishing a connection session with the server. Therefore, it is not uncommon for sessions to be shared among users, if they are all using, say, the same SMTP server. For those of you familiar with servlet sessions, please note that these sessions share no functionality with them.

Note   The session does not handle any authorization *per se;* this is done later on, as you will see, but the session can hold login information. So be careful when you decide whether or not you wish the session to be shared with every other class running in the Java Virtual Machine (JVM) at the time.

javax.mail.Session

JavaMail has the `javax.mail.Session` class that defines the mail session used for communicating with remote mail systems. The `Session` class has no public constructors to which to create a new instance. Instead you obtain one by calling one of the static methods of the class, as shown here:

```
static Session getInstance(Properties P)
```

The first method returns an unshared, private `Session` instance with the `Properties` passed in.

If, however, you wish to have a session that can be shared among other users within the JVM, you can use the following call to obtain a new instance:

```
static Session getDefaultInstance(Properties P)
```

The difference between the two calls is the method `getDefaultInstance()` uses the `Properties` object only in the initial call. When you make subsequent calls to the method, it will always return the same instance. All parameters within the `Properties` class will be ignored. If you need a new instance each time, use the `getInstance(...)` call instead.

The `Session` object uses the `java.util.Properties` class to allow for the different session parameters to be passed in. You can either obtain an instance of this class by creating a new one and filling in the necessary parameters, or by using the one returned from the call to `System.getProperties()`. The JavaMail API defines a set of parameters that are used by the core protocols as shown in Table 8-1. Please note that this list is by no means exhaustive; it is feasible that other protocol implementations, for example the Network News Transport Protocol (NNTP), may wish for additional information.

Table 8-1 **Parameters used by core protocols**		
Property	*Description*	*Default Value*
`Mail.transport.protocol`	This is the default transport protocol that will be returned when `getTransport()` is called.	The first available one from the configured protocols
`mail.store.protocol`	This is the default store protocol that will be returned when `getStore()` is called.	The first available one from the configured protocols
`mail.host`	This is the default host that both the transport and store protocols will use, should their own hosts not be specified.	The local machine
`mail.user`	This is the default user that both the transport and store protocols will use, should their own users not be specified.	*user.name*
`mail.from`	This is the return address of the current user.	*user@host*

Continued

	Table 8-1 *(continued)*	
Property	**Description**	**Default Value**
`mail.protocol.host`	This overrides `mail.host` property, for the specified protocol.	`mail.host`
`mail.protocol.user`	This overrides the `mail.user` property for the specified protocol.	`mail.user`
`mail.debug`	This is the debug setting for the session.	`false`

Going back to our quick SMTP example that sends mail (see Listing 8-1), you can see that the process we use to obtain a `Session` variable isn't steeped in as much mystery now. In the following code we are creating a new instance of the `Properties` class and populating the key properties with information detailing that when we call all the default transport mechanisms we wish to use SMTP as our delivery agent.

```
Properties p = new Properties();
p.put("mail.transport.protocol", "smtp" );
p.put("mail.smtp.host", "yourmail.yourserver.com" );
p.put("mail.smtp.port", "25" );
Session mailSession = Session.getInstance( p );
```

Our session that we have obtained is *private* to us, which means that should we make some changes to the parameters and re-obtain a `Session` variable, the session will reflect the updates. The `Session` object now enables us to access folders and stores on a remote system through the use of simple method calls. You will see this in action later on in the chapter.

javax.mail.Authenticator

In the majority of cases in which you are reading mail (or even sending it), you will need to supply a user name and password in order to authenticate the connection. The JavaMail API provides for this very cleanly with the `Authenticator` class. When a session comes to the point where it requires authentication details, it makes a call to this class for the required information. The two following variations on the static methods we used to obtain a session in the previous section make this authentication possible:

```
static Session getInstance(Properties P)
static Session getDefaultInstance(Properties P, Authenticator A)
```

The only difference between the two is the additional reference to the `Authenticator` object in the second example.

Building an authentication module is relatively straightforward as long as you implement the necessary interfaces and adhere to the simple rules. When the session comes to the point where it needs the password, it will make a call to the method

```
javax.mail.PasswordAuthentication getPasswordAuthentication()
```

from the Authenticator **abstract** class. The PasswordAuthentication class is merely a wrapper that allows the user name and password to be conveniently passed back to the calling method.

Let's work through a simple example to demonstrate this overall process. We'll assume that, when asked, we simply look up the default user within a text file of passwords. Granted this is not the most secure way of handling this situation. However, it illustrates the point without bogging us down in the complexities of connecting to a database, for example, which would be a far more sensible choice in real life.

To begin with, we simply subclass the Authenticator class, providing an implementation for the getPasswordAuthentication() method, as shown in Listing 8-2.

Listing 8-2: **A very silly authenticator**

```
import javax.mail.*;
import java.io.*;
import java.utils.*;

public class dumbAuthenticator extends Authenticator{
  Properties passwordList;

  public class dumbAuthenticator(){
    super();
    try{
      //--[ Load in the password key file
      passwordList = new Properties();
      passwordList.load( new
FileInputStreamReader("/pass.list") );
    }catch(Exception E){
      System.out.println( E );
    }
  }

  public PasswordAuthentication getPasswordAuthentication(){
    if ( passwordList.containsKey( getDefaultUserName() ) )
      return new PasswordAuthentication( getDefaultUserName(),
            (String)passwordList.get( getDefaultUserName()
) );
    else
      return null;
  }
}
```

When this class is first created, it attempts to load a key/data text file of user names and passwords using the standard `java.utils.Properties` mechanism. After that the class sits dormant until a `Session` object calls upon it using the `getPasswordAuthentication()` method, which subsequently performs a lookup in the `Properties` object and if this object is found, creates a new instance of `PasswordAuthentication` and returns. Otherwise a null is returned. To integrate this class into the session's authentication procedure, we would modify our original code to include the `stupidAuthenticator` class. Here's the code:

```
Properties p = new Properties();
p.put("mail.transport.protocol", "smtp" );
p.put("mail.smtp.host", "yourmail.yourserver.com" );
p.put("mail.smtp.port", "25" );
dumbAuthenticator sA = new dumbAuthenticator();
Session mailSession = Session.getInstance( p, sA );
```

This code would then have the desired effect of handing off all responsibility for gathering passwords to the `dumbAuthenticator` object.

Message manipulation

One of the core features of JavaMail, as you might expect, is the ability to work with messages. As we have seen earlier in this chapter, the actual procedure involved in sending an e-mail isn't that complicated. However, where things can get confusing is with the generation of the actual message to be sent; adhering to all the MIME standards to ensure safe and coherent transmission can indeed be a tricky business.

javax.mail.Message

The JavaMail API offers a rich library of classes to make the construction and deconstruction of mail messages a relatively painless process, and it all starts with `javax.mail.Message`. This abstract class provides the basic container for the representation of a mail message.

A mail message is made up of two major components, a header and some content. The `Message` class implements the `javax.mail.Part interface`, which deals with the functionality associated with constructing the header and the content.

Now, the JavaMail API might seem complicated when it comes to dealing with message contents. This is because the MIME specification allows for *multiparts*—several message parts, each with its own encoding and attributes, to be sent in one message. Multiparts are what make MIME powerful to use and, at times, such a pain to work with. We'll take a look at this array of classes and interfaces and hopefully shine some light on what might first appears to be a bewildering web of interconnecting classes. Although we are going to be using the most common message format, MIME, the JavaMail API has been designed to use any type of message. For the purposes of this chapter we'll concentrate on the standard that you are most likely to use within an Internet environment.

javax.mail.internet.MimeMessage

The `Message` class is an abstract class and therefore to actually start to use a mail message you must use a subclassed implementation. The one implementation that is part of JavaMail is the `javax.mail.internet.MimeMessage` class. We can obtain a new object instance of this class in a number of ways. The first method, shown next, calls one of its public constructors:

```
public MimeMessage(Session S)
public MimeMessage(MimeMessage M)
```

The first method creates an empty `MimeMessage` based on the session properties passed in. This is the most common method of creating a new object instance. An alternative is to use the copy-constructor, which creates a new message instance with all the same properties and content as the one passed in. This can be a very inefficient way of creating a new `MimeMessage` and ought to be avoided where possible. You might think of using this method, however, when creating a message that is a reply to an existing e-mail. Fortunately, the creators of JavaMail were one step ahead of you on that front and conveniently offer the following method:

```
public Message reply(boolean replyToAll)
```

This method enables you to easily create a new message with all the necessary headers set. It also modifies the subject line by prefixing the `RE:` if it is not already there.

Since this class is used to work with Internet mail messages, we'll take a quick look at some of the methods for accessing the common header fields that exist as part of the message specification (as detailed in RFC 822).

Here is a header plucked straight from a message received from the popular `hotmail.com` service.

```
Message-ID: <001e01c0feab$0366b7e0$8c74f5d1@computer>
From: "Noah Williamson" <noahwilliamson@hotmail.com>
To: cormac@n-ary.com
Subject: Re: thanks
Date: Thurs, 6 Mar 2003 21:46:39 -0400
MIME-Version: 1.0
Content-Type: text/plain; charset=us-ascii
X-Priority: 3
X-MSMail-Priority: Normal
X-Mailer: Microsoft Outlook Express 5.00.2615.200
```

These fields are explained in the following paragraphs.

Note   A number of fields have been removed for clarity.

From

The mail message has to have originated from at least one person and this sender(s) is detailed in the `From` header in the mail message. This field must be a valid formatted Internet mail address(es); the `Message` class provides a set of methods for setting and retrieving it. To read the field, use the following method:

```
Address[] getFrom()
```

This will return an array of `javax.mail.Address` objects that represent the e-mail addresses. We'll be using this class throughout various examples in this chapter. For the moment, consider it a wrapper class for representing a valid Internet mail address. You can set the field with either of these simple access methods:

```
void setFrom()
void setFrom(javax.mail.Address fromAddress)
```

The first method may confuse you a little. How do you set the `From` field without actually passing it anything? Well, you might remember that in the session discussion we examined the various default properties that we can associate with a given mail session. The first of the preceding methods merely uses the default property from the session for the `From` field in the message. The second method enables you to specify an alternative address to be used for the `From` field. If you want to set multiple addresses for the `From` field you can use the following method:

```
void addFrom(Address[] moreAddresses)
```

This will add the array of addresses to the existing `From` field.

TO/CC/BCC

Three broad classifications exist for addressing mail messages:

✦ `To`: The `To` field is generally intended for the recipients to whom the message is directly addressed.

✦ `CC`: CC stands for *carbon copy,* and is for public acknowledgement of recipients receiving a copy of the message.

✦ `BCC`: BCC stands for *blind carbon copy,* and is a hidden list of recipients who receive a copy of the message. Only the sender can see this list.

The `Message` class makes it easy to set and retrieve the various headers. Here's an example:

```
void setRecipient(Message.RecipientType type, Address[]
addresses)
void setRecipient(Message.RecipientType type, Address address)
Address[] getRecipients(Message.RecipientType type)
Address[] getAllRecipients()
```

In addition to the set*XXX*(...) methods, there exist derivates of the addRecipients(...) method for easily appending new addresses to existing address fields. Message.RecipientType defines the following constants:

```
Message.RecipientType.TO
Message.RecipientType.CC
Message.RecipientType.BCC
MimeMessage.RecipientType.NEWSGROUPS
```

In addition to these, MimeMessage defines an additional type for use with protocols that are servicing newsgroups via the NNTP protocol. The use of these methods to set the various fields is shown here:

```
Session mailSession = Session.getInstance( p );
Message msg = new MimeMessage( mailSession );

msg.setRecipients( Message.RecipientType.TO,
                   InternetAddress.parse("info@noah.com") );
msg.setRecipients( Message.RecipientType.CC,
                   InternetAddress.parse("info@cormac.com") );
msg.setRecipients( Message.RecipientType.BCC,
                   InternetAddress.parse("noonecansee@me.com")
);
```

Reply-To

In some instances you may want a mail message to come from a specific person, but want any reply to go somewhere else. For example, say your company CEO announces a major product: He or she can send the e-mail, but he or she may want the company's sales team to follow up on any replies. The mail standard allows for this configuration through the special Reply-To header field. The API provides two methods for the manipulation of this header field. To set the field, use the following method:

```
void setReplyTo(Address[] addresses)
```

If you do not make a call to this method, it is assumed to be null and will not be included in the resulting message header. To retrieve the Reply-To header, simply make a call to the following method:

```
Address[] getReplyTo()
```

If the header isn't present, this method will return the same information you would get if you were to call getFrom().

Subject

As you would expect, methods exist for setting the Subject header of a mail message. Here's an example:

```
void setSubject(String subject)
String getSubject()
```

Date

The `Date` field of the mail message is accessed by means of the following methods with the standard Java `Date` object. Because of this you don't have to remember the exact format of the date for the mail exchange.

```
void setSentDate(Date date)
Date getSentDate()
```

Message ID

Each mail message travelling around the Internet is meant to have a unique identifier — so if all of them ever make it to one large storage area, we'll be able to index them! The JavaMail API generates `message id` for us when the message is saved. But we can read the `MessageID` field in the messages. Here's an example:

```
String getMessageID()
```

Custom headers

The message header was designed to be flexible enough to allow any number of headers to be added. You can use this feature to send extra data with mail messages. To read and write headers we use the following:

```
void setHeader(String name, String value)
String getHeader(String name, String delimiter)
```

In addition to these methods, a whole range of methods exists that allow greater access to the information within the message header. See `http://java.sun.com/products/javamail/1.3/docs/javadocs/com/sun/mail/pop3/POP3Message.html` for more information.

javax.mail.Part

The JavaMail API offers the `javax.mail.Part` interface and its derivatives for putting together and controlling a rather complex set of message parts.

Think of the construction of mail messages as happening in logical *blocks,* or parts, where each block is in fact a unit of data. For example, a file attachment would be considered a block, as would the main body text of the message. Now consider the fact that, in its initial form, a message can only contain one block of data; so how can one attach multiple data blocks to a single message? This is what the MIME standard aims to do with its variety of MIME types. But let's go back to the JavaMail world for the moment before we look at specific implementations.

A message can contain either a single block, or a special block that itself can hold a list of blocks. In turn, that block can contain either a single block, or a special block to indicate a list. And so forth, and so forth.

In JavaMail, a message can only hold a single item content or a `javax.mail.Multipart` as its content. The `Multipart` class is a placeholder for multiple `Part` objects. There is a special class called `javax.mail.BodyPart` that is used within a `Multipart` content list to denote the blocks of data that make up the overall block of content.

Therefore, a `Multipart` class can only hold `BodyPart` classes, and a `BodyPart`, much like the `Message` class, can hold either a single block of content or a single `Multipart` class. JavaMail provides one implementation of the structure depicted in Figure 8-1, and that is the MIME implementation. The implementation follows this model and the actual classes use the same names as their abstract counterparts (except that the names of the actual classes are prefixed with `Mime`). But before we go into the classes more deeply we'll take a look at just how the content is stored. To do this we need to have a quick look at the *JavaBeans Activation Framework* (JAF).

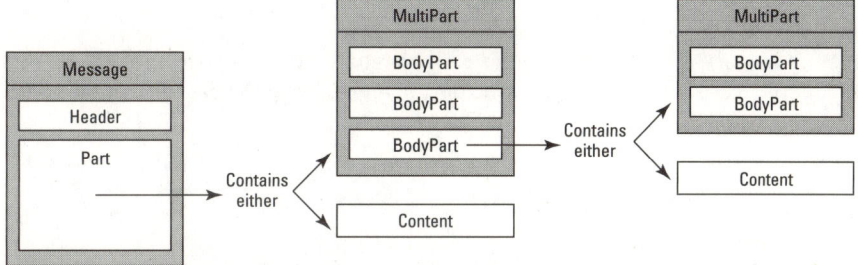

Figure 8-1: Message relationship

The JavaBean Activation Framework

If the world contained only the core data types of Java then it would be an easier environment to work in. But sadly this isn't the case. The number of data types is infinite and the good news is that the MIME standard permits this wide range of data types to be sent as content in any part as long as it's properly labeled with a label that adheres to the *xxxx/yyyy* convention. For example, we already know of at least one MIME data type, `text/plain`, which can basically be handled with a `java.lang.String` object.

However, this is probably the easiest form of content and is not representative of the bigger picture. To cope with the complexity of the data types the JavaMail API employs the services of the JavaBean Activation Framework (JAF) to give a clean and consistent interface to the wide range of data types that exist. You can learn more about the JAF by visiting `http://java.sun.com/beans/glasgow/jaf.html`

The JAF provides the `javax.activation.DataHandler` class for handling various data operations. When the `Part` class is handling content, all operations are performed through the `DataHandler` class, although the `Part` class does expose some shortcut methods, which we'll see later in this section.

Table 8-2 lists some of the more common methods of the `DataHandler` class.

Table 8-2
Common methods of the DataHandler class

Method	Description
`String getContentType()`	This method returns the MIME type of the object, including any parameters associated with it.
`Object.getContent()`	This method returns the data. If the `DataHandler` was created with an object, this method returns it. If it was created with a `DataSource` this method will attempt to find the content object and return that. Otherwise, an `InputStream` is returned.
`InputStream getInputStream()`	This method returns an input stream to the object that is holding or representing the data.
`OutputStream getOutputStream()`	This method returns an output stream to the object that is holding or representing the data so that the content may be overwritten.
`void writeTo (OutputStream OutputS)`	This is a convenient method that will write the data content to the output stream passed in.

The JavaMail API provides the following default `DataHandlers` for the MIME types:

✦ `text/plain`

✦ `text/html`

✦ `multipart/mixed`

✦ `message/rfc822`

Although you may not have realized it, in our simple and crude example of sending an e-mail the `MimePart` class was handling the `DataHandler` for us. Remember how we set the content for the text mail in Listing 8-1?

```
msg.setText( "Hello from my first e-mail with JavaMail" );
```

The `MimeMessage` class has provided some convenience methods that enable you to quickly set the data for simple content types. We could have achieved the same effect by calling all the components ourselves, as shown here:

```
String messageBody = "Hello from my first e-mail with
JavaMail";
DataHandler dh = new DataHandler( messageBody, "text/plain" );
msg.setDataHandler( dh );
```

But the above steps have been wrapped up for us in a single call to `MimeMessage`.
`setText(...)`. In this example we created a new instance of the `String` class and

set it with our message body's text. Next we created a new `DataHandler` instance, passing in a `String` object and labeling the `String` data with the type `text/plain`. Finally, we set the message content to this new `DataHandler` instance.

Getting at the information involves using the `DataHandler` class and the `Part` interface defines some shortcut methods for us. But for illustration purposes and to reinforce the notion that a specific `DataHandler` class handles the message content, we'll go the long way round. Here's the example:

```
DataHandler dh = msg.getDataHandler();
if ( dh.getContentType().equals( "text/plain" ) )
    String messageBody = (String)dh.getContent();
```

We first retrieve an instance of the `DataHandler` that is holding the data for us. We then check the content type of the data. This enables us to determine how to use the object that is returned to us from the call to `DataHandler.getContent()`. Remember, we created this instance of `DataHandler` by passing in a `String` reference to its constructor; therefore, as per the JAF API documentation, a call to `getContent()` will return the original object we used to create the content, which in this instance is the `String` reference. So we forward cast to a `String` object the `Object` reference returned from `getContent()`.

Later in this chapter in the section, "Receiving Attachments," you will see how to use the `getInputStream()` feature of the `DataHandler` class to handle data types that don't have a `DataHandler` implementation, such as the MIME type `image/jpeg` that is used to represent images.

javax.mail.Multipart

As we discussed in the previous section, a multipart is designed to manage multiple parts as a single unit. You're most likely to find a multipart when you attach a file to a mail. The message body would be one part and the file attachment would be the other. Therefore you would have to use a multipart MIME message to package this whole thing up for successful transmission. Take a quick look at Listing 8-3, which illustrates the construction of the two parts of the mail message.

Listing 8-3: **Constructing two parts of the mail message**

```
MimeMessage msg = new MimeMessage( session );
Multipart mailBody = new MimeMultipart();

//--[ Create the first part
MimeBodyPart mainBody = new MimeBodyPart();
mainBody.setText( "Here is that file we spoke of" );
mailBody.addBodyPart(mainBody);

//--[ Create the second part with the attachment
```

Continued

Listing 8-3 *(continued)*

```
FileDataSource fds = new FileDataSource( "c:\\photo.jpg" );
MimeBodyPart mimeAttach = new MimeBodyPart();
mimeAttach.setDataHandler( new DataHandler(fds) );
mimeAttach.setFileName( fds.getName() );

mailBody.addBodyPart(mimeAttach);

msg.setContent( msg );
```

Don't worry too much about the logistics of attaching a file; we'll take a much more detailed look at them in the later sections dealing with attachments. As you can see, we first created a new instance of `MimeMultipart`, the implementation for the `Multipart` abstract class. This will serve as a placeholder that will enable us to insert as many parts as we require, and in this example we only need two: one for the message text and the other for the file.

We then created an instance of `MimeBodyPart` that will hold the content for our message text and, because we know the message text is of type `text/plain`, we used the shortcut method `setText(...)` to set the text. After this we took this instance and attached it to the `MimeMultipart` by making a call to `addBodyPart(...)`, passing in our `MimeBodyPart` reference.

We repeated this for the file attachment, ending with a call to the `addBodyPart(...)` method. Finally, once we finished creating all the necessary parts that make up the multipart message, we set the content of our original `MimeMessage` to that of the `MimeMultipart`.

Internally the `Multipart` stores the various parts in a `java.utils.Vector`, and because of this the majority of the public methods of this class are merely wrappers, that enable you to manage the list of `BodyParts`. Table 8-3 lists the methods of the class `Multipart`.

Table 8-3
The methods of the Multipart class

Method Signature	Description
void addBodyPart (BodyPart bp)	This method adds the BodyPart to the end of the list of currently held BodyParts.
void addBodyPart (BodyPart bp, int index)	This method adds the BodyPart bp to the list at the specified index.
BodyPart getBodyPart (int index)	This method returns the BodyPart that is at the position passed in.

Method Signature	Description
`String getContentType()`	This method returns the MIME type for this `Multipart`.
`int getCount()`	This method returns the number of `BodyPart`s in the list.
`Part getParent()`	This method returns the parent that is presently holding this `Multipart, or null if not known.`
`boolean removeBodyPart (BodyPart bp)`	This method removes the `BodyPart` bp instance from the list. It returns `true` if successful, `false` if the instance is not found.
`boolean removeBodyPart (int index)`	This method removes the `BodyPart` instance from the list at the specified position. It returns `true` if successful, or `false` if the instance is not found.
`void setParent (Part parent)`	This method sets the parent for this `Multipart`.

As you can see the `Multipart` class isn't very complex; its main purpose is simply to manage the list of `BodyPart`s it has been asked to hold. Speaking of `BodyPart`s, let's take a closer look at the properties associated with holding data.

javax.mail.BodyPart

A `BodyPart` is the abstract class used to denote the part that makes up a `Multipart`. The `BodyPart` class is identical to the `Part` class except for the addition of one extra method to obtain the `Multipart`. The following method returns the containing `Multipart`, or null if not known: is inclusive of.

```
Multipart getParent()
```

Message content

The message has a variety of methods that enable you to determine how to handle message content and data makeup. As you have seen, a message can be made up of a number of different `Part`s, and because of this all the methods described in this section are found in the `Part` interface as opposed to the `Message` abstract class.

Recall that the MIME specification states that all content-type descriptions must be in the *xxxx/yyyy* format, where *xxxx* is the major type and *yyyy* is the subtype. Each `Part` can have its own MIME format and to determine the format we can use the following method:

```
String getContentType()
```

This might return, for example, the type `text/plain; charset=us-ascii` shown in the Internet mail message earlier in the section, "The JavaBean Activation Framework." You may think that this result is invalid, because it seems to include extra information after the *xxxx/yyyy* format, but the other data are parameter data. The MIME standard allows extra information to be transferred in this attribute that will aid in the decoding and encoding stage.

Because we make a lot of decisions based on just the *xxxx/yyyy* format, we have a helper class that assists us in determining whether a given MIME type is present. This is the method:

```
boolean isMimeType( String mimeType )
```

It makes it easy for us to determine a given type. We can pass in `text/plain` to see if that is the content type. We can even pass in `text/*` to see if the MIME type is of the `text/` type. This last is particularly useful for determining if the content is a `MultiPart/` or not.

In addition to this the MIME specification enables further description through optional attributes: `description`, `disposition`, and `filename`. This information must be packaged up according to certain rules, but because you are working through the JavaMail API you don't need to worry about them. The `description` field enables you to set some descriptive notes about this particular MIME part. Naturally, methods such as the following help you do this:

```
String getDescription()
void setDescription( String desc )
```

Another parameter that MIME permits is the `disposition` field. This is a very useful field, especially if you are using HTML-formatted e-mails. This field describes whether a particular part should be saved as an attachment or used internally to display the message. The JavaMail API defines these two constants:

```
static public ATTACHMENT
static public INLINE
```

We can use them either to set or to check the disposition of the part by calling the methods accordingly. Here's an example:

```
String getDisposition()
void setDisposition( String disp )
```

So, for example, if we want to see whether a particular `Part` containing an attachment should be used internally or saved to disk, we can use the following call:

```
String dispos = msg.getDisposition();
if ( dispos == null || dispos.equalsIgnoreCase( Part.ATTACHMENT
) )
  System.out.println( "This part is as an attachment" );
```

Lastly, the MIME specification states that if the part is a file attachment you can offer a possible name to use when the attachment is being saved. The filename passed will not contain any directory information and will be simply the name of the file, including any extension should the file have one. Methods for operating with this field are as you might expect. Here's an example:

```
String getFileName()
void setFileName( String fname )
```

In addition to these parameters, you can determine the message size and line count by calling the following methods:

```
int getSize()
int getLineCount()
```

The message size and line count is particularly useful information for clients, because it enables them to determine whether or not they should bother downloading the message if they are using a slow connection such as a wireless device. However, please note that it is not always possible to retrieve the dimensions of a mail message. If the values cannot be determined -1 is returned. If that's not enough to put you off using these methods, consider that because of message-encoding algorithms the values they return may not actually reflect the size and line count of a particular message part. So beware.

Message flags

Recall that a message has a wide range of attributes associated with it to describe its contents and addressing properties. However, none of these present attributes go anywhere to give a message a state. For example, we have no real way of telling whether a message is new, or whether it's a reply to an existing mail, or even if it has been read or answered. The JavaMail API aids the developer by providing a mechanism for easily storing this type of information within each message.

In addition to the standard flags, JavaMail API enables you to add and manipulate user-defined status flags. You can manage the flags using the wrapper class `javax.mail.Flags`. This class manages all the status flags, including the system- and user-defined statuses.

The core system flags have a broad range of characteristics and are listed in Table 8-4.

Note   Don't rely on status flags. Their implementation depends on the individual provider and in some cases it may not even be possible to determine a message's status. For example, the status of SEEN may not be available in a newsgroup (NNTP) implementation.

	Table 8-4 Core system flags	
Flag	**Description**
Flags.Flag.ANSWERED	If the message has been answered by another e-mail, this flag is set.
Flags.Flag.DELETED	If the message has been flagged for deletion, this flag is set. When a call is made to expunge the folder, all the messages with this flag set will be deleted.
Flags.Flag.DRAFT	If the message has not been sent this flag is set.
Flags.Flag.FLAGGED	If this flag has been set the client has flagged the message for some reason.
Flags.Flag.RECENT	If this flag has been set the message was received since the last time the client opened the folder.
Flags.Flag.SEEN	If the message has been read the flag is set. The client may change the state of this flag.
Flags.Flag.USER	This flag indicates whether or not the folder can support user-defined flags. (Note this isn't the actual user-defined flag, merely an indication of the existence of such flags.)

The support of these flags is up to the provider. For example, the POP protocol supports only the Flags.Flag.DELETED flag. Fortunately this arrangement is not as bad as it sounds, as you can determine which flags are supported by making a call to the following method:

```
public Flags getPermanentFlags()
```

Make this call from the javax.mail.Folder class (we will be taking a close look at the Folder class later on in the chapter in the section, "Accessing Folders"). Flags are used to track the statuses of messages and enable you to perform operations only on messages that satisfy a particular status. For example, as you will discover later on, you can easily list all the messages in a folder that have the SEEN flag set.

The javax.mail.Message class has a suite of methods that enable you to check and set the status of the flags. For example, to check whether a message has been read or not you can use the following:

```
if ( msg.isSet( Flags.Flag.SEEN ) )
    System.out.println( "This message has been read" );
```

Message flags are a wonderful addition to your ability to track messages, but be careful when you use them as they can't be relied on across implementations. Table 8-5 lists the methods of the Message class that work with message flags.

Table 8-5
Methods that work with message flags

Method signature	Description
`boolean isExpunged()`	This method checks whether or not the message has been expunged after being marked for deletion.
`boolean isSet (Flags.Flag flag)`	This method checks the status of the specified flag.
`Flags getFlags()`	This method returns a copy of the `Flags` object. Note that if you modify any of the flags within this object the modification will have no effect on the flags in the `Message` class.
`void setFlags (Flags flag, boolean set)`	This method sets or clears all the flags in the message that are in this `Flag` object. Any flags that are in the message but not in this object are unaffected.
`void setFlags(Flags.Flag flag, boolean set)`	This method sets the given flag to a given state.

javax.mail.Address

Anyone who has written classes that have had to deal with Internet e-mail addresses will know the hassles associated with all the different formats an address can take. It can be a parsing nightmare at times. Each message has at least one address associated with it, and because of this the `javax.mail.Address` is the class used to denote the address of a message.

However, JavaMail addresses can differ greatly between systems. For example, the address for a message destined for a newsgroup is not the same as that of one destined for an Internet e-mail account. Because of this the base class, `javax.mail.Address` has very little functionality with only a minimal amount of methods exposed.

Instead the subclasses provide all the real functionality. The JavaMail API ships with these two implementations:

✦ `javax.mail.internet.InternetAddress`
✦ `javax.mail.internet.NewsAddress`

javax.mail.internet.InternetAddress

An e-mail address must contain at least an address; optionally a name may be associated with it. For example, the following two e-mail addresses are valid:

```
"Ceri Moran" <ceri@n-ary.com>
<ceri@n-ary.com>
```

When you have more than one e-mail address to express, for example in the To field of a message header, you concatenate the addresses using the comma as a separator. So you do not have to continually parse and concatenate e-mail addresses, the JavaMail API provides a helper class:

```
javax.mail.internet.InternetAddress
```

This class takes all of the hard work out of this task. Methods such as the following make the creation and handling of e-mail addresses a trivial task:

```
InternetAddress MyAddress = new InternetAddress();
MyAddress.setAddress( "ceri@n-ary.com" );
MyAddress.setPersonal( "Ceri Moran" );
System.out.println( "MyAddress=" + MyAddress.toString() );
```

As you probably noticed in the previous sections, it's very rare to work with a single individual address; lists or arrays of addresses are far more common. Because of this the InternetAddress has the following static methods to make the parsing of these lists a very easy task:

```
InternetAddress to[] = InternetAddress.parse(
                        "alan@n-ary.com,ceri@n-ary.com"
                        );
for ( int x=0; x < to.length; x++ ){
  System.out.println("to["+x+"].Address="+to[x].getAddress());

System.out.println("to["+x+"].Personal="+to[x].getPersonal());
  }
```

The following derivative of InternetAddress.parse(...) takes in a Boolean value to force the tolerance of the parsing algorithm:

```
public InternetAddress[] InternetAddress.parse(String a,
boolean strict)
```

If the argument named strict is set to false, the list of addresses can be separated by either spaces or commas. If strict is set to true, the majority of the rules laid out in RFC 822 are adhered to. You would use this method if you were allowing a user to enter a list of names when creating e-mail messages.

javax.mail.internet.NewsAddress

Newsgroup addressing differs from e-mail addressing. A newsgroup message has at least a newsgroup name, and optionally a host name. The JavaMail API provides an implementation for the newsgroup addresses with the javax.mail.internet. NewsAddress class. This class operates like the InternetAddress class we discussed in the previous section, providing the following methods for easy handling of both individual addresses and lists of addresses:

```
NewsAddress MyNews = new NewsAddress(
"comp.lang.java.programmer" );
MyNews.setHost( "news.sun.com" );
System.out.println( "MyNews.newsgroup=" + MyNews.getNewsgroup()
);
System.out.println( "MyNews.host=" + MyNews.getHost() );
```

Mail storage and retrieval

So far you have seen how the JavaMail API deals with the individual message and the properties and actions associated with it. Next we'll look at the management of messages and how JavaMail provides for the handling of groups of messages.

javax.mail.Store

Messages are organized into folders and these folders are held within a single *store*. A store must by default have at least one folder in which messages can reside. This requirement allows the JavaMail API to provide a uniform access method across all the different protocols. For example, the POP protocol has no notion of folders and simply stores its messages as one list. But for the sake of abstraction any implementations of the POP protocol must provide the INBOX folder.

Before you can access folders you must first obtain a `javax.mail.Store` object instance, typically from the `javax.mail.Session` object we discussed earlier in the section, "Session Management." The `Store` class provides the access methods to the hierarchy of folders and authenticates the connection if the underlying protocol requires it. A `Store` object instance can be retrieved from the `Session` instance via any of the following methods:

```
public Store getStore()
public Store getStore( Provider provider )
public Store getStore( String protocol )
public Store getStore( URLName urlname )
```

The first version of getStore() uses the default protocol, specified in the system property `mail.store.protocol`, to create the `Store` object. The second version uses the supplied `Provider` instance to create and return an instance. The third version enables you to use a protocol other than the default one, while the fourth version uses a special object, URLName, to create the `Store` object.

Once you have obtained the `Store` object you need to connect to the mail storage before you start to retrieve and work with folders. You do this with a single call to the connect(...) method, passing in the necessary authentication details if the underlying storage requires it.

The following code snippet illustrates a typical scenario involving retrieval of the `Store` object for connection to a POP server.

```
//--[ Set up the default parameters
Properties p = new Properties();
p.put("mail.transport.protocol", "pop" );

//--[ Create the session and create a new mail message
Session mailSession = Session.getInstance( p );

//--[ Get the Store and connect to the server
Store mailStore = mailSession.getStore();
mailStore.connect( "pop.server.com",110,"myname","mypassword"
);

//--[ Proceed to manipulate folders
```

The connect(...) method can come in any one of a number of flavors, depending on the authentication required. Should the connection to the underlying
message store fail, the connect(...) method throws the javax.mail.
AuthenticationFailedException.

At this point the Store instance is ready for use, giving access to the folder
database.

javax.mail.URLName

JavaMail has introduced a very clean and uniform addressing scheme, based on
the URL syntax, to be used to access mail-storage systems. The following format,
as you can see, is not unlike a standard URL and encapsulates all the information
required to access a given resource inside a mail service.

```
<protocol>::://<username>:<password>@<server>[:<port>][/<foldern
ame>]
```

The class, javax.mail.URLName, provides the necessary methods to build and
extract information. The JavaMail API encourages the use of this class as an addressing scheme and you will see that many of the methods use the address as opposed
to carrying around up to five individual pieces of information.

The next example shows how to connect to a remote server using the URLName
object:

```
//--[ Set up the default parameters
Properties p = new Properties();
p.put("mail.transport.protocol", "pop" );

//--[ Create the session and create a new mail message
Session mailSession = Session.getInstance( p );

//--[ Get the Store and connect to the server
URLName urlname = new URLName(
"pop3://alan:ceri@www.hotmail.com" );
```

```
Store mailStore = mailSession.getStore(urlname);
mailStore.connect();

//--[ Proceed to manipulate folders
```

We will see extensive use of the URLName class in subsequent sections as we take a closer look at how to interact with individual messages inside given folders. The Store class exposes a method to obtain the URLName for a session. This method is getURLName(). As you can imagine, using this method could present a security problem because the password would be in clear view. To solve this problem, the password information is not available when obtaining the URLName object.

Note   The URLName class has absolutely no relationship to the java.net.URL class and the fact they share the URL in their names is only a coincidence. That said, as you can see, the functionality of the URLName class is very similar to that of the URL class. But do not confuse the two.

Accessing folders

It is through the Store object that we retrieve references to the folders contained within. (A folder is represented with the javax.mail.Folder class and will be discussed in the next section.) By default, the Store object must provide at least one folder. This is because some mail services don't support the notion of folders at all and this maintains a layer of abstraction for the JavaMail API. This ensures that no special cases exist, irrespective of the mail protocol. Table 8-6 lists the methods of the class Store that deal with folders.

<table>
<tr><td colspan="2" align="center">Table 8-6
Methods that deal with folders</td></tr>
<tr><td>*Method Signature*</td><td>*Description*</td></tr>
<tr><td>Folder getDefaultFolder()</td><td>This method retrieves the top-level or root folder for the store. In the instance of the POP protocol, this is the INBOX folder.</td></tr>
<tr><td>Folder getFolder
(String name)</td><td>This method returns the folder within the store, whether or not it exists. You can then in turn call the Folder.exists() method to determine that folder's state. This is useful when you wish to create new folders.</td></tr>
<tr><td>Folder getFolder
(URLName name)</td><td>This method is similar in usage to the method getFolder() listed above, except that the folder is addressed by means of the URLName object.</td></tr>
</table>

Continued

Table 8-6 *(continued)*	
Method Signature	**Description**
`Folder[] getPersonal Namespaces()`	This method returns an array of folders that are considered to be accessible by the current user.
`Folder[] getUser Namespaces(String user)`	This method returns an array of folders that are considered to be accessible by the current user and the given user passed in. This method is useful if, for example, a manager has granted access to certain folders to his secretary or another team member.
`Folder[] getShared Namespaces()`	This method returns an array of folders that are considered to be accessible by all.

Therefore, accessing the one and only folder within a POP box for a given user would take place as follows:

```
//--[ Get the Store and connect to the server
URLName urlname = new URLName(
"pop3://alan:ceri@www.hotmail.com" );
Store mailStore = mailSession.getStore(urlname);
mailStore.connect();

//--[ Proceed to manipulate folders
Folder inbox = mailStore.getDefaultFolder();

//--[ or Folder inbox = mailStore.getFolder("INBOX");
```

Note the special use of the keyword INBOX. This keyword is reserved and is a special name to denote the folder in which the user will receive his or her messages. Note that not all protocols offer the INBOX folder. For example NNTP, the newsgroup protocol, has no concept of inboxes.

When using the methods for accessing the folders, you generally have to know the name of the folder beforehand, although this isn't always the case. In addition to this, a folder can contain both messages and folders. The Folder object helps us figure out the folder names by giving us some access methods that enable us to easily list all the folders contained within. We can get the folders using the following method:

```
Folder[] javax.mail.Folder.list()
```

This method can be run on a closed folder and will return an array of all the folders contained under the present folder. This method will only list this folder's top-level folders and not drill down any deeper. However, not all folders are permitted to contain further folders. Therefore, before we do any listing it is advisable that we check that such a list can be produced, as follows:

```
Folder listOfFolders[] = null;
if ( (thisFolder.getType() & Folder.HOLDS_FOLDERS ) )
  listOfFolders = thisFolder.list();
```

The getType() method from the Folder class returns the status field for this folder, which is an integer bit-field with each bit representing a given state. The static Folder.HOLDS_FOLDERS field is but one of those statuses we can perform a check on by logically ANDing.

The Folder object doesn't stop there. We can use a specialized version of the list(...) method that enables us to pass in a search string to either narrow or broaden the set of results returned. For example, consider the following:

```
Folder listOfFolders[] = thisFolder.list("Clients%");
```

This would return all the folders within the current folder, thisFolder, that begin with the string Clients. The % is a special wildcard that enables you to scope the current folder. Now consider the following example:

```
Folder listOfFolders[] = thisFolder.list("C*");
```

This would return all the folders, including any subfolders, that start with the letter C. The asterisk (*) wildcard searches all the subfolders and, when used on its own, can list all the folders in a complete hierarchy, as shown in Listing 8-4.

Listing 8-4: **Listing folders in a hierarchy**

```
//--[ Set up the default parameters
Properties p = new Properties();

//--[ Create the session and create a new mail message
Session mailSession = Session.getInstance( p );

//--[ Get the Store and connect to the server
URLName urlname = new URLName(
"imap://alan:ceri@mail.hotmail.com" );
Store mailStore = mailSession.getStore(urlname);
mailStore.connect();

//--[ Proceed to list all the folders
Folder thisFolder = mailStore.getDefaultFolder();

if ( thisFolder != null ){
```

Continued

Listing 8-4 *(continued)*

```
if ( (thisFolder.getType() & Folder.HOLDS_FOLDERS )){
    Folder[] listOfFolders = thisFolder.list("*");
    for ( int x=0; x < listOfFolders.length; x++ )
      System.out.println( "Name=" + listOfFolders[x].getName()
);
    }
}
```

In addition to the `list(...)` methods, the following methods limit the search to just the folders that the user has subscribed to:

```
Folder[] listSubscribed()
Folder[] listSubscribed(String search)
```

Remember that many of these `listXXX(...)` methods are rendered useless in some protocol implementations — such as POP — because the underlying storage doesn't support it.

javax.mail.Folder

A folder is used as a container for a list of messages. Folders themselves can contain additional folders, thus providing a directory-like structure to the message archive. The purpose of the `Folder` object is to facilitate the communication and management of messages. Folders are by default initially retrieved in a closed state, and before any operations are executed that change the contents of the folder, the folder must first be opened.

Not all operations require the folder to be opened; for example, you can list folders, rename a folder, and monitor for new messages while the folder is closed. Once the folder is opened, you can retrieve messages, change notifications, and perform any other function that the folder object offers.

Messages within a folder are numerically addressed from 1 to a number equal to the total number of messages in the folder. This is analogous to the way the POP protocol treats its messages, with the numbering being according to the order in which they are received, with the lowest number being the oldest message. However, this ordering cannot always be relied on, and it's best to order the messages beforehand should your application call for it.

The message number is usually fixed between the time when a folder is opened and the time when it is closed. When you delete a message the numbering of the remaining messages is not recalculated until the call to `expunge()` occurs. This will permanently delete the messages marked for deletion and then cause a renumbering of the messages in the folder. Therefore, tracking messages through this numbering scheme can be problematic. If possible, refer to the message using the `Message` reference.

Opening and closing folders

Before you can list any messages you must first put the folder into an open state. You do this by making the following call:

```
void open( int mode )
```

The `open(...)` method will place the folder into either a `READ_ONLY` or a `READ_WRITE` state, depending on the mode passed in. The underlying implementation is responsible for determining whether or not a particular mode is valid. For example, some implementations, such as IMAP, will permit multiple users to read a given folder and in some cases even permit multiple users to write to the folder. But some POP implementations might not allow concurrent readers. You can see the state the folder was opened in by calling the `getType()` method as shown here:

```
if ( thisFolder.getType() == Folder.READ_ONLY )
  System.out.println( "This folder opened with READ_ONLY
access" );
else
  System.out.println( "This folder opened with READ_WRITE
access" );
```

Once a folder is opened you can begin using the majority of the access methods. After you've finished with a folder it's best to perform an explicit `close(...)` method to allow the underlying protocol to clean up any resources as opposed to leaving it for the garbage collector to clean up later.

The `close(...)` method takes in an additional Boolean parameter, which indicates whether or not an expunge operation should be performed. If this parameter is `true`, a call to `expunge()` occurs, permanently deleting any messages marked with the `Flag.DELETED` flag.

Sometimes you may be passed in a `Folder` object without knowing what state it is in. You can easily determine whether it's open or not by making the following call:

```
boolean isOpen()
```

Listing messages

The `Folder` object is designed to hold messages and to that end, a rich method list is available for retrieving messages held within the folder. Messages are returned as lists by means of arrays. The objects returned are meant to be lightweight in the sense that not all the information regarding a message is available immediately.

For example, if you were to retrieve the contents of a folder that held 10 messages, each having a 10MB file attachment, that wouldn't equate to 100MB of memory usage. Instead the message attributes and contents are retrieved when calls to the specific access methods are made. Keep in mind that this is purely up to the implementation of the underlying protocol, but in the majority of instances it is adhered to because otherwise problems with bandwidth and general memory management would result.

Table 8-7 lists the methods of the class Folder that deal with the folder's content.

Table 8-7
Methods that deal with the content of a folder

Message Signature	Description
`int getMessageCount()`	This method returns the total number of messages held in this folder, or `-1` if the total cannot be determined for some reason.
`boolean hasNewMessages()`	This method returns `true` if any of the messages held within the folder has the `Flag.RECENT` flag set. It is purely up to the underlying implementation what the definition of a new message is.
`int getNewMessageCount()`	This is much like the previous method, except that it returns the number of messages that have the `Flag.RECENT` flag set, or `-1` if this number cannot be determined for some reason.
`int getUnreadMessageCount()`	This method returns `true` if any of the messages held within the folder does not have the `Flag.SEEN` flag set.
`Message getMessage(int index)`	This method returns a lightweight version of the message at the given index.
`Message[] getMessages()`	This method returns an array of all the messages contained within this folder.
`Message[] getMessages (int start, int end)`	This method returns an array of all the messages contained within this folder that are in the range specified by `start` and `end`.
`Message[] getMessages (int index[])`	This method retrieves all the messages referenced by the array of indexes passed in.

Listing 8-5 demonstrates the listing of all the messages within a POP folder and displaying the subject field for each message.

Listing 8-5: **Listing messages in a POP folder and displaying the subject fields**

```
//--[ Set up the default parameters
Properties p = new Properties();
p.put("mail.transport.protocol", "pop" );

//--[ Create the session and create a new mail message
Session mailSession = Session.getInstance( p );

//--[ Get the Store and connect to the server
URLName urlname = new URLName(
"pop3://alan:ceri@www.hotmail.com" );
Store mailStore = mailSession.getStore(urlname);
mailStore.connect();

//--[ Proceed to get the folder
Folder rootFolder = mailStore.getDefaultFolder();
Folder inbox = rootFolder.getFolder("INBOX");
inbox.open( Folder.READ_ONLY );

Messages[] allTheMessages = inbox.getMessages();
for ( int x=0; x < allTheMessages.length; x++ ){
  System.out.println( "ID:" + x
                    + " Subject:" +
allTheMessages[x].getSubject() );
}

inbox.close( false );
mailStore.close();
```

Although JavaMail provides the necessary methods with which to determine various totals regarding a folder's status, it is not always the most efficient manner. For example, assume we wanted a count of all the messages that have recently been delivered, as per the getNewMessageCount() method. Depending on whether or not the underlying protocol can provide this functionality, this could result in a call to retrieve all the messages and then a check of the individual message-flag statuses.

What was first an innocent enough call for some numerical statistics has turned out to be quite an expensive operation. Because of this it is sometimes best just to retrieve the messages yourself and run through them once, calculating all the necessary totals in one pass.

Advancing message fetching

Recall that when we ask for a message list, this is a list of lightweight references to the actual message data, with the data being retrieved as and when they are called upon through their access methods. Although this is on the whole a very efficient system, in some instances you may wish to explicitly request that certain amounts of the message be pre-filled with data when they are retrieved from the server.

The JavaMail API supports this functionality through the use of `javax.mail.FetchProfile`, which lists the data required. The `Folder` class provides the following method:

```
void fetch( Message[] messageList, FetchProfile fProfile )
```

For a given list of messages, this method fetches the data for each one, as shown here:

```
FetchProfile fProfile = new FetchProfile();
fProfile.add("To");
fProfile.add("From");
fProfile.add("Subject");
thisFolder.fetch( thisFolder.getMessages(), fProfile );
```

This example creates a new instance of the `FetchProfile` class and adds the mail-header fields it would like to be fetched from the server for all the messages in the call from `getMessages()`. In our example we looked for the header fields `To`, `From`, and `Subject`. However, the `FetchProfile` class knows that the majority of people want groups of data to be retrieved, and to this end it enables you to express a group rather than specifying the individual fields.

The three groups of fields defined for use with the `FetchProfile` class are listed in Table 8-8.

Table 8-8 The fields of the inner class FetchProfile.Item	
Field	**Description**
`FetchProfile.Item.ENVELOPE`	This field includes the common header fields: `From`, `To`, `Cc`, `Bcc`, `ReplyTo`, `Subject`, and `Date`.
`FetchProfile.Item.CONTENT_INFO`	This field includes the information regarding the content, but not the content itself. Therefore, information such as content type, disposition, description, size, and line count are fetched.
`FetchProfile.Item.FLAGS`	This field consists of all the status flags for the message.

Modifying our current example, we could instead write the following:

```
FetchProfile fProfile = new FetchProfile();
fProfile.add( FetchProfile.Item.ENVELOPE );
thisFolder.fetch( thisFolder.getMessages(), fProfile );
```

Copying and moving messages

Chances are that if a store can support the notion of multiple folders it will permit the feature of copying and moving messages among different folders. To copy a list of messages you simply call the following method:

```
void copyMessages(Messages[] messageList, Folder toFolder )
```

This method runs through the list of messages and copies the given messages, which must be part of the present folder, to the folder given. The messages must be part of the present folder to allow the server side to optimize the transfer.

Moving messages is a simple matter of copying first and then performing a delete on each message. But remember to copy the messages first before deleting, even though the deletion isn't performed until the folder is expunged.

Searching messages

It is important to push as much processing to the server side as possible and to this end one of the most common operations of client-side applications is to search their message stores. The JavaMail API provides a very flexible search interface to build searches that can be very complex in nature. Hopefully, the underlying implementation will pass this search to the server to perform. The Folder object provides the two following methods for searching out messages:

```
Message[] search(SearchTerm term)
Message[] search(SearchTerm term, Message[] messageList )
```

These methods return a list of Messages that match the criteria, or an empty array if none matches. Consider the next example, which lists all the messages that came from noah@n-ary.com or cormac@n-ary.com:

```
SearchTerm st = new OrTerm( new FromStringTerm("noah@n-ary.com"
),
                            new FromStringTerm("cormac@n-
ary.com") );
Message messageList[] = thisFolder.search( st );
```

The javax.mail.search package provides a rich suite of classes that enable you to build up very complex search expressions. By building on the SearchTerm class, the JavaMail API offers the following logical operators:

✦ AndTerm(SearchTerm LHS, SearchTerm RHS)

✦ AndTerm(SearchTerm items[])

✦ `OrTerm( SearchTerm LHS, SearchTerm RHS)`

✦ `OrTerm( SearchTerm items[] )`

✦ `NotTerm( SearchTerm LHS )`

In addition to these, the `ComparisonTerm` object offers the following constants for building up numerical comparisons:

✦ `ComparisonTerm.EQ (Equal to)`

✦ `ComparisonTerm.GE (Greater than or Equal to)`

✦ `ComparisonTerm.GT (Greater than)`

✦ `ComparisonTerm.LE (Less than or Equal to)`

✦ `ComparisonTerm.LT (Less than)`

✦ `ComparisonTerm.NE (Not Equal to)`

The message fields that can be searched include the following:

✦ `BodyTerm( String pattern )`

✦ `FlagTerm( Flags flags, boolean set )`

✦ `FromStringTerm( String pattern )`

✦ `FromTerm( Address add )`

✦ `MessageIDTerm( String messageID )`

✦ `MessageNumberTerm( int messageNumber )`

✦ `ReceivedDateTerm( int comparison, Date date )`

✦ `RecipientStringTerm( Message.RecipientType type, String pattern )`

✦ `RecipientTerm( Message.RecipientType type, Address add )`

✦ `SentDateTerm( int comparison, Date date )`

✦ `SizeTerm( int comparison, int size )`

✦ `SubjectTerm( String pattern )`

Transportation with javax.mail.Transport

The final class in our exploratory look at the JavaMail API is the class responsible for the delivery of messages, `javax.mail.Transport`. In the majority of instances, you will be using the SMTP protocol for delivery. As a convenience, the `Transport` class offers the following static method for sending messages that we saw earlier in the chapter:

```
Transport.send( msg );
```

However, if you wish to have a little more control over the delivery of the message, consider the example shown in Listing 8-6, which implicitly gets the specific Transport object instance, manually connects, and then performs a send on the message.

Listing 8-6: **Controlling message delivery**

```
try{

    Transport myTransport = session.getTransport("smtp");
    myTransport.connect();
    myTransport.sendMessage( msg, msg.getAllRecipients() );
    myTransport.close();

} catch ( SendFailedException E ){

    Address[] list = E.getInvalidAddresses();
    for ( int x=0; x < list.length; x++ )
      System.out.println( "Invalid Address: " + list[x] );

    list = E.getUnsentAddresses();
    for ( int x=0; x < list.length; x++ )
      System.out.println( "Unsent Address: " + list[x] );

    list = E.getValidSentAddresses();
    for ( int x=0; x < list.length; x++ )
      System.out.println( "Sent Address: " + list[x] );
}
```

The advantage of this mechanism, as oppose to the static call, is that if you are sending large amounts of messages the underlying protocol doesn't require you to keep connecting to the server for each message. Instead the same connection is used. But did you notice the try ... catch block?

Should something go wrong, the send(...) methods throw a SendFailedException with a whole host of diagnostic information that gives you a clue as to which addresses got a successful delivery notification. Three lists of addresses are available to you in the event of an error:

✦ Address[] getInvalidAddresses() — This call returns the addresses that didn't get the message for some reason such as incorrect address formatting.

✦ Address[] getUnsentAddresses() — This call returns the addresses that weren't accepted for delivery.

✦ Address[] getValidSentAddresses() — This call returns the addresses that were accepted for delivery.

It is important to note that although a message is accepted for delivery, this does not guarantee it will make it to its final destination. The only thing that can be assured is the transmission from your application to the server the transport layer is communicating with. This does not equal successful delivery to the end user.

Now that we have gone through all the core classes and their relationships with respect to the manipulation of messages and folders, let us put them to use in some examples.

Using the JavaMail API

The purpose of this section is not to provide you with a complete, all-singing all-dancing mail client (that's your job!) but rather to give you real examples that show clearly what is going on without cluttering up the rest of the program with distractions.

Sending e-mail and attachments

Probably the first thing you want to do is send some e-mail. We have already demonstrated how to send a basic plain-text e-mail using the SMTP protocol, but have a look at an application that is a little more functional.

The class shown, `javamail_send`, takes the four following parameters:

✦ SMTP host

✦ to e-mail

✦ from e-mail

✦ e-mail body

As you can see in Listing 8-7, we parse out the command-line parameters and proceed to set up the session to the server.

Listing 8-7: Setting up the session to the server

```
import java.util.*;
import java.io.*;
import javax.mail.*;
import javax.mail.internet.*;
import javax.activation.*;

public class javamail_send extends Object {

    public static void main(String args[]){

        String smtpServer = null;
        String toE-mail    = null;
```

```java
        String fromE-mail  = null;
        String body        = null;

        //--[ Parse the Command line parameters
        for ( int x=0; x < args.length-1; x++ ){
          if ( args[x].equalsIgnoreCase("-S") )
            smtpServer  = args[x+1];
          else if ( args[x].equalsIgnoreCase("-T") )
            toE-mail = args[x+1];
          else if ( args[x].equalsIgnoreCase("-F") )
            fromE-mail = args[x+1];
          else if ( args[x].equalsIgnoreCase("-B") )
            body = args[x+1];
        }

        if ( smtpServer == null || toE-mail == null ||
             fromE-mail == null || body == null ){
          System.out.println( "Usage: javamail_send -S <server>
                                -T <toe-mail> -F <from> -B
<body>" );
          System.exit(1);
        }

        try{
       //--[ Set up the default parameters
          Properties props = new Properties();
          props.put( "mail.transport.protocol", "smtp" );
          props.put( "mail.smtp.host", smtpServer );
          props.put( "mail.smtp.port", "25" );

      //--[ Create the session and create a new mail message
          Session mailSession = Session.getInstance( props );
          Message msg = new MimeMessage( mailSession );

      //--[ Set the FROM, TO, DATE and SUBJECT fields
          msg.setFrom( new InternetAddress( fromE-mail ) );
          msg.setRecipients( Message.RecipientType.TO,
                          InternetAddress.parse(toE-mail) );
          msg.setSentDate( new Date() );
          msg.setSubject( "Test Mail" );

          //--[ Create the body of the mail
          msg.setText( body );

          Transport.send( msg );

          msg.writeTo( System.out );

        } catch (Exception E){
      System.out.println( E );
        }
      }
    }
```

We create the e-mail message in the usual way with the `MimeMessage` class, using as little information as possible. After all the necessary properties of the message are set, we use the static method `Transport.send(...)` to the deliver the message. That's it.

At the end of the program we do a simple dump of the core message by making a call to `Message.writeTo(...)`, which produces the following message:

```
Message-ID: <1473500.994102261928.JavaMail.Alan@host50>
Date: Fri, 7 Mar 2003 19:31:01 +0000 (GMT)
From: alan@n-ary.com
To: alan@n-ary.com
Subject: Test Mail
Mime-Version: 1.0
Content-Type: text/plain; charset=us-ascii
Content-Transfer-Encoding: 7bit

hello world this is a test
```

You can see all the headers and the actual composition of the e-mail. We'll look at one more e-mail dump when we send attachments.

Having seen how easy it is to send basic e-mail, have a look at sending something a little more complicated: file attachments. We touched on this a little earlier in the section "javax.mail.Multipart," and we build up the system using a series of different MIME bodies — one representing the message text, and the other holding the necessary information for the file we are looking to send.

Taking the example from the beginning of this section, we'll replace the `try...catch` block with the code in Listing 8-8. You can see the complete code for this example in the `javamail_send_attachment.java` file included in the source code for this book.

Listing 8-8: **Replacing the try...catch block**

```
try{
  //--[ Set up the default parameters
  Properties props = new Properties();
  props.put("mail.transport.protocol", "smtp" );
  props.put("mail.smtp.host", smtpServer );
  props.put("mail.smtp.port", "25" );

  //--[ Create the session and create a new mail message
  Session mailSession = Session.getInstance( props );
  Message msg = new MimeMessage( mailSession );

  //--[ Set the FROM, TO, DATE and SUBJECT fields
  msg.setFrom( new InternetAddress( fromE-mail ) );
  msg.setRecipients( Message.RecipientType.TO,
```

```
                         InternetAddress.parse(toE-mail) );
  msg.setSentDate( new Date() );
  msg.setSubject( "Test Mail with attachment" );

  //--[ Create the first part
  Multipart mailBody = new MimeMultipart();

  MimeBodyPart mainBody = new MimeBodyPart();
  mainBody.setText( body );
  mailBody.addBodyPart( mainBody );

  //--[ Create the second part with the attachment
  FileDataSource fds = new FileDataSource( file );
  MimeBodyPart mimeAttach = new MimeBodyPart();
  mimeAttach.setDataHandler( new DataHandler(fds) );
  mimeAttach.setFileName( fds.getName() );
  mailBody.addBodyPart( mimeAttach );

  //--[ Create the body of the mail
  msg.setContent( mailBody );

  Transport.send( msg );

  System.out.println( "The e-mail below was sent successfully"
);
  msg.writeTo( System.out );

}catch(Exception E){
  System.out.println( E );
}
```

Since this message has two different parts, we need to create the body of the core message with a `MimeMultipart` class. This enables us to put together the various parts of the e-mail. The first part is the message body and with this we use a `MimeBodyPart` class to hold the message text, which we then add to the `MimeMultipart` instance by calling `addBodyPart(...)`.

The file attachment is the next part we must tackle. We use it by creating another instance of `MimeBodyPart`, which we will use to hold our file attachment. We use the class from the Java Activation Framework, `FileDataSource`, to handle the attachment for the file. We then use this class to create our `DataHandler` instance, which we can then use to set the data handler in the `MimeBodyPart`. We can set the filename of the attachment with a call from the `FileDataSource` class. As before, we take this `MimeBodyPart` instance and add it to the list of the parts being handled by the `MimeMultipart` instance.

Finally, we take the `MimeMultipart` instance and set the main body of the message to this object with the call to `msg.setContent(...)`.

For sheer curiosity value, and because we can, let's have a quick look at the e-mail message that is generated this time. Looking at the following mail message, you can see that the mail header is pretty much the same, except for the fact that the Content-Type has been changed to reflect that this is a multipart message in which each part of the message is delimited with the string that may look as follows:

```
----=_Part_0_1472506.994107400236
```

If you seek out this string, you will see another set of Content-XXX headers. These describe the data makeup of the particular section. Notice the part that handles the file attachment: This describes all the information that was used to encode the binary data for the file attached. In this instance that information is base64. Listing 8-9 displays this code.

Listing 8-9: **Another set of Content *XXX* headers**

```
Message-ID: <1474204.994107400567.JavaMail.Alan@host50>
Date: Fri, 7 Mar 2003 19:31:01 +0000 (GMT)
From: alan@n-ary.com
To: alan@n-ary.com
Subject: Test Mail with attachment
Mime-Version: 1.0
Content-Type: multipart/mixed; boundary="----
=_Part_0_1472506.994107400236"

------=_Part_0_1472506.994107400236
Content-Type: text/plain; charset=us-ascii
Content-Transfer-Encoding: 7bit

Hot damn this is so EASY!!!
:-)

------=_Part_0_1472506.994107400236
Content-Type: image/jpeg; name=pic.jpg
Content-Transfer-Encoding: base64
Content-Disposition: attachment; filename=pic.jpg

/9j/4AAQSkZJRgABAQEASABIAAD/2wBDAAEBAQEBAQEBAQEBAQEBAQE
BAQEBAQEBAQEB
AQEBAQICAQECAQEBAgICAgICAgICAQICAgICAgL/2wBDAQEBAQEBAQEBAQE
CAQEBAgICAgIC
AgICAgICAgICAgICAgICAgICAgICAgICAgICAgL/wAA
RCABWAHMDASIA
ABgABQAP06XrPKoVRIQFAA/Qcev/2Q==
------=_Part_0_1472506.994107400236--
```

The JavaMail API handles all this mail creation for us. As you can see the overall format of the file is relatively straightforward. Ironically, one of the trickier parts is choosing a boundary string for the MIME parts. It mustn't appear apart of the data for each section; otherwise the parsing algorithm used for receiving the message will be confused.

Now that we have seen how easy it is to send messages, let us take a look at the flip side of mail management: reading mail.

Receiving e-mail

Receiving e-mail is as simple as sending e-mail as long as you follow the proper steps described earlier in this chapter in the section, "Mail storage and retrieval." We'll illustrate the majority of the concepts of dealing with mail by building a simple command-line access tool to POP3 mail. This will be a very simple tool, and it most certainly will not replace your Outlook or Eudora client! It will list all the messages held on a POP server and enable the user to interact with this list. But first of all, let's build the framework for this application. Listing 8-10 provides the code for this.

Listing 8-10: **Providing the framework**

```
import java.util.*;
import java.io.*;
import javax.mail.*;
import javax.mail.internet.*;
import javax.activation.*;

public class javamail_pop extends Object {

  public static void main(String args[]){

    if ( args.length != 1 ){
      System.out.println( "Usage: javamail_popview <urlname>"
);
      System.exit(1);
    }

    URLName urlname = new URLName( args[0] );

    try{
    //--[ Set up the default parameters
      Properties props = new Properties();
      props.put("mail.transport.protocol", "pop" );
```

Continued

Listing 8-10 *(continued)*

```java
    props.put("mail.pop.port", "110" );

    //--[ Open up the session
    Session session = Session.getInstance( props );
    Store store = session.getStore( urlname );
    store.connect();

    //--[ Open up the folder
    Folder folder = store.getDefaultFolder();
    if ( folder == null ){
      System.out.println( "Problem occurred" );
      System.exit(1);
    }

    Folder popFolder = folder.getFolder("INBOX");
    popFolder.open( Folder.READ_ONLY );

    System.out.println( "Opened with: " +
popFolder.getMessageCount() );

    BufferedReader cmdPrompt  = new BufferedReader(
                                    new InputStreamReader(
System.in ) );
    displayMessages( popFolder );

    for(;;){
      System.out.println( "Enter command (exit to end)" );
      System.out.print("% " );
      String cmd = cmdPrompt.readLine().toLowerCase();
      if ( cmd.equalsIgnoreCase("exit") )
        break;
      else
        displayMessages( popFolder );
    }

    popFolder.close(false);
    store.close();

  } catch (Exception E){
    System.out.println( E );
  }
}


  //--[ Displays the list of messages from the given folder.
  //--[ Display only the message id, from and subject fields
  private static void displayMessages( Folder folder ) throws
Exception {

    Message[] listOfMessages = folder.getMessages();
```

```
FetchProfile fProfile = new FetchProfile();
fProfile.add( FetchProfile.Item.ENVELOPE );
folder.fetch( listOfMessages, fProfile );

System.out.println( "Message List:" );

for ( int x=0; x < listOfMessages.length; x++ ){
  StringBuffer sb = new StringBuffer( 32 );

  //--[ Message ID starts from 1
  sb.append( "# " + (x+1) );

  Address[] addList = listOfMessages[x].getFrom();
  if ( addList.length > 0 )
    sb.append( "\t" +
((InternetAddress)addList[0]).getAddress() );

  sb.append( "\t\t" + listOfMessages[x].getSubject() );

  System.out.println( sb.toString() );
}

System.out.println( "End of message list\r\n" );
  }
 }
}
```

We run this application from the command line, passing in the URLName string, which describes all the information needed to make the connection to the POP3 server. For example:

```
% <javaruntime> javamail_pop

pop3://popname:poppassword@www.hotmail.com
```

The first thing this small application does is create an instance of the URLName class and use this instance to obtain access to the Store class that holds the folder hierarchy. Once we have this, we can obtain the top-level folder, which will give us access, the special INBOX folder that is the only valid folder for the POP protocol.

We will implement a simple command-line-type interface using the InputStream from System.in. By creating a BufferedReader object instance we can easily look for complete commands simply by calling the readLine() method. By putting this method inside a continuous loop, we can easily send multiple commands and have the user exit the session by typing in **exit**.

One of the most fundamental methods in this application is displayMessage(...), which takes the given folder and lists all the messages contained within, displaying the message id, From field, and Subject for each message.

Notice the use of the FetchProfile class described in the section, "Advancing message fetching." This is used to fill in the lightweight message references with all the necessary information regarding the message header. After the call to fill in the information, we simply run around the message loop extracting the necessary information.

So the next step is to add to our command-line application the ability to display the content of particular message ids. The first thing we need to do is add the ability to process the display <id> command. We make the necessary addition to make the core for(;;) loop to look like the following code:

```
for(;;){
  System.out.println( "Enter command (exit to end)" );
  System.out.print("% " );
  String cmd = cmdPrompt.readLine().toLowerCase();
  if ( cmd.equalsIgnoreCase("exit") )
    break;
  else if ( cmd.indexOf("display") == 0 )
    displaySingleMessage( popFolder, cmd );
  else
    displayMessages( popFolder );
}
```

This code simply looks for the display keyword and, when it finds that keyword, calls the displaySingleMessage(...) method as detailed next. This method then parses out the message id and attempts to retrieve the message at that given index by calling the getMessage(...) method. After that, code writes the message to the output stream by simply calling the writeTo(...) method. Here's the example:

```
private static void displaySingleMessage( Folder folder, String
cmd )
                                                      throws
Exception {
  int c1 = cmd.indexOf(" ");
  if ( c1 == -1 ){
    System.out.println( "display <id>" );
    return;
  }

  int messageID = Integer.parseInt( cmd.substring( c1+1 ) );
  Message mess  = folder.getMessage( messageID );

  mess.writeTo( System.out );
  System.out.println( "End of message\r\n" );
}
```

It doesn't take a Java genius to work out that this application is fraught with pitfalls. Very little checking is going on with respect to the ID of the desired message to check that it is indeed in the range listed by the folder. In addition to this, the error-handling is a little crude, simply allowing the exception to be thrown and caught by one try...catch block.

The purpose of this application isn't to build a fully robust POP client, but instead to illustrate some basic JavaMail principles.

Deleting mail

Let's extend our POP client to include the ability to delete a message in the folder. We can simply add to the message loop the ability to handle the `delete <id>` command, which deletion in turn calls the `deleteSingleMethod(...)` shown next.

This method parses out the `message id` and retrieves that message. We wish to delete this message, and as we know from the previous sections, no explicit `delete` method exists for the message. Instead we have to set the `DELETED` flag to `true` and then, when the folder is closed, the messages with the deleted flag will be removed. Here's the example:

```
private static void deleteSingleMessage( Folder folder, String cmd )
                                                  throws Exception {

  int c1 = cmd.indexOf(" ");
  if ( c1 == -1 ){
    System.out.println( "delete <id>" );
    return;
  }

  int messageID = Integer.parseInt( cmd.substring( c1+1 ) );
  Message mess  = folder.getMessage( messageID );

  mess.setFlag( Flags.Flag.DELETED, true );

  System.out.println( "Deleted message\r\n" );
}
```

If you run the code, you will discover one small implementation problem: It doesn't work. The message doesn't get deleted. Why not? Well it's quite subtle, really, and it's small problems like this that you have to look for when working with folders. Initially we opened the folder in the mode `READ_ONLY`. This effectively locked out all modifications to the folder and all messages contained within. By changing the opening mode we can make our application burst into life with the power to delete messages. Here's the example:

```
popFolder.open( Folder.READ_WRITE );
```

Receiving attachments

The final piece of functionality we really ought to add is the ability to save attachments to disk. We'll add the `save <id>` command, which will look up a given message, see if any attachments are associated with it, and then save it into the current directory. As before, we modify the main command-processing loop to look for the `save` command and call the `saveAttachment(...)` method. Listing 8-11 provides the example.

Listing 8-11: **Saving attachments to disk**

```
private static void saveAttachment( Folder folder, String cmd )
                                                    throws Exception {
  int c1 = cmd.indexOf(" ");
  if ( c1 == -1 ){
    System.out.println( "delete <id>" );
    return;
  }

  int messageID = Integer.parseInt( cmd.substring( c1+1 ) );
  Message mess  = folder.getMessage( messageID );

  if ( mess.isMimeType("multipart/*") ){

    Multipart multipart = (Multipart)mess.getContent();

    for (int i=0, n=multipart.getCount(); i<n; i++) {
      Part part = multipart.getBodyPart(i);

      String disposition = part.getDisposition();
      if ( disposition != null &&
          (disposition.equals(Part.ATTACHMENT) ||
           disposition.equals(Part.INLINE) ) ){
        FileWriter outFile = new FileWriter( part.getFileName() );
        BufferedReader in  = new BufferedReader(
                                new InputStreamReader(
                                  part.getInputStream() ) );
        int c;
        while ( (c=in.read()) != -1 )
          outFile.write( c );

        outFile.close();
        System.out.println("Attachment: "+part.getFileName()+" written" );
      }
    }
  }
}
```

As with our other methods, we parse out the given id and retrieve that message from the folder. Next we make the assumption that our message attachments will be part of a multipart/* message and will not appear on their own. This may not always be the case, because you can send a message with just the file and no accompanying text.

Having discovered that the MIME type is indeed a multipart/* of some kind, we cast our message content to a Multipart and run through the list of parts. We look at the disposition of the message, and if it's marked as either an ATTACHMENT or an INLINE it is saved to disk.

The saving out is a simple matter of reading a byte from the `InputStream` of the `part` object and writing it out to an appropriate `FileWriter` class.

Up until now, this chapter has dealt with JavaMail without drawing any specific attention to the other libraries of J2EE. This was on purpose, as JavaMail is a very powerful API that can be used in a variety of different applications. However, because this is a book on J2EE, we'll take a look at how you can implement some of the features of your Application server to use JavaMail features.

Integrating JavaMail into J2EE

When we were looking to send e-mail we had to get ourselves a mail `Session` object to the transport layer we wanted to communicate with, in this instance an SMTP server. This object would have the *hostname/ip* address and might even include some authentication to gain the right to relay e-mail. We don't wish to hardcode any of this information into our `WAR/EAR` files. This is the sort of information that will only be available when the system is in production and may even be liable to change.

Therefore, it is better if we keep this information out and let the administrator configure it. Naturally we can use configuration files and what have you. But a much more elegant approach is possible; we can use the Java Naming Directory Interface (JNDI).

Cross-Reference   See Chapter 11 for details about JNDI.

J2EE enables us to declare a resource at runtime under the `comp/env/mail` JNDI context name, to which we can attach our properties for SMTP. Many of the J2EE application servers will provide access to this information through their own administration tools. Failing that, look at your application server's own documentation for declaring JavaMail resource contexts.

Let's look at the example provided first thing in this chapter, but this time altered to work inside a J2EE component. Instead of creating the `Properties` object as before, we look up the `Session` object using JNDI with the context name of `mail/mySMTP`. Listing 8-12 provides this code.

> ### Listing 8-12: **Looking up the Session object**
>
> ```
> public void sendE-mail(){
>   try{
>     Context initCtx = new InitialContext();
>     Context envCtx = (Context) initCtx.lookup("java:comp/env");
> ```
>
> *Continued*

Listing 8-12 *(continued)*

```
    Session session = (Session) envCtx.lookup("mail/mySMTP");

    Message msg = new MimeMessage( session );

    //--[ Set the FROM, TO, DATE and SUBJECT fields
    msg.setFrom( new InternetAddress( "me@noah.com" ) );
    msg.setRecipients( Message.RecipientType.TO,
InternetAddress.parse("info@cormac.com") );
    msg.setSentDate( new Date() );
    msg.setSubject( "Hello World!" );

    //--[ Create the body of the mail
    msg.setText( "Hello from my first e-mail sent with
JavaMail" );

    //--[ Ask the Transport class to send our mail message
    Transport.send( msg );

  }catch(Exception E){
    System.out.println( "Oops something has gone pear
shaped!");
    System.out.println( E );
  }
}
```

This allows the component to remain completely generic and enables the administrator to decide which mail devices he or she wishes to connect to. In this respect, the JavaMail API is very much like the JDBC driver.

Summary

Hopefully, you now appreciate that JavaMail is very impressive and extremely flexible in the art of accessing and interacting with messages. The API completely abstracts away the actual implementation details of the underlying protocols to give us complete and unobstructed access to the mail messages.

In this chapter we've covered various protocols that are used for sending and receiving e-mails, discussed message attachments, multi-part messages and how to store messages in folders on a disk. We looked at the core components that make up JavaMail and how we can use them from everything from stand-alone components right through to embedded components within a J2EE application.

✦   ✦   ✦

Understanding the Java Messaging Service

✦ ✦ ✦ ✦

In This Chapter

Understanding message-oriented middleware

Using publish/ subscribe messaging

Explaining point-to-point messaging

Understanding reliable messaging

✦ ✦ ✦ ✦

J2EE isn't restricted to transaction processing with servlets and Enterprise JavaBeans. It also interoperates with non-Java-based Enterprise systems, whether they're databases or legacy business systems. One of the most popular ways to interface with these legacy systems is via messaging.

In this chapter, we'll look at how to send and receive messages. We'll also discuss the key concepts that surround messaging — the different messaging models, point-to-point and publish-subscribe, message-oriented middleware, and the various classes implemented in any application that uses messaging.

Explaining Messaging

The basic concept behind *messaging* is that distributed applications can communicate using a self-contained package of business data and routing headers. These packages are *messages*. In contrast to Remote Method Invocation (RMI) or Hypertext Transfer Protocol (HTTP), with which a client contacts a server directly and conducts a two-way conversation, messaging-based apps communicate asynchronously through a messaging server. That is, when a message is sent to another application the sender does not wait for a response. Similarly, applications that process messages are not required to provide any confirmation that the message has been received and processed. They can send another message in return to indicate successful completion of an operation, but this isn't strictly necessary. The software services that support message-based applications are referred to as *message-oriented middleware*.

Messaging is typically used in situations like enterprise-application integration (EAI) and business-to-business (B2B) communications. Most mature organizations have a variety of new and mature applications that were created independently and do not interoperate. Sometimes these organizations want to have these applications share data to better coordinate enterprise-wide activity. The process of getting these disparate applications to talk to each other is generally referred to as enterprise-application integration. A variety of techniques are used for EAI but enterprise-wide messaging is central to most of them. Data and events are exchanged among applications in the form of messages via topics or queues.

Business-to-business communication is a similar situation. Since the invention of computer networks in the 1960s, businesses have communicated via Electronic Data Interchange (EDI) using fixed, proprietary formats. The cost of entry for new participants was high and data were not exchanged in real time. With the advent of the Internet and technologies like XML, businesses can now cooperate without tightly integrating their business systems. A manufacturer can broadcast a request for bids on raw materials. Suppliers can reply with messages via a queue, indicating prices and quantities. New suppliers can be added at will and topics and queues can be used to separate the handling of requests for different types of materials or inventories. All of this is possible using loosely-coupled messaging, available in Java via the Java Messaging Service (JMS) API.

Introducing JMS

JMS is the Java Messaging Service. It is a *wrapper API* that does not provide any services directly, but instead serves to standardize the messaging functionality provided by some other service provider, like IBM's MQSeries (now WebSphere MQ) or Sonic Software's SonicMQ. Many application servers also provide their own JMS server implementations. JMS provides a single API that can be used to access the messaging facilities provided by any messaging-service provider, much as Java Database Connectivity (JDBC) is used to access any relational database that provides a JDBC driver.

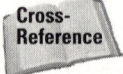
Cross-Reference   See Chapter 18 for a discussion of JDBC.

JMS versus RMI

To further help you understand JMS, let's explore the differences between systems built with JMS and those built with a synchronous protocol, like RMI. Other similar synchronous protocols include the Simple Object Access Protocol (SOAP) and CORBA's Internet Inter-Orb Protocol (IIOP). RMI tries to make a request that goes across the network appear to be the same as a method invocation in the same process. When a method call is made via RMI the caller blocks until the procedure completes. Work is performed sequentially, which ensures that tasks are completed in the specified order. Additionally, when multiple components exist each element of the system has to create an independent connection to each other component, leading to a many-to-many mapping problem between system components.

Message-oriented systems, in contrast, are asynchronous. They continue processing as soon as the message is dispatched. Messages are processed centrally by the message-oriented middleware (MOM) server, which takes care of issues like reliability, transaction processing, and message delivery. No blocking exists in messaging systems. The MOM server guarantees the delivery of messages to make sure that all messages eventually get to a consumer, even if a partial system failure occurs. Additionally, because all components in the system communicate via a centralized server, the overall architecture is a simpler one-to-many (messaging server to system components) relationship. In the specific case of JMS, the MOM server is sometimes referred to as the JMS server.

JMS provides other features like support for clustered, high-availability message servers and transaction support to ensure that related messages are either delivered together or not at all. JMS messages can also be processed in EJBs via support for message-driven beans. Message-driven beans are a special form of stateless session beans that process messages instead of processing requests that come in via RMI. A message filter is created to make sure each type of message-driven bean only receives the messages it is interested in. Message-driven beans are handled like other EJBs in which pooling, activation, and passivation are all automatically handled by the container to ensure that enough beans exist to handle the volume of incoming messages. See Chapter 17 for more on message-driven beans.

Overall, messaging and RMI are both used to connect pieces of a distributed application but they follow very different approaches. Using synchronous techniques such as RMI usually leads to more tightly coupled systems. Asynchronous techniques, such as JMS messaging, result in systems that are loosely coupled. Loose coupling is an important property of distributed systems that makes them easier to manage as they change over time.

Now that we've looked at the fundamentals of what messaging is all about, let's examine the syntax of using JMS.

A Note on Versions

J2EE 1.4 includes version 1.1 of the JMS specification. J2EE 1.3 included JMS 1.0.2b. Some significant changes have been made between these two versions of the specification. Many application servers and stand-alone JMS servers still in use implement JMS 1.0.2b.

The code examples in this chapter will not compile using a JMS 1.0.2b library. If you're having problems running the examples make sure that your JMS server implements JMS 1.1.

Message structure

The first element of JMS you need to understand is how messages are structured. A message consists of the three following parts:

✦ Headers

✦ Properties

✦ Body

The message *headers* provide a fixed set of metadata fields describing the message, with information such as where the message is going and when it was received. The *properties* are a set of key-value pairs used for application-specific purposes, usually to help filter messages quickly when they've been received. Finally, the *body* contains whatever data is being sent in the message. The contents of the body vary depending on the type of the message: The `javax.jms.Message` interface has several sub-interfaces for different types of messages. Table 9-1 lists these message types.

<table>
<tr><td colspan="2" align="center">Table 9-1
Message types</td></tr>
<tr><td>*Message Type*</td><td>*Message Contents*</td></tr>
<tr><td>`javax.jms.BytesMessage`</td><td>A stream of bytes. A number of convenience methods on the `BytesMessage` interface enable developers to deal with other primitive types or `Strings`, automatically turning these values into bytes.</td></tr>
<tr><td>`javax.jms.MapMessage`</td><td>A set of key-value pairs. Unlike a `java.util.Map` object, `MapMessage` always uses `Strings` for the keys and some primitive type for the values.</td></tr>
<tr><td>`javax.jms.ObjectMessage`</td><td>A serialized object instance. Note that the serialization mechanism will also automatically serialize any objects being referred to indirectly, so the "single object" may in fact be the root of a large graph of objects.</td></tr>
<tr><td>`javax.jms.StreamMessage`</td><td>A stream of primitives. Very similar in function to `BytesMessage`.</td></tr>
<tr><td>`javax.jms.TextMessage`</td><td>A `String` instance.</td></tr>
</table>

Most JMS providers also provide a vendor-specific `XMLMessage` interface that is usually derived from `TextMessage`. The only advantage of using these classes is that they usually have some convenience methods to automatically parse the contents of the message upon receipt.

These are all interfaces, not classes. In JMS you don't create messages (or almost any type of JMS object) directly—you use a factory class to create the instances for you. This provides a layer of independence from the particular JMS implementation you're using. Now that we've had a look at how messages are structured, let's have a look at how they're passed from message senders to message receivers.

Examining Messaging Models

For maximum compatibility with existing messaging servers, JMS supports two different messaging models: *point-to-point* (p2p) and *publish-and-subscribe* (pub/sub). Previous message-oriented middleware systems supported either the pub/sub or the p2p model. Because JMS is used as a Java-based wrapper around existing messaging systems it supports both messaging models. Most pure-Java implementations of JMS support both models.

Point-to-point messaging

In the point-to-point model messages are sent from producers to consumers via *queues.* A given queue may have multiple receivers but only one receiver may consume each message. This is illustrated in Figure 9-1. Unlike the pub/sub model, in which messages are pushed automatically to consumers, the p2p model typically uses a pull mechanism whereby consumers request messages from a queue.

JMS also supports a *p2p push model,* wherein messages are automatically delivered as in the pub/sub model. The JMS provider ensures that each message is delivered once and only once. The JMS specification makes no other guarantees about how messages are distributed among multiple receivers, although many JSM implementations implement load balancing to ensure that messages are distributed evenly among receivers. The p2p message model also allows queue browsing, whereby a receiver can examine the contents of a queue before consuming a message.

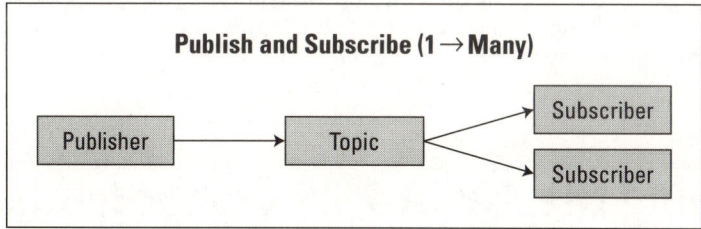

Figure 9-1: The point-to-point message distribution model

Publish-and-subscribe messaging

In the publish-and-subscribe messaging model, messages are sent (*published*) to consumers via *topics*. Messages published on a specific topic are sent to all message consumers that have registered (*subscribed*) to receive messages on that topic. This is illustrated in Figure 9-2. Messages are pushed from publishers to subscribers — subscribers receive automatic notification whenever a message is published to a topic they're subscribed to. A single message may be distributed to hundreds, even thousands, of subscribers. No coupling of producers to consumers exists — subscribers and publishers can be added dynamically at runtime. This allows systems to be easily modified and expanded without having to reconfigure existing publishers and subscribers.

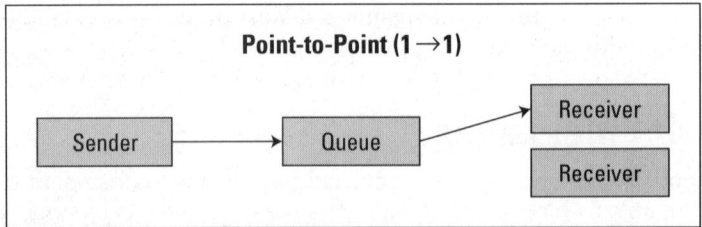

Figure 9-2: The publish-and-subscribe message distribution model

Pub/sub supports a number of other features to make messaging more reliable. A *durable* subscription is a special type of subscription that outlasts a consumer's connection to the messaging server. When a durable subscriber is disconnected from the JMS server the server will store all messages that would have gone to the subscriber and deliver them when the subscriber reconnects. This is also referred to as *store-and-forward* messaging. This type of behavior is essential for guaranteed messaging, with which a consumer can be ensured of receiving all messages regardless of application or network failures.

Which model is right for your application? It depends on how you want messages handled and, to a large extent, on how other existing applications in your organization are using messaging already. Having looked at how messages are handled, let's look at the specific components and classes used in JMS.

Understanding the Major JMS Components

Other than messages a number of classes exist that you'll need to use in almost every JMS application. Separate interfaces are available for dealing with publish/subscribe systems and point-to-point systems, but because they have so many similarities base classes encapsulate common functionality. This section discusses the following components:

✦ Destinations

✦ Connections

✦ Connection factories

✦ Sessions

✦ Producers

✦ Consumers

Destinations

A *destination* is, as its name implies, somewhere you're sending a message. Specific types of destinations are *queues* (in point-to-point systems) or *topics* (in publish/subscribe systems). Destinations are normally configured in the messaging server and are not directly instantiated in the application. Instead, you obtain them via a JNDI lookup. Queues and topics can also be created dynamically, but queues and topics so created are only valid for the lifetime of the connection with which they're associated. The destination interface is `javax.jms.Destination`, which has the four following sub-interfaces:

✦ `Queue` — Used for communicating in p2p systems, a `Queue` instance is a local proxy for the queue stored in the messaging server.

✦ `Topic` — Used for communication in pub/sub systems, a `Topic` instance is a local proxy for the topic stored in the messaging server.

✦ `TemporaryQueue` — This is a unique `Queue` object created for the duration of a `QueueConnection`. It is a system-defined queue that can only be consumed by the `QueueConnection` that created it.

✦ `TemporaryTopic` — This a unique `Topic` object created for the duration of a `TopicConnection`. It is a system-defined queue that can only be consumed by the `TopicConnection` that created it.

Connections

JMS *Connections* are similar to the `Connection` class in JDBC — it represents a connection between the application and the messaging server over which messages can be sent. The connection interface is `javax.jms.Connection`. In the JMS 1.0.2b specification, there were separate interfaces for connections to pub/sub or p2p messaging system, but in the unified model used in JMS 1.1, you only need to use the single `Connection` interface. There are still `QueueConnection` and `TopicConnection` interfaces, but they are only provided for backwards compatibility.

Connection factories

As in JDBC, connections in JMS are not directly instantiated. Instead, a connection factory creates connections. Where does the connection factory come from? From a

JNDI lookup, like a destination. Connection factories and destinations are the only types of objects in JMS that need to be obtained via JNDI. Connection factories don't do anything else other than create connection objects. The connection factory interface is `javax.jms.ConnectionFactory`. While `ConnectionFactory` has sub-interfaces, they're not necessary—the base `ConnectionFactory` interface can do everything an application needs done. The extra interfaces are, again, left over from older versions of the JMS specification.

Sessions

You don't send and receive messages directly through a connection. Instead, you need a *session*. A session serves as a factory for message objects, message producers and consumers, `TemporaryTopics`, and `TemporaryQueues`. It also does the following:

> Provides transactional behavior for the work done by its producers and consumers
>
> Defines a serial order for the messages it consumes and the messages it produces
>
> Retains messages it consumes until they have been acknowledged

`Sessions` are created using a `Connection` object. The session interface is `javax.jms.Session`. Like the `ConnectionFactory` interface, `Session` has sub-interfaces, but these aren't necessary in JMS 1.1.

Producers

Finally, having created a number of administrative objects (a `ConnectionFactory`, a `Connection`, a `Session`, and a `Destination`) we can get to the point where we're able to actually create a message and send it somewhere. The `javax.jms.Message-Producer` interface has two sub-interfaces: `QueueSender` and `TopicPublisher`. You can use whichever interface you like but the `QueueSender` and `TopicPublisher` interfaces don't add any additional functionality to `MessageProducer`. `Topic-Publisher`'s `publish()` methods do exactly the same thing as the `send()` method in `MessageProducer`. `MessageProducer` instances can be created using a `Session`.

Consumers

If you want to receive messages, use the session to create a `MessageConsumer`. The interface `javax.jms.MessageConsumer` has two sub-interfaces, `QueueReceiver` and `TopicSubscriber`. Messages can be received two different ways with a `MessageConsumer`.

JMS and Threads

Some JMS objects are safe to share between threads, specifically connection factories and connections. Sessions are single-threaded objects and, as such, should not be shared among multiple threads. If you know that a given session object will not be used in more than one thread it's safe to store it in some accessible location (like an instance variable). If the object may be shared among multiple threads (the way a servlet is), then create a new session each time the method that needs to dispatch a message is invoked. Because J2EE application servers have multiple threads, all potentially executing the same methods, it's safer not to try to share session objects outside the scope of a single method.

`MessageProducers` and `MessageConsumers`, being tied to a specific session, are also not safe to share among threads.

First, with the push approach, you can create a class that implements the `Message-Listener` interface and pass an instance of it to `MessageConsumer.setMessage-Listener()`. Whenever a message becomes available it will be automatically passed to the listener's `onMessage()` method.

Second, with the pull approach, you call `MessageConsumer.receive()`, which will return a message if one is available. If no message is available the no-argument version of `receive()` will block. You can also call `receive(int)`, which will timeout after the specified number of milliseconds, or `receiveNoWait()`, which will return null if no message is available.

The session ensures that messages sent to a `MessageListener` are serialized — if the same `MessageListener` is registered with several `MessageConsumers` that have been created using the same `Session`, it is guaranteed that `onMessage()` will not be called again until the current message is finished processing.

Now that we've seen what types of objects are needed to send and receive messages, let's look at how to set up and configure a JMS-based application along with some samples.

Configuring JMS

Much of the work in configuring a messaging-based application is done in the messaging server itself. Topics and queues are configured through the administrative interface of your MOM server, so consult your vendor's documentation to learn how to do this.

At minimum you'll need to configure a `ConnectionFactory` and a `Topic` for pub/sub applications or a `Queue` for p2p applications. These objects will be retrieved by the application via JNDI. The application will need to know the type and location of the naming service. These values can be hardcoded into the application or passed in at runtime, either via the command line or via a configuration file.

Cross-Reference   See Chapter 11 for a discussion of JNDI.

Some JMS providers require you to create either a `QueueConnectionFactory` or a `TopicConnectionfactory`, but some providers do not distinguish between the two and in some cases either type of `ConnectionFactory` can be used to create connections to both a queue and a topic.

For the example involving Connexia Airlines we will describe a point-to-point system where a meal request is passed via a queue to Connexia's catering partner. This is an example of loosely coupled business-process integration via messaging between companies. We will assume that a `ConnectionFactory` exists and that a `Queue`, `connexia.MealOrderQueue`, has been configured as well.

For the example with J2EE Publisher we'll show an order-processing system that processes orders that have been entered and then dispatches them to all the other systems in the company that need to take some action based on the orders — billing, shipping, accounting and so on. When an order is created the creator may not even know what other systems need to be notified, but by using a publish-and-subscribe messaging model we can be sure that the information is available to any interested systems. We'll assume that a `ConnectionFactory` exists and that a `Topic`, `publisher.BookOrdersTopic`, has been configured as well.

Connexia Airlines Point-to-Point Messaging Business Case

In a p2p system all messages are routed via queues. Multiple listeners may be receiving messages from the queue, but each message goes to one and only one listener. The example code here will be simplified with only one listener, but you would add additional listeners just as you added the first one. Note that deciding which queue gets which message is JMS server–specific. Some JMS servers load-balance and try to distribute the messages equally across all consumers, but this behavior is not defined by the JMS specification.

Setting up all the objects on the message-sending side is straightforward, but you must follow these steps:

1. Obtain a JNDI `InitialContext`. You don't need to do this more than once, and for performance reasons it's best to do it only once and save the result for use later.

2. Obtain the `ConnectionFactory` via a JNDI lookup. Again, JNDI lookups can be slow, so do this only once and cache the result.

3. Obtain the destination `Queue` via a JNDI lookup.

4. Use the `ConnectionFactory` to obtain a `Connection`.

Then follow these instructions in order to send a message:

1. Use the `Connection` to obtain a `Session`.

2. Use the `Session` to create a `MessageProducer`.

3. Use the `Session` to create an appropriate message.

4. Send the `Message` using the `MessageProducer`.

If you're sending multiple messages you can reuse `Message` objects without affecting the content of messages that have already been sent.

On the receiving end the steps are very similar, except that you create a `MessageConsumer` instead of a `MessageProducer`.

For the Connexia Airlines example we'll create a `MealService` class with a `request()` method that will request a specified type of meal. We'll also create a no-argument version that will request a "regular" meal. This method will use the `QueueConnection` that was created during initialization to send a `MapMessage` to the catering company, detailing the type of meal as well as the date and flight number for the given passenger. To test it we'll use a dummy `MessageListener` and a simple servlet.

Listing 9-1 contains the code to create the message.

Listing 9-1: **MealService.java**

```
import java.util.*;
import java.text.DateFormat;
import javax.jms.*;
import javax.naming.*;

public class MealService {

public static final String REGULAR = "regular";
public static final String LOW_SALT = "low salt";
public static final String VEGETARIAN = "vegetarian";
public static final String KOSHER = "kosher";
public static final String HALAL = "halal";
public static final String DIABETIC = "diabetic";

private static MealService singleton = null;
```

Continued

Listing 9-1 *(continued)*

```java
private Connection connection;
private Queue mealOrderQ;

private MealService() {

    try {
        // initialize appropriate JMS objects
        // obtain the JNDI InitialContext
        Hashtable env = new Hashtable();
        env.put(Context.INITIAL_CONTEXT_FACTORY,
            "com.swiftmq.jndi.InitialContextFactoryImpl");
        env.put(Context.PROVIDER_URL,
            "smqp://localhost:4001/timeout=10000");
        Context ctx = new InitialContext(env);

        // obtain the ConnectionFactory and
        // create the Connection
        ConnectionFactory cf = (ConnectionFactory)ctx.lookup(
            "QueueConnectionFactory");
        connection = cf.createConnection();

        // obtain the destination Queue
        mealOrderQ = (Queue)ctx.lookup(
            "connexia.MealOrderQueue");
    }
    catch(NamingException ne) {
        ne.printStackTrace();
    }
    catch(JMSException je) {
        je.printStackTrace();
    }
}

public static MealService getMealService() {
    if(singleton == null)
        singleton = new MealService();
    return singleton;
}

public void request(int flight_number, Date date) {
    request(REGULAR, flight_number, date);
}

public void request(String type, int flight_number, Date date)
{

    MessageProducer qSender;
    Session session;
```

```java
        try {
            // obtain a Session
            session = connection.createSession(false,
                Session.AUTO_ACKNOWLEDGE);

            // obtain a MessageProducer
            qSender = session.createProducer(mealOrderQ);

            // build the map message
            MapMessage msg = session.createMapMessage();
            msg.setString("mealType", type);
            msg.setInt("flightNumber",flight_number);
            msg.setString("date",
                DateFormat.getDateInstance().format(date));

            // set the message headers
            msg.setJMSDeliveryMode(DeliveryMode.PERSISTENT);

            // send the message
            qSender.send(msg);

            qSender.close();
            session.close();
        }
        catch(JMSException e) {
            e.printStackTrace();
        }
    }

    public void close() {
        try {
            connection.close();
            singleton = null;
        }
        catch(JMSException e) {
            e.printStackTrace();
        }
    }

    public static void main(String args[]) {
        MealService service = MealService.getMealService();
        service.request(234, new Date());
        service.close();
        System.exit(0);
    }

}
```

So let's have a look at what the MealService class is doing.

First of all, MealService is a singleton. The use of a singleton is unrelated to JMS, but it's important to understand that only one MealService instance will be accessible from any point in the application. It's worth noting that we are not required to make MealService a singleton—we simply want to avoid initializing multiple Connection objects, for performance reasons. Creating a separate MealService object for every request is certainly possible and will not affect our ability to send messages successfully.

The environment properties you pass in to the InitialContext will depend on what JMS provider you're using. The parameters specified here are the ones used with SwiftMQ 4.5.1 from IIT Software (http://www.swiftmq.com).

Cross-Reference See Chapter 11 for more information on using JNDI with various commercial application servers.

Once the MealService object has been initialized, sending a message in the request() method is relatively simple. It may seem that you need to create a lot of objects to perform a simple task, but each object plays a specific role in the application. One important item to note is that when the Session is created we need to specify two arguments. The first argument, a boolean, indicates whether the session is transacted. We specified false, which means that we don't want transaction support. (Transactional sessions are discussed later in the chapter in the "Transaction" section.) The second argument, an int, indicates how message-receipt acknowledgement will be handled and has one of the three values listed in Table 9-2.

<table>
<tr><td colspan="2" align="center">Table 9-2
JMS acknowledgement modes</td></tr>
<tr><td>*Mode*</td><td>*Description*</td></tr>
<tr><td>Session.AUTO_ACKNOWLEDGE</td><td>This method indicates that message-receipt responses are automatically generated. The response is provided automatically by the JMS server when an application sends a message. When an application receives a message, the response is generated by the JMS client's runtime code.

This mode provides guaranteed once-and-only-once message delivery to the JMS destination.

This is the mode used most frequently.</td></tr>
</table>

Mode	Description
Session.DUPS_OK_ACKNOWLEDGE	This mode informs the JMS provider that it is OK to send a message more than once to a destination. The idea is that in some cases the once-and-only-once delivery mechanism may incur extra overhead and reduce performance.
	Note that this mode is not guaranteed to work any faster than AUTO_ACKNOWLEDGE. Unless you have a good reason to avoid automatic message acknowledgement and your application can tolerate duplicate messages, do not use this mode.
Session.CLIENT_ACKNOWLEDGE	This mode puts the onus of message acknowledgement on the receiving client code. To acknowledge the receipt of a message, call msg.acknowledge().
	This mode gives the client the ability to inspect a message before acknowledging its receipt or to reduce overhead by acknowledging a group of messages all at once — a call to acknowledge() implicitly acknowledges all previous messages that have been received but not acknowledged.

We set only one JMS message-header property here, JMSDeliveryMode. Valid values for JMSDeliveryMode are DeliveryMode.PERSISTENT and DeliveryMode.NON_PERSISTENT. An application marks a message as persistent if it feels that the application will have problems if the message is lost in transit. If an occasional lost message is tolerable, mark the message as non-persistent. In our case we don't want to lose any meal requests so we use the persistent delivery mode. What the JMS server does with persistent messages is server-implementation-specific but they will probably be written to some persistent data store, such as a file on disk or a database. A number of other JMS message headers can be set; you can either set them directly on the message or, for some properties, specify a default value via the MessageProducer. Table 9-3 describes the different JMS message header fields.

	Table 9-3
	JMS message headers
Header	**Description**
JMSDestination	This header identifies which destination (either a Queue or a Topic) the message was sent to. This is useful for Message Listeners that consume messages from multiple destinations.
JMSDeliveryMode	This header is specified as either DeliverMode.PERSISTENT or DeliveryMode.NON_PERSISTENT.
JMSMessageID	This header is a string that uniquely identifies the message.
JMSTimestamp	This is a long value, in milliseconds, automatically set by the messageProducer, that represents when the message was sent via send().
JMSExpiration	This is a long value, in milliseconds, that specifies the maximum amount of time that the JMS server should hold on to the message. Specify zero (0) to indicate that the message doesn't expire.
JMSRedelivered	This is a Boolean that indicates whether the JMS server has already attempted to deliver this message but failed or is not certain it succeeded.
JMSPriority	This header specifies one of the 10 priority levels in JMS, 0–9. Levels 0–4 are gradations of normal priority. Levels 5–9 indicate higher, or *expedited*, priorities. The default level is 4.

Once the message has been sent we close the sender and session and when we exit the application we close the connection as well. Closing a connection also closes any open sessions, producers, or consumers associated with that connection, as well as deleting any temporary destinations. Any uncommitted transactions will be rolled back when the connection is closed.

The application that receives and processes the messages is even simpler, at least in terms of the message-handling part. Presumably some challenge remains in cooking and delivering the meals to Connexia Airlines. Listing 9-2 shows the code for the Caterer class.

Listing 9-2: **Caterer.java**

```
        import javax.naming.*;
import javax.jms.*;
import java.util.*;

public class Caterer implements MessageListener {
```

```java
    private Caterer() {
        try {
            Hashtable env = new Hashtable();
            env.put(Context.INITIAL_CONTEXT_FACTORY,
                "com.swiftmq.jndi.InitialContextFactoryImpl");
            env.put(Context.PROVIDER_URL,
                "smqp://localhost:4001/timeout=10000");
            Context ctx = new InitialContext(env);

            ConnectionFactory cf = (ConnectionFactory)ctx.lookup(
                "QueueConnectionFactory");
            Connection connection = cf.createConnection();
            Queue mealOrderQ = (Queue)ctx.lookup(
                "connexia.MealOrderQueue");
            Session session = connection.createSession(false,
                Session.AUTO_ACKNOWLEDGE);
            MessageConsumer mc = session.createConsumer(
                mealOrderQ);
            mc.setMessageListener(this);
            connection.start();
        }
        catch(Exception e) {
            e.printStackTrace();
        }
    }

    public void onMessage(Message msg) {
        try {
            MapMessage mmsg = (MapMessage)msg;
            System.out.println("Meal request for flight "+
                mmsg.getString("flightNumber")+
                " on date "+mmsg.getString("date"));
        }
        catch(Exception e) {
            e.printStackTrace();
        }
    }

    public static void main(String args[]) {
        Caterer c = new Caterer();
    }

}
```

The setup for this class is pretty much the same as it was for the `MealService` class, except that a `MessageConsumer` is created instead of a `MessageProducer`. Registering a `messageListener` isn't enough — to begin receiving messages you must also call `Connection.start()`. You can turn message delivery on and off by calling `start()` and `stop()` on the `Connection` object. Stopping message delivery has no effect on a connection's ability to send messages.

To run the example, run java `Caterer` on the command line and then, in another window, run java `MealService`. **Try running multiple** `Caterer` **instances in different windows**—notice that any message produced is sent to only one `Caterer`. Now let's look at an example using pub/sub messaging.

Magazine-Publisher Publish-Subscribe Messaging Business Case

The setup of publish-subscribe messaging systems in JMS is almost identical to that of point-to-point systems. Aside from terminology (topic instead of queue, for example) the major difference is that all messages published to a topic are broadcast to all subscribers. With queues, even if multiple receivers are connected to a single queue, only one of them will receive a message posted to the queue.

Because JMS 1.1 has unified the two messaging models virtually no difference exists between code that posts a message to a queue and code that publishes a message to a topic. In JMS 1.0.2b this was not the case—you were required to use either `QueueConnection` or `TopicConnection`, `QueueSession` or `TopicSession`, and so on. In JMS 1.1 the `Connection`, `Session`, `MessageConsumer`, and `MessageProducer` interfaces handle both messaging models.

The application shown in Listing 9-3 sends messages to the `publisher.BookOrdersTopic` topic.

Listing 9-3: **BookOrder.java**

```
import javax.naming.*;
import javax.jms.*;
import java.util.Hashtable;

public class BookOrder {

private String name;
private String isbn;

public BookOrder() {
    name = "default";
    isbn = "none";
}

public void setCustomer(String name) {
    this.name = name;
}
```

```
public void setBook(String isbn) {
    this.isbn = isbn;
}

public void dispatch() {

    try {
        Hashtable env = new Hashtable();
        env.put(Context.INITIAL_CONTEXT_FACTORY,
            "com.swiftmq.jndi.InitialContextFactoryImpl");
        env.put(Context.PROVIDER_URL,
            "smqp://localhost:4001/timeout=10000");
        Context ctx = new InitialContext(env);

        ConnectionFactory cf = (ConnectionFactory)ctx.lookup(
            "TopicConnectionFactory");
        Connection connection = cf.createConnection();

        Topic bookOrderTopic = (Topic)ctx.lookup(
            "publisher.BookOrdersTopic");

        Session session = connection.createSession(false,
            Session.AUTO_ACKNOWLEDGE);

        MessageProducer publisher = session.createProducer(
            bookOrderTopic);

        MapMessage msg = session.createMapMessage();
        msg.setString("customer",name);
        msg.setString("isbn",isbn);

        publisher.send(msg, DeliveryMode.PERSISTENT,
            5, 600000);
    }
    catch(Exception e) {
        e.printStackTrace();
    }
}

}
```

The OrderProcessor class shown in Listing 9-4 receives the messages created by BookOrder class and does something with them. In this case it simply prints the information to the user but in a real application it would perform some useful processing.

Listing 9-4: OrderProcessor.java

```java
import javax.naming.*;
import javax.jms.*;
import java.util.Hashtable;

public class OrderProcessor implements MessageListener {

String name;

public OrderProcessor(String name) {
    this.name = name;

    try {
        Hashtable env = new Hashtable();
        env.put(Context.INITIAL_CONTEXT_FACTORY,
            "com.swiftmq.jndi.InitialContextFactoryImpl");
        env.put(Context.PROVIDER_URL,
            "smqp://localhost:4001/timeout=10000");
        Context ctx = new InitialContext(env);

        ConnectionFactory cf = (ConnectionFactory)ctx.lookup(
            "TopicConnectionFactory");
        Connection connection = cf.createConnection();

        Topic bookOrderTopic = (Topic)ctx.lookup(
            "publisher.BookOrdersTopic");

        Session session = connection.createSession(false,
            Session.AUTO_ACKNOWLEDGE);

        MessageConsumer subscriber = session.createConsumer(
            bookOrderTopic);
        subscriber.setMessageListener(this);
        connection.start();
    }
    catch(Exception e) {
        e.printStackTrace();
    }
}

public void onMessage(Message msg) {
    try {
        MapMessage mmsg = (MapMessage)msg;
        System.out.println("Processor "+name+
            " received an order for "+
            mmsg.getString("isbn")+" from "+
            mmsg.getString("customer"));
    }
```

```
        catch(Exception e) {
            e.printStackTrace();
        }
    }

    public static void main(String args[]) {
        OrderProcessor accounting = new
            OrderProcessor("accounting");
        OrderProcessor shipping = new
            OrderProcessor("shipping");
        OrderProcessor sales_tracking = new
            OrderProcessor("sales_tracking");

        try {
            Thread.sleep(1000);
        }
        catch(InterruptedException e) {
        }

        BookOrder order = new BookOrder();
        order.setBook("0-7645-3966-3");
        order.setCustomer("ehenry");
        order.dispatch();
        order.setCustomer("fgeary");
        order.dispatch();

        try {
            Thread.sleep(1000);
        }
        catch(InterruptedException e) {
        }

        System.exit(0);
    }

}
```

Observe that in the `main()` method for `OrderProcessor`, which actually tests message distribution, multiple `OrderProcessor` instances are created. When you run this code you should see one message received and processed three times. Perhaps this does not seem very impressive in this small sample application, but JMS provides transparent distribution and scalability making it trivial to scale this example up into an enterprise-grade order-processing system.

In `BookOrder.dispatch()` note that the `MessageProducer.send()` method specifies three parameters in addition to the destination. The first is the delivery mode. In the point-to-point example this value was set on the message by means of calling `setJMSDeliveryMode()`. This value is set by the `MessageProducer` (via `MessageProducer.setDeliveryMode()`) unless overridden in the message header or in the call to `send()`. The second parameter is the message priority — again, this value is taken from the `MessageProducer` unless it is overridden in the message header or in the call to `send()`.

Finally, a *time-to-live* (TTL) value in milliseconds is specified. In this case, a value of `600000` represents a 10-minute time to live. Be aware that message expiration is often calculated by means of taking the current system time when the message is dispatched and adding the time-to-live value; therefore, if the clocks on the message producer and the messaging server are not synchronized messages may be prematurely expired. You can get around this by ensuring that the systems involved in message processing have synchronized clocks or by increasing the time-to-live value to ensure that messages are not prematurely removed. Now we've seen the basics of how to create, send and receive messages, let's look at extending the basic messaging model to help ensure reliability.

Explaining Reliable Messaging

JMS has a number of features that help ensure reliability. Guaranteed messaging is powerful but it doesn't happen automatically — JMS has a number of features "under the hood" that help ensure that messages are delivered consistently and reliably. Three components make up guaranteed messaging: message autonomy, store-and-forward messaging, and the message-acknowledgement semantics of JMS systems.

Autonomous messages

First of all messages are *autonomous* — they are generated by a producer, received by a consumer, and may then be retransmitted to another consumer. Once a message is created, however, it will not be modified by the messaging server — it will either be delivered or it will expire if it cannot be delivered before its time-to-live period expires.

Persistent messages

Messages marked as persistent are guaranteed to be delivered by the messaging server. Once a message is successfully received it will be stored in a persistent data store like a database or a file until it can be delivered to a consumer. In the event of a messaging-server failure, any pending messages will be held until the server is restarted and can begin attempting delivery again.

Synchronous acknowledgments

Finally, a variety of synchronous acknowledgements exist in the otherwise asynchronous message-transmission process. When a JMS client attempts to send a message, it first goes to the JMS server, which acknowledges successful receipt of the message. Because of message persistence the JMS server will safely hold on to the message until it is delivered to a message consumer and the server has received acknowledgement that the message has, in fact, been received. Think of it like a FedEx delivery — you, the sender, get a confirmation when you give a package to FedEx and FedEx, in return, gets a confirmation from the recipient when the package is delivered.

Transactions

When you need atomic delivery of several messages — that is, either all the messages are delivered or none is — you need to use a transaction. JMS supports transactions in two ways — via the JMS transaction support in the `Session` interface and via the distributed-transaction support in the Java Transaction API.

Cross-Reference

Because Chapter 10 deals extensively with the Java Transaction API, we'll only look at JMS session–based transactions here.

To create a session with transactional behavior, simply specify `true` as the first parameter passed to `createSession()`. The new session object is now transacted. You don't need to specify the beginning of the transaction; it starts automatically. All messages sent through any producer created using that session are part of the transaction until either `rollback()` or `commit()` is invoked on the session. Once a transaction is completed by either a commit or rollback a new transaction is started automatically. The following code fragment shows how a set of messages can be handled inside a transaction.

```
Session session = connection.createSession(true,
    Session.AUTO_ACKNOWLEDGE);
MessageProducer producer = session.createProducer(
    Destination);

// send some messages via producer

if(successful)
    session.commit();
else
    session.rollback();
```

Transactions are a very powerful tool and a necessity in any environment where data integrity is the primary concern. The only concept in JMS and J2EE that we haven't discussed so far are message-driven Enterprise JavaBeans.

Introducing Message-Driven Enterprise JavaBeans

Message-driven beans are a special form of stateless session beans that respond to JMS messages instead of method calls via RMI. They implement both the `javax.ejb.MessageDrivenBean` interface as well as `javax.jms.MessageListener`. The EJB container is in charge of creating the JMS connection, session, and message consumer. The destination to which the message-driven bean is connected is specified in the bean's deployment descriptor. Message-driven beans make it easy to encapsulate message-processing logic without creating all the JMS administrative objects manually.

Cross-Reference   Chapter 17 goes into much greater detail about message-driven EJBs.

Summary

This chapter aims to provide a basic overview of the capabilities of JMS and to show you how to use the core JMS classes. JMS becomes considerably more complex as you begin to explore guaranteed messaging and distributed transactions. Nevertheless, this chapter provides the essentials to help you write JMS applications.

In this chapter we've explored what message-oriented middleware (MOM) systems are good for and looked at how messaging concepts like point-to-point (p2p) messaging and publish/subscribe (pub/sub) messaging are applied to JMS.

Because there are so many interfaces used in even a simple JMS-based application, we had an overview of the JMS API and its major components: messages, destinations, connections, connection factories, sessions, producers and consumers. All of these components were shown in action in the examples provided.

Finally, we looked at the basics of making messaging reliable via message persistence and support for transactions. Messaging is a powerful model for building loosely coupled enterprise applications and with JMS it's easy to use messaging in Java.

✦   ✦   ✦

Introducing Java Transactions

✦   ✦   ✦   ✦

In This Chapter

Describing what atomic transactions are for

Illustrating ACID properties

Exploring different transaction models and how each might be useful for an application programmer

Describing important transaction standards

Reviewing a new transaction paradigm being developed for J2EE

Explaining the JTA architecture

✦   ✦   ✦   ✦

In this chapter we will introduce the notion of *atomic transactions* and show how they are integral to all enterprise-level applications. Put simply, without transactions there can be no guarantee of data consistency in the presence of failures or concurrent access. In mission-critical applications (such as banking or air-traffic control), a lack of transactional support can be the difference between successfully making a sale or not. Many people are wary of applications that can potentially lose their customers millions of dollars if a power failure occurs at just the wrong instant, for example!

The concept of atomic transactions has been around since the 1960s and several transaction-processing systems from that time continue to be used today. IBM's CICS and BEA's Tuxedo are two such systems. However, the advent of Java and J2EE truly popularized transactions, bringing them to the forefront of everyday computing. Unlike previous standardization tools, J2EE took the step of mandating transaction support: Vendors have to provide transactional capabilities for their users. This being the case, knowing what transactions are and how they can help you in your application design are of crucial importance.

What Are Atomic Transactions?

Consider the case of a distributed system where each machine provides various services, such as data storage, printing, bank accounts and so on, that can be invoked by an application program. It is natural to require that an application using a collection of these services behaves consistently in the presence of failures. Let's consider a very simple example: Imagine an online bank that allows customers to transfer funds between accounts (`CurrentAccount` and `SavingsAccount`), and let's further assume that Mr. Smith has both of these accounts whose balances are $500 and $1400, respectively. As shown, the bank is responsible for communicating with the transaction service to start and end the transaction Mr. Smith will use to manage transferring his funds.

Mr. Smith wants to transfer $400 from the `CurrentAccount` to the `SavingsAccount` and because of bank processes, this will occur in the following steps:

1. Read the amount of money in the `CurrentAccount` to determine that there are enough funds to transfer.

2. Debit $400 from the `CurrentAccount`.

3. Credit $400 to the `SavingsAccount`.

4. The bank checks that the `CurrentAccount` is still in credit and if not, charges Mr. Smith for an overdraft.

The transfer process may be affected by failures of software or hardware that could affect the overall consistency of the system in a number of ways. For example, if a failure occurs between steps 2 and 3, then it is entirely possible for the $400 to be removed from the `CurrentAccount` and to vanish into the ether rather than be credited to the `SavingsAccount`. This loss of data integrity would have dire consequences for the user and ultimately the bank!

Now let's assume that Mrs. Smith wants to withdraw $200 from the `CurrentAccount` to go shopping. Her withdrawal goes through the following steps:

1. Check the `CurrentAccount` has sufficient funds.

2. Withdraw $200.

3. The bank checks that the `CurrentAccount` is still in credit and if not, charges Mr. Smith for an overdraft.

If Mrs. Smith withdraws at the same time her husband is transferring funds then it is entirely possible for both operations to see sufficient funds in the `CurrentAccount` for their own requirements, when in fact there is insufficient funds for both. The result is that the `CurrentAccount` ends up $100 overdrawn and Mr. Smith gets an overdraft charge he didn't expect!

What Mr. Smith would like is that accesses to the account are handled in such a manner that consistency of both accounts is maintained despite failures or concurrent access. And this is in fact a more general statement of desirability for distributed applications that manipulate data or shared resources. Fortunately atomic transactions can help here.

Put simply, an atomic transaction is a unit of work that has the following properties (known as the *ACID properties*):

✦ **Atomicity** — The transaction either completes successfully (commits), making the work that was performed within its scope permanent, or it fails, and all its effects are undone (rolled back). If it rolls back, it is as though the transaction never started in the first place.

✦ **Consistency** — The transaction produces consistent results and preserves application-specific invariants.

✦ **Isolation** — Intermediate states produced while a transaction is being executed are not visible to others. Furthermore, transactions appear to be executed serially, even if they are executed concurrently (this is known as the *serialisability property* of transactions). As you will see later in this chapter, it is possible to relax isolation levels to improve application performance and throughput, but this should be done with extreme care.

✦ **Durability** — Once a computation terminates normally, the results produced are not destroyed by subsequent crashes. Any state changes produced (such as the new states of all objects modified within the transaction) are recorded on stable storage.

Therefore, an application that is structured such that all critical data are accessed within and controlled by transactions is guaranteed to preserve data consistency regardless of concurrent access by different users and arbitrary numbers of failures. The *transaction-processing system* is responsible for this guarantee and most applications will be unaware of the extra work that is going on behind the scenes on their behalf. Typically all an application programmer will have to do is start and end a transaction.

Obviously, the previous paragraphs only skim the surface of what transaction-processing systems must do in order to provide data consistency to their users. There's no such thing as a free lunch, and attendant upon transactional guarantees is overhead in terms of enforcing isolation restrictions, atomicity, and (in a distributed environment) messages. Therefore, understanding what happens when you use transactions is important, as it will help you know just when and where to use them.

In the following sections we will examine each of the ACID properties in detail. However, first we will describe the differences between *transactional objects/ services* and *transaction participants/resources*.

Examining Transactional Objects and Participants

Most transaction-processing systems make a distinction between a transactional object or service and the participants controlled by the transaction. Consider the following definitions:

✦ **Transactional object/service** — This is the object that encapsulates the work required to be conducted within the scope of a transaction. This work cannot be committed by the application; control is placed into the transaction's domain. An example of such an object would be an EJB responsible for buying a seat on a flight given user input; only if the user commits the transaction is the ticket for the flight actually purchased. This means that the EJB cannot by itself make the work it is asked to do happen; that is ultimately the responsibility of the transaction and the associated transactional participant.

✦ **Transactional participants/resources** — Under the manipulation of the transaction, this is the entity that controls the outcome of the work performed by the transactional object. In the preceding example, as illustrated in Figure 10-1, if the flight-purchasing EJB uses a database to store information on seat availability, it will typically access this information via a JDBC driver. SQL statements will be sent to the database for processing (for example, reserve seat 4A) via the driver, but these statements will be tentative and only commit when (and if) the transaction does so. In order to do this the driver/database will associate a participant with the transaction. This will inform the database of the transaction outcome.

> **Cross-Reference**   See Chapter 14 for a discussion of EJB architecture and design.

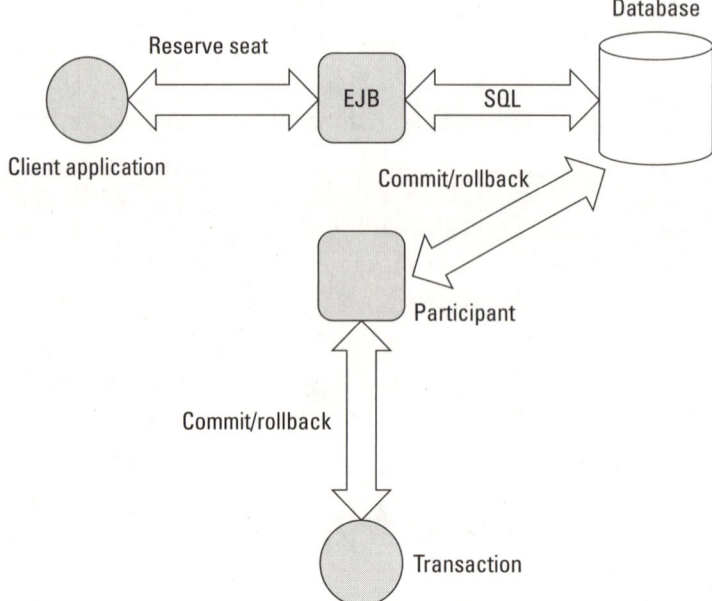

Figure 10-1: Transactional object and participant

Before we can go any further, we had better look at what exactly happens when a transaction terminates. In the next few sections, we'll look at the two-phase commit protocol and some of the various optimizations that are available in many implementations.

Reviewing Atomicity and the Two-Phase Commit Protocol

Associated with every transaction is a *coordinator,* which is responsible for governing the outcome of the transaction. The coordinator may be implemented as a separate service or may be co-located with the user for improved performance—that is, within the same Java Virtual Machine (JVM). It communicates with participants enlisted with its transaction to inform them of the desired termination requirements—whether they should commit or roll back the work done within the scope of the transaction.

In order to ensure that a transaction has an atomic (all or nothing) outcome, a two-phase commit protocol is required to obtain consensus between the various participants. Figure 10-2 illustrates the main aspects of this protocol. During the first phase, known as the *prepare phase,* the transaction coordinator, C, attempts to communicate with both transaction participants, A and B, to determine whether they can commit or roll back. A rollback response, or no response, from any participant acts as a veto on the transaction, causing it to roll back. Based upon these responses, the coordinator decides whether to commit or roll back the transaction. If the decision is to commit the transaction, the coordinator records this decision on stable storage (in the *transaction log*) and the protocol enters the second phase. In this phase the coordinator forces the participants to carry out the decision. The coordinator also informs the participants if the transaction rolls back.

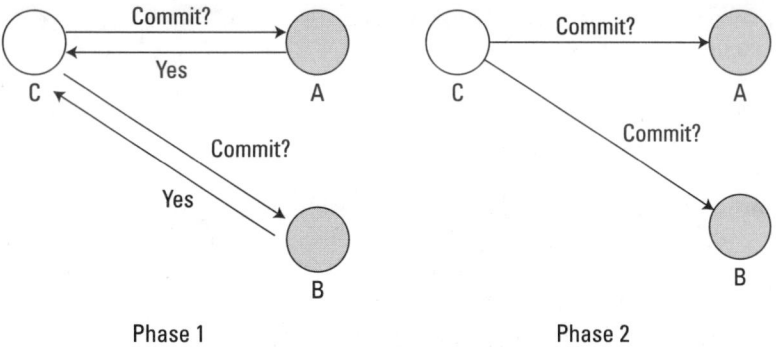

Figure 10-2: Two-phase commit protocol

When each participant receives the prepare message from the coordinator, it must determine whether or not it can commit the work that it controls. If it can, it must record sufficient information on stable storage to either commit or roll back changes made during the transaction.

After returning the prepare response, each participant that returned a commit response *must* remain blocked until it has received the coordinator's second-phase message. Until the participants receive this message, the resources they manage (such as database tables) are unavailable for use by other transactions. If the coordinator fails before delivering this message, these resources must remain blocked until the crashed machines have recovered; in this situation, specialized crash-recovery mechanisms are employed by the transaction system to ensure that any transactions or resources affected by the failures are completed (either committed or rolled back). Therefore the protocol is (eventually) unblocked.

Optimizations

The standard two-phase commit protocol has several variants, and the differences among these variants can mean significant differences in performance and recovery from failures. We will briefly describe the ones most commonly found in modern transaction-processing systems:

✦ **Presumed rollback** — The transaction coordinator need not record information about the participants in stable storage until it decides to commit — that is, until after the prepare phase has completed successfully. If the transaction rolls back either before or after prepare, the coordinator need not inform enlisted participants; it does this only as a courtesy, as failure to contact a participant has no effect on the transaction outcome. If a subsequent request for the status of the transaction occurs no information will be available in the log, and the requestor will be able to assume that the transaction has rolled back.

✦ **One-phase** — If only a single participant is involved in the transaction a prepare phase is not necessary, because consensus is implicit (a participant should be able to agree with itself, after all). Therefore, the participant will simply be told to commit. In some variants the transaction coordinator need not record information about the decision, because the outcome of the transaction is solely down to the participant.

✦ **Read-only** — If a participant is responsible for an object or service that did not do any work during the course of the transaction, or that did not do any work that modified state, it does not need to be informed about the outcome of the transaction because its fate has no effect on the transaction. This being the case, it can indicate to the coordinator during prepare that it is a *read-only participant* and it will be omitted from the second phase of the commit protocol.

Heuristics and removing the two-phase block

As you have seen, in order to guarantee atomicity the *two-phase commit protocol* is necessarily blocking. If the coordinator fails after having issued prepare, participants must remain in this state until they hear the outcome from the transaction coordinator. Since recovery may take an arbitrary amount of time, participants may remain blocked indefinitely. Obviously some applications and participants cannot tolerate being blocked.

As a result, quite early in the development of transaction-processing systems developers worked to control this problem in a controlled way: As a result, participants that have gotten past the prepare phase are allowed to make autonomous decisions as to whether they commit or roll back. A participant that makes such a decision *must* record it in case the participant is eventually contacted in order that the original transaction can be completed. If the coordinator eventually informs the participant of the fate of the transaction and it is the same as the autonomous choice the participant made, there is obviously no problem: The participant simply got there before the coordinator did! However, if the decision is contrary, a non-atomic outcome has happened — a *heuristic outcome,* with a corresponding *heuristic decision.* At this point we are no longer in the world of ACID transactions; we have entered the heuristic zone!

A participant is free to make a heuristic decision at any time after it has been told to prepare (and told the coordinator it can commit). The implementer of a participant may choose never to make an autonomous choice for fear of causing a non-atomic outcome: Just because heuristics are allowed does not mean that they have to be used.

Other implementations may choose to make autonomous decisions when they have not heard from the coordinator within a day of being asked to prepare, since most transaction commits take seconds or minutes to complete. Obviously the choice the participant makes (to commit or to roll back) will depend upon the participant implementation and possibly the application or environment in which the participant finds itself. For example, an implementation that controls a nuclear reactor's control rods may decide to always fail-safe and drop the rods back into the reactor — that is, to roll back — if it does not hear from the administrator.

The possible heuristic outcomes are as follows:

✦ **Heuristic rollback** — The commit operation failed because some or all of the participants unilaterally rolled back the transaction.

✦ **Heuristic commit** — An attempted rollback operation failed because all the participants unilaterally committed. This may happen if, for example, the coordinator was able to successfully prepare the transaction but then decided to roll it back (because it could not update its log, for instance), while in the meantime the participants decided to commit.

✦ **Heuristic mixed** — Some updates were committed while others were rolled back.

✦ **Heuristic hazard** — The disposition of some of the updates is unknown. Those that are known have either all been committed or all been rolled back.

How heuristic outcomes are reported to the application and resolved is usually the domain of complex, manually-driven system-administration tools. Attempting an automatic resolution requires semantic information about the nature of participants involved in the transaction that is normally not available to most transaction-processing systems.

It is worthwhile to check how your transaction implementation of choice manages heuristics before you use transactions in anger. Resolving heuristics without good support from the transaction system can be a long and arduous task, and further errors may occur during the resolution process. For example, imagine finding that the airline-reservation center and credit-card sites had autonomously booked your plane ticket and charged you for the pleasure when you had told the reservation transaction to roll back. Resolving this problem is not trivial even if you find out immediately that the errors have occurred, but if the transaction system does not tell you which participants did not guarantee atomicity, you may not learn about the errors until the tickets arrive in the mail — followed by your credit card bill!

Understanding Local and Distributed Transactions

So far, we haven't said anything about whether transactions are running in a local or remote application or environment. In fact we have said nothing about locality. So, let's address that in the next few sections.

Local transactions

A *local transaction* is one that is created and committed against a single resource such as a database. Local transactions can be used for a large number of applications in which the same database instance is being used. In addition, support for local transactions is mandated in order for a JDBC driver to claim full compliance. Therefore, you can generally expect the ability to create and manage local transactions against most databases you will encounter in your J2EE travels.

If we concentrate purely on local transactions within J2EE, JDBC connections have an auto-commit mode, which by default is set to "on". What this means is that every SQL statement created by the connection will be executed within its own transaction, which will be committed immediately upon completion. In order to associate more than one statement with a transaction you must disable this mode. The following code, in which `con` represents an object that implements the `java.sql.Connection` interface, shows how the auto-commit mode is disabled:

```
con.setAutoCommit(false);
```

If auto-commit is disabled, a transaction will be implicitly created and associated with the connection when the first ever statement is executed, but the transaction will not be committed until the application explicitly calls the connection's `commit()` method. At that stage *all* statements that were executed prior to the last call to `commit()` will be committed. Likewise, the application can call `rollback()` and undo all the statements. The following code illustrates the general sequence for committing multiple statements simultaneously:

```
// turn off auto-commit mode
con.setAutoCommit (false);
// create a statement
Statement update1 = con.createStatement ();
// execute an update
update1.executeUpdate (. . .);
// create a second statement
Statement update2 = con.createStatement ();
// execute a second update
update2.executeUpdate (. . .);
// commit the transaction
con.commit ();
```

In this example the auto-commit mode is disabled for the connection. Subsequently, two different updates are executed with the context of the same transaction since both statements are associated with the transactional connection. When the `commit()` method is invoked both of the updates will be made permanent in the target database.

The following are the advantages and disadvantages of using auto-commit:

> If auto-commit is enabled for a given connection and multiple statements are executed during the application, the potential exists for multiple unnecessary commits. An inherent overhead associated with database commits may degrade the performance of such an application. For example, making a backup copy of the object state prior to performing updates and then overwriting the state with the final state of the object if the transaction commits, or replacing the state with the backup. Disabling auto-commit can improve performance.

> Database locks associated with transactional processing may cause performance degradation in a situation involving multiple concurrent users. In such a situation, a developer may choose to enable auto-commit so the database locks are not held for long durations.

In general, therefore, you need to consider carefully where to place the transactional boundaries for statement execution in order to optimize an application's throughput.

Distributed transactions

In order for a transaction to span a distributed number of services or tasks, certain information has to flow between the sites or domains involved in the application. This information is commonly referred to as the *context* and includes the following elements:

Globally unique transaction identifier

Coordinator location or endpoint address so participants can be registered

As shown in Figure 10-3, the context is propagated by means of whatever distribution mechanism is appropriate to the environment in which it is used. The context is typically propagated implicitly as part of normal message interchange within an application. That is to say, the application programmer need not do anything to ensure that the context is propagated on remote invocations.

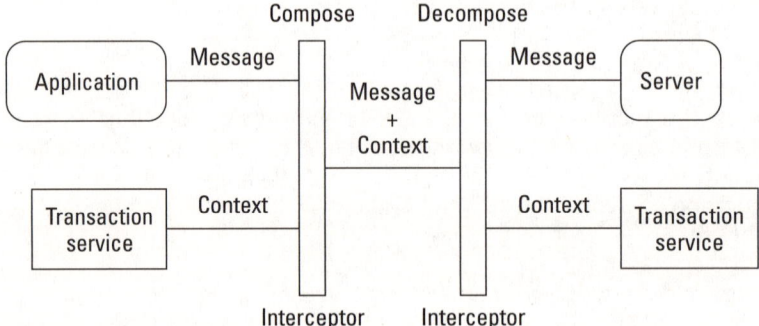

Figure 10-3: Relationship between services and contexts

Transaction-processing systems typically use interceptors to add the transaction context associated with the invoking thread to the outgoing application message. As shown in the figure, when the interceptor is called it asks the transaction service for the necessary information about the transaction (if any) associated with the application thread performing the remote-service invocation.

On the service side, the transaction context is stripped off the message and associated with the thread that is about to do the work requested. As you will see in the following section, the transaction associated may be the original transaction resident at the client, or it may entail the domain importing the transaction context to create a local transaction proxy for the remote transaction. In either event, it appears as though the transaction seamlessly crosses process/machine boundaries.

Interposition

Consider the situation depicted in Figure 10-4, which involves a transaction coordinator and three participants. Let's assume that each of these participants is on a different machine from the coordinator and from each other. Each of the lines connecting the coordinator to the participants also represents the invocations from the coordinator to the participants and vice versa. Now perform the following actions:

1. Enroll a participant in the transaction.

2. Execute the two-phase commit protocol.

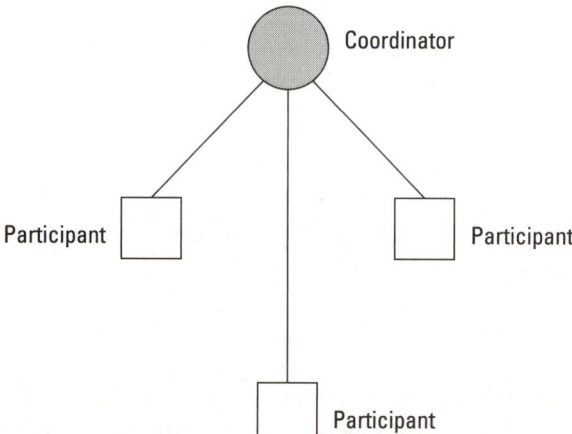

Figure 10-4: Illustration of a distributed transaction

The overhead involved in making these distributed invocations will depend upon a number of factors, including how congested the network is, the load on the respective machines, and the number of transactions being executed. In addition, as the number of participants increases, so does the overhead involved in the coordinator's executing the two-phase commit protocol.

A common way to help reduce this overhead involves first recognizing the fact that as far as a coordinator is concerned it does not matter what the participant implementation is. However, although one participant may interact with a database to commit the transaction, another may just as readily be responsible for forwarding the coordinators' messages to a number of databases — essentially acting as a coordinator itself, as shown in Figure 10-5.

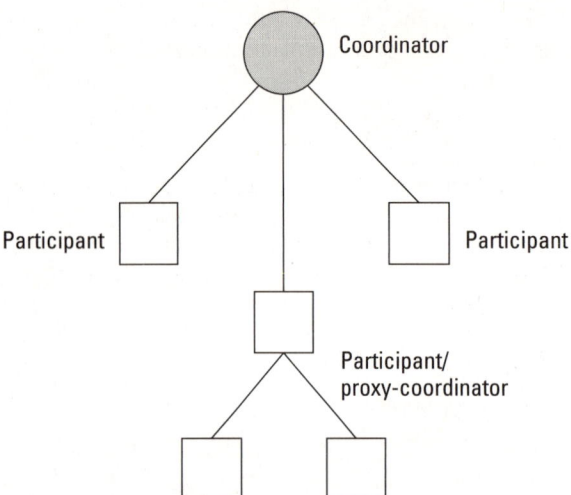

Figure 10-5: Example of a participant also acting as a subordinate coordinator

In this case, the participant is acting like a proxy for the transaction coordinator (the root coordinator). In the example, the proxy coordinator is responsible for interacting with the two participants when it receives an invocation from the coordinator and for collating their responses (and its own) for the coordinator. As far as a participant is concerned a coordinator invokes it, whereas as far as the root coordinator is concerned it only sees participants.

This technique of using proxy coordinators (also known as *subordinate coordinators* or *sub-coordinators*) is known as *interposition*. Each domain (machine) that imports a transaction context may create a subordinate coordinator that enrolls with the imported coordinator as though it were a participant. Any participants required to enroll in the transaction within this domain actually enroll with the subordinate coordinator. In a large distributed application a tree of coordinators and participants may be created, as illustrated in Figure 10-6.

Because a subordinate coordinator must execute the two-phase commit protocol on its enlisted participants, it must have its own transaction log and corresponding failure-recovery subsystem. The subordinate must record sufficient recovery information for any work it may do as a participant, *and* it must record additional recovery information in its role as a coordinator.

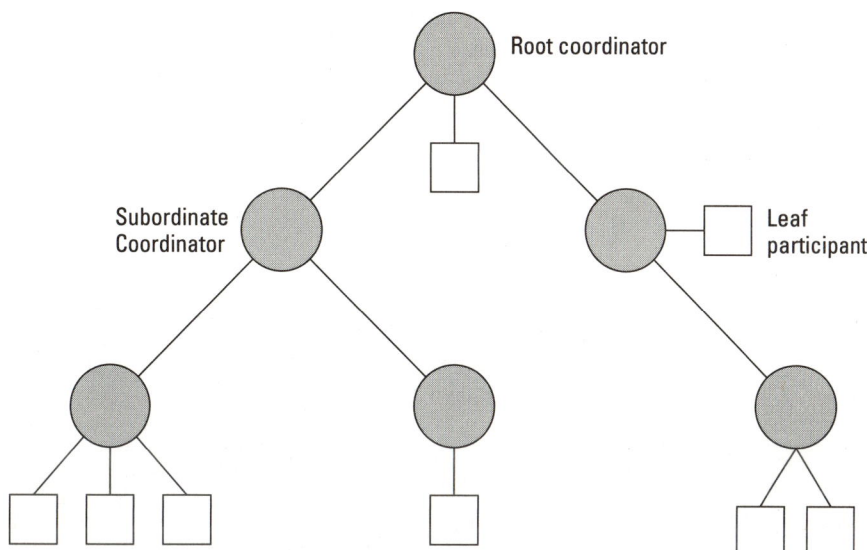

Figure 10-6: Example tree structure of a distributed transaction with interposition

Now, you may be asking yourself, "Why do I need to know this?" The answer is fairly simple and straightforward: Any decent distributed transaction system will provide you with interposition as standard, and if it does not you should look elsewhere. In our experience, the performance advantages of using interposition can be significant as soon as the number of participants from a single machine gets above one. Although you may not foresee such an occurrence, it's easy for one to happen as your applications grow with customer needs. If you don't have the support now you may not have it when you really need it, and that could leave you with just one choice: moving to another vendor implementation. Despite standards, moving from one vendor implementation to another is not trivial and gets more and more complex as your applications get bigger and bigger. Plan for the future now and don't take the risk.

So far, we've considered atomicity (the A in ACID) and some of the issues involved when using transactions in a distributed environment. Now let's look at the I (isolation) property of an ACID transaction.

Understanding Consistency

A transactional application should maintain the consistency of the resources (databases, file systems, and so on) that it uses. In essence, transactional applications should move from one consistent state to another. However, unlike the other transactional properties (atomicity, isolation, and durability), consistency is something that the transaction system cannot achieve by itself because it does not possess any semantic information about the resources it manipulates; it would be impossible for a transaction-processing system to assert that the resources are moving to (or from) consistent states. All a transaction system can ensure is that any state changes that do occur are performed in a manner that is guaranteed despite failures. It is the application programmer's responsibility to ensure consistency—in whatever way makes sense for the resources concerned.

Whereas consistency is really a property of the application, the next ACID property we'll consider (isolation) sits between the application and the transaction service. Luckily for us, it can be tied quite closely to consistency.

Introducing Isolation (Serializability)

This property ensures that the concurrent executions of programs that access common objects are free from *interference* (that is, it ensures that the concurrent execution can be shown to be equivalent to some serial order of execution). Some form of concurrency control policy is required to ensure this property. Typically this policy is implemented by means of locks associated with the resource being managed. When a data item is accessed from within a transaction a lock is acquired on it. This lock may be of either of the following types:

   ✦ **READ**—This type of lock is acquired by the resource prior to reading the data item.

   ✦ **WRITE**—This type of lock is acquired by the resource prior to updating the data item.

The most common locking rule allows for concurrent read access to a data item while requiring exclusive access for data updates. In other words, a READ lock associated with one transaction does not conflict with READ locks from other transactions, whereas a WRITE lock conflicts with all other types of lock from other transactions.

In order to ensure transaction serializability, locking must follow a two-phase policy, as illustrated in Figure 10-7. During the first phase, termed the *growing phase,* a computation can acquire locks but not release them. The second phase of the computation is the *shrinking phase,* during which time held locks can be released but no locks can be acquired.

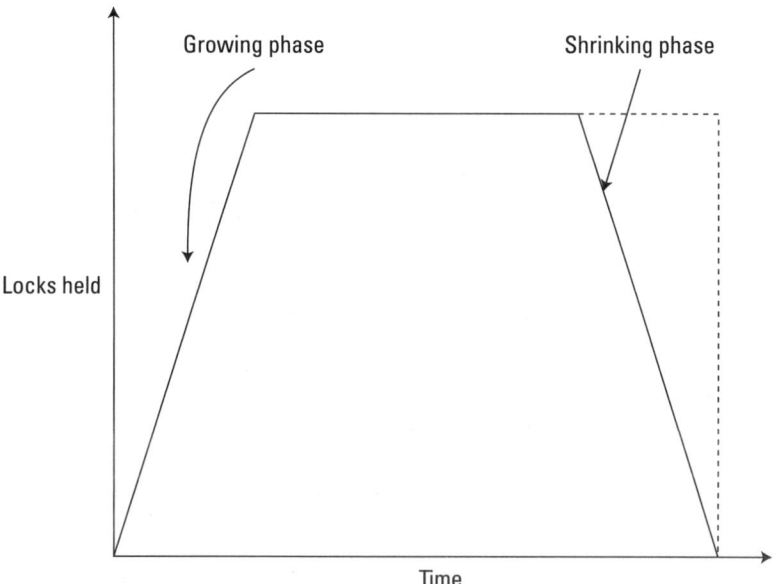

Figure 10-7: How locks are acquired during transaction

Now suppose that a transaction in its shrinking phase is to be rolled back and that some objects with write locks have already been released. If some of these objects have been locked on behalf of other transactions, rolling back of the first transaction will require these transactions to be rolled back as well. To avoid this *cascade rollback* problem, it is necessary to make the shrinking phase appear to be instantaneous, as shown in the preceding figure by the dotted lines. In effect this means that all the held locks are released simultaneously.

Optimistic versus pessimistic concurrency control

Most transaction systems use what is commonly referred to as *pessimistic concurrency control:* Whenever a data structure or other transactional resource is accessed, a lock is obtained on it. This lock will remain held for the duration of the transaction. The benefit of this is that other users will not be able to modify (and possibly not even be able to observe) the resource until the holding transaction has terminated. This style has the following disadvantages:

There can be significant overhead involved in acquiring and maintaining concurrency-control information in an environment where conflict or data sharing is not high.

Deadlocks may occur, in which one user waits for another to release a lock not realizing that that user is waiting for the release of a lock held by the first.

Optimistic concurrency control assumes that conflicts are not high and tries to ensure locks are held only briefly. It requires a means of detecting whether an update to a resource does conflict with any updates that may have occurred in the interim, and a means of determining how to recover from those conflicts. Typically detection will be made by means of timestamps: The system will take a snapshot of the timestamps associated with resources and compare them with the timestamps available when the transaction commits. Resolution is a different problem entirely, because it requires semantic information about the resources concerned. Therefore, most transaction systems that offer optimistic schemes will typically cause the detecting transaction to roll back. After rollback the application must retry, this time with new data.

Assuming both types of concurrency control are available, whether to use optimistic or pessimistic concurrency control is up to the user and the application being considered. A close examination of the environment in which the application and transactional resources reside is necessary to determine whether shared access to resources should occur, and the probability that sharing will cause a transaction to have to roll back.

Unfortunately, most J2EE transaction systems support only pessimistic concurrency control. This obviously makes the choice of which type to use easier, but it still presents performance problems. However, as you will see in the following sections, within pessimistic concurrency control are ways of removing potential performance bottlenecks.

Degrees of isolation

One of the problems with two-phase locking is that if the majority of requests on data are read-only, locks may be held for a long time and thus reduce the concurrency possible within the system to unacceptable levels. Consider for example that rather than reserving a seat on an airline, someone may decide to browse and see which seats have been allocated and to whom. If such a user does this within a single transaction, every seat he or she looks at will potentially have a READ lock obtained for it and prevent other users from reserving that seat (reservation obviously requires a WRITE lock because the state of the seat is being updated). Those seats will be unavailable for the duration of the browsing user's transaction.

In order to address this problem weaker locking rules were introduced, ranging in severity from no transactional support to very strict access control. As the transaction level gets higher greater care is taken to avoid conflicts. In addition, higher transaction levels yield slower execution times because of the need for increased database locking and the resultant decrease in concurrency between clients. Thus, because of the inherent performance implications, careful consideration is required when selecting the isolation level for a given application. In the following sections we will describe the following levels:

✦ None

✦ Read uncommitted

✦ Read committed

✦ Repeatable read

✦ Serializable

None

None is the lowest isolation level, indicating that transactions are not supported. Strictly speaking this level is not valid, because isolation is a prerequisite for transactionality.

Read uncommitted

Read uncommitted specifies that the following types of reads can occur:

✦ Dirty reads

✦ Non-repeatable reads

✦ Phantom reads

Dirty reads

A dirty read takes place when uncommitted data is read from the database. This will commonly happen when Transaction A reads information that has been modified by Transaction B before the latter has actually committed the transaction. Consequently, the information read by Transaction A may not be valid if Transaction B is rolled back.

Non-repeatable reads

A non-repeatable takes place when the data read within the scope of a transaction would be different if the query were repeated.

Phantom reads

Finally, a phantom read occurs when Transaction A queries for data satisfying a given condition, Transaction B subsequently inserts or updates data such that another row now meets the condition in Transaction A, and Transaction A later repeats the query. The new row is referred to as a *phantom row*.

This transaction level is most appropriate for situations in which an application is simply querying for data that is rarely modified, or that is designated as read-only. In this situation the application will perform optimally because little or no locking overhead is incurred.

Read committed

Read committed allows non-repeatable and phantom reads while precluding reading of uncommitted data. In other words, this isolation level ensures that an executing query sees only data that existed in the database *before* the transaction was initiated; it does not see uncommitted data or changes committed by concurrent transactions. The possibility does exist that two successive queries in the same transaction could see different results if other queries commit data between the execution of the two (see non-repeatable read above).

Note   This isolation level is supported by most databases and is generally the default level. The isolation provided by this level is adequate for many applications, but for applications that require complex database interactions a more rigorously consistent view of the database may be required.

Repeatable read

In addition to the data consistency attained with read-committed isolation, a repeatable read ensures that executing the same query multiple times will result in the same data set even if another transaction modifies the data. Transaction with this isolation level can therefore only execute repeatable reads.

Serializable

The serializable isolation level mandates that the transaction has exclusive update privileges to the database data; other concurrent transactions can neither write nor read the same data. In addition, the transaction has no view into data modifications performed by other concurrent transactions; the data view of the given transaction does not change from the view provided when the transaction is initiated.

We've looked at Atomicity, Consistency, and Isolation, so that only leaves Durability for us to consider in the next section. Along with Atomicity, Durability is perhaps the most important aspect of transactions. It can certainly have a significant impact on performance.

Understanding the Role of Durability

The durability (persistence) property requires that any state changes that occur during the transaction must be saved in a manner such that a subsequent failure will not cause them to be lost. How these state changes are made durable is dependent on the transaction system and the resources ultimately used to commit the work done by the transactional objects.

Note   The durability property can never be a guarantee, because a catastrophic failure (such as corruption of the hard disk) can ultimately result in total loss of information.

Although most users of transactions will consider durability as an aspect for the application and its objects or participants (remember what a participant must do during the commit protocol?), an aspect also exists within the transaction-system implementation itself. In order to guarantee atomicity in the presence of failures (both transaction coordinator and participant), it is necessary for the transaction service to maintain durable state. What this state comprises will depend upon the implementation. For example, the coordinator may have to remember the point in the protocol it has reached (that is, whether it is committing or rolling back), the identity of all registered participants, and what part of the protocol those participants have reached.

This information is recorded in what is typically referred to as the *transaction log*. Some implementations may maintain a separate log (file) for each transaction, which is removed when it is no longer needed. An implementation might also have a single log for all transactions, in which the transaction information is appended to the end of the log and pruned from the log when the respective transaction completes.

All of this information regarding durability is needed in case of failures so that the transaction system can eventually complete any transactions affected (whether this is to commit or rollback). In the next section, we'll look at how failure recovery uses this information.

Performing Failure Recovery

Failures occur in all computing systems, both centralized and distributed. The more components involved with an application, the greater the chance of a failure occurring. In a distributed system, failures are often independent — the failure of one component does not necessarily cause the (immediate) failure of another. In order to deal with this situation, transaction-service implementations typically possess failure-recovery subsystems that will ensure that results of a transaction are applied consistently to all resources affected by the transaction, even if some of the application processes or the machine hosting them crash or lose network connectivity. In the case of machine (system) crash or network failure, the recovery will not take place until the system or network is restored, but the original application does not need to be restarted: Recovery responsibility is typically delegated to a separate recovery process.

Recovery after failure requires that information about the transaction and the resources involved survive the failure and be accessible afterward: This information (the transaction log mentioned in the previous section) is held in some durable state-store and therefore available upon machine recovery. Typically the recovery system scans the transaction log to determine whether any transactions require recovery. If such transactions exist, the information within the log is used to recreate the transaction and continue to complete it. What action the recovery subsystem performs will depend upon which flavor of two-phase commit the transaction system uses; for example, in a presumed rollback protocol, the fact that a log entry exists implicitly means that the transaction was in the process of committing.

Until the recovery procedures are complete, resources affected by a transaction that was in progress at the time of the failure may be inaccessible. For database resources, this situation may be reported as tables or rows held by *in-doubt transactions*. Recall that resources previously prepared may make an autonomous decision about whether to commit or roll back if the coordinator fails. Upon recovery, this autonomous decision may result in a non-atomic outcome. For example, the recovered coordinator sends a participant the second-phase commit message only to find that the participant has previously rolled back; this heuristic outcome will be reported to the coordinator, which should then report it to the application or system administrator to resolve.

What we have described so far assumes that recovery occurs from the coordinator (a system known as *top-down recovery*). However, this is not necessarily always the case. In fact, recovery may have to be driven from the participant (which is known as *bottom-up recovery*). So, for example, if a machine on which a participant resides fails and then recovers, the participant may need to enquire as to the status of the transaction. If participants wait for recovery to be driven from the top down, the following problems could occur:

> If the coordinator has also failed and recovered, it may take some time before the recovery subsystem gets around to recovering the specific transaction; hence resources may be inaccessible for longer than necessary.

> If a presumed rollback protocol is used, and the participant fails after having said it could prepare, and the coordinator fails before it writes its log, no recovery will take place on behalf of that transaction — no log entry means the transaction has rolled back. Hence, the participant will never get a termination message from the recovery subsystem.

Because of these problems, most transaction systems require that a failure-recovery component exist on both the coordinator and participant machines so that recovery can be driven in a bi-directional manner.

We've seen how all of the ACID properties of transactions are provided. In the next few sections, let's turn our attention to what kind of system provides transactions (the transaction processing monitor).

Using Transaction-Processing Monitors

So far we have talked mainly about transaction systems, or transaction-processing systems. These enforce ACID properties for transactional resources by using a two-phase commit protocol in conjunction with two-phase locking. But most transaction products are sold as *transaction-processing monitors* (TPMs). A product that supports the development of transactional applications or systems is identified as a TPM and provides the following features:

Toolkits and APIs to allow transactions to be demarcated (created and terminated) and controlled in a distributed environment (given our definition of a transaction system, we can say that it is at the heart of this part of the TPM)

Security requirements are integrated. An execution environment to manage transaction load to maintain high throughput as the number of transactions to be executed increases — transactions may be automatically distributed across a number of different execution environments

Transactions are highly available. If a transaction fails it may be automatically restarted on another machine, or multiple copies (replicas) may be executed to mask failures

Administration services for configuring, monitoring, and managing transactions and transactional applications

In the world of J2EE, many of these services may seem familiar — they form the heart of application servers. A TPM is essentially a transaction-aware application server, and, in fact, many of the features found in J2EE application servers have their basis in transaction-processing monitors. Likewise, many modern-day TPMs are Java application servers with transaction-service cores.

While most transaction systems provide ACID transactions, there are places where they simply don't work: ACID is too strong. So, let's briefly look at other types of transactions and where J2EE is going in this area.

Transaction Models

The most common form of transaction that you will use is called a *top-level transaction* and it exhibits all the ACID properties. However, traditional transaction-processing systems are sufficient if an application function can be represented as a single top-level transaction. Frequently this is not the case. Top-level transactions are most suitably viewed as "short-lived" entities, performing stable state changes to the system; they are less suited when used in "long-lived" application functions (such as running for minutes, hours, or days). Long-lived top-level transactions may reduce the concurrency in the system to an unacceptable level by holding on to resources (such as locks) for a long time; furthermore, if such a transaction rolls back, much valuable work could be undone. Several enhancements to the traditional flat-transaction model have been proposed and we will briefly describe the following ones in this section:

✦ Nested transactions

✦ Nested top-level transactions

✦ Extended transaction models and the J2EE Activity Service

Nested transactions

Given a system that provides transactions for certain operations, it is sometimes necessary to combine them to form another operation, which is also required to be a transaction. The resulting transaction's effects are a combination of the effects of the transactions from which it is composed. The transactions contained within the resulting transaction are called *nested transactions* (or *sub-transactions*), and the resulting transaction is referred to as the *enclosing transaction*. The enclosing transaction is sometimes referred to as the *parent* of a nested (or *child*) transaction. A hierarchical transaction structure can thus result, as shown in Figure 10-8, in which each ellipse is a separate transaction.

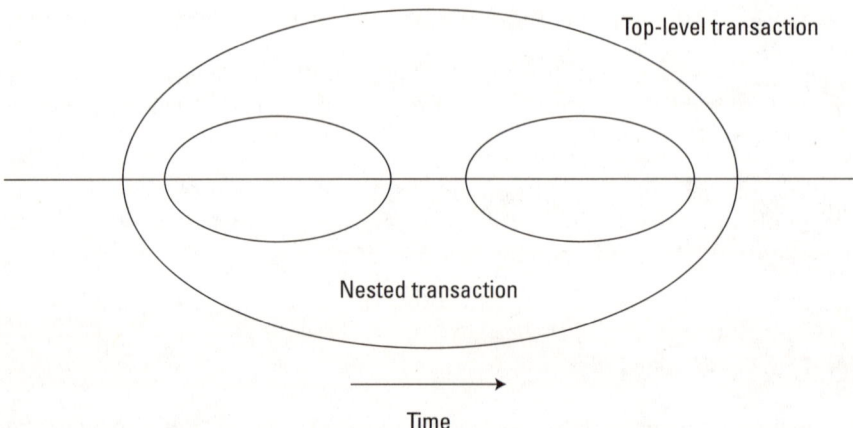

Figure 10-8: Diagrammatic representation of a nested transaction

Note   If a remote invocation is made within the scope of a nested transaction, the transaction context may contain information about the entire hierarchy and not just the most current transaction.

An important difference exists between nested and top-level transactions: The effect of a nested transaction is provisional upon the commit or rollback of its enclosing transaction(s). That is to say, the effects will be recovered if the enclosing transaction rolls back, even if the nested transaction has initially committed.

Sub-transactions are useful for two reasons:

✦ **Fault isolation** — If a sub-transaction rolls back the enclosing transaction is not required to roll back as well, so any work already done is preserved.

✦ **Modularity** — If a transaction is already associated with a call when a new transaction is begun, the transaction may be automatically nested within it. Therefore a programmer who knows that an object requires transactions can use them within the object. If the object's methods are invoked without a client transaction, the object's transactions will simply be top-level; otherwise, they will be nested within the scope of the client's transactions. Likewise, a client need not know that the object is transactional and can begin its own transaction.

Note   Because nested transactions do not make any state changes durable until the enclosing top-level transaction commits, they do not need failure-recovery mechanisms.

Nested top-level transactions

In addition to normal top-level and nested transactions are *nested top-level* transactions, which can be used to relax isolation in a controlled manner. With this mechanism it is possible to invoke a top-level transaction from within another transaction, regardless of the depth of the current transaction hierarchy. As illustrated in Figure 10-9, a nested top-level transaction can be executed from *anywhere* within another transaction and behaves *exactly* like a normal top-level transaction: Its results are made permanent when it commits and will not be undone if any of the transactions within which it was originally nested roll back. In the event that the invoking transaction rolls back compensation may be required.

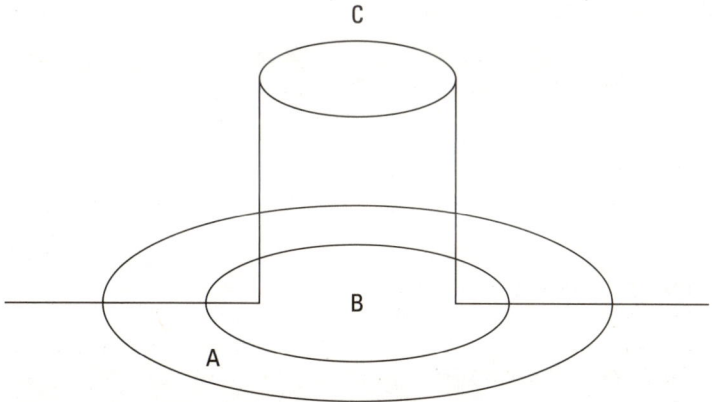

Figure 10-9: Diagrammatic representation of an independent top-level transaction

Figure 10-9 shows a typical nesting of transactions, wherein Transaction B is nested within Transaction A. Although Transaction C is logically nested within B, because it is an independent top-level transaction it will commit or roll back independently of the other transactions within the structure.

Extended transaction models and the J2EE Activity Service

Building certain activities from transactions that execute for an extended period of time (typically called *long-running transactions*) can reduce the amount of concurrency within an application or, in the event of failures, require work to be performed again. For example, in certain classes of application it is known that resources acquired within a transaction can be released "early," rather than having to wait until the transaction terminates. However, in the event of the transaction rolling back, certain compensation may be necessary to restore the system to a consistent state. One way of approaching this specific problem would be to use nested top-level transactions.

Consider the following situation. A user wants to book an entire trip, including a taxi (*t1*), reserving a table at a restaurant (*t2*), reserving a seat at the theatre (*t3*), and then booking a room at a hotel (*t4*), as shown in Figure 10-10. If all the application activity happens within a single transaction (indicated by the dotted ellipse), the taxi resource, restaurant resource, and so on will remain locked until the entire trip has been arranged. This situation will most likely be unacceptable to the individual service providers if the booking takes the user longer than a matter of minutes to conclude.

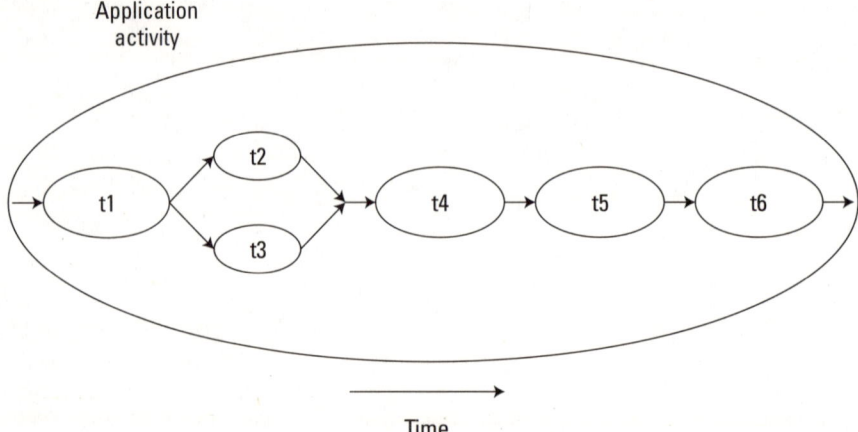

Figure 10-10: This logical long-running transaction does not encounter failure.

Therefore, as Figure 10-10 shows, we can structure each service interaction as a separate transaction (the solid ellipses) to form a logical long-running transaction. However, if failures and concurrent access occur during the lifetime of these transactional activities, the behavior of the entire logical long-running transaction may not possess ACID properties. Furthermore, some form of (application-specific) compensation may be required to attempt to return the state of the system to (application-specific) consistency.

For example, let's assume that *t4* has failed (rolls back), as shown in Figure 10-11. Further, let's assume that the application can continue to make forward progress, but that in order to do so it must now undo some state changes made prior to the start of *t4* (by *t1, t2,* or *t3*); because *t4* is a transaction, its state changes will be undone automatically by the transaction system, so no form of compensation is required. Therefore, new activities are started: *tc1,* which is a compensation activity that will attempt to undo state changes performed by, say, *t2*; and *t3,* which will continue the application once *tc1* has completed. *tc5'* and *tc6'* are new activities that continue after compensation; for example, because it was not possible to reserve the theater, restaurant, and hotel, it is decided to book tickets at the cinema. Obviously other forms of transaction composition are possible: For example, *t5'* can execute in parallel to *tc1.*

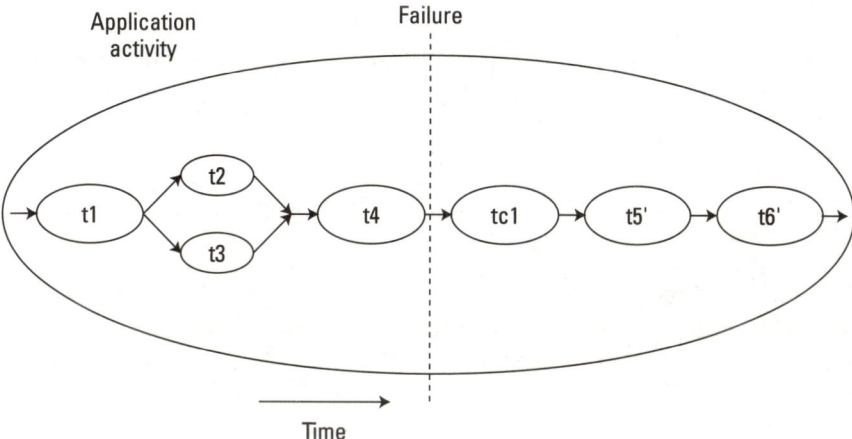

Figure 10-11: This logical long-running transaction encounters failure.

This structuring of top-level transactions in this manner is just one example of what are known as *extended transactions*. However, it is unrealistic to believe that the "one-size-fits-all" paradigm will suffice; a single-model approach to extended transactions is unlikely to be sufficient for all (or even the majority of) applications.

J2EE is tackling this problem with the *Activity Service,* which builds upon work done within the OMG on the definition of a low-level infrastructure to support the coordination and control of abstract, application-specific entities. (Activities are discussed in the next section.) These entities (*activities*) may be transactional, they may use weaker forms of serializability, or they may not be transactional at all; the important point is that the Activity Service is concerned only with their control and coordination, leaving the semantics of such activities to the application programmer.

It's worth pausing for a moment to point out that this is very new and cutting-edge stuff, so please don't expect it to be available from all vendors immediately! It will most probably take a while for this service to make its way into J2EE, but if you are either using transactions now or thinking of using them in the future you're better off knowing now what to expect.

What is an Activity?

An *Activity* is a unit of distributed work that may or may not be transactional. During its lifetime an Activity may have transactional and non-transactional periods. Every entity, including other Activities, can be part of an Activity, although an Activity need not be composed of other Activities. An Activity is used to carry transactional and other essential specifications of the application's contract with its middleware.

Demarcation signals of any kind are communicated to any registered entities (*actions*) through *signals.* For example, the termination of one activity may initiate the start/restart of other activities in a workflow-like environment. Signals can be used to infer a flow of control during the execution of an application. Actions allow an Activity to be independent of the specific work it is required to do for signals.

An Activity may run for an arbitrary length of time, and may use transactions (and sub-transactions) at arbitrary points during its lifetime. For example, consider Figure 10-12, which shows a series of connected Activities cooperating during the lifetime of an application. The solid ellipses represent transaction boundaries, whereas the dotted ellipses represent Activity boundaries. Activity *A1* uses two top-level transactions during its execution, whereas Activity *A2* uses none. Additionally, transactional Activity *A3* has another transactional Activity, *A3',* nested within it.

Just as a thread of control may require transactional and non-transactional periods and can suspend and resume its transactionality, so too may it require periods of non-Activity-related work. Thus, it is possible for an Activity thread to perform some work outside the scope of the activity before returning to Activity-related work. In the example shown in the figure, if the thread performing Activity *A3'* decides to perform some non-Activity-related work, it can do so outside the scope of *A3'* and *A3.*

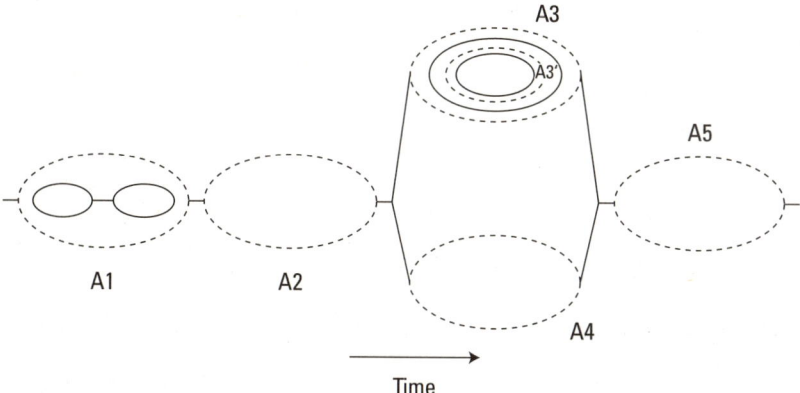

Figure 10-12: The relationship between activities and transactions

Signals, SignalSets, and Actions

An *Activity coordinator* may be implicitly associated with each Activity and is used to drive the Signal and Action interactions. If an Activity has no associated Actions, then it need not have an activity coordinator. Activities that must be informed when another Activity sends a specific Signal can register an appropriate Action with that Activity's coordinator. When the Activity sends a signal (such as at termination time), the coordinator's role is to forward this Signal to all registered Actions and to deal with the outcomes generated by the Actions.

To allow Actions to be selectively signaled, Signals are bound to SignalSets, and Actions are implicitly associated with SignalSets. When a Signal is raised it is within the context of a specific SignalSet, and only those Actions registered with that SignalSet receive the Signal. An Action may register interest in more than one SignalSet and an Activity may use more than one SignalSet during its lifetime.

With the exception of some predefined Signals and SignalSets, the majority of Signals and SignalSets are defined and provided by the higher-level applications that make use of this framework. To use the generic framework provided it is necessary for these higher-level applications to impose application-specific meanings upon Signals and SignalSets — that is, the applications must impose a structure on their abstract form. A Signal with the name foobar can mean one thing when used within one application, but the same name may have a completely different meaning when used elsewhere.

The typical coordinator logic that determines which messages to send to which participants is actually embodied within SignalSets, so the real coordinator can be fairly dumb. This setup enables the same coordinator to be used with any number of different `SignalSet` implementations and hence with any number of associated extended-transaction models. The set of Signals a given `SignalSet` can generate may change from one use to another and the actual set of Signals it sends may be a subset of these Signals. The logic that determines which Signal to send to an Action is hidden within a `SignalSet` and may be as complex or as simple as is required by the Activity implementation. When a Signal is sent to an Action, the Action acts upon the content and returns an outcome, which is passed to the `SignalSet`; the `SignalSet` may then use that information when determining the nature of the next Signal to send.

As shown in Figure 10-13, a given `SignalSet` is assumed to implement a state machine, and so it starts off in the *waiting state* until it is required by the Activity coordinator to send its first Signal, when it either enters the *first Signal state* or the *end state* if it has no Signals to send. Once in the *end state* the `SignalSet` cannot provide any further Signals and will not be reused. If the `SignalSet` enters the *first Signal state* it may then be asked for another Signal to send, and will then either enter the *next Signal state,* or the *end state* if it has no further Signals to send. Once in the *next Signal* state the `SignalSet` will be asked for a new Signal until it enters the *end state*. A new Signal is only requested from the `SignalSet` when all registered Actions have been sent the current Signal, or when an exceptional outcome is generated by an Action.

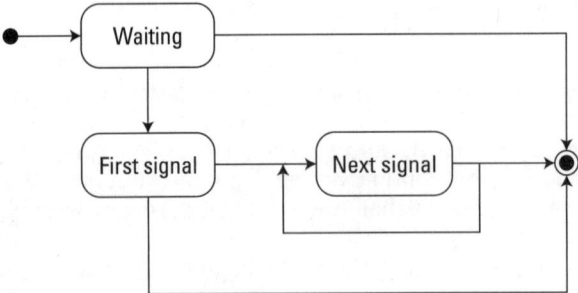

Figure 10-13: The state transitions a SignalSet goes through

For example, suppose we have two `SignalSets` to represent the possible outcomes for a transaction, Rollback and Commit and register Actions with the Activity as the transactional participants. The Signal associated with the Rollback `SignalSet` would simply be "rollback", whereas the Commit `SignalSet` would have "prepare", "commit", and "rollback" Signals. If the application decides to commit, then when called by the Activity Coordinator the `SignalSet` would generate the "prepare" Signal to be sent to the registered Actions, as shown in Figure 10-14. The Activity Coordinator would then send this Signal to each Action, and inform the

`SignalSet` of the result. Assuming none of the Actions returns an exceptional response to this Signal, then when all Actions have received the "prepare" Signal, and the Activity Coordinator asks the `SignalSet` for the next Signal, it will return the "commit" Signal.

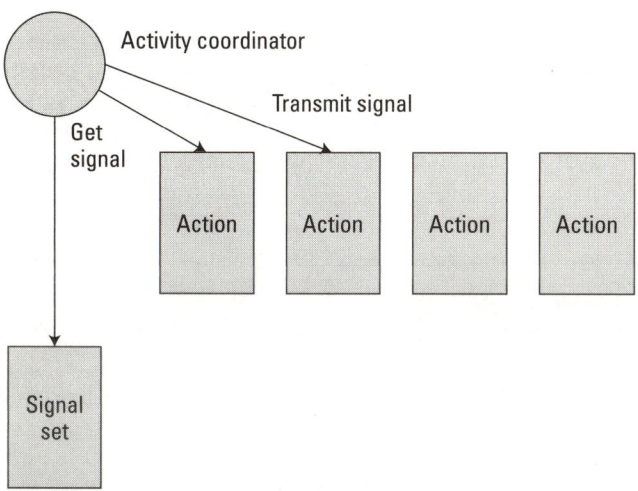

Figure 10-14: An example of the Activity coordinator signaling Actions

However, if during the "prepare" phase, an Action returns a response which indicates that there is no point in sending the "prepare" Signal to further Actions, the Activity Coordinator will be required to obtain a new Signal from the `SignalSet` (the "rollback" Signal in this case), and send this to all registered Actions. As stated previously, the intelligence about which Signal to send, and about interpreting outcomes from Actions, resides within the `SignalSet`, allowing implementations of the framework presented within this specification to be highly configurable, to match application requirements.

In the following sections, we'll look at the various transaction standards that have arisen over the years since transaction-processing technology was first developed and how they relate to J2EE.

Understanding Transaction Standards

In this section we will describe two of the more important transaction standards—X/Open Distributed Transaction Processing and the Object Transaction Service (OTS)—and how they relate to J2EE. As you will see in the section on the Java

Transaction API, these standards have influenced transactions in J2EE significantly, either explicitly (in the case of XA, discussed next) or implicitly (in the case of the OTS). Therefore, it's important to know some of their details.

X/Open Distributed Transaction Processing

X/Open is part of The Open Group, Inc., whose goal is to promote application portability through the development of API standards. In 1991 it developed a distributed transaction–processing model (XA Distributed Transaction Processing), which includes many of the features offered by traditional TP monitors. The model divides a transaction-processing system into the three following components:

✦ Transaction manager

✦ Database or other resource manager

✦ Transactional-communications manager

The transactional-communications manager interfaces among them all, as shown in Figure 10-15. It is of particular importance to us as it essentially forms the basis of the Java Transaction API (JTA).

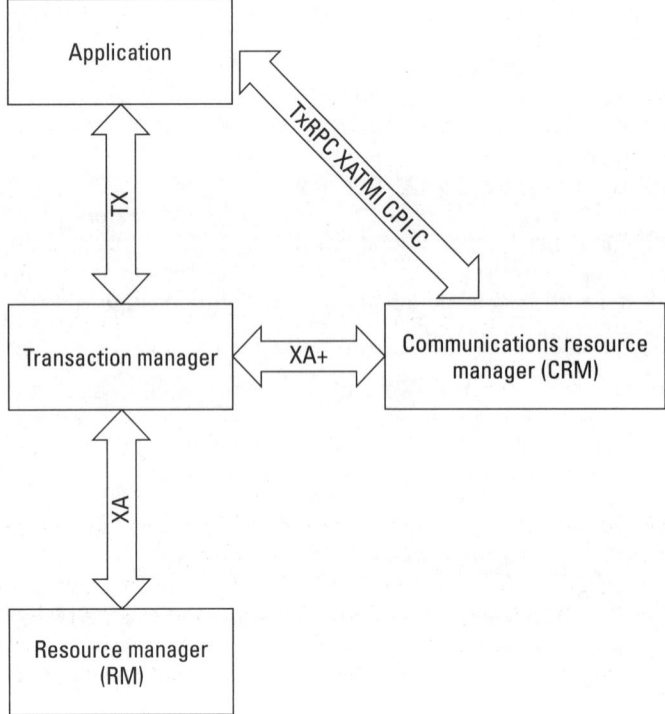

Figure 10-15: The X/Open interfaces

These are the main actors within this model:

✦ **Transaction manager** — The TM is what you would expect — the transaction coordinator and its associated systems. The X/Open specification only supports top-level transactions.

✦ **Communications-resource manager** — The CRM provides an API to a communications system that can be used for distributed transactional systems. The system ensures that remote invocations have the transaction context propagated with them.

✦ **Resource manager** — The RM represents the transactional participants, including databases, messaging queues, file systems, and so on.

✦ **XA** — This defines the interface between the RM and the TM. Most transaction-processing systems and major databases support XA. Implementations of this interface are the transactional participants driven through the two-phase commit protocol.

✦ **XA+** — This is a superset of XA that allows the CRM to inform the TM when new machines join a distributed transaction.

✦ **TX** — This defines a transaction-demarcation API and allows applications to enquire as to the status of transactions.

Most application programmers never see the X/Open DTP actors since they are hidden behind vendor-specific extensions, such as database drivers or other high-level interfaces. The fact that these actors are defined in the C programming language also restricts some of their immediate applicability.

The Object Transaction Service

The most widely accepted standard for distributed objects is the Common Object Request Broker Architecture (CORBA) from the Object Management Group (OMG). It consists of the Object Request Broker (ORB), which enables distributed objects to interact with each other, and a number of services that have also been specified by the OMG, including persistence, concurrency control, and the Object Transaction Service (OTS), which was released in 1992.

Note   The Java Transaction Service (JTS) is the Java language mapping of the OTS.

Up until this point, all the major transaction vendors had their own sets of interfaces for interacting with their transaction systems and both interoperability and portability were virtually impossible. Although some components may have supported the X/Open XA standard, support was not mandated and was typically unavailable to programmers directly anyway. Thus, the purpose of the OTS was to provide a standard set of interfaces through which vendors could expose their transaction systems and users could drive transactionality in their applications. The fact that the OTS came at the start of the object-orientation boom also made it important because no standard for transactions existed in any object-oriented environment at that time.

Note   The OTS specification also defines how to interoperate with X/Open XA and other transaction implementations. Obviously, OTS implementations are required to interoperate with other OTS implementations.

The OTS does not require all objects to have transactional behavior. Instead objects can choose not to support transactional operations at all, or to support them for some requests but not others. Furthermore, the transaction-service specification distinguishes between *recoverable objects* and *transactional objects*. Recoverable objects are those that contain the actual state that may be changed by a transaction and must therefore be informed when the transaction commits or rolls back to ensure that the consistency of the state changes. In contrast, a simple transactional object need not necessarily be a recoverable object if its state is actually implemented by means of other recoverable objects. The major difference is that a simple transactional object need not take part in the commit protocol used to determine the outcome of the transaction because it does not maintain any state itself, having delegated that responsibility to other recoverable objects that will take part in the commit process. This is essentially the same distinction we made earlier between transactional objects and participants. The fundamental architecture of the OTS is shown in Figure 10-16.

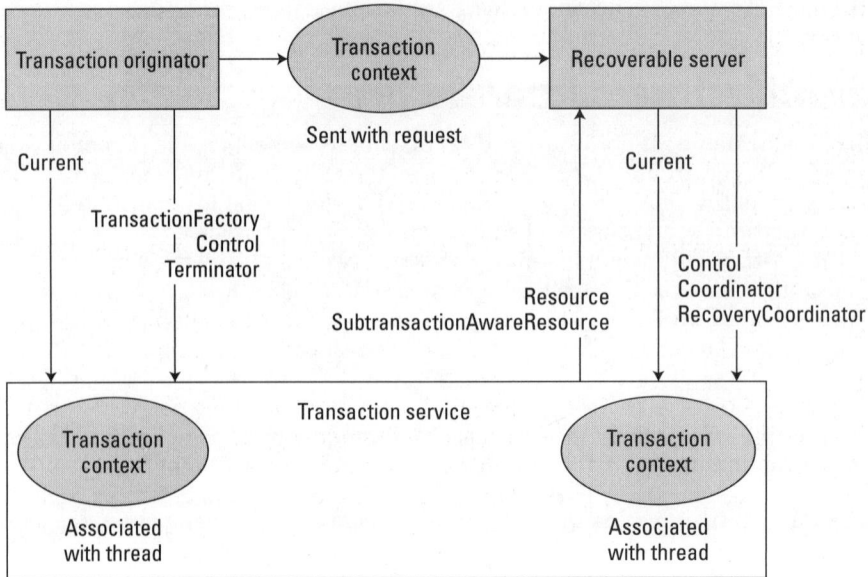

Figure 10-16: The OTS architecture

Briefly the roles are as follows:

✦ `Current` is the application programmers' typical means of interacting with the transaction implementation. It allows applications to start and end transactions. It is a per-thread object, so it must remember the transaction associated with each thread that has used it. The underlying implementation will typically use the `TransactionFactory` for creating top-level transactions. Nested transactions are an optional extra.

✦ `Control` is the interface that provides access to a specific transaction and wraps the transaction `Coordinator` and `Terminator` interfaces that are used to enlist participants and end the transaction, respectively. One of the reasons for dividing this functionality between two interfaces was to allow a transaction implementation to have finer control over the entities that could terminate the transaction.

✦ `Resource` and `SubtransactionAwareResource` represent the transaction participants and have a deliberately generic interface to allow any two-phase–compliant implementation — rather than just XA-compliant implementations — to be registered with the transaction.

✦ Each top-level transaction has an associated `RecoveryCoordinator` that is available to participants in order for them to drive failure recovery. As we mentioned earlier, recovery after a crash will almost certainly be driven from the transaction coordinators' end, but allowing participants to drive it as well can improve recovery time.

Recall that the transaction context is fundamental to any distributed-transaction system, and the OTS is no different in this respect.

It is important to realize that the OTS is simply a *protocol engine* that guarantees that transactional behavior is obeyed but does not directly support all the transaction properties. As such it requires other cooperating services that implement the required functionality, including the following:

✦ **Persistence and Recovery Service** — This is required to support the atomicity and durability properties.

✦ **Concurrency Control Service** — This is required to support the isolation property.

The OTS does not specify how these different functionalities should be provided. Because of this, it is more than likely that any vendor implementation will provide implementations (and hence APIs) that differ from those of other vendors.

To participate within an OTS transaction, a programmer must be concerned with the following:

> Creating `Resource` and `SubtransactionAwareResource` objects for each object that will participate within the transaction or sub-transaction. These resources are responsible for the persistence, concurrency control, and recovery for the object. The OTS will invoke these objects during the prepare/commit/rollback phases of the transaction, and the `Resources` must then perform all appropriate work.

> Registering `Resource` and `SubtransactionAwareResource` objects at the correct time within the transaction, and ensuring that each object is only registered *once* within a given transaction. As part of the registration process a `Resource` will receive a reference to a `RecoveryCoordinator`, which must be made persistent so that recovery can occur in the event of a failure.

> Ensuring that, in the case of nested transactions, any propagation of resources such as locks to parent transactions is correctly performed. The programmer must also manage the propagation of `SubtransactionAwareResource` objects to parents.

In the event of failures, the programmer or system administrator is responsible for driving the crash recovery for each `Resource` that was participating within the transaction.

Importantly, the OTS does not provide any `Resource` implementations. The application programmer or OTS implementer must provide these. We hope that you can begin to see that writing any kind of complex transactional application using the OTS can be extremely difficult and is beyond the scope of most programmers. Even in the case of a relatively trivial application such as one for booking a flight on an airline, a typical programmer using just the OTS would probably have to spend more time on using and driving the transaction system than on the higher-level airline-reservation application.

So, without suitable abstractions to isolate a user from these low-level details, the use of transactions would generally be limited. In the following section we will show how J2EE provided just such an abstraction through the EJB and JTA abstractions.

Understanding the Java Transaction API

The interfaces specified by the OTS are typically too low-level for most application programmers. Although the X/Open DTP XA interfaces define a higher-level abstraction for the interactions between a resource manager and a transaction manager, they do so in a very procedural (that is, non-object-oriented) way. The Java Transaction API (JTA) builds on the X/Open DTP model to define higher-level Java interfaces to assist in the development of distributed transactional applications.

The JTA's relationship to the JTS

Figure 10-17 illustrates the relationships among the JTA and possible transaction-service implementations. As shown, the JTA defines a general notion of a Transaction Manager along with the various interfaces and associated roles required to interact with it. What the JTA specification does not mandate is a specific transaction-service implementation. Thus, as long as a vendor supports the JTA interfaces, any underlying transaction service may be used.

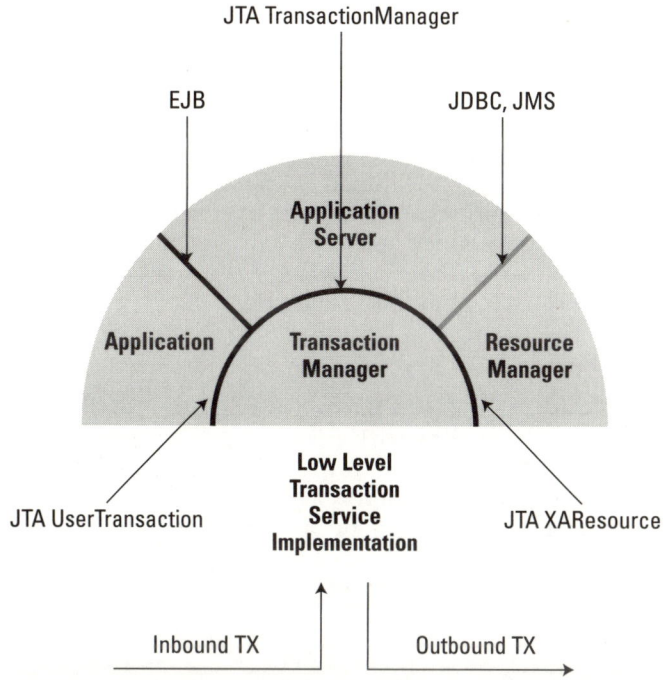

Figure 10-17: The JTA architecture

However, the ability to have clients and services participate in transactions that execute in different vendors' application servers is important. Therefore, if interoperability is required, J2EE recommends that either a JTS be used or the equivalent on-the-wire protocol be provided by the implementation.

Note   The JTA specification takes the approach of limiting the type of transaction participant to those that are XA-compliant, rather than allowing the more general resources that the OTS allows. For most applications this does not pose a problem because typically the type of resources that will be participating within your transactions will be XA-compliant databases. However, for more advanced applications it may be necessary to go beyond XA and look at the underlying transaction-service implementation — if this implementation is standards-based (such as the JTS) it will obviously make application portability easier to achieve.

The UserTransaction interface

The `javax.transaction.UserTransaction` interface provides applications with the ability to demarcate transaction boundaries. It provides typical methods for beginning, committing, and rolling back top-level transactions. Nested transactions are not supported and if the calling thread is already associated with a transaction `begin` throws a `NotSupportedException`. When a new transaction is created, `UserTransaction` automatically associates it with the invoking thread, meaning that the threads' notion of the current transaction is modified. At any given time a thread's transaction context may either be null or refer to a specific global transaction. Multiple threads may be associated with the same global transaction.

commit()

The `commit()` method is used to complete the transaction currently associated with the calling thread; after it returns, the thread is no longer associated with any transaction. If `commit()` is called when the thread has no associated transaction context, the transaction manager throws an `IllegalStateException`. In addition, some implementations restrict the commit operation to the originator of the transaction in order to guarantee integrity. Therefore, a `SecurityException` is thrown if the calling thread is not allowed to commit the transaction.

rollback()

The `rollback()` method is used to roll back the transaction associated with the current thread. As with `commit()`, after the `rollback()` method returns the thread is no longer associated with any transaction. Likewise, if the thread is not associated with a transaction, the implementation may throw an `IllegalStateException`, and if it is not allowed to terminate the transaction, the implementation may throw a `SecurityException`.

Timeout values

Whenever a top-level transaction is created, a timeout value may be associated with it, meaning that the transaction is subject to being rolled back if it has not completed within the specified number of seconds. The implementation of your transaction system is free to specify any default timeout value for transactions and it's a good idea for you to determine that number. You can use the `setTransactionTimeout` method to modify this value on a per-thread basis. *Per-thread* means that when called the value applies only to the invoking thread. In addition, any new value applies only to subsequently created transactions.

 **Note**   If a value of 0 is specified, the implementation-specified default will be restored for the calling thread.

SetRollbackOnly()

The `setRollbackOnly()` method marks the transaction so that the only possible outcome is for it to roll back. The `IllegalStateException` is raised if the transaction has already been prepared or completed, or if no transaction is currently associated with the calling thread.

The UserTransaction interface

The J2EE 1.3 specification indicates that components that may use the `UserTransaction` interface (such as EJB, Servlet, and JSP) must access the provided reference by performing a JNDI name lookup for `java:comp/UserTransaction`. Here's an example:

```
// create a JNDI Initial context
Context ctx = new InitialContext();
// obtain the UserTransaction
UserTransaction utx = (UserTransaction) ctx.lookup

("java:comp/UserTransaction");
// begin the transaction
utx.begin();
//  . . . do work
utx.commit();
```

An EJB may also access the `UserTransaction` implementation via the `EJBContext.getUserTransaction()` method. Any such reference is only valid within the component instance that performed the lookup.

The TransactionManager interface

Rather than `UserTransaction`, an application server uses the `javax.transaction.TransactionManager` interface to demarcate transaction boundaries on behalf of an application and its associated components. The `TransactionManager` is similar to `UserTransaction` in that it is responsible for maintaining the transaction-context association with the various threads of execution. (As mentioned earlier, nested transactions are not supported.) The same `begin()`, `commit()`, and `rollback()` methods are available to the application server through this interface. To determine the status of the current transaction you can use the `getStatus()` method, which will return one of the values specified in the `Status` interface.

Each transaction context is represented by a different `javax.transaction.Transaction` object, which is used to perform operations specific to a target transaction regardless of the calling thread's transaction context. In this way `Transaction` is different from `UserTransaction` and `TransactionManager`, in which the same instance can be used to control different transactions. The `getTransaction()` method returns the `Transaction` object associated with the calling thread.

Suspending and resuming a transaction

The JTA supports the concept of a thread temporarily suspending and resuming transactions to enable it to perform non-transactional work. The `suspend()` method is called to temporarily suspend the transaction that is currently associated with the calling thread. If the thread is not associated with a transaction, a null object reference is returned; otherwise, a valid `Transaction` object is returned. The `Transaction` object can be leveraged as an argument to the `TransactionManager.resume()` method to restore the associated transaction context. Suspending a transaction should be done with care, as any work performed subsequent to the `suspend` operation being called will not be recoverable. In other words, if the suspended transaction eventually rolls back, this work will not be undone.

The `resume()` method re-establishes the suspended transaction context with the calling thread. If the transaction specified is a valid transaction, the transaction context is associated with the calling thread; otherwise, the thread is associated with no transaction, as shown here:

```
Transaction tx = TransactionManager.suspend ();
. . .
TransactionManager.resume (tx);
```

If `resume()` is invoked when the calling thread is already associated with another transaction, the `TransactionManager` throws an `IllegalStateException` exception. Additionally, some transaction-manager implementations allow a suspended transaction to be resumed by a different thread: This is the only standard way in which multiple threads within the same JVM can become associated with the same transaction.

When a transaction is suspended, an application server must ensure that the resources in use by the application are no longer registered with the suspended transaction. De-listing a resource from the `TransactionManager` tells the resource manager to dissociate the transaction from the specified resource object. When the application's transaction context is resumed, the application server must ensure that the resources used by the application are re-enlisted with the transaction. Enlisting a resource as a result of a transaction's being resumed causes the `TransactionManager` to notify the resource manager that it should re-associate the resource object with the given transaction. Making the distinction between associating or re-associating is important for the resource manager to make, as it is in fact illegal for the `TransactionManager` to try to associate (rather than re-associate) the same transaction with the resource more than once.

The Transaction interface

The `javax.transaction.Transaction` interface allows applications to invoke operations on the transaction associated with the target object. Every transaction is associated with a `Transaction` object. The `Transaction` object can subsequently be used to enlist transactional resources, register synchronization callbacks, commit or roll back the transaction, or obtain the transaction's status.

The main distinction between the `Transaction` and `TransactionManager` interfaces involves thread-to-transaction association: When you use `Transaction`, the calling thread is not required to have the same transaction associated with the thread. No thread-to-transaction associations will be changed — so, for example, an invoking thread could still find itself associated with the transaction it just terminated.

In addition to the `TransactionManager` interface, the methods of the `Transaction` interface are generally used extensively by an application server to help manage the transactions for enterprise components. For example, an application server makes use of the `getStatus()` or `getTransaction()` methods to make decisions about whether a transaction should be initiated, suspended, resumed, committed, or rolled back, based on the current status and the transactional attribute assigned to the EJB method. For instance, the processing an application server may undertake if an EJB method requires a transaction to be created prior to execution may include the following:

```
Transaction tx = null;
TransactionManager tm = getTransactionManagerFromJNDI();
    // see if a transaction is initiated and is
    // associated with the invoking thread
    try
    {
        tx = tm.getTransaction();
    }
    catch(SystemException e)
    {
        // log exception
    }

    if (tx == null)
    {
        // initiate a transaction since it is required
        try
        {
            tm.begin();
        }
        catch(NotSupportedException e)
```

```
        {
            // log exception
        }
        catch(SystemException e)
        {
            // log exception
        }
    }
```

The application server first obtains the `TransactionManager` using `getTransactionManager()`, which we assume uses JNDI as mentioned earlier. The `Transaction` object is obtained from the `TransactionManager`. If the `Transaction` is null then there is no transaction currently associated with the invoking thread and it is safe to start a new transaction using the `begin()` operation on the `TransactionManager`.

The XAResource interface

Whereas the OTS interfaces define a generic `Resource` interface that can be used to register arbitrary resources with a transaction, the JTA is based on the model proposed by the X/Open CAE XA specification. The `javax.transaction.xa.XAResource` interface is a Java mapping of the `XAResource` interface.

A resource adapter that is to be used in a transactional environment implements the `XAResource` interface. For example, each database connection used by an application or its components is linked with an `XAResource` object that facilitates communication with the underlying resource-manager instance. The transaction manager obtains and uses an `XAResource` for every resource manager participating in a global distributed transaction. It uses the `start()` and `end()` methods to associate and dissociate the transaction, respectively, from the resource.

The XA specification requires that the `xa_calls` responsible for transaction association must be made from the same thread of control. This concept is central to the transaction manager's coordination of resource managers; a resource manager understands that a given work request pertains to a particular transaction branch because both the application and the transaction manager call it from the same thread.

In an object-oriented environment this concept is inappropriate because threads are generally dispatched dynamically during method invocations. In an application server, different threads may be using the same connection and associated `XAResource` object. Therefore, it is very possible that different threads will invoke the `start()` and `end()` methods on a given `XAResource`. It is the responsibility of the application server to ensure that, although multiple threads may access a transactional resource, only one transaction context is associated with that resource.

 **Note** It is possible to interleave multiple transactions using the same resource as long as each `start()` invocation is paired with an `end()` method call. In other words, each time a resource is used with a different transaction the `end()` method must be invoked for the previous transaction and then the `start()` invocation must be invoked for the current transaction.

Enrolling participants with the transaction

The application server typically manages transactional resources such as database connections by using a resource adapter in conjunction with connection pooling. For a transaction manager to coordinate the transactional work performed by the target resource managers, the application server must manage the association and dissociation of these participants with the transaction.

The enrollment process is as follows:

1. Within the two-phase commit protocol, the enlistment of participants is typically a unidirectional operation, meaning that the coordinator simply registers the fact that the participant has been enlisted by some other entity (such as a service). Recall that the JTA essentially wraps the X/Open XA protocol and hence its participants are required to be XA-compliant.

   Because of subtleties in the underlying XA protocol, association with and disassociation from the transaction are in fact bi-directional operations: The transaction manager is required to inform the resource that enlistment or delistment has occurred. Each resource is tied to a specific Resource Manager (RM) and when association or disassociation occurs the appropriate RM must be informed in order to ensure that work done using the RM is either associated (or not) with the transaction. At any given time, a connection to a Resource Manager is associated with a single transaction or with no transaction at all.

2. An application server registers each resource used by the application by invoking the `enlistResource()` method with a `javax.transaction.XAResource` object that identifies the resource.

3. An enlistment request informs the Resource Manager to start associating the transaction with the work performed through the resource. The transaction manager is responsible for passing a parameter representing the transactional state (either beginning a new transaction or joining or resuming an existing transaction, using `JMJOIN` or `JMRESUME`, respectively) in its `XAResource.start()` method call to the resource manager.

4. The `delistResource()` method dissociates the specified resource from the transaction context and informs the Resource Manager that transactional use is ended (or suspended). The application server invokes the method with the two parameters: the `XAResource` object that represents the resource, and a

flag to indicate whether the operation is the result of the transaction being suspended (TMSUSPEND), a portion of the work having failed (TMFAIL), or a normal resource release by the application (TMSUCCESS). A suspended transaction may later be resumed on the same Resource Manager. An important distinction exists between ending and suspending a transaction, because once a transaction is ended, the Resource Manager will not allow itself to be associated with that transaction again.

5. The de-list request tells the transaction manager to inform the resource manager to dissociate the transaction from the XAResource. A flag is passed as part of the invocation, indicating whether the transaction manager intends to come back to the same resource, in which case the resource states will have to be kept intact. The transaction manager passes the appropriate flag value in its XAResource.end() method call to the underlying Resource Manager.

Transaction synchronization

If an entity wishes to be informed that a transaction is about to terminate, it can register with the transaction an object that is an instance of the javax.transaction. Synchronization interface. Synchronizations are typically employed to flush volatile (cached) state (which may be being used to improve the performance of an application) to a recoverable object or database prior to the transaction committing. Once flushed, the data will be controlled by an XAResource.

For each transaction started, the application server may (and usually does) register a javax.transaction.Synchronization callback object that is invoked by the transaction manager at the appropriate time. The process is as follows:

1. beforeCompletion() is called prior to the start of the two-phase transaction-commit protocol. This call is executed in the transaction context of the caller who initiates the TransactionManager.commit() or TransactionManager. rollback(), or is executed with no transaction context if Transaction. commit() is used instead. If any beforeCompletion operation fails, the transaction will be forced to roll back.

2. afterCompletion() is called after the transaction has completed. The status of the transaction is supplied in the associated method parameter. This method is executed without a transaction context. Any failures that occur during afterCompletion processing can be safely ignored by the transaction system, as the transaction has completed.

Application servers generally use the synchronization facility to manage the pooling of transactional resources. For example, an application server may use the afterCompletion() notification to return a JDBC connection to the connection pool.

Transaction equality

The `Transaction` object's `equals()` method allows comparison between the target object and another `Transaction` object. The `equals()` method returns `true` if the given transaction object and the parameter passed in both reference the same global transaction. Here's an example:

```
Transaction tx = TransactionManager.getTransaction ();
Transaction anotherTx = . . .
. . .
boolean isSame = tx.equals (anotherTx);
```

The XID interface

The `javax.transaction.xa.XID` interface provides a Java mapping of the X/Open XA specification's XID structure. The transaction manager uses the XID and Resource Manager to identify a particular transactional. The XID is rarely if ever accessed by an application server in the context of transactional processing. The XID interface provides methods that provide the transaction's format ID, a global transaction ID, and a branch qualifier.

A transaction may have one or more branches that can be used to define separate but coordinated units of work. Each unit of work can be associated with at most one transaction branch, and once the transaction manager begins to commit a specific branch the RM can receive no additional work on behalf of that branch. However, this does not prevent it from receiving work on behalf of the same transaction but from a different branch.

In the following section, we shall see how many of the concepts we have previously discussed may be used in practice.

Airline Reservation Using Transactions Business Case

To illustrate some of the issues we have discussed in this chapter we'll build upon the airline-reservation system we proposed earlier. Assume a slightly enhanced application structure, as shown in Figure 10-18. The tourist wants to book a trip from his home city (Newcastle in the United Kingdom, say) to a conference being held in Boston, United States on the second of February. The trip involves a national flight (Newcastle to London) followed by a transatlantic flight (London to Boston). Obviously the trip cannot be made if only one of these flights is available and therefore the tourist does not want to purchase one flight without the other; assuming both flights are available, they must be purchased as an atomic unit. Therefore, the use of atomic transactions in this situation is obvious.

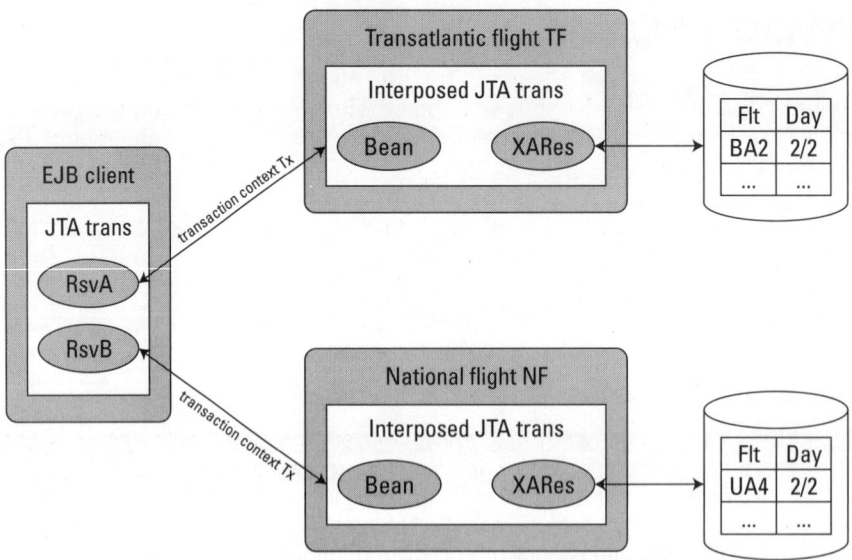

Figure 10-18: Example vacation booking using two-phase commit transactions

Luckily for the tourist, two airline reservation sites not only make their individual reservations atomic by internally using transactions but, as we shall see, enable those transactions to be coordinated as a single atomic unit.

Firstly, the client is capable of executing its own transactions (JTA transactions in this example). For simplicity we will assume that the client's transaction manager is co-located with the client application — that is, within the same JVM. When the tourist attempts to book the trip he will first start an atomic transaction (*Tx* in the figure, created via a call to `UserTransaction.begin()`) within which to perform each of the reservation attempts (*RsvA* and *RsvB*). When the reservation-invocation attempts are made, the transaction context for *Tx* is implicitly propagated with each operation to the respective airline reservation site.

Here's an example of the client's code. To make things a little simpler, we've omitted some of the error handling that you might expect. After starting a new transaction, the client obtains a list of flights that are operating on the travel date and selects the ones he wants. If the transaction commits successfully, seats on both flights will have been booked. Otherwise, no seat will have been booked and the client can try again later.

```
UserTransaction ut = getUserTransactionFromJNDI();

Date travelDate; // probably set via a GUI
```

```
if (ut != null)
{
    try
    {
        ut.begin();

        FlightInformation fi1 =
NF.getFlightInformation(travelDate);
        FlightInformation fi2 =
TF.getFlightInformation(travelDate);

        int NFNo = 0; // National Flight Number
        int IFNo = 0; // International Flight Number

        /*
         * Check that seats are available on required date and
         * assign them to variable NFNo (National Flight Number)
         * and IFNo (International Flight Number)
         * /

        fi1.bookSeat(travelDate, NFNo);
        fi2.bookSeat(travelDate, IFNo);

        ut.commit();
    }
    catch (TransactionRolledBackException ex)
    {
        System.err.println("Failed to get both seats.");
    }
    catch (Exception ex)
    {
        System.err.println("Some other error happened: "+ex);
    }
}
else
    System.err.println("Could not find UserTransaction");
```

Next, both the transatlantic reservation site (*TF*) and the national reservation site (*NF*) allow transaction contexts to be imported. In other words, when a client makes an invocation on either of the sites it is permissible for that client already to have a transaction associated with it. (How transactional properties on beans are specified within J2EE will be discussed later in Chapter 14 on Enterprise JavaBeans.) When the client application performs *RsvA*, for example, the transaction context for *Tx* is propagated to, and imported by, *TF*.

As you saw in the section "Interposition," earlier in this chapter, a good transaction-service implementation will typically employ sub-coordination when doing the import. Using this method, a subordinate transaction coordinator is created within *TF* that is enlisted with the parent (root) transaction coordinator resident at the client. How interposition is actually done will depend upon the underlying transaction-service implementation. When the context import is complete, the application-server thread in *TF* that is to do the real work is effectively associated with the client's transaction (the *global transaction*), thus ensuring that any work the thread does will be ultimately controlled by that transaction.

In this example, all airline-reservation information is held within databases independently maintained by the respective sites, and all operations such as reserving a seat or enquiring as to the availability of a seat are performed by means of appropriate SQL statements. As shown in the example program fragment below, the application therefore requests a transactional resource (a JDBC connection in this case) from a configured resource adapter (a JDBC datasource). In order to ensure that all the work performed by the reservation site is transactional, the application server intercedes in the resource request and obtains an XAResource from the resource adapter being used. It then enlists the XAResource with the global transaction (Transaction.enlistResource()). In reality, because interposition is most probably being used, the XAResource is enlisted with the subordinate transaction coordinator resident within the same JVM as the airline-reservation system.

```
TransactionManager tm = getTransactionManagerFromJNDI();
XAConnection conn = ourDataSource.getXAConnection();

if (tm != null)
{
    XAResource xaRes = conn.getXAResource();

    if (!tm.enlistResource(xaRes))
    {
        // throw an appropriate exception for application
    }
}
```

The transaction manager invokes the XAResource.start() method to associate the resource manager's work with the transaction. The application server then requests the associated connection object from the resource adapter (XAConnection.getConnection()) and returns it to the application for it to use. The reservation site can then perform operations on the relevant data held within its database; any updates will be provisional because the global transaction has yet to complete. In the case of *TF*, the only flight that matches the tourist's requirements is *BA2* and therefore issuing the relevant SQL command reserves the seat.

When the reservation-site operation has completed, it closes the connection and the application server de-lists the resource when it receives the close notification from the resource adapter (Transaction.delistResource()). The transaction manager dissociates the transaction from the resource manager by invoking the XAResource.end() method.

Assuming the transatlantic flight can be reserved, the application program can then attempt to reserve the national flight. A similar course of events will be carried out so that eventually the `XAResource` associated with the national-flight reservation will be registered with the global transaction managed by the client.

If both flights can be reserved, the client application can then instruct the global transaction to commit (`UserTransaction.commit()`). The transaction coordinator then performs the two-phase commit protocol on the registered resources — the two subordinate transaction coordinators will then each invoke `XAResource.prepare()` and `XAResource.commit()` to commit the work associated with the transaction. As you have seen, because transactions are used throughout this reservation work, either both or none of the flights will be reserved despite failures.

Summary

In this chapter we looked at the fundamentals behind atomic transactions and showed you how these transactions are a useful structuring tool for creating applications and objects that are to be both fault-tolerant and capable of being shared in a consistent manner among concurrent users. Although transactions are useful in a local environment, you have seen that they really come into their own when used in a distributed system in which multiple participants must be coordinated to ensure a consistent outcome.

We discussed the various implications of using atomic transactions (you never get something for nothing!) and showed you how most transaction-processing implementations will provide optimizations to improve performance and throughput. We also mentioned some of the different transaction models available in some systems (such as nested transactions) and others that are being developed for future use (such as the J2EE Activity Service). Although not all transaction systems support these transaction flavors, it is important to understand what they can mean to current and future developments and possibly to take this information into account when making your own purchasing or development choices.

We examined two of the most important standards in transaction processing, the X/Open XA and the OMGs Object Transaction Service. Both of these standards have heavily influenced transactions in J2EE and we illustrated this through a closer look at the Java Transaction API and an associated example.

Finally, what we have tried to illustrate in this chapter is that there is much more to atomic transactions that the well-known two-phase commit protocol — such as failure recovery mechanisms, heuristics, interposition, and so on. When considering using or buying (or possibly even developing) a transaction system, you should have all of these capabilities available to you to ensure consistency, performance, and reliability.

✦   ✦   ✦

Examining JNDI and Directory Services

✦ ✦ ✦ ✦

In This Chapter

Introducing directory services

Understanding LDAP

Accessing LDAP directories with JNDI

Accessing DNS with JNDI

✦ ✦ ✦ ✦

One of the key tasks in a distributed application is finding items such as components, resources, message queues, and databases. The Java Naming and Directory Interface (JNDI) is an essential part of J2EE applications, providing a mechanism for finding distributed components — but JNDI is good for more than just looking up EJB interfaces. It also allows access to important enterprise systems such as directory servers.

This chapter explores using JNDI to access the various naming and directory services available to J2EE applications, specifically LDAP and DNS.

Explaining Naming Services and Directory Services

Strictly speaking, a *naming service* translates human-friendly names to machine-friendly names. Most naming services are extended into *directory services,* which associate names with entries but also assign the entries additional attributes. For example, a directory might translate a user's real name into an e-mail address that also contains a phone number and physical mailing address. Some examples of directories are the Novell Directory Service (NDS), Microsoft's Active Directory (AD), and various other directory-service products that implement the Lightweight Directory Access Protocol (LDAP) standard.

While a few pure naming services are in use, most directory services are used simply as naming services. For example, the Internet Domain Name System (DNS) is a complex system; however, it is most often used simply for translating domain names (such as www.wiley.com) to IP addresses (such as 192.168.100.1).

Directory services are an important part of modern network infrastructure. They enable users and applications to look up network resources such as servers, printers, and user addresses. A directory maps the human-friendly names to something useful to an application, such as by mapping network resources to their respective network addresses. Users can take advantage of directories to find distributed resources without having to know their physical locations on the network. Applications can use directories as a database, to look up e-mail addresses corresponding to users' names.

Generally speaking, directories are organized *hierarchically.* That is, they're built in a tree structure. A corporate directory might have a single root node, with a second-level node for each state in which there is an office and, below those, a node for each department in that office. In each department would be a list of employees in the department, in that regional office. For example, if you had two regional offices, Michigan and Kansas, you might have a sales department node in each office, listing all the sales staff in that office. One major advantage of using this type of structure is that it makes distributing the directory across multiple physical servers easy. Each regional office can have its own server, which can function as the directory master for its own part of the directory tree. Each server can also replicate the contents of the other servers. This setup would allow users to connect to their local servers but still see the entire corporate directory without having to know how the directory servers were configured.

A directory can ultimately be thought of as a very sophisticated address book in which every entry contains the same types of information and the entries are organized for easy access. Why not just use an existing data-storage mechanism such as a relational database? Why have specialized directory services? Here are several reasons:

✦ *Directories are optimized for read-only access.* You look up entries in a directory far more often than you add or update entries. Relational databases need to provide a balance between query and update speed.

✦ *Directories impose a structure on the data.* All the entries have the same types of information in them, and once you've found the entry you're looking for the extra attributes are in one place in the directory. Relational databases have a more general-purpose structure than directories. Also, the restricted structure of a directory means that you don't have to worry about issues such as using first normal form, as you do in a database.

✦ *Directories are often distributed.* This makes administration easier and allows user load on the servers to be distributed as well. The simplified structure of a directory is easier to replicate than the structure of a relational database.

✦ *Directories are sorted.* However, only one sorting structure exists, and directories do not have to be very good at dealing with advanced queries. This allows them to be simpler, cheaper, and easier to administer.

Of course, like any popular technology, standards play an important role in determining how to access directory services.

Providing an Overview of X.500 and LDAP

X.500 is a set of international standards developed by the International Telecommunications Union (ITU-T) in conjunction with the International Standards Organization (ISO). These standards are principally designed to allow multiple directory systems to connect to each other and exchange information. This gives the appearance to the end user of there being a single unified directory system. In X.500 parlance, Directory Service Agents (DSAs) maintain the database of names and attributes in the directory. Directory User Agents (DUAs) make use of DSA services on a user's behalf. The DSA and DUA communicate via the Directory Access Protocol (DAP).

Although the thoroughness of the X.500 specification makes it very powerful, it is also hard to implement and difficult to use. Recognizing the need to provide a simpler way to access directory services and standardize them internationally, the University of Michigan developed the Lightweight Directory Access Protocol (LDAP) in the '90s. (See RFC 1487 et al. for details.) LDAP is based on a simple string-based approach to accessing directory services. It is widely used and is supported by a wide range of commercial and free directory products.

LDAP implementations

Some directory servers that provide a LDAP interface are the following:

✦ SunONE Directory Server

✦ Novell eDirectory (formerly NDS)

✦ Microsoft Active Directory

✦ OpenLDAP

If you want to try some of the code examples in this chapter against a sample LDAP directory, the next section, "Configuring OpenLDAP," provides a LDAP Directory Interchange Format (LDIF) file that you can import into most LDAP-compatible directory servers. If you don't already have a directory server available, you can get OpenLDAP and use that. The OpenLDAP source code is available at http://www.openldap.org and pre-compiled Windows binaries are available at http://www.fivesight.com/downloads/openldap.asp.

Configuring OpenLDAP

To use OpenLDAP to run the code in this chapter you'll need to modify the configuration file slapd.conf (shown in Listing 11-1) and import the LDIF file (shown in the subsequent listing). In the configuration file you will need to add the schema definitions for Java objects as well as for inetOrgPerson. Change the path names shown here to reflect where you've installed the OpenLDAP files.

Listing 11-1: **slapd.conf**

```
# slapd.conf - use this bare file or
# merge this with the original slapd.conf
include       c:/openldap/schema/core.schema
include       c:/openldap/schema/java.schema
include       c:/openldap/schema/cosine.schema
include       c:/openldap/schema/inetorgperson.schema

pidfile       c:/tmp/slapd.pid
argsfile      c:/tmp/slapd.args

database      ldbm
suffix        "o=Acme Inventions"
directory     c:/tmp/openldap-ldbm

index    objectClass eq
```

See *OpenLDAP 2.1 Administrator's Guide* for more information. It's available at http://www.openldap.org/doc/admin21/.

Once the configuration file is set up, start the OpenLDAP server from the command line by running slapd. Then take the LDIF file and import it into the directory with the following slapdadd command:

```
slapadd -v -f slapd.conf -l j2eebible.ldif -c
```

Listing 11-2 shows the LDIF file that contains some simple directory entries.

Listing 11-2: **j2eebible.ldif**

```
dn: o=Acme Inventions
o: Acme Inventions
objectclass: top
objectclass: organization

dn: ou=Sales, o=Acme Inventions
ou: Sales
objectclass: top
objectclass: organizationalunit

dn: ou=Engineering, o=Acme Inventions
ou: Engineering
objectclass: top
objectclass: organizationalunit

dn: cn=James McGovern, ou=Sales, o=Acme Inventions
cn: James McGovern
sn: McGovern
mail: james.mcgovern@example.com
telephonenumber: +1 610 555 6273
objectclass: top
objectclass: person
objectclass: organizationalPerson
objectclass: inetOrgPerson

dn: cn=Lee Anne Phillips, ou=Sales, o=Acme Inventions
cn: Lee Anne Phillips
sn: Phillips
mail: leeanne.phillips@example.com
mail: lee.anne.phillips@example.com
telephonenumber: +1 408 555 6273
objectclass: top
objectclass: person
objectclass: organizationalPerson
objectclass: inetOrgPerson

dn: cn=Elias Jo, ou=Sales, o=Acme Inventions
cn: Elias Jo
sn: Jo
mail: elias.jo@example.com
telephonenumber: +1 673 555 6273
objectclass: top
objectclass: person
objectclass: organizationalPerson
objectclass: inetOrgPerson
```

Continued

Listing 11-2 *(continued)*

```
dn: cn=Ethan Henry, ou=Engineering, o=Acme Inventions
cn: Ethan Henry
sn: Henry
mail: ethan.henry@example.com
userPassword: coyote
telephonenumber: +1 416 555 6273
telephonenumber: +1 905 555 6273
objectclass: top
objectclass: person
objectclass: organizationalPerson
objectclass: inetOrgPerson
```

LDAP schema

While LDAP provides a general interface to directory services, it does not specify any particular layout for the directory, also known as the directory schema. There are some standards, such as the schema for `inetOrgPerson` defined in RFC 2798 (see `http://www.faqs.org/rfcs/rfc2798.html`) but these aren't absolutely required.

While the structure of LDAP directory entries is fixed as a sequence of attributes and values, the meaning that you assign to individual attributes is not fixed anywhere outside of how you use the values in your applications. In the sample directory shown in Listings 11-1 and 11-2, the root node has the attribute `o=Acme Inventions`, which indicates that the organization's name is *Acme Inventions*. This is the standard definition of the `"o"` attribute in RFC 2798 but you could assign some other meaning to it in your directory if you wanted to define your own schema. For now, let's assume that we're using the RFC 2798 schema for entries in our directory.

Some common LDAP attributes are listed in Table 11-1.

<table>
<tr><td colspan="3" align="center">Table 11-1
Common LDAP attributes</td></tr>
<tr><td>**LDAP Attribute**</td><td>**Definition**</td><td>**Example**</td></tr>
<tr><td>o</td><td>Organization</td><td>o=Acme Inventions</td></tr>
<tr><td>ou</td><td>Organizational unit</td><td>ou=Sales</td></tr>
<tr><td>c</td><td>Country — typically the two-letter country code</td><td>c=CA</td></tr>
</table>

LDAP Attribute	Definition	Example
cn	**Common name**	cn=Ethan Henry
sn	**Surname**	sn=Henry
givenname	**First name**	givenname=Ethan
uid	**User ID**	uid=ehenry
dn	**Distinguished name**	cn=Ethan Henry, ou=Engineering, o=Acme Inventions **or maybe** uid=ehenry, dc=example, dc=com
dc	**Internet domain name**	dc=example, dc=com
mail	**E-mail address**	mail=ethan.henry@example.com

The distinguished name, or DN, specifies the complete path from the root of the directory to a particular entry. Attributes are generally expressed using the mixed-case style, such as employeeNumber. So, while the distinguished name attribute is usually written as dn in source code, we refer to it as DN in documentation. The DN is read backwards, from right to left. The hierarchy can be organized in any number of ways — in some cases it's by Internet domain name, as shown here:

    uid=ehenry, dc=example, dc=com

In other cases (and in our example) the directory may be organized according to a company's internal organization, as shown here:

    cn=Ethan Henry, ou=Sales, o=Acme Inventions

The leftmost part of the DN is referred to as the *Relative Distinguished Name (RDN)*, cn=ehenry in this case. Inside a given LDAP context, such as ou=Sales, o=Acme Inventions, the RDN is what distinguishes entries from one another.

Regardless of how your directory is structured, let's move on to seeing how you can access it via JNDI.

Reviewing the JNDI Structure

The Java Naming and Directory Interface, JNDI, is an API that provides directory and naming services to Java applications. Other Java APIs have been developed for LDAP and other types of directories. However, JNDI is a generic interface that provides access to a variety of directory services, including LDAP, NDS, DNS, and even local file systems.

JNDI provides a generic hierarchical interface with directory and naming services. The core JNDI classes listed in Table 11-2 are located in the `javax.naming` package and its subpackages.

Table 11-2	
JNDI packages	
Class	**Description**
`javax.naming`	Accesses simple naming services.
`javax.naming.directory`	Accesses directory services.
`javax.naming.event`	Handles event notification when dealing with naming and directory services.
`javax.naming.ldap`	Deals with LDAP v3 controls and extended operations.
`javax.naming.spi`	Consists of the *Service Provider Interface (SPI)* classes and interfaces used by LDAP service implementers to provide access to a specific type of naming or directory service.

A few core interfaces in JNDI are used frequently. Understanding these is essential and will help you see how JNDI maps onto the various naming and directory services to which it provides access. These interfaces are as follows:

✦ Directories and entries

✦ Names and attributes

✦ Bindings and references

✦ Contexts and subcontexts

Directories and entries

A directory consists of a number of entries or objects. Both terms are used, but for the sake of simplicity we've stuck to "entries" — both to avoid overloading the term "objects" and to make it easier to distinguish objects in the directory from objects in Java.

Names and attributes

Each entry has a name associated with it. The directory's job is to map names to entries. Entries also have additional attributes associated with them. In LDAP terms, an entry's name would be its `dn` and the entry would have multiple other attributes associated with it.

Binding and references

The association of a name to an entry is called a binding. In some cases information cannot be stored directly inside a directory, or one directory entry needs to refer, indirectly, to another. In these cases a reference can be stored inside the directory, to refer indirectly to information elsewhere in the directory or even to information outside the directory.

Contexts and subcontexts

A collection of bindings is a context. Contexts have their own naming conventions, which may be related to the names of the entries stored in them. Entries are typically manipulated via contexts — you perform lookups and add and modify operations with them. You can take a context and bind it inside another context, creating a subcontext.

File systems

Now, let's look at some examples of how these concepts map to various services that can be accessed via JNDI.

A file system can be thought of as a type of directory service. A Unix file system is hierarchical and has a single root, like a directory. The entries are files. The names are, somewhat obviously, filenames. Attributes, such as owner ID and read/write/execute permissions, are associated with each file as well. A directory such as `/usr` represents a context (defined in the previous section). Other directories inside `/usr` represent subcontexts, such as `/usr/bin` and `/usr/local`. There's a connection between the name of the context, `/usr/bin`, and the entries bound to that context, such as `/usr/bin/chmod`. Finally, a file system contains references, such as hard or soft links (created with `ln` or `ln -s`).

DNS naming conventions

DNS uses a hierarchical naming convention where contexts are ordered from right to left and separated with periods. For example, in `www.example.com`. `www` is a name in the `example.com` context, which in turn names an entry in the `com` context. DNS provides more than just a name to IP address mapping — DNS entries can have different types of records associated with them (such as A, NS, and MX). These records can in turn be expressed as attributes, making their values accessible via JNDI.

LDAP mapping

Finally, LDAP can of course be mapped into this structure as well. Each entry has a unique DN, which is composed of a set of LDAP attributes and values, such as `uid=ehenry, dc=example, dc=com`. The leftmost attribute/value pair, `uid=ehenry`, is the RDN, which is the name in JNDI terms, while the remainder of the DN, `dc=example, dc=com`, forms the context. The context in this case, `dc=example, dc=com`, might be a subcontext of `dc=com`. It might also be a single level, multi-valued context though, depending on how the directory is structured.

LDAP attributes can have multiple values, so in some cases `dc=example, dc=com` represents two entries, while `dc=example,dc=com` represents one entry with two values for the `dc` attribute. Other attributes can also be associated with the `dn`, such as an e-mail address or phone number. References can be stored inside LDAP directories as well, either to other directory entries or to external resources, such as files. This provides the ability to link data to an entry without having to copy the data into the entry. For example, you might have entries in the directory for printers and entries for different departments might have references indicating their default printer.

The interface between JNDI and these different directory structures is made with a JNDI service provider. The Java 2 SDK v1.4 includes providers for the CORBA COS Naming Service, DNS, LDAP, and Remote Method Invocation (RMI).

By far the most important use for JNDI of these different services is accessing LDAP directories, which is discussed next.

Using JNDI and LDAP

While JDNI can be used to access a variety of services, LDAP is by far the most widely used directory-service standard. It's implemented for a variety of tasks, from creating simple e-mail address books to providing user-authentication and -authorization services. Almost all commercial directory servers provide LDAP interfaces. This section gives examples of all the basic JNDI operations in the context of accessing a LDAP directory.

Connecting to the server

The first thing you'll need to do before you can perform any queries is connect to the server. You do this by creating a context that represents the root of the directory or the DN beneath the root relative to which you want your queries performed. The `Context` interface represents a context for a naming service, while a `DirContext` interface represents a directory context in which a name is bound to both an entry and a set of attributes. Here's an example:

```
Hashtable env = new Hashtable();
env.put(Context.INITIAL_CONTEXT_FACTORY,
    "com.sun.jndi.ldap.LdapCtxFactory");
env.put(Context.PROVIDER_URL, "ldap://myserver");
InitialDirContext ctx = new InitialDirContext(env);
```

Here, we're connecting to the root context in the directory service running on the machine named `myserver`. You can connect to something other than the directory root by specifying a different DN in the LDAP URL, as shown here:

```
Hashtable env = new Hashtable();
env.put(Context.INITIAL_CONTEXT_FACTORY,
        "com.sun.jndi.ldap.LdapCtxFactory");
env.put(Context.PROVIDER_URL,
    "ldap://myserver/ou=Sales,o=Acme Inventions");
InitialDirContext ctx = new InitialDirContext(env);
```

Why use `javax.naming.directory.InitialDirContext` instead of `javax.naming.ldap.InitialLdapContext`? `InitialLdapContext` is only necessary if you want to specify LDAP extended controls, which aren't required for most applications.

Specifying environment properties

A number of environment properties must be specified so that the `InitialDirContext` knows what kind of service it's connected to, where the server is located, and so on. The more commonly specified properties are listed in Table 11-3.

Table 11-3
JNDI environment properties

Constant in javax.naming.Context	Property Name	Type	Description
INITIAL_CONTEXT _FACTORY	java.naming .factory .initial	java.lang .String	This specifies the fully qualified class name of the class that will create the Context
PROVIDER_URL	java.naming .provider.url	java.lang .String	This property specifies the service's provider's URL.
SECURITY _AUTHENTICATION	java.naming .security . authentication	One of "none," "simple," or "strong"	This property specifies the type of authentication that will be used.

Continued

		Table 11-3 *(continued)*	
Constant in **javax.naming.Context**	**Property** **Name**	**Type**	**Description**
SECURITY _PRINCIPAL	java.naming .security . principal	Dependent on authentication scheme	This property specifies the identity of the user attempting authentication. For example, it can be a user name.
SECURITY _CREDENTIALS	java.naming .security . credentials	Dependent on authentication scheme	This property specifies the credentials with which the user will prove his identity. For example, it can be a password or digital certificate.
APPLET	java.naming .applet	java.applet .Applet	This property specifies an applet that will supply other properties via its PARAM tags.

The default values for unspecified properties depend on the service provider being used. In many cases, only java.naming.factory.initial and java.naming. provider.url must be specified. These are not the only environment properties that exist — other properties may be specific to the service, to some feature, or to the service provider. You'll need to consult the documentation for your specific JNDI service provider for more information.

The environment properties used to create InitialDirContext don't need to be hard-coded into the application. When you create an InitialContext, an InitialDirContext or an InitialLdapContext, the constructor determines the property values by searching through these sources in the following order:

1. In the hashtable passed into the constructor.

2. For factory and provider properties where value is not specified in the hashtable, and in the system properties passed in on the command.

3. For factory and provider properties, if the Context.APPLET property is set, then these properties will be ready from the applet's PARAM tags.

4. Any property present in the application resource files named jndi.properties located in the classpath or JAVA_HOME/lib/jndi.properties.

For single-value properties the first value found will be used, while for multi-value properties all the values found will be used and added to the value list in the order found. All properties listed in Table 11-3 are single-valued although some properties can be multi-valued. All these options give developers the ability to change servers or authentication mechanisms without having to recompile source code.

> **Tip**
>
> None of these mechanisms is very useful for Web-based applications packaged in WAR files. You probably don't want to hard-code values in the source code. You don't want to pass environment properties on the command line. Furthermore you might not have a searchable classpath depending on the application server; there are a lot of problems. One option for Web applications is to pass in JNDI environment parameters via the init-param section of the web.xml deployment descriptor.

Here's a servlet that obtains the PROVIDER_URL property from the deployment descriptor:

```
public void doGet(HttpServletRequest req,
    HttpServletResponse resp) {
    Hashtable env = new Hashtable();
    env.put(Context.INITIAL_CONTEXT_FACTORY,
        "com.sun.jndi.ldap.LdapCtxFactory");
    env.put(Context.PROVIDER_URL,
        getInitParameter("java.naming.provider.url"));
    InitialDirContext ctx = new InitialDirContext(env);
}
```

Here's how the deployment descriptor would specify the actual provider URL to use. The bold lines indicate where the parameter is being set.

```
<web-app>
  <servlet>
    <servlet-name>SomeServlet</servlet-name>
    <servlet-class>com.acme.SomeServlet</servlet-class>
    <init-param>
      <param-name>java.naming.provider.url</param-name>
      <param-value>ldap://localhost/o=Acme Inventions</param-value>
    </init-param>
  </servlet>

  <servlet-mapping>
    <servlet-name>SomeServlet</servlet-name>
    <url-pattern>/acme/*</url-pattern>
  </servlet-mapping>
</web-app>
```

Caution   While it is technically possible to configure JNDI properties by putting a `jndi.properties` file in your Web container's classpath, this is often undesirable, as multiple Web applications deployed in the same container may not all want the same property values. For this reason it's better to pass a unique set of JNDI properties to each servlet via the `<init-parm>` tag.

Once all the properties are set, you're ready to connect to your directory server — unless, of course, the directory requires authentication to prevent unauthorized access.

Implementing authentication

A LDAP server may require a user name and password to authenticate users before allowing any queries. Here's an example:

```
Hashtable env = new Hashtable();
env.put(Context.INITIAL_CONTEXT_FACTORY,
    "com.sun.jndi.ldap.LdapCtxFactory");
env.put(Context.PROVIDER_URL, "ldap://myserver");
env.put(Context.SECURITY_AUTHENTICATION, "simple");
env.put(Context.SECURITY_PRINCIPAL, "username");
env.put(Context.SECURITY_CREDENTIALS, "password");
InitialDirContext ctx = new InitialDirContext(env);
```

Simple authentication uses unencrypted, `"cleartext"` passwords. LDAP v3 servers may support more secure authentication mechanisms via *Simple Authentication and Security Layer (SASL)*. The following code finds the SASL authentication mechanisms supported by a server:

```
DirContext ctx = new InitialDirContext();
Attributes attrs = ctx.getAttributes(
    "ldap://myserver",
    new String[]{"supportedSASLMechanisms"});
```

The LDAP provider in Java 2 SDK v1.4 has built-in support for the External, Digest-MD5, and Kerberos v5 SASL mechanisms. Older versions of the LDAP provider have built-in support for the CRAM-MD5 and External SASL mechanisms. You can add support for additional mechanisms. See JSR 28 found at `http://www.jcp.org/en/jsr/detail?id=28`) for more information on the Java SASL specification.

Performing simple LDAP lookups

Once you're connected to a LDAP server and have the `DirContext` you can do a number of things with it. First, you can list all the entries in the context via `Context.list("")`. Note that the root context may possess multiple attributes. For example, even if the root context is `"dc=example,dc=com"`, there isn't necessarily a `"dc=com"`. Attempting to list the contents of `"dc=com"` in the following example would result in an exception:

```
Hashtable env = new Hashtable();
env.put(Context.INITIAL_CONTEXT_FACTORY,
    "com.sun.jndi.ldap.LdapCtxFactory");
env.put(Context.PROVIDER_URL, "ldap://myserver");

DirContext ctx = new InitialDirContext(env);
NamingEnumeration ne = ctx.list("dc=example,dc=com");

while(ne.hasMore())  {
    NameClassPair ncp = (NameClassPair)ne.next();
    System.out.println(ncp.getName());
}

ne.close();
ctx.close();
```

You can obtain the attributes associated with an entry in the context via `DirContext.getAttributes()`. You'll need to pass either the full DN of the entry for which you want to obtain the attributes, or the RDN relative to the place where you opened the `InitialDirContext`. The first example shows using the full DN:

```
Hashtable env = new Hashtable();
env.put(Context.INITIAL_CONTEXT_FACTORY,
    "com.sun.jndi.ldap.LdapCtxFactory");
env.put(Context.PROVIDER_URL, "ldap://myserver");

DirContext ctx = new InitialDirContext(env);
Attributes attrs = ctx.getAttributes(
    "cn=Lee Anne Phillips,ou=Sales,o=Acme Inventions");
NamingEnumeration ne = attrs.getAll();
while(ne.hasMore()) {
    System.out.println(ne.next());
}
ne.close();
ctx.close();
```

The following code will print out all the attributes associated with Lee Anne Phillips:

```
telephoneNumber: +1 408 555 6273
mail: leeanne.phillips@example.com, lee.anne.phillips@example.com
objectClass: top, person, organizationalPerson, inetOrgPerson
sn: Phillips
cn: Lee Anne Phillips
```

The next example shows using a RDN and obtaining Lee Anne's e-mail address. Note that in Lee Anne's case the `mail` attribute has multiple values.

```
Hashtable env = new Hashtable();
env.put(Context.INITIAL_CONTEXT_FACTORY,
    "com.sun.jndi.ldap.LdapCtxFactory");
env.put(Context.PROVIDER_URL,
```

```
          "ldap://localhost/ou=Sales,o=Acme Inventions");

    DirContext ctx = new InitialDirContext(env);
    Attributes attrs = ctx.getAttributes(
        "cn=Lee Anne Phillips");
    Attribute attr = attrs.get("mail");

    // this is the default email address
    System.out.println("default mail attribute: "
        +attr.get());

    // get all email addresses
    for(int i=0; i < attr.size(); i++)
        System.out.println("mail attribute value #"
            +i+": "+attr.get(i));

    ctx.close();
```

Note that when you call getAttributes() all attributes associated with the entry will be returned. In some cases these could be a large amount of data, which could make the query very slow. To make things more efficient you can specify which attributes you want the directory to send back, as shown here:

```
    String attr_req[] = { "mail", "ou" };
    Attributes attrs = ctx.getAttributes(
        "cn=Lee Anne Phillips", attr_req);
```

Now the directory will only return only the mail and ou attributes, reducing network traffic and memory usage.

Performing searches and comparing entries

Looking up entries in a directory given the entry's DN is fine, but what if you want to find entries that match other attributes? Or if you know part of the DN but not all of it? LDAP has a search-filter syntax for more powerful searches.

You can search in a context using the search() method to find entries that match the set of supplied attributes. Here's an example:

```
    Hashtable env = new Hashtable();
    env.put(Context.INITIAL_CONTEXT_FACTORY,
        "com.sun.jndi.ldap.LdapCtxFactory");
    env.put(Context.PROVIDER_URL,
        "ldap://localhost");

    DirContext ctx = new InitialDirContext(env);

    // passing true in the constructor specifies that
```

```
// attribute name case should be ignored
Attributes search_attrs = new BasicAttributes(true);
search_attrs.put("sn","Henry");

NamingEnumeration results = ctx.search(
    "ou=Engineering,o=Acme Inventions",search_attrs);

while(results.hasMore()) {
    SearchResult result = (SearchResult)results.next();
    System.out.println(result.getName());
    System.out.println(result.getAttributes());
}
```

This will print out the RDN of the entry (`cn=Ethan Henry`) as well as a list of all the attributes and their values for that entry.

While this is useful, sometimes you don't know the full value of the attributes you're looking for. You might know that someone's first name is James, but you might not know the full value of the `cn` attribute and `firstname` might not be an attribute in the directory (as in our example). A search filter takes the form of a regular expression specified in RFC 2254 found at `http://www.faqs.org/rfcs/rfc2254.html`.

For example, to search for anyone with a name beginning with James you might specify (`cn=James*`) as the filter. You can also combine multiple filters. For example, to specify people named James in Sales you can set the filter to (`&(cn=James*)(ou=Sales)`). Search filters use a prefix syntax — that is, the operator is specified first, followed by the arguments. The valid operators are listed in Table 11-4.

Table 11-4
LDAP search operators

Symbol	Description
&	AND means that all conditions listed must be `true` for this expression to be `true` (takes multiple conditions).
|	OR means that one or more of the conditions listed must be `true` for this expression to be `true` (takes multiple arguments).
!	NOT means that the value of this expression is the opposite of the listed condition (takes one argument).
=	Equality is used according to the matching rule of the attribute.
~=	Approximate equality is used according to the matching rule of the attribute.

Continued

Table 11-4 *(continued)*	
Symbol	**Description**
>=	Matches when the attribute is greater than the specified value.
<=	Matches when the attribute is less than the specified value.
=*	Presence means that the attribute must be present, but can have any value.
*	Wildcard means that any set of characters will match.
\	Escape is used for including *, (, and) inside attribute values.

Each item in a search filter has to be enclosed in a pair of parentheses, as in
(`"cn=James McGovern"`). Some examples of search filters that would match
entries in the sample directory are as follows:

```
(& (ou=Engineering) (sn=Jo))
(& (ou=Sales) !(sn=Smith))
(| (cn=J*) (cn=E*) (cn=L*))
```

You can further control the search via the `SearchControls` class. For example, in
the previous example the context `ou=Engineering,o=Acme Inventions` had to
be explicitly specified because by default searches only apply in the specified context. The `SearchControls` class can control the following aspects of the search:

✦ The search scope, which determines whether the search should be performed
in all subcontexts, just in the specified context (the default setting), or only in
the named entry

✦ The maximum number of entries to return

✦ How long to wait before timing out

✦ Which attributes should be returned along with each matching entry

Here's some sample code that uses the `SearchControls` class. The code relevant
to searching is highlighted in bold:

```
import javax.naming.*;
import javax.naming.directory.*;
import java.util.*;

public class Search {
public static void main(String args[]) {

    Hashtable env = new Hashtable();
    env.put(Context.INITIAL_CONTEXT_FACTORY,
        "com.sun.jndi.ldap.LdapCtxFactory");
    env.put(Context.PROVIDER_URL,
```

```
                "ldap://myserver");

        try {
            DirContext ctx = new InitialDirContext(env);

            String filter = "(cn=E*)";
            SearchControls controls = new SearchControls();
            controls.setSearchScope(
                SearchControls.SUBTREE_SCOPE);
            String ret_attrs[] = { "cn", "mail" };
            controls.setReturningAttributes(ret_attrs);

            NamingEnumeration result = ctx.search(
                "o=Acme Inventions",filter,controls);

            while(result.hasMore()) {
                System.out.println(result.next());
            }
        }
        catch(NamingException e) {
            e.printStackTrace();
        }
    }
}
```

In some cases a directory will allow you to check the value of an attribute but won't provide you with the attribute's value. This is often the case with tasks such as checking password values — cases in which you don't want to return the password to the client application. This type of security restriction is configured internally in the directory and is generally not visible to the JNDI LDAP client. If you know that you need to perform a comparison operation, perform a regular search using the following constraints:

✦ The search scope (in the `SearchControls` object) should be set to `OBJECT_SCOPE`

✦ The exact `DN`must be specified

✦ The filter string should contain no wildcards

✦ `SearchControls.setReturningAttributes` should not be invoked

For example, the following code checks a user's password in our directory:

```
SearchControls controls = new SearchControls();
controls.setReturningObjFlag(true);
controls.setSearchScope(SearchControls.OBJECT_SCOPE);
String filter = "userPassword=coyote";
NamingEnumeration answer = ctx.search("cn=Ethan Henry,
    ou=Engineering,o=Acme Inventions", filter, controls);
```

If the attributes specified in the search filter all match, `answer.hasMore()` returns `true`. Otherwise, `answer.hasMore()` returns `false`. If you directly query the value of an attribute that can only be compared, OpenLDAP will indicate that the attribute exists but will not return a value for it. Other directories should behave similarly.

Modifying the directory

Of course, simply finding entries in a directory may not be all you need to do. Sometimes new entries need to be added to the directory and sometimes out-of-date entries need to be removed. Both of these tasks are easy to carry out.

Adding new entries

Before you can add an entry you need to know two things:

✦ What context is the new entry being added to?

✦ What attributes does the new entry have?

To add a new entry you put all the attributes into a `BasicAttributes` object and then call `createSubconext`, as shown here:

```
BasicAttributes attrs = new BasicAttributes();
attrs.put("cn","Alan Williamson");
attrs.put("mail","alan.williamson@example.com");
attrs.put("telephone","+44 099 024 7226");
DirContext new_ctx = ctx.createSubcontext(
    "ou=Engineering,o=Acme Inventions",attrs);
```

Removing entries

Removing entries is even simpler than adding new entries. Removing a context removes the context, all its attributes, and all its subcontexts.

Caution   Be careful—if you delete the root context the entire database will be removed!

The following example removes an entry, all the entry's attributes, and any entries beneath it:

```
ctx.destroySubcontext(
    "cn=Alan Williamson, ou=Engineering, o=Acme Inventions");
```

Adding objects to a directory

Directory servers are powerful general-purpose tools. They're capable of storing more than just human-readable text information; you can use a directory as a storage mechanism for Java objects as well. This section covers the following approaches to adding Java objects to a directory:

✦ Storing serialized data

✦ Storing the object as a reference

✦ Storing the object data as directory attributes

Storing serialized data

The first approach to storing an object in a directory is simply to serialize the object and store the resultant string of bytes in the directory. This approach has the advantage of being simple to implement, but the information thus stored in the directory can only be understood by another Java application. The directory must be configured with the correct schema in order to store Java objects — for example, see the `ava.schema` file distributed with OpenLDAP.

This code stores an object in a directory by serializing it:

```
SomeData sd = new SomeData(); // implements Serializable
ctx.bind("cn=SomeData",sd);
```

The application that retrieves the object from the directory has to have the class file for that type of object available to deserialize the object. If you want to specify where to find the class definition for the object you can add the `javaCodeBase` attribute to the object entry, as shown here:

```
SomeData sd = new SomeData(); // implements Serializable
Basic Attributes attrs = new BasicAttributes();
attrs.put("javaCodeBase", "http://java.example.com/code");
ctx.bind("cn=SomeData",sd,attrs);
```

Once the object has been stored in the directory it can be retrieved with a call to `lookup()`, as shown here:

```
SomeData sd2 = (SomeData)ctx.lookup("cn=SomeData");
```

Storing objects as references

The second approach to storing an object in a directory is to store it as a reference. When an object is stored as a reference a number of `RefAddr` objects are stored in the directory, along with the name and location of a factory class. When it comes time to retrieve the object an instance of the factory class is created and it, in turn, retrieves the RefAddr objects from the directory and recreates the object. The location of the factory class is a URL (or a list of URLs) that specifies where to look to find the class definition for the factory class.

If this sounds more complicated than the previous approach, that's because it is. The advantage is that the information in the directory can be stored in a more compact form. More importantly, code is executed when the object is recreated, which provides the ability for the application to go out and connect to remote machines or retrieve other external information that can be used to recreate the object.

A simple example of using references should give you the general idea of how the reference mechanism works. Classes whose objects are to be stored as references must implement the Referenceable interface. The two concrete subclasses RefAddr can be used to store information in the directory: StringRefAddr and BinaryRefAddr. Here's an example:

```
public class Widget implements Referenceable {
    public String name;
    public int mass;

    public Widget(String name, int mass) {
        this.name=name; this.mass=mass;
    }

    public Reference getReference() throws NamingException {
        StringRefAddr nameRef = new StringRefAddr("Widget Name", name);
        byte bytes[] = { (byte)mass, (byte)(mass>>8) };
        BinaryRefAddr massRef = new BinaryRefAddr("Mass", bytes);
        Reference ref = new Reference(Widget.class.getName(),
            WidgetFactory.class.getName(),
            null);
        ref.add(nameRef);
        ref.add(massRef);
        return ref;
    }
}
```

When the object is stored in the directory via a call to bind() it is automatically turned into a set of RefAddr objects by calling getReference(). When the object is retrieved an instance of the factory class is created, which in turn re-creates the object. When creating a factory class be aware that sometimes a factory object is asked to instantiate an object that it doesn't know anything about. This is normal — a service provider may have many object factories on hand. If a factory is asked to instantiate something it doesn't recognize, the factory should just return null. The only time a factory should throw an exception is when it is sure that it knows how to create the type of object being asked for but is unable to. Here's an example:

```
public class WidgetFactory implements ObjectFactory {
    public Object getObjectInstance(Object info, Name name,
    Context nameCtx, Hashtable environment ) throws Exception {
        if(info instanceof Reference) {
            Reference ref = (Reference)info;
            if(ref.getClassName().equals(Widget.class.getName())) {
                String nam = (String)ref.get("Widget Name").getContent();
                byte bytes[] = (byte[])ref.get("Mass").getContent();
                return new Widget(nam,bytes[0]+(bytes[1]<<8));
            }
        }
        return null; // try another factory
    }
}
```

The JNDI provider (the LDAP provider in this case) will read the reference information stored in the directory and pass it to each of the object-factory instances it has. One of those instances should recognize the type of the object, take the information, and create a new copy of the object that was originally stored.

So to put an object into a directory using references you would do this:

```
Widget w = new Widget("ACME Rocket Booster",100);
// assuming we already have a DirContext object
ctx.bind("cn=Rocket Booster",w);
```

The service provider will store the `Widget` object by calling `getReference()` and then storing the `Reference` object n the directory. When you extract the following object

```
Widget w2 = (Widget)ctx.lookup("cn=Rocket Booster");
```

the service provider will take the `RefAddr` objects and pass them to the corresponding object factories to be converted into instances of the appropriate objects. If multiple factories are defined, the JNDI framework will check each of them until it finds a factory that can handle that type of data. The order in which the factories are searched is not defined, so you should only reference one factory for each type of object you want to read from a directory.

Note You can store a `Referenceable` object in the directory only if the underlying service provider supports it. Sun's LDAP service provider supports storing both `Reference` and `Referenceable` objects.

Storing object data as directory attributes

There may be times when you want to store a Java object inside a directory but make the object data easily accessible to non-Java applications. The easiest way do this is to store the entire object's data as attributes instead of serializing the data or using references. By implementing the `DirContext` interface on your class the service provider will store the data for instances of that class as a series of standard LDAP attributes.

 Note   The LDAP service provider may not support storing objects as attributes. Sun's LDAP service provider does support this functionality.

Implementing the `DirContext` interface requires implementing a lot of methods. For the purposes of storing objects, however, most of the methods don't need to be implemented and can be given empty method bodies. The only method that is required for storing objects is `getAttributes()`. Here's an example:

```
public class Widget2 implements DirContext {

String name;
int mass;

public Widget2(String name, int mass) {
    this.name = name; this.mass = mass;
}

public Widget2(String name, int mass) {
    // the constructor arg indicates that
    // the case for strings should be ignored
}

public Attributes getAttributes(String name)
    throws NamingException {
    // there aren't really any subcontexts so only
    // provide attributes for this context
    if(!name.equals(""))
        throw new NameNotFoundException();

    Attributes myAttrs = new BasicAttributes();
    myAttrs = new BasicAttributes(true);
    Attribute attr = new BasicAttribute("objectclass");
    attr.add("extensibleObject");
    attr.add("top");
    myAttrs.put(attr);
    attr = new BasicAttribute("name",name);
    myAttrs.put(attr);
    attr = new BasicAttribute("mass",new Integer(mass));
    myAttrs.put(attr);

    return myAttrs;
}

public Attributes getAttributes(Name name)
    throws NamingException {
```

```
        return getAttributes(name.toString());
    }

    // remainder of DirContext methods with empty bodies...

    }
```

Again, storing the object in the directory is accomplished exactly the same way as shown earlier in this chapter — by adding to the directory via `bind()`. Here's an example:

```
Widget2 w = new Widget2("ACME Canned Tornado", 2);
ctx.bind("cn=Canned Tornado", w);
```

The object can now be accessed like any other directory entry. Alternatively, if you want to retrieve the entry as an object, you can use an object factory to automatically turn the set of attributes into an object.

An object factory for an object stored as a set of attributes is similar to the `WidgetFactory` object factory shown earlier. The difference is that in this case the factory needs to implement `DirObjectFactory` instead of just `ObjectFactory`. `DirObjectFactory`'s `getObjectInstance()` method takes an additional parameter, the set of attributes representing the object. Here's an example:

```
public class WidgetFactory2 implements DirObjectFactory {
    // empty body for getObjectInstance(Object,Name,Context,Hashtable)

    public Object getObjectInstance(Object obj, Name name,
    Context nameCtx, Hashtable environment, Attributes attrs)
    throws Exception {
        if(obj instanceof DirContext) {
            try {
                // make sure both name and mass attributes are present
                if((attrs.get("name") == null) ||
                    (attrs.get("mass") == null))
                    return null;

                String name = (String)attrs.get("name").get();
                int mass = String.parseInt(
                    (String)attrs.get("mass").get());
                return new Widget2(name,mass);
            } catch(Exception e) {
                e.printStackTrace();
                throw e;
            }
        }
    return null;
    }
}
```

Two separate object-factory classes are shown to clearly demonstrate the difference between retrieving an object stored as a reference and retrieving an object stored using attributes, but it is possible to put both methods into a single factory class capable of re-creating `Widget` objects from either a reference or a set of attributes.

In addition to being storing and retrieving objects in a directory, you can store additional attributes to make finding the objects easy with the LDAP search facilities described earlier in this chapter. Attributes can be supplied when the object is put into the directory via `DirContext.bind( Name, Object, Attributes)` or modified later on with `DirContext.modifyAttributes(Name, int, Attributes)`, where the `int` parameter specifies one of the three operations listed in Table 11-5.

Table 11-5	
Attribute-modification operations	
Parameter value	**Action**
`DirContext.ADD_ATTRIBUTE`	The specified attributes will be added to the directory entry.
`DirContext.REMOVE_ATTRIBUTE`	The specified attributes will be removed from the entry.
`DirContext.REPLACE_ATTRIBUTE`	The specified attributes will have their values changed in the entry.

Attribute modification is *atomic* — either all the modifications are applied or none of them is.

These are the essentials of accessing LDAP-enabled directories with JNDI. LDAP and JNDI are a powerful combination, allowing you to access existing directory information from inside Java applications. More powerful features are available as well enabling you to store Java objects in a directory and automatic conversion between the data store in the directory and Java objects.

Connecting to DNS

LDAP isn't the only service provider available for JNDI. Another type of directly that's used frequently in Java applications is DNS — the Internet Directory Name Service. DNS is the directory that maps human-readable machine names (such as `www.example.com`) to IP addresses (such as `192.168.100.1`). DNS is more than just a simple naming service, though. It contains a number of different record types that specify different types of name-to-address translation. Table 11-6 lists some of the more commonly used record types, which are defined in RFC 1035 found at `http://www.faqs.org/rfcs/rfc1035.html`.

Table 11-6
DNS record types

Record Type	Use
A	Address: Used for basic name-to-address translation. IP addresses take the form of four eight-bit octets — for example, `192.168.100.1`.
NS	Name server: Used as the authoritative or master name server for the specified domain
CNAME	Canonical domain name: Applies to the specified server — in some cases domain names may in fact be aliases for other names
SOA	Start of authority: Contains information about the domain itself, such as a timestamp indicating the last update, a contact address, and some other information.
TXT	Text: Freeform text describing the domain
MX	Mail exchange: Specifies the servers in the domain used to receive mail. There may be multiple MX records per domain, specifying primary mail servers, secondary mail servers, and so on.
PTR	Pointer: Used for doing reverse domain-name lookups from IP addresses. The PTR record's name is not the IP address, but the IP address with its four octets reversed, followed by `.IN-ADDR.ARPA`. For example, a reverse lookup on `192.168.100.1` would use the PTR record `1.100.168.192.IN-ADDR.ARPA`.

The `java.net.InetAddress` class is capable of doing basic A-record lookups, but for anything more sophisticated, such as a Java-based mail-delivery application, you'll need to access DNS via JNDI.

To connect to a DNS server you'll need to go through the same basic set of steps you went through to connect to a LDAP server: Specify your environment parameters and then obtain an `InitalDirConext`. Sun includes a DNS service provider by default in JDK 1.4 and above. If you're using JDK 1.3 or another JVM that doesn't include a DNS service provider in its library, you can download the classes from `http://java.sun.com/products/jndi/index.html#download`.

DNS environment properties

The properties listed in Table 11-7 can be used with Sun's JNDI DNS service provider.

Table 11-7 DNS environment properties	
Property	**Description**
`java.naming.provider.url`	Specifies the host name and port number of the DNS server to use, as well as the initial context's domain name. A URL-like notation is used to represent DNS servers in the following format:
`dns:[//host[:port]][/domain]`	That is, if you do not specify a hostname `localhost` will be used as the default. If you do not specify a port number the default for DNS services is port 53.
`java.naming.factory.initial`	The initial context factory for the DNS service provider is `com.sun.jndi.dns.DnsContextFactory`. This class is always used for accessing DNS via JNDI.
`com.sun.jndi.dns.recursion`	Specifies whether the DNS server will forward queries for which it has no information. If the value is `false` the DNS server will only reply with information in its own database or cache. If the value is unspecified or `true` queries will be automatically forwarded by the DNS server.
`java.naming.authoritative`	Specifies whether the server should only return authoritative responses—that is, whether it should not return cached values but should instead forward the query to a nameserver specified in the domain's NS record.
`com.sun.jndi.lookup.attr`	Specifies the attribute to pass to an object factory when you attempt to turn the DNS entry into an object. Defaults to TXT.
`java.naming.factory.object`	Specifies a colon-separated list of class names to use as factories for transforming entries into objects. Not DNS-specific—refer to the previous section on storing objects in directories.

DNS lookups

Once you've specified the environment properties and obtained an
InitialDirContext, performing simple name-to-address translation is as simple
as calling getAttributes(). Always specify exactly what attributes you want in
the getAttributes() call—in some cases a DNS server will return only the information it has in its cache unless you explicitly ask for certain attributes. Here is a
code fragment along with the output it generates from two consecutive runs:

```
Hashtable env = new Hashtable();
env.put(Context.INITIAL_CONTEXT_FACTORY,"com.sun.jndi.dns.DnsCo
ntextFactory");
env.put(Context.PROVIDER_URL, "dns://mydnssever/");
env.put("com.sun.jndi.dns.recursion", "true");
DirContext ctx = new InitialDirContext(env);

Attributes attrs = ctx.getAttributes(args[0]);
System.out.println(attrs);

attrs = ctx.getAttributes(args[0], new String[] { "MX" } );
System.out.println(attrs);

attrs = ctx.getAttributes(args[0], new String[] { "A" } );
System.out.println(attrs);
```

Running this code results in the following output:

```
C:\>java dnsex quest.com
{ns=NS: A.NS.VERIO.NET, S.NS.VERIO.NET}
{mx=MX: 110 backupmx2.veriomail.com, 10 mail.quest.com, 30 exchange.quest.com,
100 backupmx1.veriomail.com}
{a=A: 192.77.210.55}


C:\>java dnsex quest.com
{a=A: 192.77.210.55, ns=NS: A.NS.VERIO.NET, S.NS.VERIO.NET, mx=MX: 110
backupmx2.veriomail.com, 10 mail.quest.com, 30 exchange.quest.com, 100
backupmx1.veriomail.com}
{mx=MX: 110 backupmx2.veriomail.com, 10 mail.quest.com, 30 exchange.quest.com,
100 backupmx1.veriomail.com}
{a=A: 192.77.210.55}
```

Note that the first time getAttributes() is called the DNS server returns only the
attributes it has in its cache: the NS records. Once the A and MX records have been
explicitly retrieved they are included in the full attribute set the next time.

Reverse DNS lookups

In certain situations you'd like to find the hostname of a given IP address. For example, when you're processing Web-server logs it can be useful to do a reverse lookup for the names of machines accessing your server so you can see where your users are coming from. In other cases applications need to perform reverse lookups for security reasons, to verify that servers are what they claim to be. In some cases Simple Mail Transfer Protocol (SMTP) servers will do a double reverse lookup — they'll perform a reverse lookup of the IP address of the machine attempting to deliver mail and then perform a regular lookup on that hostname. If both IP addresses match, everything is OK; otherwise the connection is rejected.

Caution   Reverse lookup is not always possible. In many cases no hostname can be retrieved for a given IP address. If no name record is available an exception will be thrown.

Reverse lookups work like regular lookups except for the following changes:

✦ The lookup is performed in the `in-addr.arpa` domain. This string has to be passed in with the provider URL or at the end of the IP address being queried.

✦ The IP address is provided backwards — that is, if the host you're looking for has the IP address `216.239.37.100`, you need to do a lookup on `100.37.239.216`.

The following code should retrieve a single PTR record with a value of `www.google.com`:

```
Hashtable env = new Hashtable();
env.put(Context.INITIAL_CONTEXT_FACTORY,
    "com.sun.jndi.dns.DnsContextFactory");
env.put(Context.PROVIDER_URL,
    "dns://mydnsserver/in-addr.arpa");
DirContext ctx = new InitialDirContext(env);

// do a reverse lookup on 216.239.37.100
Attributes attrs = ctx.getAttributes("100.37.239.216");
System.out.println(attrs);
```

JNDI provides a convenient and powerful way to access DNS information. We'll see more on accessing DNS information via JNDI in one of the examples later in the chapter.

Considering Other JNDI Service Providers

A number of JNDI service providers are available. Depending on the version of the Java SDK you're using some providers may be bundled by default. If you're looking for JNDI-provider classes you can check Sun's listing at `http://java.sun.com/products/jndi/serviceproviders.html`. This section covers the following JNDI service providers:

✦ File systems

✦ COS naming for CORBA

✦ Network Information System (NIS)

✦ Directory Services Markup Language (DSML)

✦ Application-server providers

File systems

The hierarchical nature of modern computer file systems maps naturally to the interface provided by JNDI. Sun's file-system JNDI provider is built on top of `java.io.File`, so it is only capable of doing things that are possible with the `File` class — for example, you can't get around file-system security limitations.

The file-system service provider is not meant to be used for any serious manipulation of the file system — lots of classes in the `java.io` and `java.nio` packages can enable you to do that. The file-system service provider is, however, good for learning how to use JNDI if you don't have a LDAP server handy.

COS naming for CORBA

The Common Object Services (COS) name server is the name server for storing Common Object Request Broker Architecture (CORBA) object references. CORBA is a standard for language-neutral application interoperation via the Internet Inter-Orb Protocol (IIOP). CORBA is used in a wide variety of enterprise applications, especially in systems in which not every component is written in Java.

The COS naming service provider is provided by default in Sun's JDK 1.3 and higher, but the code can also be downloaded from Sun's Web site at `http://java.sun.com/products/jndi/index.html#download`.

Network Information System

The Network Information System (NIS) is a hierarchical and secure network-information service system primarily for Unix systems. NIS is a simple distributed database that enables information managers and system administrators to manage the network information for complex and heterogeneous computer systems. NIS can be used as a distributed password file but has other, more advanced, directory functionality as well. You can download the NIS service provider from Sun.

Directory Services Markup Language

DSML is a new and evolving specification for representing directory information as XML documents. DSML v1 only specifies a XML structure for representing directory entries or query results, not queries. Sun's DSML v1 service provider provides a read-only interface to DSML files or DSML data available via an HTTP URL. The service provider reads in the entire document and makes an in-memory representation (the way a DOM parser does). Any changes you make to the information are not reflected in the original source of the DSML data.

More information on DSML is available from `http://www.oasis-open.org/committees/dsml/`. Sun's DSML service provider is available from Sun's service-providers download page.

Application-server providers

JNDI isn't just used for directory services, although all the examples shown in this chapter involve directories. Many of the other J2EE APIs use JNDI as a naming-service interface to locate distributed resources such as JDBC data sources, Enterprise JavaBeans, and JMS destinations.

Application-server providers usually have their own naming-service providers. Consult your product documentation for more information about what environment properties you need to specify. Usually you'll just need to specify the initial context factory and a provider URL, but in some cases other information may be necessary as well.

Listings 11-3 through 11-5 provide some examples of how to obtain naming contexts in the following application servers:

✦ BEA WebLogic

✦ IBM WebSphere

✦ JBoss

Listing 11-3: **BEA WebLogic server**

```
Hashtable env = new Hashtable();
env.put(Context.INITIAL_CONTEXT_FACTORY,
    "weblogic.jndi.WLInitialContextFactory");
env.put(Context.PROVIDER_URL, "t3://weblogicServer:7001");
Context ctx = new InitialContext(env);
```

Listing 11-4: **IBM WebSphere server**

```
Hashtable env = new Hashtable();
env.put(Context.INITIAL_CONTEXT_FACTORY,
    "com.ibm.websphere.naming.WsnInitialContextFactory");
env.put(Context.PROVIDER_URL,
    "iiop://myhost.mycompany.com:900");
Context initialContext = new InitialContext(env);
```

Listing 11-5: **JBoss server**

```
Hashtable env = new Hashtable();
env.put(Context.INITIAL_CONTEXT_FACTORY,
    "org.jnp.interfaces.NamingContextFactory");
env.put(Context.PROVIDER_URL, "jnp://localhost:1099");
Context ctx = new InitialContext(env);
```

Note that each of the different naming-service providers has its own initial context factory class and its own concept of how to format provider pseudo-URLs. The JNDI name for components is typically configured in the application server's administrative console or in the component's deployment descriptor. Again, refer to the product documentation for instructions about how to configure the namespace.

Exploring the Enterprise JavaBean Environment

When you're writing the code for an EJB you can use JNDI to access the enterprise bean's environment. This is a special set of values that is described in the EJB's deployment descriptor and accessed via JNDI. For example, in the code for an EJB you may have the following:

```
Context initCtx = new InitialContext();
Context myEnv = (Context)
    initCtx.lookup("java:comp/env");
Integer max = (Integer)myEnv.lookup("maxValue");
// or
Integer max2 = (Integer)initCtx.lookup(
    "java:comp/env/maxValue");
```

In this case, the application is trying to retrieve the value of the property maxValue specified in the enterprise bean's environment. This value is set in the enterprise bean's deployment descriptor as shown here:

```
<enterprise-beans>
    <session>
...
        <ejb-name>SomeBean</ejb-name>
        <ejb-class>com.company.SomeBean</ejb-class>
...
        <env-entry>
            <description>
                The maximum number of things to be done.
            </description>
            <env-entry-name>maxValue</env-entry-name>
            <env-entry-type>java.lang.Integer</env-entry-type>
            <env-entry-value>15</env-entry-value>
        </env-entry>
</enterprise-beans>
```

This deployment descriptor fragment indicates that there is a property in the enterprise bean's environment called maxValue of type Integer that has the value, 15. The environment entry values may be one of the following Java types:

✦ String

✦ Character

✦ Integer

✦ Boolean

✦ Double

✦ Byte

✦ Short

✦ Long

✦ Float

Environment properties can also be set for the following:

References to other EJBs

Web service references via the Java API for XML-based RPC (JAX-RPC) and factory references for JDBC connection factories;

JMS connection factories

JavaMail connection factories

URL connection factories

All of these types of environment properties use the same `java:com/env` JNDI syntax.

More information on enterprise bean environment references can be found in the Enterprise JavaBean 2.1 specification, section 20.

Airline Reservations Business Case

Connexia Airlines needs to create a directory that will store all the information about the users who will need to access its reservations system. The directory will have to store information about users — specifically whether a user is an agent, partner, consumer, or employee. Other pieces of information might include the user's full name, telephone number, and e-mail address.

There are two things we need to figure out here: The first is the schema and configuration of the directory server, and the second is how that server will be accessed from Java code. The first has nothing to do with Java and JNDI. However, reviewing it is necessary because it isn't possible to build the JNDI access code without knowing some details about how the directory server is configured.

For the purposes of this example we'll show a configuration file that could be used with OpenLDAP. A number of predefined object classes are provided with OpenLDAP. For the sake of convenience we can represent all the users in our system using the `InetOrgPerson` schema, which was originally defined in RFC 2798. This schema provides definitions for more attribute types than we could probably use, so we'll restrict our use of `InetOrgPerson` to these attributes:

Attribute	Description
cn	The user's full name, required by the schema
sn	The user's surname, required by the schema
uid	The user's unique ID
userPassword	The user's password, stored in cleartext for this example
employeeNumber	The employee ID (for employees)
telephoneNumber	The user's telephone number
mail	The user's e-mail address
employeeType	Either agent, partner, consumer, or employee
o	The organization (Connexia Airlines)

A definition for the InetOrgPerson schema has already been provided, so we don't have to worry about that. The only thing we do need to check is what level of access we want to give to different types of users. In this application users are not going to be looking up other users' records, so we don't need to restrict access based on user type. In situations in which users may be viewing or manipulating the contents of the directory, we would want to restrict access to read-only for non-employees. We might also want to only allow attribute comparisons and not full attribute reads for the userPassword. Finally, we might only want to allow write access only to fields such as telephoneNumber and cn so users wouldn't be able to modify their own uid or employeeType attributes.

As an example of restricting access to certain attributes, we might specify the following security restriction in the OpenLDAP configuration file:

```
access to * by * read
access to * attr=telephoneNumber, mail by * write
access to * attr=userPassword by * compare
```

This would enable users to compare userPassword attributes but not to read them, to write to the telephoneNumber and mail attributes, and to read everything else. For more information on configuring directory security, see your directory server's documentation. For OpenLDAP, see *OpenLDAP 2.1 Administrator's Guide* at http://www.openldap.org/doc/admin/.

These security considerations are determined primarily by the directory's accessibility. If the directory server is publicly accessible on the Internet, extensive security restrictions must be put in place. If the directory server is isolated behind a firewall and is only accessible to a limited number of applications (this is typical of many Web-based systems), security doesn't need to be implemented in the directory server itself as it is taken care of by the application and network architecture.

For this example we need to store passwords in cleartext and make them readable so that they can be mailed to users who have forgotten their passwords.

Next we have to determine how the directory will be organized. Because the most common use of the directory is to authenticate users with their uid and userPassword attributes, it would make sense to organize the directory by uid.

Here's a sample LDIF file showing some possible directory entries:

```
dn: o=Connexia Airlines
o: Connexia Airlines
objectclass: top
objectclass: organization

dn: uid=jmcgovern, o=Connexia Airlines
uid: jmcgovern
```

```
userPassword: red
cn: James McGovern
sn: McGovern
mail: james.mcgovern@example.com
telephonenumber: +1 610 555 6273
employeeType: agent
objectclass: top
objectclass: person
objectclass: organizationalPerson
objectclass: inetOrgPerson

dn: uid=mlittle, o=Connexia Airlines
uid: mlittle
userPassword: green
cn: Mark Little
sn: Little
mail: mark.little@example.com
telephonenumber: +1 905 555 6273
employeeType: partner
objectclass: top
objectclass: person
objectclass: organizationalPerson
objectclass: inetOrgPerson

dn: uid=radatia, o=Connexia Airlines
uid: radatia
userPassword: blue
cn: Rahim Adatia
sn: Adatia
mail: rahim.adatia@example.com
telephonenumber: +1 715 555 6273
employeeType: consumer
objectclass: top
objectclass: person
objectclass: organizationalPerson
objectclass: inetOrgPerson

dn: uid=jgordon, o=Connexia Airlines
uid: jgordon
userPassword: fuscia
cn: Jason Gordon
sn: Gordon
mail: jason.gordon@example.com
telephonenumber: +1 664 555 6273
employeeType: employee
employeeNumber: 90210
objectclass: top
objectclass: person
objectclass: organizationalPerson
objectclass: inetOrgPerson
```

Here's the OpenLDAP configuration file to use with this directory. Replace %OPENLDAP% with the name of the directory where OpenLDAP is installed.

```
include         %OPENLDAP%/schema/core.schema
include         %OPENLDAP%/schema/java.schema
include         %OPENLDAP%/schema/cosine.schema
include         %OPENLDAP%/schema/inetorgperson.schema

pidfile         %OPENLDAP%/slapd.pid
argsfile        %OPENLDAP%/slapd.args

database        ldbm
suffix          "o=Connexia Airlines"
directory       %OPENLDAP%/openldap-ldbm

access to * by * read
access to * attr=telephoneNumber,mail by * write
access to * attr=userPassword by * compare

index objectClass eq
```

This directory doesn't have much of a complex structure, but a complex structure isn't necessary for the applications we're looking at building.

Why use a directory instead of a relational database for storing user information? There are two reasons: speed and cost. A database may be busy with many complex queries. Trying to check a user's password against a busy database may take a long time. Because the directory doesn't deal with any other tasks it should always have a short response time. Also, databases are expensive. Many databases are licensed based on their size or the number of concurrent connections. There may be many users and because storing their information doesn't require a database's special capabilities it would be a waste of database resources. Finally, in the future it may be possible to integrate the user directory for Connexia Airlines' Web applications with the internal employee directory, making it easy for an employee to log in without having to set up a new account.

Another advantage of using LDAP for user-authentication data is the ability to integrate with the Java Authentication and Authorization Service (JAAS).

 **Cross-Reference**   See Chapter 12 for more information on JAAS.

Shortly you'll see some sample code that shows how an application might validate a user's password. Note that the connection to the directory is anonymous — no security is used to prevent unauthorized applications from connection to the directory. However, because userPassword attributes can't be read directly, at least that information is safe.

The following program shows a method that can be used to verify the password. To make sure it works, we test one of the user IDs with a couple of different passwords. If we attempted to read the value of the userPassword attribute the result would not have any value for that attribute.

```java
import java.util.*;
import javax.naming.*;
import javax.naming.directory.*;

public class CheckPassword {
    public static boolean checkPassword(String uid,
    String password) {
        // get initial context
        // these properties could also be specified
        // on the command line or in a jndi.properties file
        Hashtable env = new Hashtable();
        env.put(Context.INITIAL_CONTEXT_FACTORY,
            "com.sun.jndi.ldap.LdapCtxFactory");
        env.put(Context.PROVIDER_URL,
            "ldap://localhost/o=Connexia Airlines");

        try {
            DirContext ctx = new InitialDirContext(env);
            SearchControls controls = new SearchControls();
            controls.setReturningObjFlag(true);
            controls.setSearchScope(
                SearchControls.OBJECT_SCOPE);
            String filter = "userPassword="+password;
            NamingEnumeration answer = ctx.search("uid="+uid,
                filter, controls);

            return answer.hasMore();
        } catch(NamingException e) {
            e.printStackTrace();
            return false;
        }
    }

    public static void main(String args[]) {
        System.out.println(checkPassword("jmcgovern","red"));
        System.out.println(checkPassword("jmcgovern",
            "blue"));
    }
}
```

This type of directory structure provides a flexible base upon which to build a wide range of enterprise systems. In some cases, the directory used for application-based authentication may also be integrated with other enterprise systems, such as e-mail or enterprise resource planning (ERP) systems. LDAP and JNDI provide a flexible interface that allows developers to easily access this information from within custom applications.

Magazine Publisher Business Case

In the second business case, a magazine publisher wants to cut down on the number of fraudulent transactions being conducted over its Web site. One way to do this is to monitor what external sites are connecting to the publisher's e-commerce system. Two approaches are possible:

✦ The application can perform a reverse lookup on the customer's system for all transactions and log the information along with the publisher's internal record of the sale. This approach has a couple of advantages. The reverse lookup can be performed asynchronously, so the user doesn't need to wait for the reverse lookup in order to receive confirmation. Also, many machines connected to the Internet don't have reverse lookup entries in DNS, even though there isn't anything nefarious about them. This is especially true of users who use dialup Internet access.

✦ The application can perform a double reverse lookup, attempting to check the domain name from the IP address and then to turn the domain name back into an IP address to compare the two values. While it is used by some FTP and SMTP servers this is not a good approach for a consumer-oriented e-commerce application. Too many legitimate customers are likely to be turned away because of DNS configuration issues.

Even though the second option, the double reverse lookup, is out of the question, let's look at some code for it. First, here's the code for a basic reverse lookup:

```
import java.util.*;
import javax.naming.*;
import javax.naming.directory.*;

public class rdns {

/**
 * @return the name of the machine being checked or null
 *          if there is no reverse DNS entry
 **/
public static String reverseLookup(InetAddress addr) {

    byte octets[] = addr.getAddress();
    StringBuffer revName = new StringBuffer(15);

    // silly signed bytes...
    revName.append((int)octets[3] & 0xff);
    revName.append('.');
    revName.append((int)octets[2] & 0xff);
    revName.append('.');
    revName.append((int)octets[1] & 0xff);
    revName.append('.');
    revName.append((int)octets[0] & 0xff);
```

```
        try {
            Hashtable env = new Hashtable();
            env.put(Context.INITIAL_CONTEXT_FACTORY,
                "com.sun.jndi.dns.DnsContextFactory");
            env.put(Context.PROVIDER_URL,
                "dns://192.168.1.1/in-addr.arpa");
            env.put("com.sun.jndi.dns.recursion", "true");
            DirContext ctx = new InitialDirContext(env);

            Attributes attrs =
                ctx.getAttributes(revName.toString());
            return (String)attrs.get("PTR").get();

        } catch(NamingException e) {
            e.printStackTrace();
            return null;
        }
    }

    public static void main(String args[]) {
        // perform a reverse lookup on args[0]
        try {
            InetAddress addr = InetAddress.getByName(args[0]);
            System.out.println(addr.getHostAddress());
            System.out.println(addr.getHostName());
            System.out.println(reverseLookup(addr));
        } catch(UnknownHostException e) {
            e.printStackTrace();
        }
    }
}
```

Now, let's try this code on common Internet hostnames and see what happens:

```
C:\>java rdns google.com
216.239.51.100
google.com
www.google.com

C:\>java rdns 216.239.51.100
216.239.51.100
216.239.51.100
www.google.com

C:\>java rdns aol.com
64.12.187.24
aol.com
aolr-v4.websys.aol.com

C:\>java rdns 64.12.187.24
64.12.187.24
aolr-v4.websys.aol.com
aolr-v4.websys.aol.com
```

```
C:\>java rdns aolr-v4.websys.aol.com
64.12.187.24
aolr-v4.websys.aol.com
aolr-v4.websys.aol.com

C:\>java rdns 192.168.100.1
192.168.100.1
192.168.100.1
javax.naming.NameNotFoundException: DNS name not found
[response code 3]; remaining name '1.100.168.192' at
com.sun.jndi.dns.DnsClient.checkResponseCode(DnsClient.java:485
)
...
```

So, we can see that because numerous domain name aliases are in use, double reverse lookups might not always provide a match, even for safe domains. Additionally, not all addresses are in the DNS database, so sometimes a lookup will fail.

Performing a double reverse lookup is simple given the reverse lookup code, as shown here:

```
import java.net.*;
import java.util.*;
import javax.naming.*;
import javax.naming.directory.*;

public class drdns {

public static String reverseLookup(InetAddress addr) {
    // same as before...
}

public static boolean doubleLookup(InetAddress addr) {

    byte octets[] = addr.getAddress();
    StringBuffer revName = new StringBuffer(28);

    // silly signed bytes...
    revName.append((int)octets[3] & 0xff);
    revName.append('.');
    revName.append((int)octets[2] & 0xff);
    revName.append('.');
    revName.append((int)octets[1] & 0xff);
    revName.append('.');
    revName.append((int)octets[0] & 0xff);
    revName.append(".in-addr.arpa");

    try {
        Hashtable env = new Hashtable();
        env.put(Context.INITIAL_CONTEXT_FACTORY,
            "com.sun.jndi.dns.DnsContextFactory");
```

```
            env.put(Context.PROVIDER_URL,
                "dns://192.168.1.1");
            env.put("com.sun.jndi.dns.recursion", "true");
            DirContext ctx = new InitialDirContext(env);

            Attributes attrs =
                ctx.getAttributes(revName.toString());
            String name = (String)attrs.get("PTR").get();

            Attributes attrs2 = ctx.getAttributes(name);
            String address = (String)attrs2.get("A").get();

            System.out.println("  "+address);

            return address.equals(addr.getHostAddress());

        } catch(NamingException e) {
            e.printStackTrace();
            return false;
        }
    }

    public static void main(String args[]) {
        // perform a double reverse lookup on args[0]
        try {
            InetAddress addr = InetAddress.getByName(args[0]);
            System.out.println(addr.getHostAddress());
            System.out.println(addr.getHostName());
            System.out.println(reverseLookup(addr));
            System.out.println(doubleLookup(addr));
        } catch(UnknownHostException e) {
            e.printStackTrace();
        }
    }
}
```

So, while the preceding code works and is fairly straightforward, in practice DNS name mappings give us results like this:

```
C:\>java drdns 216.239.51.100
216.239.51.100
216.239.51.100
www.google.com
  216.239.51.101
false

C:\>java drdns 216.239.51.101
216.239.51.101
216.239.51.101
www.google.com
  216.239.51.101
true
```

Two addresses reverse-map to the same domain name in this instance. Although multiple A records may exist for www.google.com, that fact is not being picked up in this case. Although we might be able to write extra code to search through all the possible A records for a domain, the fundamental problem remains: the reverse-lookup database is separate from the normal DNS database and consistency between the two is not assured.

Our best bet to reduce fraud is to include the domain name of the machine used to make all purchases online and eventually begin to deny access to machines, which have historically been the source of fraudulent transactions.

Summary

This chapter described JNDI, one of the key APIs in the J2EE specification. JNDI provides the interface to a variety of directory and naming services that play important roles in connecting the different parts of your distributed enterprise applications. Because we can never be sure exactly where services are physically located in a distributed system, naming and directory services allow applications to connect to services at runtime, dynamically.

JNDI can be used to access a variety of hierarchical directory services. LDAP and DNS are the two most frequently used types of directories. We also looked at how JNDI is used as a straight naming service for the lookup of distributed resources like Enterprise JavaBeans (EJBs).

In this chapter we've introduced you to the structure of the JNDI API, the basics of LDAP directories and how to access them via JNDI as well as the basics of DNS and how to access it via JNDI. Equipped with this knowledge, you are ready to tackle developing a wide range of directory-enabled J2EE applications.

✦　　✦　　✦

Understanding Java Authentication and Authorization Services

✦ ✦ ✦ ✦

In This Chapter

Examining the importance of Java security

Providing an overview of Java Authentication and Authorization Services

Understanding security realms

Setting up for JAAS

Working with the Java Subject class

Using the JAAS login context

Authenticating users

Authorizing users

Working with predefined JAAS login handlers

Writing a login handler

Writing a callback handler

✦ ✦ ✦ ✦

J ava is among the first widely available programming environments designed to ensure security from the ground up rather than to be added in as an afterthought. As such, its security mechanisms and services are continuously evolving because the world of security never stands still. People interested in performing illicit actions are finding and exploiting ever more arcane ways of compromising system integrity while Java engineers are busily figuring out new ways to defeat them. Java Authentication and Authorization Services (JAAS) is one of the latest tools in the Java repertoire to make the task of foiling intrusions easier. Introduced as an optional package in the Java 2 SDK version 1.3, JAAS is now integrated into version 1.4 following the usual Sun Microsystems release timetable.

This chapter is an introduction to JAAS security with an emphasis on explaining how ordinary software engineers can incorporate a reasonable level of security into their projects without becoming security gurus. The new security tools introduced in Java 2, including an entirely new security model, are designed to relieve the programmer of much (but not all) of the responsibility for complex and dynamic security considerations.

One of the necessities in any security scheme is preventing unauthorized access to system resources, because the fewer potential attackers the less likely the system is to be misused. JAAS provides secure login and permissions services, limiting access to critical applications and files to authorized users and administrators and providing a needed level of defense against unauthorized incursions. JAAS also provides access to single login services, a method of allowing a user to access multiple services across many security domains with only one login interaction, for widely distributed applications, to encourage adherence to enterprise security policies and minimize user inconvenience.

Examining the Importance of Java Security

The Java enterprise is (in most cases) an inherently distributed environment. It may include one or more local-area networks (LANs) and possibly wide-area network (WAN) access as needed for access to various business systems for staff; Web access for customers and suppliers; and other specialized access points and systems designed to implement the complete business model. The standard tools used to implement security in Java systems are built into the language itself: Strong typing, byte-code verification, runtime type-checking, class loaders, and security managers all help ensure that Java code doesn't do what it shouldn't. In addition, you can fine-tune the system by granting specific levels of permissions to known code or code sources.

But even this isn't really enough in systems on which people's livelihoods, including (for the sake of argument) yours, depend. At every point where a business system touches the outside world, a potential security weakness can be found and exploited. Here are some examples:

> A point-of-sale terminal is capable of generating credits as well as generating debits, and either action may be performed fraudulently, resulting in business loss.

> Personnel and customer files are valuable business assets, and unauthorized access or dissemination can subject the enterprise to substantial liability.

> Inventory and other files may be manipulated for either fraudulent or malicious purposes, causing disruption of essential services and forcing expensive recovery procedures.

> Sensitive information can be observed by unauthorized persons, and this can compromise privacy, impair business relationships, or facilitate illegal activities.

The interesting thing about these potential exploits is that in each case some individual person is responsible, so it's essential to control individual access everywhere a potential weakness exists. Ordinary customers have no reason to access a point-of-sale terminal, unauthorized employees have no business accessing personnel and customer files, and random passers-by have no business updating your inventory records. So the enterprise as a whole gains quite a bit of safety by ensuring that certain operations can only be performed or observed by certain people. Here are some of the ways to ensure this:

By physical controls such as locking computers themselves away from casual access

By programmatic means, such as locking down virtual access points and, perhaps most importantly, restricting their use to authorized persons

By encrypting communications among vulnerable parts of the application

Java security services enable the programmer to control virtual access points with a number of APIs, of which JAAS is only one example. Of course no systems exist that can't be compromised, but judicious implementation of Java security techniques can help keep all but the most skilled and determined intruder away from your system.

Typical Java security weaknesses

Securing the Java enterprise involves many separate issues, so let's see where Java applications are most vulnerable. Table 12-1 lists the most common weakness that Java is heir to. While handling all these potential security problems is beyond the scope of this short chapter, we'll look at a few easy measures to bolster your defenses and see where JAAS fits into the overall scheme of Java security.

Table 12-1 **Java security vulnerabilities**	
Vulnerability	*Potential Exploit*
Cloning	*Cloning* enables a malefactor to create an instance of your Java object without running your constructor. Unfortunately, this possibility makes the object-oriented nature and extensibility of Java a potential weakness.
Serialization and deserialization	*Serialization* allows inspection of your code, including embedded values, by a hostile application or individual, facilitating the discovery of potential weaknesses or private data. *Deserialization* may allow an intruder to make spoofing attacks on your Java application by feeding it a fraudulently altered or wrongly initialized instance of one of your classes.

Continued

Table 12-1 *(continued)*	
Vulnerability	*Potential Exploit*
Uninitialized variables	It's possible to allocate a Java object without running its constructor. This may enable a clever programmer to manipulate the object in order to access data he or she shouldn't be able to access.
Signed code	Unsigned Java runs in the *sandbox,* a specific Java run mode designed to minimize the likelihood of malicious interference by restricting memory access and preventing file I/O, which minimizes its potential for causing damage. Signing code that doesn't absolutely need to be signed multiplies potential weaknesses with few benefits, if any.
Embedded trade secrets	No real protections exist for information embedded in Java code. *Obfuscation* disguises Java bytecodes to hinder examination and reverse engineering of the code by altering control flow, changing identifier names, manipulating data structures, replacing simple variables with complex calculations, and specific tricks designed to break known decompilers, might better be described as annoyance, because it only makes it more difficult for someone to figure out what your code does by using readily available disassemblers or decompilers. Obfuscation also increases the risk of someone stealthily introducing Java byte codes into the compiled byte- code file that do things not intended by the designer and possibly not contemplated by the original designers of Java. Since the security manager finds it almost as difficult to inspect the code as does a naïve user, these "back doors" can remain in place with little chance of discovery.
Weak or inconsistent user verification	Before JAAS was introduced in Java 2 v1.3, verification of user ID was largely left to the operating system or to the programmer, often with mixed results. Users could plausibly repudiate transactions made in their names, making it possible for them to later fraudulently deny responsibility for actions they actually performed. On the other hand, a malicious intruder could potentially enter harmful transactions in the name of an innocent user with limited exposure to detection.
Relative lack of secure logging	Many Java applications don't have secure logging, either ignoring logging completely or relying on well-known system logs with little or no security that allow security exploits to be hidden after the fact.

In most cases methods exist by which your applications may be secured, methods that involve limiting the scope or behavior of Java objects to minimize the possibility of unauthorized interference. Most enterprises today are connected to the Internet, with concomitant wider exposure to mischief and mischance, so mere verification of behavior and scope may not be enough. The programmer must also exercise due diligence in the study and practice of best coding practices to systematically minimize or eliminate potential weaknesses.

For many of the weaknesses mentioned in the preceding table, the partial solution is to explicitly override the behavior of dangerous methods to throw an exception. For example, to eliminate the possibility of your class being cloned, you'd use code something like what you see in Listing 12-1.

Listing 12-1: **Overriding the clone() method**

```
public final void clone() throws
java.lang.CloneNotSupportedException {
    throw new java.lang.CloneNotSupportedException();
    }
```

To eliminate the possibility of a malfeasant serializing or deserializing your code, you'd insert code like that shown in Listing 12-2. The first code redefines `writeObject`, the ordinary method used to serialize an object. The second redefines `readObject`, the corresponding method used to deserialize an object.

Listing 12-2: **Overriding writeObject and readObject methods**

```
private final void writeObject(ObjectOutputStream out)
    throws java.io.IOException {
    throw new java.io.IOException("Serialization forbidden.");
    }

private final void readObject(ObjectInputStream in)
    throws java.io.IOException {
    throw new java.io.IOException("Deserialization forbidden.");
    }
```

You can also redefine dangerous methods within your class to make them safer, even using cryptographic protection if high security and privacy are needed.

A systematic approach to security involves looking at every potential weakness in your code and in the environment within which your code runs, including communications paths between different sections of the code, and people who might have either legitimate or illegitimate access to any machine on which your code runs.

Figure 12-1 shows an overview of the Java security environment of which JAAS is only a part.

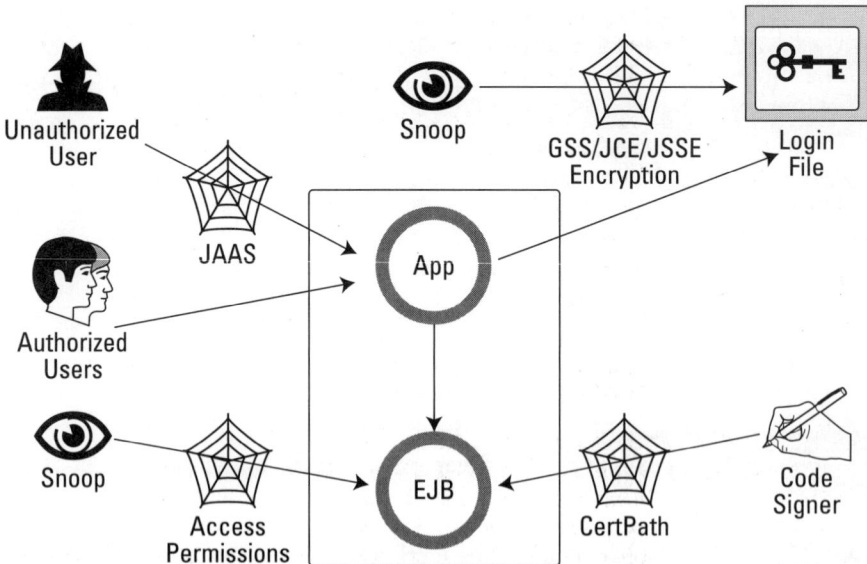

Figure 12-1: The Java security environment shows the types of barriers hindering unauthorized access.

As shown in Figure 12-1, going clockwise from the upper left corner, JAAS uses its own authentication and authorization services to prevent unauthorized users from accessing critical applications. Unauthorized persons or processes are also prevented from snooping on the login process, and its required security files, by GSS/JCE/JSSE encryption. The authenticity of the code itself, assuming that it is signed, has a valid certificate that has actually been signed by the entity trusted by the application, and not an imposter. The `CertPath` mechanism is used to ensure this process.

Standard operating system access permissions are used to protect directories and files from outside interference by persons trying to access the code for any reason, including monitoring runtime state or code structure, or replacing trusted code with modified versions. In the end, only authorized users are allowed to run the code and interact with the application, using the identity already established by the operating system. This combination of security mechanisms allows JAAS to integrate easily with preexisting applications, usually replacing a separate login process and expanding protection to foil potential security threats from a variety of sources. Although JAAS is only a part of the complete picture, it serves a central role because it forms the interface between users and the applications they need to perform their tasks.

Aside from these active measures, it may also be a good idea for the security administrator to decompile most Java applications, applets, or beans before installing them on the system, and to inspect them for security risks and then recompile them to ensure that dirty tricks haven't been inserted in among the byte codes. Further security measures are discussed on the Sun Java Security site at `http://java.sun.com/security/` and in various discussion groups on the Web.

Providing an overview of JAAS

The familiar Java *sandbox* was designed primarily to protect users, and their personal machines, from malicious interference from hostile systems in the outside world. The sandbox enables users to run Java applets without worrying too much about where they came from, by preventing the code from acting in a dangerous way.

Unfortunately, many useful activities are inherently dangerous, and so new facilities were added to enable system administrators (or users) to selectively lower the walls of the sandbox so that the code can interact with file systems, communications networks, and other resources. But this carries its own risks, because once the walls are lowered it becomes easier for an unauthorized user to exploit weaknesses. As with any security decision, system administrators must carefully assess both risks and benefits to ensure that a correct tradeoff is made between protection and ease of use. Unlike some other methods of providing active content, trust in the Java security milieu is not all or nothing, but can be fine-tuned to precisely fit business needs.

As you know, JAAS is designed to protect systems from hostile users. It does this with two basic mechanisms:

✦ **Authentication services** — These services ensure that every user is authorized to use the system and is known by name. They commonly do this by means of some sort of login mechanism, but in some environments — such as Windows 2000, Solaris, and many other operating system or network environments — user information and permissions can be found somewhere in the environment. Therefore, the JAAS login may consist primarily of JAAS checking the existence of an authorized login and copying information from that login into the Java login context.

✦ **Authorization services** — These services associate with each user a set of permissions that may grant differing levels of access to different users and may also restrict privileges to specific actions and files, relying on operating-system security features to guarantee the integrity of the application files as well as using programmatic controls to ensure disciplined access to database records and fields. In addition, authorization services can associate credentials or certificates with a user or service, to ensure that the code being executed is the same code it was when last you looked.

To ensure portability and flexibility, the actual mechanisms by which these services are provided are implemented as plugin modules defined in external files. On differing platforms, as technology improves, or when business practices change, the details of the security implementation can easily change as well. A further benefit for most enterprises is that JAAS can easily integrate Java applications into existing enterprise-security mechanisms and policies.

JAAS is usually supported by encryption or other secure-communications tools, but these tools are not, strictly speaking, part of JAAS. We'll examine these services briefly nonetheless, because they form a natural complement to JAAS.

Cross-Reference Java encryption is covered in more detail in Chapter 13.

A JAAS-enabled application performs a series of three basic functions:

1. The application obtains login information, either by requesting an explicit login sequence from the user or by obtaining the user's login context from the environment. This information may include credentials from local facilities, or from public certificate authorities by using the Java CertPath API. CertPath is actually a part of the Java Security Architecture which supports X.509 Certification Paths, allowing the programmer to create, build, and validate a chain of certificates binding the user, or program code, to an encrypted public key guaranteeing authenticity and integrity and extending back to a known and trusted certificate authority.

2. The application calls the doAs() or doAsPrivileged() method, including the user's login context and the module to be executed in the call.

3. The security manager is then called to verify that the user has all the necessary permissions to run the code. If the user does not, the call fails. If the user does, the call succeeds. Because the called module has access to the user's login information, his or her identity can be logged to facilitate surveillance and recovery.

The JAAS login process is a two-stage transaction similar (but not identical) to those discussed in Chapter 10. This ensures that the process can't be exploited to compromise correct login completion though race conditions or module failures. The entire login process is tried out to ensure that it will succeed before the commit() method is called to complete the actual login.

Handling security is arbitrarily complex, and few enterprises can afford to allocate the required resources to adequately adapt to an ever-changing playing field, so it becomes the programmer's responsibility to handle security despite the fact that this may not be among his or her strongest skills. Luckily, handling security with predefined Java APIs is not terribly hard, and indeed, as you'll see in the section "Hiding JAAS," once a login facility appropriate for your application environment is available, you can ignore JAAS completely by including in the command string a simple login utility that invokes the Java interpreter.

But what about users who have accounts on many machines? How does JAAS handle that? Read on to discover the answer to this question.

Understanding Security Realms

Most of us have accounts on more than one machine. At the very least, you probably have a default account on your personal computer and another on your connectivity provider. It's very likely that the operating systems that support these two accounts are different and that the root account on each machine refers to a different person. These two people, one of whom is probably you, may enforce widely differing policies about who can do what and who has access to each one's machine.

Quiet reflection allows the savvy developer to realize that a very large number of security regimes are available. These include the relative chaos of most user machines promiscuously connected to the Internet, the virtual privacy of networks, and the Faraday-caged Comsec/Emsec/Compusec security of military computers. Even on the Internet, the potential security barriers to outside access are numerous, with proprietary offerings making it difficult for the hacker and hapless user both to connect to virtual private networks and other protected environments.

Earlier in this chapter, in the section "Providing an overview of JAAS," we discussed some of the operating systems that JAAS supports. Different operating systems support different character sets, byte order, machine architectures, user names, and security environments, all of which may make it difficult for a single user to share information, even security information, between systems. However, even machines using the same operating system may not share security files for any number of good reasons. Even in a single enterprise, some departments may have entirely separate networks and operating environments. So when users need to access systems residing on different machines, they often require an account on each machine. The system administrator on machine A may require user names in the form, <first initial><first four letters of last name><three-digit accession number>. However, the administrator of machine B may allow free-form names chosen by the user alone like "codewiz" or "larry." Finally, the administrator of machine C may use dotted notation to present the full name. So, Lawrence B. Smith may have to remember ids and passwords for lsmit032, larry, larry7, Lawrence.B.Smith and any number of others; one for each security realm Larry has privileges in.

A JAAS *security realm* is any logical grouping of users and services that makes sense. It might be users on a particular machine, or those working for a particular company, division, or workgroup. From a Windows perspective, a realm is roughly equivalent to a Windows domain; in another environment, it might be a virtual realm located on a distributed server like a Kerberos server or Sun's X.500 Keystore (LDAP) server, with the users and services all operating on machines under their own security disciplines. The default Java security policies allow for security domains to be configured to provide different privileges to be associated with particular bits of code. Users may also be grouped into arbitrary conglomerates to ensure the ability to flexibly grant or deny particular permissions based on enterprise needs without departing completely from the sandbox-versus-unlimited-access model. The invocation of a JAAS security manager allows the full power of individual or group authentication and authorization to be added to the standard security model, but you don't have to invoke a security manager unless it's truly needed for application security.

JAAS allows each security realm to announce its requirements before the user attempts to log in, so that in the Borland implementation of JAAS, for example, a property called *reactive login* enables enterprise clients to automatically request the proper challenge and response for a particular security realm before proceeding with the login. Depending on the information gathered from the server, the user process can modify its login strategy before continuing with a login attempt. If multiple realms are supported, the client will offer the user a menu of security realms to choose from. This allows further flexibility within the total security system because it's not then necessary to authenticate the user for all the realms within which identities and passwords are held before performing a task.

Judicious use of alternative login options might accomplish similar results, or custom login modules could be written to build in this supple behavior by design. However, the inherent modularity of JAAS enables third-party vendors to add value to their offerings by foreseeing needs like this. These vendors can then supply behaviors that provide more than the handful of simple login modules furnished by Sun in the JAAS software development kit (SDK).

Single login across security domains

Anyone with more than a few accounts on several machines has cursed the need to maintain a list of user names and passwords for each account. Wouldn't it be nice to have a secure central place where you could keep a virtual key ring with all your user names and passwords tidily protected by a single login name and password? You bet it would.

The lure of *single login* is a siren call for systems administrators as well, because the other side of single login is the hope of reduced maintenance costs. So almost everyone promises it in one way or another, either by including some sort of single login capability in the OS itself, or by offering support for external single login environments. Microsoft, for example, includes a form of single login in all the recent versions of Windows, and extends that capability to untrusted networks through their Passport offering within the .NET architecture. Since many people don't completely trust Microsoft with their data, Microsoft has recently backed off from Passport slightly by offering the TrustBridge system, which moves security repositories from Microsoft servers to those owned by business partners. Sun Microsystems is leading an initiative named Liberty Alliance, which is roughly similar to TrustBridge in concept, but with a different cast of partners.

The Windows environment, for example, touts itself as a single login system, and indeed it is as long as your vision doesn't extend far beyond the Microsoft domain system. Microsoft security domains can declare their willingness to accept users from other Microsoft domains and, although the juggling of mutual trusts can get very tricky indeed, it is possible to distribute the net of users widely. In fact, one of the problems that programmers often run into is that they don't really understand the pervasiveness of the Microsoft single-login concept. So they attempt to force Microsoft environments to conform to the overlapping login domains of other operating systems' environments. But allowing layered logins to let people drop in and out of privileged states isn't safe under Windows, which doesn't allow ordinary users to initiate a login. This is anathema in the Microsoft environment, because a simple extension of this scheme can be used as an automated password cracker. Before a user process can be allowed to do this, it must be permitted to act as part of the operating system, which isn't the sort of permission one wants to give to all and sundry. A user process can *request* a login process from the Windows operating system, but the OS is responsible for making sure that request is safe by enforcing a strict login discipline. Among these disciplines is insisting on the CTRL-ALT-DELETE interrupt sequence to return the session to a known state, which then enters the administratively-configurable Windows Security Dialog.

Kerberos

Kerberos is a more robust example of single-login security, and has implementations on most platforms, including Windows. The latest incarnation of Kerberos from Microsoft seems to conform closely to the Kerberos standard. Early Microsoft implementations "extended" Kerberos slightly in ways that sometimes clashed with what other Kerberos programmers thought reasonable. For the most part, these proprietary extensions were created in an attempt to reconcile the disparate philosophies underlying Microsoft security and most of the rest of the world, especially Unix.

Kerberos was developed at the Massachusetts Institute of Technology (MIT) as part of the Athena Project, a Unix-based campus-wide facility designed to allow seamless access to resources on the MIT network. It takes its name from the fierce three-headed dog that guards the gate of Hades, although the metaphor is somewhat strained, because Kerberos only attacks people who try to escape and freely allows anyone at all to enter. This unfortunate misunderstanding probably reflects the sad lack of a classical liberal-arts education among many computer professionals.

Advantages of JAAS

Other single login security managers are available as well, such as the X.500 Keystore module supplied by Sun, or any of the many proprietary offerings created by third-party vendors. But one of the great things about JAAS is that you're not required to choose any particular scheme. Indeed, each of these schemes may return one or more JAAS `Principals`, any or all of which can be associated with a single JAAS `Subject` to create as many identities as necessary. There's an old saying among programmers that the nice thing about standards is that there are so many of them to choose from; JAAS doesn't even ask you to make that choice. Your application can have it all.

Using JAAS to conduct login processing, and using Java GSS-API and any of several distributed or local password-authentication protocols, even Windows-based Kerberos, enables system administrators to easily maintain login and password information in central locations and allows users to maintain a single login, even across differing security realms.

Setting up for JAAS

The basic foundation of any JAAS system is four properties located in the `java.security` properties file. Two properties are specifically allocated to JAAS:

✦ `login.configuration.provider` defines the basic security format expected by JAAS.

✦ `login config.url.n` where *n* is a positive integer numbered consecutively from 1 identifying each login configuration, file instance. Multiple files are concatenated.

In addition, two properties are common to all Java security:

✦ `policy.provider` defines the basic security formats expected by Java.

✦ `policy.url.n` where *n* is a positive integer numbered consecutively from 1 identifying each policy file instance. Multiple files are concatenated.

If more than one `url` file exists in either of these four categories, the contents of each file is joined with the others to form a union of properties.

JAAS itself needs only a handful of import statements, typically one or more of the `javax.security` packages added or changed for J2 v1.4 and a callback handler from the `com.sun.security.auth.module` series of packages. You might also need an I/O package or two. Listing 12-3 shows a typical selection of imported modules you might need. Exactly what you need is dependent on what your code does, of course. As you'll see later in this chapter in the section "Hiding JAAS," in many cases you don't actually have to change your code at all.

Listing 12-3: **Typical JAAS setup code**

```
import javax.security.auth.*;
import javax.security.auth.login.*;
import javax.security.auth.callback.*;
import com.sun.security.auth.callback.TextCallbackHandler;
import com.sun.security.auth.callback.DialogCallbackHandler;
```

These bring in the basic JAAS security packages plus two items identifying a toolkit used to interact with a user. This toolkit consists of *callback handlers*, which are discussed next.

Callback handlers

Callback handlers manage interaction with a user. Although they can be used to initiate a login-ID/password sequence, they are by no means limited to that function.

Simple APIs are provided in the com.sun.security.auth.callback package to allow login modules to perform various interactions with the user, including a simple login sequence that prompts for a user name and password. Two classes, shown in Table 12-2, are provided within the package to instantiate a callback handler that performs the actual prompt routines, designed for simple text I/O on standard input and output streams or, alternatively, graphical dialogs using the Swing package.

Table 12-2 JAAS predefined callback handlers	
Callback Class	**Action**
TextCallbackHandler	This class prompts and reads from the command line, offering a bare-bones user interface that works everywhere.
DialogCallbackHandler	This class uses Swing dialog windows to display prompts and read from any Swing dialog element, including check boxes, input fields, and lists, in a graphical windowing environment, offering a slightly more attractive interface.

It's often a good idea to provide hooks within your callback handlers for a variety of different callbacks, even if you foresee using your code only in environments that never use callbacks. Otherwise, if you later decide to change to an environment that does require callbacks, your code will throw an exception. During your security analysis, you should balance the possibility of your code breaking in unplanned-for environments with the potential vulnerability inherent in more complex code. But remember that your code probably shouldn't be extensible, so you might not be able to add features without rewriting and recompiling your code, a lengthy process if the code is under version control.

Text callback handlers

Text is completely reliable and has the advantage of being universal; every system supports it and it's easily accessible for users with many sorts of disabilities. Of course text is considered ugly and boring in some circles, but it's probably a mistake to eliminate it out of hand without considering the tradeoffs.

For a critical application available to the public, or to employees who require access in order to do their jobs, the likelihood is that you'll have to supply text-based access at some point. This may be a legal obligation, according to the Americans with Disabilities Act and Section 508 of the U.S. Rehabilitation Act for software developed by or sold to federal agencies. It might also be considered a moral obligation for every organization. It's neither decent nor compassionate to ignore this need, even if you are not mandated to comply with the ADA. Although Swing has accessibility mechanisms built into it, it isn't available on all devices, nor is it suitable for communicating with all disabled persons using all accessibility technologies. On the Windows platform, for example, the JAWS (Job Access With Speech) screen reader from Freedom Scientific is the only one I know of that is fully compatible with Java Swing.

In this chapter we'll use text I/O exclusively, simply because it's easier to set up, is more universal than Swing, and allows smaller and more readily understandable examples.

Dialog callback handlers

Java Foundation Classes (JFC) makes it easy to replace text with fancy buttons, lists, menus, and little boxes full of words using Swing components to create a graphical user interface (GUI). GUIs allow systems to be designed to maximize productivity and ease of use for some, but not all, users. For most enterprises the extra expense of providing such an interface is justified even though alternatives may have to be provided for some users.

Although Swing gives you enormous control over the graphical look and feel of your application, as well as a large selection of predefined widgets and tools, the use of Swing is beyond the scope of this short chapter. So, the reader is advised to consult any of several thorough discussions of this API in books covering JFC and Swing. A few recent texts are listed in Appendix C.

Pluggable/stackable authentication

Pluggable Authentication Modules (PAM) is at the heart of JAAS power. Extensibility is built into the JAAS login-configuration file, which contains a list of login modules to be invoked when an authenticating login call is made. These modules are not only pluggable, so you can easily swap out a login file designed for Unix and swap in one designed for Win2K, they're stackable, so your login sequence can consist of several steps, each of which adds information to the description of a user's identity and permissions. Each file can contain one or more callback modules in order to interact with the user on many levels, adding great flexibility and power to the entire package.

The login-configuration file consists of one or more entries having, by default, the format shown in Listing 12-4:

Listing 12-4: **Login-File format**

```
<application name> {
    <LoginModuleName> <flag> <LoginModule options>;
    <LoginModuleName> <flag> <LoginModule options>;
    . . .
    };
```

The flag defines the properties of each entry and the overall control flow of the authentication process, as shown in Table 12-3.

Table 12-3
JAAS login-module flags

Keyword	Control-Flow Meaning
required	This module is required but successive entries in the `LoginModuleName` list will be executed whether it succeeds or fails. It can be used to implement a multistage login sequence without giving away information about which step in the sequence failed.
requisite	This module is required, but if the module fails control immediately falls through to the end of the list and the process returns failure. If the login succeeds, any remaining items in the list will be executed in order. Although this may save the user extra interactions or time, it may also give away security information, facilitating step-by-step attempts to breach login security.
sufficient	This module isn't required, but if it does succeed control immediately falls to the bottom of the list and the process returns successfully.
optional	This module isn't required. Whether the login succeeds or fails, control passes down the list.

Fairly complex login scenarios can be constructed using these options. All required and requisite modules encountered must succeed in order for the overall login to succeed. At least one optional or sufficient module must succeed if no required or requisite modules are present. Each login module can have different policy files associated with it. This allows JAAS to support users who may have varying privileges. In most systems, users may carry with them not only their own individual permissions, such as read/write access to their home directories, but also permissions granted as a result of membership in certain groups, such as the database-programming group, the administrator group, and/or the department manager's group.

Note   Different `LoginModule` options are defined for each module, depending on module needs. However, all the default login modules supplied by Sun take a `debug=true` value to make the developer's life easier.

Since login information is highly attractive to snoops and uniquely vulnerable, communications are often handled by encryption methods — either the *Generic Security Services Application Program Interface* (GSS-API) or the *Java Secure Socket Extension* (JSSE). GSS-API supports Kerberos and Lightweight Directory Access Protocol (LDAP) servers using the *Simple Authentication and Security Layer* (SASL). JSSE is required by some HTTP servers because it supports Transport Layer Security (TLS, formerly known as Secure Sockets Layer or SSL) and doesn't yet support Kerberos.

It's not difficult to imagine applications that require either or both. The "Magazine-Publisher Example" section toward the end of this chapter describes a Kerberos login sequence that uses GSS encryption to hide the user name/password dialog.

JAAS login modules ultimately populate a `Subject` with one or more `Principals` that define a JAAS entity, whether that entity is an actual human or a service. The `Subject` class is discussed in the next section.

Examining the Java Subject Class

JAAS handles the multiple facets of our online login personalities by creating a `Subject` containing an array of `Principal` objects, each of which has a set of permissions associated with it, as well as any public and private keys or certificates needed by the application. A `Subject` is any entity that makes a request to access system or network resources.

Just like the language in a contract, the specific language used to describe users for security purposes has implications. A JAAS `Subject` is the actual entity authorized to request services from the Java security manager. However, a `Subject` doesn't correspond directly to any given identifier, but rather contains a set of `Principals` that contain information about the actual user. That information might be, for an individual, a personal name, an identifying number, a user ID, or any other pertinent information. Each one of these `Principals` may contain a list of permissions with associated permissions. So the total package of permissions may vary, depending on which of several alternative identifiers is included in the actual login set.

Therefore, a `Principal` might not be unique, as a personal name might be shared by many people. The name Jane Doe might describe hundreds, or thousands, of individuals, and might conceivably have one or more associated permissions. Conversely, a Social Security number should describe only one individual (absent fraud or official error) and might have another set of permissions associated with it.

A `Principal` might describe any of the following entities:

An actual user

A login ID shared by one or more users such as `root` or `Administrator`

A system-level group identification carrying a specific set of permissions with it, usually descriptive in Windows systems or a cryptic numeric under Unix or its variants

A group identification describing a user's status or role aside from or in addition to predefined system user groups, such as "returning student" or security clearances, since the needs of an application may not translate directly into system-level requirements

A system service or application module

An enterprise as a whole or a department within an organization since, in a networked world, you may know who your business partners are in a general sense without knowing their employee roster

Since a JAAS Subject consists of the set-wise union of all its Principals, the possibilities for variation and specificity are obviously very numerous.

A Subject may also contain public and private credentials such as cryptographic keys and digital signatures. You can think of a Principal as a user name or ID (including group membership IDs), and you can think of a Subject as a collection of such names, any or all of which might contribute permissions and credentials toward the fulfillment of any particular request.

Several login modules are supplied by Sun in the com.sun.security.auth. module, as shown in Table 12-4.

Table 12-4
Sun-supplied login modules

Module Name	Target Environment	Typical Features
Krb5LoginModule	Kerberos	Supports a widespread network-security tool from MIT. Requires initial login.
NTLoginModule	WinNT and Win2K	Obtains authentication and authorization information from the user's environment, and so never requires a separate login since Windows doesn't support nested logins.
UnixLoginModule	Sun, Solaris, Unix, and Linux	Obtains authentication and authorization information from the user's environment, and so may not require a separate login but does allow them, since Unix and its variants all support nested logins.
KeyStoreLoginModule	Key store	Fully supports Sun-proprietary JKS and JCEKS key stores. Partially (read access only) supports PKCS #12 with full support promised in a future release.
JndiLoginModule	JNDI	Uses a Java Naming and Directory Interface (JNDI) file-system-directory service to authenticate a user.

The Sun modules cover the great majority of environments available to the ordinary user. Each of these login modules implements at least the methods shown in the section named Writing your own login handler, Table 12-10, but we can ignore these for a while as we examine the process of authenticating a user in more detail.

Authenticating Users

At its most basic, you can enforce access security by requiring users to log in separately before using each Java service. This approach lacks flexibility, and may irritate users who hop in and out of applications during their daily activities. However, it places the least burden on the programmer and the greatest burden on the administrator, so programmers tend to favor this idea. For an administrator, though, this is a hideous nightmare, because each user requires entries in separate login and policy files for each application. So adding or deleting users is an onerous task. Users might not be thrilled either, because being forced to repeatedly log in while going about one's daily business is both irritating and tiresome.

When an operating system or other environment enforces a login discipline, it's usually sensible to use those same facilities to handle Java authentication and authorization as well. All services will be performed using the access authorizations of a particular user and the administrator will be spared most of the task of handling whatever duplication may exist.

In addition, predefined login mechanisms are often far more secure than anything the average programmer is likely to be able to create easily. For example, Kerberos uses strong cryptography to ensure secure login dialogs, even in a network environment that is not trusted. Kerberos is supplied as source code, so the canny programmer can even inspect the code to guarantee that the algorithm seems secure and that no back doors have been inserted in the code. Kerberos has been extensively tested, a prerequisite to any level of trust being bestowed on any cryptographic scheme. As with any security product, it's important to keep up with advisories and patches, but it's also possible to purchase Kerberos support from outside vendors.

The rest of this section will discuss the files needed to perform basic authentication and authorization, with simple examples offered at each step of the way. The first example in this series is the basic code needed to perform a JAAS login, shown in Listing 12-5.

Listing 12-5: **Basic JAAS-login code**

```
import javax.security.auth.*;
import javax.security.auth.login.*;
import javax.security.auth.callback.*;
import com.sun.security.auth.callback.DialogCallbackHandler;
```

```
//
// Attempt either to authenticate user or report failure
//
public class ObtainLogin {
    public static void main(String[] args) {
        // Obtain a LoginContext using the login modules listed
        // in the login configuration file named in the
        // LoginContext() call.
        // This example is chattier than most actual login
        // dialogs to ease debugging by identifying the cause
        // of any failure .
        // In an actual login context, you should volunteer as
little
        // information as possible. It would possibly be better
to
        // return a single newline if any part of the login
fails.
        // Note that a callbackHandler is supplied despite the
fact
        // that this example will use the WinNT login module,
which
        // ignores this handler. This makes it possible to change
        // the security environment without changing this code.
        LoginContext lc = null;
        try {
            lc = new LoginContext("ObtainLogin",
                                  new DialogCallbackHandler());
        } catch (LoginException le) {
            System.err.println("Cannot create LoginContext: "
                             + le.getMessage());
            System.exit(-1);
        } catch (SecurityException se) {
            System.err.println("Cannot create LoginContext: "
                             + se.getMessage());
            System.exit(-1);
        }
        try {
            // attempt authentication
            lc.login();
        } catch (LoginException le) {
            System.err.println("Authentication failed: ");
            System.err.println("   " + le.getMessage());
            System.exit(-1);
        }
        System.out.println();
        System.out.println("              ********************");
        System.out.println("              * Login Successful *");
        System.out.println("              ********************");
        System.out.println();
        // Execute a bit of privileged code
        Subject me = lc.getSubject();
```

Continued

Listing 12-5 *(continued)*

```
        PrivilegedAction pa = new GetOsName();
        Subject.doAsPrivileged(me, pa, null);
        System.out.println();
    }
}
```

This code calls another class that performs the actual privileged actions, whose content is displayed in Listing 12-6. Because the actual login process would be the same for most of your modules, separating the privileged code enables you to reuse the nuts and bolts of JAAS and also enables you to plug in different tasks as needed. Especially note that, although the code calls a `dialog` callback handler, because the code runs under Windows the requested information is read from the user's environment and no information is actually requested from the user.

Listing 12-6: **A JAAS privileged object**

```
import java.security.PrivilegedAction;

public class GetOsName implements PrivilegedAction {
    public Object run() {
        System.out.println("  OS Name: " +
                            System.getProperty("os.name"));
        System.out.println("Java Home: " +
                            System.getProperty("java.home"));
        return null;
    }
}
```

The first action lists the operating system's name, which is normally available even within the sandbox. The other reveals details of the file system that are definitely outside the sandbox. The code fails if it tries to run without this permission. Therefore, the code as it stands has three levels of diagnostic feedback built in — one announcement that the login portion of the code succeeded, another that the "privileged" code section was entered, and one more that all portions of the JAAS security features employed have worked properly.

Listing 12-7 shows the login-configuration file associated with this application.

Listing 12-7: **The ObtainLogin login-configuration file**

```
ObtainLogin {
    com.sun.security.auth.module.NTLoginModule required;
};
```

Note that module entries should be delimited by semicolons (;). This particular file contains only one entry with a single login module. Multiple named entries can be made containing any number of login modules. This allows different login methods to be used by each application with varying degrees of security complexity.

Because each module may contain full knowledge of the user's operating-system environment, it's relatively easy to add new environments as long as a potential method exists of authenticating users in that particular environment. A user in a local Solaris or Win2K context may be relatively trusted, so information on user names and groups can be used to populate an entire login context. A user entering the application via Telnet or the Web, however, is relatively anonymous and the connection itself may not be reliable. A security administrator might need to perform one or more separate login authentications, switch to a secure communications protocol, and reference internal databases to collect information similar to that found in a Windows user environment. It may even be necessary to perform sophisticated profiling of the user's online behavior and knowledge before granting access or allowing a session to continue.

Listing 12-8 shows a more complex login-configuration file that calls several login handlers for our little application.

Listing 12-8: **A more complex login-configuration file**

```
ObtainLogin {
    com.sun.security.auth.module.NTLoginModule sufficient;
    com.sun.security.auth.module.KrbLoginModule sufficient;
    VendorLoginModule optional;
};
JaasSecondExample {
    com.sun.security.auth.module.NTLoginModule required;
    VendorTwoLoginModule required;
};
JaasThirdExample {
    com.sun.security.auth.module.KrbLoginModule required;
};
```

This file contains entries for three applications with differing needs. The first runs under a standard Win2K or WinNT OS. It both uses and trusts security information from the user's environment. This file also allows both Kerberos authentication (which it also trusts) or a proprietary vendor-authentication module to obtain an alternative login context. If none of these modules obtains the required identity and permissions the login fails, but it otherwise succeeds on the first module that does succeed. The second entry uses information from both the user's Windows environment and a proprietary vendor scheme. Both modules must succeed for the login to succeed. The third entry depends entirely on the Sun-supplied Kerberos login. After a login succeeds, the user's login context is populated and execution of your application can proceed.

Authorizing users

A JAAS-enabled application may collect information from several sources before running code. It can obtain user names and associated permissions from a user's login context, and possibly credentials associated with that user. JAAS can also incorporate information obtained from external certificate authorities or databases associated with the code itself, allowing great flexibility in making security decisions and controlling program flow patterns. External certificate authorities are often accessed through a secure-socket connection using the Java Secure Socket Extension (JSSE), which implements SSL and Transport Layer Security (TLS) protocols. Although other secure-communications protocols are available in J2EE, secure-socket support is the most common on the Internet.

The authorizations or permissions associated with the user during the login process have no meaning unless they are actually used in a JAAS Policy file as described in the section immediately following.

JAAS policy files

The JAAS policy file is very similar to the standard Java policy file but has an added dimension — the users. The Java policy file refers only to code and signers of code, which is fine if any user is allowed to execute a given piece of code, but the real world doesn't usually work like that. We have keys to our cars and houses for the precise reason that we don't want just anyone to walk into our kitchen and make a sandwich, or drive to the grocery store in our car. Businesses are equally persnickety about who uses their facilities. So the standard policy file doesn't go quite far enough.

Like the standard file, the JAAS policy file enables the administrator to grant permissions to specific classes and/or specific code signers, just as the standard Java policy file does. In this sense JAAS duplicates what's already there. But JAAS also adds the ability to restrict sensitive code to specific users, just as the keys on your keyring restrict access to your home and vehicle. Listing 12-9 shows two entries in such a file — the first a code-centric permission allowing a specific class code itself to perform certain operations, and the second a user-centric permission allowing a named user to run a specific bit of code. We'll use these in our demonstration.

Listing 12-9: **Our example policy file**

```
grant CodeBase "file:./ObtainLogin.jar" {
    permission javax.security.auth.AuthPermission
                    "createLoginContext.ObtainLogin";
    permission javax.security.auth.AuthPermission
"doAsPrivileged";
};

grant CodeBase "file:./GetOsName.jar",
    Principal com.sun.security.auth.NTUserPrincipal
"Puddintane"  {
    permission java.util.PropertyPermission "java.home",
"read";
};
```

We've placed both bits of code in Java jars for verisimilitude, because many real-world applications are bundled up for convenience and security. This approach allows the entirety of an application to be signed as a single unit (if signed code is advisable in a particular instance). Therefore, it becomes more difficult to substitute malignant look-alikes in efforts to exploit weaknesses.

Like the standard Java policy file, the JAAS policy file partially relieves programmers of the need to account for their exact environments. By implementing policies, the administrator can fine-tune the security model to suit the needs of the enterprise rather than depending entirely on what the programmer thought of in the first place. Even code that, left to its own devices, would be impossibly insecure and dangerous can be tamed and brought to heel.

Compiling the example

Depending on how you've installed Java, you may need to fully qualify the path for the Java compiler and jar maker. We'll assume here that you haven't added the Java SDK binary directory to your path and that it's installed at the Windows root. Listing 12-10 shows the four steps needed to create the two jars used in the example.

Listing 12-10: **Compiling the example code**

```
\j2sdk1.4.1_01\bin\javac GetOsName.java
\j2sdk1.4.1_01\bin\jar -cvf GetOsName.jar GetOsName.class
\j2sdk1.4.1_01\bin\javac -classpath GetOsName.jar
ObtainLogin.java
\j2sdk1.4.1_01\bin\jar -cvf ObtainLogin.jar ObtainLogin.class
```

At this point you might also sign your jar files, and could then add a `SignedBy` keyword and value to the corresponding JAAS policy file entry in Listing 12-9.

This example can be run from the command line, as shown in Listing 12-11.

Listing 12-11: **Running the example code**

```
java -classpath GetOsName.jar;ObtainLogin.jar
-Djava.security.manager
-Djava.security.auth.login.config=jaas.conf
-Djava.security.policy=jaas.policy ObtainLogin
```

Figure 12-2 shows the code being run by an authorized user, while Figure 12-3 shows the same code being run by an unauthorized user. Looking carefully at these figures, note that the "Login Successful" welcome message and the Windows 2000 OS name are written on the output in both cases. This shows that the login sequence was successful, which it would have to be under Win2K, and that the non-privileged portion of the "privileged" code was also successful whether the user was authorized or not. It's only in the second case, when a truly privileged attempt is made by an *unauthorized* user to read the Java home directory, that failure occurs and error messages start spilling on the screen as shown in Figure 12-3. This proves that the failure is one of authorization rather than authentication. In real life you'd want to catch and hide all those messy errors once out of the debugging stage, but they have the advantage of telling you a little bit about what went wrong during initial development, here shown for illustrative purposes.

Of course in real life we'd probably catch those error messages and present a formatted "not authorized" message instead of giving away our hand like this.

Login-configuration files can be arbitrarily complex, as mentioned previously, and can contain entries for multiple applications. This enables a JAAS `Subject` to contain a large number of certificates, login IDs, and group memberships (on systems that support groups of users).

Next, we'll look at strategies you might want to employ during debugging of your code.

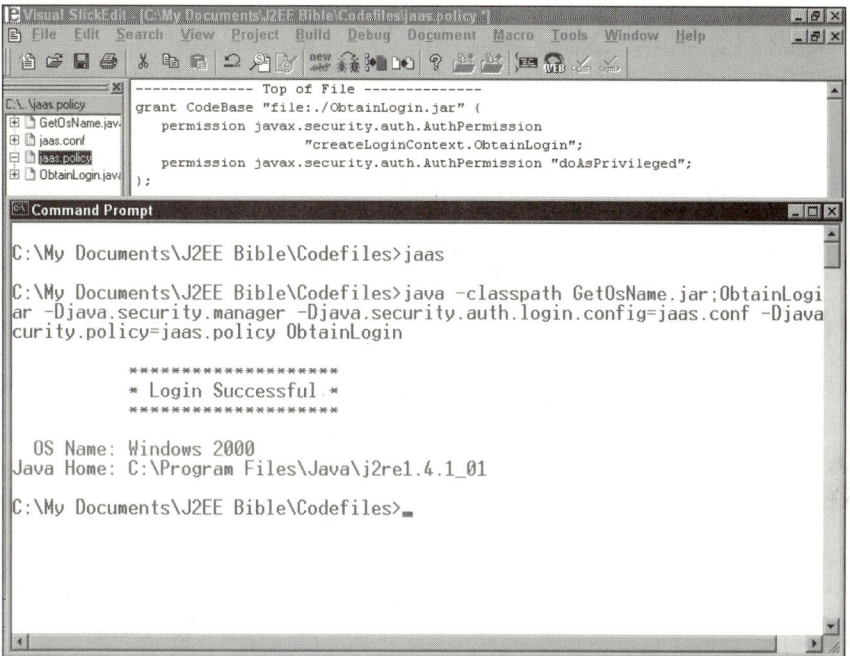

Figure 12-2: An authorized user sees a tidy little report.

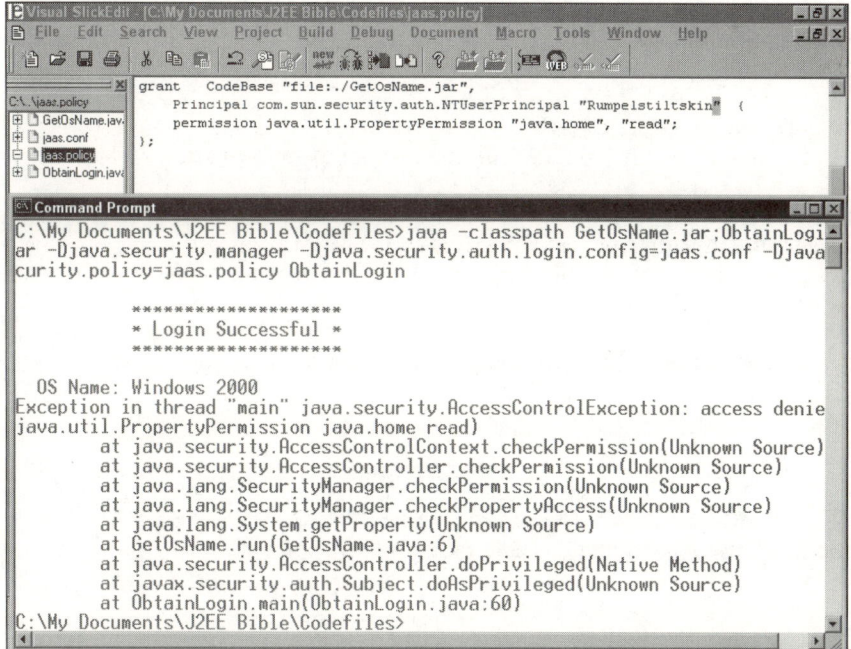

Figure 12-3: An unauthorized user sees error messages bleeding all over the screen.

Debugging the Simple JAAS Module

One of the most difficult things to deal with when creating JAAS applications is the complex interactions between the various files you absolutely need and the fact that a tiny problem in even one of those files can cause your program to fail in sometimes bewildering ways. Your first line of defense is a modern programming environment such as Sun ONE Studio or Borland Enterprise Studio for Java. However, if your budget doesn't stretch quite that far, a good alternative is a modern programmer's editor, such as Visual SlickEdit. This editor interfaces to your Java development kit and knows what Java looks like, simplifying early development and eliminating many gross coding errors.

In addition, many programmers' editors, including SlickEdit, work closely with JBuilder and other integrated development suites. In addition, SlickEdit is particularly interesting for programmers with visual disabilities, as it is compliant with the accessibility requirements of the U.S. Rehabilitation Act, Section 508, and supports the JAWS screen reader. Figure 12-4 shows Java code under development with an interactive debugging session in progress.

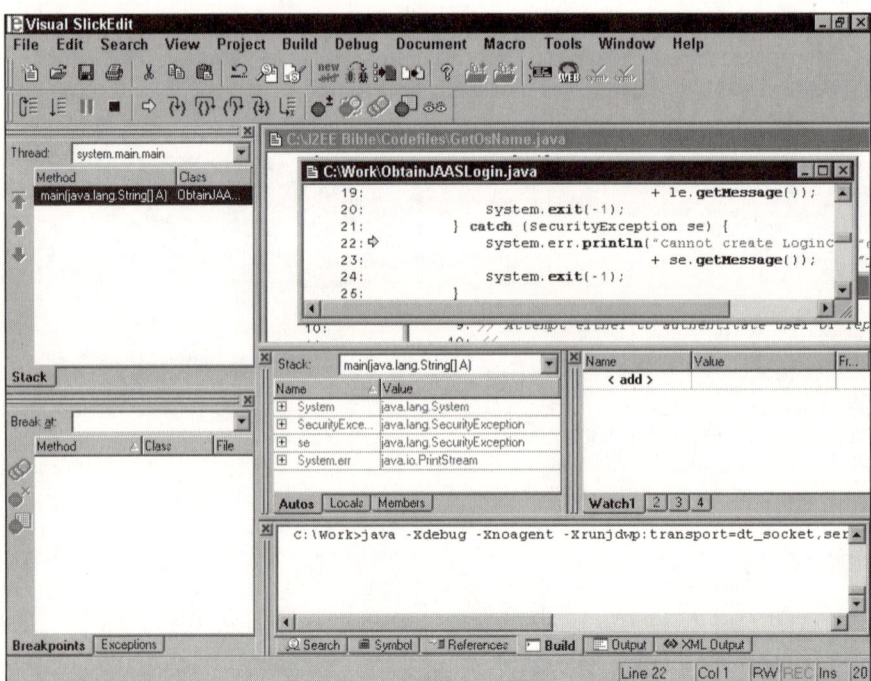

Figure 12-4: Use a programmer's editor for Java development.

As a general rule, during development, set up the policy file(s) to grant infinite access, get the application running under these loose conditions, and then gradually tighten security.

You might set up a standard Java policy pile, for development only, like that shown in Listing 12-12. You might also set up a `jaas.policyjava.policy` development file like that shown in Listing 12-13. These specifically grant all permissions to the code and allow all users to do anything, so they won't be useful once you get your code working properly, but they simplify the process of development by eliminating many possibilities for initial failure.

Listing 12-12: **The java.policy development file**

```
grant {
    permission java.security.AllPermission;
};
```

Listing 12-13: **The jaas.policy development file**

```
grant   CodeBase "file:./GetOsName.jar",
    Principal com.sun.security.auth.NTUserPrincipal "Everyone"
{
    permission java.util.PropertyPermission "java.home",
"read";
    permission java.util.PropertyPermission "os.name", "read";
};
```

This approach enables you to first develop your code as if you were in the Java sandbox, get it running, and then gradually bring it fully under JAAS security. It's much easier to get one or two things right at a time than to get a hundred things right all at once.

It goes without saying, of course, that leaving the policy files in that initial state would be unwise. Listing 12-14 and 12-15 show more fully developed versions of these files.

Listing 12-14: **The finished Java policy file**

```
grant   CodeBase "file:./GetOsName.jar",
    Principal com.sun.security.auth.NTUserPrincipal
"Puddintane" {
    permission java.util.PropertyPermission "java.home",
"read";
    permission java.util.PropertyPermission "os.name", "read";
};

grant   CodeBase "file:./GetOsName.jar",
    Principal com.sun.security.auth.NTSidGroupPrincipal
"Booking Agents" {
    permission java.util.PropertyPermission "java.home",
"read";
    permission java.util.PropertyPermission "os.name", "read";
};
```

Listing 12-15: **The finished JAAS policy file**

```
grant CodeBase "file:./ObtainLogin.jar" {
    permission javax.security.auth.AuthPermission
                    "createLoginContext.ObtainLogin";
    permission javax.security.auth.AuthPermission
"doAsPrivileged";
};

grant   CodeBase "file:./GetOsName.jar",
    Principal com.sun.security.auth.NTUserPrincipal
"Puddintane"   {
    permission java.util.PropertyPermission "java.home",
"read";
};
```

When you run your development code, point to the temporary files as shown in Listing 12-16. Note that this approach uses the Windows semicolon (;) scheme to separate `jar` files in the `classpath`. On Unix systems, use a colon (:) to separate these files instead.

> ### Listing 12-16: **Running the simple JAAS module**
>
> ```
> java -classpath GetOsName.jar;ObtainLogin.jar
>         -Djava.security.manager
>         -Djava.security.auth.login.config=jaas.conf
>         -Djava.security.policy=jaas.policy ObtainLogin
> ```

The preceding discussion has assumed that you're developing code from scratch, but in the real world, you often inherit code from antiquity. Luckily, JAAS has techniques for using old code as well as new. We'll look at these in the next section.

Hiding JAAS

By now you've seen that JAAS requirements are pretty simple. The steps required to log in are pretty much the same no matter what the application does. So why not write one login class to perform logins for all your code modules and be done with it?

Not surprisingly, JAAS is designed to permit just that, allowing a simple login utility to invoke other classes. This enables you to "JAAS up" your applications by a few administrative steps, adding entries to the login configuration and JAAS policy files and then changing the commands that invoke your application classes. While not a perfect JAAS implementation, something like this is a definite start and can be a useful interim measure while the total system is under revision.

Predefined JAAS login callbacks and their handlers

In the preceding sections, we've used standard login modules without really looking under the hood. We'll start this section by looking more closely at the modules that form the standard offering. Later in this chapter, we'll discuss what might be added by custom work.

When a login context is not available from the environment, or when that context doesn't extend to special permissions used by a JAAS-enabled application, JAAS has the ability to request a login from a user by issuing a callback. The default handlers for Unix and WinNT/2K environments don't really need callbacks because users have to be logged in anyway. However, other environments, including Kerberos and JNDI, may not have a useful login context available. This is because the user may be on a machine in a different security realm, connecting to an application over the Internet or local network.

The standard callbacks enable you to request information from the user in a variety of ways, and also provide a method for presenting announcements to the user during the login process. This last method might be used to tell prospective users about things they should be aware of even before logging on. It might also be used to format a plain-language error message telling the user what went wrong. Table 12-5 lists the seven predefined callbacks you can use without writing your own, along with short descriptions of their intended purposes.

Table 12-5
JAAS predefined callbacks

Callback Class	Action
ChoiceCallcack	Presents a choice to the user, optionally allowing multiple selections
ConfirmationCallback	Obtains a confirmation response from a user
LanguageCallback	Obtains or sets a user locale to determine whether a different language or display format should be used
NameCallback	Obtains a user name
PasswordCallback	Obtains a password
TextInputCallback	Obtains unformatted text from the user
TextOutputCallback	Presents a text message to the user; this facility is usually used to present information needed by the user, or to present warning or error messages

These seven callback choices allow wide flexibility for your callback handler and you might consider providing stubs for each in your own interactive callback-handler instance. You never know when an application will wind up requiring more information from the user. Of course handlers designed for automated services can't use any but the most basic callback classes, usually NameCallback and PasswordCallback. However, the cost of providing all of them is small, because you don't have to supply any you don't need right then. Indeed, providing a stub callback that does nothing at all might be a useful way of making room in your application for support of unforeseen problems by enabling you to swap in a specialized callback when the need arises.

You simply pass the callback handler an array containing the callback methods you want to use. The callback handler then iterates through the array looking for supported callbacks and tries to execute them. If any of your callbacks aren't supported, the handler throws an UnsupportedCallbackException. It's really pretty simple except for the fact that the seven callbacks require different arguments and need to be treated differently.

Kerberos login handler

Kerberos is a good module to start with, because it works consistently across many platforms. Also, it always does something, unlike the Win2K and Unix modules, which merely inspect an existing user's environment. Kerberos requires several mandatory arguments that point to the location of the ticket server and, usually, to the port(s) associated with it, unless these arguments are hardwired into the code. Kerberos listens by default on well-known port 88, and responds on ephemeral ports above 1024. Kerberos might also require several other well-known ports, including 543, 749-754, and 2105, for various housekeeping functions. Table 12-6 shows the various arguments used to define Kerberos login behavior.

Table 12-6
Kerberos configuration options

Option Name	Purpose	Action
useTicketCache	Set login behavior	This option is Boolean — it must be present if `ticketCache` is set. If this option is set and `ticketCache` is also set, use `ticketCache`. If it is set and `ticketCache` is not set, search for a `ticketCache` in default locations.
TicketCache	Locate ticket cache	This option specifies the location of a ticket cache.
doNotPrompt	Set login behavior	This option is Boolean — if it is set, do not prompt for a user name or password.
UseKeyTab	Set login behavior	This option is Boolean — if it is set, search for a key tab using `keyTab`, if one is set, or obtain the location of the file from the Kerberos configuration file, or look in the user's home directory for the file `krb5.keytab`.
KeyTab	Set login behavior	This option specifies the location and name of a key tab file containing the user's secret key.
StoreKey	Set login behavior	This option is Boolean — it is set if the user's private key should be stored with the user's private credentials.
Principal	Specify principal name	This option specifies the name of the principal.

Continued

	Table 12-6 *(continued)*	
Option Name	**Purpose**	**Action**
`UseFirstPass`	Set login behavior	This option is Boolean — after a `Subject` has logged in, retrieve the login-name and password information from the login module's shared state and use that information when re-authenticating. If re-authentication fails, fail the authentication and do not attempt to log in again.
`TryFirstPass`	Set login behavior	This option is Boolean — after a `Subject` has logged in, retrieve the login-name and password information from the login module's shared state and use that information when re-authenticating. If re-authentication fails, collect a new login name and password using the callback handler and attempt to authenticate again.
`StorePass`	Set login behavior	This option is Boolean — after authentication and commit, store the login name and password in the login module's shared state. (Note that this option must be set to enable `useFirstPass` and `tryFirstPass` to have any effect.)
`ClearPass`	Set login behavior	This option is Boolean — after authentication and commit, clear the login name and password from the login module's shared state. (Note that this option makes `useFirstPass` and `tryFirstPass` moot.)

The magazine-publisher example later in this chapter uses Kerberos to authenticate a user, so we needn't go into great detail about Kerberos here.

The default Kerberos login module returns a single `Principal`:
`KerberosPrincipal`

However, the possibilities are endless. Microsoft, for example, "extends" Kerberos by allowing the user to skip the login stage if he or she already possesses a valid credential from a trusted domain, or by permitting a Java Card holder to accomplish login through a card reader.

WinNT/Win2K login handler

Although the callback handler should be specified in the options for this module, its value will be ignored and the supplied handler doesn't actually interact with the user. This module obtains all of its information from the WinNT or Win2K environment. (Note that this means that the predefined NT/Win2K login will always succeed if the user is logged into an NT/Win2K machine.) So if you want any special handling of the login process based on a login response, you'll have to write your own login module and provide a real callback handler. This doesn't mean that the login is only useful for authentication. You can examine the user's Win2K environment and use it to set locale options, for example, so you know what language to use for prompts and error messages, as well as the proper format for dates, times, and monetary units.

Note   The NT login-handler interface contains no options or actions.

The simple example discussed in the previous section "Authenticating Users" does a complete WinNT/Win2K login, so we needn't go into this login further here.

The WinNT login module may return any or all of the following `Principal`s:

   ✦ `NTUserPrincipal`

   ✦ `NTDomainPrincipal`

   ✦ `NTSidUserPrincipal`

   ✦ `NTSidDomainPrincipal`

   ✦ `NTSidGroupPrincipals`

   ✦ `NTSidPrimaryGroupPrincipal`

   ✦ `NTNumericCredential`

Unix login handler

This module obtains all of its information from the Unix environment, much like WinNT/2K. As with NT, the configuration options are minimal. The Unix login handler contains no arguments or actions.

The Unix login module returns the following `Principal`s:

   ✦ `UnixPrincipal`

   ✦ `UnixNumericUserPrincipal`

   ✦ `UnixNumericGroupPrincipal`

Key-store login handler

Like Kerberos, key-store services enable distributed login authentication but are tailored for the LDAP /ISO X.500 environment. If you're in such an environment you probably know about this, but these services are encountered infrequently by most programmers. A predefined `UserPassword` attribute is available in X.500 directory entries, so the addition of any unique alias or unique CN within the DN makes a potential user name/password pair.

X.500 values are handled by keyword/value pairs, and may look rather odd to the uninitiated. Instead of the simple user name one might expect, or the relatively concise flat namespace of RFC 822/2822 e-mail addresses, you'll find something like this: C=<*Country Code*>, O=<*Organization Name*>, OU=<*Organizational Unit*>, OU=<*Another Organizational Unit*>, CN=<*Any Name*>. A real person in Germany might be `C=DE, O="Trolls Inc.", OU="Weavers Division", OU="Straw Into Gold Group", CN=Rumpelstiltskin`. The entire path is termed a Distinguished Name (DN) and is order dependent, although an application can define whether to read the path from left to right or right to left. So if you swapped the order of the two OU entries in the DN for Rumpelstiltskin, you'd have a different DN. An interesting feature of X.500 directories is that they allow multiple aliases to be defined for every user. These directories can contain great quantities of information (including what type of beer an individual prefers) that can be operated on in a fully relational manner.

While this feature makes ISO directories very powerful, it also makes human interactions with them tedious in the extreme. Most users wind up hating the lengthy process of entering X.500 addresses if they have to deal with them directly. The directory Distinguished Name is commonly hidden behind aliases guaranteed to be unique, such as RFC-822 e-mail addresses or standard fully qualified filenames so users may think they're interacting with a simpler directory scheme. Thoughtful programmers and systems administrators take pains not to disabuse their users of this naïve notion if at all possible.

So X.500 directories are quite often used as backbones to connect disparate file systems or namespaces and are often invisible to the user. Because they are hierarchical, you can handle differences in directory or data format transparently by knowing just where in the hierarchy a particular file or name lives. If you collect information about local root nodes in the worldwide X.500 hierarchy, you can identify a file format or communications protocol used for that file or name by knowing which local root it descends from. Table 12-7 shows the options that can be set for key-store logins.

Table 12-7
Key-store-configuration options

Option Name	Purpose	Action
KeyStoreURL	Locate key-store file	This option specifies the location of the key-store file.
KeyStoreType	Specify key-store type	This option specifies the key-store type. If it is absent, call KeyStore.getDefaultType()
KeyStoreProvider	Identify key-store provider	This option specifies the key-store provider. If it is absent, look for a provider in the search path.
KeyStoreAlias	Identify key-store login name (alias)	This option specifies a login name. It is required if no callback handler is supplied.
KeyStorePasswordURL	Locate key-store password	This option specifies the location of the key store password. It is required if no callback handler is supplied.
privateKeyPasswordURL	Locate private-key password	This option specifies the location of the private-key password required by the application to access the private key for this alias. If it is absent, use the key-store password.

Because LDAP sends any required password in clear text, use of an underlying secure-communications protocol is recommended. Possible LDAP X.500 attribute types are listed in Table 12-8.

Table 12-8
LDAP/X.500 attribute types

X.500 Attribute String	Attribute Type	Description
CN	commonName	A personal name. Because personal names are often shared, X.500 directories may require other identification attributes to find a unique entry.

Continued

Table 12-8 *(continued)*

X.500 Attribute String	Attribute Type	Description
L	localityName	Typically, a city or other political subdivision. There may be more than one, since a city may be known by different names to different people. So
		L=Chicago, L="Windy City" might both refer to the same locality in the USA, or L=Zurich, L=Zuerich, L=Z\cdurich (with T.61 escape sequence to add the umlaut) all refer to the same German city, properly named Z_rich.
ST	stateOrProvinceName	A state or province name. Outside the USA, Canada, and a few other countries, a major political subdivision of a country.
O	organizationName	A company name or other organizational identifier.
OU	organizational UnitName	An organizational subdivision. There may be more than one in a single directory entry. X.500 attributes are parsed in order of distance from the root, so the corporate hierarchy is traversed downward by each successive OU.
C	countryName	A country name, actually a two-letter country code as defined in ISO 3166. In X.500 proper, C may be supplemented by a friendlyCountry identifier, so relatively obscure country codes like DZ can be supplemented by the more recognizable "Algeria."
STREET	streetAddress	A street address or postal direction.
DC	domainComponent	A DNS or NRS domain name. There may be more than one.
UID	userid	A userid. User names are usually unique within a single organization or domain, but since X.500 is fully relational, a unique ID may be constructed from a join of almost any fields, for example, UID and DC, which may be used to construct or deconstruct an RFC 822/2822 e-mail address.

The key-store login module returns a single `Principal`, as shown here:

```
X500Principal
```

JNDI login handler

The Java Naming and Directory Interface (JNDI) is really a Sun-specific login handler, as few outside the Sun environment bother with it. The options available are shown in Table 12-9.

Table 12-9
JNDI configuration options

Argument Name	Purpose	Action
`user.provider.url`	Locate JNDI provider	This mandatory option points to a URI and access protocol: `ldap://<uri>` or `nis://<uri>`
`group.provider.url`	Locate JNDI provider	This mandatory option points to a URI and access protocol: `ldap://<uri>` or `nis://<uri>`
`UseFirstPass`	Set login behavior	This option is Boolean — after a `Subject` has logged in, retrieve the login name and password information from the login module's shared state and use that information when re-authenticating. If re-authentication fails, fail the authentication and do not attempt to log in again.
`TryFirstPass`	Set login behavior	This option is Boolean — after a `Subject` has logged in, retrieve the login name and password information from the login module's shared state and use that information when re-authenticating. If re-authentication fails, collect new login name and password using the callback handler and attempt to authenticate again.

Continued

Table 12-9 *(continued)*		
Argument Name	**Purpose**	**Action**
StorePass	Set login behavior	This option is Boolean — after authentication and commit, store the login name and password in the login module's shared state. (Note that this argument must be set in order for useFirstPass or tryFirstPass to have any effect.)
ClearPass	Set login behavior	This option is Boolean — after authentication and commit, clear the login name and password from the login module's shared state. (Note that this option makes the use of useFirstPass or tryFirstPass moot.)

The JINDI login module returns the following Principals:

✦ UnixPrincipal

✦ UnixNumericUserPrincipal

✦ UnixNumericGroupPrincipal

Cross-Reference See Chapter 11 for a discussion of JNDI and directory services.

Custom login modules

There is, however, nothing to prevent vendors from supplying login modules with their products, or to prevent you from writing your own login module to handle enterprise-specific requirements. You could introduce biometric security logins, SmartCard access (with optional PIN), or other means as they're developed.

Note The former JAAS login module supporting Sun Solaris only is now deprecated and should be replaced by the generic Unix module. We'll see a simple login routine later in this chapter in the section "Authenticating a Web user against a Windows NT domain."

An administrator might choose first to check the user's own environment for login and permissions information. If this succeeds, all is well, so this module might be flagged sufficient. If not, other attempts to obtain a valid login might be made before a particular application is executed.

Alternatively, an administrator might choose first to check a distributed authentication service like Kerberos before looking at the user's own environment for login and permissions information. Because it's not clear that either source of login information is necessarily present, both login modules would probably be flagged `optional`. If either succeeds, the user might then be prompted to enter further information to verify that he or she is who he or she seems to be, or to enter a specially privileged state. By the addition of layers of security, critical or dangerous applications can be made arbitrarily more difficult to access.

Writing your own login handler

In many situations, you might want to create your own login handler. If your application will be distributed as a package to many different systems, you might want to create a handler that automatically adjusts to the OS it's used under. Alternatively, a series of login modules can be dropped into packaged versions of the code for each supported environment.

Because JAAS expects login modules to obey certain rules, you'll have to implement its `LoginModule` interface in order to integrate your handler with JAAS. A login module requires the methods shown in Table 12-10, shown in roughly the order in which they might be used.

Table 12-10
JAAS login-module methods

Method	Action
`public void initialize(Subject subj, CallbackHandler callback, Map sharedState, Map options)`	This method initializes the login module, identifying the `Subject`, naming the callback handler, allocating storage for shared information, and passing through option arguments from the login configuration file.
`public boolean login()`	This method tries to authenticate a `Subject`.
`public boolean commit()`	This method is called if the login should be committed. The JAAS login process has two steps. First, the path though the module list is tried to see whether it will succeed in its entirety, and then the already tested login path is committed. This prevents unscrupulous users from attempting to race the login process, using a security exploit to trick the system into granting momentary access during an operation that will later be rescinded.

Continued

Table 12-10 *(continued)*

Method	Action
`public boolean abort()`	This method is called when the login fails any required step, doesn't fulfill any of the available optional steps, or encounters problems. Like the `logout` method, `abort` should clean up any sensitive stored information.
`public boolean logout()`	This method allows a `Subject` to logout, cleans up any stored `Principals`, and explicitly zeros any sensitive information that would otherwise be released for the garbage collector.

The `initialize` method in particular requires a particular set of arguments needed to properly set up the login module. This collection of arguments is shown in Table 12-11.

Table 12-11
Login initialize arguments

Argument Name	Purpose	Action
`Subject`	Identify the `Subject`	This argument names the `Subject` this login module will populate with one or more `Principals`. Note that these are not necessarily user IDs but may reference a role or other ephemeral identity that an authorized user or process may take on. The `Subject` may, in fact, be populated with several `Principals` representing actual user IDs, groups, and so on, in context.
`callbackHandler`	Identify the `CallbackHandler`	This argument names the callback handler used with this login module.
`sharedState`	Map the shared `LoginModule` state	This argument is an array containing login and authorization information shared between modules.
`Options`	Map the `LoginModule` options	This argument contains the options read in from the login-configuration file.

A login module requires several characteristics besides the ability to implement the necessary methods. Most importantly, any `Principal` or `Subject` associated with a particular login module must be serializable. This is necessary because your application may be used to contact a remote server. If your `Principal` isn't serializable, you won't be able to present it to the remote server for authorization.

Let's suppose that we want to write a custom login module supporting the Java Card smart card, a physical device one can carry around in a purse or pocket. Several APIs are written for such devices, but in the interest of keeping the example short we'll imagine a fictional API that listens for a card insertion and does all the necessary housekeeping.

We'll define a `Principal` class that is essentially a collection of methods used to return information from the login context and call it `JavaCardPrincipal`. A simple implementation is shown in Listing 12-17. You'll note, as ever, that it doesn't do much in the way of error handling, so before using it you might want to add a few output statements to let you know what's happening and what might have gone wrong. The same is true for all the code in this section. Because referring to line numbers is awkward, we'll often describe the code in comments within the code itself rather than by referencing it from the outside.

Listing 12-17: **JavaCardPrincipal**

```
import java.security.*;
import java.io.*;
// Note that this code is serializable. Because JAAS is
designed
// operate in a network environment, Principals and Subjects
must
// always be serializable, or they can't be presented to a
server.

public class JavaCardPrincipal implements Principal,
Serializable {

    private String name;

    public JavaCardPrincipal(String s) {
    name = s;
    }

    public String getName() {
    return name;
    }

    // Compare object names to determine identity
    public boolean equals(Object o) {
```

Continued

Listing 12-17 *(continued)*

```
     if (o == null)
         return false;
     if (!(o instanceof JavaCardPrincipal))
         return false;
         return ((JavaCardPrincipal) o).name.equals(name);
     }

     public String toString() {
     return name;
     }

     public int hashCode() {
     return name.hashCode();
     }
}
```

As you can see, the most care has been lavished on the equality test, because that
little bit is very important when you're trying to iterate through a Subject with
several Principals.

Listing 12-18 shows an example launcher for a Java Card login. Because the classes
associated with the login are probably stored on the card itself, the code has to be
accessed before it can be run. The code must either be extracted from the card and
run on a host or initiated on the card itself. A practical example in the real world
would be far more complex, because different types of smart card exist, some of
which have no actual processing power. Also, the login methods would have to
accommodate several variations in platform.

Listing 12-18: **Java Card launcher**

```
import java.lang.reflect.Method;
import java.lang.reflect.InvocationTargetException;
import java.security.PrivilegedAction;

// Launch a Java <module> from a Java Card
public class JavaCardLauncher implements PrivilegedAction {

    private Class module = null;

    public JavaCardLauncher (Class module) {
        this.module = module;
    }

    public Object run() {
        invokeMain(module);
```

```
            return null;
        }

    private void invokeMain (Class javaCardClass) {
        Class argArray [] = new Class [] {String[].class};
        Object arg [] = {new String[0]};
        Method mainMethod = null;
        try {
            mainMethod =
javaCardClass.getMethod("main",argArray);
        } catch (Exception e) {
            System.exit(-1);
        }
        try {
            mainMethod.invoke(null,arg);
        } catch (Exception e) {
        }
    }
}
```

Listing 12-19 shows the code that describes the virtual Java Card itself. It talks to the card proper and uses the launcher to start up the proper module from the card.

Listing 12-19: **Java Card**

```
import java.security.Principal;
import javax.security.auth.*;
import javax.security.auth.callback.*;
import javax.security.auth.login.*;
import javax.security.auth.spi.*;
import com.sun.security.auth.*;
import java.net.URLClassLoader;
import java.net.URL;
import java.util.*;
import java.io.*;

public class JavaCard {

    public static void main(String[] s) {

        LoginContext lc = null;
        while (true) {
            try {
                try {
                    lc = new LoginContext("JavaCard");
                } catch (Exception e) {
                }
```

Continued

Listing 12-19 *(continued)*

```
                lc.login();
                break;
            } catch (Exception e) {
            }
            try {
                Thread.currentThread().sleep(0);
            } catch (Exception e) {
            }
        }
        try {
            URL u[] = new URL[1];
            u[0] = new URL((String)
(lc.getSubject().getPublicCredentials().toArray())[0]);
            URLClassLoader ucl = new URLClassLoader(u);
            Class module = null;
            module = ucl.loadClass((String)
(lc.getSubject().getPublicCredentials().toArray())[1]);
            Subject.doAs(lc.getSubject(),
                        new JavaCardLauncher(module));
        } catch (Exception e) {
        }
        try {
            lc.logout ();
        } catch (Exception e) {
        }
        System.exit(0);
    }
}
```

Listing 12-20 shows the skeleton of the actual login module itself. Since we can't distribute the code for an actual proprietary Java Card API, most of the activity needed is described in comments, or a generic approximation of actual code is commented out.

Listing 12-20: Java Card login module

```
import java.util.*;
import java.io.IOException;
import javax.security.auth.*;
import javax.security.auth.callback.*;
import javax.security.auth.login.*;
import javax.security.auth.spi.*;
// import proprietary.JavaCardAPI.*;
```

```
// Note that there isn't any such thing as the above API

public class JavaCardLoginModule implements LoginModule /*,
JavaCardMonitor */ {
// Note that there isn't any such class as
// the above "JavaCardMonitor."
// If there were such a class, it would handle the details of
waiting
// for the insertion of a Java Card in a reader and accessing
it.
// The best part about an imaginary API is that it can do
whatever we
// want it to do. If you were actually programming for a Java
Card,
// though, you'd probably want to use a real API

    // Set up initial state
    private Subject subject;
    private Map sharedState;
    private Map options;

    // Keep track of login progress.
    // You have to try the entire process to be sure that it
will
    // succeed before doing it "for real."
    private boolean loginOk = false;
    private boolean commitOk = false;

    // username
    private String username;

    // Java Module stuff
    private String url;
    private String className;

    private JavaCardPrincipal userPrincipal;
    // Keep track of the Java Card
    private static Object monitor = "synchronization monitor";
    private JavaCard jc;


    public void initialize(Subject subject,
                    CallbackHandler callbackHandler,
                    Map sharedState, Map options) {
        this.subject = subject;
        this.sharedState = sharedState;
        this.options = options;
        try {
            //          if (JavaCard.started () == false) {
            //              JavaCard.start ();
            //          }
        } catch (Exception e) {
```

Continued

Listing 12-20 *(continued)*

```
        }
        // Begin polling for CARD_INSERTED or CARD_REMOVED
events
        //      EventGenerator.getGenerator().addJavaCardMonitor
        //                   (new JavaCardLoginModule());
    }

    // Get the url of the Java module to be launched.
    public boolean login() throws LoginException {
        try {
            System.out.println ("Please insert your Java
Card(tm)!");
            // wait for the user insert their Java Card
            // Do some magic on the card using the Java Card
API
            // Get the user name
            // Get the Url for the class
            // Get the class name
        } catch (Exception e) {
            throw new LoginException("");
        }

        // verify the PIN using a magical technique found below
        try {
            if (verifyPIN()) {
                loginOk = true;
                return true;
                // Assert: at this point we are ready
                // to commit the login transaction
            }
        } catch (Exception e) {
            throw new LoginException("");
        }
        loginOk = false;
        throw new FailedLoginException("");
    }

    public boolean commit() throws LoginException {
        if (!loginOk) {
            // While we may not have verified a login,
            // someone else might have, so clean up nicely.
            username = null;
            return false;
        } else {
            // Perform more magic to populate the Subject
        }
        // then clean up.
        username = null;
        commitOk = true;
        shutdown ();
```

```
            return true;
        }


    public boolean abort() throws LoginException {
        try {
            synchronized (monitor) {
                System.out.println ("Please remove your Java
Card(tm) now.");
                // Check the status of the terminal here
            }
        } catch (Exception e) {
        }
        if (!loginOk) {
            return false;
        } else if (loginOk && !commitOk) {
            loginOk = false;
            username = null;
            userPrincipal = null;
        } else {
            logout();
        }
        shutdown ();
        return true;
    }

    public boolean logout() throws LoginException {
        // Clean up
        // Remove the User's Principal, URL and classname
        loginOk = false;
        commitOk = false;
        username = null;
        userPrincipal = null;
        url = null;
        className = null;
        shutdown ();
        return true;
    }

    // A Java card has been inserted.
    // public void javaCardInserted (JavaCardTerminalEvent
jcte) {
    // Perform magic
    // }

    // A Java card has been removed.
    public void javaCardRemoved (/*JavaCardTerminalEvent
jcte*/) {
        synchronized (monitor) {
            monitor.notifyAll();
        }
```

Continued

Listing 12-20 *(continued)*

```
        }

    private static void shutdown () {
        try {
            // Do some magic to the card
        } catch (Exception e) {
        }
    }

    private boolean verifyPIN () {
        //    abracadabra();
        // Perform magical communications with the Java Card
and then
        return true;
    }
}
```

Although we specified a callback handler when we called the login module, we don't actually use it. This is because the actual login is performed by our magic API, which only accepts a PIN from the user to verify his or her identity. The API bases its idea of who the user actually is, and what credentials or certificates the user might hold, on the mere fact that he or she possesses the card and knows the PIN.

Writing your own callback handler

When a login context is not available from the environment, or when that context doesn't extend to special permissions used by a JAAS-enabled application, JAAS has the ability to request a login from a user by issuing a callback. The default handlers for Unix and WinNT/2K environments don't usually need callbacks because users have to be logged in anyway. However other environments, including Kerberos and JNDI, may not have a useful login context available. In addition, the default login handlers supplied by Sun are environment-specific, so you'll have to write your own if you want to distribute code without OS dependencies.

A callback handler may look something like the code shown in Listing 12-21, with a simple loop checking for the presence of a given callback and calling it if needed. Not every choice in the example is fully expanded into code, but hints are given that makes this step a straightforward exercise left to the reader.

Listing 12-21: **CallbackHandler framework**

```
import java.io.*;
import java.util.*
import javax.security.auth.callback.*;

class CBH implements CallbackHandler {
    private String username;
    private String password;
    public void handle(Callback[] cb)
    throws IOException, UnsupportedCallbackException {
        // iterate through the callbacks, if any
        for (int i = 0; i < cb.length; i++) {
            // ChoiceCallback -- Options are supplied in the
prompt string
            // The choice callback may be used to specify a
security realm,
            // or any other selection or selections from a list.
            if (cb[i] instanceof ChoiceCallback) {
                ChoiceCallback ccb = (ChoiceCallback) cb[i];
                System.out.print(ccb.getPrompt() + " ");
                System.out.flush();
                String choice = new BufferedReader
                                (new
InputStreamReader(System.in)).readLine();
                // Note that both buffered readers and readLine may
cause
                // problems when used without care. Not all
environments
                // allow more than one buffered read from a single
input
                // stream. It may be necessary to share a single
buffer
                // between your callback handlers, an advanced
technique
                // slightly beyond the scope of this chapter.
            }
            // Confirmation Callback
            else if (cb[i] instanceof ConfirmationCallback) {
                ConfirmationCallback cc =
                        (ConfirmationCallback)cb[i];
                // Typically, you'd implement a switch here for
                // each type of confirmation you want to support.
                //    case ConfirmationCallback.YES_NO_OPTION: ...
                //    case
ConfirmationCallback.YES_NO_CANCEL_OPTION: ...
                // and so on.
```

Continued

Listing 12-21 *(continued)*

```
                }
                // LanguageCallback
                else if (cb[i] instanceof LanguageCallback) {
                    LanguageCallback lc =
                             (LanguageCallback)cb[i];
                    // The LanguageCallback is used to get a locale
from
                    // the user's environment or to set a locale based
                    // on the user's response to a prompt.
                    //    lcb.setLocale( Locale.getDefault());
                    // or
                    //    lcb.setLocale(Locale.US);
                    // The above format uses one of the constants
defined
                    // in the Locale class which create common Locales
                    // of the form Locale(String language="en",
                    //                    String country="US")
                    // Inspect the Locale class in java.util

                } // end LanguageCallback
                // NameCallback
                else if (cb[i] instanceof NameCallback) {
                    NameCallback ncb = (NameCallback)cb[i];
                    ncb.setName(username);

                } // end NameCallback
                // PasswordCallback
                else if (cb[i] instanceof PasswordCallback) {
                    PasswordCallback pcb = (PasswordCallback)cb[i];
                    pcb.setPassword(password.toCharArray());

                } // end PasswordCallback
                // TextInputCallback
                else if (cb[i] instanceof TextInputCallback) {
                    TextInputCallback tic =
                             (TextInputCallback)cb[i];
                  // proceed with a prompt and read sequence

                } // end TextInputCallback
                // TextOutputCallback
                else if (cb[i] instanceof TextOutputCallback) {
                    // display the message according to the specified
type
                    TextOutputCallback toc = (TextOutputCallback)cb[i];
                    switch (toc.getMessageType()) {
                    case TextOutputCallback.INFORMATION:
                        System.out.println(toc.getMessage());
                        break;
                    case TextOutputCallback.ERROR:
```

```
                    System.out.println("ERROR: " +
toc.getMessage());
                    break;
                case TextOutputCallback.WARNING:
                    System.out.println("WARNING: " +
toc.getMessage());
                    break;
                default:
                    throw new IOException("Unsupported message type:
" +
                                    toc.getMessageType());
                } // end TextOutputCallback
            } // next callback or fall through
        } // end handle
    } // end CallbackHandlerFramework
}
```

It's a simple matter to vary the I/O behavior of your code dynamically, by feeding it an array of handlers and data in whatever order seems best. They'll be executed in sequence. For example, your code could check for the existence of an announcement file when entering a login sequence. It could then present the announcement to the user before (or instead of) allowing the login to proceed. Or it could call a language-callback handler to see what language to use by looking at or prompting for a user locale. It could then set an accessible locale variable, and continue the login process with a selection of prompts and messages that make sense to your user. This is better than assuming, as so many do, that everyone speaks English.

Authenticating a Web user against a Windows NT domain

The magazine-publisher application will require database access to allow subscribers to access their subscription accounts to check the remaining number of issues or renew for an integral number of years. Since this information is private, a subscriber has to supply a user name and password to access this feature. The publisher runs a Microsoft-only shop, and insists on using Microsoft servers for handling Web requests.

Brief security analysis

This is a low-value transaction, so it doesn't make sense to devote a lot of resources to it. The only significant exposures are the possibility of sniffing a user's credit-card information and the possibility of hacking into the subscription database itself, possibly causing damage or economic loss. Subscribers will log in to the server through a browser screen. They will then continue interaction with the application through HTTPS and Java Server Pages (JSP), which are typically seen as sufficient for credit-card interactions on the Web. The encrypted user-ID/password dialogue adds another layer of security to the process, since we might not want our magazine subscriptions widely known.

Security limitations

Because the terminals live on the open Internet, the application remains vulnerable to any exploits discovered by malicious or mischievous persons unknown to the system. Because this is not a text on computer security, we have the luxury of ignoring any potential impingements from the real world.

Implementation

There are several reasonable ways to implement remote logins to a Microsoft machine. The simplest way is probably to use Microsoft's Kerberos support, which only requires running the built-in Win2K Server Kerberos server. Presto chango! Windows-domain login made simple. Kerberos is well understood in the Web-enabled-application-developer community and has a rich set of resources available. It's also designed to be used by a distributed user base and doesn't have expectation possessed by native-mode Windows systems that the rest of the world consists exclusively of Windows systems.

The code samples used in this section omit error handling and feedback for the most part, to bring the samples down to a reasonable size. Remember to catch exceptions and do something with them, even if it's just silently ignoring them. And it will be handy for debugging purposes to print out a few chatty messages at significant points, just so you know where you are.

You'll need some server code to handle the secure-socket communication link, as shown in Listing 12-22.

Listing 12-22: **Magazine-publisher server code**

```
import org.ietf.jgss.*;
import java.net.Socket;
import java.io.IOException;
import java.io.DataInputStream;
import java.io.DataOutputStream;

public class Subscriber {

    public static void main(String[] args)
    throws IOException, GSSException  {

        String krbServer = args[0];
        String hostName = args[1];
```

```
int portnumber = Integer.parseInt(args[2]);
Socket s = new Socket(hostName,
                        portnumber);
DataInputStream i =
new DataInputStream(s.getInputStream());
DataOutputStream o =
new DataOutputStream(s.getOutputStream());
// kerberos_v5 OID
// This OID number is predefined by Sun for Kerberos
Oid krb5Oid = new Oid("1.2.840.113554.1.2.2");
GSSManager m = GSSManager.getInstance();
GSSName n = m.createName(krbServer,
                            null);
GSSContext c = m.createContext(n,
            krb5Oid,
            null,
            GSSContext.DEFAULT_LIFETIME);
c.requestMutualAuth(true);
c.requestConf(true);
c.requestInteg(true);
byte[] token = new byte[0];
while (!c.isEstablished()) {
    token = c.initSecContext(token,
                0,
                token.length);
    if (token != null) {
        o.writeInt(token.length);
        o.write(token);
        o.flush();
    }
    if (!c.isEstablished()) {
        token = new byte[i.readInt()];
        i.readFully(token);
    }
}
byte[] byteArray = "Wazzup?\0".getBytes();
MessageProp mp =  new MessageProp(0, true);
token = c.wrap(byteArray, 0, byteArray.length, mp);
o.writeInt(token.length);
o.write(token);
o.flush();
c.dispose();
s.close();
    }
}
```

Then you'll need a client to do the actual login, as shown in Listing 12-23.

Listing 12-23: **Magazine-publisher client code**

```
import java.io.*;
import java.lang.reflect.*;
import java.util.Arrays;
import javax.security.auth.callback.*;
import javax.security.auth.login.*;
import javax.security.auth.Subject;
import com.sun.security.auth.callback.TextCallbackHandler;

public class Login {

    public static void main(String[] args) {
        LoginContext lc = null;
        try {
            lc = new LoginContext(args[0], new
TextCallbackHandler());
        } catch (Exception e) {
            System.exit(-1);
        }
        try {
            lc.login();
        } catch (Exception e) {
            System.exit(-1);
        }
        try {
            Subject.doAsPrivileged(lc.getSubject(),
                                   new  KRBPrivilegedAction(args),
                                   null);
        } catch (Exception e) {
            System.exit(-1);
        }
        System.exit(0);
    }
}

class KRBPrivilegedAction implements
    java.security.PrivilegedExceptionAction {

    String[] argArray;
    public KRBPrivilegedAction(String[] argArray) {
        this.argArray = (String[])argArray.clone();
    }

    public Object run() throws Exception {
        ClassLoader cl =
Thread.currentThread().getContextClassLoader();
        try {
            Class c = Class.forName(argArray[0], true, cl);
            Class[] PARAMS = { argArray.getClass()};
            java.lang.reflect.Method mainMethod =
                    c.getMethod("main", PARAMS);
```

```
        String[] saveArgArray = new String[argArray.length -
1];
        System.arraycopy(argArray, 1, saveArgArray, 0,
argArray.length - 1);
        Object[] argArray = { saveArgArray};
        mainMethod.invoke(null, argArray);
    } catch (Exception e) {
        // This class should only throw one exception type
        throw new java.security.PrivilegedActionException(e);
    }
    return null;
  }
}
```

And finally, you'll need the standard JAAS configuration and policy files, as shown grouped in Listing 12-24.

Listing 12-24: **Magazine-publisher configuration and policy files**

Login Configuration File

```
Login {
   com.sun.security.auth.module.Krb5LoginModule required;
};

Subscriber {
   com.sun.security.auth.module.Krb5LoginModule required
   storeKey=true
         principal="KRBServer@krb.testmag.com";
};
```

Client Policy File

```
grant CodeBase "file:./Login.jar" {
   permission java.security.AllPermission;
};

grant CodeBase "file:./Subscriber.jar",
Principal javax.security.auth.kerberos.KerberosPrincipal
   "Puddintane@krb.testmag.com" {

   permission java.net.SocketPermission "*", "connect";

   permission javax.security.auth.kerberos.ServicePermission
   "krbtgt/krb.testmag.com@krb.testmag.com",
```

Continued

Listing 12-24 *(continued)*

```
    "initiate";

    permission javax.security.auth.kerberos.ServicePermission
    "KRBServer@krb.testmag.com ",
    "initiate";
};
```

Server Policy File

```
grant CodeBase "file:./Login.jar" {
    permission java.security.AllPermission;
};

grant CodeBase "file:./Subscriber.jar"
Principal javax.security.auth.kerberos.KerberosPrincipal
"KRBServer@krb.testmag.com" {

    permission java.net.SocketPermission "*", "accept";

    permission javax.security.auth.kerberos.ServicePermission
    "KRBServer@krb.testmag.com", "accept";
};
```

Be sure to start the server before you run the client, as the attempt to connect with the server will fail if it's not running. Listing 12-25 shows the Java run commands used to start up your system. The server will ask only for the password, because the `Principal` is specified in the server-policy file. The client will ask for both a user name, which ought to be `Puddintane`, since I like that name, and a password. You should have created these entries on your Kerberos server beforehand.

Listing 12-25: Magazine-publisher run command and arguments

Start the Server

```
java -classpath Login.jar;Subscriber.jar
    -Djava.security.manager
    -Djava.security.krb5.realm=krb.testmag.com
    -Djava.security.krb5.kdc=KRBKdc.testmag.com
    -Djava.security.policy=KRBServer.policy
    -Djava.security.auth.login.config=KRBServer.conf
    Login Subscriber 6702 <or any unused port>
```

Start the Client

```
java -classpath Login.jar
    -Djava.security.manager
    -Djava.security.krb5.realm=krb.testmag.com
    -Djava.security.krb5.kdc=KRBKdc.testmag.com
    -Djava.security.policy=KRBClient.policy
    -Djava.security.auth.login.config=KRBServer.conf
    Login Subscriber KRBServer@krb.testmag.com
                gold.testmag.com 6702
```

If you're running on a Unix box, the semicolon (;) used as a separator in the classpath is replaced with a colon (:), as always. In a normal administrative environment, the server is usually named by means of concatenating the name of the service with the name of the machine it runs on, so the simple name in the preceding code might be replaced with something like this: KRBServer/gold@ krb.testmag.com.

Alternative methods

The more interesting way to log in to a Windows domain is also the more difficult. It involves using the built-in Windows security APIs to access "real" Windows login facilities. But that's a rather thorny problem: The APIs are not easily used from "outside the box," and the programmer has to account for the fact that not all of them work in quite the manner one might expect.

But one of the nice things about the Java development community is that a great number of excellent programmers are still dedicated to the proposition that life is easier when we cooperate with each other. Among them are Andy Armstrong of Tagish, Ltd. and Thomas Restrepro, who've come up with two essential bits of code that make life much easier for other programmers trying to fiddle with Windows security from the outside. This is a task that Microsoft understandably hasn't paid a great deal of attention to.

If you want to explore a "native-mode" Windows login technique, I highly recommend the pages of Messrs. Armstrong and Restrepro, which are listed in Appendix C. You could also use the Java Virtual Machine to issue the JAAS challenge and response directly, or create a highly Windows-specific routine using the Windows Active Directory as a data store.

The Connexia Airlines business case uses a directory service on a Sun server, but is otherwise very similar to the first example.

Connexia Airlines Business Case

In this example, we'll examine the JAAS environment one might encounter when setting up an airline scheduling system accessible over the Web or on a private network.

Authenticating a Web user against a directory service

The airline application will require database access to obtain flight and fare information and make reservations. Booking agents, whether in-house agents employed by the airline or those employed by outside travel agencies, require equal and non-preferential access to all functions of the system in order for federal regulations to be met. In addition, provisions must be made for collecting payment by credit card or company purchase order (for pre-qualified accounts) before confirming a booking. When the booking is confirmed, the system offers a choice of an electronic ticket or a hard-copy ticket delivered to a physical address or printed on official ticket stock at selected remote locations. All tickets are encoded with a unique identifier to allow confirmation of ticket validity at any point in the check-in and boarding process.

Brief security analysis

Agents will have to log in to use the system, because they may enter transactions with real-world value. Since the agents may not be located at secure or trusted locations, a central login service will have to be provided to ensure login-ID and password integrity.

Eavesdropping on a communications path might reveal agent login IDs and passwords, compromising the integrity of the ordering and payment system, so every login transaction will have to be encrypted to make life arbitrarily difficult for snoops. LDAP is a widely supported standard that supports encrypted communications and would be especially appropriate for this application since it will run on a Sun Solaris server, which supports X.500 directories directly.

Also, personal information will be collected to verify passenger identity and contact information, as well as to obtain credit-card details, which the airline is obliged to keep secret, so this transaction chain requires encryption as well. Since it has been determined that managing a Virtual Private Network (VPN) would be difficult, given the very large number of potential agent/users, a Web application based on the Secure HyperText Transfer Protocol (HTTPS) will be used for communication after the initial login. This means that JAAS and LDAP will be used only once, to initiate the session, and that normal Web logic can be used to continue the interaction between the agent/user and his or her terminal.

The outbound data stream may include personal information as well as confidential authorization information, and the data required to print encoded ticket media at remote locations, so all portions of the outbound and inbound data stream will require encryption. HTTPS satisfies this requirement as well.

Since the airline application requires distributed access by agents in varied network environments, as well as transmission of personal information, including credit-card numbers, addresses, and telephone numbers, all incoming transactions will have to be encrypted. Additionally, interception of ticket information would allow duplicate tickets to be forged, possibly interfering with orderly boarding as dozens of passengers show up, each assigned to the same seat. HTTPS satisfies this requirement as well, since ticket media can be printed directly from a Web page displayed in a browser window.

No further authorization calls need be made until the agent/user signs off, which he or she does simply by ending the secure session, because the unreliable nature of Web sessions makes it impossible to guarantee that sessions can be ended formally. This lack of predictability implies that Web sessions should be periodically timed out if there is no activity, to avoid allowing an agent/user session to remain active indefinitely, causing a security exception if the user later attempts to login to the system twice or offering a point of attack for a hacker browsing for inactive sessions.

Security limitations

Since JAAS is not continuously "in the loop, the entire Web application must be deployed on a single server. This means that logins will have to be periodically timed out and there is no easy way to offer "single sign-on" to the agents if, in fact, one or more alternative servers exist in the system. While this is a limitation, it doesn't seem too serious, because the alternative, retaining security context on a user's machine, isn't all that attractive either. User machines are, by definition, both unreliable and risky places to place important information about your security techniques.

Implementation

Surprisingly, this is essentially the same problem as in the magazine-publisher example. While we might change the communications protocol in the program, using a key-store directory instead of a Windows directory is basically an administrative task. The appropriate login module has to be called, different arguments passed, and different entries made in the configuration and policy files, but that's about it. Listings 12-26 and 12-27 show the sorts of entries required.

Listing 12-26: **Airline reservation configuration and policy files**

```
Login Configuration File

Login {
   com.sun.security.auth.module.KeyStoreLoginModule required;
};

Subscriber {
   com.sun.security.auth.module.KeyStoreLoginModule required
   storeKey=true
           principal="KeyStoreServer@x500.testair.com";
};

Client Policy File

grant CodeBase "file:./Login.jar" {
   permission java.security.AllPermission;
};

grant CodeBase "file:./Passenger.jar",
Principal javax.security.auth.X500.X500Principal
   "cn=Puddintane" {

   permission java.net.SocketPermission "*", "connect";
};

Server Policy File

grant CodeBase "file:./Login.jar" {
   permission java.security.AllPermission;
};

grant CodeBase "file:./Subscriber.jar"
Principal javax.security.auth.X500.X500Principal
"x500server.testair.com" {

   permission java.net.SocketPermission "*", "accept";

   Permission
   "x500server.testair.com", "accept";
};
```

Listing 12-27: **Airline reservation run command and arguments**

Start the Server

```
java -classpath Login.jar;Subscriber.jar
    -Djava.security.manager
    -Djava.security.policy=X500Server.policy
    -Djava.security.auth.login.config=X500Server.conf
    Login Subscriber 636 <or any unused port>
```

Start the Client

```
java -classpath Login.jar
    -Djava.security.manager
    -Djava.security.policy=X500Client.policy
    -Djava.security.auth.login.config=X500Server.conf
    Login Subscriber X500Server.testair.com
                    gold.testair.com 636
```

Summary

In this chapter we looked at the Java Authentication and Authorization Service (JAAS) introduced in Java 2 V1.3 in the context of the Java security environment. We've seen how JAAS can be used to extend standard Java security methods down to the user level, incorporating support for user certificates, encrypted secure communications, and single sign-on techniques such as Kerberos. We've also seen how JAAS pluggable authentication hides environment and implementation details from the application, allowing an administrator to easily change the system security environment for entire classes of users. JAAS stackable authentication allows multiple or alternative authentication modules to be layered and used based on application need or environment, so users can be offered a very flexible path through the login process or, alternatively, be locked into multiple layers of security challenge and response protocols to ensure arbitrary levels of system security.

JAAS provides user-based authorization as opposed to code-based authorization, which guarantees that intrinsic accountability and auditing can be incorporated into secure systems with little chance of spoofing or later repudiation. While not a guarantee of good security design in every system, it's definitely an invaluable tool in every system architect's engineering kit or security administrator's repertoire of methods.

✦ ✦ ✦

Exploring Java Cryptography Extensions

In This Chapter

Exploring one-way versus two-way encryption

Understanding algorithms

Introducing shared secret cryptography

Introducing public-key cryptography

Examining digital certificates

Reviewing the Java cryptography package

The previous chapter covered Java Authentication and Authorization Services (JAAS); this chapter is a primer on Java Cryptography Extensions (JCE). Starting with J2SE 1.4, JCE is integrated as a part of the standard API. (Using JCE in earlier versions of Java SDK involved downloading the JCE package from `http://www.javasoft.com/jce` and integrating it into the application yourself.)

JCE provides a cryptographic framework for the Java language. A framework usually is a set of jointly acting classes (java term of a package) that make up a reusable design for a specific software classification. On the same definition, a cryptographic framework provides a package of classes that provides cryptographic functionality to the Java language. This framework incorporates implementations for encryption, generating keys for encryption, and key agreement, as well as algorithms for message-authentication codes. The various implementations of encryption available in the JCE framework include in alphabetical order asymmetric, block, stream cipher and symmetric classes. JCE has a plug-and-play architecture where libraries implemented by third-party vendors can be integrated seamlessly into the existing JCE architecture. They are more like the service providers. Support for secure streams and sealed objects are available.

Before we delve into the details of JCE, we will present the basic terminology of cryptography, the various algorithms in cryptography, and the widely used forms of cryptography (shared-key cryptography, public/private-key cryptography, and digital-certificate cryptography). We will end the chapter with a couple of examples simulating one-way and two-way hashes, respectively, with the JCE package.

Grasping the Basic Terminology

Cryptography involves the securing of messages exchanged between a sender and receiver. The people who specialize in this field are called *cryptographers*. Figure 13-1 depicts a complete process involving encryption and decryption of messages.

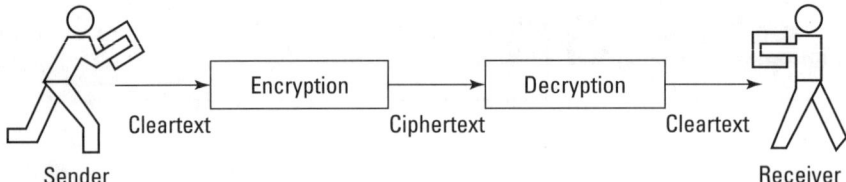

Figure 13-1: Standard cryptography process

In Figure 13-1, a sender wants to disguise a message that he or she sends over the Internet to a receiver. The message is usually referred to as the *cleartext* or *plaintext*. To become disguised, the message first undergoes a process called *encryption*, which renders the actual message text invisible. (The encrypted message is sometimes referred to as *ciphertext*.) When the message reaches the receiver, a process called *decryption* takes place, in which the encrypted message is converted to plaintext. A *key* can be used for encryption; we will discuss this method of encryption later in the section "One-way encryption versus two-way encryption."

Following are the important characteristics that the process of encrypted-message passing must have:

✦ **Authentication** means that the receiver must be able to determine the origin of the message. Tapers of messages should not be able to act as senders.

✦ **Integrity** means that the receiver must be able to ascertain that the message was not modified in transit and that the taperer (for example, the person who taps the message) must not be able to substitute parts of the message in transit.

✦ **Nonrepudiation** means that the sender must not at any time be able to deny that a message was not sent by him or her. That is, the sender trying to deny falsely that he did not send the message.

One-way encryption versus two-way encryption

Cryptographic algorithms are also referred as *ciphers*. Mathematically, they represent functions for encryption and decryption. A *restricted* algorithm is one in which security is based on retaining the algorithm's mechanism. These algorithms have no quality control or standardization, and ROIs (Return on Investments) for these algorithms are poor and insecure because if somebody leaves the group they have to switch to a new algorithm. The other obvious reason being if somebody reveals the logic of the algorithm then the algorithm is compromised. Restricted algorithms are popular in low-security applications, because in low-security applications users do not care or realize that there are security problems inherent within the system.

In modern cryptographic algorithms the problems of no quality control and no standardization is solved with a key that holds a large number of values. The range of the possible values of the key is called the *keyspace*. Both the encryption and decryption processes use this key, as shown in Figure 13-2. The key is usually a large number value.

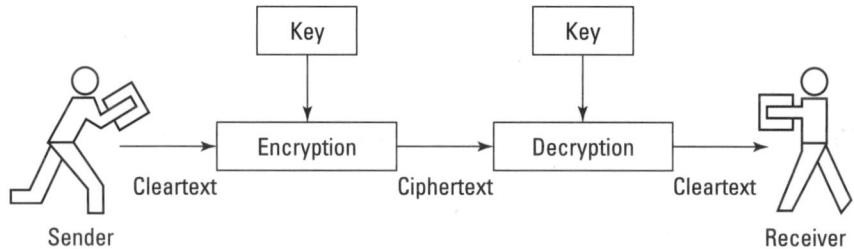

Figure 13-2: Cryptography through a key

Most cryptographic algorithms can be divided into two main categories: *one-way encryption* and *two-way encryption*. We'll explain both of these in the following sections.

One-way encryption and hash functions

In a one-way encryption scenario, encryption and decryption each involve a different key. The Rivest, Shamir & Adleman (RSA) algorithm is a good example of one-way encryption. Figure 13-3 shows how different keys are used for encrypting and decrypting the ciphertext, respectively, in one-way encryption.

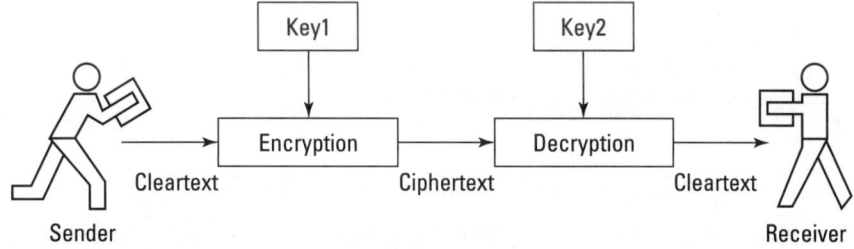

Figure 13-3: Cryptography using different keys

Now, consider a *one-way hash function*, H(c), which operates on a ciphertext of arbitrary length. It also generates a hash value of fixed length c, h=H(c), where the length of h is c. Following are the properties of the security of the algorithm, represented mathematically:

Given c, it is easy to calculate h.

Given h, it is difficult to compute c such that H(c) = h.

Given c, it is hard to find another ciphertext c1, such that H(c) = H (c1).

In addition to RSA, examples of one-way hashes include MD4, MD5 and SHA. These algorithms are discussed later in this chapter.

Two-way encryption

In a *two-way encryption*, the same key is used for encryption and decryption, as shown in Figure 13-4.

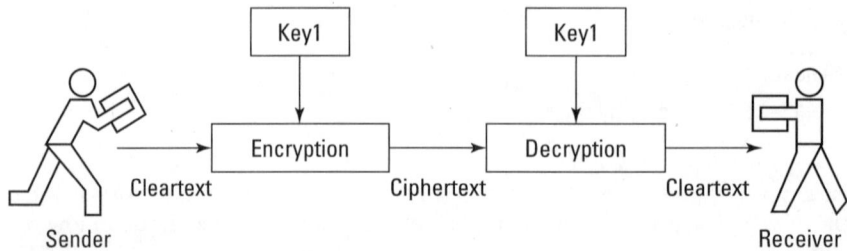

Figure 13-4: Two-way encryption

Algorithms

Let's take a look at some of the standard algorithms used in cryptography today that are available with the JCE package:

✦ DES

✦ Triple DES

✦ Blowfish

✦ MD5

✦ SHA

Data Encryption Standard (DES)

DES is the Federal Information Processing Standard that describes the Data Encryption Algorithm (DEA) and also appears in ANSI standard X9.32. (Actually, DEA is an improvement of IBM's implementation of LUCIFER, which was developed in the early '70s.). The following URL is a good place to start learning about the cryptographic algorithms: http://www.rsasecurity.com/.

DES is a *block cipher;* it encrypts 64-bit blocks of plaintext as cipher text. The same key is used for both encryption and decryption of data, so DES is referred to as a *symmetric algorithm.*

Two types of encryption techniques are used in this algorithm: *confusion* and *diffusion.* These techniques are combined and followed by a substitution and a permutation of the plaintext based on a 56-bit key. This process is usually referred to as a *round* and 16 rounds exist in DES.

Standard arithmetic and logical operations are used throughout the algorithm. Its characteristics are as follows:

✦ Provides a high level of security

✦ Efficient, valid, complete and exportable

✦ Bases security on a key and not on algorithm secrecy

✦ Is accessible to the general public

✦ Has diverse applications

✦ Can be implemented economically in hardware

Figure 13-5 shows an implementation of the DES:

The algorithm implemented in Figure 13-5 works as follows. The plain text undergoes a permutation and is separated into 32bits of left and right blocks. Then there is a function that is applied 16 times on these blocks of text after which both the blocks are combined to generate the ciphertext. Some of the primary uses of DES are for single-user encryption and storing files in encrypted form. DES is re-certified every five years by the National Institute of Standards and Technology (NSIT). Many attempts have been made to crack DES and the latest succeeded in 22 hours with a cracking machine. This hack on DES was possible because the 56-bit key is easily broken. DES is no longer used, but instead has been replaced with triple DES.

Triple DES

Triple DES encrypts the plaintext three times using three different keys — Key1, Key2, Key3. While Triple DES can be implemented in different ways, DES-EDE is the most common. So far, attacks on Triple DES have been unsuccessful.

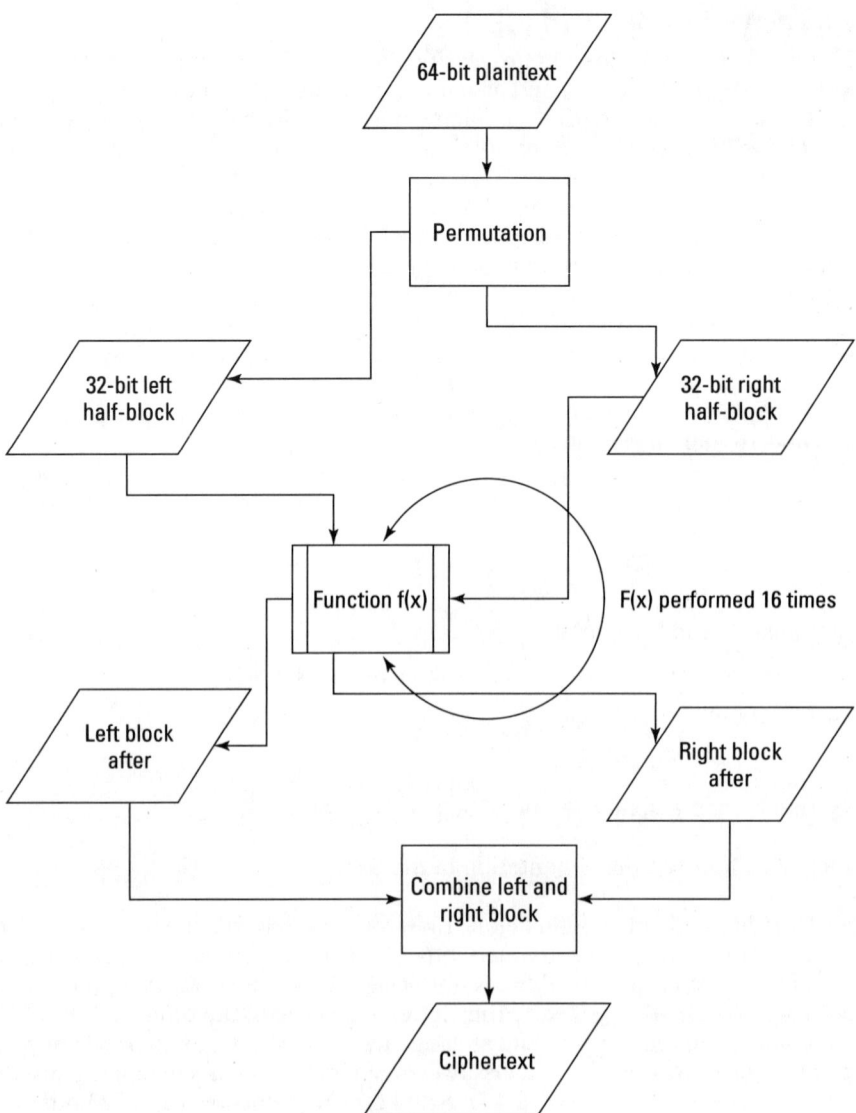

Figure 13-5: Algorithmic implementation of DES

Blowfish

Blowfish was designed specifically for large microprocessors. Its creator, Bruce Schneier, says that he designed this algorithm based on the following design criteria:

✦ Speed

✦ Compactness

✦ Simplicity

✦ Variably Secure

In Blowfish, the key can be as many as 448 bits in length and more processor-intensive than other algorithms that have been implemented in hardware. Analysis has shown that the algorithm provides optimal performance in systems in which the key does not change frequently. Like DES Blowfish is a 64 bit–block cipher. There are two steps in the algorithm: *key expansion* and *data encryption*. In the key-expansion phase a key is converted to 448 bits and several subkey arrays of 4,168 bytes each are created and iterated 16 times each over a function. Each iteration step consists of key-dependent permutation and key-data substitution.

The Blowfish algorithm is most secure if implemented with more numbers of iterations during the data-encryption phase of the implementation.

Message Digest 4 and Message Digest 5

This algorithm was developed by Rivest in 1991 as an improvement over MD4. Plaintext is processed in three different steps in MD4 but undergoes four steps in MD5. The plaintext is processed in blocks of 512 bits each. Each of these blocks is then divided into 16 sub-blocks of 32 bits each. The output is a 128-bit hash out of four encrypted blocks, each 32 bits in length.

Though attacks have been made on MD5, the only place where weakness has been detected is in the compression function. This weakness does not compromise the security of the hash function.

Secure Hash Algorithm (SHA)

SHA was developed jointly between NIST and NSA (National Security Agency). The output of SHA is a 160-bit hash. In this algorithm the plaintext is padded out to a multiple of 512 bits. The padding of the plaintext starts with a 1 followed by additional zeroes until the number of bits is 64 short of a multiple of 512. In the final step before padding a 64-bit representation of the plaintext is created. Cryptanalysis has shown that SHA is resistant to all brute-force attacks and is more secure because of the 160-bit hash output.

Shared-key cryptography

Shared-key cryptography is also known as *secret-key cryptography* and *symmetric encryption*. This is a two-way encryption model because the same key is used for both encryption and decryption. Prior to shared-key cryptography, if both the parties shared communication channels, they also shared the same key. The inherited problem with this encryption scheme is the distribution of the key. If a third party knows the key it can hack into message exchanges between the two parties. Figure 13-6 summarizes secret-key cryptography:

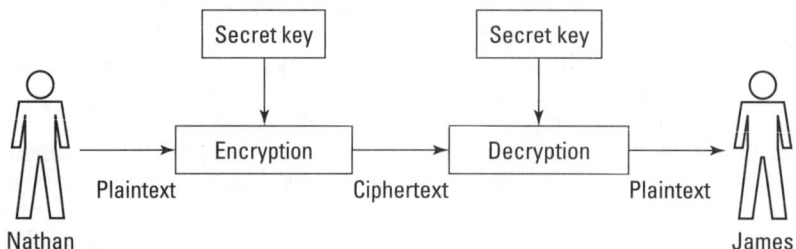

Figure 13-6: Shared-key cryptography

Figure 13-6 follows these steps:

1. A secret key is shared between Nathan and James.

2. Nathan encrypts the plaintext using the secret key.

3. The ciphertext is sent to James.

4. James decrypts the ciphertext using the secret key.

5. James retrieves the plaintext that Nathan sent.

This secret-key encryption is fast and efficient and can be found in algorithms such as DES and triple DES.

Public-key cryptography

Public-key cryptography is also known as *asymmetric cryptography.* In this encryption scheme two keys (the public and private key) are used for encrypting and decrypting data, respectively. The public key is exchanged and the private key is not exchanged.

Conceptually, public-key cryptography is a one-way hash. Some famous algorithms that implement public-key cryptography are the RSA (Rivest, Shamir and Adleman) algorithm and the Rjindael algorithm.

If the public key is used for encryption then the private key will be used for decryption. This solves the problem that shared-key cryptography creates, the problem of key dispersal. However, public-key cryptography is costly, because of extensive processor-oriented computations, and slow in execution. Optimal performance has been realized by sending minimal bits of data in blocks. Figure 13-7 summarizes public-key cryptography:

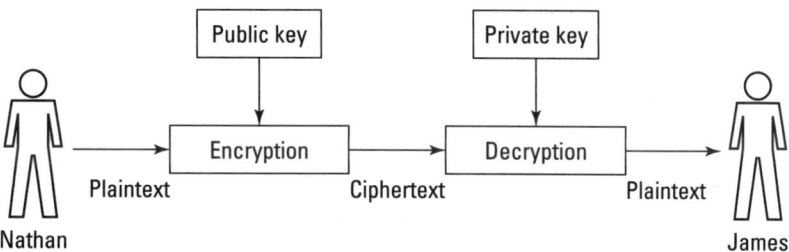

Figure 13-7: Public-key cryptography

Figure 13-7 follows these steps:

1. James holds the private key.

2. Nathan encrypts the plaintext using the public key.

3. The ciphertext is sent to James.

4. James decrypts the ciphertext using the private key.

5. James retrieves the plaintext that Nathan sent.

Digital certificates

These certificates are specified in the X.509 format and are useful when digital documents need to be signed. A digital certificate is based on a digest created according to the content of the document that needs to be digitally signed.

Certificate authorities such as Verisign issue digital certificates. To validate that the document has not been tampered with, the recipient can use an algorithm to calculate the digest on the document and match that digest against the one sent with the document. If the digests match the document has not been tampered with; otherwise, it has been tampered with. In the first example of using one-way hash for passwords we will be looking at a variation of digital signatures called message digest.

Protocols

A protocol that uses cryptography is called a *cryptographic protocol*. Protocols formalize behavior and abstract the process of accomplishing a task from the mechanism of how a task is accomplished.

Before we discuss some specific protocols we'll define the roles we're going to use to explain the protocols in detail:

✦ **Nathan** — First party involved in the protocol.

✦ **James** — Second party involved in the protocol.

✦ **Michael** — Trusted lawyer.

In all the cases, let us that assume Nathan is selling a computer notebook to James. James and Nathan do not know each other. James wants to pay Nathan by check, but Nathan cannot validate the integrity of the check that James gives him. The best course of action is for Nathan to have the check cleared before shipping the notebook. Since the level of trust between James and Nathan is equivalent, James wants the notebook before he sends the check.

Now let's go into detail about the following general classifications of protocols represented in cryptography:

✦ Adjudicated protocol

✦ Arbitrated protocol

✦ Self-enforcing protocol

Adjudicated protocol

In this protocol Michael, the lawyer, becomes involved only if a dispute arises between Nathan and James. Figure 13-8 sums up the adjudicated protocol between Nathan and James:

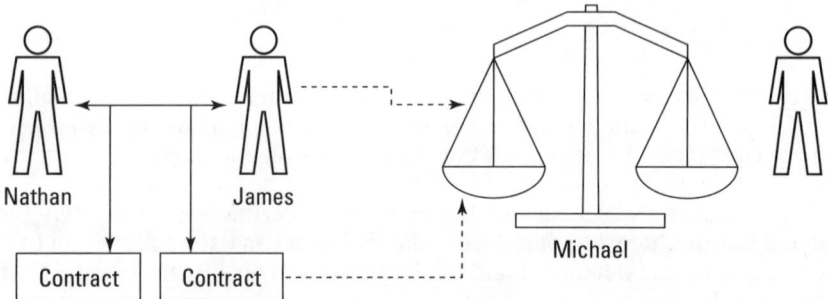

Adjudicated Protocol

Figure 13-8: Adjudicated protocol

This protocol can be divided into two sub-protocols, non-arbitrated and adjudicated, the division is based on being executed every time and executed only on dispute. The following actions take place in a non-arbitrated sub-protocol:

1. Nathan and James negotiate the terms of the contract.

2. Nathan signs the contract.

3. James signs the contract.

If a dispute occurs between Nathan and James, lawyer Michael will settle the dispute. The adjudicated sub-protocol comes into play as follows:

1. Nathan and James appear before Michael.

2. Nathan presents his contract.

3. James presents his contract.

4. Michael rules on the contract.

Arbitrated protocol

In this protocol, every transaction between Nathan and James is conducted through Michael. This protocol is costly, therefore, because of the fees associated with hiring an attorney. MIT's Kerberos system architecture is based on the concept of arbitrated protocol, which is depicted in Figure 13-9.

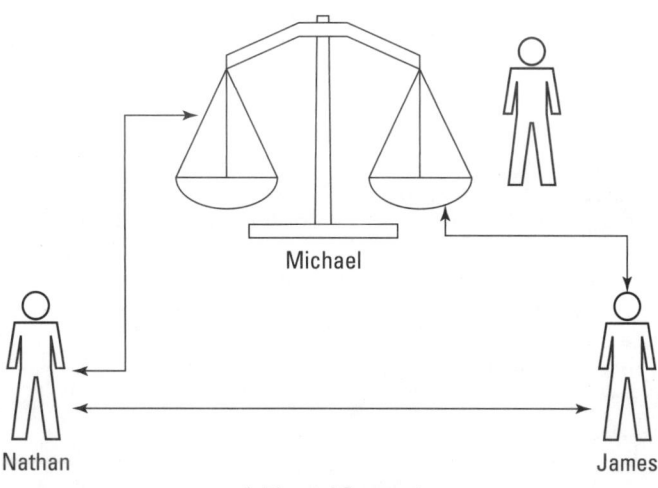

Michael

Nathan

James

Arbitrated Protocol

Figure 13-9: Arbitrated protocol

In this protocol the following steps occur:

1. Nathan gives the notebook to Michael.

2. James gives the check to Nathan.

3. Nathan deposits the check.

4. If the check clears, Michael gives the notebook to James. If the check does not clear, Nathan shows proof of this to Michael, and Michael returns the notebook to Nathan.

Self-enforcing protocol

In this protocol Nathan and James execute their tasks with fairness without involving Michael. This is the best type of protocol available and it ensures that no dispute occurs. If a dispute does occur, the other party (for example, either James or Nathan) can detect the cheating and the protocol can stop any further transaction. Figure 13-10 summarizes the self-enforcing protocol.

Nathan   James

Figure 13-10: Self-enforcing protocol

Reviewing the Java Cryptography Package

The Java platform already supports digital signatures and message digest. The JCE framework extends the Java cryptography architecture and includes implementations of cryptography algorithms that were regulated earlier (for example, a couple of years ago) by U.S. export restrictions. The current version of JCE is 1.2.2 and can be exported outside of the U.S. The beauty of this version is that it has policy files that regulate the encryption schemas that can be used and controlled by third parties, so only qualified providers can be plugged into the architecture.

Following are the important features of the JCE as mentioned on Sun's site at `http://java.sun.com/products/jce/index-122.html`:

✦ 100-percent pure Java implementation

✦ Plug-and-play architecture

✦ Exportation outside the U.S. in binary form only

✦ Single distribution of the software locally and globally

✦ Ciphers, key agreements, and MACs (Message Authentication Codes) are implemented

In addition to DES, DES-EDE, and Blowfish, which were discussed earlier in this chapter, the following algorithms are provided out of the box by SunJCE providers:

✦ PBEWithMD5AndDES

✦ PBEWithMD5AndTripleDES

✦ Diffie-Hellman key agreement among multiple parties

✦ HmacMD5

✦ HmacSHA1

Following are the packages available in JCE:

✦ `javax.crypto`—Contains classes and interfaces for cryptographic operations.

✦ `javax.crypto.interfaces`—Provides Diffie-Hellman key, Diffie-Hellman private-key, and Diffie-Hellman public-key encryption.

✦ `javax.crypto.spec`—Provides classes and interfaces for algorithm-parameter specification and key specification.

The following classes are used by JCE in the base `java.security` package. The javadoc with the classes describes the functionality of each class.

✦ `Cipher`

✦ `Cipher InputStream`

✦ `Cipher OutputStream`

✦ `KeyAgreement`

✦ `Key Generator`

✦ `Mac`

✦ `SecretKeyFactory`

✦ `SealedObject`

The next section details how to write code using the JCE framework and applies it to the case studies in the book.

Writing a Java Program Using JCE

Following are the steps involved in writing a simple JCE program. Both of the case studies in this chapter will follow them.

1. Get an instance of the `KeyGenerator` of the algorithm being used.

2. Generate the secret key.

3. Get an instance of the cipher for the algorithm to be used.

4. Initialize the Cipher object with the appropriate mode like `ENCRYPT_MODE` or `DECRYPT_MODE`.

5. Encrypt or decrypt the plaintext or ciphertext.

Magazine Publisher Business Case

This case study implements a one-way hash for user passwords. The code is well documented and has a main `main` method that shows the following methods being called:

✦ `OneWayHash` — A constructor setting two messages.

✦ `doCalculateDigest` — Calculates the digest for the two messages.

✦ `MatchMessages` — Compares the two digests to determine whether they match or not.

Listing 13-1 contains the complete code for the program.

Listing 13-1: One-way hash for user passwords

```
/**
 * Created by IntelliJ IDEA.
 * User: vnathan
 * Date: Jan 20, 2003
 * Time: 10:31:19 PM
 * This class is used to create oneway hash for user passwords
in the Magazine Publisher hash.
 */
import java.io.*;
import java.security.*;

public class OneWayHash {
    private static byte[] digest1;
    private static byte[] digest2;
    private static String message1;
    private static String message2;
    //default constructor to set the messages.
    public OneWayHash(String msg1, String msg2){
        message1 = msg1;
        message2 = msg2;
    }
    /**
     * Method that calculates the digest based on the SHA-1
algorithm
     */
    public static void doCalculateDigest(){
        byte[] buf = new byte[message1.length()];
        message1.getBytes(0,message1.length(),buf,0);
        //
        MessageDigest algorithm = null;
```

```
        try{
            //get the message digest for SHA-1 algorithm
            algorithm = MessageDigest.getInstance("SHA-1");
        }catch(NoSuchAlgorithmException e){
            System.out.println(e);
        }
        algorithm.reset();
        algorithm.update(buf);
        //calculate digest1
        digest1 = algorithm.digest();

        algorithm.reset();
        buf = new byte[message2.length()];
        message2.getBytes(0,message2.length(),buf,0);
        algorithm.update(buf);
        //calculate digest2
        digest2 = algorithm.digest();
    }
    /**
     * Method that matches the digests of the message and
prints out whether they match or not.
     */
    public static void matchMessages(){
        if(digest1.length != digest2.length){
            System.out.println("Digests do not match!");
            System.exit(0);
        }
        for (int i=0; i<digest1.length;i++){
            if (digest1[i]!= digest2[i]){
                System.out.println("Digests do not match");
                System.exit(0);
            }
        }
        System.out.println("Digest match!");
    }
    //main method of the program
    public static void main(String args[]){
        OneWayHash owh = new OneWayHash("password","password");
        owh.doCalculateDigest();
        owh.matchMessages();

    }

}
```

Figure 13-11 shows the output when two messages do not match.

Figure 13-12 shows the output when two messages match.

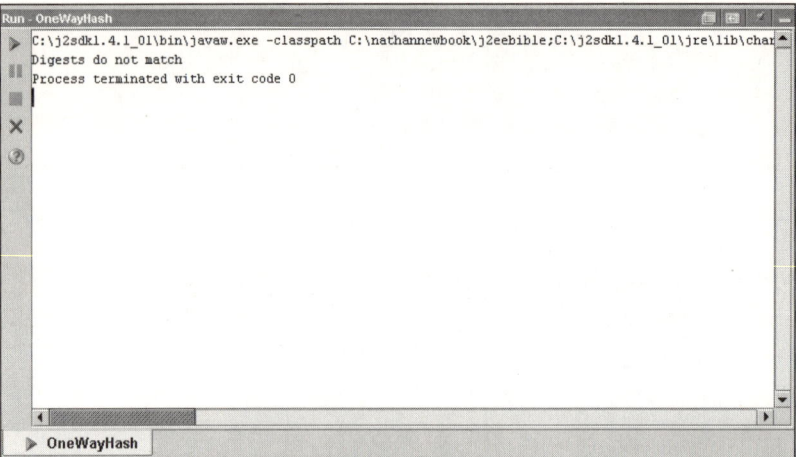

Figure 13-11: These two messages don't match.

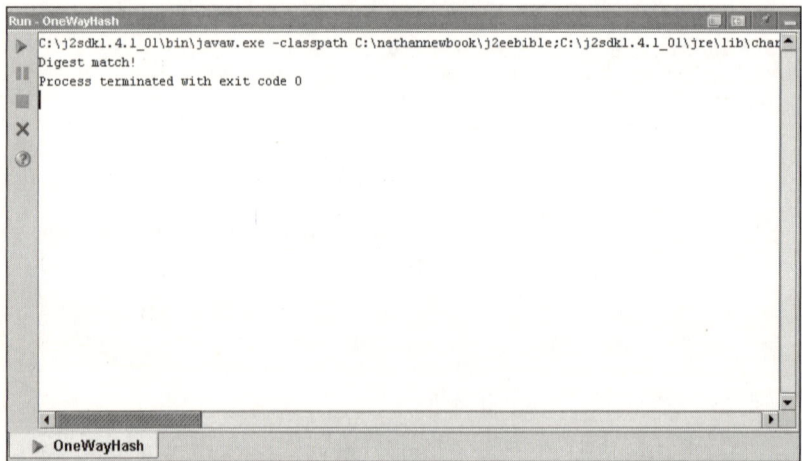

Figure 13-12: These two messages match.

Airline Reservations Business Case

This case study implements a two-way hash for credit card–number processing. The code is well documented and has a main `main` method that shows the various methods being called. Remember: Always convert to a byte array the string that needs to be encrypted.

Listing 13-2 contains the following methods that are executed in the main `main` method to set credit-card numbers, perform encryption using Blowfish, and decrypt the data back, respectively: The source code is available from the Wiley site.

✦ setCreditCardNumber(String creditCardNumber)

✦ doEncryption(String algorithm)

✦ doDecryption()

Listing 13-2 contains the complete code listing for the program. It is also available as a separate Java file from the Wiley site.

Listing 13-2: **Two-way hash for processing of credit-card numbers**

```java
import java.security.*;
import javax.crypto.*;
import javax.crypto.spec.*;

public class TwoWayHash{
  private byte[] creditCardNumber;

  public void setCreditCardNumber(String creditCardNo){
        creditCardNumber = creditCardNo.getBytes();
  }
  public byte[] getCreditCardNumber(){
        return creditCardNumber;
  }

  public static void main(String args[]){
        try{
                KeyGenerator kGenerator = KeyGenerator.getInstance( "Blowfish"
);

                System.out.println("Generating Key ... ");
            SecretKey secretKey = kGenerator.generateKey();
            byte[] bytes = secretKey.getEncoded();
                SecretKeySpec specKey = new SecretKeySpec(bytes,"Blowfish");

                System.out.println("Creating cipher ...");
                Cipher cipher = Cipher.getInstance( "Blowfish" );

                System.out.println("Encrypting ... " );
                cipher.init(Cipher.ENCRYPT_MODE, specKey);
                String target = "Encrypt this buddy.";
                byte[] encrypted = cipher.doFinal(target.getBytes());

                System.out.println("before:" + target);
                System.out.println("after: " + new String(encrypted));

                //Decrypt
                cipher.init(Cipher.DECRYPT_MODE, specKey);
                byte[] decrypted = cipher.doFinal(encrypted);
```

Continued

Listing 13-2 *(continued)*

```
                System.out.println("\n after decrypt: " + new
String(decrypted));
        }catch(Exception e){
                System.out.println("Exception caught: " + e);
        }

    }

}
```

Figure 13-13 shows the output of the program.

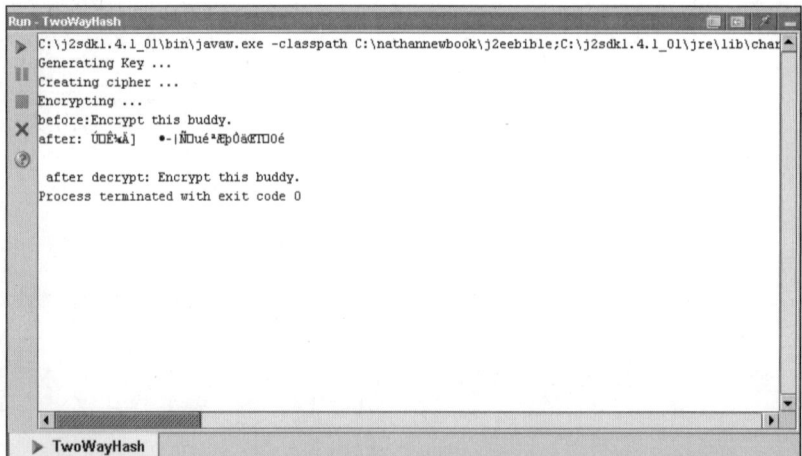

Figure 13-13: Output from a two-way hash

Summary

In this chapter we covered the basics of cryptography, the differences between a one-way versus two-way encryption. Key cryptographic algorithms like DES, Triple DES, Blowfish, MD5, MD4 and SHA. We also talked about different cryptography key technologies like Public key and Shared key. Digital Certificates and the various Security Protocols were discussed. We also covered on standard data-encryption methods, the Java cryptography extension model, and examples that implemented the one-way and two-way hashes.

✦   ✦   ✦

The Service Tier

◆ ◆ ◆ ◆

In This Part

Chapter 14
Understanding EJB
Architecture and
Design

Chapter 15
Explaining
Session Beans and
Business Logic

Chapter 16
Working with
Entity Beans

Chapter 17
Using Message-
Driven Beans

◆ ◆ ◆ ◆

Understanding EJB Architecture and Design

✦ ✦ ✦ ✦

In This Chapter

Learning about roles and relationships

Understanding portability

Explaining EJBs

Examining persistence transactions

Exploring CORBA and EJB legacy systems

Developing EJB applications and components

✦ ✦ ✦ ✦

So far in the book we have described various components of the J2EE architecture. In the following chapters we're going to consider Enterprise JavaBeans (EJB), the typical way in which you will interact with J2EE. However, before describing EJB, we're going to give an overview of the entire architecture in this chapter. The intention is to show you some of the J2EE components we've already seen fit in and lay the groundwork for more detailed descriptions in subsequent chapters.

As well as trying to give an overview of most of the EJB architecture, we'll also discuss some related issues such as where the Object Management Groups CORBA architecture fits in and what strategies application server vendors are currently offering for their high-availability offerings (allowing them to tolerate machine failures). We'll also talk about some of the performance issues related to using EJBs and try to give you some help in addressing these if they come up in your application development.

Explaining the EJB Component Model

You are probably familiar with Java objects and interfaces, but may not be so familiar with Java *components*. A Java component is a set of interfaces and classes that have been assembled into a single package to provide a specific functionality. A component is typically designed to be used in a variety of different applications as an independent piece of software.

A major advantage components offer over objects is that only the business logic of an application needs to be addressed by a programmer; any required support services are incorporated into the application at deployment time. *Containers* that host components are responsible for providing the underlying middleware services they require (such as persistence to ensure object durability or transactions).

It is worth examining here briefly why this component-oriented abstraction has been considered necessary when the industry has been using object-orientation for many years. Although object-oriented middleware provides type-checked remote invocations and standard ways of using commonly required services (such as naming, persistence, transactions, and so on), application developers still have to worry about application logic as well as technically complex ways of using a collection of services.

For example, using transactions on distributed objects requires concurrency control and persistence and the transaction services have to be used in a particularly intricate manner. Component-oriented middleware makes the developer's job easier with components that are composed of objects, and containers that host component instances. Containers take on the responsibility of using the underlying middleware services for communication, persistence, transactions, security, and so forth; the developer's task is simplified to declaring the services required by components.

Modern client-server distributed-computing systems such as EJB can be seen as implementations of a **3**-tier architecture that is organized as follows:

- ✦ **First or client tier** — This tier consists of client applications containing browsers, stand-alone application clients, and so on (The remaining tiers deployed within an enterprise represent the server side.)

- ✦ **Second or business tier** — This tier is capable of hosting distributed applications and is typically called the *application server*. Application servers host containers.

- ✦ **Third or enterprise information systems tier** — This tier contains *Enterprise Resource Planning Systems* (ERPS), mainframe-transaction-processing systems, databases, and legacy applications of the enterprise.

An application server typically deploys a variety of object-oriented middleware services using an *object request broker* (ORB). However, the application server provides applications with a higher level of abstraction than object-orientation: component-oriented middleware.

Enterprise JavaBeans (EJB) is the component model for enterprise applications that has quickly become the *de facto* standard for developing mission-critical enterprise software. It leverages best-of-breed technologies from standards organizations such as the Object Management Group (OMG) and years of experience from vendors such as IBM, BEA, Sun, and Oracle in building enterprise applications in other languages. The result is a development and deployment environment that allows scalable applications to be created without compromising performance. It enables a clearer separation between functional and non-functional aspects of an application's development, such that the programmer does not typically need to worry about issues such as security, transactions, concurrency, persistence, and resource pooling: These are automatically taken care of by EJB, so the programmer can concentrate on more important issues.

> **Note** This chapter is intended to lay the groundwork for the next few chapters and place them into context within the overall J2EE framework. As a result, in the rest of this chapter we may have to use some terms and references to method names that we don't fully explain. Don't worry too much, as we will provide references to the relevant chapters for you to examine if the need arises.

Enterprise applications have existed for decades in languages as diverse as COBOL and C++, and in environments ranging from telecommunications to banking. Hence some form of application server existed prior to Java and the development of EJB. Unfortunately, as a result of this, and the fact that until relatively recently companies tended to purchase most software from a single vendor, it was incredibly difficult (and often impossible) to take an application, component, or object developed to run within one vendor's application server and deploy it within another vendor's application server. This situation is often known as *vendor lock-in*: Your application code is tied to a particular vendor's software, with all of the disadvantages that this implies. What if the vendor goes out of business or does not provide bug fixes quickly enough for you? In addition, what if you want to sell your components or application to someone else who has already invested time and money in using an application server from a different vendor? Persuading that customer to move vendors as well as buy your component may be a tough sell! In general, removing critical dependencies on one vendor's product is a good thing.

One of the major benefits of developing any standard is that it improves the likelihood of interoperability and portability. We deliberately used the word "improves" in that last sentence because some standards are written to allow vendors some leeway in their implementations, so watch out. The EJB and J2EE architectures are comprised of a set of standards that have been developed in open standards bodies such as the Java Community Process from Sun, or leverage standards from other bodies such as the OMG. Therefore, one of the advantages of EJB is that it provides a framework within which applications can be developed in a portable manner. In theory, at least, it is possible to develop a component using one vendor's application server and sell it to someone who is dependent upon another vendor's application server. Watch out for those vendor-specific enhancements to the product that go beyond what the EJB specification defines or you could easily stray into "lock-in land" again!

Having given an overview of why component-orientated middleware has rapidly overtaken the more traditional object-oriented approaches, now let's look at the EJB architecture in more detail. In the next sections we'll consider the application development and deployment phases of using EJB and the various roles EJB defines as being involved in each phase.

Reviewing Roles, Relationships, and Responsibilities

EJB achieves portability by defining a number of roles and responsibilities required for the development and deployment of application components within the application server. The interactions among these different roles are carefully laid out through the definition of contracts (rules that are agreed to by all parties involved) that each actor (implementer of a specific role) must follow. As in a movie or TV production, EJB allows a given actor to play multiple roles; however, the advantage of splitting roles is that individuals and companies can concentrate their efforts on just those areas where they have (or wish to acquire) expertise. It is no longer necessary to become dependent on a single vendor for all your enterprise needs.

In this section we will briefly consider the following roles, relationships, and responsibilities in EJB (we will expand on some of these in subsequent sections):

- ✦ The deployment descriptor
- ✦ The bean provider
- ✦ The server/container provider
- ✦ The application assembler
- ✦ The EJB deployer
- ✦ The system administrator

The deployment descriptor

The deployment descriptor is part of the EJB contract between the EJB developer and the EJB container. It defines the declarative information that is necessary to the use of the bean but that is not encoded directly within the bean implementation. For example, it defines whether the methods of the bean must be invoked within the scope of transactions, whether or not a bean's methods are re-entrant (whether a thread within a specific method can invoke the same method), and so on.

A deployment descriptor is similar to traditional Java property files in that the information contained within the descriptor may be used to configure the component or application either when the component or application is initially deployed or at runtime. An EJB's deployment descriptor is represented as an XML document, which is both human-readable and writeable by means of standard XML tools or even text editors.

The bean provider

As its name implies, the bean provider is the source of *enterprise beans* (not to be confused with EJBs!), which are essentially the software components that do application-specific work (such as reserving a seat on a specific flight). These components are intended to be individually deployable and can be combined into a complete solution to a specific problem. In our *3*-tier architecture, enterprise beans are server-side components.

Note
As we have already mentioned, it is entirely possible for a vendor to provide functionality over and above what the EJB specification requires. If you use such functionality then it is highly unlikely that the component will be reusable. Just because a vendor claims to be compliant with a given specification does not mean that its code or yours will necessarily be portable. Don't fall into the "specification implies portability" trap.

Designing enterprise beans is very similar to designing any software entity, whether a component, object, or subroutine. If you want your bean to be reused within different applications and to have a longer useful lifetime, you need to design reusability and reconfigurability into it from the start. For example, beans whose functionality can be configured at runtime will be more useful to customers than those that require recompilation.

The bean provider is responsible for creating the deployment descriptor associated with the bean. Typically this will occur through the use of a popular graphical-development tool. Once the deployment descriptor has been created, it and the bean can be packaged for deployment within a Java Archive (JAR) file.

In order to ensure the portability of beans across deployment environments, the EJB specification places certain restrictions on what the bean provider may do. We will enumerate these restrictions in the section on EJB container functionality, because many of them are related to portability among container implementations.

The server/container provider

This provider supplies the application-server functionality to deploy, contain, and manage components. The container provides the environment in which your enterprise beans live out their lives; in general, the container is responsible for life-cycle management, security management, deployment, transactions, threading, and so on, on behalf of components. Recall that the benefit of containers is that bean providers do not need to explicitly incorporate support for these types of functionality within their application code. A good relationship between container and component will allow the application to be modified through the container without the need to change the code.

Within a deployment descriptor, the developer specifies information describing the appropriate system services required and how they are to be applied to an EJB. A container is responsible for hosting components and ensuring that middleware services are made available to components at runtime as described in deployment descriptors of components. Containers mediate all client/component interactions. A container vendor provides automatic code-generation tools that will produce the appropriate mechanisms to integrate a component into a container.

As shown in Figure 14-1, the relationship of server to container is similar to that of container to bean: The server provides the runtime environment in which a container executes, managing lower-level resources. As shown, each server may encapsulate more than on the container. The container is responsible for mediating all interactions with the enterprise beans, managing the lifecycle of the beans and also providing the various services that it requires, such as transactions or messaging. In the figure, a persistent data store is shown because as we shall see, some types of bean may save (and restore) their states to a durable storage system so that they may be used over many interactions and across a long duration. As we saw in Chapter 10, the transaction system may also use the persistent store.

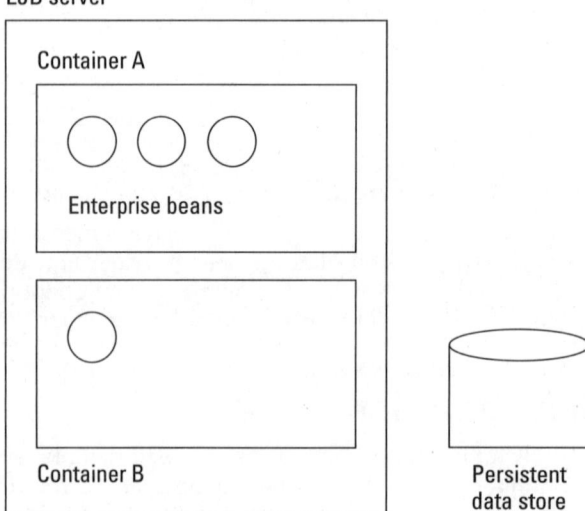

Figure 14-1: The relationship between server, container and enterprise beans

The application assembler

If a bean provider supplies the reusable components, it is the job of the application assembler to take these components and convert them into an application that can solve a business problem. The application assembler is the architect who has intimate knowledge of the components and of the problem that needs a solution.

Obviously, the way in which the components are "glued" together will depend upon the application requirements: For example, there may be no inherent distribution within the application and all of the required beans may reside within the same JVM. As a result, the components may interact directly via other Java classes. An example of such structuring would be an enterprise bean that represents an airplane that uses many individual seat enterprise beans.

Alternatively, the interactions between components may be structured as a workflow, whereby the result of an invocation on one distributed component may cause an invocation on another distributed component. For example, an online travel booking system may use an airline bean within one container, travel insurance beans within another container (and server) and an alternative airline reservation bean in the event the prime site fails.

All of this structuring and tying together of individual components is the domain of the application assembler.

The EJB deployer

So far we have considered the roles that are necessary for building the entire application. Obviously software that just sits on a hard drive or floppy disk is of very little use in solving real-world business problems! Therefore, the EJB deployer is responsible for converting the application into a running execution environment such as a corporate intranet. This is obviously a distinctly different job from that of the application assembler because the application assembler individual may not know the specifics of the execution environment in which the application must run. For example, where are the firewalls? What are the security restrictions placed on business divisions?

The EJB deployer knows how to deploy enterprise beans within application servers and how to customize the beans and/or server environment for a specific problem domain. In addition, the deployer is responsible for mapping the access level of a bean to fit any deployment domain's security settings.

The system administrator

The system administrator's role is to oversee the application once it is up and running. It is the administrator who will monitor the application and its interactions and may make changes to the runtime deployment configuration based on feedback from the application, the server, and the container.

In the next few sections we will concentrate more on the bean provider and container provider, as they are the roles that you will typically encounter in your use of EJBs.

In the next sections we'll take a closer look at exactly what constitutes an EJB. As we'll see, there are a variety of different bean types, each aimed at a specific problem area. We'll also look at how some of the services offered by containers (such as persistence or transactions) are used by enterprise beans.

The Enterprise JavaBean

Recall that an enterprise bean is a component that may be deployed within a container to form part of a distributed enterprise application. Every bean has a *component interface* that defines the business methods callable by the clients, and a *home interface* that defines the methods with which the client can create, remove, and find EJB components of a specific type. All client-to-entity bean and client-to-session bean communications are normally made via the *Java Remote Method Invocation* (RMI).

Three types of EJBs have been specified in J2EE:

✦ Entity beans

✦ Session beans

✦ Message-driven beans

They are discussed in the following sections.

Entity beans

Entity beans represent and manipulate the persistent data of an application, providing an object-oriented view of data that are frequently stored in relational databases. This is an important advantage to users, because the underlying format in which data may well be stored in a database is via relational tables accessed through SQL queries and stores. Encapsulating this state behind an object isolates the users from the implementation details of how the state is represented in memory and in the persistent store: The entity bean is then responsible for loading the state from the store and saving it back later.

As shown in Figure 14-2, it's much better for the user of a bean to be able to call a `reserveSeat` method on an airline-reservation object than have to deal with the persistent store directly (which will typically involve SQL) Once the state is loaded into volatile memory—meaning that the entity bean has been activated—the application can manipulate the bean state. However, until the state is saved back to persistent storage it is susceptible to machine failures or application-server crashes: The state on persistent (stable) store will survive crashes unless there is a catastrophic failure of the persistent store, whereas the state within the entity bean will definitely be lost. All of the interactions between the bean and the data store are mediated by the container and hidden from the client. Imagine if this was not the case and the user had to drive state management directly!

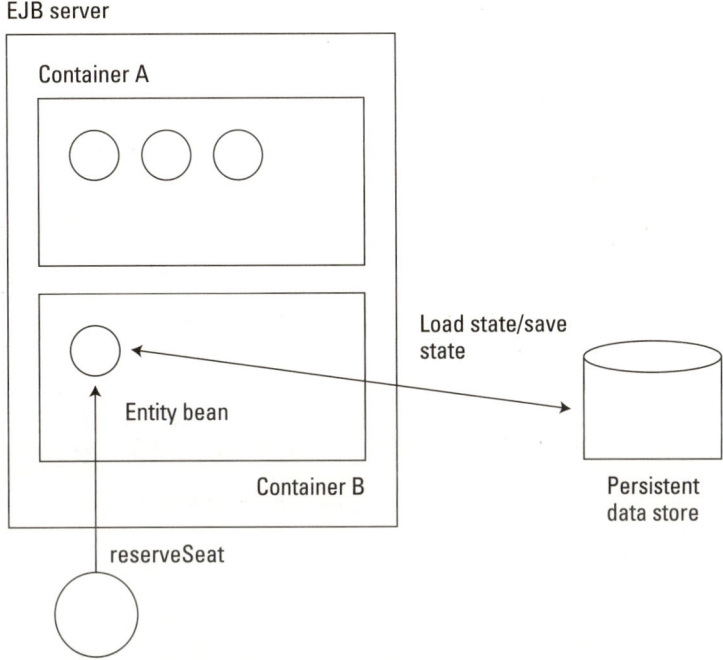

EJB server

Container A

Load state/save state

Entity bean

Container B

Persistent data store

reserveSeat

Bespoke client, Web browser, and so on

Figure 14-2: An example of a client's interactions with an airline EJB

Another important point is that entity beans can be shared among multiple concurrent clients. Thus, in the example in Figure 14-2, different users can be calling the reserveSeat method simultaneously. If concurrent data manipulation is not allowed by the application, the bean should use transactions to ensure data consistency. For example, as you saw in Chapter 10, if the methods of an entity bean are called within the scope of a transaction, it is possible to set the sharing level of the transaction such that concurrent conflicting write operations are not possible. The transactions associated with each client invocation are serializable, such that all of the work for one client happens before the work for the other client.

Two subtypes of entity bean exist:

✦ Bean-managed persistent (BMP)

✦ Container-managed persistent (CMP)

Bean-managed persistence (BMP)

In BMP, the persistence of an entity bean to persistent storage (called *synchronization*) is the responsibility of the bean provider. An entity bean synchronizes its state to the underlying store or, database through the ejbLoad and ejbStore methods that are part of all entity beans. The bean provider is responsible for implementations of these methods that are relevant to the particular persistent store used. So, for example, although databases are typically used to store a bean's state, it is entirely possible for implementations to use the file system provided by the operating system.

The bean provider is given flexibility in how state is managed between the persistent-store representation and the bean instance. Some types of bean may have state split across a number of different databases: For example, our airline stores specific passenger information such as name, address, dietary habits, and so on in one database and seat assignments in another. However, these stores might use a single entity bean (such as the FlightBean, say) to present both sets of information to the travel agent.

Consider the airline-reservation example and assume you have a SeatBean that manages information about a specific seat on a flight. Further assume that the relevant fields in this bean are a value, isReserved, indicating whether or not the seat is reserved, and a name, representing the name of the person who has the seat assignment. The SeatBean also knows the flight it is assigned to via the flightId integer identifier. The ejbStore method for this bean would be as follows:

```
public void ejbStore () throws RemoteException
{
    Connection conn = null;
    PreparedStatement prepStmnt = null;

    try
    {
        conn = getConnection();
        prepStmnt = conn.prepareStatement("update Seat set
reserved = ?, name = ?, where flight = ?");

        prepStmnt.setBoolean(1, isReserved);
        prepStmnt.setString(2, name);
        prepStmnt.setInt(3, flightId);

        if (premStmnt.executeUpdate() != 1)
            throw new RemoteException("A failure occurred while
writing the flight seat!");
    }
    catch (SQLException sqlExp)
    {
        throw new RemoteException(sqlExp.toString());
    }
    finally
    {
        try
        {
            if (prepStmnt != null)
                prepStmnt.close();

            if (conn != null)
```

```
                    conn.close();
            }
          catch (SQLException sqlExp)
          {
          }
      }
  }
```

Cross-Reference Don't worry about the fact that so far we have ignored issues such as how to locate or create the entity bean in the first place: We'll cover a lot of the specifics behind entity beans in Chapter 16.

Obviously, persisting the state of an entity bean can be a complex task, especially if the bean has a lot of state. Therefore, EJB provides *container-managed persistence*, which is the means whereby the bean provider can concentrate on the functional aspects of the bean and leave persistence to someone else.

Container-managed persistence (CMP)

With CMP, the bean provider does not take a role in persisting the state of the entity bean: it is now the responsibility of the container to provide the code necessary to map the bean's state to the underlying persistence store. All that the bean provider has to do is describe precisely what state needs to be persisted and the container then does the necessary work. This has obvious advantages over the BMP setup as it can save much valuable implementation time for the bean provider, and it removes one possible area of error.

Note Use of container-managed persistence and transactions are strongly recommended for entity beans. This is because the container and transaction service cooperate to ensure that the state of the entity bean is loaded from and saved to the data store automatically on transaction boundaries.

In CMP, the bean's container-managed fields are automatically synchronized with the persistent storage implementation. Therefore, the `ejbLoad` and `ejbStore` methods that you used in BMP are typically not required. However, regardless of whether CMP or BMP is being used, the container will still invoke these methods during loading and saving of the bean's state. As a result, it is entirely possible to take advantage of these callbacks from the container if sophisticated synchronization management is required.

For example, suppose the `SeatBean` from the previous example is extended to include all of the information about the passenger, including name, address, method of payment, dietary requirements, and so on. Furthermore, let's also assume that the bean provider decides to use CMP. Now, the information maintained by the bean may be large (several kilobytes, for example) and may potentially be sensitive. Rather than just synchronize the state of the bean to and from the datastore, the bean provider can use the fact that `ejbStore` will be called prior to synchronization of the state to the datastore to compress and encrypt the state (perhaps using some of the techniques we saw in Chapter 13). By means of the `ejbLoad` method the state may then be decrypted and uncompressed.

Session beans

Session beans, on the other hand, do not use persistent data and are instantiated on a per-client basis with an instance of a session bean available for use by only *one* client, in contrast to entity beans. In general, whereas an entity bean represents persistent data, a session bean performs calculations. Session beans are intended to encapsulate business logic. For example, in the airline-reservation system you might employ a session bean to help display a list of all available seats in the business-class cabin.

Note   Because entity beans represent business data rather than process, they typically achieve a higher level of reuse than session beans.

A session bean may be *stateless,* meaning that it does not maintain conversational state, or *stateful,* meaning that it maintains conversational state. Conversational state is needed to share state information across multiple requests from a client.

Cross-Reference   We will briefly give details of these two bean subtypes next and follow up in Chapter 15.

Stateless session beans

Stateless session beans do not maintain any state and are not specific to a particular client. Session beans can handle two types of transaction:

✦ **Container-managed transactions (CMT)** — In these transactions, the deployment descriptor is used to specify the transactional qualities associated with the EJB on a per-business method basis. The bean provider does not have to identify transactional boundaries (such as `begin` and `commit`) within the bean's code: The container uses the deployment descriptor to set the boundaries of a transaction, beginning a transaction immediately before an enterprise bean method starts and committing a transaction just before the method exits.

✦ **Bean-managed transactions (BMT)** — In this case the container has minimal control over transactions: The bean provider must explicitly manage transaction boundaries (starting and terminating of the transactions).

Don't worry if you want a bit more detail about transactions and beans. We'll have much more to say about them the section "Container Managed Transactions" later in this chapter.

Stateful session beans

Each stateful session bean is typically allocated to a specific client. Requests are always routed to the same session bean within the container. State information is retained on behalf of the client across multiple bean-method invocations. Like stateless session beans, stateful session beans support both CMT and BMT.

Stateful versus stateless session beans

You may well be asking yourself just when would you use a stateful session bean instead of a stateless one (or vice versa). If the business process inherently requires state to be maintained between client invocations, the use of stateful beans seems obvious. For example, a diary bean that keeps track of a users schedule will obviously require updating periodically over time.

However, you should consider one important thing before deciding to go with stateful session beans: *application fault-tolerance*. The fact that the same stateful bean is required to service all requests from the same client can severely limit your application's ability to tolerate failures. Since all data are maintained by the bean, if the application server hosting the data were to fail (for example, if the machine it runs on were to crash), the data will obviously be lost and the client will have to start again from scratch. Re-routing the client's request (as can happen for stateless session beans) won't help the client in this situation and can even lead to application inconsistencies!

But what if you really need to share state between invocations? The only way to do this currently is to shift the burden of state management from the session bean to the client. For example, you can use a stateless session bean so that a different instance can be used for each invocation from the same client and have the client send all state to the bean that it will require in order to deal with the client's request. However, this method has its own drawbacks, not least of which is the fact that the client can obviously fail. As you will see in the Distribution Support section, the cost of doing remote invocations from client to server is directly related to the amount of information that must be conveyed from the client to the server. If a lot of state must be shipped, the performance of the application will suffer adversely.

Entity beans versus session beans

Given that more than one type of bean exists, how do you decide which type is appropriate for a particular problem? As we have shown, the main difference between session and entity beans is that the former represent business processes (workflow) whereas the latter represent business data. Obviously, a session bean may be used to interact with an entity bean.

For example, consider the airline-reservation system shown in Figure 14-3. The system employs a session bean to enquire of the specific airline about the availability of seats on the plane requested by the tourist; the data returned by the session bean can then be displayed graphically at the client frontend. This particular interaction is a one-shot and the same client is not required to have subsequent interactions with the airline system to share information.

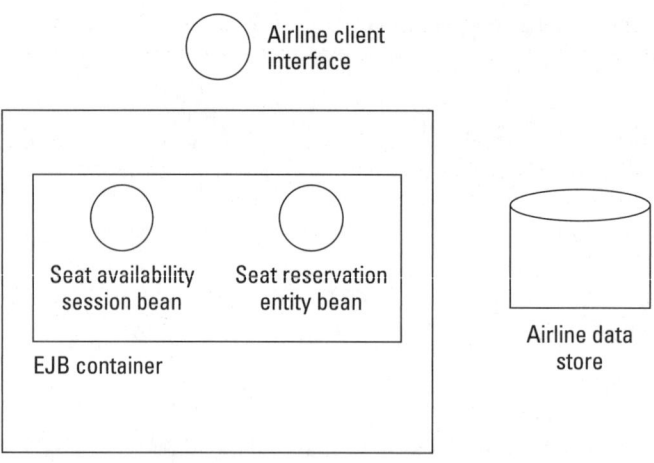

Figure 14-3: Airline reservation example using session and entity beans

Now, once the client (tourist) has chosen the seat required, the frontend attempts to reserve that seat by invoking the reserveSeat method on the entity bean. If the bean developer is interested in consistency and fault-tolerance then the bean will use transactions to load in the state of the plane or individual seat from the data store. The bean should then mark that seat as being reserved on behalf of the tourist before committing the transaction. If the transaction commits successfully then the transaction will force the new state back to the data store. In this case the work is being performed directly on the persistent representation of the airline data, and an entity bean is the only choice available to the bean developer.

Really no competition between entity and session beans exists. Each is well suited to specific requirements. If you do not need to manipulate (read, write, or update) persistent state, do not use entity beans: They are the heavyweight tool in terms of overhead. Session beans are lightweight and provide a means of conversational state-sharing.

Take a good long look at your application and its requirements before deciding which type of bean to use. Also, remember that while you may be able to reuse entity beans from other applications, in all likelihood you will have to write your session beans from scratch.

Message-driven beans (MDB)

Message-driven beans were introduced in the EJB 2.0 specification to provide asynchronous processing by acting as message-listeners for Java Messaging Service (JMS). A traditional request-response procedure call is termed synchronous because the requester waits for the response before proceeding. In an asynchronous model, the requester may perform other work before receiving the response.

As we'll see in Chapter 17, like stateless session beans, MDBs do not maintain conversational state for clients, although instance variables of a message-driven bean can maintain state across multiple client messages. Unlike session and entity beans, MDBs have no direct client-interaction interface: Clients must interact with MDBs via JMS topics and queues.

MDBs reside in an application server's EJB container and act as asynchronous message listeners. They can leverage all of the facilities afforded by the container, such as security and transactioning, while simultaneously supporting the JMS programming model for message consumers. Additionally, the MDB model can support concurrent processing of a stream of messages by means of container supplied pooling of bean instances.

Recall that MDBs are stateless and have no client visible identity. A client application has no direct knowledge of an MDB but rather sends messages to a given JMS destination for which the MDB acts as a message consumer. Since the bean has no business methods that are invoked directly by EJB clients there is no need for the home and remote interfaces required of other enterprise bean types.

Creating a message receiving application using MDBs is simpler than a pure JMS application since the container performs a number of the required steps. While an MDB is instantiated and initialized the container creates a message consumer (`TopicSubscriber` or `QueueReceiver`) to receive the bean's messages based on the configured destination and connection factory. The bean is subsequently registered with the given message consumer.

The runtime management of messaging interactions is also simplified. The container is responsible for handling message acknowledgement for the deployed bean. The form of message acknowledgement is dependent on the transaction mode utilized by the bean. If the bean is using container-managed transactions the container will perform the message acknowledgement as part of the transaction commit. However, if bean managed transactions are used the container will perform the acknowledgement as dictated by the mode specified in the deployment descriptor.

What does an EJB contain?

So far we have described what an enterprise bean is in terms of roles and relationships. Now, take a brief look at what classes and interfaces an EJB actually contains. The following interfaces and classes are important:

✦ **Component interface** — This defines the bean's business methods and constitutes its public representation to the outside world. Although the bean provider specifies this interface, it is the container that creates a class that implements it. The component interface is either *remote* (in which case it extends `javax.ejb.EJBObject`, which also extends `java.rmi.Remote`) or it is *local* (in which case it extends `javax.ejb.EJBLocalObject`). Typically this interface is referred to as the *EJB object*.

✦ **Home interface** — This defines the bean's lifecycle methods for creating, removing, and finding beans. As with the component interface, this interface comes in two flavors: remote (extending `javax.ejb.EJBHome`) and local (extending `javax.ejb.EJBLocalHome`).

✦ **Bean class** — This class provides implementations of the business methods, such as reserving a seat on a particular flight. The bean class typically does not implement the home or component interfaces; however, it must have matching methods for the component interface and corresponding methods for some of the home interface. Each bean type has its own interface, all of which extend `javax.ejb.EnterpriseBean`. This being the case, you won't be surprised to learn of the `javax.ejb.SessionBean`, `javax.ejb.EntityBean` and `javax.ejb.MessageDrivenBean` interfaces.

✦ **Primary key** — This class is the route to uniquely identifying a bean. A primary key can be very simple and provide a pointer into a database. The only real requirement is that it be serializable and override the equals method. Only entity beans need a primary key, because they represent persistent state. If two entity beans have the same home and primary keys they are considered identical.

Figure 14-4 shows the relationship among the interfaces, the EJB object, and the EJB class; the primary key is not shown though it is used by the `EJBObject`.

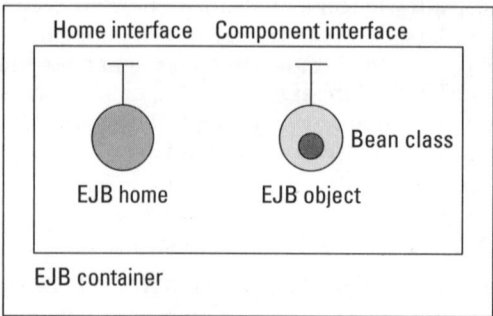

Figure 14-4: The relationship between EJB object and EJB home

Now you know what comprises a bean; the remaining chapters in Part IV will expand on these brief descriptions and give some concrete examples of how the components interact to create a real enterprise bean.

The lifecycle methods

In the rest of Part IV, we will examine the various enterprise-bean interfaces in much more detail and show lifecycle diagrams for each type of bean. However, for this chapter it is sufficient to enumerate the important methods used to manage the lifecycle of a bean instance, as shown in Table 14-1.

Table 14-1
Enterprise-Bean lifecycle methods

Name	Description	Entity Bean	Session Bean	Message Driven Bean
ejbCreate	Creates the bean instance	Yes	Yes	Yes
ejbPostCreate	Initializes the instance	Yes	No	No
ejbRemove	Informs the instance it is no longer required	Yes (also used to notify the instance that state is about to be deleted from datastore)	Yes	Yes
ejbLoad	Indicates that state is about to be loaded from datastore	Yes	No	No
ejbStore	Indicates that state is about to be saved to datastore	Yes	No	No
ejbActivate	Indicates that the bean is about to be activated (for example, removed from a pool)	Yes	Yes (conversational state is to be saved)	Yes
ejbPassivate	Indicates that the bean is about to be deactivated	Yes	Yes (conversational state has been loaded)	Yes

Every bean class must provide implementations of the methods defined in its interface. However, the implementations themselves do not have to do anything meaningful; it is perfectly correct to leave the bodies of some or all of these methods empty.

The EJBContext interface

Implementations of the `javax.ejb.EJBContext` interface are used to provide an enterprise bean with information about its environment, including its container, the client using it, and the bean instance itself. Other information available through the context includes a handle on the current transaction and the client's security-context information.

As with most things in EJB, there are actually three subtypes specific to the type of bean:

- ✦ `javax.ejb.EntityContext`
- ✦ `javax.ejb.SessionContext`
- ✦ `javax.ejb.MessageDrivenContext`

The context is your bean's route into the container that houses it — it encapsulates the bean's environment. The EJB context is a part of the container and in effect represents a handle on the container that can be accessed from within your beans. The fact that beans have a reference to the environment means that they can do interesting things such as determining (and modifying) their status.

Note   A bean's state may change over its lifetime and therefore the context object may also change dynamically. The container is responsible for changing the context to reflect any status changes in the bean.

We've described the various types of EJB and associated interfaces and classes such as the context. Now let's dive down into how the container drives the beans, providing the services they require and ensuring that they are used in a consistent manner, despite simultaneous access by many clients.

Understanding EJB Container Functionality

Recall that EJB containers are responsible for managing enterprise beans and providing an environment in which they can run. It is through the container that enterprise beans are made available to remote clients. In addition to threading, the container manages the following items (this is not an exhaustive list):

✦ **Lifecycle for a component** — The container instantiates the component (bean) upon demand when a client invocation arrives and passivates it when it is no longer needed.

✦ **Security** — The container ensures that only clients with the correct credentials can access a particular bean's methods.

✦ **Transactions** — The container starts a new transaction when the client invocation is received.

A container is expected to provide such functionality as persistence and transactions. The container provider can also assist in the construction of enterprise applications through various tools. In order to discuss the exact functionality you can expect from an EJB container, we will consider the simplified J2EE application-server architecture shown in Figure 14-5 in the rest of this section.

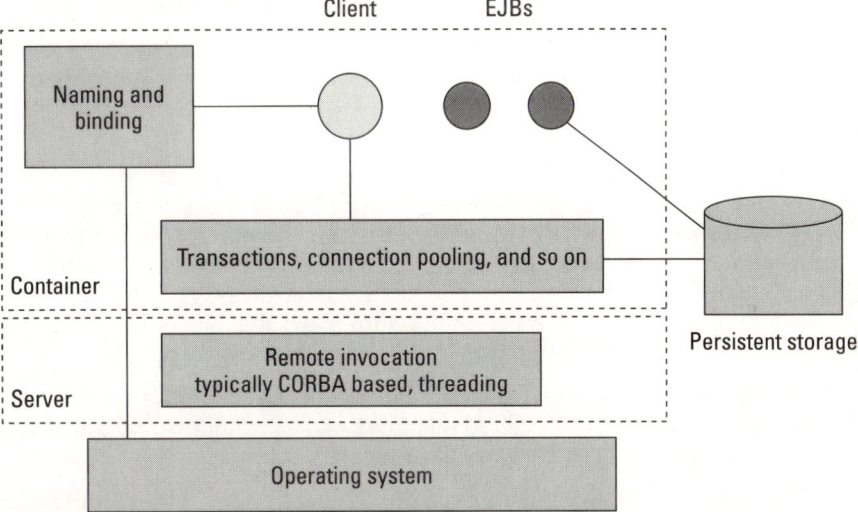

Figure 14-5: A simplified application server architecture

Restrictions on the bean provider

Recall that portability of EJB code was of paramount importance during the designing of the EJB specification. Therefore, in order to achieve portability certain restrictions were placed on the bean provider:

✦ **Static data fields**—If an enterprise bean has static data fields then these must be read-only; this is to allow container implementations to distribute bean instances across multiple JVMs (processes). If static fields could be written to, it would be mandatory to ensure that all copies of those fields were consistently updated *simultaneously,* regardless of which processes they resided in. As you can imagine, this would not be a trivial problem to solve. It involves keeping track of all copies of the objects across the distributed environment, intercepting updates to each field no matter in which object they occur, and then distributing these updates to all object instances; and this doesn't even take into account concurrent updates that might conflict!)

✦ **Synchronized keyword**—For the same reason just mentioned, an enterprise bean must not use the `synchronized` keyword to synchronize execution of multiple instances—otherwise deadlocks may occur.

✦ **Runtime interaction**—Most EJB servers do not allow runtime interaction between an application and an input device such as a keyboard; as a result, an EJB must not use the AWT functionality for input or output.

✦ **File I/O**—File I/O via the `java.io` package is notoriously prone to platform and environment peculiarities. Therefore, EJBs must not manipulate the file system through classes in this package. Rather, a resource manager such as JDBC should be used to store and retrieve data.

✦ **Networked servers**—An enterprise bean may be a network-socket client, but it is not allowed to be a network server because that would conflict with the basic function of the EJB: to serve EJB clients. An enterprise bean must not, therefore, listen on a socket, accept connections on a socket, or use a socket for multicast (where the sender sends the same message to multiple recipients simultaneously). It must not attempt to set the `Socket`, `ServerSocket`, or socket factory, or the stream-handler factory used by the URL.

✦ **Reflection**—An EJB must not use reflection or any other means to obtain information about the declared members of a class that would otherwise be inaccessible given the Java language-security rules.

✦ **ClassLoader**—An EJB must not create a `ClassLoader`, obtain the current loader, or set the context `ClassLoader` or `SecurityManager`. In addition, it must not attempt to change the I/O or error streams. Otherwise security and the container's ability to efficiently manage the runtime environment for EJBs could be compromised.

✦ **Thread management**—An enterprise bean must not manage threads, including starting, stopping, suspending, or resuming threads, or change the priority or name of an existing thread.

✦ **Security restrictions**—To protect security restrictions, an enterprise bean must not directly read or write a file descriptor. Furthermore, to prevent security being compromised, the bean must not obtain security information for a particular code source, load a native library, define a class in a package, or access or modify security-configuration objects.

This may sound like quite a few restrictions on what you can do. However, if you examine them you'll find that you would never want to do most of the things you're prevented from doing anyway. So, knowing that the same restrictions holds true for all well-behaved bean and container implementations should give you some added feeling of security that your own enterprise beans aren't going to be compromised by another bean implementation.

Why restrict threading?

Writing multi-threaded applications is an inherently complex task. For example, you must make sure that your classes are *thread-safe*, meaning that concurrent use of a specific instance of the class by multiple threads does not compromise data consistency. You must also be certain that deadlocks and livelocks do not occur.

In a centralized, single JVM environment it can often be difficult enough to ensure that your application is thread-safe. In a distributed system, where components from different vendors and implementers interact across heterogeneous deployments, it can be orders of magnitude more complex to ensure that an application will behave as you wish in the presence of many threads.

As a result, the designers of the EJB specification tried to simplify application composition where threads are concerned; therefore, EJBs must be *single-threaded*. The container automatically instantiates a new instance of an enterprise bean whenever a client invocation is received. This makes the life of the bean developer easier: They don't need to worry about making the class thread safe, or about deadlocks or livelocks, since each instance will only ever have a single thread running through it. The container handles all load-balancing of client requests to multiple instances of the single-threaded component, providing a highly scalable environment.

The disadvantage of the EJB threading model is that some problems are best handled by multi-threading. Unfortunately, in these cases EJB is not the best tool.

Concurrency control and re-entrance

The restriction that all enterprise beans must be single-threaded makes the issue of concurrency control of beans much simpler. Because multiple clients (threads) cannot access the same bean instance at the same time, they can't perform conflicting operations simultaneously. So, for example, if you take your SeatBean, in the reserveSeat method you would obviously like to prevent a situation in which one tourist (Fred) reserves the seat and simultaneously so does another (John). Since the container guarantees that each client (tourist) has exclusive access to the bean instance, this situation is prevented.

Re-entrance occurs when a thread attempts to re-enter a class or procedure it has already traversed. In the case of EJB, as shown in Figure 14-6, this situation occurs when a thread attempts to re-enter an enterprise bean. In EJB enterprise beans are non-re-entrant by default, and so loopbacks are not allowed. This is an important concept to understand because in general it can be difficult to guarantee that loop-backs will not occur. Formation of applications through the composition of components (beans) that have been created by different users, possibly for other applications, almost invariably lead to complex interactions among those components. So, although you may not think that re-entrance is going to happen, it can.

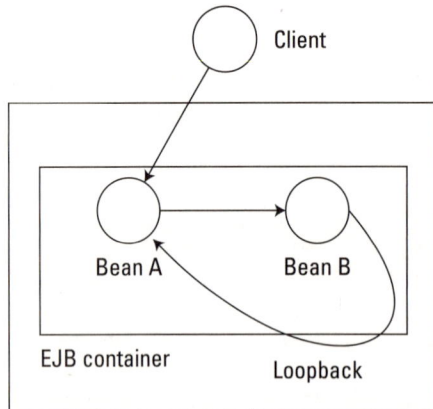

Figure 14-6: An example of re-entrance in an EJB

All interactions with an enterprise bean occur through remote references: Clients and beans do not interact directly with one another, whether the client is another bean or a bespoke frontend. The real problem with re-entrance is that the container or bean has no way to differentiate between an invocation made by a "pure" client (as in Figure 14-6) and a re-entrant call being made by the bean (Bean B). Thus, allowing re-entrance is effectively the same as allowing multi-threading and the possibility of corrupting data and the application.

With session beans, if a loopback attempt is made, a `RemoteException` will be thrown. Entity beans, on the other hand, can be configured at deployment time to allow re-entrance. However, we do not recommend it.

Achieving scalability by pooling resources

Recall that EJB provides a scalable platform for the development and deployment of enterprise applications. But how does this work? You may have seen descriptions of applications using application servers that can cope with hundreds or thousands of clients simultaneously. Surely the fact that each client has a corresponding bean within the container places a limiting factor on the number of simultaneous client requests?

To a certain extent this is true. However, as we mentioned at the start of this chapter, EJB is based on the collective experiences of many companies who have deployed many enterprise-level applications into the field in other (non-EJB) environments. One of the common characteristics that existing applications share that helps to make them scalable is that of *resource pooling*: Rather than resources being created for each client, a smaller pool of resources is used and shared among them. This pool typically grows and shrinks on demand to cope with changing client load. EJB uses a similar technique to achieve its own scalability goals.

All beans have a well-defined lifecycle. Typically a bean goes from a *passive* state (such as the state of the entity bean when it is on disk) to an *active* state when a client uses it. Eventually it is passivated again when it is no longer required. (Recall that the EJB container is responsible for managing and directing the lifecycle of a bean.)

Also remember that clients interact with enterprise beans via their remote (component) interfaces. This being the case, a client never has a direct view of the underlying bean implementation. So why should the same bean instance be used for every one of the client's interactions? Obviously, if the bean is preserving state that must span a given client's invocations (because it is being used within a transaction, for example), that client is effectively bound to that specific bean for the duration. However, in many cases, beans are used once only or for only short periods. In those cases, there is no reason that the instance of the bean cannot change for the same client. This is because the client does not need to know and will not be able to differentiate between this situation and one in which it always uses the same instance implementation. The container need only keep a pool of beans (known as *instance pooling*) and copy state into and out of them as required.

The time when a bean is not actively servicing a client's request is unproductive, and instance pooling minimizes this period by making the bean instance available to as many clients as possible during its lifetime. This decreases resource use and improves performance.

The life of an entity bean

The lifecycles of all beans are similar, but probably the most important one to consider first is that of the entity bean. At any given time, an entity bean is in one of the following states:

✦ **Nonexistence** — The bean has not yet been instantiated in this state.

✦ **Pooled** — The bean has been instantiated by the container in this state, but has not been associated with any particular EJB object.

✦ **Ready** — The instance has been associated with an EJB object in this state, and is ready to be used by a client.

A logical instance pool may exist for each type of bean (each class). To create an instance pool, the container generates a number of instances of the class and places them within the pool until they are needed. The initial size of the pool will be vendor-specific. However, your favorite application-server implementation may enable the system administrator to configure the size of the pool at runtime to improve performance.

As clients make requests on the business logic, the container assigns instances from the pool. Because all instances in the pool are equivalent, any instance may be selected to service a particular client request. Once the EJB object no longer requires the bean instance, the instance is returned automatically to the pool. Obviously, the initial size of the pool may be inadequate for the throughput of client requests. In this case the container may increase and/or decrease the size of the pools to better suit the runtime environment.

Figure 14-7 illustrates what happens when a new client invocation arrives. When the pool of bean instances is created, each bean is given a reference to a `javax.ejb.EJBContext` instance by the container. Recall that it is through this context that the bean can obtain information on, and interact with, its environment.

The code fragment below shows how an EJB for an airline reservation application might be implemented. The `setEntityContext` method is called by the container at initialization time.

```
public AirlineBean implements EntityBean
{
public void setEntityContext (EntityContext ctx) throws
RemoteException
{
  myContext = ctx;
  myEnvironment = ctx.getEnvironment();
}

public EntityContext myContext;
public Properties myEnvironment;
}
```

Initially all that exists is the EJB home object that the client can use to obtain a remote interface to the bean. The container then creates the corresponding EJB object, which is empty, in that it has not been assigned a bean instance.

As shown in Figure 14-8, once created, the EJB object is assigned any instance from the pool. That instance moves from the pooled state to the ready state. At this point the enterprise bean can receive invocations from the client on its business logic by means of the remote interface. The container can manage this bean further — for its persistence or transaction requirements, for example.

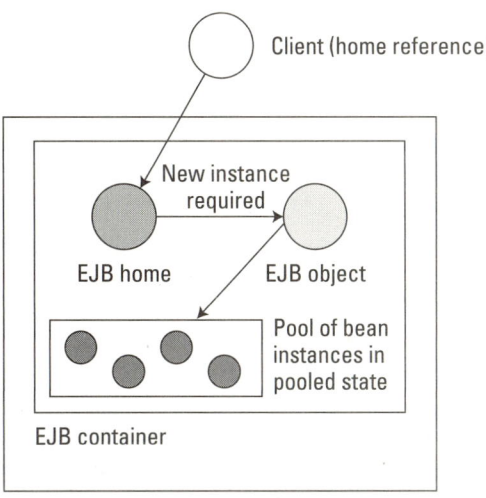

Figure 14-7: How the container activates an EJB from the pool of instances

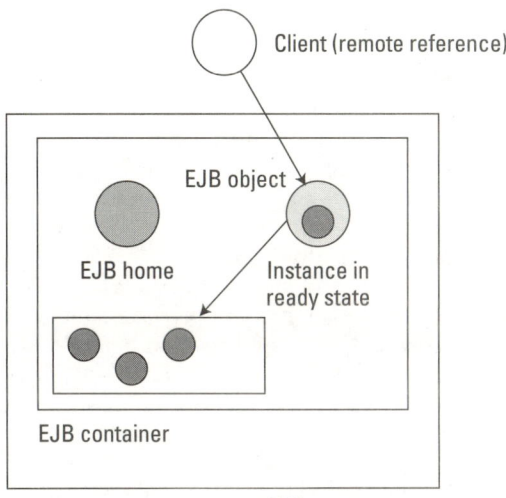

Figure 14-8: The client uses the bean instance now that it has been activated.

Note   When a bean instance moves from the pooled state to the ready state, the `javax.ejb.EJBContext` instance it was given when it was created then allows it to access its own EJB object and home and determine information about the client. It is through this interface that the bean can also create, locate, and remove beans of its own type.

When the client is finished with the bean's remote reference, it can let the reference pass out of scope and become garbage, or call one of the bean's `Remove` methods. Once removed or marked as not being needed, the instance is disassociated from the EJB object and returned to the pool. Its state is therefore moved back to pooled.

The life of a session bean

Since instance pooling seems like such a good idea, can it be applied to session beans? Fortunately the answer is yes, but as we will now show, only if those beans are stateless session beans.

Pooling of stateless session beans

Stateless session beans can be pooled in the same way as entity beans. However, the container can use pooling in a more powerful manner simply because the bean instances are stateless. Furthermore, every method invocation by a client can be serviced by a completely different stateless session-bean instance if necessary. Therefore, the container can swap stateless session beans into and out of the pool between each method invocation made by a client. Typically the time taken to perform a method invocation is much shorter than the time between method invocations. As a result, pooling of stateless session beans allows the container to keep a much smaller number of instances in the pool than if it were pooling entity beans.

What about stateful session beans?

Earlier in this chapter you saw that stateful session beans can maintain conversational state between client invocations; this state is typically maintained in the same datastore as your entity beans. Furthermore, this state must remain consistent for the duration of the client's interactions with a specific bean instance. As a result, stateful session beans cannot participate in pooling techniques in the same way that stateless session beans and entity beans do.

However, this is not to say that the EJB specification has not provided a means for achieving scalability and performance when using stateful session beans. Instead, the container uses a process known as activation and passivation. When the container needs to conserve resources it can evict (passivate) those stateful session beans from memory that are not currently servicing a client's requests.

As shown in Figure 14-9, when the bean is instructed that it is to be passivated by means of the `ejbPassivate` method, its state is serialized to secondary storage to preserve any conversational state it has.

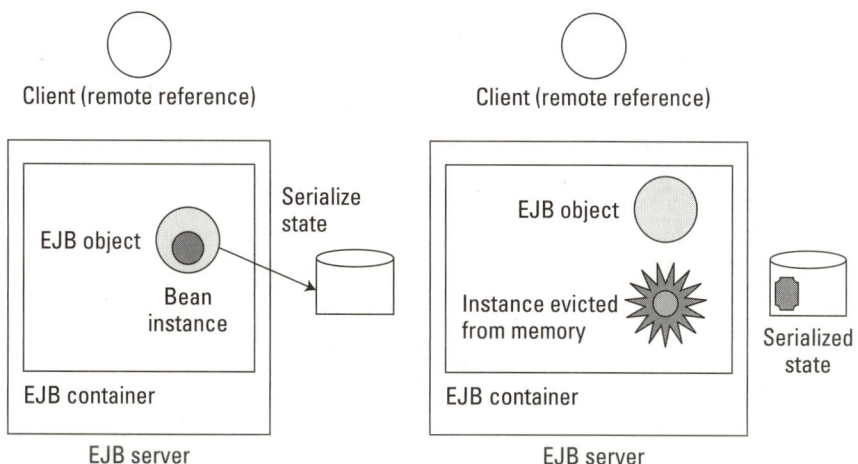

Figure 14-9: An illustration of a stateful session bean being passivated

The following fragment illustrates what may occur during ejbActivate and ejbPassivate for our Airline bean (changed to a SessionBean for the purposes of this example). In this example, the Airline has a JDBC Connection and associated DataSource; the connection is obtained during ejbActivate (the bean needs to supply a user and password login) and closed during ejbPassivate, since the bean implementer knows that signifies the end of the bean's lifecycle.

```
public class AirlineBean implements SessionBean
{
  public void ejbActivate ()
  {
      conn = dataSource.getConnection("user", "password");
  }

  public void ejbPassivate
  {
      try
      {
          conn.close();
      }
      catch (Exception ex)
      {
      }
  }

  private DataSource dataSource;
  private Connection conn;
}
```

Importantly, this preserved state is associated with the bean's EJB object. When a subsequent invocation from the client arrives on the EJB object, a new bean instance is created and its state is loaded from the previously serialized form. At this point, the bean is activated; once it is loaded, `ejbActivate` is called. Fortunately for the client, as with instance pooling, all of this activation and passivation of stateful session beans happens transparently. The client continues to use the EJB object interface and is blissfully unaware of the state changes going on within the container.

The `ejbPassivate` method is called immediately prior to the state of the bean being serialized. The bean implementation can use this method to close connections, free other resources, and so on. Likewise, `ejbActivate` is called immediately after the state has been loaded from the datastore, and the bean can use this to reset connections, transient fields (data this is not persisted), and so forth.

Transactions and EJBs

The EJB XML deployment descriptor allows session beans to be defined as having either bean- or container-managed transactions. Transaction type is defined in the EJB 1.1 and EJB 2.0 XML DTDs as follows:

```
<!ELEMENT transaction-type (#PCDATA)>
```

The `transaction-type` is also a required child element for the session element. This means that session bean with container-managed transactions have a structure like this:

```
<session>
...
  <transaction-type>container</transaction-type>
...
```

Entity beans always have container-managed transactions. If a bean is declared to have container-managed transactions, the DTD specifies a `container-transaction` element defined as follows:

```
<!ELEMENT container-transaction (description?, method+, trans-
attribute)>
```

This example indicates that the `container-transaction` element may have an optional description, one or more methods specified, and a single transaction attribute.

Container-managed transactions

Container-managed transactions (CMTs) are the core of the EJB component model. Writing system code to create and control distributed transactions can be difficult and error-prone. Fortunately the EJB model allows the container to handle the initiation, termination, and recovery of transactions. In fact, the container still plays an important role with beans that are labeled as bean-managed, handling error recovery and management of state-transaction association in stateful session beans.

This separation of concerns is a particularly important strength of the EJB model, because it enables developers to concentrate on the functional aspects of their business logic and leave the transactional aspects of the code to the container writers. As you saw in Chapter 10, using the OTS isn't exactly a trivial thing to do, and so any help that users can get to move them further up the development stack can only be a benefit to development efficiency and application reliability.

The declarative semantics of container-managed transactions are relatively straightforward. The following transaction attributes may be specified for a method on a bean that is declared as having container-managed transaction attributes for its methods:

✦ NotSupported

✦ Supports

✦ Required

✦ RequiresNew

✦ Mandatory

✦ Never

They are defined in the following sections.

NotSupported

This attribute indicates that the container should ensure that a business method should never be executed in the context of a transaction. However, the caller is allowed to invoke the bean's remote (or local) interface with an active transaction context. In that case, the container will suspend the transaction for the duration of the method dispatch and resume the transaction when the method completes.

Technically, the method is executed in an unspecified transaction context, which provides the container with several options for dealing with access to underlying resource managers from a transactional standpoint. In practice, many containers will simply assume that no container intervention is required or desired. However, according to the EJB specification it is entirely permissible for the container to follow one of the following strategies, or a combination of two or more:

The container may invoke the method without any transaction context.

The container may treat each call of an instance to a resource manager as a single transaction. In the case of JDBC, this means that the container would set the auto-commit flag to `true` on the connection.

The container may merge multiple calls of an instance to a resource manager into a single transaction.

The container may merge multiple calls of an instance to multiple resource managers into a single transaction.

If the bean instance invokes other EJBs that run in an unspecified transaction context, the container may merge the resource-manager calls for all EJBs into a single transaction.

The EJB specification recommends that bean developers write beans "conservatively" so as not to rely on a particular container's behavior. Also, keep in mind that any nested EJB calls within the business method will be executed without a current transaction context's being associated with the calling client.

Supports

This attribute indicates that the container should allow the invocation of the business method within the transaction context of a caller. However, the method may also be called with no transaction context associated with the caller. In that case the method will be invoked in an unspecified transaction context according to the semantics we explained for the NotSupported transaction attribute.

The Supports transaction attribute allows the calling client to control the transactional characteristics of the business method. This can be a powerful construct for gaining operational efficiency from a business method used in different contexts. On the other hand, it means that required transactional behavior can be compromised by client misuse — and this can lead to data inconsistencies within an application.

Some people mistakenly believe that this attribute can be used to eliminate all interaction between the container and the transaction manager during a method invocation in which no transactional context is associated with the client. Regardless of the container's strategy for handling the unspecified transaction context, this is never the case; the container must still interact with the manager even in the simplest case. The efficiency is gained in the interaction with the database connections or Enterprise Integration System (EIS) adapters, which do not need to involve the XA transaction manager in their interactions (as we saw in Chapter 10).

Required

This attribute indicates that the business method must be invoked in the context of a transaction. If a transaction is associated with the caller, that transaction will be associated with the method invocation. If the caller does not have an associated transaction, the container will start a new transaction prior to invoking the business method on the bean instance, and will terminate the transaction when the business method has returned. This attribute guarantees that access to multiple transactional resource managers will be made in the context of a single global transaction — and helps to ensure that data consistencies are maintained across heterogeneous systems.

RequiresNew

This indicates that the bean will always be invoked in the context of a new transaction. If the caller invokes the method within a transaction, the container will suspend that transaction and start a new transaction before calling the actual business method. When the business method completes, the container will terminate the existing transaction and resume the caller's transaction. This means that the outcome of the transaction associated with the business method has no effect on the transaction of the caller.

The benefit of `RequiresNew` is that the business method itself is an atomic transaction, independent of other business logic within the system. This quality can guarantee the consistency of an operation, regardless of the state of other business methods in the system. For example, a method that enables employees to change personal information in an Enterprise Resource Planning (ERP) system may require success independently of the success or failure of a larger transaction in which the personal-information update is a part.

Mandatory

In this case, callers without a transaction context will receive a subclass of `java.rmi. RemoteException`, the Java Transactions API (JTA) exception `javax.transaction. TransactionRequiredException`. The container will not attempt to start a transaction on behalf of the caller. This is useful when failure of the business method must be correlated closely with the transactional integrity of resources associated with the caller's transaction. A transaction attribute like `Required` cannot enforce this behavior. The `Mandatory` attribute could be used, for example, to ensure that fund transfers cannot happen independently of the success of a larger business operation in an e-commerce application.

Never

The `Never` attribute was added to the component model in EJB 1.1. If a `Never` attribute is invoked while the caller is part of a transaction, the container will throw a `RemoteException` and the bean's method will never execute. However, if the caller is not associated with a transaction, the container will dispatch the method on the bean instance and it will execute normally. The bean's method will be invoked in an unspecified transaction context according to the semantics we described for the `NotSupported` transaction attributes. The `Never` attribute can be used when you want to signal a usage error to the calling client if the method is invoked in a transaction context.

Specifying container-managed transactions

A typical container-transaction element looks like this:

```
<container-transaction>
  <method>
    <ejb-name>EmployeeBean</ejb-name>
    <method-name>provideRaise</method-name>
```

```
</method>
<trans-attribute>Required</trans-attribute>
<container-transaction/>
```

It is possible to omit the transaction attribute of a method; the DTD does not enforce rules that specify that all methods must be mapped, because technically this mapping is the responsibility of the application assembler rather than the bean developer. The resulting behavior may be container-dependent.

Recall that the EJB specifications go to great length to define roles for each stage of the development and deployment lifecycle of an EJB. They do this in an attempt to provide great flexibility and separation of concerns. This design is also aimed at trying to ensure reusability of components, but often doesn't map to real-life scenarios. Bean developers should take care to ensure that beans developed for a specific project have completed deployment descriptors. The container will generally assume that omissions in the deployment descriptor are intended.

Bean-managed transactions

As the name implies, EJBs that use bean-managed transactions manage their own transaction initiations and terminations. However, the container still plays an important role, because it enforces well-defined rules that limit how bean developers can use transactions, principally to ensure that transactions initiated by bean developers are terminated correctly. It's critical to note that only session beans may use the bean-managed transaction demarcation; the container always manages transactional semantics for entity beans.

With bean-managed transactions, bean instances establish and manage transactions via the JTA javax.transaction.UserTransaction interface, which can be acquired from either the EJBContext associated with the bean instance or the environment via a JNDI lookup. The container is responsible for ensuring enlistment of resource-manager drivers and for the coordination of the commit or rollback. The code looks like this:

```
Context initCtx = new InitialContext();
UserTransaction utx = (UserTransaction)initCtx.lookup(
"java:comp/UserTransaction");
utx.begin();
//access resource manager(s)...
utx.commit();
```

When a client uses the home, remote, or local interface to invoke a business method on a bean with bean-managed transactions, the container will always suspend any transaction associated with the client's request. However, with bean-managed transactions the container has different behavior for managing transactions for stateful session beans and stateless session beans.

Stateful session beans

If the bean instance for a stateful session bean previously initiated a transaction, the transaction is associated with the request after the caller's transaction is suspended. This condition occurs when a business method completes without terminating the transaction it has initiated. Remember that stateful session beans are associated with a single client and maintain conversational state, and hence this situation is allowed. When the method returns, the container must suspend any transaction associated with the bean instance, and if a transaction was associated with the original client request the container must resume the original transaction. The container is responsible for managing and maintaining the associations, illustrating that the container has a lot of work to do in bean-managed transaction scenarios.

Stateless session beans

On the other hand, a stateless session bean must terminate any transactions it initiates within a business method prior to returning. Stateless session-bean instances are interchangeable between business-method invocations and may, for example, be pooled. (Pooling was discussed earlier in the Section Scalability by Pooling Resources.) Maintaining an association between the instance and a transaction across multiple requests would be a serious error and would damage data integrity. For example, a pooled stateless session bean that maintains a transaction association across requests can modify data for two clients in the context of the same transaction. So if the container finds that a stateless session bean returns from a business method without committing or rolling back a transaction it has initiated, the container must do the following, in the following order:

1. Log an application error to alert the system administrator (no standard mechanism for doing this exists at present, but in practice containers often simply log an error message to the console or a file).

2. Roll back the started transaction.

3. Discard the instance of the session bean because it is erroneously maintaining state associated with a client.

4. Throw `java.rmi.RemoteException` to the client.

Stateful versus stateless session beans

For either stateful or stateless session beans, the container must allow the bean instance to start and terminate any number of transactions serially within the business method. If a bean instance attempts to start a new transaction by invoking `begin` on the `UserTransaction` interface or any other method, the container will throw a `javax.transaction.NotSupportedException` from the `begin` method. This means that the container supports nested transactions, which are disallowed for EJBs. If a bean attempts to use the `setRollbackOnly( )` or `getRollbackOnly( )` methods on the `EJBContext` object, the container will generate a `java.lang.IllegalStateException`, because these methods are reserved for beans with container-managed transaction demarcation.

Examining a transactional EJB example

The main elements required for supporting transactional EJB applications deployed in an application server are shown in Figure 14-10. An application server usually manages a few containers, with each container hosting many (hundreds of) EJBs; only one container, hosting three EJBs, is shown in the figure.

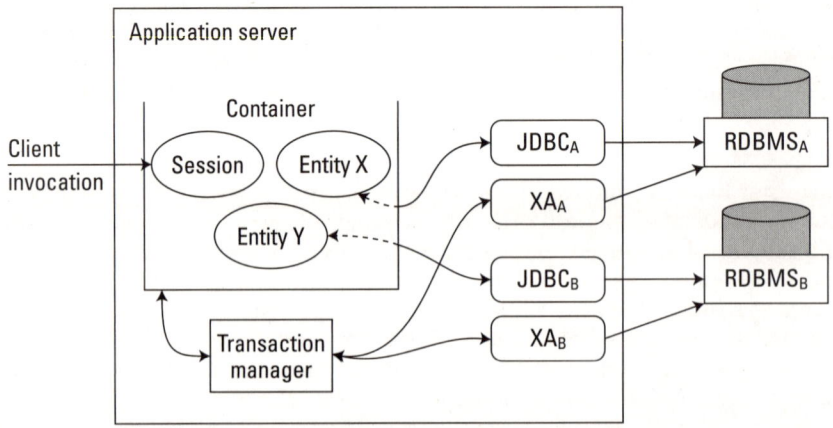

Figure 14-10: Illustrating the various components involved in an EJB transaction

The application server is a multi-threaded program that runs in a single process. Of the many middleware services provided by an application server to its containers, we explicitly show just the transaction service. A transaction manager is hosted by the application server and assumes responsibility for enabling transactional access to EJBs. The transaction manager does not necessarily have to reside in the same address space as the application server, but this is frequently the case in practical systems. At least one *resource manager* (persistence store) is required to maintain persistent state of the entity beans supported by the application server; we show two in the figure. In particular, we have shown relational database management systems (RDBMSes) as our resource managers (Entity X stores its state on $RDMS_A$ and Entity Y does the same on $RDMS_B$).

Communications between an RDBMS and a container takes place by means of a Java DataBase Connectivity (JDBC) driver. Another interface is required to enable a resource manager to participate in transactions originated in EJBs. In Chapter 10, you saw that this is the XAResource interface (shown as XA in Figure 14-10). As you also saw in Chapter 10, there is a clear separation of concerns between transaction management via the XAResource interface and resource manager read/write operations via JDBC. In simple terms, the transaction manager interoperates with the resource manager via the XAResource interface to drive the resource manager through the two-phase commit protocol, and the application interoperates with the resource manager via the JDBC driver.

We'll now describe a sample scenario with a single transaction involving three enterprise beans (using CMT) and two resource managers. A session bean receives a client invocation. The reception of the client invocation results in the session bean starting a transaction, T1, and issuing a number of invocations on two entity beans, X and Y.

When entity beans are required by the session bean, the session bean will first have to activate these beans via their home interfaces, which results in the container retrieving their states from the appropriate resource managers to initialize the instance variables of X and Y. The container is responsible for passing the transaction context of T1 to the JDBC drivers in all its interactions, which in turn guarantee that the resource managers are kept informed of transaction starts and ends. Note the following, in particular:

> Retrieving the persistent state of X (Y) from $RDMS_A$ ($RDMS_B$) at the start of T1 will lead to the associated resource manager obtaining a write-lock on the resource (the persistent state, stored as a row in a table); this prevents other transactions from accessing the resource until T1 ends (commits or rolls back).

> XA resources (XA_A and XA_B) "register" themselves with the transaction manager so that they can take part in the two-phase commit.

Once the session bean has indicated that T1 is at an end, the transaction manager attempts to carry out the two-phase commit to ensure that all participants either commit or roll back T1. In the current example, the transaction manager will poll $RDBMS_A$ and $RDBMS_B$ (via XA_A and XA_B, respectively) to ask if they are ready to commit. If either $RDBMS_A$ or $RDBMS_B$ cannot commit, it informs the transaction manager and rolls back its own part of the transaction. If both $RDBMS_A$ and $RDBMS_B$ can commit, the transaction manager informs all participants to commit the transaction and the modified states of X and Y become the new persistent states.

In our example, all the beans are in the same container. Support for distributed transactions involving beans in multiple containers (on possibly distinct application servers) is straightforward if the transaction manager is built atop a CORBA transaction service (Java Transaction Service), because such a service can coordinate both local and remote XA resources. Such a transaction manager will also be able to coordinate a transaction that is started within a client and spans EJBs, provided the client is CORBA-enabled.

Naming objects

In a distributed system it is obviously important to be able to name objects in order to identify them and use them. All distributed systems, from the Distributed Computing Environment (DCE) to the Common Object Request Broker Architecture (CORBA), provide a naming service. (CORBA is discussed later the Section Integrating with CORBA.) In J2EE, as you saw in Chapter 11, this naming service is provided through the Java Naming and Directory Interface (JNDI), since JNDI supports pretty much any kind of implementation you could possibly want. Both clients and servers, as containers and EJBs, respectively, are expected to use JNDI. Luckily for us, the various J2EE specifications clearly define the names that services such as JTA are expected to use in order to publish into JNDI.

In order to support interoperable access to naming services for looking up `EJBHome` objects, the EJB specification requires naming implementations to be based on the Object Management Group's CosNaming service, which itself must follow the CORBA Interoperable Name Service (INS) specification. As you will see in the Section Distribution Support, all remote invocations with the naming-service implementation must occur by means of OMG's Internet Inter-ORB Protocol (IIOP).

The security infrastructure

The EJB security infrastructure uses a role-driven access-control paradigm as defined in the EJB 2.0 specification. Roles are mapped to an EJB's methods using the deployment descriptor. When a user accesses a protected resource, his or her principal is established and associated with the role. Similarly, distributed clients are authenticated by means of JAAS APIs, as you saw in Chapter 12. If the user invokes an EJB method, the principal is passed with the request. If the principal's role is mapped to the requested method, the method is invoked. If the EJB method subsequently invokes another EJB method, the principal is passed with the request and will be verified by the EJB being called.

The EJB 2.0 specification ensures that any EJB type can establish a security context prior to the execution of the bean's methods. The EJB developer does this by setting a *run-as* role under the *security-identity* section of the deployment descriptor for a given EJB.

The Timer service

Most operating systems give you the ability to schedule tasks to be executed at certain times of day or at regular intervals. For example, you may want a housekeeping service that archives unused files at 12:00am on the first day of every month. It is natural therefore to expect the EJB container to provide similar functionality. With EJB 1.4, the new *Timer service* provides a watchdog service that allows you to schedule time-specific events (timed notifications) for all enterprise beans with the exception of stateful session beans.

In order to be able to receive timer events, the enterprise bean must implement the `javax.ejb.TimedObject` interface. When a timer event occurs (the timer expires), the container invokes the `ejbTimeout` method of the `TimedObject`, which may handle the event in an implementation specific manner (e.g., archiving your files). The `Timer` that has just triggered is passed to the bean via `ejbTimeout`. Timers for entity beans are associated with the specific bean instance. However, stateless session beans and message-driven beans do not have unique timers for each bean instance: the timer may be called on any bean instance in the pooled state.

Timers are serializable and persistent. So, if the server crashes or shuts down cleanly, then upon restart all timers will be re-activated. Luckily for us, if a timer goes off while the server is down, the `ejbTimeout` method will be called upon re-activation.

> **Note** Although the timer service appears to provide the capability of setting timer events with a resolution of milliseconds, you shouldn't expect this level of timer granularity in practice: the timer service is meant for business applications that typically measure events in hours or days. So, if you do try to get millisecond (or possibly even second) resolution, don't rely on your `ejbTimeout` method being invoked precisely when you set the alarm. In addition, the container will interleave calls to `ejbTimeout` with the bean's business and lifecycle methods, so the time at which `ejbTimeout` is called may not correspond exactly with the time specified when the timer was created.

Timer creation is handled by the `javax.ejb.TimerService`, which has a number of `createTimer` methods for different purposes (for example, create a timer to go off after a specific duration). When the bean invokes one of the `createTimer` methods of the `TimerService`, a timer is created and begins to count down. For example:

```
TimerService ourTimerService = ctx.getTimerService();
Timer theTimer =
ourTimerService.createTimer(archiveFileDuration, "archiver
timer created");
```

In the example, the bean's `EJBContext` is used to obtain the container's `TimerService`. Then we create a timer for our file archive bean. The additional string that we have given can actually be any serializable object and is intended to allow client-specific information to be passed to the timer: the bean can retrieve this information when the timer expires to recognize the significance of the event.

We can create single-event timers (the container calls `ejbTimeout` once and then cancels the timer), or multi-event timers that execute until explicitly removed. For example, when an entity bean instance is removed, the container cancels the bean's timer. Alternatively when a bean invokes the `Timer's cancel` method, the container will cancel the timer.

If you use `Timers` then you'll probably want your beans to be able to find out how much time is left on a timer, when the next timeout is going to occur etc. The `Timer` interface gives you access to these functions. For example, in the code fragment below we decide to have our bean involved in a number of timers. Therefore, our enterprise bean checks the user-supplied information on the `Timer` to determine whether or not it is the archiver timer and acts accordingly.

```
public void ejbTimeout (Timer timer)
{
    if (timer.getInfo().equals("archiver timer created"))
    {
        // archive files
    }
```

```
        else
            // do something else
    }
```

> **Note**   If you want to check `Timers` for equality then you must only use the `equals` method to compare them.

Timers are transaction-aware. What this means is that if a bean creates a timer within a transaction and that transaction rolls back, the timer creation will also be rolled back. Likewise, if the bean cancels a timer within a transaction that is subsequently rolled back, the timer's duration is reset as if the cancel attempt had never happened.

In the case of CMT, the `ejbTimeout` method typically uses the `RequiresNew` attribute, and the container starts a new transaction before calling `ejbTimeout`.

Persistence in BMP and CMP

You've already seen how persistence of entity beans and stateful session beans is important to the EJB architecture. In BMP, the bean provider is solely responsible for managing the reading and writing of a bean instance's state from and to a datastore. In CMP, the container is responsible for this and may provide a variety of different datastore implementations to choose from (such as a file system–based implementations, or an implementation based on a database). Whatever the underlying implementation for the persistence service, the container-persistence relationship must still invoke the various EJB callback methods and transactions that you saw in the section "The Life of an Entity Bean."

> **Note**   Many different implementations are possible for a persistence service and your favorite application-server implementation may support more than one. As you will see in the section "Persistence", your choice of implementation can have a critical impact on your application's performance. Your choice of implementation will vary by vendor, but will usually involve the deployment descriptor.

Distribution support

In Chapter 4, you saw how distributed invocations occur through the use of client and server stubs, which make the distributed application appear to be executing locally. As shown in Figure 14-11, the client stub object (CSO) appears to the user as if it were the real object O; however, when its methods are invoked, it performs a remote-method invocation or Remote Procedure Call (RPC) on the server stub object (SSO) residing on the other node. This in turn invokes the real method invocation on O.

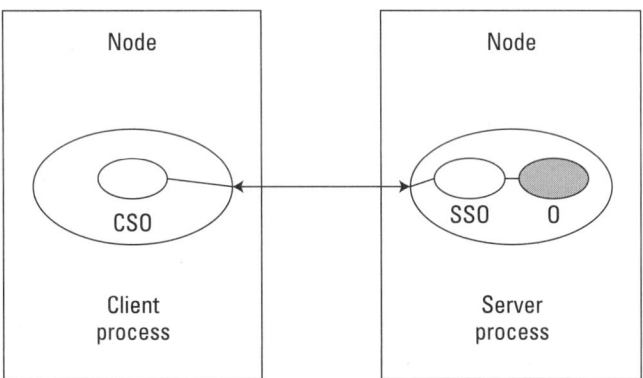

Figure 14-11: Client and server stub implementations using Java RMI

In early versions of the EJB specification, the on-the-wire protocol was not mandated and vendors were free to use a range of different implementations, including Java RMI and CORBA. Now, as you can imagine, the problem with this was that interoperability between different vendor implementations was extremely hard to set up.

For this reason, and because of other interoperability issues that we'll cover later in this chapter, the latest version of the EJB specification now mandates that the protocol be based on CORBA IIOP. This does not mean that your application suddenly has to know about CORBA, an ORB, or the Interface Definition Language (IDL), which CORBA uses: It is only the on-the-wire protocol format that is required to be CORBA IIOP (version 1.2). CORBA is discussed in the following section.

Note   EJB enables vendors to support other distribution protocols, but to be compliant and to achieve interoperability they must at least support CORBA IIOP. You should be careful when selecting a distribution protocol in case you later find that it restricts the clients and services you can interact with.

Integrating with CORBA

Up to this point you've heard us mention the Object Management Group (OMG) and the Common Object Request Broker Architecture (CORBA), but we have not yet described fully what these things are and how they are important to J2EE and, in particular, to the application server. In this section we will address these issues directly.

Don't worry about having to understand yet another distributed-object model. We're not going to go into a great deal of detail about CORBA; enough books are on the market that can do that subject more justice than we have space for here. Typically, you won't need to know about CORBA in order to take advantage of the functionality it provides within J2EE. However, it's useful to know something about CORBA for a number of reasons including: interoperability (two different vendor application servers that are based on CORBA have a better chance of interoperating than not) and performance (CORBA is typically slower than Java RMI, so if you're not interested in interoperability you may want some way of circumventing CORBA.)

Why is CORBA important to J2EE?

Since its inception in the late 1980s, the OMG has successfully released specifications addressing issues ranging from transactions to medical services. All of the specifications released have had multi-vendor support and inherent interoperability. The amount of work involved in defining any specification is immense. This is especially true if you want to have multiple vendors endorse it without their jeopardizing their existing investments and products in that area! Getting agreement from vendors for one such specification is good work. The OMG has obtained agreement for dozens of specifications, which is impressive to say the least.

However, one of the main problems with CORBA is its complexity. Although the OMG is in the business of assisting in the development of open standards, these standards are typically at a very low level in the application architecture — for example, concerning transactions or concurrency control. Until the release of the CORBA Component Model (which was heavily influenced by EJB), no effort had been made to define a standard that would allow the various object services to be composed to create applications or components. Furthermore, the OMG is not in the business of defining APIs because these are, by their very nature, programming language–specific.

As a result, when J2EE started, some made a conscious effort not to use the CORBA specifications. CORBA was seen as complex, and some people believed that anything tied to it must also be complex. However, it quickly became obvious that reinventing the wheel was a pointless and time-consuming task. This was especially true given that many of the same companies involved in J2EE were involved in CORBA's development!

At roughly the same time, work began in the OMG to define a language mapping to Java. Its purpose would be to enable CORBA applications to be written in Java and for those applications to transparently use services, such as transactions or persistence, written in other languages. Up to that point, all distributed-object invocation in Java was conducted via Java RMI, which is explicitly a single-language protocol. Users who needed to interact with services and systems written in other languages had to do so in a proprietary manner. Despite what you might have been led to believe, a lot of components out there are written in languages other than Java. In an enterprise application you'll typically have to interact with these components sooner rather than later.

Therefore, in order to achieve interoperability with multi-language systems and to benefit from the experiences of the OMG, later versions of J2EE recommend CORBA as the interoperability platform of choice. This is not to say that services had to be written using CORBA Interface Definition Language (IDL) or that the services you might use had necessarily been written to use an ORB: This recommendation was made purely for the sake of on-the-wire interoperability. As long as the wire format for distributed invocations is identical to that specified by the CORBA standard (currently 2.3), it does not matter whether ORBs are at the client or server: You cannot tell the difference between them being present or not being present.

At the level of the application programmer and EJB provider, whether or not a J2EE implementation is using CORBA is typically not apparent. However, interoperability with legacy CORBA applications comes for free and that's no small bonus.

When J2EE met CORBA

So you've seen how CORBA is important in J2EE for interoperability and for leveraging previously developed open standards. But what exactly does the "CORBA-effect" mean to you in practice? Which CORBA specifications have had an impact on J2EE and which are going to in the future? In this section we give a brief description of the following components within the J2EE architecture, which owe a lot to the OMG, and of the components that OMG specifications are likely to contribute to its future development:

- ✦ Internet Inter-ORB Protocol (IIOP)
- ✦ Transactions
- ✦ Naming
- ✦ Security
- ✦ Notification service
- ✦ Activity service

The Internet Inter-ORB Protocol (IIOP)

IIOP is the standard remote method–invocation protocol for CORBA and was developed specifically to allow different ORB implementations to communicate and use each other's services. As you know, Java has its own protocol, called RMI, that was developed to be a lightweight, language-specific invocation mechanism that supports distributed garbage collection. Its on-the-wire format is the Java Remote Method Protocol (JRMP). Although RMI does not have multi-language support, it is particularly well suited for distributed Java applications.

Despite the fact that these two protocols are intended to solve the same problem, that of using remote objects, their on-the-wire formats and language bindings are significantly different. So much so that a client written to use Java RMI would not be able to interact with a corresponding service written using CORBA IIOP. They simply wouldn't be able to understand each other, let alone locate one another.

We've said several times that interoperability of applications and services is important. So the obvious solution to this mismatch would be to require every Java programmer to stop using RMI and use CORBA instead. However, this isn't going to happen for the following reasons:

CORBA is difficult to use and developing applications can be time-consuming.

Java programmers don't want to have to learn CORBA IDL.

RMI is perfectly suited to pure-Java distributed applications and solves the problem of distribution transparency for Java better than CORBA does.

No distributed garbage collection is available in CORBA: Determining which objects are garbage and can be removed from the system is sometimes difficult enough in a single VM, but when objects can be referenced by multiple clients/services in a distributed environment it's a very hard problem to solve in general and particularly if your distributed application uses different languages that might not support asynchronous garbage collection.

So the "obvious" solution isn't going to work after all!

However, IIOP is the *de facto* network standard for distributed invocations. This leaves us with the problem of how to integrate IIOP with RMI. Fortunately the OMG and Sun Microsystems worked hard on this problem and came up with the following solution: *RMI over IIOP.*

In a nutshell, RMI over IIOP replaces the JRMP protocol that RMI uses with IIOP. Importantly, this replacement is completely transparent to users. At the client side, the client RMI stub generates an IIOP-specific invocation by contacting a local ORB for server communication. On the server side, the ORB receives the IIOP request. In fact, the ORB can't distinguish between an IIOP request and one generated by a "pure" CORBA client, and it passes the request to the server RMI stub that can then invoke the real object method. This flow of events is illustrated in Figure 14-12.

Note   Although we've talked about Java clients and Java servers in the preceding example, because we are using IIOP we could just as easily replace the client with a CORBA application or the server with a legacy CORBA component written in a completely different language. That's the beauty of using IIOP: We don't need to care about the implementation at either end of the protocol.

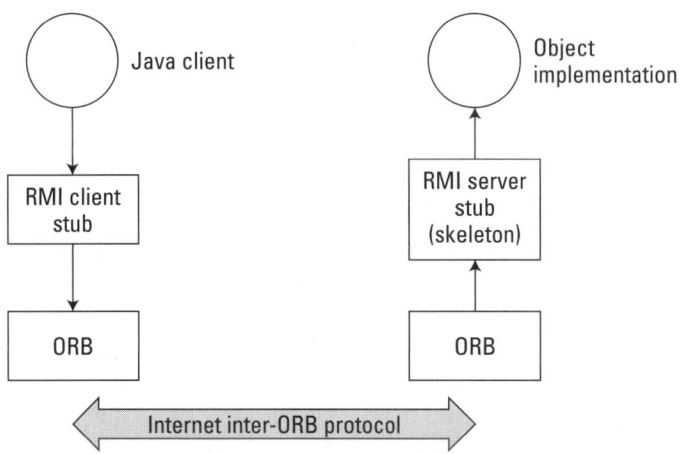

Figure 14-12: How RMI over IIOP works at the architecture level

Transaction interoperability

Transaction interoperability between application-server implementations is achieved by means of the OMGs Object Transaction Service (OTS) specification. Unfortunately, transaction interoperability is still only an optional feature of J2EE, so you should be careful when choosing a vendor if interoperability is one of your requirements.

As you saw in Chapter 10, the Java Transaction Service (JTS) is simply a mapping into the Java language of the OTS. The OTS defines the roles and relationships for a transaction-service implementation, such as the relationship between a coordinator and participant, and the format of the transaction context. That context is an instance of the `CosTransactions::PropagationContext` structure, which, in the case of J2EE, is implicitly propagated with remote-method invocations. Containers that support transaction interoperability must be able to produce and consume JTS contexts in IIOP messages.

Note   Although the JTS protocol is required for interoperability, an implementation need not conform to the OTS interfaces. Only the on-the-wire format is required to conform, and as with RMI over IIOP, how the end-users in the protocol care to implement the actual services is up to them.

The Naming specification

You saw earlier in the section "Naming objects" how the CORBA CosNaming specification has been incorporated within the EJB specification to achieve interoperable naming. In addition, the naming service must follow all the requirements laid out in the CORBA Interoperable Name Service (INS) specification. Security of the service access is achieved by means of mandating that the implementation support the CORBA security-interoperability protocol.

Secure interoperability

The secure-interoperability requirements for the latest versions of EJB are based on Conformance Level 0 of the OMGs Common Secure Interoperability version 2 (CSIv2) Final Available specification. All EJBs, Web-client containers, and application-client containers must support all requirements of Conformance Level 0.

The Notification Service

The CORBA Event Service provides support for the producer/consumer pattern of interactions. It supports a channel that gives the producer the ability to create events for any valid IDL or data type, and that gives the consumers the ability to receive these events. The Notification Service extends the Event Service and adds several new kinds of functionality.

There are many successful cases of companies using implementations of the notification service either directly or embedded within other applications. However, with the advent of J2EE and JMS users have begun to move away from CORBA for some of their messaging requirements. Instead, many people see the notification service, with its robustness, as providing a backbone for messaging interaction within the enterprise, with JMS implementations "feeding off" it. This being the case, a lot of work has recently been done on JMS notification-service interoperation.

The Activity Service

You saw in Chapter 10 how traditional transaction semantics are not sufficient for all cases and how J2EE is attempting to address this problem through the *Activity Service*. The Activity Service is a framework for supporting a wide range of extended transaction models. Its specification was originally developed within the OMG and has been successful there. Watch out for this service, as we believe its incorporation into J2EE represents a significant advancement over other component models.

So, you've seen the EJB architecture and the various services it offers to bean developers. There are a lot of variables involved and as with anything, if not used properly it's very easy to end up with something that either doesn't work as expected or is less than optimal. In the following sections we'll try to give you some hints and tips on what pitfalls to look out for and how to avoid them when building your EJB applications.

Performance and Scalability Issues

Application performance is important both to a developer and to an end user. In critical areas such as business-to-business interactions it can be the deciding factor between competing systems. In addition, while equipment costs are coming down, so too are profit margins; hence, businesses are looking to support more users with less equipment. In this section we will examine the following components in an enterprise application and how they may affect performance and scalability:

✦ Application-server availability strategies

✦ Transaction concerns

✦ The threading model

✦ Performance-analysis tools

 Note We will obviously only be able to talk about general aspects of application servers. It would be advisable to check out any additional features your favorite implementation might provide.

Application-server availability strategies

We saw in Chapter 10 how transactions can guarantee consistency of application data in the presence of concurrent users and failures. By using transactions, you can make sure that your data isn't corrupted should a machine failure occur in the middle of an update. However, transactions can't guarantee forward progress. A persistent machine failure, for example, will mean that a transaction will be forced to rollback, but each retried transaction will simply rollback too.

It is possible to improve the probability of forward progress by increasing the availability of an application's objects by replicating them on several machines or application servers and managing them through replica-consistency protocols. The failure of a subset of these replicas may then be masked, allowing the application to continue.

In addition, what happens when all of the really important beans are contained in a single application server that is being accessed by hundreds or even thousands of clients simultaneously? Even the most powerful of machines can only support a finite number of client requests before you would start to see deterioration in performance. Distribution client requests (processing load) across a number of machines and application servers would help to reduce the load on a single instance and so allow you to cope with the requests without affecting the overall performance of your application.

Unfortunately although there have been a lot of standardization efforts in areas such as transactions, concurrency control etc. there has been very little in the area of load balancing or replication. There's been even less attention paid to this in J2EE; at the time of writing there is some effort underway in the Java Community Process, but it could be quite a while before this comes to fruition. So, although you'll find vendors who offer solutions to these problems, you won't find any that are standards compliant: there simply aren't any standards!

What we'll outline in the next few sections are some of the ways in which current vendors try to provide ways of load balancing requests or replicating application servers. However, although no standards exist, this is an active area for vendor differentiation and solutions change frequently. As such, all we can do is try to offer some insight into the types of solutions you're likely to find. You should obviously be aware of vendor lock-in too!

Commercial application servers make use of multiple application-server instances deployed over a cluster of machines. In this configuration, specialist router hardware masks server failures and relies on propriety replication mechanisms of database vendors for database availability. In order to improve availability by masking individual machine failures, application servers are typically deployed over a cluster of machines. A locally distributed cluster or set of machines with the illusion of a single IP address and that is capable of working as a single unit to host a Web site provides a practical way of scaling up processing power and sharing the load at a given site.

Load distribution

Commercially available application-server clusters typically rely on a specially designed gateway router to distribute the load using a mechanism known as *network address translation* (NAT). The mechanism operates by editing the IP headers of packets to change the destination address before the IP-to-host-address translation is performed. Similarly, return packets are edited to change their source IP address. Such translations can be performed on a per-session basis so that all IP packets corresponding to a particular session are consistently redirected.

Load distribution can also be performed by means of a group communication system; The JBoss open-source application server has such a mechanism. In this scheme multiple application server instances are formed into a group so that requests sent to one instance are seen by all instances.

The two market leaders in the application-server space, WebSphere from IBM and WebLogic from BEA, have very similar approaches to clustering. They typically use clustering for the following reasons:

✦ **Scalability** — The proposed configuration should allow the overall system to service more clients than the basic single-machine configuration. Ideally, it should be possible to service any given load simply by adding the appropriate number of machines.

✦ **Load-balancing** — The proposed configurations should ensure that each machine or server in the configuration processes a fair share of the overall client load that is being processed by the system as a whole. Furthermore, if the total load changes over time, the system should adapt itself to maintain this load-balancing property.

✦ **Fail-over** — If any one machine or server in the system fails for any reason, the system should continue to operate with the remaining servers. The load-balancing property should ensure that the client load is redistributed to the remaining servers, each of which will process a slightly higher percentage of the total load than before. *Transparent fail-over,* whereby failures are masked from a client, which minimally might need to retransmit the current request, is ideal. However, it is rarely achievable with the current technology, for reasons outlined later in this section. The important consideration in current systems is that progress is possible eventually and in less time than would be the case if only a single machine were used.

Transparent fail-over

Transparent fail-over is easy to achieve for stateless session beans. This is because any server in the cluster can service any request and if a client makes multiple requests in succession, each may well be serviced by a different server. Fail-over support in this case is trivial because if the server fails while it is doing work for the client, the client will get an exceptional response and will have to retransmit the request.

The situation is more complicated for a stateful session, in which the same server instance must be used for requests from the client, and in which the server failure will lead to loss of state. The approach adopted in some commercial systems to avoid loss of state is to use the stateless session approach with a twist. The stateful session bean is required to serialize its state to a datastore at the end of each client request; the subsequent bean instance in the other server must then de-serialize the state before servicing the new request. Obviously, the servers must have access to the same datastore.

The replication of the datastore is assumed to be the domain of the datastore itself. This way, some of the functionality available for stateless sessions can be regained. However, even in this case, a failure during serialization of the bean's state (which could result in the state being corrupted) is not addressed. A more serious limitation also exists: Transactions cannot be supported. If transactional access to a bean is used, the same server instance must be used for every invocation on that bean.

Transaction concerns

Before using transactions, think about whether you really need them. This may sound obvious, but we have seen many enterprise applications in which transactions were used "just in case," even though they weren't necessary. The functionality provided by transactions does not come at zero cost. Atomicity, isolation, and durability all require additional resources, CPU cycles, or disk accesses that can quickly bring an application's performance to its knees.

Where does the overhead come from? Just to give you an idea, we've outlined these four potential bottlenecks:

> Before a transaction can commit, it must execute the two-phase commit protocol to reach consensus between participants; for *n* participants, this obviously requires $2n$ remote invocations!

Whenever a remote invocation is made within a transaction, the transaction context must be propagated from the caller to the entity being called. The context represents additional information that must be carried and can, in some circumstances, be quite large.

Some transaction-service implementations do not support interposition. Without it, distributed transactions among many services can be costly. (See Chapter 10 for details.)

In order to make a particular transaction tolerate failures, the transaction coordinator must persist certain information to durable storage in the transaction log. Not only can the amount of information be large, but the coordinator must also wait for the durable store to indicate that it has successfully written the data. For example, if the store is based on the file system, the file must be sync-ed.

All right, the fact that transactions make your beans tolerant of concurrent access by users and certain types of failures sounds cool and useful. But you need to ask yourself whether your beans need transactions. The fact that the EJB threading model limits the number of threads accessing a bean to one removes some isolation problems. However, this is the case only if your beans are used in a "one-shot" way. BMP or CMP will give you persistence without requiring a separate transaction service.

We're not trying to prevent you from using transactions. Like many tools, when used correctly they can be invaluable to the reliability and availability of an application.

You should definitely look at your transaction-service implementation and determine what (if any) control it gives you over performance-affecting characteristics such as the size of the transaction log, interposition, and so on.

Threading model

Although EJB is limited to a single-threaded model, this limit obviously only applies at the bean level: Within a bean you can start your own threads or attempt to access some local or remote shared object. Threads should be used with care. Throwing more resources (in this case threads) at a problem does not necessarily help, especially if you inadvertently run up against deadlock or livelock.

In most cases, the default threading model of EJB should be used and capitalized on: For example, if you know that only a single thread can ever access your code, you can remove those pesky `synchronized` statements. Doing so always helps performance!

Pooling of resources

We saw earlier how resource pooling (with entity beans) can be used to improve performance and scalability. Fortunately, the application server typically performs pooling transparently for users. However, the initial size of the pool is often of critical important as is the *quanta* ("chunks") that the container increases or decreases it by: For example, if your pool continually has too few resources for the amount of client requests it receives, then the container may spend more time creating resources than servicing requests. Likewise, if the pool has too many resources in it, then the size of the container (the amount of physical memory is requires) will be larger than required and this will affect performance (the operating system's virtual memory manager may have to swap physical memory to disk in order to service other processes, and disk access is extremely slow compared to main memory).

The kinds of resources that you can typically expect to have equivalent pools include:

✦ Threads

✦ JDBC connections

✦ Enterprise beans

Many commercial application servers allow the size of resource pools and the quanta to be configured at runtime. Obviously one configuration may not be suitable for all use cases, so not only is configuration going to be an iterative process (change it and watch the effect and then revisit your decision if necessary), but it may well have to be done on a per usage basis as well.

Persistence

We have seen how persistence is integral to many aspects of EJBs: transactionality, fail-over support, conversational state and entity beans, for example. Persistence implementations are many and varied, including:

✦ The file system.

✦ A database.

✦ Non-volatile RAM (NVRAM), though even this will have a secondary storage as backup.

✦ Replicated volatile (or non-volatile) RAM. If volatile, then a catastrophic failure of all replicas will result in loss of data unless it is backed to one of the other implementations.

All of the implementations require a hard disk in one form or another. Unfortunately it is a fact that disk access speed is substantially slower than main memory (RAM) access and will continue to remain so for the foreseeable future. As a result, the performance of your application or component can be affected directly by the amount of persistence they use, either directly (for example, entity bean persistence) or indirectly (for instance, the transaction log).

There is obviously very little you can do about other services that you require which also require persistence. However, you should be aware that they exist and can have an effect on your own performance. In addition, you should carefully examine where you are considering using persistence and whether or not it is appropriate. If the answer to the latter is that you do require persistence, then the next questions are as follows:

✦ **Which persistence implementation?** This will obviously depend on your deployment environment and the characteristics of the component that requires persistence. Every system will typically possess a file system, so you won't necessarily need extra expense. However, does your application server support it for CMP? If not, then you will have to look at BMP.

✦ **Does the persistence implementation cache write in memory to try to improve performance and not flush them to disk until the cache is full or explicitly signaled to do so?** If the answer is yes, then the failure characteristics are significantly different. You may well think that your bean has been made persistent and tolerant of failures when in fact it has not (yet).

✦ **How much data do you really need to persist?** The amount of time you spend using the persistence service will depend upon the amount of data you need to read/write from/to disk. Keeping this small will improve performance. So, you should ask yourself how much of the information actually needs to be written and how much of it can be regenerated. For example, a spreadsheet does not need all rows and columns to be persisted, since some (the totals, for example) can be recreated from the other cells.

Security

As with transactions, security tends to be used more often than it is actually required. There are significant performance overheads associated with security and you should carefully examine your requirements before assuming security should be enabled.

CORBA

The OMG's CORBA architecture has become the platform of choice for interoperability for J2EE. Whether implementers actually use a full-blown CORBA ORB or emulate its distribution capabilities to obtain RMI over IIOP is up to the vendor. However, the different approaches can have a significant impact on your application's overall performance and scalability.

As we have seen, distributed invocations are not as fast as local method calls on an object. This is due to the slower nature of the distribution medium (for example, Ethernet) and to the additional costs of marshalling requests and un-marshalling responses. Therefore, using a remote object will be slower than using the same object when it is co-located (located in the same process/JVM as the user).

Now, the necessity for distribution is often unavoidable and the performance hit you take will simply have to be suffered. The relative performance differences between native CORBA and RMI over IIOP are not as significant as it once was.

Paradoxically, the real problem with application server implementations that use a CORBA ORB is to do with local (co-located) invocations! In recent years the OMG has spent a lot of time and effort on improving the architecture's location transparency functionality. With the advent of the Portable Object Adapter (POA) and Portable Interceptors (PI) it is now possible to configure a purely local CORBA application so that it behaves identically to its remote counterpart in terms of:

✦ **Threading** — A separate thread from the user can be used to service the actual object request (this happens implicitly in a distributed environment when the client's thread blocks waiting for the remote server thread to complete its work and return the result).

✦ **Memory management** — When doing remote invocations, parameters are marshaled into and results un-marshaled from buffers that network friendly (so called network byte order).

✦ **Object activation** — In order to use a CORBA object it must be registered with the POA so that remote invocations can be directed to it.

Distribution transparency sounds nice in principle, but in practice it is not needed all of the time. It also imposes a significant overhead on users when most of their objects or services are local: imagine marshalling and un-marshalling all of your requests to a component for a single thread and then multiply this overhead by the actual number of clients you might expect!

If your application server implementation uses an ORB that ensures transparency by default, and none of your objects are remote and none of the underlying system's services are remote (for example, transactions or security), then there is very little point in having the potential overhead shown above. Luckily most ORB implementations allow you to turn off this feature and talk to your objects or services directly (this is a runtime modification and no change is required to the component code or the application server).

Tools

The more you know about the inner workings of your application and the container(s) that host its components, the better armed you will be to tackle issues relating to performance and scalability. In Table 14-2 we mention several tools that you may find invaluable when tracking down bottlenecks.

	Table 14-2
	Performance-analysis tools

Tool	Description
sar	The sar tool is a Un*x system activity–reporter utility that gathers data on the file system, disk I/O, CPU use, swapping, and context-switching.
vmstat	This is a Un*x virtual-memory reporter, useful for obtaining queuing, paging, scheduling, and CPU-use data.
perfmon	The perfmon Windows utility monitors resource use for the CPU, disk I/O, paging, network, threads, and so on.
netstat	This useful utility provides information on network I/O, collisions, errors, and network-related memory use.
taskmgr	The taskmgr Windows utility displays information on active processes, CPU, and memory.
iostat	This Un*x utility displays disk and other I/O statistics.

For example, if you look at Figure 14-13, you'll see a sample from perfmon on Windows. This tool allows you to track statistics on a number of different resources and display only those that interest you. In this example, we're looking at the interrupts that are occurring per second as the processor operates amongst other things. By interpreting the graph, it is possible to determine where your applications are spending a lot of their time.

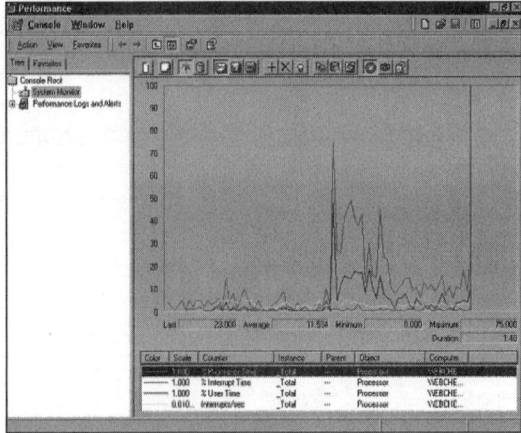

Figure 14-13: Sample output from perfmon.exe

If you use the Windows task manager, then you can examine the individual characteristics of the processes that are executing on a specific machine. For example, if you look at Figure 14-14 you will be able to see the name of each process on the machine, the percentage of the processor (CPU) that it is using, how much of the lifetime of the CPU it has used in total, and the amount of memory it is consuming. This information can be extremely useful in determining things such as memory leaks and performance bottlenecks.

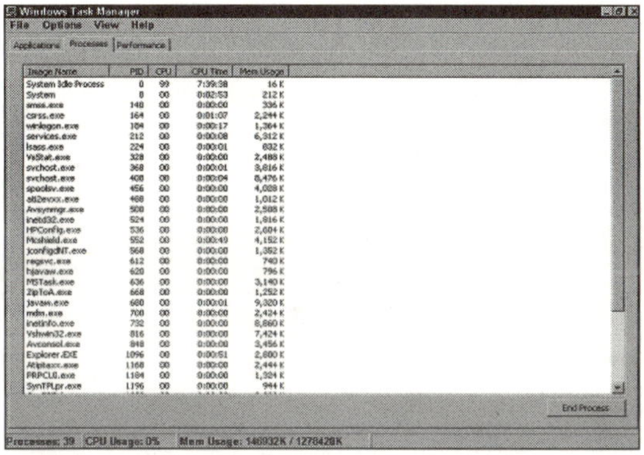

Figure 14-14: Windows task manager output

Summary

In this chapter we looked at the fundamentals behind the EJB architecture. We showed how it breaks down the various roles involved in implementing and deploying an EJB application. Throughout the chapter we considered the issue of application-server portability and how EJB has attempted to achieve this for a number of reasons, not least of which is reducing the chance of vendor lock-in.

We then gave an overview of exactly what an Enterprise JavaBean is, addressing issues such as persistence, transactions, and security. We discussed the various types of Enterprise bean, from the most commonly used, the entity bean, through stateless and stateful session beans and finally the relatively new message-driven beans. Furthermore, we saw how each bean type has been carefully developed to offer a different kind of functionality in order to fulfill different roles for the application developer.

We considered some of the more important issues related to developing beans, such as restrictions on the threading model and disallowance of re-entrant code. We considered the reasons behind these limitations. We then considered the various component services provided by an application server and how they cooperate to provide the fully featured application-server technology that we use today.

An important recent development in the EJB specification has been the adoption for distribution of the OMG's CORBA architecture. This allows Java applications and components to transparently make use of other objects or services written in non-Java languages, and provides a valuable integration point for legacy systems.

Finally, we discussed a number of different aspects of the EJB architecture and the design of application servers that may affect the performance and scalability of your applications. We also gave tips on finding and eliminating performance bottlenecks.

✦   ✦   ✦

Explaining Session Beans and Business Logic

✦ ✦ ✦ ✦

In This Chapter

Introducing EJB
classes and interfaces

Understanding
stateless session
beans

Writing an EJB client

Understanding
stateful session beans

Explaining
passivation and
activation

Implementing the
SessionsSynchroniz-
ation interface

Storing a handle

Choosing between
stateless and stateful
beans

✦ ✦ ✦ ✦

Session beans represent a conversation with a client and are intended to execute *business processes*. A business process can involve searching or ordering a book online, booking a flight, checking your bank balance, or paying your credit-card bill online, for example.

A session bean may be stateful or stateless. *Stateless* session beans are generally used to provide a service. They do not store any conversation state between calls. If you invoke a method on a stateless session bean, it executes the method and returns the result without being affected by any previous or subsequent requests. Each call to a stateless bean is considered an independent unit of work; each instance of a stateless bean has no identity and is equivalent to any other instance. Therefore, a small number of instances can serve a large number of users or requests.

Stateful session beans can store a conversation state. Each instance of a stateful session bean is associated with a particular client. They should be considered an extension of the client application. A stateful session bean performs tasks on behalf of the client and maintains state related to that client.

Both types of session beans are *non-persistent*. This means that they are not stored in any permanent storage. They live in the memory, and if the server or the machine dies, the beans are destroyed too.

In this chapter we will discuss session beans in detail, covering their lifecycle, what is involved in writing a session bean, and how to invoke a session bean from a client.

Writing a Session EJB

As per the EJB specifications, session beans have the following characteristics:

Execute on behalf of the client

Can be transaction-aware

Update shared data in an underlying database

Do not represent directly shared data in the database, although they may access and update such data

Are relatively short lived

Are removed when the EJB container crashes (the client has to re-establish a new object to continue computation)

If you write your business logic within an enterprise bean you implicitly get lot of services such as location transparency, fail-over, security, and transaction management, to name a few. But all of this doesn't come completely free. To be able to take advantage of it, you are expected to write a little bit more than just your logic. The simplest of the EJBs consists of at least the following four elements:

✦ Home interface

✦ Component interface

✦ Bean class

✦ Deployment descriptor

In the following sections we are going to look into each of these elements in detail, examining what they require and how they are bound to each other.

The home interface

The home interface is responsible for controlling the lifecycle operations of a bean. These include the creation, removal, and location of the bean. The home interface works as the EJB's factory and contains only the signature for the methods. The container provides the implementation of these methods. Enterprise beans that provide a remote client view provide a remote home interface; enterprise beans that provide a local client view provide a local home interface. (See the sidebar "EJB Client Views," later in this chapter, for details.)

The remote home interface

The remote home interface extends the `javax.ejb.EJBHome` interface. A session bean's remote interface must define one or more `create()` methods. Each `create()` method defined in the home interface must match one of the `ejbCreate()` methods defined in the session bean's implementation class. The matching `ejbCreate()` method in the bean class must have the same number and types of arguments as the `create()` method declared in the home interface. The return type for a `create()` method must be the session bean's remote-interface type. The `throws` clause of the `create()` method must throw the `javax.ejb.CreateException`.

The following code illustrates the remote home interface for the FlightService bean (defined later in the chapter):

```
public interface FlightServiceHome extends EJBHome {
    public FlightService create() throws CreateException,
                                          RemoteException;
            }
```

The local home interface

The local home interface extends the `javax.ejb.EJBLocalHome` interface. Like a remote home interface, a local interface must define one or more `create()` methods. The return type for a `create()` method declared in the local home interface must be the session bean's local interface. The `throws` clause of the `create()` method must include the `javax.ejb.CreateException`.

The following code snippet shows a sample of local home interface:

```
public interface FlightServiceLocalHome extends EJBLocalHome {
    public FlightService create() throws CreateException;
}
```

As we will explore later in the section 'Writing an EJB client', a client locates an enterprise bean's home interface through the standard Java Naming and Directory Interface (JNDI) API.

The component interface

When the client calls the `create()` method on the home interface, it will get a reference to the component interface that implements the `EJBObject` or `EJBLocalObject`. The component interface is the element in which the bean provider declares the business methods callable by the client. Like the home interface, the component interface contains only the signature of the methods. The implementation of these methods is provided in the bean class. The component interface can be either a remote interface or a local interface.

Cross-Reference   Both the remote and local interfaces are allowed to have super-interfaces. Therefore, they can use the benefits of inheritance. We will discuss this more in Chapter 24.

The remote interface

The remote interface extends the `javax.ejb.EJBObject` interface. For each method defined in the remote interface a matching method must exist in the session bean's class. The matching method must have the following:

Same name

Same number and types of arguments, and same return type

Same exceptions in the `throws` clause; in addition, each method in the remote interface must include the `java.rmi.RemoteException` in the `throws` clause

The following code segment illustrates a remote interface:

```
public interface FlightService extends EJBObject {
    public FlightData[] searchFlights(String origin,
                          String destination,
                          String departureDate,
                          String arrivalDate)
                          throws RemoteException;
    public boolean bookFlight(FlightData flightData,
    PassengerData passengerData) throws RemoteException;
```

The local interface

The local interface extends the `javax.ejb.EJBLocalObject` interface. Unlike in the remote interface, the `throws` clause of the methods defined in the local interface does not include the `java.rmi.RemoteException`. For each method defined in the local interface a matching method must exist in the session bean's class. The matching method must have the following:

Same name

Same number and types of arguments, and the same return type

Same exceptions in the `throws` clause

The following code segment illustrates a local interface:

```
public interface FlightServiceLocal extends EJBLocalObject {
    public FlightData[] searchFlights(String origin,
                        String destination,
                        String departureDate,
                        String arrivalDate);
    public boolean bookFlight(FlightData flightData,
    PassengerData passengerData;
```

EJB Client Views

The client view of an Enterprise JavaBean is represented by the home and component interfaces. Prior to the EJB 2.0 release, the specifications listed only the *remote client view.* In the remote view, the client makes no assumption about the location of the EJB. A client running in the same JVM as the bean uses the same API as a client running in a different JVM on the same machine or a different one. The remote view does provide location transparency to the client but behind the scenes—the container has to marshal and unmarshal the data for each client request. Even though the client and the EJB are co-located on the same server, the container still has to have the overhead for each client request.

EJB 2.0 specifications introduced the concept of the *local client view.* The local client view assumes that the client and the bean are collocated on the same server. A local client to the bean uses the bean's local interface and local home interface and the arguments and the results are passed by reference.

EJB 2.1 specifications also introduced the Web service endpoint interface for stateless session beans in which Java clients can access the end point using JAX-RPC.

While it is possible to provide more than one client view for a session bean, typically only one will be provided. If the client of your bean is going to be co-located within the same container as the bean, the local client view should be considered as their performance is likely to be better than that of the remote view.

The session bean class

The session bean class must implement the `javax.ejb.SessionBean` interface. The class is instantiated at runtime by the container and thus the class must be defined as public and must not be an abstract class. The bean implementation contains two types of methods, the callback methods required by the `javax.ejb.SessionBean` interface and the business methods declared in the bean's component interface (local or remote). The callback methods are called by the container at appropriate times during the lifecycle of the bean.

The following code snippet shows a sample of a bean class:

```
public class FlightServiceBean implements SessionBean {
    //Callback methods
    public void ejbRemove(){};
    ...

    //Business methods
    public boolean bookFlight(PassengerData passengerData,
                             FlightData flightData) {
...
}
```

The deployment descriptor

Recall that each EJB needs a deployment descriptor. The specifications require that the deployment-descriptor file be named `ejb-jar.xml` and that it be placed under a directory named `META-INF`. The deployment-descriptor file contains several tags used to specify the various components that we discussed in the preceding sections. Figure 15-1 lists the elements that can be specified in the deployment descriptor for a session bean.

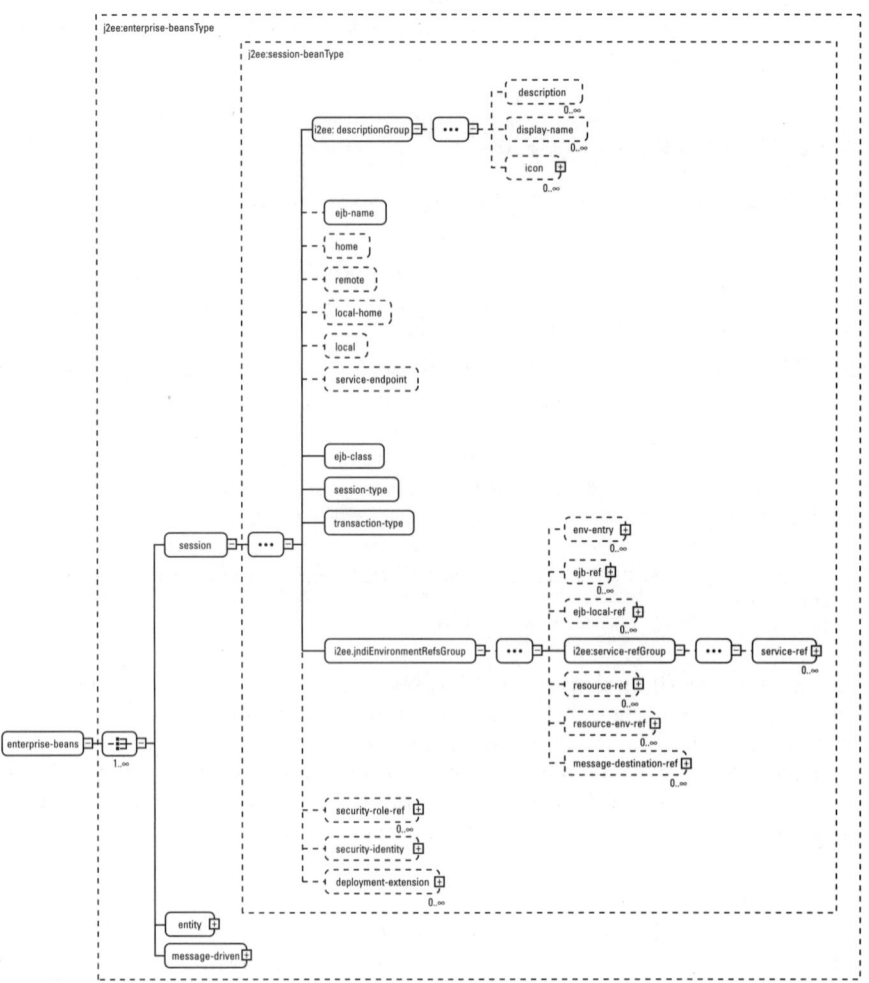

Figure 15-1: Session-bean deployment descriptor

`<home>` / `<local-home>` elements specify the fully classified names of the classes representing the bean's home interface. Similarly `<remote>` / `<local>` elements are used to specify the classes that implement the component interface of the bean.

The `<service-endpoint>` element contains the fully classified name of the enterprise bean's Web service endpoint interface. `<ejb-class>` element specifies the fully classified name of the bean class.

`<session-type>` describes whether the session bean is a stateful session bean or a stateless session bean. The valid values are "`Stateful`" or "`Stateless`." `<transaction-type>` element specifies an enterprise bean's transaction management type. The valid values are "`Bean`" or "`Container`."

`<security-role-ref>` and `<security-identity>` elements are used to restrict access to the bean's methods.

The elements in the `<jndiEnvironmentRefsGroup>` are used to declare references to other resources such as data sources or other enterprise beans.

The stateless session bean

Stateless session beans are often used to perform services that are fairly generic and reusable. These session beans are lightweight, efficient, and relatively easy to develop. They are neither persistent not dedicated to one client, and thus they require few server resources. They supply business logic for one client at a time without keeping track of the state of the client across method invocations. Because stateless session beans do not maintain the conversational state of the client, multiple clients can share the same instance of a bean. However, this means that everything the bean instance needs to know has to be passed via the method's parameters.

The stateless session bean's lifecycle

It is important to understand that the container determines the lifecycle of a stateless session bean. The container is allowed to create and destroy bean instances as it deems appropriate. The stateless session bean has two primary states in its lifecycle: Does Not Exist and Method-Ready Pool. Figure 15-2 shows the states and transitions of a stateless session bean instance.

Does Not Exist
When a bean is in the Does Not Exist state it's not yet instantiated and it does not exist in memory. This is generally the case when the application server first starts up and no call has been made to the bean. The actual behavior of the application is dependent on the implementation and tuning parameters.

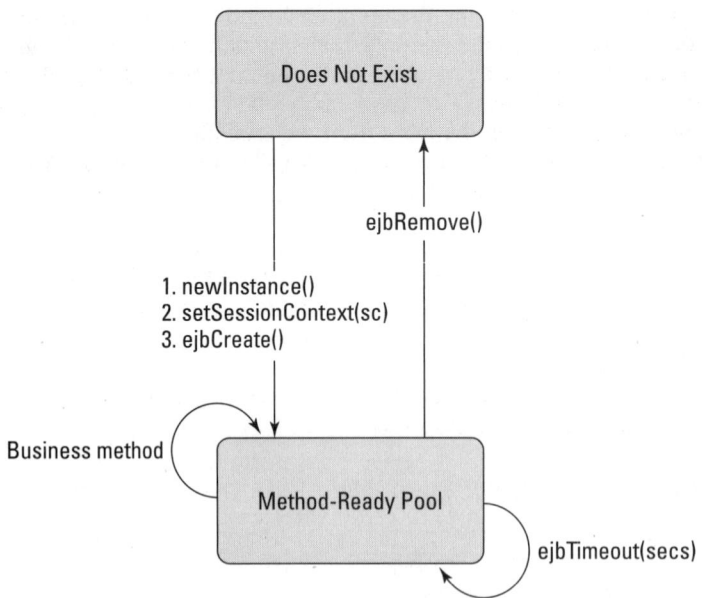

Figure 15-2: Stateless session bean lifecycle

Method-Ready Pool

Stateless bean instances enter the Method-Ready Pool state as the container needs them. When a bean instance goes from the Does Not Exist state to the Method-Ready Pool state, the following three operations are performed on it:

1. **Instantiation** — The container invokes the newInstance() method on the session-bean class to create a new instance. The Class.newInstance method requires a call to the no-argument constructor; because of this, the bean writer should never define constructors in the bean class.

2. setSessionContext — The container calls the setSessionContext method on the bean instance. The container passes the EJBContext as a parameter to this method. The EJBContext can later be used by the bean for various reasons. For instance, the identity of the bean's caller can be determined by calling the SessionContext.getCallerPrincipal() method.

3. **Create** — Finally, the container invokes the method ejbCreate() on the bean instance.

Once an instance is in the Method-Ready Pool state it is ready to service any client requests. When a client calls a business method on a stateless session object or invokes a method on a stateless session bean through its Web-service client view, the container selects an instance from the Method-Ready Pool to serve the request.

During the execution of the method call, the instance is dedicated to the client that invoked the method. Once the instance has finished servicing the client it is disassociated from the request and returned to the Method-Ready Pool state. EJB 2.1 also introduced the concept of Timer Services (explained in Chapter 14). If the bean instance takes a long time in serving the request, the container can call the `ejbTimeout` method on the bean instance. In that case the bean instance will terminate the request and be returned to the pool.

At its own discretion the container may decide to reduce the total size of the Method-Ready Pool. It can do this by calling `ejbRemove()` on the bean instance. When the `ejbRemove()` method is called on the bean instance that instance is removed from the memory and goes from the Method-Ready Pool state to the Does Not Exist state. The bean writer is still responsible for providing the implementation of the `ejbRemove()` method; it is generally used to perform the clean-up of resources, such as closing any open resources.

The ejbCreate() and ejbRemove() methods

The home interface for a stateless session bean is required to have a single `create()` method with no arguments, and the bean class supplies a corresponding `ejbCreate()` method that takes no arguments.

When a client calls the create method on the home interface, the container does not necessarily create an instance of the EJB. It merely needs to return an instance of the remote interface. It can be a brand-new instance or it can be an instance from the pool. The `ejbCreate()` method is invoked only once during the lifecycle of the stateless session bean. Similarly, the `ejbRemove()` method is invoked only once during the lifecycle of the bean. When a client calls the remove method on the home interface the container might not remove the bean instance from the memory. The client's invocation of the home interface's `remove` methods is only an indication to the container that the client no longer needs the bean.

Member variables in stateless session beans

Recall that stateless session beans are not expected to maintain any client state between method calls. Since a stateless session-bean instance is used by several clients, any member variable that stores information (such as user ID or account number) can cause serious problems. Stateless session beans should not store any client-specific state, but they can still store a state if it is common to all clients, such as, for example, if it is a bean-specific state.

For example, you might use a bean to connect to a backend legacy system. Each instance of the bean can maintain a connection with the backend system. When the client makes a call to the bean, it does not care what instance of the bean it receives. Though each instance of the bean has a state (that is, a connection to the legacy system), that state is the same for each client request.

Pooling stateless session bean instances

A stateless session bean instance does not take any arguments during instantiation. Thus, each instance of the stateless session bean is exactly the same as every other instance for the same type of stateless session bean. EJB containers can use this characteristic and pre-create the instances of the stateless session beans. When a client calls a method the container can retrieve the instance from the pool, serve the request, and then return the instance back to the pool. Because of this the EJB container can save the time required to create new instances and is able to concurrently serve a large number of clients.

The Web-service endpoint interface for the stateless session bean

EJB 2.1 specifications defined a new component interface for the stateless session bean — the Web-service endpoint interface. The Web-service endpoint interface is another type of remote client view that extends the `java.rmi.Remote` interface. (See the sidebar "EJB Client Views," earlier in this chapter.) In addition, the Web-service endpoint interface should also follow the requirements for WSDL (Web Services Definition Language) to Java mapping.

 **Cross-Reference**   Refer to Chapter 21 for details about WSDL.

The argument and the return values for all the methods must be of valid types for the JAX-RPC. From the perspective of the client, the existence of the stateless session bean is completely hidden behind the Web-service endpoint that the bean implements. Java clients can access the endpoint interface as a JAX-RPC service using the JAX-RPC client-view APIs. The J2EE Web-service client uses JNDI to look up the service object that implements the `javax.xml.rpc.Service` interface. The client then uses the service object to obtain a stub or proxy that implements the stateless session bean's Web-service endpoint interface.

You now have a good understanding of stateless session beans. It's time to put this knowledge into practice. We will build on our example of Connexia Airlines and add some functionality in the process.

Connexia Airlines Business Case

Our Connexia application enables a user to make a reservation (flight, hotel, and so on). But before making a reservation, the user would like to search for available flights.

We will develop a bean that will help us search for flights that best fit the itinerary of the passenger. For the purpose of our discussion here, we will assume that the client is remote.

FlightServiceHome — The home interface

The home interface of a stateless session bean must declare a single `create()` method with no arguments. The method is required to return a reference to the remote object. The `create()` method is required to include the `CreateException` in the `throws` clause. It will be thrown if any error occurs during the creation of the bean.

The following code segment illustrates the home interface for the `FlightServiceBean`.

```
package com.connexia.ejb.FlightServiceBean
import java.rmi.CreateException;
import java.rmi.RemoteException;
public interface FlightServiceHome extends javax.ejb.EJBHome {
    public FlightService create() throws CreateException,
RemoteException;
}
```

FlightService — The remote interface

In the remote interface of our `FlightServiceBean` we declare two methods, `searchFlights` and `bookFlight`. The `searchFlight` method will be used to search for flights based on the data passed as arguments. Once the user has selected a flight he can use the method `bookFlight` to make a reservation. The remote interface only lists the signature of the methods; the actual implementation is left for the bean class. Each method defined in the remote interface is completely independent of the others. All the data required to process the request are passed through the method arguments.

The following code segment illustrates the remote interface for the `FlightServiceBean`.

```
import java.rmi.RemoteException
import javax.ejb.EJBObject;
public interface FlightService extends EJBObject {

public FlightData[] searchFlights(String origin,
                                  String destination,
                                  String departureDate,
                                  String arrivalDate)
                throws RemoteException;
public boolean bookFlight(FlightData flightData,
                          PassengerData passengerData)
                throws RemoteException;
```

Cross-Reference

`FlightData` **and the other classes are listed in Appendix A.**

FlightServiceBean — The bean class

Recall that stateless session beans are used to provide services that are generic and reusable. The user of our system would like to search for available flights and eventually book one. The `FlightServiceBean` thus is an excellent candidate for a stateless session bean as it provides a reusable service and need not maintain any state during subsequent requests.

The bean class implements the `SessionBean` interface. The bean-class defines all the callback methods that are required by the `SessionBean` interface and the business methods as they are listed in our remote interface.

The following code segment illustrates the bean class for the `FlightServiceBean`.

```
import javax.ejb.*;
public class FlightServiceBean implements SessionBean {

// Callback Methods
public void ejbRemove()
public void ejbActivate()
public void ejbPassivate()
public void setSessionContext(SessionContext sc) {}
public void ejbCreate() throws CreateException {}

// Business Methods


/**
* This method is used to search for flights that meet
* the user criterion for origin, destination, departure
* date and arrival date.
* @param String origin
* @param String destination
* @param String departure date
* @param String arrival date
* @return FlightData[] An array of FlightData objects.
*/
public FlightData[] searchFlights(String origin,
                                  String destination,
                                  String departureDate,
                                  String arrivalDate) {

...
// Code implementation
...

}


/**
* This method is used to reserve flight for the
* passenger based on the passed arguments.
* @param PassengerData Passenger Information.
```

```
* @param FlightData    Flight Information.
* @return boolean  true if the reservation was successful
*/
public boolean bookFlight(PassengerData  passengerData,
                          FlightData flightData) {
...
// Code implementation
...
}
```

For the sake of simplicity the preceding example doesn't include the actual implementation of the business logic. As our focus here is to illustrate the classes and interfaces required to write a session bean, we are going to skip the logic required to search and book the user's flight.

The ejb-jar.xml deployment descriptor

The deployment descriptor is comprised of information used by the EJB compiler and by the container at runtime. In the deployment descriptor the `<home>` and `<remote>` tags define the home and remote interfaces, respectively, that we defined earlier. The `<ejb-class>` tag defines the name of the bean class. The `<session-type>` declares that the bean is stateless. And the `<transaction-type>` specifies that the transaction will be managed by the container.

The following is a segment from the deployment descriptor of the FlightServiceBean.

```
<?xml version="1.0"?>
<!DOCTYPE ejb-jar PUBLIC '-//Sun Microsystems, Inc.//DTD Enterprise JavaBeans
2.0//EN' 'http://java.sun.com/dtd/ejb-jar_2_0.dtd'>

<ejb-jar>
<description>Stateless Session Bean Example</description>
<enterprise-beans>
<session>
<ejb-name>FlightServiceBean</ejb-name>
<home>
com.connexia.ejb.FlightServiceBean.FlightServiceHome
</home>
<remote>
com.connexia.ejb.FlightServiceBean.FlightService
</remote>
<ejb-class>
com.connexia.ejb.FlightServiceBean.FlightServiceBean
</ejb-class>
<session-type>Stateless</session-type>
<transaction-type>Container</transaction-type>
</session>
</enterprise-beans>
</ejb-jar>
```

Deployment

Once you have written the preceding components it is time to compile and deploy the bean. This step varies a little by application server although the basic concept remains the same. The home interface, remote interface, bean class, deployment descriptor, and any other files required by your application server are packaged in a `.jar` file. Generally your application server will provide a tool or a script to compile these files, verify the elements in the deployment descriptor, and generate the necessary stubs and skeletons. Once you have completed these steps, deploy the bean on the server. You may have a vendor tool to assist you in doing this; otherwise, simply copy the files into a special directory per your application server's instructions.

Writing an EJB client

For a client, a session object is a non-persistent object that implements some business logic running on the server. The session may provide a remote interface and/or a local interface. A client needs to get a reference to the component interface and execute the method call. Behind the scenes, the call is delegated to the bean-class. Briefly, a client needs to perform the following tasks:

1. Get the initial context.

2. Look up the home interface using the bean's JNDI name. This name is specified in the deployment descriptor for the bean. For more details on JNDI, refer to Chapter 11.

3. Use the home object to get a reference to the component object.

4. Set up the data to call the business method on the bean.

5. Use the component object to call the business method.

6. Remove the bean.

Now that we have a bean up and running and you understand how to write a Java client to invoke it, it's time to put everything together. Figure 15-3 illustrates the `FlightServiceBean` runtime objects.

```
package com.connexia.client;

import java.rmi.RemoteException;
import java.util.Properties;
import javax.ejb.CreateException;
import javax.naming.Context;
import javax.naming.InitialContext;
import javax.naming.NamingException;

import com.connexia.data.FlightData;
import com.connexia.ejb.FlightServiceBean.FlightService;
import com.connexia.ejb.FlightServiceBean.FlightServiceHome;
```

```
public class StatelessBeanClient {
    public static void main(String args[]) {
    Context ctx = null;
    FlightServiceHome home = null;
    FlightService remote = null;
```

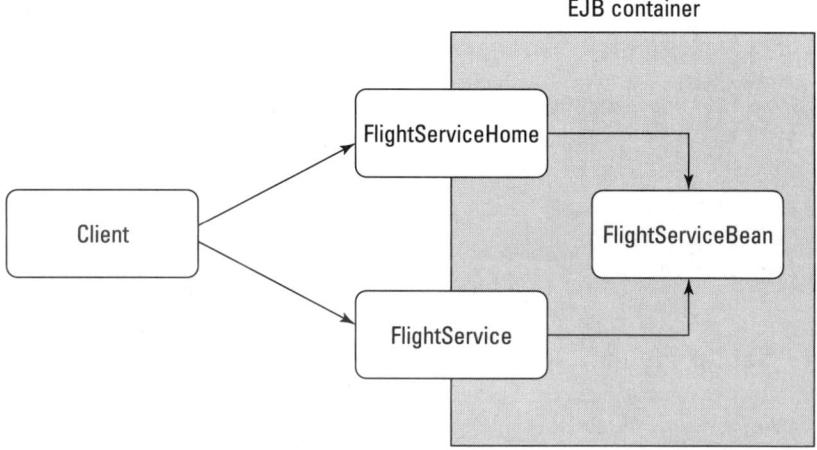

Figure 15-3: Client view

Step 1 – Get the InitialContext

Perform this task as follows:

```
try {
    Properties props = System.getProperties();
    ctx = new InitialContext(props);
} catch (NamingException ne) {
    System.out.println("Exception in getting the context");
    ne.printStackTrace();
    return;
}
```

Step 2 – JNDI Lookup to get the bean's home interface

Perform this task as follows:

```
try {
    home =(FlightServiceHome)    ctx.lookup(
"com.connexia.ejb.FlightServiceBean.FlightServiceHome");
} catch (NamingException ne) {
    System.out.println("Exception in getting the home interface");
    ne.printStackTrace();
    return;
}
```

Step 3 — Get the remote interface of the bean

The client always accesses bean's methods by using the component (remote or local) interface. If there is an error in the bean creation, the client will get a CreateException.

```
try {
      remote = (FlightService) home.create();
} catch(CreateException ce) {
    System.out.println("CreateException while creating the bean
instance");
    ce.printStackTrace();
    return;
} catch (RemoteException re) {
    System.out.println("RemoteException while creating the bean
instance");
    re.printStackTrace();
    return;
}
```

Step 4 — Set up the data to call the bean's business methods

In our example, these values are specified in the code itself. In reality, these values might be retrieved from the screen (html/jsp) or by any other input means.

```
String origin = "Boston";
String destination = "London";
String departureDate = "12152003";
  String arrivalDate = "12182003";
```

Step 5 — Invoke the business method on the bean using the input data from the previous step

The searchFlight method will provide a list of FlightData objects that match the search criterion. Note that any business method invoked on the remote interface can throw a RemoteException.

```
try {
    FlightData[] flightList = remote.searchFlights(origin,
    destination, departureDate, arrivalDate);
if (flightList != null) {
    for (int i = 0; i < flightList.length; i++) {
        System.out.println(flightList[i]);
    }
} else {
    System.out.println("No matching flight found");
}
```

```
    } catch(RemoteException re) {
        System.out.println("Error in calling searchFlights");
        re.printStackTrace();
        return;
    }
```

Step 6 — Remove the bean

As mentioned in the earlier section on stateless session bean lifecycle, the bean instance is moved back to the instance pool.

```
try {
    remote.remove();
} catch (RemoveException re) {
    System.out.println("RemoveExcepton while removing the bean");
    re.printStackTrace();
        return;
} catch (RemoteException e) {
    System.out.println("RemoteException while removing the bean");
    e.printStackTrace();
    return;
    }


} // END main
}
```

Stateful-session-bean model

In theory, no code change is required to convert a stateless session bean into a stateful session bean. Both EJB types must implement the `javax.ejb.SessionBean` interface and have the same basic requirements for the home and component interfaces. The only change required is in the deployment descriptor associated with the EJB. However, the stateful programming model is quite different from the stateless one. The biggest difference is that each stateful session bean is associated with a particular client. When a client calls the create method on the home interface of the EJB, the container instantiates a new instance and associates it with the client. In the case of a stateless session bean, the container merely selects an instance from the pool. Stateful session beans do not use the concept of instance pooling. As depicted in Figure 15-4, stateful session beans are dedicated to one client for their entire lives, and no swapping or pooling of instances takes place.

If the client makes multiple business-method calls on the bean's component (remote or local) interface, the container must dispatch the calls to the same instance of the bean.

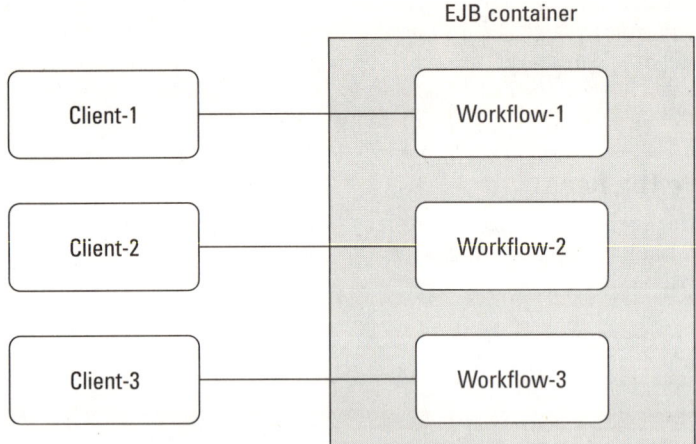

Figure 15-4: Stateful-session-bean model

The lifecycle of the stateful session bean

Figure 15-5 illustrates the lifecycle of the stateful session bean, which has the three following states:

✦ Does Not Exist

✦ Method-Ready

✦ Passivated

The Does Not Exist state

This state is similar to its counterpart in the stateless session bean. When a stateful bean instance is in the Does Not Exist state, it has not been instantiated yet and does not exist in the memory.

The Method-Ready state

When a client invokes the `create()` method on the home interface of a stateful session bean, the container does the following:

1. Invokes `newInstance()` on the bean class and creates a new instance.

2. Invokes `setSessionContext()` on the instance and passes it the reference to the `SessionContext`. At this point the bean instance is assigned to its EJB Object.

3. Invokes the `ejbCreate()` method on the instance that matches the `create()` method invoked by the client. Unlike the stateless session bean, the stateful session bean can have multiple create methods, each with a different set of arguments. Once `ejbCreate()` is completed the container returns the EJB object's reference to the client. The instance is not ready to service any business method invoked by the client.

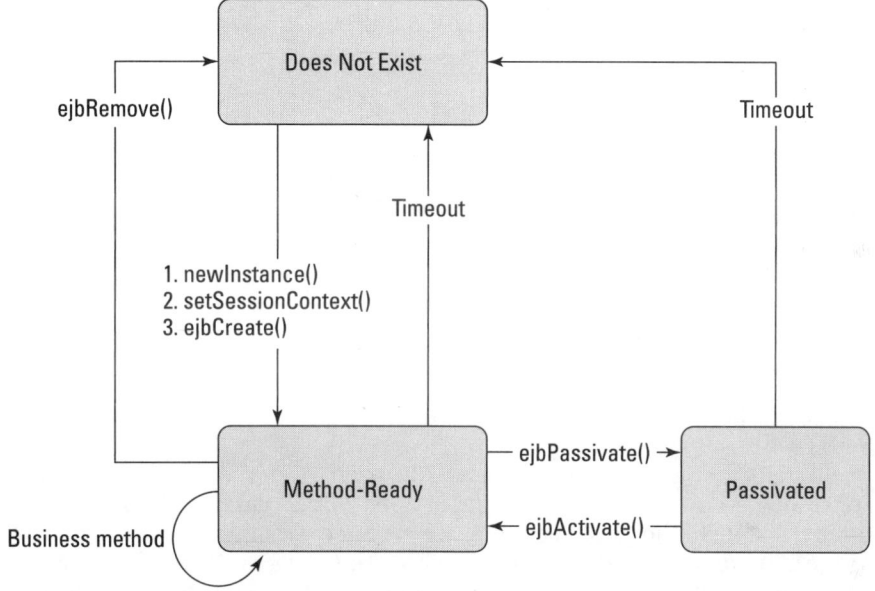

Figure 15-5: Stateful-session-bean lifecycle.

From the Method-Ready state the bean can either transfer to the Does Not Exist state or to the Passivated state. The bean can enter the Does Not Exist state under the following conditions:

The client application calls the remove method on the client interface (it translates to the `ejbRemove()` invocation on the bean instance).

OR

The container decides to remove the bean either to preserve resources or because the bean instance has timed out. When no client activity exists for the particular bean instance, it becomes eligible for passivation.

Passivation is the process by which the application server removes the bean from memory while preserving the EJB's state on disk.

The passivated state

If a bean instance has not been used for a long time the container may decide to passivate it. In the passivated state, the bean's state is stored in a secondary storage area such as a disk and the bean instance itself is removed from memory. If the client calls a method on this bean, the container activates the bean when the bean instance is back in the Method-Ready state and serves the request.

Let's take a look at the concepts of passivation and activation in more detail and at how they can be used with stateful session beans.

Passivation and activation

In the stateful programming model, the state of the client is stored in the bean as member variables, and each client has its own associated instance of bean. The number of clients for a large enterprise application can be high and it is not always feasible to store a corresponding instance of the bean in memory. To help deal with this issue, the specifications provide the concepts of passivation and activation. Swapping out a bean out of the memory is called passivation. Before a passivated bean can be used again, the container has to activate the instance. That process is called activation.

Passivation

The container may passivate the bean to preserve resources or based on the timeout parameters specified by the bean provider. During passivation the container stores the state of the bean, including the instance variables, on a secondary storage area and removes the bean instance from the memory. Before passivating the bean the container invokes the method `ejbPassivate()`, alerting the bean instance that it about to enter the passivated state. This provides time for the bean instance to close any open resources and to do other cleanup work. The EJB specification requires that the container cannot passivate a stateful session bean while it is in use or participating in a transaction.

Activation

When a client calls a business method on a stateful session bean's component interface, the EJB container needs to locate the corresponding bean instance. If the bean is in memory, it is used to serve the request. If the bean has been passivated, the container first activates the instance — it reads the state from secondary storage and creates an instance in memory. When a bean's conversational state has been successfully restored the `ejbActivate()` method is invoked on the bean instance. This is the EJB's chance to reacquire any resources. Once `ejbActivate()` is complete the bean is back in the Method-Ready state and available to service client requests.

The processes of passivation and activation are transparent to the client. As far as the client is concerned it calls a business method on the bean's component interface and is serviced by a bean instance in memory.

Implementing the Session Synchronization Interface

Session beans can use either the container-managed transactions or the bean-managed transactions. Stateful session beans with container-managed transactions can optionally implement the `javax.ejb.SessionSynchronization` interface. This interface defines an additional set of callback methods that notify the bean of its participation in transactions. This interface contains three methods: `afterBegin()`, `beforeCompletion()` and `afterCompletion(boolean)`. The container calls the `afterBegin()` method when the stateful session bean enters a transaction. The `beforeCompletion()` call occurs before the transaction is prepared to commit. The `afterCompletion(boolean)` method takes a boolean as an argument. If the container passes `true` to `afterCompletion() method`, the transaction was committed; a value of `false` indicates that there was a rollback.

Storing a Handle

The `EJBHome` interface provides a method `getHomeHandle()` to get a handle to the home interface of the bean. Similarly, the `EJBObject` interface supports a method `getHandle()` that can be used to get a handle to the bean's remote interface. A *handle* is basically a persistent reference to an object and can be used to reconstruct the object. A handle extends the `java.io.Serializable` interface and thus it is possible to serialize the handle to local storage for later use or to pass it to another client running on a different virtual machine. The handle acts as a ready reference and therefore if the client needs access to the home interface, it can use the `HomeHandle.getEJBHome()` method and does not need to do the JNDI lookup. Similarly, if the client application requires a reference to the remote interface, it does not need to call the `create()` method and can simply use the `Handle.getEJBObject()` method to do the same.

Handles are especially useful for stateful session beans. For example, our user can use our `WorkFlow` bean to make flight reservations and decide to come back later for the hotel reservations. If the user disconnects and comes back later, he can do a JNDI lookup to get the home interface and then invoke the `create()` method to get the bean instance. But in doing so, the user will get a brand new instance of the `WorkFlow` bean. Storing a handle to the remote interface ensures that the user can come back at a later time and get the same instance of the `WorkFlow` bean, which knows about the user's existing reservations.

Keep in mind, though, that the handle is only a reference to an object in memory. Therefore, if the server goes down between the two requests, the handle is of no use.

Collecting Payment Business Case

In the earlier section we developed a stateless session bean, FlightService, that can be used to book a flight. Suppose we also have a bean, PaymentService, that we will use to collect the payment for the flight booking. In a normal operation the client would reserve the flight using the FlightService bean and, if the flight reservation was successful, then use the PaymentService bean to make the payment. Between the two calls (FlightService for booking and PaymentService for payment) the user would expect our server-side components to store the common data — passenger information in this case. Here we develop a stateful session bean, WorkFlow, that will do this for us.

WorkFlowHome — The home interface

Like our stateless bean from earlier in the chapter, the home interface of the stateful session bean extends from the EJBHome interface. But unlike the stateless bean, the stateful bean can define a create method that can take arguments. Thus we can pass an identity to our stateful bean at the time of creation, and the bean will maintain it across several business-method calls. In the following case we are going to pass the information about the passenger:

```
package com.connexia.ejb.WorkFlowBean

import java.rmi.RemoteException;
import java.rmi.CreateException

public interface WorkFlowHome extends javax.ejb.EJBHome {
    public WorkFlow create(PassengerData passengerData)
                        throws CreateException,RemoteException;
}
```

WorkFlow — The remote interface

Again like the FlightService bean of our earlier example, the remote interface is derived from the EJBObject interface. The remote interface specifies only the signature of the methods; implementation is left for the bean class. In the remote interface we declare the following two business methods — submitReservation and submitPayment:

```
package com.connexia.ejb.WorkFlowBean;

import java.rmi.RemoteException;
import javax.ejb.EJBObject;


import com.connexia.data.CreditCardData;
import com.connexia.data.FlightData;
```

```
public interface WorkFlow extends EJBObject {
    public boolean submitReservation(FlightData flightData)
        throws RemoteException;
    public boolean submitPayment(CreditCardData creditCardData)
        throws RemoteException;

} // END WorkFlow
```

WorkFlowBean — The bean class

In our `WorkFlowHome` interface we declared a create method that takes an argument of `PassengerData`. For each `create()` method in our home interface we need to provide an `ejbCreate` method in our bean-class. In the case of a stateful session bean, when the client calls the create method on the home interface, the container in turn calls the `ejbCreate` method on the bean class. Therefore `ejbCreate` can be used to initialize a bean's state. In our case, we assign `PassengerData` passed as an argument, to the bean's member variable `passengerData`. In stateful session beans we can define member variables to store client-specific information.

Our bean provides two business methods, `submitReservation()` and `submitPayment()`. The first method, `submitReservation()`, takes `FlightData` as the argument and invokes the `bookFlight()` method on our stateless session bean to make the flight reservations. You already know from our earlier example how to invoke a method on the bean. In real life, `submitReservation()` method will do more than just a single call to another bean's method. For instance, it can call the `FlightService` bean to make a flight reservation and invoke another bean (say `HotelService`) to make hotel reservations.

Our `submitPayment()` method takes `CreditCardData` as the argument and invokes the `process()` method on the `PaymentService` bean.

Each of the preceding invocations on the `WorkFlow` bean require more than what is passed as an argument to the method call. They both require `PassengerData`, which is not supplied in the request. That is the beauty of the stateful programming model. We passed `PassengerData` at the creation of the bean and the bean is smart enough to store the information during its lifecycle.

Listing 15-1 illustrates the `WorkFlowBean` class.

Listing 15-1: **WorkFlowBean class**

```
package com.connexia.ejb.WorkFlowBean;

import java.rmi.RemoteException;
import java.util.Properties;
```

Continued

Listing 15-1 *(continued)*

```java
import javax.ejb.CreateException;
import javax.ejb.SessionBean;
import javax.ejb.SessionContext;
import javax.naming.Context;
import javax.naming.NamingException;
import com.connexia.data.CreditCardData;
import com.connexia.data.PassengerData;
import com.connexia.data.FlightData;
import com.connexia.ejb.FlightServiceBean.FlightService;
import com.connexia.ejb.FlightServiceBean.FlightServiceHome;

public class WorkFlowBean implements SessionBean {

// Callback methods. In this code snippet, these are defined as
empty methods. But they can be used to get and remove other
resources as explained in the section on stateful session bean
lifecycle.

    public void ejbActivate() {}
    public void ejbRemove() {}
    public void ejbPassivate() {}
    public void setSessionContext(SessionContext ctx) {}

// Member variable of the bean class. It is used to store
client information between method calls.

private PassengerData  passengerData= null;


/**
* This method matches the create method defined in the
* home interface that accepts PassengerData. It stores
* PassengerData in the bean member variable for future
* method calls.
* @param PassengerData Passenger information.
* @throws CreateException
*/

public void ejbCreate(PassengerData passengerData)
                    throws CreateException {
    System.out.println(" + ejbCreate ");
    this.passengerData = passengerData;
    System.out.println(" - ejbCreate ");
}


/* This method invokes the bookFlight method on the
* FlightService bean to reserve the flight.
* @param FlightData
* @return Boolean true if the reservation is successful.
```

```
* @see FlightService
*/
public boolean submitReservation(FlightData flightData) {
   System.out.println(" + submitReservation");
   boolean result = false;
   Context ctx = null;
   FlightServiceHome home = null;
   FlightService remote = null;

   // Get the initial context
   try {
           Properties props = System.getProperties();
     ctx = new InitialContext(props);
   } catch (NamingException ne) {
       System.out.println("Exception in getting the context");
       ne.printStackTrace();
       return;
   }

    // Get the home interface
   try {
      home =
      (FlightServiceHome)
ctx.lookup(com.connexia.ejb.FlightServiceBean.FlightServiceHome
");
              } catch (NamingException ne) {
                  System.out.println("Exception in getting the
home");
                  ne.printStackTrace();
                  return;
              }

    // Get the remote interface
    try {
     remote = (FlightService) home.create();
    } catch (CreateException ce) {
       System.out.println("CreateException while creating");
       ce.printStackTrace();
       return;
    }  catch (RemoteException re) {
       System.out.println("RemoteException while creating");
       re.printStackTrace();
       return;
    }

    // Call the business method on the bean's remote interface

try {
           result = remote.bookFlight(flightData, passengerData);
} catch (RemoteException e) {
```

Continued

Listing 15-1 *(continued)*

```
        System.out.println("RemoteExcepton");
        e.printStackTrace();
        return;
    }
    System.out.println(" - submitReservation ");
    return result;
}


/**
* Method submitPayment.
* This method is used to collect the credit card
* payment. It retrieves passenger information
* from the bean's member variable that was populated
* by ejbCreate(). It uses PaymentService bean
* services to collect the payment.
* @param CreditCardData
* @return boolean true if the operation is successful.
* @see PaymentService
*/
public boolean submitPayment(CreditCardData creditCardData) {
    System.out.println(" + submitPayment ");
    boolean result = false;
    Context ctx = null;
    PaymentServiceHome home = null;
    PaymentService remote = null;


        // Get the initial context
    try {
        Properties props = System.getProperties();
        Context ctx = new InitialContext(props);
    } catch (NamingException ne) {
        System.out.println("Exception in getting the context");
        ne.printStackTrace();
        return;
    }


        // Get the home interface
    try {
        home =
        (PaymentServiceHome)
ctx.lookup("com.connexia.ejb.PaymentServiceBean.PaymentServiceH
ome");
            } catch (NamingException ne) {
```

```
                        System.out.println("Exception in getting the
        home");
                        ne.printStackTrace();
                        return;
                }

        // Get the remote interface
        try {
          remote = (PaymentService) home.create();
        } catch (CreateException ce) {
            System.out.println("CreateException while creating");
            ce.printStackTrace();
            return;
        }   catch (RemoteException re) {
            System.out.println("RemoteException while creating");
            re.printStackTrace();
            return;
        }


        // Call the business method on the bean's remote interface
        result = remote.process(creditCardData, passengerData);
    } catch (RemoteException e) {
        System.out.println("RemoteExcepton");
        e.printStackTrace();
    }
    System.out.println(" - submitPayment ");
    return result;
}
```

Choosing between Stateless and Stateful Beans

Now that you have a good understanding of stateless and stateful beans, you might be wondering how to choose between them. This choice should be dictated by your business requirements. If your business process requires several invocations with common information to be shared, the stateful model fits nicely. If your business requirement is to provide services that are independent enough of each other, the stateless paradigm is better. In a real-world situation you would probably use a combination of both models. One common approach is to use stateless beans to provide services and stateful beans to control the process flow between the stateless bean's invocations.

The stateless model

The stateless model provides two big advantages. The first is the ability to scale. With stateless beans the container is able to pool and reuse beans easily. Stateless beans thus require fewer resources and are more efficient than stateful beans. The second advantage is fault tolerance.

However, the stateless model has some disadvantages too. The biggest one is the requirement to pass all client-specific data for each method invocation. Stateless beans have no means of remembering data between calls, so even common information such as PassengerData in the earlier stateful session bean example must be supplied anew with every request. One way to do this is to pass the information as method arguments. This leads to performance degradation, however, as the data must be marshaled and unmarshaled in the process. The performance impact is directly proportional to the amount of data being passed.

The stateful model

Because the stateful session bean caches client conversation in memory, a bean malfunction owing to the failure of the application server or the machine results in loss of data. In a stateful model all data are maintained by the bean; therefore the failure of the bean essentially means that the user has to start over.

Summary

Session beans are server-side Java components that leverage the standard transaction, fail-over, resource-pooling, and security services provided by the EJB container. In this chapter, we studied the various components that comprise a session bean. We discussed the lifecycle of both stateless and stateful session beans and when to use one versus the other. We considered the several steps required to invoke a method on the session bean. We also built on the Connexia Airlines business case and created a stateless and a stateful session bean to implement its business logic.

✦   ✦   ✦

Working with Entity Beans

✦ ✦ ✦ ✦

In This Chapter

Understanding entity beans

Reviewing classes and interfaces of entity beans

Explaining container-managed persistence

Working with EJB QL

Explaining bean-managed persistence

Defining exceptions

✦ ✦ ✦ ✦

In this chapter, we will study the lifecycle of an entity bean. We will also examine the several callback methods that are supported by the entity-container contract. We will explain the container-managed persistence (CMP) model and how it defines the persistence and relationship fields. To illustrate the CMP model, we will develop a `PassengerBean` and later enhance it to include relationships. We will write a client to `PassengerBean` to demonstrate how to access an entity bean. Finally, we will examine the bean-managed persistence (BMP) model and develop the `AircraftBean` bean.

Understanding Entity Beans

In a typical multi-tier e-commerce application, the persistence data are stored in one or more databases. The presentation state is represented by HTML, servlets, and JSPs. Session EJBs provide the business logic between the Web tier and the database. As we discussed in the previous chapter, the session beans can take advantage of the container services, such as transactions, security, and fail-over. Although session beans can use the Java Database Connectivity (JDBC) code to access the database, they cannot directly represent the persistent data. Java is an object-oriented language but databases store data relationally in the form of rows and tables. Moreover, session beans are associated with the client and thus they cannot share state across multiple clients.

Cross-Reference Session beans and JDBC are discussed in Chapters 15 and 18, respectively.

An entity bean represents an object-oriented view of the data. It should be thought of as a single point of access to the data; any client that accesses the data will go through that entity bean. Unlike session beans, which are only accessible to a single client, entity beans are shared among multiple clients. Thus the lifecycle of a session bean is dependent upon the lifecycle of the client, whereas the lifespan of an entity bean is determined by the existence of the data it represents.

Using entity beans instead of accessing the database directly provides you with many advantages. It provides developers with a simple mechanism for accessing and changing data. As you will see later in our `PassengerBean` example, it is much easier to change the address of a passenger by calling `passenger.setAddress()` than by executing an SQL command against the database.

Entity beans come in two basic types, distinguished by how they manage persistence. They are as follows:

✦ **Container-managed persistence beans** — Here, the persistence of the bean's state to the underlying database is automatically managed by the container.

✦ **Bean-managed persistence beans** — Here, the bean provider writes the SQL code to persist the data to the database.

Entity beans have come a long way since their first introduction. The programming model (especially for container-managed persistence, or CMP) has changed drastically between the EJB 1.x and EJB 2.x specifications. Because most of the current application-server vendors support the EJB 2.x specification, we will be discussing only the EJB 2.x programming model in this chapter.

Remote and local client views

Entity beans support both the *remote* and *local client views*. The client view of an entity bean is independent of the implementation of the entity bean and its container. A remote client accesses an entity bean through the entity bean's remote and remote home interfaces. The remote client view of an entity bean is location-independent and thus a client running in the same JVM as an entity-bean instance uses the same API to access the entity bean as a client running in a different JVM on the same or a different machine.

A local client, on the other hand, is co-located with the entity bean and is tightly coupled with the bean. A local client accesses an entity bean through the entity bean's local and local home interfaces. The arguments for the methods of the local interface and the local home interface are passed by reference. Later in this chapter in the section "Introduction to CMR" we will discuss the concept of container-managed relationships for entity beans. In order to be the target of a container-managed relationship, an entity bean with container-managed persistence must provide a local interface.

Entity-bean components

An entity bean is comprised of the following components:

✦ Home interface (remote and/or local)

✦ Component interface (remote and/or local)

✦ Entity-bean class

✦ Primary-key class

✦ Deployment descriptors

In this section we are going to examine each of the components, the methods it provides, and its purpose in the entity-bean model.

Home interface

The home interface of an entity bean is responsible for controlling its lifecycle operations: creating, removing, and locating the bean. It acts as a factory for the entity bean's instances. The home interface may also provide home-business methods, which are not specific to a particular entity-bean object.

Enterprise beans that provide a remote client view also provide a remote home interface; enterprise beans that provide a local client view provide a local home interface. The remote home interface extends the `javax.ejb.EJBHome` interface. The local home interface extends the `javax.ejb.EJBLocalHome` interface.

Let's explore the methods defined in the bean's home interface.

Create

An entity bean's home interface can define zero or more `create()` methods, one for each way to create an entity object. The arguments of the `create()` methods are typically used to initialize the state of the created entity object.

The return type of a `create()` method on the remote home interface is the entity bean's remote interface. The return type of a `create()` method on the local home interface is the entity bean's local interface.

The `throws` clause of every `create()` method on the home interface includes the `javax.ejb.CreateException`. It may include additional application-level exceptions. For the remote home interface, the `throws` clause must include the `javax.rmi.RemoteException` too. (We will explain more about these exceptions in the section "Exceptions" later in this chapter.) In this chapter we will be developing a `PassengerBean` to represent the passenger of Connexia Airlines.

The following code snippet shows the `create()` method for our `PassengerBean`

```
public Passenger create(Integer passengerID,
                        String firstName,
                        String lastName,
                        int age) throws RemoteException,
                                        CreateException
```

Finder methods

An entity bean's home interface defines one or more finder methods, one for each way to find an entity object or collection of entity objects within the home. The arguments of a finder method are used by the entity-bean implementation to locate the requested entity objects. The return type of a finder method is the bean's component interface (remote or local) or a collection of them. Based on their return type, the finder methods can be divided into the two following types:

✦ Single-object finders

✦ Multi-object finders

Single-object finder methods are designed to return at most one entity object. A special type of single-object finder method is the `findByPrimaryKey()` method. Each home-interface definition must include the `findByPrimaryKey()` method. The implementation of this method is provided by the container.

The following code illustrates a single-object finder method for our `PassengerBean`:

```
Passenger findByPrimaryKey(Integer passengerID)
        throws FinderException,
               RemoteException
```

Finder methods that return more than one entity object are known as multi-object finders. The result type of a multi-object finder is a collection of objects implementing the bean's component interface.

The following is an example of a multi-object finder from our `PassengerBean`:

```
java.util.Collection findFirstClassPassengers(String classCode)
                throws FinderException,
                       RemoteException
```

The `throws` clause of every finder method includes the `javax.ejb.Finder Exception`. If the method is defined on the remote home interface it must also include the `java.rmi.RemoteException`.

remove methods

The `remove` method allows the client to remove the entity object. Remember that in the context of entity beans, this means removing the data from the underlying data source. The `throws` clause of every `remove()` method on the home interface must include the `javax.ejb.RemoveException`. For the remote home interface it should also include the `javax.rmi.RemoteException`.

The following code snippet shows the `remove` method for our `PassengerBean`:

```
void remove(Object primaryKey) throws RemoteException,
                                       RemoveException
```

home methods

An entity bean's remote home interface may define one or more `home` methods. These are methods that the bean provider supplies for business logic that is not specific to an entity-bean instance. The arguments of a `home` method are used by the entity-bean implementation in computations that do not depend on a specific entity-bean instance.

The component interface

When the client calls the `create()` method on the home interface, it will get a reference to the component interface that implements the `EJBObject` or `EJBLocalObject`. The *component interface* is the element in which the bean provider declares the business methods that are callable by the client. As with the home interface, the component interface only contains the signature of the methods; the implementation of these methods is provided by the container. The component interface can either be a remote interface or a local interface. Both the remote and local interfaces are allowed to have super-interfaces.

For instance, we might want to provide a business method to upgrade the class of our Connexia Airlines passenger. Here's an example:

```
void upgrade(String class) throws java.rmi.RemoteException
```

The entity-bean class

The *entity-bean class* must implement the `javax.ejb.EntityBean` interface. The class is instantiated at runtime by the container and thus the class must be defined as public with a no-argument constructor. For a container-managed persistence (CMP) bean, the container generates the class and thus it must be `abstract`.

The bean implementation contains these two types of methods:

✦ **Callback methods** — These are required by the `javax.ejb.EntityBean` interface.

✦ **Business methods** — These are declared in the bean's component interface (local or remote).

We will explain more about the callback methods in the section 'The entity container contract' when we discuss the lifecycle of an entity bean.

The primary-key class

Entity beans must include a *primary-key class*. Just like the primary-key column in a relational database, the primary-key class for an entity bean uniquely identifies the bean instance. The primary-key class can be either a Java primitive wrapper type (such as `Integer`, `Long`, or `String`) or a custom primary-key class written by the bean provider. Because the primary key may be used in remote invocations, the type of the primary-key class must be a valid type in RMI-IIOP (Remote Method Invocation — Internet Inter-ORB Protocol). The primary-key class must provide suitable implementations of `public int hashCode()` and `public boolean equals(Object)`.

There are two kinds of primary-key class for entity beans:

    ✦ Single-field primary keys

    ✦ Compound primary keys

Single-field primary keys

A single-field primary key maps to a single persistence field defined in the bean class. The key can be defined as a Java primitive wrapper type such as `Integer` or `String`. However, it cannot be defined as a Java primitive type such as `int`, `char`, or `long`. The finder method on the bean's instance is allowed to return a `Collection` of primary-key instances and `Collection` only works with `Object` types. The specifications also dictate that the primary-key class should implement the `hashCode` and `equals` methods (to verify their uniqueness) and Java primitive types do not have `equals` or `hashCode` method implementations because they are not of type `Object`. Also, the method `EJBObject.getPrimaryKey()` is declared as returning a value of type `Object`, so the primary keys must be `Object`s.

The `<primkey-field>` element in the deployment descriptor is used to specify the container-managed field of the entity-bean class that contains the primary key. The `<prim-key-class>` element of the deployment descriptor specifies the type of the object used for the primary-key class.

Compound primary keys

The bean provider is allowed to create a custom object that maps to multiple fields in the entity-bean class. This approach is used when the bean instance does not have a field that can be used to uniquely identify the bean. The class must be declared public and must have a public no-argument constructor. All the fields in the primary key class must also be declared public.

The fields declared in the primary-key class must be a subset of the container-managed fields in the bean class with matching names and data types. This is required so that the container can match the variables declared in the compound key to the correct CMP fields in the bean class.

Unknown primary keys

The entity-bean provider may choose not to specify the primary-key class or the primary-key fields for an entity bean with container-managed persistence. It will usually do this when the entity bean does not have a natural primary key or when the bean is expected to support multiple persistence data stores. In such instances the entity bean's primary key will be derived from the primary-key type used by the underlying data-storage system. This model allows the bean provider to defer declaring the primary key to the deployer. Using this model, the bean provider can develop an entity bean that can be used with multiple backend systems even if they require different primary-key structures.

In such cases the `findByPrimaryKey` method must be declared to accept the argument type of `java.lang.Object`, and in the deployment descriptor the element `<prim-key-class>` should list `java.lang.Object` as the value.

The deployment descriptor

Each entity bean requires a deployment descriptor (or a set of deployment descriptors, depending on the application-server vendor). It is required by the specifications that the main deployment-descriptor file should be named `ejb-jar.xml` and placed under a directory named `META-INF`. The deployment-descriptor file consists of several tags used to specify the various components that we discussed in the preceding sections. For a CMP bean, it is also used to declare the fields and relationships that need to be persisted. It also defines the security roles for the application, the authentication information, and the access-control list for the various business methods. Figure 16-1 lists the elements that can be specified in the deployment descriptor for an entity bean.

The `<persistence-type>` element is used to specify the persistence type of the entity bean. The valid values are `Container` or `Bean`. The value of `Container` means that it's a container-managed persistence (CMP) bean and that the container will handle the persistence logic. The value of `Bean` indicates bean-managed persistence (BMP) and that the bean provider must provide the persistence logic in the bean class.

The `<cmp-field>` and `<field-name>` elements identify the fields that need to be persisted. (This is only applicable for beans with container-managed persistence.)

The entity-container contract

Each entity-bean class (CMP or BMP) must implement the `EntityBean` interface. The `EntityBean` interface defines a number of callback methods that are called during the lifecycle of the bean. In this section we will explain each of those callback methods. We will also discuss the lifecycle of an entity bean.

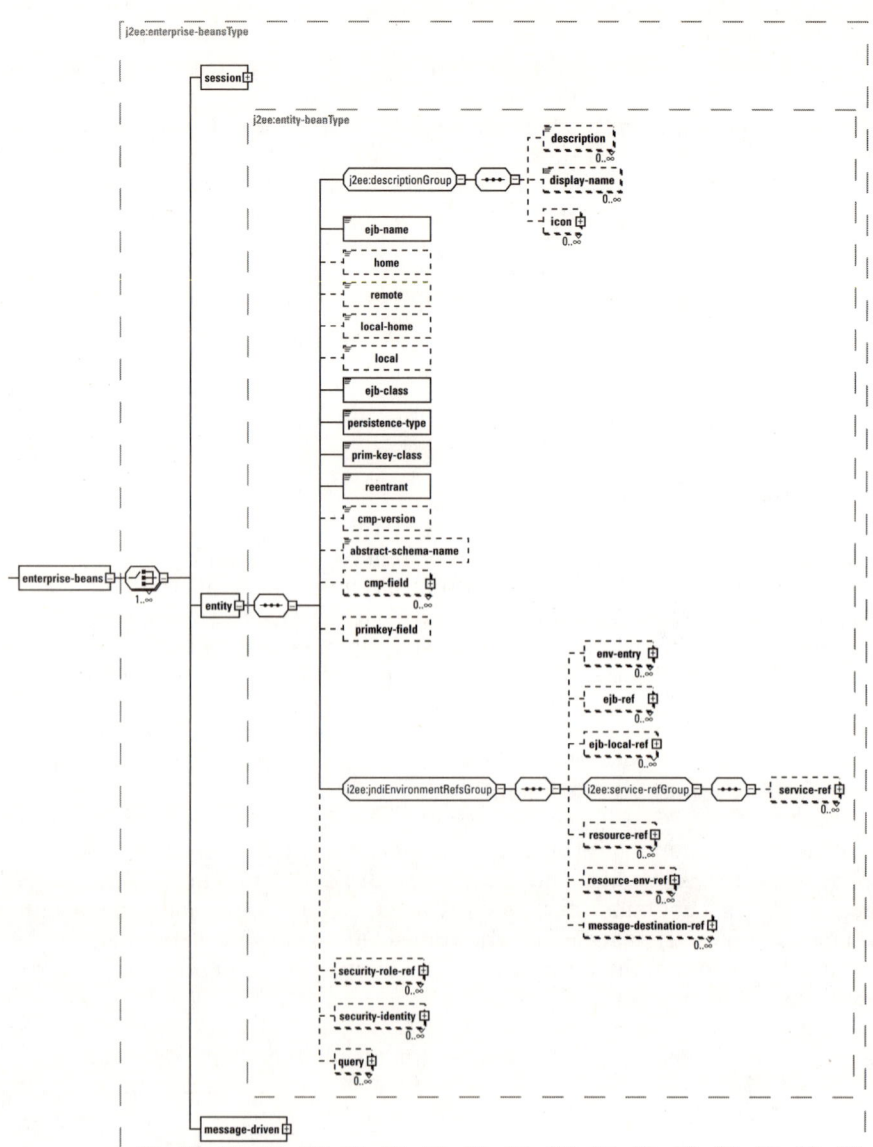

Figure 16-1: Deployment descriptor — entity bean

The following code segment illustrates the `EntityBean` interface and lists the methods that are required by this interface:

```
package javax.ejb;
import java.rmi.RemoteException;
```

```
public interface EntityBean extends EnterpriseBean {
    public abstract void ejbActivate()
            throws EJBException, RemoteException;

    public abstract void ejbLoad()
            throws EJBException, RemoteException;

    public abstract void ejbPassivate()
            throws EJBException, RemoteException;

    public abstract void ejbRemove()
            throws EJBException, RemoteException;

    public abstract void ejbStore()
            throws EJBException, RemoteException;

    public abstract void setEntityContext()
            throws EJBException, RemoteException;

    public abstract void unSetEntityContext ()
            throws EJBException, RemoteException;
```

In addition to the preceding methods, the bean class should also define the `ejbCreate()` and `ejbPostCreate()` methods.

The callback methods

Entity beans are object representation of the data. The main operations that could be performed on the data are as follows:

✦ create

✦ read

✦ update

✦ delete

The EJB specifications provide the equivalent callback methods for each of these operations, as shown here:

```
Create   ejbCreate() and ejbPostCreate()
Read     ejbLoad()
Update   ejbStore()
Delete   ejbRemove()
```

Each callback method is invoked on an entity-bean instance at a specific time during its lifecycle. For a CMP bean most of these methods can be empty implementations, because the state of a CMP bean is automatically persisted by the container. BMP beans, on the other hand, must use these methods to manage the bean's persistent state.

setEntityContext()

The `setEntityContext()` method is the first to be called after the bean instance is instantiated. The container uses this method to pass a reference to the `EntityContext` interface to the entity-bean instance. If the entity-bean instance needs to use the `EntityContext` interface during its lifetime, it must remember the `EntityContext` interface in an instance variable. It is not uncommon for a bean provider to have an implementation like the following in the bean-implementation code:

```
private EntityContext ctx;
public void setEntityContext(EntityContext ctx) {
    this.ctx = ctx;
}
```

The bean instance can take advantage of the `setEntityContext()` method to allocate any resources to be held by the instance for its lifetime. The `setEntity Context()` method is called only once during the life of an instance, so the resources cannot be specific to an entity bean's identity because the instance might be reused during the bean's lifetime. An example of such a resource could be a reference to a mainframe system or to an external resource.

unsetEntityContext()

A container invokes this method before terminating the life of the instance. The invocation of `unsetEntityContext` indicates that the bean instance is about to be evicted from memory by the container. The bean instance can take advantage of the `unsetEntityContext()` method to free any resources obtained in the `setEntityContext()` method.

ejbCreate()

When the client application calls a `create()` method on the bean's home interface, the container invokes a matching `ejbCreate()` method on the entity-bean instance. The bean class can contain definitions for zero or more `ejbCreate()` methods but each one's signature has to match a corresponding `create()` method in the bean's home interface. The `create()` and `ejbCreate()` methods are responsible for initializing the bean instance so that the container can insert a record into the database.

Remember that invoking `create()` for an entity bean is equivalent to inserting a row in the database. This is unlike what happens with session beans, with which calling `create()` simply means instantiating an instance of the bean in the container.

In the CMP model, the `ejbCreate()` method is called before the bean's state is written to the database. Arguments passed to the `ejbCreate()` method are used to initialize the CMP fields of the bean instance. In the BMP model, the bean provider must write some code to insert its data into the database.

Once the record has been inserted into the database, the bean instance is ready to be assigned to an EJB object. Once the bean is assigned to an EJB object, the bean's identity is available and the `ejbPostCreate()` method is invoked.

ejbPostCreate()

For each `ejbCreate()` method is a matching `ejbPostCreate()` method that has the same input parameters but whose return type is `void`. The container invokes the matching `ejbPostCreate()` method on an instance after it has invoked the `ejbCreate()` method with the same arguments.

The `ejbPostCreate()` method gives the bean an opportunity to perform any post-processing tasks prior to servicing the client requests. In the CMP model, it can be used to set the values in the container-managed relationship fields. The primary key is not available during the execution of the `ejbCreate()` method. To maintain referential integrity, the primary key is required if the mapping for the relationship uses it as a foreign key. Thus the assignment of relationships is done in the `ejbPostCreate()` method, where the instance can discover its primary key by calling the `getPrimaryKey()` method on its entity-context object.

ejbActivate()

The container invokes this method on the instance to notify that the entity bean has returned from the pool, is not associated with an EJB object, and has been assigned an identity. The `ejbActivate()` method gives the entity-bean instance the chance to acquire additional resources that it needs while it is in the ready state.

ejbPassivate()

The container invokes this method on an instance when the container decides to disassociate the instance from an entity-object identity and to put the instance back into the pool of available instances. Once in the pool, the instance can be reused by some other EJB object. The `ejbPassivate()` method gives the instance the chance to release any resources that it should not hold while in the pool.

ejbRemove()

When the client application calls the `remove` operation on the entity bean's home or component interface, the container invokes the `ejbRemove()` method on the instance. Remember that invoking `remove()` method on an entity bean is equivalent to deleting a row in the database. This is unlike what happens with session beans, with which calling `remove()` simply means deleting the bean instance.

In the CMP model the container is responsible for deleting the data from the database. The `ejbRemove()` method is called before the container actually deletes the data, which gives the bean provider an opportunity to do any cleanup. In the BMP model the bean provider must write some code to remove data from the database.

Once the record has been inserted into the database the bean instance is ready to be assigned to an EJB object. Once the bean is assigned to an EJB object, the bean's identity is available and the ejbPostCreate() method is invoked.

ejbLoad()

Entity beans are object representation of the data in the persistence-data store. The ejbLoad() method is equivalent to the read functionality. When the container needs to synchronize the state of an entity-bean instance with the bean's state in the database, the container calls the ejbLoad() method.

With container-managed persistence, the EJB container takes care of the synchronization or reading of the data from the database. The ejbLoad() method is called after the bean's state has been loaded, and so the ejbLoad() method can be left blank. However, the ejbLoad() method for CMP can be used to provide some custom logic. For instance, the bean might store the state in a binary or compressed format, and the ejbLoad() method can be used to reformat or decompress the data as appropriate to the bean's state.

With bean-managed persistence, the bean provider is responsible for reading the bean's state from the database. The container is responsible for managing the transaction and invoking the ejbLoad() method at appropriate times, but the bean provider is expected to write the logic to read the data in the ejbLoad() method.

ejbStore()

The ejbStore() method is equivalent to the update 'update' functionality for entity beans. When the container needs to synchronize the state of the entity object in the database with the state of the enterprise bean instance, the container calls the ejbStore() method on the instance.

With container-managed persistence the EJB container takes care of the synchronization or writing the data to the database. The ejbStore() method is called before the entity bean's state is written to the database, so the ejbStore() method can be left blank. But like ejbLoad(), the ejbStore() method provides an opportunity for the CMP bean developer to pre-process the data — for example, by formatting or compressing the data before the synchronization takes place.

With bean-managed persistence the bean provider is responsible for writing the bean's state to the database and must provide the logic to write the data in the ejbStore() method.

ejbFind()

When the client application calls a finder method on the bean's home interface, the container invokes the corresponding ejbFind() method on the bean instance. During the execution of the ejbFind() method the bean instance remains in the pool; the container is not required to move it to the ready state. If the ejbFind() method is declared to return a single primary key, the container creates a single

EJB object reference for the primary key and returns it to the client. If the `ejbFind()` method is declared to return a collection of primary keys, the container creates a collection of EJB-object references for the primary key and returns the collection to the client.

The bean provider does not provide the implementation of the finder methods for CMP beans. Instead, the bean writer provides a query for each finder. Queries are written in the EJB QL language and are included in the deployment descriptor. (We will discuss the EJB QL language in the section on EJB QL later in this chapter.)

ejbHome()

Bean providers can define home methods to perform operations that are not specific to an entity-bean instance. The home methods are defined in the home interface of the bean and each must have a matching `ejbHome()` method defined in the bean class.

When the client application calls the home method on the bean's home interface, the container invokes the corresponding `ejbHome()` method on the bean instance. The `ejbHome()` methods execute on the instance when it's in the *pooled* state, meaning that it does not have any identity. When the home method is called the container simply picks an instance from the instance pool, executes the `ejbHome()` method, and returns the instance to the pool.

ejbSelect()

A `select` method is a query method that is not directly exposed to the client in the home or component interface. The bean provider typically calls a `select` method within a business or home method. We will cover the details of the `select` method in the section on EJB QL later in this chapter.

ejbTimeout()

The container invokes the `ejbTimeout()` method on the instance when a timer with which the bean has been registered expires. The `ejbTimeout()` method notifies the instance of the time-based event and allows the instance to execute the business logic to handle it.

The entity-bean lifecycle

Now that you understand the basic purpose of each of the callback methods, let's explore the lifecycle of an entity bean. The entity bean has the three following states in its lifecycle:

✦ Does not exist

✦ Pooled state

✦ Ready state

Figure 16-2 shows the states and transitions of an entity-bean instance.

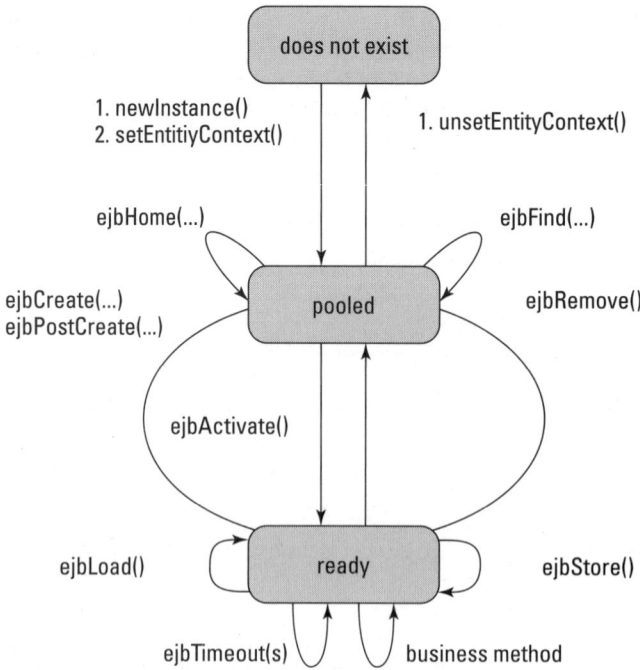

Figure 16-2: Lifecycle of an entity bean

Does not exist
When a bean is in the does-not-exist state, it's not yet instantiated and it does not exist in the memory. This is generally the case when the application server first starts up (the actual behavior is dependent on the implementation and tuning parameters) and no call has been made to the bean.

Pooled
An entity-bean instance's life starts when the container creates the instance by calling the Class.newInstance() method on the bean class. The newInstance() method creates an instance using the default constructor, which has no arguments. The container then invokes the setEntityContext() method to pass the instance a reference to the EntityContext interface. The EntityContext interface allows the instance to invoke services provided by the container and to obtain the information about the caller of a client-invoked method. After the instance has been assigned its context, it is entered into the instance pool.

In the instance pool the bean instance is available to the container as a candidate for servicing client requests. All instances in the pooled state are considered equivalent. None of the instances is assigned to an EJB object, and none has any state.

Therefore, any instance can be assigned by the container to any entity-object identity at the transition to the ready state.

While the instance is in the pooled state, the container may use the instance to execute any of the entity bean's finder or home methods. The instance does not move to the ready state during the execution of a finder method or a home method. Therefore, if a finder method returns an entity bean (or a collection of entity beans), the instance does not move to the ready state until it is accessed directly by the client.

The entity-bean instance can move from the pooled state to the ready state in two ways. The first involves the following process:

1. A client application invokes a `create()` method on the EJB home.

2. An EJB object is created in the container.

3. An entity-bean instance is taken from the instance pool and assigned to the EJB object.

The second occurs when an instance that had been passivated earlier is accessed by the client application. Activation and passivation facilitates resource management by allowing a few bean instances to service many EJB objects. In order to preserve resources, or if the bean instance has not been used for a long time, the container passivates the instance and moves it back to the pool. However, the EJB object maintains its stub connection with the client and thus this process is completely transparent to the client application. When the client application invokes a business method on the EJB object, the container picks an instance from the pool and assigns it to the EJB object. When a bean instance is activated it leaves the pooled state and moves to the ready state. The container calls the callback methods `ejbActivate()` and `ejbLoad()` on the bean instance before the instance is ready to service the client requests.

Ready

When an entity-bean instance is in the ready state the instance is associated with a specific entity-object identity and is ready to accept client requests. While the instance is in the ready state the container can synchronize the state of the instance with the state of the entity in the underlying data source. The container does this by invoking the `ejbActivate()` and `ejbLoad()` callback methods.

A bean can move from the ready state to the pooled state in one of the following three ways:

✦ Passivation

✦ Removal

✦ Rollback

Passivation

Recall that the container might decide to passivate the bean to preserve resources. While doing so it invokes the `ejbStore()` and `ejbPassivate()` callback methods on the bean instance. The `ejbPassivate()` method can be used to release any resources. The `ejbStore()` method is called to synchronize the bean instance's state with the underlying datasource prior to the passivation of the bean.

Removal

When the client application invokes a `remove()` method on the entity object's component interface or the home interface, the container calls the `ejbRemove()` method on the bean instance and removes the entity. Once the `ejbRemove()` method has finished, the bean instance is moved back to the instance pool.

Rollback

The container calls `ejbCreate()`, `ejbPostCreate()`, or `ejbRemove()` in response to create or remove invocations by the client. If a problem arises during the instantiation or removal of the instance, the container rolls back the transaction and moves the instance back to the pooled state.

Container-managed persistence (CMP)

One of the goals of the Enterprise JavaBeans technology is to allow the EJB component developer to focus on the business logic of the application. The container provides the system-level services such as transaction, security, and fail-over that are not only complex to write but also of less relevance to the main business of the application. The CMP model follows the same paradigm and it allows the bean provider to focus on the business logic rather than on writing SQL statements or JDBC code. The container takes care of implementing the persistence logic. The EJB 2.*x* CMP model provides a flexible object model, a full-featured standard-based query language, and extensive support for relationships among the entities.

The abstract-programming model

With container-managed persistence, the state of the entity beans is managed by the container. The enterprise-bean developer is responsible for defining the attributes and relationships of the bean, and the container is responsible for managing and persisting this state to the database. The bean developer defines the state of the bean by writing the abstract methods. Abstract methods are part of bean's implementation class and are used to access the bean's persistence state. However, the bean developer cannot declare any container-managed fields in the bean class. Instead the bean developer declares the abstract get and set methods for each container-managed field. For instance, instead of declaring a `private String name` field in the bean class, the bean provider writes `public abstract String getName()` and `public abstract String setName()`. Abstract methods are defined for use by the container and not by the client application. They may or may not be exposed in the bean's component interface. They are defined as public and abstract because their actual implementation is provided by the EJB container.

Declaring the container-managed fields

From the perspective of the bean provider, the container-managed persistent fields and container-managed relationship fields are virtual fields and can only be accessed through the get and set accessor methods. The bean provider is responsible for specifying the container-managed persistent fields and container-managed relationships in the deployment descriptor and for specifying the corresponding accessor methods in the bean class. The accessor methods must be public and abstract and must follow JavaBean-naming conventions.

The naming convention for abstract accessors corresponds to the standard naming convention for the JavaBean accessors. The first letter of the state-variable name is capitalized and prefixed by either get or set. Getter methods take no arguments and have a return type corresponding to the type of the state variable. Setter methods take one argument with a type corresponding to the type of the state variable, and return void. Finally, a CMP field represents a persistence state, and a CMR field represents the endpoint of a persistence relationship.

Writing a simple CMP

In this section we will write a basic CMP to demonstrate the simplicity of this model. In the following few sections, we will enhance our CMP to illustrate other advanced concepts.

PassengerHome – the home interface

The home interface of an entity bean is used to create, locate, and remove the entities. The home interface defines three kinds of methods:

    Home business methods

    Zero or more create methods

    One or more finder methods

In the following example, we will write two create() methods and a find() method. The find() method locates a specific instance of PassengerBean using the primary key.

```
package com.connexia.ejb.PassengerBean;

import java.rmi.RemoteException;
import javax.ejb.CreateException;
import javax.ejb.EJBHome;
import javax.ejb.FinderException;

public interface PassengerHome extends EJBHome {

    public Passenger create(
        Integer id,
        String lastName,
        String firstName,
```

```
            int age,
            String category,
            String foodCode)
            throws CreateException, RemoteException;

        public Passenger create(
            Integer id,
            String lastName,
            String firstName,
            int age)
            throws CreateException, RemoteException;

        public Passenger findByPrimaryKey(Integer primaryKey)
            throws FinderException, RemoteException;

    }
```

The home interface must define a findByPrimaryKey() method that takes the entity bean's primary-key type as its only argument. The findByPrimaryKey() method does not need a matching method in the bean class. At runtime the findByPrimaryKey() method will automatically locate and return a reference to the entity bean's component interface with the matching primary key.

Passenger — the remote interface

The remote interface of the bean defines the business methods that clients can use to interact with the bean. Any method defined in the remote interface must have a corresponding method in the bean class with the same signature. When the remote-interface methods match the persistence-field methods, the client has direct access to the bean's persistence fields. And thus, in our case, the client can invoke the method setLastName() and it will change the passenger's last name in the database.

The remote interface can be independent of the abstract programming model and can provide other business methods that are not mapped to the abstract accessor methods. For instance, our remote interface defines a method upgrade() that does not map to any accessor method. We will see the implementation of this method in the next section.

The following code segment illustrates the remote interface:

```
package com.connexia.ejb.PassengerBean;

import java.rmi.RemoteException;
import javax.ejb.EJBObject;

public interface Passenger extends EJBObject {

    public boolean upgrade(String category) throws
RemoteException;
```

```
      public String getName() throws RemoteException;
      public void setFoodCode(String foodCode) throws
RemoteException;
      public void setCategory(String category) throws
RemoteException;
}
```

PassengerBean — the bean class

The implementation class implements the `EntityBean` interface. The bean-implementation class defines all the callback methods as listed in the `Entity` interface and all the business methods as listed in our remote interface. The bean class must also declare the accessor methods for each persistence and relationship field defined in the deployment descriptor. The class is declared as an abstract class because the container generates the concrete implementation. The container uses the abstract methods defined in the bean class and the fields specified in the deployment descriptor to generate a concrete entity-bean class.

Listing 16-1 shows the implementation of `PassengerBean` class.

Listing 16-1: **PassengerBean**

```
package com.connexia.ejb.PassengerBean;

import javax.ejb.CreateException;
import javax.ejb.EntityBean;
import javax.ejb.EntityContext;
import javax.ejb.RemoveException;
import javax.naming.Context;
import javax.naming.InitialContext;
import javax.naming.NamingException;

abstract public class PassengerBean implements EntityBean {
    final static boolean VERBOSE = true;
    private EntityContext ctx;

    public PassengerBean() {
    }

    /*
     * @see
javax.ejb.EntityBean#setEntityContext(javax.ejb.EntityContext)
     */
    public void setEntityContext(EntityContext ctx) {
        this.ctx = ctx;
    }

    /*
```

Continued

Listing 16-1 *(continued)*

```
 * @see javax.ejb.EntityBean#unsetEntityContext()
 */
public void unsetEntityContext() {
    this.ctx = null;
}

/**
 * container managed fields
 */
abstract public Integer getPassengerId();
abstract public void setPassengerId(Integer val);

abstract public String getLastName();
abstract public void setLastName(String val);

abstract public String getFirstName();
abstract public void setFirstName(String val);

abstract public int getAge();
abstract public void setAge(int val);

abstract public String getCategory();
abstract public void setCategory(String val);

abstract public String getFoodCode();
abstract public void setFoodCode(String val);

/*
 * @see javax.ejb.EntityBean#ejbActivate()
 */
public void ejbActivate() {
}

/*
 * @see javax.ejb.EntityBean#ejbPassivate()
 */
public void ejbPassivate() {
}

/*
 * @see javax.ejb.EntityBean#ejbLoad()
 */
public void ejbLoad() {
}

/* (non-Javadoc)
 * @see javax.ejb.EntityBean#ejbStore()
 */
public void ejbStore() {
}
```

```
    public void ejbRemove() throws RemoveException {
    }

/** This method creates the passenger in the database
 * with the passed values.
  * @param Integer id
  * @param String lastName
  * @param String firstName
  * @param int age
  * @param String category
  * @param String foodCode
  * @return Integer PrimaryKey
  * @throws CreateException
  */
  public Integer ejbCreate(
      Integer id,
      String lastName,
      String firstName,
      int age,
      String category,
      String foodCode)
      throws CreateException {
      setPassengerId(id);
      setLastName(lastName);
      setFirstName(firstName);
      setAge(age);
      setCategory(category);
      setFoodCode(foodCode);

      return null;
  }

  /** This method creates the passenger in the database
   * with the passed values.
   * @param Integer id
   * @param String lastName
   * @param String firstName
   * @param int age
   * @return Integer Primary Key
   * @throws CreateException
   */
  public Integer ejbCreate(
      Integer id,
      String lastName,
      String firstName,
      int age)
      throws CreateException {
      setPassengerId(id);
      setLastName(lastName);
      setFirstName(firstName);
      setAge(age);
```

Continued

Listing 16-1 *(continued)*

```
        return null;
    }

    /** This method gives the bean an opporutunity to
     * perform any post-processing tasks.
     * @param Integer id
     * @param String lastName
     * @param String firstName
     * @param int age
     * @param String category
     * @param String foodCode
     */
    public void ejbPostCreate(
        Integer id,
        String lastName,
        String firstName,
        int age,
        String category,
        String foodCode) {
    }

  /** This method gives the bean an opporutunity to
   * perform any post-processing tasks.
     * @param Integer id
     * @param String lastName
     * @param String firstName
     * @param int age
     */
    public void ejbPostCreate(
        Integer id,
        String lastName,
        String firstName,
        int age) {
    }

    /**This method upgrades the flight category
     * for the passenger.
     * @param String category
     * @return boolean true if the upgrade was successful.
     */
    public boolean upgrade(String category) {

        // check if upgrade can be done...
        setCategory(category);

        return true;
    }
```

```
/** This method return the name (first + last) of
 * the passenger.
 * @return String name of the passenger
 */
public String getName() {
    return getFirstName() + "  " + getLastName();
}


}
```

ejb-jar.xml — the deployment descriptor

The deployment descriptor is comprised of information used by the EJB compiler and the container at runtime. In the deployment descriptor the <home> and <remote> tags define the home and remote interfaces, respectively, that we defined earlier. The <ejb-class> tag defines the name of the bean class. The <persistence-type> tag declares that the bean uses container-managed persistence. And the <cmp-field> tag provides the list of persistent fields. Listing 16-2 shows the deployment descriptor for the PassengerBean.

Listing 16-2: **Deployment descriptor**

```
<ejb-jar>
   <enterprise-beans>
      <entity>
         <ejb-name>PassengerBean</ejb-name>

<home>com.connexia.ejb.PassengerBean.PassengerHome</home>

<remote>com.connexia.ejb.PassengerBean.Passenger</remote>
         <ejb-class>
            com.connexia.ejb.PassengerBean.PassengerBean
         </ejb-class>
         <persistence-type>Container</persistence-type>
         <prim-key-class>java.lang.Integer</prim-key-class>
         <reentrant>False</reentrant>
         <cmp-version>2.x</cmp-version>
         <abstract-schema-name>PassengerBean</abstract-schema-
name>
         <cmp-field>
            <field-name>passengerId</field-name>
         </cmp-field>
         <cmp-field>
            <field-name>lastName</field-name>
         </cmp-field>
         <cmp-field>
            <field-name>firstName</field-name>
```

Continued

Listing 16-2 *(continued)*

```
            </cmp-field>
            <cmp-field>
                <field-name>age</field-name>
            </cmp-field>
            <cmp-field>
                <field-name>category</field-name>
            </cmp-field>
            <cmp-field>
                <field-name>foodCode</field-name>
            </cmp-field>
            <primkey-field>passengerId</primkey-field>
        </entity>
```

Client — invoking the PassengerBean

A client needs to get a reference to the component interface and execute the method call. Behind the scenes the call is delegated to the bean-implementation class. The following code illustrates our client application. It shows how to invoke the `create()`, `findByPrimaryKey()`, and `remove()` methods for an entity bean. In summary, our client is performing the following tasks:

1. Getting the initial context.

2. Looking up the bean's home using the bean's JNDI name (the bean's JNDI name is specified in the deployment descriptor for the bean).

3. Using the home object's `create()` method and the primary key to create a bean instance.

4. Using the bean instance to call any business methods.

5. Using the primary key and the home interface to locate the entity-bean instance.

6. Removing the bean.

Cross-Reference   For more details on JNDI, refer to Chapter 11.

Listing 16-3 displays the client application illustrating the preceding steps.

Listing 16-3: **PassengerBeanClient**

```
package com.connexia.ejb.PassengerBean;

import java.rmi.RemoteException;
import java.util.Properties;
```

```
import javax.ejb.CreateException;
import javax.ejb.FinderException;
import javax.ejb.RemoveException;
import javax.naming.Context;
import javax.naming.InitialContext;
import javax.naming.NamingException;

public class PassengerBeanClient {
    private static final String URL = "t3://localhost:7001";
    public static void main(String args[]) throws
NamingException {

        Context ctx = null;
        PassengerHome home = null;
        Passenger remote = null;

        /*
         * Get the initial context
         */
        Properties props = System.getProperties();
        try {
            ctx = new InitialContext(props);
        } catch (NamingException ne) {
            System.out.println("Error: NamingException");
            ne.printStackTrace();
            return;
        }

        /*
         * Get the home interface
         */
        try {
            home =
                (PassengerHome) ctx.lookup(

"com.connexia.ejb.PassengerBean.PassengerHome");
        } catch (NamingException ne) {
            System.out.println("Error: NamingException");
            ne.printStackTrace();
            return;
        }

        /*
         * Create a passenger.
         */
        Integer primaryKey = new Integer(1);
        String firstName = "John";
        String lastName = "Smith";
        int age = 30;

        try {
```

Continued

Listing 16-3 *(continued)*

```
        remote =
            (Passenger) home.create(primaryKey, firstName,
lastName, age);
        remote.setFoodCode("VEGGIE");
        remote.setCategory("Econ");
    } catch (RemoteException re) {
        System.out.println("Error: RemoteException");
        re.printStackTrace();
        return;
    } catch (CreateException ce) {
        System.out.println("Error: CreateException");
        ce.printStackTrace();
        return;
    }

    /*
     * Find the passenger
     */
    Integer key = new Integer(1);
    Passenger passenger = null;
    try {
        passenger = home.findByPrimaryKey(key);

        System.out.println("Name   : " +
passenger.getName());
    } catch (RemoteException re) {
        System.out.println("Error: RemoteException");
        re.printStackTrace();
        return;
    } catch (FinderException fe) {
        System.out.println("Error: FinderException");
        fe.printStackTrace();
        return;
    }

    /*
     * Remove the passenger
     */
    try {
        passenger.remove();
    } catch (RemoteException re) {
        System.out.println("Error: RemoteException");
        re.printStackTrace();
        return;
    } catch (RemoveException rme) {
        System.out.println("Error: RemoveException");
```

```
        rme.printStackTrace();
        return;
    }

}

}
```

Introduction to Container Managed Relationships (CMRs)

One of the most powerful aspects of the CMP model is its comprehensive support for relationships. In the earlier section we discussed the abstract programming model, and how the container can persist the fields defined by means of the abstract accessor methods. In addition to that, two or more CMP beans can be in a relationship and the container will handle the persistence logic necessary to manage the relationship. Again, the bean developer has to provide the abstract accessor methods to define these relationship fields.

The following types of relationships exist:

✦ One-to-one

✦ One-to-many

✦ Many-to-many

Also, relationships may be either *bidirectional* or *unidirectional*. If a relationship is bidirectional it can be navigated in both directions, whereas a unidirectional relationship can be navigated in one direction only. (Both of these terms are discussed later in this section.) Before we discuss the different kind of relationships, let's understand the deployment descriptor that brings all this together.

The entity beans that have relationships with each other have to be defined in the same deployment descriptor. When they share a deployment descriptor they are deployed together and are seen as a single deployment unit, sharing the same database and the same Java virtual machine (JVM). The bean developer is responsible for defining the beans in the relationship, their *cardinality* (one-to-one, one-to-many, or many-to-many) and their direction (unidirectional or bidirectional). This information is specified in the deployment descriptor. The deployment descriptor for a CMP bean has a `<relationships>` element used to specify the persistence schema for the entity beans in the relationship. Figure 16-3 shows the sub-elements of the `<relationships>` section.

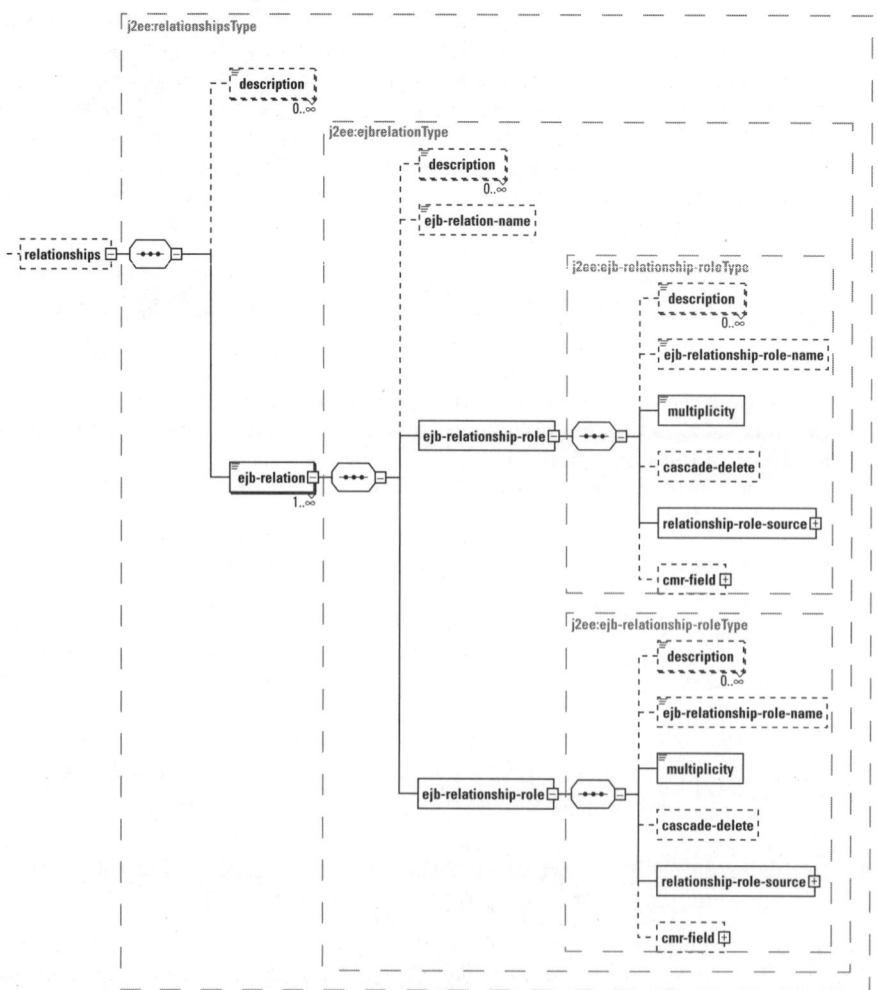

Figure 16-3: Deployment descriptor relationships

Defining relationship fields involves adding an ⟨ejb-relation⟩ element to the XML deployment descriptor for each entity-to-entity relationship. The ⟨ejb-relation⟩ element has the following sub-elements:

✦ ⟨ejb-relation-name⟩ — This element can be used to identify the relationship for someone reading the deployment descriptor or for deployment tools. This element is not required.

✦ ⟨description⟩ — This element can be used to provide more information about the relationship. Like ⟨ejb-relation-name⟩, this element is optional.

✦ `<ejb-relationship-role>` — A relationship is defined between two entities, and thus each `<ejb-relation>` has exactly two `<ejb-relationship-role>` elements, one for each participant in the relationship. Each `<ejb-relationship-role>` element includes a `<relationship-role-source>` element that specifies the name of the entity bean in the relationship. The name of the entity bean should match the name in the original declaration of the entity bean in the `<enterprise-beans>` section. The `<ejb-relationship-role>` element also declares the cardinality, or multiplicity, of the role. The `<multiplicity>` element can be either `One` or `Many`.

✦ `<cmr-field>` — The `<ejb-relationship-role>` also defines the `<cmr-field>` element that lists the reference of the other bean in the relationship. The `<cmr-field>` element includes the `<description>`, `<cmr-field-name>`, and `<cmr-field-type>` elements. For every relationship field defined using the `<cmr-field>` element there must be a pair of matching abstract accessor methods in the bean class.

✦ `<cascade-delete>` — When this element is specified for a particular relationship, the lifetime of one entity object depends on another. When the client application invokes a `remove()` method on an entity bean that bean is removed from the underlying datasource. But if the entity is in a relationship with other entity bean(s), they might be affected too. For example, say we have our `PassengerBean` in a relationship with an `AddressBean` (we will explain more about this relationship later in the section). The `PassengerBean` represents our airline's passenger and the `AddressBean` is used to store the address of the passenger. If we invoke `remove()` method on the `PassengerBean`, we may have created a situation in which we have an `AddressBean` representing the address of a passenger that no longer exists in our system. To avoid this, we can specify the `<cascade-delete>` element with our relationship. This ensures that whenever we remove a `PassengerBean`, the corresponding `AddressBean` will also be removed.

In the next few sections, we will explain different types of relationships that can be defined using the bean's deployment descriptor. To illustrate these relationships, we will use `PassengerBean`, `AddressBean` and the `FlightBean` entities. `PassengerBean` is already defined in the preceding section and stores information about a passenger. `AddressBean` stores information about a passenger's address whereas `FlightBean` represents a Flight and therefore stores flight information such as flight no, flight destination and arrival locations. In order to focus on the relationships, we will only show the relationship section of the deployment descriptor and not the complete source code of the bean.

Unidirectional relationships

Unidirectional relationships only navigate in one direction. For example, if Entity A and Entity B are in a one-to-one, unidirectional relationship and the direction is from Entity A to Entity B, than Entity A is aware of Entity B, but Entity B is unaware of

Entity A. (One-to-one relationships will be discussed shortly.) This type of relationship is implemented when you specify a `cmr-field` deployment-descriptor element for the entity bean from which navigation can take place and do not specify a related `cmr-field` element for the target entity bean. The `get` method for a `cmr-field` must return either the local interface of the entity bean or a collection of the same. The `set` method for the relationship must take as an argument the entity bean's local interface or a collection of the same. Figure 16-4 represents a unidirectional relationship.

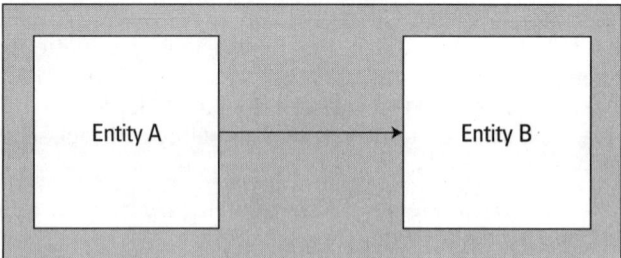

Figure 16-4: Unidirectional relationship

Bidirectional relationships

Bidirectional relationships navigate in both directions. These types of container-managed relationships can exist only between beans whose abstract persistence schemas are defined in the same deployment descriptor and therefore managed by the same container. If Entity A and Entity B are in a bidirectional relationship each is aware of the other and the changes made to one participant in the relationship are instantly reflected in the other participant. For instance, `ReservationBean` and `PassengerBean` are in a bidirectional relationship with each other. Given a reservation bean, we should be able to find the passenger(s), and given a passenger we should be able to find the details of his or her reservation. Relationships that are bidirectional have abstract accessors for both participants in the relationship. Figure 16-5 represents a bidirectional relationship.

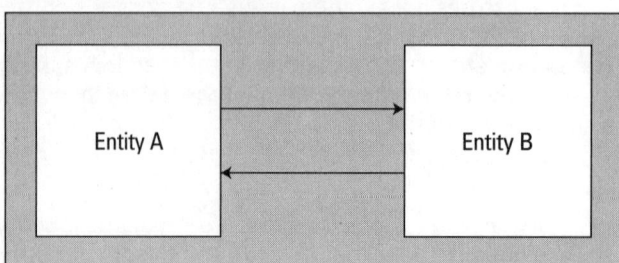

Figure 16-5: Bidirectional relationship

One-to-one relationships

A one-to-one relationship is one in which one and only one Entity B exists for each Entity A. In database terms, a one-to-one relationship involves the physical mapping from the foreign key in one bean to the primary key in another bean. For example, our `PassengerBean` developer from earlier in the chapter might reference an `AddressBean` to store the address information for the passenger. Figure 16-6 illustrates a one-to-one relationship.

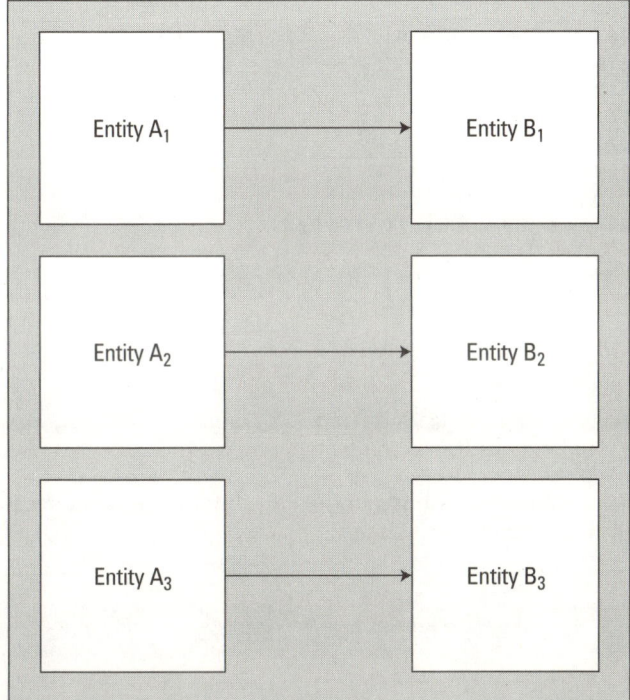

Figure 16-6: One-to-one relationship

Listing 16-4 shows a one-to one relationship mapped between the `PassengerBean` and the `AddressBean`.

Listing 16-4: **Deployment descriptor/one-to-one**

```
<relationships>
    <ejb-relation>
        <ejb-relation-name>Passenger-Address<ejb-relation-name>
        <ejb-relationship-role>
```

Continued

Listing 16-4 *(continued)*

```
        <ejb-relationship-role-name>
           Passenger-has-an-Address
        </ejb-relationship-role-name>
        <multiplicity>One<multiplicity>
        <relationship-role-source>
           <ejb-name>PassengerBean</ejb-name>
        </relationship-role-source>
        <cmr-field>
          <cmr-field-name>address</cmr-field-name>
        </cmr-field>
     </ejb-relationship-role>
     <ejb-relationship-role>
        <ejb-relationship-role-name>
           Address-belongs-to-Passenger
        </ejb-relationship-role-name>
        <multiplicity>One</multiplicity>
        <relationship-role-source>
           <ejb-name>AddressBean</ejb-name>
        </relationship-role-source>
     </ejb-relationship-role>
   <ejb-relation>
</relationships>
```

Listing 16-5 illustrates the additional methods in the `PassengerBean` that set the address of the passenger using the `AddressBean`.

Listing 16-5: More methods using AddressBean

```
/*
   * Abstract methods for passenger's address.
   */
   abstract public Address getAddress();
   abstract public void setAddress(Address val);


  /** This method sets the address of the passenger.
    * This method is also exposed in the bean's remote
    * interface. Therefore, the client can call
    * PassengerBean's setAddressData() method to set
    * the address of the passenger.
    * @param String passengerId
    * @param Integer addressId
    * @param String street
```

```
 * @param String city
 * @param String zip
 * @param String state
 * @param String country
 */
public void setAddressData(
    String passengerId,
    String addressId,
    String street,
    String city,
    String zip,
    String state,
    String country) {
    try {
        Context ctx = new InitialContext();
        AddressHome home =
            (AddressHome) ctx.lookup(

"com.connexia.ejb.PassengerBean.AddressHome");
        Address address =
            home.create(
                passengerId,
                addressId,
                street,
                city,
                zip,
                state,
                country);
        this.setAddress(address);
    } catch (NamingException e) {
      System.out.println("Error: NamingException");
        e.printStackTrace();
    } catch (CreateException e) {
        System.out.println("Error: NamingException");
        e.printStackTrace();
    }

}
```

One-to-many relationships

A one-to-many relationship is one in which multiple Entities B can exist for a single Entity A. A one-to-many relationship involves the physical mapping from the foreign key in one bean to the primary key of another. However, in a one-to-many relationship the foreign key is always contained in the "many" role of the relationship.

Figure 16-7 represents a one-to-many relationship.

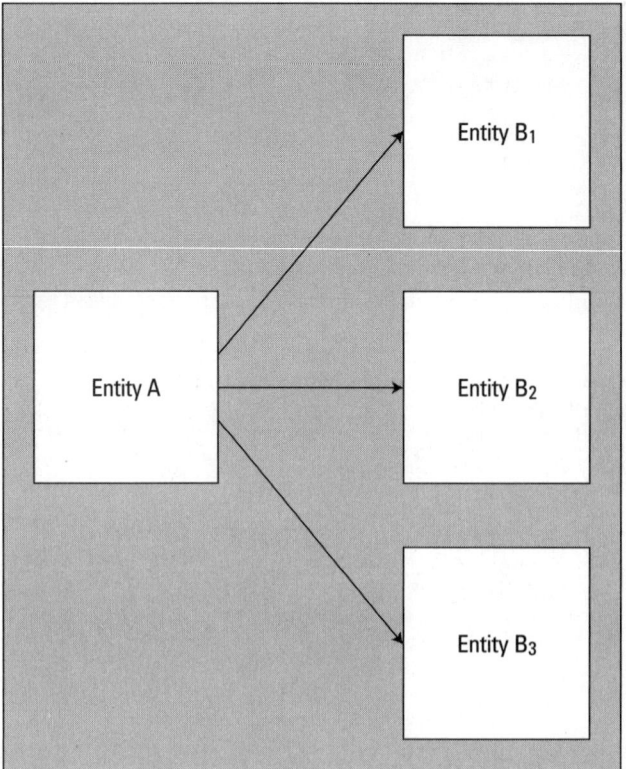

Figure 16-7: One-to-many relationship

For instance, we might allow more than one address for a passenger and change the relationship between the `PassengerBean` and the `AddressBean` as one-to-many. Listing 16-6 displays the deployment descriptor that defines the relationship. Note that the `<cmr-field-type>` is defined as `java.util.Set` because a single `PassengerBean` can refer to multiple `AddressBean` references.

Listing 16-6: **Deployment descriptor/one-to-many**

```
<relationships>
   <ejb-relation>
      <ejb-relation-name>Passenger-Address<ejb-relation-name>
      <ejb-relationship-role>
         <ejb-relationship-role-name>
            Passenger-has-many-Addresses
         </ejb-relationship-role-name>
         <multiplicity>One<multiplicity>
         <relationship-role-source>
            <ejb-name>PassengerBean</ejb-name>
         </relationship-role-source>
```

```
      <cmr-field>
        <cmr-field-name>addressList</cmr-field-name>
        <cmr-field-type>java.util.set</cmr-field-type>
      </cmr-field>
    </ejb-relationship-role>
    <ejb-relationship-role>
      <ejb-relationship-role-name>
        Addresses-for-Passenger
      </ejb-relationship-role-name>
      <multiplicity>Many</multiplicity>
      <relationship-role-source>
        <ejb-name>AddressBean</ejb-name>
      </relationship-role-source>
    </ejb-relationship-role>
  </ejb-relation>
</relationships>
```

Many-to-many relationships

In a many-to-many relationship both participating beans maintain a collection relationship with each other. In the database terms, a many-to-many relationship involves the physical mapping of a join table. Each row in the join table contains two foreign keys that map to the primary keys of the entities involved in the relationship. Consider for example the relationship between the `FlightBean` and the `PassengerBean`. A Flight has many passengers and a passenger can be booked on many flights. Figure 16-8 represents a one-to-many relationship.

Listing 16-7 shows a many-to-many relationship mapped between the `FlightBean` and the `PassengerBean`.

Listing 16-7: **Deployment descriptor/many-to-many**

```
<relationships>
  <ejb-relation>
    <ejb-relation-name>Flight-Passenger<ejb-relation-name>
    <ejb-relationship-role>
      <ejb-relationship-role-name>
        Flight-has-many-Passengers
      </ejb-relationship-role-name>
      <multiplicity>Many<multiplicity>
      <relationship-role-source>
        <ejb-name>FlightBean</ejb-name>
      </relationship-role-source>
      <cmr-field>
        <cmr-field-name>passengerList</cmr-field-name>
        <cmr-field-type>java.util.Collection</cmr-field-type>
      </cmr-field>
```

Continued

Listing 16-7 *(continued)*

```
        </ejb-relationship-role>
        <ejb-relationship-role>
           <ejb-relationship-role-name>
              Passengers-has-many-Flights
           </ejb-relationship-role-name>
           <multiplicity>Many</multiplicity>
           <relationship-role-source>
              <ejb-name>PassengerBean</ejb-name>
           </relationship-role-source>
           <cmr-field>
              <cmr-field-name>flights</cmr-field-name>
              <cmr-field-type>java.util.Collection</cmr-field-
type>
           </cmr-field>
        </ejb-relationship-role>
     <ejb-relation>
</relationships>
```

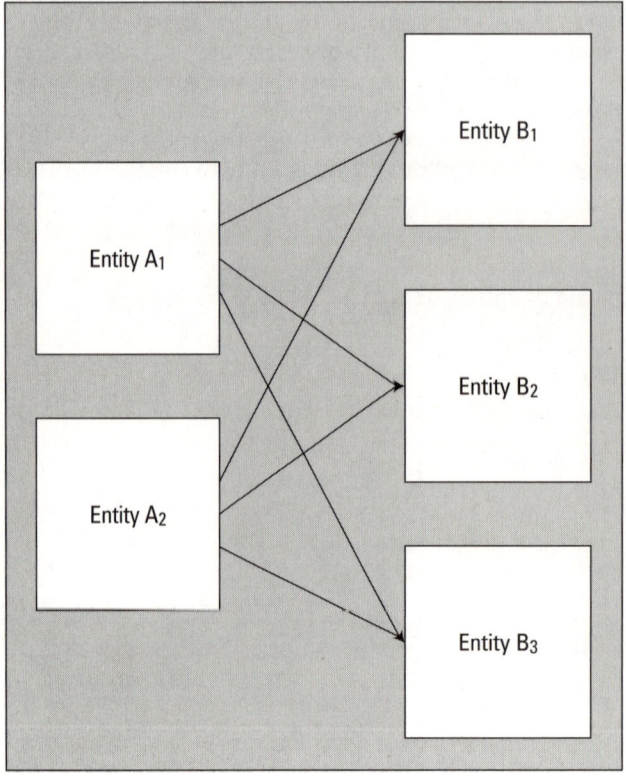

Figure 16-8: Many-to-many relationship

The EJB Query Language (EJB QL) – An Example

The Enterprise JavaBeans Query Language (EJB QL) is used to define queries for CMP beans. Its structure is very similar to SQL's and thus it should look very familiar to database users. Earlier in the section on callback methods, we mentioned finder and `select` methods. The EJB QL is used to define queries for the finder and `select` methods of the entity beans with container-managed persistence.

EJB QL queries use the abstract-persistence schema of entity beans for their data model. Thus they are independent of the underlying data store and are portable across databases or other persistent stores. At runtime the query methods can use the native language of the underlying data store. As a result, query methods defined using EJB QL are both optimizable and portable.

An EJB QL query is a string that consists of the following clauses:

✦ `SELECT` — This clause determines the type of the object or values to be selected.

✦ `FROM` — This clause specifies the domain or entity beans to be queried.

✦ `WHERE` — This clause is optional and may be used to restrict the results of the query.

✦ `ORDER BY` — This clause is optional and may be used to order the results of the query.

The EJB QL query statements are specified with the `<query>` tag in the deployment descriptor. The `<query>` element contains two primary elements, the `<query-method>` element that declares the finder or `select` method and the `<ejb-ql>` element that specifies the actual query. Here's an example:

```
<query>
  <query-method>
    <method-name>findByName</method-name>
    <method-params>
        <method-param>java.lang.String</method-param>
    <method-params>
  </query-method>
  <ejb-ql>
    SELECT FROM PassengerBean a WHERE a.firstName = ?1
  </ejb-ql>
    </query>
```

Query methods

Recall that the EJB QL is used for two types of query methods: finder methods and `select` methods.

Finder methods

Finder methods are defined in the home interface (remote or local) of an entity bean and return either entity objects or local entity objects. A finder method defined on the remote home interface must return either an EJBObject or a collection of EJBObjects. A finder method defined on the local home interface must return either an EJBLocalObject or a collection of EJBLocalObjects.

The query for the finder methods is specified in the deployment descriptor. The exception is the findByPrimaryKey() method, which always returns a single entity that matches the supplied primary key and for which the query is generated by the container. The bean providers are expected to write the query for other finder methods that can return either a single entity or a collection.

The following listing illustrates a query for the findByName() finder method for the PassengerBean. The method returns a list of passengers matching the supplied first and last name. Add this code segment to the home interface, PassengerHome.

```
    public Passenger findByName(String lastName, String
firstName)
        throws FinderException, RemoteException;
```

Change the deployment descriptor to include the following section:

```
<query>
  <query-method>
     <method-name>findByName</method-name>
     <method-params>
        <method-param>java.lang.String</method-param>
        <method-param>java.lang.String</method-param>
     <method-params>
  </query-method>
  <ejb-ql>
     SELECT OBJECT(a) FROM PassengerBean a
     WHERE a.firstName = ?1
     AND a.lastName = ?2
  </ejb-ql>
</query>
```

Select methods

select methods are a special type of query method not directly exposed through the client view. The result type of a select method can be an EJBLocalObject (or a collection of EJBLocalObjects), an EJBObject (or a collection of EJBObjects), a cmp-field value (or a collection of cmp-field values), or the result of an aggregate function.

The WHERE clause and conditional expressions

The WHERE clause is used to restrict the results of a query by specifying a conditional expression. Only the objects or values that satisfy the expression are returned as the result. In this section we will look at a few constructs that you can use in building the WHERE clause

Literals

Literals can be string literals, such as VEGGIE; numeric literals, such as 22; approximate numeric literals, such as 22.35; or boolean literals, such as TRUE.

If we want to get a list of customers that are vegetarians, we can execute a SQL like the following:

```
SELECT  OBJECT(a) FROM PassengerBean a
WHERE a.foodCode = 'VEGGIE';
```

Input parameters

Query methods that use EJB QL statements may specify method arguments. Input parameters allow these method arguments to be mapped to EJB QL statements. The input parameters are designated by a question-mark (?) prefix followed by an integer.

For instance:

```
SELECT OBJECT (a) FROM PassengerBean a
WHERE a.firstName = ?1
```

The corresponding finder method will look like the following:

```
public Collection findByFirstName(String firstName)
throws FinderException
```

Operators

The WHERE clause can use several logical and conditional operators. They are listed here in decreasing order of precedence:

✦ Navigation operator (.)

✦ Arithmetic operators:

- +, - (unary)

- *, / (multiplication and division, respectively)

- +, - (addition and subtraction, respectively)

✦ Comparison operators: =, >, >=, <, <=, <> (not equal to)

✦ Logical operators: NOT, AND, OR

For instance, the following code segment will retrieve a list of passengers with age > 25.

```
SELECT OBJECT(a) from PassengerBean a
WHERE a.age > 25;
```

BETWEEN expressions

The `BETWEEN` clause can be used to specify a range. Here's an example:

```
SELECT OBJECT(a) from PassengerBean a
WHERE a.age BETWEEN 25 AND 30;
```

Semantically this is equivalent to the following:

```
SELECT OBJECT(a) from PassengerBean a
WHERE a.age >= 25 AND a.age <=30 ;
```

The IN expression

This is used to specify the condition as a list of literal string values. Here's an example:

```
SELECT OBJECT(a) from PassengerBean a
WHERE a.firstName in ("John", "Joe") ;
```

The LIKE expression

This allows the query to select `String`-type CMP fields that match a specified pattern. For example:

```
SELECT OBJECT(a) from PassengerBean a
WHERE a.firstName like 'J%' ;
```

The NULL comparison

The null comparison expression tests whether or not the single-valued path expression or input parameter is a NULL value. For instance, you would do the following to find out which passengers do not have an address:

```
SELECT OBJECT(a) from PassengerBean a
WHERE a.address IS NULL;
```

The EMPTY comparison

The IS EMPTY operator allows the query to see whether a collection-based relationship is empty. It has the same objective as a test to see whether a single CMP or CMR field is null. For instance, here's how you would find the flights that do not have any reservations:

```
SELECT OBJECT(a) from FlightBean a
WHERE a.reservations IS EMPTY;
```

Functional expressions

EJB QL includes the following built-in functions for `String` manipulations:

- ✦ `CONCAT(String, String)` **returns a concatenated** `String`.
- ✦ `SUBSTRING(String, start, length)` **returns a substring of the original** `String`.
- ✦ `LOCATE(String, String [, start] )` **returns the location of the** `String`.
- ✦ `LENGTH(String)` **returns an** `int` **indicating the length of the** `String`.

EJB QL also includes the following built-in functions for arithmetic operations:

- ✦ `ABS(number)` **returns the absolute value of the number.**
- ✦ `SQRT(double)` **returns the square root of a double.**
- ✦ `MOD(int, int)` **returns the mod value.**

The SELECT clause

`DISTINCT` is used to specify that duplicate values must be eliminated from the query result. The following aggregate functions can also be used in the `SELECT` clause of an EJB QL query:

- ✦ `AVG`
- ✦ `COUNT`
- ✦ `MAX`
- ✦ `MIN`
- ✦ `SUM`

The ORDER BY clause

The `ORDER BY` clause allows the objects or values returned by the query to be ordered. The order can be specified as ascending or descending. For instance, here's how we could get a list of the passengers sorted according to their last names:

```
SELECT OBJECT(a) from PassengerBean a
ORDER BY a.lastName;
```

Bean-managed persistence (BMP)

The data-access protocol for transferring the state of the entity between the entity-bean instances and the underlying database is referred to as *object persistence*. In the last few sections we looked at the container-managed persistence model, wherein entity beans rely on the container to provide the persistence logic. The EJB specifications also support entity beans with bean-managed persistence (BMP) wherein the entity beans write explicit code to access the persistence store. For most users, accessing the persistence store involves writing JDBC code to access a relational database.

From a bean provider's perspective, this is more effort than the CMP model, because he or she must provide the logic to create, update, and remove the bean's state; but bean-managed persistence is a viable choice in some circumstances. One benefit of BMP comes when mapping a bean's attributes to database fields proves to be difficult. This may occur if the bean state is defined by data in different databases. It can also occur if you are using a target data store that is a legacy system: You will probably need to access the store using a vendor-specific protocol rather than SQL commands, and the EJB container might not support the protocol. Bean-managed persistence is a good alternative to container-managed persistence when the container tools are inadequate for mapping the bean's instance state to the underlying data source.

One major disadvantage of using a BMP (other than that it makes more work for the bean provider) is that it ties the bean to a specific database type and structure. Any change in the database schema will require a coding change in the bean class and it may not be a trivial change. With CMP, it is managed by the abstract persistence schema and thus is easier to accommodate.

Note   BMP gives you more flexibility in terms of how the state is managed between the bean instance and the database, while CMP speeds up bean development and increases bean flexibility.

Writing a BMP

In this section we will write an entity bean with the BMP model. Unlike the CMP model, the bean provider has to write code to insert, delete, read, and update data from the database. `AircraftBean` of the following example represents an aircraft and stores information such as model number, make, year built and seating capacity of the aircraft.

AircraftHome — the home interface

The home interface is used to create, remove, and locate the entity-bean instances. The home interface must also define the `findByPrimaryKey()` method. For a CMP bean the implementation of the `findByPrimaryKey()` method is generated by the container, whereas in the case of BMP beans the bean provider must provide the implementation in the bean class.

The following code segment illustrates the home interface for the `AircraftBean`:

```
package com.connexia.ejb.AircraftBean;
import java.rmi.RemoteException;

import javax.ejb.CreateException;
import javax.ejb.FinderException;

public interface AircraftHome extends javax.ejb.EJBHome {
    public Aircraft create(
        Integer serialNo,
        String modelNo,
        String make,
        String yearBuilt,
        int seatCount)
        throws CreateException, RemoteException;
    public Aircraft findByPrimaryKey(Integer primaryKey)
        throws FinderException, RemoteException;

}
```

Aircraft — the remote interface

As is the case with the CMP entity beans, the remote interface must extend the `javax.ejb.EJBObject` interface. It defines the business methods that clients can use to interact with the bean. Each method defined in the remote interface should have a matching method in the bean class. The remote interface only provides the signature, whereas the bean class provides the actual implementation of the methods.

The following listing illustrates the remote interface for the `AircraftBean`:

```
package com.connexia.ejb.AircraftBean;
import java.rmi.RemoteException;

public interface Aircraft extends javax.ejb.EJBObject {
    public String getModelNo() throws RemoteException;
    public void setModelNo(String modelNo) throws
RemoteException;
    public String getMake() throws RemoteException;
    public void setMake(String make) throws RemoteException;
    public String getYearBuilt() throws RemoteException;
    public void setYearBuilt(String yearBuilt) throws
RemoteException;
    public int getSeatCount() throws RemoteException;
    public void setSeatCount(int seatCount) throws
RemoteException;
}
```

AircraftBean — the bean class

For a BMP bean, the bean provider is responsible for writing code to synchronize the state of the bean with the underlying data source. As we mentioned earlier in the section on the callback methods, using `ejbCreate()` is equivalent to inserting into the database, using `ejbLoad()` is equivalent to reading from the database, using `ejbStore()` is equivalent to updating the database, and using `ejbRemove()` is equivalent to deleting a record from the database. The container calls all these methods at the appropriate times, but the bean provider is responsible for implementing them in the bean class. Listing 16-8 illustrates the bean class for `AircraftBean`.

Listing 16-8: **The Bean class for AircraftBean**

```
package com.connexia.ejb.AircraftBean;

import java.sql.Connection;
import java.sql.PreparedStatement;
import java.sql.ResultSet;
import java.sql.SQLException;

import javax.ejb.*;
import javax.naming.Context;
import javax.naming.InitialContext;
import javax.naming.NamingException;
import javax.sql.DataSource;

public class AircraftBean implements EntityBean {
    public Integer serialNo;
    public String modelNo;
    public String make;
    public String yearBuilt;
    public int seatCount;

    private static final String ORACLE_JNDI_NAME =
        "examples-dataSource-demoPool";

    public EntityContext context;

    /**
     * This method gets a database connection and inserts a
     * record in the AIRCRAFT table with the passed data.
     * @param Integer    serialNo
     * @param String     modelNo
     * @param String     make
     * @param String     yearBuilt
     * @param int        seatCount
     * @return Integer   Primary key
     * @throws CreateException
     */
    public Integer ejbCreate(
```

```
                    Integer serialNo,
                    String modelNo,
                    String make,
                    String yearBuilt,
                    int seatCount)
                    throws CreateException {
                    this.serialNo = serialNo;
                    this.modelNo = modelNo;
                    this.make = make;
                    this.yearBuilt = yearBuilt;
                    this.seatCount = seatCount;

                    Connection conn = null;
                    PreparedStatement ps = null;

                    try {
                        conn = this.getConnection();
                        String sql =
                            "insert into Aircraft(serial_no, model_no,
        make, year_built, seat_count) "
                                    + "values(?, ?, ?, ?, ?)";
                        ps = conn.prepareStatement(sql);
                        ps.setInt(1, serialNo.intValue());
                        ps.setString(2, modelNo);
                        ps.setString(3, make);
                        ps.setString(4, yearBuilt);
                        ps.setInt(5, seatCount);

                        int result = ps.executeUpdate();
                        if (result != 1) {
                            throw new CreateException("Can not create
        Aircraft");
                        }
                        return serialNo;
                    } catch (SQLException se) {
                        throw new EJBException(se);
                    } finally {
                        closeStatement(ps);
                        closeConnection(conn);
                    }
                }

            /**
             * This method gives the bean an opportunity to perform any
             * post-processing tasks.
             * @param Integer    serialNo
             * @param String     modelNo
             * @param String     make
             * @param String     yearBuilt
             * @param String     seatCount
             * @throws CreateException
             */
```

Continued

Listing 16-8 *(continued)*

```java
    public void ejbPostCreate(
        Integer serialNo,
        String modelNo,
        String make,
        String yearBuilt,
        int seatCount)
        throws CreateException {
    }


    /**
     * This method gets a database connection and retrieves the
     * Aircraft entity matching with the passed serial no.
     * @param Integer serialNo
     * @return Integer Primary Key (Serial No)
     * @throws FinderException
     */
    public Integer ejbFindByPrimaryKey(Integer serialNo)
        throws FinderException {
        Connection conn = null;
        PreparedStatement ps = null;
        ResultSet rs = null;

        try {
            conn = this.getConnection();
            String sql = "select serial_no from Aircraft where
serial_no = ?";
            ps = conn.prepareStatement(sql);
            ps.setInt(1, serialNo.intValue());
            rs = ps.executeQuery();

            if (rs.next() == false) {
                throw new ObjectNotFoundException(
                    "Can not find Aircraft with serial no: " +
serialNo);
            }
        } catch (SQLException se) {
            throw new EJBException(se);
        } finally {
            closeResultSet(rs);
            closeStatement(ps);
            closeConnection(conn);
        }
        return serialNo;
    }


    /**
     * @see
javax.ejb.EntityBean#setEntityContext(javax.ejb.EntityContext)
```

```
    */
    public void setEntityContext(EntityContext ctx) {
        context = ctx;
    }

    /** This method is invoked just before the instance is
evicted from
     * memory.
     * @see javax.ejb.EntityBean#unsetEntityContext()
     */
    public void unsetEntityContext() {
        context = null;
    }

    /**
     * @see javax.ejb.EntityBean#ejbActivate()
     */
    public void ejbActivate() {
    }


    /**
     * @see javax.ejb.EntityBean#ejbPassivate()
     */
    public void ejbPassivate() {
    }

    /**
     * This method retrieves data from the AIRCRAFT table
     * and updates the entity's state.
     * @see javax.ejb.EntityBean#ejbLoad()
     */
    public void ejbLoad() {
        Integer primaryKey = (Integer) context.getPrimaryKey();
        Connection conn = null;
        PreparedStatement ps = null;
        ResultSet rs = null;

        try {
            conn = this.getConnection();
            String sql =
                "select model_no, make, year_built, seat_count
from Aircraft where serial_no = ?";
            ps = conn.prepareStatement(sql);
            ps.setInt(1, serialNo.intValue());
            rs = ps.executeQuery();
            if (rs.next()) {
                serialNo = primaryKey;
                modelNo = rs.getString("model_no");
                make = rs.getString("make");
                yearBuilt = rs.getString("year_built");
                seatCount = rs.getInt("seat_count");
```

Continued

Listing 16-8 *(continued)*

```java
            } else {
                throw new EJBException();
            }
        } catch (SQLException se) {
            throw new EJBException(se);
        } finally {
            closeResultSet(rs);
            closeStatement(ps);
            closeConnection(conn);
        }
    }

    /**
     * This method updates the AIRCRAFT table with the
     * entity's state.
     * @see javax.ejb.EntityBean#ejbStore()
     */
    public void ejbStore() {
        Connection conn = null;
        PreparedStatement ps = null;
        try {
            conn = this.getConnection();
            String sql =
                "update Aircraft set model_no = ?, make = ?,
year_built = ?, seat_count = ?";
            ps = conn.prepareStatement(sql);
            ps.setString(1, modelNo);
            ps.setString(2, make);
            ps.setString(3, yearBuilt);
            ps.setInt(4, seatCount);

            int result = ps.executeUpdate();
            if (result != 1) {
                throw new EJBException("Exception in
ejbStore");
            }
        } catch (SQLException se) {
            throw new EJBException(se);
        } finally {
            closeStatement(ps);
            closeConnection(conn);
        }
    }

    /**
     * This method removes the aircraft record from the
database.
     * @see javax.ejb.EntityBean#ejbRemove()
     */
    public void ejbRemove() {
        Connection conn = null;
```

```
            PreparedStatement ps = null;

            try {
                conn = this.getConnection();
                String sql = "delete from Aircraft where serial_no
= ?";
                ps = conn.prepareStatement(sql);
                ps.setInt(1, serialNo.intValue());
                int result = ps.executeUpdate();
                if (result != 1) {
                    throw new EJBException("Exception in removing
the aircraft");
                }
            } catch (SQLException se) {
                throw new EJBException(se);
            } finally {
                closeStatement(ps);
                closeConnection(conn);
            }
        }

    /**
     * This method gets a connection to the database.
     * @return java.sql.Connection
     * @throws SQLException
     */
    private Connection getConnection() throws SQLException {
        DataSource ds = null;
        Connection conn = null;
        try {
            Context ctx = new InitialContext();
            ds = (DataSource) ctx.lookup(ORACLE_JNDI_NAME);

        } catch (NamingException ne) {
            System.out.println("Error: DataSource lookup
failed");
            ne.printStackTrace();
        }
        return ds.getConnection();
    }

    /**
     * This method closes the Connection with the database.
     * @param java.sql.Connection conn
     */
    private void closeConnection(Connection conn) {
        try {
            if (conn != null)
                conn.close();
        } catch (SQLException e) {
            System.out.println("Error in closing Connection");
            e.printStackTrace();
```

Continued

Listing 16-8 *(continued)*

```java
        }
    }

    /**
     * This method closes the PreparedStatement.
     * @param java.sql.PreparedStatement ps
     */
    private void closeStatement(PreparedStatement ps) {
        try {
            if (ps != null)
                ps.close();
        } catch (SQLException e) {
            System.out.println("Error in closing
PreparedStatement");
            e.printStackTrace();
        }
    }

    /**
     * This method closes the ResultSet.
     * @param java.sql.ResultSet rs
     */
    private void closeResultSet(ResultSet rs) {
        try {
            if (rs != null)
                rs.close();
        } catch (SQLException e) {
            System.out.println("Error in closing ResultSet");
            e.printStackTrace();
        }
    }


    /*
     * Business Methods. These methods are declared in
     * the remote interface of the bean.
     *   They are used to get and set the bean's state.
     */

    public String getModelNo() {
        return modelNo;
    }
    public void setModelNo(String val) {
        modelNo = val;
    }
    public String getMake() {
        return make;
    }
    public void setMake(String val) {
        make = val;
    }
```

```
    public String getYearBuilt() {
        return yearBuilt;
    }
    public void setYearBuilt(String val) {
        yearBuilt = val;
    }
    public int getSeatCount() {
        return seatCount;
    }
    public void setSeatCount(int val) {
        seatCount = val;
    }

}
```

Listing 16-9 contains the deployment descriptor for the `AircraftBean`. The `<persistence-type>` is defined as `Bean` and no fields are defined in the deployment descriptor. In the BMP model, the fields are defined in the bean class itself.

Listing 16-9: **The deployment descriptor for AircraftBean**

```
<ejb-jar>
    <enterprise-beans>
        <entity>
            <description>BMP Example </description>
            <ejb-name>AircraftBean</ejb-name>

<home>com.connexia.ejb.AircraftBean.AircraftHome</home>

<remote>com.connexia.ejb.AircraftBean.Aircraft</home>
            <ejb-class>
                com.connexia.ejb.AircraftBean.AircraftBean
            </ejb-class>
            <persistence-type>Bean</persistence-type>
            <prim-key-class>java.lang.Integer</prim-key-class>
            <reentrant>False</reentrant>
        </entity>
    </enterprise-beans>
    <assembly-descriptor>
    ...
    </assembly-descriptor>
</ejb-jar>
```

```
public String getMake() throws RemoteException;
```

Exceptions

The following is a list of the standard application exceptions defined by the EJB specifications:

- ✦ CreateException
- ✦ DuplicateKeyException
- ✦ FinderException
- ✦ ObjectNotFoundException
- ✦ RemoveException

Each exception has its own meaning and the related methods must include these exceptions in their throws clause. For a CMP bean, the container handles the part of throwing these exceptions. But for a BMP, the bean provider must throw these exceptions in the bean class as appropriate. The client application can handle these exceptions just like any other application exception.

CreateException

CreateException indicates that an application error has occurred during the create operation. This exception must be listed in the throws clause of the create(), ejbCreate(), and ejbPostCreate() methods.

DuplicateKeyException

Each entity-bean instance is associated with a unique primary key. If the client application attempts to create an entity bean with an existing primary key, the DuplicateKeyException is thrown. DuplicateKeyException is a subclass of CreateException, and it is thrown by the container to the client to indicate that the entity object cannot be created because an entity object with the same key already exists.

FinderException

The container throws the FinderException if an application error occurs during the find or select operation. All the finder and select methods must include the FinderException in their throws clause.

ObjectNotFoundException

If the client application invokes a single-object finder or select method and no matching entity is found, the container throws the ObjectNotFoundException. Only single-object finder or select methods throw this exception. If the client application invokes a multi-object finder or select method and no matching entity is found, the container simply returns an empty list.

RemoveException

`RemoveException` indicates that an application error has occurred during the `remove` operation.

Summary

Entity beans provide a powerful abstraction from Java objects to persistent, transactional business logic. In this chapter, we studied the development of entity beans. We looked at the lifecycle of entity beans and several callback methods. We discussed the distinction between the CMP and BMP entity beans. We developed a CMP `PassengerBean` to represent a passenger for our Connexia Airlines example and explained how to declare relationships in the CMP model. We also examined the query language (EJB QL) and the different constructs that it supports. The CMP model allows for rapid development, where the bean provider can focus on the business logic while leaving the infrastructure to the EJB container. We also developed BMP `AircraftBean` that included the logic to access the database.

The BMP model requires more work for the bean provider but it also allows for more flexibility than the CMP model.

✦   ✦   ✦

Using Message-Driven Beans

✦ ✦ ✦ ✦

In This Chapter

Using Enterprise
JavaBeans for
messaging

Bringing together EJB
and MOM

Noting changes to
MDB in the EJB 2.1
specification

Working with EJBs
asynchronously

✦ ✦ ✦ ✦

The message-driven beans are the EJB components, which perform one specific function — retrieve messages from a message-oriented middleware (MOM). As opposed to session or entity beans, client programs do not access these beans directly. These beans use message listeners and are activated by the EJB container when the message arrives. The client programs could be written using Java or any other language that can send messages to the MOM of your choice, which makes messaging in general and MDB in particular a good component for integration of the J2EE systems with the legacy applications.

We've briefly mentioned message-driven beans (MDBs) in Chapter 14 while discussing the Enterprise JavaBeans architecture. You also learned in Chapter 9 how Java programs send messages to each other using the Java Messaging Service (JMS) API. In this chapter we'll discuss how the EJB technology in general, and MDB in particular, fits in the J2EE messaging architecture. But before going into details, let's see why the need for MDB has arisen in the EJB world.

Understanding the Need for MDB

One of the most important benefits of message-oriented systems is that the messages can be sent and received *asynchronously* (there could be a time gap between these two actions). This process is very similar to sending or receiving an e-mail. A person can send an e-mail and immediately continue working on some other task without waiting for a reply. The recipient may not have his or her mail reading program up and running when the message is sent, but he or she will get the message later.

Enterprise JavaBeans are controlled by an EJB container that creates, pools, activates, passivates, and removes them. Using an EJB for sending messages is straightforward. For example, you can create a JMS `Connection` object in the `ejbCreate()` method and close it in the `ejbRemove()` method. You may also need to repeat these operations in the methods `ejbActivate()` and `ejbPassivate()`. After you've done this, any business method of an EJB can create a JMS `Session`, a `QueueSender`, or a `TopicPublisher`, and send or publish a message.

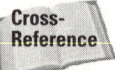

Cross-Reference   See Chapter 9 for a discussion of JMS.

Things get complicated if you want a receiving session bean that will "wait" for the messages asynchronously. Even though nothing stops you from declaring that a session bean implement a `MessageListener` interface, the container's action may not guarantee that this listening thread will work properly because the bean is not an independent Java program. The EJB specification in general strongly discourages developers from using any threads that are not created by the container. It also specifically states that "session and entity beans are not permitted to be message listeners." For details, see section 15.4.2 in the EJB specification 2.1, which can be downloaded from `http://java.sun.com/products/ejb/docs.html`).

That's why a special class called message-driven beans has been introduced in the EJB specification 2.0. The first design of MDB supported only JMS messaging. Starting from version 2.1, message-driven beans can be also used for other types of messaging, such as the lightweight SOAP-based messaging which is widely used in Web services.

Message-oriented middleware is still required for MDB. In some cases the EJB vendor of your choice may provide the implementation of the MDB and the MOM. For example, the application server WebSphere 5.0 from IBM supports EJB 2.0, and it also provides a very robust MOM called WebSphere MQ (formerly MQSeries). The application server WebLogic from BEA Systems also supports EJB 2.0 starting from version 6.1. BEA also provides its own implementation of MOM. Application-server vendors often enable you to use the MOM of another vendor even if they provide their own. For example, WebLogic explains how to do this in its white paper called "Using Foreign JMS Providers with WebLogic Server." For details, see `http://dev2dev.bea.com/resourcelibrary/whitepapers/jmsproviders.jsp`.

A sample scenario of ticket reservations system that uses MDB is shown in Figure 17-1. For simplicity, the same clients send orders and receive confirmations. In real life senders and receivers could be different. The MDB receives the messages from the `Reservation` queue, passes them for further processing to a session bean, which creates a reservation and sends confirmations or rejections back to the `Confirmation` queue.

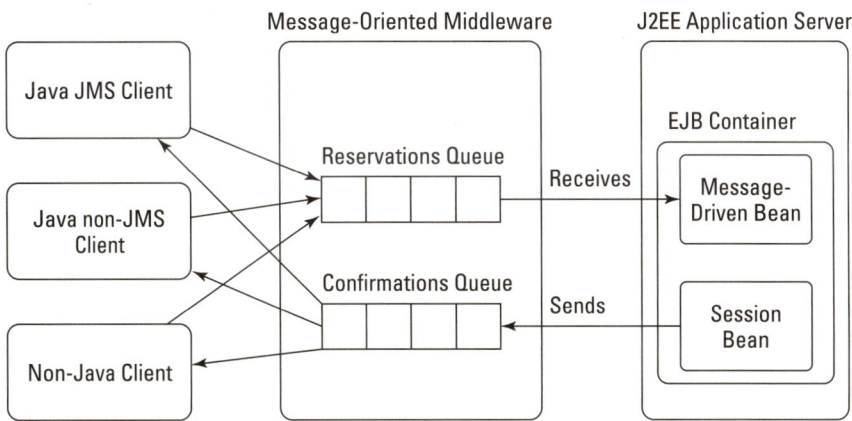

Figure 17-1: A sample ticket reservation system

An MDB has neither home nor remote interfaces, because its clients do not need to access the bean — it just sits in the EJB container's memory and listens to a particular queue or a topic. Such a bean must implement two interfaces: `MessageDrivenBean` and some message listener, such as `javax.jms.MessageListener`. When a message appears in the queue the EJB container picks one of the message-driven beans from the pool and passes the message to that bean's `onMessage()` method. Listing 17-1 shows how the `Caterer` class from Chapter 9 could be implemented as an MDB.

Listing 17-1: **Message-driven bean caterer**

```java
import javax.jms.*;
import javax.ejb.*;
public class Caterer
            implements MessageDrivenBean, MessageListener{
  MessageDrivenContext ctx;
  //  A no-argument  constructor is required
  public Caterer() {}
  public void onMessage(Message message){
 try {
        MapMessage mmsg = (MapMessage)msg;
        System.out.println("Meal request for flight "+
            mmsg.getString("flightNumber")+
            " on date "+mmsg.getString("date"));
    }
    catch(Exception e) {
        e.printStackTrace();
    }
  }
```

Continued

Listing 17-1 *(continued)*

```
public void ejbRemove()throws javax.ejb.EJBException {
}
public void setMessageDrivenContext(
 MessageDrivenContext ctx)throws javax.ejb.EJBException {
   this.ctx = ctx;
}
public void ejbCreate()  {
}
}
```

If you use MDB instead of independent Java message consumers, an EJB container gives you the following excellent freebies:

✦ **Transaction services** — Like other beans, transactions can be handled either in the code (bean-managed transactions) or by the container (container-managed transactions).

✦ **Automatic pooling** — Because MDBs are controlled by a container, you can easily configure the number of MDBs by specifying pool size in the deployment descriptor (described in the next section). In high-volume systems you can easily increase the number of consumers by changing the pool size.

✦ **Co-location of receivers and other beans** — MDBs, session and entity beans live in the same EJB container, which eliminates the need for the network communication between the message receiver and the beans that implement business processing logic.

✦ **Simple association of queues or topics to an MDB in deployment descriptors** — See the section, "MDB deployment descriptors," later in this chapter.

✦ **Security services** — Security of the MDB can be specified in the deployment descriptor of the bean.

As you see, message-driven beans become very handy for any EJB application that needs to receive messages from another system. Existence of MDBs allows you to perform more work inside of the EJB container. Similarly to session and entity beans, the EJB container controls the lifecycle of MDBs as well. During the lifecycle of an MDB, a container calls various methods on the bean, which are described in the next section.

Reviewing MDB Lifecycle Methods

Every MDB must implement the `javax.ejb.MessageDrivenBean` and the appropriate message-listener interface, for example `javax.jms.MessageListener`. As of EJB specification 2.1, besides the JMS messaging, vendors of EJB containers must also support MDBs based on the Java Connector Architecture 1.5.

 **Cross-Reference**   See Chapter 19 for a discussion of the Java Connector Architecture.

An EJB container calls several methods during the lifecycle of an MDB. The `javax.ejb.MessageDrivenBean` interface declares two callback methods that are invoked by the container: `ejbRemove()` and `setMessageDrivenContext()`.Each MDB must have a no-argument `ejbCreate()` method. After creating an instance of the bean's class, the container calls the `setMessageDrivenContext()` method, and then `ejbCreate()`. The `ejbRemove()` method is called when the bean's instance is being removed from memory by the container. The `setMessageDrivenContext()` method is called to associate the bean instance with its context maintained by the container. The bean's context can be used for transaction management, security, and the EJB timer services.

If an MDB implements the `javax.jms.MessageListener` interface it can be called a *JMS message-driven bean*. In this case the bean must implement the `onMessage()` method, as shown in Listing 17-1. This method is called by the EJB container when a message has been placed into the queue or published to a topic specified in the bean's deployment descriptor. The `onMessage()` method has to contain the business logic that handles the processing of the message.

If an MDB implements either the `javax.xml.messaging.OnewayListener` or `javax.xml.messaging.ReqRespListener` interface, it can be called a *JAXM message-driven bean* (JAXM stands for *Java API for XML Messaging*).

Like any other EJB, message-driven beans can implement an optional interface, `javax.ejb.TimedObject`. This interface is a container-provided EJB timer service that allows an EJB to be registered for timer callback methods that will be invoked by the container after a specified interval. This interface has a single method, `ejbTimeout()`, and if an MDB is registered with the EJB timer service this method will be called when the timer expires.

Besides the ability to control the lifecycle of an MDB, the container needs to have the means to associate the MDB with a particular message producer, set the acknowledgement, mode, transactional behavior and some other configurable attributes. Such attributes are specified in the MDB deployment descriptors that are discussed next.

Examining MDB Deployment Descriptors

Configurable attributes of message-driven beans are located in the same XML-based deployment descriptors where the session or entity beans store their attributes. The EJB specification 2.0 has defined the major MDB attributes, and the EJB specification 2.1 added new functionality to MDBs and some new descriptor elements. Let's talk about how we can configure message-driven beans.

Deployment descriptors as per EJB 2.0

If you compare the code in Listing 17-1 with the `Caterer` class from Chapter 9 you'll notice that the MDB version does not create a JMS connection, session, or receiver, and that the names of the queues are not specified in the code. These JMS objects are specified in the deployment descriptors of the MDB. Some of the values have to be specified in the `ejb-jar.xml` descriptor that must be implemented by all EJB `Container` vendors, and some MDB parameters are listed in a vendor-specific descriptor(s).

Listing 17-2 shows a sample deployment descriptor, `ejb-jar.xml`, for the `Caterer` MDB. This descriptor contains the `message-driven` element that marks the bean as an MDB. It also states that the `Caterer` MDB will use container-managed transactions, and that the JMS messages will be acknowledged by means of the `auto-acknowledge` mode explained in Table 9-2 in Chapter 9. This bean will listen to a topic in a nondurable way: If the bean is not listening when a message is published to the topic, the bean won't get the message.

Listing 17-2: The deployment descriptor of the Caterer MDB

```
<!DOCTYPE ejb-jar PUBLIC "-//Sun Microsystems, Inc.//DTD
Enterprise JavaBeans 2.0//EN" "http://java.sun.com/dtd/ejb-
jar_2_0.dtd">
<ejb-jar>
    <enterprise-beans>
        <message-driven>
            <ejb-name>Caterer</ejb-name>
            <ejb-class>Caterer</ejb-class>
            <transaction-type>Container</transaction-type>
            <transaction-scope>Local</transaction-scope>
            <jms-acknowledge-mode>
                auto-acknowledge
            </jms-acknowledge-mode>
            <message-driven-destination>
              <jms-destination-type>
                  javax.jms.Topic
              </jms-destination-type>
              <jms-subscription-durability>
                  nondurable
              </jms-subscription-durability>
```

```
            </message-driven-destination>
          </message-driven>
        </enterprise-beans>
        <assembly-descriptor>
          <container-transaction>
            <method>
              <ejb-name>Caterer</ejb-name>
               <method-name>onMessage</method-name>
                <method-params>
                  <method-param>
                    javax.jms.Message
                  </method-param>
                </method-params>
            </method>
            <trans-attribute>NotSupported</trans-attribute>
          </container-transaction>
        </assembly-descriptor>
      </ejb-jar>

</ejb-jar>
```

The `ejb-jar.xml` deployment descriptor does not include queue or topic names —
these values are specified in the vendor-specific descriptors, for example in
`weblogic-ejb-jar.xml`, shown in Listing 17-3. The `MealOrders` object that represents a JMS topic has to be created, configured, and bound to the application
server's JNDI tree in advance. Decoupling the MDB code from the consumer type
and name has another benefit; should we decide to use the same bean for getting
messages from a queue instead of a topic, we do not need to change the code. We
just modify the deployment descriptor and restart the server.

Listing 17-3: **The WebLogic deployment descriptor weblogic-ejb-jar.xml**

```
<?xml version="1.0"?>
<!DOCTYPE weblogic-ejb-jar PUBLIC
    "-//BEA Systems, Inc.//DTD WebLogic 6.0.0 EJB//EN"
   "http://www.bea.com/servers/wls600/dtd/weblogic-ejb-
jar.dtd">
<weblogic-enterprise-bean>
    <ejb-name>Caterer</ejb-name>
      <message-driven-descriptor>
        <destination-jndi-name>
            MealOrders
        </destination-jndi-name>
      <pool>
       <max-beans-in-free-pool>100</max-beans-in-free-pool>
        <initial-beans-in-free-pool>20</initial-beans-in-free-pool>
```

Continued

Listing 17-3 *(continued)*

```
    </pool>
    </message-driven-descriptor>

</weblogic-enterprise-bean>
```

Note   The WebLogic application server creates and maintains a pool of message-driven beans. If the size of the pool is not specified (see the `max-beans-in-free-pool` element in Listing 17-3) the number of beans in the pool is limited only by the size of the memory.

Changes in MDB 2.1 deployment descriptors

As the step toward support for Web services, MDBs 2.1 can process not only the JMS but also other types of messages. Please note that any particular MDB can process only a single messaging type. Changes that allow you to specify the type of messages have been made in some of the deployment descriptor elements. The new `<messaging-type>` element defines whether the MDB uses JMS or some other type of messaging. For JMS messages this element will look as follows:

```
<messaging-type>javax.jms.MessageListener</messaging-type>
```

For messaging other than JMS this element must contain a fully qualified name of the appropriate class. If the `<messaging-type>` element is missing, the default value `javax.jms.MessageListener` is used.

A new generic element, `<activation-config>`, has to contain the values of the expected configuration properties of the message-driven bean — such as message acknowledgement, message selector, expected destination type, and whatever else might be needed by the messaging environment. The presence of the `<jms-acknowledge-mode>` property is no longer a given. Properties that are specific to MOM have to be specified now with the key-value pairs `<activation-config-property-name>` and `<activation-config-property-value>`. For example, the `<jms-acknowledge-mode>` element from Listing 17-2 will look as follows:

```
<activation-config>
 <activation-config-property>
    <activation-config-property-name>
       jms-acknowledge-mode
    </activation-config-property-name>
    <activation-config-property-value>
       auto-acknowledge
    </activation-config-property-value>
 </activation-config-property>

</activation-config>
```

The message-selector values are specified in a similar fashion:

```
<activation-config-property-name>
    messageselector
</activation-config-property-name>
<activation-config-property-value>
    meal_type='veg'

</activation-config-property-value>
```

The `<jms-destination-type>` element becomes `<message-destination-type>`, as follows:

```
<message-destination-type>
  javax.jms.Topic
<message-destination-type>
```

The connector-based MDBs require the URL of a remote connection factory in the following format:

```
url=corbaname:iiop:server-name:1050# server -name
```

Let's say that the server name is `April25`. The appropriate element in the descriptor file will look like this:

```
<activation-config-property-name>
        url
</activation-config-property-name>
<activation-config-property-value>
        corbaname:iiop:April25:1050#April25
</activation-config-property-value>
```

Internal messaging within EJB applications

One of the new features of EJB 2.1 is the ability to link session and entity beans that send messages with MDBs that consume them by matching producers and consumers in the deployment descriptor. The new `<message-destination-link-ref>` element specifies the usage, name, and type, and the destination to which messages have to be sent. If this element includes the `<message-destination-link>` element, the sending bean and the receiving MDB will become "linked." This linking can be done only for the beans in the same application. The rest of the fragment of the deployment descriptors in this section demonstrates how the session bean `MealOrderSender` can be linked with the MDB `Caterer` by means of the JMS topic `MealOrders`.

```
<session>
 <ejb-name>MealOrderSender</ejb-name>
  ...
 <message-destination-ref>
   <message-destination-ref-name>
```

```
        MealOrders
      </message-destination-ref-name>
      <message-destination-type>
          javax.jms.Topic
      </message-destination-type>
      <message-destination-usage>
          Produces
      </message-destination-usage>
      <message-destination-link>
          MealServiceTopic
      </message-destination-link>
    </message-destination-ref>
    ...

    </session>
```

The EJB producer can locate and get a reference to this JMS topic by executing code that might look like this:

```
Context ctx = new InitialContext();
Topic mealTopic = (Topic) ctx.lookup("MealOrders");
```

The MDB that receives meal orders must have the same value in its `<message-destination-link>` descriptor element, as the sending session bean, for example:

```
<message-driven>
  <ejb-name>Caterer</ejb-name>
   ...
  <messaging-type>

        javax.jms.MessageListener

  </messaging-type>
    <message-destination-link>
        MealServiceTopic
    </message-destination-link>
  </message-destination-ref>
  ...

  </message-driven>
```

The name of this link must also be specified in the `<message-destination>` element, as shown here:

```
    <assembly-descriptor>
    ...
    <message-destination>
      <message-destination-name>
        MealServiceTopic
      </message-destination-name>
```

```
</message-destination>
...
</assembly-descriptor>
```

In general, deployment descriptors allow an easy mapping of the message-driven beans to the message sources, specify acknowledgment modes, control the number of message consumers and work with many other configurable bean's attributes. After the beans are deployed, they can be accessed by the clients, and this is the next topic of our chapter.

Understanding Clients and MDB

Message-driven beans are special in that the clients never need to access them. The clients just send or publish messages, and from their perspective an MDB is just a consumer of these messages. That's why there are no such things as home or remote interfaces used by the clients of session or entity beans. From the perspective of the client MDBs are stateless, because they do not know who their clients are. The only state that MDBs may store is references to other objects, for example open database connections.

Application servers usually create and maintain a pool of MDBs, which may improve the speed of message consumption tremendously because the beans will retrieve messages concurrently. In some scenarios, however, this process might present a problem for the clients that need to ensure that the messages are retrieved in the same order in which they were sent. Imagine an online stock-trading system that enables customers to place their orders to buy or sell securities 24 hours a day. Let's say a customer enters an order to sell 100 shares of IBM at 8:30 a.m., and it's placed in the application's queue. At 8:31 a.m. some good news about IBM is broadcast on the radio, and the customer decides to keep the stock and places a *cancel* order that goes to the same queue. The message-driven beans will start consuming the messages concurrently from this queue at 9:30 a.m. when the stock market opens. The chances are that the *cancel* order will be picked up before the order to sell! No general solution for such problems exists — each application has to implement some processing logic specific to the business.

The fact that the clients and MDBs are decoupled makes it impossible for the beans to know anything about the transaction context of their clients. Besides, transactions lock up the system resources and should be executed quickly, but the possible time gaps between the sending and receiving messages can lead to a long running transaction. That's why the only options for the `<trans-attribute>` element in the MDB deployment descriptor are either `NotSupported` or `Required` (the bean can start its own transaction).

The next section will discuss the relationships between the clients, message-driven and session beans from a different perspective — asynchronous versus synchronous processing.

Working with EJBs Asynchronously

As opposed to asynchronous processing offered by MDBs, session and entity beans work only in a synchronous mode. For example, a client gets a remote reference to the `OrderProcessor` session bean and calls its method `placeOrder()` to buy 100 shares of stock with a symbol SUNW and waits till the method is complete. The process of placing such an order can consist of the following steps:

1. Creating a new order in the database.

2. Connecting and passing the order to the system running on the stock exchange.

3. Receiving the confirmation or a rejection of the order from the stock exchange.

4. Updating the order status in the database.

If the method `placeOrder()` returns a result to the client only after all of the above steps are complete, we call it a synchronous processing. But in a distributed application these steps are performed on different computers and multiple clients should to be able to place the orders fast, regardless of the delays that may happen during any of these steps. That's why it could be a good idea to introduce the asynchronous messaging to this process. For example, instead of a direct connection to the stock exchange, the `OrderProcessor` session bean can send the orders as messages to a queue, while the `StockExchangeOrder` MDB retrieves the messages from this queue. Now the `placeOrder()` method will complete much faster, and the orders can be accumulated in the message queue in case of delays in the stock exchange. Another MDB (namely, `StockExchangeConfirmation`) will listen to the confirmations and rejections coming back from the stock exchange and initiate the order status update in the database.

If your application server does not support MDBs, you can arrange such asynchronous work with the session or entity beans using one of the J2EE design patterns called *Service Activator*. The service activator can be implemented as an independent Java class that receives the client messages asynchronously, and then locates and invokes the required business methods (namely, the session bean's methods) to fulfill the request. The service activator class must implement the proper listener interface to be able to consume the messages, for example:

```
public class OrderServiceActivator implements
MessageListener{...}
```

On the message arrival this class finds the `OrderProcessor` session bean and calls its `placeOrder()` method. You can find more information on the service-activator pattern at http://java.sun.com/blueprints/corej2eepatterns/Patterns/ServiceActivator.html.

Usually J2EE application servers allow you to specify the classes that have to be automatically instantiated on the server's startup. If the `OrderServiceActivator` class is specified as such startup class, it will be instantiated by the server and in a daemon-like manner will listen to the incoming messages until the server is shut down. The other alternative is to instantiate this class independently outside of the application server's JVM.

During your business processing the session beans could also be clients to another session or entity beans, and you can always break this synchronous link in your business chain by introducing either an MDB or a custom-made service activator class.

Summary

Messaging is an elegant way to connect different components of distributed applications. Message-driven beans enable you to take advantage of the benefits of EJB containers while integrating J2EE applications with Java-based or non-Java-based systems.

In this chapter we've covered such topics as the benefits of using message-driven beans as opposed to independent Java programs, relationships between the clients and MDBs, and how to configure an MDB using deployment descriptors. We've also discussed the asynchronous nature of the message-driven beans.

MDB should definitely be considered for real-time systems that require high-performance and concurrent message processing. The introduction of non-JMS message-driven beans into EJB specification 2.1 makes them even more valuable components for distributed enterprise applications.

✦　　✦　　✦

The Data Tier

◆   ◆   ◆   ◆

In This Part

Chapter 18
Reviewing Java
Database
Connectivity

Chapter 19
Understanding the
J2EE Connector
Architecture

◆   ◆   ◆   ◆

Reviewing Java Database Connectivity

In This Chapter

Introducing the different types of JDBC drivers

Working with result sets

Using the RowSet interface

Explaining database connection pooling

Business applications usually store data in databases. Currently, relational-database-management systems (RDBMSes) are the most popular ones. They store data in tables that consist of rows and columns, and understand Structured Query Language (SQL) (which is beyond the scope of this book). The major commercial relational RDBMSes are Oracle, DB2, SQL Server, and Sybase.

Two technologies are available for accessing relational databases from Java programs. The first is SQLJ, which is an American National Standards Institute (ANSI) and International Organization for Standardization (ISO) standard for embedding SQL in Java. Next is JDBC (Java Database Connectivity), which is defined by the Java Community Process.

J2SE and J2EE include the packages `java.sql` and `javax.sql`, which contain all classes required for a Java program that access a database by means of JDBC. Please refer to the vendor's documentation for your DBMS or J2EE application server to see what version of JDBC drivers is implemented.

The best thing about the JDBC Application Programming Interface (API) is that it's the same for all databases; it does not require any proprietary calls, and it provides easy access to the information. If you use standard SQL or stored procedures and need to switch from Oracle to SQL Server, for example, you need change only the name of the driver or a data source in your Java programs.

In this chapter we'll discuss JDBC technology and its current specification, 3.0. We'll also cover the following topics:

Various JDBC driver types.

Different methods of executing SQL queries and processing database result sets.

How to update the data stored in a database using SQL or stored procedures.

What are the benefits and how to use database connection pools and data sources.

How to perform batch updates, use the savepoints and transactions.

Disconnected result sets.

All examples in this chapter have been tested against the Oracle database server, version 9.2. An evaluation version of this product is available at http://otn. oracle.com/software/products/oracle9i/content.html. The JDBC drivers can be found under the installation directory in the file jdbc\lib\classes12.jar, which must be added to the CLASSPATH variable.

Introducing JDBC Driver Types

JDBC drivers play the role of middleman between a Java program and an RDBMS. Drivers are available from database vendors and from the vendors of J2EE application servers. Sun also provides a reference implementation of drivers for each JDBC specification. The list of available JDBC drivers can be found at the following URL: http://industry.java.sun.com/products/jdbc/drivers.

Regardless of what RDBMS you use, you should understand the four following types of JDBC drivers and be aware of their pros and cons as you decide which one is most suitable for your application:

✦ **Type 1**—This driver is a JDBC-ODBC bridge that allows Java programs to work with a database using widely available ODBC drivers. For example, if you have an ODBC driver for Oracle installed on your computer, no additional Java classes are required for database access. The major drawbacks of the ODBC drivers are that they are slower than the other types, and must be installed and configured on each user's machine—on Windows computers installation and configuration are done via a special icon in the Control Panel (see more details in the section "Configuring the JDBC-ODBC Bridge"). If you access databases from Java applets, access to the hard disk is restricted and type 1 drivers may not be an option.

✦ **Type 2**—This driver consists of Java classes that work in conjunction with the non-Java native drivers, provided by the database vendors, that are installed on the client's machines. These drivers work much faster than type 1 drivers, but they also require installation and configuration on the machine on which the Java programs run. These drivers convert JDBC requests to calls to the client's portion of the native DBMS drivers.

A type 2 driver is a partly-Java driver. In the client-server applications, when multiple clients are working directly with a database, the fact that these drivers must be installed on each client's machine is a downside of the type 2 drivers. In J2EE applications these drivers are installed only on the machines that run application servers.

✦ **Type 3** — This driver is a pure Java network driver (JDBC-Net driver) that is provided by some application servers and consists of two parts. The first part is the client's portion, which performs a DBMS-independent SQL call. The second part is the SQL call itself, which is then translated to a specific protocol according to the middleware vendor. This driver has the flexibility of working with different databases. The downside of using this driver is that you have to deal with a middleware vendor (or application server vendor) which created these flexible drivers, and that can be expensive. All other types of drivers are usually provided by the database vendors for free.

✦ **Type 4** — This driver is a pure Java driver, which comes as a `.jar` or a `.zip` file containing Java classes that perform direct calls to the database server. It does not need any configuration on the client's machine and can be dynamically downloaded to the client. The applets can be packaged with this driver by means of the `archive` attribute of the `<applet>` HTML tag, which automatically downloads the `.jar` file with the drivers to the user machine's memory.

The best way to learn how to work with JDBC drivers is by writing the Java program that accesses the data stored in the database. That's why the next section will show you an example of such program.

Creating Your First JDBC Program

In this section we'll go over several simple steps that must be performed in any Java program that works with a relational database using JDBC. We'll identify the required steps and then implement them in a sample program that displays the list of registered users of Connexia Airlines (described in Appendix A).

We assume that the reader knows that in relational databases data is stored in tables as *rows* and *columns*. One row represents one database record, for example, one customer, one order, and so on. A column corresponds to a field from a record, i.e. last name, age, and so on. The SQL *select* statement is used to retrieve data from the database, for example:

```
select lastname, firstname from customer
```

The SQL *insert* statement is used to add a new row to the table, for example:

```
Insert into customer values("Lee", "Mary")
```

The SQL *update* statement modifies the data. The next example will change the last name of a customer with id=123. The new last name will become Smith after execution of the following statement:

```
Update customer set lastname="Smith" where custid=123
```

Finally, the SQL *delete* removes a row(s) from the database:

```
Delete from customer where custid=123
```

Our example will use the tables air_user and login that must be created in Oracle or another relational database by means of SQL *create* statements, as shown in Listing 18-1.

Listing 18-1: **The database tables air_user and login**

```
CREATE TABLE air_user (
    id                    NUMBER NOT NULL,
    lastname      VARCHAR2(20)      NOT NULL,
    firstname     VARCHAR2(20)      NOT NULL,
    street  VARCHAR2(30)      NOT NULL,
    city    VARCHAR2(30)         NULL,
    state   VARCHAR2(2)          NULL,
    zip     NUMBER(5)     NOT NULL,
    country       VARCHAR2(10)      NOT NULL,
    phone         VARCHAR2(10)         NULL,
    fax           VARCHAR(12)          NULL,
    email         VARCHAR2(40)         NULL,
    user_type     varchar2(1)          NULL,
    emloyeeID     VARCHAR2(10)         NULL,
        PRIMARY KEY (id),
        FOREIGN KEY (id) references login(userID)
);
insert into  air_user values (1,'Queen','Larry','123 Main St.',
'Princeton','NJ','08068','USA',6091235566',  '6091235567',
'ql123@somemail.com','A',null);
insert into  air_user values (2,'Nelson','Mary', '30 Broadway',
  'New York','NY','10001','USA','2121035566',  '2121205567',
'nm@somemail.com','P','1398' );

CREATE TABLE login (
    userID          NUMBER          NOT NULL,
    username        VARCHAR2(10)    NOT NULL,
    password        VARCHAR2(10)    NOT NULL,
    hint_question    VARCHAR2(50) NULL,
    hint_answer      VARCHAR2(50) NULL,
    role             VARCHAR2(10) NOT NULL
            CHECK (role IN ('A', 'P', 'C', 'E')),
                PRIMARY KEY (userID)
);
```

```
insert into login values(1, 'LQueen', 'spring',
    'What is the name of your pet?','Sharick','consumer');
insert into login values(2, 'MNelson', 'fall',
   ' What is the name of your boyfriend?','Joe','employee');
```

After the table is created, two rows are inserted for the logins LQueen and MNelson. To simplify conversion to other relational DBMSes, only two data types have been used in the tables air_user and login — all text columns have the data type VARCHAR2, and all numeric data are represented by the type NUMBER.

Retrieving data

The following is a typical sequence of actions for a Java program to perform to retrieve data from a database table or tables:

1. Load a JDBC driver using the method Class.forName(). You'll have to find out the name of the class to be loaded by using the method forName() from the driver's documentation. Please note that so-called XA drivers support distributed transactions and the two-phase commit — you can easily recognize them because the name of the class always contains XA.

2. Obtain the database connection. You can do this by calling the DriverManager. getConnection() method. Because obtaining a connection to the database is a slow process, we recommend using database connection pools, which are described later in this chapter in the section, "Explaining Database Connection Pools and Data Sources."

3. Create a Statement object by calling Connection.createStatement(). As an alternative, you could create a PreparedStatement or a CallableStatement; these are explained a little bit later in the sections, "The PreparedStatement Class" and "The CallableStatement Class" respectively.

4. For SQL select statements call the Statement.executeQuery() method. For SQL insert, update, or delete statements call the Statement. executeUpdate() method. For SQL queries, which produce more than one result set, use the execute() method.

5. Write a loop to process the database result set, if any. For example:

```
ResultSet rs=
        stmt.executeQuery("select lastname from air_user");
    while (rs.next()) {
        String lastName=rs.getString("lastname");
    }
```

6. Release the system resources by closing the ResultSet, Statement, and Connection objects.

The UserList class shown in Listing 18-2 performs all the preceding steps. This class displays the users' data from the table air_user shown in Listing 18-1 using Oracle JDBC drivers of type 2 (described earlier in this chapter).

Listing 18-2: The UserList program

```
import java.sql.*;
class UserList {
  public static void main(String argv[]) {
   Connection conn=null;
   Statement stmt=null;
   ResultSet rs=null;

   try {
    // Load the Oracle JDBC driver
    Class.forName("oracle.jdbc.driver.OracleDriver");

    // Connect to locally installed Oracle database using
    // JDBC driver of type 2 and default user
    // credentials scott/tiger.
    // Type 4 driver would have been loaded using
    // "jdbc:oracle:thin:scott/tiger@"

    conn = DriverManager.getConnection(
         "jdbc:oracle:oci:scott/tiger@");

    String sqlQuery=
            "select id,lastname,firstname from air_user";
    stmt = conn.createStatement();

    // Execute SQL and get the ResultSet object
    rs = stmt.executeQuery(sqlQuery);

    // Process the result set - print user id and name
    while(rs.next()){
      int id = rs.getInt("id");
      String lastName = rs.getString("lastname");
      String firstName= rs.getString("firstname");
      System.out.println(" User Id: " + id +
                  ", Last Name: " + lastName +
                  ", First Name: " + firstName + "\n");
    }

   } catch( SQLException se ) {
      System.out.println ("SQLError: " + se.getMessage()
         + " code: " + se.getErrorCode());
   } catch( Exception e ) {
      e.printStackTrace();
   } finally{
      // clean up system resources
      try{
```

```
        rs.close();
        stmt.close();
        conn.close();
    } catch(Exception e){
      e.printStackTrace();
    }
  }
 }
}
```

After compilation and running, the UserList program's command-prompt window should look like this:

```
User Id: 1, Last Name: Queen, First Name: Larry
User Id: 2, Last Name: Nelson, First Name: Mary
```

Database-error processing

The UserList class processes possible database errors by catching an SQLException. You can retrieve the original database-error code by calling the getErrorCode() method, and the error text by calling the getMessage() method. Sometimes a DBMS will return more than one error. The following example prints all errors that may have been returned by a database:

```
catch( SQLException se ) {
    do{
        System.out.println ("SQLError: " + se.getMessage()
            + " code: " + se.getErrorCode() +
            + " SQL state: " + se.getSQLState());
        se.getNextException();
    } while (se !=null);
    }
```

You can retrieve database warning messages by calling the getWarnings() method. This method is available in the classes Statement, PreparedStatement, and CallableStatement.

Processing result sets

After execution of the line rs = stmt.executeQuery(sqlQuery), the cursor rs points at the very first row of the result set in memory. Each row contains as many columns as were specified in the SQL select statement. A program can extract each column's value based on the data type of the column by calling such methods as getString(), getInt(), and so on. JDBC drivers are smart enough to convert the data from database-specific types to the corresponding Java types; for example, Oracle's varchar2 becomes a Java String.

If you know the names of columns in the result set, specify them as method arguments, as in the following example:

```
String lastName = rs.getString("lastname");
String firstName= rs.getString("firstname");
```

You can get the same values by specifying the relative position of the column from the SQL select clause, as shown here:

```
String lastName = rs.getString(2);   // second column
String firstName= rs.getString(3);   // third column
```

Columns are numbered from the left starting with 1. In some cases, the only choice you have is the column numbers. For example, the following SQL query does not produce a column name:

```
stmt.executeQuery("Select count(*) from air_user");
```

The UserList class just prints the retrieved data in a loop, but a result set can also be placed in a Java collection object for further processing. The ResultSet object holds the database connection and is not serializable. If you need to send the result set over a network, either use a RowSet (explained later in this chapter in the section "Using the RowSet Interface"), or create a class representing a row from the result set (see Listing 18-3) and populate a Vector or other Java collection object with its instances, as shown in Listing 18-3.

Listing 18-3: **Creating a collection of AirUsers**

```
class AirUser{
  private int userId;
  private String lastName;
  private String firstName;
  public void setUserId(int value){userId=value;}
  public void setLastName(String value){lastName=value;}
  public void setFirstName(String value){firstName=value;}
  public int getUserId(){return userId;}
  public String getLastName(){return lastName;}
  public String getFirstName(){return firstName;}
}
class UserList2 {
  // the code to connect to a database and get
  // the result goes here
  Vector airUsers = new Vector();
  while (rs.next()){
    AirUser currentUser = new AirUser();
    currentUser.setEmpNo(rs.getInt("id"));
    currentUser.setEName(rs.getString("lastName"));
    currentUser.setJob(rs.getString("firstname"));
    airUsers.add(currUser);
  }
```

```
    // Now you can serialize the Vector airUsers to a stream
    // pointing to a remote computer, if needed.
}
```

The ResultSetMetaData class

JDBC enables you to process a result set even if the database-table columns are not specified in the SQL query. Imagine that you need to write a program that will accept any SQL `select` statement and display the retrieved data. The `java.sql.ResultSetMetaData` class can dynamically find out the structure of the underlying database table—how many columns it contains, and the types and names of the columns. Here's an example:

```
String sqlQuery = "select * from AirUser ";
ResultSet rs = stmt.executeQuery(sqlQuery);

ResultSetMetaData rsMeta = rs.getMetaData();
int colCount = rsMeta.getColumnCount();

for (int i = 1; i <= colCount; i++)  {
  System.out.println(
      " Column name: " + rsMeta.getColumnName(i) +
      " Column type: " + rsMeta.getColumnTypeName(i));
}
```

The `ShowAnyData` class from the upcoming listing prints a result set based on any SQL `select` statement passed from a command line, as in the following example:

```
java ShowAnyData "select * from air_user"
```

The output of such a command will look like this:

```
ID LASTNAME FIRSTNAME STREET CITY STATE ZIP COUNTRY PHONE FAX
EMAIL EMLOYEEID AGENTID
1 Queen Larry 123 Main St. Princeton NJ 8068 USA 6091235566
6091235567 ql123@somemail.com A null
2 Nelson Mary 30 Broadway New York NY 10001 USA 2121035566
2121205567 nm@somemail.com  P 1398
```

The code for `ShowAnyData.java` appears in Listing 18-4.

Listing 18-4: **ShowAnyData.java**

```
import java.sql.*;
class ShowAnyData {
```

Continued

Listing 18-4 *(continued)*

```java
public static void main(String args[]) {
 Connection conn=null;
 Statement stmt=null;
 ResultSet rs=null;
 if (args.length==0){
  System.out.println(
         "Usage: java ShowAnyData SQLSelectStatement");
  System.out.println(
  "For example: java ShowAnyData \"Select * from EMP\"");
  System.exit(1);
 }
 try {
    Class.forName("oracle.jdbc.driver.OracleDriver");
    conn = DriverManager.getConnection(
      "jdbc:oracle:oci:scott/tiger@");
    stmt = conn.createStatement();
     rs = stmt.executeQuery(args[0]);
   // Find out the number of columns , their names,
   // and display the data
   ResultSetMetaData rsMeta = rs.getMetaData();
   int colCount = rsMeta.getColumnCount();
    for (int i = 1; i <= colCount; i++)  {
     System.out.print(rsMeta.getColumnName(i) + " ");
     }
   System.out.println();
    while (rs.next()){
       for (int i = 1; i <= colCount; i++)  {
         System.out.print(rs.getString(i) + " ");
       }
       System.out.println();
    }
  } catch( SQLException se ) {
     System.out.println ("SQLError: " + se.getMessage ()
                       + " code: " + se.getErrorCode ());
  } catch( Exception e ) {
     System.out.println(e.getMessage());
     e.printStackTrace();
  } finally{
      try{
    rs.close();
    stmt.close();
    conn.close();
      } catch(Exception e){
          e.printStackTrace();
      }
  }
 }
}
```

Scrollable result sets

So far we've been navigating JDBC result sets using the `next()` method, which enables us to move forward only. Another option is to create a scrollable result set, so the cursor can navigate the result set both backward and forward. A two-argument version of the `createStatement()` method exists. The first argument specifies the type of scrolling (TYPE_FORWARD_ONLY, TYPE_SCROLL_INSENSITIVE, or TYPE_SCROLL_SENSITIVE), and the second enables you to make the result set either read-only or updateable (CONCUR_READ_ONLY or CONCUR_UPDATABLE, respectively), as in the following example:

```
Statement stmt = con.createStatement(
                ResultSet.TYPE_SCROLL_INSENSITIVE,
                        ResultSet.CONCUR_READ_ONLY);
ResultSet rs = stmt.executeQuery("select * from air_user");
```

The TYPE_FORWARD_ONLY argument allows the cursor to move forward only. By using either TYPE_SCROLL_INSENSITIVE or TYPE_SCROLL_SENSITIVE you can determine whether the scrolling should reflect the changes that might have been made to the result-set data. The next example sets the cursor at the end of the result set and moves the cursor backward:

```
rs.afterLast();
while (rs.previous()){
     int id = rs.getInt("id");
     String lastName = rs.getString("lastname");
     String firstName= rs.getString("firstname");
     System.out.println(" User Id: " + id +
                      ", Last Name: " + lastName +
                      ", First Name" + firstName + "\n");
}
```

You can also move the cursor to a specific row, as shown in the following examples:

```
rs.absolute(25);   // moves the cursor to the 25th row
rs.relative(-4);   // moves the cursor to the 21st row
rs.first();
rs.last();
rs.beforeFirst();
```

The CONCUR_UPDATABLE option makes the result set updatable and enables you to modify the underlying database table while scrolling. For example, the following statements will update the phone of the user based on the cursor's current position:

```
rs.updateString("phone","8001234567");
rs.updateRow();
```

The PreparedStatement class

This is a subclass of the `Statement` class: It compiles the SQL statement before execution and can also take parameters. Let's say we need to execute the same query—for example `select * from air_user where id=...`—multiple times. The user IDs come from the `userId[]` array. If we use the `Statement` class, this SQL query will be compiled in each iteration of the loop, like this:

```
for (int i=0; i< userId.length; i++){
  sqlQuery="select * from air_user where id=" + userId[i];
  stmt.executeQuery(sqlQuery);
}
```

The class `PreparedStatement` gives us a different solution:

```
PreparedStatement stmt=
  conn.prepareStatement("select * from air_userwhere id =?");

for (int i=0; i< userId.length; i++){
  // pass the id as a parameter to  replace the question mark
  stmt.setInt(1, userId [i];)
  ResultSet rs=stmt.executeQuery(sqlQuery);
  // Process the result set here
}
```

In this case the SQL statement is compiled only once and parameters are provided by the appropriate `setXXX()` method, depending on the data type of the underlying column. The first argument of such methods is the parameter number. If a query needs to take two parameters, for example, you could arrange it as follows:

```
PreparedStatement stmt=conn.prepareStatement(
    " select * from air_user where lastname =? and city=?");
for (int i=0; i < userName.length; i++){
  stmt.setInt(1,userName[i];)
  stmt.setString(2,"New York");
 ResultSet rs=stmt.executeQuery(sqlQuery);
}
```

A special method, `setNull()`, enables you to use the null value in a query.

Theoretically you can expect better performance from the `PreparedStatement` class than from the `Statement` class, but in real life performance varies depending on the vendor's implementation of the particular JDBC driver.

The CallableStatement class

This class extends the `PreparedStatement` class and is used for executing database stored procedures from a Java program. Let's say a stored procedure called `changeEmpTitle` takes two parameters: `employeeId` and `title`. Here's the code with which to execute this stored procedure:

```
CallableStatement stmt = conn.prepareCall(
                ("{call changeEmpTitle(?,?) }");
stmt.setInt(1,7566);
stmt.setString (2,"Partner");
stmt.executeUpdate();
```

If a stored procedure returns some values using output parameters, each of these values must be registered before the statement is executed. The next example shows how to execute a stored procedure, getEmpTitle, which takes an employee's ID and returns her title through the second output parameter:

```
CallableStatement stmt = conn.prepareCall(
                ("{call getEmpTitle(?,?) }");
stmt.setInt(1, 7566);
stmt.registerOutParameter(2,java.sql.Types.VARCHAR);
 stmt.executeQuery();
String title=stmt.getString(2);
```

In general, stored procedures should be used to encapsulate business processing that consists of multiple steps that involves SQL. For example, to get an employee title the stored procedure getEmpTitle may need to log this request (insert a row into another table), and only after that execute the SQL select statement. The stored procedure changeEmpTitle may need to update multiple tables as a single transaction. The batch updates that are explained in the section below are yet another way of performing multiple database updates in a transactional mode.

Performing Batch Updates

Sometimes several database modifications have to be processed as a batch; in this case, if one of the updates fails the whole transaction has to be rolled back. A well known definition states that transaction is a logical unit of work. You can find more information about database transactions in Chapter 10. In batch updates database operations must be explicitly committed in case of success or rolled back in case of failure, as in the following example:

```
 try{
  con.setAutoCommit(false);
  Statement stmt = con.createStatement();
stmt.addBatch("insert into Flight " +
        " values(1608,'PHL','MIA','13:45','18:25'");
stmt.addBatch("insert into pilot_flight values(1608,145");
  stmt.executeBatch();
  con.commit ();    // Transaction succeeded
  con.setAutoCommit(true);
}catch(Exception e){
  con.rollback ();  // Transaction failed
  e.printStackTrace();
}
```

The next section shows how to execute the same SQL statements in the same transaction with a partial rollback in case of failure.

Using Savepoints

JDBC supports savepoints starting from version 3.0. A savepoint is a marker within a transaction that allows you to rollback a part of the transaction. A `java.sql.Savepoint` interface enables you to set designated transaction savepoints so that in case of an error a Java program does not have to roll back the whole transaction — it can undo changes only up to a particular savepoint without affecting the preceding work.

Savepoints are set via the `Connection.setSavePoint()` class. The overloaded version of the `rollback()` method takes the savepoint name as a parameter. The following code will insert a row into the table `flight` even if the insert into the table `pilot_flight` should fail:

```
con.setAutoCommit(false);

Statement stmt = con.createStatement();
stmt.executeUpdate("insert into flight " +
  " values(1608,'CAN','PHL','13:45','18:25'");

Savepoint svpFlight = con.setSavepoint("AfterFlight");

try{
stmt.executeUpdate("insert into pilot_flight " +
  " values(1608,145");
}catch(Exception e){
 System.out.println("Insert into pilot_flight is rolled back"
   + e.getMessage();
   con.rollback(svpFlight);
}

con.commit();
```

At this point we've spent quite a bit of a time explaining various features of JDBC, and it may be a good idea to try to compile and run these examples. You need to have J2SE or J2EE installed, any relational database that has JDBC drivers. The next section contains detailed instructions on how to configure the JDBC drivers of type 1 for Oracle.

Configuring the JDBC-ODBC Bridge

If you already have ODBC drivers installed on your computer, the easiest way to start working with RDBMSes from a Java program is to configure the JDBC-ODBC bridge or type 1 JDBC driver. Follow these steps to perform the configuration:

1. In Windows, create a new Data Source Name (DSN) by selecting ODBC Data Sources from the Control Panel.

2. Press the Add button. You'll see a list of the ODBC drivers installed on your machine. To be consistent, we'll use the Oracle example.

3. Select the Oracle ODBC driver, as shown in Figure 18-1.

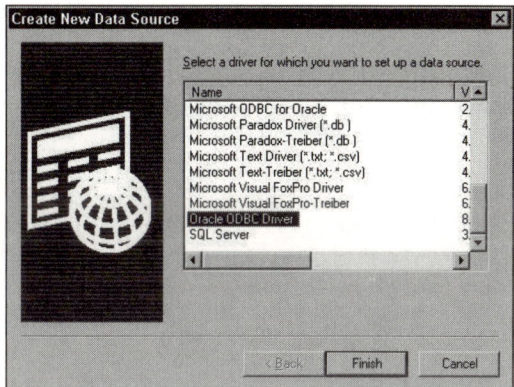

Figure 18-1: How to create a new data source

4. If Oracle runs on this computer, press the Finish button. Then enter the data source name, such as `MyOracleData` as shown in Figure 18-2. Press the OK button.

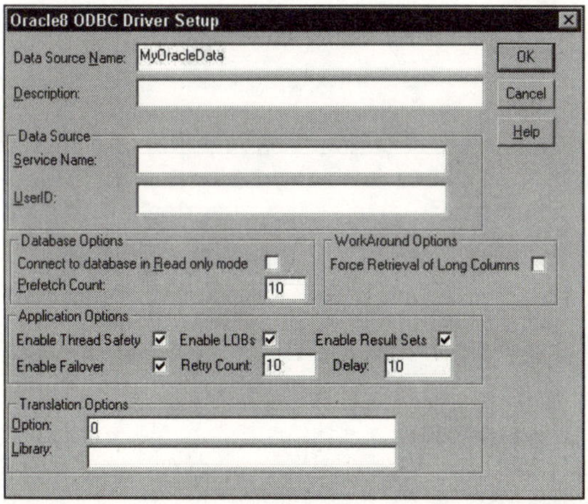

Figure 18-2: How to configure the Oracle ODBC driver

5. To create a DSN pointing to a remote Oracle database, enter the name of the computer, the port, and the remote Oracle service in the Service Name field.

After ODBC DSN is created, the Java programs are ready to access the data from the database. You do not need to install any additional software as long as you have J2SE available. The following three lines of code create the connection to the newly configured Oracle data source:

```
Class.forName("sun.jdbc.odbc.JdbcOdbcDriver");
String dsn = "jdbc:odbc:MyOracleData";
Connection con = DriverManager.getConnection(dsn,
                                    "scott", "tiger");
```

JDBC-ODBC drivers are not widely used; they work slower than the native drivers because they have one extra layer (an ODBC driver) between Java and the native driver. On the other hand, the JDBC-ODBC bridge is an easy way to get you going with JDBC technology.

In all previous examples we were getting the connection to the database using the method getConnection() from the class DriverManager. The next section will show you a more efficient way of managing database connections by means of connection pools.

Explaining Database Connection Pools and Data Sources

When a program works with a database, the most time-consuming operation is creating a Connection object. When a program closes a connection this object becomes a candidate for garbage collection, which can affect the program's performance.

Object pools in general enable you to reuse objects and minimize the need for Java garbage collection. The idea of object pooling is simple: Create a collection of objects that you'd like to reuse (such as Connection objects) and keep the reference variable that points to this collection alive for the lifetime of the application. You also need to maintain a single instance of a class that deals with this collection — such a class is usually called a *singleton*. This class should have a method, such as getConnection(), to return the next available object from the collection, and the close() method to return the object back to the collection. The good news is that connection pools are usually implemented by the major database and application-server vendors.

J2EE-compliant application servers provide a simple way to configure connection pools. You need to create two entries in the JNDI tree used by your application server: *connection pool* and *data source*. The process of creating these entries is described in this section.

Configuring connection pools

Connection pools are usually configured by means of a GUI administration tool provided by the vendor (you can also manually edit the XML file with connection attributes). For example, in WebLogic this tool is called Administration Console; in WebSphere it's Administrative Console. Typically you enter the pool's name, the minimum and maximum number of connections allowed, and the name of the database-driver class. Figure 18-3 is a snapshot of a screen that shows a sample configuration for a JDBC type 2 Oracle driver in WebLogic. Distributed-transaction support requires the XA driver, such as WebLogic's jDriver for Oracle/XA.

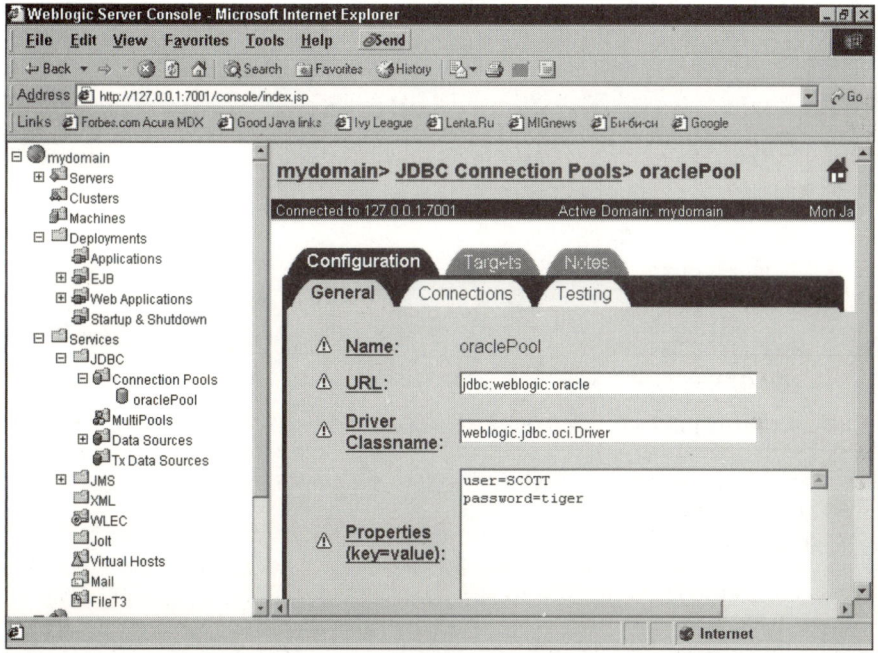

Figure 18-3: Configuring connection pools in WebLogic

After the connection pool is configured you should create the data source object that will use this connection pool.

Creating Data Source objects

The JDBC specification defines the `javax.sql.DataSource` and `javax.sql.XADataSource` classes, which represent a particular database and typically work with database-connections pools (the latter provides connections that can participate in distributed transactions). The data source is usually created with the application server's administrative tool. If you are using WebLogic, do the following:

1. Start a default WebLogic console and select the option JDBC@>DataSources, as shown in Figure 18-3. For distributed transactions select TxDataSources.

2. Enter the name of the data source (such as oracleDS) and the name of the pool to be used for database connections (such as oraclePool, created in the previous section).

After you have done this you can access the data source from a session bean, servlet, or other Java program by performing a JNDI lookup, as demonstrated here:

```
Connection con = null;
ResultSet rs   = null;
Statement stmt = null;
try {
    ctx = new InitialContext();
    DataSource ds  = (DataSource) ctx.lookup ("oracleDS");
    con = ds.getConnection();

    stmt = con.createStatement();
    stmt.execute("select * from air_user");

    rs = stmt.getResultSet();
    while (rs.next){
        // process the result set here
    }
} catch(Exception e){
    // error processing goes here
}
finally {
    try{
        rs.close();
        stmt.close();
    } catch(Exception e) {
        e.printStackTrace();
    }

    // return the Connection object to the pool.
    // It won't be garbage collected!
    try{
        con.close();
    } catch(Exception ex) {
     ex.printStackTrace();
    }
  }
```

From the application viewpoint, connection pooling is transparent. The above example just calls the getConnection() method on the DataSource object that is implemented by the J2EE application server. Behind the scenes, the DataSource object deals with a middle-tier's transaction manager that in turn uses the following classes and interfaces: `ConnectionPoolDataSource`, `PooledConnection`, `ConnectionEvent`, and `ConnectionEventListener`.

You can call a transaction distributed if it uses two or more `DataSource` objects. Distributed transactions are supported by the interfaces `XADataSource` and `XAConnection` that allow application to process data in multiple servers as a single transaction. Since distributed transactions are controlled by the transaction manager of the application server, the application can not call `commit()` or `rollback()` on the `Connection` object (this will throw a `SQLException`).

Cross-Reference   See the section, "Distributed Transactions," in Chapter 10 for additional information on this topic.

The following code fragment illustrates the use of two `DataSource` objects in a session EJB:

```
UserTransaction tx= ejbContext.getUserTransaction();
DataSource ds1 = (DataSource) ctx.lookup ("oracleDS");
Connection con1 = ds.getConnection();

tx.begin(); // begin transaction

DataSource ds2 = (DataSource) ctx.lookup ("sybaseDS");
Connection con2 = ds.getConnection();

// A regular JDBC code that works with both con1 and con2
// objects goes here, i.e. con1.getStatement(),
// stmt.executeUptdate(), and so on.
// When the processing is finished,
// the distributed transaction is committed and
// changes are applied to both databases

tx.commit();  // commit the transaction
```

The next section contains yet another example that works with the `DataSource` object.

Revisiting DBProcessor

Listing 18-5 shows the `DBProcessor` class, which is a modified version of the class shown in Listing 6-15, in Chapter 6. This code obtains the pooled database connection using the previously created data source `oracleDS`, generates the next unique database ID for the tables `air_user` and `login`, and inserts the data into these two tables in one transaction (batch).

Listing 18-5: **DBProcessor.java, Version 2**

```java
package com.connexiaair;
import java.sql.*;
import javax.sql.DataSource;
import javax.naming.*;
public class DBProcessor {
    Statement stmt = null;
    Connection con = null;
  public DBProcessor() {
  }
 public void addUser(RegisterBean rb)
       throws NamingException, SQLException{
    Statement stmt = null;
    Connection con = null;
    ResultSet  rs=null;
    int dbId=0;
    String sql="";
    try {
      // Get DB Connection from a pool using the DataSource
      Context ctx = new InitialContext();
      DataSource  ds = (DataSource) ctx.lookup("oracleDS");
      con = ds.getConnection();
      stmt = con.createStatement();
      // Get the next unique user ID
      rs = stmt.executeQuery("select max(id)+1 from air_user");
      while (rs.next()){
        dbId=rs.getInt(1);
      }

      // Perform the batch update to ensure data integrity
      con.setAutoCommit(false);
      // Insert statement for the login table
      stmt.addBatch("insert into login values("+ dbId +
        ",'" + rb.getUserId()+"'" +
        ",'" + rb.getPwd()+"'" +
        ",null,null"  +  // hint qst/answer
        ",'" + rb.getUserType()+"'" +
        ")");
      // Insert statement for the air_user table
      stmt.addBatch("insert into  air_user values (" + dbId +
        ",'" + rb.getLastName()+"'" +
        ",'" + rb.getFirstName()+"'" +
        ",'" + rb.getStreet()+"'" +
        ",'" + rb.getCity()+"'" +
        ",'" + rb.getState()+"'" +
        ",'" + rb.getZip()+"'" +
        ",'USA'" +
        ",'" + rb.getZip()+"'" +
        ",null,null" +             // phone, fax
        ",'" + rb.getEmail()+"'" +
        ",'" + rb.getUserType()+"'" +
        ",'" + rb.getUserId()+"'" +
```

```
              ")");
        stmt.executeBatch();
        con.commit();  // success
        con.setAutoCommit(true);
      } finally{
        try{
        rs.close();
        stmt.close();
        con.close();
        }catch (Exception e) {
          con.rollback();  // // success
          e.printStackTrace();}
      }
    }
}
```

All of the examples that retrieved data used JDBC `ResultSet` to process result sets. The next section will introduce you to `RowSet` interface that will be a part of Java 1.5. as defined in the Java Specification Request (JSR) 114.

Using the RowSet Interface

The `javax.sql.RowSet` interface is a subclass of the `ResultSet` class, and also includes some of the properties of such interfaces as `Connection` and `Prepared Statement`. The `RowSet` interface decouples the tabular data from a result set, which greatly simplifies sending data over a network. It also enables you to use the scrollable result sets even if the underlying JDBC driver does not support them.

Look at how simple it is to get the data from a database using the `RowSet` interface:

```
rowset.setUrl ("jdbc:oracle:oci:@");
rowset.setUsername ("scott");
rowset.setPassword ("tiger");
rowset.setCommand (
   "select id,lastname,firstname from air_user where id= ?");
rowset.setInt(1,2);  // first parameter's value is 2
rowset.execute();
```

When you work with JDBC drivers from a particular vendor, find out which classes implement the `RowSet` interface, and where are they located. For example, Oracle classes that implement the `RowSet` interface are located in the file `ocrs12.jar`.

`RowSet` objects come in two major flavors — connected and disconnected. The disconnected objects are implemented by means of the `CachedRowSet` or `WebRowSet` classes, whereas connected objects are implemented with the help of the `JDBCRowSet` class. `JDBCRowSet` is a wrapper for the `ResultSet` class.

Working with CachedRowSet

CachedRowSet is a serializable object that keeps the result set in memory and does not maintain a connection to the database; hence it can be sent to a remote client. Obviously, this might not be the best system for result sets having millions of rows, but it may come in very handy, for example, if a CEO of Connexia Airlines wants to work with the airline's data on the road using his or her laptop.

The following two code fragments show how to create and populate a CachedRowSet object using Oracle drivers. Please note that these examples work with a pooled connection using a DataSource.

The following example first creates an instance of the OracleCachedRowSet class, which is Oracle's implementation of the CachedRowSet class, and then connects to the database and executes and processes a query.

```
RowSet cachedRs = new OracleCachedRowSet ();
cachedRs.setDataSourceName("oracleDS");
cachedRs.setUsername ("scott");
cachedRs.setPassword ("tiger");
cachedRs.setType (ResultSet.TYPE_SCROLL_INSENSITIVE);
cachedRs.setCommand(
        "select  id,lastname,firstname from air_user");
cachedRs.execute ();
while (cachedRs.next ()) {
System.out.println(
    " User Id: " + cachedRs.getInt("id") +
    ", Last Name: " + cachedRs.getString("lastname") +
    ", First Name" + cachedRs.getString("firstname") + "\n");
}
The second  example populates a RowSet from an existing
ResultSet.
Context ctx=new InitialContext();
        DataSource ds  = (DataSource) ctx.lookup ("oracleDS");
        Connection con = ds.getConnection();
Statement stmt=con.createStatement();
ResultSet rs=stmt.executeQuery(
        "select  id,lastname,firstname from air_user");
OracleCachedRowSet cachedRs = new OracleCachedRowSet ();
cachedRs.populate (rs);
```

After the cached row set is populated you can send it over the network, say to a Java servlet that will prepare an HTML table and send it to a user, as in the next code fragment:

```
public void doPost(HttpServletRequest req,
                   HttpServletResponse res){

    res.setContentType("text/html");
PrintWriter out = res.getWriter();
```

```
// The class SomeClass encapsulates work
// with the airline's database
RowSet cachedRs = SomeClass.getAirUsers();

   StringBuffter sb=new StringBuffer();
   sb.append("<TABLE >");
   while (cachedRs.next()){
    sb.append("<TR>");
    sb.append("<TD>"+ cachedRs.getInt("id")+"</TD>");
    sb.append("<TD>"+ cachedRs.getString("lastname")+"</TD>");
    sb.append("<TD>"+ cachedRs.getString("firstname")+"</TD>");
    sb.append("</TR>");
   }
   sb.append("</TABLE >");
   out.println(sb);
  }
```

Cross-Reference

Java servlets are discussed in Chapter 5.

Using Enterprise JavaBeans technology in a distributed application, you can create a session bean with a method that returns a disconnected RowSet:

```
public RowSet getFlights () throws RemoteException,
SQLException {
   Connection con = null;
            try { DataSource ds  = (DataSource) ctx.lookup
("oracleDS");
                Connection con = ds.getConnection();
     Statement stmt=con.createStatement();
     ResultSet rs=stmt.executeQuery(
     "select flightNo,origin,destination, departure from
flight");
     OracleCachedRowSet cachedRs = new OracleCachedRowSet ();
     cachedRs.populate (rs);
     return cachedRs;
   } finally {
     // Close JDBC resources here
   }
}
```

Cross-Reference

Part IV, "The Service Tier" discusses EJB technology.

Using a CachedRowSet object with JSP

The following code fragment shows how to use a CachedRowSet object as a bean within a JSP. The CachedRowSet object is populated within the <jsp:useBean> tag, and the rest of the code just extracts the data from the bean and sends it over the network to the Web client as an HTML table.

```
<%@ page import="oracle.jdbc.rowset.CachedRowSet" %>
<HTML>
<BODY>
<jsp:useBean id="airUsers"
      class="oracle.jdbc.rowset.CachedRowSet" scope="session">
<%
airUsers.setUrl ("jdbc:oracle:oci:@");
airUsers.setUsername ("scott");
airUsers.setPassword ("tiger");
airUsers.setCommand (
        "select id,lastname,firstname from air_user");
airUsers.execute();
airUsers.first();
%>
</jsp:useBean>
<%
 StringBuffter sb=new StringBuffer();
 sb.append("<TABLE>");
  while (airUsers.next()){
    sb.append("<TR>");
    sb.append("<TD>"+ airUsers.getInt("id")+"</TD>");
    sb.append("<TD>"+ airUsers.getString("lastname")+"</TD>");
    sb.append("<TD>"+ airUsers.getString("firstname")+"</TD>");
    sb.append("</TR>");
    }
    sb.append("</TABLE >");
    out.println(sb);
%>
</BODY>
</HTML>
```

Cross-Reference The `<java:useBean>` tag is discussed in Chapter 6.

Updating the database using a RowSet

Imagine a CEO of Connexia Airlines sitting in a limo with his laptop. The laptop has a GUI program that displays in a `JTable` the flight schedule that came as a `CachedRowSet`. The third row shows the flight from New York to Miami, but the CEO decides to change the flight origin to Philadelphia. When the cursor has been moved to the third row, the program performs the following line:

```
cachedRs.absolute(3);
```

When the CEO modifies the flight origin to `PHL`, which is the value of the column number 2, the program performs this action:

```
cachedRs.updateString(2, "PHL");
cachedRs.updateRow();
```

Since we work with the disconnected RowSet object, the actual database update will be initiated only after the program executes the following code:

```
cachedRs.acceptChanges();
```

The preceding line can be placed under actionPerformed() for the Save button.

Updatable row sets must meet certain requirements: The SQL query cannot contain joins, the data must come from a single table, and the primary key of this table must be included in the SQL query.

In addition to acceptChanges(), the application has to call different saving procedures depending on whether the CEO works on the laptop in a stand-alone mode, or from the office connected to the database server. In "office mode" the code has to reconnect to the database and apply the changes. In "limo mode" the changes can be saved in a local file, as in the following example:

```
FileOutputStream fos = new FileOutputStream ("flights.ser");
ObjectOutputStream oos = new ObjectOutputStream (fos);
oos.writeObject (cachedRs);
oostream.close ();
fos.close();
```

The following code snippet loads a serialized RowSet from the file flights.ser:

```
FileInputStream fis = new FileInputStream("flights.ser");
ObjectInputStream ois = new ObjectInputStream(fis);
RowSet cachedRs = (RowSet) ois.readObject();
istream.close();
fis.close();
```

Processing RowSet events

If you have a class that has to be notified of the user's action while the user is browsing or updating the RowSet object, this class has to implement the RowSetListener interface. This interface has the following three methods:

✦ rowChanged — This method will be called when the user changes a row in the RowSet object, for example if the GUI class calls the cachedSet.updateRow() object.

✦ rowSetChanged — This method will be called when a user changes the command string that has been used to create the RowSet object, for example if the SQL statement has changed.

✦ cursorMoved — This method is called to notify the listener that the user has moved the cursor on the RowSet object, for example if the method cachedRs.next() is called.

The `addRowSetListener()` method registers a class responsible for the reaction on the updates. For example, if the flight origin has been changed, the spreadsheet detailing the Connexia Airlines staff requirements has to be recalculated and a bar chart has to be refreshed on the screen. If the `FlightBarChart` class contains the logic to generate a spreadsheet and draw a bar chart, it has to be registered as a listener, as shown here:

```
cachedRs.addRowSetListener(FlightBarChart);
```

The WebRowSet class

Finally, the `WebRowSet` is a wrapper class that internally uses a servlet that supports communication between the Web clients and a database. `WebRowSet` stores the data as XML and communicates with the client using HTTP.

Summary

In this chapter we've explained the use of JDBC technology and the types of drivers, and provided examples of the most important database operations performed via a Java program. JDBC is a generic and elegant way of accessing relational databases from Java programs. JDBC allows Java programs to execute any SQL command or a database-stored procedure. It has an ability to control transactions, process data result sets, perform batch updates and support pools of database connections. Various types of JDBC drivers are widely available from all major vendors of database managements systems. The vendors of J2EE application servers also offer JDBC drivers with support of distributed transactions. JDBC is a vital component of any J2EE application.

✦   ✦   ✦

Understanding the J2EE Connector Architecture

✦ ✦ ✦ ✦

In This Chapter

Examining the system-level lifecycle contract

Investigating the system-level connection Management contract

Understanding the system-level transaction-management contract

Looking at the system-level work-management contract

Going over the system-level message-inflow contract

Reviewing the application-level CCI contract

Understanding packaging

✦ ✦ ✦ ✦

In the real world, a lot of enterprise applications contain their data and functionality in enterprise information systems (EISes). Examples of EISes include enterprise resource planning (ERP), mainframe transaction processing (TP), and database systems. Although many of these systems are mature and stable, they don't necessarily provide Web enablement, location transparency, failover support, and other critical functionalities that have made the J2EE domain such a popular one. The J2EE Connector architecture defines a standard architecture for connecting the Java 2 platform to such heterogeneous EISes. Prior to the existence of the Connector architecture, the Java platform had no such standard architecture. It was up to each of the EIS vendors and application-server vendors to determine its own EIS-integration approach.

The J2EE Connector architecture provides a Java solution to the problem of connectivity among the multitude of application servers and EISes. The Connector architecture is made of two parts. One is implemented by the application-server vendors and allows them to connect seamlessly to multiple EIS systems. If they conform to the J2EE Connector architecture, the application-server vendors do not need to add custom code to extend their support connectivity to a new EIS.

The other part is implemented by the EIS vendors and is called a *resource adapter*. A resource adapter is a system-level software driver that is used by a Java application to connect to an EIS. The resource adapter is specific to the EIS and can use native calls, but it can plug into any application server that supports the Connector architecture. Because of this it is no longer necessary for EIS vendors to customize their products for each application server.

Version 1.5 of the Connector architecture defines several system-level contracts and an application-level contract. In this chapter, we are going to look into each of the contracts in detail and at how it fits into the J2EE Connector architecture.

Examining the Contracts

Figure 19-1 provides an overview of the Connector architecture and the relationships among the application server, resource adapter, and EIS system.

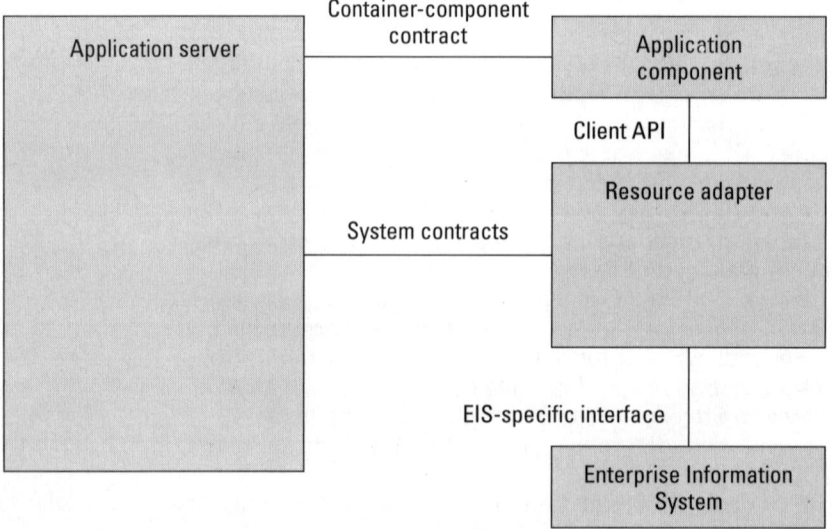

Figure 19-1: Overview of the Connector architecture

The system-level contracts are specified between the application server and the EIS resource adapter. An application server and an EIS collaborate to keep all system-level mechanisms, such as transactions, security and connection management, transparent from the application components. Therefore, the application component provider does not need to worry about the system level issues related to the EIS integration. The application component provider can focus on the business logic of the application. The application server and the EIS vendors handle the connectivity issues.

The J2EE Connector architecture defines the following set of system-level contracts between an application server and EIS, which enables outbound connectivity to an EIS.

✦ **Connection-management contract** — This contract allows an application server to pool connections to the underlying EIS and enables application components to connect to the EIS. This leads to a scalable application environment that can support a large number of clients requiring access to EISes.

✦ **Transaction-management contract** — This contract allows an application server to use a transaction manager to manage transactions across multiple resource managers. This contract also supports transactions that are managed internal to an EIS resource manager without the necessity of involving an external transaction manager.

✦ **Security contract** — This contract allows for a secure access to an EIS by extending the security model for the J2EE based applications to include EIS integration.

The J2EE Connector architecture defines the following set of system-level contracts between an application server and EIS, which enables inbound connectivity from an EIS. In inbound communication, the resource adapter allows an EIS to call application components and perform work. All communication is initiated by the EIS.

✦ **Message-inflow contract** — This contract allows a resource adapter to asynchronously deliver messages to message endpoints residing in the application server, independent of the specific messaging style, the messaging semantics, and the messaging infrastructure used to deliver messages. This contract also serves as the standard message provider pluggability contract that allows a wide range of message providers such as Java Message Service (JMS) and Java API for XML Messaging (JAXM) to be plugged into any J2EE compatible application server via a resource adapter.

✦ **Transaction-inflow contract** — This contract allows a resource adapter to propagate an imported transaction to an application server and ensures that the ACID properties of the imported transaction are preserved.

Cross-Reference

For a detailed discussion of the ACID properties and other aspects of transactions, refer to Chapter 10.

The J2EE Connector architecture defines the following set of system-level contracts between an application server and EIS, which enables resource adapter lifecycle management and thread management.

✦ **Lifecycle-management contract** — This contract allows an application server to manage the lifecycle of a resource adapter.

✦ **Work-management contract** — This contract allows a resource adapter to do work (monitor network endpoints, call application components, and so on) by submitting work instances to an application server for execution.

The J2EE Connector architecture also defines an application contract between an application component and a resource adapter. In particular, this contract defines a client API that an application component can use to access the EIS. The client API may be the Common Client Interface (CCI) or an API specific to a resource adapter. The CCI defines a standard client API for application components and Enterprise Application Integration (EAI) frameworks to drive interactions across heterogeneous EISes using a common client API.

If you are an application component provider, you should be able to use one of the adapters provided by the tool vendors or EIS vendors and not worry about the integration issues between the application server and EIS. You can simply use the adapter's client API and get access to the underlying system. The section on CCI provides a sample of an application accessing an EIS using a resource adapter.

However, in order to develop your own adapter, you need to define classes that implement the interfaces as required by the several contracts listed in the J2EE connector specification. In the following sections, we will discuss and explain each of these contracts and interfaces. Once you have implemented these interfaces, you can package your classes along with the deployment descriptor to generate a deployable resource adapter. Deployment descriptors and packaging are explained in the section, "Packaging and Deployment," later in this chapter.

The lifecycle-management contract

The lifecycle management contract provides the means for an application server to manage the lifecycle of a resource adapter instance. As we mentioned in the previous section, a resource adapter is a system-level software driver. A resource adapter is the core piece of the J2EE Connector architecture. It is deployed within the application server and is used by the application server or an application client to connect to the EIS. The lifecycle management contract allows an application server to bootstrap a resource adapter instance during resource adapter deployment or during the application server startup. It also provides a mechanism to notify the resource adapter instance while it is undeployed or during an orderly shutdown of the application server.

The ResourceAdapter JavaBean

Let's take a quick look at the implementation class before examining the deploy/undeploy process. To create a resource adapter, we need to define a class that implements the `ResourceAdapter` interface. The specifications require this class to follow the conventions of a JavaBean. As you will see in the section on packaging and deployment later in this chapter, the resource adapter also needs a deployment descriptor. The name of the class and other properties can be configured in the deployment descriptor. During deployment, the resource-adapter deployer creates a `ResourceAdapter` JavaBean and configures it with the appropriate properties. The `ResourceAdapter` JavaBean represents a resource-adapter instance and contains the configuration information pertaining to the resource-adapter instance. At runtime, the resource-adapter instance may contain several objects (for example, `ManagedConnectionFactory` or `ActivationSpec`) to do the application processing. Such objects may be created or discarded during the life-time of the resource-adapter instance.

Resource-adapter bootstrapping

When a resource adapter is deployed or during application-server startup, an application server bootstraps an instance of the resource adapter in its address space. In order to bootstrap a resource-adapter instance, the application server uses the configured `ResourceAdapter` JavaBean and calls its start method. The application server must instantiate at least one `ResourceAdapter` JavaBean per resource-adapter deployment. Also, the application server must not reuse the same `ResourceAdapter` JavaBean object to manage multiple incarnations of a resource adapter. During the start method call, the following happens:

1. The application server provides a `BootStrapContext` instance containing references to the application server's facilities.

2. The resource-adapter instance initializes itself, and may use the `WorkManager` to submit `Work` instances for execution. (The `WorkManager` and Work are explained later in the section on the work-management contract.)

Resource-adapter shutdown

The application server uses a two-phase process to shut down the resource-adapter instance. This process is invoked if the application server is being shut down or if the resource adapter is being undeployed. During phase one, the application server ensures that all the applications using the specific resource-adapter instance in question are stopped. In phase two, the application server calls the `stop` method on the `ResourceAdapter` JavaBean. This call acts as a shutdown notification from the application server to the resource-adapter instance, instructing it to stop functioning.

The following code listing illustrates a sample implementation of a resource adapter. It implements the `start()` and `stop()` methods to provide support for the lifecycle management contract.

```
package com.connexia.adapter;

import javax.resource.spi.ResourceAdapter;
import javax.resource.spi.BootstrapContext;
import javax.resource.spi.work.*;

public class MyResourceAdapter implements ResourceAdapter {
    void start(BootstrapContext context) {
        // setup network points and get Work instances.
    }

    void stop() {
        // release Work instances, do clean up and return.
    }
```

Figure 19-2 lists the various stages in the lifecycle of a resource adapter. The resource adapter deployer configures the resource adapter by assembling the required classes and deployment descriptors. In the next step, the resource adapter is deployed in the application server. The application server vendor might provide a tool to facilitate the deployment process. The deployed resource adapter is still non-functional till the application server calls the `start()` method on the resource adapter. Once the `start()` method has been called, the resource adapter is ready for use by the application.

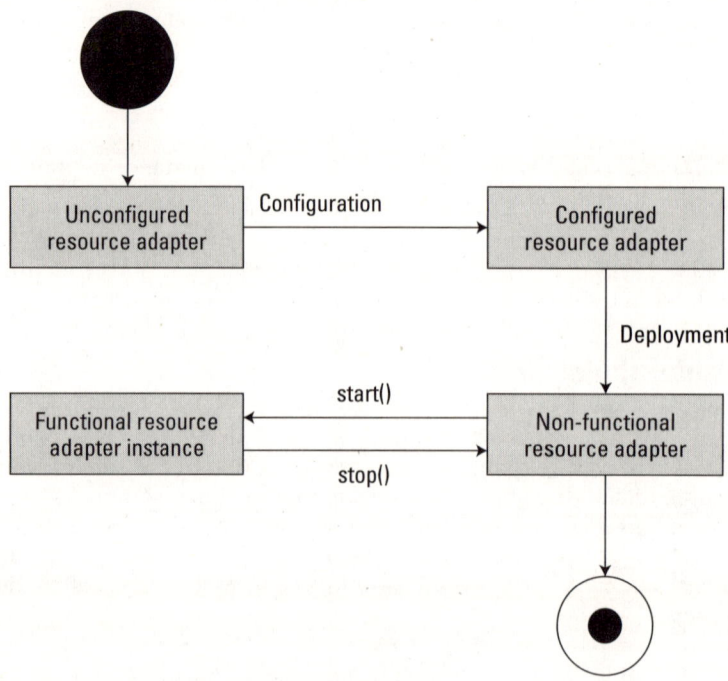

Figure 19-2: Resource-adapter lifecycle

Work management contract

A simple resource adapter merely functions as a passive library that executes in the context of an application thread. But in some cases the resource adapter might need threads to function properly—such as to listen to network endpoints, to process incoming data, to communicate with a network peer, to do its internal work, or to dispatch calls to application components.

It's not a good idea to have the resource adapter create its own Java threads. An application server is optimally designed to manage such resources. An application server knows the overall state of its runtime environment (remember that the resource adapter runs within the application server). Therefore it may make better decisions about granting threads to a resource adapter. Using it also leads to better manageability of its runtime environment.

The work-management contract allows a resource adapter to submit Work instances to an application server for execution. The application server dispatches threads to execute submitted Work instances. This allows a resource adapter to avoid creating or managing threads directly, provides a mechanism for the resource adapter to do its work, and allows an application server better control over its run-time environment.

The work-management model

Figure 19-3 illustrates the work management model and the interaction between the application server and resource adapter.

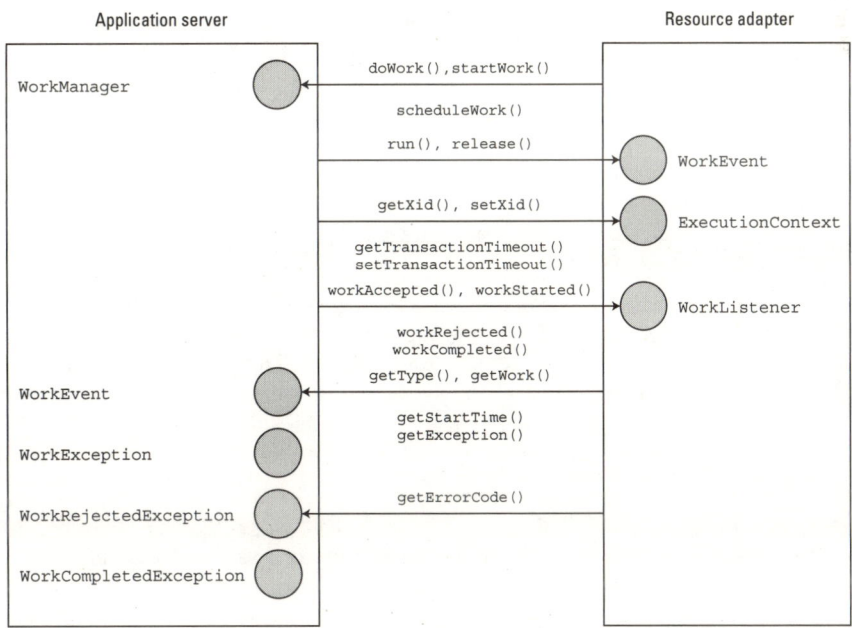

Figure 19-3: Work-management interfaces

A resource adapter obtains a WorkManager instance from the BootstrapContext instance provided by the application server during its deployment. The resource adapter may create Work instances to do its work and submit them to the WorkManager along with an optional ExecutionContext for execution.

The application server has a pool of free threads waiting for a Work instance to be submitted. When a Work instance is submitted, one of the free threads picks up the instance, sets up an appropriate execution context, and calls the run method on the Work instance. The application server is free to choose an appropriate thread to execute the Work instance. However, the application server is required to use threads of the same thread-priority level to process Work instances submitted by a specific resource adapter.

If the resource adapter has implemented the WorkListener interface, the application server sends Work processing event notifications to the WorkListener.

Interfaces and classes

Take a look at the various classes and interfaces defined as part of the work-management contract.

✦ Work — The Work interface models a Work instance to be executed by a WorkManager upon submission. The Work interface is implemented by the resource adapter.

✦ WorkManager — The WorkManager interface provides a mechanism for submitting Work instances for execution. It is implemented by the application server. You can obtain a WorkManager instance by calling the getWorkManager method on the BootstrapContext instance. The WorkManager interface supports both synchronous and asynchronous submission of Work instances. It provides several methods (doWork(), startWork(), and scheduleWork()) with which to submit the Work instance for execution. A submitted Work instance can go through several states: work accepted, work rejected, work started, or work completed.

✦ WorkListener — The WorkListener interface is optionally implemented by the resource adapter. It is supplied to the WorkManager during Work submission and provides an event-listener callback mechanism in order to be notified when the various Work-processing events (work accepted, work rejected, work started, work completed) occur. When a WorkListener instance is provided by the resource adapter, the application server must send event notifications to it.

✦ ExecutionContext — The ExecutionContext class allows a resource adapter to specify an execution context (transaction, for example) with which the Work instance must be executed. It is the responsibility of the resource adapter to populate the ExecutionContext instance with an appropriate execution context.

Work submission

Figure 19-4 depicts the work-submission procedure. The WorkManager submits a Work instance for submission. It can do so by calling either the doWork method, the startWork method, or the scheduleWork method. With the doWork method, the call blocks until the Work instance completes execution. With the startWork method, the call blocks until the Work instance starts execution. With the scheduleWork method, the call does not block and returns immediately. When the Work instance is submitted, it can either be accepted or rejected with a WorkRejectedException set to an error code.

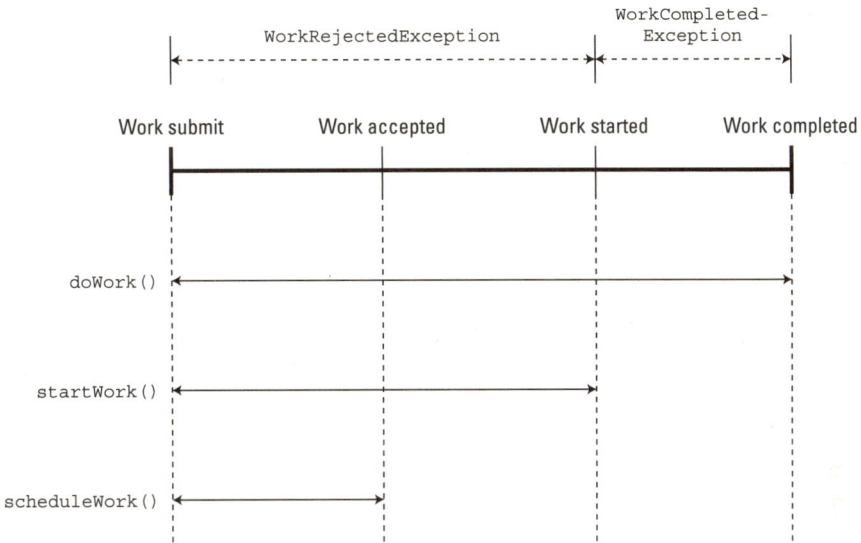

Figure 19-4: Work-submission procedure

Listing 19-1 enhances our sample resource adapter from the previous section by submitting the Work instances.

Listing 19-1: **Submitting the Work instances**

```
package com.connexia.adapter;

import javax.resource.spi.ResourceAdapter;
import javax.resource.spi.BootstrapContext;
import javax.resource.spi.work.*;

public class MyResourceAdapter implements ResourceAdapter {
    void start(BootstrapContext context) {
        // setup network points and get Work instances.

        WorkManager wm = context.getWorkManager();
        Work work = new MyWork();
        try {
            wm.startWork(work);
        } catch (WorkException we) {
            // handle exception and wrap it with a
            // WorkCompletedException set to an appropriate
            // error code.
        }
    }
}
```

Continued

Listing 19-1 *(continued)*

```
void stop() {
    // release Work instances, do clean up and return.
}

public class MyWork implements Work {
    /**
     * The WorkManager calls this method to hint the active Work
     * instance to complete execution. This is called on a
separate
     * thread other than the one actually executing the Work
instance.
     */
    void release() {
        // set a flag to hint the Work instance to complete.
    }

    void run() {
        // do work (call application components, monitor network
        // ports etc.)
    }
}
```

Outbound communication

In outbound communication, the resource adapter allows an application to connect to an EIS system and perform work. All communication is initiated by the application. The resource adapter serves as a passive library for connecting to an EIS, and executes in the context of the application threads. Let's look at the following contracts that are specified by the architecture pertaining to outbound communication: connection management, transaction management, and security.

The connection-management contract

Applications require connections to access the EIS resources. A connection can be a database connection, a Java Message Service (JMS) connection, a SAP R/3 connection, and so forth. An application obtains a connection, uses it to access an EIS resource, and then closes the connection. But these connections are expensive to create and destroy. Creating and destroying a connection each time an application needs an EIS resource affects scalability and performance adversely. The J2EE Connector architecture specifies the connection-management contract between the application server and the resource adapter. The connection-management contract defines the fundamentals for the management of connections between applications and the underlying EISes. It provides support for connection pooling. It also provides consistent application programming for connection acquisition.

Connection-management classes and interfaces

Take a look at the various classes and interfaces defined as part of the connection-management contract. For the purpose of our discussion here, we are only going to focus on the *managed environment*. A managed environment defines a J2EE-based multi-tier environment wherein the Web-enabled applications access the EIS systems. A *non-managed environment* defines a two-tier environment wherein an application client directly uses a resource adapter (without the application server) to access an EIS system.

Connection factories and connection interfaces

A connection factory provides an interface with which to get a connection to an EIS instance. A connection provides connectivity to an underlying EIS. The `javax.resource.cci.ConnectionFactory` and `javax.resource.cci.Connection` interfaces are both implemented by the resource adapter. An application can invoke the `getConnection` method of the `ConnectionFactory` to get a connection to an underlying EIS. The connection factory implementation class delegates the `getConnection` method invocation to the associated `ConnectionManager` instance. The connection factory implementation class also takes the connection-request information and passes it to the `ConnectionManager.allocateConnection` method. The `ConnectionRequestInfo` parameter to the `ConnectionManager.allocateConnection` method enables a resource adapter to pass its own request-specific data structure across the connection-request flow.

The following code segment illustrates the above interfaces:

```
public interface javax.resource.cci.ConnectionFactory
        extends java.io.Serializable,
javax.resource.Referenceable {

    public javax.resource.cci.Connection getConnection() {
    ...
}

public interface javax.resource.cci.Connection() {
    public void close() throws javax.resource.ResourceException;
    ...
}
```

The connection manager

The `javax.resource.spi.ConnectionManager` provides a hook with which a resource adapter can pass a connection request to an application server. The `ConnectionManager` interface is implemented by the application server. Through this interface the server provides its additional services, including security, connection-pool management, transaction management, and error logging. The `ConnectionManager` interface defines the `allocateConnection` method. Listing 19-2 illustrates these interfaces.

Listing 19-2: **The ConnectionManager interfaces**

```
public interface javax.resource.spi.ConnectionManager
        extends java.io.Serializable {

        /** The method allocateConnection gets called by the
resource
        * adapter's connection factory instance
        * @param ManagedConnectionFactory
        * @param ConnectionRequestInfo
        * @return Object
        */
public Object allocateConnection (
        ManagedConnectionFactory mcf,
        ConnectionRequestInfo cxRequestInfo)
        throws ResourceException;
}


public interface javax.resource.spi.ConnectionRequestInfo {

        /** Checks whether this instance is equal to another.
        * @param Object
        * @return boolean
        */
    public boolean equals(Object other);


    /** Returns the hashCode of the ConnectionRequestInfo.
    * @param Object
    */
    public int hashCode();
}
```

The ManagedConnectionFactory interface

The ManagedConnectionFactory interface is a factory of both ManagedConnection instances and connection-factory instances. The interface supports methods for creating factory instances. It also provides methods with which to create a new physical connection (represented by a ManagedConnection instance) to an underlying EIS instance. The matchManagedConnection method enables the application server to use a resource adapter–specific criterion for matching. The ManagedConnectionFactory interface is required to be implemented by the resource adapter. Listing 19-3 illustrates the ManagedConnectionFactory interface.

Listing 19-3: **ManagedConnectionFactory**

```
public interface javax.resource.spi.ManagedConnectionFactory
       extends java.io.Serializable {

   /** Creates a Connection Factory instance.
    * @param ConnectionManager
    * @return Object
    * @throws ResourceException
    */
   public Object createConnectionFactory(
               ConnectionManager connectionManager)
               throws ResourceException;


   /** Creates a Connection Factory instance.
    * @return Object
    * @throws ResourceException
    */
   public Object createConnectionFactory() throws
ResourceException;


   /** Creates a new physical connection to the underlying
    * EIS resource manager
    * @param Subject
    * @param ConnectionRequestInfo
    * @return ManagedConnection
    * @throws ResourceException
    */
   public ManagedConnection createManagedConnection(
       javax.security.auth.Subject subject,
       ConnectionRequestInfo cxRequestInfo)
       throws ResourceException;


   /** Returns a matched connection from the candidate set
    * of connections.
    * @param Set
    * @param Subject
    * @param ConnectionRequestInfo
    * @return ManagedConnection
    * @throws ResourceException
    */
   public ManagedConnection matchManagedConnection(
       java.util.Set connectionSet,
       javax.security.auth.Subject subject,
       ConnectionRequestInfo cxRequestInfo)
       throws ResourceException;
```

Continued

Listing 19-3 *(continued)*

```
    /** Check if this ManagedConnectionFactory is equal to
another
     * ManagedConnectionFactory.
     * @param other
     * @return boolean
     */
    public boolean equals(Object other);


    /** Returns the hash code for the ManagedConnectionFactory
     * @return int
     */
    public int hashCode();


}
```

The ManagedConnection interface

An instance of the ManagedConnection interface represents a physical connection to the underlying EIS. This interface provides the method getConnection to create a new application-level connection handle. A connection handle is tied to an underlying physical connection represented by a ManagedConnection instance.

The interface also supports methods to add and remove the ConnectionEventListener to the ManagedConnection. The ManagedConnection interface is implemented by the resource adapter. The event callback mechanism (ConnectionEventListener) enables an application server to receive notifications to manage its connection pool, to clean up invalid or terminated connections, and to manage local transactions. Listing 19-4 illustrates the ManagedConnection interface.

Listing 19-4: ManagedConnection

```
public interface javax.resource.spi.ManagedConnection {
    /**
     * Adds a connection event listener to the
ManagedConnection
     *instance.
     * @param ConnectionEventListener
     */
    void addConnectionEventListener(
        ConnectionEventListener listener);


    /**
     * Used by the container to change the association of an
```

```
    * application-level connection handle with a
ManagedConnection
    * instance.
    * @param Object
    */
    void associateConnection(java.lang.Object connection);


    /**
    * Application server calls this method to force any
cleanup
    * on the ManagedConnection instance.
    */
    void cleanup();


    /**
    * Destroys the physical connection to the underlying
resource
    * manager.
    */
    void destroy();

    /**
    * Creates a new connection handle for the underlying
physical
    * connection represented by the ManagedConnection
instance.
    * @param Subject
    * @param ConnectionRequestInfo
    * @return Object
    */
    java.lang.Object getConnection(
        Subject subject,
        ConnectionRequestInfo cxRequestInfo);

    /**
    * Returns an javax.resource.spi.LocalTransaction instance.
    * @return LocalTransaction
    */
    LocalTransaction getLocalTransaction();

    /**
    * Gets the log writer for this ManagedConnection instance.
    * @return PrintWriter
    */
    java.io.PrintWriter getLogWriter();


    /**
    * Gets the metadata information for this connection's
    * underlying EIS resource manager instance.
```

Continued

Listing 19-4 *(continued)*

```
 * @return ManagedConnectionMetaData
 */
ManagedConnectionMetaData getMetaData();


/**
 * Returns an javax.transaction.xa.XAresource instance.
 * @return XAResource
 */
XAResource getXAResource();


/**
 * Removes an already registered connection event listener
 * from the ManagedConnection instance.
 * @param ConnectionEventListener
 */
void removeConnectionEventListener(
    ConnectionEventListener listener);

/**
 * Sets the log writer for this ManagedConnection instance.
 * @param PrintWriter
 */
void setLogWriter(java.io.PrintWriter out);

}
```

Error logging

The connection-management contract provides support for error logging and tracing
for both the managed and non-managed environments. This enables the application
server to detect resource-adapter errors and to use error information for debugging
purposes. The ManagedConnectionFactory interface defines two methods for
error logging. The setLogWriter method registers a character output stream, or log
writer, with a ManagedConnectionFactory instance, while the getLogWriter
method returns the current log writer for the ManagedConnectionFactory
instance.

Application steps for establishing a connection

The following is a list of steps that happens when an application establishes a connection with the EIS (in a managed environment). Most of these steps are part of
the handshake between the application server and resource adapter (and the
underlying EIS). The application component has to implement only a subset of
these steps and we will examine those under the section, "Using the CCI," later in
this chapter.

Figure 19-5 illustrates the following steps as well as the interaction between the application component, resource adapter, and the application server.

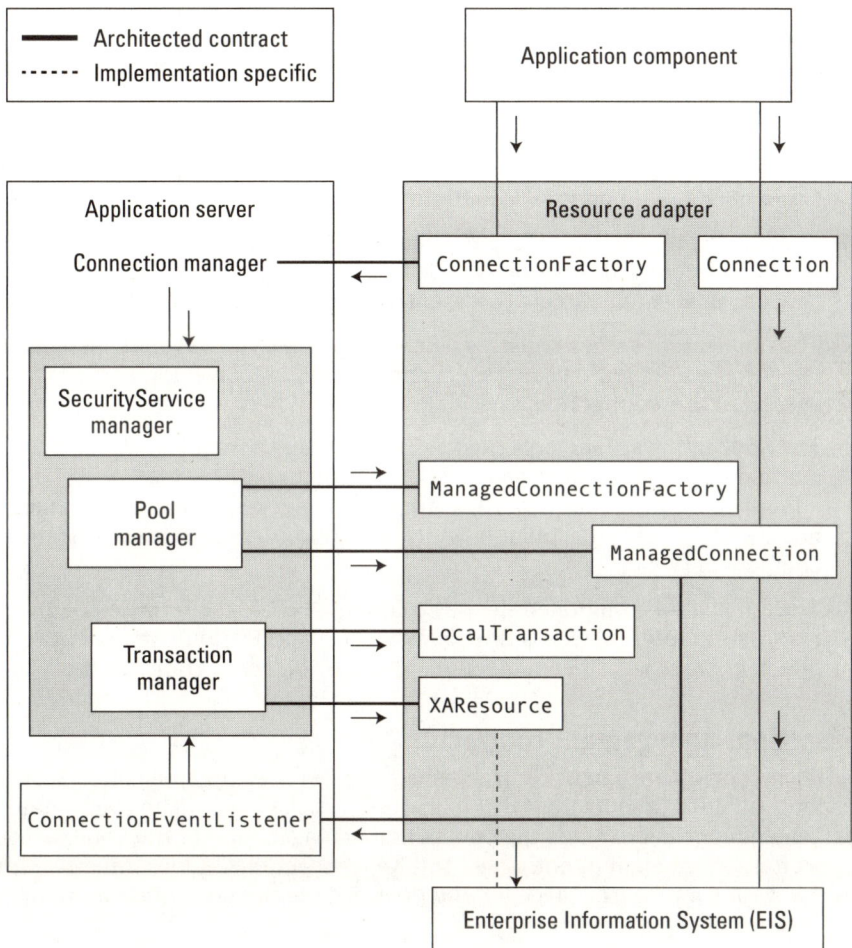

Figure 19-5: Connection management interfaces

1. The application component does a JNDI lookup for the ConnectionFactory.

2. The application component calls the getConnection method on the ConnectionFactory to get a connection to the underlying instance.

3. The ConnectionFactory delegates the connection request to the associated ConnectionManager instance. The ConnectionFactory instance calls the allocateConnection method on the ConnectionManager and passes the ConnectionRequestInfo parameter.

4. After receiving the request the `ConnectionManager` instance attempts to find a suitable existing connection in the application server's connection pool. The interaction between a `ConnectionManager` instance and the Connection pool manager is internal and specific to an application server.

5. If the application server finds a connection in the pool that it considers suitable, it uses that matching `ManagedConnection` to satisfy the application's connection request.

6. If the application server finds no matching `ManagedConnection` instance, the application server calls the `ManagedConnectionFactory.createManagedConnection` method.

7. The `ManagedConnectionFactory` instance creates a new physical connection to the underlying EIS instance and returns it to the application server. This new physical connection is represented by a `ManagedConnection` instance.

8. The application server registers a `ConnectionEventListener` instance with the `ManagedConnection` instance, enabling it to receive notifications for events on this connection.

9. The application server calls the `ManagedConnection.getConnection` method to get an application-level connection handle of type `javax.resource.cci.Connection`. The application server returns this connection handle to the resource adapter, which in turn returns it to the application component.

10. The application component uses the connection handle returned by the resource adapter to access the EIS. When the application component completes its work with the connection, it closes the connection handle.

Transaction-management contract

The transaction-management contract is defined between an application server and a resource adapter (and its underlying EIS resource manager). The transaction-management contract extends the connection-management contract and provides support for management of both local and XA transactions. A *local transaction* is managed within a resource manager and does not require coordination by an external resource manager.

An *XA transaction* (also called a JTA or global transaction) can span multiple resource managers. This type of transaction requires transaction coordination by an external transaction manager. The transaction manager also provides additional low-level services that enable transactional context to be propagated across systems.

Cross-Reference   Refer to Chapter 10 for more details on transactions.

As shown in Figure 19-6, the transaction-management contract specifies these three key interfaces:

✦ `javax.resource.spi.ManagedConnection`

✦ `javax.transaction.xa.XAResource`

✦ `javax.resource.spi.LocalTransaction`

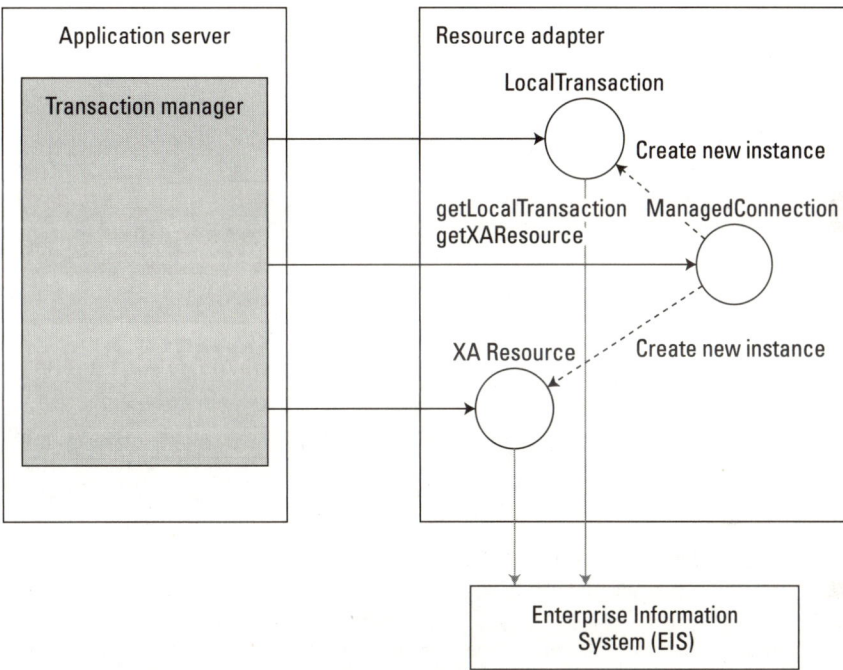

Figure 19-6: Transaction-management interfaces

A `ManagedConnection` interface represents a physical connection to the underlying EIS. It defines two methods that pertain to the transaction-management contract:

✦ `getLocalTransaction` is used to create a new `LocalTransaction` instance.

✦ `getXAResource` is used to create a new `XAResource` instance.

Local-transaction management contract

Transactions managed within a resource manager are local transactions. The application server uses the `javax.resource.spi.LocalTransaction` interface to manage local transactions transparently to an application component. The `LocalTransaction` interface defines the following three methods:

✦ begin

✦ commit

✦ rollback

An application server invokes the LocalTransaction begin method to explicitly start a local transaction. The application server can either call the commit method to complete the transactional changes made to the EIS, or it can call the rollback method to undo the changes.

The local-management contract also specifies the local transaction-related event notifications. An application server implements the javax.resource.spi. ConnectionEventListener interface. The ConnectionEventListener interface specifies the following three methods that pertain to local-transaction management:

✦ localTransactionStarted

✦ localTransactionCommitted

✦ localTransactionRolledback

When a local transaction starts, a ManagedConnection instance calls the localTransactionStarted method to notify its registered listeners that the transaction has started. Similarly, a ManagedConnection instance calls the localTransactionCommitted method to notify its listeners that the transaction has committed, and it calls localTransactionRolledback to notify its registered listeners that the transaction has been rolled back.

The XAResource transaction-management contract

The XAResource transaction-management contract is based on the X/Open transaction model. The javax.transaction.xa.XAResource interface is a Java mapping of the industry-standard XA interface based on the X/Open CAE (Common Applications Environment) specification.

The XAResource interface is implemented by the resource adapter for an EIS resource manager. This interface enables the resource manager to participate in transactions controlled and coordinated by an external transaction manager. The application server uses a transaction manager to support a transaction-management infrastructure that enables an application component to perform transaction access across the multiple EIS resource managers. The XAResource transaction-management contract supports a two-phase commit protocol that ensures that a transaction across the multiple resource managers either entirely commits or entirely rolls back. If even one resource manager is not ready to commit, the transaction manager rolls back the transaction across all the participating resource managers.

Figure 19-7 illustrates a scenario where the transaction context is propagated across multiple resource adapters. An application client invokes EJB component X. EJB X accesses transaction programs managed by a TP system and calls EJB Y to access an ERP system. The resource adapters for both systems implements the

XAResource interface that enables the two resource managers to participate in transactions that are coordinated by the application server's transaction manager. When the transaction commits, the transaction manager ensures that all read/write access to resources managed by both TP system and ERP system is either entirely committed or entirely rolled back.

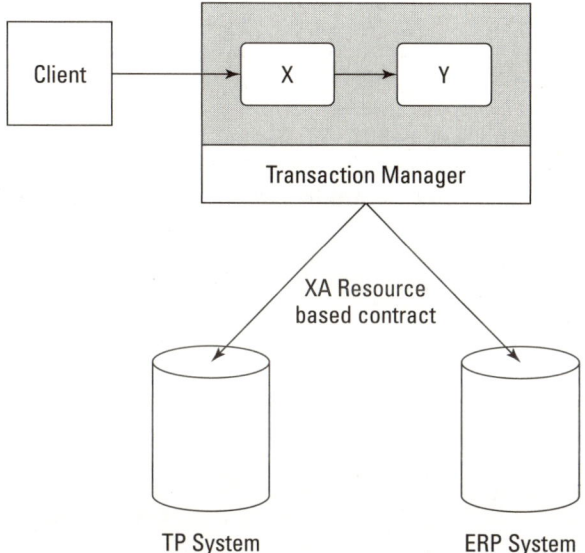

Figure 19-7: XAResource transaction contract

Security management contract

It is critically important for an enterprise application to protect the integrity of the business information. The J2EE security model defines the security that is applied to client access to the Web tier, and then from the Web tier to the EJB tier.

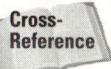 **Cross-Reference** For a detailed explanation of the J2EE security model, refer to Chapter 12.

The Connector architecture defines a security-management contract that extends the J2EE security model to include support for secure connectivity to EISes. The security-management contract is both security-mechanism-independent and technology-independent. Thus application servers and EISes can support the contract regardless of their own levels of support for security. The contract provides support for both the authentication and authorization of users.

The term *authentication* refers to the security mechanism by which the requester and the service provider establish their identities to one another. *Authorization* is defined as a security mechanism through which it is verified that the user has the authority to access the requested resource or service.

When an application component requests a connection in the J2EE environment, it is established under the security context of a resource principal. Once the connection is established all the application-level invocations occur under the same context. An application component can sign on to an EIS system using one of the following two approaches: container-managed or component-managed. As explained later in this chapter, in the section "Packaging and Deployment," the application-component provider uses a deployment-descriptor element such as `res-auth` for EJB to indicate the sign-on approach. A value of `Container` indicates container-managed sign-on and a value of `Application` indicates component-managed sign-on.

With container-managed sign-on the application component lets the container take the responsibility of configuring and managing the EIS sign-on. The container determines the user name and password for establishing a connection to an EIS instance. The component code invokes the `getConnection` method on the `ConnectionFactory` instance with no security-related parameters. Here's an example:

```
// Container Managed sign-on
Context ctx = new InitialContext();

//JNDI look up
javax.resource.cci.ConnectionFactory cxf =
(javax.resource.cci.ConnectionFactory)ctx.lookup("java:comp/env
/eis/MyEIS");

// No security-related parameters.
javax.resource.cci.Connection cx = cxf.getConnection();
```

In the component-managed sign-on the application component code manages the EIS sign-on by including code that performs the process of signing on to an EIS. In this case the application component must pass the security information (user name, password) to the `ConnectionFactory` when invoking the `getConnection` method. Here's an example:

```
//Component Managed sign-on
Context ctx = new InitialContext();

//JNDI look up
javax.resource.cci.ConnectionFactory cxf =
(javax.resource.cci.ConnectionFactory)ctx.lookup("java:comp/env
/eis/MyEIS");

// set the security information
com.myeis.ConnectionSpecImpl properties = ..
properties.setUserName("John");
properties.setPassword("Doe");
javax.resource.cci.Connection cx =
cxf.getConnection(properties);
```

Understanding EIS sign-on

Creating a new physical connection requires signing on to the EIS instance. EIS sign-on typically requires the execution of one or more of the following steps:

1. Determining a resource principal under whose security context a physical connection to an EIS will be established.

2. Authenticating a resource principal if it is not already authenticated.

3. Authorizing a resource principal.

4. Establishing a secure communication between the application server and the EIS. Once such communication is established, additional security mechanisms, such as data confidentiality and data integrity, may be applied.

Let's discuss these steps in more detail.

Setting a resource principal

When an application component requests a connection from a resource adapter, the connection request is always made under the security context of a resource principal. The deployer can set the resource principal using one of the following approaches:

✦ Configured identity

✦ Principal mapping

✦ Caller impersonation

✦ Credentials mapping

With the configured-identity approach a resource principal has its own configured identity and security attributes, and these can be independent of the identity of the principal initiating the connection request. The connection to the mainframe is always established under the security context of a valid EIS user account. This account is always used, regardless of the initiating or caller principal, which is set to be the user accessing the system.

With the principal-mapping approach the container manages the mapping of the resource principal from the identity or security attributes of the initiating or caller principal. When this approach is used the resource principal does not inherit the identity or security attributes of the principal from which it is mapped. Instead the resource principal gets its identity and security attributes based on the principal mapping. For example, if the caller principal has identity A, a mapped resource principal can be `mapping(A, EIS1)` and `mapping(A, EIS2)` on two different EIS instances.

With caller impersonation a resource principal acts on behalf of an initiating/caller principal. When a resource principal impersonates a caller principal, the caller's identity and credentials are delegated to the EIS instance.

The credentials-mapping mechanism can be used when an application server and the EIS support different authentication domains. In this case the mapped resource principal has the same identity as the initiating/caller principal. For example, a principal with Identity A has initial credentials `cred (A, mech1)` and has credentials `cred (A, mech2)` after mapping. The `mech1` and `mech2` represent different mechanism types.

Authenticating a resource principal

An application server and an EIS collaborate to ensure the proper authentication of a resource principal that establishes a connection to an underlying EIS. Although the Connector's security architecture is independent of any particular security mechanism, the architecture does identify these two commonly supported authenticated mechanisms:

A basic user password–based authentication mechanism specific to an EIS

A Kerberos version 5–based authentication mechanism

Authorizing a resource principal

Authorization ensures that the principal has properly authorized access to the EIS resources. It can be applied either at the EIS level or at the application-server level. If it is done at the EIS level it can be done in an EIS-specific manner. Application servers that use J2EE containers such as EJB and servlet containers can define their security-authorization policies either programmatically or declaratively.

Establishing a secure communication

A secure association is shared security information that allows a component on the application server to communicate securely with an EIS. The establishment of a secure association can include the following steps:

1. Authenticating the resource principal to the EIS. (This may require mutual authentication.)

2. Negotiating a quality of protection, such as confidentiality or integrity.

3. Establishing a shared security context using the credentials of the resource principal, by means of a pair of communicating entities — an application server and an EIS instance.

A secure association between an application server and an EIS is always established by the resource-adapter implementation. The resource-adapter library runs within the address space of the application server. Once a secure association is established successfully the connection is associated with the security context of the resource principal. Subsequently, all application-level invocations to the EIS instance using the connection happen under the security context of the resource principal.

Inbound communication

Version 1.5 of the J2EE Connector architecture provides support for inbound communication. It enables a resource adapter initiated call to invoke EJBs (session, entity and message-driven beans) residing in the application server. It also provides the mechanism to propagate transaction information from an EIS to an application residing in an EJB container. Let's look at the following contracts that are specified by the architecture pertaining to inbound communication: message inflow and transaction inflow.

Message inflow and message endpoint

The-message-inflow contract between an application server and a resource adapter allows a resource adapter to asynchronously deliver messages to message endpoints residing in the application server. It also serves as the standard message-provider "pluggability" contract that allows a wide range of message providers to be plugged into any J2EE-compatible application server via a resource adapter. Figure 19-8 gives an overview of the message-inflow contract.

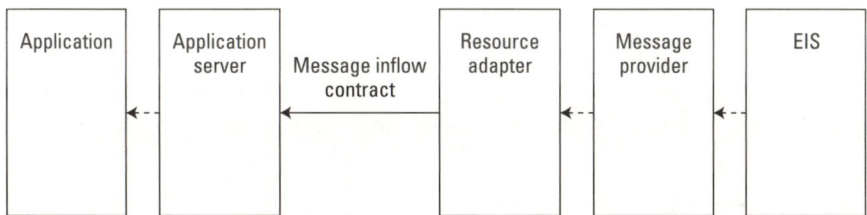

Figure 19-8: The message-inflow contract

The message endpoint is a message-driven bean application deployed on the application server. The resource adapter uses the `MessageEndpointFactory` instance to obtain message-endpoint instances for delivering messages. The resource adapter also provides a configured `ActivationSpec` JavaBean class for each supported endpoint message–listener type. Message-endpoint lifecycle has the following stages:

✦ **Endpoint deployment** — To deploy, you need to select a suitable resource adapter (capable of delivering messages), configure the `ActivationSpec` JavaBean instance obtained from the resource adapter, and pass that instance to the endpoint application. The application server activates the message endpoint by calling the chosen resource adapter via the `endPointActivation` method, and passes a `MessageEndpointFactory` instance and the configured `ActivationSpec` JavaBean instance.

✦ **Message delivery** — Once message endpoints are activated they are ready to receive messages from a message provider. When messages arrive, the resource adapter uses the `MessageEndpointFactory` to create an endpoint instance. Since the resource adapter knows the endpoint type from the `ActivationSpec`, it narrows the endpoint instance to the actual message-listener type and delivers the message to the endpoint instance.

✦ **Endpoint undeployment** — The application server notifies the resource adapter, via `endpointDeactivation`, about the undeployment of the message endpoint. It also passes the `ActivationSpec` JavaBean instance used during endpoint activation.

EJB invocation

A resource adapter may need to call session or entity beans. The J2EE Connector architecture suggests using the resource adapter's bean to dispatch logic to such invocations. The resource adapter can use the message-inflow contract to call a message-driven bean, and use the message-driven bean to dispatch calls to session and entity beans using the EJB client-view model. Thus, the message-driven bean can be used as a replaceable unit of the resource adapter that serves the job of a bean dispatcher. The message-inflow contract allows the creation of multiple endpoint instances (message-driven beans) at runtime, so it is possible to do concurrent bean dispatches.

The transaction-inflow contract

The transaction-inflow contract provides a mechanism with which a resource adapter can propagate an imported transaction to an application server. It also allows transaction completion (two-phase commit) and crash recovery, and ensures that the atomicity, consistency, isolation, and durability (ACID) properties of the imported transaction are preserved.

Cross-Reference   For a detailed discussion on the ACID properties of a transaction, refer to Chapter 10.

Transaction propagation

When the EIS makes a transaction call to the resource adapter, the resource adapter imports the transaction context and represents it in a standard form using the `javax.transaction.xa.Xid` instance. It creates a `Work` instance and an `ExecutedContext` instance containing the constructed `Xid` instance. It then submits the `Work` instance to the application server. The application server's `WorkManager` accepts the submitted `Work` instance and recreates the execution context for the `Work` instance and calls the run method on the `Work` object.

Transaction completion

On receiving the prepare message from the EIS, the resource adapter obtains an `XATerminator` instance from the application server. The resource adapter then calls the `prepare` method on the `XATerminator` instance with an appropriate `Xid` instance, and returns the outcome of the prepare operation to the EIS. When the EIS sends a commit message for the transaction, the resource adapter calls the `commit` method on the `XATerminator` instance with an appropriate `Xid` instance.

The Common Client Interface (CCI)

So far we have looked at the system contracts between the application server and the resource adapter. The Connector architecture also defines an application contract between the application components and the resource adapters. This contract is referred to as the Common Client Interface (CCI). The CCI simplifies the problem of writing code to connect to an EIS. The CCI provides an API that is common across heterogeneous EISes. It provides a set of interfaces and classes whose methods allow a client to perform typical EIS connection, remote-function execution, and data-access operations in a generic way not specific to any particular EIS.

The EIS vendors can use the CCI to write a generic interface to their products. With this one interface, an application deployed on any J2EE compliant platform will be able to access their product. Likewise, application developers only need to learn one API to connect to any EIS system. Additionally, even if the enterprise changes its underlying EIS system, the application code does not need to change.

Functionally, the CCI interfaces and classes are divided into the four following categories:

- ✦ Connection
- ✦ Interaction
- ✦ Data
- ✦ Metadata

Table 19-1 lists the four categories and the supported interfaces.

<table>
<tr><td colspan="3" align="center">Table 19-1
Categories and supported interfaces for CCI</td></tr>
<tr><td>*Categories*</td><td>*Description*</td><td>*Interfaces*</td></tr>
<tr><td>Connection</td><td>This category includes the interfaces to represent connection, specifically a connection factory and an application level connection.</td><td>`javax.resource.cci.`
  `ConnectionFactory`
`javax.resource.cci.Connection`
`javax.resource.cci.`
  `ConnectionSpec`
`javax.resource.cci.`
  `LocalTransaction`</td></tr>
</table>

Continued

Table 19-1 (continued)		
Categories	*Description*	*Interfaces*

Interaction	This category includes the interfaces, which enables a component to execute or drive an interaction with an EIS instance.	`javax.resource.cci.Interaction`
		`javax.resource.cci.`
		`    InteractionSpec`

Data	This category includes the interfaces that represent the data structures involved in an interaction with an EIS instance.	`javax.resource.cci.Record`
		`javax.resource.cci.`
		`    MappedRecord`
		`javax.resource.cci.`
		`    IndexedRecord`
		`javax.resource.cci.`
		`    RecordFactory`
		`javax.resource.cci.Streamable`
		`javax.resource.cci.ResultSet`
		`javax.sql.ResultSetMetaData`

Metadata	This category includes the interfaces that provide basic metadata information about a resource adapter implementation and an EIS connection.	`javax.resource.cci.`
		`    ConnectionMetaData`
		`javax.resource.cci.`
		`    ResourceAdapterMetaData`
		`javax.resource.cci.`
		`    ResultSetInfo`

Connection interfaces

Connection interfaces encompass the following connection-related interfaces:

✦ `ConnectionFactory` — The `ConnectionFactory` interface provides an application component with an interface for getting a connection to an EIS instance. An application component uses JNDI APIs first to look up a `ConnectionFactory` instance from the JNDI namespace and then to get a connection to the EIS instance. It provides the method `getConnection` to obtain a connection to the EIS instance. It supports two variants of the `getConnection` method — one used if the application is using the container-managed sign-on and the other one used if the application is using the component-managed sign-on.

✦ `Connection` — The `Connection` interface represents an application-level connection handle for accessing an EIS instance. It only represents a logical connection to the EIS; the actual physical connection is represented by a `ManagedConnection`. It provides the method `createInteraction` to create an `Interaction` instance. An `Interaction` enables a component to access EIS data and functions. It also provides the method `getLocalTransaction`, which enables the application components to use their own transactions.

✦ ConnectionSpec — The ConnectionSpec interface is used to pass properties specific for a connection request to the getConnection method. The CCI specification defines two standard properties for the ConnectionSpec interface: UserName and Password. A resource adapter that implements the ConnectionSpec interface can add its own additional properties.

Interaction interfaces

The following interaction interfaces enable a component to drive an interaction with an EIS instance:

✦ Interaction — The Interaction interface defines methods that enable an application component to execute EIS functions. It provides two variants of the execute method. One takes three parameters, an input Record, an output Record and an InteractionSpec instance. This method executes the EIS function represented by the InteractionSpec and updates the output Record. The other variant takes two parameters, an input Record and an InteractionSpec. This method executes the EIS function represented by InteractionSpec and produces the output Record as a return value.

✦ InteractionSpec — The InteractionSpec instance is used to hold the properties that are used by the Interaction instance to interact with the EIS. The CCI defines a set of standard properties for the InteractionSpec interface, but the implementation class is only required to support a property if the property is relevant to the underlying EIS. Standard properties include FunctionName (a string representing the name of the EIS function) and InteractionVerb (an integer representing the mode of interaction with an EIS instance).

Data interfaces

The following data-related interfaces represent the data structures involved in an interaction with an EIS instance:

✦ RecordFactory — Just as the ConnectionFactory interface is used to create connections, a RecordFactory interface is used to create Record instances. It provides methods for creating the MappedRecord and IndexedRecord. The methods only take the name of the Record as the parameter. The name of the Record acts as a pointer to the meta information. The implementation class uses the meta information to create the Record instance.

✦ Record — A Record interface acts as a data structure used to pass the data between the application component and the EIS. It is a base interface and can be implemented by a MappedRecord, an IndexedRecord, or a ResultSet. The MappedRecord represents a key-value map based collection of Record elements and is based on the java.util.Map. IndexedRecord is an ordered and indexed collection of Record elements and is based on the java.util. List. ResultSet represents tabular data and is based on the java.sql. ResultSet.

Metadata interfaces

The following interfaces provide basic meta information about a resource adapter implementation and an EIS instance:

✦ `ConnectionMetaData` — The `ConnectionMetaData` interface provides basic meta information about the EIS connection. An application component that has a connection with the EIS instance can call the method `getMetaData()` on the `Connection` instance to get a `ConnectionMetaData` instance. The `ConnectionMetaData` interface holds information like the EIS name, EIS version, and the name of the user for the connection.

✦ `ResourceAdapterMetaData` — The `ResourceAdapterMetaData` interface provides information about the capabilities of a resource-adapter implementation. An active connection to the EIS instance is not required to retrieve this information. The interface provides information about the version of the specifications implemented by the resource adapter, the variants of `execute` (on `Interaction` interface) implemented, and whether the resource adapter supports local-transaction demarcation.

Using the CCI

A client or application component that uses the CCI to interact with an underlying EIS does so in a prescribed manner. The following basic programming steps are required to use the CCI API:

1. Perform a JNDI lookup to locate the `ConnectionFactory` for the resource adapter.

2. Call the `getConnection()` method of the `ConnectionFactory` to obtain a connection. The `Connection` instance represents a connection handle to the EIS and is used for subsequent interactions with the EIS.

3. Call the `createInteraction()` method on the `Connection` instance to create a new `Interaction` instance.

4. Instantiate an object representing the `InteractionSpec` interface. The `InteractionSpec` object is used to specify properties related to the target interaction with the EIS.

5. Call the `getRecordFactory()` method of the `ConnectionFactory` to get a reference to the `RecordFactory`.

6. Use the `RecordFactory create` methods to create `Record` instances. The application components read and write data to the EIS using a particular type of `Record` (`MappedRecord`, `IndexedRecord`, or `ResultSet`).

7. Start the transaction if the application component is managing its own transaction.

8. Perform the desired operation.

9. Close the transaction (`commit` or `rollback`), if the application component is managing its own transaction.

10. Close the connection to the EIS.

Listing 19-5 illustrates an application example that uses the CCI to access an EIS.

Listing 19-5: **Accessing an EIS with the CCI**

```
package com.connexia.client;

import javax.naming.Context;
import javax.naming.InitialContext;
import javax.naming.NamingException;
import javax.resource.ResourceException;
import javax.resource.cci.*;
import javax.resource.cci.Connection;
import javax.resource.cci.ConnectionFactory;
import javax.resource.cci.Interaction;
.
.
.

public void connecttoEIS() {

        ConnectionFactory connectionFactory = null;
        Connection conn = null;
        Interaction interx = null;
        RecordFactory recordFactory = null;
        IndexedRecord inputRecord = null;
        IndexedRecord outputRecord = null;

        // 1. Obtain a ConnectionFactory.
        // Establish a JNDI initialcontext and use the lookup
method
        // to locate the ConnectionFactory for the resource
adapter.

        try {
            Context context = new InitialContext();
            connectionFactory =
                (ConnectionFactory)
context.lookup("java:comp/env/CCIEIS");
        } catch (NamingException e) {

            e.printStackTrace();
            // clean up...
            return;
        }
```

Continued

Listing 19-5 *(continued)*

```
        // 2. Obtain a Connection.
        // Call the getConnection() method to get a connection
  to
        // the EIS instance. You can also call
        // getConnection(ConnectionSpec) method and pass
        // user/password information in the ConnectionSpec
  object.

        try {
            conn = connectionFactory.getConnection();
        } catch (ResourceException re) {
            System.out.println(
                "ResourceException thrown: Could not
                  create connection");
            re.printStackTrace();
            return;
        }

        // 3. Create a Interaction object to enable the
        // application to execute EIS functions.

        try {
            interx = conn.createInteraction();
        } catch (ResourceException re) {
            System.out.println(
                "ResourceException thrown: Could not create
                  interaction");
            re.printStackTrace();
            // clean up...
            return;
        }

        // 4. Create an object implementing the  InteractionSpec
        // interface.
        // This object will hold properties such as schema name
  and
        // function name. The interaction object will use these
        // properties to interact with the EIS instance.

        MyInteractionSpec myInteractionSpec = new
  MyInteractionSpec();
        myInteractionSpec.setFunctionName("Search");

        // 5. Get a RecordFactory

        try {
            recordFactory =
  connectionFactory.getRecordFactory();
        } catch (ResourceException re) {
            System.out.println(
```

```
                    "ResourceException thrown: Could not create
RecordFactory");
                re.printStackTrace();
                // clean up...
                return;
        }

        // 6. Get a Record instance to pass the input data.

        try {
                inputRecord =
recordFactory.createIndexedRecord("InputRecord");
        } catch (ResourceException re) {
                System.out.println(
                    "ResourceException thrown: Could not create
Record");
                re.printStackTrace();
                // clean up...
                return;
        }

        // 7. Start a transaction.
        // This step is optional. If the application is using
the
        // container managed transaction, then this step is not
        // needed. If the application is managing the
transaction
        // itself, then get the LocalTransaction object from
the
        //connection object and start the transaction.

        // for example :
        //   transaction = conn.getLocalTransaction();
        //   transaction.begin();

        .
        .
        .




        // 8. Perform the operation
        // myInteraction is used to pass the properties and
        // inputRecord is used to pass the data for the
operation.
        // outputRecord contains the result of the operation.

        try {
            outputRecord =
                (IndexedRecord)
interx.execute(myInteractionSpec, inputRecord);
        } catch (ResourceException re) {
```

Continued

Listing 19-5 *(continued)*

```
            System.out.println(
                "ResourceException thrown: Could not create get
the transaction");
            re.printStackTrace();
            // clean up...
            return;
        }

        // 9. Close the transaction.
        // If you used the transaction in the earlier step, you
need
        // to close the transaction (commit or rollback)
        // for example: transaction.rollback() or
        // transaction.commit();

        // 10. Close the connection
        try {
            conn.close();
        } catch (ResourceException re) {
            System.out.println(
                "ResourceException thrown: Could not close
connection");
            re.printStackTrace();
        }

    }
```

Packaging and Deployment

In most regards a resource-adapter module is just like any other J2EE module, such as an enterprise-bean module or a Web-application module. It must be deployed on the application server before it can be accessed by other J2EE components and applications. The J2EE Connector architecture supports the modular and portable deployment of a resource adapter. The resource-adapter module can be deployed either as a stand-alone unit or as part of a J2EE enterprise application. When it is deployed as a stand-alone unit, multiple J2EE applications running on the same application server can share a single resource adapter. When it is deployed as part of a J2EE enterprise application, the resource adapter is available only to modules and components within the same application.

Typically, a resource adapter module includes the following elements:

Java classes and interfaces that implement the contracts and the functionality of the resource adapter

Utility Java classes for the resource adapter

Platform-dependent native libraries required by the resource adapter

Help files and documentation

A deployment-descriptor file containing meta information about the resource adapter

A resource adapter is packaged into a Resource Adapter Archive (RAR) format. The RAR format uses the standard Java archive (JAR) format. A RAR file is identified by the `.rar` file extension. The following is a sample directory structure for a resource adapter module:

```
META-INF/ra.xml
readme.html
Images/icon.jpg
eis.jar
utilities.jar
windows.dll
solaris.so
```

The `ra.xml` deployment descriptor contains the meta information about the resource adapter. The J2EE model dictates that the file should be under the directory `META-INF`. The files `ra.jar` and `cci.jar` contain the Java interfaces and implementation classes for the resource adapter. The `win.dll` and `solaris.so` libraries are examples of native libraries.

Let's examine some of the important elements that can be configured in the deployment descriptor. The deployment descriptor specifies the interfaces and the implementation classes for the resource adapter.

The element `<resourceadapter-class>` specifies the fully qualified name of the Java class that implements the `javax.resource.spi.ResourceAdapter` interface. The elements related to the connection contract specify the fully qualified names of the Java classes that implement their respective interfaces. Listing 19-6 provides an example.

Listing 19-6: `<resourceadapter-class>` implementing
`javax.resource.spi.ResourceAdapter`

```
<?xml version="1.0" encoding="UTF-8"?>

<!DOCTYPE connector PUBLIC '-//Sun Microsystems, Inc.//DTD
Connector 1.5//EN'
```

Continued

Listing 19-6 *(continued)*

```
'http://java.sun.com/j2ee/dtds/connector_1_5.dtd'>

<connector>
    <display-name>MyJCA</display-name>
    <vendor-name>MyJCA</vendor-name>
    <spec-version>1.5</spec-version>
    <eis-type>My Data</eis-type>
    <version>1.0</version>
    <resourceadapter>
       <resourceadapter-class>
       com.connexia.adapter.MyResourceAdapter
       </resourceadapter-class>
      <outbound-resourceadapter>
        <connection-definition>
        <managedconnectionfactory-class>
            com.connexia.adapter.MyManagedConnectionFactory
        </managedconnectionfactory-class>
        <connectionfactory-interface>
            javax.sql.DataSource
        </connectionfactory-interface>
        <connectionfactory-impl-class>
            com.connexia.adapter.MyDataSource
        </connectionfactory-impl-class>
        <connection-interface>
            java.sql.Connection
        </connection-interface>
        <connection-impl-class>
            com.connexia.adapter.MyConnection
        </connection-impl-class>
       </connection-definition>


             .
             .
             .

    </outbound-resourceadapter>
    <inbound-resourceadapter>
    ...
    </inbound-resourceadapter>

    </resourceadapter>
</connector>
```

The resource adapter can be configured to provide appropriate transaction support. The valid values for transaction level are `NoTransaction`, `Local Transaction` and `XATransaction`. Here's an example:

```
<transaction-support>LocalTransaction</transaction-support>
```

The deployment-descriptor also specifies the authentication mechanism that the resource adapter supports. The valid values for the authentication types are `BasicPassword` and `Kerbv5`. Here's an example:

```
<authentication-mechanism>
    <authentication-mechanism-type>
        BasicPassword
    </authentication-mechanism-type>
    <credential-interface>
        javax.resource.security.PasswordCredential
    </credential-interface>
</authentication-mechanism>
```

The inbound resource adapter section of the deployment descriptor allows specifying the attributes for the messaging resource adapter. Here is an example:

```
<inbound-resourceadapter>
    <messageadapter>
        <messagelistener>
            <messagelistener-type>
                javax.jms.MessageListener
            </messagelistener-type>
        <activationspec ">
            <activationspec-class>
                com.connexia.adapter.MyActivationSpec
            </activationspec-class>
        </activationspec>
        </messagelistener>
    </messageadapter>
</inbound-resourceadapter>
```

During resource adapter deployment, the deployer configures the resource adapter based on the properties defined in the deployment descriptor. Generally, you package and deploy a resource adapter using the tools that are provided with your application server.

Summary

The J2EE Connector architecture defines a standard architecture for connecting the J2EE platform to heterogeneous EISes. It defines contracts and responsibilities for various roles for standard bi-directional connectivity to an EIS. The J2EE Connector architecture extends the benefits of J2EE beyond the application server and provides a way for the EIS vendors to plug into the J2EE space. In this chapter, we examined the system-level contracts between the J2EE server and the resource adapter. By adhering to the terms of these contracts when developing their components, EIS vendors no longer need to customize their product for each application server. Application server vendors who conform to the J2EE Connector architecture do not need to add custom code when they add connectivity to a new EIS. We also looked at the Common Client Interface (CCI), a common client API for accessing multiple heterogeneous EISes. The CCI sample code illustrated how to use the different interfaces and classes defined by CCI to access a resource adapter for an underlying EIS.

The Connector architecture is currently supported by a significant number of J2EE compliant application servers and EIS vendors. The J2EE Connector architecture provides a very flexible API. But in order to provide support for flexibility, it has also become a complex API and is more oriented towards commercial software vendors. A lot of companies have taken the initiative of implementing adapters for various EISes. You can either leverage an off-the-shelf adapter to connect to your legacy system or implement your own. If your enterprise changes the backend legacy system, you only need to replace the adapter.

✦   ✦   ✦

Web Services

✦ ✦ ✦ ✦

In This Part

Chapter 20
Introducing Web Services

Chapter 21
Digging Deeper into SOAP, WSDL, and UDDI

Chapter 22
Understanding J2EE Web Services

✦ ✦ ✦ ✦

Introducing Web Services

In This Chapter

Defining
Web services

Explaining why we
need Web services

Examining some
Web-service
scenarios

Understanding the
technologies behind
Web services

There was once a time when an 8 megahertz CPU and a 300 baud modem was all you needed to spend an entire day playing games, sending e-mail, or participating in a news-group. Your friendly Bulletin Board System (BBS) was your portal to education, adventure, and mischief, and everything was quite simple. Then in the mid-'90s, the Internet exploded and changed the face of computing, information exchange, and eventually business, forever.

While Hypertext Markup Language (HTML), JavaScript, and Common Gateway Interface (CGI) were relatively powerful technologies, they were not easy to work with, and they were limited in their flexibility. In the late '90s, technologies like Microsoft's Active Server Pages (ASP), and Sun's Java Servlets and JavaServer Pages (JSP) offered more flexible, more efficient, and more dynamic frameworks for building Web sites. The next evolutionary phase was from marking data for display (HTML) to marking data for content by means of the eXtensible Markup Language (XML). XML is more intelligent than HTML because it is capable of describing data context and data types, as well as describing the meaning, or purpose of a particular piece of data. Additionally, the structure of an XML document is more tightly defined and is capable of being understood by any application with access to an appropriate XML parser. XML has thus paved the way for mobile devices and other embedded systems to join the World Wide Web.

In the same way that XML represents a more intelligent and more flexible evolution of HTML, Web services can be thought of as a more intelligent and more flexible evolution of XML. In this chapter we will introduce you to Web services and the effect they are having on the industry. We will also discuss a high-level view of the technologies behind Web services, Simple Object Access Protocol (SOAP), Web Services Definition Language (WSDL), and Universal Description, Discovery, and Integration (UDDI).

Defining Web Services

Web services extend the Extensible Markup Language (XML) that enables us to share data and functionality. That's right, you can use existing applications that expose methods as Web services to create new applications. Web services are quite complex and provide more flexibility than this definition implies. Let's take a look at a more detailed definition of the term *Web service:*

> The W3C Web Services Architecture group refers to a Web service as a software system identified by a URI, whose public interfaces and bindings are defined and described using XML. Its definition can be discovered by other software systems. These systems may then interact with the Web service in a manner prescribed by its definition, using XML-based messages conveyed by Internet protocols.

We believe this is the most complete definition available. It captures the dynamic nature of a Web service and mentions the use of open technologies, XML, and Internet protocols. However, it can be confusing, so let's take a closer look at it.

Universal Resource Identifiers

Webopedia.com defines a *Universal Resource Identifier* (URI) as "The generic term for all types of names and addresses that refer to objects on the World Wide Web." Currently there are two types of URIs, Universal Resource Locators (URLs) and Universal Resource Names (URNs). These terms are defined as follows:

✦ **URLs** — Uniform Resource locators point to a specific location or address and have a prefix such as ftp, http, or mailto. You must know the entire URL in order to obtain the information you are looking for.

✦ **URNs** — Universal Resource names require only the name of the resource in order to work.

XML-based technologies

Communication via XML-based messages is commonly achieved by means of the Simple Object Access Protocol (SOAP) and HTTP. It is important to note that SOAP, WSDL, UDDI, and HTTP are not required in a Web-service environment. We will discuss SOAP, WSDL, and UDDI in more detail later in the chapter.

Finally, because XML-based technologies and HTTP make up a Web-service environment, you do not need to specify a programming language or platform. Web services are language-independent and vendor-neutral. These are very important points because historically the most popular technologies and protocols for distributed computing have been proprietary in some way. They have not fully met the needs of the distributed-computing industry; we will discuss these problems in the next section.

Why Do We Need Web Services?

Traditional distributed-computing environments have been tightly coupled, meaning that they do not deal with a changing environment well. For instance, if the purpose of an application is to exchange data, it might not be able to dynamically handle the varying data types of new applications across multiple platforms without a considerable change in architecture. Let's take a look at some of the common problems associated with traditional architectures in a real-world situation.

Let's say our company has software that handles monetary transactions for an airline-reservation system. A customer decides to purchase a ticket for $10,000. The client software that handles purchases sends the request to the server. The server receives the request and the order is placed. The server may or may not send a response back. How does the requestor know that the order was placed? What if one of the servers failed, possibly causing total application failure? Errors can prove to be very costly.

The most popular "I'm not sure I understand what you mean" technologies for traditional computing are the following:

✦ Remote Method Invocation (RMI)

✦ Distributed Component Object Model (DCOM)

✦ Common Object Request Broker Architecture (CORBA)

RMI, CORBA, and DCOM all have one common theme: *dependency*. Whether the technology is dependent on the vendor or language doesn't matter; the result is the same. Systems made with these technologies do not interoperate or communicate effectively with multiple systems in varying environments. The lack of effective communication usually means that a developer will take on the role of watchdog to make sure everything goes smoothly. Most importantly, the traditional architectures for distributed computing use RMI, CORBA, and DCOM, and thus do not take full advantage of the Internet because they were created before the Internet became mainstream. The Internet provides standards that are recognized worldwide and any technologies that incorporate these standards can be used to create highly interoperable applications.

Let's take a closer look at RMI, DCOM, and CORBA.

Remote Method Invocation

RMI allows applications to communicate across a network by allowing Java objects to remotely invoke each other. RMI is a great technology but it requires every application in the environment that wants to communicate to use Java.

 **Cross-Reference** For more information on RMI, please refer to Chapter 4 or visit `http://java.sun.com/products/jdk/rmi/`.

DCOM

DCOM is Microsoft's distributed version of the Component Object Model (COM). You can use the language of your choice; the only requirement is that you implement the COM interfaces. This technology is a "Microsoft-standard," meaning that you can use it on most Windows platforms with no problems. Overall, support for COM is limited to specific platforms. For more information please visit `http://www.microsoft.com/com/tech/DCOM.asp`.

CORBA

The Common Object Request Broker Architecture (CORBA) was created by the Object Management Group to help increase interoperability within distributed-computing environments. CORBA is platform- and language-independent. Sounds great, huh? Unfortunately, CORBA requires each application in an environment to have the same Object Request Broker. An ORB facilitates communication between a client seeking a service and servers that host a service, so interacting with many different applications can become very expensive and inefficient. Lastly, CORBA does not interact well with firewalls, primarily because it was created before the WWW was widely used. Currently, CORBA does have some support for firewall interaction, but with the emergence of Web services, focus has shifted away from CORBA. For more information on CORBA please visit `http://www.corba.org/`.

Web-service architecture

By now we have taken enough shots at the prominent technologies for distributed computing. We can't blame the current state of distress solely on the technologies; after all, they are only part of a larger architecture. In this section we'll take a look at two of the most important architectures for current distributed computing, remote procedure call–based architectures and message-based architectures. We will also examine the architecture that Web services use.

Remote procedure call–based architecture

As you may know, a remote procedure call–based architecture allows an application to use the functionality of an application on an RPC server. During the application request the required arguments are passed to the RPC server, the arguments are processed, and a value is returned to the requesting application. The RPC architecture does not allow an application to discover services or information about the type of service provided. The requestor has to know the required information in order to make a call, which severely limits interoperability.

Message-based architecture

A message-based architecture tends to handle load balancing and fail-over much better than an RPC-based architecture. Typically, message-based architectures use *asynchronous messaging,* by means of which data are transferred using messages that are sent to a *queue.* The queue handles processing from there. There's no need for the requestor to wait for a response. Message-based architectures are usually created with proprietary middleware products, and you know the problem with using proprietary products; however, in a J2EE application this can be mitigated using JMS-compliant products. All participants must have the messaging software and any other software required to communicate with other messaging environments. So what happens when you are communicating with 100 different environments? That can become very expensive!

If you haven't noticed, I haven't mentioned HTTP, XML, or any other open standard. Why? Because the traditional software architecture does not take full advantage of Internet standards. Traditional software architectures are primarily object-based models and use proprietary protocols. Web services typically use the open standard of HTTP and a service-oriented architecture.

Service-oriented architectures

The service-oriented architecture (SOA) consists of these three parts:

- ✦ **Requestor** — This role is responsible for discovering a service by searching through the service descriptions given by the service broker. It is also responsible for binding to services provided by the service provider.

- ✦ **Provider** — This role allows access to services, creates a description of a service, and publishes the service to the service broker.

- ✦ **Broker** — This role hosts a registry of service descriptions. It is responsible for linking a requestor to a service provider.

Figure 20-1 illustrates the service-oriented architecture.

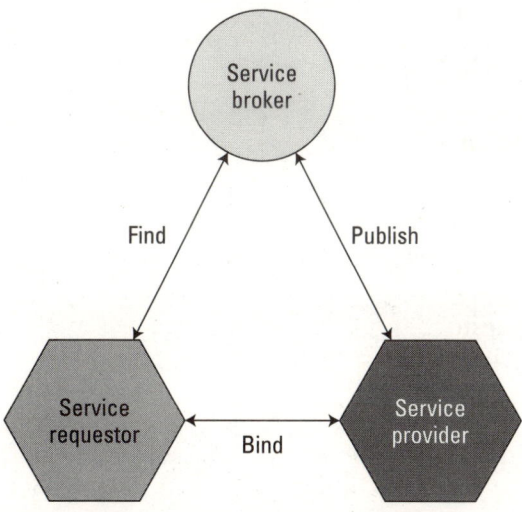

Figure 20-1: A service-oriented architecture

Some of the advantages of an SOA are that it is loosely coupled, dynamic, and efficient. For instance, if a requestor requests a service from a service provider, and the provider's system fails, the requestor can dynamically find a new provider through the broker. The provider may also redirect the requestor to a backup system. Below is a list of some of the principles of a software-oriented architecture.

✦ **Platform independence** — In an SOA, the platforms that are used are not as important as you might think. The main focus is on finding, binding, and publishing services. The platform doesn't matter because the services are accessed via a common interface.

✦ **Flexibility** — An SOA must be flexible enough to handle a changing environment and changing business requirements.

✦ **Design independence** — The design of a service and the system that hosts or accesses a service should not be dependent upon each other.

We have examined the drawbacks of using some of the traditional architectures for distributed computing, and looked at the advantages of implementing a service-oriented architecture. In the next section we will take a look at some of the advantages of Web services.

Advantages of Web services

Web services provide several significant benefits for distributed enterprise systems. Some of the most notable benefits include the following:

✦ Interoperability

✦ Efficiency

✦ Standardization

We will briefly explore each of these in this section.

Interoperability

Interoperability is the ability of software on different systems to communicate by sharing data and functionality. Above all, Web services are built with interoperability in mind. Most companies will have numerous business partners; instead of writing a new addition to your applications every time you gain a new partner, you can write one interface using Web-service technologies like SOAP. Now your partners can dynamically find the services they need using UDDI, and bind to them using SOAP. (UDDI and SOAP are discussed in greater detail later in this chapter.)

You can also extend the interoperability of your systems by implementing Web services within your corporate intranet. With the addition of Web services to your intranet systems and to your extranet, you can reduce the cost of integration and increase communication. It is also important to note that the industry has established the Web Services Interoperability Organization (WS-I).

The WS-I consists of approximately 51 vendors, including IBM, Microsoft, Accenture, BEA, HP, and Oracle. It determines whether a Web service conforms to WS-I standards as well as industry standards. In order to establish integrity and acceptance, companies will seek to build their Web services in compliance with the WS-I standards. You can visit the WS-I at `www.ws-i.org`.

In addition to the WS-I, the Organization for the Advancement of Structured Information Standards (OASIS) helps promote standardization within the realm of Web services. The organization consists of more than 600 members including IBM, Sun Microsystems, Microsoft, BEA Systems and Computer Associates. The OASIS is involved in the development of UDDI, ebXML, CMG Open, LegalXML, and PKI.

Quality attributes

When we think of *quality attributes,* we think of saving money, time, and energy. Web services enable you to save all these things. Web services enable you to increase scalability by allowing you to reuse your existing applications: Instead of creating totally new applications "from scratch", you can create new applications using various combinations of services exposed by your existing applications. Developers can be more efficient because they can focus on learning industry-standard technology, instead of wasting time learning every new technology that arises. Web services are also fairly simple to learn and implement; for a manager this means a reduction in the cost of buying new software. Web services enable developers to meet changing business requirements and complete projects faster.

Standardization

For something to be a true standard, it must be accepted and used by the majority of the industry. One vendor or small group of vendors must not control the evolution of the technology or specification in question. Most if not all of the industry leaders are involved in the development of Web-service specifications. Almost all businesses use the Internet and World Wide Web (WWW) in one form or another. The underlying protocol for the WWW is of course the Hypertext Transfer Protocol (HTTP). Web services are built upon a foundation of HTTP and XML.

Examining Some Web-Service Scenarios

So far we have determined what Web services are and we have looked at some of the benefits of using them. In this section we will look at when and where you should implement them. Currently many companies are focused on implementing Web services for the following:

✦ Enterprise-application integration

✦ Application-service providers

✦ Smart Web services

✦ Mobile e-services

Enterprise-application integration (EAI)

Whether because of a merger or a partnership with a company that runs on "dinosaur technology," we have all had to deal with the pain of enterprise-application integration, or EAI. For the IT staff it can prove to be a nightmare. You may be dealing with older, tightly coupled systems that can go down with the slightest change in code. You may also have to deal with systems built with differing technologies and data types.

Many companies are finding that Web services are complementary to enterprise-application integration. In an EAI environment you generally have varying systems such as Customer Relationship Management (Peoplesoft), Enterprise Resource Planning (Siebel), databases, and legacy applications interacting to share data and business processes. They all connect to a common EAI system that allows the actual communication to take place. Typically, the EAI system is created with old proprietary technology that requires *mirror integration,* meaning that once integration is achieved, changes on one end must be made on the other end. With Web services you don't have to worry about this. The requestor of the Web service is accessing an XML-based interface to a system and not the system directly. If changes are made to the system, the requestor doesn't malfunction and does not need to make the same change made by the system providing the service.

Another benefit of using Web services in an EAI environment is that they give you the ability to create wrappers for the individual application components. (In the past, EAI systems weren't able to provide this type of functionality; they could only provide application-level services.)

Application-service providers (ASPs)

In the past, an ASP would typically allow consumers to use an application that was hosted by the ASP or downloaded. For many ASPs the cost of building an infrastructure to host all the applications could become very expensive. In many situations you would have to pay a fee for the use of a complete application even when you only needed certain parts of it.

Frequently, there was also the problem that one application could not adequately cater to all industries. An ASP must respond to the needs of consumers by building additional functionality into its application. ASPs spent a lot of money trying to customize applications and consumers couldn't find one application that fit all their needs. Web services are having a tremendous effect on the way ASPs do business. Web services allow an ASP to provide component services. With a Web service–based model, an ASP can expand its offerings.

The term *component services* refers to businesses exposing various components within their applications as services. With Web services an ASP can now offer a single application composed of a variety of interchangeable services. ASPs can also offer individual services and allow consumers to assemble their own customized applications. Figure 20-2 depicts a service-oriented architecture that can be used by a news service.

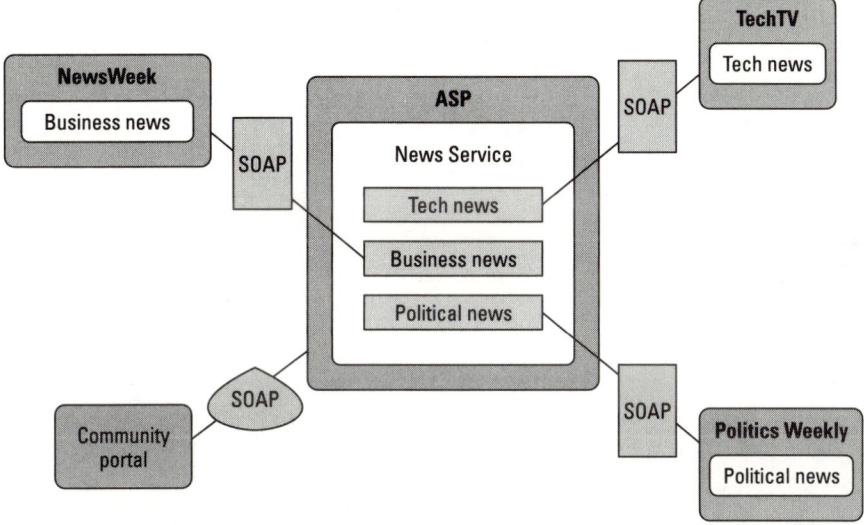

Figure 20-2: Architecture for an ASP-style Web service

Currently, if a community portal wants to display breaking news on its Web site, it must find a company that sells access to a news-information system. In order to gain access to those, the news portal must use the particular programming language and API the system requires. If the news company were to provide an interface described by WSDL and accessible by SOAP, any XML-capable consumer would be able to access the news information systems.

Smart Web services

So far we have discussed the ability of a consumer to dynamically find services published to a registry by the service provider; the interaction among the Web-service components has been simple. What happens when you introduce Web services into a real-time environment, one in which things are constantly changing? Sun Microsystems is currently addressing this issue with *smart Web services* that are context-sensitive. For instance, if you, your doctor and dentist make your electronic scheduler accessible via smart Web services, the schedulers can automatically schedule appointments with each other. Smart services will surely boost competition and improve the end value received by consumers.

Mobile e-services

In the U.S., many mobile devices do not have the memory or processing power to run robust applications locally. In Europe, some manufacturers have enabled cellular telephones to purchase snacks from vending machines, and to purchase various products online. In the future mobil e-services may enable doctors to perform real-time queries to compare a patient's symptoms with known diagnoses, and provide access to your home's computer system, your bank account, and your travel arrangements. These examples are depicted in Figure 20-3.

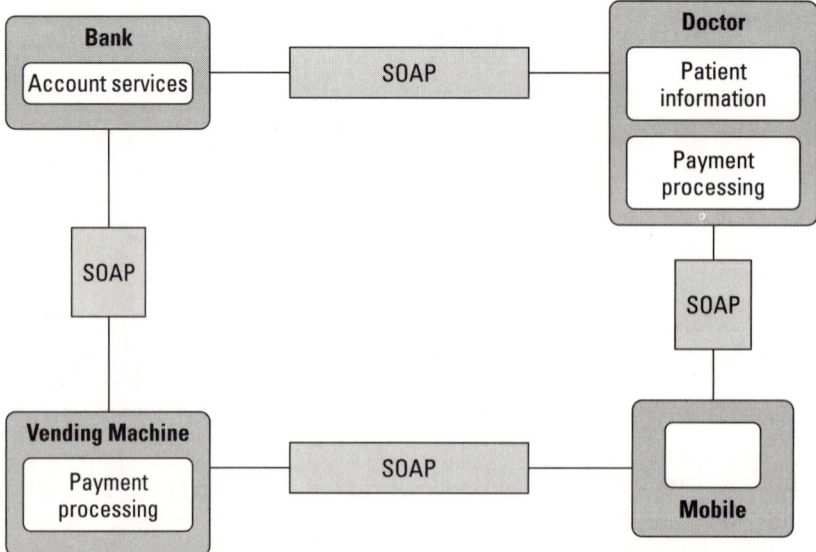

Figure 20-3: A wireless Web services mobile e-services environment

Ultimately, Web services will enable the entire wireless industry to provide the end user with the ability to access rich applications regardless of manufacturer platform. So far we have examined the advantages of Web services in general and in specific scenarios. In the next section we will take a closer look at the actual technologies that make the advantages of Web services possible.

Understanding the Technologies behind Web Services

In Web services, The Universal Distribution, Discovery and Integration (UDDI) registry serves as the service broker. The publish, find, and bind interactions are typically performed with the Simple Object Access Protocol (SOAP). The Web-service requestor can be any client with the ability to find Web-service descriptions and invoke these services using the parameters and protocol supported by the service. The Web-service provider is responsible for creating a description for the service, generally using the Web Service Description Language (WSDL), and for publishing that description to the registries of the discovery agency.

Now let's take a look at the following technologies behind Web services:

✦ Simple Object Access Protocol (SOAP)

✦ Web Services Description Language (WSDL)

✦ Universal Distribution, Discovery, and Interoperability (UDDI)

SOAP

According to the W3C, SOAP is "a lightweight protocol for exchange of information in a decentralized, distributed environment." The latest version of the SOAP specification can be found at `http://www.w3c.org/TR/soap12-part1 /`

SOAP is the key to the binding operation between the service requestor and the service provider. According to the SOAP 1.1 note, SOAP consists of these three parts:

✦ **SOAP envelope** — The envelope contains the message exchanged between providers. It also contains information needed to process a message. Within the envelope are a header and a body. The header is optional and enables a SOAP message to have additional functionality such as support for security or transactions. The body is not optional and contains the actual data being requested.

✦ **SOAP encoding rules** — According to the W3C, these rules define "a serialization mechanism that can be used to exchange instances of application-defined data types" (see `www.w3.org`). The encoding rules are built around XML Schema structures and XML Schema data types.

✦ **SOAP RPC** — The SOAP RPC allows remote procedure calls and responses via XML.

Now we have looked at SOAP and how it is used to access Web services. In order for SOAP to access the correct services, the services need a way of describing themselves. That's where WSDL comes in.

WSDL

WSDL provides a way for Web services to be described. The WSDL document provides a description of the service, which helps the service requestor to find a compatible service from the discovery agency. A WSDL document provides the following information as a service description:

The functionality provided by the service

The information needed to access the service (such as encoding and transport information)

Location information

The latest version of the WSDL specification can be found at `http://www.w3.org/TR/wsdl`.

A WSDL document is composed of the following elements:

✦ **Data types** — These contain information about the data types needed to access the service. A WSDL document typically uses XML schemas as the type system.

✦ **Message** — The message is an abstract description of the data being accessed or requested.

✦ **Operation** — This describes what a service can do and is comprised of messages. It is similar to a function.

✦ **Port type** — The port type is used to map a set of operations to one or more endpoints.

✦ **Binding** — This enables you to specify a concrete protocol (such as HTTP) and a data format (such as SOAP) to bind a port type.

✦ **Port** — The port is a combination of a binding and a physical network address.

✦ **Service** — The service is a collection of related ports.

UDDI

UDDI is like the Yellow Pages for Web services. It enables service discovery through queries to the UDDI registry at design time or at runtime. It also enables providers to publish descriptions of their services to the registry. The registry typically contains a URL that locates the WSDL document for the Web services and contact information for the service provider. Within UDDI business information is placed into these three categories:

✦ **White pages** — The white pages contain general information (such as name, address, and other contact information) about the company providing the service.

✦ **Yellow pages** — The yellow pages list businesses according to the industries their services cater to.

✦ **Green pages** — The green pages are primarily for you hardcore techies! They provide technical information that will enable a client to bind to the service being provided.

The latest version of the UDDI specification can be found at `http://www.uddi.org/specification.html`

So far we have looked at the key technologies behind individual Web services, but how do they interact? We'll explore this topic in the next section.

Web services in a service-oriented architecture

To better understand how the technologies behind Web services interact, take a look at the services in the context of the service-oriented architecture depicted in Figure 20-4. We will also examine the following Web-service stacks:

✦ Wire stack

✦ Description stack

✦ Discovery stack

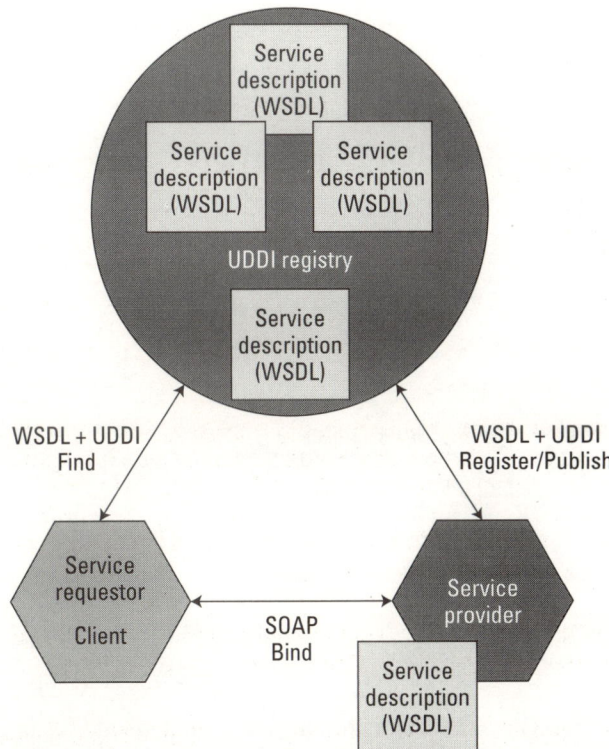

Figure 20-4: SOAP, WSDL, and UDDI combine to create a robust, service-oriented systems architecture.

The wire stack

The wire stack, illustrated in Figure 20-5, contains the technologies that enable communication among the UDDI registry, the Web-service provider, and the client requesting the service. It consists of the following three layers:

✦ Transport layer

✦ Packaging layer

✦ Extensions layer

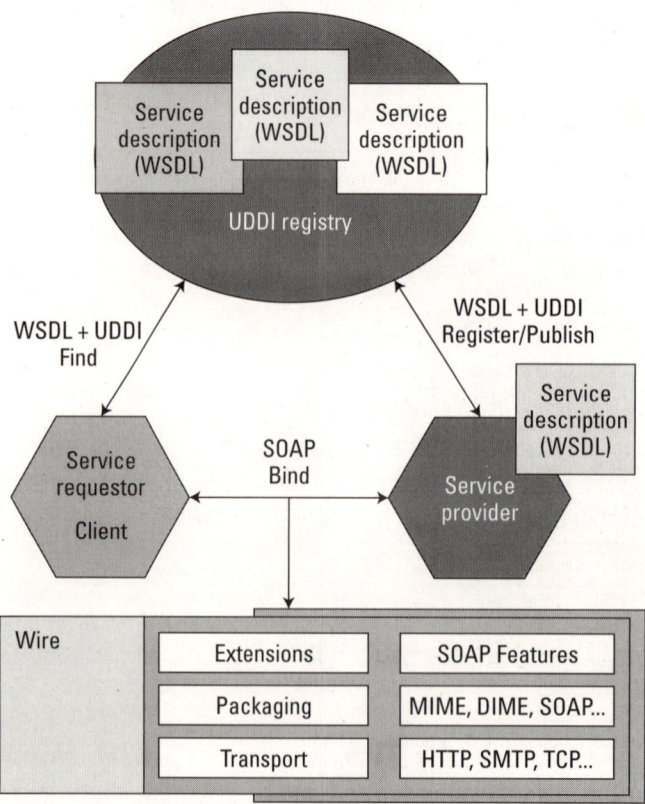

Figure 20-5: The Web-services wire stack

Transport

The transport layer consists of the network protocols that can be used to send or receive services. Some of the protocols that can be used include Hypertext Transfer Protocol (HTTP), SMTP (Simple Mail Transfer Protocol), Transmission Control Protocol (TCP) and File Transfer Protocol (FTP). Also, if your system requires the use of proprietary technologies, protocols like Internet Inter-ORB Protocol (IIOP) and IBM MQseries can be used as well.

Packaging

The packaging layer consists of the technologies used to encapsulate the data used to find, bind, and publish services. Packaging is typically handled by SOAP, which takes care of the XML messaging and data encoding.

Extensions

The extensions layer provides the ability to support additional functionality that allows Web services to adapt and evolve. There are numerous things that the layer can provide, I'm not sure about functionality being singular. Of course, the extensions layer is handled by SOAP.

The description stack

The description stack, shown in Figure 20-6, is key to the success of Web services. Within this are the following layers:

✦ **XML schema** — This layer sits at the base of the stack because it defines the entire stack.

✦ **Interface description** — This layer describes the functionality supported by a service and provides binding information.

✦ **Implementation description** — This layer describes the location of a service and how the provider implements the service.

✦ **Policy** — This layer allows the stack to include business-specific information, as well as information about such things as security, quality of service, and management.

✦ **Presentation** — This layer allows the stack to describe how a service should be presented or rendered to the client. This layer is great for addressing a user base that consists of multiple devices.

All the layers consist of XML-based description documents (typically WSDL).

The discovery stack

The discovery stack, illustrated in Figure 20-7, contains the mechanisms that facilitate the discovery of services. It consists of these layers:

✦ Inspection layer

✦ Publication layer

✦ Discovery layer

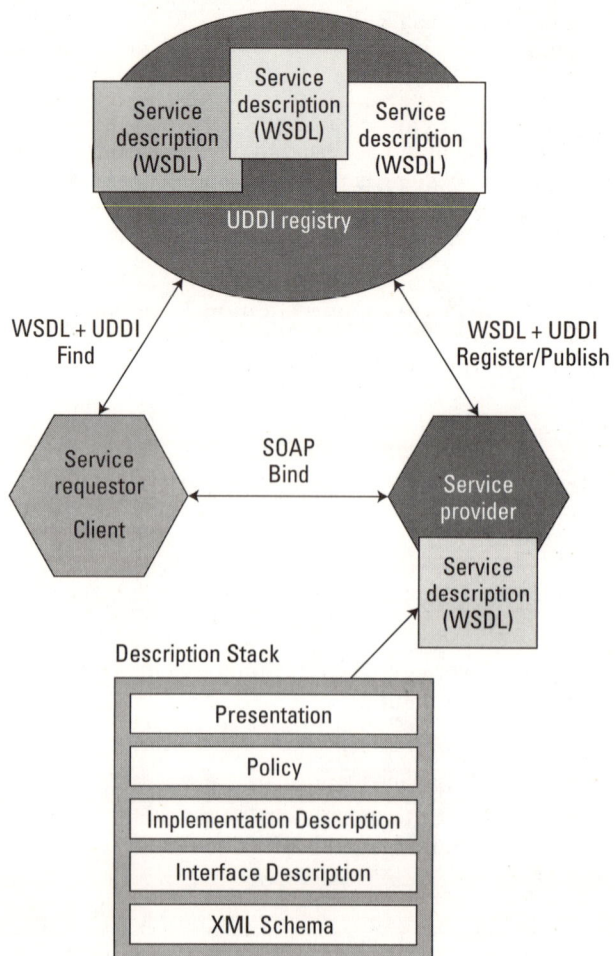

Figure 20-6: The Web-services description stack

Inspection

The inspection layer allows services to be discovered in areas other than a single UDDI registry. For instance, you can find a service directly from a provider. One of the most popular technologies for inspection is the Web Service Inspection Language (WSIL).

Publication

Publication can occur in various ways. For instance, a service provider can e-mail a description to a requestor or provide it by other means; this is called a *direct publish*. Of course you can use WSIL to retrieve the description via a URL. Recall that you can also publish the service to a UDDI registry.

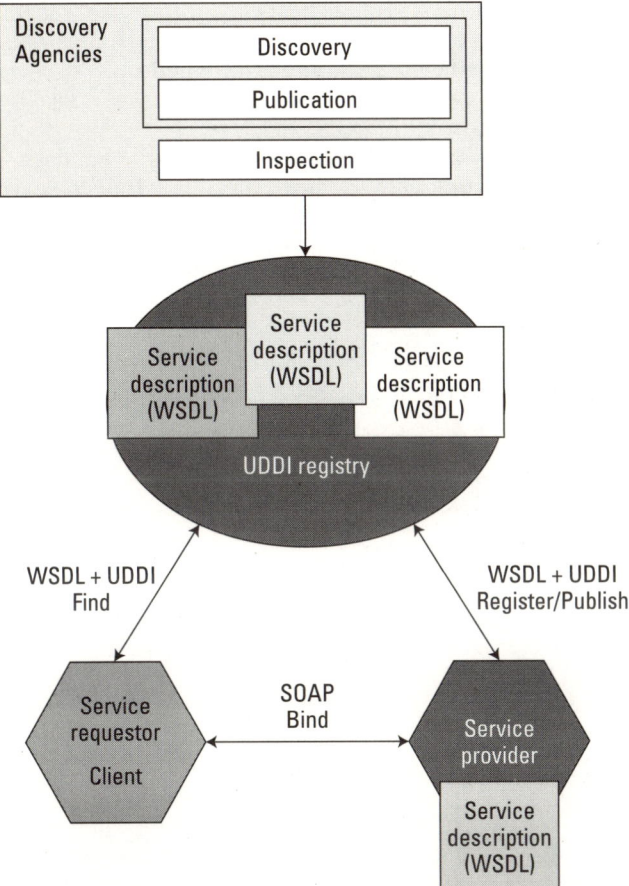

Figure 20-7: The Web-services discovery stack

Discovery

Discovery can occur at design time or at runtime. At runtime, a requestor will search a registry or access it from a Web site. At design time, the description can be hard-coded or possibly stored in a separate local file.

Summary

We've come a long way since ancient times (circa 1990-1995). Now CPUs are measured in gigahertz, modem speeds in thousands of baud per second, and the Internet is being used for everything from commerce, to research, to communication, to entertainment. Initially, the Internet was used to fulfill very simple tasks.

Content was valued over graphics because the Web's primary purpose was information exchange. Now, the order of the day is on-demand, distributed enterprise computing, that is delivered via a vendor, language, and platform-neutral, service-oriented architecture. In short, Web services.

In this chapter we discussed the downfall of older technologies that are used in traditional distributed computing environments. We introduced you to Web services and the interoperability, efficiency and standardization that Web services provide. We also looked at the advantages of implementing Web service solutions in various scenarios such as ASP, EAI and mobile phone scenarios. Finally, we gave you a brief overview of the technologies behind Web services.

In the next chapter, we will take our general knowledge of Web services and service-oriented architecture, and overlay this with the Java 2 Enterprise computing platform and architectural design model.

✦   ✦   ✦

Digging Deeper into SOAP, WSDL, and UDDI

✦ ✦ ✦ ✦

In This Chapter

Understanding the SOAP message architecture

Explaining the Web Services Description Language (WSDL)

Examining the Universal Description and Discovery Interface (UDDI)

✦ ✦ ✦ ✦

In this chapter we dig deeper into the three core Web-service specifications: the Simple Object Access Protocol (SOAP), the Web Services Description Language (WSDL), and the Universal Description and Discovery Interface (UDDI). Each section stands independently, so you can use this chapter as a reference for finding details about these three technologies.

We'll begin with the Web-service message layer by exploring SOAP. In the SOAP section we will examine the architecture of SOAP messages and the role of XML schema in defining SOAP data types. We will also look at SOAP message styles and, finally, introduce SOAP intermediaries.

Next, we will turn our attention to describing services with WSDL. We'll begin this section by looking at a WSDL document for our Connexia Airlines case study. After examining that sample document, we will address the various WSDL bindings.

We will conclude the chapter with a section on UDDI. This section will begin with an assessment of the evolution of UDDI from version 1 to version 3, followed by an examination of the UDDI data model. We will explore the application-programming interfaces (APIs) and then look at the integration between WSDL and UDDI. Finally, we will pull all the information in the chapter together by applying it to our Connexia Airlines case study.

Understanding the SOAP Message Architecture

A SOAP message is comprised of these three elements:

✦ Envelope

✦ Header

✦ Body

These elements are discussed in the following sections.

The SOAP *envelope* is the root element of a SOAP message. The `envelope` tag itself consists of an xml namespace, and optional `encodingStyle` attribute. The SOAP message also contains the header and body elements. (The header element is also optional.) Here's an example of an envelope:

```
<?xml version="1.0"?>
<soap:Envelope
xmlns:soap=" http://schemas.xmlsoap.org/soap/encoding/"
soap:encodingStyle="http://schemas.xmlsoap.org/soap/encoding/">
</soap:Envelope>
```

The namespace must have a value of `http://www.w3.org/2001/12/soap-envelope` or an error will be generated.

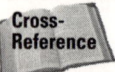

Cross-Reference   For more information on namespaces, take a look at Chapter 2.

The value of the optional `encodingStyle "Deleted, if so WHY?---JG"` attribute — the Uniform Resource Identifier (URI) — specifies the serialization rules for the SOAP message and therefore defines the data types used within the message.

The header

Recall that the SOAP *header* is an element within the SOAP message. The SOAP header is optional but plays a very important role customizing messages. It enables you to include elements that relate to your specific application. Additionally, the SOAP header must be namespace qualified. More importantly, the header allows the SOAP message to extend its capabilities by enabling features like security and transaction handling. Any elements within the header element are part of the SOAP *header block*.

The header block contains these four main attributes:

✦ `mustUnderstand` — This attribute is another very important part of processing. It determines whether a header entry is mandatory or optional. When its value is 0, this means that the processing is optional, if its value is 0, the recipient must process the header entry. (See "SOAP Messaging" later in this chapter for an example of its use.)

✦ `Actor` — This attribute indicates which SOAP node a header block points to.

✦ `encodingStyle` — This attribute functions as in the `envelope` element.

In the following example, the `actor` attribute is using a special URI. When this particular URI is used, the first application that processes the message will receive the header element. The value of the `mustUnderstand` attribute equals 1, which indicates that the receiver of the message is required to process the reservation element. The reservation and passenger elements consist of their respective namespaces in order to prevent conflict with element names. The remaining elements contain the actual data that will be exchanged.

```
<SOAP-ENV:Header>
   <m:reservation xmlns:m="http://www.j2eebible.com/reservation"
          SOAP-
ENV:actor="http://schemas.xmlsoap.org/soap/actor/next"
          SOAP-ENV:mustUnderstand="1">
    <m:reference>uuid:abc123-def456-ghi789</m:reference>
    <m:dateTime>2003-06-01T13:20:00.000-05:00</m:dateTime>
   </m:reservation>
   <n:passenger xmlns:n="http://mycompany.example.com/employees"
          SOAP-ENV:
actor="http://schemas.xmlsoap.org/soap/actor/next"
          SOAP-ENV:mustUnderstand="1">
    <n:name>Jason Gordon</n:name>
   </n:passenger>
</SOAP-ENV:Header>
```

The body

The SOAP *body* contains the main and mandatory information that must be transported from sender to receiver. In Listing 21-1, the body contains the arrival and departure information — which is the most important information when you're flying. The two main elements are the itinerary and lodging elements. The itinerary element contains the departure and return elements. The departure and return elements contain the seating preference, departure dates, departure times, departing, and arriving cities. The lodging element contains the hotel preference of the passenger.

Listing 21-1: **A sample body**

```
<SOAP-ENV:Body>
  <p:itinerary
    xmlns:p="http://www.j2eebible.com/reservation/travel">
    <p:departure>
      <p:departing>Dallas </p:departing>
      <p:arriving>New York</p:arriving>
      <p:departureDate>2003-06-01</p:departureDate>
      <p:departureTime>late afternoon</p:departureTime>
      <p:seatPreference>aisle</p:seatPreference>
    </p:departure>
    <p:return>
      <p:departing> New York </p:departing>
      <p:arriving>Dallas</p:arriving>
      <p:departureDate>2003-06-15</p:departureDate>
      <p:departureTime>mid-morning</p:departureTime>
      <p:seatPreference/>
    </p:return>
  </p:itinerary>
  <q:lodging
    xmlns:q="http://www.j2eebible.com/reservation/hotels">
    <q:preference>none</q:preference>
  </q:lodging>
</SOAP-ENV:Body>
```

XML schemas and SOAP data types

An *XML schema* describes and defines the elements, attributes, data types, and overall structure of an XML document. Take a look at Listing 21-2, which should give you an idea of what a typical XML-schema document looks like.

Listing 21-2: **An XML schema**

```
<?xml version="1.0"?>
<schema targetNamespace="http://www.j2eebible.com/"
xmlns="http://www.w3.org/2001/XMLSchema"
xmlns:Conexia="http://www.j2eebible.com/"
elementFormDefault="qualified">
<element name='
</xs:schema>
```

Now take a look at how XML schema documents are used in SOAP.

SOAP encoding and data types

Encoding is one of the most important topics in creating interoperable Web services. The SOAP specifications include encoding rules that define how data types are to be formatted or expressed within SOAP messages. According to the SOAP 1.1 specifications, SOAP encoding provides the following:

✦ Simple-type values

✦ Polymorphic accessors

✦ Compound-type values

Simple-type values

Simple types can include strings, decimals, integers, enumerations, array of bytes and doubles. Here's an example of a string:

```
<airlineName>Eagle Airlines </airlineName>
```

This is an example of a decimal:

```
<flightCost>234.09 </flightCost>
```

Enumeration can be described as a set of names related to a base type. In the following example, the `FlightClass` element contains a `simpleType` element that contains three enumeration elements. The elements are related to the `FlightClass` element in that they are different kinds of flight classes.

```
<xs:schema xmlns:xs=http://www.w3.org/2001/XMLSchema>
 <xs:element name="FlightClass">
  <xs:simpleType base="xsd:string">
     <xs:enumeration value="First"/>
     <xs:enumeration value="Business"/>
     <xs:enumeration value="Coach"/>
  </simpleType>
 </xs:element>
 </xs:schema>
```

Array of Bytes

Section 5.2.3 of the SOAP 1.1 specifications recommends that you use base64 to represent an opaque array of bytes, as shown here:

```
<confirmation xsi:type="enc:base64">
  wHsdfF64534vdFb45m544233m2
</confirmation >
```

Polymorphic accessor

The *polymorphic accessor* enables you to use polymorphism to access values at runtime.

In order for you to successfully use the polymorphic accessor, an instance must contain a `xsi:type` attribute, as shown here:

```
<flightmiles xsi: type= "xsd:float">4567.08</ flightmiles>
```

Compound-type values

In SOAP, structures and arrays are kinds of compound-type values. *Structures* are accessors that are distinguished by their names. The following sequence element simply implies that the data must be in a certain order. Structures support simple and complex member interaction. Different members can interact, or rather reference each other, by using the `href` attribute. The `href` attribute functions as a link that points to a corresponding id attribute of the member being referenced. Listing 21-3 shows an XML schema for a structure.

Listing 21-3: An XML schema for a structure

```
<xs:element
name="ReturnInfo"xmlns:xs="http://www.w3.org/2001/XMLSchema">
<xs:complexType>
<xs:sequence>
      <xs:element name=" departing " type="xsd:string"/>
      <xs:element name=" arriving " type="xsd:string"/>
      <xs:element name=" departureDate" type="xsd:date"/>
      <xs:element name=" departureTime" type="xsd:string"/>
</xs:sequence>
 </xs:complexType>
</xs:element>
```

Listing 21-4 shows an example of an XML instance for a structure.

Listing 21-4: XML instance for structure

```
<p:departing> New York </p:departing>
<p:arriving>Dallas</p:arriving>
<p:departureDate>2003-06-15</p:departureDate>
<p:departureTime>mid-morning</p:departureTime>
```

Arrays

As in most programming languages, *arrays* in SOAP are referred to as `arrayTypes` and are used to deal with large amounts of information. Table 21-1 lists various arrayType values and their descriptions. For the remainder of the array section we will take a look at the various ways arrays function in SOAP.

Table 21-1
arrayType values and descriptions

arrayType Value	Description
A:Airline[10]	An array of ten airlines
xsd:int[3]	An array of three integers
xsd:int[,][3]	An array of three two-dimensional arrays of integers
xsd:float[4,5]	A four-by-five, four-dimensional array of floats

The array types available in SOAP 1.1 include the following:

✦ Single-dimensional arrays

✦ Multidimensional arrays

✦ Partially-transmitted arrays

✦ Sparse arrays

These array types are discussed in the following sections.

Single-dimensional Arrays

The following XML schema fragment provides an example of a single-dimensional array:

```
<element name="FlightNumbers"type="SOAP-ENC:Array"/>

XML
<FlightNumbers SOAP-ENC:arrayType="xsd:int[2]">
    <flight>1191</flight>
    <flight>788</flight>
</FlightNumbers>
```

Multidimensional arrays

Here is an example of a *multidimensional array* consisting of three rows and three columns. This particular array contains strings.

```
<SOAP-ENC:Array SOAP-ENC:arrayType='xsd:string[3,3]'>
<Item>1stRow 1stColumn</Item>
<Item>1stRow 2ndColumn</Item>
<Item>1stRow 3rdColumn</Item>
```

```
<Item>2ndRow 1stColumn</Item>
<Item>2ndRow 2ndColumn</Item>
<Item>2ndRow 3rdColumn</Item>
<Item>3rdRow 1stColumn</Item>
<Item>3rdRow 2ndColumn</Item>
<Item>3rdRow 3rdColumn</Item>
</SOAP-ENC:Array>
```

Partially-transmitted arrays

Partially-transmitted arrays include the `SOAP-ENC:offset` attribute. So how does this offset work? Let's take a look at the example below. In this example you have an array of size 8 and an offset of 4.

In this case data are only transmitted after the fourth position in the array. Remember that the first element is zero, not one.

```
<SOAP-ENC:Array SOAP-ENC:arrayType='xsd:string[8]'
                SOAP-ENC:offset='[4]'>
  <Item>Fourth String </Item>
  <Item>Fifth String    </Item>
  <Item>Sixth String    </Item>
  <Item>Seventh String</Item>
</SOAP-ENC:Array>
```

Sparse arrays

If you hadn't noticed, the syntax for different arrays only differs according to the type of attribute used. With *sparse arrays* that attribute is `SOAP-ENC:position`. The `position` attribute indicates which elements will be provided. In the following code fragment elements 2, 4, and 9 are available, and their corresponding values are returned.

```
<SOAP-ENC:Array SOAP-ENC:arrayType='xsd:int[8]'>
  <Item SOAP-ENC:position="[2]">Two</Item>
  <Item SOAP-ENC:position="[4]">Fourth </Item>
  <Item SOAP-ENC:position="[9]">Ninth</Item>
</SOAP-ENC:Array>
```

SOAP RPC

The SOAP 1.1 specifications define a mechanism for encapsulating and exchanging remote procedure calls (RPCs) using XML. As you may already know, in SOAP *remote procedure calling* involves the following components:

✦ Client application

✦ Client SOAP implementation

✦ Server application

✦ The server's SOAP implementation

Figure 21-1 illustrates the entire process of SOAP remote procedure calling.

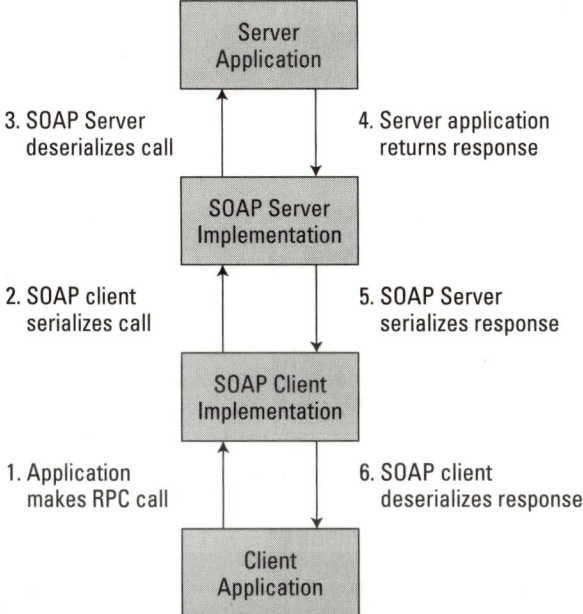

Figure 21-1: The SOAP RPC process

So here's what you need to use SOAP RPC:

✦ The URI of the target object

✦ A method name

✦ A method signature (optional)

✦ Parameters

✦ Header data and contextual information, such as security (optional)

Here's what's required for the request:

The compound-type value, `struct`, represents the method invocation within the SOAP message. Because `struct` represents the method invocation it must have the same name and return value as the method.

SOAP uses child elements to represent method parameters. The child elements' names and data types are identical to the parameters'. Note that the parameters can be in or in/out parameters.

The response requires the following:

> A `struct` also represents the response; its name really doesn't matter but the specifications encourage naming it after the method and appending `"Response"`. More specifically, the first child element contains the return value followed by the out or in/out parameters in the same order as in the method signature.

> The out or in/out parameters must have the same name and type as the method.

> If an error occurs during the request, the SOAP `Fault` element must be returned. We will get to SOAP faults later in the "Soap Binding" section.

Here is a sample SOAP RPC request:

```
<SOAP-ENV:Envelope
xmlns: SOAP-ENV ="http://schemas.xmlsoap.org/soap/envelope/"
SOAP-
ENV:encodingStyle="http://schemas.xmlsoap.org/soap/encoding/">
  <SOAP-ENV:Body xmlns:m="http://www.wiley.com/fare">
    <m:GetFlightPrice>
      <m:FlightName>DFW TO LAX</m:FlightName>
    </m:GetFlightPrice>
  </SOAP-ENV:Body>
</SOAP-ENV:Envelope>
```

The preceding example is a SOAP RPC request in which `GetFlightPrice` is used to retrieve the price of a flight called "DFW TO LAX". The price is retrieved from a SOAP server with a namespace of `"http://www.wiley.com/fare"`.

The following example is a SOAP RPC response, which in this scenario will process the SOAP request from `GetFlightPrice` and return the price of the flight using the price parameter.

```
<SOAP-ENV:Envelope
xmlns:SOAP-ENV="http://schemas.xmlsoap.org/soap/envelope/"
SOAP-ENV:encodingStyle="
http://schemas.xmlsoap.org/soap/encoding/">
  <SOAP-ENV:Body >
    <m:GetFlightPriceResponse
xmlns:m="http://www.wiley.com/fare">
      <m:Price>300.00</m:Price>
    </m:GetFlightPriceResponse>
  </SOAP-ENV:Body>
</SOAP-ENV:Envelope>
```

SOAP messaging

SOAP messaging is another form of communication that involves transferring SOAP messages that contain XML documents within the envelope. A SOAP message consists of a *sender* and a *receiver* and must have identical schemas for the envelope, the optional encoding, and the application-specific data.

SOAP *intermediaries* enable additional processing to take place between the requestor and the provider of the service. Intermediaries are able to manipulate the SOAP message themselves or forward it to another destination. SOAP headers allow SOAP intermediaries to be included in the processing of the message. Before sending or forwarding a message to the next destination, an intermediary must remove any header entry that was intended for it. Figure 21-2 illustrates how intermediaries fit into a SOAP message exchange model.

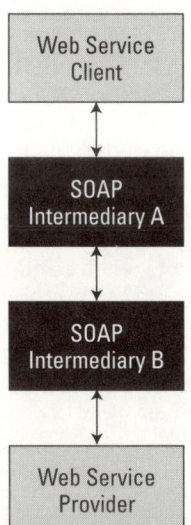

Figure 21-2: Intermediaries are part of the SOAP message exchange model.

The `actor` attribute of the SOAP header has a URI whose value indicates either an intermediary or an ultimate destination. Also, if the URI is equal to `http:// schemas.xmlsoap.org/soap/actor/next` the header element is intended for the first SOAP application that will process the message. The following example shows the `actor` attribute in use. It also tells you what section of the SOAP header entry will be sent and who should handle it.

```
<SOAP-ENV:Header>
<c:Flight
xmlns:m="http:// www.j2eebible.com /conexiaws/"
```

```
SOAP-ENV:actor="http://www.j2eebible.com/flightinfo/" SOAP-
ENV:mustUnderstand="0">
7779311
</c:Flight>
</ SOAP-ENV:Header >
```

The `mustUnderstand` attribute is very important in processing. It determines whether a header entry is mandatory or optional. When its value is 0 the processing is optional; if its value is 0 the recipient must process the header entry.

SOAP and Java

As you know, SOAP is *language independent*, which means that implementation and integration with a programming language and its environment is the responsibility of the developer. There are many Java-based SOAP implementations. One of the most popular open-source implementations is Apache Axis by the Apache Software Foundation. In the upcoming example we will use the Java API for XML-Based RPC (JAX-RPC) through Axis. As with many APIs, JAX-RPC provides a layer of abstraction for implementing SOAP-based Web services. Simply put, as a developer you won't have to deal directly with SOAP itself. The runtime environments provided by JAX-RPC takes care of the mapping between SOAP and remote procedure calls.

Listing 21-5 consists of the Search for Flights, List Connections and Book Flights operations. The `Reservation` constructor accesses `Flight.java` and creates an array of `Flight` objects. This array includes three `Flight` objects, each containing one or more `Connection` objects from `Connection.java`. The `search` method takes `depart` and `arrive` as strings and searches arrays of flights for a match. In our simple example, the constructor populates the flight arrays. The `book` method passes in the necessary information needed to purchase tickets and generates a `reservationID`. The `list` method takes an `id` and matches it with the `connexiaID` of the `flightArray`.

Listing 21-5: The Connexia Reservation service (Reservation.java)

```java
package com.wiley.j2eebible.services;

import java.util.ArrayList;
import java.util.Date;
import java.util.Iterator;
import java.util.Vector;

public class Reservation {

    Connection          connect, connect2;
    Flight              flight;
    Flight[]            flightArray = new Flight[3];
```

```
   ArrayList            reservations = new ArrayList();

 public Reservation() {

        connect = new Connection( 123456, "Dallas", "New
York",
        "Boeing 757", "6:35am", "10:00am" );
        flight = new Flight();
        flight.addConnection( connect );
        flight.setPrice( 356.00 );
        flight.setConnexiaID( 13579 );
        flightArray[0] = flight;

        connect = new Connection( 246810, "Sacramento",
"Phoenix",
        "Faulker 100", "10:06am", "12:00pm" );
        connect2 = new Connection( 289213, "Phoenix",
"Denver",
        "Faulker 100", "12:42pm", "2:39pm" );
        flight = new Flight();
        flight.addConnection( connect );
        flight.addConnection( connect2 );
        flight.setPrice( 289.00 );
        flight.setConnexiaID( 67538 );
        flightArray[1] = flight;

        connect = new Connection( 1497365, "Detroit",
"Chicago",
        "Faulker 100", "3:11pm", "4:24pm" );
        connect2 = new Connection( 3395641, "Chicago", "Salt
Lake
        City", "Boeing 737", "4:52pm", "6:29pm" );
        flight = new Flight();
        flight.addConnection( connect );
        flight.addConnection( connect2 );
        flight.setPrice( 265.00 );
        flight.setConnexiaID( 23850 );
        flightArray[2] = flight;
  }

  public Flight[] search( String depart, String arrive ) {

        Flight[] searchResults = null;

        for( int x = 0; x < flightArray.length; x++ ) {
                Vector connections =
flightArray[x].getConnections();
                Iterator iterate = connections.iterator();
                boolean connectDepart = false, connectArrive =
false;

                while( iterate.hasNext() ) {
```

Continued

Listing 21-5 *(continued)*

```
                Connection c = (Connection)iterate.next();
                if( c.getDepartCity().equals( depart ) )
                    connectDepart = true;
                if( c.getArriveCity().equals( arrive ) )
                    connectArrive = true;
                }//end while( iterate.hasNext() )

                if( connectDepart && connectArrive ) {
                    searchResults = new Flight[0];
                    searchResults[0] = flightArray[x];
                    break; // This simple implementation
returns
                        the first match
            }//end while
            }//end for()

            return searchResults;
    }

    public String book( long departID, long arriveID, int
        numPassengers, long ccNum ) {
            String reservationID = "ABC" + ( new Date()
).getTime();
            reservations.add( reservationID );
            return reservationID;
    }

    public Connection[] list( long id ) {
            Flight flight = new Flight();

            for( int x = 0; x < flightArray.length; x++ ) {
                    if( flightArray[x].getConnexiaID() == id )
                        flight = flightArray[x];
            }

            return
(Connection[])flight.getConnections().toArray();
    }
}
```

In Listing 21-6, we see the `ConnexiaClient.java` file. This file is responsible for defining the endpoint of the service, creating the actual instance of the service that will be used and creating the SOAP request call. It is also responsible for invoking the service, sending the request and retrieving the results. For a line-by-line explanation, please view the comments in the code. All of the files required to run the example including deployment descriptors can be found on the CD.

```java
package com.wiley.j2eebible.services;

import org.apache.axis.client.Call;
import org.apache.axis.client.Service;
import org.apache.axis.encoding.ser.BeanSerializerFactory;
import org.apache.axis.encoding.ser.BeanDeserializerFactory;
import javax.xml.namespace.QName;
import javax.xml.rpc.ParameterMode;
import java.util.Date;
import java.util.Vector;

public class ConnexiaClient {
    public static void main(String [] args) {
      System.out.print( "\nSearching for a flight from Sacramento
to Denver... " );

        try {
                String endpoint =
"http://localhost:8080/axis/services/ReservationService";
 //Endpoint definition of the service

                Service  service = new Service();
    //Creating the new service

                Call     call    = (Call) service.createCall();
    //SOAP request call creation

                call.setTargetEndpointAddress( new
java.net.URL(endpoint) );
    //Setting the target of the provider location.

                call.setOperationName( new QName(
"http://www.wiley.com/j2eebible/connexia", "search" ) );
    //The service operation name and methods are set.

               QName qname = new QName(
"http://www.wiley.com/j2eebible/connexia" );

call.registerTypeMapping( Flight.class,
                               new QName(
"http://www.wiley.com/j2eebible/connexia", "flight" ),
                               new
BeanSerializerFactory( Flight.class, qname ),
                               new
BeanDeserializerFactory( Flight.class, qname ) );
    //The service operation name and methods are set for Flight.
```

Continued

Listing 21-6 *(continued)*

```
call.registerTypeMapping( Connection.class,
                                    new QName(
"http://www.wiley.com/j2eebible/connexia", "connection" ),
                                    new
BeanSerializerFactory( Connection.class, qname ),
                                    new
BeanDeserializerFactory( Connection.class, qname ) );
//The service operation name and methods are set for
Connection.

          Object[] flights = (Object[]) call.invoke( new
Object[]{ "Sacramento", "Denver" } );
//Service invocation occurs and a Java object is returned.

        Connection[] connects;
        Flight       f;

        call.setOperationName( new QName(
"http://www.wiley.com/j2eebible/connexia", "list" ) );
//The service operation name and methods are set

        for( int x = 0; x < flights.length; x++ ) {
            f = (Flight)flights[x];
            System.out.println( "flight FOUND" );
             System.out.println( "--Flight " + x + 1 + "--"
);
              System.out.println( "ConnexiaID - " +
                f.getConnexiaID() );
              System.out.println( "Price - $" + f.getPrice()
);
              connects = (Connection[]) call.invoke( new
Object[] { new Long(f.getConnexiaID()) } );
              for( int y = 0; y < connects.length; y++ ) {
                    System.out.println( "-Connection " + x +
1 );
                    System.out.println( "Departure " +
connects[x].getDepartCity() + " -- " +
connects[x].getDepartTime() );
                    System.out.println( "Arrival " +
connects[x].getArriveCity() + " -- " +
connects[x].getArriveTime() );
                  }
//Itinerary displayed to user at command line.

          }

        System.out.print( "Booking Flight... " );

        call.setOperationName( new QName(
"http://www.wiley.com/j2eebible/connexia", "book" ) );
```

```
//The service operation name and methods are set
        String reservation = (String) call.invoke( new
Object[]{ new Long(12345), new Long(67890),
                                                       new
Integer(1), new Long(123456) } );

        if( reservation != null )
            System.out.println( "flight RESERVED" );
        else {
            System.out.println( "reservation failed" );
            System.exit(0);
        }

        } catch( Exception e ) {
            e.printStackTrace();
        }
    }
}
```

Explaining WSDL

As discussed in the previous chapter, a Web Services Description Language (WSDL) document consists of the following elements:

✦ Definition—The definition element is the root element of the WSDL document, containing the namespaces to be used and the name of the Web service.

✦ Types—This element contains information about the data types needed to access the service. It typically uses XML schemas as the type system.

✦ Message—This is an abstract description of the data being accessed or requested.

✦ Operation—This element describes what a service can do and is comprised of messages. It's similar to a function.

✦ Port type—This is used to map a set of operations to one or more endpoints.

✦ Binding—This element enables you to specify a concrete protocol, such as HTTP, and a data format, such as soap, to bind a port type. The WSDL 1.1 specifications provide support for HTTP, MIME, and SOAP.

✦ Port—This is a combination of a binding and a physical network address.

✦ Service—A collection of related ports.

Now, let's take a look at Listing 21-7. Reservation.wsdl gives an example of how a WSDL document could look for Connexia Airlines. The actual code is available on the accompanying CD. The definition element is self-explanatory; it contains the namespaces to be used in the document.

Listing 21-7: The Reservation.wsdl Document for Connexia Airlines

```
<?xml version="1.0" encoding="UTF-8"?>
<wsdl:definitions
targetNamespace="http://localhost:8080/axis/services/Reservatio
nService" xmlns="http://schemas.xmlsoap.org/wsdl/"
xmlns:apachesoap="http://xml.apache.org/xml-soap"
xmlns:impl="http://localhost:8080/axis/services/ReservationServ
ice"
xmlns:intf="http://localhost:8080/axis/services/ReservationServ
ice" xmlns:soapenc="http://schemas.xmlsoap.org/soap/encoding/"
xmlns:tns1="http://www.wiley.com/j2eebible/connexia"
xmlns:wsdl="http://schemas.xmlsoap.org/wsdl/"
xmlns:wsdlsoap="http://schemas.xmlsoap.org/wsdl/soap/"
xmlns:xsd="http://www.w3.org/2001/XMLSchema">
    <wsdl:types>
<schema
targetNamespace="http://www.wiley.com/j2eebible/connexia"
xmlns="http://www.w3.org/2001/XMLSchema">
        <import
namespace="http://schemas.xmlsoap.org/soap/encoding/" />

        <complexType name="connection">
            <sequence>
                <element name="aircraftType" nillable="true"
type="xsd:string" />

                <element name="arriveCity" nillable="true"
type="xsd:string" />

                <element name="arriveTime" nillable="true"
type="xsd:string" />

                <element name="connectID" type="xsd:long" />

                <element name="departCity" nillable="true"
type="xsd:string" />

                <element name="departTime" nillable="true"
type="xsd:string" />
            </sequence>
        </complexType>

        <complexType name="flight">
            <sequence>
                <element name="connections" nillable="true"
type="apachesoap:Vector" />

                <element name="connexiaID" type="xsd:long" />

                <element name="price" type="xsd:double" />
```

```
            </sequence>
        </complexType>

        <complexType name="flightArray">
            <complexContent>
                <restriction base="soapenc:Array">
                    <attribute ref="soapenc:arrayType"
wsdl:arrayType="tns1:flight[]" />
                </restriction>
            </complexContent>
        </complexType>
    </schema>

    <schema targetNamespace="http://xml.apache.org/xml-soap"
xmlns="http://www.w3.org/2001/XMLSchema">
        <import
namespace="http://schemas.xmlsoap.org/soap/encoding/" />

        <complexType name="Vector">
            <sequence>
                <element maxOccurs="unbounded" minOccurs="0"
name="item" type="xsd:anyType" />
            </sequence>
        </complexType>
    </schema>
</wsdl:types>

<wsdl:message name="confirmRequest">
    <wsdl:part name="in0" type="xsd:string" />
</wsdl:message>

<wsdl:message name="searchResponse">
    <wsdl:part name="searchReturn" type="tns1:flightArray" />
</wsdl:message>

<wsdl:message name="bookResponse">
    <wsdl:part name="bookReturn" type="xsd:string" />
</wsdl:message>

<wsdl:message name="searchRequest">
    <wsdl:part name="in0" type="xsd:string" />

    <wsdl:part name="in1" type="xsd:string" />

    <wsdl:part name="in2" type="xsd:dateTime" />

    <wsdl:part name="in3" type="xsd:dateTime" />
</wsdl:message>

<wsdl:message name="bookRequest">
    <wsdl:part name="in0" type="xsd:long" />
```

Continued

Listing 21-7 *(continued)*

```xml
        <wsdl:part name="in1" type="xsd:long" />

        <wsdl:part name="in2" type="xsd:int" />

        <wsdl:part name="in3" type="xsd:long" />
    </wsdl:message>

    <wsdl:message name="confirmResponse">
        <wsdl:part name="confirmReturn" type="tns1:flightArray" />
    </wsdl:message>

    <wsdl:portType name="Reservation">
        <wsdl:operation name="search" parameterOrder="in0 in1 in2
in3">
        <wsdl:input message="intf:searchRequest"
name="searchRequest" />

        <wsdl:output message="intf:searchResponse"
name="searchResponse" />
    </wsdl:operation>

        <wsdl:operation name="book" parameterOrder="in0 in1 in2
in3">
        <wsdl:input message="intf:bookRequest"
name="bookRequest" />

        <wsdl:output message="intf:bookResponse"
name="bookResponse" />
    </wsdl:operation>

        <wsdl:operation name="confirm" parameterOrder="in0">
        <wsdl:input message="intf:confirmRequest"
name="confirmRequest" />

        <wsdl:output message="intf:confirmResponse"
name="confirmResponse" />
    </wsdl:operation>
    </wsdl:portType>

    <wsdl:binding name="ReservationServiceSoapBinding"
type="intf:Reservation">
        <wsdlsoap:binding style="rpc"
transport="http://schemas.xmlsoap.org/soap/http" />

        <wsdl:operation name="search">
        <wsdlsoap:operation soapAction="" />

        <wsdl:input name="searchRequest">
            <wsdlsoap:body encodingStyle="http://schemas
.xmlsoap.org/soap/encoding/" namespace="http://localhost:8080/
axis/services/ReservationService" use="encoded" />
```

```
        </wsdl:input>

        <wsdl:output name="searchResponse">
            <wsdlsoap:body
encodingStyle="http://schemas.xmlsoap.org/soap/encoding/"
namespace="http://localhost:8080/axis/services/Reservation
Service" use="encoded" />
        </wsdl:output>
    </wsdl:operation>

    <wsdl:operation name="book">
        <wsdlsoap:operation soapAction="" />

        <wsdl:input name="bookRequest">
            <wsdlsoap:body
encodingStyle="http://schemas.xmlsoap.org/soap/encoding/"
namespace="http://localhost:8080/axis/services/Reservation
Service" use="encoded" />
        </wsdl:input>

        <wsdl:output name="bookResponse">
            <wsdlsoap:body
encodingStyle="http://schemas.xmlsoap.org/soap/encoding/"
namespace="http://localhost:8080/axis/services/Reservation
Service" use="encoded" />
        </wsdl:output>
    </wsdl:operation>

    <wsdl:operation name="confirm">
        <wsdlsoap:operation soapAction="" />

        <wsdl:input name="confirmRequest">
            <wsdlsoap:body
encodingStyle="http://schemas.xmlsoap.org/soap/encoding/"
namespace="http://localhost:8080/axis/services/Reservation
Service" use="encoded" />
        </wsdl:input>

        <wsdl:output name="confirmResponse">
            <wsdlsoap:body
encodingStyle="http://schemas.xmlsoap.org/soap/encoding/"
namespace="http://localhost:8080/axis/services/Reservation
Service" use="encoded" />
        </wsdl:output>
    </wsdl:operation>
  </wsdl:binding>

  <wsdl:service name="ReservationService">
    <wsdl:port binding="intf:ReservationServiceSoapBinding"
name="ReservationService">
        <wsdlsoap:address location="http://localhost:8080/
axis/services/ReservationService" />
```

Continued

Listing 21-7 *(continued)*

```
        </wsdl:port>
      </wsdl:service>
    </wsdl:definitions>
```

The `Types` element contains five `complexType` elements, including `Connection`, `flight`, `flightArray`, and `vector`.

Now let's look at the message elements. `ConfirmRequest` serves as the input message for the confirm operation. The `confirm` operation references the `confirmRequest` message via parameter `"in0"`. `ConfirmResponse` is the output for the `confirm` operation. `SearchRequest` and `searchResponse` are the input and output for the `search` operation.

As you can see, the `search` operation has the attribute `parameterOrder="in0 in1 in2 in3"`. This attribute specifies which parts of the messages will be processed and in what order. The `book` operation works the same way. All operations are contained within the `portType` element.

The next major element in the `binding` element is `ReservationServiceSoapBinding`. It tells you that in order to bind to the service you can use SOAP-RPC. It also gives you specific information about which namespace and encoding style will be used for each individual operation.

The last element is the `service` element, which tells you that the service is located at `http://localhost:8080/axis/services/ReservationService`.

SOAP binding

SOAP binding enables the developer to specify which protocol will be used to send the message and the style of communication that will be used. Take a look at the following example:

```
<wsdl:binding name="ReservationServiceSoapBinding"
    type="intf:Reservation">
  <wsdlsoap:binding style="rpc"
    transport="http://schemas.xmlsoap.org/soap/http" />
</wsdl:binding>
```

The `style` attribute specifies that RPC will be used. The value of the `style` attribute can be set to `rpcRPC` or `document`. Of course with `rpcRPC` you will send parameters and return values. With `document` documents will be sent.

The `transport` attribute indicates that HTTP will be used as a transport.

<soap:operation>

The `operation` element gives you information about SOAP action headers and can contain the `style` attribute to reveal the type of communication to be used (RPC or document).

<soap:body>

This element provides information about how the parts of a message will be displayed in the `body` element of the SOAP message. The required use attribute can be set to `"literal"` or `"encoded"`. You specify `"literal"` when you want the parts in the `<soap:body>` to conform to the specified schema; `"encoded"` if you want the parts of the `<soap:body>` to be serialized in some manner.

<soap:fault>

This element gives you information about how the `fault` element fits into SOAP.

<soap:address>

This element enables you to specify a port address.

Note   Only one address may be indicated if you are using SOAP binding.

HTTP GET and POST binding

It is common for Web-based applications to use a browser to access information. Of course HTTP is usually the choice of transport and information is sent and received using the `GET` and `POST` verbs. For example, a user may fill out a form to make reservations. The user information is processed through some parameters passed by means of a form or through the query string. The process is just that easy for consuming Web services as well, but not all the applications you build will be Web-based. This is where the HTTP `GET` and `POST` binding elements come in. They allow applications that are not browser-based to take advantage of the `GET` and `POST` verbs by allowing the binding of port types to SOAP.

Here is an example of what a partial `GET` implementation might look like:

```
<binding name="ReservationServiceHTTPBinding" type="ReservationServicePortType" >
       <http:binding verb="GET"/>
       <operation name="search" >
          <http:operation location="search"/>
          <input>
              <http:urlencoded/>
          </input>
          <output>
              <mime:content type="text/xml"/>
          </output>
       </operation>
    </binding>
```

MIME binding

WSDL also provides support for binding for various Multipurpose Internet Mail Extensions (MIME) types, such as `gifs` and `jpegs` within the binding elements. The WSDL 1.1 specifications define the following MIME bindings:

✦ `multipart/related`

✦ `text/xml`

✦ `application/x-www-form-urlencoded`

✦ Others supported through the use of MIME-type strings

In order for the search portion of Reservation.wsdl to support the MIME type `jpeg`, we will need to change the `searchResponse` message element as follows:

```
<wsdl:message name="searchResponse">
  <wsdl:part name="searchReturn" type="tns1:flightArray" />
  <wsdl:part name="photo" type="xsd:binary" />
  </wsdl:message>
```

Now take a look at Listing 21-8, which shows how the `binding` element itself will change.

Listing 21-8: **MIME binding**

```
<wsdl:binding name="ReservationServiceSoapBinding"
type="intf:Reservation">
     <wsdlsoap:binding style="rpc"
transport="http://schemas.xmlsoap.org/soap/http" />

<wsdl:operation name="search">
     <wsdlsoap:operation soapAction="" />

<wsdl:input name="searchRequest">
  <wsdlsoap:body
    encodingStyle="http://schemas.xmlsoap.org/soap/encoding/"
namespace="http://localhost:8080/axis/services/ReservationServi
ce" use="encoded" />
</wsdl:input>

<wsdl:output name="searchResponse">

<mime:multipartRelated>
<mime:part>

<wsdlsoap:body
encodingStyle="http://schemas.xmlsoap.org/soap/encoding/"
namespace="http://localhost:8080/axis/services/ReservationServi
ce" use="encoded" />
```

```
</mime:part>
<mime:part>
<mime:content part="photo" type="image/jpg">
</mime:part>
</mime:multipartRelated>
</wsdl:output>
</wsdl:operation>

</wsdl:binding>
```

In the preceding listing, the only element that changes is the `searchReponse` element. We have added the `<mime:multipartRelated>` and `<mime:part>` elements in order to support the JPEG format.

WSDL and Java

You're probably wondering why we haven't talked much about Java in the WSDL section. Well, the truth is that you rarely deal with WSDL directly. For instance, the WSDL document above was generated using the Java2WSDL utility available with Axis. The Web service implementation was created first and then the WSDL document was generated. With some tools it is actually possible to generate Java classes from WSDL documents. For more information, check out WASP by Systinet at `www.systinet.com/wasp`, **IBM Web Services Toolkit** at `www.alphaworks.ibm.com/tech/webservicestoolkit/`.

Examining UDDI

The Universal Description, Discovery and Integration (UDDI) specification has undergone some substantial changes during its short life. Consequently, we will begin this section with a brief overview of the three versions of UDDI and the relevant differences among them. Afterwards we will examine the data model, the query, publish, and subscription APIs, and the integration between WSDL and UDDI. Finally, we will pull all the information together by applying this knowledge to our Connexia Airlines case study.

UDDI versions 1, 2, and 3

Versions 2 and 3 of the UDDI specification have really expanded to incorporate more of its broader enterprise-level features and capabilities.

The following sections certainly do not cover every feature defined within the UDDI specification, but they do identify the key aspects of each version. With the release of UDDI version 3, many Web-services experts now regard UDDI as having reached an important stage of maturity within the marketplace. As best practices continue to be refined and tool vendors bring their development, management, and registry tools up to date with the latest UDDI spec, the adoption of UDDI is expected to grow steadily.

> **Note**   Versions 1 and 2 of the UDDI spec were originally released by the UDDI organization (`www.uddi.org`). In the summer of 2002 the UDDI project was absorbed by OASIS (`www.oasis-open.org`) and version 3 of the specification was made available as well.

UDDI version 1

UDDI version 1, which went into effect in September 2000, includes the following features:

✦ Essential XML grammar

✦ Definition of core registry entry types: business organizations, business services, service bindings, and technical models

✦ Basic Inquiry "Okay — JG" API

✦ Basic Publish API

UDDI version 1 established a foundation that addressed the need for a central registry for various business services. UDDI version 1 provides us with an Inquiry API that allows us to find basic information about businesses and services as well as more detailed information. This version of UDDI also provides us with a Publish API that gives the ability to save and delete information about businesses and services. Basic security such as authentication, and establishing credentials is also provided.

These APIs and the operations within them are listed in Table 21-2. While very advantageous, it is important to note that UDDI version 1was not flexible enough to address the need of large businesses to relate to their partners or to individual entities within the company. UDDI version 2 takes care of this issue.

Table 21-2
Inquiry and Publishing APIs available in UDDI version 1

Inquiry Operations	Publishing Operations
Find	Save
find_business	save_business
find_service	save_service
find_binding	save_binding
find_tModel	save_tModel

Inquiry Operations	Publishing Operations
Get Details	Delete
get_businessDetail	delete_business
get_serviceDetail	delete_service
get_bindingDetail	delete_binding
get_tModelDetail	delete_tModel
get_registeredInfo	
	Security
	get_authToken
	discard_authToken

UDDI version 2

UDDI version 2, which went into effect in June 2001, includes the following features:

Definition of an additional registry-entry type: publisher assertions

Support for publishing and querying these relationships

The UDDI information model (introduced in UDDI version 2) supports defining relationships between businesses.

Recall that one of the most important enhancements available in UDDI version 2 is the support for relationships within and between businesses. The Publishing API in version 2 features publisher assertions. Publisher assertions allow businesses to define and manipulate relationships with each other. The Inquiry API includes the find_relatedBusinesses operation, which allows you to search the relationships that are established. Version 2 also allows a business to feature services of other businesses as if the services were its own, a concept referred to as service projections. Some other enhancements include the ability to describe services in different languages, improved categorization and improved searching options. Table 21-3 lists the APIs. The asterisks (*) denote new operations.

Table 21-3	
Inquiry and Publishing APIs available in UDDI version 2	
Inquiry Operations	Publishing Operations
Find	Save
find_business	save_business

Continued

Table 21-3 *(continued)*	
Inquiry Operations	*Publishing Operations*
find_service	save_service
find_binding	save_binding
find_tModel	save_tModel
*find_relatedBusinesses	
Get Details	Delete
get_businessDetail	delete_business
get_serviceDetail	delete_service
get_bindingDetail	delete_binding
get_tModelDetail	delete_tModel
get_registeredInfo	
*get_businessDetailExt	Security
	get_authToken
	discard_authToken
	Publisher Assertions
	*add_publisherAssertions
	*delete_publisherAssertions
	*get_publisherAssertions
	*set_publisherAssertions

UDDI version 3

UDDI version 3, which went into effect in July 2002, includes the following features:

✦ Definition of an additional registry-entry type: operational info

✦ Introduction of the subscription API

✦ Support for tracking, monitoring, and responding to changes made to registry entries

✦ Support for user-defined registry keys

✦ Introduction of new key format: domain keys

✦ Support of key derivation from existing keys

✦ Support for organizations defining policies for domain-key generation and derivation

✦ Support for digital signatures

The enhancements in UDDI version 3 focus on concepts of how registries in the public, private, and shared domains interact and maintain the integrity of information efficiently. It also defines roles for publishing and subscribing services.

The UDDI information model

As we discussed in the previous chapter, UDDI is used to publish and discover services. The UDDI information model consists of the following basic data structures:

✦ businessEntity

✦ businessService

✦ bindingTemplate

✦ tModel

Figure 21-3 identifies the relationships among the four basic data structures and publisher assertions. We will define and analyze each structure in turn. (We will address the UDDI version 3 operational-info structures separately.)

The businessEntity data structure

This top-level structure provides information about the business or service provider. The information given about a service provider can vary from simple contact information to a description of what the provider's line of business is. This is the type of information that is defined as "White Pages level" information. Here is the businessEntity-structure according to uddi.org:

```
<element name="bindingTemplate" type="uddi:bindingTemplate" />

<complexType name="bindingTemplate">

  <sequence>

    <element ref="uddi:description" minOccurs="0"
             maxOccurs="unbounded" />

    <choice>

      <element ref="uddi:accessPoint" />

      <element ref="uddi:hostingRedirector" />

    </choice>

    <element ref="uddi:tModelInstanceDetails" />

  </sequence>

<attribute name="serviceKey" type="uddi:serviceKey" use=
"optional" />
```

```
<attribute name="bindingKey" type="uddi:bindingKey"
use="required" />

</complexType>
```

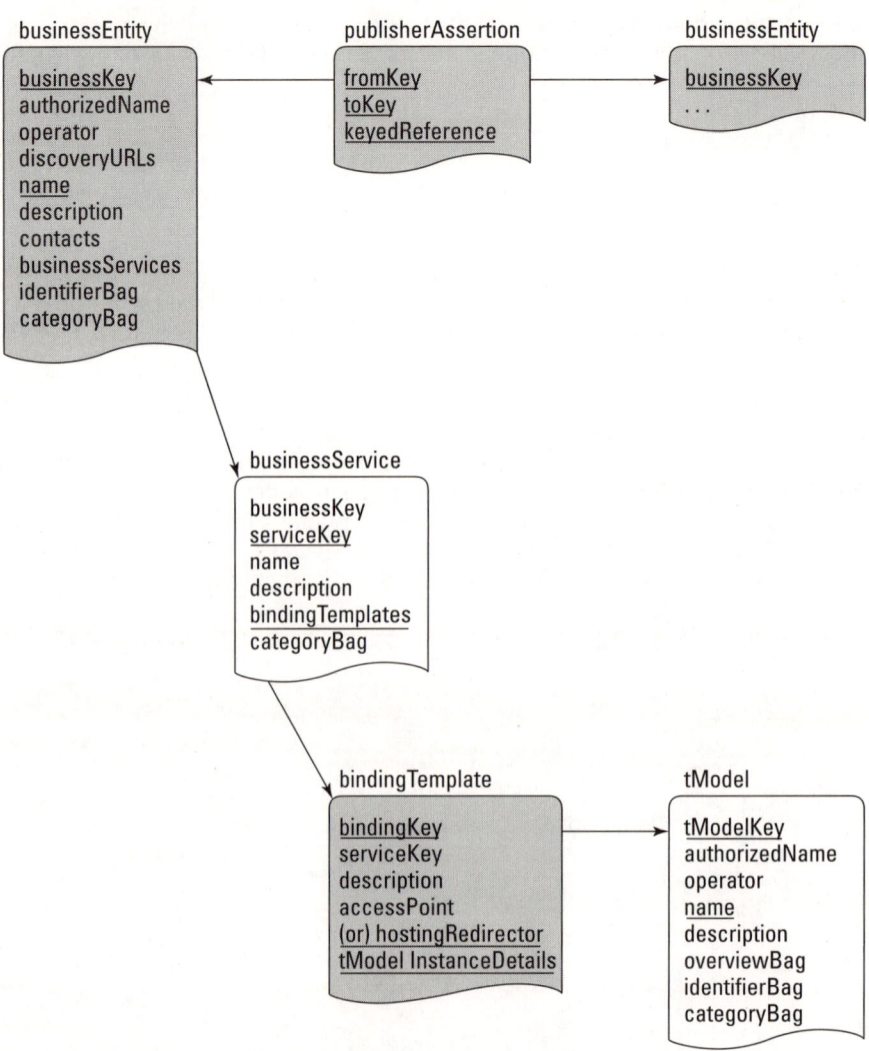

Figure 21-3: The relationship between the basic UDDI data structures

The businessService data structure

This data structure represents the services offered by a provider. It provides information such as the service name or a description of the service; this is typically referred to as "Yellow Pages level" information. A businessService data structure is also the logical child of a businessEntity structure.

Since a business can offer more than one service, the businessEntity structure can contain more than one businessService. Each businessService can also be used by more than one businessEntity. Here is the businessService-structure according to uddi.org:

```
<element name="businessService" type="uddi:businessService" />

<complexType name="businessService">

  <sequence>

    <element ref="uddi:name" minOccurs="0"
maxOccurs="unbounded" />

      <element ref="uddi:description" minOccurs="0"
              maxOccurs="unbounded" />

      <element ref="uddi:bindingTemplates" minOccurs="0" />

      <element ref="uddi:categoryBag" minOccurs="0" />

  </sequence>

  <attribute name="serviceKey" type="uddi:serviceKey"
              use="required" />

  <attribute name="businessKey" type="uddi:businessKey"
              use="optional" />

</complexType>
```

The bindingTemplate data structure

This structure is found within the businessService data structure. It gives you technical descriptions such as the address information required for accessing the service. Here is the bindingTemplate-structure according to uddi.org:

```
<element name="bindingTemplate" type="uddi:bindingTemplate" />

<complexType name="bindingTemplate">

  <sequence>

    <element ref="uddi:description" minOccurs="0"
              maxOccurs="unbounded" />
```

```
<choice>

  <element ref="uddi:accessPoint" />

  <element ref="uddi:hostingRedirector" />

</choice>

<element ref="uddi:tModelInstanceDetails" />

</sequence>

<attribute name="serviceKey" type="uddi:serviceKey"
           use="optional" />

<attribute name="bindingKey" type="uddi:bindingKey"
           use="required" />

</complexType>
```

The tModel data structure

A tModel defines flexible, reusable data structures that are roughly equivalent to a WSDL type. This data structure appears all over UDDI-registry data. In binding templates tModels identify the interface and protocol to be expected, in category tags they define the specific taxonomy, in identifier tags they define the type of identifier. The tModel is even used within publisher assertions to define the type of relationship the assertion represents. Here is the tModel-structure according to uddi.org:

```
<element name="tModel" type="uddi:tModel" />

<complexType name="tModel">

  <sequence>

    <element ref="uddi:name" />

    <element ref="uddi:description" minOccurs="0"
             maxOccurs="unbounded" />

    <element ref="uddi:overviewDoc" minOccurs="0" />

    <element ref="uddi:identifierBag" minOccurs="0" />

    <element ref="uddi:categoryBag" minOccurs="0" />

  </sequence>

  <attribute name="tModelKey" type="uddi:tModelKey"
use="required" />
```

```
<attribute name="operator" type="string" use="optional" />

<attribute name="authorizedName" type="string" use="optional"
/>

</complexType>
```

Additions to the UDDI information model (UDDI v3)

Although UDDI version 3 has been out for a while now, many vendors will still lag behind in supporting the latest bells and whistles laid out in the specification. And even if your vendor supports version 3, you may not have any need for the additional features it defines. If the diagram and registry data described in the previous pages are sufficient to meet your needs, you don't need to concern yourself with this last section. If, however, you are interested in taking full advantage of the UDDI version 3 specification, then keep reading.

The subscription API provides clients, known as *subscribers,* with the ability to register their interest in one or more entries within a UDDI registry. When changes are made to an entry, an `operationalInfo` element is created that represents the changes made. The subscription API can then be used by the subscriber to retrieve any changes that have been made to subscribed entries. Alternatively, the API can be used to set up an asynchronous notification. The subscription API will be discussed in greater detail later in this chapter under the section "Subscribing with UDDI".

Figure 21-4 illustrates how the `operationalInfo` registry entry relates to the other registry entries.

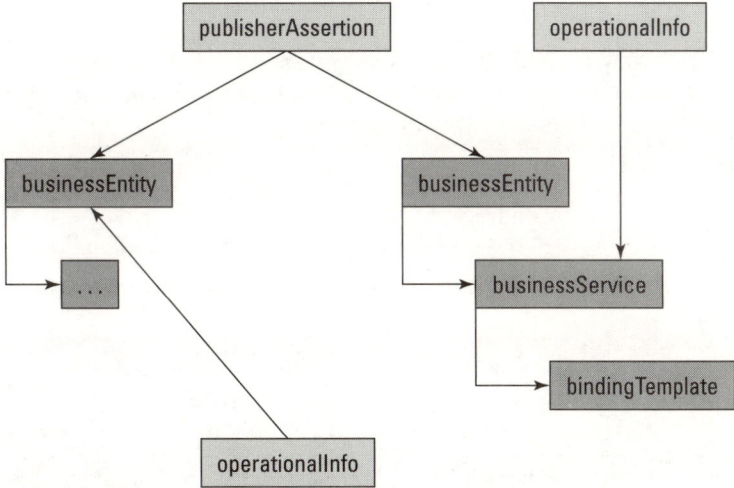

Figure 21-4: The operationalInfo registry entry relates to the other registry entries.

When UDDI data structures are published, information about the change is captured and an `operationalInfo` element is created. The element includes data such as the identity of the publisher, the date and time that the data structure was created and modified, and the identifier of the UDDI node that was published. Here is the `operationalInfo`-structure according to `uddi.org`:

```
<element name="operationalInfo"
type="uddi:operationalInfo"final="restriction"/>
<complexType name="operationalInfo" final="restriction">
    <sequence>
        <element name="created"
type="uddi:timeInstant"minOccurs="0"/>
        <element name="modified"
type="uddi:timeInstant"minOccurs="0"/>
        <element
name="modifiedIncludingChildren"type="uddi:timeInstant"

minOccurs="0"/>
        <element name="nodeID" type="uddi:nodeID" minOccurs="0"/>
        <element name="authorizedName" type="xsd:string"
minOccurs="0"/>
    </sequence>
<attribute name="entityKey" type="uddi:uddiKey"
use="required"/>
</complexType>
```

Searching with UDDI

UDDI defines an inquiry API to support the programmatic discovery of registry data contained within a UDDI registry. This API primarily consists of *finder* methods and *retriever* methods. The finder methods (`find_XXXX`) are used to return result sets based upon general criteria, while retriever methods (`get_XXXX`) return detailed information about a specific registry entry. Table 21-4 lists the finder methods that are available and Table 21-5 displays the retriever methods.

Table 21-4 Finder methods	
Method	**Action**
`find_binding`	Locates specific bindings within a registered business service
`find_business`	Locates one or more business entities
`find_relatedBusiness`	Locates one or more business entities based upon relationships asserted within `publisherAssertion` elements
`find_service`	Locates one or more business services
`find_tModel`	Locates one or more `tModel`s

Here are some examples of the finder methods:

```
find_service

<find_business generic="2.0" xmlns="urn:uddi-org:api">
    <name>IBM</name>
</find_business>


find_service

<find_service businessKey="6112-4T17-8X" generic="2.0"
xmlns="urn:uddi-org:api">
    <name>delayed stock quotes</name>
</find_service>
```

Table 21-5
Retriever methods

Method	Action
get_bindingDetail	Returns the runtime binding-template information
get_businessDetail	Returns one or more complete business-entity objects
get_operationInfo	Returns operational information pertaining to one or more entities
get_serviceDetail	Returns a complete service object
get_tModelDetail	Returns a complete tModel object

Here are some examples of the retriever methods:

```
get_bindingDetail

<get_bindingDetail generic="2.0" xmlns="urn:uddi-org:api">
    <bindingKey>RJ12-6397-B2</bindingKey>
</get_bindingDetail>

get_businessDetail

<get_businessDetail generic="2.0" xmlns="urn:uddi-org:api">
    <businessKey>6112-4T17-8X</businessKey>
</get_businessDetail>

get_serviceDetail

<get_serviceDetail generic="2.0" xmlns="urn:uddi-org:api">
    <serviceKey>38AN-4E98-Q77</serviceKey>
</get_serviceDetail>
```

The UDDI specification also defines three usage patterns for use with the finder and retriever methods. These three patterns are often used in combination with each other; the first two are particularly complementary.

✦ **Browse** — The browse pattern is familiar to many of us. Its use typically involves starting with some broad information such as a subject, category, or geographic location, performing a search that produces general result sets, and then retrieving more specific information via the drill-down pattern. This scenario commonly plays out during searches through large quantities of information such as browsing through book categories on Amazon or through chat-room categories on Yahoo. In UDDI, finder methods return result sets with corresponding unique identifiers, enabling you to use the drill-down pattern to get more complete information.

✦ **Drill-down** — The drill-down pattern allows specific information to be retrieved based upon some type of key or unique identifier. On Amazon this would be the equivalent of retrieving book information via an International Standard Book Number (ISBN), rather than by browsing through the Information Technology (IT) category. In a Web-based search the unique identifier would be a URL, in a UDDI registry a UDDI key. With the key, all the relevant registry data can be retrieved.

✦ **Invocation** — The invocation pattern is easily the least commonly used of the three usage patterns, but it is potentially the most powerful. One of the dreams of Web services from the beginning has been the concept of discovering and binding to a service at runtime, rather than coding a static client application and then accessing a service. The `bindingTemplate` element for a service contains sufficient information for a client application to bind to a Web service and invoke its operations. The binding information can be obtained from the registry by means of the browse and drill-down patterns and then cached on the client and used to contact the Web service at the registered address whenever it needs to communicate with the service instance.

Publishing with UDDI

UDDI defines a publishing API to support the programmatic publication of registry data to a UDDI registry. This API consists of four sets of methods used for the following purposes:

Adding or updating registry entries (`save_XXXX`)

Removing registry entries (`delete_XXXX`)

Managing `publisherAssertions` (`add_XXXX` and `set_XXXX`)

Retrieving the status of published entries (`get_XXXX`).

Table 21-6 lists the methods used to add or update registry entries.

<table>
<tr><td colspan="2" align="center">Table 21-6
Methods for adding or updating registry entries</td></tr>
</table>

Method	Action
save_binding	**Registers new** bindingTemplate **or updates existing one**
save_business	**Registers new** businessEntity **or updates existing one**
save_service	**Registers new** businessService **or updates existing one**
save_tModel	**Registers new** tModel **information or updates existing information**

Here are some method examples for adding and updating registry entries:

```
save_binding
<save_binding generic="2.0" xmlns="urn:uddi-org:api">
   <bindingTemplate>
      <accessPoint useType="endpoint">
         https://connexia.example/reservation.html
      </accessPoint>
      <tModelInstanceDetails>
         <tModelInstanceInfo
         tModelKey="uddi:ubr.uddi.org:transport:http">
      </tModelInstanceInfo>
      </tModelInstanceDetails>
   </bindingTemplate>
   <categoryBag>
     <keyedReference

tModelKey="uddi:uddi.org:categorization:general_keywords"

keyName="connexia.example:categorization:transportation"
      keyValue="c"/>
   </categoryBag>
</save_binding>

save_business

<save_business generic="2.0" xmlns="urn:uddi-org:api">
   <businessEntity businessKey="1764a-0c20">
  <name>IBM</name>
   </businessEntity>
</save_business>

save_service

<save_service generic="2.0" xmlns="urn:uddi-org:api">
   <businessService>
  <name> </name>
   </businessService>
</save_service>
```

Table 21-7 lists the methods used to remove registry entries.

<table>
<tr><td colspan="2" align="center">Table 21-7
Methods for removing registry entries</td></tr>
<tr><td>*Method*</td><td>*Action*</td></tr>
<tr><td>`delete_binding`</td><td>Removes existing `bindingTemplate` entry</td></tr>
<tr><td>`delete_business`</td><td>Removes existing `businessEntity` entry</td></tr>
<tr><td>`delete_service`</td><td>Removes existing `businessService` entry</td></tr>
<tr><td>`delete_tModel`</td><td>Removes existing `tModel` entry</td></tr>
</table>

Here are some method examples for removing registry entries:

```
delete_binding

<delete_binding generic="2.0" xmlns="urn:uddi-org:api">
    <bindingKey>RJ12-6397-B2</bindingKey>
</delete_binding>

delete_business

<delete_business generic="2.0" xmlns="urn:uddi-org:api">
    <businessKey>6112-4T17-8X</businessKey>
</delete_business>

delete_service

<delete_service generic="2.0" xmlns="urn:uddi-org:api">
    <serviceKey>38AN-4E98-Q77</serviceKey>
</delete_service>
```

Table 21-8 lists the methods used to modify publisher assertions.

<table>
<tr><td colspan="2" align="center">Table 21-8
Methods for modifying publisher assertions</td></tr>
<tr><td>*Method*</td><td>*Action*</td></tr>
<tr><td>`add_publisherAssertions`</td><td>Adds a new relationship assertion to the current set of assertions</td></tr>
<tr><td>`delete_publisherAssertions`</td><td>Removes a specific `publisherAssertion`</td></tr>
<tr><td>`set_publisherAssertions`</td><td>Saves a new complete set of assertions for a publisher, completely replacing any previous assertions</td></tr>
</table>

Table 21-9 lists the methods used to retrieve status information about registry data.

Table 21-9	
Methods for retrieving status information about registry data	
Method	*Action*
get_assertionStatusReport	Retrieves a report identifying all registered assertions and their current status for the request publisher
get_publisherAssertions	Retrieves a list of all assertions for a particular publisher
get_registeredInfo	Saves a new complete set of assertions for a publisher, completely replacing any previous assertionsgetInfo

Subscribing with UDDI

UDDI defines an *optional* subscription API to enable clients to monitor changes to specified registry entries. Because the API is optional, support is determined on a node-by-node basis. Table 21-10 lists the methods defined by the specification.

Table 21-10	
Methods provided by Subscription API	
Method	*Action*
delete_subscription	Removes (cancels) one or more subscriptions
get_subscriptionResults	Synchronously returns registry data related to a particular subscription
get_subscriptions	Returns current list of subscriptions associated with the subscriber
notify_subscriptionListener	Receives asynchronous notifications of changes to data that the subscriber is monitoring (this method is optional for a client)
save_subscription	Registers a new subscription, or modifies or renews an existing one

Here are some method examples:

```
delete_subscription

<delete_subscription generic="2.0" xmlns="urn:uddi-org:api">
      <subscriptionKey>RY67-1009-4</subscriptionKey>
</delete_subscription>

save_subscription

<save_subscription generic="2.0" xmlns="urn:uddi-org:api">
      <subscription>
   <subscriptionFilter>
         <find_service businessKey="6112-4T17-8X" generic="2.0"
                       xmlns="urn:uddi-org:api">
                  <name>delayed stock quotes</name>
         </find_service>
   </subscriptionFilter>
      </subscription>
</save_subscription>
```

Finally, the subscription API supports two monitoring patterns:

✦ **Asynchronous notification** — This pattern is sometimes referred to as *subscriber listener*. It enables subscribers to inform the UDDI node that they wish to be directly notified when subscribed registry data changes.

✦ **Synchronous notification** — This pattern is sometimes referred to as *change tracking*. It enables subscribing clients to issue a synchronous request to retrieve registry changes that match their subscription preferences.

UDDI and Java

Support for UDDI in Java can be achieved through the use of the Java API for XML Registries (JAXR). JAXR provides a way to interact with XML registries without having to deal with the complexity of UDDI. The JAXR information model (the type of information supported by a registry) is primarily based upon ebXML's information model but provides support for UDDI. The architecture of JAXR also allows the developer to create one client application that will work with a variety of registries.

JAXR Architecture

The JAXR architecture consists of the following:

✦ **JAXR client** — This client uses the JAXR API to access a registry through the JAXR provider.

✦ **JAXR provider** — This provider consists of a JAXR pluggable provider that allows interaction with any registry. The JAXR provider also consists of a JAXR registry-specific provider that supplies a JAXR implementation for a particular registry. The registry-specific provider usually plugs into the pluggable

provider and transforms client requests so that the intended registry understands the request. The registry-specific provider also transforms registry-
specific responses to JAXR responses and sends the response to the client.
The JAXR Bridge provider is similar to the registry-specific provider but
adheres to a registry specification such as UDDI or ebXML.

Figure 21-5 illustrates the JAXR architecture.

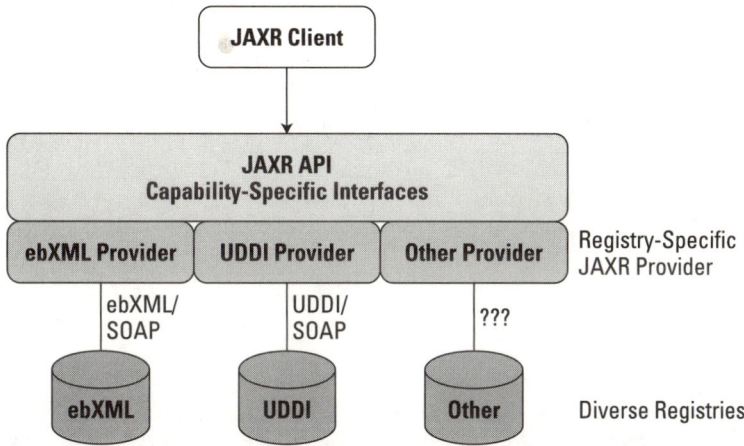

Figure 21-5: The JAXR architecture

JAXR capability profiles

In order to support a wide variety of registries the JAXR API defines capabilities and
capability profiles. A capability is a set of similar features and a capability profile is
a categorization of API methods that have the same level. The JAXR defines level 1
and level 0 capability profiles. Level 0 is required and provides basic registry capabilities. Level 1 is optional, and provides advanced registry capabilities and support
for Level 0 capabilities. It is also important to note that each API method is
assigned a capability level.

JAXR API

The JAXR API consists of two main packages, `javax.xml.registry` and
`javax.xml.registry.infomodel`. The `javax.xml.registry.infomodel` contains interfaces that control the relationship between registry objects and what
type of objects are in the registry. The javax.xml.registry package contains access
interfaces that define how registry objects are handled. Figure 21-6 and Figure 21-7
illustrate some of the primary interfaces in JAXR API. A brief description of the
offerings of the two main packages follows.

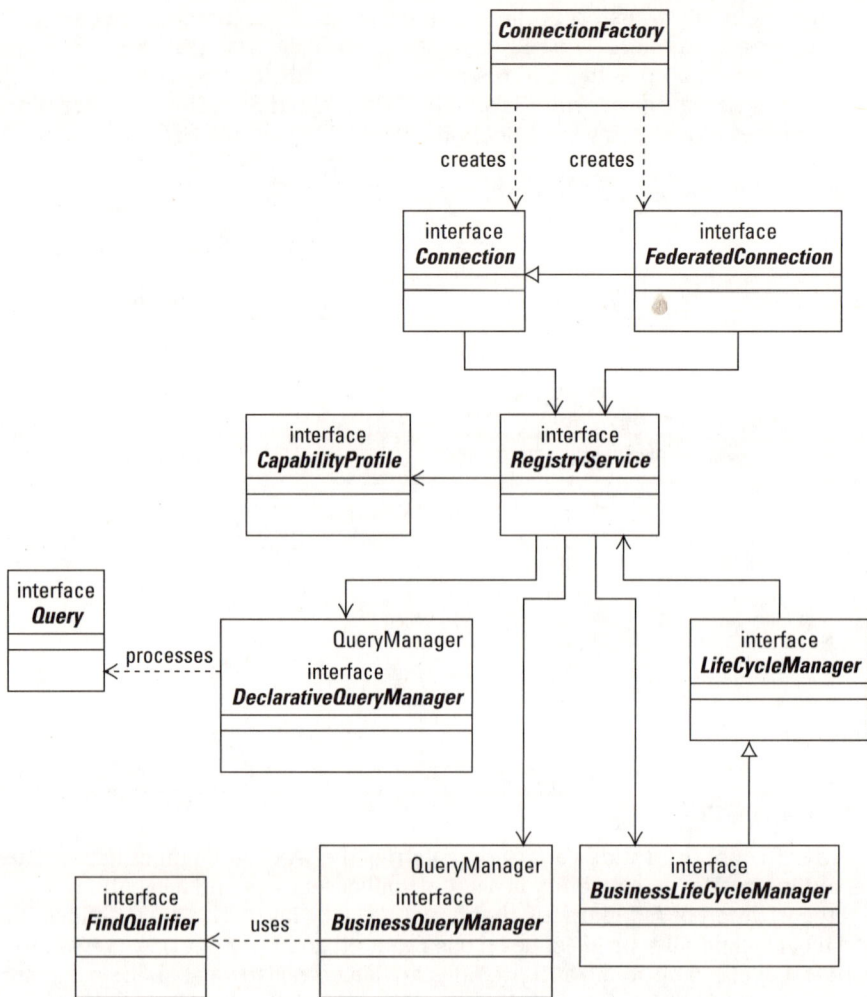

Figure 21-6: The primary interfaces of the JAXR API

`javax.xml.registry` consists of the following elements:

✦ `Connection` represents a session that a client has with the registry provider.

✦ `BusinessLifeCycleManager`- allows the saving or updating of information in a registry and generally consists of level 1methods.

✦ `LifeCycleManager`- supports the creating, updating, deprecating and deleting of registry objects and generally consists of level 0 methods.

✦ BusinessQueryManager- supports for basic searching of the JAXR information model and generally consists of level 1 methods.

✦ DeclarativeQueryManager- supports searching of the JAXR information model via SQL queries and generally consists of level 0 methods.

javax.xml.registry.infomodel consists of these elements:

✦ RegistryObject provides metadata for registry objects and is a base class used by most classes in the JAXR information model.

✦ Organization provides information about organizations, the services offered and can have relationships with other organization types.

✦ Service provides information on services offered by an organization.

✦ ServiceBinding provides technical details about how to access service interfaces.

✦ Association defines associations between objects.

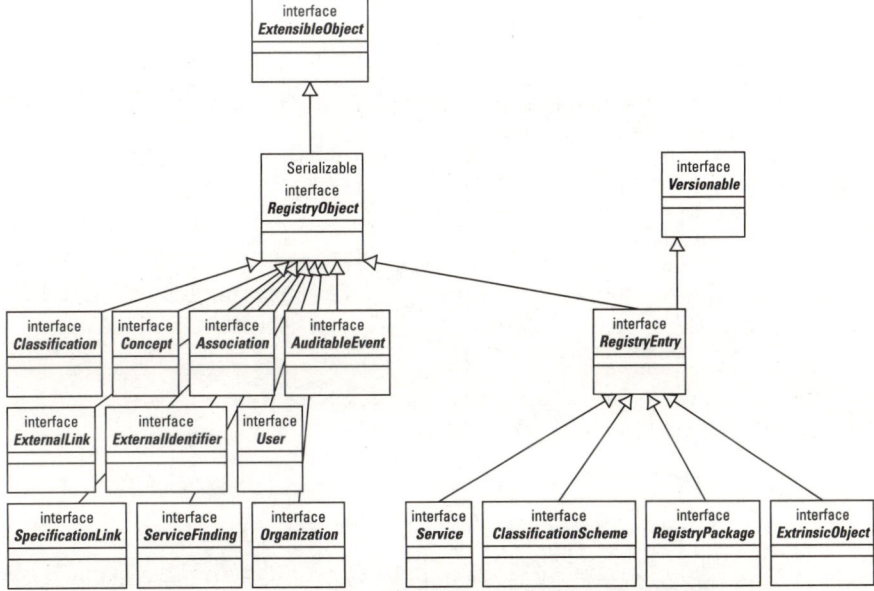

Figure 21-7: Inheritance within the javax.xml.registry.infomodel package

Listing 21-9 is an example of a JAXR client. It will give you a better idea of how some of the interfaces we discussed work together. First, we create an instance of the ConnectionFactory class. Next, we specify which registry we will be accessing and set the connection configuration properties. Then, we obtain access to the `RegistryService` object and `BusinessQueryManager` in order to prepare for a query. After that, we define find qualifiers and name patterns, then execute the query. Finally, we obtain the search results.

Listing 21-9: A sample JAXR client

```
package wiley.simplejaxr;

import javax.xml.registry.*;
import java.util.*;

public class JAXRClient {

    public static void main( String[] args ) throws Exception {
//Creating an instance of ConnectionFactory
        ConnectionFactory connFactory =
ConnectionFactory.newInstance();
//Specify registry access
        Properties props = new Properties();
        props.setProperty(
            "javax.xml.registry.queryManagerURL",
            "http://localhost/registry-
server/RegistryServerServlet");
        props.setProperty(
            "javax.xml.registry.lifeCycleManagerURL",
            "http://localhost/registry-
server/RegistryServerServlet");
//Set connection properties
        connFactory.setProperties(props);
        Connection connection = connFactory.createConnection();
//Get access to the RegistryService object and
BusinessQueryManager to prepare for a query
 BusinessQueryManager
        BusinessQueryManager bqm;

    bqm =
connection.getRegistryService().getBusinessQueryManager();

        // Define find qualifiers and name patterns
        Collection findQualifiers = new ArrayList();
        findQualifiers.add(FindQualifier.SORT_BY_NAME_DESC);
        Collection namePatterns = new ArrayList();
        namePatterns.add("Connexia");

        // Find using the name
        BulkResponse response =
            bqm.findOrganizations(
```

```
              findQualifiers,
              namePatterns,
              null,
              null,
              null,
              null);
// obtain the search results.
        Collection orgs = response.getCollection();
        System.out.println("orgs returned " + orgs.size());

    }

}
```

In this section, we looked at the evolution of UDDI from version 1 to version 3 and discussed the internal workings of UDDI. Version 1 serves as a basic foundation that provides a central location for services to be published and searched.

Version 2 includes enhancements to the Inquiry API and Publishing API. The enhancements focus on the ability to make complex relationships between and within businesses. We examined how version 3 focuses on the interaction with registries. We looked at the UDDI information model and its basic data structures. We also examined tracking changes within the registry with the `operationalInfo` entry. We discussed the subscription API and the monitoring patterns it supports. Finally, we examined how UDDI and Java interact by introducing the JAXR API.

Summary

In this chapter, we took a closer look at SOAP, WSDL and UDDI. We began this chapter by discussing the architecture of SOAP messages, the encoding and the processing of SOAP messages. We looked at the datatypes available and the structures that handle them. We learned that RPC based communication in SOAP can occur by using SOAP-RPC. SOAP also provides the ability to communicate by exchanging SOAP messages that contain XML documents. Next we discussed the basics of WSDL and examined an actual wsdl document. We then walked through the WSDL bindings. We ended our discussion with an in-depth look at UDDI and its evolution.

✦   ✦   ✦

Understanding J2EE Web Services

✦ ✦ ✦ ✦

In This Chapter

Using servlets in a Web-services architecture

Exposing EJBs as Web services

Using JMS as a transport layer

Exploring products and tools for Web Services

Locating Web-service components via JNDI

Examining JSR 109

Explaining the client-side programming model

Explaining the server-side programming model

Reviewing Web-service deployment descriptors

✦ ✦ ✦ ✦

The intersection between the world of Java 2 Enterprise Edition and the newly forming world of Web services is a vast expanse of opportunities, possibilities, and potential conflicts. This chapter provides a general overview and addresses the matter of building Web service–enabled J2EE architectures.

We will begin by looking at how Web services fit into the J2EE platform. Next we will look at howvarious J2EE components (servlets, EJBs, and JMS) can participate in a Web-services exchange. This discussion will be a very general one in which a high-level architectural perspective of J2EE Web services will be provided. In the second half of the chapter we will drill down into the details of J2EE Web services as we explore JSR 109, which is a specification that explains how to incorporate Web services into a J2EE architecture in a consistent and standardized way.

Integrating J2EE and Web Services

SOAP is designed to address only the description and basic delivery of a message. The protocol was intentionally designed without any details regarding higher-level concerns like security, session handling, transactions, or guaranteed delivery.

See Chapter 21 for a discussion of SOAP.

In order to build truly enterprise-grade Web services you need to combine lightweight XML Web-service components with robust enterprise components. This is not always easy. Some components are better suited for this task than others. As we address various J2EE components throughout this section, you will notice that they have different strengths and weaknesses within a Web services context. We will identify those strengths and weaknesses on a component-by-component basis within each subsection.

Using Java servlets in a Web-services architecture

Java servlets are by far the most popular J2EE technology for building Web-service applications, for the following reasons:

Web services require accessibility via lightweight, standardized Internet protocols such as HTTP. Java servlets were designed as a server-side component model for communicating by means of such protocols.

Web services are typically implemented by means of a request/response-programming model. Java servlets were designed to support this model.

Applications exposing Web-service interfaces must be able to respond simultaneously to multiple requests. The Java-servlet architecture incorporates an inherently lightweight threading model that easily scales to handle increasing demand for services.

The majority of J2EE developers are much more proficient with Java servlets than with some of the more complex components such as EJB or JMS. Thus developers are generally more inclined to use servlets for implementing Web-service applications.

The last factor is mitigated to some extent by tools (BEA Workshop, IBM's WSAD, Cape Clear Studio, and so forth) that make it fairly easy to expose EJBs or JMS components as Web services. Some of the tools that support Web services are listed in the "Web Services Tools" section. Taking advantage of these tools still presumes that developers have enough knowledge of these more advanced J2EE components to create the J2EE business logic that exists behind the XML interface. Consequently, many teams choose to implement their XML service layers using Java servlet technology.

As far as the programming model is concerned, having servlets process Web service requests is quite simple. A servlet can be set up to do the following:

1. Receive an HTTP request (containing an XML SOAP request in the POST body) at a particular URL on a given port

2. Parse the SOAP request somewhere within the servlet's doPost() method (this often involves passing the SOAP request to a helper component as a Java string and having the component handle the parsing of the message)

3. Execute the request locally and access one or more business services, or even other Web services, to fulfill the client's request

4. Finally, synchronous services package the response as a SOAP message and return it to the client; asynchronous services might send the response data as a new SOAP request to a Web service exposed by the client of the original request or might not send the response at all

One drawback of servlets is that they are somewhat limited in terms of enterprise capabilities such as security, transactions, legacy-resource integration, and so on. These tasks are best handled by JMS and/or EJB components. The catch is that Web-service requests are typically sent over HTTP, but HTTP is not required. Because servlets are the only components designed to handle HTTP requests, they will often wrap EJB and JMS components when such enterprise business services are required.

In short, Java servlets are ideally suited to process Web-service requests and interact with the Web-service client. It is often a good idea to delegate processing to helper components. In some cases, doing this may even involve accessing the EJB container and/or a JMS messaging provider.

Exposing EJBs as Web services

Enterprise JavaBeans provide a robust framework for encapsulating business logic and enterprise services.

EJB technology provides the following key benefits:

Developers can focus upon writing business logic without regard for the deployment platform or for the semantics of accessing enterprise services.

Enterprise beans are portable across platforms. They are managed and maintained by the EJB container that is supplied by the EJB vendor. The container's interfaces are specified; the implementation is left to the vendor.

Deployment information — such as security settings, property values, database locations, component references, and transaction semantics — are all declared within an XML file that is read at deployment time.

Because developers are writing business-logic components that run in a standard container environment, EJB vendors can fine-tune their tools to provide optimizations for loading and managing beans as well as the resources that those beans access.

EJBs are capable of smoothly scaling to handle increasing demand.

From a Web-services standpoint, EJBs are most useful for fulfilling complicated backend business processes requiring transactions and communication with multiple enterprise resources. Currently no EJB is capable of directly handling an HTTP request, so most companies choose to use a servlet to handle the HTTP and SOAP side of the communication and then delegate the fulfillment of the client's request to an EJB whenever enterprise-grade functionality is required.

With the advent of message-driven beans, the door has been opened to allow EJBs to interact directly with Web services via SOAP.

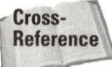 **Cross-Reference**   For a discussion of message-driven beans see Chapter 17.

So EJBs provide the robust enterprise functionality that some Web services may need. Currently Web services do not often require this level of sophistication and so using EJB can introduce an unnecessary layer of complexity. This lack of sophistication is largely because of the immaturity of the Web-services specifications and a lack of standardization for handling higher-level-service semantics such as transactions, sessions, and advanced security concepts like authorization, federation, privacy and trust. Until these issues are resolved, EJBs will be used less extensively than servlets for fulfilling Web-service requests.

Using JMS as a transport layer

The Java Message Service (JMS) is a robust enterprise-messaging technology supported across the industry by companies like IBM, Sun, BEA, and Sonic Software.

JMS defines a standard way to send and receive enterprise messages from the Java platform. Enterprise messaging requires the following:

✦ Reliable messaging

✦ Security

✦ Transaction support

✦ Guaranteed message delivery

✦ Multiple message-delivery paradigms

SOAP has none of these features. JMS, on the other hand, does.

The SOAP protocol is designed to facilitate a binding to any transport layer. The most common layers are the Hypertext Transfer Protocol (HTTP) and the Simple Mail Transport Protocol (SMTP). Although JMS is technically an application-layer technology and not a lower-level transportation-layer technology, from the perspective of a SOAP message it looks like the transport layer because JMS shields the SOAP protocol from the lower-level transportation issues.

When SOAP uses JMS as the transport mechanism, many more options are available for the messaging architecture. Because JMS can operate on top of message-oriented middleware products, SOAP messages sent via JMS can be sent using a point-to-point paradigm, a publish-subscribe paradigm, or any other paradigm supported by the product. The flexibility of SOAP as a messaging format is one of the reasons it has gained so much popularity in such a short period of time.

In sum, if you are looking to build asynchronous Web services, JMS and SOAP make a perfect combination. JMS can provide the transport layer and manage the messaging semantics, while SOAP can be used to encode the payload of the message itself. So far we have discussed how Web services can be integrated with various components of the J2EE platform. In the next section, we will discuss some of the products and tools that support the integration and development of Web services in a J2EE environment.

Exploring Products and Tools for Web Services

We will discuss the following products and tools in this section:

- ✦ AXIS
- ✦ BEA WebLogic
- ✦ Sun's offerings
- ✦ WebSphere
- ✦ Cape Clear Studio and Cape Connect

AXIS

AXIS is an open source tool that is an ongoing project maintained by the Apache Software Foundation. Some of the features of Axis 1.1 (release candidate 2 version) are listed here:

JavaBeans can be automatically serialized or de-serialized.

Availability of support for JMS-based and HTTP-servlet-based transport.

Allows access to EJBs as Web services.

Provides the functionality to generate proxies and skeletons from WSDL documents.

Inclusion of a SOAP 1.1–compliant engine. Partial support for SOAP 1.2 is included.

For more information on Axis please visit the Axis Web site at `http://ws.apache.org/axis/`.

BEA WebLogic

WebLogic Server 8.1 is includes support for Web service ANT tasks, an implementation for SAAJ, portable stubs, JMS transport protocol, SOAP 1.2, reliable SOAP messaging, digital signatures and encryption.

Sun's offerings

Sun provides a variety of support for Web services. The foundation of Sun's offerings includes the Java APIs for XML. The Java Web Services Developer Pack version 1.1 includes support for the following:

✦ Java Server Pages Standard Tag Library (JSTL)

✦ Apache Tomcat 4.1.2 container

✦ Ant Build Tool 1.5.1

✦ SOAP with Attachments API for Java (SAAJ) v1.1.1

✦ Java Architecture for XML Binding (JAXB) v1.0

✦ Java API for XML Registries (JAXR) v1.0.3

✦ Java API for XML Messaging (JAXM) v1.1.1

✦ Java API for XML Processing (JAXP) v1.2.2

✦ Java API for XML-based RPC (JAX-RPC) v1.0.3

✦ Java WSDP Registry Server v1.0_04

✦ Tomcat the Java Architecture for XML Binding

Sun also offers the Sun Open Net Environment (Sun One) Application server 7.0 and Studio 4.0. Together, the application server and studio offer an environment to develop enterprise applications and Web services.

IBM's WebSphere

IBM offers WebSphere Application server version 5. WebSphere supports J2EE 1.3, XML, WSDL, SOAP and JMS. WebSphere Application server currently provides support for transforming existing applications into Web service-based applications. IBM also provides the WebSphere SDK for Web services (WSDK) for creating Web services with existing Java components. Here is a partial list of components and features included in the WSDK:

Support for Web services of J2EE (JSR109), SOAP 1.1, UDDI 2.0, WSDL 1.1, JAX-RPC 1.0, WSDL4J, UDDI4J and EJB 2.0

The WebSphere Application Server-Express, version 5 is included.

The ability to publish stateless-session EJBs and JavaBeans as Web services.

A private registry that supports UDDI 2.

For more information on IBM's WebSphere, please visit http://www-3.ibm.com/software/info1/websphere/index.jsp?tab=highlights.

Cape Clear Studio and Cape Connect

Cape Clear Studio allows you to build both client and server interfaces to new and pre-existing business logic. It also allows developers to develop applications that reference external WSDL documents and allows you to expose their interfaces. Cape Connect is a server that allows you to deploy, test, and host Web services. Some of the key benefits of Cape Clear products are as follows:

XML Schema support for WSDL

Point and click business integration.

The ability to expose J2EE, MQSeries, CORBA, database, and COBOL systems as Web services without changing your existing code.

Fast implementation and modular architecture

In this section we introduced various products and tools that facilitate the integration of J2EE and Web services. In the next section, we will take a look at the overall architectural aspects of integrating Web services and J2EE.

JSR 109 – J2EE Web Services

Web Services for J2EE (Java Specification Request 109) defines an architectural relationship of technologies for the J2EE platform that is designed to facilitate the use of Web services. The specification defines client- and server-side programming models. It also outlines standard procedures for describing Web service–enabled J2EE components and ultimately how to deploy those components based upon declarative statements embedded in deployment descriptors.

We will begin our study of JSR 109 with a brief overview of the specifications goals and a high-level look at the overall architecture of J2EE Web services. Once this foundation is laid we will examine the client-side programming model, the server-side programming model, and finally the deployment of J2EE Web services.

Before diving into the gory details, it is helpful to begin with an understanding of the goals that the specification's authors had when crafting JSR 109. Here are some of the main objectives of JSR 109, according to the specification:

Providing a basic model for defining and deploying a Web service onto a J2EE application server

Using current Web-service standards like WSDL and SOAP as a foundation

Defining the interaction between the J2EE platform roles and the roles that are specific to JSR 109

Taking advantage of existing J2EE technology

Specifying the functions that must be provided by the J2EE application vendors

Making sure that the various vendor implementations of the specification interoperate

According to the specification, a Web service can be as simple as a Java class running in the Web container. A more sophisticated example is an implementation of a stateless EJB that lives in the EJB container. Figure 22-1 illustrates the typical contents of the Web, application, applet, and EJB containers.

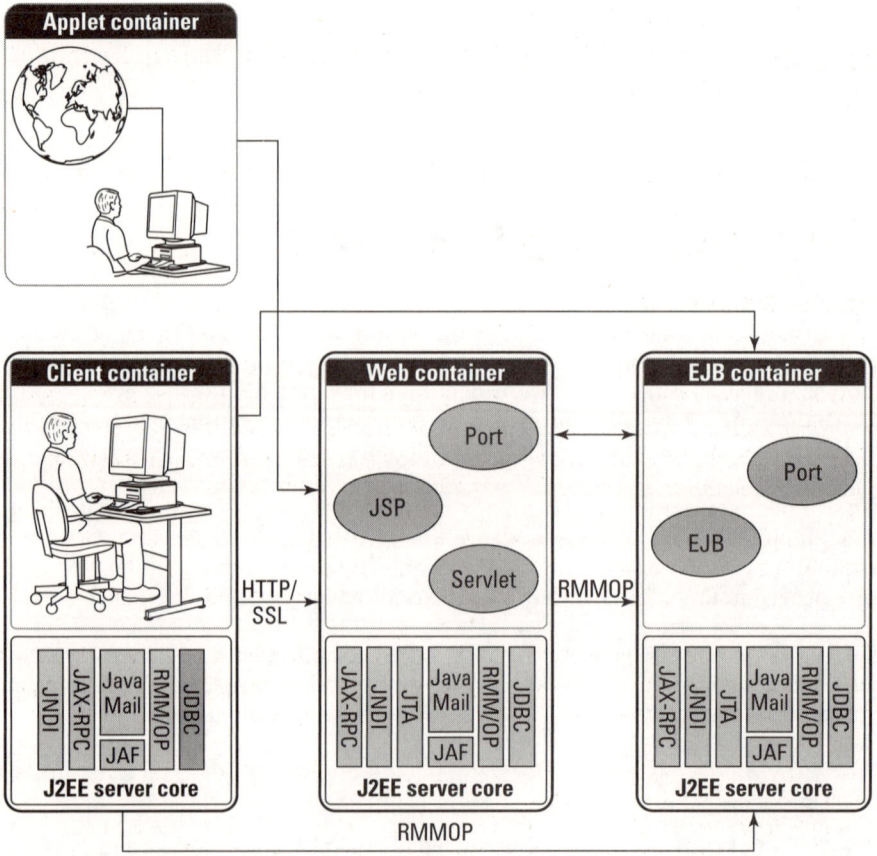

Figure 22-1: The J2EE platform supports Web services, and various APIs fit into the J2EE architecture.

Figure 22-1also shows how the Web service specific APIs fit into the J2EE 1.4 architecture. The J2EE 1.4 platform architecture provides an excellent environment for developing, accessing and providing Web services. J2EE 1.4 includes the Java API for XML-based RPC (JAX-RPC) to develop SOAP based Web service clients. It also includes SOAP with attachments API for Java (SAAJ) for creating and consuming messages according to the SOAP 1.1 and the SOAP with Attachments note. J2EE 1.4 provides the Java API for XML Registries for UDDI manipulation and the Web Services for J2EE specifications (JSR 109). As in earlier versions of J2EE, the rest of the Java APIs for XML processing are included.

The client-side programming model

The client programming indicated in the Web services for J2EE specification discusses the use of the *JAX-RPC* client-programming model in the context of a J2EE environment. In this model, a client should interact with a Web service through methods accessible via a service-endpoint interface.

So what actually happens in this model? A service implements the service interface by means of a client using JNDI lookup. The service generates a *stub* or *proxy* that functions as an instance of the Web service. An instance of a Web service is referred to as a *port*.

Finding a service

The Java Naming and Directory Interface (JNDI) is used to look up Web services according to the JSR 109 specifications. The developer creates a JNDI name that is used as a service reference and used in the deployment descriptor. In the following code fragment the name of the service reference is `ReservationService`. The job of the container is to make sure that the location specified in the JNDI namespace has an implementation of the `Service` interface bound to it.

```
InitialContext ic = new InitialContext();
Service res = (Service)ic.lookup
    ("java:comp/env/service/ReservationService");
```

The following code fragment doesn't require the container to do the same work that is required by the preceding fragment. It provides access to an object that implements a `Generated Service` interface. In our case the interface is `ReservationService`.

```
InitialContent ic = new InitialContext();
ReservationService res = (ReservationService)ic.lookup
    ("java:comp/env/service/ReservationService");
```

 **Cross-Reference**   See Chapter 11 for a discussion of JNDI.

The Service interface

The `Service` interface provides us with what we need in order to bind to the service. It represents a Web Services Description Language (WSDL) document that has been deployed. Recall that the interface supplies the client with a dynamic proxy, a stub, or a Dynamic Invocation Interface (DII) for a port. The Service interface has many methods to provide clients with a variety of features.. The methods available for the `Service` interface are as follows:

```
Call createCall()
Call createCall(Qname portName)
Call createCall(Qname portName, String operationName)
Call createCall(Qname portName, Qname operationName)
Call[] getCalls(Qname portName)

HandlerRegistry getHandlerRegistry()
TypeMappingRegistry getTypeMappingRegistry()

Iterator getPorts()
Remote getPort(Class SEI)
Remote getPort(Qname port Class SEI)

QName getServiceName()

URL getWSDLDocumentLocation()
```

 **Cross-Reference** See Chapter 21 for a discussion of WSDL.

If a client wants dynamic port access and to obtain a `Call` object DII, he or she can use the following methods:

```
Call createCall()
Call createCall(Qname portName)
Call createCall(Qname portName, String operationName)
Call createCall(Qname portName, Qname operationName)
Call[] getCalls(Qname portName)
```

In compliance with JSR 109, the container has to give support for the methods found in the `Generated Service` interface by providing one or more dynamic proxies or static stubs. The container must make sure that it can handle an environment in which ports cannot be determined at the time of development. It must also be able to handle multiple WSDL ports with the same invoking information. In order for the client to actually receive a stub or proxy, it can access the following methods of the `Service` interface:

```
java.rmi.Remote getPort(java.lang.class
serviceEndpointInterface) throws ServiceException;

java.rmi.Remote getPort(Qname portName, Class
serviceEndpointInterface) throws ServiceException;
```

The `Service` interface has methods that behave differently depending on their deployment configurations. Table 22-1 is from the specifications. It shows some of the differences between using full, partial, and no WSDL.

Table 22-2 Service-interface method behavior			
Method	**Full**	**Partial**	**None**
Call `createCall()`	Normal	Normal	Normal
Call `createCall(Qname portName)`	Normal	Unspecified	Unspecified
Call `createCall(Qname portName, String operationName)`	Normal	Unspecified	Unspecified
Call `createCall(Qname portName, Qname operationName)`	Normal	Unspecified	Unspecified
Call `[ ] getCalls(Qname portName)`	Normal	Unspecified	Unspecified
`HandlerRegistry getHandlerRegistry()`	Exception*	Exception*	Exception*
Remote `getPort(Class SEI)`	Normal	Normal	Unspecified
Remote `getPort(Qname port Class SEI)`	Normal	Unspecified	Unspecified
Iterator `getPorts()`	Bound ports	Bound ports	Unspecified
`QName getServiceName()`	Bound service name	Bound service name	Unspecified
`TypeMappingRegistry getTypeMappingRegistry()`	Exception*	Exception*	Exception*
URL `getWSDLDocumentLocation()`	Bound WSDL location	Bound WSDL location	Unspecified

The server-side programming model

Currently Web services for J2EE gives support for services that run in the Web container and in the EJB container. If you want to use Web services in the Web container you can use the JAX-RPC servlet-container-based Java-class-programming model. In the JAX-RPC servlet-container-based model, a JAX-RPC service endpoint is used and the service implementation is a Java class in the Web container. EJB requires the stateless-session EJB programming model. In the EJB model, an EJB service endpoint is used and the service implementation is a stateless session bean in the EJB container. The two models supply support for *port components* — or *ports* for short — which provide the server view of a Web service. Here are some of the things that port components do:

✦ Take advantage of the current J2EE-container offerings as well as using popular programming models

✦ Ensure a set plan for growing into more complex runtime service requirements

✦ Present a common client view by hiding the details of how the service is actually implemented

✦ Ensure a Web-services programming model that is portable

Now let's take a look at the following important sections that are defined by the Port:

✦ WSDL

✦ Service-implementation bean

✦ EJB container

✦ Web container

WSDL

As you know, WSDL actually describes the service and includes binding information, providing a platform and language-neutral declaration of the service interface and how to invoke the service. It essentially serves as the contract between clients and the service. So long as the service upholds the contract by not changing the interface, clients can access the service without regard for changes that may have been made to the service implementation.

Service Endpoint interface

The `Service Endpoint` interface defines the methods of a Web service. The methods are implemented by the service-implementation bean and are accessible to various clients.

Service-implementation bean

The service-implementation bean is best described as a Java class that describes the contract a port has for a container. It is similar to the `Service Endpoint` interface (SEI) but it doesn't have to implement the SEI. The service-implementation bean also handles the interaction between the services provided by the container and the actual business logic. The service-implementation bean can be implemented by a JAX-RPC service endpoint or a stateless session EJB.

EJB container

An EJB container is a Java environment (either part of the main JVM, or a separate JVM instance) designed to manage enterprise beans and provide them with managed access to enterprise resources. You will only have an EJB container if your architecture includes Enterprise JavaBeans.

Here is a list of the requirements for establishing a service-implementation bean (SIB) as a stateless session EJB:

> A default public constructor is required.
>
> All the method signatures of the `Service Endpoint` interface must be implemented.
>
> None of the business methods can be final or static and have to be declared as public.
>
> Any state relating to the client cannot be saved throughout method calls; an SIB must be a stateless object.
>
> The class cannot define the `finalize()` method and the class has to be declared as public.
>
> An SIB also has to implement the `ejbRemove()` and `ejbCreate()` methods. Empty implementations can be used as well. Following is an example of an EJB-service-endpoint implementation.

If you plan on exposing an existing EJB, the exposed business methods of the EJB must meet the requirements for SIB (discussed earlier). According to the specifications, the SEI methods have to be a subset of the remote-interface methods of the EJB.

The JAX-RPC specification for Java-to-WSDL mapping defines requirements that the `Service Endpoint` interface must adhere to. The SEI methods have transaction attributes that cannot include `Mandatory`.

Lastly, the port in the Web-services deployment descriptor needs an ejb-link to your EJB and the entire Web service has to be packaged as defined in Section 5.4 of the Web services for J2EE specifications. For more detailed coverage of implementing EJBs and Web services please refer to Chapter 15.

The Web container

A J2EE Web container is similar to an EJB container in that it is a Java environment (part of the main JVM, or a separate instance) designed to manage Java components. J2EE Web containers do not manage EJBs. Instead, they manage the lifecycles of servlets and JSPs. You will only have a Web container if your architecture includes servlets, JSPs, or both.

The JAX-RPC service endpoint is used for Web services that run within the Web container. The requirements are very similar to those of the EJB container. Here is the only major difference that the specifications note in the requirements:

"The Service Implementation Bean may implement the Service Endpoint Interface as defined by the JAX-RPC Servlet model. The bean must implement all the method signatures of the SEI. In addition, a Service Implementation Bean may be implemented that does not implement the SEI. This additional requirement provides the same SEI implementation flexibility as provided by EJB service endpoints. The business methods of the bean must be public and must not be static. If the Service Implementation Bean does not implement the SEI, the business methods must not be final. The Service Implementation Bean may implement other methods in addition to those defined by the SEI, but only the SEI methods are exposed to the client."(Java Specification Request 109, section 5.3.2.2)."

The following is an example of a `Service` interface:

```
import java.rmi.Remote:
import.java.rmi.RemoteException;
public interface FlightName extends Remote {
        public String sendName() throws RemoteException;
}
```

An optional but important part of the Web-container environment is the ability to implement the `ServiceLifeCycle` interface. The `ServiceLifeCycle` interface informs the service-implementation bean when there are changes in its state. If `ServiceLifeCycle` is implemented, the container has to call the `init` method before making requests. If the container wants to delete an instance of the bean from the working set, it must call the `destroy` method. The following example is a JAX-RPC servlet-endpoint implementation of the `FlightName` interface:

```
import java.rmi.*;
import javax.xml.rpc.*;
import javax.xml.rpc.server*;

public class FlightNameService implements FlightName,
ServiceLifecycle {

    public void init(Object context) throws JAXRPCException {}

public String sendName()throws RemoteException {

    return ("DFWtoLAX");

 }
 public void destroy(){}
}
```

So far we have discussed the server and client programming models. In the next section we will discuss the important topic of Web-service deployment descriptors.

Web-service deployment descriptors

The Web-services deployment descriptor describes the Web services that will be deployed in the container. It may include the following information:

✦ **Port name** — A unique port name needs to be created for use in the `<port-component-name>` element.

✦ **Bean class** — The `<service-impl-bean>` element holds the implementation information. The bean identified here must refer to a class that implements methods of the `Service Endpoint` interface. As you know, the JAX-RPC service endpoint can be implemented for Web (servlet) applications and the stateless session bean for EJB.

✦ `Service Endpoint` **interface** — The class name of the `Service Endpoint` interface is specified here in the `<service-endpoint-interface>` element.

✦ **WSDL definition for port** — The `<wsdl-file>` element contains the location of the WSDL description.

✦ **QName for port** — Allows the `QName` for each individual `<wsdl-port>` to be described.

✦ **JAX-RPC mapping** — This is where the association between the WSDL definition and the interfaces is specified. The element used is `<jaxrpc-mapping-file>`.

✦ **Handler** — The `handler` element enables you to specify optional handlers.

✦ **Servlet mapping** — For a JAX-RPC service endpoint, a servlet mapping may be specified in the deployment descriptor.

The Web Services for J2EE v1 specifications provide a DTD for the Web-services deployment descriptor that can help explain the descriptor in detail. For more information, download JSR 109 at `ftp://www-126.ibm.com/pub/jsr109/spec/1.0/websvcs-1_0-fr.pdf`. The DTD is found in Section 7.1.5.

Summary

We began this chapter by observing how various J2EE components can participate in a Web-services exchange. We showed that HTTP servlets are a natural choice for exposing Web-service interfaces because they already understand HTTP, incorporate a request-response programming model, scale easily and smoothly to handle an increasing load, and enjoy the widest support among the development community in terms of skills, tools, and best practices. We also discussed JMS as an excellent Web service–enabling component. The enterprise messaging aspects of JMS (guaranteed delivery, message delivery models like publish-subscribe, and the inherent support for asynchronous communication) make it a particularly compelling choice if you need to support asynchronous service exchanges and/or adopt a message-delivery model. Finally, we introduced the idea of directly exposing EJBs as Web-service components. We identified the strength that EJBs provide with respect to accessing enterprise resources, but also recognized the lack of an HTTP-handling mechanism, and the increased complexity that EJBs introduce into a J2EE architecture. We also discussed various tools that facilitate the integration of Web services and J2EE.

In this chapter we also introduced one of the first significant milestones in the formation of J2EE Web services, JSR 109, the first significant attempt by the industry to specify how to incorporate Web services into a J2EE architecture in a standardized way. We identified the goals of JSR 109, as well as the various programming models, significant components, and architectural concepts defined by the specification.

The Web-services landscape is in a state of constant transition. The J2EE world, although dynamic, is much more mature, and thus not as fluid. In this chapter we have identified the current way in which Web services fit into the J2EE platform. While this is an accurate picture of how J2EE systems currently participate in a Web-services exchange, the picture is likely to change in the following months and years as Web services begin to mature.

✦   ✦   ✦

Patterns

P A R T

VII

◆ ◆ ◆ ◆

In This Part

Chapter 23
Reviewing
Presentation-Tier
Patterns

Chapter 24
Working with
Service-Tier Patterns

Chapter 25
Using Data-Tier
Patterns

◆ ◆ ◆ ◆

Reviewing Presentation-Tier Patterns

✦ ✦ ✦ ✦

In This Chapter

Providing an overview of patterns

Explaining the session pattern

Understanding the router pattern

Reviewing the model-view-controller pattern

Using the front-controller pattern

Working with the view-helper pattern

Using the composite-view pattern

Explaining the intercepting-filter pattern

✦ ✦ ✦ ✦

This chapter and the subsequent ones introduce you to design patterns that can be used for developing J2EE applications. Design patterns are efficient solutions for recurring problems. Enterprise applications designed with design patterns provide a common vocabulary to the team members, and they help to leverage a proven solution by constraining the solution space. We are going to start with a definition of the word *pattern*. We will then review when patterns were used first. Finally, we will define our model of the Web and apply patterns to the different components of the Web model that we propose.

Providing an Overview of Patterns

According to *The American Heritage Dictionary*, a *pattern* is "A plan, diagram, or model to be followed in making things." Leonard Da Vinci's Notebook captures some of the patterns used in his time for civil engineering. The inspiration for software design patterns stems from the documentation of architectural patterns used in Civil Engineering and Architecture in the classic work by Christopher Alexander, *A Pattern Language: Towns, Buildings, Construction* (Alexander, Ishikawa, and Silverstein 1977, Oxford Press). This book strongly influenced the book *Design Patterns Elements of Reusable Object-Oriented Software* (Erich Gamma, Richard Helm, Ralph Johnson, John Vlissides, 1995, Addison-Wesley), by the so-called Gang of Four (GOF). The Gang of Four (Erich Gamma, Richard Helm, Ralph Johnson, and John Vlissides) are internationally recognized experts in the field of Object Oriented Technology. Dr. John Vlissides currently serves as the series editor for *The Software Pattern Series* (Addison-Wesley publications).

As we use the concept of patterns in designing software systems hence the name design patterns. A design pattern describes a problem, which occurs consistently in the domain of the problem and describes the core solution of the problem enabling the reuse of this solution across similar problems encountered in the domain without reinventing the wheel.

There are many books on design patterns including finitely countable for Java Programming Language. Different authors have classified design patterns according to the intent of the pattern. We are going to classify design patterns based on the simplified view of the Web-tier model as depicted in Figure 23-1. As you can see, this figure simplifies the overall Web tier into three tiers.

Figure 23-1: Simplified Web-tier model

Note   The terms *pattern* and *design pattern* will be used interchangeably throughout this book.

Presentation-tier patterns represent solutions to the most common problems in the presentation tier of a Web model. Therefore, they can be used as blueprints for solving those problems. Some of the common presentation-tier problems are controlling code in multiple views, exposing data structures in presentation tier directly to service tier, allowing duplicate submission of forms and exposing sensitive resources to direct client access.

We will present the following patterns in this chapter:

✦ **Session pattern** — Helps in the creation of an association of state between client-server systems communication.

✦ **Router pattern** — Decouples multiple information sources from the information target.

✦ **Model-view-controller pattern** — Helps in breaking the enterprise system into three logical parts, namely model, view, and controller, for maintainability and extensibility.

✦ **Front-controller pattern** — Helps in coordinating access to system services, content views and navigation views across multiple requests in a centralized or decentralized manner.

✦ **View-helper pattern** — Helps in designing systems in which the presentation content must process dynamic business data and in which the intermingling of presentation and business processing must be avoided.

✦ **Composite-view pattern** — Helps enterprise applications containing Web pages, which gather data from numerous sources and use multiple views that map to a single Web page by providing multiple atomic sub-views where each sub-view can be included dynamically into the whole Web page and the page layout can be maintained independently of the content.

✦ **Intercepting-filter pattern** — Provides a mechanism for intercepting requests and responses and does pre-processing and post-processing actions before passing them to the appropriate handler.

The patterns covered in this chapter and the next two are organized into the following sections:

✦ **Forces** — Describes the considerations you need to take into account while documenting the pattern. These considerations include environmental, linguistic, organizational, and platform issues. Recognizing forces that cause the problem is an extremely complex process.

✦ **Implementation** — Deals with the solution to the problem in context.

✦ **Strategies** — Describes the various collaborations that can be implemented in using the pattern apart from the regular way.

✦ **Results** — Includes any issues that still need to be resolved after the pattern is applied.

✦ **Sample code** — Describes through a skeleton sample code of how to implement the pattern or sometimes the class diagram is presented on how the pattern can be modeled or designed.

✦ **Related patterns** — Describes other patterns that are related to this pattern. Sometimes you can use a combination of patterns to resolve a recurring problem. You might even form a new pattern.

Having provided the template on how we are going to catalog the patterns in this and subsequent chapters, we are going to present next the patterns that can be used in the presentation tier. Sessions are an important concept in any client-server enterprise system. We continue with the discussion of the session pattern.

Explaining the Session Pattern

Most enterprise client-server and peer-to-peer (P2P) systems need to differentiate between clients and requests. This distinction becomes more challenging when the client-server is a distributed system. The session pattern enables you to associate state between the server and client for enterprise client-server and P2P systems using the Web as their infrastructure.

The session pattern also maintains an association of state between client-server communications or requests.

Forces

The following forces encourage the use of the session pattern:

If multiple clients are updating the information on the server, the server needs a way to track and to service different client requests.

Updates to information by different clients can create a state of flux on the server, and results in the server making wrong updates to different client information.

The need to distinguish clients in a multi-user environment

Client-server communications are transactional.

The persistence of data between client-server communications

Implementation

The session pattern provides a means by which the server can differentiate among different clients. In a transaction, this pattern helps the server track information about the client; for performance improvement on the server this pattern can cache the user information.

Figures 23-2 and 23-3 depict the structure of the session pattern. Figure 23-2 depicts a client-managed session, and Figure 23-3 depicts a server-managed session.

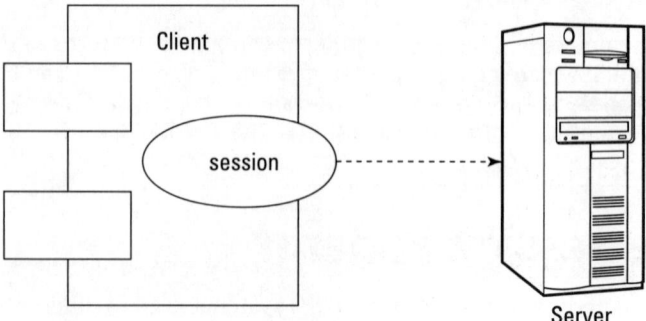

Figure 23-2: Client-maintained session

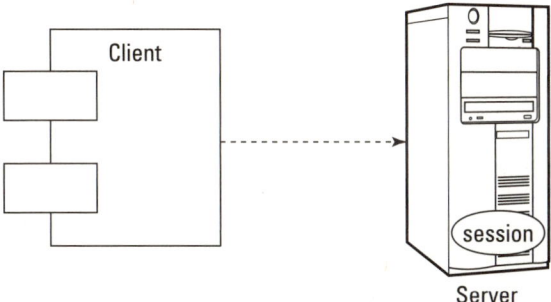

Figure 23-3: Server-managed session

Figure 23-2 represents how clients track their session with the server and Figure 23-3 is the opposite and it represents how servers manage sessions across from multiple clients.

Figure 23-4 shows the sequence diagram for the interaction between different components involved in a session pattern.

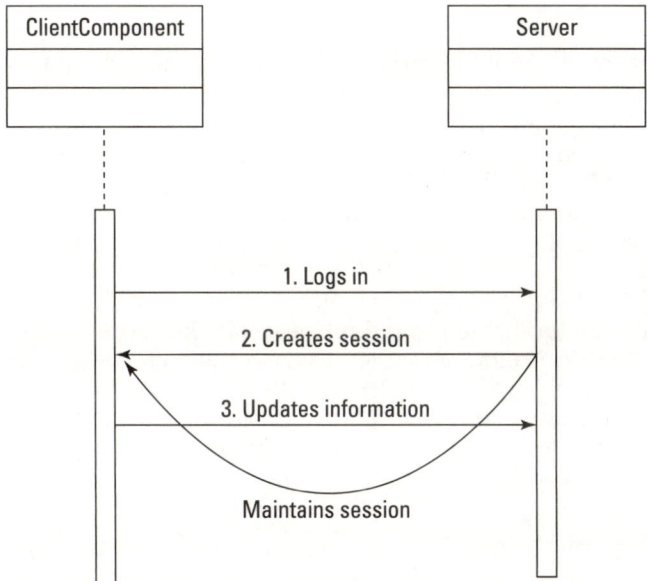

Figure 23-4: Sequence diagram for a session pattern

ClientComponent

`ClientComponent` is the client piece of client-server architecture; it can be an HTML document, a JavaServer page (JSP), or a servlet presenting information to the user, and the user can use it to update any information to the server.

Server

The server can be a Web server or an application server that services the requests of a client and maintains identification among different clients. It is the server part of the client-server architecture.

Strategies

According to the system requirements, the session pattern can be implemented as a stateful or stateless communication.

Stateful communication

The best example of stateful communication is the File Transfer Protocol (FTP) program, in which a socket connection is set up between the FTP client and the FTP server. Not every step in this transaction is sequential, and the server is aware of the client calls.

Session patterns and stateful communication occur when multiple interactions between client and server take place and information from the client is updated on the server. You can implement a session by setting an ID on the client browser or the machine. This ID is called a *session cookie* and it is sent across to the server with each client request. The cookie allows the server to identify the client for which it is fulfilling the request. An example of this procedure is Hotmail, where cookies are used for maintaining user sessions with the server. Banking sites are another good example.

Stateful communication can be implemented through *session identification* and *representation*. For session identification the server needs to maintain the state of the session over the lifetime of the application. For example, if somebody accesses Yahoo mail, session identification takes place through the user-provided login id. Session representation represents the state of the application. For example, the user might be in the *state* of a shopping cart.

Stateless communication

In stateless communication the server does not know which client it serviced. The HTTP protocol of the Web is an example of stateless communication. This implementation is good when a Web site is made of static pages and session tracking need not be implemented.

Results

The session pattern enables the following consequences:

> The important advantage is servicing requests and maintaining states of the application.

> If the client identity is established, the Session can assume the role of managing accountability and prioritize any access to the server side access need to process the request of the client.

> The main drawback of this pattern is an increase in the server workload. This workload can arise from different cases, the most common being validation of each client for each request. This kind of scenario is common in Web services in which the user accesses a portal and is connected to another site to track his or her 401(K) options, for example.

Session pattern – UML diagram and sample code

The UML class diagram shown in Figure 23-5 shows how a session can be used to create and destroy sessions. Notice how `SessionHandler` can create either zero or more sessions' objects of the session class.

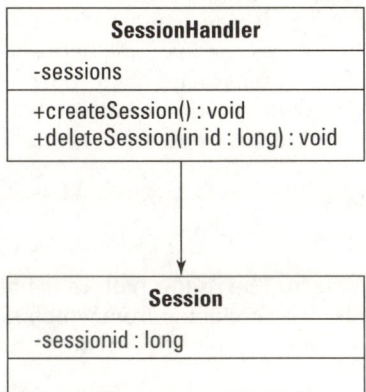

Figure 23-5: Class diagram for implementing the session pattern

Related patterns

No related patterns exist for the session pattern.

With the session pattern we have seen how we can provide state between client and server requests. Next, we move to the router pattern whose functionality is similar to the router in a network switch.

Understanding the Router Pattern

A router pattern helps to decouple multiple information sources from their information targets. A router pattern is used much like the network router that routes traffic based on the message and its intended recipient.

Forces

The following forces encourage the use of the router pattern:

Multiple sources of information exist for an enterprise application.

Multiple destinations have to receive information from these sources.

Implementation

The router pattern incorporates logic to route requests from their sources to the appropriate destinations. The function of the router pattern is similar to that of the router in the network traffic. The router usually captures the mapping between different sources and destination. Based on the incoming message from a source, the router directs it to the appropriate destination. The router pattern, rather than the source, can provide methods with which to add and remove different destinations.

 Note   Multiple sources can have different destinations.

Figure 23-6 depicts the structure of the router pattern. The router pattern is used to process the client requests. Based on what needs to be collected from which data storage source, this pattern routes requests to the appropriate type of data storage.

Figure 23-7 shows the sequence diagram for the interaction among different components involved in a router pattern.

ClientComponent

`ClientComponent` can be any HTML, JSP, or servlet requesting information from two different data sources.

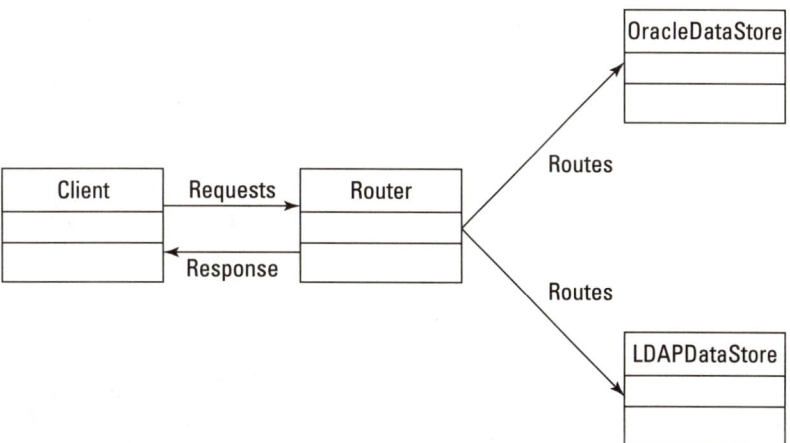

Figure 23-6: Implementing the router pattern

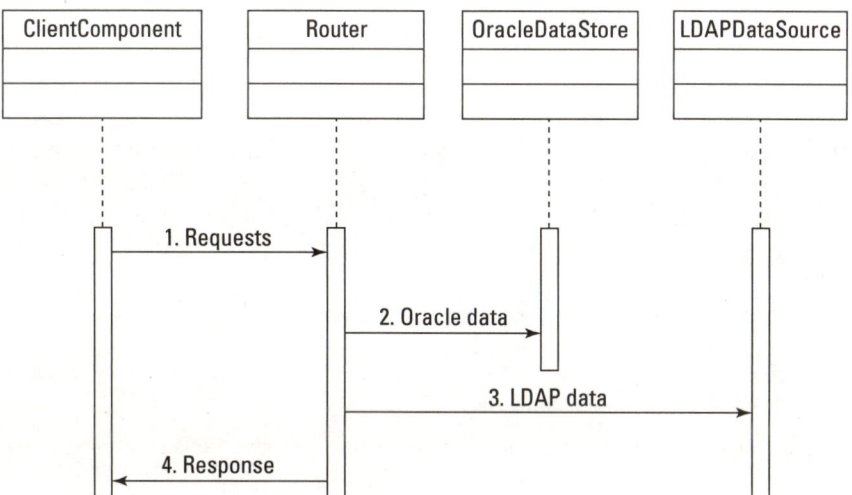

Figure 23-7: Sequence diagram for the router pattern

Router

Based on client requests the router has logic built in to route the requests to both the Oracle and the Lightweight Directory Access Protocol (LDAP) data stores and present the information back to the client.

OracleDataStore

`OracleDataStore` has information stored in an Oracle database. It also has a business component that processes router requests and sends back the information.

LDAPDataStore

`LDAPDataStore` has information stored in the LDAP database. It also has a business component that processes router requests and sends back the information.

Strategies

The router can track the sources and their destinations through a mapping. Methods can be provided to add destinations and delete destinations rather than registering the destinations with the source. Based on the bytes of information passed, the throughput of the information should be handled as fast as possible. If throughput is not handled fast, the application slows down. The router should have the intelligence built in to drop target if failure in throughput occurs. This guarantees the quality of service (QOS) for other destinations that do not have this problem.

A variation of the router pattern involves making the mapping between arbitrary key and destinations. In a normal implementation of the router pattern for any source one route always exists. By registering an arbitrary key with the router, it is possible to have more than one route for a source.

Results

The router pattern enables the following consequences:

> Source and destination can be decoupled, enabling the input to know the router and not the destination.

> Trouble in one channel does not affect the other channels in the system.

> The router can associate a new thread with a channel.

> Client logic is simplified because of the message-distribution role assumed by the router.

> Reliability in messaging is enhanced.

The router pattern — sample code

The skeleton code in Listing 23-1 shows how to implement a router pattern.

Listing 23-1: **Code for the router pattern**

```
public class RouterPattern implements OutputChannel{
  //constructor
public RouterPattern(){
  }
  public synchronized void deliverMessage(Message msg){
  }
  //can store a internal HashMap to store these destinations.
public void addRoute(InputChannel source, OutputChannel[ ]
destinations){
  }
}
```

Listing 23-2 includes the code for the interface implemented by the Router class.

Listing 23-2: **Code for OutputChannel**

```
public class OutputChannel extends Remote{
  public void deliverMessage(Message msg);
}
```

Listing 23-3 includes the code for the InputChannel that is used by the Message class.

Listing 23-3: **Code for InputChannel**

```
public interface InputChannel extends Serializable{;}
```

As shown in Listing 23-4, the Message class creates the instance of the InputChannel and returns it whenever the getSource method is called.

Listing 23-4: **Code for Message**

```
//as EJB 2.0 requires data store classes to implement
serializable interface
public class Message implements Serializable{
```

Continued

Listing 23-4 *(continued)*

```
   private InputChannel src;
   private String message;
   //constructor
public Message(InputChannel source, String msg){
   //set the InputChannel and message attributes here.
   }
   //method to return the source.
   public InputChannel getSource( ){
        return src;
        }
        //method to return the msg
        public String getMessage(){
             return message;
             }
}
```

Related patterns

Patterns that can be used in combination with this pattern include the following:

✦ Mediator

✦ Observer

✦ WorkerThread

More information about the patterns is available in *Applied Java Patterns* by Stephen Stelting (Olav Maassen, 2002, PH PTR).

The next section describes the model-view-controller pattern, which is also known as the Web2 pattern. This pattern is primarily useful for designing client-server systems as separate components.

Reviewing the Model-View-Controller Pattern

A model-view controller (MVC) enables an enterprise system to be broken into these three logical parts:

✦ Model

✦ View

✦ Controller

This scheme greatly enhances maintenance, code extensibility, scalability, and modifiability of enterprise systems. Interweaving presentation, business logic, and data access is better for a single type of client, but given the way the Internet has evolved, Figure 23-8 suggests the requirements for developing an enterprise system nowadays.

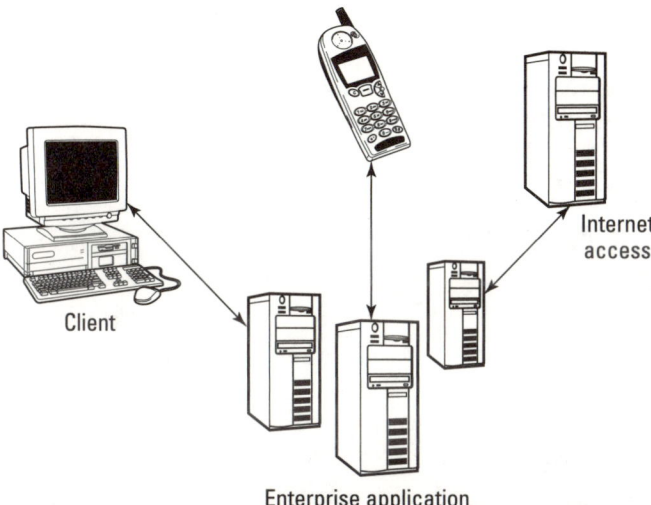

Figure 23-8: Example of the model-view-controller pattern

Nowadays we have to develop applications for different lines of users, such as Web browsers, Wireless Devices and Web services. Having a single monolithic system do all the processing is cumbersome, so the MVC approach is called for.

An enterprise system can be broken into three logical parts, model, view, and controller, for maintainability and extensibility. The software team doing design, implementation, and maintenance will be comprised of individuals with different skills.

Forces

The following forces encourage the use of the model-view-controller pattern:

> Components or subsystems can be viewed in different ways, for example as HTML, as WML, as XML, and so on.
>
> Multiple sources can invoke different behavior on the same component.
>
> The behavior of the component changes with the use of the component.
>
> Representation of the component changes with the use of the component.

The component can be reused with minimum recoding.

Supporting multiple views and interactions should not affect components that process and provide the core functions in the enterprise system.

Implementation

MVC provides decoupling of business components from the view or presentation and the controller, which uses the business component. Different presentation models can use the same underlying data model so that multiple clients like Hypertext Markup Language (HTML), Wireless Markup Language (WML), and the eXtensible Markup Language (XML) can all be implemented and easily maintained.

Figure 23-9 depicts the structure of the model-view-controller pattern. The Controller component provides different views based on what data needs to be shown.

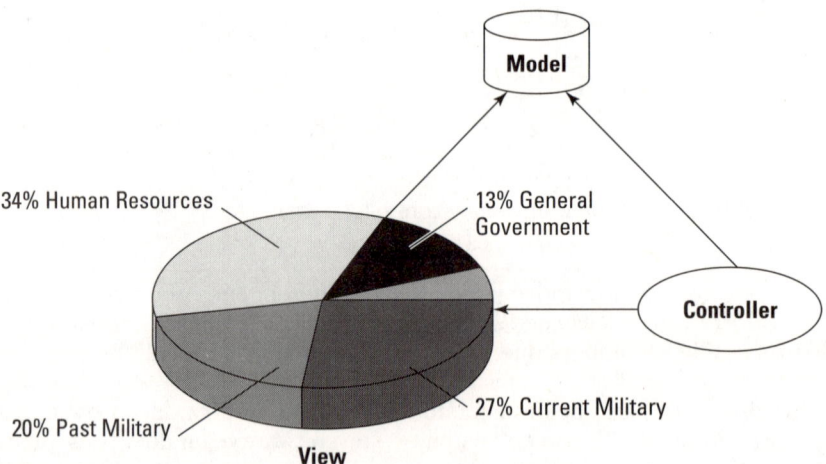

Figure 23-9: Example of model-view-controller pattern

Figure 23-10 shows the sequence diagram for the interaction among different components involved in an MVC pattern.

View

The view displays the model. Push or pull technology can be used with the view to show the updated model. In the push model, as in the delegation model of AWT (Abstract Window Toolkit), the view can register with the model and the model will notify the view whenever there is an update. In the pull model, the view can get updates from the model whenever necessary.

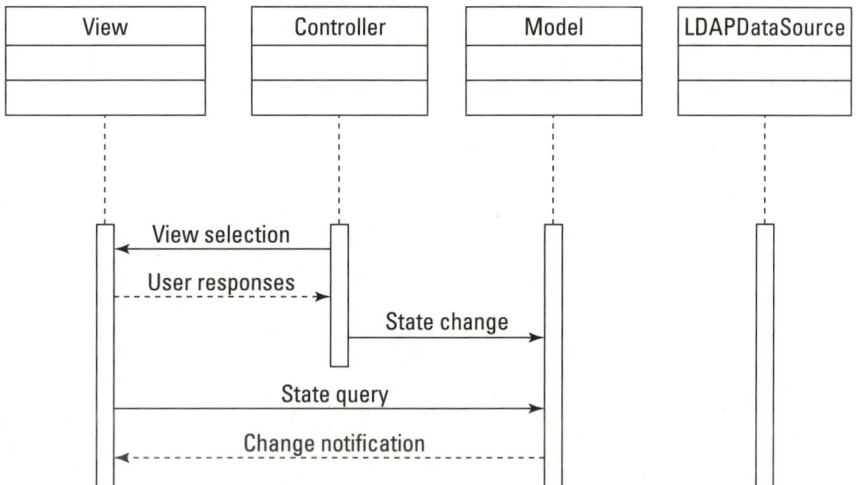

Figure 23-10: Sequence diagram for the MVC pattern

Controller

The controller manages the flow between the view and the model. Based on the action in the view the controller translates it to the action that is to be performed by the model. For example let us consider a Web application form where a participant of the Web application is updating his personal information. Hitting an update button on participant information can cause the controller to notify the participant model to fetch the data for the database.

Model

The model represents both the business logic and the data used to represent the view. Business logic manipulates data and the view queries the model in order to display information to the user.

Strategies

The view can be implemented using HTML, JavaServer Pages (JSP), or servlets. The controller can be a servlet that translates the requests from the view to the model. The model can be split into two components: a business-logic component, often implemented as an EJB, and data represented in a database like Oracle.

Results

The MVC pattern enables the following consequences:

Separating the various components of the application into layers enables the reuse of the model components across applications. Teams can also work independently in completing the layer and integrate it later. The MVC pattern works well with Xtreme programming. *Xtreme programming* is a software methodology that is applied in projects involving small teams. One of the main principles of this methodology is splitting the team on a role-based activity. Sub-teams then interact with each other in a way that all the members of the development team have a hands-on experience with the different parts of the application. In a way, this is effective because all the members of the team own the application. It was developed to provide collaboration within the team.

Any new client can be easily wired into the architecture, as only the view and some logic for the controller need be written.

The complexity of the design and architecture increase with the additional layers.

The model-view-controller pattern — sample code

The skeleton code in Listing 23-5 shows how a controller for a MVC pattern can be implemented.

Listing 23-5: **Code for the controller**

```
public class Controller extends HttpServlet{
Map actionClasses = new HashMap();
Map routingClasses = new HashMap();
static{
  //wire code for mapping action classes for example
  actionClasses.put("Login" ,"LoginServlet");
  // wire code for the routing class for example
  routingClasses.put("ChangePassword","ChangePasswordSpecificActions");
}
public void init() throws ServletException{
}
public void service(HttpServletRequest request,
HttpServletResponse response) throws ServletException, IOException {
String pgActions = actionClasses.get("Login");
//invoke the logic for model class as below.
Class actionClass = Class.forName(pgActions);
//note that the LoginServlet implements a common interface.
actionClass.process(request,response);
  }
}
```

Listing 23-6 provides the code for the model part of the model-view-controller pattern.

Listing 23-6: **Code for the model**

```
public class LoginServlet implements RequestHandler{
  //default constructor
  public LoginServlet(){
  }
  //method in the RequestHandler interface
  public void process(HttpRequest request, HttpResponse response){
  //write processing code here.
  }
}
```

In the sample code in Listing 23-6, look at how `LoginServlet` is called. `LoginServlet` implements an interface, which is a strategy pattern. The `Controller` servlet functions as the gateway for the application forwarding requests to the needed models from the view, which is a JSP page; the code is not shown here. (More details on the strategy pattern can be found in the book *Design Patterns Elements of Reusable Object-Oriented Software* by Erich Gamma, Richard Helm, Ralph Johnson, John Vlissides, 1995, Addison-Wesley.)

Listing 23-7 provides the method for the Request Handler that is implemented by the Model component in Listing 23-6.

Listing 23-7: **Code for the interface**

```
public  interface RequestHandler{
  public void process(HttpRequest request, HttpResponse response){
  }
}
```

Related patterns

Patterns that can be used in combination with this pattern include the following:

✦ Observer

✦ Strategy

Please refer to the *Design Patterns* by GOF for more details.

Next, we move to discussing another important pattern of the presentation tier namely, the front-controller pattern, which forms the controller part of the MVC pattern.

Using the Front-Controller Pattern

The front-controller pattern plays the controller role in the MVC pattern. Consider the following scenario: An airline reservation Web site, with views for flight arrivals, flight reservations, and so on as menu items. The view navigation is going to be the same across these different views. If each view were to maintain its own system services and navigation then there would be duplication of code across different views. This would mean that a change in navigation would have to be updated in the view. A front-controller pattern is used to avoid this scenario. It coordinates processing of multiple requests for each user accessing the site in a centralized or decentralized manner.

The front-controller pattern coordinates access to system services, view content, and view navigation across multiple requests in a centralized or decentralized manner based on how you want to design the access coordination.

Forces

The following forces encourage the use of front-controller pattern:

> Common application processing is made per request.

> Processing logic can be centralized in a single controller rather than duplication occurring across numerous views.

> Request handling is centralized.

> System services and view management are complex.

> Different views might have code duplication for the same navigation items that is same across all these views.

Implementation

The front controller acts as the gateway to the enterprise application. It can handle authentication, delegate business processing, manage views (based on servlet or JSP), handle errors, and log access. Usually a dispatcher pattern can be used in conjunction with the front controller; in such a scenario the dispatcher will maintain view management and navigation. An enterprise application can have multiple controllers, each providing a distinct set of system services. For example, a controller might provide role-based access to a system, and a controller might log messages within the application.

Figure 23-11 depicts the structure of the front-controller design pattern. Note the front controller to which all the client requests are forwarded and which generates based on whether it is a flight arrival or a flight reservation.

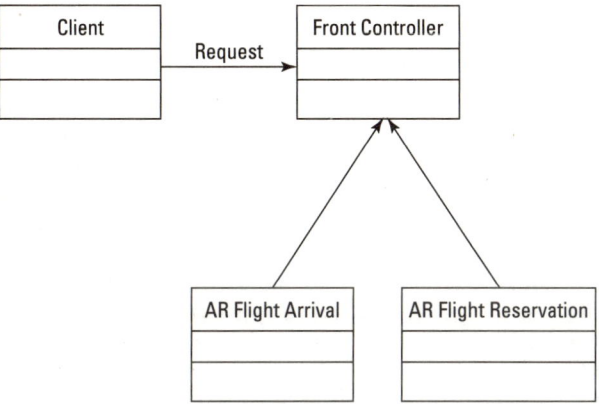

Figure 23-11: Example of the front-controller pattern

Figure 23-12 shows the sequence diagram for the interaction between different components involved in a front-controller pattern.

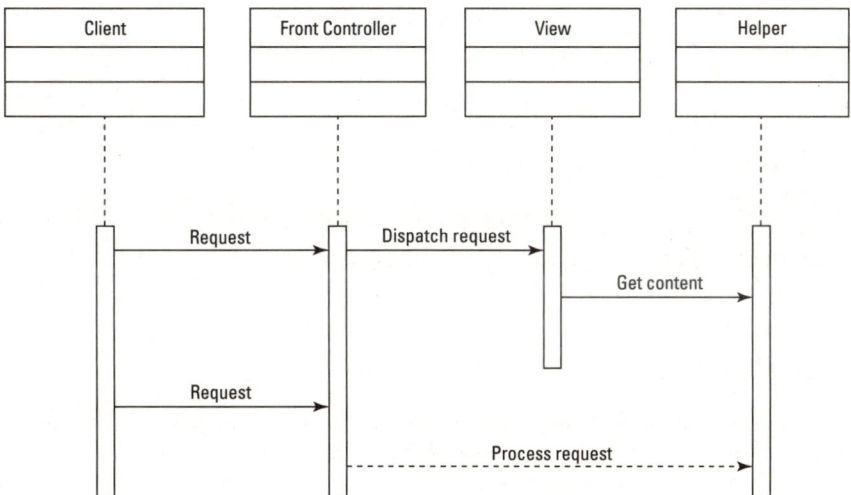

Figure 23-12: Sequence diagram for the front-controller pattern

The various components that participate in the sequence diagram are explained next.

Front controller

The front controller is the gateway to handle the entire request to any views or backend systems. It may implement a dispatcher to delegate requests to a helper to complete system services or retrieve information.

View

The view corresponds to the view component in a MVC. The view may retrieve data from a model and display the information. Helpers encapsulate the data model and help the view use the model for presentation.

Helper

The helper helps either a front controller or a view complete requests. The helper encapsulates the underlying data model and provides data to the view and the view can manipulate and display data. For example, in an application the Extensible Stylesheet Language Transformations (XSLT) template serves as the view and the servlet can generate the XML, which is raw data. The template engine can merge the XML data with the XSLT template and render the HTML page.

Strategies

Several different strategies for implementing a controller are possible. We list all of them but will be discussing only a couple of important ones.

✦ The multiplexed-resource-mapping strategy

✦ The command-and-controller strategy

✦ The servlet-front strategy

✦ The physical-resource-mapping strategy

✦ The logical-resource-mapping strategy

The multiplexed-resource-mapping strategy

In this strategy the front-controller pattern can be used to map two different resources to the same servlet. For example, a servlet serves information for a person within the U.S. and also for a person sitting on the other side of the globe, say in Germany like an offshore client. Then the servlet can be given two different names, such as `USProcessServlet` and `OffshoreProcessServlet`, but can be mapped to the same underlying class in both instances.

The command-and-controller strategy

This is a combination of the command-pattern and front-controller patterns. It is a very powerful pattern that provides a generic interface to which the front controller may delegate the responsibility. Using the command pattern requires minimal or no changes to the controller and the helper. As command processing and invocation are decoupled the command processor can be used with various clients.

The servlet-front strategy

In this strategy the front controller is implemented as a servlet. This servlet manages request handling, business logic, and application flow. Display formatting is separate. This strategy has a drawback: It does not leverage automatic population of request parameters into helper properties.

Results

The front-controller pattern enables the following consequences:

Improves security management; thereby controlling hacks into the Web application. Auditing is made simple.

All the request-handling processes are managed by a centralized control access. This enables easy tracking and logging of requests.

Promotes code reusability.

The front-controller pattern – sample code

The skeleton code in Listing 23-8 shows how to implement a front controller using the command-and-controller strategy.

Listing 23-8: Code for the command-and-front-controller strategy

```java
public class FrontController extends HttpServlet{
  public void init() throws ServletException{
  }
  public void service(HttpServletRequest request,
          HttpServletResponse response) throws
ServletException, IOException {
        String displayPage;

        try{
                Helper h = new Helper(request);
                CommandPattern cmd = h.getCommandPattern();
                displayPage = cmd.execute(request,response);

        }catch(Exception e){
                //a wrapper for log4j.jar from apache open source.
                Log4jWrapper.log("FrontController Pattern", e);
                //take the user to a error page.
        }
        dispatch(request, response, displayPage);
  }
}
```

The front-controller servlet calls the command pattern to process the command. The command pattern in turn creates the corresponding display page that is to be passed to the dispatcher. The output result is sent to the dispatcher to display the appropriate view.

Related patterns

Patterns that can be used in combination with this pattern include the following:

- ✦ View helper
- ✦ Intercepting filter
- ✦ Dispatcher view and service to worker

The intercepting-filter and view-helper patterns are discussed in this chapter. For more details on the dispatcher-view and service-to-worker patterns, consult *Core J2EE Patterns* by Deepak Alur, John Crupi and Dan Malks (Sun Microsystems Press, 2001).

Next, we will move on the view-helper pattern. As the name suggests, this pattern solves the problem of views that change frequently. For example, in a Web site the look and feel might change based on different users of the system.

Working with the View-Helper Pattern

In an enterprise system, in which presentation and business processing are combined, changes occur frequently and are costly to maintain when the presentation formatting changes. This makes the enterprise application less reusable, less modular, and less flexible to changes. No clear distinction exists between Web-production and software-development teams.

The view-helper pattern is useful in places in which presentation content must process dynamic business data, and in which the intermingling of presentation and business processing needs to be avoided.

Forces

The following forces encourage the use of the view-helper pattern:

View (each) processes a specific business request.

The business-data-requirement-gathering process is complex.

Differentiate between roles in an application team like the Web-production team and the software-development team.

A maintenance problem exists because of the intermingling of presentation and business followed by code duplication all over the system.

Implementation

The view usually contains code for formatting and presenting data. It may delegate the processing of data to the view-helper pattern. This pattern stores the intermediate data model and serves the purpose of a business-data adapter. It makes code more reusable, modular, and flexible to changes. A front controller can be used with this pattern to handle requests; otherwise the view handles them.

Figure 23-13 depicts the structure of the view-helper design pattern.

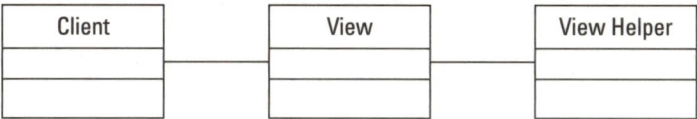

Figure 23-13: Example of view-helper pattern

Figure 23-14 shows the sequence diagram for the interaction among different components involved in a view-helper pattern.

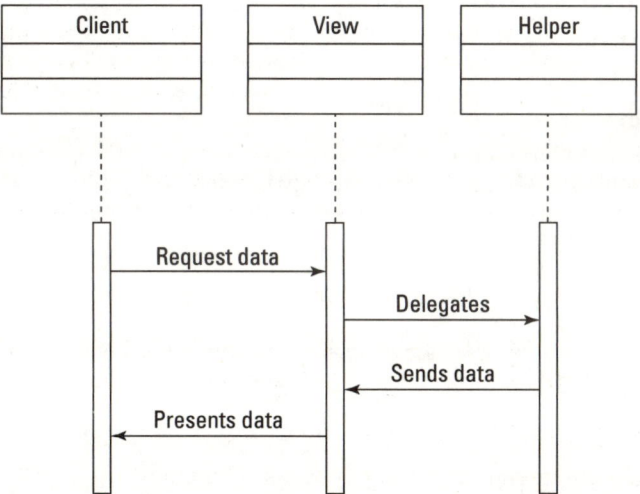

Figure 23-14: Sequence diagram for the view-helper pattern

Client

The client is typically a Web browser that requests the view to format and display data.

View

The view formats and displays the data to the client. The business data to display is retrieved from the underlying data model.

Helper

The helper is responsible for helping the viewer or controller complete processing. The helper gathers data and formats them as necessary for the Web content. Helpers can service requests for data from the view by providing raw data either as XML or as format data.

Strategies

Several different strategies can be used to implement a view-helper pattern. We list all of them but will be discussing only a couple of important ones.

✦ The JSP-view strategy

✦ The servlet-view strategy

✦ The JavaBean-helper strategy

✦ The custom-tag-helper strategy

✦ The business-delegate-helper strategy

✦ The transformer-helper strategy

The JSP-view strategy

In this strategy a JSP is the view component. Both Java code and markup language are intermingled. The only problem with this strategy is that no clear distinction is made between roles, and consequently it is easier to introduce problems into the system.

The servlet-view strategy

The servlet-view strategy uses servlets for a view. Intermingling of Java and markup code is done within the servlet. JSP is preferred over the servlet because of the compilation efforts.

The JavaBean-helper strategy

In this strategy a JavaBean is used in the JSP or servlet view and can be directly called to get data from the backend systems. This strategy is easier to construct because less development effort is required to construct a JavaBean. This results in a cleaner separation of code between business logic and application.

Results

The view-helper pattern enables the following consequences:

> All applications can be easily partitioned, reused and maintained. Business logic is factored out of JSPs (Java Server Pages) into the view-helper pattern.

> Separating business logic enables clear distinction among roles in an enterprise-development team.

The view-helper pattern — sample code

The skeleton code in Listing 23-9 shows how to implement a view helper using the JSP and the JavaBean-helper strategy.

Listing 23-9: Implementing a view helper using JSP and the JavaBean-helper strategy

```
<jsp:useBean id="loginHelper" scope="request"
class="LoginHelper" />
<HTML>
<head>
<title>Welcome Message</title>
</head>
<body>
  <% if (loginHelper.isValidUser())
  {
  %>
  <center><H2>Hi<b>
  <jsp:getProperty name="loginHelper" property="name"/>
  </b><br><br><br><H2></center>
  %>
  <H3><p align = center>Welcome to the world of Java Patterns
Site !</p></H3>
</body>
</html>
```

The JSP-view strategy is combined with the JavaBean-helper strategy to display messages to a valid user logging into a virtual Java-patterns site. If people are using the Apache Struts framework for development they can see a combination of the MVC and View-Helper strategies spread across the framework.

Related patterns

Patterns that can be used in combination with this pattern include the following:

✦ Business delegate

✦ Dispatcher view and service to worker

✦ Front controller

The business-delegate pattern is discussed in more detail in Chapter 24. The front controller is discussed in this chapter. More details on the dispatcher-view and service-to-worker patterns can be found in *Core J2EE Patterns* by Deepak Alur, John Crupi and Dan Malks, Sun Microsystems Press, 2001.

The next section covers the composite-view pattern, which creates an aggregrate view from subcomponents.

Using the Composite-View Pattern

Enterprise applications contain Web pages, which gather data from numerous sources and use multiple views that map to a single Web page. The enterprise-development team involves people with different skills to the development and hosting of the Web pages within the enterprise application.

In a composite-view pattern, the modules and atomic portions of a view are combined and embed directly into the view the code used to format the data. The important reason for using this pattern is because of the duplication of code for the same context across different views and fixing an error at one view has to be duplicated to other views.

Forces

The following forces encourage the use of the composite-view pattern:

Embedding the frequently changing code in the enterprise system, such as changing the header and footer on a view, affects the administration of the system. As a result of embedding the code the server has to be shut down and restarted for the changes to take place.

In Enterprise applications, atomic portions of the view change frequently.

Layout changes are difficult to maintain when they are embedded directly into the code, as these changes involves duplication of the code.

Implementation

In the composite-view pattern the views are composed of multiple sub-views that involve atomic contents of the enterprise application. This enables you to decouple the page layout from the content. This pattern also enables prototyping the layout for a site by plugging in static data and later replacing it with the actual contents for the site.

Figure 23-15 depicts the structure of the composite-view design pattern.

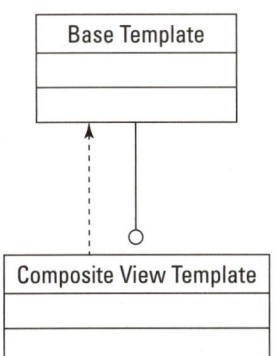

Figure 23-15: Example of the composite-view pattern

Figure 23-16 shows the sequence diagram for the interaction among different components involved in a composite-view pattern.

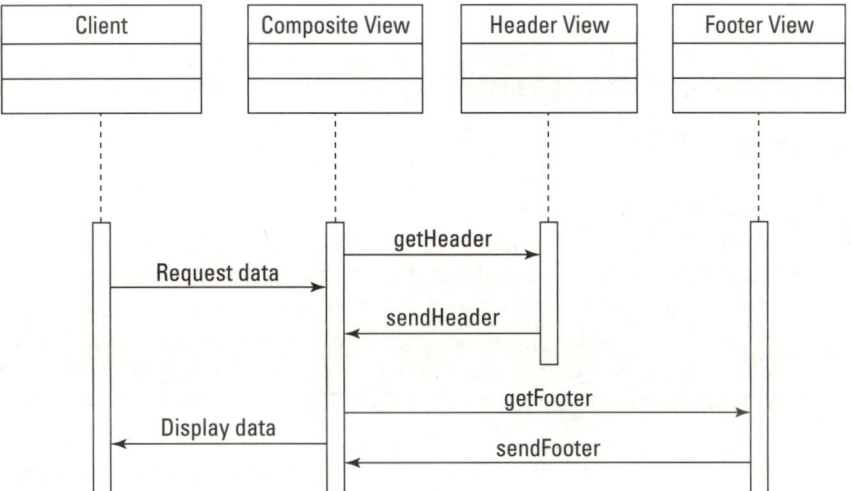

Figure 23-16: Sequence diagram for the composite-view pattern

Client

The client is typically a Web browser that requests view to format and display data.

Composite view

The composite view is a combination of different atomic components viewed in an enterprise application.

Header view

The header view is responsible for serving the static header data to the composite view.

Footer view

The footer view is responsible for serving the static footer data to the composite view.

Strategies

Several different strategies can be used to implement a composite-view pattern. We list all of them here but will be discussing only a couple of important ones:

- ✦ JSP-view strategy
- ✦ Servlet-view strategy
- ✦ Custom-tag-view-management strategy
- ✦ JavaBean-view-management strategy
- ✦ Standard-tag-view-management strategy
- ✦ Transformer-view-management strategy
- ✦ Early-binding-resource strategy
- ✦ Late-binding-resource strategy

The JSP-view strategy

In this strategy a JSP is the view component. Both Java code and markup language are intermingled. The only problem with this strategy is that no clear distinction is made between roles, and consequently it is easier to introduce problems into the system.

The servlet-view strategy

The servlet-view strategy uses servlets for a view. Intermingling of Java and markup code is done within the servlet. JSP is preferred over the servlet because of the compilation efforts.

The custom-tag-view-management strategy

In this strategy the management of the view is implemented through the custom tags in JSP. View layout and composition are controlled by the code within the custom tags. Based upon the user roles and security policies, page layout and composition can be designed. Building this strategy involves more development effort and more complexity is involved with respect to code integration and management. But this is the preferred strategy of all the strategies we have mentioned so far.

Results

The composite-view pattern enables the following consequences:

There is an increase in the flexibility of the content display, as it can be based on rules and roles within the security model used in the enterprise system.

Portions of the template can be easily changed, thereby increasing maintainability and manageability.

The pattern also promotes reuse and modularity within the existing code.

A runtime overhead is associated with this pattern because of the cohesion of different display pieces, which may also reduce manageability.

The composite-view pattern — sample code

The skeleton code in Listing 23-10 shows how to implement a composite-view pattern using the custom-tag-view-management strategy.

Listing 23-10: **Custom-tag-view-management strategy**

```
<region:render template='/classes/login.jsp'>
<region:put section='header' content='/classes/header.jsp'>
<region:put section='footer' content='/classes/footer.jsp'>
<region put section='mainContent'
content='/classes/maincontent.jsp'>
```

This example can be used with the Airline Reservation system in which the composite-view pattern can be used to present different atomic-content views within one single view using the custom-tag strategy.

Related patterns

Patterns that can be used in combination with this pattern include the following:

✦ View helper

✦ Composite

We next move to the last design pattern in the chapter—the intercepting-filter pattern. Filters are a new concept that were introduced with the Servlet API 2.3 specification.

Using the Intercepting-Filter Pattern

Client requests and responses have to be pre-processed and sometimes post-processed too. Typical checking mechanisms involve validating sessions, checking the content length, encoding types, version of the browser used by the client making the request, and so on. Most of these checks are usually performed by means of a typical if/else logic block. Some of the request headers need to be parsed before they are sent for further request handling, so an intercepting-filter pattern can be used. It provides a simple mechanism for adding and removing the processing of components. Each of these processing requests is associated with a filter-specific action.

The presentation tier gets different requests; some are to be handled as is, while others need to be modified. The intercepting-filter pattern can be applied in situations in which a request must be modified before being sent to a handler. Note that the introduction of filters in servlet API 2.3 is a good example of the use of the intercepting-filter pattern.

Forces

The following forces encourage the use of intercepting-filter pattern:

Some of the common application-request-checking mechanisms like logging, checking for appropriate headers, validating user sessions, and so on.

Common logic across the application needs to be centralized such as parsing header information to validate each request from a client.

Components can be easily added and removed. This in-turn helps to group a wide variety of components together.

Implementation

In the intercepting-filter pattern, incoming requests and outgoing responses are intercepted and pre- and post-processing actions are done. Using this filter pattern creates a pluggable architecture and they can be removed without any change to the rest of the application code. For example, it is possible in WebLogic Server to define a set of filters that map to URLs; when a request matches, one of these filters will be called before the appropriate handler processes the request.

Figure 23-17 depicts the structure of the intercepting-filter design pattern.

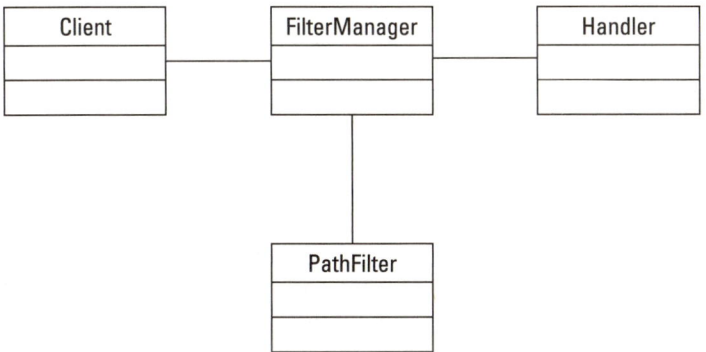

Figure 23-17: Example of the intercepting-filter pattern

Figure 23-18 shows the sequence diagram for the interaction between different components involved in an intercepting-filter pattern.

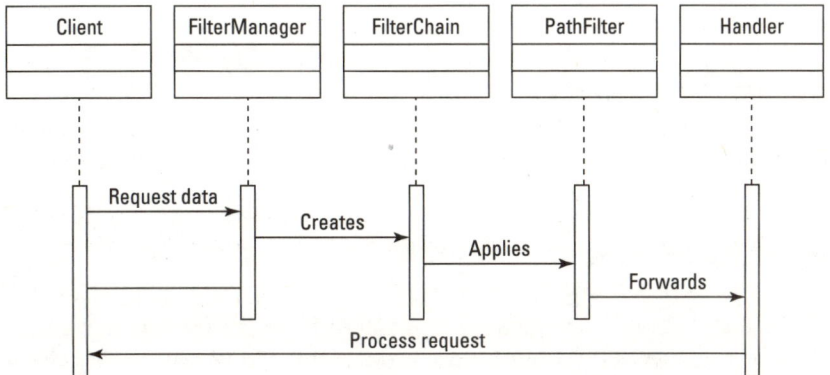

Figure 23-18: Sequence diagram for the intercepting-filter pattern

Client

The client is typically a Web browser that requests view to format and display data.

FilterManager

FilterManager manages filter processing, and usually creates the filter chain and loads the appropriate filters.

FilterChain

`FilterChain` contains the collection of filters for the application.

PathFilter

`PathFilter` checks for the path validation of incoming requests before forwarding the request to the handler.

Handler

The handler processes the client request.

Strategies

Several different strategies can be used to implement a custom-filter pattern. We list all of them but will be discussing only the important ones.

- ✦ The standard-filter strategy
- ✦ The base-filter strategy
- ✦ The custom-filter strategy
- ✦ The template-filter strategy

The standard-filter strategy

Filters can be declared in a deployment descriptor and added or removed just by means of modifying this deployment descriptor. In the standard-filter strategy filters are built around interfaces.

The base-filter strategy

A base filter serves as an abstraction for all common functionality across different filters in an application. This functionality can be shared across all filters. The base filter can include default behavior for all the servlet-container callback methods.

Results

The intercepting-filter pattern enables the following consequences:

Using filters creates a cleaner partition of application and promotes reusability of these filters across different applications. For example, an authentication filter checking for valid sessions and content length can be used across different applications.

Configuring filters is easy and centralizes control logic.

Sharing of information across filters is inefficient.

The intercepting-filter pattern – sample code

Listing 23-11 shows how to implement an intercepting-filter pattern using the base-filter strategy.

Listing 23-11: **Code for the base-filter strategy**

```
public class BaseFilter implements javax.servlet.Filter{
  private javax.servlet.FilterConfig filterConfig;

  //constructor
  public BaseFilter(){
  }

  //code for setting default container behavior
public void doFilter(ServletRequest req, ServletResponse res,
FilterChain fchain) throws IOException, ServletException{
  fchain.doFilter(req,res);
}
//get method
public FilterConfig getFilterConfig(){
  return filterConfig;
}
//set method
public void setFilterConfig(FilterConfig fconfig){
  filterConfig = fconfig;
}

}
```

This code is from a base filter that can be used in the airline reservation site for abstracting all the common filters used in the site.

Related patterns

Patterns that can be used in combination with this pattern include the following:

✦ Front controller

✦ Decorator

✦ Template method

✦ Interceptor

✦ Pipes and filters

Summary

In this chapter we discussed the presentation tier. Presentation-tier patterns play an important role in managing the presentation logic, providing a single control point for various systems, providing a decoupled Web design through MVC (which is the basis for the Apache's Struts framework), and using the composite view to manage different atomic contents in sub-views in a single Web page. More details on the Struts framework can be found from the Apache site at www.apache.org.

✦   ✦   ✦

Working with Service-Tier Patterns

In This Chapter

Introducing service-tier patterns

Using the business-delegate pattern

Understanding the value-object pattern

Exploring the session-facade pattern

Explaining the composite-entity pattern

Utilizing the service-locator pattern

Working with the half-object-plus-protocol pattern

In the previous chapter, we briefly explained the simplified Web model that we will be using for all the chapters on design patterns. We also provided a template that we have used to catalog the different patterns. This chapter is about service-tier patterns, which form the second layer in the simplified Web model. We present the simplified Web model in this chapter again as a handy reference.

Introducing Service-Tier Patterns

Some of the bad design practices in the service tier include the following:

- ✦ Mapping the object model directly to entity beans.
- ✦ Mapping the relational model directly to entity beans.
- ✦ Mapping use cases in an enterprise application to a session bean.
- ✦ Embedding lookup services in clients. The best way to do this is to provide a service-locator pattern, which will be discussed in this chapter.
- ✦ Using entity beans as read-only and fine-grained objects.
- ✦ Designing complex security mechanisms for authentication between Web services.

Service-tier patterns represent solutions to the most common problems encountered in the service tier of a Web model. These patterns can be used as a blueprint for solving those problems. We are going to classify design patterns based on the simplified view of the Web depicted in Figure 24-1.

Figure 24-1: Simplified Web-tier model

Note   We will use the terms *pattern* and *design pattern* interchangeably throughout this book.

We are going to present the following patterns in this chapter:

✦ **Business-delegate** — This pattern helps in decoupling presentation and service tiers.

✦ **Value-object** — This pattern helps establish data exchange between tiers and helps network performance.

✦ **Session-facade** — This pattern provides a centralized way to access EJB's complex workflow.

✦ **Composite-entity** — This pattern helps to construct coarse-grained beans from dependent beans.

✦ **Service-locator** — This pattern helps to segregate EJB lookup and creation.

✦ **Half-object-plus-protocol** — This pattern provides a single object that can live in more than two address spaces and, with a combination of methods, can be invoked locally and executed remotely.

✦ **Session-authenticator** — This pattern provides a mechanism for authentication in portal sites that use Web service to exchange messages.

✦ **Stateless-service-provider** — This pattern provides a mechanism for stateless communication between sites exchanging information through Web services.

Session authenticator and stateless service provider are the author's own creation and were created as part of a Web-services design for an electronic commerce site. We already presented our own template pattern to describe all the patterns in the previous chapter and the next two chapters.

We are going to start this chapter with the business-delegate pattern, which helps to couple the presentation and service tiers. Enterprise applications need to be coupled loosely because if tight coupling were introduced, the application would lose scalability, maintainability, and reusability. The business-delegate pattern also provides interfaces to the underlying services in the enterprise application.

Using the Business-Delegate Pattern

Most of the presentation-tier clients that need to use business services' application programming interface (API) must directly invoke remote methods; the lack of a proper caching mechanism on the presentation tier can therefore cause network traffic. As the remote method interfaces (RMIs) change frequently, the presentation-tier pattern must be updated. This causes a tight coupling between the presentation tier and business services. To prevent this tight coupling, a business-delegate pattern can be used.

In multi-tiered enterprise applications, methods usually have to be invoked remotely on server objects, and the data that is generated as a result of these methods' execution must be received across tiers. Because of this, clients need to deal with the complexity of these method invocations.

Forces

The following forces encourage the use of the business-delegate pattern in enterprise applications:

> The presentation tier needs access to business services.
>
> The business-processing interface changes with the business requirements.
>
> Coupling between presentation tier and service tier has to be minimal.
>
> In-built caching mechanisms must be incorporated in clients so that clients can avoid making frequent calls. This will reduce network traffic.

Implementation

The business-delegate pattern reduces coupling between the presentation tier and business services. This pattern encapsulates the lookup and access to the business services. In addition, the business-delegate pattern acts as an abstraction for the presentation tier (that is, the clients). Finally, the business-delegate pattern can cache business-service-call result sets.

Structure

Figure 24-2 depicts the structure of the business-delegate pattern:

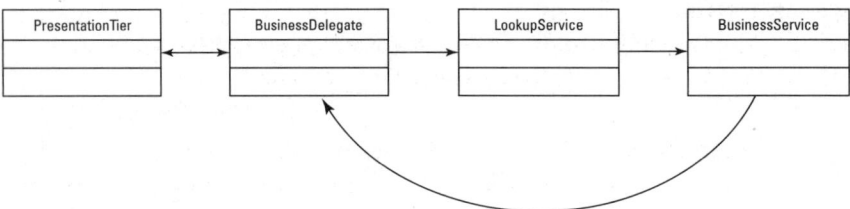

Figure 24-2: Example of the business-delegate pattern

The presentation tier would correspond to the any of the front-end HTML or Java server pages. The business-delegate class implements the business-delegate pattern and provides methods to access the business service. The business service component usually represents entity beans that have methods for querying the database. They can be either bean-managed or container-managed entity beans. The business-delegate implementation class does incorporate `LookupService` to look up the needed entity beans. The lookup-service pattern is discussed in detail later in this chapter. Figure 24-3 shows the sequence diagram for the interaction among the different components involved in a business-delegate pattern:

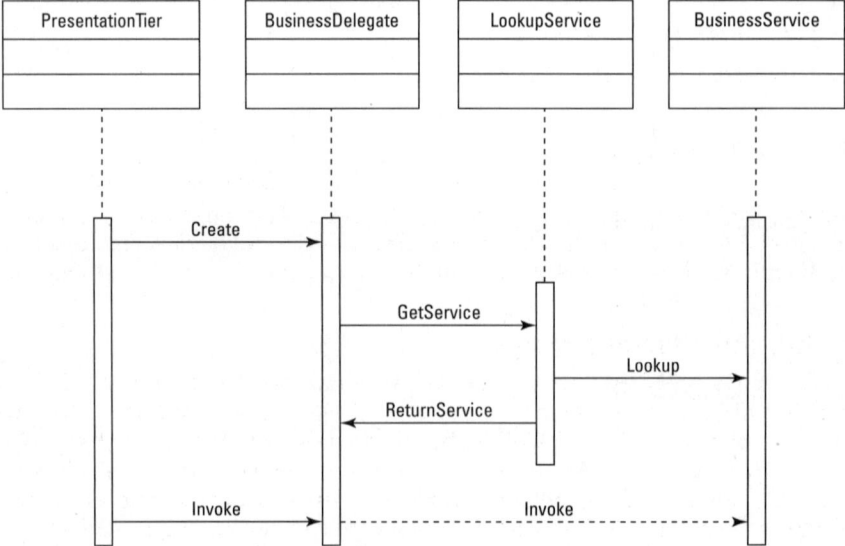

Figure 24-3: Sequence diagram for the business-delegate pattern

The various components in the sequence diagram are explained briefly in the following sections.

PresentationTier

PresentationTier is typically a client, like JSP pages, that creates BusinessDelegate and calls business-service methods.

BusinessDelegate

BusinessDelegate provides control and protection for the business services. It encapsulates the lookup and invocation of business methods.

LookupService

BusinessDelegate uses LookupService to locate the business services.

BusinessService

BusinessService is a service-tier component, such as an EJB, that provides the required service.

Strategies

The business-delegate pattern can be implemented through one of two strategies:

✦ The delegate-proxy strategy
✦ The delegate-adapter strategy

The delegate-proxy strategy

Here the business-delegate pattern acts as a proxy, providing a wrapper for the methods provided by the remote business interface. Any request of the client is proxied by the business-delegate pattern. Here for the lookup the business-delegate pattern can either use lookup or provide its own lookup.

The delegate-adapter strategy

In this scenario, a B2B adapter acts between the B2B client and BusinessDelegate. A common XML language can be used as the communication mechanism between the client and BusinessDelegate. In the Stateless-Service-Provider pattern (this pattern is the author's own creation and is explained in detail at the end of this chapter), we provide a combination of this B2B (Business-to-Business) and the business-delegate pattern. This kind of strategy is useful in Web-service applications.

Results

Using the business-delegate pattern has the following consequences:

This pattern reduces coupling between the presentation tier and the business service. This pattern also reduces coupling in other tiers.

Business-service expectations are converted to more user-friendly messages for the presentation-tier patterns.

Because of built-in caching services this pattern affects performance but hides remoteness (looking up and invoking services).

This pattern implements automatic failure recovery and thread-synchronization mechanisms.

Business-delegate pattern — sample code

Listing 24-1 shows how a business-delegate pattern can be implemented.

Listing 24-1: **Implementing the business-delegate pattern**

```
public class BusinessDelegate{
  //constructor
  public BusinessDelegate() {
  }
//method used to create beneficiary accounts using account
number.
public static int createBene ( String actno) {
   int actID = -1;
   InitialContext ctx = null;
   try{
     ctx = new InitialContext();
     // get ejb
     Enrollment enrol = ((EnrollmentHome)
ctx.lookup("EnrollmentHome")).create();
     actID = enrol.createBene( actno );
   } catch (Exception e){
   //handle exception
   }finally {
      try{
        ctx.close();
      }catch(NamingException ne){;}
   }
   return actID;

  }
}
```

In the preceding code, an interface to the creation of a beneficiary account is provided through the class implementing the business-delegate pattern. Inside the method, the `Enrollment Bean` entity bean method is used to create the beneficiary account.

Related patterns

The business-delegate pattern can be used in combination with the following patterns:

- ✦ Service locator
- ✦ Proxy
- ✦ Adapter
- ✦ Broker
- ✦ Stateless-service provider

The service-locator and stateless-service-provider patterns are cataloged in this chapter. A *proxy* pattern is often used to represent another object. The Remote Method Invocation (RMI) services within the Java kit are a good example of using proxy patterns. The Stubs and Skeletons that are used in RMI to communicate between the client and server are good examples of proxy objects. The adapter pattern acts as an intermediary between two classes converting the interfaces of one class so that it can be used with the other class. A broker pattern — more like the meaning attached to the word broker — performs the role of a broker between presentation and service tiers.

Next, we are going to catalog the value-object pattern, which facilitates the exchange of data as a result of querying the databases between the entity beans.

Understanding the Value-Object Pattern

When a client makes a request to an enterprise bean it usually invokes multiple calls through attributes for executing the front-end logic to get the data it needs. Each of these calls is costly and could have an effect on network traffic and performance. Using a *value-object pattern* it is possible to group certain attributes into a class, use this class to store all the needed values for the client, and invoke the class through a single method call to the enterprise bean.

Presentation-tier components need to exchange data with EJBs because presentation tier components can capture data through Web forms and this data needs to be sent to the backend system for storing. For example, in the airline reservation system a passenger can provide his information for booking tickets, and this needs to be stored in the backend database.

Forces

The following forces encourage the use of the value-object pattern:

Access to EJBs is provided through bean remote interfaces.

Read transactions are more than update transactions in an enterprise application.

The client may need more than one attribute and can invoke multiple remote calls.

Multiple calls made by the client to the remote object result in decreased network performance.

Implementation

In a value-object pattern a single method call is used to send information to and retrieve information from the Enterprise JavaBean using a value object. The Enterprise bean can create the value object or the client can pass the value object to the bean method and the method can populate the values for the object.

Figure 24-4 depicts the usage structure of the value-object pattern.

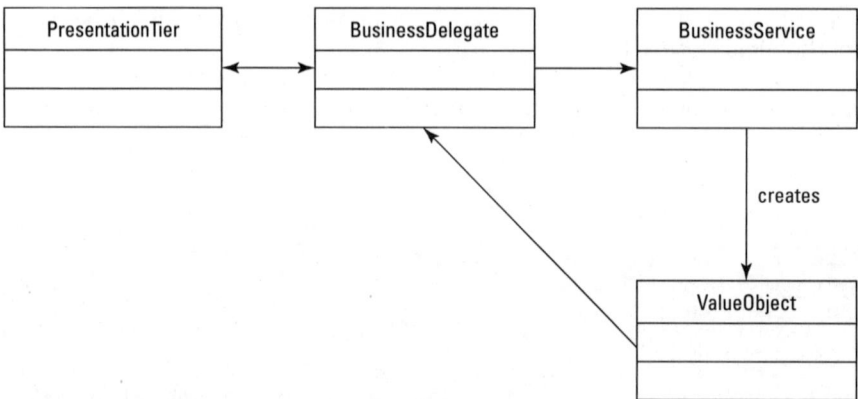

Figure 24-4: Example of a value-object pattern

Figure 24-5 shows the sequence diagram for the interaction among different components involved in a value-object pattern.

The various components depicted in the sequence diagram are explained in the following sections:

PresentationTier

PresentationTier is typically a client, such as JSP, which creates BusinessDelegate and calls business-service methods.

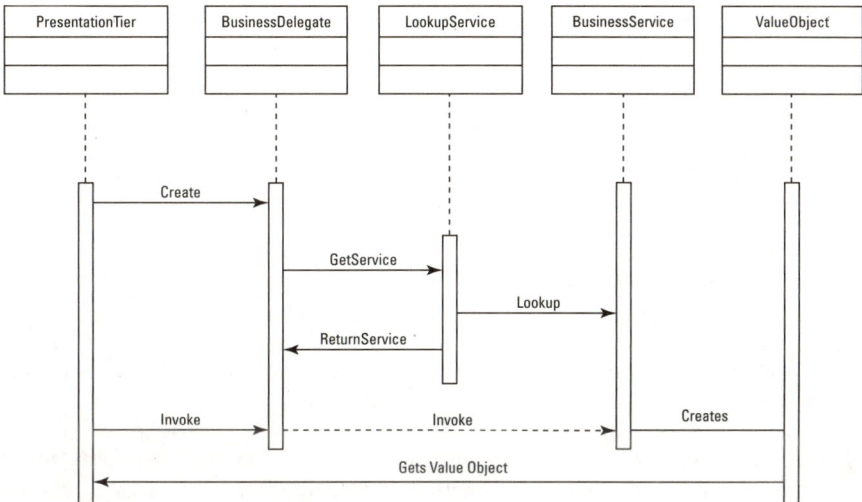

Figure 24-5: Sequence diagram for value-object pattern

BusinessDelegate

BusinessDelegate provides control and protection for the business services. It encapsulates the lookup and invocation of business methods.

LookupService

BusinessDelegate uses LookupService to locate the business services.

BusinessService

BusinessService is a service-tier component, such as an EJB, that provides the required service.

ValueObject

ValueObject encapsulates some of the common attributes that can be returned as part of a remote-method call, thus making unnecessary numerous requests to retrieve different attributes.

Strategies

The following strategies can be used in variance with the value-object pattern:

  ✦ The updateable-value-objects strategy
  ✦ The multiple-value-objects strategy

✦ The entity-inherits-value-object strategy

✦ The value-object-factory strategy

The first two strategies are applicable when the EJB is either a session or an entity bean. The last two are applicable when the EJB is an entity bean. We will discuss only the updateable and value-object-factory strategies, as they are the most common in enterprise applications.

Updateable-value-objects strategy

In this strategy, the client can call a `getData` method on the EJB to get the value object and uses a `SetData` method to update the value object. The value object must provide set methods with which the client can update attributes. Field-level validations can be performed in these methods. A flag can be set to notify the entity bean, which attributes to update, rather than comparing against the already existing values to see which attributes have changed. The only problem with this strategy is the creation of stale value objects that do not contain updated attribute values.

Value-object-factory strategy

In this strategy, the EJB creates value objects on demand using reflection. This is a more dynamic strategy than the updateable option. The best way to implement this approach is to have an interface and have all the value objects implement this handler. In the client call use the instance of operator to check for the particular instance of the value object and then invoke the appropriate methods on the value object.

Results

Using the value-object pattern has the following consequences:

Simplifies the calls to the EJBs by transferring more data in a single method call

Reduces network traffic and code duplication

Increases complexity with synchronization and version control

Clients can usually update value objects and invoke methods on EJBs to update the database, but other similar value objects may have outdated values, resulting in more stale value objects.

Value-object pattern – sample code

Listing 24-2 shows how a value object can be implemented.

Listing 24-2: **Implementing a value object**

```
public class Beneficiary implements java.io.Serializable {
  private int beneId=0;
  private String beneSSN="";
  private String beneFirstName="";
  private String beneMiddleInitial="";
  private String beneLastName="";
  private Date birthDate;
  //other attributes
  public void setBeneId(String beneId) throws
BeneIdNotFoundException{
        if (beneId == null){
              throw new BeneIdNotFoundException("Bene ID not
found");
        }
        this.beneId = beneId;
  }
  //define other set methods.
  //...........
  }
```

In the preceding code, we define a class that implements a value-object and provides set and get methods to set the attributes and get method to query the values of the attributes. This value-object can be used in an entity bean to be populated with values or use the values that are in the object to do updates to the database.

Related patterns

Patterns that can be used in the combination with this pattern include the following:

✦ Session facade

✦ Value-object assembler

✦ Value-list handler

✦ Composite entity

The session-facade and composite-entity patterns are discussed in this chapter. A value object assembler helps to build composite value objects from different data sources it is more like a factory pattern. The value-list-handler pattern is used to provide lists of dynamically constructed value objects.

The session facade is the next pattern that is cataloged. It is used to expose complex underlying distributed services. These services are implemented as entity beans to the presentation tier.

Exploring the Session-Facade Pattern

In enterprise applications a tight coupling exists between the client and business objects. As the whole application is implemented as EJBs, too many method invocations from the client to the server occur, the chattiness of the application increases, and severe network performance problems result. Besides, no uniform strategy exists for accessing the EJBs. Using a session-facade pattern decreases the complexity described above by providing a simple interface to these services.

Enterprise JavaBeans expose their interfaces, encapsulate business logic, and persist business data, increasing the complexity for clients in a distributed-enterprise system.

Forces

The following forces encourage the use of session-facade pattern:

> Reducing the number of business objects exposed to the client over the network

> Hiding from the client the internal intricacies of various interactions between the business components, thus making a centralized strategy to these business objects

> Providing an abstraction between business-service abstractions from business service implementation

> Reducing coupling between the client and the business objects

Implementation

A session-facade pattern provides a uniform centralized service-access layer to clients, encapsulating the complexity of interactions between various business objects.

Structure

Figure 24-6 depicts the structure of the session-facade pattern.

Figure 24-7 shows the sequence diagram for the interaction among the different components involved in a session-facade pattern.

The different components participating in the sequence diagram for session facade are discussed below:

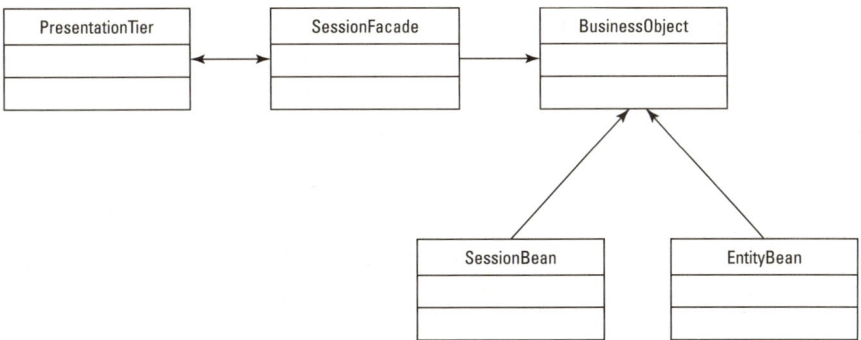

Figure 24-6: Example of the session-facade pattern

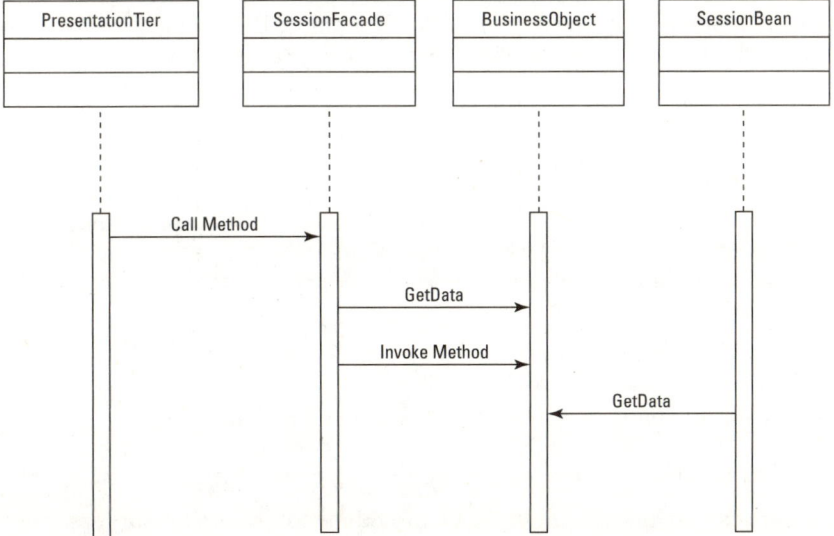

Figure 24-7: Sequence diagram for the session-facade pattern

PresentationTier

PresentationTier is the client that needs access to business services.

SessionFacade

SessionFacade is usually implemented as a session bean. It manages relationships among different business objects and provides coarse-grained access to the underlying business objects.

BusinessObject

BusinessObject is a role that can be constructed with various strategies; it can also be used to construct a session facade. It provides data access and services to the SessionFacade.

Strategies

SessionFacade can be implemented by means of two strategies:

✦ The stateless-session-facade strategy

✦ The stateful-session-facade strategy

The stateless-session-facade strategy

When a client needs only one method call to complete the business transaction, a stateless session bean can be applied. Usually using cases and scenarios in a UML diagram enables you to decide when a stateless-session-facade strategy should be applied.

The stateful-session-facade strategy

When a client needs multiple method calls to complete a business transaction, a stateful session facade can be used. In this strategy the conversational state between the client and the bean must be saved for each method invocation.

Results

The session-facade pattern enables the following consequences:

Increases manageability, reduces coupling by providing a uniform interface

Improves network performance by providing coarse-grained access

Centralizes security management and transaction control

Session-facade pattern — sample code

Listing 24-3 shows how to implement a session-facade pattern.

> Listing 24-3: **Implementing a session-facade pattern as a stateless strategy**

```
public class WebServicesBean extends SessionBean {
  //encapsulates method to authenticate the web service
  public String authenticateWebServiceUser(String username,
String password){
```

```
        //internally calls another EJB to complete the webservice
   call.
       }
       //retrieve service call
       public String getNewsService (String newsId){
       //internally calls another EJB to complete the news service
   call.
       }
   }
```

In the preceding code, a simple Web services class provides the Web service call getNewsService; the underlying complexity of calling the entity bean that provides the service is hidden.

Related patterns

Patterns that can be used in the combination with this pattern include the following:

✦ Facade

✦ Data-access object

✦ Service locator

✦ Business delegate

✦ Broker

The data-access-object pattern is catalogued in Chapter 25. The service-locator and business-delegate patterns are explained in this chapter. The broker pattern is explained in the "Related Patterns" section of the business-delegate coverage in this chapter. A facade pattern is used to provide a simplified interface to a complex subsystem.

The composite entity is the next pattern that we are going to catalog. It enables us to design coarse-grained entity beans by grouping objects dependent on the parent bean into a single entity bean.

Explaining the Composite-Entity Pattern

The composite-entity pattern is a solution to the common problem of mapping object to EJB model. Entity beans represent coarse-grained objects. The mapping of back-end (namely, database objects) objects to EJB model does not take into consideration the concept of coarse-grained versus dependent objects. Not recognizing these dependent objects affects areas such as entity relationships, manageability, network performance, and database-schema dependency. Entity beans form a better implementation for coarse-grained persistent objects, though not for every object.

Forces

The following forces encourage the use of the composite-entity pattern:

Enterprise applications that directly map each row in a table to an entity-bean instance

Mapping directly data objects to EJB model does not distinguish between coarse-grained beans and dependent beans

Clients need not know the underlying complexity involved with lookup, invocation, and execution of entity beans

Increase in chattiness because of communication among dependent beans; this can be noted among the beans as well as between the client and the beans

Implementation

The composite-entity pattern enables representation and management of a set of interrelated persistent objects. It is usually a graph of these interrelated persistent objects.

Figure 24-8 depicts the structure of the composite-entity design pattern.

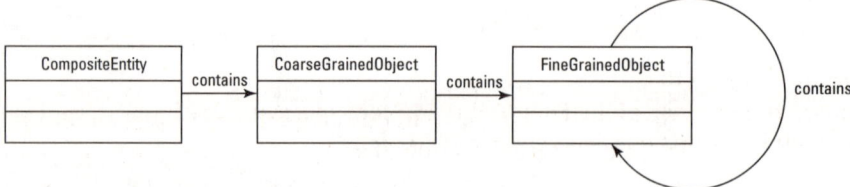

Figure 24-8: Example of the composite-entity pattern

Figure 24-9 shows the sequence diagram for the interaction between different components involved in a composite-entity pattern.

The different components in the sequence diagram are explained next.

CompositeEntity

This is the coarse-grained entity bean. It may hold references to other coarse-grained objects.

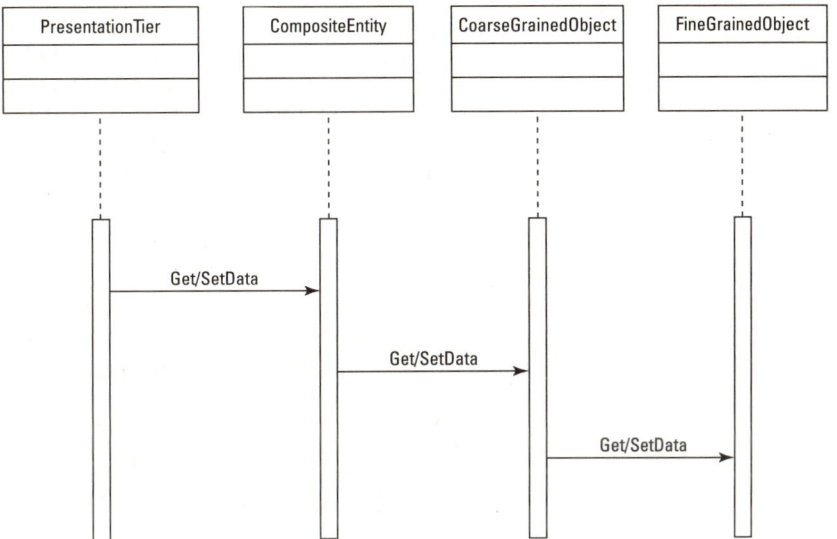

Figure 24-9: Sequence diagram for the composite-entity pattern

CoarseGrainedObject

This object has its own lifecycle and maintains the relationships with other objects on its own. `CoarseGrainedObject` can hold dependent objects or fine-grained objects.

FineGrainedObject

Manages the lifecycle of the Fine-Grained Object, is managed by the Coarse-Grained object, and depends on `CoarseGrainedObject`.

Strategies

Several different strategies can be used to implement a composite-entity pattern. We will be discussing the most important ones:

✦ The lazy-loading strategy

✦ The composite-value-object strategy

✦ The composite-entity-contains-coarse-grained-object strategy

✦ The-composite-entity-implements-coarse-grained-object strategy

✦ The dirty-marker strategy

The lazy-loading strategy

In this strategy the composite-entity pattern can be thought of as a tree of objects. Loading all the dependent objects during the `ejbLoad()` method can be costly and time-consuming. So for the call of `ejbLoad()` only the important ones are loaded; all the other objects are loaded as needed from the database. Any subsequent calls to `ejbLoad` must include those dependent objects to synchronize any change with the persistent storage.

The composite-value-object strategy

In this strategy the client can request information in one method remote call. As the composite-entity pattern holds the graph of coarse-grained objects and dependent objects it can create the required value object and return it to the client.

Results

The composite-entity pattern enables the following consequences:

> Relationships existing internally between entities are eliminated and the relationships become more manageable because of the elimination

> Reduces database-schema dependency and increases object granularity

> There is overhead in multi-level dependent objects in the tree structure

Composite-entity pattern — sample code

Listing 24-4 shows how to implement a composite entity using the composite-value-object strategy.

Listing 24-4: **Implementing a composite entity using the composite-value-object strategy**

```
public class CompositeValueObject{
    private CompositeVO cvo;
    private Collection plans;
    private Collection funds;

    // value object constructors

    // mutator and accessor methods.
}
```

```
//creating the Composite Value Object
public CompositeValueObject getPlanDetails(){
   CompositeValueObject cvo = new
CompositeValueObject(getCompositeVO(),getPlans(),getFunds());
return cvo;
      }
```

In the preceding code, the composite value object is being used to combine get plans and funds that corresponds to these plans in a single call.

Related patterns

Patterns that can be used in combination with this pattern include the following:

✦ Value object

✦ Session facade

✦ Value-object assembler

The value-object and session-facade patterns are cataloged in this chapter. The value object assembler is discussed in the "Related Patterns" section of the value-object coverage in this chapter.

The service-locator pattern is the next one that we will catalog.

Using the Service-Locator Pattern

When clients need to invoke entity beans in an enterprise system, they need to locate the service component and then do a lookup. Usually, clients do this through the Java Naming and Directory Interface (JNDI). As this JNDI lookup is available across the whole system, code is duplicated in a lot of places. In addition, this lookup involves a significant amount of resources. It is the case of using Java Messaging Service components. Looking up and creating components involves vendor-supplied implementation, and this creates a dependency on a vendor. Using a service-locator pattern simplifies the lookup services for entity beans.

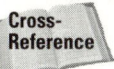 **Cross-Reference** See Chapter 11 for a discussion of JNDI.

Service lookup and the creation of enterprise beans are complex and involve heavy network operation.

Forces

The following forces encourage the use of the service-locator pattern:

EJB clients use the JNDI API to lookup the registered EJBs.

The initial context factory used to look up an EJB Home Interface is vendor-provided, so a dependency is created.

The lookup and creation process is complex and resource-consuming.

Clients need to reestablish connections for a previously accessed bean instance.

Implementation

The service-locator pattern abstracts all JNDI-specific complexities, including EJB-home lookup and re-creation. Multiple clients can use the service locator, as it provides a single point of control and can improve performance by providing a caching facility. Figure 24-10 depicts the structure of the service-locator design pattern:

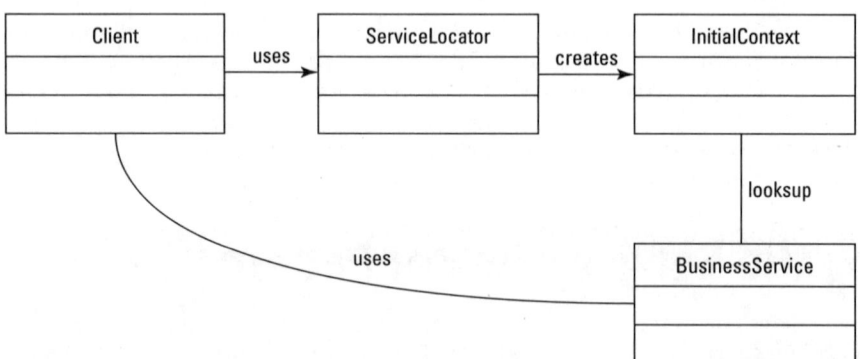

Figure 24-10: Example of the service-locator pattern

Figure 24-11 shows the sequence diagram for the interaction between different components involved in a service-locator pattern.

The various components involved in the sequence diagram for a service-locator pattern are discussed next.

Client

Client is typically a Web browser that requests access to business services through ServiceLocator.

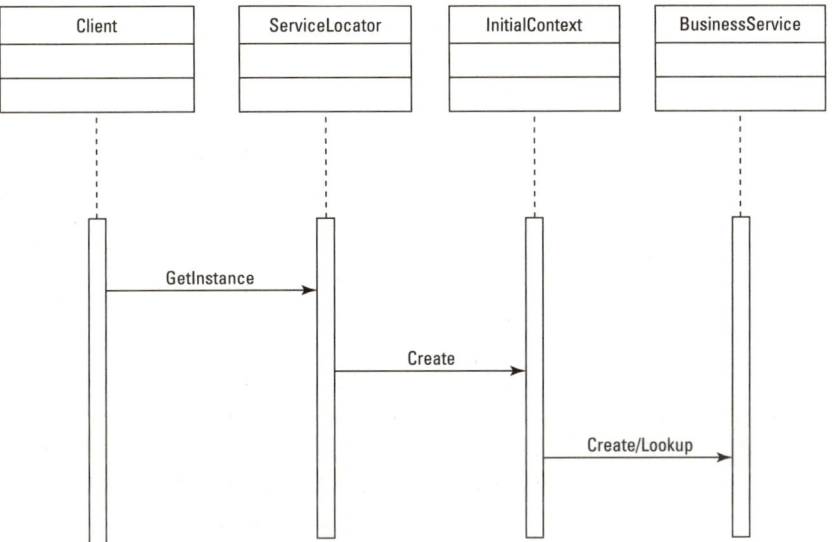

Figure 24-11: Sequence diagram for the service-locator pattern

ServiceLocator

`ServiceLocator` abstracts the JNDI lookup access, encapsulates lookup complexities and business-service creation, and provides a simple interface to the client.

InitialContext

This is the first step in the lookup and creation process. Service providers usually provide this context object, which is used for lookup and creating service.

Strategies

There are several different strategies for implementing a service-locator pattern. We list all of them as follows but will be discussing only the important one.

✦ The EJB-service-locator strategy

✦ The JMS-queue-service-locator strategy

✦ The JMS-topic-service-locator strategy

✦ The combined EJB and JMS service-locator strategy

✦ The type-checked service-locator strategy

✦ The service-locator-properties strategy

The EJB-service-locator strategy

In this strategy, the service locator can be used to get a reference to the
EJBHomeEJB Home object and can be cached in the service locator for future use,
thus rendering JNDI lookup unnecessary. This Home object can be used by the client
to look up, create, and remove EJBs. Otherwise the service locator can act as a
proxy for all client requests.

Results

The service-locator pattern enables the following consequences:

> Abstracts complexity, providing clients with centralized access to services

> Enables easy addition of new lookup for business components, which
> improves network performance

> Enhances client performance by providing caching mechanisms

Service-locator pattern — sample code

Listing 24-5 shows how to implement a service locator. Observe the different ways
in which EJBs are looked up.

Listing 24-5: Implementing a service locator

```
import javax.naming.*;
import java.rmi.RemoteException;
import java.util.Hashtable;
public class ServiceLocator{
   public ServiceLocator(Hashtable env) throws
javax.naming.NamingException{
        //set up all the environment variables.
   }
   public ServiceLocator throws javax.naming.NamingException(){
}
   public ProviderHome getProviderHome(){
        try{
                return
(ProviderHome)lookup("example.application.ejb. ProviderHome");
        }catch(javax.naming.NamingException ne){
                ne.printStackTrace();
        }
   return null;
   }
```

```
public PortalAuthenticatorHome getPortalAuthenticatorHome(){
      try{
            return
(PortalAuthenticatorHome)lookup("example.application.ejb.Portal
AuthenticatorHome");
      }catch(javax.naming.NamingException ne){
            ne.printStackTrace();
      }
      return null;
}
//other ejb lookup....
}
```

In the preceding sample code, the method PortalAuthenticatorHome internally looks up the entity bean PortalAuthenticator and returns the home context.

Related patterns

Patterns that can be used in combination with this pattern include the following:

✦ Business delegate

✦ Session facade

✦ Value-object assembler

The business-delegate and session-facade patterns are cataloged in this chapter. The value-object-assembler pattern is discussed under the "Related patterns" section of the value object coverage.

The half-object-plus-protocol is the next pattern that we are going to catalog. As the name suggests, this pattern acts as a half-object and half- protocol mechanism.

Working with the Half-Object-Plus-Protocol Pattern

In a typical RMI application, clients invoke methods locally on the stub of the server, which passes across the network to be executed on the server, and the requests go through the skeleton of the server before the actual execution takes place on the server. In this model all method calls are sent to the server. Sometimes certain methods can be executed locally without being sent to the server. A half-object-plus-protocol pattern enables you to implement this behavior.

Forces

The following forces encourage the use of half-object-plus-protocol pattern:

An entity needs to be in two different address spaces and cannot be split according to functionality.

Some methods must be invoked locally and others must be executed remotely.

The acts of caching and combining multiple requests into one single network call should made transparent to the client.

Implementation

The half-object-plus protocol creates an object implementing the remote interface of the server and also has reference to the original stub of the remote object. The new object handles methods that are to be executed locally and the server handles remote methods. Figure 24-12 depicts the structure of the half-object-plus-protocol pattern.

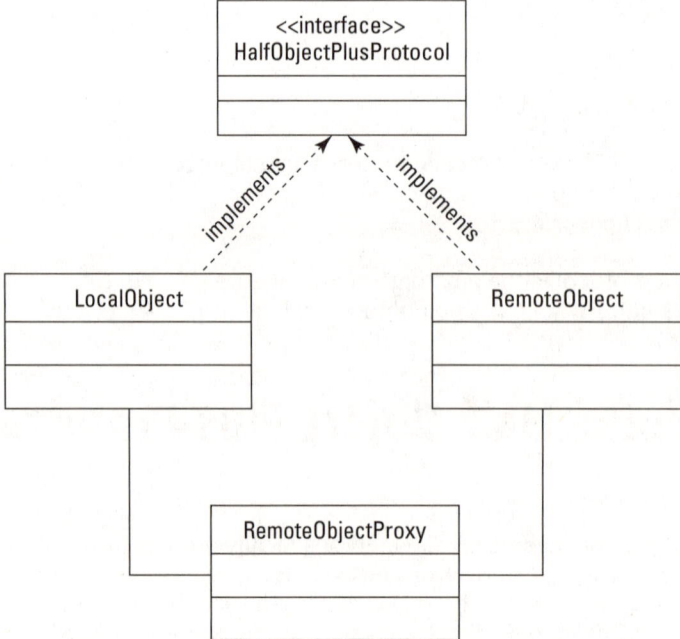

Figure 24-12: Example of the half-object-plus-protocol pattern

Figure 24-13 shows the sequence diagram for the interaction between different components involved in a half-object-plus-protocol pattern:

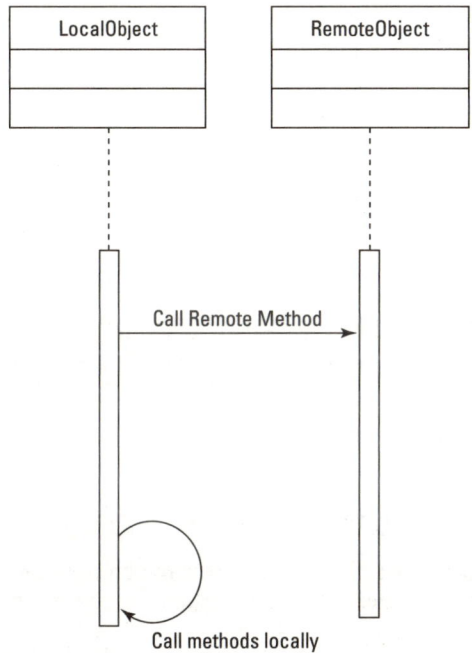

Figure 24-13: Sequence diagram for the half-object-plus-protocol pattern

The various components that participate in the sequence diagram of the pattern are described next.

LocalObject

LocalObject implements the HalfObjectPlusProtocol interface; some of the methods are executed locally and some remotely.

RemoteObject

RemoteObject implements the HalfObjectPlusProtocol interface and implements methods that will be executed remotely.

Strategies

This is how the half-object-plus-protocol pattern must be implemented:

1. Create an object that implements the required remote interfaces and that contains a reference to the generated stub of the remote object.

2. Make this object implement any local methods necessary.

3. Send remote method calls to the remote server, which will implement the `HalfObjectPlusProtocol` interface. This new object will execute all the local methods.

Results

The half-object-plus-protocol pattern enables the following consequences:

Each object resides in two address spaces.

Provides transparency for the client using one part of the pattern.

Each part of the pattern has the capacity to decide when and how to communicate with the other half.

Duplication of code exists between the two halves.

Half-object-plus-protocol pattern — sample code

Figure 24-14 depicts how the half-object-plus-protocol pattern can be implemented. `RemoteObjectProxy` contains the protocol and forwards all the remote calls to the remote object.

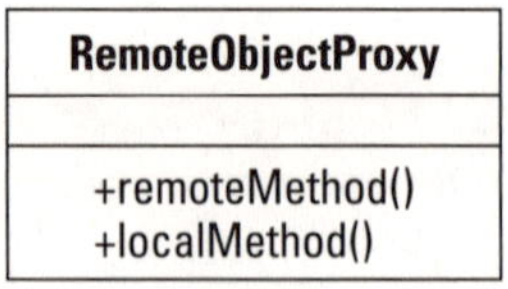

RemoteObjectProxy
+remoteMethod() +localMethod()

Figure 24-14: Class diagram for the half-object-plus-proxy pattern

Related patterns

Patterns that can be used in the combination with this pattern include the following:

✦ Session authenticator

✦ Stateless-service provider

✦ Mediator

✦ Proxy

We are going to look at two new patterns straight out of the author's own pattern catalog. These two patterns are solutions to common problems in Web services and have been implemented successfully in several Web-services-architecture designs.

Session authenticator

One of the common problems that portal sites face is that of authenticating the user requesting data when that user has logged in and authenticated on one portal and is trying to retrieve information from another portal. Things become more complex when these portals are in different domains and the validity and authenticity of the user must be determined before the user can be allowed to access information.

Consider the scenario depicted in Figure 24-15, in which the client authenticates on Domain A and requests Domain B. Say the client is signed with an online bank. He or she signs on to the bank domain. However, the bank has an agreement with a statement provider to supply statements for its user based on the user's account number. So when the client wants to retrieve his or her bank statement the request has to be forwarded to Domain B. Now, Domain B acts as a Web-service host and must somehow validate the authenticity of the request and the user, and determine whether the session is still valid for the user.

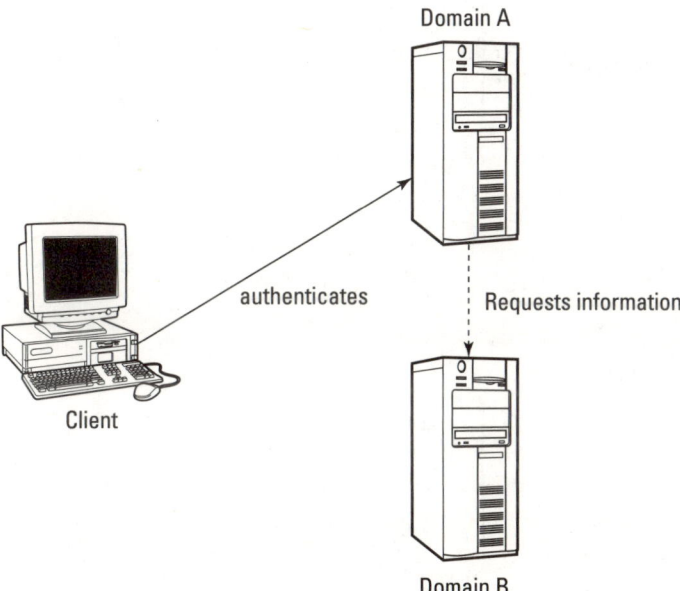

Figure 24-15: Example of the session-authenticator pattern

Using a session-authenticator pattern Domain B can authenticate the user from Domain A and enable the user to access statements on its server. The session-authenticator pattern can be implemented in the following way:

1. The client session ID in Domain A is encrypted and sent as a part of the request to Domain B.

2. Domain B makes a HTTP request to Domain A with the encrypted session ID to validate the authenticity of the client.

3. Domain A's permission program takes the incoming requests, decrypts the session ID, and validates the session and credentials of the client. It then sends a XML response to Domain B.

4. Based on the response, Domain B decides whether to allow the client to retrieve or show the necessary information.

Figure 24-16 shows the communication mechanism.

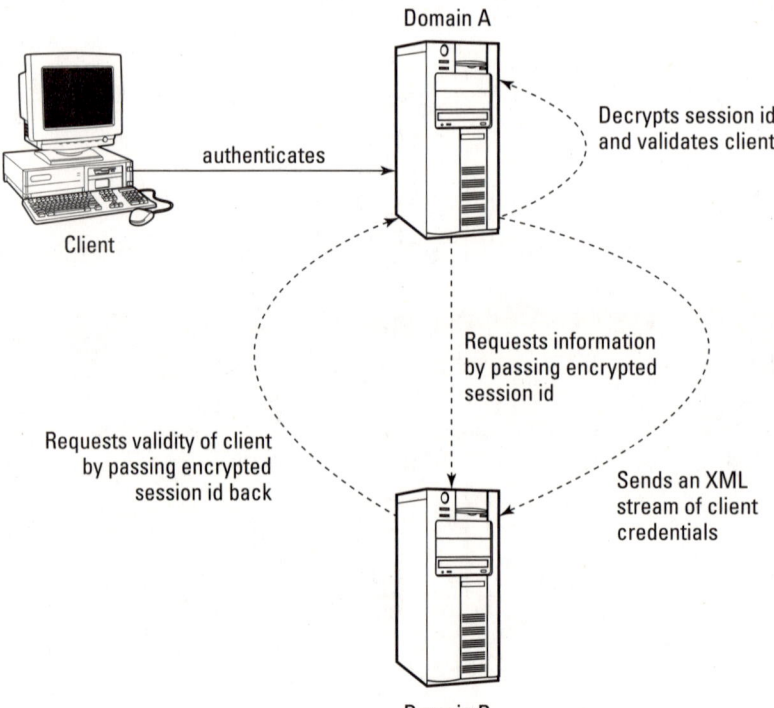

Figure 24-16: Implementation of the session-authenticator pattern

If this mechanism is implemented in Java it works on a single machine as well as in a cluster. To establish and encrypt a session there will one servlet and for decrypting and forwarding the requesting to the session establishing servlet there will be a separate servlet. Because the servlet API does not allow a servlet to call itself passing an ID, servlets can be chained while verifying the credentials of the client from the request sent from Domain B to Domain A.

Listings 24-6 and 24-7 show the usage of the session-authenticator pattern. They show two JSPs called gateway.jsp and permission.jsp, respectively. The gateway.jsp page acts as the gateway to the application-establish session and cookie and permission.jsp calls the gateway to validate the user session and displays appropriate information. These two pages act as different domains. The gateway.jsp contains code to create a session and parses the session when a call is made by the permission. jsp. The gateway.jsp acts as an authenticator of the session that it created for the permission.jsp code.

Listing 24-6: **gateway.jsp**

```
<html>
<%
String password = request.getParameter("password");
String action = request.getParameter("act");

if (action != null && action.equals("session")){
 String pwd = (String)session.getValue("password");
 out.println("Request for session... <br>");
 out.println("password=" + pwd + "<br>");
 return;
}

if (action != null && action.equals("proxy")){
 Cookie [] cooks = request.getCookies();
 String val = null;
    for (int i=0; i<cooks.length; i++){
       Cookie c = cooks[i];
       if (c.getName().equals("sessionauthenticator")){
          val = c.getValue();
          String aid = val.substring(3);
          out.println("aid=" + aid + "<br>");
  String theurl = "http://" + localhost +
":7001/j2eebible/gateway.jsp?action=session";
   out.println("Calling " + theurl + " from j2eebible
server<br>");
   java.net.URL url = new java.net.URL(theurl);
    java.net.HttpURLConnection conn =
(java.net.HttpURLConnection) url.openConnection();
    conn.setRequestProperty("Cookie", "exampleUser=" + aid);
    int rtnCode = conn.getResponseCode();
    if (rtnCode == 200){
```

Continued

Listing 24-6 *(continued)*

```
java.io.InputStream is = conn.getInputStream();
    byte [] chunk = new byte[1024];
    StringBuffer buf = new StringBuffer(1024);
    int num = -1;
    while ((num = is.read(chunk, 0, chunk.length)) != -1)
    {
      buf.append(new String(chunk, 0, num));
    }
    is.close();
    out.println(buf.toString());
  } else
  out.println("return code = " + rtnCode);


      }
    }
  return;
}

if (password != null && password.equals("test")){
String sid = session.getId();
String newsid = "jinx" + sid;
session.putValue("password",password);
Cookie c = new Cookie("sessionauthenticator",newsid);
//set your appropriate domain here.
//c.setDomain(".test.com");
//c.setPath("/");
response.addCookie(c);
out.print("Session id = " + sid + "<br />\n");
out.print("Session authenticator cookie is: " + newsid + "<br
/>\n");
out.print("<a target=\"localhost\"
href=\"http://localhost:7001/j2eebible/permission.jsp\">Go to
localhost</a>\n");
} else {
    Cookie [] cooks = request.getCookies();
 out.print("<br />Printing all cookies: <br />\n");
 String val = null;
    for (int i=0; i<cooks.length; i++){
      Cookie c = cooks[i];
      if (c.getName().equals("sessionauthenticator")){
        val = c.getValue();
 String wsid = val.substring(3);
 out.println("aid=" + aid + "<br>");
      }
      out.println(c.getName() + " = " + c.getValue() + "<br
/>\n");
    }
}
```

```
  %>
</html>
```

Listing 24-7: **permission.jsp**

```
<html>
<%
    String val = null;
    Cookie [] cooks = request.getCookies();
    for (int i=0; i<cooks.length; i++){
      Cookie c = cooks[i];
      if (c.getName().equals("sessionauthenticator")){
        val = c.getValue();
      }
      out.print(c.getName() + " = " + c.getValue() + "<br
/>\n");
    }

    out.println("<br> Here is the output from localhost <br>");

    java.net.URL url = new
java.net.URL("http://localhost:7001/j2eebible/gateway.jsp?actio
n=proxy");
    java.net.HttpURLConnection conn =
(java.net.HttpURLConnection) url.openConnection();
    conn.setRequestProperty("Cookie", "sessionauthenticator=" +
val);
    int rtnCode = conn.getResponseCode();
    if (rtnCode == 200){
  java.io.InputStream is = conn.getInputStream();
    byte [] chunk = new byte[1024];
    StringBuffer buf = new StringBuffer(1024);
    int num = -1;
    while ((num = is.read(chunk, 0, chunk.length)) != -1)
    {
      buf.append(new String(chunk, 0, num));
    }
    is.close();
    out.println(buf.toString());
  } else
  out.println("return code = " + rtnCode);

%>

</html>
```

Certainly, this pattern can benefit Web sites that exist in different domains and want to share information based on user credentials.

The stateless-service-provider pattern

The other common problem with Web sites using Web-service architecture is exchange of data between the two sites in a seamless way. Enough complexity is involved in this data-exchange mechanism in terms of proprietary ways to pass messages and parse them and display them to the user.

As XML is the lingo for Web services, the stateless-service-provider pattern provides a means of exchanging mechanisms seamlessly with little development effort and a lot of portability. This pattern can be used in scenarios in which the user logs in to a portal and wants to access information from another portal. When the user selects a link on the information page, that page will be served from the other portal.

To facilitate exchange of information through the stateless-service-provider pattern you should define a stateless session bean with the needed methods. The caller portal will call the `authentication` method followed by the `service` method. Finally, when deploying the stateless session bean deploy it as a Web service and the descriptor file for the EJB will need to be configured as shown in Listings 24-8 and 24-9. In Listing 24-8, see how the stateless-session bean is used to provide the authentication between Web portals when one portal passes the user information. In Listing 24-9, note how we define an admin role that has access to the methods. Nobody outside the admin role can invoke this method.

Listing 24-8: The stateless-service-provider pattern EJB

```
public class StatelessServiceProviderBean extends
javax.ejb.SessionBean{
  //method to authenticate the user can be based on any input
parameter specific to the site.
  public String authenticateUser(String username, String
password){
  }
  //retrieves user information from ldap providing a username.
  public String getUserInformation(String username){
  }
}
```

Listing 24-9: **The EJB deployment descriptor**

```
<!DOCTYPE ejb-jar PUBLIC '-//Sun Microsystems, Inc.//DTD
Enterprise JavaBeans 2.0//EN' 'http://java.sun.com/dtd/ejb-
jar_2_0.dtd'>
<!-- Generated XML! -->
<ejb-jar>
  <enterprise-beans>
    <session>
      <ejb-name>example.j2eebible.ejb.
StatelessServiceProviderHome</ejb-name>
      <home>example.j2eebible.ejb.
StatelessServiceProviderHome</home>
      <remote>example.j2eebible.ejb.
StatelessServiceProvider</remote>
      <ejb-class>example.j2eebible.ejb.
StatelessServiceProviderBean</ejb-class>
      <session-type>Stateless</session-type>
      <transaction-type>Container</transaction-type>
      <env-entry>
        <env-entry-name>realm</env-entry-name>
        <env-entry-type>java.lang.String</env-entry-type>
        <env-entry-value>j2eebible</env-entry-value>
      </env-entry>
      <env-entry>
        <env-entry-name>pool</env-entry-name>
        <env-entry-type>java.lang.String</env-entry-type>
        <env-entry-value>j2eebiblePool</env-entry-value>
      </env-entry>
      <env-entry>
        <env-entry-name>acl</env-entry-name>
        <env-entry-type>java.lang.String</env-entry-type>
        <env-entry-value>j2eebible.admin</env-entry-value>
      </env-entry>
    </session>
  </enterprise-beans>

  <assembly-descriptor>
    <security-role>
      <role-name>j2ee_user</role-name>
    </security-role>

  <method-permission>
      <role-name>j2ee_user</role-name>
    <method>
        <ejb-
name>example.j2ee.session.StatelessServiceProviderHome
</ejb-name>
```

Continued

Listing 24-9 *(continued)*

```
            <method-intf>Remote</method-intf>
            <method-name>*</method-name>
        </method>
    </method-permission>

    <container-transaction>
        <method>
            <ejb-name>
example.j2ee.session.StatelessServiceProviderHome </ejb-name>
            <method-intf>Remote</method-intf>
            <method-name>*</method-name>
        </method>
        <trans-attribute>Required</trans-attribute>
    </container-transaction>
    </assembly-descriptor>

</ejb-jar>
```

The two Web-services patterns have been tested in several Web-portals that have been designed as information providers. These patterns have worked effectively for both authentication and service providing. The two things that are often over-worked in Web-service portal design are the authentication mechanism and providing of information. When one conducts a study on Web portals in the Internet space, they can see how many portals have been re-designed to fit themselves in the Web service space because they provided proprietary mechanism for Web service. Now Simple Object Access Protocol (SOAP) has simplified and has provided a common protocol mechanism for Web services.

Summary

In this chapter we discussed service-tier patterns and the important role they play in decoupling presentation and service logic, facilitating data exchange among different tiers, providing a centralized means of accessing complex EJB workflows, helping to construct coarse-grained beans, helping to segregate EJB lookup and creation, constructing a single object that exists in multiple addresses, creating an authentication mechanism for portal sites, and providing a mechanism for stateless communication between two portal sites.

✦   ✦   ✦

Using Data-Tier Patterns

In This Chapter

Introducing the data-access-object pattern

Using the service-activator pattern

Examining the transfer-object pattern

The data tier is the last tier in the simplified Web-tier model that we first presented in Chapter 23. We will discuss some of the problems that occur commonly in this tier. Some of the problems happen when the application has to access multiple datasources. Other problems are the result of having to introduce asynchronous activation without the use of Java Messaging Service (JMS) in the already existing EJB model. Another example of a typical problem involves applications that have to access related attributes.

Introducing the Data-Access-Object Pattern

For your convenience, we present the diagram highlighting the data tier.

The following patterns will be discussed in this chapter:

✦ **Data-access-object pattern** — This pattern provides a core solution to the problem of applications that have to access multiple datasources in order to present and process information.

✦ **Service-activator pattern** — This pattern provides a core solution to the problem of applications that already have their business services built using EJBs and wants to use the concept of asynchronous activation.

✦ **Transfer-object pattern** — This pattern provides a core solution to the problem of applications that want to access a group of related attributes from database calls.

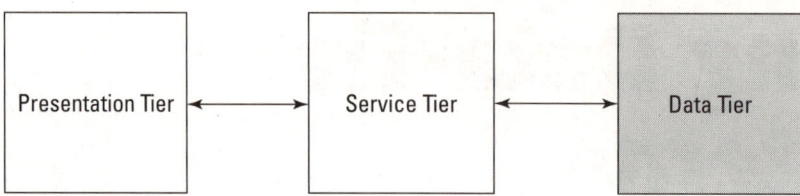

Figure 25-1: Simplified Web-tier model

Enterprise applications need to access data from various sources. The mechanism for accessing data across the various sources varies with the vendor API and type of storage. The data-access-object pattern provides a core solution to this problem for applications having to access different datasources to process and present information. The data-access-object pattern (DAO) abstracts access to datasources.

For example, an enterprise application may use Netscape's Directory Server to store user-related information to allow user access to the system and store enterprise-related system data in a relational database. The core of the problem arises because the system data were stored in Sybase and now need to be moved to an Oracle database. SQL implementations and data-access mechanisms, such as application-programming interfaces (APIs) vary between these databases. Even accessing data from legacy systems involves programming in proprietary APIs. Including code in business components like EJBs would necessitate reengineering of the code when deployed to a different datasource, for example, like moving from an Oracle database to a Sybase database. To avoid such underlying deficiencies the data-access-object pattern abstracts the concept of accessing data across different sources and provides a core solution to the problem of data-source access.

Note   Access to different sources of data is dependent on the data-storage type (flat files, RDBMS, ODBMS, LDAP, and so on) and vendor implementation. Data-storage and -access implementations vary across vendors providing data-source software.

The data-access-object pattern has the following characteristics:

Enables transparency for the presentation or business component. These components can then use the datasource without having knowledge of the underlying vendor implementation or access mode.

Makes migration between datasources easier, as only the underlying implementation of the data-access object layer, not the interface, must be changed.

Adds a layer to the business model and reduces code complexity. This layering feature centralizes access to different datasources within one unified factory model. A factory pattern helps to define an interface for creating an object and has control on which class needs to be instantiated. A detailed catalog of this pattern can be found in *Design Patterns* by Erich Gamma et al.

The data-access-object pattern is not useful for container-managed persistence because the container controls access to the datasource.

Keep in mind the following facts that pertain to using the data-access-object pattern:

Presentation-tier components such as Java Server Pages, servlets, and business-tier components like EJBs (both entity and session) need to access data from multiple sources.

Components that access data from datasources and use proprietary APIs need to be designed to be portable.

Access needs to be transparent between components accessing datasources. Transparency allows easy migration from one datasource to another datasource.

Implementation

The data-access-object pattern also encapsulates all access mechanisms to the datasource, including connectivity, querying the database, and creating different data-access objects based upon the datasource needed for the application. The interface that DAO provides to its clients does not change when data migrate from one datasource to another. The role of DAO is like that of the adapter pattern acting as an intermediary between two participating classes, converting the interface of one class to be used with the other participating class. This promotes reusability of older functionality. The adapter pattern provides the interface a client expects, utilizing the services provided by a class that implements a different interface.

Figure 25-2 depicts the usage structure of the data-access-object pattern, and abstracts the access to the underlying datasource. It also creates transfer objects for the business component and presentation component. Both these components can use the transfer object for processing.

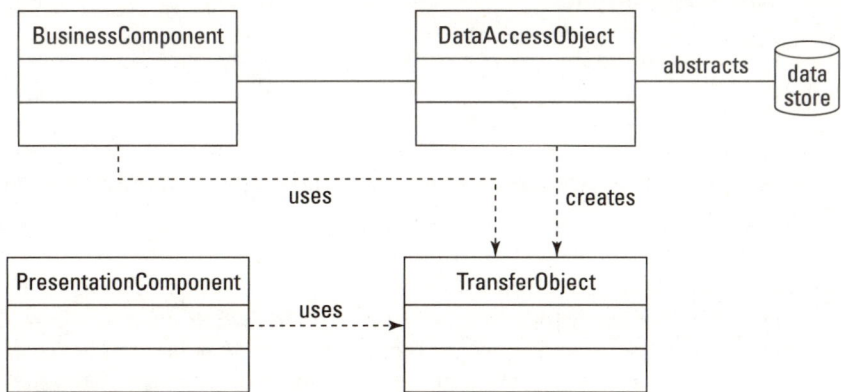

Figure 25-2: Example of the data-access-object pattern

Figure 25-3 shows the sequence diagram for the interaction among different compo-nents. For simplicity we use one view of the sequence diagram as seen by the pre-sentation component:

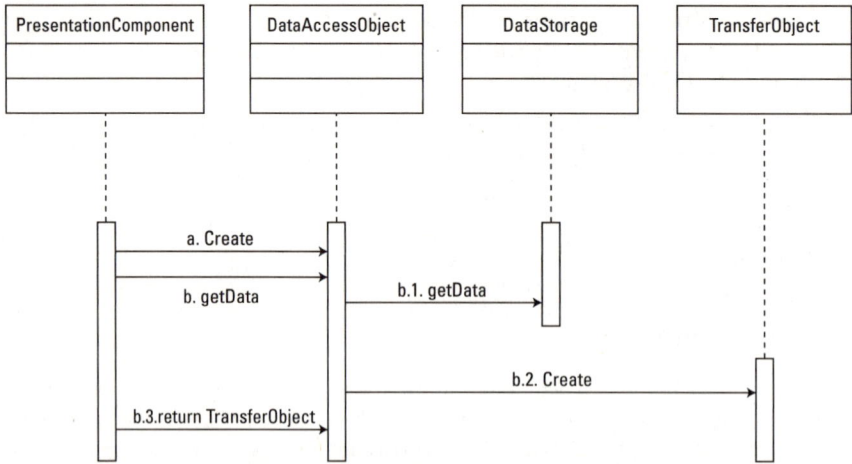

Figure 25-3: Sequence diagram for the data-access-object pattern

The following elements of this figure are discussed in the subsequent sections:

✦ PresentationComponent

✦ DataAccessObject

✦ DataStorage

✦ TransferObject

PresentationComponent

PresentationComponent is mainly the frontend component, such as JSP or servlets, that processes the data and presents information to the user. Note that BusinessComponent, a business component, can replace PresentationComponent, a presentation component here. The Business component refers to any component from the service tier, and the presentation component represents any component from the presentation tier. The presentation component acts as the client for the data-access object.

DataAccessObject

DataAccessObject is the primary component of the data-access-object pattern. It abstracts datasource access. Also, it encapsulates the mechanism to access data, enabling transparent access to data by the presentation or business component.

DataStorage

DataStorage can be an RDBMS, flat file, ODBMS, or native-XML database providing data to the presentation or business component.

TransferObject

TransferObject is the data carrier. In Figure 25-3 the data-access object uses the transfer object TransferObject to send a group of related attributes so that the presentation component could process the necessary data and present data to the client requesting the data.

Implementing the Data-Access-Object Pattern

Two different strategies can be used for implementing this pattern, depending on whether or not the datasource is going to be the same across different enterprise-application implementations. When the datasource is the same, the base implementation uses the factory Design pattern to make the data-access-object pattern produce a finite number of DAOs. Those DAOs are based on the requirement of the enterprise application, as illustrated in Figure 25-4.

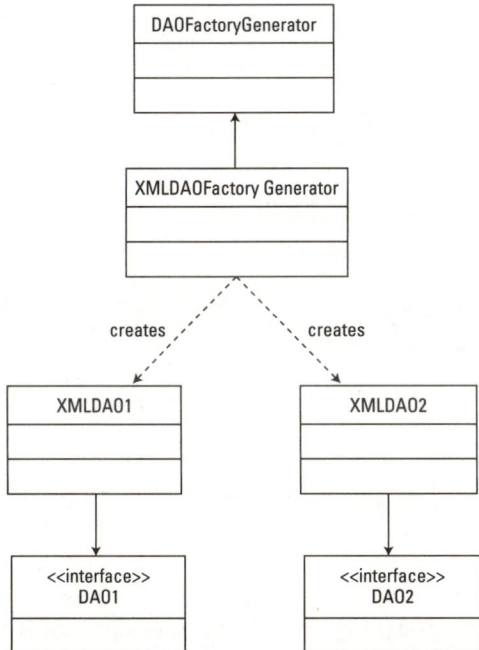

Figure 25-4: Example implementation of the data-access-object pattern (XML Source)

Figure 25-4 shows an XMLDAOFactoryGenerator that creates concrete objects XMLDAO1 and XMLDAO2. These objects are based on the DAOs and can be created by means of a descriptor file or can introspect the native-XML database to construct these objects. The interfaces are implemented by the DAO objects and are specific to the objects. For example, in the Airline Reservation business case there could be a DAO object for Flight Arrival times and another for Flight Reservations and each could implement an interface that defines specific methods that are used for the DAO objects.

When the datasources are different across enterprise applications, using a combination of abstract factory along with factory design pattern carries the base implementation. Figure 25-5 shows how the data-access-object pattern can be implemented if the connection is between two different datasources. More details of abstract factory pattern can be found in the book, *Design Patterns* by Erich Gamma et al.

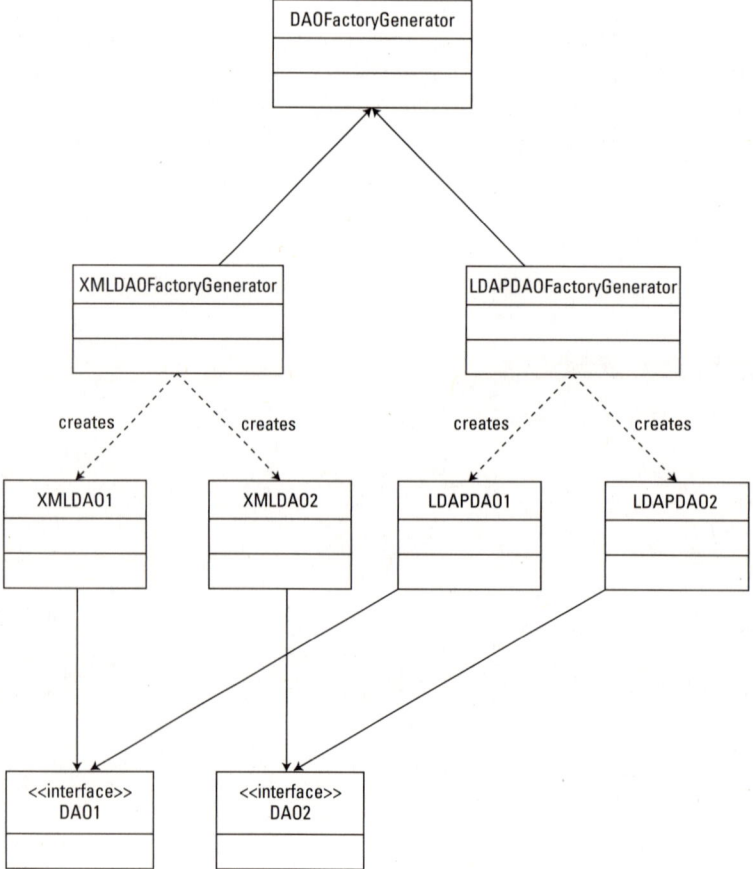

Figure 25-5: The data-access-object pattern accessing multiple data sources

Figure 25-5 is an example of the data-access-object pattern accessing multiple data-sources. Here, an LDAP and an XML datasource are being accessed.

Applying the data-access-object pattern

Listings 25-1 through 25-4 use the DAOFactoryGenerator abstract factory pattern with the XMLDAOFactoryGenerator concrete factory pattern to generate XMLAccountOwnerDAO. Both the interface and AccountOwnerDAO will be common between the two factories, which is also the case with LDAPFactoryGenerator.

Listing 25-1: **Abstract DAOFactory class**

```
public abstract class DAOFactoryGenerator{
  //available datasource
  public static final int LDAP = 1;
  public static final int ORACLE = 2;

  //generate the necessary DAO's to be implemented by the
specific DAO generators.
  public abstract AccountOwnerDAO getAccountOwnerDAO();
  public abstract BeneficiaryDAO  getBeneficiaryDAO();

  //method to get the concrete DAO factories
  public static DAOFactoryGenerator getDAOFactory(int
dataSourceIndicator){
        switch(dataSourceIndicator){
                case ORACLE:
                        return new XMLDAOFactoryGenerator();
                case LDAP:
                        return new LDAPDAOFactoryGenerator();
                default:
                        return null;
        }
  }
}
```

Listing 25-2: **Concrete DAOFactory class**

```
//import all the necessary libraries
public class XMLDAOFactoryGenerator extends
DAOFactoryGenerator{
  public static Connection createConnection(){
        //code to connect to oracle database.
  }
```

Continued

Listing 25-2 *(continued)*

```
//implement methods of the abstract class
public AccountOwnerDAO getAccountOwnerDAO(){
       return new AccountOwnerDAO();
}
public BeneficiaryDAO getBeneficiaryDAO(){
       return new BeneficiaryDAO();
}
} OK
```

Listing 25-3: Interface for the Account Owner

```
// interface for the account owner
public interface AccountOwnerDAO{
  public int insertAccountOwner();
  public int getAccountOwnerSSN();
  public int insertAccountOwnerAddress(AccountOwner
accountOwner);
  //other needed methods.
} OK
```

Listing 25-4: Implementation of AccountOwnerDAO

```
//implementation of accountowner DAO
public class XMLAccountOwnerDAO implements AccountOwnerDAO{\
  //default constructor
  public XMLAccountOwnerDAO(){
  }
  //implement methods of the interface.
  public int insertAccountOwner(){
  }
  public int getAccountOwnerSSN(){
  }
  public int insertAccountOwnerAddress(AccountOwner
accountOwner){
  }
}
```

Applying related patterns

Following are the patterns used in combination with the data-access-object pattern:

✦ Abstract factory pattern

✦ Factory pattern

✦ `PresentationComponent`

✦ `BusinessComponent`

✦ `TransferObject`

The abstract factory and factory patterns are discussed in more detail in *Design Patterns* by Erich Gamma et al.

Using the Service-Activator Pattern

Consider the typical EJB call, in which a lookup gets a remote-interface reference to the necessary EJB and then calls the methods on that EJB. The process is *synchronous,* meaning that one follows the other. Some clients may need *asynchronous* access to data. The existing EJB model, 1.0 (or) 1.1, does not allow asynchronous calls. Therefore, if the existing application needs the functionality for asynchronous calls you can use the service-activator pattern. With EJB 2.0, message-driven beans solve the problem of having asynchronous models (asynchronous means not happening at the same time, but happening later) built into enterprise applications. EJBs coded with the version 1.0 and version 1.1 specification need to be invoked asynchronously by means of message-driven beans without the existing code's being converted to an EJB 2.0 model.

The service-activator pattern has the following characteristics:

Allows the JMS and EJB 1.0 and 1.1 version implementations to interact.

Provides the concept of asynchronous message processing, which is available only from EJB 2.0 onward, to the EJB 1.0 and 1.1 implementations through message-driven beans.

Can be used either as a stand-alone component, or can be used as a plug-and-play pattern into the current EJB 1.0 and 1.1 implementations, or as a part of the application-server services.

 **Cross-Reference** See Chapter 17 for a discussion of message-driven beans.

Keep in mind the following facts that pertain to using the service-activator pattern:

Existing EJB models enable invoking them by means of a method invocation after a lookup for remote reference.

Implementation of the JMS model is not possible because it would cause a violation of the EJB specification and the EJB container controls access to the EJBs.

The EJB 2.0 model supports message-driven beans for asynchronous EJB invocation and existing models must have similar functionality.

EJB containers may make EJBs inactive, usually to conserve resources. The client will need to go through a lookup followed by method invocation to activate the EJB.

Clients want to use the JMS but the EJB container does not support it.

Implementation

The service-activator pattern can process asynchronous calls from the client. This pattern locates the necessary business component, such as an EJB, and invokes methods to fulfill the requests of the client.

This pattern is a JMS (Java Messaging Service) listener and delegation service that implements the JMS message-listener interface. The service-activator pattern receives the message from the client, unmarshals the client request, activates the necessary business component, and finally sends acknowledgement to the client. You might notice the influence of the Abstract Window Toolkit (AWT) delegation-design model in this service-activator design pattern because both use the delegation process in their model. In case you're curious, this is what happens in the AWT delegation model: Clients register with listeners and listeners notify the clients once events are triggered. For a brief description of the AWT event-delegation model refer to *Java in a Nutshell* by David Flanagan (O'Reilly and Associates; 4th Edition, March 2002).

Figure 25-6 depicts the structure of the service-activator pattern:

In Figure 25-6, the Presentation Component sends an Asynchronous request and the Request class implements the Java Messaging Service (JMS) message and the service-activator pattern receives it and invokes the necessary Business Component, asynchronously.

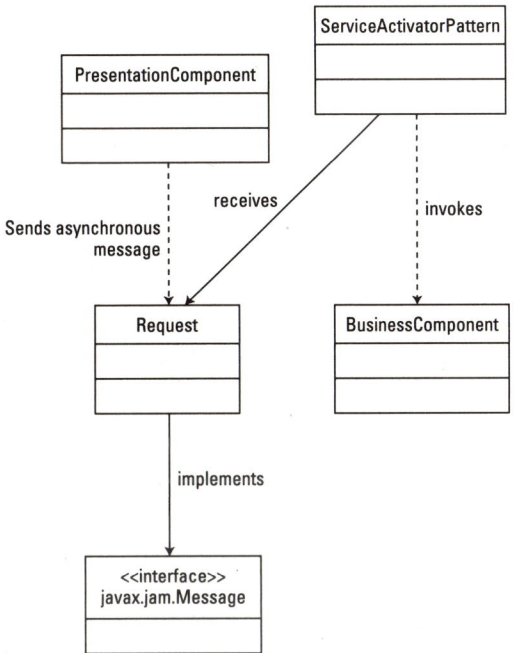

Figure 25-6: Example of the service-activator pattern

Figure 26-7 shows a snapshot of the sequence diagram for the service activator:

The word *Create* in Figure 25-7 refers to the creation of the appropriate object.

The following elements of this figure are discussed in the subsequent sections:

✦ PresentationComponent

✦ Request

✦ ServiceActivator

✦ BusinessComponent

✦ Acknowledgment

PresentationComponent

PresentationComponent is mainly the front-end component, like JSP or servlets, that needs to call BusinessComponent. So it creates a Request to use the services offered by the service-activator pattern.

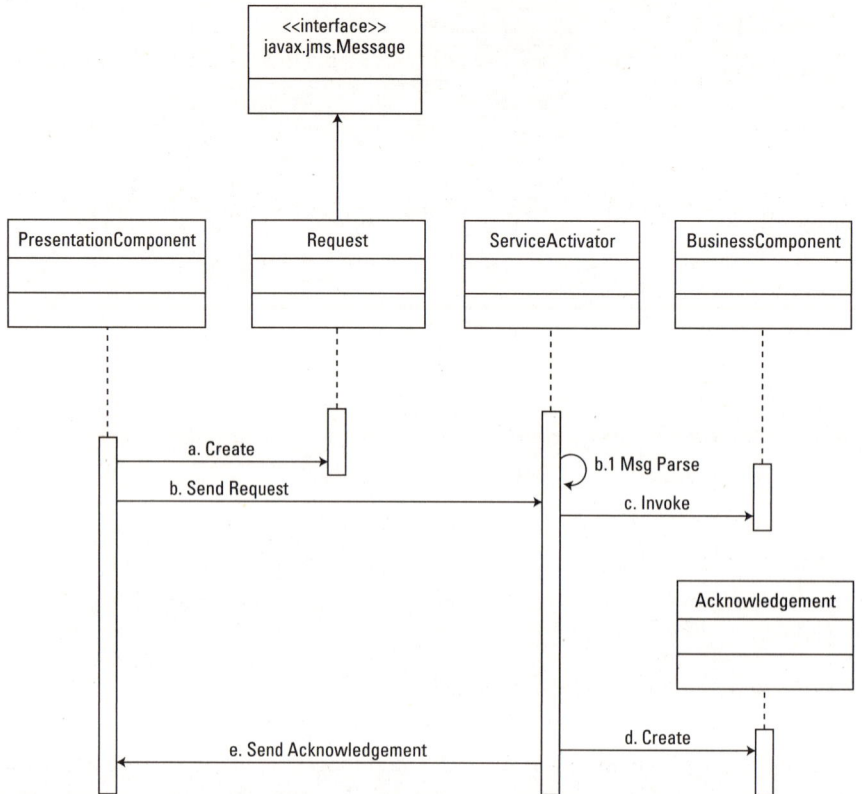

Figure 25-7: Sequence diagram for the service-activator pattern

Request

The Request is an implementation of the Message object that is created by PresentationComponent so that the service activator can process client requests.

ServiceActivator

ServiceActivator unmarshals the message sent, the client looks up the necessary business component and invokes the message. If successful, Service Activator object creates an instance of the Acknowledgment object and acknowledges the requesting client. Note that ServiceActivator implements the javax.jms. MessageListener interface as defined by the JMS specs.

BusinessComponent

This component is an EJB that processes the request sent by ServiceActivator.

Acknowledgment

`Acknowledgment` corresponds to the acknowledgement created by `ServiceActivator` to acknowledge client requests.

Implementing the Service-Activator Pattern

The service-activator pattern can be implemented in a few different ways. We will discuss the following in order:

✦ The service-activator-server strategy

✦ The EJB-server strategy

✦ The EJB-client strategy

The service-activator-server strategy

This pattern can be implemented either as a stand-alone application or as part of the application-server services. The main advantage of this strategy comes when you implement it as an application-server service. This is because the server can monitor and control the state of the pattern (that is, start, stop, and restart) through manual or automatic configuration.

The EJB-server strategy

The business-component element of the service-activator pattern can use either a session or an entity bean. For simple-flow applications an entity bean can be the business component. For complex applications a session-facade-design pattern can provide access for the service-activator pattern. For invoking multiple methods on the business component it is advisable to use a stateful session bean instead of a stateless session bean because stateful session is needed.

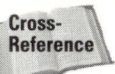

See Chapter 24 for a discussion of the session-facade design pattern. See Chapter 15 for an explanation of session beans.

The EJB-client strategy

The client need not be a presentation component; it can also be another business component such as an EJB. For integration with legacy systems, the client should generate the message based on the transaction with the legacy system. The service activator can unmarshal the message and invoke the necessary business component for processing the legacy system's request.

Applying the service-activator pattern

Figure 25-8 shows a high-level class diagram depicting how the service-activator pattern can be used to glue JMS and EJB together to provide asynchronous business invocation. One real-life scenario in which this can be used is an online shopping mall taking orders from clients and sending the requests to companies that completes the process. The online shopping mall acts as a placeholder with which different stores can set up their businesses.

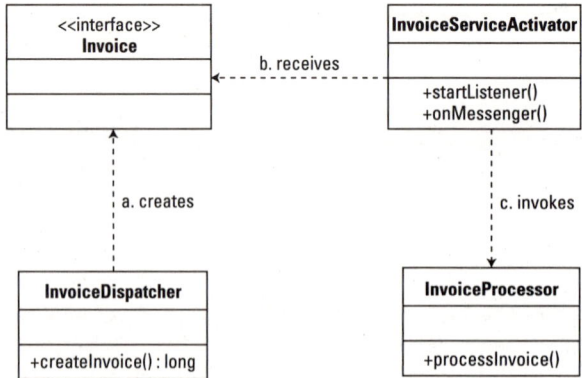

Figure 25-8: Class diagram for implementing the service-activator pattern

`InvoiceDispatcher` creates an invoice along with the store that needs to process it. The invoice-service activator receives the invoice and invokes `InvoiceProcessor` to create an e-mail based on the invoice and sends it to the necessary store so that store will process the invoice.

Applying related patterns

Following are the patterns that can be used in combination with the data-access-object pattern:

✦ Session facade

✦ Business delegate

✦ Service locator

✦ Half-sync/half-async [POSA2]

The session-facade, business-delegate, and service-locator patterns are cataloged in Chapter 24. A discussion of the half sync half-async discussion can be found in

Pattern-Oriented Software Architecture, Volume 2: Patterns for Concurrent and Networked Objects by Douglas Schmidt, Michael Stal, Hans Rohnert and Frank Buschmann (Wiley Press, 2000.)

Examining the Transfer-Object Pattern

Every call to an EJB involves a lookup to get a reference to the remote interface and then execute the necessary method. It is costly every time the EJB method is invoked to get a value and heavy network overhead is associated with such calls. Applications must exchange data with the EJBs and data must be available at different points within the application.

It is a good design principle to group related attributes and populate them all at once during a method call. A transfer-object pattern helps you do this by providing access to related attributes.

The transfer-object pattern has the following characteristics:

> More data are transferred between the presentation tier and business tier components.
>
> Network overhead and code duplication are reduced because of fewer EJB calls.
>
> Stale `TransferObjects` can result from the updateable strategy of this pattern. These are components that have old copies of the `TransferObject` values.

`TransferObject` provides concurrent access and transactions.

The transfer-object pattern introduces complexity for synchronization of data; the best way to resolve this problem is to use version-control numbers during updating of data by the business component.

Keep in mind the following facts that pertain to using the transfer-object pattern:

> EJB method calls to get values from database tables are costly as they involve a lookup and an invocation. Several calls could cause network overhead in bandwidth and productivity.
>
> Enterprise applications involve read, delete, and update transactions. Read-only access is needed for presentation components. Business components need read, delete, and update transactions in any combination.
>
> Enterprise applications require more than one attribute and this involves invoking multiple calls on the business component to get different attribute values.
>
> Enterprise applications involving more data being transferred across the presentation and business components can cause overhead and network performance bottlenecks.

Implementation

TransferObject is a serializable class grouping related attributes and encapsulating the business data. A single method can be used to send and retrieve TransferObject. The EJB can take a transfer object already created or create a new transfer object TransferObject, and populate it with values from the datasource for attributes within the TransferObject, and send the TransferObject. Figure 25-9 depicts the structure of the transfer-object pattern:

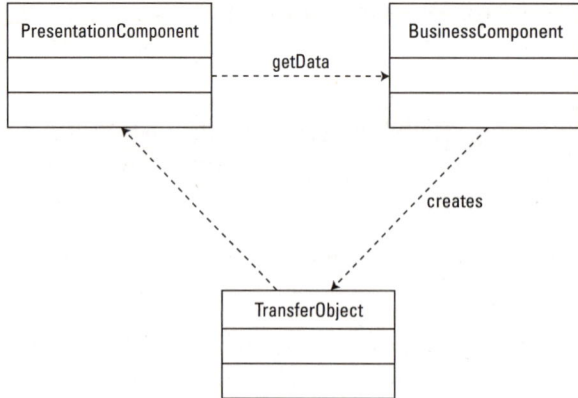

Figure 25-9: Example of the transfer-object pattern

Figure 25-10 shows a snapshot of the sequence diagram for TransferObject:

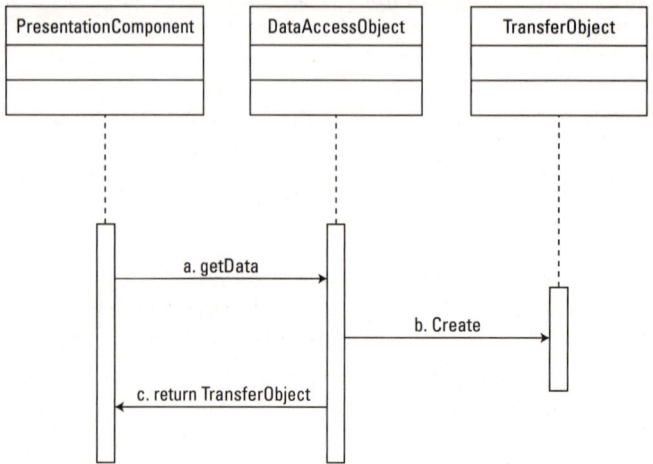

Figure 25-10: Sequence diagram for the transfer-object pattern

The following elements of this figure are discussed in the subsequent sections:

✦ `PresentationComponent`

✦ `BusinessComponent`

✦ `TransferObject`

PresentationComponent

`PresentationComponent` is mainly the frontend component, like JSP or servlets, that calls the business component to get related data attributes.

BusinessComponent

`BusinessComponent` is typically an EJB that creates a `TransferObject`, populates it with necessary data, and sends it to `PresentationComponent`.

TransferObject

`TransferObject` is a serializable class that contains groups of related attributes filled with data as a result of the call to `BusinessComponent`.

Note   We can add one more layer through a data-access-object pattern, which generates `TransferObject`. Figure 25-2 shows how a business component requests data through a data-access-object pattern. The data-access-object pattern in turn constructs the transfer object.

Implementing the transfer-object pattern

The transfer-object pattern can be implemented in a few different ways. We will discuss the following in order:

✦ The updateable `TransferObject` strategy

✦ The multiple-`TransferObject`s strategy

✦ The `TransferObject`-factory strategy

The updateable TransferObject strategy

This strategy is useful when `PresentationComponent` wants to update the data in `TransferObject`. Instead of using the JavaBeans way of having mutator and access methods, `PresentationComponent` can directly update the data in `TransferObject` and pass them to `BusinessComponent`, which can then update the row in the database.

The multiple TransferObjects strategy

Sometimes `PresentationComponent` may need multiple `TransferObjects`. For example, say `PresentationComponent` needs an `AccountOwner` transfer object and a `SuccessorOwner` transfer object. Then `BusinessComponent` can provide separate methods for generating both `TransferObjects`.

The TransferObject-factory strategy

In this strategy, `PresentationComponent` invokes `BusinessComponent`, which calls a `TransferObject` factory that generates the needed `TransferObject`. For example, a factory can generate both the `AccountOwner` and `SuccessorOwner` `TransferObjects`.

Applying the transfer-object pattern

Listing 25-5 presents the transfer-object pattern and entity bean code with which to provide `TransferObject` to the calling `PresentationComponent`:

Listing 25-5: Account Owner interface

```
//Transfer Object Pattern
public interface AccountOwner extends java.io.Serializable{
  public String getFirstName();
  public String getLastName();
  public String getAddress();
  public void setFirstName(String firstName);
  public void setLastName(String lastName);
  public void setAddress(String address);
}

//Transfer Object Pattern implementing the AccountOwner
Interface.
public class AccountOwnerTransferObject implements
AccountOwner{
  public String firstName;
  public String lastName;
  public String address;

  //implement the interface methods
  public void setFirstName(String firstName){
        this.firstName = firstName;
  }
  public void setLastName(String lastName){
        this.lastName = lastName;
  }
  public void setAddress(String address){
        this.address = address;
  }
  public String getFirstName(){
```

```
        return firstName;
    }
  public String getLastName(){
        return lastName;
    }
  public String getAddress(){
        return address;
    }
}

//EJB code to populate the AccountOwner Transfer Object Pattern
object
public class AccountOwnerEntity implements EntityBean{
  public String firstname;
  public String lastname;
  public String address;

  //method to get the AccountOwner Transfer Object.
  public AccountOwnerTransferObject getAccountOwnerData(){
        return createAccountOwnerTransferObject();
    }

  public AccountOwnerTransferObject
createAccountOwnerTransferObject(){
        private AccountOwnerTransferObject tobj = new
AccountOwnerTransferObject();
        tobj.firstName = firstname;
        tobj.lastName = lastname;
        tobj.address = address;
    }
}
```

In the preceding code, we define an `Account Owner` encapsulating the common attributes used to gather account owner details from the database. We use it within an `Account Owner` entity bean to populate the account owner attributes as a part of a single method call rather than calling each time to get an attribute.

Applying related patterns

Following are the patterns that can be used in combination with the transfer-object pattern:

✦ Session facade

✦ The value-object assembler

✦ The value-list handler

✦ The composite entity

✦ The data object access

The session-facade and composite-entity patterns are cataloged in Chapter 24. The value-object assembler and value-list handler are cataloged in *Core J2EE Patterns* by Deepak Alur, John Crupi, and Dan Malks (Sun Microsystems Press, 2001). The Data-Object-Access pattern is discussed in this chapter.

Summary

Data-tier patterns play an important role in managing access to datasources, transferring data through grouping of related attributes, and enabling asynchronous invocations on business components.

✦   ✦   ✦

Advanced Topics

P A R T

VIII

♦ ♦ ♦ ♦

In This Part

Chapter 26
Exploring
Frameworks and
Application
Architecture

Chapter 27
Using ANT to Build
and Deploy
Applications

Chapter 28
Creating High-
Performance Java
Applications

♦ ♦ ♦ ♦

Exploring Frameworks and Application Architecture

✦ ✦ ✦ ✦

In This Chapter

Explaining
frameworks

Understanding the
pains of J2EE and
why developers need
more than just the
J2EE application
server and an IDE to
be successful

Reviewing
application
architectures

Building frameworks

Exploring alternatives
to frameworks

Predicting the future
of frameworks

Evaluating
frameworks

✦ ✦ ✦ ✦

Sun and the Java Community Process have vastly improved the world of distributed computing by defining the Java 2 Enterprise Edition. Software vendors have been gracious enough to implement the J2EE specification, providing a variety of fully-functional application servers from which to choose. All that is left is for someone to acquire one of those application servers and nothing would stand in their way of successfully creating new business applications . . . right? Unfortunately, that is not the case.

J2EE improves the runtime environment for applications by standardizing a large part of the infrastructure, much of what used to be either developed by companies internally or provided by a proprietary single vendor product. There are many benefits of this standardization. Vendor neutral applications can be deployed in one application server today and redeployed in a different application server tomorrow. Companies providing other enterprise products, such as databases or security systems, only need to provide one integration with their technology that all application servers can use. This openness that comes from standardization gives J2EE adopters much freedom and creates a good market for J2EE technology.

While J2EE does do some great things, it has one big problem: it is not easy for inexperienced developers to successfully create applications. And even for experienced developers it is not trivial to have continued success, especially if the experienced and inexperienced are mixed together on the development team. What is needed is an approach to make success with J2EE less of an art and more of a science—an approach that an entire team can adopt and with it consistently deliver quality J2EE applications.

In this chapter we will introduce frameworks—what they are, why they are needed, and how to make them part of your environment. We will also discuss other technologies that include alternatives to frameworks or advancements beyond frameworks. By the end of the chapter, you should have a good understanding of the options available to help you be successful with J2EE.

What are Frameworks?

The software industry is notorious for having multiple definitions for the same terms. If you have tried having a discussion about frameworks, components, or services, before defining the concept up front, you're probably familiar with the confusion that can ensue. So it is very important to come to a common understanding of what is meant by *framework* before we can move forward. It is also important to understand that the definition we agree upon here isn't one that you can assume in another conversation. We will use the following definition for our purposes:

> Frameworks provide a set of classes that interact in a predefined manner to address a particular problem area.

That is the simplest explanation of what a framework is. It is often the assumed default definition because it is the lowest-common-denominator definition with the broadest applicability. The problem is that frameworks come in many flavors, but the ones we're interested in for this chapter are the *business-application frameworks*. So we're going to take it a step further and provide the following, richer definition of this particular type of framework:

> Business-application frameworks the creation of business applications and control the execution of the applications built on that structure. The structure includes defining interfaces, providing classes, and employing external configuration that interact in a well-known manner. The classes, interfaces, and configuration are extended to create the business application. Business-application frameworks apply the principles of *inversion of control, separation of concerns, and loose coupling* to provide flexibility, increase reusability, and improve productivity. (These concepts are discussed in the "Understanding Framework Principles" section in this chapter.) Most importantly, these frameworks are aligned with business-developer skills and business requirements.

In this chapter we will use the terms *framework* and *business-application framework* interchangeably. However, it is important to keep the distinction between generic "framework" and "business-application framework" in mind when you discuss frameworks with a larger audience.

Now, maybe you're wondering about the other types of frameworks. Here are a few examples:

✦ **Technical frameworks** (such as a logging or distribution framework) solve low-level problems

✦ **Industry-vertical frameworks** (such as a retail-banking or airline framework) solve a category of high-level business problems

This chapter covers business-application frameworks because J2EE is most widely used for business applications and adopting a business-application framework would have the biggest impact on the success of J2EE.

Frameworks versus class libraries

How does a framework differ from a class library? A business-application framework is implemented as a collection of classes that are packaged together, so in that one way the two are similar. Other than that, however, frameworks are as different from class libraries as J2EE application servers (which also share the packaging commonality).

Two qualities that can quickly distinguish a class library from a framework are completeness and extendibility. A class library performs a complete task, such as opening a file or calculating the area of a circle. A business-application framework provides the structure but not the complete solution for a category of problems. The complete solution is formed when the user adds behavior to the framework. Examples of the application areas business-application frameworks might focus on are presentation, business logic, and persistence.

Extendibility is useful for distinguishing between broadly defined "frameworks" (not just business-application frameworks) and class libraries. Log4J is an open-source framework from Apache that does logging. Even though Log4J is a complete solution, which you can install and start using immediately, it is not a class-library because it is extendable. Log4J allows you to create custom classes and modify configurations to extend the behavior of the framework. Class libraries are usually used as-is with a "black-box" nature that does not expose the workings of the class library and is not extendable. Before we go into more detail about the framework qualities, we'll take a look at why frameworks are needed.

The pains of J2EE

Frameworks have been around since early in the adoption of object-oriented-software. They are definitely not new and are not only applicable to J2EE development. But you may be asking yourself, "Why do I need frameworks when I have J2EE?" Early on in the history of J2EE that might have been a more common question: J2EE was new and was such a large improvement over what had existed previously (for example, complex CORBA systems, vendor dependent application servers such as Kiva, or custom in-house built application servers) that those adopting it thought it was all they needed. However, the mere fact that you are reading this book implies that J2EE is not the easiest technology to understand and use correctly. For all of the problems that J2EE does address, there are still places where frameworks can add value.

J2EE is infrastructure technology for creating distributed applications, an inherently difficult task that requires much expertise. Many different people acting in a variety of roles are usually involved in creating an enterprise J2EE application. Satisfying the needs of this audience is the source of many pains that frameworks can eliminate. Table 26-1 provides a glimpse of what these pains might be.

Table 26-1 **The pains of J2EE**	
Role	*Pain*
New J2EE developer	Fear of the unknown in adopting J2EE
	Too much to learn too quickly
	Steps to successfully using J2EE are not clear
Experienced J2EE developer	Bored with repetitive tasks
	Drained from extensive mentoring of new team members
Architect	Wants uniform way to address similar problem areas across multiple projects (as an example, Struts demonstrates the need for more structure in the presentation layer)
	Fear of making wrong decisions that will be expensive to change by the time decisions are validated (or invalidated) late in development
	Needs to be able to accommodate constantly changing requirements
Project manager	Not sure how to divide up work among team members
	Not sure how to determine quality of work
	Not sure how to determine work progress
	Too long a delay before any progress can be shown to business owner
Business owner	Success with J2EE development requires team of expensive J2EE experts
	Every change is a slow, expensive redevelopment effort
	Doesn't realize economies of scale in building suite of J2EE applications (applications do not go down in cost to create even though company continues to build more)

The first step in solving many problems is first admitting that the problem exists. Although ideally you would have had great success with J2EE, it is very likely that some of the pains we mentioned resonate with your experiences. We have already introduced frameworks and now we will go into more detail on business-application frameworks and why they can help companies succeed with J2EE.

Understanding Framework Principles

In this section we are going to delve into more detail about the following principles and concepts related to frameworks:

- ✦ Inversion of control
- ✦ Separation of concerns
- ✦ Loose coupling
- ✦ Extensibility
- ✦ Configurability
- ✦ Alignment
- ✦ Design patterns

Inversion of control

Inversion of control, sometimes referred to as the Hollywood Principle ("don't call us, we'll call you"), refers to the flow of control and how it passes through the framework. Frameworks distinguish themselves by retaining control of the application execution, calling out in a pre-determined manner to be custom defined by the framework structure. In contrast, a class library is called in to perform a particular function before returning control back to the caller. An analogy would be an EJB container: The container is in control and administers calls to EJBs, which are the custom components. It is this principle that allows the framework to define the environment and that lays the foundation for creating reusable classes that are "plug-and-play." Adopting the inversion-of-control principle makes the following two principles much easier to adhere to.

Separation of concerns

This principle refers to the need to compartmentalize deliverables by the skills required to create them. The three main benefits of applying this principle to framework design are as follows:

People with particular skills can be assigned to the deliverable where they will be most productive.

Work on the deliverables, instead of being sequential, can happen simultaneously.

The deliverables created should be more reusable because they address particular needs, as opposed to coarse-grained results that address many requirements. Components that address many requirements become more complex, making them difficult to understand and more dependent on the exact scenario for which they were originally built — both of which lead to less reuse.

An application of this principle that you may be familiar with is the model-view-controller (MVC) design pattern. Very briefly, the model-view-controller design pattern describes an approach for cleanly separating those three areas related to creating user interfaces. That clean distinction enables the people with the most relevant skills to create views, models, and controllers, and to work independently of each other. Views and models are reusable and all three can be changed with minimal (or at least known) impact on each other.

Loose coupling

This principle describes the need for independence among the classes involved in the framework. This independence involves *late binding* among the classes involved, meaning that the relationship among the classes is established at run-time. Loose coupling is the opposite of *tight coupling,* wherein the relationship is established during the compile. Loose coupling and late binding are powerful concepts that enable the framework to be fluid and to accommodate the changing requirements that are a natural part of application development and maintenance.

Extensibility

Extensibility is the ability to significantly change or enhance the behavior of the framework by providing new classes for the framework to use. These classes can be subclasses of existing classes or new implementations of the interfaces defined by the framework. By supporting extensibility, the framework opens itself to the variety of customizations that may be required initially or in the future. This openness to change is critical if the framework is to have a long life — no matter how completely or exactly a framework fulfills current requirements, those requirements are destined to change.

Configurability

Configurability is the capacity of the framework to use external metadata to affect the behavior of the framework. Unlike extensibility, configurability is not used to change the core algorithm employed by the framework but rather to influence or provide input to the algorithm to reflect the desired application behavior. This configuration should not become so complex as to become a replacement for coding; that kind of extreme customization should be accomplished through extensibility.

One of the challenges of trying to make a framework configurable is knowing where it is best applied. A process can be applied to determine those areas. The process is similar to determining equations from story problems in algebra, when you attempt to find an algorithm that contains variables and produces the correct results when values for those variables are plugged in. In the case of configurability, the algorithm is captured in code while the value for the variables comes from external metadata.

The process consists of following these straightforward steps:

1. Find classes that contain behaviors that are identical except for slight variances. Often those variances will be based on data (that is, variables or constants) as opposed to code variances, although that is not always the case.

2. Attempt to derive a common algorithm that could be used to replace the custom code with the variables now being read in from some external source (usually an XML configuration file).

3. Test and refine your algorithm if necessary. This is also the point at which you can use your experience to decide whether the configuration makes sense. Is it something that would actually be used in a real application? Does it make sense — is the goal of the configurability evident?

4. Be wary of configurations that actually make things more complicated and cumbersome as opposed to simplifying the problem — sometimes extensibility, even though it seems repetitive, is the better approach.

The benefits of configurability are as follows:

Less custom code to write, debug, and maintain

Easier to review and maintain configuration than custom code

Ensures that the algorithm remains consistently applied; this is in contrast to extensions, where the algorithm can be drastically modified by the user (for better or worse)

Alignment

One of the most important principles of a business-application framework is that it must be *aligned* with developer skill sets and business requirements. One of the biggest challenges in adopting J2EE is that not many J2EE experts are available, especially not when compared to the large numbers of developers for legacy applications (such as COBOL) or departmental-level applications (such as Visual Basic, Web CGI, and so on). A business-application framework should enable a team of non-J2EE experts to successfully map their business requirements to the functionality that satisfies those requirements. This happens when the framework makes it very clear, almost in a step-by-step fashion, how specific requirements are implemented and when the framework makes the most of the existing developer skills.

You may be thinking that J2EE should be the source for this alignment. However, J2EE is usually focused on solving lower-level technical problems, not aligning with the developer skills or business application requirements. An easy example of where J2EE is not aligned with developers creating business applications is the complexity of both session and entity Enterprise JavaBeans (EJBs). Session and entity EJBs are some of the core components of J2EE where developers will spend much of their time, yet it is much easier to make mistakes with them than it is to use them correctly. These mistakes originate both in design (for example, how many EJBs should be used, what should the interface be) and development (for example, correctly developing the Home Interface, Remote Interface, EJB Implementation, and deployment descriptors).

Java ServerPages (JSPs) are an example of where J2EE is more aligned with the developer skills. JSPs were added to J2EE because much servlet (of which JSPs are a subclass) development was being done to output HTML. Before JSPs were introduced, creating an HTML user interface from servlets involved coding in Java to output HTML strings. This coding required Java developers and the code itself is difficult to create and maintain because the format of the code doesn't match the traditional HTML file. With JSPs the user interface files are formatted like traditional HTML files. HTML developers with existing skills can be more successful, eliminating the need to train HTML developers Java or Java developers HTML. However, even with the benefits of JSPs, it is not clear how page navigation, data validation, and business logic should be structured. The Struts framework (discussed shortly) builds on JSPs and servlets by making it easier to translate business application requirements directly to the required implementation. So even though JSPs are better aligned with developer skills than servlets, more is needed to create alignment with application requirements.

Design patterns

At this point it is useful to mention design patterns and how they apply to frameworks. Frameworks are a valuable source of industry best practices; using design patterns can only improve the quality of the framework.

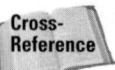 **Cross-Reference** See Chapters 23 through 25 for discussions of patterns.

In addition to the design patterns discussed in Part VII of this book, object-oriented (OO) design patterns are also available, such as those listed in *Design Patterns* by the Gang of Four (Erich Gamma, Richard Helm, Ralph Johnson, and John Vlissides; Addison-Wesley, 1995). In the context of a framework for J2EE applications, the J2EE and OO categories of design patterns have different purposes. The framework should employ OO design patterns in its construction, and it should apply J2EE design patterns to the problems it solves.

This is an important distinction best illustrated by a quick example. If you were using more than one framework, let's say one for navigation and one for persistence, they could both employ the same OO patterns — such as facade, flyweight, and singleton — in their construction. However, because these frameworks are addressing different application areas, they would use different J2EE design patterns. The navigation framework might use the model-view-controller pattern while the persistence framework might use the value-object and data-access-object patterns.

Codifying design patterns in a framework results in several benefits, including the following:

> Consistent implementation of the design pattern will be used by everyone, as opposed to each person using his or her own implementation

> Team members can all benefit from the design pattern without having to be experts in design patterns or going through the effort of translating the concepts into practice

> Team members will benefit from the understanding of the design patterns gained by using an expert implementation

Examining the Struts framework example

The best way to illustrate the framework principles is to go through an example of their implementation. We will be using Struts as an example because it is an open-source product that you can download and go through in more detail on your own. For those not familiar with Struts, it is a framework for the presentation layer of a Web application. Struts is available from Apache as part of the Jakarta Project. For more information go to `http://jakarta.apache.org/struts/index.html`.

Design patterns

We will first cover the design patterns that Struts implements because that will make it easier to discuss the other aspects of the framework. Struts is an implementation of the model-view-controller (MVC) design pattern as it applies to Web applications. Using the MVC design pattern for server side based user interfaces is informally known as MVC2 or *Model 2*. The MVC design pattern was introduced briefly earlier in this chapter in the section "Separation of concerns." It is an old design pattern that originated in the Smalltalk graphical user interface (GUI) world. It describes how a user interface should be divided into the following components:

✦ **Model** represents the data for the user interface

✦ **View** determines how those data will be displayed

✦ **Controller** orchestrates the user interaction with the views and models

You can read about this design pattern by going to the Sun site at `http://java.sun.com/blueprints/patterns/MVC-detailed.html`.

Inversion of control

When you are using Struts, all incoming Hypertext Transfer Protocol (HTTP) requests are intercepted by a controller servlet. This servlet has the following responsibilities:

✦ Analyzing the request

✦ Accessing the Struts configuration

✦ Determining which action class to execute

This combined behavior is the logical controller described as part of MVC. It is a classic example of the inversion-of-control design principle. (Inversion of control was introduced earlier in this chapter in the section of the same name.) The incoming request is handed off to the Struts framework, which determines which custom class is the correct one to execute. Figure 26-1 shows this flow of control and illustrates how the Struts controller retains control, even though it calls out to custom classes determined by its configuration. Figure 26-2 goes into more detail by showing a sequence diagram that identifies specific Struts classes and where they are involved in the execution flow.

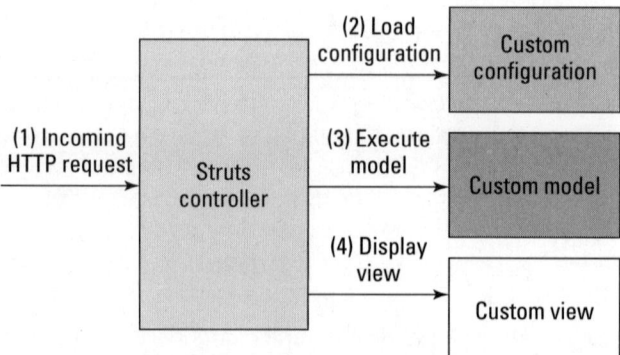

Figure 26-1: This high-level Struts-processing flow shows the interaction of the model, view, and controller, with the Struts controller retaining control throughout.

Separation of concerns

Struts provides an easy example of the separation of concerns introduced earlier in this chapter because its guiding MVC design pattern is based on that concept. The model, view, and controller are distinguished entities that should have minimal or no knowledge of each other. That allows them to be created independently by the respective expert in each area as well as leading to greater reuse. In Struts, the controller expert will be responsible for organizing the struts-config.xml; the view expert will spend time creating JavaServer Pages (JSPs), and the model expert will work with the Struts Action classes. The skills required in the different areas of Struts are shown at a high level in Figure 26-3.

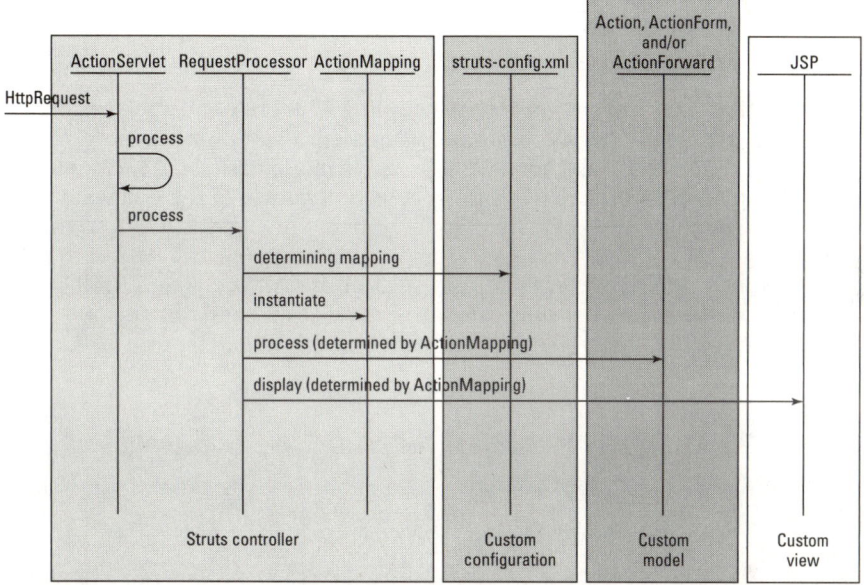

Figure 26-2: The behavior that takes place when processing a request is shown in this simplified sequence diagram of Struts.

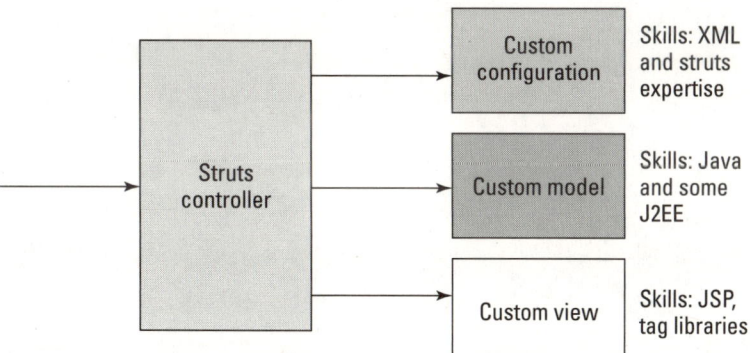

Figure 26-3: Different skills are required to develop in the various areas of Struts.

Loose coupling

Loose coupling was introduced earlier in this chapter and Struts achieves it by using the controller as a mediator. The controller is the component that determines which models and views are involved in a user interaction. Because the components (the JSPs, actions, and so on) do not directly refer to each other, they can easily be changed and reused. And because the controller uses the configuration to determine which custom classes to load, and only refers to the Struts defined superclass, the custom classes can be changed without this change affecting the controller.

However, Struts does not provide loose coupling with the controller mechanism. If you want to change the behavior of the Struts controller you need to delve into the Struts source code and make somewhat invasive modifications. If the controller logic is encapsulated you can potentially change the logic of the controller by plugging in a new implementation instead of directly modifying the Struts source code.

Listing 26-1 is from the `RequestProcessor` class and shows the controller-execution path, how the controller only refers to base classes (and not specific classes), and how the flow is determined by the configuration.

Listing 26-1: **Struts RequestProcessor code snippet**

```
/**
 * <p>Process an <code>HttpServletRequest</code> and create the
 * corresponding <code>HttpServletResponse</code>.</p>
 *
 * @param request The servlet request we are processing
 * @param response The servlet response we are creating
 *
 * @exception IOException if an input/output error occurs
 * @exception ServletException if a processing exception occurs
 */
public void process(HttpServletRequest request,
                    HttpServletResponse response)
    throws IOException, ServletException {

    .... code removed from example ....

    // Identify the mapping for this request
    ActionMapping mapping = processMapping(request, response, path);
    if (mapping == null) {
        return;
    }

    // Check for any role required to perform this action
    if (!processRoles(request, response, mapping)) {
        return;
    }
```

```
// Process any ActionForm bean related to this request
ActionForm form = processActionForm(request, response, mapping);
processPopulate(request, response, form, mapping);
if (!processValidate(request, response, form, mapping)) {
    return;
}

// Process a forward or include specified by this mapping
if (!processForward(request, response, mapping)) {
    return;
}
if (!processInclude(request, response, mapping)) {
    return;
}

// Create or acquire the Action instance to process this request
Action action = processActionCreate(request, response, mapping);
if (action == null) {
    return;
}

// Call the Action instance itself
ActionForward forward =
    processActionPerform(request, response,
                         action, form, mapping);

// Process the returned ActionForward instance
processActionForward(request, response, forward);

}
```

Extensibility

You should be able to extend frameworks by changing classes or adding new implementations of interfaces. Struts enables you to do this by providing classes, such as `Action` or `ActionForm`, that can be subclassed and then used by Struts once they are added to the configuration.

One way in which Struts could improve is by using more interfaces as an extension mechanism as opposed to just subclassing. In Java requiring subclassing as an extension approach is an especially constraining limitation: In Java an object can only have one superclass because of the single-inheritance restriction.

Listing 26-2 is from a Struts example and shows a custom `Action` class that extends the Struts `Action` class.

Listing 26-2: **Custom Action-class code snippet**

```java
public final class LogonAction extends Action {
    ... code removed ...

    /**
     * Process the specified HTTP request, and create the corresponding HTTP
     * response (or forward to another web component that will create it).
     * Return an <code>ActionForward</code> instance describing where and how
     * control should be forwarded, or <code>null</code> if the response has
     * already been completed.
     *
     * @param mapping The ActionMapping used to select this instance
     * @param form The optional ActionForm bean for this request (if any)
     * @param request The HTTP request we are processing
     * @param response The HTTP response we are creating
     *
     * @exception Exception if business logic throws an exception
     */
    public ActionForward execute(ActionMapping mapping,
                                 ActionForm form,
                                 HttpServletRequest request,
                                 HttpServletResponse response)
        throws Exception {

        // Extract attributes we will need
        Locale locale = getLocale(request);
        MessageResources messages = getResources(request);
        User user = null;

        // Validate the request parameters specified by the user
        ActionErrors errors = new ActionErrors();
        String username = (String)
            PropertyUtils.getSimpleProperty(form, "username");
        String password = (String)
            PropertyUtils.getSimpleProperty(form, "password");
        UserDatabase database = (UserDatabase)
          servlet.getServletContext().getAttribute(Constants.DATABASE_KEY);
        if (database == null)
            errors.add(ActionErrors.GLOBAL_ERROR,
                       new ActionError("error.database.missing"));
        else {
            user = getUser(database, username);
            if ((user != null) && !user.getPassword().equals(password))
                user = null;
            if (user == null)
                errors.add(ActionErrors.GLOBAL_ERROR,
                           new ActionError("error.password.mismatch"));
        }
```

```
    // Report any errors we have discovered back to the original form
    if (!errors.isEmpty()) {
        saveErrors(request, errors);
        return (mapping.getInputForward());
    }

    // Save our logged-in user in the session
    HttpSession session = request.getSession();
    session.setAttribute(Constants.USER_KEY, user);

    if (log.isDebugEnabled()) {
        log.debug("LogonAction: User '" + user.getUsername() +
                "' logged on in session " + session.getId());
    }

    // Remove the obsolete form bean
    if (mapping.getAttribute() != null) {
        if ("request".equals(mapping.getScope()))
            request.removeAttribute(mapping.getAttribute());
        else
            session.removeAttribute(mapping.getAttribute());
    }

    // Forward control to the specified success URI
    return (mapping.findForward("success"));
    }

.... code removed ....
}
```

Configurability

The Struts configuration plays a central role in how the framework executes. (We have talked about it already in the earlier sections "Loose coupling" and "Extensibility.") The control Struts provides through configuration as opposed to coding is probably the most important factor in the popularity of Struts. Note is that it is not making everything a configuration parameter that matters, but understanding which aspects of the framework to make configurable.

Another aspect of configuration is the tradeoffs between human readability and complexity—this tradeoff places an emphasis on a quality configuration design. It is very easy to have configuration that is so complex that working with the configuration directly is at best very error prone and at worst almost impossible. While that complexity may allow a dramatic improvement in capabilities, it may not be worth the tradeoff in successfully managing the configuration. Unless the framework comes with a tool for creating and managing its configuration, the design of the configuration format itself is just as important as the functional-class and interaction designs.

Listing 26-3 is a snippet of the struts-config.xml file. From this action mapping, you can see how an `Action` class, `LogonAction`, is configured to handle a request for the "/logon" URL. If an exception takes place, the mapping routes the user to `changePassword.jsp`.

Listing 26-3: Struts struts-config.xml configuration snippet

```
... config removed ...
<!-- Process a user logon -->
<action    path="/logon"
           type="org.apache.struts.webapp.example.LogonAction"
           name="logonForm"
           scope="session"
           input="logon">
  <exception
           key="expired.password"
           type="org.apache.struts.webapp.example.ExpiredPasswordException"
           path="/changePassword.jsp"/>
</action>
... config removed ...
```

Alignment

The alignment of Struts with the functional requirements and the requirements of the business developer is a reflection of its core MVC design pattern as well as the quality of the implementation. When using Struts, it is easy for a novice J2EE developer to successfully translate user-interface specifications into a working application. Imagine making that attempt with nothing but the servlet and JSP J2EE specifications. It is not that servlets and JSPs are flawed—on the contrary, they are essential to the Struts framework—but they are not aligned with the needs of the business developer. Figure 26-4 shows the alignment provided by Struts between the business requirements that Struts addresses and the skills possessed by the development team.

This concludes our discussion of framework principles and the walkthrough of Struts as an example of those principles. Struts was chosen as an example because it can be easily downloaded from the Apache Web site and because it is an open-source framework. An open-source framework allows scrutinizing of both the user experience with the framework and also the framework implementation internals. Going through Struts in more detail on your own will provide a thorough understanding of framework principles.

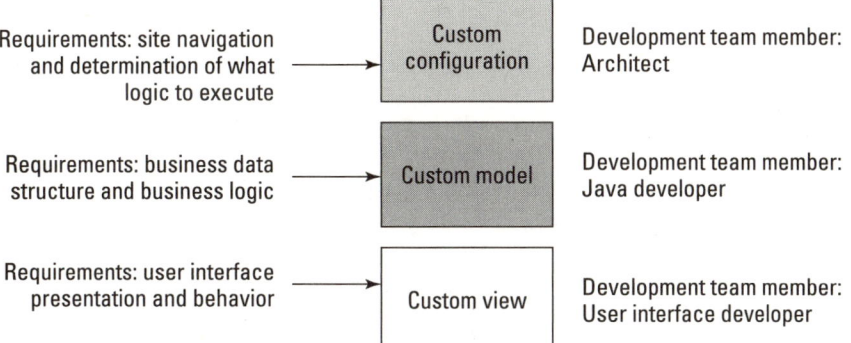

Figure 26-4: Struts aligns business requirements with the skills of the development team.

Understanding Framework Objectives and Benefits

So far we have described frameworks and covered some of the pains of J2EE that a framework might address. Now we will bring those two topics together by detailing the objectives of a framework. We will do this by categorizing the objectives based on the following stages in the software lifecycle:

✦ Design

✦ Development and testing

✦ Production and maintenance

These objectives are discussed in the following sections.

Design

Adopting a framework streamlines the design process. Because the framework is aligned with the business requirements, the designs are vastly simplified. Much of what would have had to be designed now comes as part of the framework. As a result, the designs are focused on the business problem and business details, and less complicated by the mapping of those requirements to the underlying technology.

Development and testing

Frameworks improve development and testing by providing the following benefits:

✦ **Greater developer productivity** — A framework aligns with the business developer and requirements to enable the developer to be productive immediately.

✦ **Less coding** — Much of what was custom code is now replaced entirely by the framework or has become framework configuration; this is a benefit in terms of development as well as testing, as there is less code to test.

✦ **Greater consistency** — Many similar development challenges are usually encountered by different team members and solved in different ways; by employing a framework you create a consistent approach for use across the application.

✦ **Immediate results** — By streamlining the mapping of requirements to functionality, you reduce the time necessary for development. This allows for more and faster iterations, which produce a higher-quality product.

✦ **Greater flexibility** — The loose coupling provided by the framework creates flexibility, in response to both changing business requirements and a changing technology landscape.

✦ **More effective architects** — The structure provided by the framework enables the architects to spend their time making critical decisions instead of being stretched thin in an effort to enforce best practices (which the framework does for them).

✦ **More effective managers** — A big challenge for a project manager is dividing up the work and assigning the right resources to the right people, both of which are more easily done within the structure of the framework.

Production and maintenance

Frameworks are valuable for production and maintenance because of the flexibility and consistency they provide. If you employ a framework, the application can easily respond to changing business requirements and technology. Changes to production applications have historically required finding out how an individual developer solved a particular problem and then invasively changing that behavior. A common solution to the invasive historical approach is to use members of the original development team to maintain the application in production, which is not a very efficient use of resources. With a framework in place, a consistent approach is used across the application and has flexibility as one of its core principles. This means that it is easy to locate the part of an application that is affected by new requirements and, just as important, to make changes in a controlled manner.

Application portfolios

The previous objectives are relevant to a single application going through the development lifecycle. But what if your company has many applications that are being slated for development? The benefits of employing a business-application framework are greatly amplified when the framework is applied across a portfolio of applications. These benefits increase because of the vastly lowered development and production costs and more importantly because of the improved ability of the applications to respond to business changes.

Frameworks are grounded in their objectives and it is hard to argue that the benefits they propose are worthwhile. This is because frameworks are often a few steps ahead of the application development; they are often based on applying yesterday's experience to tomorrow's projects. How to take a leap forward with architecture is the next topic.

Reviewing Application Architecture beyond Frameworks

While frameworks provide a great advantage over using J2EE alone, they are not the end of the evolution of best practices. Architecture is growing in prominence and promises to raise the bar for the benefits already achievable with frameworks. In this section we will introduce architecture and discuss two application architectures.

Overview of architectures

Like *framework*, *architecture* is a word that has many definitions or levels of meaning. In general, it refers to the guiding principles that form the foundation of how elements are organized. You can think of the architecture of a bridge, which is the design and structure that keeps the bridge from crumpling into an unorganized mass of steel and concrete.

In our industry, *architecture* by itself is not a specific enough term because it is applied to many concepts. Two that everyone may be familiar with are *enterprise architecture* and *application architecture*. Enterprise architecture is concerned with detailing the whole of an enterprise's information-technology resources and configurations, including such things as network topology, security, production applications, and data-center hardware. The Zachman Framework for Enterprise Architecture is one of the most renowned attempts to define enterprise architecture. The Software Productivity Consortium provides an overview of the Zachman Framework on their Web site (`http://www.software.org/sysmigweb/framework/fwk-home.asp`). Application architecture, on the other hand, is concerned with the needs of a particular application. Application architecture is the topic of this section.

When discussing architectures it is necessary to distinguish between architectures as concepts described on paper and architectures that have been realized (or are realizable) in a software implementation. Both types of architecture are necessary and they are equally important. Even when the architecture is a software product it should be fully documented and described so that the architecture can be understood and communicated. The Zachman Framework for Enterprise Architecture mentioned earlier is an example of an architecture that exists only as a documented concept. The application architectures discussed in this section are software products.

A common question here may be "Isn't J2EE an application architecture?" J2EE is an infrastructure technology that will definitely play a part in helping to define your application architecture, but by itself it is not an application architecture. Already in this chapter we have discussed some of the pains of adopting J2EE. We discussed them in the context of frameworks but they also apply to application architecture. These pains do not illustrate that J2EE is not a solid infrastructure, but they do illustrate that there is a gap between what J2EE provides and the needs of the teams who are using J2EE. This gap is addressed by application architecture.

The next two sections will explain the following architectures:

✦ Traditional application architecture

✦ Services-oriented architecture (SOA)

Traditional application architecture

The first architecture we want to discuss is *traditional* application architecture. This architecture is concerned with the design, development, and production characteristics of a traditional all-in-one application — usually an application with a user interface, transactional business logic, and backend data stores.

Building a traditional application architecture requires:

1. Layering the application so that the user interface is separate from the business logic, which is separate from the data-access functionality

2. Structuring the user interface; a typical approach applied here is the use of the model-view-controller design pattern

3. Structuring the business logic so going from design requirements to implementation is easy

4. Creating reusable components

5. Structuring the data access and persistence behavior to isolate the intricacies of the data handling from the business logic; the data-access layer also needs to take into account transactional and object-relational mapping concerns; ideally the data layer will be reusable across applications

6. Supporting partitioning the application between multiple tiers that may be deployed in different physical locations

7. Providing an approach for integrating with legacy or third-party applications; the details of this integration should be encapsulated

8. Defining the application components and the interfaces among those components where necessary in the previous requirements

9. Describing an approach for unit-testing and integration-testing the application

10. Describing how the application will be monitored in production

11. Describing how the application can be upgraded in production

12. Describing how security can be applied to the application

13. Describing how other applications will integrate with the application

Even from this brief list, it is easy to see that the requirements for building a traditional application architecture are very comprehensive. These requirements are beyond the scope of a business-application framework. Later in this section we will go over those differences in more detail.

Services-oriented architecture

Services-oriented architecture (SOA) is a relatively new incarnation of application architecture. It is sometimes also referred to as *Web-services architecture* or *services-oriented application architecture.* SOA is distinct from the traditional application architecture in that it regards a service, as opposed to the entire application, as the deliverable. Individual services may be federated to form what is traditionally thought of as an application. (*Services* in this context refers to software functionality that has a network-addressable interface; Web services may be one technology approach to building services but you can use other approaches as well, such as Common Object Request Broker Architecture (CORBA), Enterprise JavaBean (EJB), or Java Message Service (JMS)-based services.)

An example of decomposing an application into services should make things more clear. Say an airline has services for searching for available flights, booking flights, checking in for flights, and determining current flight status. Many different types of interfaces could then be built to access these services, such as a Web-based interface for the customer or a thick-client application for the airline agents.

Advantages of SOA

SOA provides much more than just the architecture for a single application. One of the biggest advantages of SOA is that it enables you to break away from the mindset of traditional applications and instead start thinking in terms of services. SOA more closely aligns the application architecture with the enterprise architecture. With traditional application architecture, the development process emphasizes the requirements and design of the application above all else. The first concern is building and delivering the application; determining how the application fits into the enterprise is secondary. The result is an enterprise comprised of many disparate applications with fragile integration or no integration at all. Reuse in that environment is nearly impossible, which causes the enterprise to make redundant investments in similar functionality. This slows information-technology (IT) responsiveness to changing requirements, which reduces the agility of the business, resulting in lost opportunities. Instead of being an asset, the enterprise's growing portfolio of applications becomes an anchor, which slows the business down.

SOA, on the other hand, is focused on providing *services*. Services are defined by contracts; contracts describe the interface of the service, how to call it, where it resides, and other details. The implementation of a contract is called a *service provider*. The user of that contract is called a *service consumer*. The idea of providing services is not confined to the scope of a single application, but applies to all of the IT software assets. SOA can be alternately thought of as an application architecture, an enterprise architecture, or an integration architecture. This should not cause confusion, but rather reinforce how an SOA reflects the true concerns of building IT assets. Integration cannot be an afterthought and the enterprise cannot afford to invest in monolithic all-in-one applications that slow down the business.

Web-service implementation

We mentioned how services can be implemented as Web services or using other technologies. A Web-service implementation refers to services that use the Simple Object Access Protocol (SOAP), Web Services Definition Language (WSDL), and Universal Description, Discovery, and Integration (UDDI) protocol standards. In the Java environment, programmers often have questions about services and how they relate to the J2EE connector architecture. Is the connector architecture a good technology to use as the basis for an SOA or is it an alternative to an SOA? The answer has to do with granularity and coupling. Most discussions about SOA revolve around document-centric (course-grained) business services that are loosely coupled. Loose coupling is when a service consumer can use a service provider even though they are not using the same platform or development language and they were probably built with no knowledge of each other.

The connector architecture is used for building API-centric (fine-grained), J2EE-specific resource adapters for point-to-point integration with non-Java systems. This integration is usually tightly coupled in the sense that the connector architecture supports strict transaction, security, and connection management, which are not normally part of the loosely coupled SOA environment.

Here is an example of how they might work together. In an SOA you might have a Java-based service provider that in its own implementation uses the connector architecture to integrate with a backend legacy system. A consumer of that service wouldn't care that the service provider was written in Java or that it uses the connector architecture.

Application architecture versus frameworks

Now that you have a better understanding of application architecture, we can form a comparison with frameworks. Two common distinctions exist between business-application architectures and business-application frameworks. The first is the coverage of functional requirements. Frameworks usually address a small slice of the application functionality while architecture provides a holistic structure for building the entire application. The second distinction is the breadth of the offering. Frameworks are usually focused on the development of the application while architecture is not only concerned with improving development but also with all the other facets of the application-development lifecycle, even when the application is in production and maintenance.

One effect of the framework only supporting a slice of the requirements is that in order to address the entire application, you will probably need more than one business-application framework. While this is a common situation, it is not ideal for two reasons. First, a lot of work can be involved in integrating the frameworks. This integration should not be taken lightly because the frameworks may have differences that cause them to be less than compatible. Second, the resulting application may look like a collage assembled from different materials. This can result in increased development costs and higher ongoing maintenance costs.

In the fast moving world of application development, we often look just one step ahead because we have our heads down doing the demanding work of today. The intention of this discussion of application architecture was to shed some light on the landscape ahead of frameworks. You won't start looking for a better solution until you know it is out there! Now we continue forward and discuss how you can come to have a framework.

Building Your Own Framework

If you are familiar with IT, it should not be a surprise that many frameworks are built in house. This is a reflection of the ingenuity of software engineers faced with a completely custom technology stack. Remember that frameworks have been around for a long while, much longer than J2EE. Before J2EE, many enterprises also built their own runtime infrastructures in lieu of using J2EE application servers. In that completely custom environment, the likelihood of finding a framework on the open market that could be brought in was minimal if not nonexistent. However, now that Java and J2EE comprise the common enterprise infrastructure, the marketplace can deliver frameworks based on a standard foundation.

Building versus buying

So the question becomes, "Do you build your own framework (or possibly continue to invest in one you've already built) or do you bring in a framework from the outside?" This isn't necessarily a buy-versus-build decision, because some open-source options do not have an initial price tag. You can answer this question in two ways — either from the business point of view or from the technology point of view. On the business side, you have to ask yourself if building frameworks is one of your differentiators. If it is not, then why spend time there when you should be spending it on features with which you can create differentiation. On the technology side, you have two factors to consider: Is there something unique about your requirements or your environment such that you don't think you're a fit for a framework from the outside, and just as importantly, do you have the time it takes to design, develop, test, document, maintain, and train resources on your own frameworks in addition to performing all your other tasks?

A healthy comparison exists between the build-versus-buy considerations for frameworks and those for application servers. In the early days of the Internet, a demand existed for a platform for building Web applications. In the absence of any products, many enterprises built their own platforms. Once J2EE emerged as the standard for this platform vendors started offering productized application servers. At that point enterprises switched from considering building their own application servers to determining which application server they should bring in from outside. This same evolution also occurred with operating systems, office-productivity applications, and databases, and will continue to occur in the future.

So while it may be possible to build your own framework, the wise decision is to do some research and find a product on the market that satisfies your needs. This enables you to spend your time and effort where they add the most value to your business. If you decide to bring in a framework, there are three sources for obtaining them: open-source development, software vendors, and included with the offerings of a system integrator. In the following sections we'll cover the pros and cons of each of these sources.

Open source

Struts and Log4J were introduced earlier in this chapter in the section "Frameworks versus Class Libraries." Recall that they are a couple of open-source frameworks. Also recall that even though Log4J is a framework, it is not a business-application framework. Open-source frameworks are similar to other open-source products such as the Linux operating system or the JBoss application server. In order for a product to be considered open source you must be able to download and use it for free, as well as have access to the source code. The most obvious indication that a product is open source is that it subscribes to either the GNU General Public License (GPL, http://www.gnu.org/copyleft/gpl.html) or Apache Software License (http://www.apache.org/LICENSE.txt). As always, the buyer should beware of unscrupulous vendors who claim their product is open source but who have not made that status official through the adoption of an open-source license. This may lead you to adopt what you thought to be an open-source product only to have the vendor later recant.

Advantages of open source

Let's first discuss some of the positive qualities of the open source movement. Open source products have the advantage of becoming ubiquitous because they carry no upfront cost. Download the open-source framework and start using it. With this easy availability, open-source frameworks that are useful become popular and are adopted by the community. This means that books are written about them, developers contribute to their continued evolution, they can have further influence on the evolution of the J2EE specification, and people off the street may already be able to work with them.

Disadvantages of open source

Now let's cover some of the downsides of using open-source products. A couple of times now we have referred to open source as having no "initial" or "upfront" costs. This is because some cost is always involved in bringing in a product. This cost is incurred when you need to support the open-source product. This support can take the form of training people, making enhancements, debugging, and handling production problems. While having access to the source code sounds like a good thing (because it gives you the feeling of full control over your destiny), it can cause its own problems.

It is possible to take an open-source product and enhance it in such a way that you can no longer use new versions as they become available, or worse yet, different departments in the enterprise can enhance it independently until it essentially becomes two different products. Either way, you have gone from "build versus bring in," to "bring in and then build." The end result is that you now "own" the open-source product and have to continue to invest in its support and evolution.

A final concern with regard to open source is that, because there is no price tag, these products often slip by a company's official process for bringing in third-party software. While this can be a good thing from the point of view of the developer (who may need the software right away and be unable to afford a lengthy approval process), it can often come back to haunt you for the reasons we mentioned earlier.

Software vendor

Next is the option of purchasing a framework from a software vendor. Vendors offering frameworks for J2EE have been increasing in number as J2EE has matured and become more widely adopted. Some of these vendors have grown up around Java and J2EE and others have made the transition from a previous technology.

Advantages of using software vendors

The pros of going with a vendor are that you will get a fully documented product supported by the vendor and the vendor will continue to invest in the product evolution. The vendor should also articulate a product road map, support old product versions, and maintain backward compatibility as you move from one version to the next.

Disadvantages of using software vendors

The con of using a vendor offering is that you have to pay to license the product. Justifying this upfront cost can require some work but is usually worth it in the long run. If nothing else, going through the process should clarify your requirements, which are themselves valuable for whichever framework option you decide upon. Something you should keep in mind when contemplating a vendor offering is that the product should be usable without requiring extensive use of the vendor's consultants. In other words, make sure that the product is actually a product, and not just a sales tool for the vendor's professional-services group.

System Integrators (SIs)

Finally, framework offerings are available from *system integrators* (SIs). From the small SIs to the big ones (such as IBM and Accenture), professional-services teams may bring to the table a framework that they built in house. These frameworks may appear as line items on the project proposal with an associated cost, they may be used as talking points to differentiate the SI from their competition, or the SI may just use them behind the scenes. One big variable is whether or not a real framework exists. Often the framework may be a conglomeration of code that the SI takes from one project to the next and that exists as a framework only in his or her sales and marketing.

Advantages of using SIs

Using an SI framework has two pros. Let's make the assumption that the SI actually has a quality framework. Under that assumption, the quality of the deliverables from the SI will probably be better than they would have been had the SI not used a framework. In addition, the SI should be more productive with his or her framework. The end result is that you get a higher-quality product for less money. While this may sound great, the cons may outweigh these pros.

Disadvantages of using SIs

The cons of this situation depend on a single factor. Does the SI make the framework product available on the open market, either as a product that can be purchased or as open source? If the answer is yes, then refer to the previous sections on those sources for frameworks. Otherwise, you should have serious doubts about using the framework. Why? First, the quality and competitiveness of the framework cannot be verified unless a developer engages with the SI. Second, using the SI framework will build a dependence on the SI. To realize many of the benefits of a framework you should use it uniformly on all projects. This will not be possible if the only way to obtain the product is to use the SI services — unless you are willing to make that commitment.

Third, products take serious commitment to build and support; if the SI hasn't made this investment, you may be getting a shell of a framework that is really just a selling point for services.

Finally, if the product isn't available on the open market, the only source for expertise and support for the framework will be the SI. There is very little likelihood that you will find someone who knows the framework to join your company or that you will find other SIs who know the framework.

As you can see, there are many ways to acquire a framework. Which one is right for you depends on your environment. What are the costs and benefits and risks on which you are willing to trade off? One of the risks for any technology is the future; once you bring in frameworks and make them part of your application, you will have to live with them for some time. This is the topic of the next section where we look into the future of frameworks.

Predicting the Future of Frameworks

Predicting the future is always a gamble. But as with anything else, it helps to have some foresight, or at least an educated guess, as to what will happen in the near and long term. Frameworks are here today, but will they be around tomorrow? And if not, what happens to the features they offer?

At least two possible occurrences might start to chip away at frameworks. One is the inclusion of framework features in the J2EE specification. The other is the large application-server vendors, such as IBM and BEA, expanding their offerings beyond standard J2EE and including frameworks.

The Java Community Process (JCP), the standards body that guides the evolution of Java and J2EE, could continue to develop the specifications for J2EE and include features that were previously part of custom frameworks. Once part of the J2EE specification, these features would be provided as part of the standard application server. While this may happen with small features that are refinements of existing specifications, it is not likely that J2EE will branch into new areas where frameworks currently exist. This is because JCP is focused on standardizing the infrastructure, not with trying to completely specify everything involved with business applications.

The JCP realizes that J2EE can be used for many purposes and that too much specification might limit its broad applicability, and also that room needs to be made for value-added offerings in the marketplace. As an example, database-connection pooling is likely to become part of the J2EE specification; however, user-interface construction the likes of which Struts provides is not likely to be standardized.

In addition, large application-server vendors may begin to offer frameworks in their products. These vendors are not restricted to offering just the application server. Much consolidation has already taken place and the application-server vendors have broadened their offerings to include integrated developer environments (IDEs), portals, workflow, personalization, and the like. Because you are already getting your application server from these vendors, why not get your frameworks from them as well? The immediate reaction to this line of thinking is to wonder why the vendor would offer frameworks. Would they be competitive products that benefit the consumer or just a tactic to lock the consumer into the vendor's line of products? Enforcing this suspicion is the big vendors' need to create some lock-in. Their application-server offerings make it easy for the consumer to switch to another vendor's products, because the application-server products must conform to the J2EE specification and applications are meant to be portable among different application-server implementations.

The application-server vendors seem to have chosen to pursue comprehensive Integrated Development Environments (IDEs) as a solution to the problems addressed by frameworks: BEA has Workshop, Oracle has JDeveloper/BC4J, and IBM has the WebSphere product line. You can read more about this alternative in the following Alternatives to Frameworks section.

Note   The future of application architecture may also be of value if you are taking that approach. While the future is always uncertain, application architecture has a good chance of becoming another well-established layer in the application stack in its own right. A good analogy is to draw parallels with the establishment of the application server layer. Both the application architecture and application server are functions that used to be mixed in with the application development. As we gain more experience with building applications it only makes sense to evolve our operating environment.

Alternatives to Frameworks

Those familiar with the challenges of J2EE or who are pondering them for the first time may be wondering if they have other options. Sure, frameworks are good, but isn't there a better approach? One alternative that we already covered is application architecture. In this section we'll briefly cover the following J2EE alternatives:

✦ All-in-one proprietary environments

✦ Model-driven architecture (MDA)

✦ Minimal J2EE

✦ Advanced IDEs

All-in-one proprietary environments

If you're looking on the market for a commercial product, you'll find no shortage of companies who claim they'll solve all your problems if you adopt their product stacks. These product stacks encompass everything from the tools down to the execution environment. Often they introduce a new development methodology and language. The resulting application will run within a J2EE application server, but that may be the only thing it has in common with an application not developed using the vendor's product. Examples of vendors with this type of approach include Versata, AltoWeb, and M7.

Usually these products give an initial boost to the application development. Results can be seen immediately for the "standard" parts of an application—creating a new user interface or accessing a database. These products excel with the 80 percent of your application that is similar to all other applications.

Products in this category have two critical shortcomings: *vendor lock-in* and *application coverage*. Vendor lock-in occurs because the applications developed and the team skills acquired are only useful in the context of that vendor; if the vendor goes away, you'll have to rebuild your applications using another technology with a team whose skills are no longer useful. Application coverage refers to the vendor's support for the unique 20 percent of your application. The 80/20 rule is helpful in understanding the impact of this 20 percent; the 80/20 rule when applied to software development states how it is common to spend 80 percent of your time in 20 percent of the application. With the poor coverage of the unique application requirements, developers will find themselves spending 80 percent of their time in that unique 20 percent of the application, because they'll have to dig their way out of the proprietary environment before they can begin the real work.

Model-driven architecture

Model-driven architecture (MDA) is a standard that the Object Management Group (OMG) is driving forward. The emphasis in this method is on creating a valid model of the application that then becomes the enterprise's most valuable asset; this technology-independent model can then be translated into a working application for a particular technology stack, in our case J2EE. Coming from the OMG, the model would be described in the Unified Modeling Language (UML).

Modeling is an important phase of enterprise software development and the models should be treated as a valued asset that isn't immediately outdated once development begins. That being said, good (or even great) modeling alone isn't going to overcome the challenges presented by J2EE. The best result will come from a combination of frameworks and MDA. MDA will make modeling more useful while frameworks will improve the development and execution environments.

At this point, you may be asking how MDA compares with the Computer Aided Software Engineering (CASE) approaches of the past. This is a typical first reaction that often hides some negativity. CASE wasn't successful, so why will MDA be any different? The distinguishing factor between CASE and MDA is that MDA is being driven in an open standard process through the OMG. The primary focus of MDA is on modeling information and the mechanisms for translating that modeling information into an application. Depending on which translator was chosen, the application created could be for the J2EE, Microsoft .Net, or some other standard or proprietary environment. CASE products, on the other hand, were all proprietary: The focus was on creating a proprietary model that could be used to create an application that only ran in a proprietary environment. MDA is (we hope) creating a lasting foundation for increasing the value of modeling that also has some benefits in the short term.

Minimal J2EE

One of the knee-jerk reactions to the challenges of J2EE is to only use the minimal required parts. An example is a Web-based application that only uses JSPs and JDBC — the minimal requirement for creating a user interface that needs to communicate with the database. While this minimalist approach is not really an effective response, it is so common that it should be addressed. As attested to by this book, J2EE has many technology offerings, from Java database connectivity (JDBC) to servlets for Web connectivity to EJBs for distributed objects. Using all of them can be daunting, so why not use just the minimum? You're building a Web application that uses a relational database, the required technologies are servlets and JDBC — why go any further?

Stopping there may be a valid option if what you want is a small departmental application. However, if the objective is a large-scale long-term enterprise application, it is an injustice to what J2EE has to offer. The sacrifices of application development and production quality aspects such as flexibility, reuse, ease of maintenance, scalability, performance, and manageability can end up being very costly. If the application server was purchased for a large dollar amount, you are probably not realizing the benefits of that investment — benefits that come with leveraging the entire application server feature set. Are these tradeoffs you are willing to make?

Advanced Integrated Development Environments

More and better tooling has always been viewed as a valid response to the complexities of software development. Tool suites, which usually include code editors, step-by-step wizards, and debugging facilities, are referred to as Integrated Development Environments (IDEs). IDEs are not new; they have been around for quite a while in other technologies. A couple that you may have used are Microsoft Visual Basic tools and Sun SPARCworks tools for C and C++. In the Java and J2EE environment, IDEs have been maturing and growing in features.

Are IDEs really a replacement for frameworks? That is a good question. On one hand, if you decide to use frameworks, you'll still need to use some editor to write your code. That editor can be something as simple as EditPlus on Windows or vi on Unix, but you can also use an IDE if you want. So if you know you want to use frameworks, you can still use an IDE as well.

On the other hand, you could decide that all you want to use is an IDE, not a framework. Feature-rich IDEs can provide wizards to automate the construction of standard J2EE components (for example, to create Enterprise JavaBeans or JavaServer Pages) and model environments that enable you to drag and drop design patterns. You can think of these features as providing the same development-time benefits as a framework, so why do you need a framework at all? The answer is that using an IDE, even a very feature-rich IDE, is not a replacement for frameworks. First, frameworks are not just about development improvements. In "Understanding Frameworks Objectives and Benefits" we discussed the benefits of frameworks for design, development, testing, and production.

Second, even in the development phase frameworks are not about rapid development, they are about taking a consistent approach that should minimize coding but, more importantly, that incorporates best practices. Using an IDE may let you do "more coding faster," but is it going to lead your team to provide a high-quality result?

Finally, even though IDEs can do wonders in the hands of an expert, they do not translate to a uniform approach for the whole team. Individual experts can correctly drag and drop design patterns and use the wizards, but the resulting application will be a quilt of the experts' work stitched together. That does not lead to lower maintenance or repeatability.

A continuing trend in the IDE market is that of J2EE application-server vendors providing IDEs as part of their product suites. The major application-server vendors and their tools are BEA with Workshop, IBM with WebSphere Studio, and Oracle with JDeveloper. The IDEs from these vendors stray from the traditional IDE by incorporating some features that require runtime components. These features, such as Business Components for Java (BC4J) from Oracle or the Workshop runtime from BEA, cannot be independently compared with frameworks because they can only be used through the IDE. Also very important is that these features and their associated runtimes can only be used with the respective vendor's application server.

The resulting combination of IDE, runtime components, and application server makes an offering similar to the all-in-one proprietary environment that we already discussed. Is this a bad path to choose? That depends on your requirements for independence — both from the IDE and from the application server. You can always stop using any given traditional IDE because all the artifacts, such as classes and deployment descriptors, are usable in different IDEs or with no IDE at all. When you use an IDE with custom extensions, you build a dependency on that IDE that you can only break by starting from scratch with a different IDE. The custom extensions also result in vendor lock-in.

If you don't think you'll ever need to change the application server, none of this may be a problem. However, many enterprises may use one application server in development (possibly one with low or zero cost) and a different one in production (possibly a high-end one with clustering behavior); some enterprises are also shifting to open-source application servers (such as JBoss) in production. Do you really want your choice of IDE to limit your ability to choose these options? That is up to you.

Note Some might put MDA in this category; however, MDA is distinct in that it is about a new paradigm for software development that may require some new tools, as opposed to IDEs in which the tools themselves are the focus. Please refer to the previous section on MDA for details.

It is obvious from this discussion that software development is difficult. Otherwise, there wouldn't be so many options for improving the experience! However, maybe it isn't so obvious, which is the best option for your environment; much of that decision rests on the tradeoffs only you can make. If you do decide to continue with frameworks (which is a great choice) the next section will help you in the process of framework evaluations.

Evaluating Frameworks

If you have decided that frameworks are a good fit for your environment, you'll need to decide which ones make sense. This decision should be based on an understanding of your requirements, your price range and the costs of the frameworks, the quality of the framework products, and the position of the framework vendor. In this section, we will cover those topics to help you make an educated decision.

Requirements

Recall that frameworks are focused on a slice of the application. Frameworks are available for Web-user interfaces, object-relational mapping, data validation and transformation, and many more. Only you understand the requirements of your application. By taking the effort to gather, document, and analyze your requirements you can decide which frameworks you need for your application. Doing some market research will provide you with a list of potential candidates for your required framework categories. Once you have that list, you can begin going through the rest of this section to determine the framework(s) that are the best fit.

Cost

When you're shopping for frameworks, it is not as simple as "I have x dollars to spend, therefore I can only get a product that costs y (which is less than x)." While the equation in this story problem would be simple if we were shopping for a new CD or a pair of jeans, with software it is not so easy. Lets talk about each variable in the equation.

Estimating cost

Say you know that you have x dollars to spend. To get the value for x you simply look at your development budget (or possibly your lack thereof), and come back with a number greater than or equal to zero, right? Not so fast. The number for x should really reflect the full value of getting a product that meets your requirements. Since a framework has benefits for design, development, testing, production, and maintenance, shouldn't you look beyond the development budget to determine what it is worth? If your development budget has only a few spare dollars, but your testing budget is pretty high because historically your applications are buggy, wouldn't it be wise to take some of those testing dollars and purchase a framework that could lower testing costs? Applying this line of thinking, shifting the potential savings from using a framework to apply towards the purchase of the framework, will probably give you more money to spend.

Determining the true cost

Say you know that you can only get a product that costs *y*. Once you know how much you can spend, the next part is easy: You just need to find a product that costs less than your limit. What is so obscure about that? Well, the tricky part is determining the true cost of the framework. This is especially important considering the popularity of open source in today's environment. Many might think that using open source means bringing in a product with zero cost. However, that is not the case.

The true cost of a product is a reflection not just of the dollars you spend (or in the case of open source, don't spend) to get a product license, but also of the investment you need to make in the successful implementation of a product. That investment could include marketing the product internally to get buy-in and clearance to use it, training the people who will use the product, development-team support, production support, product-upgrade support, and many other costs. Understanding all these investments and determining which ones come with the product, which ones you can hire someone else to do, and which ones you will end up doing yourself will help you arrive at the true cost of the product.

Framework checklist

This section contains a list of categories for qualifying the framework. Because these categories are meant to apply to all frameworks, specifics about application layers such as user interface, persistence, and so on are not included. The following detailed questions will most likely apply to those application layers, but new categories may need to be added for your particular situation:

✦ **Extensible (business-application framework principle)** — Can you extend the framework through subclassing framework classes, or (preferably) through implementing framework interfaces?

✦ **Configurable (business-application framework principle)** — Does the framework use external configuration that replaces custom code, allows strong control of framework behavior, and allows tuning of the often-changed aspects of the business requirements?

✦ **Loosely coupled (Business-application framework principle)** — Are the different elements of the framework loosely coupled so that you can make changes in one area without affecting other areas?

✦ **Separation of concerns (business-application framework principle)** — Is the framework structure separated along the boundaries of skill requirements, so that everybody doesn't have to know everything about how things work and can focus only on his or her area of expertise?

✦ **Alignment with business requirements and developers (business-application framework principle)** — Does the framework make it easy to see how you are going to turn your requirements and designs into framework components and how you are going to assign team members to the work to be done?

✦ **Design patterns** — Does the framework leverage object-oriented design patterns and include implementations of the J2EE design patterns that are particular to your domain (such as a persistence framework that includes an implementation of the data-access-object design pattern)?

✦ **Documentation** — Does the framework include up-to-date API-level documentation (often in the Javadoc format) as well as more comprehensive external documentation such as architect and developer-level user guides?

✦ **Samples and examples** — Does the framework come with sample applications and more focused partial examples that can be used to illustrate how to use the framework?

✦ **Kick-start** — Is there any kick-start approach to using the framework so that you don't have to read documentation and reach inner enlightenment before you are productive with the framework?

✦ **Upgradeability** — What approach does the framework provide for upgrading to new versions of the framework or new versions of dependent software (such as JDK or J2EE)?

✦ **Maturity and stability** — Has the framework been used in a variety of environments for long enough for the framework to reflect the incorporation of use in multiple environments and over long durations into a mature API and structure that does not change, and a quality implementation that is not buggy?

✦ **Testability** — Does the framework provide an approach for determining the quality of the functionality you build with it? The more proprietary the framework, the more important this is.

✦ **Performance and scalability** — Was the framework designed to meet your performance and scalability requirements?

✦ **Production impact** — Does the framework impose new requirements on your production environment and/or provide production benefits? How will you manage the framework once it is in your production environment?

✦ **Integrations** — Does the framework come with integrations to products that you already have in your environment or that you think may be introduced into your environment later on? Does the framework have a structure that supports integration?

✦ **Technological concurrency** — Is the framework concurrent with recent versions of dependent technology (such as application servers and JDKs)?

✦ **Currency with best practices** — Does the framework incorporate mature best practices from the industry, where appropriate (possibly including design patterns that we have already mentioned but also such things as XML)?

✦ **J2EE-compliance** — Does the framework leverage your investment and the features of your J2EE application server? Does the framework allow you to use all of J2EE? Does the framework violate any of the J2EE specifications or principles? Was the framework built for J2EE or ported to J2EE? Ports can be a source of concern because the framework may include behavior that is redundant with what J2EE offers, or because the problems that existed in the previous environment are not the same ones that exist in J2EE.

✦ **Reusability** — Does the framework promote reusability (including reuse of the framework across projects, of framework components in development, and of runtime functionality that has already been built and deployed)?

✦ **Consistency** — Is the structure of the framework consistent, such that once one aspect of the framework is understood, the structure of other aspects makes sense?

Vendor questions

While evaluating the framework is essential to determining if it is a good product that meets your requirements, evaluating the vendor is just as important. The vendor is essential to your success with the framework today, and can also mitigate your risks for the future. If the framework you are considering is from a systems integrator (SI), the SI is considered the vendor. If you are looking at an open-source framework, the vendor could be the open-source community, a specific vendor you engage to assist you with the framework, or a combination of the two. Consider the following questions as you make decisions about working with vendors:

✦ **Support** — Does the vendor have a responsive support system for development as well as production issues?

✦ **Training** — How will the vendor train your team once the framework has been adopted? Does the vendor have onsite or Web-based training or both? (Web-based training is good because it is quicker and cheaper, but onsite training is good for getting access to experts.)

✦ **Community** — Do you have access to a community of framework users? Establishing an open community has proven to provide significant benefits when combined with official vendor support for resolving issues, exchanging ideas, or learning more about the framework.

✦ **Process to evaluate** — Does the vendor have a process for evaluating just the framework? Is the evaluation free and without obligation? Is there a way to engage the vendor (sometimes for a fee) to do a more in-depth evaluation?

✦ **Product versus consulting** — Is the framework a product you can adopt without being required to use vendor services? This is very important, even if you are thinking about using the vendor services, because once adopted, the framework may be beneficial for other projects on which you are not going to use those services.

✦ **Customer references** — Can the vendor provide customer references and/or case studies?

✦ **Industry involvement** — Is the vendor involved in the industry, whether standards bodies or other groups? If the vendor is on the front lines and staying abreast of current developments, few surprises and a better product should be the result.

✦ **Thought leadership** — Is the vendor a thought leader in his or her field, as reflected by press coverage, published articles, and/or book authoring? This reinforces that the vendor is not only aware of what the industry is doing, but is active in giving it direction.

✦ **Product road map** — Does the vendor have a product road map that he or she will share with you and that is aligned with your visions of the direction the product should be taking? This helps ensure that the framework you bring in today will be one that you'll be happy using in the future.

✦ **Backward compatibility** — What are the vendor's plans for backward compatibility among releases? A mature product should be backward-compatible with only a few exceptions. Those exceptions, as well as the process for moving from the old approach to the new approach, should be made explicit by the vendor.

✦ **Sunsetting plans** — What is the vendor's approach to ceasing to support old product versions? Does that plan align with your schedules and needs?

✦ **Product management** — Does the vendor incorporate your feedback, with regard to both improving existing features and introducing new features, into the framework?

✦ **Engineering** — Does the vendor have an engineering team working on the product? This reflects an investment in improving the product.

✦ **Company viability** — Does the vendor have a viable business that will be around after you've adopted the framework and are using it in production? Does the vendor run a profitable business or a venture-funded business? Does he or she have other paying customers?

Summary

In this chapter we looked at frameworks — what they are and the value they bring to the table. We clarified that although many types of frameworks are available, both historically and for Java and J2EE, the one type that we are interested in is business-application frameworks. What distinguishes this type from the others is that it provides structure for building business applications — structure that needs custom components before it can do anything useful — and that the framework is aligned with the requirements and skills of the business developer, as opposed to frameworks that expose technical details and require an expert in order to be used correctly.

We introduced architecture, with its many shapes and variances, and emphasized that if frameworks are good, architecture represents advancement to the next level. While business-application frameworks address only a slice of the problem, architectures address the breadth of the application-development lifecycle and all the application layers. The architectures we discussed were application architecture and services-oriented architecture. Application architecture is for traditional applications that encompass everything from the user interface to the database access and are often deployed as a single unit. Services-oriented architecture focuses on creating discrete, reusable business services that can then be orchestrated to create federated applications.

Finally, we discussed how to determine which framework is the right framework for you. This involves determining your requirements, your budget, and the framework cost, and evaluating the framework and the framework vendor. Only by understanding each of these areas can you make a decision about which is the right product for your situation.

✦　　✦　　✦

Using ANT to Build and Deploy Applications

In This Chapter

Introducing ANT

Getting comfortable with ANT vocabulary

Understanding tasks

Putting it all together

O nce in a while, a utility such as (ANT) comes along and becomes essential to your toolbox. The name *ANT* is attributed to it being a tiny thing that is capable of building grand applications, while ANT is also often referred to as a short form for "Another Neat Tool". Take your pick. What is also remarkable in this day of the graphical user interface (GUI), ANT is largely a command-line tool. This chapter provides an overview of this utility, including a very straightforward example. You will also learn the vocabulary of ANT, and finally, you will look at some of the ways in which ANT can benefit you as a developer. The chapter also covers many of the ANT tasks that you are required to understand to be able to create your own ANT build files.

Introducing ANT

ANT is a Java-based *make* utility, although this definition covers only a small fraction of what it is capable of. Before the advent of the Integrated Development Environment (IDE), code was developed with basic text editors, with custom-built shell scripts taking the source code and compiling it into the necessary executable. These shell scripts soon grew into a more formal approach known as the *makefile,* which became associated with all variants of Unix. The makefile enabled the designer to describe the necessary compilation logic that allowed code to be compiled successfully. In the days when compilation order was important, these makefiles allowed user control over the processing order for the compiler. The makefile itself was just a series of commands, closely resembling a shell script.

ANT is a lot more than just a Java alternative to make. It provides all the functionality of make while not suffering from the drawbacks of it. ANT is a drastic improvement over make as regards the ease of use and the minimal learning curve. With ANT, all that a Java developer needs to understand is Java and some basic XML; this wasn't true with makefiles. Makefiles involved quite a lot of non-Java learning on the part of the developer, something that is not really expected of him/her. As ANT uses Java, it can also boast of platform independence, something that was missing with makefiles.

Like many projects controlled by Apache, ANT was the result of necessity, not the desire for luxury. ANT's creator, James Duncan Davidson, the man behind Sun's reference implementation of the Servlet/JSP specifications known as Tomcat, needed a reliable means of compiling the source files over a variety of different platforms. Since Davidson didn't use any IDE, shell scripts were performing all compilation. Realizing that this was introducing more problems than it solved, he set out to write a tool that would enable him to easily control the process. This tool was introduced to the Apache group of projects in January 2000, where it was formally known as ANT.

The first release of the tool as a stand-alone Apache project was the following summer in July 2000. From that point forward it has become enormously popular, with developers from all over the world contributing to its core feature set. ANT is used in all areas of development and has become the de facto standard for multi-teamed projects, particularly open-source projects. Once you have experienced the power ANT can add to your development you'll wonder how you ever worked without it.

The actual compilation of a single Java class file isn't the most difficult task that has to be done; simply throw it at the javac compiler and a .class file is easily produced. However, it doesn't take long for this process to get a little more complicated.

Add in package paths and dependent JAR files with external code, and before you know it you need to create a custom shell script to speed up the whole process. Now consider the fact that you may need to do this in both Microsoft Windows and Unix environments, even though path-name separators in the two are different, and you need to start looking at supporting a whole suite of shell scripts. This is before you consider the problems that come when someone decides to change the directory where all the source code lives, or wishes to build to another location or JAR file.

You may argue that your present IDE is taking care of all these problems for you, and for the most part it probably is. However, in a team environment you have to assume that everyone is using the IDE in order for you to share project files, which of course assumes that the actual IDE makes it easy for you to do that. But even if everyone in the team is using the same IDE, everyone may not be using the same directory structure to store source files. Before you know it, each of your team is building JAR files of different sizes and you can't fully trust any of them to be the correct build.

Finally, anyone who has been involved with manual J2EE deployment also knows the joys that come from building a Web application archive (WAR), which requires strict adherence to known path names and naming conventions. A well written ANT build file can get you this, consistent deployment adhering to any standards you have set for the project.

These are the sorts of problems ANT can solve, without introducing a huge administration cost to manage it.

ANT can be used on any Java 1.1+ system, which makes it extremely portable to pretty much any operating system in use today. ANT is a command line–driven program that uses an eXtensible Markup Language (XML) file to describe the build process. This file is known as the *build file,* and is just an XML file that describes the various tasks ANT has to complete. If you leave off the filename, the default is to look for the file `build.xml` in the present directory.

The key to ANT's success is the fact it was built in Java. So an important cause for ANT's popularity is the support it has received from the strong Java developer and open source Java community worldwide. Developers from around the world have contributed a rich array of new tasks that makes ANT go way beyond what it began with. ANT is an official Apache open-source project that is freely available from Apache's main Web site at `http://ant.apache.org/`.

Without further ado let us take a whistle-stop tour of a typical ANT project. In this section we'll perform the following tasks:

1. Download and install ANT.

2. Build a simple `build.xml` file for compilation and JAR-file packaging.

3. Run ANT.

This will give you a feel for what ANT can do. Subsequent sections will delve deeper into the specifics.

Installing ANT

The first thing you must do is retrieve the latest version of ANT from the main Apache Web site at `http://ant.apache.org/`. Follow the Download link and select the correct binary for your system. (Typically this will be either a `.ZIP` or `.TAR.GZ` file.) Installation is a simple matter of unpacking the downloaded archive into a directory and setting up these two environment variables:

✦ ANT_HOME — This environment variable points to the directory to which you unpacked ANT. It is also a good idea to add `$ANT_HOME\bin` to your system path. This enables you to easily call the `ant` script that encapsulates all the calls to Java.

✦ JAVA_HOME — This environment variable points to the directory in which you installed JDK. It is a very handy variable to enable anyway, as it enables you to easily upgrade your JDK without having to go around and change all your scripts.

That's it. To test your installation, simply enter the command **ant -version** and you should see the following output:

```
C:\>ant -version
Apache Ant version 1.5
```

This verifies that ANT is correctly installed and you are ready to use it. If for any reason this command does not work, make sure you have your environment variables set correctly. Depending on your operating system you may have to restart your console session.

Simple build.xml

Now that you have ANT installed, the next stage is to use it. If you simply enter **ant** you'll receive the following output:

```
C:\>ant
Buildfile: build.xml does not exist!
Build failed
```

ANT gets its instructions from a build file, usually named `build.xml`. You can specify a different name for your build file and simply pass it in as an argument to the script. For example, to use a file named `test.xml` as your build file, you can either of the options `-buildfile`, `-file`, and `-f`. All three work in a similar fashion. You could use any of the following three commands, where the file `test.xml` is located in the same directory.

```
ant -buildfile test.xml
ant -file test.xml
ant -f test.xml
```

Before you take a look at this file, let's define exactly what it is you are attempting to do. Assume you have a directory underneath the current directory, /src/, that contains all your Java source files. You want to keep the source files separate from the class files, and to make things easier, you want to compile into the /classes/ directory that also sits within the current directory. Therefore, to complete a successful compile you probably want to clean out the /classes/ folder from any previous compiles, and then run the Java compiler (javac) on all the files in the source directory.

The build file is an XML file with blocks of instructions meant to run in a specific order. The basic build file for this basic scenario is shown in Listing 27-1.

Listing 27-1: **Simple ANT build file build.xml**

```xml
<project name="antbook" default="compile" basedir=".">
  <property name="src" value=".\src\"/>
  <property name="build" value=".\classes\"/>

  <target name="init">
    <mkdir dir="${build}"/>
  </target>

  <target name="compile" depends="init">
    <javac srcdir="${src}"
           destdir="${build}"
           optimize="on"
           debug="on">
      <classpath>
        <pathelement location="${build}"/>
      </classpath>
    </javac>
  </target>

  <target name="clean">
    <delete dir="${build}"/>
  </target>
</project>.
```

Let's look at this code from the inside out, starting with the `<target>` blocks. As you can see you name each one, and for one you'll notice the `depends` attribute. Each target represents a logical block of tasks, which is treated as a single unit. The `depends` attribute controls the order in which these blocks are executed. For example, before you compile the source code, you may wish to make sure that the output directory actually exists and create it if it doesn't.

Near the top of the file you will notice the `<property>` elements, which define some variables that will be used throughout the build process. Here you are defining the source and output directory. The ability to do this is a particularly powerful feature of ANT, as you can easily change the output directory without having to manually edit the whole file for every occurrence. When you run this file through ANT, here's what happens:

```
C:\>ant
Buildfile: build.xml
```

```
init:
    [mkdir] Created dir: C:\classes

compile:
    [javac] Compiling 1 source file to C:\classes

BUILD SUCCESSFUL
Total time: 6 seconds
```

So the first thing ANT printed out was the name of the build file it was processing. By default, the ANT script will look for a `build.xml` file in the current directory. If it doesn't find one, it will stop any further processing.

Then ANT started running through the targets. Which one did it know to run first? Looking back at the `build.xml` file you will notice that in the top-level tag, `<project>`, is an attribute, `default`, that defined the target to be run first. However, this attribute had the value `"compile"`, but `"init"` was the first target that was actually run. How come?

You have just witnessed the power of ANT and its ability to have dependencies based on the order in which targets are run. If you look at the `"compile"` target you will notice that the `depends="init"` attribute is defined. This states that before this target executes, the target `"init"` should be run. This is good for the purpose of the current example, as you want to ensure that the output directory exists before you compile your Java source files into it.

As you can see from the rest of the output, the directory for the class files is created, and then the source file is compiled. But what if you run the build file again? See what happens this time:

```
C:\>ant
Buildfile: build.xml

init:

compile:

BUILD SUCCESSFUL
Total time: 2 seconds
```

It starts out the same, but notice how the `"init"` target output has nothing written in it this time? This is because the default action of the `<mkdir>` task within the `"init"` target is to not do anything if the directory already exists. The next target processed is the `"compile"` target, which again has no output. This is because the timestamp on the class file is the same as the timestamp on the source file, so there is no need to recompile, according to the rules of the `javac` task.

However, what if you wish to force a compilation? How do you signal that? That is where the final target in the build file, the `"clean"` target, comes into play. As you can probably guess from its name, this target deletes the files in the directory defined by the property `${build}`. But how do you run it? Simple—you pass in the name of the target you want to trigger to the ANT script, like this:

```
C:\>ant clean
Buildfile: build.xml

clean:
    [delete] Deleting directory C:\classes

BUILD SUCCESSFUL
Total time: 2 seconds
```

This will override the default target defined in the project element and run the "`clean`" target. After you have done this you can then run the ant script again to compile your Java code. Alternately, you could stack up the trigger targets in one call at the command line, as shown here:

```
C:\>ant clean compile
```

This will run the "`clean`" target and then the "`compile`" target immediately afterwards.

That's it—your first ANT project file. ANT is made up of a series of targets, each of which defines a sequence of tasks that make up the whole build process for a particular project. Depending on the circumstances you can change the execution order of these targets, which in turn enables you to move around the building blocks of your development process.

The real power of ANT is in its ability to marry the flexibility of its core/optional tasks with the framework that controls the overall flow. The section `Common Ant Tasks` will take you through the more common tasks with which you can control the J2EE development environment.

Getting Comfortable with ANT Vocabulary

You might already be familiar with the following ANT vocabulary:

✦ Projects

✦ Properties

✦ Targets

✦ File matching

✦ Tasks

Just in case they are new to you, this section will run through these top-level terms.

Projects

A project defines one or more *targets* and any number of *properties*. (Properties and targets will be discussed shortly.) Only one project block exists in any one build file.

Table 27-1 details the attributes associated with the `project` tag.

Table 27-1 Project attributes	
Attribute	**Description**
name	The name of the project
default	The default target that will be run if none is specified in the command line (The default is main)
basedir	The directory from which all the relative paths are calculated (The default is the directory from which the script was run).

```
<project name="antbook" default="compile" basedir=".">
```

The `project` tag used in Listing 27-1 denotes that the project name is `antbook`, and the default target is `compile`. The value "." for the attribute `basedir` denotes the directory in which the build file resides. This would be taken as the base directory, irrespective of where the build file is executed from.

Properties

One of the most powerful features of the ANT framework is the ability to define properties inside or outside the project file. These properties can then be used in any attribute throughout the project file. A property has a name and a value and can be defined as follows:

```
<property name="build" value="classes\"/>
```

The property can then be accessed by means of the notation ${<*propertyname*>}, for example:

```
${build}
```

Note   Be careful when defining and using properties, as they are case-sensitive. In addition to this, if a property is defined inside the main project element and outside a target, it is evaluated before any targets are executed.

ANT defines a number of built-in properties, listed in Table 27-2, which can be accessed just like any user-defined properties.

Table 27-2
Built-in properties

Name	Value
basedir	The absolute directory the ANT script is running from
ant.file	The absolute path of the current build file
ant.version	The present version of the ANT build
ant.project.name	The name of the project, as defined in the name attribute of the project tag
ant.java.version	The version of the JDK from which this ANT session is running

Some tasks can be triggered that will result in properties being defined. For example, `</tstamp>` results in the properties DSTAMP, TSTAMP, and TODAY being created with the current date and time as the value. In addition to the properties defined by ANT and the project you can also access any of the Java system properties using the full property name $`{file.separator}`.

Targets

The target defines a sequence or block of tasks that are to be executed. The target block is a very powerful part of the ANT framework, as it is from the target block that dependencies occur. For example, in the previous example you wanted to make sure the directories existed before you made any attempt to compile. You therefore made the `"compile"` target dependent on the `"init"` target.

A project can have any number of targets contained within it, thus there can be any number of possible combinations of target execution. It is important to note that no matter how many times a target is asked to run in any given pass, it is only executed once per session.

Take a look at the following more complicated example adapted from the core ANT documentation. It will serve to illustrate the power of the dependency feature of ANT.

```
<target name="A">
  <echo message="I am Target A"/>
</target>
<target name="B" depends="A">
  <echo message="I am Target B"/>
</target>
```

```
<target name="C" depends="B">
  <echo message="I am Target C"/>
</target>
<target name="D" depends="C,B,A">
  <echo message="I am Target D"/>
</target>
```

What if you choose to run `Target-D`? What will be echoed out?

```
C:\>ant D
Buildfile: build.xml

A:
     [echo] I am Target A

B:
     [echo] I am Target B

C:
     [echo] I am Target C

D:
     [echo] I am Target D

BUILD SUCCESSFUL
Total time: 2 seconds
```

This is a *tiered dependency tree*, so when it is traced back you can see that every target ultimately needs A to be run, then B, and so on until D is successfully run. While this method is very powerful, using it is not the only way you can control the flow of execution through the targets.

In addition to the `depends` attribute, two more attributes enable you to execute a target depending on the status of variables. These attributes are `if` and `unless`. The `if` attribute will look for a given property. If that property has been defined the target will be triggered for execution. Conversely, if the property defined in `unless` is not found, the target will be triggered for execution. Here's an example:

```
<target name="B" if="somePropertyName">
  <echo message="I am Target B"/>
</target>
<target name="C" unless="somePropertyName2">
  <echo message="I am Target C"/>
</target>
```

Please refer to Table 27-3 for a complete list of attributes that can be associated with a target.

Table 27-3
Target attributes

Attribute	Description
name	This is the case-sensitive name of the target.
depends	This is a comma-separated list of targets that must be executed before the target is executed.
if	This means that if the given property has been defined the target will be executed.
unless	This means that if the given property has not been defined the target will be executed.
description	This determines whether or not the target is defined as `internal`. An `internal` target is one that is not publicly available when queried from the script command line.

File matching

At the heart of ANT's power and flexibility is the ease with which it handles files and directories. With extreme ease you can include or exclude any combination of files based on relatively simple rules. Many of the tasks act on files or directories; we'll take a quick look at the sort of techniques you can employ to control which files are considered for use.

You can specify which files are used by defining `include` or `exclude` (or both) filters. Files (or directories) are matched if they satisfy the `include` filter and do not match the `exclude` filter. Consider the following scenario, in which you want to compile all the Java files underneath the `com/wiley/j2ee` package except for the Java files within the `com/wiley/j2ee/javamail` package.

```
<javac srcdir="${src}"
       destdir="${build}"
       includes="com/wiley/j2ee/**"
       excludes="com/wiley/j2ee/javamail/**"/>
```

You can specify the `includes` attribute to match the `com/wiley/j2ee` package and everything underneath it. The double asterisk (**) is a special wildcard used to match directories and any subdirectories. The normal directory-listing wildcards can be used to filenames — one asterisk (*) for any number of characters and a question mark (?) for a single character.

The mastering of these simple techniques will ensure that you will be able to customize ANT tasks to include the precise files you want and exclude the ones you do not.

Tasks

The task is where all the real work is performed. This is the actual command executed inside the target. A task can take any number of attributes, and can be any legally formatted XML tag. ANT has three different types of tasks:

✦ **Core tasks** — These are tasks that are shipped with the core distribution of ANT. They include all common tasks normally associated with the core JDK and the build process in general. For example, <javac> is used for general compilation, <jar> for packaging up JAR files.

✦ **Optional tasks** — These are official tasks that require additional JAR files in order to be executed. For example, <ftp> is used to upload files to or download files from a remote FTP server.

✦ **User-defined tasks** — These are unofficial tasks that have been developed by users.

Although these task distinctions do exist, in all probability you would not need to go beyond the common tasks that we will delve into in the next section.

Over 100 core and optional tasks are available and they cover a wide range of tasks and activities. We'll highlight the following in this section:

✦ javac

✦ jar

✦ junit

✦ war

✦ cvs

javac

One of the most common tasks to be invoked is the command to compile the source. You saw it briefly in Listing 27-1, but now take a closer look at this task. The javac task will take a given set of source files and compile them into a specified output directory. This task will compile all source files that do not have corresponding class files or that have class files older than the source files themselves.

The most basic example is to give javac a directory in which all the source files are located, and the corresponding output directory. Let's use (${src} and ${build} as two properties that refer to the source directory and the build directory respectively.

```
<javac srcdir="${src}" destdir="${build}"/>
```

In this example, `javac` will recursively go through all the `.java` files in the directory specified by `${src}` and compile them, creating the class files in the directory that the property `build` refers to. Naturally there is a little more to compilation, such as classpath rules, warnings, and selective compilation of files (as opposed to blindly compiling the whole tree). The `javac` task has many properties to control all of these.

The `classpath` attribute enables you to specify a comma-separated list of directories and JAR files in which to find classes for use in compilation. For example, assume that the current example requires the JavaMail JAR file `mail.jar`. You would modify the example as follows:

```
<javac srcdir="${src}" destdir="${build}"
classpath="mail.jar"/>
```

It is not difficult to see that this type of modification can get out of hand very quickly as more JAR files are linked in. Fortunately ANT is a step ahead of you on that front and provides a mechanism to enable you to group together all the necessary classpath parameters in one place and address them from `javac` using a symbolic reference as shown in Listing 27-2.

Listing 27-2: **Using <path> to specify the classpath**

```
<path id="class.path">
  <pathelement location="${build}"/>
  <pathelement location="${jarpath}servlet23.jar"/>
  <pathelement location="${jarpath}crimson.jar"/>
  <pathelement location="${jarpath}activation.jar"/>
  <pathelement location="${jarpath}mail.jar"/>
  <pathelement location="${jarpath}junit.jar"/>
</path>

<javac srcdir="${src}" destdir="${build}"
classpathref="class.path"/>
```

This enables you to specify all the necessary components that make up the classpath without cluttering up the `javac` task, which reduces the chances of making an error. The classpath information is used by a number of components in the Java process. (We'll demonstrate a similar technique with the `junit` task later in this section.) Notice how the JAR-file locations in the `path` reference aren't even hard-coded. You merely reference their names with the actual locations of the files, using the `${jarpath}` property. Again, doing this gives you only one item in the build file to change should you move the JAR files.

With the `classpath` now sorted, take a look at pulling together source files from various locations as opposed to just blindly compiling everything under one source tree. You can specify the locations to be compiled by using the `include` attribute with the task. However, a cleaner way is to use the nested tags `src` and `include`, as shown in Listing 27-3.

Listing 27-3: **Specifying different Java source locations**

```
<javac destdir="${build}" classpathref="class.path">
  <src path="${src}"/>
  <src path="${srctocustomlibrary}"/>
  <include name="com/wiley/j2ee/**/"/>
  <exclude name="com/wiley/swing/**/"/>
</javac>
```

Here you specify the two separate directories where your source is located, making sure you include all the ".java." files in the package `com.wiley.j2ee`. Notice the `exclude` tag. It is used just like the `include` tag, but instructs the `javac` task to leave out all files that match the specified pattern, in this instance the `com.wiley.swing` package. (Typically you use the `exclude` tag to remove, for example, all the testing classes from a final build.)

Many more options are associated with the `javac` task, including simple attributes to turn on the debug information or to suppress warnings. The `javac` task has a very cool feature that enables you to compile for different versions of the JDK by specifying different compilers. This may be useful if you have to support an older application server that is still using an older application-programming interface (API).

jar

The `jar` task is used to create archive files. It makes the creation of JARs, including the insertion of any manifest files you wish to use, a trivial matter. The `jar` task takes at least two attributes: the file you wish to create and the directory in which to create the jar file. Here's an example:

```
<jar destfile="${lib}/wiley.jar" basedir="${build}"/>
```

As with the `javac` task, you can use the `include` and `exclude` nested tags to control which files make it to the final JAR file and which do not. For example, you can use the `include` task to ensure that you only place `.class` files in your archive. By default the `jar` task will compress all the files it places in the archive, but you can turn this behavior off by specifying an attribute named `compress`, with the value as `false`.

You can create a manifest file for your JAR file by including the `manifest` nested tag, as shown in Listing 27-4.

Listing 27-4: **Creating a JAR file with a manifest file**

```
<jar destfile="${lib}/wiley.jar" basedir="${build}">
  <manifest>
    <attribute name="Built-By" value="${user.name}"/>
    <section name="common">
      <attribute name="Specification-Title" value="Ant
Chapter"/>
      <attribute name="Specification-Version"
value="${version}"/>
      <attribute name="Specification-Vendor" value="Wiley"/>
    </section>
  </manifest>
</jar>
```

This will place a manifest file inside the jar file created. The manifest file will contain the following information:

```
Manifest-Version: 1.0
Built-By: alan
Created-By: Apache Ant 1.5

Name: common
Specification-Title: Ant Chapter
Specification-Version: 1.9
Specification-Vendor: Wiley
```

There isn't much more to the `jar` task, which makes using it an absolute breeze.

junit

As the complexity of software increases, so do the possible number of different execution paths through the system. Although the notion of unit testing isn't new, what is relatively new is the introduction of this practice into mainstream programming.

One of the biggest problems with asking a developer to test his or her code is more social than technical. Developers don't like to admit that they are developing bad or buggy code. Most take the moral high ground, claiming that their code is above testing. In order that code can be tested, the framework has to be very easy and nonintrusive. Enter `junit` (http://www.junit.org/), an open-source initiative that makes creating tests a very trivial task, but adds in a whole a new level for conformance testing that should bring a smile to any project manager's face.

For those of you not familiar with any unit-testing methodologies, `junit` is a great place to start, and its integration into ANT makes the whole process completely painless. An in-depth review of `junit` is outside the scope of this book, but Listing 27-5 shows a quick example of how you might use it, and then how you would use it to test a completely contrived example. The class in the example will simply maintain an integer, but badly: When we ask it to decrement the value it will decrement 2 instead of 1.

Listing 27-5: **A very poorly implemented class**

```
public class integerClass extends Object {
  int X;

  public integerClass( int X ){
   this.X = X;
  }

  public int getX(){ return X; }

  public void decrement(){
    X += 2;
  }
}
```

Granted this is the sort of thing that you can easily spot when the code is laid out like this, but such a fundamental error can be missed if a class has many methods inside it. Compiling this class will not throw any errors because, syntax-wise, it is correct. What you must do now is create a separate class that will test this class in a runtime scenario.

Using the `junit` framework you can simply create a class, as shown in Listing 27-6. Simply extend the `junit.framework.TestCase` class and create a constructor that will pass the given string down to the base class.

Listing 27-6: **Test class for integerClass**

```
import junit.framework.*;

public class integerClassTest extends TestCase {
  public integerClassTest( String _string ){
    super( _string );
  }

  public void testDecrement(){
    corruptClass cC = new integerClass( 4 );
    cC. decrement();
```

```
    assertEquals( cC.getX(), 3 );
  }
}
```

The `junit` framework uses Java Reflection to determine the tests that must be run. You define a series of tests by declaring a separate method with the following signature:

```
public void testXXX()
```

where *XXX* is any valid method. Inside these methods you place your test cases.

So, how do you signal when something isn't right? You use the underlying `assertXXX(...)` methods to perform tests on various conditions. In the current example, you want the test to fail if the return value isn't equal to 3. Now that you have your testing class, you need to integrate it into ANT using the `junit` task, as shown in Listing 27-7. The first thing to do is set up a simple target that will manage the compilation of your tests. Because you don't want to compile everything, you limit the compilation to the classes that begin with the pattern `integerClass`.

Listing 27-7: **ANT tasks for controlling junit**

```
<target name="compiletests">
  <javac srcdir="${src}" destdir="${build}"
         includes="intergerClass*.java" optimize="off"
debug="on"/>
</target>

<target name="junit1" depends="compiletests">
  <junit printsummary="on" showoutput="yes">
    <classpath>
      <pathelement path="${build}"/>
    </classpath>
    <test name="integerClassTest"/>
  </junit>
</target>
```

When we run this task it will inevitably fail, with `junit` reporting the line number it failed on.

Note   One of features of the `junit` task is the ability it gives you to run your test in a separate JVM from the one controlling ANT. This has a number of advantages, specifically that you can run tests in a clean environment with a controlled classpath. Also, if something should go completely wrong with your test classes, it won't crash the ANT build process.

One of the great features of the junit task is its ability to collate information pertaining to the tests that it has just run. It can format these data in an XML format for later use with the junitreport task. This task is very useful for consolidating the entire XML file set, generated by the junit task, into viewable HTML files for easy dissemination. If you feel that wading through reams of log files to look at the results of your testing is a little tedious, you will thoroughly enjoy the output from this task.

The example illustrated in Listing 27-7 only tested one class. The junit task enables you to group together class files for batch testing using the batchtest nested tag. Consider Listing 27-8, which runs all the available test classes, collating the output in XML files to be passed onto the task junitreport for final HTML production of a report.

Listing 27-8: **Batch test**

```
<target name="junit" depends="compiletests">
  <delete dir="${junit.output}"/>
  <mkdir dir="${junit.output}"/>

  <junit fork="yes" printsummary="yes" showoutput="yes">
    <classpath>
      <path refid="class.path"/>
        <pathelement location="${jarpath}xalan.jar"/>
    </classpath>

    <formatter type="xml"/>
    <batchtest haltonfailure="yes" todir="${junit.output}">
      <fileset dir="${src}">
        <include name="com/wiley/junit/**Test.java" />
      </fileset>
    </batchtest>
  </junit>

  <junitreport todir="${junit.output}">
    <fileset dir="${junit.output}">
      <include name="TEST-*.xml"/>
    </fileset>
    <report format="frames" todir="${junit.output}/html"/>
  </junitreport>
</target>
```

This target starts off by deleting any log files from previous tests by removing and creating the directory. Then you fork a new JVM to run the tests.. You set the output of the junit task to XML, which will be used when the report is produced. You then create a series of tests using the batchtest nested tag that looks for all class names that end in Test.java. Finally you run the junitreport task, which will run through all the log files and produce all the HTML files, which you can then view with the full results of your recently run test.

The `junit` tool is very powerful and it should be used throughout the development process, not just near the end of a project. It is a great tool for making sure that nothing will get broken during any future development or refactoring.

Note   The use of the `junit` tasks will require that you download the `junit` and the `X-alan` JAR files for use within your ANT distribution.

war

A WAR file is basically just a ZIP file with special directories placed inside it so the application server can deploy it successfully. ANT makes creating WAR files very easy. The `war` task takes input for the specific positions in the structure `/WEB-INF/web.xml`, `/WEB-INF/lib/`, `/WEB-INF/classes/`, and `/WEB-INF/web.xml` and produces the resulting WAR file, which is then ready for deployment.

The `war` task makes it easy to build the WAR file from a variety of disparate parts. For example, your main `web.xml` file may be created out of a file that might not even be named `web.xml`; thus you are able to build up WAR files using different targets. Listing 27-9 depicts and example of creating a WAR file using the `war` task.

Listing 27-9: Building up a WAR file

```
<war destfile="myapp.war" webxml="src/metadata/myapp.xml">
  <fileset dir="src/html/myapp"/>
  <fileset dir="src/jsp/myapp"/>
  <lib dir="thirdparty/libs">
    <exclude name="jdbc1.jar"/>
  </lib>
  <classes dir="build/main"/>
  <zipfileset dir="src/graphics/images/gifs"
              prefix="images"/>
</war>
```

One of the major advantages of the `war` task is that it builds a legal file. For example, the specification insists that the name of the directory `/WEB-INF/` be in uppercase, but sometimes Windows will not maintain the case of the directory when you manually create the archive.

CVS

The majority of developers maintain their code in Concurrent Versions System (CVS); those who do not should consider it. CVS is one of the more popular version-control systems, largely because it comes preinstalled in the majority of Unix-distribution systems and because of its easy-to-use interface. Developers use CVS differently depending on the policy of the particular project each is working on. Generally speaking, the rule of thumb is never to check in buggy code or half-complete code. Following this rule enables you to build ANT scripts, for example, to build the latest WAR file for a particular project. The ANT script can automatically pull the latest source code from a CVS repository.

ANT provides a couple of tasks that enable interaction with the CVS server. The first and most important task, cvs, sends commands straight to the CVS server specified by means of the CVS root. If you are familiar with CVS commands you will have no problems integrating CVS operations into your ANT script. For example, if you want to check out the module com/wiley/j2ee from your CVS root we can include the following command:

```
<cvs cvsroot=":pserver:${cvsuser}@myserver.com:/home/src"
    command='checkout com/wiley/j2ee' dest="${checkout.dir}"/>
```

As you can see, by doing this you are simply passing the CVS command to the server and specifying the output directory as an ANT property.

Now take a quick look at a more practical example. Assume that you want to extract the latest revision number from a given source file that has the CVS $Revision: $ tag in it somewhere. You can write an ANT target to pull the latest version from CVS, extract it, and then set it as an ANT property for later use. Listing 27-10 illustrates the ANT target for this operation.

Listing 27-10: **Extracting the revision**

```
<target name="getrevision">
  <cvspass cvsroot=":pserver:${cvsuser}@myserver.com:/home/src"
          password="${cvspassword}"/>
  <cvs cvsroot=":pserver:${cvsuser}@myserver.com:/home/src"
      command='update ${src}/com/wiley/j2ee/main.java'
      output="cvsoutput.txt"/>
  <replaceregexp byline="false"
      match="(.)+\n(.)+\n(new revision:) (.+);(.)+\n(.)+"
      replace ="buildversion=\4" file="cvsoutput.txt"/>
  <property file="cvsoutput.txt"/>
</target>
```

The first thing you will notice is the cvspass task. If your CVS server requires a password for access, this task sets the necessary .cvspass file with the given password. Next you pull out the latest version of the com/wiley/j2ee/main.java file, with the output of that operation saved into the file cvsoutput.txt. Taking the contents of cvsoutput.txt, you run a regular expression on it, using the replaceregexp task, which finds the revision and replaces it with the single line "buildversion=x". Finally you pass the file cvsoutput.txt to the property task, which parses this file as a set of key/data pairs and makes those pairs available in the ANT file.

Putting It All Together

We have taken a look at the most common tasks and techniques of ANT with this chapter. This chapter is by no means an exhaustive look at what ANT can do; it is an overview of ANT's most common uses. To round this off, take a look at a typical build file (Listing 27-11) that you may use during various parts of a project's development cycle.

Listing 27-11: **A sample build.xml file**

```xml
<project name="wiley" default="compile" basedir=".">

  <!-- Define the properties for this project -->
  <property name="src"          value=".\src"/>
  <property name="build"        value=".\classes"/>
  <property name="dest"         value=".\lib"/>
  <property name="jarpath"      value=".\jars"/>
  <property name="junit.output" value=".\junitreport\"/>

  <path id="project.class.path">
    <pathelement location="${build}"/>
    <pathelement location="${jarpath}activation.jar"/>
    <pathelement location="${jarpath}mail.jar"/>
    <pathelement location="${jarpath}xalan.jar"/>
  </path>

  <!-- initialise some directories -->
  <target name="init">
    <tstamp/>
    <mkdir dir="${build}"/>
    <mkdir dir="${junit.output}"/>
  </target>

  <target name="clean">
    <delete dir="${build}"/>
  </target>

  <!-- Compile the java code from ${src} into ${build} -->
  <target name="compile" depends="init">
```

Continued

Listing 27-11 *(continued)*

```
      <javac srcdir="${src}"
             destdir="${build}"
             includes="com/wiley/j2ee/**"
             optimize="off" debug="on"
             classpathref="project.class.path"/>
   </target>

   <!-- JUnit tests: Compilation -->
   <target name="compiletests" depends="init">
      <javac srcdir="${src}"
                        destdir="${build}"
                        includes="com/wiley/junit/j2ee/**"
                        optimize="off"
                        debug="on"
                        classpathref="project.class.path"/>
   </target>

   <!-- JUnit tests: Running and producing output -->
   <target name="runtests" depends="compiletests">
      <delete dir="${junit.output}"/>
      <mkdir dir="${junit.output}"/>

      <junit fork="yes" printsummary="yes" showoutput="yes">
        <classpath>
           <path refid="project.class.path"/>
         </classpath>
        <formatter type="xml"/>
          <batchtest haltonfailure="yes" todir="${junit.output}">
             <fileset dir="${src}">
               <include name="com/wiley/junit/j2ee/**Test.java" />
             </fileset>
          </batchtest>
      </junit>

      <junitreport todir="${junit.output}">
         <fileset dir="${junit.output}">
            <include name="TEST-*.xml"/>
         </fileset>
         <report format="frames" todir="${junit.output}/html"/>
      </junitreport>
   </target>

   <!-- Build JAR file -->
   <target name="buildjar" depends="compile">
      <jar destfile="${dist}wiley_j2ee.jar">
         <fileset dir="${build}"
                  includes="com/wiley/j2ee/**/*.class"/>
      </jar>
   </target>
</project>
```

As you glance through the build file you will quickly see how it all comes together. You set up all your properties at the top of the build file, which ensures that you won't have to hardcode any directory paths anywhere. It is important that you stay away from hard coding any paths, filenames, directory names, etc. into your ANT tasks; as otherwise you are not seeing the full benefit ANT can bring to your development environment.

You define all your paths from the `basedir="."`, which is the directory in which the `build.xml` file is saved. Then you define some simple housekeeping-type targets that ensure that the necessary directories exist before you try compiling into them.

You run the main targets, `compile`, `runtests`, and `buildjar`, by specifying the target name as a command-line argument to ANT when you trigger the script. There is no limit to the number of targets you can have in one file. However, the key thing is to document your targets well so that anyone maintaining your build file can do so with relative ease.

Summary

In this chapter we had a quick look at ANT and saw how you can make use of it in your own development environment. We tried to understand the structure of an ANT build file and also touched on some of the commonly used ANT tasks and ANT's possible integration with JUnit and CVS.

ANT can minimize the housekeeping activities involved in managing your J2EE environment, and free you to get on with building robust and scalable enterprise applications. ANT has revolutionized J2EE deployment, and considering the ever-growing complexity of J2EE, ANT can only get more relevant and more useful in the future.

✦　　✦　　✦

Creating High-Performance Java Applications

✦ ✦ ✦ ✦

In This Chapter

Understanding
performance metrics
for J2EE

Introducing J2EE
performance tools

Logging

Managing memory-
usage problems

✦ ✦ ✦ ✦

O ne of the marvelous things about Java is that it is a
very resilient runtime environment. Because no direct
access to memory is available via pointers, and because memory is not manually de-allocated, many problems that would
crash programs written in other languages will not crash a
Java application. This doesn't mean that Java is immune to
problems — what happens instead is what computer scien-
tists call *graceful degradation*, where the performance gets
worse over time although the application doesn't crash
outright.

Understanding Different Types of Problems

This section discusses some of the most common types of
problems that occur in Java applications, how to identify
them, and how to isolate them. It's not possible to describe
every possible solution to every possible problem, but once a
problem has been clearly identified and isolated the solution
is usually straightforward.

Before we can start looking at techniques for diagnosing and
fixing problems, we need to understand what kinds of problems we can encounter in J2EE applications. When we talk
about *applications* in this chapter, we mean *distributed* J2EE
applications — ones that are built using servlets, JSPs, EJBs,
or JMS. These applications are all similar in that they are

accessed via some network protocol, like the Hypertext Transfer Protocol (HTTP) for servlets and JavaServer Pages (JSPs), or remote method invocation (RMI) for Enterprise JavaBeans (EJBs).

All of these systems have a similar basic setup—some component provides a response to requests coming in from a remote user. In many cases there may be a chain of these requests, as with a servlet calling one or more EJBs that in turn make Java Database Connectivity (JDBC) queries. In these cases the exact source of the problem can be difficult to identify. However, the basic performance-tuning principles hold true for each component in the system as well as for the system overall. Performance-tuning desktop GUI applications is similar, but many of the performance metrics discussed in this chapter don't apply to them.

 **Cross-Reference**   See Chapter 18 for a discussion of JDBC.

It's worth noting that from a performance standpoint J2EE systems are quite similar to other types of distributed applications, like client-server systems and mainframe transaction-processing systems. All these systems have multiple pieces that communicate over a network and deal with multiple simultaneous users. If you are familiar with performance testing and tuning on these types of systems, some of this chapter will be familiar to you.

Functional problems

First of all we can have *functional problems*. Every developer is familiar with functional errors. They happen when your application gives you the wrong result. Functional errors are easy enough to identify once they occur—the trouble is the process of rigorously going through every possible use case and verifying that the correct results are produced. It's impossible for this book to even scratch the surface of the subject of doing functional testing. Suffice it to say that the field of software quality assurance is broad and deep, and that most developers have some familiarity with it.

Performance problems

Once we're past functional problems we get into the more difficult-to-diagnose realm of *performance problems*. These problems affect applications in the following ways:

Requests complete too slowly.

Slow-downs occur as the number of users increases

Requests arrive faster than they can be completed

Let's define and then discuss the following performance metrics:

✦ Response time

✦ Throughput

✦ Scalability

Response time

Response time is the amount of time it takes to complete a single request. Request time can be defined a number of ways. For example, does the response time include the amount of time it takes to transmit the request from the client browser to the server? In most cases this end-to-end user-centric view of the system is the metric we use to measure response time. When users and developers talk about poor performance, a poor response time is usually what they mean. Sometimes poor response time is the result of some sort of inefficiency or problem in the application. More often, however, a poor response time is a symptom of some other problem that has yet to be revealed.

When looking at response time it is useful to think of it as a statistical measure. The response time for one request in isolation says next to nothing about the system's overall performance. In most systems you'll want to use a load-testing tool to help generate a large number of requests to simulate real-world usage patterns. (Load testing is discussed later in this chapter.)

Once you have a large number of requests you'll be able to talk about *average response time* (ART), *maximum response time,* and various other statistical measures such as *standard deviation.* Some people also calculate the *aggregate average response time* (AART) of a set of load tests to compare test suites with respect to the total amount of load they generate (see *J2EE Performance Testing* by Peter Zadrozny, Expert Press, 2002).

Throughput

Throughput refers to the number of requests that can be processed by the application in some period of time. Throughput is typically measured in requests per second, or kilobytes per second if the size of the requests is highly variable.

Throughput can be measured at any point in time, but what most people are usually interested in is the maximum throughput. At any given point in time the current throughput is usually lower than the maximum because there's some unused processing capacity in the system.

Scalability

Scalability refers to the number of users who can access the application before response time starts to increase. In an ideal world your application maintains a uniform response time regardless of how many users are accessing it. In reality an application can handle only a finite number of requests before its performance starts to degrade. No separate measure of scalability exists — a system's maximum possible throughput determines its scalability.

In an ideal world response time is zero, maximum throughput is infinite, and scalability is a non-issue. However, in reality, this is never the case. No simple, linear relationship exists among response time, current throughput, and maximum throughput (scalability), but in most applications we can observe the behavior depicted in Figure 28-1.

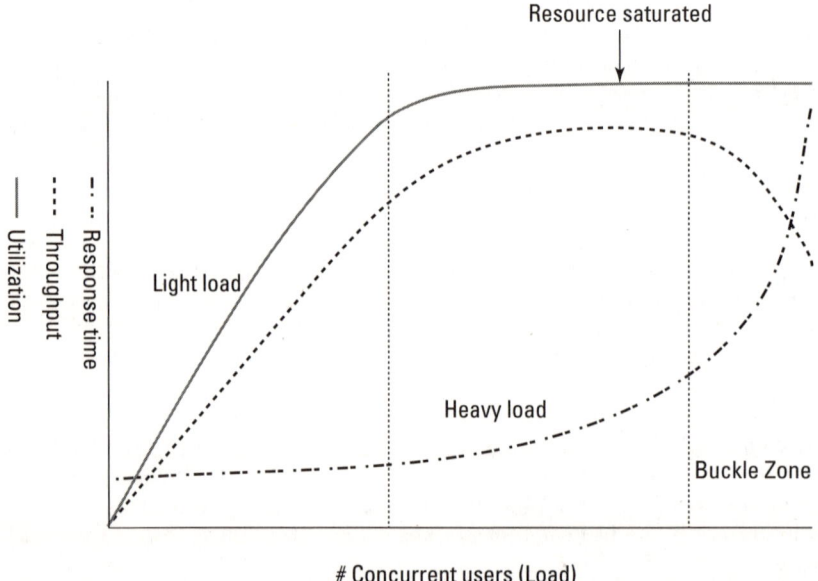

Figure 28-1: The relationship between load and response time, throughput, and utilization

The way to interpret this graph is to watch what happens to the various performance metrics as users connect to the system (moving right on the *x*-axis). The x-axis can be described as either the number of connected users or the request arrival rate. However, the most common term for it is simply *load*. This term has been used for a long time in engineering as an indicator of how much work the system is trying to do.

We see that at the beginning response time is constant as the number of users increases. The larger the *light-load* zone, the better the system's scalability.

Response time doesn't usually start to increase until the system enters the *heavy-load* zone, wherein the system is processing at the maximum possible rate (in other words, the throughput line has leveled off). The response time isn't increasing because we've reached the maximum throughout for our application—instead they're both correlated to a hidden third factor: *resource use.*

Finally we get to the point where the system spends more time coordinating the access to this shared resource than it spends actually using it—the *buckle zone.* In some cases the system will recover once the rate of request arrivals drops, but in many cases the system will crash.

Resource use refers to any number of resources shared among users in the application. For example, most applications have only one database, so all the users have to compete to access it. Other examples of shared resources are as follows:

✦ **Threads**—Most application servers have a finite number of threads available to handle incoming HTTP, RMI, and JMS requests.

✦ **Memory**—While it is not typically viewed as a resource, many Java Virtual Machines have a single shared heap, which means that only one thread at a time can allocate objects, leading to contention.

✦ **CPU time**—While most applications are limited by the network bandwidth available or by the speed of the database, some applications need to do heavy processing and the CPU can become a bottleneck.

✦ **EJB instances**—Many application servers pool stateless session beans, so a finite number are available to respond to requests.

✦ **Locks**—Any synchronized method or synchronized block in your code represents a resource that can be used by only one thread at a time. If the code block is very small this probably won't be a problem, but as the size of the code block grows, so does the possibility for conflict. Many hidden locks are also present in your application, like the one used to manage the shared servlet session-management data structures.

✦ **Database connections**—These are also typically pooled by the application server.

✦ **Disk bandwidth**—Some application servers will passivate EJBs directly to disk, queue JMS messages on disk, and so on, making the disk a potential bottleneck.

So with this model for application performance, what can we do to improve the performance of our application? If response times are slow, two possible reasons exist. First, our application could be moving into the heavy-load zone or the buckle zone too quickly. This means the problem is really a scalability problem. Or, more probably, the response-time line is simply too high on the graph. Even under low load, the response time is poor. In either case what we need to do is streamline the application, and determine which resource is becoming saturated and in turn limiting our throughput or reducing the maximum throughput. Determining where the problem occurs and what resource is involved is not easy, but some structured approaches and tools can help us. Let's look at some techniques that can help us track down the source of performance problems.

Isolating Problems

We can use the following techniques to try and identify where problems are coming from:

✦ Guessing

✦ Critical-path analysis

✦ Load testing

✦ Benchmarking

✦ Profiling

The first technique, guessing, doesn't merit a lot of discussion for technical reasons, but it is certainly popular. Anytime you don't have enough data to make a complete diagnosis of the problem, anytime you make a code change based on a "hunch," you're really just guessing. Developers can be pretty good guessers and their guesses can be right sometimes, but when you have a few million lines of code and deadlines to worry about it's not a sufficiently reliable technique.

Critical-path analysis

Critical-path analysis is a technique in which you analyze application code statically. You identify certain use cases based on the application requirements or on whichever use cases are presenting performance problems. Then you manually trace through the sequence of system components and method calls, looking for potential problems and generally optimizing the code along those paths of execution.

Critical-path analysis is slow, tedious and error-prone. It is, however, a more rigorous method than simply guessing and will yield better results. The key first step is identifying the use case to be analyzed, as well as every method executed during that use case. Extensive use of logging (discussed later) is very helpful in this regard, as it can be difficult to statically trace every possible path of execution through the code.

Load testing

Here is where we enter the world of tools. Not every problem can be solved by a smart developer and a text editor alone. Most developers are fully aware of this, of course, and love using the wide variety of debugging and analysis tools at their disposal. As the old saying goes, however, "A fool with a tool is still a fool." You need to have a clear understanding of what tools are capable of doing for you and what information you expect them to provide.

A load-testing tool simulates a large number of users connecting to the system and using the application. It's a critical part of final system tests to determine the overall capability of the system and help with capacity planning. Some examples of commercial load-testing tools are Benchmark Factory from Quest Software (`http://benchmarkfactory.com`), LoadRunner from Mercury Interactive (`http://www-svca.mercuryinteractive.com/products/loadrunner/`), and SilkPerformer from Segue (`http://www.segue.com/html/s_solutions/ s_performer/s_performer.htm`). Freely available tools include The Grinder (`http://grinder.sourceforge.net/`) and Apache JMeter (`http://jakarta. apache.org/jmeter/`). Some of these tools are not only capable of generating HTTP requests but can also test EJBs over RMI or generate JMS messages. Some may also have support for testing Web services via SOAP.

These tools are useful not only because they can simulate anywhere from a dozen to thousands of users connecting to your system, but also because they're script-able so that they can replay complex series of requests and change their behavior dynamically. For example, in an e-commerce application users might be required to log in with unique user names before they can add items to their shopping carts. Tests wouldn't be realistic if all 200 simulated users were logging in using the same user name, so many tools can parameterize their test scripts and bring in a list of user names from a file, spreadsheet, or database.

What is a load-testing tool going to tell you? It depends on the complexity of the tool. At the very least a load-testing tool is going to give you a response-time curve—the response time versus time, or the response time versus number of con-nected users. More complex tools can monitor other aspects of the application and provide other metrics versus time or user load. For example, IBM WebSphere has its own monitoring API called PMI. The JMX application-programming interface (API) makes a number of internal application-server metrics available for applica-tion servers that support it. Possible JMX metrics are things like number of pooled EJB instances, number of `HTTPSession` instances, number of JMS messages in a queue, and other metrics as well. More information is available at `http://java. sun.com/products/JavaManagement/`.

What a load tester isn't going to do is tell you *why*. Why is the problem you're see-ing occurring? If the response time is unacceptable, what is the root cause of the problem? For this you're going to have to go back to critical-path analysis or move on to using a profiling tool that will identify bottlenecks within the application. Load-testing individual components (like EJBs and databases) in the system can be a help in this regard—at least you can pin the performance problem down to a spe-cific component in the system. Then you'll be able to move on and use a more spe-cific tuning tool.

Benchmarking

One issue that faces J2EE development teams is choosing what application server to use. This is partly a non-technical issue; some developers may prefer to use open-source products like Tomcat and JBoss. Other developers may choose to select a commercial vendor because of improved support or support for specific operating systems, or because the salesperson took them out for lunch. While the

J2EE specification attempts to make application servers into interchangeable commodities, significant technical differences still exist among them. Which application server will run your code the fastest? How can you tune and configure the application server to run your code as fast as possible?

The first question is mostly unanswerable. If you remove all other variables from the system you may be able to make a fair comparison, but this is often difficult to do. If you compare several app servers all on identical hardware with the same application with the same load tests and the same database, one application server will be better than the others according to some metric. Of course, you have to choose your performance criteria as well. Perhaps one application server provides more consistent and lower response times while another provides higher throughput.

Application-server vendors are fond of publishing benchmark statistics using industry-standard benchmarks. Various vendors use benchmark applications like SPECjAppServer2002 and SPECjvm98 to tout their technical superiority. (Visit the site at `www.specbench.org/` for details about these applications.) Of course, no two vendor benchmarks are ever run on the same hardware platform.

Also consider how closely the execution profile of the benchmark application matches the characteristics of your application. Benchmark numbers provided by vendors, while interesting, are ultimately useless for the practical job of making your particular application run faster.

Lastly, the question of what application server to choose is often out of any individual developer's hands. The decision has often already been made by management or some technical-selection committee, and the developer's task is to take the environment at hand and make the best of it.

So the second question is much more relevant to most developers: How can you tune and configure the application server to make your code run as fast as possible? This sort of performance tuning is, without a doubt, an art, not a science. Anywhere from a few dozen to several hundred settings exist on a commercial J2EE application server. The vendor's documentation will provide you with some guidance as to what you can change, but these settings are very application server specific.

You cannot simply blindly change values and expect to see performance improvements. Also, the optimal value for these settings will vary from application to application. You can't just copy what's working well for another development group. How can you determine which values are optimal for your application? You can embark on the long, slow process of benchmarking.

A typical benchmarking setup consists of hardware that resembles that which will actually be used in production, the same Java Virtual Machine (JVM), the same application server, the same database (although not necessarily the same data, although the data should be realistic), and a load-generation tool with some scripts to exercise the application. You'll need to define what metric you're trying to optimize — response time, throughput, perhaps peak memory usage.

You run an initial test with the default settings for everything to create a baseline. Then you change the value of a single parameter (or a very small number of parameters), rerun the test, and compare the results to your baseline. Were the new settings better or worse? In many cases optimal values for configuration settings are neither the maximum nor the minimum value but somewhere in between. If increasing the maximum heap memory from 512MB to 1024MB resulted in a 5 percent improvement in response time, that doesn't necessarily mean that increasing it further to 2GB or 3GB will be better still. In some cases extremely large heaps result in garbage collections that, although they take a very long time, happen less frequently; this can reduce the average response time.

Tunable parameters

Aside from changing application code, you can often improve overall system performance by tuning various parameters on your application server and Java Virtual Machine.

Application-server parameters

Unfortunately, there are too many application server parameters to get into in this book. Even more frustratingly, the parameters vary greatly between different application servers as the tunable parameters reflect the unique internal architecture of the different application servers.

However, some common parameters include the following:

✦ **Execute Thread Pool Size** — This is equal to the number of requests that the application server will process at once–any other requests will be queued. Note that there's a limit to the improvement you get from increasing this value.

✦ **JDBC Connection Pool Size** — This is the number of connections the application server will open to the database. This value should typically be equal to or greater than the number of execute threads.

✦ **Stateful Session EJB Pool Sizes** — Depending on the number of beans used in each request this value will typically be some multiple of the thread pool size. The value will usually have to be adjusted for each type of EJB used in the application.

For more detailed information, refer to the performance documentation for your application server.

JVM parameters

The JVM may require some tuning, depending on which JVM you're using and what features it supports. The three major commercial JVM vendors are Sun, IBM, and BEA with its JRockit JVM. The set of available parameters varies among vendors and from release to release so it's difficult to state exactly what options will be available on the JVM you're using.

It's worth noting that in the future we'll see JVMs becoming more and more "self-aware" and capable of automatically determining the optimal values for the different parameters described here. This is roughly analogous to what has happened with cars over the last 50 years: The user-adjustable choke has disappeared, and many cars come with automatic transmissions, automatic traction-control systems, anti-lock brakes, and climate-control-luxury automobiles that will even tell you via GPS where you are and how to get where you're going. We can only hope that it doesn't take JVM designers 50 years to make analogous progress.

Here are some of the major tunable elements in current-generation JVMs:

✦ The bytecode compiler

✦ Heap size

✦ The garbage-collection algorithm

These elements are discussed in the following sections.

The bytecode compiler

The bytecode compiler is the engine that translates Java bytecodes into native machine instructions. This is in contrast to javac and similar tools that translate source code into Java bytecodes. All the optimizations are done at runtime in the JVM and not by javac. It's therefore important to use a highly optimizing bytecode compiler.

Early bytecode compilers were referred to as "JITs" because they performed what is known as *just-in-time compilation,* wherein the bytecode is recompiled when the class is loaded into the JVM. Newer JVMs, like Sun's HotSpot, use more sophisticated techniques. This product starts by interpreting the bytecodes and collecting runtime data, which allows it to decide more intelligently than a simple JIT, which methods need to be compiled. It's also capable of performing more aggressive optimizations that result in faster code. Most JVMs only come with a single bytecode compiler, but Sun's HotSpot comes with two versions, referred to as *client* and *server.* While the server version is designed for J2EE applications, some developers have reported that their applications run faster in the client version. You will have to benchmark your own code to find out.

The command-line options for the Sun JVM since Sun's JDK 1.2 are `-client` and `-server`. These options actually affect a number of settings, including how heap memory is configured, so performance differences resulting from using one option or the other may not be the result of the different compiler alone.

Heap size

Heap size is probably the single most important JVM setting. While the JVM will allocate more heap memory from the operating system when it's required, it is conservative in doing so and may not allocate the optimal amount. Setting the initial heap size improves the startup time for your application and can improve steady-state performance as well. Setting the initial size of the heap too large can cause problems, however: If the heap gets paged out this can cause virtual memory thrashing and slow down memory access for garbage collection. Setting the maximum size of the heap prevents the JVM from consuming excessive system resources. Additionally, you may be required to set the maximum size if you set the minimum size to a large value, as the default maximum size may be lower than the initial size you've set.

In some cases you may want or need to set the size of other memory regions as well. Some JVMs enable you to adjust the size of the stacks that are associated with each thread. If your application has a shallow call-tree structure and does not store a lot of data in local variables you can save some memory by reducing the size of the stacks. Some JVMs enable you to adjust the size of the permanent area, or method area, wherein bytecode and static variables are stored. This may be required for very large applications in which the size of all the loaded classes exceeds the default maximum amount of permanent-area space. This is, however, perhaps a bug and not a feature.

Some heaps use more complex structures, such as a *generational heap.* In generational heaps the heap is broken down into two regions: one for the allocation of new objects and another for objects that have been around for a while. These are usually referred to as the "new" and "old" regions respectively. The *new* region allocates and disposes of objects more quickly but is less efficient in its use of space. The *old* region uses space efficiently but is slow to allocate and garbage collect. Some J2EE applications that create large numbers of transient objects benefit from having the size of the new region increased from the default. Doing this is usually more expedient than trying to reduce object allocation activity.

In Sun's JVM the overall heap size is controlled via the `-Xms` and `-Xmx` flags—for example, `java -Xms128m -Xmx512m`.

The garbage-collection algorithm

Some JVMs have multiple garbage collectors available. The difference between them is usually some sort of tradeoff between pause time and throughput. Some garbage collectors require that all threads in the system be suspended when garbage is being collected (these are referred to as *stop-the-world* collectors). This results in a pause in the application's processing of anywhere from a few milliseconds to several seconds. The pause time is proportional to the number of objects on the heap, which is in turn usually proportional to the overall size of the heap—so as a rule of thumb, the bigger the heap, the longer the pause. While small pauses typically do not cause problems for J2EE systems, large pauses can cause problems like transaction failures or browser timeouts.

In order to reduce the pause time a number of different strategies are available. Parallel garbage collectors distribute the GC activity across multiple processors concurrently. This is only a benefit in multiprocessor systems, however. Other garbage collectors are concurrent where the garbage collector does not require that other threads have to be suspended for the entire time the garbage collector is running. In both cases the reduction in pause time comes at a price: throughput. Although the individual pauses are smaller, more time is spent overall in garbage collection than would be spent with a stop-the-world collector.

Not all garbage collectors are equal — you get to pick two out of three: low pause time, high throughput, and simple architecture. As JVM vendors spend more time implementing better and more complex garbage collectors, performance improves for both pause time and throughput. Again, it's difficult to make specific statements about garbage-collector performance outside the context of a particular JVM and a particular application. If you have a choice of multiple garbage collectors, it's worthwhile to benchmark them and see if there is any difference.

The following documents have some useful performance-tuning information, but may not be the most up to date. It is often difficult to find information on new JVM features, but these documents should provide a good starting point:

- ✦ http://java.sun.com/docs/performance/
- ✦ http://wireless.java.sun.com/midp/articles/garbagecollection2/
- ✦ www-106.ibm.com/developerworks/ibm/library/i-garbage1/
- ✦ www-106.ibm.com/developerworks/library/i-gctroub/
- ✦ www-106.ibm.com/developerworks/ibm/library/j-berry/
- ✦ http://edocs.bea.com/wljrockit/docs70/tuning/

Profiling

A *profiler* is a tool that measures how much time is spent in each method in your applications. The most popular profiler is probably Quest Software's JProbe (found at http://java.quest.com/jprobe), but profilers are also available from Borland and Compuware among others.

Profiling is an essential part of any performance-tuning strategy, because without it you're reduced to guessing which methods are causing performance problems or to going through the laborious process of tracing through the critical path(s) by hand. With a profiler you can see exactly which methods are executed for a particular use case and how much time is spent in each of them. Some profilers can also monitor object-allocation activity so you can make correlations between excessive object creation and excessive timing values.

One thing that profiling is not good at is correlating the internal activity of an application with the user's perception of it. That is, you can not simply run through a random series of operations in your application, collect some profiling data, tune the most expensive method, and expect to see any significant improvement. A good performance-tuning strategy identifies specific application-use cases to be analyzed and collects data on just those use cases. Profiling information that isn't collected in the context of some operation that's relevant to the end user is just useless data.

Profiling, like benchmarking, works well in conjunction with an organized load-testing strategy. Load testing will identify which use cases are problematic and a profiler will provide the data that break down what's happening inside the application in those situations. Profilers are sometimes referred to as *white-box* tools, which is a reference to the contrast between their approach and the *black-box* approach of a load tester.

In many cases, however, you'll be forced into situations where you're trying to diagnose a problem that's already occurred without an easy way to reproduce it or evaluate it within a tool like a profiler. What you need in those situations is a record of what happened — a log.

Logging

One way to isolate problems is to carefully track every activity in your application. Recording every action taken in an application is referred to as *logging* and it is an extremely powerful debugging technique.

The concept behind logging is as old as software development — every time an application does something it also prints a message saying what it just did. The trouble then becomes adding these statements to and removing them from the source code. You don't want customers or users to see all the details of the application's internal operation, but sometimes it's useful to have the information available to help diagnose difficult-to-reproduce bugs. What's needed is a technique that enables you to turn debugging output on and off dynamically without having to recompile the application.

Finally, developers do sometimes want to display messages to the end user — for example, if the network is unavailable the user should receive a message letting him or her know that the application hasn't failed at random but for a specific reason. The logging APIs available for Java provide all of these features.

One issue that faces developers who decide to use logging in their applications is the question of what to log. How can you make sure you're logging every piece of information you will want to see? There is no easy answer to this question. Here are some approaches:

✦ **Log everything** — This is usually impractical. In certain critical sections of an application, however, it may be the best approach to help make sure everything is working perfectly.

✦ **Log every method** — This is a useful approach, as it helps the developer track chains of method calls at runtime. Often the exact sequence of method calls may be difficult to determine *a priori* because of dependencies on the inputs to the system. The major difficulty with logging every method call is that it requires a lot of discipline to log each and every method. Once you start making exceptions for small or "unimportant" methods you lose the certainty of being able to see everything that's going on.

✦ **Log the border** — By *border* I mean the entry points to major components of your system. For J2EE applications the border would consist of servlets, JPSs, and EJB methods. JDBC calls would also be a logical border point, but modifying JDBC-driver code to add logging statements isn't usually possible. In some cases you may want to take the less convenient path of logging every call to JDBC method call. Monitoring the border is a good tactic, though, as it is an easy way to identify the entry points into the major components of your application.

✦ **Log critical operations** — With this approach you log only those operations that are deemed "critical" by some measure. The problem is that often methods that seem innocuous during development end up playing a major role in some problem that occurs once the application is deployed. There's really no way to effectively define "critical" for every possible set of circumstances. Being selective about what you log does, however, cut down on both the amount of logging code in the application and the amount of logging output.

The most common approach is to log most, but not all, methods. The problem is that too much logging information is generated when developers choose to log every method call. However, by using the concept of logging levels, developers can get the best of border logging as well as method logging.

Logging APIs

Two logging APIs are available. One is the standard logging API provided with JDK 1.4 and higher, defined in JSR 47 and found at www.jcp.org/en/jsr/detail?id=47. The other API is the Apache Jakarta project's Log4J, found at http://jakarta.apache.org/log4j. Why do two logging APIs exist when one of them is a standard? Partly for historical reasons — Log4J was developed before JSR 47 was finalized and became popular enough that many developers didn't switch to the new standard API when it became available. The other reason is that the two APIs provide different capabilities and in some cases developers have found that the extra features provided by Log4J are worth the trouble of including another third-party library in the application.

The JSR 47 logging specification was first implemented in the Java 2 SDK (JDK) 1.4 release. No official release of the JSR 47 logging classes exists for earlier JDK releases. However, an open-source package called Lumberjack can be found at `http://javalogging.sourceforge.net/`. This package provides the JSR 47 for JDK 1.2 and JDK 1.3. All the JSR 47 logging classes are defined in the `java.util.logging` package.

Note Log4J has been under development for a long time (since 1999). It originated as a project at IBM, though it is now a fully open-source member of the Apache Jakarta project. The Log4J classes are defined in the `org.apache.log4j` package.

If the two APIs seem similar, it's because the architecture of JSR 47 was influenced by Log4J and other hierarchical logging packages. Because many concepts are shared by both APIs, it's easy to explain them both at the same time. Choosing one is not really a technical issue — if you're using JDK 1.4 or higher exclusively, use the JSR 47 logging classes that come in the JDK standard library. If you need to support earlier JDK releases, Log4J may be a better choice.

Logging is all about messages. A *message* is some piece of information that you want to record for the purpose of monitoring the activity of your application. Figure 28-2 shows how messages are processed by the logging framework with Loggers, Handlers and Formatters.

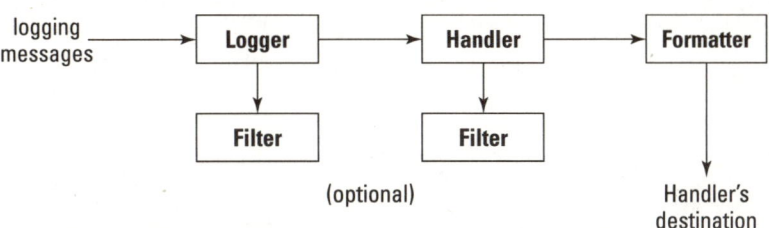

Figure 28-2: Logging architecture

The JSR 47 specification represents messages using strings with optional extra objects that are provided as arguments to the message. Log4J represents messages using any type of object and converts them into some sort of human-readable format via a formatter. In practice you'll primarily log single-string messages when using either API. Messages can optionally have a `Throwable` object associated with them to encapsulate call-stack information about where the message was generated.

The important thing about logging APIs is that they're not going to simply print out every logging message generated by the application — messages also have a priority level associated with them. This enables you to dynamically adjust which messages are being logged by monitoring only certain levels of messages. The following priority levels are defined in JSR 47 and Log4J:

	JSR 47/JDK 1.4	**Log4J**
Most Detail	FINEST	n/a
Least Important	FINER	n/a
Lowest	FINE	DEBUG
	CONFIG	INFO
	INFO	WARN
Least Detail	WARNING	ERROR
Most Important	SEVERE	FATAL
Highest		

These priority levels are simply mapped to integer values, so you can define additional levels if you wish. So when we talk about high priority messages, these are messages that we always want to log because they're very important. Low priority messages may be logged, but we might also want to disable them to prevent an excessive number of messages from being logged when the system is functioning normally.

Once you've created a message you want to log and have decided what priority it is, what do you do with it? You pass it to a logger. The logger is responsible for taking the message, checking its priority level to see if it should be logged, and, if so, sending it to some destination. Every logger has a priority level associated with it and will automatically discard messages with lower priority levels. In both JSR 47 and Log4J the logger class is simply called Logger — either java.util.Logger or org.apache.log4j.Logger.

Loggers are hierarchical and this is a very powerful feature. Every logger has a name in a hierarchical namespace associated with it, just as classes are organized into packages in Java. Most applications create a logger for each class with the same name as the class, although any structure can be used. This hierarchical setup enables you to easily filter or sort through messages according to where they were generated, on either a per-package or per-class basis. For example, we might have two code packages com.acme.foo and com.acme.bar, as shown in Figure 28-3. By changing the priority for the logger named com.acme you implicitly change the priority associated with both the com.acme.foo and com.acme.bar loggers that correspond to the two code packages.

Priority levels are inherited, so if you don't set a priority level for a logger explicitly, the priority level will be inherited from the nearest parent that has its level set. In this example, if there is already a logger for com.acme with its priority level set to INFO, the com.acme.Foo logger will automatically inherit the same priority level (INFO). Also, messages sent to a child logger are sent to the parent as well, so messages can be handled at any point in the hierarchy.

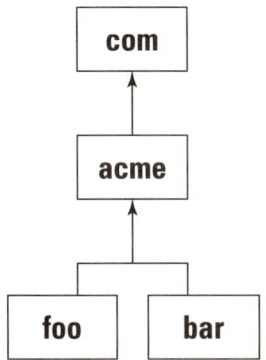

Figure 28-3: A possible logger hierarchy mirrors class names.

One important difference between the two logging APIs is how they handle the order of initialization. The following code will work the same in both APIs:

```
Logger parent = Logger.getLogger("com.acme");
Logger child = Logger.getLogger("com.acme.Foo");

parent.setLevel(HIGHER); // where HIGHER is FATAL or SEVERE
child.setLevel(LOWER);   // where LOWER is DEBUG or FINE
```

But the following code will work differently:

```
Logger parent = Logger.getLogger("com.acme");
Logger child = Logger.getLogger("com.acme.Foo");

child.setLevel(LOWER);   // where LOWER is DEBUG or FINE
parent.setLevel(HIGHER); // where HIGHER is FATAL or SEVERE
```

In JSR 47 new children copy the parent's level until their own level is changed. When the level is changed on a parent logger, the level of all children loggers will be changed. In contrast, Log4J dynamically walks the logger tree each time a level determination is required.

Caution   In JDK 1.4, order of configuration for loggers matters — always configure parents before children.

The `Logger` class in both APIs has a number of methods to handle messages. Each class has `Logger.log` methods that take a priority level and a message and optionally a `Throwable` object. Here's an example:

```
// JSR 47 / JDK 1.4
// these classes are in java.util.logging
```

```
Logger logger = Logger.getLogger("com.acme.Foo");
Logger.log(Level.WARNING, "A message");
Logger.log(Level.FINE, "Another message", new
RuntimeException());

// Log4J
// these are different classes in org.apache.log4j
Logger logger = Logger.getLogger("com.acme.Foo");
Logger.log(Level.ERROR, "A message");
Logger.log(Level.DEBUG, "Another message", new
RuntimeException());
```

You can see the similarity between these two APIs. Convenience methods such as the following, which have the same names as the priority levels, are also available.

```
Logger logger = Logger.getLogger("com.acme.Foo");

// in JSR 47
Logger.config("A CONFIG priority message");
Logger.fine("A FINE priority message");

// in Log4J
Logger.info("A INFO priority message");
Logger.debug("A DEBUG priority message");
```

When a message is sent to a logger, the message's priority level is compared to the logger's priority level. If the message's priority is equal to or higher than the logger's priority level, the logger generates a LogRecord (in JSR 47) or LoggingEvent (in Log4J) object. This is an internal logging object that generally isn't visible to the developer. It is in turn passed to a Handler (in JSR 47) or Appender (in Log4J), which takes the new log entry and puts it in the log. LogRecords (and LoggingEvents) are also sent to the parent logger so that in a typical application you need to attach only a Handler (or Appender) to the root logger (whose name is an empty string). Loggers can also have multiple Handlers attached, allowing them to log messages of different priority levels to different destinations.

JSR 47 Handlers

In JSR 47 the following Handlers are included:

- ✦ StreamHandler
- ✦ ConsoleHandler
- ✦ FileHandler
- ✦ SocketHandler
- ✦ MemoryHandler

You can also define your own Handlers by subclassing Handler or StreamHandler.

StreamHandler

StreamHandler is a base class that provides common functionality to the Handlers that send output to some subclass of java.io.OutputStream. ConsoleHandler, FileHandler, and SocketHandler are all subclasses of StreamHandler.

ConsoleHandler

ConsoleHandler sends output to the OutputStream provided by System.err. This means that the messages will usually show up in the console that started the JVM. In some application servers the System.err output will be collected in a special application-server log that can be viewed in the application server's administration console.

FileHandler

FileHandler sends logging output to a file or a set of files. This code fragment demonstrates writing to a single file:

```
// in some initialization code
Logger rootLogger = Logger.getLogger("");
Logger logger = Logger.getLogger("com.acme.Foo");
FileHandler handler = new FileLogger("logfile");
rootLogger.addHandler(handler);

// later on
logger.log(Level.INFO, "A Message");
```

Note also that in this example the Handler is attached to the root logger so that even though no logger is explicitly attached to the com.acme.Foo logger the output will still be logged. FileLogger can also automatically start a new log file when the current file reaches a certain size. This feature is useful as it can be used to prevent the log files from filling up all the available drive space.

```
// in some initialization code
Logger rootLogger = Logger.getLogger("");
Logger logger = Logger.getLogger("com.acme.Foo");
// use 3 files of 50K each
FileHandler handler = new FileLogger("logfile", 50*1024, 3);
rootLogger.addHandler(handler);

// later on
logger.log(Level.INFO, "A Message");
```

SocketHandler

SocketHandler writes all its output to a socket. You'll need to specify a machine name and a destination port in its constructor. No corresponding server classes are provided—you'll have to write your own classes that listen on a ServerSocket and process the incoming messages.

MemoryHandler

`MemoryHandler` is a terminal destination for messages—a proxy that buffers a finite number of `LogRecords` in memory using a circular buffer until a predefined condition is met. This condition is typically met when a message arrives that has a priority level higher than the `MemoryHandler`'s (set in the `pushLevel` property). So the `Memoryhandler` will buffer messages, discarding old ones as new ones arrive, until something important happens.

Log4J Appenders

In Log4J `Appenders` serve the same role that `Handlers` do in JSR 47. Log4J is much more powerful than JSR 47 in one way—it provides a large number of `Appenders` "out of the box." It's difficult to imagine a situation in which one of the provided `Appenders` isn't sufficient. Another difference between JSR 47 and Log4J is that Log4J makes no assumptions about where you want logging output to go, so no default `Appenders` exist. You'll have to explicitly create an `Appender`, either by instantiating one or placing one in the configuration file. See the sections on JSR 47 configuration and Log4J configuration, later in this chapter.

Log4J provides the following wide variety of `Appenders`:

✦ `AsynchAppender` collects `LoggingEvents` in a separate thread and then dispatches them to other `Appenders` asynchronously.

✦ `JDBCAppender` sends `LoggingEvents` to a database.

✦ `JMSAppender` sends `LoggingEvents` out via a JMS topic (such as publish/subscribe).

✦ `LF5Appender` sends messages to a Swing-based console application.

✦ `NTEventLogAppender` sends messages to the NT Event Log service.

✦ `SMTPAppender` sends an e-mail.

✦ `SocketAppender` transmits a serialized `LoggingEvent` object via a socket.

✦ `SocketHubAppender` listens on a socket as opposed to opening a remote server.

✦ `SyslogAppender` sends events to a syslog daemon.

✦ `TelnetAppender` creates a socket you can telnet into to monitor logging messages. It defaults to port 23, the telnet port.

✦ `ConsoleAppender` logs to `System.out` or `System.err`.

✦ `FileAppender` sends messages to a file.

✦ `RollingFileAppender` backs up the log file automatically when it reaches a certain size.

✦ `DailyRollingFileAppender` rolls over the log file at a fixed frequency.

Consult the Log4J documentation for more details about how to use each of these different `Appenders`, `http://jakarta.apache.org/log4j/docs/documentation.html`.

Formatting output

The last thing that both logging frameworks do is format the messages into something suitable for saving. They do this via a `Formatter` (JSR 47) or `Layout` (Log4J) that transforms the message into an appropriate binary or human-readable format.

In JSR 47 the two available Formatters are `SimpleFormatter` and `XMLFormatter`. `SimpleFormatter`, the default formatter, formats a `LogRecord` into a simple, human-readable one- or two-line output. `XMLFormatter` outputs a standard XML format as defined in the DTD supplied in Appendix A of JSR 47 (`www.jcp.org/aboutJava/communityprocess/review/jsr047/spec.pdf`).

Consider, for example, in JDK 1.4.1, a `SimpleFormatter` configured like this:

```
// create a Logger & a ConsoleHandler
Logger logger = Logger.getLogger("com.acme.Foo");
Handler handler = new ConsoleHandler();
// This next step is optional as SimpleHandler is the default
handler.setFormatter(new SimpleFormatter());
logger.addHandler(handler);

logger.severe("Whoa!");
```

This produces the following output:

```
Feb 18, 2003 9:47:25 PM LogTest main
SEVERE: Whoa!
Feb 18, 2003 9:47:25 PM LogTest main
SEVERE: Whoa!
```

Why is the message printed out twice? Because a `ConsoleHandler` is already attached to the root logger by default. The logging classes are configured so that you will get logging output without having to do any more than create a logger. One message comes from the root logger's `ConsoleHandler` and the other from the `com.acme.Foo` logger's `ConsoleHandler`.

You can define new `Formatter`s simply by subclassing the `Formatter` class and overriding the `format(LogRecord)` method.

Log4J layouts

Log4J comes with a much wider variety of pre-defined layouts. This is because Log4J uses the more general approach of allowing any type of object to be logged as a message. The defined Log4J layouts are as follows:

✦ `DateLayout` formats `Date` objects.

✦ `HTMLLayout` outputs messages in an HTML table.

✦ `PatternLayout` uses a pattern string to generate message output.

✦ `SimpleLayout` prints only the message priority and the message as a string.

✦ `XMLLayout` is similar to JSR 47's `XMLLayout`, but has a different DTD.

New layouts can be defined by means of subclassing `Layout` and overriding `format(LoggingEvent)`.

Multi-threaded logging

Logging messages in a complex multi-threaded system is a challenge. Messages may arrive in any order and are not necessarily logged in the order in which they arrived. Additionally, many threads may be executing the same method (as in a servlet or EJB container) and it may be difficult to distinguish one thread's activity from another. Also, you may want to distinguish all the activity coming from one client machine separate from activity generated by other machines, which may be handled by multiple threads on the server.

Log4J makes this last task easy with the Nested Diagnostic Context (NDC) class. The NDC is set up like a stack: Whenever you enter a new context you push the context information onto the stack and when you leave the context you pop it off again. What defines a context? You could set up a servlet's `doGet()` method as a new context and call `push()` at the beginning and `pop()` at the end. The entry point for an important EJB method might be another possible context. The power of nested contexts lies in their ability to let you track the activity from the servlet to the EJB and back again. You do this by watching the NDC information that's automatically included in each logged message.

All the NDC methods are static and the data structures inside the NDC class manage the information on a per-thread basis. This all happens transparently to the developer.

Here's a code fragment showing how to use a NDC:

```
public class StockServlet extends HttpServlet {
Logger logger = Logger.getLogger("StockServlet");

public void init( ) {
   logger.setLevel(org.apache.log4j.Level.INFO);
   org.apache.log4j.BasicConfigurator.configure();
}

public void doGet(...) {
   NDC.push("From: "+request.getRemoteHost());
```

```
  // do some stuff
  logger.info("some message");

  NDC.pop();
}
```

This code fragment would produce output like this:

```
0 [HttpProcessor[8080][4]] INFO StockServlet From: 127.0.0.1 - some message
```

The message includes the following elements:

> ✦ [0] is a timestamp.
>
> ✦ [HttpProcessor[8080][4]] is the thread name.
>
> ✦ [INFO] is the logging level.
>
> ✦ [StockServlet] is the logger name.
>
> ✦ [From: 127.0.0.1] is the NDC message.
>
> ✦ [some message] is the actual message logged.

Runtime configuration

The final advantage of using a structured logging API instead of plain old println() statements is that you can dynamically change the amount of data being logged without having to recompile — or in some cases restart — your application.

JSR 47 configuration

In JSR 47 logging configuration is managed via the LogManager class. By default the LogManager reads its initial configuration from the properties file lib/logging. properties in the JRE directory. If you edit that property file you can change the default logging configuration for all uses of that JRE. In addition, the LogManager uses the two following optional system properties that give you more control in reading the initial configuration:

> ✦ java.util.logging.config.class
>
> ✦ java.util.logging.config.file

These two properties may be set via command-line property definitions to the java command, as shown here:

```
java -Djava.util.logging.config.file=logging.config SomeClass
```

The configuration file uses the simple key/value format shown in Listing 28-1.

Listing 28-1: **JSR47 configuration file**

```
# "handlers" specifies a comma separated list of log Handler
# classes.  In this case, a single ConsoleHandler is
# configured
handlers= java.util.logging.ConsoleHandler

# To also add the FileHandler, use the following
# line instead.
#handlers= java.util.logging.FileHandler,
java.util.logging.ConsoleHandler

# Default global logging level.
# This specifies the priority level of the root logger
# Note that the ConsoleHandler also has a separate level
# setting to limit messages printed to the console.
.level= FINEST

# default file output is in user's home directory.
java.util.logging.FileHandler.pattern = %h/java%u.log
java.util.logging.FileHandler.limit = 50000
java.util.logging.FileHandler.count = 1
java.util.logging.FileHandler.formatter =
java.util.logging.XMLFormatter

# Limit the messages that are printed on the console
# to INFO and above.
java.util.logging.ConsoleHandler.level = INFO
java.util.logging.ConsoleHandler.formatter =
java.util.logging.SimpleFormatter


############################################################
# Facility specific properties.
# Provides extra control for each logger.
############################################################

# For example, set the com.acme.Foo logger to only log SEVERE
# messages:
com.acme.Foo.level = SEVERE
```

These properties can also be defined in any location accessible by an
InputStream and passed to the LogManager class at runtime via LogManager.
readConfiguration(InputStream).

Different properties are available for the different classes. The properties are set up
to mirror the Java class names like java.util.logging.ConsoleHandler, but
with the limitation that only one instance of each class can exist because of naming
conflicts.

Log4J configuration

Log4J configuration is managed via a `Configurator`. The `Configurator` interface has two primary implementations, which allow the configuration settings to come from a file, a `Properties` object (`PropertyConfigurator`), or a XML DOM (`DOMConfigurator`).

`PropertyConfigurator` works much like JSR 47's `LogManager`, with one interesting additional feature: It can be configured to open a file and re-check it at whatever interval you define. This is very useful, as it enables you to change the logging properties without even having to restart your application — you can start getting extra logging information about problems on the fly without having to try to reproduce the problem.

Listing 28-2 is an example of a servlet that monitors a local configuration file for logging settings.

Listing 28-2: **Log4J configuration file**

```
public class MyServlet extends HttpServlet {

Logger logger;

public void init() {
// configure Log4J
// check for changes every 60 seconds
PropertyConfigurator.configureAndWatch("local_config_file",
    60);
// convenience method to create a logger with the same
// name as a class
logger = Logger.getLogger(this.class);
}

public void doGet(HttpServletRequest request,
    HttpServletReponse response) {

// do some stuff
logger.info("INFO Message");
// etc
}
}
```

Note that you don't want to invoke `PropertyConfigurator` in the `init` method for every servlet in your system — this would result in the logging system being initialized multiple times, which may not be what you want. Tomcat will automatically initialize Log4J as part of its startup procedure, but in other systems you'll want to create a class that tracks whether logging has been initialized and makes sure that it only happens once. Alternatively, you can avoid the problem of multiple initializations by creating the appenders and layouts you want to use in your initialization code and not using a `Configurator`.

Having looked at logging, let's move on and look at a separate topic related to managing the performance of your applications — memory management.

Managing Memory-Usage Problems

While the garbage-collection system in Java makes memory management much easier to deal with for developers, garbage collection is not a panacea. The potential to waste memory still exists. Memory-management problems can manifest a number of symptoms ranging from benign excessive memory usage and performance loss owing to excessive garbage collections all the way to application failures owing to an out-of-memory condition.

Before we can discuss memory problems in Java, let's discuss how memory management and the garbage collector work. Objects are allocated on the heap by means of the new operator and accessed via references. Probably the easiest way to think about memory in Java is to picture the heap forming a directed graph, wherein objects form the nodes and the references between objects make the edges. This is shown in Figure 28-4.The garbage collector sees the memory this way, as a graph of objects and references.

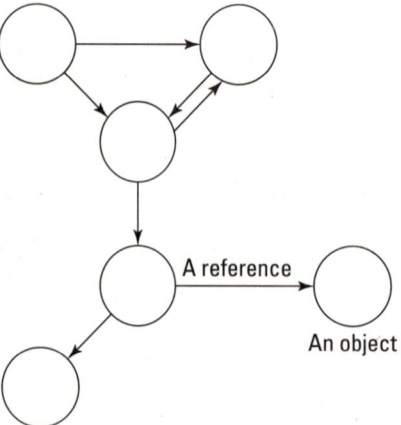

Figure 28-4: Memory in Java

The purpose of the garbage collector is to remove from memory objects that are no longer needed. But how does it determine which objects are no longer needed? This is a hard problem to solve — the garbage collector can't tell whether or not you need any particular object, so it uses an approximation and looks for objects that are no longer reachable. If we use the directed-graph analogy, it looks for objects that can't be reached by any path starting from a root. *Roots* are the starting points for the garbage collector, fixed places that are always guaranteed to exist. In Java, the roots include static fields in classes and locals on the stack. This is shown in Figure 28-5. Anything that the garbage collector can't reach from one of the program's roots by any path is considered garbage.

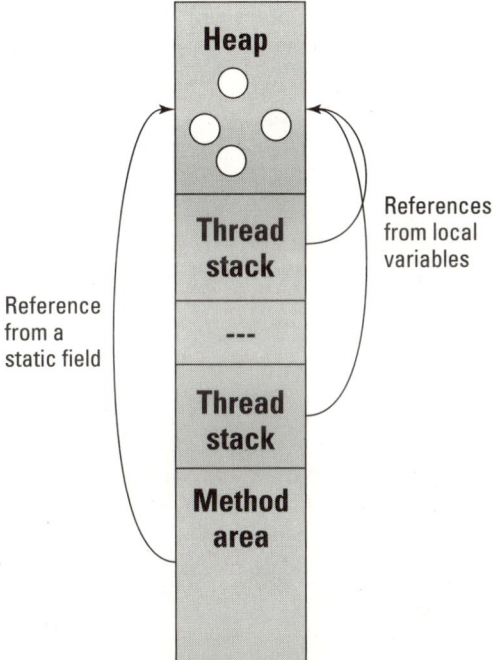

Figure 28-5: Memory regions and roots in Java

For an example of how the garbage collector evaluates what is and isn't garbage look at the following code:

```
Public void useless() {
MyObject m1 = new MyObject();   // object A
MyObject m2 = new MyObject();   // object B
m1.ref = m2;
global.ref = m2;
return;
}
```

This method has two local references on the stack, m1 and m2. Another variable, called global is also created, outside the scope of this method. m1 and m2 are, temporarily at least, two roots for the garbage collector. Two objects, A and B, are created and two references, or edges, are created to them from the locals on the stack (m1 and m2). Another reference is added from m1 to m2 and a reference is added from the global object to m2. When the method returns, m1 and m2 are no longer on the stack, so object A is no longer reachable while object B can still be reached via the reference `global` See Figure 28-6 for an illustration of this.

Because the garbage collector can no longer reach that object by some path it will, at some point in the future, clean up that object. It's important to note that garbage collection does not happen immediately, but at some indeterminate point in the future. In practice the garbage collector runs every few seconds but there are no guarantees if and when it will run. Even though the object will stay in memory for some period of time until the garbage collector releases it, it remains unreachable and can't be reused.

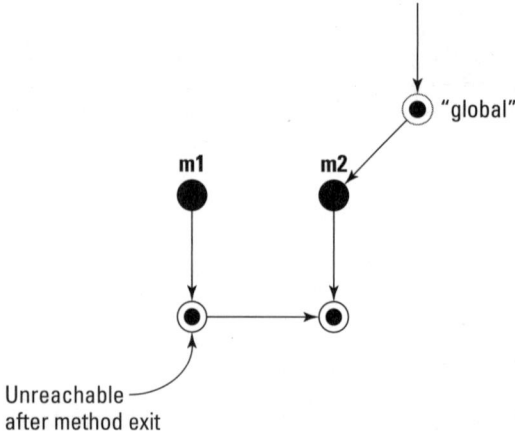

Figure 28-6: Determining reachability for garbage collection

Loiterers

Now that we've talked about what the garbage collector is and what it does, let's look at what it means to have a memory leak in Java. An object can exist in any of the three following states:

- ✦ Allocated
- ✦ Reachable
- ✦ Live

Figure 28-7 shows objects on the heap and the references between them, dividing objects into the three states. The set of *allocated* objects contains all objects that have been created but not yet removed by the garbage collector. *Reachable* objects are all the allocated objects that can be reached from one of the garbage collector roots. *Live* objects are reachable objects that are being actively used by your program.

Dispelling Myths About Garbage Collection in Java

Some common myths about garbage collection in Java are worth "cleaning up." The first is that the garbage collector can't handle cycles — it can. That is, if you have three objects, A, B, and C, with references from A to B, from B to C, and from C to A, and if these are the only references to those objects, the garbage collector will clean those objects up. In this respect Java is unlike other systems that use reference-counting techniques, such as Microsoft's COM, that do have problems handling cycles in the object-reference graph.

The second myth (and this is really for people who've moved to Java from C++) is that the finalizer is the same as a C++ destructor. A number of subtle differences exist, but the most important one is that the finalizer is not guaranteed to be called, unlike a destructor in C++, which is always called when the object is removed. You can't reliably depend on the finalizer in Java. One interesting piece of trivia, however, is that if the finalizer is called, it's possible for it to "resurrect" the object by making a reference to the object that's about to be garbage-collected from another object, thus making it reachable again. While this is a bad thing to do in practice, the garbage collector is aware of the fact that it can, in theory, happen.

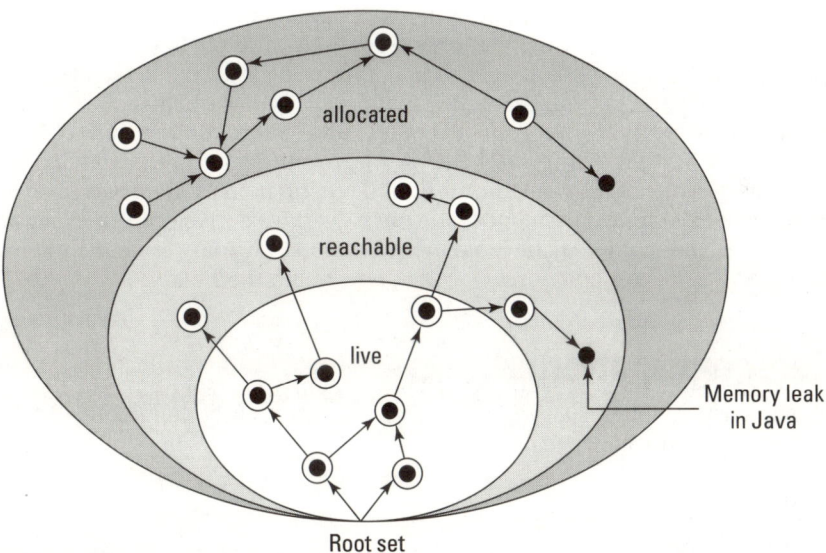

Figure 28-7: Finding memory leaks in Java

The garbage collector takes care of the allocated but unreachable objects for you, so a Java memory leak is an object that's reachable but not live. Even though you have a reference to that object somewhere and a path to that object from some root exists, the object isn't needed by the program and could be disposed of — if there wasn't a reference to it.

One possible complication is that while the object itself can be reached, the code that manages the object may not be accessible to you — for example, the reference to the unneeded object might be from a private field in a class for which you don't have the source code. On the other hand, if the reference itself is accessible the program should be able to take some action to remove all the references to the object, thus making it unreachable and eligible for garbage collection.

When an object is being unnecessarily held in memory it's rarely the case that a single object is there alone. That object will have references to other objects, which will have more references, and so on, forming a large subgraph of objects that are leaked just because one reference wasn't properly cleared. For example, in Swing or AWT programming containers, such as panels or frames, include other child components, such as buttons, text fields, and so on. The container can reach all of its children, as it has references to them (to lay them out), and at the same time each component has a reference back to its parent. A path, therefore, exists from every object in the user interface to every other object. Compounding the problem, user interface (UI) objects are often subclassed, adding additional references and objects to the subgraph. The result is that the memory leak is not just a small set of components; a very large collection of objects may be leaking.

It has become popular to refer to these unused objects in Java as *loiterers,* as opposed to *memory leaks,* which denotes a different problem in C/C++ development community. The Dictionary.com definitions of loitering are "to delay an activity with aimless idle stops and pauses" (which will happen as the garbage collector has more and more objects to check on each pass) and "to remain in an area for no obvious reason" (you're not using them, so why are they there?), both fairly apt descriptions of what's going on. Another good reason to use a different term is that the Java virtual machine and many of the libraries have native code in them, written in C++, and that code may have memory leaks in it, leading to confusion as to whether a leak is in Java code or C++ code underneath the Java.

Loiterer anti-patterns

So, knowing what a loiterer is, what are some common situations that lead to loitering objects? Here are a few examples:

✦ Lapsed listeners

✦ Large sessions

✦ Lingerers

✦ Limbo

Lapsed listeners

A lapsed listener refers to an object being added to a collection and never removed. The most common example of this is an event listener in Swing or AWT, where the object is added to a listener list but never removed once it is no longer needed. The object's usefulness has lapsed because although it's still in the list, receiving events, it no longer performs any useful function.

One of the side effects of lapsed listeners is that the collection of listeners may be growing without bound. You can keep adding listeners to a collection, but they are never removed. This causes the program to slow down as events have to be propagated to more and more listener objects, causing each event to take longer and longer to process. This is probably the most common memory-usage problem in Java — Swing and AWT are very susceptible to this problem and it can occur easily in any large framework.

Large sessions

Configuring your application server for long session timeouts can lead to excessive memory consumption, which is much like a loitering-object problem. The good news is that this is an easy problem to fix — simply reduce the session timeout period. If you're allowing sessions to persist for several hours before they're removed you're going to require a lot of extra memory to hold the session data.

Alternately, sometimes large sessions are caused by programmer carelessness and not long timeouts — perhaps an object was stored in a session that had a reference to some other large set of objects that weren't being used. In this case you'll need to analyze what exactly is being stored in the `HttpSession` objects and remove any unnecessary objects.

Stateful session beans can also lead to excessive memory consumption if not managed properly. A common occurrence is that as users connect to the system, a stateful session bean is created for each new user. As users leave the system the beans are not removed immediately — they have to time out. Before the timeout limit is reached, however, more users connect, so the application server needs to reuse that memory, so the beans are *passivated,* which means that their data are written to persistent storage, typically disk. This passivation can be a time- and resource-consuming activity and is only necessary if the same user is going to return to the system and expect to see it in the same state as when he or she left it. When `HttpSessions` are removed via timeout any stateful session beans associated with that user should be manually removed from the system as well.

Lingerers

A lingerer is an object that hangs on for a while after the program is finished with it. Specifically, it appears when a reference is used transiently by a long-lived object but isn't cleared when finished with. The next time the reference is used it will probably be reset to refer to a different object, but in the meantime the previous object loiters about.

The following print service in an application is one example of a lingerer:

```
public class PrintService {

static PrintService singleton;
Printable target;

public PrintService getPrintService() {
  return singleton;
}

public void setTarget(Printable p){
  target = p;
}

public void doPrint() {
  // set stuff up
  // print target
}
}
```

The print service can be implemented as a singleton because there isn't usually any need to have multiple print services in an application (at least for the sake of this example). The print service contains a field called `target`, and when the program calls `doPrint()` the print service goes and prints the object referred to by `target`. The important thing is that when the print service is done printing the target reference is not set to null. The object that was being printed can't be garbage-collected now, as a reference to it from the printer object is still lingering. You have to make sure that transient references are set to null once you've finished using them.

Here's another example of a lingerer in a class that implements a stack:

```
public class Stack {
Object stack[] = new Object[10];
int index = 0;

public void push(Object o) {
    stack[index] = o;
    index++;
}

public Object pop() {
    index--;
    return stack[index];
}
}
```

So, if we ignore the possibility for `ArrayIndexOutOfBounds` exceptions, what's wrong with this code? Imagine what happens after you push three objects on the stack and then pop them off. While the stack is empty, it still contains the references to those three objects, preventing those objects from being garbage-collected.

One strategy for dealing with lingerers is to encapsulate state in a single object as opposed to having a number of objects maintaining state information. This makes changing state easier, as you have only one reference to deal with. Lingerers often occur when objects with multiple states hold onto references unnecessarily when the object is in a quiescent or inactive state, so you have to carefully consider the state-based behavior of your objects.

Another strategy is to avoid early exits in methods — you should set up methods so that they do their setup first, then the processing, and finally any cleanup necessary. If you exit before the method has a chance to clean up, references may be left holding onto objects that are no longer needed.

Limbo

In our final anti-pattern, things in limbo are caught between two places, occupying neither of them fully. Objects in limbo may not be long-term loiterers, but they can take up a lot of memory at times when you don't want them to.

Limbos occur when an object being referenced from the stack is pinned in memory by a long-running thread. The problem is that the garbage collector can't perform *liveness analysis,* by which it would be able to find out that an object won't be used anywhere in the rest of a method, thus making it eligible for garbage collection.

Consider this code fragment, in which the method is supposed to read through a file, parse items out of it, and deal with certain elements in it:

```
Void method() {
   // this creates a large object
   // perhaps a XML DOM tree
   Biggie big = readIt();

   // this condenses it
   // assume item has no references to big
   Item item = findIt(big);

   // we'd really like to reuse big's memory
   // this method is going to run a long time
   parseIt(item);
}
```

This might happen if you were looking for a specific piece of data in an XML file, for instance. So the first thing the method does is call readIt(), which reads in the whole file, which would consume a lot of memory. Then the method findIt() goes through and searches for the particular information you're looking for, condensing all the information from the big object into something much smaller. From this point on you don't need big anymore and you'd probably like to reuse the memory it's occupying. But when you call parseIt(), which may take a long time, the memory for big can't be reused because there's still a reference to it from the stack in method()'s stack frame—big can't be garbage-collected until method() returns. You need to help the garbage collector out by setting the reference to big to null before the call to parseIt().

One way to deal with limbos is to be aware of long-running methods and to watch where large allocations are occurring, to make sure that you're not creating large objects that are being held on the heap by a reference on the stack. Tools such as profilers and memory debuggers can help determine what methods take a long time to run and what objects are very large.

Explicitly adding statements to set references to null in cases where large objects are being needlessly held can make a big difference by allowing objects to be garbage collected earlier. While it's not practical or necessary to null out every reference after you're done with it, it helps where appropriate.

Finally, a blocked thread can also be a problem; for example, when a thread is blocked waiting on I/O, no object referenced from the stack in that thread can be garbage-collected. In these cases, resolving the thread blockage will also resolve a loitering object problem.

Summary

Overall this chapter has touched on a number of different topics all relating back to the core idea of creating high-performance applications. When analyzing performance problems, or any type of problem, you need to go through three steps: detect, diagnose, and resolve.

Detecting the problem can be difficult, especially since you, the developer, want to detect problems before your users do. Various types of testing tools, like load testing tools, can help to detect problems before your application is deployed into production.

Diagnosing the problem requires another set of tools—things profilers and logs of application activity generated via a structured logging API. The information provided by these tools helps you to determine where exactly the problem originates.

Finally, resolving the problem requires an understanding of what the root cause of the problem is—in some cases it may be obvious, but in other cases, like excessive memory usage ("Loiterers"), the problem may be more difficult to track down and you'll need knowledge of how the garbage collector operates to help fix the issue. In other cases it may be quicker to make a change to the execution environment by tuning parameters associated with the JVM or the application server.

Using the tools and concepts explained in this chapter you should be well equipped to detect, diagnose and resolve performance problems in Java applications.

✦   ✦   ✦

Airline Reservations Business Case

Any examples of companies, organizations, products, domain names, e-mail addresses, people, places, or events depicted herein are fictitious. No association with any real company, organization, product, domain name, e-mail address, person, place, or event is intended or should be inferred.

Executive Summary

Connexia Airlines is a new startup consumer airline that will take advantage of a specific gap in the short-haul domestic-travel market. This gap exists in low-cost service in the following metros:

✦ Hartford/Springfield, Connecticut

✦ Milwaukee, Wisconsin

✦ Toledo, Ohio

✦ Atlantic City, New Jersey

✦ Wilmington, Delaware

✦ Baltimore, Maryland

The lack of availability of cheap service in and out of these locations, coupled with the demand for such service, indicates that a new airline could capture a significant market share of current air travel in and out of these locations.

Management-consulting firm Aspectsoft.com has conducted extensive market research and predicts that air travel to and from the preceding destinations is sufficient to provide a new carrier with annual revenues of $250 million in its first year of operation. The sales figures are based on two factors: first, achieving a load factor of 65 percent in the first year, and second, achieving a 75 percent booking rate for tickets through electronic means.

Based on the stated revenue, Connexia can produce a net profit of between $1 million and $2 million in its first year of operations, and $16 million dollars in its second year. The first year of operations will drain cash until revenue can commence, because of regulatory and organizational obligations in the first year for any new carrier.

Mission Statement

Connexia Airlines has the following mission statement:

> We will provide safe, low-cost, on-time consumer air travel. We will stress safety as our highest priority. Connexia will operate the newest aircraft and best information-technology systems available. We will never shortcut maintenance at any time for any reason. We will make every effort to operate our flights on time. We will provide friendly and courteous no-frills service.

The Management Team

These are the members of Connexia's management team:

Mattie Lee Mitchell, president and CEO — Mattie Lee successfully founded three different regional airlines in a fifteen-year period. She is an accomplished pilot and businessperson. Prior to starting airlines she was the corporate pilot for United Express, Kelon Piano Company, Planet Fruit, and Flute Bank. Mattie Lee attended the University of Carlisle.

Fong Sai Yuk, chief financial officer — Fong Sai Yuk was the vice president and treasurer for Roti Resorts Limited. He previously was president of a $40 million martial-arts-film company. Sai Yuk has successfully raised capital for two different public companies and has written strategic growth plans as both an executive and a member of the board of directors. Fong has a BA in finance from the College of Plumitan and an MBA in finance from Biche University.

Sherry Ann Rattan, chief technology officer — Sherry Ann has over seven years of information-technology experience, including distinguished military service. She has been director of operations, chief architect, and a technical writer. She has also served as chief information officer for Rio Claro Airlines.

Technology Overview

The key to obtaining profitable customers and keeping expenses in line is using information technology to obtain competitive advantage. Connexia's CTO, Sherry Ann Rattan, has asked her team to focus their primary efforts on making the reservations process more efficient.

Sabre and Apollo are the two predominant reservations systems used in the airline industry today, but they are outmoded and obsolete. The major airline carriers are slow to change their information systems because of the huge expense involved. Hence, they keep operating with old and outdated systems.

Sabre is in the process of testing a new system that leverages Java Messaging Service (JMS), and Apollo is testing a new system that uses Web services. Sherry Ann would like to support these new interfaces in pilot mode but would require the older RMI and proprietary interfaces to be supported. Since Sabre is a mainframe system, she wants the team to consider using the Java Connector Architecture (JCA) to encapsulate all Sabre logic.

The Connexia reservations system will have the three following advantages, which will contribute to reduced expenses:

- ✦ Speed
- ✦ Learning curve
- ✦ Easy integration with current and future business partners

Since many of its business partners' systems were developed more than 20 years ago, Connexia constantly needs to retransmit records from one system to another. Retransmission should happen without human intervention.

One of the biggest issues facing Connexia is compliance. The Federal Aviation Administration (FAA) requires exacting record keeping. Connexia will be periodically audited and must have clearly defined procedures and documented internal accountability.

Examples in this Book

This book contains the following examples.

Developing a login page — JSP Basics (Chapter 6)

This will demonstrate a simple login page that prompts the user to enter his or her user ID, password, and role (agent, partner, consumer, employee). Each user is given five attempts to login. After the fifth failed attempt a user is locked out of the system and redirected to a page that will let him or her contact an administrator.

Developing a lost-password page – JSP Basics (Chapter 6)

This screen will prompt users to enter hints. Employees will enter their employee IDs; all others will enter their e-mail addresses. If they are known to Connexia, they will be redirected to a page that will tell them that their IDs and passwords will be e-mailed to them.

Developing a registration screen – JSP Basics (Chapter 6)

This screen will enable agents, partners, consumers and employees to register their Web sites. Users will enter their names, e-mail addresses, and phone numbers. Simple validation will occur. Employees will be required to enter their employee IDs, agents will be required to enter their agent IDs, and partners will be required to enter their partner IDs.

Sending e-mail – JavaMail (Chapter 8)

The marketing department will have a screen that will enable its members to enter a subject and a message and to select a group of recipients (agents, partners, consumers, employees) to whom to send a message. When the composer of the message clicks Send, the system will display a page that shows how many recipients were e-mailed and how many initially known failures occurred.

Sending e-mail to newsgroups – Java e-mail (Chapter 8)

The marketing department would like a screen that enables its members to enter a subject and a message and to select a group of Usenet newsgroups to which to send a marketing message. Members will be able to select up to five newsgroups at any one time.

Sending a request for food to the caterer – JMS (Chapter 9)

Every time a reservation request is booked, the airline will send a request for food based on the passenger's dietary requirements (regular, low salt, vegetarian, kosher, halal, or diabetic) along with the itinerary to the caterer that serves the flight.

Receiving a request to book a ticket – Java Transactions (Chapter 10)

Sometimes a customer will have an itinerary that involves airlines other than Connexia. In this scenario, we want to make sure that all airlines in the itinerary accept any reservation requests; otherwise, the customer may be left stranded. Of course, each partner may use different connection mechanisms.

Storing registration information in LDAP – JNDI and Directory Services (Chapter 11)

All registration information is stored within an LDAP-based directory service and replicated between its two data centers (Bloomfield, Connecticut and Biche, Trinidad).

Authenticating requests against the directory – JAAS (Chapter 12)

Connexia would like to validate all incoming requests from JMS, servlets, and RMI calls against LDAP. It has expressed a preference to tie this functionality into the J2EE container it uses.

Encrypting Credit-Card Information – JCE (Chapter 13)

Connexia requires payment information for all reservations booked through its consumer and agent Web site whereby the customer is required to enter credit-card information. It is important that credit-card information be stored in an encrypted format to avoid breaches. Connexia also requires support for pluggable encryption algorithms, as computers get faster over time and that increases the odds that any one algorithm will eventually be broken. Connexia stores all credit-card information using reversible encryption, and the key is based on the user ID and role (agent, consumer, and so on).

Searching for the cheapest flight – Session Beans and Business Logic (Chapter 15)

Connexia has standardized on the use of stateless session beans for its architecture wherever practical. It uses one session bean that holds the business logic for searching for flight information for a customer's itinerary. It also interacts with other session beans to determine pricing and tax information to develop the total itinerary.

Receiving a request from another airline to book — Message-Driven Beans (Chapter 17)

Several of Connexia's airline partners have the ability to send reservation requests in a transactional manner via JMS. One of their partners sends a serialized object while another uses a prearranged textual format to indicate flight information. When a request is received, it first checks that the information is correct and then makes the reservation.

Storing reservation information — JDBC (Chapter 18)

When a reservation request enters the system, the system updates multiple data-sources including passenger/flight tables, the general ledger (payment information), and frequent-flyer-information systems.

Booking accompanying car rental — Java Connector Architecture (Chapter 19)

Sometimes a customer would like to book a hotel room and/or rental car at his or her destination. Connexia gives customers the ability to do this through its main-frame links with Sabre, Apollo, and Worldspan.

Sending a message to various law-enforcement agencies — SOAP (Chapter 21)

Because of recent terrorist acts all airlines are required to send passenger information to various law-enforcement agencies, including the Federal Aviation Administration (FAA), the Federal Bureau of Investigation (FBI), the state police of the state in which the departure takes place, and customs and immigration officials at the flight's destination. Each of the government agencies has exposed its systems via Web services.

Creating WSDL for the reservation system — WSDL (Chapter 21)

Connexia would like to create WSDL for its reservation system so that external part-ners can interact with the system's various functionalities to search for flights, book tickets, and so on. Agents would like to determine their monthly commissions online.

Concierge services – UDDI (Chapter 21)

In the future Connexia would like to add concierge services as part of the reservation process. This service may enable a user to make reservations at restaurants, arrange for cabs and limousines, or get tickets to sports venues and theaters at his or her destination. Connexia publishes services information in a public UDDI registry based on industry classification and geographic location.

✦   ✦   ✦

Magazine Publisher Business Case

Any examples, companies, organizations, products, domain names, e-mail addresses, people, places, or events depicted herein are fictitious. No association with any real company, organization, product, domain name, e-mail address, person, place, or event is intended or should be inferred.

Executive Summary

J2EE Publishers is the publisher of multiple technology magazines including *Hackers Daily, Agile Architect's Journal,* and *J2EE Standard.* Each of its magazines is directed at the information-technology community at all levels of business throughout the United States, Canada, the United Kingdom, and Easter Island. All of its publications have a combined total circulation of 2,222,000 copies and it hopes to reach the three million mark by the end of the next fiscal year. Each of the magazines is published bimonthly. To increase exposure and build subscription volume, J2EE Publishers will use sample distribution and direct mail to targeted lists of information-technology professionals.

Publishing magazines is highly profitable and has a high margin. Success depends on successful marketing. J2EE Publishers maintains a multidimensional sales and marketing plan to increase its circulation quickly. Successful execution of the J2EE Publishers business plan will produce an annual revenue of $35 million this fiscal year. Margins are in excess of 40 percent after taxes.

Mission Statement

J2EE Publishers is for the technologist who is capable of designing and developing at any level in any language. The company's mission statement is as follows:

> Our magazines are committed to be a voice for technologists who represent the creative and technical vision in the marketplace and who can give confidence to other information-technology professionals. J2EE Publishers, through its books, magazines and syndicated editorial content, will be a vehicle for informing and enlightening the world about technology principles in everyday business. Our prime directive is to promote the concept of "community" in society.

Technology Overview

J2EE Publishers is looking to further increase its competitive lead and margin by using state-of-the-art information-technology systems. The executive team has decided the following are priorities in making the information system meet the strategic business goals:

> Learn more about the subscribers by storing preferences within the databases to their buying habits.

> Integrate the subscription-management system and accounts-receivable system so that all financial information can be analyzed up to the minute and nightly batch feeds can be eliminated.

> Reduce the amount of fraudulent orders placed for magazine subscriptions.

Examples in this Book

This book contains the following examples.

Develop a login page — Servlet Programming (Chapter 5)

This will demonstrate a simple login page that prompts the user to enter his or her user ID, password, and role (agent, partner, consumer, employee). Each user is given five attempts to login. After the fifth failed attempt a user is locked out of the system and redirected to a page that will let him or her contact an administrator.

Develop a lost password page — Servlet Programming (Chapter 5)

This screen will prompt users to enter hints. Employees will enter their employee IDs; all others will enter their e-mail addresses. If they are known to Connexia, they will be redirected to a page that will tell them that their IDs and passwords will be e-mailed to them.

Demonstrating required and optional fields — JSP Tag Extensions (Chapter 7)

The user-interface group for J2EE Publishers requires that for Web sites all required fields be preceded by a green oval and all optional fields by an orange diamond.

Showing how long a user has been logged in — JSP Tag Extensions (Chapter 7)

The user-interface group for J2EE Publishers requires that all pages display in the upper right-hand corner of the screen the date and the time the user has been logged in, as well as how much time he or she has before the session expires.

Sending a message to the accounting system — JMS (Chapter 9)

Whenever J2EE Publishers receives an order, it is required to send additional information via JMS to its general ledger, indicating customer information, amount received, payment method, and items ordered.

Checking for fraud using DNS — JNDI and Directory Services (Chapter 11)

J2EE Publishers frequently receives fraudulent orders from people using stolen credit cards. One of the steps it has decided to take is to look at referrer information and use DNS to reverse the host name and IP address to see if they match. This will help the company determine potential fraudulent activities.

Authenticating requests against the directory — JAAS (Chapter 12)

J2EE Publishers would like to validate all incoming requests servlets against an internally maintained database. It wants to tie this functionality in to the J2EE container it uses.

Password encryption — JCE (Chapter 13)

J2EE Publishers wants to have all passwords stored in its database by means of one-way non-reversible encryption. It will use a fixed key for all operations.

Publications, authors, and orders — Entity Beans (Chapter 16)

The persistence mechanism of choice for J2EE Publishers is the use of entity beans. Each publication can have one or more authors. Authors can work on one or more publications. An order can include one or more publications.

✦   ✦   ✦

Additional Reading and References

The author team has collated a listing of additional books and references that we believe should make a good addition to any J2EE book collection. This list is not meant to be complete, as there are more books than we could possibly list, and is only meant to point one in the right direction.

Architecture

Fowler, M.; Rice, D.; Foemmel, M.; Hieatt, E.
Patterns of Enterprise Application Architecture
Addison Wesley, November 2002

McGovern, J.; Ambler, S.; Stevens, M.; Linn, J.;
Sharan, V.; Jo, E.
Practical Guide to Enterprise Architecture
Prentice Hall, May 2003

BEA WebLogic

Mueller, S.; Weber, S.
BEA WebLogic Server Administrator's Guide
John Wiley & Sons, May 2003

Zuffoletto, J.; Wells, G.; Gill, B.; Schneider, G.; Tucker, B.;
Helton, R.; Madrid, M.; Makhijani, S.
BEA WebLogic Server Bible
John Wiley & Sons, February 2002

Corba

Bolton, F.
Pure Corba
Sams Publishing, July 2001

Pritchard, J.
COM and Corba Side by Side: Architectures, Strategies and Implementations
Addison Wesley, July 1999

Slama, D.; Garbis, J.; Russell, P.
Enterprise Corba
Prentice Hall, March 1999

Frameworks

Husted, T.
Struts in Action: Building Web Applications with the Leading Java Framework
Manning Publications, November 2002

IBM WebSphere

Kelly, B.
Getting Started with WebSphere
29th Street Press, March 2002

Kataoka, B.; Ramirez, D.; Sit, A.
WebSphere Application Server Bible
John Wiley & Sons, July 2002

Jakarta

Goodwill, J.
Apache Jakarta-Tomcat
APress, December 2001

Goodwill, J.
Mastering Jakarta Struts
John Wiley & Sons, September 2002

Hightower, R.; Lesiecki, N.
Java Tools for Extreme Programming: Mastering Open Source Tools including Ant, JUnit and Cactus
John Wiley & Sons, December 2001

Husted, T.; Dumoulin, C.; Franciscus, G.; Winterfeldt, D.; McClanahan, C.
Struts in Action: Building Web Applications with the Leading Java Framework
Manning Publications, November 2002

Java

Bloch, J.
Effective Java
Addison Wesley, June 2001

Grosso, W.
Java RMI
O'Reilly & Associates, October 2001

Melton, J.; Eisenberg, A.; Cattell, R.
Understanding SQL and Java Together
Morgan Kaufmann Publishers, May 2000

Neward, T.
Server-Based Java Programming
Manning Publications, July 2000

Shirazi, J.
Java Performance Tuning
O'Reilly & Associates, January 2000

Tate, B.
Bitter Java
Manning Publications, April 2002

J2EE

Bayern, S.
JSTL in Action
Manning Publications, July 2002

Fleury, M.; Lindfors, J.
JMX: Managing J2EE Applications with Java Management Extensions
Sams Publishing, January 2002.

Hunter, J.
Java Servlet Programming
O'Reilly & Associates, January 2001

Price, J.
Oracle 9i JDBC Programming
McGraw Hill, May 2002

Roman, E.; Ambler, S.; Jewell, T.; Marinescu, F.
Mastering Enterprise JavaBeans
John Wiley & Sons, December 2001

Sharma, R.; Stearns, B.; Ng, T.; Dietzen, S.
J2EE Connector Architecture and Enterprise Application Integration
Addison Wesley, December 2001

Singh, I.; Stearns, B.; Johnson, M.
Designing Enterprise Applications with the J2EE Platform
Addison Wesley, June 2002

JMS

Erdogan, L.
Java Message Service (JMS) for J2EE
New Riders Publishing, August 2002

Haefel, R.; Chappell, D.
Java Message Service
O'Reilly & Associates, December 2000

Terry, S.
Enterprise JMS Programming
John Wiley & Sons, February 2002

Patterns

Alur, D.; Crupi, J.; Malks, D.
Core J2EE Patterns: Best Practices and Design Strategies
Prentice Hall, June 2001

Gamma, E.; Helm, R.; Johnson, R.; Vlissides, J.
Design Patterns
Addison Wesley, January 1995

Marinescu, F.; Roman, E.
EJB Design Patterns: Advanced Patterns, Processes and Idioms
John Wiley & Sons, February 2002

UML

Ambler, S.
The Elements of UML Style
Cambridge University Press, December 2002

Fowler, M.; Scott, K.
UML Distilled
Addison Wesley, August 1999

Schmuller, J.
Teach Yourself UML in 24 Hours, 2nd Edition
Sams Publishing, August 2001

Web Services

Apshankar, K.; Sadhwani, D.; Samtani, G.; Siddiqui, B.; Clark, M.; Fletcher, P.;
Hanson, J.; Irani, R.; Waterhouse, M.; Zhang, L.
Web Services Business Strategies and Architectures
Expert Press, August 2002

McGovern, J.; Tyagi, S.; Stevens, M.; Mathew, S.
Java Web Services Architecture
Morgan Kaufmann Publishers, April 2003

XML

McGovern, J.; Bothner, P.; Cagle, K.; Linn, J.; Nagarajan, V.
XQuery Kick Start
Sams Publishing, March 2003

Ray, E.
Learning XML
O'Reilly & Associates, February 2001

Miscellaneous Java Books

Brill, G.
Codenotes for Web Based UI
Random House, January 2002

Pepperdine, K.; Williamson, A.; Gibson, J.; Wu, A.
Ant Developer's Handbook
Sams Publishing, October 2002

Vermeulen, A.; Ambler, S.; Bumgardner, G.; Metz, E.; Misfeldt, T.; Shur, J.;
Thompson, P.
The Elements of Java Style
Cambridge University Press, January 2000

Other

Adams, S.
Dogbert's Top Secret Management Handbook
Harper Collins, October 1997

Buckingham, M.; Coffman, C.
First, Break all the Rules: What the World's Greatest Managers Do Differently
Simon & Schuster, May 1999

Collins, J.; Porras, J.
Built to Last: Successful Habits of Visionary Companies
Harper Collins, September 1994

Lundin, S.; Paul, H.; Christensen, J.
Fish! A Remarkable Way to Boost Morale and Improve Results
G K Hall & Co, December 2001

Pirsig, R.
Zen and the Art of Motorcycle Maintenance: An Inquiry into Values
Bantam Books, April 1984

Spencer, J.
Who Moved My Cheese?
Putnam Publications, November 2001

Covey, S.
Seven Habits of Highly Effective People
Simon & Schuster, January 1989

References by Chapter

For your convenience, we have organized the following resources by chapter.

Chapter 4, "Understanding Remote Method Invocation"

✦ **RMI specification** — `http://java.sun.com/products/j2se/1.4/docs/guide/rmi/spec/rmiTOC.html`

✦ **RMI tutorial** — `http://java.sun.com/docs/books/tutorial/rmi`

Chapter 5, "Studying Servlet Programming"

✦ **HTML Tutorial** — `http://www.w3schools.com/html/`

✦ **Servlets Tutorial from Sun Microsystems** — `http://java.sun.com/docs/books/tutorial/servlets/`

✦ **Java BluePrints — session state in the client tier** — `http://java.sun.com/blueprints/qanda/client_tier/session_state.html`

✦ **Java Servlet 2.4 Specification (Proposed Final Draft)** — `http://jcp.org/aboutJava/communityprocess/first/jsr154/`

Chapter 6, "Going Over JSP Basics"

✦ **JSP Tutorial** — `http://java.sun.com/products/jsp/docs.html`

✦ **JSP Fundamentals by jGuru** — `http://developer.java.sun.com/developer/onlineTraining/JSPIntro`

✦ **JSP specification** — `http://java.sun.com/products/jsp/download.html`

Chapter 11, "Examining JNDI and Directory Services"

✦ RFCs (Request for Comments — Internet standards documents) referenced in this chapter are available at `http://www.faqs.org/rfcs/`.

✦ A comprehensive tutorial on using JNDI is available from Sun at `http://java.sun.com/products/jndi/tutorial/`.

✦ OpenLDAP, a free LDAP directory server, is available at `http://www.openldap.org`. Compiled binaries for Windows 2000 are available at `http://www.fivesight.com/downloads/openldap.asp`.

Chapter 12, "Understanding Java Authentication and Authorization Services"

✦ **The Sun Java Web site** — `http://java.sun.com/`

✦ **Gamelan.com** — `http://www.gamelan.com/`

✦ **MIT Kerberos Web site** — `http://web.mit.edu/kerberos/www/`

✦ **Kerberos from outside the USA and Canada** — `http://www.crypto-publish.org/`

✦ **Andy Thompson** — `http://free.tagish.net/jaas/doc-1.0.3/`

✦ **Tomas Restrepo** — `http://www.mvps.org/windev/security/sspi.html`

✦ **Section 508 Accessibility Requirements** — `http://www.section508.gov/`

✦ **JAWS Screen Reader** — `http://www.freedomscientific.com/`

✦ *Swing* by Matthew Robinson and Pavel Voroblev, Manning Publications, February, 2003.

✦ *Java Swing, Second Edition*, Marc Loy, Robert Eckstein, David Wood, James Elliott, and Brian Cole, O'Reilly and Associates, 2002.

Chapter 17, "Using Message-Driven Beans"

✦ **A message-driven bean example** — `http://java.sun.com/j2ee/tutorial/1_3-fcs/doc/MDB.html`

✦ **Using foreign JMS providers with a WebLogic server** — `http://dev2dev.bea.com/resourcelibrary/whitepapers/jmsproviders.jsp`

✦ **Core J2EE Patterns — Service Activator** — `http://java.sun.com/blueprints/corej2eepatterns/Patterns/ServiceActivator.html`

Chapter 18, "Reviewing Java Database Connectivity"

✦ **JDBC driver from Sun Microsystems** — `http://java.sun.com/products/jdbc`

✦ **SQL Tutorial** — `www.sqlcourse.com`

✦ **JDBC Tutorial** — `http://java.sun.com/docs/books/tutorial/jdbc/basics/index.html`

Chapter 20, "Introducing Web Services"

For more in-depth coverage of Web services, you can check out "Developing Java Web Services" by Wiley. Some Web sites you may want to check out include IBM Developer Works (`http://www-106.ibm.com/developerworks/webservices/`) and `http://www.webservices.org`.

✦　　✦　　✦

Index

SYMBOLS AND NUMERICS

<> (angle brackets)
  enclosing XML prologue, 20
  for HTML comments (<!- -), 119
  for JSP comments (<%- -), 119
  for JSP declarations (<%!), 117
  for JSP directives (<%@), 118
  for JSP expressions (<%=), 114, 117
  for JSP scriptlets (<%), 119
* (asterisk) in DTDs, 24
@ (at sign) for JSP directives (<%@), 118
[ ] (brackets) in DTDs, 24
, (comma) concatenating e-mail addresses, 204
= (equals sign) for JSP expressions (<%=), 114, 117
! (exclamation mark)
  for HTML comments (<!- -), 119
  for JSP declarations (<%!), 117
500 error code, 124
404 error code, 124
9iAS application server (Oracle), 49
(number sign) in #PCDATA keyword, 25
% (percent sign)
  for JSP comments (<%- -), 119
  for JSP declarations (<%!), 117
  for JSP directives (<%@), 118
  for JSP expressions (<%=), 114
  for JSP scriptlets (<%), 119
+ (plus sign) in DTDs, 24
? (question mark) in DTDs, 24

A

A DNS record type, 329
abort() method, 386
AbstractDAOFactory class, 803
abstract-programming model (CMP), 526
acceptChanges() method, 605
Account Owner interface, 814–815
ACID transaction properties, 256–257
acknowledgement modes (JMS), 244–245
Acknowledgment component, 809
Action class (Struts), 831–833
actionPerformed() method
  RowSet object and, 605
  of Send button, 108
actions (JSP)
  forward, 120, 121
  include, 120
  overview, 120–121
  param, 120
  plugin, 120, 121
  useBean, 125–126
activation of stateful session beans, 502
Activity coordinator, 281, 282–283
Activity Service for CORBA, 472

actor attribute of SOAP header, 675–676
ADD_ATTRIBUTE operation of DirContext interface, 328
addBodyPart() method, 198
addFrom() method, 192
add_publisherAssertions method, 702
addRecipients() method, 193
Address class, 203–205
AddressBean bean class
  CMR examples, 541–546
  methods, 542–543
addresses for JavaMail messages, 203–205
addRowSetListener() method, 606
adjudicated cryptographic protocol, 418–419
Aircraft remote interface, 553
AircraftBean bean class, 554–561
AircraftHome home interface, 552–553
Airline Reservations application
  Airline User JavaBean, 124–125
  airline-registration screen, 133–141
  authenticating Web users against directory
    service, 404–407
  BMP, 552–561
  business case, 915–921
  client policy file, 406
  CMP, 527–537
  CMRs, 539–546
  delivering messages between systems, 27–28
  entity beans for, 436–437, 438–439, 452
  entity beans versus session beans for, 441–442
  error page (JSP), 123
  executive summary, 915–916
  external DTD specification, 26
  internal DTD specification, 25
  JAAS security for, 404–407
  JCE for, 424–426
  JMS point-to-point messaging, 240–248
  JNDI for, 337–341
  login configuration file, 406
  management team, 916
  mission statement, 916
  namespace examples, 28–30, 33–34
  OpenLDAP configuration file, 337–340
  password verification method, 341
  payment collection stateful session bean, 504–509
  pushing data from the RMI server, 68–72
  registering objects in RMI, 62–63
  remote interface for RMI, 57–60
  resource adapter (Connector architecture), 615–616
  RMI Flight Server application, 65–68
  security analysis, 404–405
  security limitations, 405
  SOAP for, 676–681

Continued

Airline Reservations application *(continued)*
 starting the login client, 407
 starting the login server, 407
 stateless session beans, 492–499
 summary of examples, 917–921
 technology overview, 917
 transactions in, 297–301
 WML document, 38–40
 WSDL for, 681–686
 XML Schema for, 32–34
 XSLT for, 35–38
`Airline User` JavaBean
 instantiating, 125–126
 overview, 124–125
airline-registration screen
 `DBProcessor` class for database, 138–139
 deploying using Tomcat, 141
 error page, 139–140
 overview, 133
 `registerBean.java` JavaBean, 137–138
 `register.html` registration page, 133–135
 `register.jsp` controller, 135–137
`AirUser` class, 588
`air_user` database table, 584
Alexander, Christopher (*A Pattern Language*), 729
algorithms (cryptography)
 block ciphers, 413, 415
 Blowfish, 414–415
 DES, 413, 414
 Message Digest, 415
 one-way hash function, 412
 restricted, 410–411
 RSA, 411
 SHA, 415
 SunJCE, 420–421
 symmetric, 413
 Triple DES, 413
alignment
 frameworks for, 825–826
 Struts framework, 834–835
all-in-one proprietary environments, 846–847
`allocateConnection()` method, 617
Alur, Deepak (*Core J2EE Patterns*), 750, 754
angle brackets (<>)
 enclosing XML prologue, 20
 for HTML comments (<!- -), 119
 for JSP comments (<%- -), 119
 for JSP declarations (<%!), 117
 for JSP directives (<%@), 118
 for JSP expressions (<%=), 114, 117
 for JSP scriptlets (<%), 119
ANT
 core tasks, 868
 `cvs` task, 875–877
 development of, 858
 downloading, 859
 environment variables, 860
 file matching, 867
 installing, 859–860

`jar` task, 870–871
 `javac` task, 868–870
 `junit` task, 871–875
 optional tasks, 868
 overview, 857–859
 projects, 864
 properties, 864–865
 simple `build.xml` file for, 860–863
 targets, 865–867
 tiered dependency tree, 866
 typical `build.xml` file for, 877–879
 user-defined tasks, 868
 `war` task, 875
 Web site, 859
`ant.file` built-in property (ANT), 865
`ANT_HOME` environment variable, 860
`ant.java.version` built-in property (ANT), 865
`ant.project.name` built-in property (ANT), 865
`ant.version` built-in property (ANT), 865
Apache. *See also* ANT; Log4J logging API; Tomcat
  servlet containers
 AXIS Web services tool, 715
 JMeter, 887
 Taglibs, 145
APIs. *See also specific APIs*
 application component APIs, 13
 implementing the J2EE platform, 43–45
 J2EE standard services, 11–13
 J2EE XML-based APIs, 40
 overview, 10–13
`Appenders` (Log4J), 900–901
`APPLET` property (JNDI), 314
applets
 applet-servlet communication, 107–111
 overview, 7
 RMI clients, 65
 servlets versus, 77–78
applet-servlet communication
 code examples, 109–111
 design considerations, 107
 receiving data from servlets, 107–108
 steps for applet/servlet object serialization, 108
application architecture. *See also* SOA (service-
  oriented architecture)
 defined, 837
 frameworks versus, 841
 overview, 837–838
 traditional, 838–839
 Zachman Framework for Enterprise Architecture, 837
application assembler
 defined, 8
 EJB, 434–435
application clients
 J2EE APIs required for, 12–13
 overview, 6
application component provider, 8
application components. *See also specific components*
 APIs, 13
 overview, 6–7

application contract, 610
application coverage, 847
application fault-tolerance, 441
application portfolios, 837
`application` scope of JavaBeans, 127
application servers. *See also* servers
    architecture for EJB container examples, 447
    availability strategies, 473–475
    avoiding vendor lock-in, 53–54
    client agnosticism, 46
    clustering, 474–475
    development support, 47
    EJB, 430
    fail-over, 474–475
    features provided by, 45
    full implementations, 47–50
    load distribution, 474–475
    load-balancing, 474
    methods native to, 53
    partial implementations, 51–53
    proxy interface for, 53–54
    resource pooling and, 477
    scalability, 46, 474
    server management, 47
    service providers, 334–335
    transparent fail-over, 475
    tunable parameters, 889
`application` variable (JSP), 122
application-service providers (ASPs), 654–655
Applied Java Patterns (Stelting, John), 740
arbitrated cryptographic protocol, 419
architecture
    EJBs, 430
    further information, 927
    JAXR, 704–705
    JTA, 289
    J2EE, 5, 6
    logging, 895
    Web services, 650–652
array of bytes (SOAP), 669
arrays (SOAP)
    `arrayType` values and descriptions, 671
    multidimensional, 671–672
    overview, 670–671
    partially-transmitted, 672
    single-dimensional, 671
    sparse, 672
ASPs (application-service providers), 654–655
asterisk (*) in DTDs, 24
asymmetric cryptography, 416–417
asynchronous messages, MDB and, 565–566
asynchronous notification pattern (UDDI), 704
asynchronous processing (MDB), 576–577
asynchronous versus synchronous request-response,
    442–443
at sign for JSP directives (<%@), 118
atomic transactions. *See* transactions
atomicity
    in ACID properties of transactions, 257
    two-phase commit protocol and, 259–262

attachments (e-mail)
    receiving, 227–229
    sending, 221
`attribute` method (TLD), 150
attributes
    ANT projects, 864
    ANT targets, 867
    CMT, 457–459
    `DirContext` attribute-modification operations, 328
    dynamic (JSP), 174–176
    HashMap attributes of TagSupport classes, 169
    `InetOrgPerson` schema, 337
    JNDI, 310–311
    LDAP, 308–309
    printing for LDAP lookups, 317
    storing object data as directory attributes, 325–328
    XML, 21, 25
authentication. *See also* JAAS (Java Authentication and
        Authorization Service)
    defined, 627
    encrypted, 316
    encrypted-message passing and, 410
    JAAS services, 353
    LDAP implementation by JNDI, 316
    Pluggable Authentication Modules, 360–363
    of resource principal, 630
    SASL, 316
    of users with JAAS, 364–371
`Authenticator` class, 188–190
authorization. *See also* JAAS (Java Authentication and
        Authorization Service)
    defined, 627
    JAAS services, 353
    JavaMail sessions and, 186
    of resource principal, 630
    of users with JAAS, 368
auto-commit mode of transactions, 262–264
autonomous messages (JMS), 252
AXIS Web services tool (Apache), 715

B

`basedir`
    built-in property (ANT), 865
    project attribute (ANT), 864
`BasicTag.java` tag handler, 157–159
batch updates using JDBC, 593–594
`BCC` JavaMail header field, 192–193
BEA jRockit JVM, 48
BEA WebLogic. *See* WebLogic application server
bean provider for EJBs
    overview, 433
    restrictions on, 447–449
bean-managed persistence. *See* BMP
bean-managed transactions. *See* BMTs
`begin()` method, 291
Benchmark Factory (Quest Software), 887
benchmarking, 887–889
`BETWEEN` clause (EJB QL), 550
bidirectional relationships (CMR), 537, 540

bind() method
  JNDI, 324, 327
  RMI, 61
binding
  JNDI, 311
  registering objects in RMI, 61–63
bindingTemplate data structure (UDDI), 695–696
block ciphers, 413, 415
Blowfish algorithm, 414–415
BluePrints, 9
BMP (bean-managed persistence). *See also* entity beans
  Airline Reservations application, 552–561
  bean class, 554–561
  CMP versus, 466, 512
  deployment descriptor, 561–562
  disadvantages, 552
  home interface, 552–553
  overview, 437–439, 552
  remote interface, 553
  writing a BMP, 552–561
BMTs (bean-managed transactions)
  CMTs versus, 440
  defined, 440
  JTA and, 460
  overview, 460
  stateful session beans and, 461
  stateless session beans and, 461
  stateless versus stateful session beans, 461
body (SOAP), 667–668
<body-content> element (TLD), 151
body-content method (TLD), 150
BodyPart class, 199
BodyTag interface
  constant, 163
  JSP for, 165
  methods, 163
  TLD for, 164–165
  TryBodyTag.java tag handler, 165–167
BodyTagSupport class
  HashMap attributes, 169
  methods, 169
  need for, 167–168
bookFlight() method, 493
BookOrder class, 248–249
BootStrapContext instance, 611
bootstrapping a resource adapter, 611
Borland
  Enterprise AppServer Edition, 48
  Enterprise Studio for Java, 372
  reactive login, 356
bottom-up recovery for transactions, 274

 (line break) tags (HTML), 21
brackets ([ ]) in DTDs, 24
browse pattern (UDDI), 700
B2B (business-to-business) messaging, 232
build.xml files (ANT)
  defined, 859
  simple, 860–863
  typical, 877–879

Buschmann, Frank (*Pattern-Oriented Software Architecture, Volume 2*), 810–811
business methods
  Airline Reservations application, 504, 505
  BMTs and, 460–461
  CMTs and, 457–459
  EJB client and, 498–499
  EJB component interface, 436, 444
  entity-bean class, 515
  FlightServiceBean session bean, 494
  MDB bean class, 444
  session bean component interface, 485
  session-bean class, 487
  stateful session beans, 499, 501, 502
  stateless session beans, 440, 490
business processes, 483
business tier (EJBs), 430
business-application frameworks. *See* frameworks
BusinessComponent component
  service-activator pattern, 808
  transfer-object pattern, 813
BusinessDelegate component
  business-delegate pattern, 767
  value-object pattern, 771
business-delegate pattern
  BusinessDelegate component, 767
  BusinessService component, 767
  described, 764
  forces, 765
  implementation, 765–767, 768
  LookupService component, 767
  overview, 764–765
  PresentationTier component, 767
  related patterns, 769
  results, 767–768
  sample code, 768
  sequence diagram, 766
  strategies, 767
  structure, 765–766
businessEntity data structure (UDDI), 693–694
BusinessObject component, 776
BusinessService component
  business-delegate pattern, 767
  value-object pattern, 771
businessService data structure (UDDI), 695
business-to-business (B2B) messaging, 232
bytecode compiler (JVM), 890
bytecodes, 4

C
c LDAP attribute, 308
CachedRowSet object
  with JSP, 603–604
  overview, 602–603
  processing RowSet events, 605–606
  updating the database, 604–605
CallableStatement class, 592–593
callback handlers (JAAS). *See also* login handlers (JAAS)
  dialog, 360
  framework, 395–397

operating systems and, 394
overview, 358–359
predefined callback handlers, 359
predefined login callbacks, 375–376
text, 359–360
writing your own, 394–397
callback methods (entity beans)
  `ejbActivate()`, 521
  `ejbCreate()`, 520–521
  `ejbFind()`, 522–523
  `ejbHome()`, 523
  `ejbLoad()`, 522
  `ejbPassivate()`, 521
  `ejbPostCreate()`, 521
  `ejbRemove()`, 521–522
  `ejbSelect()`, 523
  `ejbStore()`, 522
  `ejbTimeout()`, 523
  overview, 515, 519
  `setEntityContext()`, 520
  `unsetEntityContext()`, 520
callback methods (MDB), 569
`callbackHandler` login initialize argument, 386
capability profiles (JAXR), 705
Cape Clear
  Connect tool, 717
  Studio tool, 717
Cascading StyleSheets (CSS), 34–35
case-sensitivity of XML, 21
`Caterer` class
  deployment descriptor (MDB), 570–571
  JMS, 246–248
  MDB, 567–568
Caucho Technology's Resin servlet container, 51, 52
CC JavaMail header field, 192–193
CCI (Common Client Interface)
  categories and interfaces, 633–634
  Connection interfaces, 633, 634–635
  Data interfaces, 634, 635
  EIS access with, 637–640
  Interaction interfaces, 634, 635
  Metadata interfaces, 634, 636
  overview, 633
  programming steps, 636–637
`CDATA` keyword, 25
`CertPath` security mechanism, 352
chaining servlet filters, 98, 106
`checkCredentials()` method, 129
`ChoiceCallback` class (JAAS), 376
ciphers. *See* algorithms (cryptography)
class diagrams
  service-activator pattern, 810
  user-created servlet, 80
class libraries versus frameworks, 821
classes. *See also specific classes*
  classic tag handlers as, 153
  connection-management, 616–622
  EJB, 444
  entity beans, 515–517

JAAS predefined callbacks, 376
JCE, 421
thread-safe, 449
work-management, 614
classic tag handlers
  `BodyTag` interface, 163–167
  `BodyTagSupport` class, 167–169
  defined, 153
  `IterationTag` interface, 159–163
  JSP versions and, 153
  `Tag` interface, 154–159
  `TagSupport` class, 167–169
`ClassLoader`, bean provider restrictions for, 448
`ClearPass`
  JDNI configuration option, 384
  Kerberos configuration option, 378
client agnosticism in application servers, 46
`Client` class, 109–110
client tier (EJBs), 430
`ClientComponent` component
  router pattern, 736
  session pattern, 734
client-maintained session, 732
clients
  CMP entity bean, 534–537
  composite-view pattern, 755
  entity bean views, 512
  intercepting-filter pattern, 759
  JAXR, 704, 707–709
  MDB and, 575
  scalability and number of, 46
  session bean views, 487
  thin client advantages, 77–78
  view-helper pattern, 752
  writing an EBJ client, 496–499
  writing RMI clients, 63–65
client-side programming model (Web services)
  JNDI lookup for services, 719
  overview, 718
  `Service` interface, 720–721, 724
`clone()` method, overriding, 351
cloning security vulnerability
  described, 349
  overriding the `clone()` method, 351
`close()` method, 211
closing folders (JavaMail), 211
closing tags (XML), 21
clustering application servers, 474–475
CMP (container-managed persistence). *See also* CMRs
        (Container Managed Relationships); EJB QL
        (EJB Query Language); entity beans
  abstract-programming model, 526
  Airline Reservations application, 527–537
  bean class, 529–533
  BMP versus, 466, 512
  client, 534–537
  Container Managed Relationships, 537–546
  data-access-object pattern and, 799

Continued

CMP *(continued)*
    declaring container-managed fields, 527
    deployment descriptor, 533–534
    EJB QL, 547–551
    home interface, 527–528
    overview, 439
    remote interface, 528–529
    writing a simple CMP, 527–537
CMRs (Container Managed Relationships), 537
    Airline Reservations application, 539–546
    bidirectional, 537, 540
    deployment descriptors, 537–539, 541–542, 544–546
    many-to-many, 545–546
    one-to-many, 543–545
    one-to-one, 541–543
    overview, 537
    unidirectional, 537, 539–540
CMTs (container-managed transactions)
    advantages of, 456–457
    BMTs versus, 440
    declarative semantics, 457
    defined, 440
    `Mandatory` attribute, 459
    `Never` attribute, 459
    `NotSupported` attribute, 457–458
    `Required` attribute, 458
    `RequiresNew` attribute, 459
    specifying, 459–460
    `Supports` attribute, 458
cn attribute (`InetOrgPerson` schema), 337
cn LDAP attribute, 309
CNAME DNS record type, 329
`CoarseGrainedObject` component, 779
comma (,) concatenating e-mail addresses, 204
comments
    in JSPs, 119
    in XML Schema, 31
`commit()` method
    auto-commit mode and, 263
    JAAS login process and, 354
    JAAS login-module, 385
    `TransactionManager` interface, 291
    `UserTransaction` interface, 290
Common Client Interface. *See* CCI
Common Object Request Broker Architecture.
    See CORBA
Common Object Services (COS) naming for
    CORBA, 333
communications-resource manager (CRM), 285
`ComparisonTerm` object, 216
Compatibility Test Suite (CTS), 45
compiling
    JAAS login code, 369–370
    `javac` task (ANT) for, 868–870
component interface
    entity beans, 515
    session beans, 485–486
component services, 655
component-managed sign-on, 628

`CompositeEntity` component, 778
composite-entity pattern
    `CoarseGrainedObject` component, 779
    `CompositeEntity` component, 778
    described, 764
    `FineGrainedObject` component, 779
    forces, 778
    implementation, 778–779, 780–781
    overview, 777
    related patterns, 781
    results, 780
    sample code, 780–781
    sequence diagram, 778, 779
    strategies, 779–780
    structure, 778
composite-view pattern
    client, 755
    composite view, 755
    described, 731
    footer view, 756
    forces, 754
    header view, 756
    implementation, 754–756
    overview, 754
    related patterns, 757
    results, 757
    sample code, 757
    sequence diagram, 755
    strategies, 756–757
    structure, 755
compound primary keys, 516
compound-type values (SOAP), 670
`com.sun.jndi.dns.recursion` property (DNS), 330
`com.sun.jndi.lookup.attr` property (DNS), 330
`com.sun.security.auth.callback` package
    (JAAS), 359
concurrency
    EJB concurrency control, 449
    entity beans and, 437
    optimistic versus pessimistic concurrency control,
        269–270
Concurrency Control Service for OTS, 287
Concurrent Versions System (CVS), 875–877
conditional expressions (EJB QL), 549–551
conditional operators (EJB QL), 549–550
config variable (JSP), 122
configurability
    frameworks for, 824–825
    Struts framework, 833–834
`ConfirmationCallback` class (JAAS), 376
`connect()` method, 205–206
Connect tool (Cape Clear), 717
connection factories
    Connector architecture, 617
    JMS, 237–238
`Connection` interface (CCI), 634
connection interfaces (CCI), 633, 634–635
connection pools (JDBC), 596–597, 889
`ConnectionFactory` interface (CCI), 634

connection-management contract
    application steps for establishing connections, 622–624
    classes, 616–622
    connection factories, 617
    connection interfaces, 617
    ConnectionManager interfaces, 617–618
    described, 609
    error logging, 622
    ManagedConnection interface, 620–622
    ManagedConnectionFactory interface, 618–620
    overview, 616
ConnectionManager interfaces, 617–618
ConnectionMetadata interface (CCI), 636
connections (JMS), 237
ConnectionSpec interface (CCI), 635
Connector architecture. See also CCI (Common Client
        Interface); specific contracts
    application contract, 610
    client API, 610
    Common Client Interface, 633–640
    connection-management contract, 609, 616–624
    contracts overview, 608–610
    inbound communication, 609, 631–632
    as J2EE standard service, 11, 12
    lifecycle-management contract, 609, 610–612
    message-inflow contract, 609, 631–632
    outbound communication, 609, 616–630
    overview, 607–608
    packaging and deployment, 640–643
    resource adapter, 607–608, 610–612
    security-management contract, 609, 627–630
    system-level contracts, 608–609
    transaction-inflow contract, 609, 632
    transaction-management contract, 609, 624–627
    work-management contract, 609, 612–616
Connexia Airlines example. See Airline Reservations
        application
ConnexiaClient.java SOAP example, 678–681
consistency property of transactions
    defined, 257
    overview, 267–268
ConsoleHandler (JSR 47), 899
constants
    BodyTag interface, 163
    IterationTag interface, 160
    Tag interface, 155
consumers (JMS), 238–239
Container Managed Relationships. See CMRs
container-managed persistence. See CMP
container-managed sign-on, 628
container-managed transactions. See CMTs
containers
    J2EE platform, 44
    servlet, 51–53
context
    distributed transactions and, 264
    JNDI, 311, 312

JNDI environment properties, 313–315
    servlet, 84–85, 95–96
Context interface (JNDI), 312
contracts (Connector architecture). See also specific
        contracts
    application, 610
    connection-management, 609, 616–624
    lifecycle-management, 609, 610–612
    message-inflow, 609, 631–632
    overview, 608–610
    security-management, 609, 627–630
    system-level, 608–609
    transaction-inflow, 609, 632
    transaction-management, 609, 624–627
    work-management, 609, 612–616
Control role (OTS), 287
controller in MVC pattern
    defined, 827
    JSPs for, 116, 135–137
    overview, 10, 743
    sample code, 744
controllers
    airline-registration screen JSP, 135–137
    online store servlet, 132–133
cookies, 88–89
copying messages (JavaMail), 215
copyMessages() method, 215
CORBA (Common Object Request Broker
        Architecture)
    Activity Service, 472
    complexity of, 468
    COS naming for, 333
    CosNaming naming specification, 471
    distribution transparency, 479
    EJB integration, 467–472
    Event Service, 472
    further information, 928
    IIOP protocol for, 469–471
    importance of, 468–469
    limitations of, 650
    Notification Service, 472
    performance and, 478–479
    RMI versus, 56, 73, 468–469
    RMI-IIOP and, 11, 72–73
    secure interoperability, 472
    transaction interoperability, 471
    Web site, 650
Core J2EE Patterns (Alur, Deepak and Crupi, John and
        Malks, Dan), 750, 754
core library (JSTL), 147
core tasks (ANT), 868
CosNaming naming specification for CORBA, 471
counters, instance variable for, 172
create() method
    Airline Reservations application, 493
    home interface for entity beans, 513–514
    local home interface for session beans, 485
                                              Continued

create() method *(continued)*
　PassengerHome home interface, 527–528
　remote home interface for session beans, 485
　stateful session beans, 500–501
createCall() method, 720, 721
CreateException EJB exception, 562
createInteraction() method, 636
createStatement() method, 585, 591
createTimer() method, 465
critical-path analysis, 886
CRM (communications-resource manager), 285
Crupi, John (*Core J2EE Patterns*), 750, 754
cryptography. *See also* encryption; JCE (Java
　　　Cryptography Extensions)
　algorithms, 411–415
　characteristics of encrypted message-passing, 410
　decryption, 410
　defined, 410
　digital certificates, 417
　keys for encryption, 411
　keyspace, 411
　one-way versus two-way encryption, 410–412
　protocols, 417–420
　public-key, 416–417
　shared-key, 415–416
CSS (Cascading StyleSheets), 34–35
CTS (Compatibility Test Suite), 45
Current role (OTS), 287
cursorMoved() method, 605
custom tags (JSP). *See* JSP tag extensions
CVS (Concurrent Versions System), 875–877
cvs task (ANT), 875–877

D

Data Encryption Algorithm (DEA), 413
Data Encryption Standard, 413, 414
data interfaces (CCI), 634, 635
data types
　SOAP, 669–670
　XML Schema, 31
　XML Schema versus DTDs, 31
DataAccessObject component, 800
data-access-object pattern
　AbstractDAOFactory class, 803
　accessing multiple data sources, 802–803
　AccountOwnerDAO implementation, 804
　applying, 803–804
　characteristics, 798
　CMP and, 799
　ConcreteDAOFactory class, 803–804
　DAOs, 801–802
　DataAccessObject component, 800
　DataStorage component, 801
　described, 797
　further information, 802, 805
　implementation, 799–804
　interface for AccountOwner, 804
　overview, 798–799
　PresentationComponent component, 800
　related patterns, 805

sample code, 803–804
sequence diagram, 800
structure, 799
　TransferObject component, 801
database-error processing (JDBC), 587
databases. *See also* JDBC (Java Database
　　　Connectivity); relational databases
　DBProcessor class, 138–139, 599–601
　EJB transactional example, 462–463
　J2EE platform requirement, 44
data-centric XML documents, 20
DataHandler class, 195–197
DataSource objects (JDBC), 597–599
DataStorage component, 801
data-tier patterns. *See also* patterns; *specific patterns*
　data-access-object, 797–805
　overview, 797
　service-activator, 797, 805–811
　transfer-object, 797, 811–816
Date JavaMail header field, 194
Davidson, James Duncan (ANT creator), 858
DBProcessor class, 138–139, 599–601
dc LDAP attribute, 309
DCOM, 650
DEA (Data Encryption Algorithm), 413
debugging JAAS, 372–375
declaring
　container-managed fields (CMP), 527
　JSP variables and methods, 117
　remote interfaces for RMI, 57–58
　XML attributes in DTDs, 25
　XML elements in DTDs, 24–25
decryption, 410
default project attribute (ANT), 864
Delete statement (SQL), 584
delete_binding method, 702
delete_business method, 702
delete_publisherAssertions method, 702
delete_service method, 702
deleteSingleMessage() method, 227
delete_subscription method, 703, 704
delete_tModel method, 702
deleting
　e-mail (JavaMail), 227
　LDAP directory entries with JNDI, 322
delistResource() method, 295–296
depends target attribute (ANT), 867
deployer
　defined, 8
　EJB, 435
deploying
　airline-registration screen, 141
　FlightServiceBean session bean, 496
　login JSP, 129–130
　RMI Flight Server application, 68
　servlets, 103
deployment descriptors. *See also* web.xml
　　　deployment descriptor
　BMP entity bean, 561–562
　CMP entity bean, 533–534

for CMRs (many-to-many), 545–546
for CMRs (one-to-many), 544–545
for CMRs (one-to-one), 541–542
for CMRs (overview), 537–539
EJB, 336, 432, 456, 464, 795–796
EJB QL and, 547
entity beans, 517, 518
error page implementation, 124
internal messaging with EJB applications, 573–575
MDB (EJB 2.0), 570–572
MDB (EJB 2.1), 572–575
property files and, 432
resource adapter, 641–643
session beans, 488–489
Web service, 725
DES (Data Encryption Standard), 413, 414
description method (TLD), 150
description stack (SOA), 661
description target attribute (ANT), 867
deserialization security vulnerability
described, 349
overriding the writeObject() and readObject()
  methods, 351
design patterns. See patterns
Design Patterns (Gamma, Erich and Helm, Richard and
  Johnson, Ralph and Vlissides, John), 729,
  745, 802, 805
design streamlining, frameworks for, 835
destinations (JMS), 237
destroy() method
of servlet Filter interface, 98
of servlets, 81
development
application server support for, 47
frameworks and, 836
dialog callback handlers (JAAS), 360
digital certificates, 417
DirContext interface (JNDI), 312, 326, 328
directives (JSP)
overview, 118
taglib, 146, 147, 152
directories
adding in LDAP with JNDI, 322
hierarchical organization of, 304
JavaMail folders, 207–213
JNDI, 310
removing from LDAP with JNDI, 322
for TLD files, 151, 156
WAR directory structure, 103–104
Web application, 155
directory services. See also JNDI (Java Naming and
  Directory Interface); LDAP (Lightweight
  Directory Access Protocol)
adding objects in LDAP with JNDI, 323–328
advantages of, 304–305
authenticating Web users against, 404–407
data structured by, 304
defined, 303
distributed, 305
hierarchical organization of, 304

importance of, 304
naming services and, 303–304
read-only optimization, 304
relational databases versus, 304–305, 340
sorting of directories in, 305
storing object data as directory attributes, 325–328
storing objects as references, 323–325
storing serialized data, 323
X.500 standard, 305
Directory Services Markup Language (DSML), 334
dirty reads, 271
discovery layer (discovery stack), 663
discovery stack (SOA), 661–663
displaySingleMessage() method, 226
distributed directories, 305
distributed transactions
context and, 264
interposition, 265–267
overview, 264–265
proxy coordinators, 266
distribution support for EJBs, 466–467
distribution transparency for CORBA, 479
dn LDAP attribute, 309
DNS (Domain Name System)
connecting to a server, 329
double reverse lookups, 343–346
environment properties, 330
JNDI with, 328–332
lookups, 331
naming conventions in JNDI, 311
overview, 328–329
record types, 329
reverse lookups, 332, 342–343
use as naming service, 304
doAfterBody() method
IterationTag interface, 159, 160, 165
TagSupport class, 168
doCalculateDigest() method, 422–423
Document Object Model (DOM) parsers, 22–23
document-centric XML documents, 20
doDecryption() method, 425
doEncryption() method, 425
doEndTag() method
Tag interface, 155
TagSupport class, 168
Does Not Exist state
stateful session beans, 500
stateless session beans, 489–490
does-not-exist state (entity beans), 524
doFilter() method
Filter interface, 98
FilterChain interface, 99
wrappers for, 100–102
doGet() method
destroy() method and, 81
Get method (HTML) and, 84
println() method in, 113
service() method and, 81
session tracking using, 92

doInitBody() method
    BodyTag interface, 163, 165
    BodyTagSupport class, 169
DOM (Document Object Model) parsers, 22–23
Domain Name System. *See* DNS
doNotPrompt Kerberos configuration option, 377
doPost() method
    destroy() method and, 81
    if statement in, 97
    of LoginServlet class, 82
    parsing SOAP requests in, 712
    Post method (HTML) and, 84
    service() method and, 81
doStartTag() method
    BodyTagSupport class, 169
    Tag interface, 155, 165
    TagSupport class, 168
doTag() method
    SimpleTag interface, 170, 173
    SimpleTagSupport class, 173
downloading ANT, 859
doWork() method, 614
drill-down pattern (UDDI), 700
DSML (Directory Services Markup Language), 334
DTDs (Document Tag Definitions)
    external specification, 26
    implementing, 24–26
    internal specification, 25
    special characters in, 24
    valid XML documents and, 18, 24
    web.xml deployment descriptor element for, 104
    XML Schema versus, 30, 31
DuplicateKeyException EJB exception, 562
durability property of transactions
    defined, 257
    overview, 272–273
DynaAttribs.jsp JSP tag extension example, 175
dynamic attributes, 174–176
DynamicAttributes interface
    JSP for, 175
    method, 174
    TLD for, 175
    TrySimpleDynamic tag handler, 175–176
dynamic-attributes method (TLD), 150

E

EAI (enterprise-application integration)
    messaging in, 232
    Web services for, 654–656
Eclipse development environment (IBM), 49
EIS (enterprise information systems)
    access with the CCI, 637–640
    EJB tier, 430
    JMS for messaging, 714–715
    sign-on, 629
EJB client
    data setup for business methods, 498
    getting the InitialContext, 497
    getting the remote interface, 498
    invoking the business method, 498–499
    JNDI lookup for home interface, 497
    removing the bean, 499
    runtime objects, 496–497
    tasks, 496
EJB QL (EJB Query Language)
    BETWEEN clause, 550
    conditional expressions, 549–551
    deployment descriptors and, 547
    EMPTY comparison, 550–551
    finder methods, 548
    FROM clause, 547
    functions, 551
    IN expression, 550
    LIKE expression, 550
    NULL comparison, 550
    ORDER BY clause, 547, 551
    overview, 547
    SELECT clause, 547, 551
    select methods, 548
    WHERE clause, 547, 549–551
ejbActivate() method
    entity bean callback, 521
    overview, 445
    stateful session beans, 455
ejbCreate() method
    entity bean callback, 520–521
    MDB, 569
    overview, 445
    remote home interface and, 485
    service-implementation bean, 723
    stateful session beans, 501, 505
    stateless session beans, 490, 491
ejbFind() callback method, 523
ejbHome() callback method, 523
EJBHome interface, 485, 503
ejb-jar.xml deployment descriptor
    BMP entity bean, 561–562
    CMP entity bean, 533–534
    for CMRs (many-to-many), 545–546
    for CMRs (one-to-many), 544–545
    for CMRs (one-to-one), 541–542
    for CMRs (overview), 537–539
    EJB QL and, 547
    entity beans, 517, 518
    FlightServiceBean session bean, 495
    internal messaging with EJB applications, 573–575
    MDB (EJB 2.0), 570–571
    MDB (EJB 2.1), 572–575
    session beans, 488–489
ejbLoad() method
    entity bean callback, 522
    overview, 445
ejbPassivate() method
    entity bean callback, 521
    overview, 445
    stateful session beans, 454–456
ejbPostCreate() method
    entity bean callback, 521
    overview, 445

`ejbRemove()` method
    entity bean callback, 521–522
    MDB, 569
    overview, 445
    service-implementation bean, 723
    stateful session beans, 501
    stateless session beans, 491
EJBs (Enterprise JavaBeans). *See also* entity beans;
        MDB (message-driven beans); session beans
    advantages for Web services, 713–714
    application assembler, 434–435
    as application component APIs, 13
    application-server availability strategies, 473–475
    bean class, 444
    bean provider, 433, 447–449
    client views, 487, 512
    component interface, 444
    component model, 429–431
    conservative recommendation for, 458
    container functionality, 446–447
    CORBA integration, 467–472
    deployer, 435
    deployment descriptor, 336, 432, 456, 464, 795–796
    distribution support, 466–467
    `EJBContext` interface, 446
    exceptions, 562–563
    home interface, 444
    interoperability and portability of, 431
    invocation, 632
    JNDI with, 335–337, 463–464
    J2EE APIs required for, 12–13
    lifecycle methods, 445–446
    load distribution for, 474–475
    naming objects, 463–464
    overview, 13
    performance and scalability issues, 472–481
    performance-analysis tools, 479–481
    persistence and, 466, 477–478
    primary key class, 444
    resource pooling for, 450–451, 476–477
    restrictions on bean provider, 447–449
    roles, 432–436
    scalability, 450–451
    security and, 478
    security infrastructure, 464
    as server components, 7
    server/container provider, 433–434
    system administrator, 435–436
    threading model and, 476–479
    3-tier architecture, 430
    `TimedObject` interface, 464–466
    timer service, 464–466
    `TimerService` interface, 465
    transactional example, 462–463
    transactional objects and, 258
    transactional participants and, 258
    transactions and, 456
    transactions and performance, 475–476
    transparent fail-over for, 475
    types of, 13, 436
    Web service-implementation bean, 722
    Web services using, 713–714
    writing an EBJ client, 496–499
`ejbSelect()` callback method, 523
`ejbStore()` method
    entity bean callback, 522
    overview, 445
    `SeatBean` entity bean, 438–439
`ejbTimeout()` method
    entity bean callback, 523
    MDB, 569
    `TimedObject` interface, 464–466
elements
    declaring XML, in DTDs, 24–25
    of JSPs, 116–122
    of XML documents, 20–21, 24–25
e-mail. *See* JavaMail
embedded trade secrets, 350
`employeeNumber` attribute (`InetOrgPerson`
        schema), 337
`employeeType` attribute (`InetOrgPerson`
        schema), 337
EMPTY comparison (EJB QL), 550–551
encryption. *See also* cryptography; JCE (Java
        Cryptography Extensions)
    algorithms, 411–415
    for authentication, 316
    decryption, 410
    defined, 410
    filters for servlet parameters, 100
    keys for, 411
    login methods, 361–362
    one-way versus two-way, 410–412
    terminology, 410–420
end() method, 294–295
`enlistResource()` method, 295
enterprise applications, 430–431
Enterprise AppServer Edition (Borland), 48
enterprise information systems. *See* EIS
Enterprise JavaBeans. *See* EJBs
Enterprise Studio for Java (Borland), 372
enterprise-application integration. *See* EAI
entity beans. *See also* BMP (bean-managed
        persistence); CMP (container-managed
        persistence); EJBs (Enterprise JavaBeans)
    advantages of, 436–437
    Airline Reservations application, 436–437, 438–439
    callback methods, 519–523
    component interface, 515
    components, 513–517
    defined, 436
    deployment descriptor, 517, 518
    does-not-exist state, 524
    EJB transactional example, 462–463
    entity-bean class, 515

Continued

entity beans *(continued)*
    `EntityBean` interface, 517–519
    entity-container contract, 517–526
    `EntityContext` interface, 446
    exceptions, 562–563
    home interface, 513–515
    instance pooling, 452, 453, 524–525
    lifecycle, 451–454, 523–526
    lifecycle methods, 445–446
    local client view, 512
    overview, 511–512
    passivation, 526
    pooled state, 524–525
    primary-key class, 516–517
    ready state, 525–526
    remote client view, 512
    removal, 526
    rollback, 526
    session beans versus, 441–442
entity-bean class, 515
`EntityBean` interface, 517–519
entries (JNDI), 310
envelope (SOAP), 657, 666
environment properties
    DNS, 330
    for EJBs with JNDI, 336–337
    JNDI, 313–316
equality of transactions, 297
`equals()` method, 297
equals sign for JSP expressions (<%=), 114, 117
error logging, 622
error pages (JSP)
    for airline-registration screen, 139–140
    overview, 123–124
error processing (JDBC), 587
`EVAL_BODY_AGAIN` constant, 160
`EVAL_BODY_BUFFERED` constant, 163, 164
`EVAL_BODY_INCLUDE` constant, 155
`EVAL_PAGE` constant, 155
event listeners. *See* listeners (servlet)
Event Service (CORBA), 472
`exception` variable (JSP), 121, 123
exceptions
    entity beans, 562–563
    JSP error pages for, 123–124, 137, 139–140
exclamation mark (!)
    for HTML comments (<!- -), 119
    for JSP declarations (<%!), 117
execute thread pool size, 889
`executeQuery()` method, 585, 587
`ExecutionContext` interface, 614
expressions in JSPs, 115, 117–118
extended transaction models with J2EE Activity
        Service
    Actions, 281–283
    Activities, 280–281
    Activity coordinator, 281, 282–283
    extended transactions, 279–280
    long-running transactions and, 278–279

    Signals, 281–283
    `SignalSets`, 281–283
extensibility
    frameworks for, 824
    Struts framework, 831–833
eXtensible Markup Language. *See* XML
eXtensible Stylesheet Language Transformations.
            See XSLT
extensions layer (wire stack), 661
external DTD specification, 26

F

fail-over, 474–475
failure recovery for transactions, 273–274
fault isolation, 277
`FetchProfile` class, 214–215, 226
`FetchProfile.Item.CONTENT_INFO` field, 214
`FetchProfile.Item.ENVELOPE` field, 214
`FetchProfile.Item.FLAGS` field, 214
File I/O, bean provider restrictions for, 448
file matching (ANT), 867
file systems (JNDI), 311, 333
`FileHandler` (JSR 47), 899
`Filter` interface, 98
`FilterChain` interface, 99, 760
`FilterConfig` interface, 98
`FilterManager` component, 759
filters (servlet)
    chaining, 98, 106
    for encrypting parameters, 100
    for intercepting and logging requests, 99–100
    interfaces, 98–99
    introduction of, 97
    response wrapper, 100–102
    reusable tasks for, 98
    Servlet Specification 2.4 and, 111
    `web.xml` deployment descriptor elements, 106–107
`finalize()` method, 723
`find()` method, 527–528
`findAncestorWithClass()` method
    `SimpleTagSupport` class, 173
    `TagSupport` class, 168
`find_binding` method, 698
`find_business` method, 698, 699
`findByPrimaryKey()` method
    EJB QL, 548
    entity beans, 514
finder methods
    EJB QL, 548
    entity beans, 514
    UDDI, 698–699
`FinderException` EJB exception, 562
`find_relatedBusiness` method, 698
`find_service` method, 698, 699
`find_tModel` method, 698
`FineGrainedObject` component, 779
500 error code, 124
flags
    JAAS login-module, 361
    JavaMail message, 201–203

Flags class, 201–202
Flags.Flag.ANSWERED system flag, 202
Flags.Flag.DELETED system flag, 202
Flags.Flag.DRAFT system flag, 202
Flags.Flag.FLAGGED system flag, 202
Flags.Flag.RECENT system flag, 202
Flags.Flag.SEEN system flag, 202
Flags.Flag.USER system flag, 202
Flanagan, David (*Java in a Nutshell*), 806
FlightBean bean class, 545–546
FlightClient class, 62–63
FlightClient2 class, 69–70
FlightServer interface (RMI), 57–58
FlightServerImpl class, 58–60
FlightServerImpl_skel class, 61
FlightServerImpl_stub class, 61
FlightService remote interface, 493
FlightServiceBean stateless session bean
    bean class, 494–495
    deploying, 496
    deployment descriptor, 495
    EJB client, 496–499
    home interface, 493
    remote interface, 493
    runtime objects, 496–497
FlightServiceHome interface, 493
Folder class
    listing messages, 211–212
    methods for folder content, 212
    methods for folders, 207–208
    opening and closing folders, 211
    overview, 210–211
folders (JavaMail)
    accessing, 207–210
    advanced message fetching, 213–215
    copying and moving messages, 215
    listing in a hierarchy, 209–210
    listing messages, 211–213
    methods dealing with content, 212
    methods for accessing, 207–208
    opening and closing, 211
    overview, 210–211
    searching messages, 215–216
FooterFilter class, 101–102
forces for patterns
    business-delegate pattern, 765
    composite-entity pattern, 778
    composite-view pattern, 754
    defined, 731
    front-controller pattern, 746
    half-object-plus-protocol pattern, 786
    intercepting-filter pattern, 758
    MVC pattern, 741–742
    router pattern, 736
    service-locator pattern, 782
    session pattern, 732
    session-facade pattern, 774
    value-object pattern, 769–770
    view-helper pattern, 750–751

<FORM> tag (HTML), 78, 84
formatNumber tag (JSTL), 146
formatting library (JSTL), 147
forName() method, 585
forward action (JSP), 120, 121
forward() method
    JSP forward action and, 120
    of RequestDispatcher class, 86, 120
    sendRedirect() method versus, 86, 87
404 error code, 124
frameworks. *See also* JAF (JavaBeans Activation
        Framework)
    alignment, 825–826, 834–835
    alternatives to, 846–850
    application architecture versus, 841
    for application portfolios, 837
    building your own, 841–845
    business-application, 820
    buying versus building, 841–842
    callback handlers (JAAS), 395–397
    checklist for, 851–853
    class libraries versus, 821
    configurability, 824–825, 833–834
    costs, 850–851
    defined, 820
    design patterns, 826–828
    for design process streamlining, 835
    for development and testing, 836
    e-mail reception (JavaMail), 223–225
    evaluating, 850–854
    extensibility, 824, 831–833
    further information, 928
    future of, 845–846
    inversion of control, 823, 828
    loose coupling, 824, 830–831
    need for, 819–820, 821–823
    objectives and benefits, 835–837
    open source, 842–843
    principles, 823–827
    for production and maintenance, 836
    requirements, 850
    separation of concerns, 823–824, 828–829
    from software vendors, 843–844
    Struts example, 827–835
    from system integrators (SIs), 844–845
    types of, 821
    vendor questions, 853–854
FROM clause (EJB QL), 547
From JavaMail header field, 192
front-controller pattern
    described, 730
    forces, 746
    front controller, 748
    further information, 750
    helper, 748
    implementation, 746–748
    overview, 746
    related patterns, 750

Continued

front-controller pattern *(continued)*
    results, 749
    sample code, 749–750
    sequence diagram, 747
    strategies, 748–749
    structure, 747
    view, 748
`function` method (TLD), 150
functional problems, 882
`function-class` method (TLD), 150
functions (EJB QL), 551
`function-signature` method (TLD), 150

G

Gamma, Erich (*Design Patterns*), 729, 745, 802, 805
Gang of Four (GOF), 729, 745
garbage collection (Java). *See also* memory-usage
        problems (Java)
    algorithm (JVM), 891–892
    myths about, 909
    overview, 906–908
`gateway.jsp` authenticator, 791–793
Generic Security Services Application Program
        Interface (GSS-API), 361–362
Get method (HTML), 84
GET verb (HTTP), 687
`getAllRecipients()` method, 192
`getArrivalTime()` method, 57–58
`get_assertionStatusReport` method, 703
`getAttribute()` method, 85
`getAttributeNames()` method, 85
`getAttributes()` method
    `DirContext` interface, 317, 318, 326
    for DNS lookups, 331
`get_bindingDetail` method, 699
`getBodyContent()` method, 169
`getBodyPart()` method, 198
`get_businessDetail` method, 699
`getCalls()` method, 720, 721
`getConnection()` method, 585, 598–599, 636
`getContent()` method, 196
`getContentType()` method, 199–200
    `DataHandler` class, 196
    `Multipart` class, 199
`getCount()` method, 199
`getDefaultFolder()` method, 207
`getDefaultInstance()` method, 188
`getDepartureTime()` method, 57–58
`getDescription()` method, 200
`getDisposition()` method, 200
`getEJBObject()` method, 503
`getEmployee()` method, 125
`getFileName()` method, 201
`getFilterName()` method, 98
`getFlags()` method, 203
`getFlightArrivals()` method, 60
`getFolder()` method, 207
`getFrom()` method, 192
`getHeader()` method, 194

`getHomeHandle()` method, 503
`getID()` method, 168
`getInitParameter()` method
    `init()` method and, 81
    of servlet `FilterConfig` interface, 98
`getInitParameterNames()` method, 98
`getInputStream()` method, 196
`getInstance()` method, 188
`getJspBody()` method, 174
`getJspContext()` method, 174
`getLineCount()` method, 201
`getMessage()` method, 212
`getMessageCount()` method, 212
`getMessageDrivenContext()` method, 569
`getMessageID()` method, 194
`getMessages()` method, 212
`getNewMessageCount()` method, 212, 213
`get_operationInfo` method, 699
`getOutputStream()` method, 196
`getParameter()` method, 83
`getParameterNames()` method, 83
`getParameterValues()` method, 83
`getParent()` method
    `BodyPart` class, 199
    `Multipart` class, 199
    `SimpleTag` interface, 170
    `SimpleTagSupport` class, 174
    `Tag` interface, 155
    `TagSupport` class, 168
`getPasswordAuthentication()` method, 189–190
`getPermanentFlags()` method, 202
`getPersonalNamespaces()` method, 208
`getPort()` method, 720, 721
`getPorts()` method, 720, 721
`getPreviousOut()` method, 169
`getProperties()` method, 187
`get_publisherAssertions` method, 703
`getRecipient()` method, 192
`getReference()` method, 324, 325
`get_registeredInfo` method, 703
`getReplyTo()` method, 193
`getSentDate()` method, 194
`get_serviceDetail` method, 699
`getServiceName()` method, 720, 721
`getServletContext()` method, 98
`getSession()` method, 91–92
`getSharedNamespaces()` method, 208
`getSize()` method, 201
`getStatus()` method
    `Transaction` interface, 293
    `TransactionManager` interface, 291
`getStore()` method, 205
`getSubject()` method, 193
`get_subscriptionResults` method, 703
`get_subscriptions` method, 703
`get_tModelDetail` method, 699
`getTransaction()` method
    `Transaction` interface, 293
    `TransactionManager` interface, 291

getTransactionManager() method, 294
getType() method, 209
getTypeMappingRegistry() method, 720, 721
getUnreadMessageCount() method, 212
getUserNamespaces() method, 208
getValue() method, 168
getValues() method, 168
getWorkManager() method, 614
getWSDLDocumentLocation() method, 720, 721
givenname LDAP attribute, 309
GOF (Gang of Four), 729, 745
green pages (UDDI), 658
The Grinder, 887
group.provider.url JDNI configuration option, 383
GSS-API (Generic Security Services Application
        Program Interface), 361–362

H

half-object-plus-protocol pattern
    described, 764
    forces, 786
    implementation, 786–787
    LocalObject component, 787
    overview, 785
    related patterns, 788
    RemoteObject component, 787
    results, 788
    sample code, 788
    sequence diagram, 787
    strategies, 787–788
    structure, 786
handler (intercepting-filter pattern), 760
Handlers (JSR 47), 898–900
handlesPost() method, 81
HashMap attributes of TagSupport classes, 169
hasNewMessages() method, 212
header fields (JavaMail), 191–194
header (SOAP), 666–667
heap size (JVM), 890–891
Hello.jsp JSP tag extension example, 157
HelloWorld e-mail example, 181–183
HelloWorld Web page, 113, 114
Helm, Richard (Design Patterns), 729, 745, 802, 805
helper
    front-controller pattern, 748
    view-helper pattern, 752
heuristic outcomes of two-phase commit protocol,
    261–262
home interface for entity beans
    BMP bean, 552–553
    CMP bean, 527–528
    create() method, 513–514
    finder methods, 514
    home() methods, 515
    overview, 513–515
    remove() method, 514–515
home interface for session beans
    Airline Reservations application, 493, 504
    JNDI lookup for EJB client, 497

    local home interface, 485
    overview, 484
    remote home interface, 485
home() methods, 515
<HR> (horizontal line) tags (HTML), 21
HTML (HyperText Markup Language)
    bad example, 19
    data entry elements and components, 78–79
    HelloWorld page, 113
    hidden fields, 90–91
    JSP versus, 114
    limitations of, 19–20
    login screen, 79–84, 127–128
    producing documents with XSLT, 34–38
    register.html page, 133–135
    well-formed document, 19
    XML roots in, 18
HTTP (HyperText Transfer Protocol)
    as J2EE standard service, 11, 12
    servlets and HTTP requests, 712, 713
    Struts framework and, 828
    WSDL GET and POST binding, 687
HttpServletResponse class, 86–87
HttpSession object
    creating or finding, 91
    getSession() method, 91–92
    servlet listeners for events, 94, 95, 96–97
    session tracking using, 91–93
HttpSessionAttributeListener interface, 95
HttpSessionBindingEvent class, 95
HttpSessionEvent class, 95
HttpSessionListener interface, 95
human-readable documents, 34
HyperText Markup Language. See HTML
HyperText Transfer Protocol. See HTTP
HyperText Transfer Protocol Secure (HTTPS), 11, 12

I

IBM
    Eclipse development environment, 49
    LUCIFER algorithm, 413
    Web Services Toolkit, 689
    WebSphere application servers, 48, 335, 474–475,
        716, 928
IDEs (Integrated Development Environments), 846,
    848–850, 858–859
IDL (Interface Definition Language), 72
if statement in doPost() method, 97
if target attribute (ANT), 867
IIOP (Internet Inter-Orb Protocol)
    overview, 469–471
    RMI-IIOP, 11, 12, 72–73, 470–471
IMAP (Internet Message Access Protocol), 184–185
implementation
    business-delegate pattern, 765–767, 768
    composite-entity pattern, 778–779, 780–781
    composite-view pattern, 754–756
    data-access-object pattern, 799–804

Continued

implementation *(continued)*
    DTDs, 24–26
    error pages (JSP), 124
    front-controller pattern, 746–748
    half-object-plus-protocol pattern, 786–787
    intercepting-filter pattern, 758–760
    J2EE platform, 43–45
    MVC pattern, 742–743
    persistence, 477
    remote interfaces for RMI, 58–60
    ResourceAdapter interface, 641–643
    router pattern, 736–738
    service-activator pattern, 806–810
    service-implementation bean, 722, 723
    service-locator pattern, 782–783, 784–785
    session pattern, 732–734
    session-authenticator pattern, 790
    session-facade pattern, 774–777
    SOA for Web services, 840
    transfer-object pattern, 812–815
    value-object pattern, 770–771, 772–773
    view-helper pattern, 751–752, 753
implementation description layer (description
        stack), 661
implicit objects (JSP), 121–122
importing
    JSP page directives for, 118
    JSTL tag libraries, 147–148
IN expression (EJB QL), 550
include action (JSP), 120
include directive (JSP)
    jsp:include action versus, 120
    online store example, 131
    overview, 118
in-doubt transactions, 274
InetOrgPerson schema, 337–340
init() method
    Filter interface, 98
    of servlets, 81
InitialContext component, 783
INITIAL_CONTEXT_FACTORY property (JNDI), 313
initialize() method, 385
input parameters for EJB QL, 549
Insert statement (SQL), 583
inspection layer (discovery stack), 662
installing
    ANT, 859–860
    RMI Flight Server application, 66
instance pooling. *See also* resource pooling
    entity beans, 524–525
    overview, 451
    stateless session beans, 492
instance scope of variables (JSP), 122
instantiating
    Airline User JavaBean, 125–126
    stateless session beans, 490
Integrated Development Environments (IDEs), 846,
        848–850, 858–859
integrity, encrypted-message passing and, 410

Interaction interface (CCI), 635
interaction interfaces (CCI), 634, 635
InteractionSpec interface (CCI), 635
intercepting-filter pattern
    client, 759
    described, 731
    FilterChain component, 760
    FilterManager component, 759
    forces, 758
    handler, 760
    implementation, 758–760
    overview, 758
    PathFilter component, 760
    related patterns, 761
    results, 760
    sample code, 761
    sequence diagram, 759
    strategies, 760
    structure, 759
Interface Definition Language (IDL), 72
interface description layer (description stack), 661
interfaces
    application server proxy, 53–54
    BodyTag (JSP tag handler), 163–167
    CCI, 633–634
    Connection (JMS), 237
    ConnectionFactory (JMS), 238
    connection-management (Connector architecture),
        616–622, 623
    Context (JNDI), 312
    Destination (JMS), 237
    DirContext (JNDI), 312, 326, 328
    EJB, 444, 464
    EJBContext, 446
    EntityBean, 517–519
    IterationTag (JSP tag handler), 159–163
    JAXR, 706–708
    MDB, 569
    Message (JMS), 234–235
    MessageConsumer (JMS), 238–239
    MessageProducer (JMS), 238, 251–252
    MVC pattern, 745
    Part (JavaMail), 190, 194–195
    Referenceable (JNDI), 324
    ResourceAdapter (Connector architecture), 610
    RMI RefreshScreen, 68–69
    RMI registry, 64
    RMI remote, 57–60
    RowSet (JDBC), 601–606
    Service Endpoint (Web services), 722, 723
    Service (Web services), 720–721, 724
    ServiceLifeCycle (Web services), 724
    servlet filter, 98–99
    servlet listener, 95
    session bean component, 485–486
    session bean home, 484–485
    Session (JMS), 238
    SessionBean (EJB), 487

`SessionSynchronization` (stateful session beans), 503

`SimpleTag` (JSP tag handler), 170–173

stateless session beans Web-service endpoint, 492

`Synchronization` (JTA), 296

`TagSupport` (JSP tag handler), 167–169

`TimedObject` (EJB), 464

`Transaction` (JTS), 293–294

transaction-management (Connector architecture), 625

`TransactionManager` (JTA), 291

`UserTransaction` (JTA), 290–291

work-management (Connector architecture), 613, 614

`XAResource` (JTA), 294–295

`XID` (JTA), 297

X/Open Distributed Transaction Processing, 284

internal DTD specification, 25

International Standards Organization (ISO), 305

International Telecommunications Union (ITU-T), 305

Internet Inter-Orb Protocol. *See* IIOP

Internet Message Access Protocol (IMAP), 184–185

Internet resources

    ANT, 859

    Apache Taglibs, 145

    Apache Tomcat, 52

    AXIS (Apache), 715

    BEA WebLogic, 48

    Borland Enterprise AppServer Edition, 48

    Caucho Technology Resin servlet container, 52

    CORBA information, 650

    COS naming service provider, 333

    cryptographic algorithms, 413

    DCOM, 650

    DNS record types RFC, 329

    DSML, 334

    IBM Eclipse development environment, 49

    IBM WebSphere information, 48, 716

    IMAP information, 185

    JAAS information, 933–934

    Java Adventure Builder, 9

    Java Verification Program, 45

    JBoss application server, 49

    JCE, 420

    JCP, 15

    JDBC drivers, 582

    JDBC information, 934

    JNDI information, 933

    JNDI search filter RFC, 319

    JNDI-provider classes, 333

    JProbe (Quest Software), 892

    JSP information, 933

    JSR 47 (logging specification), 894

    JSTL specification, 145

    load-testing tools, 887

    Log4J, 894

    MDB information, 934

    MIME information, 185

    MVC information, 828

    New Atlanta ServletExec servlet container, 52

OpenLDAP information, 306

Oracle 9iAS application server, 49

Orion application server, 50

POP3 RFC, 184

resources by chapters in this book, 932–934

RMI information, 932

SASL specification, 316

security-policy file information, 65

servlet information, 933

SMTP RFC, 184

Software Productivity Consortium, 837

Struts framework, 827, 828

Sun Java Security site, 353

Sun ONE application server, 50

UDDI specification, 659

vendors providing J2EE implementations, 54

WASP (Systinet), 689

Web services information, 934

Web services specification (JSR 109), 725

Web Services Toolkit (IBM), 689

WSDL specification, 658

Zachman Framework for Enterprise Architecture, 837

`InternetAddress` class, 203–204

interoperability

    CORBA and, 469, 471, 472

    EJBs and, 431

    transaction, 471

    as Web services advantage, 652–653

invalidating sessions, 92–93

inversion of control

    frameworks for, 823

    Struts framework, 828

invocation pattern (UDDI), 700

`invoke()` method, 173

iostat performance-analysis tool, 480

`isEmployee()` method, 125

`isExpunged()` method, 203

`isMimeType()` method, 200

ISO (International Standards Organization), 305

isolation property of transactions

    cascade rollback and, 269

    defined, 257, 268

    degrees of isolation, 270–272

    optimistic versus pessimistic concurrency control, 269–270

    overview, 268–269

    two-phase locking policy for, 268–269

`isSet()` method, 203

`IterateBuf.jsp` JSP tag extension, 165

`Iterate.jsp` JSP tag extension, 160

`IterateSimple.jsp` JSP tag extension, 171

`IterationTag` interface

    constant for, 160

    JSP for, 160

    method for, 159

    overview, 159

    TLD for, 160

    `TryIterationTag` tag handler, 161–163

itrArray tag
    BodyTag interface, 164–167
    IterationTag interface, 160–163
ITU-T (International Telecommunications Union), 305

J

JAAS (Java Authentication and Authorization Service)
    advantages of, 357
    Airline Reservations application, 404–407
    authenticating users, 364–371
    authenticating Web users against directory
        service, 404–407
    authenticating Web users against WinNT domain,
        397–403
    authentication services, 353
    authorization services, 353
    basic login code, 364–366
    callback handlers, 358–360, 394–397
    compiling the login code, 369–370
    custom login modules, 384–385
    debugging, 372–375
    dialog callback handlers, 360
    functions of JAAS-enabled applications, 354
    import statements, 358
    JNDI login handler, 383–384
    as J2EE standard service, 12
    Kerberos login handler, 377–378
    key-store login handler, 380–383
    login initialize arguments, 386
    login process, 354
    login-configuration files, 360–361, 367–368
    login-module flags, 361
    login-module methods, 385–386
    Magazine Publisher application, 397–403
    operating systems and authentication, 353
    overview, 353–354
    Pluggable Authentication Modules, 360–363
    policy files, 368–369, 373–374
    portability and, 353
    predefined login callbacks, 375–376
    privileged object, 366
    reactive login (Borland), 356
    running the login code, 370–371
    running the module, 375
    setup, 358
    single login across security domains, 356–357
    single login class for all modules, 375
    Subject class, 362–364
    Sun-supplied login modules, 363
    text callback handlers, 359–360
    Unix login handler, 379
    Web sites, 933–934
    WinNT/Win2K login handler, 379
    writing a callback handler, 394–397
    writing a login handler, 385–394
jaas.policy file, 373–374
JACC (Java Authorization Service Provider Contract
        for Containers), 12, 13

JAF (JavaBeans Activation Framework)
    JavaMail and, 195–197
    as J2EE standard service, 11, 12
Jakarta, 928–929
JAR files
    jar task (ANT) for, 870–871
    TLDs in, 151
jar task (ANT), 870–871
Java
    further information, 929, 931
    history, 3–4
    J2SE, 5
    policy files, 373–374
    sandbox, 350, 353
    SOAP and, 676–681
    UDDI and, 704–709
    WSDL and, 689
Java Adventure Builder application, 9
Java API for XML Binding (JAXB), 40
Java API for XML Messaging. *See* JAXM
Java API for XML Parsing. *See* JAXP
Java API for XML Registries. *See* JAXR
Java API for XML-RPC. *See* JAX-RPC
Java Authorization Service Provider Contract for
        Containers (JACC), 12, 13
Java BluePrints, 9
Java Community Process. *See* JCP
Java Cryptography Extensions. *See* JCE
Java Database Connectivity. *See* JDBC
Java Development Kit (JDK), 5
Java in a Nutshell (Flanagan, David), 806
Java Management Extensions (JMX), 12, 13
Java Messaging Service. *See* JMS
Java Naming and Directory Interface. *See* JNDI
Java Secure Socket Extension (JSSE), 361–362
Java Specification Requests. *See* JSRs
Java Transaction API. *See* JTA
Java 2 Standard Edition (J2SE), 5
Java Verification Program, 45
Java Web Services Developer Pack, 716
JavaBeans. *See also* EJBs (Enterprise JavaBeans)
    Airline User JavaBean, 124–125
    for airline-registration screen, 137–138
    defined, 124
    in JSP, 124–130
    login JSP using, 127–130
    login screen using JSP, 127–130
    scope, 127
    ShoppingCartBean, 131
JavaBeans Activation Framework. *See* JAF
javac task (ANT), 868–870
JavaCard class, 389–390
JavaCardLauncher class, 388–389
JavaCardPrincipal class, 387–388
JAVA_HOME environment variable, 860
JavaMail. *See also* sessions (JavaMail)
    accessing folders, 207–210
    Address class, 203–205

addresses for messages, 203–205
advanced message fetching, 213–215
authenticating connections, 188–190
Authenticator class, 188–190
BodyPart class, 199
ComparisonTerm object, 216
components, 185–186
controlling message delivery, 217
copying and moving messages, 215
core protocol parameters, 187–188
DataHandler class, 195–197
deleting mail, 227
FetchProfile class, 214–215, 226
flags, 201–203
Flags class, 201–202
Folder class, 207–213
framework for e-mail reception, 223–225
integrating into J2EE, 229–230
InternetAddress class, 203–204
JAF, 11, 12, 195–197
javamail_send class, 218
as J2EE standard service, 11, 12
listing folders in a hierarchy, 209–210
listing messages, 211–213
looking up the Session object, 229–230
mail storage and retrieval, 186, 205–216
Message class, 190
message content, 199–205
message manipulation, 186, 190–199
message storage and retrieval, 186, 205–216
MIME content-type descriptions, 199–201
MimeMessage class, 191–194
Multipart class, 197–199
NewsAddress class, 204–205
opening and closing folders, 211
parsing e-mail addresses, 204
Part interface, 190, 194–195
protocols, 183–185
receiving attachments, 227–229
receiving e-mail, 223–227
searching messages, 215–216
SearchTerm class, 215–216
sending e-mail and attachments, 218–223
Session class, 186–188
session management, 186–190
setting up sessions to the server, 218–220
Store class, 205–206
Transport class, 216–218
transportation, 186, 216–218
try...catch block for sending messages, 217, 220–221
URLName class, 206–207
using the API, 218–229
javamail_send class, 218
java.naming.authoritative property (DNS), 330
java.naming.factory.initial property (DNS), 330
java.naming.factory.object property (DNS), 330
java.naming.provider.url property (DNS), 330
java.policy file, 373–374

java.rmi.registry.Registry interface, 64
java.rmi.Remote interface, 57, 60
java.rmi.RemoteException declaration, 57, 60
java.security properties file, 358
JavaServer Pages. See JSPs
java.sql.ResultSetMetaData class, 589–590
java.util.Properties class, 187–188
javax.activation.DataHandler class, 195–197
javax.crypto package (JCE), 421
javax.crypto.interfaces package (JCE), 421
javax.crypto.spec package (JCE), 421
javax.ejb.EJBContext interface, 446
javax.ejb.EJBHome interface, 485, 503
javax.ejb.EJBLocalHome interface, 485
javax.ejb.EJBLocalObject interface, 485, 486
javax.ejb.EJBObject interface, 485, 486
javax.ejb.SessionBean interface, 487
javax.ejb.TimedObject interface, 464
javax.ejb.TimerService interface, 465
javax.jms.BytesMessage interface, 234–235
javax.jms.Connection interface, 237
javax.jms.ConnectionFactory interface, 238
javax.jms.Destination interface, 237
javax.jms.MapMessage interface, 234–235
javax.jms.Message interface, 234–235
javax.jms.MessageConsumer interface, 238–239
javax.jms.MessageProducer interface, 238, 251–252
javax.jms.Session interface, 238
javax.jms.StreamMessage interface, 234–235
javax.jms.TextMessage interface, 234–235
javax.jsp.SessionSynchronization interface, 503
javax.mail.Address class, 203–205
javax.mail.Authenticator class, 188–190
javax.mail.BodyPart class, 199
javax.mail.FetchProfile class, 214–215, 226
javax.mail.Flags class, 201–202
javax.mail.Folder class. See Folder class
javax.mail.internet.InternetAddress class, 203–204
javax.mail.internet.MimeMessage class. See MimeMessage class
javax.mail.internet.NewsAddress class, 204–205
javax.mail.Message class, 190, 202–203
javax.mail.Multipart class, 197–199
javax.mail.Part interface, 190, 194–195
javax.mail.Session class, 186–188
javax.mail.Store class, 205–206
javax.mail.Transport class, 216–218
javax.mail.URLName class, 206–207
javax.naming package (JNDI), 310
javax.naming.directory package (JNDI), 310
javax.naming.event package (JNDI), 310
javax.naming.ldap package (JNDI), 310
javax.naming.spi package (JNDI), 310
javax.sql.RowSet interface. See RowSet interface
javax.transaction.Synchronization interface, 296
javax.transaction.Transaction interface, 293–294
javax.transaction.TransactionManager interface, 291

`javax.transaction.UserTransaction` interface, 290–291

`javax.transaction.xa.XAResource` interface, 294–295

`javax.transaction.xa.XID` interface, 297

`javax.xml.registry` package (JAXR), 705–707

`javax.xml.registry.infomodel` package (JAXR), 705, 707

JAXB (Java API for XML Binding), 40

JAXM (Java API for XML Messaging)
   described, 40
   JAXM MDB, 569

JAXP (Java API for XML Parsing)
   described, 40
   as J2EE standard service, 11, 12

JAXR (Java API for XML Registries)
   API, 705–708
   architecture, 704–705
   capability profiles, 705
   client, 704, 707–709
   described, 40
   interfaces, 706–708
   as J2EE standard service, 12, 13
   packages, 705–708
   provider, 704–705

JAX-RPC (Java API for XML-RPC)
   described, 40
   as J2EE standard service, 12, 13
   `Service Endpoint` interface and, 723

JBoss application server, 49, 335, 474

JBuilder programmer's editor, 372

JCE (Java Cryptography Extensions). *See also* cryptography; encryption
   Airline Reservations application, 424–426
   classes, 421
   cryptography terminology, 410–420
   features, 420
   Magazine Publisher application, 422–424
   overview, 409
   packages, 421
   policy files, 420
   steps for writing programs, 421
   Sun Web site, 420
   SunJCE algorithms, 420–421

JCP (Java Community Process)
   frameworks and, 845
   overview, 14
   Web site, 15

JDBC (Java Database Connectivity)
   `AirUser` class, 588
   batch updates, 593–594
   `CallableStatement` class, 592–593
   connection pools, 596–597, 889
   creating a program, 583–593
   database-error processing, 587
   `DataSource` objects, 597–599
   `DBProcessor` class, 599–601
   driver types, 582–583
   EJB transactional example, 462

JDBC-ODBC bridge configuration, 594–596
   J2EE platform requirement, 44
   as J2EE standard service, 11, 12
   loading a driver, 585
   overview, 581–582
   `PreparedStatement` class, 592
   processing result sets, 587–589
   `ResultSetMetaData` class, 589–590
   retrieving data, 585–587
   `RowSet` interface, 601–606
   savepoints, 594
   scrollable result sets, 591
   `ShowAnyData.java` example, 589–590
   `UserList` class, 586–587
   `UserList2` class, 588–589
   Web sites, 934

JDK (Java Development Kit), 5

JMeter (Apache), 887

JMS (Java Messaging Service). *See also* MDB (message-driven beans); point-to-point (p2p) messaging; publish-and-subscribe messaging
   acknowledgement modes, 244–245
   autonomous messages, 252
   `BookOrder` class, 248–249
   `Caterer` class, 246–248
   components, 236–239
   configuring, 239–240
   connection factories, 237–238
   `Connection` interface, 237
   `ConnectionFactory` interface, 238
   connections, 237
   consumers, 238–239
   `Destination` interface, 237
   destinations, 237
   enterprise messaging using, 714–715
   further information, 930
   interfaces, 234–235, 237–238
   JNDI lookup and, 237–238
   as J2EE standard service, 11, 12
   `MealService` class, 241–246
   message headers, 246
   `Message` interface, 234–235
   message structure, 233–234
   message types, 233
   `MessageConsumer` interface, 238–239
   message-driven beans and, 254
   message-driven beans introduced for, 442–443
   `MessageProducer` interface, 238, 251–252
   messaging overview, 231–232
   `OrderProcessor` class, 249–251
   overview, 232
   persistent messages, 252
   point-to-point example, 240–248
   point-to-point messaging model, 235
   producers, 238
   publish-and-subscribe example, 248–252
   publish-and-subscribe messaging model, 236
   queues, 237

reliability features, 252–253
RMI versus, 232–233
`Session` interface, 238
sessions, 238
synchronous acknowledgments, 253
transactions support, 253
versions, 233
as Web services transport layer, 714–715
`JMSDeliveryMode` message header, 246
`JMSDestination` message header, 246
`JMSExpiration` message header, 246
`JMSMessageID` message header, 246
`JMSPriority` message header, 246
`JMSRedelivered` message header, 246
`JMSTimestamp` message header, 246
JMX (Java Management Extensions), 12, 13
JNDI (Java Naming and Directory Interface). *See also*
          LDAP (Lightweight Directory Access
          Protocol)
    adding directory entries with LDAP, 322
    adding objects to LDAP directories, 323–328
    Airline Reservations application, 337–341
    attributes, 310–311
    authentication in LDAP, 316
    binding, 311
    callback handler for, 394–397
    connecting to LDAP server, 312–313
    `Context` interface, 312
    contexts and subcontexts, 311
    `DirContext` interface, 312, 326, 328
    directories, 310
    DNS double reverse lookups, 343–346
    DNS lookups, 331
    DNS naming conventions, 311
    DNS reverse lookups, 332, 342–343
    DNS with, 328–332
    EJBs with, 335–337, 463–464
    entries, 310
    environment properties, 313–316, 336–337
    file systems, 311, 333
    JMS and JNDI lookup, 237–238
    `jndi.properties` file, avoiding, 316
    as J2EE standard service, 11, 12
    LDAP lookups, 316–318
    LDAP mapping, 312
    LDAP with, 312–328
    login handler for JAAS, 383–384
    lookup for home interface, 497
    Magazine Publisher application, 342–346
    mapping in JNDI, 312
    names, 310–311
    overview, 303
    packages, 310
    `Referenceable` interface, 324
    references, 311
    removing directory entries in LDAP, 322
    `SearchControls` class, 320–322
    searching for entries in LDAP, 318–322
    service component lookup, 781

service providers, 332–335
storing object data as directory attributes, 325–328
storing objects as references, 323–325
storing serialized data in directories, 323
structure, 309–312
Sun-supplied login module, 363
for Web services lookup, 719
Web sites, 933
`JndiLoginModule` login module, 363
`jndi.properties` file, avoiding, 316
Johnson, Ralph (*Design Patterns*), 729, 745, 802, 805
JProbe (Quest Software), 892
jRockit JVM (BEA), 48
JSP Standard Tag Library. *See* JSTL (JSP Standard Tag
          Library)
JSP tag extensions. *See also* JSTL (JSP Standard Tag
          Library)
    advantages of, 143–144
    `BodyTag` interface, 163–167
    difficulties developing custom tags, 145
    dynamic attributes, 174–176
    importing a tag library, 147–148
    `IterationTag` interface, 159–163
    overview, 144
    tag handlers, 145, 153–174
    `Tag` interface, 154–159
    `taglib` mapping, 152
    TLDs, 145, 148–150
`jsp:forward` action (JSP), 120, 121
`JspFragment` interface, 173
`jsp:include` action (JSP), 120
`jsp:param` action (JSP), 120
`jsp:plugin` action (JSP), 120, 121
JSPs (JavaServer Pages)
    actions, 120–121
    airline-registration screen using, 133–141
    as application component APIs, 13
    `BodyTag` example, 165
    `CachedRowSet` object with, 603–604
    comments, 119
    declarations, 117
    directives, 118, 146
    `DynamicAttributes` example, 175
    elements, 116–122
    error pages, 123–124
    expressions, 115, 117–118
    HelloWorld example, 113–114
    HTML versus, 114
    implicit objects, 121–122
    `IterationTag` example, 160
    Java expressions in, 115
    JavaBeans in, 124–130
    login screen using JavaBeans, 127–130
    MVC pattern and, 115–116
    `MyFirstJSPPage.jsp` example, 114–115
    online store design using, 130–133
    overview, 13, 113
    `register.jsp` controller, 135–137

Continued

JSPs *(continued)*
  repeating headers for, 118
  scriptlets, 119
  `SimpleTag` example, 171
  `Tag` interface example, 156–157
  version 2.0, 115
  as Web components, 7
  Web sites, 933
`jspService()` method
  automatic generation of, 114
  scriptlets and, 119
`jsp:useBean` action (JSP), 125–126
JSR 47 (logging specification). *See also* logging
  formatting output, 901
  `Handlers`, 898–900
  initialization order and, 897
  Log4J versus, 894–895, 896, 897
  `Logger` class methods, 897–898
  messages, 895, 898
  priority levels, 895–896
  runtime configuration, 903–904
  Web site, 894
JSR 109 (Web services specification)
  client-side programming model, 719–721
  goals, 717–718
  server-side programming model, 721–724
  Web service APIs, 718–719
  Web service deployment descriptors, 725
JSRs (Java Specification Requests)
  JCP process for, 14–15
  logging specification (JSR 47), 894–901, 903–904
  Web services (JSR 109), 717–725
JSSE (Java Secure Socket Extension), 361–362
JSTL (JSP Standard Tag Library)
  Apache Taglibs reference implementation, 145
  core library, 147
  formatting library, 147
  importing a tag library, 147–148
  JSP versions and, 145
  `NumberFormat.jsp` example, 146
  specification, 145
  SQL library, 147
  `taglib` mapping, 152
  TLDs, 145, 148–150
  XML library, 147
JTA (Java Transaction API). *See also* transactions
  architecture, 289
  BMTs and, 460
  enrolling participants, 295–296
  JTS and, 289
  as J2EE standard service, 11, 12
  suspending and resuming transactions, 292
  `Synchronization` interface, 296
  transaction equality, 297
  `Transaction` interface, 293–294
  transaction synchronization, 296
  `TransactionManager` interface, 291
  `UserTransaction` interface, 290–291
  `XAResource` interface, 294–295

`XID` interface, 297
  X/Open DTP model and, 288
JTS, JTA and, 289
J2EE Connector architecture. *See* Connector architecture
J2EE (Java 2 Enterprise Edition). *See also specific APIs*
  APIs, 10–13
  application components, 6–7
  architecture, 5, 6
  avoiding vendor lock-in, 53–54
  Compatibility Test Suite, 45
  components and services, 44
  containers, 44
  CORBA's importance to, 468–469
  full implementations, 47–50
  further information, 929–930
  future of, 14
  implementing the platform, 43–45
  improvements in version 1.4, 13–14
  JavaMail integration, 229–230
  licensees, 44
  minimal, 848
  origin of, 5
  pains of, 821–823
  partial implementations, 51–53
  standard services APIs, 11–13
  Web services integration with, 711–717
J2EE product provider, 7
`j2eebible.ldif` file (OpenLDAP), 306–308
`j2eebible-taglib.tld` file, 156
`junit` task (ANT), 871–875
JVMs (Java Virtual Machines)
  applets and, 7
  bytecode compiler, 890
  garbage-collection algorithm, 891–892
  heap size, 890–891
  RMI and, 55, 56
  tunable parameters, 889–892

K

Kerberos
  advantages for authentication, 364
  callback handler for, 394–397
  login handler for JAAS, 377–378
  Microsoft implementation, 357
  security realm, 357
  Sun-supplied login module, 363
key store
  LDAP/X.500 attribute types for, 381–382
  login handler for JAAS, 380–383
  login-handler configuration options, 381
  Sun-supplied login module, 363
keys for encryption
  keyspace, 411
  overview, 411
  public-key cryptography, 416–417
  shared-key cryptography, 415–416
keyspace, 411
`KeyStoreAlias` key-store configuration option, 381

`KeyStoreLoginModule` login module, 363
`KeyStorePasswordURL` key-store configuration
     option, 381
`KeyStoreProvider` key-store configuration
     option, 381
`KeyStoreType` key-store configuration option, 381
`KeyStoreURL` key-store configuration option, 381
`KeyTab` Kerberos configuration option, 377
`Krb5LoginModule` login module, 363

L

`LanguageCallback` class (JAAS), 376
launcher for JAAS login handler, 388–389
LDAP Directory Interchange Format (LDIF) file,
     306–308, 338–340
LDAP (Lightweight Directory Access Protocol). *See
     also* JNDI (Java Naming and Directory
     Interface)
     adding directory entries with JNDI, 322
     adding objects to directories with JNDI, 323–328
     attribute types for key-store login module, 381–382
     attributes, 308–309
     authentication, 316
     development of, 305
     environment properties for JNDI, 313–316
     implementations, 305–306
     JNDI with, 312–328
     lookups by JNDI, 316–318
     mapping in JNDI, 312
     OpenLDAP configuration, 306–308
     removing directory entries with JNDI, 322
     schema, 308–309
     search filters, 319–320
     search operators, 319–320
     searching for entries by JNDI, 318–322
     server connection by JNDI, 312–313
     storing object data as directory attributes, 325–328
     storing objects as references, 323–325
     storing serialized data in directories, 323
     X.500 standard and, 305
`LDAPDataStore` component, 738
LDIF (LDAP Directory Interchange Format) file,
     306–308, 338–340
licensees (J2EE), 44
lifecycle
     EJB container functionality, 447
     EJB lifecycle methods, 445–446
     EJB resource pooling and, 451
     of entity beans, 451–454, 523–526
     MDB lifecycle methods, 569
     resource adapter (Connector architecture), 612
     servlet lifecycle methods, 80–81
     of session beans, 454–456
     of simple tag handler, 170
     stateful session beans, 500–502
     of stateless session beans, 489–491
lifecycle-management contract
     described, 609
     overview, 610

resource-adapter bootstrapping, 611
     `ResourceAdapter` JavaBean, 610–611
     resource-adapter shutdown, 611–612
Lightweight Directory Access Protocol. *See* LDAP
`LIKE` expression (EJB QL), 550
line break (`<BR>`) tags (HTML), 21
Linux login module, 363
`list()` method, 208–209
listeners (servlet)
     defined, 94
     event classes, 95
     for `HttpSession` events, 94, 95, 96–97
     interfaces, 95
     introduction of, 94
     Servlet Specification 2.4 and, 111
     for `ServletContext` events, 94–96
     `web.xml` deployment descriptor elements, 105
listing
     folders in a hierarchy (JavaMail), 209–210
     messages (JavaMail), 211–213
literals in EJB QL, 549
load
     defined, 884
     load testing, 886–887
     performance and, 474–475, 884–885
LoadRunner (Mercury Interactive), 887
local client view
     entity beans, 512
     session beans, 487
local interface for session beans
     local component interface, 486
     local home interface, 485
local scope of variables (JSP), 122
local transactions
     auto-commit mode, 262–264
     defined, 262
     disabling auto-commit mode, 263
`LocalObject` component, 787
`LocalTransaction` interface, 625–626
local-transaction management contract, 625–626
`LogFilter` class, 99
Log4J logging API (Apache). *See also* logging
     `Appenders`, 900–901
     development of, 894, 895
     initialization order and, 897
     JSR 47 versus, 894–895, 896, 897
     layouts, 901–902
     `Logger` class methods, 897–898
     messages, 895, 898
     multi-threaded logging, 902–903
     Nested Diagnostic Context (NDC), 902–903
     priority levels, 895–896
     runtime configuration, 905–906
     Web site, 894
logging. *See also* JSR 47 (logging specification); Log4J
          logging API (Apache)
     architecture, 895
     deciding what to log, 893–894

Continued

logging *(continued)*
    defined, 893
    JSR 47 (logging specification), 894–901, 903–904
    Log4J, 900–903, 905–906
    messages, 895
    multi-threaded, 902–903
    security vulnerability, 350
logical operators
    EJB QL, 549–550
    for searching messages (JavaMail), 215–216
`login` database table, 584–585
login handlers (JAAS). *See also* callback handlers
    (JAAS)
    Java Card module, 390–394
    JNDI, 383–384
    Kerberos, 377–378
    key-store, 380–383
    launcher, 388–389
    login initialize arguments, 386
    login-module methods, 385–386
    `Principal` class, 387–388
    Unix, 379
    virtual Java Card, 389–390
    WinNT/Win2K, 379
    writing your own, 385–394
`login()` method, 385
login screen (HTML)
    deploying JSP version using Tomcat, 129–130
    HTTP `Get` and `Post` requests, 84
    `Login.html` screen, 127–128
    `pub_login.html` screen, 79–80
    servlet structure and lifecycle methods, 80–81
    using JSP and JavaBeans, 127–130
    writing the servlet, 81–83
login security. *See* authentication; authorization; JAAS
    (Java Authentication and Authorization
    Service)
`login.configuration.provider` property
    (JAAS), 358
`login.config.url.n` property (JAAS), 358
`Login.java` JavaBean, 127, 128–129
`LoginServlet` class
    with access counter, 93–94
    creating, 81–83
`logout()` method, 386
`lookup()` method
    for directory objects, 323
    `java.rmi.Naming` class, 64
lookups
    in DNS with JNDI, 331–332
    for home interface with JNDI, 497
    in LDAP with JNDI, 316–318
    for Magazine Publisher application, 342–346
    service component with JNDI, 781
    for Web services with JNDI, 719
`LookupService` component
    business-delegate pattern, 767
    value-object pattern, 771
loopbacks, EJB single-thread restriction and, 449–450

loose coupling
    frameworks for, 824
    Struts framework, 830–831
`LostPasswordServlet` example, 87–88

M

machine-readable documents, 34
Magazine Publisher application
    applet-servlet communication, 107–111
    authenticating Web users against WinNT domain,
        397–403
    business case, 923–926
    client code for login, 399–401
    client policy file, 401–402
    client side, 79
    creating using servlets, 77–84
    double reverse lookup for, 343–346
    executive summary, 923
    JAAS security for, 397–403
    JCE for, 422–424
    JMS publish-and-subscribe messaging, 248–252
    JNDI for, 342–346
    login configuration file, 401
    mission statement, 924
    reverse lookup for, 342–343
    security analysis, 397–398
    security limitations, 398
    server code for secure-socket communication link,
        398–399
    server policy file, 402
    server side, 78–79
    servlet filter for logging requests, 99–100
    servlet-context listener, 95–96
    servlet-session listener, 96–97
    starting the login client, 403
    starting the login server, 402
    summary of examples, 924–926
    technology overview, 924
`MagPublisherContextListener` class, 96
`MagPublisherSessionListener` class, 96–97
`mail` attribute (`InetOrgPerson` schema), 337
`mail` LDAP attribute, 309
mail storage and retrieval (JavaMail)
    accessing folders, 207–210
    advanced message fetching, 213–215
    copying and moving messages, 215
    `Folder` class, 207–213
    listing folders in a hierarchy, 209–210
    listing messages, 211–213
    opening and closing folders, 211
    overview, 186
    searching messages, 215–216
    `Store` class, 205–206
    `URLName` class, 206–207
`mail.debug` parameter (JavaMail), 188
`mail.from` parameter (JavaMail), 187
`mail.host` parameter (JavaMail), 188
`mail.protocol.host` parameter (JavaMail), 188
`mail.protocol.user` parameter (JavaMail), 188

`mail.store.protocol` parameter (JavaMail), 187
`mail.transport.protocol` parameter (JavaMail), 187
`mail.user` parameter (JavaMail), 187
maintenance, frameworks and, 836
make utility. *See* ANT
Malks, Dan (*Core J2EE Patterns*), 750, 754
`ManagedConnection` interface, 620–622, 625
`ManagedConnectionFactory` interface, 618–620
`Mandatory` CMT attribute, 459
many-to-many relationships (CMR), 545–546
`matchManagedConnection()` method, 618
`matchMessages()` method, 422, 423
MDA (model-driven architecture), 847–848
MDB (message-driven beans). *See also* EJBs
    (Enterprise JavaBeans); JMS (Java
    Messaging Service)
  advantages of, 568
  asynchronous messages and, 565–566
  asynchronous processing, 576–577
  `Caterer` class, 567–568
  clients and, 575
  deployment descriptors (EJB 2.0), 570–572
  deployment descriptors (EJB 2.1), 572–575
  interfaces, 569
  internal messaging with EJB applications, 573–575
  JAXM, 569
  lifecycle methods, 445–446, 569
  `MessageDrivenContext` interface, 446
  need for, 565–568
  overview, 442–443
  ticket reservation example, 566–567
  Web sites, 934
MD4 and MD5 algorithms, 415
`MemoryHandler` (JSR 47), 900
memory-usage problems (Java)
  garbage collector and, 906–908, 909
  lapsed listeners, 910–911
  large sessions, 911
  limbo, 913–914
  lingerers, 911–913
  loiterer anti-patterns, 910–914
  loiterers, 908–910
Mercury Interactive LoadRunner, 887
`Message` class, 190, 202–203
message content (JavaMail)
  `Address` class, 203–205
  addresses for messages, 203–205
  flags, 201–203
  `Flags` class, 201–202
  `InternetAddress` class, 203–204
  `NewsAddress` class, 204–205
Message Digest algorithms, 415
message endpoint, 631–632
message flags (JavaMail)
  core system flags, 202
  `Message` class methods that work with, 203
  overview, 201–202
message headers (JMS), 246

message manipulation (JavaMail)
  `BodyPart` class, 199
  `DataHandler` class, 195–197
  JavaBeans Activation Framework, 195–197
  `Message` class, 190
  `MimeMessage` class, 191–194
  `Multipart` class, 197–199
  overview, 186, 190
  `Part` interface, 194–195
message-based Web-service architecture, 650–651
message-driven beans. *See* MDB
`Message-ID` JavaMail header field, 194
message-inflow contract
  described, 609
  EJB invocation, 632
  endpoint deployment, 631
  endpoint undeployment, 632
  message delivery, 631–632
  message endpoint, 631–632
  overview, 631
message-oriented middleware (MOM), 231, 233, 566
messages. *See* JavaMail; JMS (Java Messaging Service)
messaging (SOAP), 675–676
metadata interfaces (CCI), 634, 636
Method-Ready Pool state (stateless session beans),
  490–491
Method-Ready state (stateful session beans), 500–501
methods. *See also specific methods*
  for accessing folders (JavaMail), 207–208
  `BodyTag` interface, 163
  `BodyTagSupport` class, 169
  CMT attributes and business methods, 457–459
  `DataHandler` class, 196
  `DynamicAttributes` interface, 174
  EJB lifecycle, 445–446
  EJB QL, 547–548
  entity bean callback methods, 515, 519–523
  for folder content handling (JavaMail), 212
  home interface for entity beans, 513–515
  `IterationTag` interface, 159
  JAAS login-module methods, 385–386
  `JspFragment` interface, 173
  MDB lifecycle methods, 569
  `Message` class, for flags, 203
  `Multipart` class, 198–199
  native to application servers, 53
  `RowSetListener` interface, 605–606
  `Service` interface, 720–721
  servlet lifecycle, 80–81
  `SimpleTag` interface, 170
  `SimpleTagSupport` class, 173–174
  `Tag` interface, 154–155
  `TagSupport` class, 168–169
  TLD, 150
  `Transaction` interface (JTA), 293–294
  `TransactionManager` interface (JTA), 291, 292
  UDDI finder methods, 698–699

Continued

methods *(continued)*
    UDDI publishing API, 701–703
    UDDI retriever methods, 699
    UDDI subscription API, 703–704
    UserTransaction interface (JTA), 290–291
    WorkManager interface, 614
    XAResource interface (JTA), 294–295
Microsoft
    Kerberos implementation, 357
    single-login concept, 356–357
MIME (Multipurpose Internet Mail Extension)
    content-type descriptions, 199–201
    MimeMessage class, 191–194
    Multipart class, 197–199
    multipart messages, 190, 194–195, 197–199, 200–201
    overview, 185
    WSDL binding, 688–689
MimeMessage class, 191–194
minimal J2EE, 848
mirror integration, 654
mobile e-services, 656
model in MVC pattern
    defined, 827
    JSPs and, 116
    overview, 9–10, 743
    sample code, 745
model-driven architecture (MDA), 847–848
model-view-controller pattern. *See* MVC pattern
modularity, 277
MOM (message-oriented middleware), 231, 233, 566
moving messages (JavaMail), 215
multidimensional arrays (SOAP), 671–672
Multipart class, 197–199
Multipurpose Internet Mail Extension. *See* MIME
mustUnderstand attribute of SOAP header, 676
MVC (model-view-controller) pattern
    controller in, 10, 743
    described, 730
    forces, 741–742
    further information, 745
    implementation, 742–743
    Java Swing components and, 116
    JSPs and, 115–116
    long-lived applications and, 9
    model in, 9–10, 743
    overview, 9, 740–741
    related patterns, 745
    results, 743–744
    sample code, 744–745
    sequence diagram, 743
    strategies, 743
    Struts framework, 827
    view in, 10, 742
    Web applications and, 115–116
    Web site, 828
    XSLT and, 34
MX DNS record type, 329
myErrors.jsp error page, 137, 139–140
MyFirstJSPPage.jsp example, 114–115

N
name
    project attribute (ANT), 864
    target attribute (ANT), 867
name method (TLD), 150
NameCallback class (JAAS), 376
name-given method (TLD), 150
names (JNDI), 310–311
namespaces (XML)
    Airline Reservations application, 28–30, 33–34
    defined, 26
    for grouping tags using URIs, 28
    identification in prologue, 28
    including in tags, 29–30
    in XSL files, 36–37
naming services. *See also* JNDI (Java Naming and Directory Interface)
    defined, 303
    directory services and, 303–304
    for EJBs, 463–464
    overview, 303–304
    RMI registry, 56, 61–63
NAT (network address translation), 474
NDC (Nested Diagnostic Context), 902–903
nested transactions
    overview, 276
    top-level, 277–278
    uses for sub-transactions, 277
netstat performance-analysis tool, 480
network address translation (NAT), 474
Network Information System (NIS), 333
networked servers, 448
Never CMT attribute, 459
New Atlanta
    ServletExec Debugger, 53
    ServletExec servlet container, 51, 52–53
NewsAddress class, 204–205
newsgroup addressing (JavaMail), 204–205
9iAS application server (Oracle), 49
NIS (Network Information System), 333
non-repeatable reads, 271
nonrepudiation, 410
Notification Service for CORBA, 472
notify_subscriptionListener method, 703
NotSupported CMT attribute, 457–458
NS DNS record type, 329
NTLoginModule login module, 363
NULL comparison (EJB QL), 550
number sign (#) in #PCDATA keyword, 25
NumberFormat.jsp JSTL example, 146

O
o attribute (InetOrgPerson schema), 337
o LDAP attribute, 308
Object Management Group (OMG), 467–469, 847
object persistence, 552
object pools (JDBC), 596
object request broker (ORB), 430
Object Transaction Service. *See* OTS
ObjectNotFoundException EJB exception, 562

ObtainLogin login-configuration file, 367–368
ODBC driver configuration for JDBC-ODBC bridge, 594–596
OMG (Object Management Group), 467–469, 847
ONE application server (Sun), 50
ONE Studio programming environment (Sun), 372
one-phase optimization of two-phase commit, 260
one-to-many relationships (CMR), 543–545
one-to-one relationships (CMR), 541–543
one-way encryption
    hash function for, 412
    Magazine Publisher application, 422–424
    RSA algorithm, 411
OneWayHash() constructor, 422
online store
    actions needed for, 130
    designing using JSP, 130–133
    partial controller servlet, 132–133
    ShoppingCartBean, 131
onMessage method (MDB), 569
The Open Group (API standards developers), 284
open() method, 211, 227
opening folders (JavaMail), 211
OpenLDAP
    Airline Reservations configuration file, 337–340
    configuring, 306–308
    InetOrgPerson schema, 337
    Internet resources, 306
    LDIF file for, 306–308, 338–340
    slapd.conf file for, 306
    starting the server, 306
OpenLDAP 2.1 Administrator's Guide (OpenLDAP publication), 306
open-source frameworks, 842–843
operationalInfo element (UDDI v3), 697–698
optimistic concurrency control, 270
optional login-module flag (JAAS), 361
optional tasks (ANT), 868
Options login initialize argument, 386
Oracle
    JDBC-ODBC bridge configuration, 594–596
    9iAS application server, 49
OracleCachedRowSet class, 602
OracleDataStore component, 738
ORB (object request broker), 430
ORDER BY clause (EJB QL), 547, 551
OrderProcessor class, 249–251
OrderProcessor session bean, 576–577
OrderServlet class, 110–111
Orion application server, 50
OTS (Object Transaction Service)
    cooperating services, 287
    development of, 285–286
    participating within, 288
    recoverable objects, 286
    roles, 287
    transactional objects, 286
ou LDAP attribute, 308
out variable (JSP), 121

P
packages
    JAAS callback handlers, 359
    JAXR, 705–708
    JCE, 421
    JNDI, 310
packaging layer (wire stack), 661
packaging TLDs in JARs, 151
page directive (JSP)
    error pages and, 123
    overview, 118
page scope of JavaBeans, 127
page variable (JSP), 121
PageContext class, 122
pageContext variable (JSP), 121
pains of J2EE, 821–823
PAM (Pluggable Authentication Modules), 360–363
param action (JSP), 120
parsers (XML). See XML parsers
parsing e-mail addresses (JavaMail), 204
partially-transmitted arrays (SOAP), 672
Passenger remote interface, 528–529
PassengerBean bean class
    CMR examples, 539–546
    overview, 529–533
PassengerBeanClient CMP entity bean client, 534–537
PassengerHome home interface, 527–528
passivation
    ejbPassivate method, 445, 454–456
    entity beans, 526
    stateful session beans, 454–456, 502
PasswordCallback class (JAAS), 376
passwords
    LostPasswordServlet example, 87–88
    verification method, 341
PathFilter component, 760
A Pattern Language (Alexander, Christopher), 729
Pattern-Oriented Software Architecture, Volume 2 (Schmidt, Douglas and Stal, Michael and Rohnert, Hans and Buschmann, Frank), 810–811
patterns. See also specific patterns
    business-delegate, 764–769
    composite-entity, 764, 777–781
    composite-view, 731, 754–757
    data-access-object, 797–805
    defined, 729
    forces defined, 731
    frameworks and, 826–827
    front-controller, 730, 746–750
    further information, 729, 930
    half-object-plus-protocol, 764, 785–788
    implementation defined, 731
    intercepting-filter, 731, 758–761
    MVC (model-view-controller), 9–10, 34, 115–116, 730, 740–745
    overview, 729–731

Continued

patterns *(continued)*
    proxy, 769
    related patterns defined, 731
    results defined, 731
    router, 730, 736–740
    sample code defined, 731
    service-activator, 797, 805–811
    service-locator, 764, 781–785
    servlet filters for Wrapper pattern, 101–102
    session, 730, 731–736
    session-authenticator, 764, 789–794
    session-facade, 764, 773–777
    stateless-service-provider, 764, 794–796
    strategies defined, 731
    Struts framework, 827–828
    transfer-object, 797, 811–816
    value-object, 764, 769–773
    view-helper, 730, 750–754
    Web-tier model, 730
#PCDATA keyword, 25
percent sign (%)
    for JSP comments (<%- -), 119
    for JSP declarations (<%!), 117
    for JSP directives (<%@), 118
    for JSP expressions (<%=), 114
    for JSP scriptlets (<%), 119
perfmon performance-analysis tool, 480–481
performance (EJBs)
    analysis tools, 479–481
    application-server availability strategies, 473–475
    CORBA and, 478–479
    importance of, 472–473
    load distribution for, 474–475
    persistence and, 477–478
    resource pooling for, 476–477
    security and, 478
    threading model and, 476–479
    transaction concerns, 475–476
    transparent fail-over for, 475
performance (Java applications)
    benchmarking, 887–889
    common problems, 881–885
    critical-path analysis, 886
    functional problems, 882
    isolating problems, 886–893
    load testing, 886–887
    logging for analyzing, 893–906
    memory-usage problems, 906–914
    profiling, 892–893
    response time problems, 883
    scalability problems, 883–885
    shared resources and, 885
    throughput problems, 883
    tunable parameters, 889–892
permission.jsp JSP example, 791, 793
persistence
    bean-managed (BMP), 437–439, 466, 512
    container-managed (CMP), 439, 466, 512

    durable transactions, 257, 272–273
    implementations, 477
    JMS messages, 252
    object, 552
    performance and, 477–478
    session beans and, 483
Persistence and Recovery Service for OTS, 287
pessimistic concurrency control, 269
phantom reads, 271
PI (Portable Interceptors), 479
placeOrder() method, 576
Pluggable Authentication Modules (PAM), 360–363
plugin action (JSP), 120, 121
plus sign (+) in DTDs, 24
POA (Portable Object Adapter), 479
point-to-point (p2p) messaging (JMS)
    Airline Reservations application, 240–248
    Caterer class, 246–248
    creating a message, 241–246
    JMS acknowledgement modes, 244–245
    JMS message headers, 246
    MealService class, 241–246
    overview, 235
    push model, 235
    receiving messages, 241
    setting up objects on sending side, 240–241
    steps for sending messages, 241
policy files
    Airline Reservations application, 406
    JAAS, 368–369, 373–374
    Java, 373–374
    JCE, 420
    Magazine Publisher application, 401–402
    RMI, 65
policy layer (description stack), 661
policy.provider property (JAAS), 358
policy.url.n property (JAAS), 358
polymorphic accessor (SOAP), 669–670
pooled state (entity beans), 524–525
POP3 (Post Office Protocol), 184
Portable Interceptors (PI), 479
Portable Object Adapter (POA), 479
ports (RMI registry), 64
Post method (HTML), 84
Post Office Protocol. *See* POP3
POST verb (HTTP), 687
prefix attribute of taglib directive, 147
prepare phase of two-phase commit protocol, 259
PreparedStatement class, 592
presentation layer (description stack), 661
PresentationComponent component
    data-access-object pattern, 800
    service-activator pattern, 807
    transfer-object pattern, 813
PresentationTier component
    business-delegate pattern, 767
    session-facade pattern, 775
    value-object pattern, 770

presentation-tier patterns. *See also* patterns; *specific patterns*
    composite-view, 731, 754–757
    front-controller, 730, 746–750
    intercepting-filter, 731, 758–761
    MVC (model-view-controller), 9–10, 34, 115–116, 730, 740–745
    overview, 730–731
    router, 730, 736–740
    session, 730, 731–736
    view-helper, 730, 750–754
presumed rollback optimization of two-phase commit, 260
primary-key class of entity beans
    compound primary keys, 516
    overview, 516
    single-field primary keys, 516
    unknown primary keys, 517
`Principal class` for JAAS login handler, 387–388
`Principal` Kerberos configuration option, 377
`Principal` objects
    for JAAS login modules, 362–363
    for JNDI login module, 384
    for Kerberos login module, 378
    for key-store login module, 383
    for Unix login module, 379
    for WinNT login module, 379
`println()` method
    in `doGet()` method, 113
    of `PrintWriter` object, 82
`privateKeyPasswordURL` key-store configuration option, 381
processors (XML). *See* XML parsers
producers (JMS), 238
`ProductCatalog` class, 133
production, frameworks and, 836
profiling, 892–893
projects (ANT), 864
prologue
    namespaces in, 28
    of XML documents, 20, 28
    of XSL files, 36
`Properties` class, 187–188
provider (JAXR), 704–705
`PROVIDER_URL` property (JNDI), 313, 315
proxy coordinators for distributed transactions, 266
proxy interface for application servers, 53–54
proxy patterns, 769
PTR DNS record type, 329
p2p messaging. *See* point-to-point messaging (JMS)
publication layer (discovery stack), 662
public-key cryptography, 416–417
publish-and-subscribe messaging (JMS)
    `BookOrder` class, 248–249
    durable subscriptions, 236
    Magazine Publisher application, 248–252
    `OrderProcessor` class, 249–251
    overview, 236

    `send()` method parameters, 251–252
    setup, 248
publishing with UDDI, 700–703
`pub_login.html` HTML login screen, 79–80
pub/sup messaging. *See* publish-and-subscribe messaging (JMS)

Q
quality attributes as Web services advantage, 653
query methods (EJB QL), 547–548
Quest Software
    Benchmark Factory, 887
    JProbe, 892
question mark (?) in DTDs, 24
queues (JMS), 237

R
RAR (Resource Adapter Archive) files, 641
`ra.xml` deployment descriptor, 641–643
RDBMS. *See* relational databases
reactive login (Borland), 356
read committed transaction isolation, 272
read uncommitted transaction isolation, 271
`readObject()` method, overriding, 351
read-only optimization of two-phase commit, 260
ready state (entity beans), 525–526
`rebind()` method (RMI), 62
receiving
    attachments (JavaMail), 227–229
    e-mail (JavaMail), 223–227
    messages (JMS), 241
`Record` interface (CCI), 635
`RecordFactory` interface (CCI), 635
`RecoveryCoordinator` role (OTS), 287
re-entrance, EJB single-thread restriction and, 449–450
`Referenceable` interface (JNDI), 324
references (JNDI)
    overview, 311
    storing objects as, 323–325
reflection, bean provider restrictions for, 448
`refreshFlightInfo()` method, 69
`RefreshScreen` interface (RMI), 68–69
`registerBean.java` JavaBean, 137–138
`registerClient()` method, 70, 71
`register.html` airline-registration page, 133–135
`register.jsp` controller, 135–137
`registerUser()` method, 137
registry (RMI), 56, 61–63, 64
relational databases. *See also* databases; JDBC (Java Database Connectivity)
    directory services versus, 304–305, 340
    EJB transactional example, 462–463
    JDBC and, 581
`release()` method
    `Tag` interface, 155
    `TagSupport` class, 168
remote client view
    entity beans, 512
    session beans, 487

Remote interface, 57, 60
remote interface for entity beans
    BMP bean, 553
    CMP bean, 528–529
remote interface for session beans
    Airline Reservations application, 493, 504–505
    getting for EJB client, 498
    remote component interface, 486
    remote home interface, 485
Remote Method Invocation to Internet Inter-ORB
        Protocol. *See* RMI-IIOP
remote procedure call-based Web-service
        architecture, 650
RemoteObject component, 787
remove() method
    EJB client, 499
    entity beans, 526
    home interface for entity beans, 514–515
removeAttribute() method, 85
REMOVE_ATTRIBUTE operation of DirContext
        interface, 328
removeBodyPart() method, 199
RemoveException EJB exception, 563
removeValue() method, 169
repeatable read transaction isolation, 272
REPLACE_ATTRIBUTE operation of DirContext
        interface, 328
reply() method (JavaMail), 191
Reply-To JavaMail header field, 193
Request component, 808
request scope of JavaBeans, 127
request variable (JSP), 121
RequestDispatcher class, 86, 120
RequestProcessor class (Struts), 830–831
Required CMT attribute, 458
required login-module flag (JAAS), 361
required method (TLD), 150
RequiresNew CMT attribute, 459
requisite login-module flag (JAAS), 361
ReservationErrors.jsp error page, 123
Reservation.java SOAP example, 676–678
Reservation.wsdl WSDL example, 681–686
Reset button (HTML), 79
Resin servlet container (Caucho Technology), 51, 52
Resource Adapter Archive (RAR) files, 641
resource adapters, 607–608
    Airline Reservations application, 615–616
    bootstrapping, 611
    deployment descriptor, 641–643
    EJB invocation, 632
    elements, 640–641
    lifecycle, 612
    packaging, 641
    ResourceAdapter JavaBean, 610–611
    shutdown, 611–612
    submitting Work instances, 615–616
resource manager (RM), 285
resource pooling. *See also* instance pooling
    EJB, 451
    entity beans, 451, 452, 453, 524–525

instance pooling, 451
    performance and, 476–477
    scalability and number of, 450–451
    stateless session beans, 454, 492
resource principal, 629–630
Resource role (OTS), 287, 288
resource use and performance, 885
ResourceAdapter interface, 610, 641–643
ResourceAdapter JavaBean, 610–611
ResourceAdapterMetadata interface (CCI), 636
response time, 883, 884
response variable (JSP), 121
response wrapper, servlet filter for, 100–102
restricted cryptography algorithms, 410–411
result sets (JDBC)
    processing, 587–589
    ResultSetMetaData class, 589–590
    scrollable, 591
results from patterns
    business-delegate pattern, 767–768
    composite-entity pattern, 780
    composite-view pattern, 757
    defined, 731
    front-controller pattern, 749
    half-object-plus-protocol pattern, 788
    intercepting-filter pattern, 760
    MVC pattern, 743–744
    router pattern, 738
    service-locator pattern, 784
    session pattern, 735
    session-facade pattern, 776
    value-object pattern, 772
    view-helper pattern, 753
ResultSetMetaData class, 589–590
resume() method, 292
resuming transactions, 292
retriever methods (UDDI), 699
retrieving data using JDBC, 585–587
reverse DNS lookups, 332
RFCs
    DNS record types, 329
    IMAP, 185
    InetOrgPerson schema, 337
    JNDI search filters, 319
    POP3, 184
    SMTP, 184
Rivest, Shamir & Adelman (RSA) algorithm, 411
RM (resource manager), 285
RMI Flight Server application
    components, 66
    deploying within Connexia Airlines, 68
    installing, 66
    overview, 65
    running, 66–68
RMI (Remote Method Invocation)
    compiler (rmic), 56, 61, 70
    components, 56
    CORBA versus, 56, 73, 468–469
    declaring remote interfaces, 57–58
    defined, 55

Flight Server application, 65–68
implementing remote interfaces, 58–60
JMS versus, 232–233
JVMs and, 55, 56
limitations of, 649
overview, 55–56
pushing data from the server, 68–72
`RefreshScreen` interface, 68–69
registering remote objects, 61–63
remote exceptions, 57, 60
RMI over IIOP, 11, 12, 72–73
rules for remote interfaces, 57
security-policy files, 65
skeletons, 60–61
steps in developing applications, 57
stubs, 60, 61
typical applications, 56
wait mode of servers, 56
Web sites, 932
writing RMI clients, 63–65
rmic (RMI compiler), 56, 61, 70
RMI-IIOP (Remote Method Invocation to Internet Inter-ORB Protocol)
as J2EE standard service, 11, 12
overview, 72–73, 470–471
Rohnert, Hans (*Pattern-Oriented Software Architecture, Volume 2*), 810–811
roles
application assembler, 8
application component provider, 8
defined, 7
deployer, 8
J2EE product provider, 7
model-view-controller pattern and, 9
system administrator, 8
system-component provider, 8
tool provider, 8
`rollback()` method
auto-commit mode and, 263
JDBC, 594
`TransactionManager` interface, 291
`UserTransaction` interface, 290
router pattern
`ClientComponent` component, 736
described, 730
forces, 736
further information, 740
implementation, 736–738
`LDAPDataStore` component, 738
`OracleDataStore` component, 738
overview, 736
related patterns, 740
results, 738
sample code, 738–740
sequence diagram, 737
strategies, 738
`rowChanged()` method, 605
`RowSet` interface
`CachedRowSet` object, 602–606
getting data from a database, 601

overview, 601
processing events, 605–606
updating the database using, 604–605
`WebRowSet` class, 606
`rowSetChanged()` method, 605
`RowSetListener` interface, 605–606
RSA (Rivest, Shamir & Adelman) algorithm, 411
`rtexprvalue` method (TLD), 150
running
JAAS login code, 370–371
JAAS module, 375
RMI Flight Server application, 66–68
runtime interaction, bean provider restrictions for, 448

S
SAAJ (SOAP for attachments API for Java), 12, 13
sandbox (Java), 350, 353
sar performance-analysis tool, 480
SASL (Simple Authentication and Security Layer), 316, 361–362
`saveAttachment()` method, 227–228
`save_binding` method, 701
`save_business` method, 701
savepoints (JDBC), 594
`save_service` method, 701
`save_subscription` method, 703, 704
`save_tModel` method, 701
saving e-mail attachments to disk (JavaMail), 227–229
SAX (Simple API for XML) parsers, 22–23
scalability
in application servers, 46
clustering application servers and, 474
defined, 46, 883
EJB resource pooling and, 450–451
performance problems, 883–885
`scheduleWork()` method, 614
schemata
LDAP, 308–309
XML Schema, 18, 31–34, 668–670
Schmidt, Douglas (*Pattern-Oriented Software Architecture, Volume 2*), 810–811
Schneier, Bruce (Blowfish creator), 414
scope
JavaBeans, 127
for `SearchControls` object, 321
variables (JSP), 122
scriptlets (JSP), 119
`search()` method
`Folder` class, 215
for LDAP in JNDI, 318–319
`SearchControls` class, 320–322
`searchFlights()` method, 493
searching
LDAP entries with JNDI, 318–322
LDAP search operators, 319–320
messages (JavaMail), 215–216
`SearchTerm` class, 215–216
`SeatBean` entity bean, 438, 439
secret-key cryptography, 415–416
Secure Hash Algorithm (SHA), 415

security. *See also* JAAS (Java Authentication and
        Authorization Service)
    bean provider restrictions for, 448
    CORBA secure interoperability, 472
    EJB container functionality, 447
    EJB infrastructure, 464
    importance of, 348–349
    Java advantages for, 347–348
    Java sandbox, 350, 353
    Java security environment, 351–352
    Java vulnerabilities, 349–353
    LDAP authentication by JNDI, 316
    performance and, 478
    policy files for RMI, 65
    SASL specification, 316
    security realms, 355–357
    Sun Java Security site, 353
security realms
    defined, 355
    JAAS advantages, 357
    Kerberos, 357
    overview, 355–356
    reactive login (Borland), 356
    single login across security domains, 356–357
SECURITY_AUTHENTICATION property (JNDI), 313
SECURITY_CREDENTIALS property (JNDI), 314
security-management contract
    authenticating a resource principal, 630
    authentication defined, 627
    authorization defined, 627
    authorizing a resource principal, 630
    component-managed sign-on, 628
    container-managed sign-on, 628
    described, 609
    EIS sign-on, 629
    establishing secure communication, 630
    overview, 627–628
    setting a resource principal, 629–630
security-policy files, 65
SECURITY_PRINCIPAL property (JNDI), 314
Segue SilkPerformer, 887
SEI (Service Endpoint interface), 722, 723
SELECT clause (EJB QL), 547, 551
select methods (EJB QL), 548
select statement (SQL), 583
self-enforcing cryptographic protocol, 420
send() method
    MessageProducer interface, 251–252
    Transport class, 216–218
sending
    e-mail and attachments (JavaMail), 218–223
    messages (JMS), 241
sendRedirect() method
    forward() method versus, 86, 87
    of HttpServletResponse class, 86–87
separation of concerns
    frameworks for, 823–824
    Struts framework, 828–829

sequence diagrams
    business-delegate pattern, 766
    composite-entity pattern, 778, 779
    composite-view pattern, 755
    data-access-object pattern, 800
    front-controller pattern, 747
    half-object-plus-protocol pattern, 787
    intercepting-filter pattern, 759
    MVC pattern, 743
    router pattern, 737
    service-activator pattern, 807, 808
    service-locator pattern, 782, 783
    session pattern, 733
    session-facade pattern, 774, 775
    Struts framework, 829
    transfer-object pattern, 812
    value-object pattern, 770, 771
    view-helper pattern, 751
serializable transaction isolation, 272
serialization
    applet/servlet object, 108
    isolation property of transactions, 257, 268–272
    security vulnerability, 349, 351
    storing serialized data in directories, 323
server/container provider for EJBs, 433–434
server-managed session, 733
servers. *See also* application servers
    components, 7
    EJB, 444
    EJBs as components, 7
    JNDI connection to LDAP server, 312–313
    pushing data from (RMI), 68–72
    session pattern, 734
    setting up JavaMail sessions, 218–220
    starting OpenLDAP server, 306
    wait mode (RMI), 56
server-side programming model (Web services)
    EJB container, 722–723
    overview, 721–722
    Service Endpoint interface (SEI), 722, 723
    service-implementation bean, 722
    Web container, 723–724
    WSDL port section, 722
Service Endpoint interface (SEI), 722, 723
Service interface, 720–721, 724
service() method of servlets
    jspService() method and, 114
    overview, 81
ServiceActivator component, 808
service-activator pattern
    Acknowledgment component, 809
    applying, 810
    asynchronous data access and, 805
    BusinessComponent component, 808
    characteristics, 805
    class diagram, 810
    described, 797
    further information, 806, 810–811

implementation, 806–810
overview, 805–806
PresentationComponent component, 807
related patterns, 810
Request component, 808
sequence diagram, 807, 808
ServiceActivator component, 808
strategies, 809–810
structure, 806–807
service-implementation bean (SIB), 722, 723
ServiceLifeCycle interface, 724
ServiceLocator component, 783
service-locator pattern
described, 764
forces, 782
implementation, 782–783, 784–785
InitialContext component, 783
overview, 781
related patterns, 785
results, 784
sample code, 784–785
sequence diagram, 782, 783
ServiceLocator component, 783
strategies, 783–784
structure, 782
service-oriented architecture. See SOA
service-tier patterns. See also patterns; specific patterns
bad design practices, 763
business-delegate, 764–769
composite-entity, 764, 777–781
half-object-plus-protocol, 764, 785–788
overview, 763–764
service-locator, 764, 781–785
session-authenticator, 764, 789–794
session-facade, 764, 773–777
stateless-service-provider, 764, 794–796
value-object, 764, 769–773
ServletContext class
servlet listeners for events, 94–96
using the servlet context, 84–85
ServletContextAttributeEvent class, 95
ServletContextAttributeListener interface, 95
ServletContextEvent class, 95
ServletContextListener interface, 95
ServletExec servlet container (New Atlanta), 51, 52–53
servlets
access counter example, 93–94
advantages for Web services, 711
applets versus, 77–78
applet-servlet communication, 107–111
as application component APIs, 13
browser/servlet interaction, 83
cached row sets with, 602–603
class diagram for user-created servlet, 80
context, using, 84–85
cookies with, 88–89
deploying, 103
encrypting parameters sent to, 100

filters, 97–102
HTML login screen using, 79–84
HTTP requests and, 712, 713
JSP generation of, 114
JSP page directives for, 118
JSP scriptlets and, 119
listeners, 94–97
Lost Password screen example, 87–88
Magazine Publisher application using, 77–84
online store controller, 132–133
overview, 13, 77
response wrapper, 100–102
servlet engines, 51–53
Servlet Specification 2.4, 111
session tracking using, 88–94
structure and lifecycle methods, 80–81
URL redirection using, 85–88
WAR file for, 103–104
in Web services architecture, 711–712
Web sites, 933
web.xml deployment descriptor, 104–107
session beans. See also EJBs (Enterprise JavaBeans);
        stateful session beans; stateless session
        beans
Airline Reservations application, 492–499
application fault-tolerance and, 441
characteristics, 484
component interface, 485–486
defined, 440
deployment descriptor, 488–489
EJB transactional example, 462–463
elements, 484
entity beans versus, 441–442
home interface, 484–485
lifecycle, 454–456
lifecycle methods, 445–446
returning a disconnected RowSet object, 603
SessionBean interface, 487
SessionContext interface, 446
stateful versus stateless, 441, 461, 483, 509–510
storing a handle, 503
writing, 484–492
writing an EBJ client, 496–499
Session class, 186–188
session management (JavaMail)
Authenticator class, 188–190
core protocol parameters, 187–188
overview, 186
Session class, 186–188
session defined, 186
Session object, looking up, 229–230
session pattern
ClientComponent component, 734
client-maintained session, 732
described, 730
forces, 732
implementation, 732–734

Continued

session pattern *(continued)*
    overview, 731–732
    results, 735
    sample code, 735
    sequence diagram, 733
    server, 734
    server-managed session, 733
    stateful communication, 734
    stateless communication, 734
    strategies, 734
    UML diagram, 735
session scope of JavaBeans, 127
session tracking
    closing sessions, 92
    cookies for, 88–89
    defined, 88
    hidden fields for, 90–91
    HttpSession object for, 91–93
    in LoginServlet with access counter, 93–94
    overview, 88
    servlets for, 88–94
    servlet-session listeners, 96–97
    timeout for sessions, 93
    URL rewriting for, 90
session variable (JSP), 121
session-authenticator pattern
    communication mechanism, 790–791
    described, 764
    example, 789
    implementation, 790
    overview, 789–790, 796
    sample code, 791–794
Session.AUTO_ACKNOWLEDGE mode (JMS), 244
SessionBean interface, 487
Session.CLIENT_ACKNOWLEDGE mode (JMS), 245
Session.DUPS_OK_ACKNOWLEDGE mode (JMS), 245
SessionFacade component, 775
session-facade pattern
    BusinessObject component, 776
    described, 764
    forces, 774
    implementation, 774–777
    overview, 773–774
    PresentationTier component, 775
    related patterns, 777
    results, 776
    sample code, 776–777
    sequence diagram, 774, 775
    SessionFacade component, 775
    strategies, 776
    structure, 774, 775
sessions (JavaMail)
    authorization and, 186
    core protocol parameters, 187–188
    defined, 186
    looking up the Session object, 229–230
    obtaining private instances, 186, 187
    obtaining shared instances, 187

    passing parameters, 187
    setting up to the server, 218–220
sessions (JMS), 238
sessions (JSP), 118
SessionSynchronization interface, 503
setAttribute() method, 85
setAutoCommit() method, 263
setBodyContent() method
    BodyTag interface, 163
    BodyTagSupport class, 169
setCreditCardNumber() method, 425
setDescription() method, 200
setDisposition() method, 200
setDynamicAttribute() method, 174
setEntityContext() entity bean callback
        method, 520
setFileName() method, 201
setFlags() method, 203
setFrom() method, 192
setHeader() method, 194
setID() method, 169
setJspBody() method
    SimpleTag interface, 170
    SimpleTagSupport class, 174
setJspContext() method
    SimpleTag interface, 170
    SimpleTagSupport class, 174
setMessageDrivenContext() method, 569
setNull() method, 592
setOutput() method, 82
setPageContext() method, 154
setParent() method
    Multipart class, 199
    SimpleTag interface, 170
    SimpleTagSupport class, 174
    Tag interface, 154
    TagSupport class, 169
set_publisherAssertions method, 702
setRecipient() method, 192
setReplyTo() method, 193
setRollbackOnly() method, 291
setSavePoint() method, 594
setSentDate() method, 194
setSessionContext method, 490
setSubject() method, 193
setValue() method, 169
SGML (Standard Generalized Markup Language), 18
SHA (Secure Hash Algorithm), 415
shared resources, 885
shared-key cryptography, 415–416
sharedState login initialize argument, 386
ShoppingCartBean JavaBean, 131
short-name method (TLD), 150
ShowAnyData.java JDBC example, 589–590
SIB (service-implementation bean), 722, 723
Signals, 281–283
SignalSets, 281–283
signed code, security vulnerability from, 350

SilkPerformer (Segue), 887
Simple API for XML (SAX) parsers, 22–23
Simple Authentication and Security Layer (SASL), 316,
    361–362
Simple Mail Transport Protocol. *See* SMTP
Simple Object Access Protocol. *See* SOAP
simple tag handlers
    defined, 153
    `JspFragment` interface, 173
    `SimpleTag` interface, 170–173
    `SimpleTagSupport` class, 173–174
`SimpleExample.xsd` XML Schema, 30
`SimpleTag` interface
    JSP for, 171
    methods, 170
    overview, 170
    tag handler lifecycle, 170
    TLD for, 171
    `TrySimpleTag` tag handler, 171–173
`SimpleTagSupport` class, 173–174
simple-type values (SOAP), 669
single-dimensional arrays (SOAP), 671
single-field primary keys for entity beans, 516
SIs (system integrators), 844–845
skeletons (RMI), 60–61
`SKIP_BODY` constant, 155
`SKIP_PAGE` constant, 155
`slapd.conf` file for OpenLDAP, 306
SlickEdit programmer's editor (Visual), 372
smart Web services, 655
SMTP (Simple Mail Transport Protocol)
    overview, 183–184
    sending a mail message using, 181–183
    `try...catch` block for, 220–221
`sn` attribute (`InetOrgPerson` schema), 337
`sn` LDAP attribute, 309
SOA DNS record type, 329
SOA (service-oriented architecture). *See also*
        Web-service architecture
    advantages of, 652, 839–840
    broker role, 651
    description stack, 661
    discovery stack, 661–663
    overview, 839
    provider role, 651
    requester role, 651
    SOAP, WSDL, and UDDI in, 659
    Web-service implementation, 840
    wire stack, 660–661
SOAP for attachments API for Java (SAAJ), 12, 13
SOAP RPC
    components, 672
    defined, 657
    process, 673
    request example, 674
    request requirements, 673
    requirements for using, 673
    response example, 674
    response requirements, 674

SOAP (Simple Object Access Protocol)
    Airline Reservations application, 676–681
    arrays, 670–672
    binding in WSDL, 686–687
    body, 667–668
    `ConnexiaClient.java` example, 678–681
    data types, 669–670
    encoding rules, 657
    envelope, 657, 666
    header, 666–667
    header attributes, 675–676
    intentional limitations of, 711
    Java and, 676–681
    JMS as transport mechanism, 714–715
    messaging, 675–676
    overview, 657
    request parsing by servlets, 712–713
    `Reservation.java` example, 676–678
    SOAP RPC, 657, 672–676
    XML instance for structure, 670
    XML schema for structure, 670
    XML schema (typical), 668
`<soap:address>` element (WSDL), 687
`<soap:body>` element (WSDL), 687
`<soap:fault>` element (WSDL), 687
`<soap:operation>` element (WSDL), 687
`SocketHandler` (JSR 47), 899
software design patterns. *See* patterns
Software Productivity Consortium, 837
software-vendor frameworks, 843–844
Solaris (Sun) login module, 363
sparse arrays (SOAP), 672
SQL library (JSTL), 147
SQLJ, 581
Stal, Michael (*Pattern-Oriented Software Architecture,
        Volume 2*), 810–811
Standard Generalized Markup Language (SGML), 18
standard services APIs, 11–13. *See also specific APIs*
standardization as Web services advantage, 653
`start()` method
    resource-adapter shutdown, 611–612
    `XAResource` interface, 294–295
`StartFlightServer` class, 62
starting
    Airline Reservations application login client, 407
    Airline Reservations application login server, 407
    Magazine Publisher application login client, 403
    Magazine Publisher application login server, 402
    OpenLDAP server, 306
`startWork()` method, 614
stateful communication (session pattern), 734
stateful session beans. *See also* session beans
    activation, 502
    Airline Reservations application, 504–509
    BMTs and, 461
    defined, 440, 483
    Does Not Exist state, 500
    lifecycle, 454–456, 500–502

Continued

stateful session beans *(continued)*
    Method-Ready state, 500–501
    model, 499–500, 510
    as non-persistent, 483
    overview, 440
    passivated state, 502
    passivation, 454–455, 502
    pool size, 889
    `SessionSynchronization` interface, 503
    stateless session beans versus, 441, 461, 483,
        509–510
stateless communication (session pattern), 734
stateless session beans. *See also* BMTs (bean-managed
        transactions); CMTs (container-managed
        transactions); session beans
    Airline Reservations application, 492–499
    BMTs and, 461
    CMTs versus BMTs, 440
    defined, 440, 483
    Does Not Exist state, 489–490
    `ejbCreate()` method, 490, 491
    `ejbRemove()` method, 491
    instance pooling, 492
    instantiation, 490
    lifecycle, 454, 489–491
    member variables, 491
    Method-Ready Pool state, 490–491
    model, 510
    as non-persistent, 483
    resource pooling, 454
    `setSessionContext` method, 490
    stateful session beans versus, 441, 461, 483, 509–510
    uses, 489
    Web-service endpoint interface, 492
stateless-service-provider pattern
    described, 764
    EJB, 794
    EJB deployment descriptor, 795–796
    overview, 794, 796
    sample code, 794–796
static data fields, bean provider restrictions for, 448
Stelting, John *(Applied Java Patterns)*, 740
`stop()` method, 611–612
`Store` class, 205–206
store-and-forward messaging. *See* publish-and-
    subscribe messaging
`StoreKey` Kerberos configuration option, 377
`StorePass`
    JDNI configuration option, 384
    Kerberos configuration option, 378
strategies for using patterns
    base-filter, 760, 761
    business-delegate pattern, 767
    command-and-controller, 748, 749–750
    composite-entity pattern, 779–780
    composite-value-object, 780
    composite-view pattern, 756–757
    custom-tag-view-management, 756–757

    defined, 731
    delegate-adapter, 767
    delegate-proxy, 767
    EJB-client, 809
    EJB-server, 809
    EJB-service-locator, 784
    front-controller pattern, 748–749
    half-object-plus-protocol pattern, 787–788
    intercepting-filter pattern, 760
    JavaBean-helper, 752
    JSP-view, 752, 756
    lazy-loading, 780
    multiple `TransferObjects`, 814
    multiplexed-resource-mapping, 748
    MVC pattern, 743
    router pattern, 738
    service-activator pattern, 809–810
    service-activator-server, 809
    service-locator pattern, 783–784
    servlet-front, 749
    servlet-view, 752, 756
    session pattern, 734
    session-facade pattern, 776
    standard-filter, 760
    stateful-session-facade, 776
    stateless-session-facade, 776
    transfer-object pattern, 813–814
    `TransferObject`-factory, 814
    updateable `TransferObject`, 813
    updateable-value-objects, 772
    value-object pattern, 771–772
    value-object-factory, 772
    view-helper pattern, 752
`StreamHandler` (JSR 47), 899
`string` data type (XML Schema), 31
Struts framework example
    `Action` class, 831–833
    alignment, 834–835
    configurability, 833–834
    design patterns, 827–828
    extensibility, 831–833
    inversion of control, 828
    loose coupling, 830–831
    processing flow, 828
    `RequestProcessor` class, 830–831
    separation of concerns, 828–829
    sequence diagram, 829
    `struts-config.xml` configuration file, 834
    Web sites, 827, 828
`struts-config.xml` configuration file, 834
stubs (RMI), 60, 61
Studio tool (Cape Clear), 717
stylesheets. *See also* XSLT (eXtensible Stylesheet
    Language Transformations)
    CSS versus XSLT, 34–35
    defined, 34
`Subject` class, 362–364
`Subject` JavaMail header field, 193

`Subject` login initialize argument, 386
`Submit` button (HTML), 79
`submitPayment()` method, 504–505
`submitReservation()` method, 504–505
subordinate coordinators for distributed transactions, 266
subscribing with UDDI, 703–704
`SubscriptionOrder` class, 108, 109
`SubtransactionAwareResource` role (OTS), 287, 288
`sufficient` login-module flag (JAAS), 361
Sun
    COS naming service provider, 333
    file-system service provider, 333
    Java Security site, 353
    JCE site, 420
    login modules supplied by, 363
    NIS, 333
    ONE application server, 50
    ONE Studio programming environment, 372
    Web services support, 716
`Supports` CMT attribute, 458
`suspend()` method, 292
suspending transactions, 292
symmetric encryption, 415–416
synchronization
    in BMP, 437
    of transactions, 296
`Synchronization` interface, 296
`synchronized` keyword, 448
synchronous acknowledgments (JMS), 253
synchronous notification pattern (UDDI), 704
synchronous versus asynchronous request-response, 442–443
system administrator
    defined, 8
    EJB, 435–436
system integrators (SIs), 844–845
system-component provider, 8
system-level contracts. See Connector architecture
Systinet WASP, 689

T

tag extensions. See JSP tag extensions
tag handlers. See also specific interfaces
    `BasicTag.java` example, 157–159
    `BodyTag` interface, 163–167
    `BodyTagSupport` class, 167–169
    classic, 153–169
    defined, 145, 153
    dynamic attributes, 174–176
    `IterationTag` interface, 159–163
    JSP versions and, 153
    `JspFragment` interface, 173
    lifecycle of simple tag handler, 170
    overview, 153
    simple, 153
    `SimpleTag` interface, 170–173
    `SimpleTagSupport` class, 173–174
    `Tag` interface, 154–159
    `TagSupport` class, 167–169

`TryBodyTag.java` example, 165–167
`TryIterationTag` example, 161–163
`TrySimpleDynamic` example, 175–176
`TrySimpleTag` example, 171–173
`Tag` interface
    `BasicTag.java` tag handler, 157–159
    constants, 155
    hierarchy and support classes, 154
    JSP for, 156–157
    methods, 154–155
    overview, 154
    simple example, 155–159
    TLD for, 156
    Tomcat output for example, 159
tag libraries, 145. See also JSTL (JSP Standard Tag Library)
`tag` method (TLD), 150
`tag-class` method (TLD), 150
`taglib` directive (JSP)
    mapping, 152
    `NumberFormat.jsp` example, 146
    `prefix` attribute, 147
tag-library descriptors. See TLDs (tag-library descriptors)
Taglibs (Apache), 145
tags (XML)
    case-sensitivity, 21
    closing, 21
    including namespaces in, 29–30
    `xsd:element` tags, 31
`TagSupport` class
    `HashMap` attributes, 169
    methods, 168–169
    need for, 167–168
`targetNamespace` keyword, 34
targets (ANT), 865–867
`taskmgr` performance-analysis tool, 480
`telephoneNumber` attribute (`InetOrgPerson` schema), 337
templates (XSLT), 37
testing
    ANT installation, 860
    frameworks and, 836
    J2EE Compatibility Test Suite, 45
    `junit` task (ANT) for unit-testing, 871–875
text callback handlers (JAAS), 359–360
text fields (HTML), 78
`TextInputCallback` class (JAAS), 376
`TextOutputCallback` class (JAAS), 376
thin clients, 77–78
threading
    bean provider restrictions on, 448, 449
    CORBA distribution transparency and, 479
    execute thread pool size, 889
    multi-threaded logging, 902–903
    performance concerns, 476–479
    persistence and, 477–478
    re-entrance and, 449–450
    resource pooling and, 476–477
    security and, 478

thread-safe classes, 449
3-tier architecture (EJBs), 430
throughput, 883, 884
TicketCache Kerberos configuration option, 377
tiered dependency tree (ANT), 866
TimedObject interface (EJB), 464, 569
timeout values, 290
timer service for EJBs, 464–466
TimerService interface (EJB), 465
TLDs (tag-library descriptors)
    <body-content> element, 151
    BodyTag example, 164–165
    defined, 145
    DynamicAttributes example, 175
    example, 149–151
    as independent files, 151
    IterationTag example, 160
    in JARs, 151
    JSP versions and, 149
    location of, 151
    methods, 150
    role of, 148
    SimpleTag example, 171
    Tag interface example, 156
TM (transaction manager), 285
tModel data structure (UDDI), 696–697
To JavaMail header field, 192–193
Tomcat servlet containers (Apache)
    default exception output, 140
    deploying airline-registration screen using, 141
    features comparison, 51
    login JSP deployment using, 129–130
    overview, 52
    tag handler output, 159
tool provider, 8
top-down recovery for transactions, 274
top-level transactions
    nested, 277–278
    overview, 275
TPMs (transaction-processing monitors), 274–275
trade secrets, embedded, 350
traditional application architecture, 838–839
Transaction interface, 293–294
transaction manager (TM), 285
transaction models
    extended models with J2EE Activity Service, 278–283
    nested top-level transactions, 277–278
    nested transactions, 276–277
    top-level transactions, 275
transactional objects/services, 258
transactional participants/resources
    defined, 258
    EJBs and, 258
    enrolling participants, 295–296
    heuristic decisions by, 261–262
transaction-inflow contract, 609, 632
transaction-management contract
    described, 609
    interfaces, 625

local transactions, 624
local-transaction management contract, 625–626
overview, 624–625
XA transactions, 624
XAResource transaction-management contract, 626–627
transaction-processing monitors (TPMs), 274–275
transactions. See also BMTs (bean-managed transactions); CMTs (container-managed transactions); JTA (Java Transaction API)
    ACID properties, 256–257
    Airline Reservations application, 297–301
    atomic, defined, 255–257
    atomicity and the two-phase commit protocol, 259–262
    auto-commit mode, 262–264
    consistency, 257, 267–268
    dirty reads, 271
    distributed, 264–265
    durability, 257, 272–273
    EJB container functionality, 447
    EJB transactional example, 462–463
    EJBs and, 456
    enrolling participants, 295–296
    equality, 297
    extended models with J2EE Activity Service, 278–283
    failure recovery, 273–274
    in-doubt, 274
    interoperability, 471
    interposition, 265–267
    isolation, 257, 268–272
    Java Transaction API, 288–297
    JMS support for, 253
    local, 262–264
    long-running, 278
    models, 275–283
    nested, 276–277
    nested top-level, 277–278
    non-repeatable reads, 271
    optimistic versus pessimistic concurrency control, 269–270
    OTS, 285–288
    performance concerns, 475–476
    phantom reads, 271
    suspending and resuming, 292
    synchronizing, 296
    top-level, 275
    transactional objects and participants, 257–258
    transaction-processing monitors, 274–275
    transaction-processing system, 257
    two-phase locking policy, 268–269
    X/Open Distributed Transaction Processing, 284–285
TransferObject component
    data-access-object pattern, 801
    transfer-object pattern, 813

transfer-object pattern
    `Account Owner` interface, 814–815
    applying, 814–815
    `BusinessComponent` component, 813
    characteristics, 811
    described, 797
    further information, 816
    implementation, 812–815
    overview, 811
    `PresentationComponent` component, 813
    related patterns, 815–816
    sample code, 814–815
    sequence diagram, 812
    strategies, 813–814
    structure, 812
    `TransferObject` component, 813
transparent fail-over, 475
`Transport` class, 216–218
transport layer (wire stack), 660–661
`Travelinfo_External.xml` listing, 26
`Travelinfo_InternalDTD.xml` DTD specification, 25
`Travelinformation.dtd` DTD specification, 26
`TravelinformationNS.xml` namespace, 28–29
`TravelinformationNS2.xml` namespace, 29–30
`TravelinformationSchema.xml` XML Schema, 32–33
`TravelinformationSchema.xsd` namespace, 33–34
`Travelinformation.xsl` XSLT stylesheet, 35–38
Triple DES, 413
try, 5
`TryBodyTag.java` tag handler, 165–167
`try...catch` block for JavaMail messages, 217, 220–221
`TryFirstPass`
    JDNI configuration option, 383
    Kerberos configuration option, 378
`TryIterationTag` tag handler, 161–163
`TrySimpleDynamic` tag handler, 175–176
`TrySimpleTag` tag handler, 171–173
tunable performance parameters
    application-server, 889
    JVM, 889–892
two-phase commit protocol
    heuristic outcomes, 261–262
    optimizations, 260
    overview, 259–260
    prepare phase, 259
    transaction log, 259
two-phase locking policy for transactions, 268–269
two-way encryption
    Airline Reservations application, 424–426
    overview, 412
TX transaction-demarcation API, 285
TXT DNS record type, 329
Type 1 through 4 JDBC drivers, 582–583

U

UDDI (Universal Description and Discovery
    Interface), 694
    additions to information model (version 3),
        697–698
    asynchronous notification pattern, 704
    `bindingTemplate` data structure, 695–696
    browse pattern, 700
    `businessEntity` data structure, 693–694
    `businessService` data structure, 695
    drill-down pattern, 700
    finder methods, 698–699
    green pages, 658
    information model, 693–698
    inquiry and publishing APIs (version 1), 690–691
    inquiry and publishing APIs (version 2), 691–692
    invocation pattern, 700
    Java and, 704–709
    methods, 701–704
    `operationalInfo` element (version 3), 697–698
    overview, 658–659
    publishing with, 700–703
    relationship between data structures, 694
    retriever methods, 699
    searching with, 698–700
    specification, 659
    subscribing with, 703–704
    synchronous notification pattern, 704
    `tModel` data structure, 696–697
    versions, 689–693
    white pages, 658
    yellow pages, 658
`uid` attribute (`InetOrgPerson` schema), 337
`uid` LDAP attribute, 309
UML, 930–931
`unbind()` method (RMI), 62
unidirectional relationships (CMR), 537, 539–540
unit-testing with `junit` task (ANT), 871–875
Universal Description and Discovery Interface.
    See UDDI
Universal Resource Identifiers. *See* URIs
Universal Resource Locators. *See* URLs
Universal Resource Names (URNs), 648
Unix
    callbacks not needed for, 394
    login handler for JAAS, 379
    Sun-supplied login module, 363
`UnixLoginModule` login module, 363
unknown primary keys for entity beans, 517
`unless` target attribute (ANT), 867
`unsetEntityContext()` entity bean callback
        method, 520
`Update` statement (SQL), 584
`updateFlightInfo()` method, 69, 70–72
`uri` method (TLD), 150
URIs (Universal Resource Identifiers). *See also* URLs
    (Universal Resource Locators)
    defined, 648
    grouping tags in namespaces using, 28
    overview, 648
    `taglib` mapping and, 152
    URNs, 648
`urlEncode()` method, 86–87
`URLName` class, 206–207

URLs (Universal Resource Locators)
  defined, 648
  for JavaMail addressing, 206–207
  for JSPs, 114
  redirection using servlets, 85–88
  URL rewriting, 90
URNs (Universal Resource Names), 648
useBean action (JSP), 125–126
UseFirstPass
  JDNI configuration option, 383
  Kerberos configuration option, 378
UseKeyTab Kerberos configuration option, 377
user-defined tasks (ANT), 868
UserList class, 586–587
UserList2 class, 588–589
userPassword attribute (InetOrgPerson
           schema), 337
user.provider.url JDNI configuration option, 383
users
  authenticating with JAAS, 364–368
  authorizing with JAAS, 368
  verification (security vulnerability), 350
UserTransaction interface, 290–291
useTicketCache Kerberos configuration option, 377

V

valid XML documents
  defined, 18
  DTD implementation for, 24–26
ValueObject component, 771
value-object pattern
  BusinessDelegate component, 771
  BusinessService component, 771
  described, 764
  forces, 769–770
  implementation, 770–771, 772–773
  LookupService component, 771
  overview, 769
  PresentationTier component, 770
  related patterns, 773
  results, 772
  sample code, 772–773
  sequence diagram, 770, 771
  strategies, 771–772
  structure, 770
  ValueObject component, 771
variable method (TLD), 150
variables
  environment variables for ANT, 860
  for implicit JSP objects, 121–122
  instance variable for counters, 172
  scopes in JSP, 122
  stateless session bean member variables, 491
  uninitialized, as security vulnerability, 350
Vector class, 131
vendor lock-in
  all-in-one proprietary environments and, 847
  avoiding, 53–54
  enterprise applications and, 431

vendors
  frameworks from, 843–844, 853–854
  for full J2EE implementations, 47–50
  for partial J2EE implementations, 51–53
  Web site for J2EE vendors, 54
version method (TLD), 150
view
  front-controller pattern, 748
  MVC pattern, 10, 116, 742, 827
  view-helper pattern, 752
view-helper pattern
  client, 752
  described, 730
  forces, 750–751
  further information, 754
  helper, 752
  implementation, 751–752, 753
  overview, 750
  related patterns, 753–754
  results, 753
  sample code, 753
  sequence diagram, 751
  strategies, 752
  structure, 751
  view, 752
virtual Java Card, 389–390
virtual machine, 4. *See also* JVMs (Java Virtual
           Machines)
Visual SlickEdit programmer's editor, 372
Vlissides, John (*Design Patterns*), 729, 745, 802, 805
vmstat performance-analysis tool, 480

W

war task (ANT), 875
WAR (Web-application archive)
  directory structure, 103–104
  for servlets, 103–104
  war task (ANT) for, 875
WASP (Systinet), 689
Web applications
  MVC pattern and, 115–116
  standard directories for, 155
Web browser interaction with servlets, 83
Web components. *See also* JSPs (JavaServer Pages);
           servlets
  J2EE APIs required for, 12–13
  overview, 7
Web services. *See also* specific protocols
  advantages of, 652–653
  APIs in J2EE architecture, 718–719
  architecture, 650–652
  ASPs, 654–655
  client-side programming model, 719–721
  defined, 648
  deployment descriptors, 725
  for EAI, 654–656
  EJB container, 722–723
  EJBs, exposing for, 713–714
  intelligence of, 647

JMS as transport layer for, 714–715
JNDI lookup for, 719
J2EE integration with, 711–717
mobile e-services, 656
need for, 649
products and tools, 715–717
scenarios, 653–656
server-side programming model, 721–724
Service Endpoint interface (SEI), 722, 723
Service interface, 720–721, 724
service-implementation bean, 722, 723
ServiceLifeCycle interface, 724
service-oriented architecture, 659–663
servlets for, 711–712
smart, 655
SOA implementation, 840
SOAP for, 657, 666–681
specification (JSR 109), 717–725
support as J2EE standard service, 12
technologies behind, 656–663
UDDI for, 658–659, 693–709
Web container, 723–724
Web site, 934
WSDL for, 657–658, 681–689
as XML extension, 648
Web Services Architecture Group (W3C), 648
Web Services Description Language. *See* WSDL
Web Services Toolkit (IBM), 689
Web sites. *See* Internet resources
Web-application archive. *See* WAR
WEB-INF directory
taglib mapping and, 152
TLD files in, 151
WebLogic application server (BEA)
clustering, 474–475
connection pool configuration, 597
further information, 927
obtaining naming context, 334
overview, 48
Web services support, 715
weblogic-ejb-jar.xml deployment descriptor,
571–572
WebRowSet class, 606
Web-service architecture. *See also* SOA (service-
oriented architecture)
message-based, 650–651
remote procedure call-based, 650
service-oriented, 651–652
Web-service endpoint interface, 492
WebSphere application servers (IBM)
clustering, 474–475
further information, 928
obtaining naming context, 335
overview, 48
web.xml deployment descriptor
DOCTYPE element, 104
error page implementation, 124
mandatory servlet elements, 104–105

optional XML tags, 105
servlet filter elements, 106–107
servlet listener elements, 105
Servlet Specification 2.4 and, 111
for servlets, 104–107
taglib mapping in, 152
Welcome.jsp JSP page, 127, 128
well-formed XML documents, 18
WHERE clause (EJB QL), 547, 549–551
white pages (UDDI), 658
WinNT/Win2K
authentication for WinNT domain, 397–403
callbacks not needed for, 394
login handler for JAAS, 379
Sun-supplied login module, 363
using built-in security APIs for login, 403–404
wire stack (SOA), 660–661
WML (Wireless Markup Language), 38–40
Work interface, 614
WorkFlow remote interface, 504–505
WorkFlowBean stateful session bean
bean class, 505–509
home interface, 504
overview, 504
remote interface, 504–505
WorkFlowHome home interface, 504
WorkListener interface, 614
work-management contract
classes, 614
described, 609
interfaces, 613, 614
overview, 612–613
work-management model, 613–615
work-submission procedure, 614–616
WorkManager interface, 614
World Wide Web Consortium. *See* W3C
wrapper classes, servlet filters for, 101–102
writeObject() method, overriding, 351
writeTo() method, 196
WSDL (Web Services Description Language)
Airline Reservations application, 681–686
document elements, 658
elements, 681
HTTP GET and POST binding, 687
Java and, 689
MIME binding, 688–689
overview, 657–658
Reservation.wsdl example, 681–686
Service interface and, 720–721
SOAP binding, 686–687
<soap:address> element, 687
<soap:body> element, 687
<soap:fault> element, 687
<soap:operation> element, 687
specification, 658
W3C (World Wide Web Consortium)
Web Services Architecture Group, 648
XML standard adoption, 17

X

XA transaction processing, 285
XA+ transaction processing, 285
XAResource interface, 294–295, 625, 626–627
XAResource transaction-management contract, 626–627
X.500
   attribute types for key-store login module, 381–382
   LDAP and, 305
XID interface, 297
XML (eXtensible Markup Language)
   attributes, 21
   case-sensitivity, 21
   closing tags, 21
   data-centric documents, 20
   document structure, 20–21
   document-centric documents, 20
   elements, 20–21
   further information, 931
   human-readable versus machine-readable
            documents, 34
   implementing DTDs, 24–26
   importing a tag library, 148
   J2EE XML-based APIs, 40
   namespaces, 26–30
   overview, 17–18
   parsers, 21–23
   prologue of documents, 20
   roots of, 18
   terminology misuse for, 18
   valid documents, 18
   Web services as extension of, 648
   well-formed documents, 18
   W3C standard, 17
XML library (JSTL), 147
XML parsers
   defined, 21
   DOM, 22, 23
   DOM versus SAX, 23
   overview, 21–22
   SAX, 22–23

XML Schema
   Airline Reservations application, 32–34
   comments in, 31
   data types, 31
   DTDs versus, 30, 31
   overview, 30–34
   simple example, 30–31
   SOAP data types and, 668–670
   using in XML documents, 31–32
   valid XML documents and, 18
XML schema layer (description stack), 661
XML-based technologies, 648
X/Open Distributed Transaction Processing, 284, 285
xsd:annotation tag, 31
xsd:documentation tag, 31
xsd:element XML tags, 31
xsl:output tag (XSLT), 37, 40
xsl:stylesheet tag (XSLT), 36, 40
XSLT (eXtensible Stylesheet Language
            Transformations)
   Airline Reservations application, 35–38
   applying XSL files to documents, 35
   CSS versus, 34–35
   MVC pattern and, 34
   namespace specification, 36–37
   output method specification, 37
   overview, 34–40
   producing simple HTML with, 35–38
   producing WML documents with, 38–40
   templates, 37
xsl:template tag (XSLT), 37, 40

Y

yellow pages (UDDI), 658

Z

Zachman Framework for Enterprise Architecture, 837